The IEBM Encyclopedia of Marketing

Titles from the International Encyclopedia of Business and Management series

International Encyclopedia of Business and Management
6 volume set, hardback, 0-415-07399-5

Concise International Encyclopedia of Business and Management
1 volume edition, hardback, 1-86152-114-6

Pocket International Encyclopedia of Business and Management
Paperback, 1-86152-113-8

The IEBM Encyclopedia of Marketing
Edited by Michael J Baker
Hardback, 1-86152-304-1

The IEBM Regional Encyclopedia of Business and Management
4 volume set, hardback 1-86152-403-X

IEBM Handbook Series

The IEBM Handbook of Human Resource Management
Edited by Michael Poole and Malcolm Warner
Hardback, 1-86152-166-9

The IEBM Handbook of Information Technology in Business
Edited by Milan Zeleny
Hardback, 1-86152-308-4

The IEBM Handbook of Management Thinking
Edited by Malcolm Warner
Hardback, 1-86152-162-6

The IEBM Handbook of Organizational Behaviour
Edited by Arndt Sorge and Malcolm Warner
Hardback, 1-86152-157-X

The IEBM Handbook of International Business
Edited by Rosalie L. Tung
Hardback, 1-86152-216-9

The IEBM Encyclopedia of Marketing

Edited by
Michael J. Baker

INTERNATIONAL THOMSON BUSINESS PRESS
I(T)P® An International Thomson Publishing Company

London • Bonn • Boston • Johannesburg • Madrid • Melbourne • Mexico City • New York • Paris • Singapore • Tokyo • Toronto • Albany, NY • Belmont, CA • Cincinnati, OH • Detroit, MI

The IEBM Encyclopedia of Marketing

Copyright ©1999 International Thomson Business Press

First published by International Thomson Business Press

I(T)P®   A division of International Thomson Publishing Inc.
The ITP logo is a trademark under licence

All rights reserved. No part of this work which is copyright may be reproduced or used in any form or by any means – graphic, electronic, or mechanical, including photocopying, recording, taping or information storage and retrieval systems – without the written permission of the Publisher, except in accordance with the provisions of the Copyright Designs and Patents Act 1988.

Whilst the Publisher has taken all reasonable care in the preparation of this book the Publisher makes no representation, express or implied, with regard to the accuracy of the information contained in this book and cannot accept any legal responsibility or liability for any errors or omissions from the book or the consequences thereof.

Products and services that are referred to in this book may be either trademarks and/or registered trademarks of their respective owners. The Publisher/s and Author/s make no claim to these trademarks.

British Library Cataloguing-in-Publication Data
A catalogue record for this book is available from the British Library

---

First edition 1999

Typeset by Hodgson Williams Associates, Cambridge
Printed in China

ISBN 1-86152-304-1

International Thomson Business Press
Berkshire House
168–173 High Holborn
London WC1V 7AA
UK

http://www.itbp.com

Contents

List of contributors. vii
Preface, *Michael J. Baker* xii

The nature and scope of marketing
Marketing – philosophy or function?, *Michael J. Baker* 3
Historical research in marketing, *D. G. Brian Jones* 18

The theoretical foundations
The economics basis of marketing, *Roger M. Heeler and Edward K. Chung* 35
The psychological basis of marketing, *Gordon R. Foxall* 52
The sociological basis of marketing, *Kjell Grønhaug* 64
Cultural aspects of marketing, *Kam-hon Lee* 76
Quantitative methods in marketing, *John Saunders* 85
Channels of distribution, *Bert Rosenbloom* 100
Consumer behaviour, *R. W. Lawson* 114
Organizational buying behaviour, *Stephen Parkinson* 128
Purchasing management, *Lars-Erik Gadde* 138
Relationships and networks, *Lars-Gunnar Mattson* 150

Marketing management
Marketing strategy, *Robin Wensley* 161
Strategic marketing planning, *John O'Shaughnessy*. 175
Marketing organization and management, *Nigel F. Piercy and David W. Cravens* 186
Marketing budgeting and resource allocation, *Richard M. S. Wilson* 208
Information technology and marketing, *Robert D. Buzzell and Rajendra S. Sisodia* 225
Environmental analysis, *Douglas Brownlie* 238
Marketing and public policy, *Stephen A. Greyser* 251
Marketing research, *Christopher West* 255
The marketing audit, *Aubrey Wilson* 268
Sales forecasting, *J. Scott Armstrong* 278
Market segmentation, *Yoram (Jerry) Wind* 291
Positioning, *Graham J. Hooley* 309

The marketing mix
The marketing mix, *Walter van Waterschoot* 319
Product policy, *Susan J. Hart* 331
New product development, *Robert G. Cooper* 342
Product life-cycle management, *Peter Doyle* 356
Packaging and design, *Peter Dart* 368
Branding and brand management, *Mark Sherrington* 376
Pricing, *Katia Campo and Els Gijsbrechts* 390
Channel management, *Bert Rosenbloom* 407
Logistics and value creation, *Donald J. Bowersox and David J. Closs* 420
Wholesaling: the role of marketing intermediaries, *Adel I. El-Ansary and Louis W. Stern* . . 432
Retailing, *Peter J. McGoldrick* 444

The IEBM Encyclopedia of Marketing

Direct marketing: Advancing to integrated (Internet)
   communications, *Arch G. Woodside and Rahul Rosha* 462
Marketing communications, *Keith Crosier*. 486
Advertising, *Simon Broadbent* 494
Sales promotion, *Ken Peattie*. 505
Personal selling and sales management, *Bill Donaldson*. 518
Public relations, *Roger Haywood*. 531
Exhibitions, *Gillian Rice* 541
Customer care and satisfaction, *David J. Carson* 550
Developing and implementing a marketing plan, *Malcolm H. B. McDonald* 562

Marketing in practice
Commodity marketing, *David H. Buisson* 579
Business marketing, *Kristian Möller and David Wilson* 592
Marketing of services, *Evert Gummesson* 604
Franchising, *Christina Fulop* 613
Exporting, *Philip Rosson* 624
Global marketing, *Susan P. Douglas and C. Samuel Craig* 639
Marketing ethics, *N. Craig Smith*. 653
Strategic marketing for non-profit organizations, *Philip Kotler and Alan R. Andreasen* . . . 668

Special topics
Total quality management (TQM), *John S. Oakland*. 685
Green marketing, *Heribert Meffert and Manfred Kirchgeorg* 702
Product-country Images, *Nicolas Papadopoulos*. 719
Corporate identity, *John Balmer* 732
Internal marketing – a relationship perspective, *Christian Grönroos and Paivi Voima* 747
The assessment of marketing performance, *Tim Ambler and Flora Kokkinaki* 752
Qualitative research in marketing, *Andy Lowe*. 765
Strategic alliances and supplier partnerships, *Prathap Oburai and Michael J. Baker*. 776
Marketing theory, *Michael Saren* 794
Postmodern marketing, *Stephen Brown* 810
The future of marketing, *Michael J. Baker*. 816

List of Contributors

Tim Ambler
Senior Research Fellow
London Business School
London
England

Professor Alan R. Andreasen
Professor of Marketing and Associate Dean for Faculty Affairs
School of Business
Georgetown University
Washington, DC
USA

Professor J. Scott Armstrong
Professor of Marketing
The Wharton School
University of Pennsylvania
Philadelphia
USA

Professor Michael J. Baker
Department of Marketing
University of Strathclyde
Glasgow
Scotland

Dr John Balmer
Department of Marketing
University of Strathclyde
Glasgow
Scotland

Professor Donald J. Bowersox
John H. McConnell University Professor of Business Administration
Eli Broad Graduate School of Management
Michigan State University
East Lansing
USA

Dr Simon Broadbent
Founding Partner
The Brand Consultancy
London
England

Professor Stephen Brown
Professor of Retailing
School of Commerce and International Business Studies
University of Ulster at Coleraine
Coleraine
Northern Ireland

Professor Douglas Brownlie
Professor of Marketing
University of Stirling
Stirling
Scotland

Professor David H. Buisson
Professor of Marketing
University of Otago
Dunedin
New Zealand

Professor Robert D. Buzzell
School of Business Administration
George Mason University
Virginia
USA

Dr Katia Campo
Postdoctoral Fellow of the Fund for Scientific Research – Flanders (Belgium) University Faculties Saint-Ignatius (UFSIA)
University of Antwerp
Belgium

Professor David J. Carson
Professor of Marketing
University of Ulster at Jordanstown
Newtonabbey
Northern Ireland

Professor Edward K. Chung
Norbert College
DePere, Wisconsin
USA

Professor David J. Closs
Professor of Marketing and Logistics
Eli Broad College of Business
Michigan State University
East Lansing
USA

Professor Robert G. Cooper
DeGroote School of Business
McMaster University
Hamilton
Ontario
Canada

Professor C. Samuel Craig
Professor of Marketing and International
Business and Chairman of the Marketing
Department
Leonard N. Stern School of Business
New York University
New York
USA

Professor David W. Cravens
Eunice and James L. West Chair of American
Enterprise Studies and Professor of
Marketing
M.J. Neeley School of Business
Texas Christian University
Fort Worth
USA

Dr Keith Crosier
Department of Marketing
University of Strathclyde
Glasgow
Scotland

Peter Dart
Added Value Group
Hampton Wick
Surrey
England

Dr Bill Donaldson
Strathclyde Graduate Business School
University of Strathclyde
Glasgow
Scotland

Professor Susan P. Douglas
Professor of Marketing and International
Business
Leonard N. Stern School of Business
New York University
New York
USA

Professor Peter Doyle
Professor of Marketing and Strategic
Management
Warwick Business School
University of Warwick
Coventry
England

Professor Adel I. El-Ansary
Paper and Plastics Educational Research
(PAPER) Foundation Endowed Research
Chair in Wholesaling
College of Business Administration
University of North Florida
South Jacksonville
Florida
USA

Professor Gordon R. Foxall
Department of Management
University of Keele
Keele
England

Emeritus Professor Christina Fulop
formely Deputy Director, Centre for
Franchise Research
City University Business School
London
England

Professor Lars-Erik Gadde
Professor of Industrial Marketing
Chalmers University of Technology
Gothenburg
Sweden

Professor Dr Els Gijsbrechts
Professor of Marketing
University Faculties Saint-Ignatius (UFSIA)
University of Antwerp
Belgium

Professor Peter Graham
Graduate College of Management
Southern Cross University
Lismore
Australia

Professor Stephen A. Greyser
Professor of Marketing
Graduate School of Business Administration
Harvard University
Boston
Massachusetts
USA

List of Contributors

Professor Christian Grönroos
Department of Marketing and Economic Geography
Hanken Swedish School of Economics
Helsinki
Finland

Professor Kjell Grønhaug
Norwegian School of Economics and Business Administration
Bergen-Sandviken
Norway

Professor Evert Gummesson
Professor of Service Management and Marketing
Stockholm University
Stockholm
Sweden

Dr Jim Hamill
Department of Marketing
University of Strathclyde
Glasgow
Scotland

Professor Susan J. Hart
Professor of Marketing
Department of Business Organization
University of Stirling
Stirling
Scotland

Roger Haywood
International Director
Kestrel Communications
London
England

Professor Roger M. Heeler
Schulich School of Business
York University
Toronto
Canada

Professor Graham J. Hooley
Professor of Marketing and Research Director
Aston Business School
Aston University
Birmingham
England

Professor Brian Jones
Professor
School of Business
University of Prince Edward Island
Charlottetown
Prince Edward Island
Canada

Professor Dr. Manfred Kirchgeorg
Associate Professor
Institut für Marketing
Wesfäloscje Wilhelms-Universität
Münster
Germany

Dr Flora Kokkinaki
Research Fellow
London Business School
London
England

Professor Philip Kotler
S. C. Johnson & Son Distinguished Professor of International Marketing
Kellogg Graduate School of Management
Northwestern University
Evanston
Illinois
USA

Professor Rob Lawson
Department of Marketing
University of Otago
Dunedin
New Zealand

Professor Kam-hon Lee
Professor of Marketing
The Chinese University of Hong Kong
Shatin
Hong Kong
China

Dr Andy Lowe
Department of Marketing
University of Strathclyde
Glasgow
Scotland

Professor Lars-Gunnar Mattsson
Professor of Business Administration
Stockholm School of Economics
Sweden

Professor Malcolm McDonald
Professor of Marketing Strategy
Cranfield School of Management
Cranfield University
Bedford
England

Professor Peter J. McGoldrick
Professor of Retailing
Manchester School of Management
UMIST
Manchester
England

Professor Heribert Meffert
Chairman
Institut für Marketing
Wesfälische Wilhelms-Universität
Münster
Germany

Professor Kristian Möller
Professor of Marketing
Director of the Finnish Doctoral Programme of Marketing
Helsinki School of Economics and Business Administration
Finland

Professor John O'Shaughnessy
Professor Emeritus of Business
Columbia University
New York
USA
and Senior Associate
Judge Institute of Management
University of Cambridge
England

Professor John Oakland
Executive Chairman
Oakland Consulting PLC
Leeds
England

Prathap Oburai
Doctoral Researcher
Department of Marketing
University of Strathclyde
Glasgow
Scotland

Professor Nicolas Papadopoulos
School of Business
Carleton University
Ottawa
Canada

Professor Stephen Parkinson
Ulster Business School
University of Ulster at Jordanstown
Newtonabbey
Northern Ireland

Dr Ken Peattie
Senior Lecturer in Strategic Management
Cardiff Business School
University of Wales, Cardiff
Wales

Professor Nigel Piercy
Sir Julian Hodge Professor of Marketing
Cardiff Business School
University of Wales, Cardiff
Cardiff
Wales

Professor Gillian Rice
Associate Professor of Marketing
Thunderbird – The American Graduate School of International Management
Glendale
Arizona
USA

Professor Bert Rosenbloom
The G. Behrens Ulrich Professor of Marketing
College of Business and Administration
Drexel University
Philadelphia
Pennsylvannia
USA

Rahul Rosha
DMB & B
New York
USA

Professor Philip Rosson
Dean of Management
Dalhousie University
Halifax
Canada

List of Contributors

Professor Michael Saren
Department of Marketing
University of Strathclyde
Glasgow
Scotland

Professor John Saunders
Director
Aston Business School
Aston University
Birmingham
England

Mark Sherrington
Added Value Group
Hampton Wick
Surrey
England

Professor Rajendra S. Sisodia
Trustee Professor of Marketing
Bentley College
Waltham
Massachusetts
USA

Professor N. Craig Smith
Associate Professor
McDonough School of Business
Georgetown University
Washington
USA

Professor Louis W. Stern
John D. Gray Distinguished Professor of Marketing
Kellogg Graduate School of Management
Northwestern University
Evanston
Illinois
USA

Paivi Voima
Department of Marketing
CERS Centre for Relationship Marketing and Service Management
Hanken Swedish School of Economics
Helsinki
Finland

Professor Walter van Waterschoot
Professor of Marketing
University Faculties Saint-Ignatius (UFSIA)
University of Antwerp
Belgium

Professor Robin Wensley
Warwick Business School
University of Warwick
Coventry
England

Christopher West
Managing Director
Marketing Intelligence Services Ltd.
London
England

Dr Aubrey Wilson
Independent Consultant
Aubrey Wilson Associates
London
England

Professor David T. Wilson
Alvin H. Clemens Professor of Entrepreneurial Studies
Smeal College of Business Administration
Pennsylvania State University
Pennsylvania
USA

Professor Richard M. S. Wilson
Professor of Business Administration
The Business School
Loughborough University
Loughborough
England

Professor Yoram (Jerry) Wind
SEI Center for Advanced Studies in Management
The Wharton School
University of Pennsylvania
Philadelphia
USA

Professor Arch G. Woodside
Malcolm S. Woldenburg Professor of Marketing
A. B. Freeman School of Business
Tulane University
New Orleans
Louisiana
USA

Preface

This second edition of the *Encyclopedia of Marketing* signifies both the success of the first edition published by Routledge in 1995 as well as a significant expansion of the marketing entries contained in the *International Encyclopedia of Business and Management*. Edited by Professor Michael Baker of the Department of Marketing at the University of Strathclyde, this major reference book is intended to reflect the growing maturity of the marketing discipline.

During the past decade the need for more effective marketing has become accepted as a necessary condition for success in almost every kind of organization – manufacturing businesses, service organizations such as banks, insurance companies and airlines, and even not-for-profit institutions like charities, hospitals and universities. However, the scope, nature and practice of marketing are not well understood. Indeed, many would-be disciples of the craft and practice mistake two of its less central activities – advertising and promotion – for a concept that is concerned with the creation of mutually satisfying exchange relationships. An authoritative and comprehensive reference book such as this should do a great deal to dispel the confusion as well as provide much needed guidance on the origins, scope and practice of marketing.

As defined, 'encyclopedia' connotes the comprehensive treatment of the aspects of a subject. It follows that people turn to encyclopedias as a first point of reference to help them define a topic or issue, to establish its relationship to other associated or connected subjects, and, possibly, for guidance as to where to go for more detailed exposition. The title 'encyclopedia' also suggests a more rigorous and authoritative treatment than one would expect from a handbook, and indeed there are already several handbooks in circulation. Yet another distinguishing feature of an encyclopedia is that its emphasis is upon the accepted body of knowledge at its time of publication. Thus, while it may anticipate new trends and developments, its primary function is to summarize what is known about a subject and provide insight and understanding of it.

Given these characteristics one may identify two primary audiences for such a work – business persons and students. For both audiences the need is perceived as the same – a concise, authoritative, comprehensive and clear summary of the topic, with advice on how to apply or use the information and where to look for greater detail if this is required.

The perspective of the editor is that 'marketing is marketing'. In other words, there is a body of knowledge and a series of generalizations that are of universal validity and so may be used to inform and enlighten any specific marketing issue and problem. It is also believed that, like medicine and engineering, marketing is a synthetic discipline. It has sound foundations in the long established and recognized social sciences such as economics, psychology and sociology, but it differs from them in its holistic approach to understanding the nature and satisfaction of human needs. Also, like medicine and engineering, marketing embraces a body of knowledge as well as a professional practice dependent upon that body of knowledge.

The *Encyclopedia* seeks to recognize both these facets in a comprehensive and rigorous way. The work starts with an exposition and justification of the proposition that marketing is a universal discipline. This introductory entry seeks to define the nature of the marketing concept and establish the distinction between marketing as a business philosophy, guiding an organization's direction and development, and as a business function, enhancing both efficiency and effectiveness in the execution of an organization's mission. The following entry addresses the history of marketing thought in order to provide perspective and establish the origins of and linkages with other disciplines that form the basis of current marketing thinking.

Next the *Encyclopedia* addresses the theoretical foundations that underpin and support the subject. Taken together these entries explore the origins, nature and functions of marketing.

The third section is concerned mainly with marketing management and seeks to define and describe the issues and tasks associated with the management of the marketing function. Entries in this section are largely concerned with the ways and means whereby the theoretical foundations have been shaped and developed to help solve practical marketing problems.

The fourth section develops the theme that the marketing manager's role is to select and integrate the available mix of marketing 'ingredients' to maximum effect. Here will be found treatment of the distinctive subfields of marketing which deal with the product, its pricing, promotion and distribution.

The fifth section looks at marketing in practice, examining the deployment of the marketing mix in a variety of specific contexts, such as the marketing of industrial goods and of services.

Finally, the last section includes a number of special topics that have emerged as of particular significance and importance as we approach the millennium. Eight new entries have been added to this section covering topics as diverse as the assessment of marketing performance (identified as the most important research theme for the period 1998–2000 by the prestigious Marketing Science Institute), Product-Country Images, Strategic Alliances and Postmodernism. (The author asked if this entry might be the last given its suggestion that we need an alternative paradigm of marketing. However, the editor asserted his right to have the last word.)

In preparing the second edition each author was selected on the basis that he or she is recognized internationally as an expert on the topic of his or her entry. In order to ensure some comparability in treatment each author was asked to ensure that his or her contribution:

- defines clearly the scope and nature of the topic;
- explains where it fits into the body of marketing knowledge;
- identifies, defines and describes the key concepts and ideas associated with the topic;
- provides a summary of current issues and potential future developments that bear upon the topic;
- suggests the most important sources of reference for further reading.

All of the contributors to the first edition have reviewed their original entry. Many have made extensive revisions to accommodate the dynamic changes in their topic area while others have made only minor corrections reflecting the maturing of much of the body of knowledge which underpins the practice of marketing.

Taken together the contributions amply meet the editor's specification set out above. In doing so it also satisfies the criteria for an encyclopedia in that it is authoritative, comprehensive, rigorous and up-to-date. We trust you will find it an invaluable work of reference.

The nature and scope of marketing

Marketing – philosophy or function?

1 Introduction
2 Exchange and economic growth
3 The rediscovery of marketing
4 The marketing management school
5 The European perspective
6 So what is marketing?
7 Summary

Overview

This opening entry seeks to define what might be considered the true essence of marketing: that it is the establishment of mutually satisfying exchange relationships. The modern marketing concept would appear to have undergone at least three major phases of evolution – the emergence of the mass market, the articulation of the modern marketing concept, and the transition from an emphasis upon the transaction to the relationship.

The paper concludes with a review of specific definitions of marketing to document how these have changed over time and to speculate as to the possible nature and direction of future change in order to ponder the question, what is marketing?

1 Introduction

On first introduction to a subject it is understandable that one should seek a clear and concise definition of it. If nothing else this definition should enable one to distinguish the domain of that subject from all others while also giving an indication of its scope and nature. Of course, none of us expect that a short definition will be able to encompass the complexity of a subject which, in the case of this Encyclopedia, extends to over 900 printed pages. This said, it does seem reasonable that persons who profess or claim expertise on a subject should be able to define it.

In this introductory article it will become clear that there is no scarcity of definitions of marketing and we will review a number of them. In doing so it will also become clear that views as to the scope of the subject tend to polarize in the manner implied by the title of this article between those who perceive marketing as a philosophy of business, or state of mind, and those who regard it as a managerial function responsible for particular activities in much the same way as production, finance or human resource management.

To throw light on this dichotomy it will be helpful first to review what is seen to be the true essence of marketing – mutually satisfying exchange relationships – and its evolution over time in parallel with stages of economic growth and development. On the basis of this review it will be argued that marketing has always been an intrinsic element of the commercial exchange process but that its importance has waxed and waned with shifts in the balance between supply and demand. Without anticipating unduly Brian Jones' discussion of historical research in marketing (see HISTORICAL RESEARCH IN MARKETING) it will be suggested that we can detect at least three major phases in the evolution of the modern marketing concept – the emergence of the mass market *ca* 1850, the articulation of the modern marketing concept *ca* 1960, and the transition from an emphasis upon the transaction to the relationship *ca* 1990. To conclude this article we then review specific definitions of marketing to document how these have changed over time and speculate as to the possible nature and direction of future change in order to answer our opening question, Marketing – philosophy or function?

2 Exchange and economic growth

Since time immemorial humans have had to live with scarcity in one form or another. In its most acute form scarcity threatens the very existence of life itself but, even in the most affluent and advanced post-industrial societies its existence is still apparent in the plight of the homeless and the poor. Indeed, in some senses it is doubtful whether mankind will ever overcome scarcity, if for no other reason than that there appears to be no upper limit to human wants.

The use of the noun 'wants' is deliberate for early on in any study of marketing it is important to distinguish clearly between 'needs' and 'wants'. Needs have been classified as existing at five levels by Abraham Maslow (1943) and his 'hierarchy of human needs' (Figure 1) is a useful starting point for a discussion of the nature of marketing. As can be seen from Figure 1, Maslow's hierarchy conceives of human needs as resting on a foundation of physiological needs, essential for existence, and ascending through a series of levels – safety, love and esteem – to a state of self-actualization in which the individual's specification of a need is entirely self-determined. According to this conceptualization one can only ascend to a higher level once one has satisfied the needs of a lower level and the inference may be drawn that scarcity will only cease to exist once every individual has attained the highest level of self-actualization.

From this description it is clear that 'needs' are broadly based and defined and act as a summary statement for a whole cluster of much more precisely defined wants which reflect the exact desires of individuals. In a state of hunger the Westerner may want bread or potatoes but the Easterner is more likely to want rice. Both of these wants are fairly basic. While they have the ability to satisfy the need 'hunger', they offer little by way of variety. The desire for variety, or choice, is another intrinsic element of human nature and much of human development and progress may be attributed to a quest for variety – of new ways of satisfying basic needs. Indeed, the process appears to be self-sustaining which prompted us to propose that a maxim of marketing is that 'the act of consumption changes the consumer' (Baker 1980). In other words, each new experience increases and extends the consumer's expectations and creates an opportunity for a new supplier to win their patronage by developing something new and better than existing solutions to the consumer's need.

Faced with an apparent infinity of wants the challenge to be faced is in determining what selection of goods and services will give the greatest satisfaction to the greatest number at any particular point in time. Indeed, the purpose of economic organization has been defined as 'maximizing satisfaction through the utilization of scarce resources'. Marketing is the function which facilitates achievement of this goal. To understand how it does this, it will be helpful to review the process of economic development. Rostow's (1962) Stages of Economic Growth model provides an excellent basis for such a review.

Rostow's model is shown in Figure 2 and proposes that human societies progress from the lowest level of subsistence or survival through a series of clearly identified stages until they achieve the sophistication and affluence of the modern post-industrial state. In grossly simplified terms certain key events appear to be associated with the transition from one stage to the next.

Figure 1 Maslow's hierarchy of human needs
Source: Maslow (1943: 370–96)

Marketing – philosophy or function?

```
                Beyond
              high mass
             consumption
            ─────────────
              Age of high
            mass consumption
           ───────────────────
              Drive to maturity
          ─────────────────────
                Take-off
          Preconditions for take-off
         ─────────────────────────────
              Traditional society
```

Figure 2 Rostow's Stages of Economic Growth model
Source: Rostow (1962)

At the lowest level of all is the subsistence economy based upon hunting, gathering and collecting. Such economies are nomadic and entirely dependent upon nature for their survival. While members of such nomadic tribes may share food and shelter, and band together for safety, they are societies which are devoid of any recognizable form of commercial exchange.

With the domestication of animals and the development of primitive agriculture man begins to exercise a degree of control over his environment. At the same time new activities create new roles and the potential for the first step towards increased productivity and economic progress – task specialization. Once it becomes recognized that some people are better suited to some tasks than others then the potential for task specialization exists. For it to be realized, however, an agreed system of exchange must be developed. Indeed, it seems likely that the creation of a system of exchange was a necessary prerequisite for task specialization to flourish.

A fundamental law of economics is that beyond a certain point each additional unit of any good or service becomes worth progressively less and less to its owner (the law of diminishing marginal utility). Given a surplus of any specific good its owner will be able to increase his overall satisfaction by exchanging units of his surplus for another good which he wants. Thus hunters can exchange meat for vegetables with farmers to their mutual and enhanced satisfaction.

For an exchange to occur there must be at least two persons, each with a surplus of one good which is desired by the other. Once contact has been established between the two persons they can then negotiate an exchange which will increase their overall satisfaction by swapping units until the marginal utility of the two goods is equal (i.e. one would receive less satisfaction by acquiring one additional unit of the other person's surplus than by retaining a unit of one's own output). While this concept is easy to understand in principle, especially when discussing only one exchange, its implementation in practice poses numerous problems. To reduce these problems three additional developments are called for.

First, in order that those with surpluses to exchange can be brought together it will be helpful to set aside a specific place for the purpose – a market. Second, one needs an accepted store of value that will act as a universal medium of exchange – money. Third, because marketing is a separate task from production it will further increase productivity and add value if specialist intermediaries – merchants and retailers – come into existence to perform these functions. Clearly, markets, money and intermediaries have existed since the earliest civilization. Indeed, it would be no exaggeration to claim that the development of formal commercial exchange relationships was the foundation for civilization as we know it today. It would seem that marketing is perhaps not such a recent phenomenon as many believe it to be!

The creation of markets and the development of exchange provide the preconditions for take-off. For take-off itself to occur task specialization has to be taken a stage further to what economists call the division of labour. One of the earliest and best-known examples of the division of labour is provided by Adam Smith's description of the pin-making industry.

> To take an example, therefore, from a very trifling manufacture; but one in which the division of labour has been very often taken notice of, the trade of the pin maker; a workman not educated to this business (which the division of labour has rendered a distinct trade), nor acquainted with the use of the machinery employed in it (to the invention of which the same division of labour has probably given occasion), could scarce, perhaps, with his utmost industry, make one pin in a day, and certainly could not make 20. But in the way in which this business is now carried on, not only the whole work is a peculiar trade, but it is divided into a number of branches, of which the greatest part are likewise peculiar trades. One man draws out the wire, another straights it, a third cuts it, a fourth points it, a fifth grinds it at the top receiving the head; to make the head requires 3 distinct operations; to put it on is a peculiar business, to whiten the pins is another; it is even a trade by itself to put them into the paper; and the important business of making a pin is, in this manner, divided into about 18 distinct operations, which, in some manufactories, are all performed by distinct hands, though in others the same man will sometimes perform 2 or 3 of them. I have seen a small manufactory of this kind where 10 men only were employed and where some of them consequently performed 2 or 3 distinct operations. But though they were very poor, and therefore but indifferently accommodated with the necessary machinery, they could, when they exerted themselves, make among them about 12 pounds of pins in a day. There are in a pound upwards of 4000 pins of the middling size. These 10 persons, therefore, could make among them upwards of 48,000 pins in a day. Each person, therefore, making a tenth part of 48,000 pins, might be considered as making 4800 pins in a day. But if they had all wrought separately and independently, and without any of them having been educated to this peculiar business, they could certainly not each of them have made 20, perhaps not 1 pin in a day; that is, certainly, not the 240th, perhaps not the 4800th part of what they are at present capable of performing, in consequence of a proper division and combination of their different operations.
>
> (Smith 1970 [1776])

It seems reasonable to assume that under conditions of craft industry, where each craftsman was responsible for all the tasks associated with the production of a particular good, the number of craftsmen in a community would be approximately sufficient to satisfy the demands of that community. Indeed, the medieval craft guilds (and, more recently, trade unions) strictly controlled the number of apprentices that could be trained in the craft to ensure that a satisfactory balance between supply and demand be maintained. Clearly, the enormous increase in productivity associated with the division of labour destroyed this control and flooded the market with the product in question driving the price down and making many craftsmen redundant. One new pin factory employing 10 pin makers could match the output of 240 craftsmen and so service the needs of 240 times as many customers. As a result production became concentrated in locations possessing natural advantages associated with the product – sources of power and raw material, labour, good channels of communication – and it became necessary to employ sales persons to help sell the output into a greatly enlarged market.

Because of the enormous increase in output associated with factory production, standards of living improved substantially with a consequential increase in life expectancies and the numbers of children surviving infancy. As the size of a market is determined ultimately by the size of the population, an expanding population represented an expanding market and further fuelled the rapid economic growth associated with take-off. This growth was to receive even greater impetus with the spate of scientific and technological innovation of the eighteenth century, which gave birth to what has become known as the Industrial Revolution and formed the foundation for Rostow's fourth stage of economic growth – the age of high mass consumption

In his original conceptualization Rostow (1962) perceived that some of the more advanced and affluent industrialized economies were approaching the limits of mass consumption. While population growth had slowed to a near steady state further improvements in productivity had created saturated markets and the potential for excess supply. John Kenneth Galbraith (1958) designated this the post-industrial society while Rostow merely termed it the Age Beyond High Mass Consumption. Eight years later, in 1970, Rostow revised his model and designated the final stage The Search for Quality – the inference being that if a static population could not physically consume more then the only way growth could be sustained would be to consume 'better'.

Elsewhere (Baker 1994) we have discussed the way in which the stages in Maslow's need hierarchy correspond closely to the stages in Rostow's economic stages model, e.g. subsistence economies are concerned primarily with physiological needs; the search for quality with self-actualization, etc. Clearly, human needs (demand) motivate supply creation and the matching of supply and demand is achieved through a process of exchange and marketing. It is also clear that these processes have existed for a very long time indeed, so why is marketing often represented as a twentieth-century phenomenon? We turn to this question in the next section but, before doing so, will summarize some of the key points that have emerged from our greatly simplified account of economic development.

First, exchange adds value and increases satisfaction. It also encourages variety and improves choice. Second, the parties to a commercial exchange are free agents so that for an exchange to occur both parties must feel that they are benefiting from that exchange. It is from these observations that we derive our basic definition of marketing as being concerned with mutually satisfying exchange relationships. Third, task specialization and the division of labour greatly increase productivity and increase the volume of goods available for consumption. In turn this increased supply results in an improved standard of living and an increase in the population thereby increasing demand and stimulating further efforts to increase supply. Fourth, the concentration of production and the growing size and dispersion of the market increases the need for specialized channels of distribution and of intermediaries to service and manage them. Fifth, improved standards of living lead to a stabilization of population growth and absolute market size (demand) but accelerating technological innovation continues to enhance our ability to increase supply. It was this which was to lead to the 'rediscovery' of marketing.

3 The rediscovery of marketing

As we have seen markets and marketing are as old as exchange itself yet many people regard marketing as a phenomenon which emerged in the second half of the twentieth century – to be precise about 1960 when Professor Ted Levitt published an article entitled 'Marketing myopia' in the *Harvard Business Review* in which he addressed the fundamental question of why do firms, and indeed whole industries, grow to a position of great power and influence and then decline. Taking the American railroad industry as his main example Levitt showed that this industry displaced other forms of overland transportation during the nineteenth century because it was more efficient and effective than the alternatives it displaced. By the beginning of the twentieth century, however, development of the internal combustion engine and the building of cars and trucks had provided an alternative to the railroads for both personal and bulk transportation. In the early years this challenge was limited because of the high cost of the substitute product, their lack of sophistication and reliability and their low availability. However, their potential was clear to see – if you owned a car or truck you had complete personal control over your transportation need and could travel from door to door at your own convenience. Henry Ford perceived this market opportunity, invented the concept of mass assembly and began to produce a reliable, low-cost motor car in constantly increasing numbers. From this time on the fortunes of the railroad began to decline so that by the 1950s this once great industry appeared to be in terminal decline.

What went wrong? Levitt's thesis is that those responsible for the management of the railroad were too preoccupied with their product to the neglect of the need that it served which was transportation. Because of their myopia or 'production orientation' they lost sight of the fact that the railroad product had been a substitute for earlier, less attractive products so that, offered a choice, consumers had switched from the old to the new to increase their personal satisfaction. It should have been obvious, therefore, that if a new, more convenient mode of transportation was developed then consumers would switch to it too. Thus, if the railroad management had concentrated on the need served – transportation – rather than their product they might have been able to join the infant automobile industry and develop a truly integrated transportation system. In other words the railroads failed because they lacked a marketing orientation.

At almost the same time as the appearance of Levitt's seminal paper, Robert Keith (1960) published an article in which he described the evolution of marketing in the Pillsbury Company for which he worked. In Keith's view the company's current marketing approach was the direct descendant of two earlier approaches or eras, which he termed production and sales. This three eras or stages model – production, sales, marketing – was widely adopted by what has come to be known as the marketing management school whose ideas have dominated the theory and practice of marketing for the past thirty years or more.

The essence of the production orientation – a preoccupation with the product and the company – and the marketing orientation – a focus on the consumer's need and the best way to serve it – have already been touched on in reviewing Levitt's 'Marketing Myopia'. Keith's contribution then was to propose an intermediate or transitional phase he termed the sales era. In the sales era firms were still largely production orientated but as demand stabilized supply continued to grow, resulting in fierce competition between suppliers. One aspect of this was that producers committed more effort to selling their products with an emphasis on personal selling, advertising and sales promotion – hence the 'sales orientation'.

Chronologically the production era was dated from the mid-1850s and lasted until around the late 1920s, which saw the birth of the sales era that lasted to around the mid-1950s, when the marketing era commenced. This conceptualization is now seen to be seriously flawed in terms of its historical accuracy but none the less remains a useful pedagogical device for reasons we will return to momentarily. First, however, it will be helpful to set the record straight.

As we have noted on several occasions there has been a tendency to date the emergence of marketing to the late 1950s and early 1960s. In an article entitled 'How modern is modern marketing?' Fullerton (1988) provides a rigorous analysis based on historical research.

At the outset it will be helpful to summarize the three key facets of the historical approach. First, there is 'a philosophical belief that historical phenomena such as markets are intrinsically rich and complex; efforts to simplify or assume away aspects of such phenomena are deeply distrusted' (Fullerton 1988: 109). Second, the historical research tradition emphasizes 'systematic and critical evaluation of historical evidence for accuracy, bias, implicit messages, and now extinct meanings' (Fullerton 1988: 109). The third facet of historical research is the process itself through which the researcher seeks to synthesize and recreate what actually happened in the past.

While there is considerable evidence that supports the existence of a production era there are also strong arguments to support a contrary view. Fullerton summarizes these as follows:

1 It ignores well-established historical facts about business conditions – competition was intense in most businesses, over-production common, and demand frequently uncertain.
2 It totally misses the presence and vital importance of conscious demand stimulation in developing the advanced modern economies. Without such stimulation the revolution in production would have been stillborn.
3 It does not account for the varied and vigorous marketing efforts made by numerous manufacturers and other producers.
4 It ignores that dynamic growth of new marketing institutions outside the manufacturing firm.

(Fullerton 1988: 111)

Each of these arguments is examined in detail and substantial evidence is marshalled to support them. A particularly telling point concerns the need for active demand stimulation and the need for production and marketing to work in tandem.

> Some of the famous pioneers of production such as Mathew Boulton and Josiah Wedgwood were also pioneers of modern marketing, cultivating large-scale demand for their revolutionary inexpensive products with techniques usually considered to have been post-1950 American innovations: market segmentation, product differentiation, prestige pricing, style obsolescence, saturation advertising, direct mail campaigns, reference group appeals, and testimonials among others.
>
> (Fullerton 1988: 112)

In Fullerton's view 'demand-enhancing marketing' spread from Britain to Germany and the USA. In the USA it was adopted with enthusiasm and Americans came to be seen as 'the supreme masters of aggressive demand stimulation', a fact frequently referred to in contemporary marketing texts of the early 1990s. Numerous examples support Fullerton's contention that producers of the so-called production era made extensive use of marketing tools and techniques as well as integrating forward to ensure their products were brought to the attention of their intended customers in the most effective way. That said, the examples provided (with one or two possible exceptions) do not, in my opinion, invalidate the classification of the period as the 'production era' in the sense that it was the producer who took the initiative and differentiated his product to meet the assumed needs of different consumer groups based on economic as opposed to sociological and psychological factors. In other words, producers inferred the consumers' behaviour but they had not yet developed techniques or procedures which would enable them to define latent wants and design, produce and market products and services to satisfy them.

Similarly, while the period from 1870 to 1930 saw the emergence and development of important marketing institutions in terms of physical distribution, retailing, advertising and marketing education, which are still important today, it does not seem unreasonable to argue that all these institutions were designed to sell more of what was being produced. This is not to deny the 'rich marketing heritage' documented by Fullerton but to reinforce the point that the transition to a 'marketing era' was marked by a major change in business philosophy from a producer-led interpretation of consumer needs to a consumer-driven approach to production.

As to the existence of a sales era (rejected by Fullerton) this seems as convenient a label as any to give to the transitional period between a production and marketing orientation. In addition to the reality of a depressed world economy in the 1930s, which required large-scale producers to sell more aggressively to maintain economies of scale, the period saw the migration of many behavioural scientists from a politically unstable Europe to the safety of the USA. In retrospect it appears that it was this migration that led to the more rigorous analysis of consumer behaviour which was to underpin the emergence of a new 'marketing era'.

Combined with this greater insight into consumer behaviour were a period of great economic growth and prosperity following the Second World War, together with a major increase in the birth rate, which was to result in a new generation of consumers brought up in a period of material affluence (the baby boomers). It was this generation which sought to reassert consumer sovereignty and so initiated the change in the balance of power between producer and consumer which heralded the 'marketing era'.

Fullerton's argument that the production-sales-marketing era framework is a 'catastrophic model' 'in which major developments take place suddenly, with few antecedents' (1988: 121) is not without merit. Certainly, it could and has had the effect of disguising the evolutionary nature of marketing thought and practice. In place of a catastrophic model, or, indeed, a continuity model which tends to observe differences over time, Fullerton suggests a 'complex flux model'. Such a complex flux model has the ability to incorporate dramatic changes but it also 'stresses that even dramatic change is based on and linked to past phenomena' (Fullerton 1988: 121). It is also neutral in the sense that it does not automatically equate development or evolution with 'improvement', leaving such judgements for others to make.

Fullerton's complex flux model embraces four eras:

1 *Setting the stage: the era of antecedents* A long gestational period beginning around 1500 in Britain and Germany, and the 1600s in North America. A period of low levels of consumption in which '75–90% of the populace were self-sufficient, rural, and viscerally opposed to change' (1988: 122). Commerce was generally discredited but its standing improved as the benefits of trade became apparent.

2 *Modern marketing begins: the era of origins* Britain 1759; Germany and USA *ca* 1830. 'This period marked the beginning of *pervasive* attention to stimulating and meeting demand among *nearly all of society*' (1988: 122) Precipitated by the Industrial Revolution and the mass migration from the countryside to an urban environment potential markets had to be created through marketing techniques and activities.

3 *Building a superstructure: the era of institutional development* Britain 1850; Germany and USA *ca* 1870 – until 1919. 'During this period most of the major institutions and many of the practices of modern marketing first appeared' (1988: 122).

4 *Testing, turbulence, and growth: era of refinement and formalization* From 1930 to the present day. 'The era's most distinguishing characteristic, however, has been the further development, refinement, and formalisation of institutions and practices that were developed earlier' (1988: 122).

Fullerton's analysis reflects a growing interest in the history of marketing thought and confirms that 'modern marketing has a rich heritage worthy of our attention' (1988: 123). Whether one should substitute his conceptualization as contained in his complex flux model for the widely accepted production–sales–marketing eras model is not seen as an either/or choice. Indeed, Fullerton's emphasis on the origins and evolution of marketing thought and practice reflects the historical research approach and merits attention in its own right. By contrast the 'eras model' is seen, at least by this author, as serving a different purpose in that it seeks to distinguish between marketing as a practice and clearly present in both the production and sales eras, and marketing as a philosophy of business which shifts the emphasis from the producer's pursuit of profit as the primary objective to the achievement of customer satisfaction which, in the long run, is likely to achieve the same financial reward.

In other words the three eras model provides a convenient framework for summarizing changes in the dominant orientation of business management Thus it is a useful, albeit oversimplified model of the evolution of modern marketing or what I prefer to designate 'the rediscovery of marketing' (Baker 1976). In truth marketing has been around since the very first commercial exchange but there can be little doubt that until comparatively recently it has been of secondary or even tertiary importance to other more pressing imperatives in terms of increasing supply to meet the needs and wants of a rapidly expanding population. The objective of authors and teachers in using the three-stage evolutionary model has been to highlight major changes in the dominant orientation of business rather than to analyse in detail the much more complex processes which underlay and resulted in these changes. What is beyond doubt is the fact that from around 1960 onwards marketing thinking and practice has been dominated by the marketing management school of thought.

4 The marketing management school

The marketing management school which evolved in the late 1950s and early 1960s is inextricably linked with the concept of the marketing mix and an analytical approach to marketing management following the positivist sequence of Analysis, Planning, Control. As with most major paradigm shifts no single author/researcher can claim sole credit for the new phenomenon. Among those who contributed significantly to the new school of thought were Joel Dean, Peter Drucker, Ted Levitt, E. Jerome McCarthy, Neil Borden and Philip Kotler. Dean and Drucker writing in the early 1950s paved the way but it was McCarthy's *Basic Marketing* (1960) which first promoted what came to be known as the four Ps of marketing – the idea that the marketing manager's task was to develop unique solutions to competitive marketing problems by manipulating four major marketing factors – Product, Price, Place and Promotion. This idea of a 'marketing mix' (the four Ps) was elaborated on by Neil

Borden (1964), building on an earlier idea of James Culliton (1948), and confirmed by the appearance in 1967 of the first edition of Philip Kotler's bestselling *Marketing Management: Analysis, Planning and Control*. Levitt's contribution in distinguishing the essence of the marketing orientation/concept – a focus on customer needs – has already been referred to.

An authoritative review of the marketing management school is to be found in Frederick E. Webster Jnr's 1992 article in the *Journal of Marketing* ('The changing role of marketing in the corporation'). In his own words, 'the purpose of this article is to outline both the intellectual and the pragmatic roots of changes that are occurring in marketing, especially marketing management, as a body of knowledge, theory, and practice and to suggest the need for a new paradigm of the marketing function within the firm' (Webster 1992: 1).

While Webster's article recognizes the need for 'a new paradigm of the marketing function within the firm', in the opinion of many European scholars a much more radical reappraisal is called for which challenges the very roots of the marketing management school.

5 The European perspective

One of the leading critics of the marketing management school is French professor Giles Marion. Marion's views are contained in a paper 'The marketing management discourse: what's new since the 1960s?' (1993), which is 'an attempt to describe the formalisation of ideas which make up marketing management as a school of thought' (1993: 143), based upon the content of the most popular marketing textbooks (American and European).

Marion argues that 'marketing as a discipline, should show greater humility by presenting its prescriptions in a more prudent manner, and by describing more systematically the interaction between supply and demand and the organisational consequences that follow' (1993: 166). In conclusion he expresses the view that, while the normative theory of marketing management may well have had a useful impact on managerial thinking and practice 'there has been nothing new since the 1960s or even well before' (1993: 166).

While Marion's critique strikes at the very heart of the marketing management school promoted by Americans it is comparatively mild compared with the trenchant criticism expressed by Evert Gummesson, a leading member of the Scandinavian School. In Gummesson's view 'the traditional textbooks do not satisfactorily reflect reality' and he proposes six objections to support his thesis (1993):

1 Textbook presentations of marketing are based on limited real world data – specifically, they are largely concerned with mass marketed, packaged consumer goods.
2 Goods account for a minor part of all marketing, but the textbook presentations are focused on goods; services are treated as a special case.
3 Marketing to consumers dominates textbooks, while industrial/business marketing is treated as a special case.
4 The textbook presentations are a patchwork; new knowledge is piled on top of existing knowledge, but not integrated with it.
5 The textbooks have a clever pedagogical design; the form is better than the content.
6 The Europeans surrender to the USA and its marketing gurus and do not adequately promote their own original contributions.

In sum, Gummesson argues that US textbooks represent a colonization of thought and that this thought excludes or ignores much of the development in marketing thinking which has occurred in the fields of industrial and services marketing in Europe in the past twenty years or more. To some extent the blame must rest with the Europeans for failing to promote their ideas in the USA but the dismissive, not-invented-here attitudes of American academics who act as gatekeepers to US-based publications must also bear some of the blame.

Many of the views expressed by Marion and Gummesson are echoed in the work of Christian Gronröos (another leading member of the Scandinavian School). In Grönroos' view (1994) the majority of marketing academics and textbooks treat marketing as a subject which emerged in the 1960s and is founded upon the concept of the marketing mix and the four Ps of Product, Price, Place and Promotion (McCarthy 1960) which comprised it. As a consequence 'empirical studies of what the key marketing variables are, and how they are perceived and used by marketing managers have been neglected. Moreover, structure has been vastly favoured over process considerations' (Kent 1986).

While McCarthy's simplification of Borden's original conceptualization of the marketing mix has obvious pedagogical attractions, its application appears best suited to mass markets for consumer packaged goods underpinned by sophisticated distribution channels and commercial mass media. Indeed, this is the context or setting of many marketing courses and texts, but it is clearly representative of a limited aspect of the domain and process of marketing.

However, the concept of the marketing mix is more seriously flawed. To begin with the paradigm is a production-oriented definition in the sense that its approach is that customers are persons *to* whom something is done rather than persons *for* whom something is done. (See Dixon and Blois 1983; Grönroos 1989, 1990.) A second deficiency is that while McCarthy recognized the interactive nature of the four Ps 'the model itself does not explicitly include any interactive elements. Furthermore, it does not indicate the nature and scope of such interactions' (Grönroos 1994).

However, perhaps the major deficiency of the four Ps approach is that it defines marketing as a functional activity in its own right and so creates the potential for conflict with other functional areas, discourages persons from becoming involved in marketing because it is the preserve of the marketing department and, as a result, can frustrate or compromise the adoption of the marketing concept.

Grönroos sees the four Ps as a direct development from the microeconomic theory of imperfect competition developed by Robinson and Chamberlin in the 1930s, but argues that the separation of the four Ps model from its theoretical foundations left it without roots. Indeed, Grönroos goes even further and argues that 'the introduction of the 4 Ps of the marketing mix with their simplistic view of reality can be characterised as a step back to the level of, in a sense equally simplistic, microeconomic theory of the 1930s'. This observation is largely prompted by the apparent failure of marketing academics in the USA to detect the evolution of the 'Copenhagen School's' *parameter theory*. Building upon the work of Frisch (1933), Von Stackelberg (1939), Kjaer-Hansen (1945) and Rasmussen (1955), Gosta Mickwitz observed:

When empirically based works on marketing mechanisms show that the enterprise uses a number of different parameters markedly distinct from each other, a theory of the behaviour of the enterprise in the market will be very unrealistic if it is content to deal only with ... (a few) ... of them. We have therefore tried throughout to pay attention to the presence of a number of different methods which firms employ to increase their sales.
(Mickwitz 1959: 217)

Grönroos (1994) explains further: 'The interactive nature of the marketing variables was explicitly recognised and accounted for in parameter theory by means of varying market elasticities of the parameters over the life of the product life cycle'.

At the same time that the four Ps was becoming the established 'theory' or normative approach to marketing in the USA and many other countries, new theories and models were emerging in Europe – specifically, the interaction network approach to industrial marketing and the marketing of services (1960s) and, more recently, the concept of relationship marketing.

The interaction/network approach originated in Uppsala University in Sweden during the 1960s and was subsequently taken up in many countries following the establishment of the IMP (Industrial Marketing and Purchasing) Group. As Grönroos explains:

Between the parties in a network various interactions take place, where exchanges and adaptation to each other occur. A flow of goods and information as well as financial and social exchanges takes place in the network. (See, for example, Håkansson 1982 Johanson and Mattson 1985 and Kock 1991.) In such a network the role and forms of marketing are not very clear. All exchanges, all sorts of interactions have an impact on the position of the parties in the network. The interactions are not necessarily initiated by the seller – the marketer according to the marketing mix paradigm – and they may continue over a long period of time, for example, for several years.
(Grönroos 1994)

The interaction/network model recognizes that exchanges are not the exclusive preserve of professional marketers and may, indeed, involve numerous other members of the interacting organizations, some of whom may well have more influence and impact on the relationship than the functional specialists.

In the 1970s interest in the marketing of services developed simultaneously in the USA and Europe. But, while the four Ps framework continued to prevail in the USA, in Scandinavia and Finland the Scandinavian School of Services saw the marketing of services as an integral element of overall management. Grönroos and Gummesson have been strong proponents of this School and have written extensively on the subject.

The interaction and network approach to industrial marketing and modern service marketing approaches 'clearly views marketing as an interactive process in a social context where *relationship building* is a vital cornerstone' (Grönroos 1994). Grönroos argues that this approach is similar to the system-based approaches to marketing of the 1950s (e.g. Alderson 1957) and contrasts strongly with the clinical approach of the four Ps paradigm which makes sellers active and buyers passive. As noted earlier, the latter emphasis tends to put exchange relationships into the hands of the professional marketers which may psychologically alienate other members of an organization from becoming involved. This is a far cry from Drucker's (1954) observation that the sole purpose of the business is to create customers!

As a consequence of rapid advances in both manufacturing (flexible manufacturing, CAD, CAM) and information technology, the mass consumer markets suited to the four Ps approach have become fragmented and call for flexible and adaptable marketing approaches. In the 1980s the response to this need has been the emergence of *relationship marketing*. Grönroos refers to his own (1990) definition of relationship marketing: 'Marketing is to establish, maintain, and enhance relationships with customers and other partners, at a profit, so that the objectives of the parties involved are met. This is achieved by a mutual exchange and fulfilment of promises'. While more extended and explicit this definition is essentially similar to that proposed by Baker (1976) a number of years earlier: 'Marketing is concerned with mutually satisfying exchange relationships'. Similarly, Baker (and other authors) have argued consistently for the need to regard marketing both as a philosophy of business and a business function. As a business function responsible for coordinating and executing the implementation of a marketing plan, marketing is likely to continue to find the marketing mix model a useful one, albeit that the four Ps is an oversimplified version of the original concept. It is, of course, important to emphasize that continuing to use such an organizational and planning framework is in no way inimical to the newly fashionable emphasis on relationship marketing as contrasted to the prior emphasis on a transactional model.

Although Grönroos and others see relationship marketing as being at an early stage of its conceptual development, there can be no doubt that its very existence has only recently been recognized in the USA, this is not to say that the practice is new. In fact, it is the very essence of the true marketing concept and can be identified as intrinsic to buyer-seller interactions since commercial exchanges were first initiated. Buyers have always looked for reliable sources of supply at a fair price as this reduces the dissonance and uncertainty of having to consider every single transaction as an entirely new decision. Similarly, sellers recognize that there are increased opportunities for long-term survival and profit if they can establish a customer franchise and repeat purchasing behaviour. That said, there can be no doubt that there are radically different interpretations of capitalism and the market economy, one of which emphasizes long-term relationships, the other the one-off transaction.

It is perhaps only with the collapse of the centrally planned and controlled command economies of Eastern Europe and the Soviet Union that the existence of two models of capitalism has come into sharper relief and focus. Based on a book by Michel Albert (1991), Christian Dussart (1994) highlights the differences between the Anglo-Saxon model of capitalism, as practised in the UK and USA, which is essentially short-term and transactionally based and the Alpine/Germanic model, which also embraces Scandinavia (and Japan), that emphasizes long-term relationships as the source of buyer satisfaction and seller profitability.

6 So what is marketing?

At the 1993 UK Marketing Education Group Conference a group of researchers from the Henley Management College (Gibson et al. 1993) presented their findings of a content and correspondence analysis of approximately 100 definitions of marketing in an attempt to answer the question 'What is marketing?' Specifically, the authors set out to 'shed some light on the nature of the process of defining marketing, to identify strong and emerging themes, and to develop a map of the territory'. By using content analysis to evaluate the definitions collected and using these findings as input to a correspondence analysis the authors provide both a qualitative and quantitative analysis of how scholars have defined marketing over the years.

To begin with a collection of approximately 100 explicit marketing definitions were collected from textbooks, journals and institute/association publications which spanned the twentieth century. The vast majority of these definitions were academic and originated in the USA, UK and Europe. Themes were selected as the unit of assessment and five clusters were established as:

1. object of marketing;
2. nature of the relationship;
3. outcomes;
4. application;
5. philosophy or (versus) function.

The authors describe in some detail how each of these themes was derived and how definitions falling within them have changed in approach and emphasis over time. However, 'in order to simplify the definitions of various authors, and give more relevance to the five themes identified earlier, some of the definitions gathered and analysed for content were subjected to a process of correspondence analysis'. In essence, correspondence analysis is a graphical technique which enables one to develop a two-dimensional plot indicating the degree of similarity or correspondence between rows or columns of data which have similar patterns or counts. Using the authors as rows and their perspectives on the themes as columns the map reproduced as Figure 3 was produced.

Figure 3 Marketing definitins: a map of the territory

They explain:

> The authors' perspectives on the original themes were constructed as dichotomies and include, first 'profit and non-profit', which related to the outcomes and application themes; secondly, 'micro and macro', which translated across to philosophy or function; thirdly, 'static and dynamic' and 'open and closed' which referred to the relationship theme and to some extent provided some insight into the content and nature of the whole definition; and, finally, two additional dichotomies were included, 'positive and normative', namely, whether the definitions described what exists or prescribed what 'ought' to happen, and whether the definition was 'explicit or implicit'.
>
> (Gibson *et al.* 1993)

Based upon both the qualitative and quantitative analyses certain conclusions may be derived.

1. Changes have occurred across all five content themes indicating significant evolution in the concept of marketing since its earliest definition.
2. The greatest change has occurred in the 'nature of the relationship' theme (i.e. between provider and user, from one-way narrow, discrete transactions to the recognition and positioning of relationships as a key strategy resource'). This change is also reflected in the other themes, particularly 'philosophy or function', and marks the moderation of economic explanations of consumption behaviour through the admission of concepts derived from psychology and sociology.
3. Changes in the marketing environment have resulted in a broadening and softening of the original concept and its transfer into other domains – services, not for profit, etc.
4. 'Marketing' has shown itself to be adaptable, flexible, international and open. But Gibson *et al.* warn that 'this latitude has allowed ambiguity to creep into its definition and cause confusion. Definitional clarity is essential in the future'.

In conclusion, Gibson *et al.* offer three further points prompted by their analysis:

1. Marketing and its guardians continue to foster its open and innovative culture.
2. A single definition is not aimed for as its existence would probably discourage future development of the subject.
3. None the less, greater rigour should be given to the formulation of definitions in future.

7 Summary

In this article we have endeavoured to shed some light on the nature and scope of 'marketing'. As we have seen, and as is apparent from the sheer size of this Encyclopedia, marketing is a large and complex subject which covers a multitude of economic and social activities. Many of these are described in some detail in the following entries. That said, the practice of marketing is founded on a very simple philosophy, that of 'mutually satisfying (commercial) exchange relationships'.

In the 1990s 'Relationship marketing' has become the dominant theme almost everywhere, despite its somewhat belated recognition in the USA. As our review has attempted to show it was ever so but, depending upon the existing balance between supply and demand at any point in time, one or other of the parties to an exchange is likely to exercise more control over the relationship than the other. If this is the producer/seller it does not necessarily mean that they are production or sales oriented and insensitive to consumer needs. Indeed, it is a truism that all successful businesses are marketing orientated – if they were not meeting and satisfying customer needs profitably they would not be successful. What matters is the state of mind of the producer/seller – their philosophy of business. If this philosophy includes a concern for the customers' needs and wants, an appreciation of the benefits and satisfactions which are looked for, a genuine effort to establish a dialogue and build a long-term relationship then this is a marketing philosophy irrespective of whether or not the organization possesses any personnel or function designated as 'marketing'.

In the articles which follow many facets and aspects of the subject are examined and explored by internationally recognized experts. Taken together these provide a comprehensive overview of and introduction to the body of knowledge and practice of marketing.

While personal perspectives may vary the core proposition remains – marketing is concerned with the identification, creation and maintenance of mutually satisfying exchange relationships.

MICHAEL J. BAKER
UNIVERSITY OF STRATHCLYDE

References

(References cited in the text marked *)

* Albert, Michel (1991) *Capitalisme contre Capitalisme*, Paris: Seuil, L'Histoire Immédiate.
* Alderson, W. (1957) *Marketing Behavior and Executive Action*, Homewood, IL: Irwin.
* Baker, Michael J. (1976) 'Evolution of the marketing concept', in Michael J. Baker (ed.) *Marketing Theory and Practice*, London: Macmillan.
* Baker, Michael J. (1980) 'Marketing maxims', *Advertising* 66: Winter.
* Baker, Michael J. (ed.) (1994) *The Marketing Book*, 3rd edn, Oxford: Butterworth-Heinemann Ltd.
* Borden, Neil H. (1964) 'The concept of the marketing mix', *Journal of Advertising Research/*
* Chamberlin, E. J. (1933) *The Theory of Monopolistic Competition*, Cambridge, MA: Harvard University Press.
* Culliton, James W. (1948) *The Management of Marketing Costs*, Andover, MA The Andover Press Ltd.
* Dean, Joel (1951) *Managerial Economics*, Englewood Cliffs, NJ: Prentice-Hall.
* Dixon, D. F. and Blois, K. J. (1983) 'Some limitations of the 4 Ps as a paradigm for marketing', *Proceedings*, Marketing Education Group Conference, Cranfield.
* Drucker, Peter (1954) *The Practice of Management*, New York: Harper & Row.
* Dussart, Christian (1994) 'Capitalism versus capitalism', in Michael J. Baker (ed.) *Perspectives on Marketing Management*, Vol. 4, Chichester: John Wiley & Sons.
* Frisch, R. (1933) 'Monopole – Polypole – la notion de la force dans l'économic', *Nationalokonomisk Tidskrift* Denmark.
* Fullerton, Ronald A. (1988) 'How modern is modern marketing? Marketing's evolution and the myth of the production era', *Journal of Marketing* 52, January: 108–25.
* Galbraith, J. K. (1958) *The Affluent Society*, Harmondsworth: Penguin.
* Gibson, Helen, Tynan, Caroline and Pitt, Leyland (1993) 'What is marketing?: a qualitative and quantitative analysis of marketing decisions', *Proceedings*, Marketing Education Group Conference, Loughborough.
* Grönroos, C. (1989) 'Defining marketing: a market-oriented approach', *European Journal of Marketing* 23: 52–60.
* Grönroos, C. (1990) *Service Management and Marketing. Managing the Moments of Truth in Service Competition*, Lexington, MA: Free Press/Lexington Books.
* Grönroos, Christian (1994) 'Quo vadis marketing? Toward a relationship marketing paradigm', *Journal of Marketing Management* 10.5: 1–13.
* Gummesson, E. (1993) 'Broadening and specifying relationship marketing', invited paper, Monash Colloquium on Relationship Marketing, Monash University, Melbourne, Australia, 1–4 August 1993.
* Håkansson, H. (ed.) (1982) *International Marketing and Purchasing of Industrial Goods*, New York, NY: Wiley.
* Johanson, J. and Mattson, L.-G. (1985) 'Marketing investments and market investments in industrial networks', *International Journal of Research in Marketing* 4.
* Keith, R. J. (1960) 'The marketing revolution', *Journal of Marketing* 24: 35–8.
* Kent, R. A. (1986) 'Faith in 4 Ps: an alternative', *Journal of Marketing Management* 2.
* Kjaer-Hansen, M. (1945) *Afsaetningsokonomi* [Marketing], Copenhagen: Erhvervsokonomisk Forlag.
* Kock, S. (1991) *A Strategic Process for Gaining External Resources through Long-lasting Relationships*, Helsingfors/Vara, Finland: Swedish School of Economics and Business Administration.
* Kotler, Philip (1967) *Marketing Management: Analysis, Planning and Control*, Englewood Cliffs, NJ: Prentice-Hall.
* Levitt, T. (1960) 'Marketing myopia', *Harvard Business Review* July–August.
* McCarthy, E. Jerome (1960) *Basic Marketing: A Managerial Approach*, Homewood, Ill: Irwin.
* Marion, G. (1993) 'The marketing management discourse: what's new since the 1960s?', in Michael J. Baker (ed.) *Perspectives on Marketing Management*, Vol. 3, Chichester: John Wiley & Sons.
* Maslow, A. H. (1943) 'A theory of human motivation', *Psychological Review* July: 370–96.
* Mickwitz, Gosta (1959) *Marketing and Competition*, Helsingfors, Finland: Societas Scientarium Fennica.
* Rasmussen, Arne (1955) *Pristeori eller parameterteori – studier ombring virksomhedens afsaetning*, Copenhagen: Erhvervsokonomisk Forlag.
* Robinson, Joan (1933) *The Economics of Imperfect Competition*, London: Macmillan.
* Rostow, W. W. (1962) *The Process of Economic Growth*, 2nd edn, New York: W.W. Norton.

* Smith, Adam (1776) *The Wealth of Nations*, Andrew Skinner (ed.) (1970), Harmondsworth: Pelican Books.
* Stackelberg, H. von (1939) 'Theorie der Vertreibspolitik and der Qualitätsvariation' *Schmollers Jahrbuck* 63/1.
* Webster, Frederick E. Jr (1992) 'The changing role of marketing in the corporation', *Journal of Marketing* 56: 1–17.

Historical research in marketing

1 Introduction
2 Recording the facts
3 Laying the foundations
4 The emerging discipline
5 Conclusion

Overview

The purpose of this entry is to review historical research in marketing. This includes not only the history of marketing thought (e.g. ideas, theories, schools of thought), but also of marketing content (the activities, practices and processes of marketing). Of course, marketing thought is often practice-driven and marketing practice is (hopefully) not thoughtless! However, this initial categorization is a useful one when reviewing the larger field of historical research in marketing (Savitt 1980).

This review includes research that deals with marketing from an historical perspective, which involves the description, analysis or explanation of events through time (Savitt 1980: 53). An historical perspective also includes a thorough, systematic and sophisticated awareness of change or continuity over time, and of the contexts of place, situation and time in which change or continuity occurs (Fullerton 1987: 98). That perspective characterizes most of the research reviewed here. In some instances it was difficult to assess the extent to which a publication dealt with change or explained events through time, since it may have essentially described marketing at some point in history (rather than through time) and only implicitly was there comparison with some other era.

Historical research in marketing or, more specifically, by marketing scholars published primarily in marketing or marketing-related publications, provided the literature base for this review. The search included all of the major marketing journals, business and economics history periodicals, a computerized bibliographic search, and a survey of participants at the first three Marketing History Conferences (1983, 1985, 1987). This produced a bibliography of approximately 400 publications. Because of space limitations, however, all but key citations of conference proceedings and of journal articles have been omitted. It was a thorough, yet not exhaustive review of the literature. Without the relatively narrow definition of historical research in marketing used here, the bibliography could have been longer. Nevertheless, this more restricted set is thought to reflect the mainstream of historical research in marketing.

1 Introduction

The structure of this review loosely follows three themes: chronological, topical and historiographic. The first theme is, perhaps, not surprising. The discussion throughout the review follows chronologically the development of historical research in marketing, starting with a publication in 1933 by Paul Converse.

The second theme followed here is, of course, the topical one including marketing and marketing thought (referred to above) as well as methodology. Furthermore, within the history of marketing thought are works examining the development of the literature, biographies of pioneer scholars, the roles played by important organizations and institutions, the history of university teaching, and, of course, the development of concepts, theories and schools of thought. Marketing history (practices, activities and processes) includes the various marketing functions (the four Ps) and their component activities, marketing research, retailing, wholesaling, company or industry histories where the focus is on marketing, biographies of important marketing practitioners and macromarketing issues such as the regulation of marketing. Finally, methodology includes historiographic issues such as data sources, historical method, philosophy of history and the justification of historical research in marketing.

Within this topical theme there are some noteworthy omissions from this review. First, many company and industry histories include discussion of marketing practices, especially histories of retailing institutions (e.g. Hower's

History of Macy's of New York, 1858–1919 (1946)). However, such histories seldom have as their primary purpose an examination of marketing. Therefore, except for some recent examples from conference proceedings and from the periodic literature, these have been excluded from this review. Also, although not that recent, Hidy (1970) presented an excellent review of such work. A second (qualified) exception is advertising history. Again, a somewhat dated bibliography and review of this topic has been published (Pollay 1979). Since then several books on advertising history have been written, although mostly by historians outside the marketing discipline (Pollay 1988a: 195). Therefore, the attention was restricted here primarily to the advertising history which has appeared more recently in the marketing and marketing-related literature. Finally, the history of consumption has also been reviewed more recently and quite thoroughly by a number of scholars (Rassuli and Hollander 1986a; McCracken 1987; Sheth and Gross 1988; Rassuli 1991; Smith and Lux 1993).

Therefore, the topics mentioned above will not be given the attention otherwise warranted in a complete review of historical research in marketing. One final exception is also noteworthy. A good deal of the earliest research by marketing scholars in this century, for example, Nystrom's (1915) *The Economics of Retailing*, followed an historical perspective. However, since this research appeared before there were well recognized traditions of business and marketing history, and has also been reviewed elsewhere (Jones 1987a; Jones and Monieson 1990) it has been excluded from this survey.

The final theme followed in this review is an historiographic or methodological one. In fact there is a strong correlation between the chronological development of this literature (mentioned above) and the sophistication of the historical analysis employed. So, for instance, during the 1930s when historical research in marketing began to be published, the work focused mainly on identifying and collecting historical facts – putting things on the record, so to speak. More recently some of the historical research being done is quite sophisticated in its analysis, synthesizing more sources of primary data and providing a higher level of interpretation both in the traditional story-telling approach and the social scientific approach (Jones 1993).

2 Recording the facts

With the founding in 1915 of the National Association of Teachers of Advertising (NATA) leading to the formation of the American Marketing Association (AMA) in 1937, there emerged an important impetus for historical work. These first attempts formally to organize marketing scholars led naturally to reflection about the origins and development of this emerging discipline. At the same time, these events provided specialized outlets for the publication of such historical reflection. Thus, there were a number of attempts to put things on the record.

History of marketing thought

From the early 1930s to the late 1950s historical research in marketing was dominated by the study of marketing thought. During this period attention was focused on tracing the earliest literature (Converse 1933, 1945; Applebaum 1947, 1952; Coolsen 1947; Bartels 1951; Maynard 1951) and marketing courses taught in American universities (Hagerty 1936; Maynard 1941; Weld 1941; Litman 1950; Bartels 1951; Hardy 1954). The earliest historical study included in this review was Converse's (1933) 'The first decade of marketing literature' published in the *NATMA Bulletin*. Converse's article was typical in its attempt to identify historically significant events. In his opinion the 'first modern books on marketing' were Nystrom's (1915) *Economics of Retailing* and A.W. Shaw's (1915) *Some Problems in Market Distribution* (Converse 1933: 1).

Other early historical studies focused on the individuals and organizations that pioneered the development of the discipline (Agnew 1941; Bartels 1951; Converse 1959b), and a series of 23 biographical sketches published in the *Journal of Marketing* between 1956 and 1962 was later compiled in book form (Wright and Dimsdale 1974). Bartels' (1951) article entitled 'Influences on the development of marketing thought, 1900–1923' was seminal in that it was an early attempt to go beyond a simple chronicle of 'firsts'. It drew upon numerous interviews of pioneer scholars in order to examine some of the sources of early marketing ideas. Bartels' article was also the most ambitious historical analysis at that time based, as it was, on his (1941) doctoral dissertation at Ohio State University.

During the 1950s a trend began towards focusing on the history of marketing concepts (Kelley 1956; Breen 1959), theories (McGarry 1953), and schools of thought (Brown 1951). Cassels (1936) had earlier examined the influence of significant schools of economic thought on marketing, but it was not until the 1950s that marketing ideas were developed enough to warrant a retrospective. An important collection of such articles was published in 1951 under the title *Changing Perspectives in Marketing*. It claimed to be 'one of the few, if not the only one, in which a series of papers has been compiled to give historical treatment and perspective to the development of marketing [thought]' (Wales 1951: v). This included topics such as retailing, sales management, marketing research and marketing theory. Its contributors were eminent scholars in marketing – most had been recipients of the AMA's prestigious Paul D. Converse Award.

Marketing history

There was less research done during this early period on marketing history, most of which focused on the history of retailing and wholesaling (Jones 1936; Marburg 1951; Nystrom 1951; Barger 1955). Barger's (1955) book, entitled *Distribution's Place in the American Economy Since 1869*, examined the changing role of wholesale and retail sectors in the American economy from 1869 to 1950. It was a unique study of the cost and output of distribution, and of the relative importance of wholesale and retail sectors as measured by the proportion of the labour force engaged in each.

A more general history of marketing which was distinctive both in its scope of subject matter and in its historical perspective was Hotchkiss's (1938) *Milestones of Marketing*. Using the American Marketing Association's definition of marketing to guide his choice of topics, Hotchkiss traced 'the most important steps in the evolution of marketing' (Hotchkiss 1938: vii) back to ancient Rome and Greece through medieval England to modern North American practices (mostly retailing, advertising and merchandising). Only recently have marketing historians again attempted to examine the marketing practices of such early periods in history (e.g. Dixon 1979; Friedman 1984).

Another marketing history which complemented the Hotchkiss book by focusing on marketing practices of the twentieth century was Converse's (1959a) *Fifty Years of Marketing in Retrospect*. This was written as a companion to his (1959b) study of the beginnings of marketing thought. Converse described his marketing history book as 'the story of business and particularly of market distribution as I have seen it and as I have studied it' (Converse 1959a: vi). In addition to marketing practices such as advertising and promotion, pricing, merchandising and others, Converse described the changing economic conditions and technological developments during the early twentieth century which influenced such practices.

Throughout this early period historical research was mostly descriptive as marketers focused on recording the facts of marketing history and the history of marketing thought. The most prolific and perhaps the most important contributor during this era was Paul D. Converse, whose two monographs published in 1959 seemed to typify historical research in marketing to that point in time.

3 Laying the foundations

The 1960s was a transition period with fewer, but more in-depth, publications. A number of significant works and events laid the foundation for the growth of interest in historical research evident today. For example, during the early 1960s successive conferences of the American Marketing Association featured tracks on historical research (Greyser 1963; Smith 1965). Most of the papers published from those sessions offered justifications for doing such work and in that way may have helped to legitimate subsequent historical studies. Although there was a noticeable decline in the number of published works in the periodic literature, a number of important books were published. Four books appeared in succession on the history of marketing thought and an important collection of work on seventeenth-, eighteenth-, and nineteenth-century marketing practices.

History of marketing thought

Converse's (1959b) *The Beginnings of Marketing Thought in the United States* served as a transition point, both in time and in depth of analysis, in the history of marketing thought. One of Converse's students, Frank Coolsen, followed with a dissertation on the marketing ideas of nineteenth-century liberal economists, which was published in 1960 under the title *Marketing Thought in the United States in the Late Nineteenth Century*. Essentially, this was an expansion of some of the material in Converse's book.

Two other books on the history of marketing thought which complemented each other were Bartels' (1962) *The Development of Marketing Thought*, and Schwartz's (1963) *Development of Marketing Theory*. Bartels' book was essentially a chronology of published literature, university courses and events that had played a role in the development of marketing thought since 1900. Schwartz was more concerned with specific theories in marketing. His was a more concentrated and rigorous follow-up to the 1951 collection edited by Hugh Wales. In addition to examining the historical development of well-recognized marketing theories such as retail gravitation, regional theory, marketing functions and Alderson's functionalist theory, Schwartz included chapters examining the potential contribution of fields such as social physics and game theory. This made the book somewhat unorthodox and may explain why it has been largely ignored by students of the history of marketing thought. Bartels' book, on the other hand, has since been updated twice (1976, 1988) and has become a staple of most doctoral seminars in North America.

In addition to those general works, there were studies of specific concepts and theories during the 1960s. Examples included Hollander's historical analysis of retailing institutions (1960, 1963a, 1966), and historical examinations of marketing management by Keith (1960), Lazer (1965), and La Londe and Morrison (1967).

During the 1960s some researchers began to integrate marketing history with the history of marketing thought. Such work went beyond the simplistic approach of earlier writings by using the history of marketing practice to interpret the development of marketing thought. An example of this was Hollander's work cited above, and more recently his reexamination of the origins of the marketing concept (1986b). That distinctive approach to historical research has recently been described by Rassuli (1988).

Marketing history

As the marketing discipline moved away from the institutional and commodity schools of thought and began to popularize marketing functions through the managerial approach, research in marketing history reflected that trend. This included historical research in advertising and promotion (McKendrick 1960; Curti 1967), product innovation (Silk and Stern 1963), and personal selling (Hollander 1963b, 1964).

A broad range of marketing history, especially in economic development, regulation, institutions and advertising was covered in Shapiro and Doody's (1968) *Readings in the History of American Marketing: Settlement to Civil War*. As editors of this extensive collection, Shapiro and Doody stated that their objective was to 'awaken the interest of students of marketing in history and historical analysis' (1968: 12). Their book of readings and Bartels' (1962) *Development of Marketing Thought* were undoubtedly the most important publications during the 1960s. In both of those books the level of interpretation and scale of effort were unprecedented.

Ironically, as the 1960s drew to a close there seemed to be a decline of interest in historical research in marketing. The marketing discipline had been moving during the 1960s in a more quantitative, scientific direction and perhaps historical research seemed less rigorous.

4 The emerging discipline

The quantity and quality of historical research in marketing have grown enormously since the early 1980s. Of course, much of this work is accounted for by the Marketing History Conferences.

In 1983 Michigan State University began hosting the Marketing History Conference in an effort to provide a biannual platform for the growing number of scholars interested in the subject. At that time one of the conference organizers suggested that historical research was something marketing professors did only after they had received tenure! If this was ever true it is certainly no longer the case. The conference regularly includes the work of senior and junior faculty as well as doctoral students. Attendance has grown with each successive conference and has truly become an international gathering. There is also a regularly published newsletter, *Retrospectives in Marketing*, which is affiliated with the Conference.

Even if we exclude the papers published in the Proceedings of the Marketing History Conferences, the increase in the number of publications in this emerging discipline is significant. Top journals in marketing such as the *Journal of Marketing*, *Journal of Consumer Research*, and *Journal of the Academy of Marketing Science* have been regularly publishing historical research. The *Journal of the Academy of Marketing Science* (1990) featured a special issue on the history of marketing thought and the *Journal of Macromarketing* now regularly publishes historical research. There is a new maturity in this emerging discipline and a breadth to the research evident in developments across all three major topical categories of historical research in marketing.

Methodology

If one were looking for a single publication which signalled the emergence (or rather, the revival) of history as a 'legitimate' field within the marketing discipline, it might be Ronald Savitt's (1980) 'Historical research in marketing' published in the *Journal of Marketing*. In substance it was a statement of the rationale and method for historical research, although in the latter, only one of a range of possible approaches. In spirit, however, it was both a symbol of the legitimacy of doing historical research by marketing scholars, and a challenge to them to do so. As a statement on method, Savitt's article initiated a much needed discussion in the marketing literature about the theory and methods of historical scholarship.

There is a wide range of methodological approaches within historiography from positivistic (e.g. Hempel 1959) to hermeneutic (e.g. Collingwood 1974: 17–40). These approaches have recently been summarized as they apply to historical research in marketing by Jones (1993). Savitt proposed what was essentially a positivistic method of historical research based on hypothesis testing (1980, 1982, 1984) and a search for causal relations (1988: 119). Kumcu (1987) has also outlined an historical method close to Savitt's in its concern with probable causes, hypothesis testing and relative validity of laws. A more recent, and perhaps more thorough, presentation of this social scientific approach to historical research is given by Smith and Lux (1993). They discuss the ontological and epistemological assumptions of social scientific history and present a model of research design and analysis in the context of historical research into consumer behaviour.

On the other hand, Firat (1986) suggested going beyond such methods – that explanation and understanding of marketing history requires the interpretation and reflection characteristic of a hermeneutic approach. Fullerton (1987) distinguishes between the philosophy of history, which is concerned with epistemological and ontological issues, and historical method, which follows from the philosophy of history in which one believes. Fullerton's own approach to history is derived from the philosophy of German historicism (Fullerton 1986) which is based on assumptions very different from those of a positivistic historical method. For Fullerton, the basic elements of historical method include systematic doubt, flexible use of analytical tools, use of multiple data sources, creative and critical synthesis and a narrative form of description (Fullerton 1987: 112). Consistent with the traditional approach, Stern (1990) has described the use of literary criticism as an analytical tool which complements historical method by providing additional insights when interpreting historical data.

In the echoes of those discussions about the philosophy and method of marketing history there have also been voices calling for more historical research (Savitt 1980, 1982; Fullerton 1987) and providing rationales for using marketing history in teaching (Nevett 1989; Witkowski 1989). Nevett (1991) has also described how historical method relates to marketing decision making and offered recommendations for applying historical thinking to marketing practice. Finally, rounding out the discussion of methodology are descriptions of various data sources for historical research in marketing (Rassuli and Hollander 1986a; Pollay 1988a).

Marketing history

Until the 1980s historical research in marketing was dominated by interest in the history of marketing thought. That emphasis has since changed, with a good deal of research now being conducted on the history of marketing activities and functions such as advertising (Nevett 1982; Pollay 1985; Stern 1988; Gross and Sheth 1989), product simplification strategy (Hollander 1984a), channel relations (Marx 1985), retailers' pricing strategies (Dickinson 1988) and segmentation strategy (Fullerton 1985; Tedlow 1990; Hollander and Germain 1992).

Two important historical studies of marketing segmentation strategy were presented in Tedlow's (1990) *New and Improved: The Story of Mass Marketing in America* and Hollander and Germain's (1992) *Was There a Pepsi Generation Before Pepsi Discovered it?* In its subject matter Tedlow's book, in fact, goes well beyond the history of segmentation strategy. In his words the book is about 'how some of America's most important corporations have battled for dominance in key consumer product markets during the past hundred years' (Tedlow 1990: 4). Those corporations include Coca-Cola and Pepsi, Ford and General Motors, A&P, and Sears, Montgomery Ward. Nevertheless, Tedlow's main theme is the evolution of market structure in America from a fragmented market in the nineteenth century, to a mass market, and then to market segmentation. For example, with respect to the soft drink industry Tedlow concludes 'There was no such thing as the Pepsi Generation until Pepsi created it' (1990: 372). It is that statement which is turned around in the title of Hollander and Germain's (1992) in-depth examination of the history of segmentation practices. They disagree with Tedlow's three-phase theory and provide detailed evidence of earlier (than those documented by Tedlow) segmentation practices as well as conceptualizations of segmentation by early marketing scholars.

Tedlow's books also led to two important collections of work on marketing history. *The Rise and Fall of Mass Marketing* (Tedlow and Jones 1993) presents a collection of 11 articles by a distinguished group of international scholars which examines the similarities and differences between the evolution of mass marketing in the USA and other nations. This comparative marketing history focuses on the UK and the USA, but includes Australia and Japan as well. In that way it marks for the first time a significant collection of marketing history which is truly international in content and authorship. The range of industries covered is equally broad and includes automobiles, computers, banking, wheat marketing, food retailing and Scotch whisky. The latter two subjects help set the stage for the second collection of work stimulated, albeit indirectly, by Tedlow's book. *Adding Value: Brands and Marketing in Food and Drink* (Jones and Morgan 1994) is similarly international and comparative in its focus, but takes a more in-depth look at the history of branding. More specifically, this volume focuses on food and drink, exploring the marketing histories of Coca-Cola, Kellogg, Johnnie Walker, Foster's Lager, Sainsbury's and Carlsberg. Additional articles round out the collection by dealing historically with conceptual dimensions of branding such as the nature and functions of branding as well as its value to society.

Within marketing history, advertising has become a leading topic of interest. A number of individuals have contributed to this research, but the work of two authors is especially prominent. Terence Nevett has written extensively about the history of British advertising (1982, 1985, 1988a, 1988c, 1988d). Much of Nevett's work is comparative and cross cultural, for example, his study with Fullerton of societal perceptions of advertising in Britain and Germany (Fullerton and Nevett 1986), and of American influences on British advertising (Nevett 1988a), as well as British influences on American advertising (1988c). At times his work has taken on a macromarketing perspective (Nevett 1985, 1988b; Fullerton and Nevett 1986) by looking at the impact of advertising on society.

Others have also contributed to the study of British advertising history, focusing on specific companies (Ferrier 1986; Seaton 1986), professional sales promotion organizations (Legh 1986), and self-regulation in the advertising industry (Miracle and Nevett 1988).

A second individual whose work on advertising history has been prominent is Richard Pollay. During the late 1970s Pollay observed that there were very few significant sources of advertising history (1979: 8) and those had been written outside the marketing discipline. To correct that situation, he outlined an ambitious research programme for advertising history, including the justification, research methods and data sources required for such work (Pollay 1977, 1978, 1979). Having identified and developed important archival sources (Pollay 1979, 1988a), he conducted a rigorous content analysis of twentieth-century American print advertising in order to identify the portrayed values (Belk and Pollay 1985; Pollay 1984a, 1988b), the extent of informativeness (Pollay 1984b), and the creative aspects of advertising strategy (Pollay 1985). More recently, his work has taken on a macromarketing perspective (Pollay 1988c; Pollay and Lysanski 1990), specifically his study of the history of cigarette advertising and its impact on society. This interest in the history of cigarette advertising is shared by others such as Wilcox (1991) who examined the correlation between advertising and cigarette consumption for the period from 1949 to 1985.

The complete range of methodological approaches to historical research is evident in recent studies of advertising history. Pollay's use of quantification, content analysis, and hypothesis testing is representative of the social scientific approach to historical research. In a similar fashion, Gross and Sheth (1989) performed content analysis of advertisements spanning 100 years in the *Ladies Home Journal* to investigate the use of time-oriented appeals. On the other hand, Stern (1988) has used literary criticism to examine the medieval tradition of allegory in relation to the development of contemporary advertising strategies. Nevett also used biographical data and a qualitative interpretation of advertisements to examine the development of British advertising (1982, 1983, 1985, 1988a, 1988c, 1988d).

In addition to activities and functions, three other subcategories of marketing history have attracted considerable attention. First, corporate and industry marketing practices have emerged as a popular topic of study (Erb 1985; Clark 1986; Tedlow 1990). Second, marketing systems – whole economies or systems of marketing – emerged during the 1980s as a significant topic for historical research (Corley 1987; Kaufman 1987; Fisk 1988; Fullerton 1988b; Speece 1990; Pirog 1991; Kitchell 1992) and is undoubtedly related to the rising interest in macromarketing (see also Hollander 1984b, 1988). Pirog's (1991) study of changes in the structure and output of the US distribution system builds on Barger's (1955) seminal work mentioned earlier in this review. Of course, an essential aspect of the history of marketing systems is the relationship between marketing and economic development (Dixon 1981; McCarthy 1988; Savitt 1988), and that the fundamental importance of marketing history to the study of economic development has been used as a justification for more historical research in marketing since the late 1950s (Myers and Smalley 1959).

A third subcategory of marketing history that continues to hold interest for marketing historians is retailing. After marketing thought, retailing may have the longest consistent tradition of historical research. What we now know about retailing history, however, remains largely as scattered threads, focusing on selected firms and specific individuals. In a proposal for American retailing history Savitt (1989) agreed with Hollander's (1983; 1986a) assessment of the need for a 'synthesizing' history of retailing, one which went beyond simple, descriptive chronology to identify patterns and integrate marketing practice with marketing thought. Examples of such an approach include Hollander's study of the effects of industrialization on retailing in the twentieth century (1980c) and his evaluation of hypothesized patterns of retail institutional evolution (1980a). The testing of hypotheses about retail institutional evolution has also been a focus in Savitt's work. Having developed specific hypotheses from McNair's wheel of retailing theory, Savitt (1984) used single-firm, total-product line data for a ten-year period to test them. Recent work by others has also contributed to the tracing of retail institutional evolution (Cundiff 1988: 149–62; Kotler 1988; Ortiz-Buonofina 1992).

History of marketing thought

It is a natural progression for any discipline to begin with isolated 'how-to' writings and university courses of instruction, then to develop concepts, theories and eventually schools of thought. This same pattern is evident in the development of the history of marketing thought.

Recently there has been less research on the history of the marketing literature. In addition to Grether's (1976) forty-year review of the *Journal of Marketing* there have been retrospectives of other major journals in the field (Muncy 1991; Berkman 1992). Likewise there has been less research into the history of marketing teaching (Schultz 1982; Lazer and Shaw 1988). There is a need, however, to examine developments that occurred outside the USA, such as in Jones' (1992) study of early marketing courses in Canada.

There has been some renewed interest in biographical research (Jones 1987, 1989, 1993; Wright 1989; Kreshel 1990). In that connection, the third edition of Bartels' (1988) *History of Marketing Thought* is notable for its addition of biographical information about important scholars of the 1960s, 1970s and 1980s. The *Journal of Macromarketing* has also begun a series of autobiographies of eminent scholars in marketing.

However, the development of ideas now dominates research in the history of marketing thought. For example, both Hollander (1986b) and Fullerton (1988a) have given critical historical accounts of the development of the 'so-called' marketing concept. Both scholars concluded that serious and sophisticated marketing has been practised much longer than received doctrine suggests. That conclusion was also supported by Droge et al. (1990). Taken together these studies also point to the value, and in some cases the necessity, of historical research in evaluating existing theory. More importantly perhaps, they have contributed to a more critical perspective and to a rewriting of the history of marketing thought. This has included an extensive reevaluation of the schools of thought from which marketing emerged as a discipline (Jones 1987; Jones and Monieson 1990) and an extension of our historical perspective beyond the twentieth century (Dixon 1978, 1979, 1981, 1982).

Another concept which has attracted recent attention is marketing productivity. Both Shaw (1987, 1990) and Dixon (1990, 1991) have done extensive work on the historical development of the concept and measurement of marketing productivity. Shaw's historical review of empirical studies concludes that marketing productivity in the USA during the past century has increased, but he points to the continuing lack of clear concepts and measures of marketing costs and effectiveness (Shaw 1990: 290).

Schools of thought within the discipline have attracted increasing attention from marketing historians. Discussions of the so-called classical schools – institutional (Hollander 1980b), functional (Hunt and Goolsby 1988) and commodity (Zinn and Johnson 1990) – have been complemented by studies of more contemporary schools of thought including consumer behaviour (Sheth and Gross 1988; Mittelsteadt 1990), macromarketing (Savitt 1990) and others (Sheth et al. 1988).

The most extensive of these studies is the book by Sheth et al. (1988), *Marketing Theory: Evolution and Evaluation*, which identifies, classifies and evaluates twelve schools of marketing thought which have emerged during the twentieth century. These include the classical schools – functional, institutional and commodity – which most marketing historians would agree qualify as schools of thought, and nine others with which, even using the authors' criteria, some historians might disagree. The classification and evaluation of all of these schools could easily be debated, but are not essential to the historical theme which provides the bulk of the presentation. There are also some striking similarities between this book and the earlier one by Schwartz (1963) on *The Development of Marketing Theory*. Several of the 'theories' included in the latter have become 'schools of thought' in Sheth et al. (1988) and both books have a distinctly scientific perspective (especially evident in the form of metatheoretic evaluations of each theory or school of thought). Whereas the Schwartz book should have, perhaps, become the companion to the Bartels work, the Sheth et al. book will surely fill that role.

5 Conclusion

The recent growth of interest in historical research in marketing is surely a natural development in a maturing discipline. Parallel discussions about philosophies of science have focused the attention of marketing scholars on their discipline and have increased their tolerance of different methodologies and perspectives. A more mature marketing discipline has recognized the legitimacy of, as well as the need for, historical research.

At the conference level there has been widespread acceptance by the academic associations. During 1988 the American Marketing Association (AMA), Academy of Marketing Science (AMS), and Association of Consumer Research (ACR) all devoted significant portions of their conferences to historical perspectives. In addition to being the major outlet for historical research in marketing, the Marketing History Conferences have been a vital catalyst and promoter of research in the field and have served to institutionalize historical research in marketing. The success of the History Conferences (held every two years since 1983), the invisible college of marketing historians (becoming more and more visible), a regularly published newsletter (*Retrospectives in Marketing*), and a special issue (1990) in a major journal (*Journal of Academy of Marketing Science*), are all convincing evidence of the pattern Ziman has identified for the development of an academic specialty (1984: 94).

It is no coincidence that those active in marketing history tend to overlap with the group of scholars working in macromarketing. Macromarketing issues, for example, economic development, tend to require a longer term perspective. Therefore, the institutionalization of macromarketing during the late 1970s through an annual seminar and subsequent publication of the *Journal of Macromarketing* has also helped to justify and stimulate historical research in marketing.

Future history?

As for the nature of future historical research in marketing, this review seems to suggest trends in some key directions. For example, we have seen a synthesis of marketing history and the history of marketing thought which, hopefully, will continue. One natural and desirable outcome of this synthesis is an increase in theory development and testing. Many marketing concepts and theories are inherently historical in nature and must be tested with historical evidence.

Another recent trend has been that of identifying and describing sources of historical data and various methodologies of historical research. A better understanding is needed of the various philosophies of history, historical methods, types of primary historical data, and how to use them. Continued efforts in this direction will help improve the quality of historical research in marketing.

Increasingly marketing historians have drawn upon business history, the history of business education, and the history of science to provide a context for historical research in marketing. This trend should be expanded to include economic, social and political history as well as the history of economic thought and other disciplines with connections to marketing.

Finally, there is exciting work being carried out by younger scholars trained at the doctoral level in marketing history and the history of marketing thought. This next generation of scholars will ensure continued growth of interest in historical research in marketing.

D. G. BRIAN JONES
UNIVERSITY OF PRINCE EDWARD ISLAND

Acknowledgement

The author would like to acknowledge the contributions of David D. Monieson to an earlier version of this entry which appeared in the *Journal of the Academy of Marketing Science* Fall, 1990.

Further reading

(References cited in the text marked *)

* Agnew, Hugh E. (1941) 'The history of the American Marketing Association', *Journal of Marketing* 5: 374–9.
* Applebaum, W. (1947) 'The *Journal of Marketing*: the first ten years', *Journal of Marketing* 11: 355–63.
* Applebaum, W. (1952) 'The *Journal of Marketing*: post war', *Journal of Marketing* 16: 294–300.
* Barger, Harold (1955) *Distribution's Place in the American Economy Since 1869*, Princeton: Princeton University Press.
* Bartels, Robert (1951) 'Influences on the development of marketing thought, 1900–1923', *Journal of Marketing* 16: 1–17.
* Bartels, Robert (1962) *The Development of Marketing Thought*, Homewood, IL: Irwin.
* Bartels, Robert (1976) *The History of Marketing Thought*, 2nd edn, Columbus, OH: Grid.
* Bartels, Robert (1988) *The History of Marketing Thought*, 3rd edn, Columbus, OH: Publishing Horizons Inc.
* Belk, Russell W. and Pollay, Richard W. (1985) 'Images of ourselves: the good life in twentieth

century advertising', *Journal of Consumer Research* 11: 887–97.
* Berkman, Harold W. (1992) 'Twenty years of the Journal', *Journal of the Academy of Marketing Science* 20: 299–300.
* Breen, John (1959) 'History of the marketing management concept', in L. Stockman (ed.) *Advancing Marketing Efficiency*, Chicago: American Marketing Association, 458–61.
* Brown, George H. (1951) 'What economists should know about marketing', *Journal of Marketing* 16: 60–6.
* Cassels, J.M. (1936) 'The significance of early economic thought on marketing', *Journal of Marketing* 1: 129–33.
* Clark, Paul (1986) 'The marketing of margarine', *European Journal of Marketing* 20: 52–65.
* Collingwood, R.G. (1974) 'Human nature and human history', in Gardiner, Patrick (ed.) *The Philosophy of History*, London: Oxford University Press.
* Converse, Paul D. (1933) 'The first decade of marketing literature', *NATMA Bulletin Supplement*, November: 1–4.
* Converse, Paul D. (1945) 'The development of the science of marketing – an exploratory survey', *Journal of Marketing* 10: 14–23.
* Converse, Paul D. (1959a) *Fifty Years of Marketing in Retrospect*, Texas: Bureau of Business Research, The University of Texas.
* Converse, Paul D. (1959b) *The Beginnings of Marketing Thought in the United States*, Texas Bureau of Business Research, University of Texas.
* Coolsen, Frank (1947) 'Pioneers in the development of ativertising', *Journal of Marketing* 12: 80–6.
* Coolsen, Frank (1960) *Marketing Thought in the United States in the Late Nineteenth Century*, Texas: Texas Technical Press.
* Corley, T.A.B. (1987) 'Consumer marketing in Britain, 1914–1960', *Business History* 29: 65–83.
* Cundiff, Edward (1988) 'The evolution of retailing institutions across cultures', in Nevett, Terence and Fullerton, Ronald (eds), *Historical Perspectives in Marketing: Essays in Honor of Stanley C. Hollander*, Lexington: Lexington Books.
* Curti, Merle (1967) 'The changing concept of human nature in the history of American advertising', *Business History Review* 41: 355–7.
* Dickinson, Roger (1988) 'Lessons from retailers' price experiences of the 1950s', in Nevett, Terence and Fullerton, Ronald (eds), *Historical Perspectives in Marketing: Essays in Honor of Stanley C. Hollander*, Lexington: Lexington Books.
* Dixon, Donald F. (1978) 'The origins of macromarketing thought', in Fisk, George and Nason, Robert W. (eds), *Macromarketing: New Steps on the Learning Curve*, Boulder: University of Colorado, Business Research Division.
* Dixon, Donald F. (1979) 'Medieval macromarketing thought', in Fisk, George and White, Phillip (eds), *Macromarketing: Evolution of Thought*, Boulder: University of Colorado, Business Research Division.
* Dixon, Donald F. (1981) 'The role of marketing in early theories of economic development', *Journal of Macromarketing* 1: 19–27.
* Dixon, Donald F. (1982) 'The ethical component of marketing: an eighteenth century view', *Journal of Macromarketing* 2: 38–46.
* Dixon, Donald F. (1990) 'Marketing as production: the development of a concept', *Journal of the Academy of Marketing Science* 18: 337–44.
* Dixon, Donald F. (1991) 'Marketing structure and the theory of economic interdependence: early analytical developments', *Journal of Macromarketing* 11l: 5–18.
* Droge, Cornelia, Germain, Richard and Halstead, Diane (1990) 'A note on marketing and the corporate annual report: 1930–1950', *Journal of the Academy of Marketing Science* 18: 355–64.
* Erb, Lyle C. (1985) 'The marketing of Christmas: a history', *Public Relations Quarterly* 24–8.
* Ferrier, R. W. (1986) 'Petroleum advertising in the twenties and thirties: the case of the British Petroleum Company', *European Journal of Marketing* 20: 29–51.
* Firat, A. Fuat (1986) 'Historiography, scientific method and exceptional historical events', in Wallendorf, Melanie and Anderson, Paul (eds), *Advances in Consumer Research*, Association for Consumer Research, 14: 435–8.
* Fisk, George (1988) 'Interactive systems frameworks for analyzing spacetime changes in marketing organization and processes', in Nevett, Terence and Fullerton, Ronald (eds), *Historical Perspectives in Marketing: Essays in Honor of Stanley C. Hollander*, Lexington: Lexington Books.
* Friedman, H.H. (1984) 'Ancient marketing practices: the view from Talmudic times', *Journal of Public Policy and Marketing* 3: 194–204.
* Fullerton, Ronald A. (1985) 'Segmentation strategies and practices in the 19th century German book trade: a case study in the development of a major marketing technique', in Tan, C.T. and Sheth, Jagdish N. (eds), *Historical Perspectives in Consumer Research: National and International Perspectives*, Singapore: National University of Singapore.
* Fullerton, Ronald A. (1986) 'Historicism: what it is, and what it means for consumer research', in Wallendorf, Melanie and Anderson, Paul (eds), *Advances in Consumer Research*, Association for Consumer Research, 14: 431–4.
* Fullerton, Ronald (1987) 'The poverty of ahistorical analysis: present weakness and future cure in U.S. marketing thought', in Firat, Fuat, Dholakia, Nikhilesh and Bagozzi, Richard P. (eds), *Philosophical and Radical Thought in Marketing*, Lexington: Lexington Books.

* Fullerton, Ronald (1988a) 'How modern is modern marketing? Marketing's evolution and the myth of the production era', *Journal of Marketing* 52: 108–25.
* Fullerton, Ronald A. (1988b) 'Modern Western marketing as a historical phenomenon: theory and illustration', in Nevett, Terence and Fullerton, Ronald (eds), *Historical Perspectives in Marketing: Essays in Honor of Stanley C. Hollander*, Lexington: Lexington Books.
* Fullerton, Ronald A. and Nevett, Terence R. (1986) 'Advertising and society: a comparative analysis of the roots of distrust in Germany and Great Britain', *International Journal of Marketing* 5: 225–41.
* Grether, E.T. (1976) 'The first forty years', *Journal of Marketing* 40: 63–9.
* Greyser, Stephen (ed.) (1963) *Toward Scientific Marketing*, American Marketing Association Proceedings Series, Chicago: American Marketing Association.
* Gross, Barbara L. and Sheth, Jagdish N. (1989) 'Time oriented advertising: a content analysis of United States magazine advertising, 1890–1988', *Journal of Marketing* 53: 76–83.
* Hagerty, J.E. (1936) 'Experiences of an early marketing teacher', *Journal of Marketing* 1: 20–7.
* Hardy, Harold (1954) 'Collegiate marketing education since 1930', *Journal of Marketing* 19: 325–30.
* Hempel, Carl G. (1959) 'The function of general laws in history', in Gardiner, Patrick (ed.), *Theories of History*, Glencoe, IL: The Free Press.
* Hidy, Ralph W. (1970) 'Business history: present status and future needs', *Business History Review* 44: 483–97.
* Hollander, Stanley C. (1960) 'The wheel of retailing', *Journal of Marketing* 25: 37–42.
* Hollander, Stanley C. (1963a) 'A note on fashion leadership', *Business History Review* Winter: 448–51.
* Hollander, Stanley C. (1963b) 'Anti-salesman ordinances of the mid-nineteenth century', in Greyser, Stephen (ed.), *Toward Scientific Marketing*, Chicago: American Marketing Association.
* Hollander, Stanley C. (1964) 'Nineteenth century anti-drummer legislation in the United States', *Business History Review* 38: 479–500.
* Hollander, Stanley C. (1966) 'Notes on the retail accordion', *Journal of Retailing* 42: 29–40.
* Hollander, Stanley C. (1980a) 'Oddities, nostalgia, wheels and other patterns in retail evolution', in Stampfl, R.W. and Hirschman, E. (eds), *Competitive Structure in Retail Marketing: The Department Store Perspective*, Chicago: American Marketing Association.
* Hollander, Stanley C. (1980b) 'Some notes on the difficulty of identifying the marketing thought contributions of the early institutionalists', in Lamb, C.W. and Dunn, P.M. (eds), *Theoretical Developments in Marketing*, Chicago: American Marketing Association.
* Hollander, Stanley C. (1980c) 'The effects of industrialization on small retailing in the United States in the twentieth century', in Bruchey, S. (ed.), *Small Business in American Life*, New York: Columbia University Press.
* Hollander, Stanley C. (1983) 'Who and what are important in retailing and marketing history: a basis for discussion', in Hollander, Stanley C. and Savitt, Ronald (eds), *First North American Workshop on Historical Research in Marketing*, Lansing: Michigan State University.
* Hollander, Stanley C. (1984a) 'Herbert Hoover, Professor Levitt, simplification and the marketing concept', in Anderson, Paul and Ryan, Michael (eds), *Scientific Method in Marketing*, Chicago: American Marketing Association.
* Hollander, Stanley C. (1984b) 'Sumptuary laws: demarketing by edict', *Journal of Macromarketing* 4: 3–16.
* Hollander, Stanley C. (1986a) 'A rearview-mirror might help us drive forward: a call for more historical studies in retailing', *Journal of Retailing* 62: 7–10.
* Hollander, Stanley C. (1986b) 'The marketing concept: a déjà-vu', in Fisk, George (ed.), *Marketing Management Technology as a Social Process*, New York: Praeger.
* Hollander, Stanley C. (1988) 'Dimensions of marketing reform', in Shapiro, Stanley and Walle, A.H. (eds), *Marketing: A Return to the Broader Dimensions*, Proceedings of the Winter Educators' Conference, Chicago: American Marketing Association: 142–6.
* Hollander, Stanley C. and Germain, Richard (1992) *Was There a Pepsi Generation Before Pepsi Discovered it?*, Lincolnwood, IL: NCT Business Books.
  Hollander, Stanley C. and Rassuli, Kathleen (eds) (1993) *Marketing*, Cheltenham: Edward Elgar Publishing.
* Hotchkiss, George Burton (1938) *Milestones of Marketing*, New York: Macmillan.
* Hower, Ralph M. (1946) *History of Macy's of New York, 1858–1919*, Cambridge: Harvard University Press.
* Hunt, Shelby D. and Goolsby, Jerry (1988) 'The rise and fall of the functional approach to marketing: a paradigm displacement perspective', in Nevett, Terence and Fullerton, Ronald (eds), *Historical Perspectives in Marketing: Essays in Honor of Stanley C. Hollander*, Lexington: Lexington Books.
* Jones, D.G. Brian (1987a) 'Origins of marketing thought', doctoral dissertation, Kingston, Ontario: Queen's University.
* Jones, D.G. Brian (1987b) 'Edward David Jones: a pioneer in marketing', in Nevett, Terence and

Hollander, Stanley C. (eds), *Marketing in Three Eras*, Lansing: Michigan State University.
* Jones, D.G. Brian (1989) 'Henry Charles Taylor: a pioneer in marketing', in Nevett, Terence, Whitney, Kathleen and Hollander, Stanley (eds), *Marketing History: The Emerging Discipline*, Lansing: Michigan State University.
* Jones, D.G. Brian (1992) 'Early development of marketing thought in Canada', *Canadian Journal of Administrative Science* 9: 126–33.
* Jones, D.G. Brian (1993) 'Historiographic paradigms in marketing', in Hollander, Stanley and Rassuli, Kathleen (eds), *Marketing*, Cheltenham: Edward Elgar Publishing.
* Jones, D.G. Brian and Monieson, David D. (1990) 'Early development of the philosophy of marketing thought', *Journal of Marketing* 54: 102–13.
* Jones, Fred (1936) 'Retail stores in the United States, 1800–1860', *Journal of Marketing* 1: 135–40.
* Jones, Geoffrey and Morgan, Nicholas J. (eds) (1994) *Adding Value: Brands and Marketing in Food and Drink*, London: Routledge.
* *Journal of the Academy of Marketing Science* (1990) 'The history of marketing thought', Special Issue (Fall).
* Kaufman, Carol J. (1987) 'The evaluation of marketing in a society: the Han Dynasty of Ancient China', *Journal of Macromarketing* 7: 52–64.
* Keith, Robert J. (1960) 'The marketing revolution', *Journal of Marketing* 24: 35–8.
* Kelley, William T. (1956) 'The development of early thought in marketing and promotion', *Journal of Marketing* 21: 62–76.
* Kitchell, Susan (1992) 'Foundation of the Japanese distribution system: historical determinants in the Tokugawa Period (1603–1868)', in Duhaime, Carole (ed.), *Marketing Proceedings*, Administrative Sciences Association of Canada Conference, 108–16.
* Kotler, Philip (1988) 'The convenience store: past developments and future prospects', in Nevett, Terence and Fullerton, Ronald (eds), *Historical Perspectives in Marketing: Essays in Honor of Stanley C. Hollander*, Lexington: Lexington Books.
* Kreshel, Peggy J. (1990) 'John B. Watson at J. Walter Thompson: the legitimation of "science" in advertising', *Journal of Advertising* 19: 49–59.
* Kumcu, Erdogan (1987) 'Historical method: toward a relevant analysis of marketing systems', in Firat, Fuat, Dholakia, Nikhilesh and Bagozzi, Richard P. (eds), *Philosophical and Radical Thought in Marketing,* Lexington: Lexington Books.
* La Londe, Bernard J. and Morrison, Edward J. (1967) 'Marketing management concepts, yesterday and today', *Journal of Marketing* 31: 9–13.
* Lazer, William (1965) 'Marketing theory and the marketing literature', in Halburt, Michael (ed.), *The Meaning and Sources of Marketing Theory*, New York: McGraw-Hill.
* Lazer, William and Shaw, Eric (1988) 'The development of collegiate business and marketing education in America: historical perspectives', in Shapiro, Stanley and Walle, A.H. (eds), *Marketing: A Return to the Broader Dimensions*, Proceedings of the Winter Educators' Conference, Chicago: American Marketing Association, 147–52.
* Legh, Faith (1986) 'Half a century of professional bodies in sales promotions', *European Journal of Marketing* 20: 27–40.
* Litman, Simon (1950) 'The beginnings of teaching marketing in American universities', *Journal of Marketing* 15: 220–3.
* Marburg, Theodore (1951) 'Domestic trade and marketing', in Williamson, H.F. (ed.), *The Growth of the American Economy*, New York: Prentice Hall.
* Marx, Thomas G. (1985) 'The development of the franchise distributive system in the United States auto industry', *British History Review* 59: 465–74.
* Maynard, H.H. (1941) 'Marketing courses prior to 1910', *Journal of Marketing* 5: 382–4.
* Maynard, H.H. (1951) 'Developments of science in selling and sales management', in Wales, Hugh G. (ed.), *Changing Perspectives in Marketing*, Urbana: University of Illinois Press.
* McCarthy, E. Jerome (1988) 'Marketing orientedness and economic development', in Nevett, Terence and Fullerton, Ronald (eds), *Historical Perspectives in Marketing: Essays in Honor of Stanley C. Hollander*, Lexington: Lexington Books.
* McCracken, Grant (1987) 'The history of consumption: a literature review and consumer guide', *Journal of Consumer Policy* 10: 139–66.
* McGarry, E.D. (1953) 'Some new viewpoints in marketing', *Journal of Marketing* 18: 33–40.
* McKendrick, N. (1960) 'Josiah Wedgwood: an eighteenth century entrepreneur in salesmanship and marketing techniques', *Economic History Review* 12: 408–31.
* Miracle, Gordon E. and Nevett, Terence (1988) 'A comparative history of advertising self-regulation in the United Kingdom and the United States', *European Journal of Marketing* 22: 7–23.
* Mittelstaedt, Robert (1990) 'Economics, psychology, and the literature of the subdiscipline of consumer behaviour', *Journal of the Academy of Marketing Science* 18: 303–12.
* Muncy, James A. (1991) 'The *Journal of Advertising*: a twenty year appraisal', *Journal of Advertising* 20: 1–12.
* Myers, K. and Smalley, D. (1959) 'Marketing history and economic development', *Business History Review* 33: 387–401.

The nature and scope of marketing

* Nevett, Terence (1982) *Advertising in Britain, A History*, London: Heinemann.
* Nevett, Terence (1983) 'Blood, sweat, tears and biography', in Hollander, Stanley and Savitt, Ronald (eds), *Proceedings of the First North American Workshop on Historical Research in Marketing*, Lansing: Michigan State University.
* Nevett, Terence (1985) 'The ethics of advertising, F.P. Bishop reconsidered', *International Journal of Advertising* 4.
* Nevett, Terence (1988a) 'American influences in British advertising before 1920', in Nevett, Terence and Fullerton, Ronald (eds), *Historical Perspectives in Marketing: Essays in Honor of Stanley C. Hollander*, Lexington: Lexington Books.
* Nevett, Terence (1988b) 'Reform in Great Britain – the Scapa society', in Shapiro, Stanley and Walle, A.H. (eds), *Marketing: A Return to the Broader Dimensions*, Chicago: American Marketing Association.
* Nevett, Terence (1988c) 'The early development of marketing thought: some contributions from British advertising', in Shapiro, Stanley and Walle, A.H. (eds), *Marketing: A Return to the Broader Dimensions*, Chicago: American Marketing Association.
* Nevett, Terence (1988d) 'Thomas Barratt and the development of British advertising', *International Journal of Advertising* 7: 267–76.
* Nevett, Terence (1989) 'The uses of history in marketing education', *Journal of Marketing Education*, Summer: 48–53.
* Nevett, Terence (1991) 'Historical investigation and the practice of marketing', *Journal of Marketing* 55: 13–23.
* Nevett, Terence and Fullerton, Ronald A. (eds) (1988) *Historical Perspectives in Marketing: Essays in Honor of Stanley C. Hollander*, Lexington: Lexington Books.
* Nystrom, Paul H. (1915) *The Economics of Retailing*, New York: Ronald Press.
* Nystrom, Paul H. (1951) 'Retailing in retrospect and prospect', in Wales, Hugh G. (ed.), *Changing Perspectives in Marketing*, Urbana: University of Illinois Press.
* Ortiz-Buonofina, Marta (1992) 'The evolution of retail institutions: a case study of the Guatemalan retail sector', *Journal of Macromarketing* 12l: 16–27.
* Pirog, Stephen F. (1991) 'Changes in U.S. distribution output, 1947–1977: the effects of changes in structure and final demand', *Journal of Macromarketing* 11: 29–41.
* Pollay, Richard W. (1977) 'The importance, and the problems of writing the history of advertising', *Journal of Advertising History* 1: 3–5.
* Pollay, Richard W. (1978) 'Maintaining archives for the history of advertising', *Special Libraries* 69: 145–54.
* Pollay, Richard W. (1979) *Information Sources in Advertising History*, Riverside, CT: Greenwood Press.
* Pollay, Richard W. (1984a) 'The identification and distribution of values manifest in print advertising 1900–1980', in Pitts, E. Jr. and Woodside, Arch (eds), *Personal Values and Consumer Behavior*, Lexington: Lexington Press.
* Pollay, Richard W. (1984b) 'Twentieth century magazine advertising: determinants of informativeness', *Written Communication* 1: 56–77.
* Pollay, Richard (1985) 'The subsiding sizzle: a descriptive history of print advertising, 1900–1980', *Journal of Marketing* 49: 24–37.
* Pollay, Richard W. (1988a) 'Current events that are making advertising history', in Nevett, Terence and Fullerton, Ronald (eds), *Historical Perspectives in Marketing: Essays in Honor of Stanley C. Hollander*, Lexington: Lexington Books.
* Pollay, Richard W. (1988b) 'Keeping advertising from going down in history – unfairly', *Journal of Advertising History* 1, Autumn.
* Pollay, Richard W. (1988c) 'Promotion and policy for a pandemic product: notes on the history of cigarette advertising', unpublished paper, History of Advertising Archives, Vancouver: University of British Columbia.
* Pollay, Richard W. and Lysanski, Steven (1990) 'Advertising sexism is forgiven, but not forgotten: historical, cross cultural and individual differences in criticism and purchase boycott intentions', *International Journal of Advertising*.
* Rassuli, Kathleen M. (1988) 'Evidence of marketing strategy in the early printed book trade: an application of Hollander's historical approach', in Nevett, Terence and Fullerton, Ronald (eds), *Historical Perspectives in Marketing: Essays in Honor of Stanley C. Hollander*, Lexington: Lexington Books.
* Rassuli, Kathleen M. (1991) 'An interpretation of events in the recent history of consumer research: implications for paradigms and theories', in Taylor, Charles, Kopp, Steven, Nevett, Terence and Hollander, Stanley C. (eds), *Marketing History: Its Many Dimensions*, Lansing: Michigan State University.
* Rassuli, Kathleen M. and Hollander, Stanley C. (1986a) 'Comparative history as a research tool in consumer behaviour', in Wallendorf, Melanie and Anderson, Paul (eds), *Advances in Consumer Research*, Association for Consumer Research, 14: 442–6.

Rassuli, Kathleen M. and Hollander, Stanley C. (1986b) 'Desire – induced, innate, insatiable?', *Journal of Macromarketing* 6l: 4–24.

Robins, George W. (1947) 'Notions about the origins of trading', *Journal of Marketing* 11: 228–36.
* Savitt, Ronald (1980) 'Historical research in marketing', *Journal of Marketing* 44: 52–8.
* Savitt, Ronald (1982) 'A historical approach to comparative retailing', *Management Decision* 20: 16–23.
* Savitt, Ronald (1984) 'The wheel of retailing and retail product management', *European Journal of Marketing* 18: 43–54.
* Savitt, Ronald (1988) 'A personal view of historical explanation in marketing and economic development', in Nevett, Terence and Fullerton, Ronald (eds), *Historical Perspectives in Marketing: Essays in Honor of Stanley C. Hollander*, Lexington: Lexington Books.
* Savitt, Ronald (1989) 'Looking back to see ahead: writing the history of American retailing', *Journal of Retailing* 65: 326–55.
* Savitt, Ronald (1990) 'Pre-Aldersonian antecedents to macromarketing: insights from the textual literature', *Journal of the Academy of Marketing Science* 18: 293–302.
* Schultz, Quentin J. (1982) 'An honourable place: the quest for professional advertising education 1900–1917', *Business History Review* 56: 16–32.
* Schwartz, George (1963) *Development of Marketing Theory*, Cincinnati, OH: South-Western Publishing.
* Seaton, A.V. (1986) 'Cope's and the promotion of tobacco in Victorian England', *European Journal of Marketing* 20: 5–26.
* Shapiro, Stanley and Doody, Alton F. (1968) *Readings in the History of American Marketing: Settlement to Civil War*, Homewood, IL: Irwin.
* Shaw, Arch (1915) *Some Problems in Market Distribution*, Cambridge: Harvard University Press.
* Shaw, Eric (1987) 'Marketing efficiency and performance: an historical analysis', in Nevett, Terence and Hollander, Stanley (eds), *Marketing in Three Eras*, Lansing: Michigan State University.
* Shaw, Eric (1990) 'A review of empirical studies of aggregate marketing costs and productivity in the United States', *Journal of the Academy of Marketing Science* 18: 285–92.
* Sheth, Jagdish N. and Gross, Barbara L. (1988) 'Parallel development of marketing and consumer behaviour: a historical perspective', in Nevett, Terence and Fullerton, Ronald (eds), Historical Perspectives in Marketing: Essays in Honor of Stanley C. Hollander, Lexington: Lexington Books.
* Sheth, Jagdish N., Gardner, D. M. and Garrett, D. (1988) *Marketing Theory: Evolution and Evaluation*, New York: Wiley and Sons.
* Silk, A. and Stern, Louis (1963) 'The changing nature of innovation in marketing: a study of selected business leaders, 1852–1958', *Business History Review* 37: 182–99.
* Smith, George L. (ed.) (1965) *Reflections on Progress in Marketing*, Proceedings Series, Chicago: American Marketing Association.
* Smith, Ruth Ann and Lux, David S. (1993) 'Historical method in consumer research: developing causal explanations of change', *Journal of Consumer Research* 19: 595–610.
* Speece, Mark (1990) 'Evolution of ethnodominated marketing channels: evidence from Oman and Sudan', *Journal of Macromarketing* 10: 78–93.
* Stern, Barbara B. (1988) 'Medieval allegory: roots of advertising strategy for the mass market', *Journal of Marketing* 52: 84–94.
* Stern, Barbara B. (1990) 'Literary criticism and the history of marketing thought: a new perspective on "reading" marketing theory', *Journal of the Academy of Marketing Science* 18: 329–36.
* Tedlow, Richard (1990) *New and Improved: The Story of Mass Marketing in America*, New York: Basic Books.
* Tedlow, Richard S. and Jones, Geoffrey (eds) (1993) *The Rise and Fall of Mass Marketing*, London: Routledge.
* Wales, Hugh (ed.) (1951) *Changing Perspectives in Marketing*, Urbana, IL: University of Illinois Press.
* Weld, L.D.H. (1941) 'Early experience in teaching courses in marketing', *Journal of Marketing* 5: 380–1.
* Wilcox, Gary B. (1991) 'Cigarette brand advertising and consumption in the United States: 1949–1985', *Journal of Advertising Research*, August–September: 61–7.
* Witkowski, Terrence H. (1984) 'History's place in the marketing curriculum', *Journal of Marketing Education*, Summer: 54–7.
* Wright, John S. (1989) 'Return biography to the "Journal of Marketing": a polemic', in Nevett, Terence, Whitney, Kathleen and Hollander, Stanley C. (eds), *Marketing History: The Emerging Discipline*, Lansing: Michigan State University.
* Wright, John S. and Dimsdale, Parks B. (1974) *Pioneers in Marketing*, Atlanta, Georgia: Georgia State University.
* Ziman, John (1984) *An Introduction to Science Studies: The Philosophical and Social Aspects of Science and Technology*, Cambridge: Cambridge University Press.
* Zinn, Walter and Johnson, Scott D. (1990) 'The commodity approach in marketing research: is it really obsolete?', *Journal of the Academy of Marketing Science* 18: 345–54.

See also: ADVERTISING, BRANDING AND BRAND MANAGEMENT; RETAILING

The theoretical foundations

The economics basis of marketing

1 Introduction
2 The consumer
3 Marketing strategy
4 Product
5 Price
6 Place
7 Promotion
8 International marketing
9 Summary

Overview

The origins of marketing are to be found in economics, indeed marketing began as a form of *applied* economics. Fundamental to the study of marketing are such economics-based concepts as exchange, profit maximization, utilities, specialization, the economic man and rationality. Central to marketing is a study of consumer behaviour, marketing strategy and the four Ps of customer satisfaction.

The role of the marketer, essentially, is to achieve better results than the competition. Marketers must encourage consumers to buy their products or services, and economics factors can impact on consumers and the buying choices they make. A vital part of marketing strategy is segmentation of the market, and here, again, economics comes into play in the concepts of pricing, product differentiation and positioning.

Economics can also assist marketing when considering products, what makes consumers buy particular products and why they do or do not continue to buy those products as time goes on. Economics teaches the marketer how to consider a product as a bundle of attributes which may satisfy the needs of the end-user. From economics come the concepts of supply and demand and price elasticity, both of which can affect marketing decision making. At the present time, there are great opportunities for firms to expand on to the international stage, and organizations must decide whether they will operate at the macro-level or micro-level, and here, clearly, macroeconomics and microeconomics have a role to play.

1 Introduction

> If we want economic development in freedom and responsibility, we have to build it on the development of marketing.
> (Drucker 1958: 259)

This entry examines the relationship between marketing and economics. Since this is an encyclopedia of marketing the approach will be to examine how economics interacts with the key functions of marketing, rather than the other way round. We shall explore some of the origins and central concepts of marketing thought, and their relationship with the older discipline of economics. Armed with this knowledge, we then examine how marketing works in unison with economics. Other entrie saddress in detail the major elements of marketing. Consequently, the following discussion offers but a necessarily brief look at important marketing concepts.

The economics foundation of marketing

The German Historical School of Economics provided much of the philosophical foundation of the discipline of marketing. Both Harvard and the University of Wisconsin, considered two of the original centres of influence in the development of marketing thought in the USA, built their marketing departments around German-trained economists (Jones and Monieson 1990). This so-called Historical School was concerned with solving real economic problems and its 'practitioner' perspective still exerts a major influence on marketing scholarship today. As Bartels (1988: 186) remarks, 'economic theory has provided more concepts for the development of marketing thought than has any other social discipline'. Indeed, particularly since early marketing scholars were essentially economists, marketing was for a long time held as a branch of economics (Bartels 1988). Around the turn of the century, when the first marketing courses began to appear on American university campuses, the majority

Table 1 Economics, utilities and marketing

	Fundamental economic problems	
	Production	Distribution
Manufacturing	Form	XXX
Marketing	XXX	Time, place, possession

were based on the study of economics (Ferrell et al. 1991).

Inasmuch as economics 'is the study of how men and society choose ... to employ scarce production resources to produce various commodities over time and distribute them for consumption' (Samuelson 1961: 6), it is chiefly concerned with two fundamental problems: production and distribution. Where does marketing come in? According to McCarthy and Shapiro (1983), customer satisfaction is premised on four kinds of economic utilities – form, time, place and possession. Marketing provides the latter three kinds of utilities, while form utility falls into the domain of manufacturing. As depicted in Table 1, it is easy to see the role that marketing plays in addressing economic problems.

Marketing as exchange

Whereas economics emphasizes resource allocation in determining production and distribution, marketing focuses on the process of exchange which underlies this allocation (Houston and Gassenheimer 1987). Indeed, exchange has been offered as 'the defining concept underlying marketing' (Kotler and Turner 1993: 7, and its particular formation is under debate (Deligonul and Cavusgil 1997).

In a market economy, individuals enjoy a freedom to choose whom they will buy from and sell to. There is thus an exchange process for which marketing, with its emphasis on customer wants and needs, is the primary conduit. While Bagozzi (1975) identifies various kinds of exchange, he acknowledges that the 'utilitarian' or economic exchange is implicit in much of marketing literature. Underlying this concept of exchange is the idea of the 'economic man'.

Central to this notion of the 'economic man' is full and complete information, which a person uses in a rational manner to assess his or her choices and make a decision accordingly (Halbert 1964). This rational, economic being has been, for example, the predominant perspective in consumer behaviour studies until quite recently (Mittelstaedt 1990) when psychological and sociological concepts began to take hold.

In an exchange relationship, it is commonly assumed in marketing that the producer seeks to maximize profits (Anderson 1982) while the consumer seeks to maximize utilities (Houston and Gassenheimer 1987). Maximization, be it profits or utilities, is of course a widely recognized economics concept. Enabling this maximization to take place is specialization, as manifested in division of labour, which has greatly affected marketing thinking (Bartels 1988). An obvious example of this is the study of marketing channels which regularly presupposes specialization of distributive functions (see CHANNEL MANAGEMENT).

Summary

Marketing owes much of its heritage to economics, and indeed emerged less than a century ago basically as *applied* economics. To this

Table 2 Contrasting economics and marketing

	Marketing	Economics
Factors of production	Little attention	Beginning point
Goals	Meet needs	Allocate resources
Success criteria	Marketers' needs met	Efficiency and fairness in allocation
Desired form of competition	Monopolistic competition	Perfect competition
Unit of analysis	Exchange	Aggregation of buyers and sellers

Source: Houston and Gassenheimer (1987)

day, marketers still borrow heavily from economics in formulating their own theories and applications. Fundamental to the study of marketing are such economics-based concepts as exchange, profit maximization, utilities, specialization, the economic man and rationality.

To borrow and build upon concepts from economics, however, does not mean copying them. Table 2, adapted from Houston and Gassenheimer (1987), provides a summary of some of the contrasting features between the two disciplines.

We shall now turn to more specific areas within the marketing discipline, where the contrast depicted in Table 2 will become clearer. Inasmuch as the consumer is often the focal point of marketing endeavours, we shall next consider how economics has influenced the study of consumer behaviour.

2 The consumer

> Positive economics can be used to analyze any form of known consumer behavior no matter how immoral, misguided or chauvinistic it may seem to be to the person conducting the analysis
>
> (Lipsey 1966: 202)

As we mentioned earlier, the study of consumer behaviour was highly economics-based until recently. According to Bennett and Kassarjian (1972: 11), 'the economic theory of consumer behavior is one of the most completely refined bodies of theory in the social sciences'. Indeed, to the extent that what consumers choose to buy and what producers choose to sell reflect the economic fundamentals of demand and supply, consumer behaviour is of major concern to economists. Bartels (1988) remarks that the economic concepts of marginal utility, opportunity costs, and rationalism are some of the more popular tools that marketers have borrowed in the study of consumer behaviour. It is to the economic law of diminishing marginal utility that we shall now turn.

Choice is assumed to be universal in the economists' view of the consumer (Bennett and Kassarjian 1972), as reflected in their focus on resource allocation. Lancaster (1979: 7) notes that 'to the economist, individuals are represented in the system by their preferences ... these preferences are, in fact, the individual's economic *persona*'. In microeconomics, the law of diminishing marginal utility governs consumer choice. Some economists choose to call it a 'principle', others a 'hypothesis', but, for our purpose, we shall follow Samuelson (1961: 439) and refer to it as 'law'. Essentially, the law of diminishing marginal utility suggests that an individual's enjoyment of an additional unit of a good diminishes as more and more of that good is consumed. As a result, the individual's total utility increases at a reducing rate as he or she consumes more of the product. Given that individuals are assumed to maximize their utilities (see earlier discussion), and given that an individual's resources (i.e. budget) are limited, the consumer thus faces a quandary. Of the amount of resources at his or her disposal, which goods and how much of each should the person choose? (see CONSUMER BEHAVIOUR).

To solve this question of choice, the economist turns to the concept of indifference curve for help (see, for example, Lancaster 1980). The indifference curve portrays the combinations of goods which give the consumer the same degree of satisfaction, or the same amount of total utility. A series of these curves form the indifference map. Thus, the individual is indifferent as to the different combinations on any particular curve. The reader will perhaps have noticed how indifference maps provide the rationale behind the technique of conjoint analysis so widely used in marketing. Colvin et al. (1980) present a useful example of how conjoint analysis can be used to help build an advertising strategy. Green and Wind (1975) provide more details on the technique, and Jedidi et al. 1996 show how to operationalize conjoint analysis for segments.

Inherent in this concept of indifference are the opportunity costs that an individual must face. By choosing one thing over another, the person forgoes the enjoyment that may be derived from the object not chosen. Only if the opportunity cost associated with one alternative is no greater than the total utility achieved from another alternative would the consumer be in a state of equilibrium – in this case, indifferent.

Economics is, of course, not the only discipline from which consumer researchers have borrowed concepts. Other entries discuss consumer research, and marketing in general, through the lens of psychology and other related fields. Hence, economics does not provide the ultimate answer to the marketer's questions. But as Bennett and Kassarjian (1972: 11) point out, while the economic theory of consumer behaviour may be incomplete, 'it does make important contributions. We therefore do not wish to be guilty of "throwing out the baby with the bathwater"'. As Bartels (1988) reminds us, it is largely because of Adam Smith's notion that the objective of all economic activity is the satisfaction of consumption that led to marketing's proclamation of the consumer as king (or queen).

3 Marketing strategy

> Market segmentation and its counterpart, positioning, must rank as marketing's most important contributions to strategic management.
> (Biggadike 1981: 623)

Market segmentation involves identifying subgroups that share common properties within the total market. The objective is to discern viable target markets that the company can profitably enter. Having targeted these market segments, the marketer seeks to establish competitive advantages by positioning (which in many instances means differentiating) the company's products. This process of segmenting, targeting and positioning represents the 'heart of modern strategic marketing' (Kotler and Turner 1993: 278) (see MARKET SEGMENTATION; MARKETING STRATEGY; POSITIONING).

By now, we should not be surprised to find a strong economics underpinning in this crucial area of marketing strategy. As Dickson and Ginter (1987) point out, the economics theory of monopolistic competition is the basis behind market segmentation and product differentiation. As we saw in Table 2, marketers are particularly concerned with achieving monopolistic competition. Indeed, the economics of segmented pricing provides much of the rationale behind the idea that the marketplace consists of various segments which can be appealed to differently. Essentially, in recognizing the existence of multiple segments and attempting to position its offerings accordingly, the marketer is in the process of creating what may be seen as 'mini-monopolies'. Lipsey (1966: 336) notes that in this scenario, 'the short-run equilibrium of the firm is exactly the same as that of a monopolist' – a scenario achieved by product differentiation, which involves constructing a less elastic demand curve for the firm's product. The theory of monopolistic competition predicts that more non-price competition will take place in industries characterized by monopolistic competition. Of course, non-price competition (as manifested in product differentiation) is arguably the bread and butter of marketers.

Industrial organization (IO) economists have also extensively investigated this approach to strategy. For example, Porter suggests that a firm's success depends on attaining sustainable competitive advantages, and these latter result 'from a firm's ability to perform the required activities at a collectively lower cost than rivals, or perform some activities in unique ways that create buyer value and hence allow the firm to command a premium price' (1991: 102). This is the essence of Porter's 'generic' strategies of low-cost versus differentiation, which have had considerable impact on the study of marketing strategies (e.g. see Day and Wensley 1988). But marketing has also picked up from economics the criticism of the classic equlibrium paradigm (Dickson 1996). This IO concept of sustainable competitive advantage is also behind marketing researchers' recent interest in the study of 'market orientation' (e.g. see Narver and Slater 1990) as a key conduit to creating superior value for customers, and performance for the organization (Jaworski and Kohli 1993.

Table 3 provides a synopsis of how the theory of monopolistic competition has impacted the study of marketing strategy. On the left are ideas borrowed from micro- and IO economics. On the right are marketing's version of these ideas. The final objective is to achieve superior performance.

Monopolistic competition, however, is not the only economics theory that has affected the study of marketing strategy. For example, Kerin et al. (1992), attempting to integrate the literature on first-mover advantage, note that marketers have been affected by the theoretical and analytical literature in IO economics, particularly in viewing a first-mover's ability to create entry barriers. By contrast Shankar et al. (1998) show how these barriers may be surmounted by innovation. Lambkin and Day

Table 3 Strategy and economics

Theory of monopolistic competition	
Economics	*Marketing*
Different demand functions	Market segmentation
Less elastic demand curve	Product positioning
Non-price competition	Differentiation
Sustainable competitive advantage	Market orientation
Performance	

(1989), seeking to develop a framework for understanding market evolution, argue that three 'forces' – the demand system, supply system, and resource environment – impact the way markets evolve. Sen (1997) shows how both demand and supply side factors affect advertising intensity in the soft drinks industry. The economics concepts of complementary and substitute goods play a large role in both the demand and supply systems. Furthermore, Eliashberg and Chatterjee (1985) state that economists, investigating competition under various market structures – perfect competition, monopolistic competition, oligopoly – are traditionally concerned with the efficiencies of structures. On the other hand, marketers focus more on the conduct of the competitors. The similarity between this and IO economics' structure–conduct–performance paradigm is unmistakable. On a more fundamental level, moreover, the microeconomics assumption of profit maximization is the premise for much of the normative literature on marketing management (Anderson 1982).

In the mid-1990s game theory became an important component of economics. It was used to analyze traditional market mechanisms (Bulow and Klemperer 1996). Game theory was used in marketing for a deeper understanding of the strategy of competition and for the development of new exchange mechanisms (McAfee and McMillan 1996).

At a more operational (or 'management') level, marketing is also heavily influenced by economics in the organization of marketing activities. Microeconomics has been most useful in conceptualizing the role of marketing management (Webster 1992). Transaction cost analysis (also see the section on Place) can be a useful theoretical tool for evaluating whether certain marketing activities should be undertaken internally or by third parties (Rindfleisch and Heide, 1997). Ruekert *et al.* (1985) have used transaction cost analysis as their basic framework from which to build a contingency theory of marketing organization. Such an approach, for instance, has been found useful in studying the evolution of the marketing function in the developing economy of China (Heeler *et al.* 1992). Even as Webster (1992) notes that the recent shift from a transaction to a relationship focus requires marketers to go beyond the microeconomics paradigm and place increasing emphasis on relationship management, the fact that marketing is in essence an economic activity underscores the importance of economics concepts to any analysis of marketing organization.

Critical to the success of any strategy is information. Drucker's (1958) idea of entrepreneurial judo as a strategic management concept, for example, necessitates extensive information gathering and processing. And market intelligence takes a central role in promoting a 'market orientation' in an organization (e.g. Narver and Slater 1990). Thus, while economists generally assume a world of perfect information, marketers seek to actualize this assumption by engaging in market research. Without information, managers' behaviour may deviate from economic norms (Brodie *et al.* 1996).

4 Product

Individuals are interested in goods not for their own sake but because of the characteristics they possess.

(Lancaster 1979: 17)

Lancaster's 'Characteristics Approach' to analysing goods as a bundle of attributes was first published in 1966 in the *Journal of Political Economy*, and has been the cornerstone of marketing's application of multi-attribute choice models (Horsky and Sen 1980). A product therefore goes beyond its physical properties and is seen as a collection of characteristics, each being preferred in varying degrees by different individual consumers. Thus, individuals react differently to the same product not because of their different perceptions of the product's properties, but because they have different preferences with respect to the bundle of attributes that the product represents.

In marketing, a product can be seen as 'the needs-satisfying offering of the firm' (McCarthy and Shapiro 1983: 310). (Though we use the term 'product' here, the discussion is also largely relevant for services. For the sake of parsimony, we will not make the distinction between the two. Zeithaml *et al.* (1985) and Bitner and Zeithaml (1987) provide interesting discussions on the issues facing the service marketer.) In other words, it is not so much how the product is manufactured or what other technical properties the product has, but rather how it can best satisfy the customer's needs that matters. Since, as proposed by Lancaster, a product has many different attributes, the same product is therefore capable of satisfying the different needs of various consumers, and different needs of the same consumer (Wansink and Ray, 1996).

This idea of 'bundle of attributes' is also related to the marketing concept of product (and brand) positioning (see BRANDING AND BRAND MANAGEMENT; POSITIONING; PRODUCT POLICY). As McCarthy and Shapiro have noted, positioning usually focuses on specific product features, which is only possible if there are multiple attributes. Brand concept management (Park *et al.* 1986), a framework concerned with selecting, implementing and controlling a brand's image over time, largely hinges on a product's ability to satisfy a multitude of needs among consumers, and integrating these with the process orientated view of quality in manufacturing (Karmarkar and Pitbladdo, 1997).

Another major contribution of economics is the discipline's classification of goods into substitutes and complements. For example, marketers have been interested in the effects on a product's purchase patterns caused by stimulating demand for its complement (e.g. see Walters 1991). And as Howard (1965) notes, the concepts of substitutes and complements are also useful in planning the addition or deletion of brands (see PRODUCT LIFE-CYCLE MANAGEMENT).

Insofar as a marketer's job is to try to create monopolies, new product introduction takes on increasing importance as competitive products begin breaking down the differentiation walls that set the existing product apart. Because of this, marketing researchers have devoted much energy to the study of new product introduction (see NEW PRODUCT DEVELOPMENT). The economics of product innovation timing are discussed by Dhebar (1994). Pretest marketing models are among the heavily researched phenomena (for a detailed discussion, see Shocker and Hall 1986) (see MARKETING RESEARCH).

In the area of adoption and diffusion, marketers and economists have also been active in their research, though at different levels of analysis (Gatignon and Robertson 1989). While marketers have focused their attention mainly at the consumer level, for example the effect of a new entrant to a market on product demand (Mahajan *et al.* 1993), economists have studied the phenomenon at the organizational level. Reviewing the economics literature on the subject, Gatignon and Robertson suggest that adoption of innovations, for example, may be a way to create entry barriers, and may be particularly attractive for firms in highly concentrated industries. The level of price competition is also posited by Gatignon and Robertson to have a negative impact on adoption.

5 Price

> Any business transaction in our modern economy can be thought of as an exchange of money – the money being the Price – for Something... The nature and extent of this Something will determine the amount of money to be exchanged.
>
> (McCarthy and Shapiro 1983: 584)

To the economist, price is set by the market forces of demand and supply in a world of perfect competition. Indeed, the point where demand meets supply (and where marginal costs equal marginal revenues) is the 'equilibrium', where profit maximization is to be found. But as Samuelson (1961) has noted, this is applicable only in the presence of perfect competition and for certain kinds of standardized commodity such as wheat. He also indicates, however, that although other forces (e.g. imperfect competition, government interference) can and do affect prices, they do so by working through their effects on demand and supply. The forces of demand and supply not only govern market prices, but also are important determinants of quantity discounts and surcharges, which are common pricing tools in marketing. Quantity discounts appear to be intuitively appropriate, particularly in view of the conventional downward-sloping demand curve. Heeler (1989) has demonstrated that surcharges also fall into the realms of economics theory. In addition, as we shall see, imperfect information on the part of the consumer may further contribute to the existence of surcharges. Nagle (19840 points out that although economics models are abstractions and do not prescribe specific pricing actions, 'the marketer's task [of pricing] should prove less strenuous when he stands on a sound foundation of economic theory' (1984: S4). He offers three general areas of economics theory that are particularly useful in the study of pricing: the economics of information, the economics of spatial competition and the economics of segmented pricing.

The economics of information

Pricing one's products based on buyers' perceptions of the products' values is called perceived-value pricing (Smith and Nagle 1995). In this case, price reflects value as perceived by customers. A problem may arise when, because of insufficient or inaccurate information, customers may over- or underevaluate the value of a product. This phenomenon, for example, is quite common in the used automobile market where consumers substantially discount the value of a used car because they are unsure as to the car's condition. A related, though conceptually distinct, concept is the 'price–quality effect'. Scitovsky (1944) is considered the origin of the now familiar 'price–quality' effect which suggests that lacking perfect information, consumers may infer higher quality to higher priced products. Thus, Menon and Varadarajan (1992) suggest that this effect may cause marketers to place greater faith in information that has been gathered at high cost, and buyers may be willing to pay more for an assurance of quality (Rao and Bergen 1992).

This asymmetry of information has important implications for marketing, especially when it comes to branding. A brand name is often used by consumers as the major indicator of product quality (McCarthy and Shapiro 1983). Because 'consumers should pay more of a premium for a high-quality brand' (Nagle 1984: S8), marketers who are able to create and sustain a high-quality image for their brands would reap the benefits.

The value that consumers place on a brand, as an indication or guarantee of quality, as an indicator of social correctness, as a store of information that economizes on shopping time in turn gives value to brands for marketers. Indeed in the 1990s brand names were often the real value sought in corporate takeovers and major brands emerged as global assets. These values accumulated as the interaction of all the elements of the marketing mix through time, and obviously reflected the expenditures made on such things as advertising.

Traditional accounting shows expenses such as advertising, but does not show the resultant brand asset. Similarly, economics has recognized tangible resources such as plant but not the intangible resource of brand. In marketing the concept of brand equity has developed to allow representation of this important resource and its use in marketing (Aaker 1991, 1997).

In addition to asymmetrical information, economists have studied how consumers acquire information. Recognizing that 'perfect information' is not realistic in the real world, we may consider that price sensitivity is determined not so much by the actual number of competitive products (or substitutes) in the market, but by how many of these the consumer is aware. Because humans are limited in their cognitive abilities, we often do not make decisions in a systematic, comprehensive manner. This is the essence of the concept of 'bounded rationality' (see e.g. Simon 1976). As Drummond (1992: 2) puts it: 'Choice is based on intelligent guess work, the aim being to find something that "will do"'. At first glance, this

The theoretical foundations

may appear to contradict the basic economics assumption of rationality. But as Samuelson so succinctly points out, the 'economic man' need not be a perfect processor of limitless information, that 'he can even make most of his decisions unconsciously or out of habit ... as long as he is fairly consistent in his tastes and actions' (Samuelson 1961: 449).

Marketers, too, recognize that consumers do not necessarily consider (or are even aware of) all the alternatives 'out there'. The distinction between 'choice set', 'consideration set' and 'total set' of alternative products (e.g. Kotler and Turner 1993: 193) is an example of the application of the above discussion on imperfect information acquisition.

Also as a result of imperfect information, some economists posit that the fewer alternatives the consumers are aware of, the less price sensitive they will be. This has important implications for the marketer, particularly with respect to whether advertising promotes or retards price sensitivity, and consequently, consumer welfare (Kanetkar *et al.* 1992).

The economics of spatial competition

Just as marketers use spatial representations (e.g. multidimensional scaling) to analyse product positioning, economists have been using spatial competition models to study the effects of product variety on price competition since the late 1920s. Nagle (1984) suggests that these two approaches can be integrated, so that marketers may investigate not only positioning and product entry to maximize market potential, but also where (relative to the competition) to introduce the product so as to minimize potential competition from later entrants.

The economics of segmented pricing

Segmented pricing involves charging different prices to different groups of customers. Practices such as tie-ins, metering and product bundling are examples of segmented pricing. Segmented pricing can also be seen as price discrimination (Lipsey 1966), which is a standard topic in most intermediate economics textbooks. Segmented pricing is possible because different consumers exhibit different demand elasticities for the product in question. In order for the firm successfully to implement segmented pricing, then, it would have to know, *a priori*, the factors that affect the price elasticity of different consumers. This, however, may not be a feasible task. One of the (more practical) ways to overcome this problem is by way of product bundling (Yadav and Monroe, 1993). An increasing number of companies are using discriminatory pricing, partly as a result of deregulation (Kotler and Turner 1993: 526). It should be noted, however, that discriminatory pricing, as used in our present context, is not necessarily illegal even for regulated industries. Examples abound: for instance, airlines have been charging different fares for the same class for years and automobile manufacturers have long been offering option packages as a form of product bundling. The topic is just as popular in marketing textbooks as it is in economics texts. We saw above how segmented pricing contributes to the fundamental concept of market segmentation.

The contributions made by microeconomics notwithstanding, we must be cognizant of the fact that economic theory does not always fully explain human reactions towards the price element. Not satisfied with standard economics theory of the consumer, which 'omit virtually all marketing variables except price and product characteristics', Thaler (1985: 200) uses Kahneman and Tversky's (1979) 'prospect theory' as a basis to develop a new model of consumer behaviour that incorporates cognitive psychology and microeconomics. Prospect theory is an alternative to classical economic utility theory, and it posits that economic agents make choices relative to a neutral outcome or a 'frame'. People are more averse to losses than to gains, and value is judged as a proportional gain or loss rather than an absolute amount. In other words, relative to the reference point, losses are perceived as larger than gains that are equal in absolute terms. Winer (1988) offers a good discussion of prospect theory in the context of 'reference price'. Thaler (1985) thus derives his theory of transaction utility, stating that consumers gain utility not just from consumption, but also from the 'transaction' of acquiring the product, especially at a bargain price. The amount of this latter utility is directly related to the difference between the perceived special or regular prices. The value to consumers of their own time has been found to depend on the characteristics of the decision situation (Leclerc *et al.* 1995).

It is worth mentioning that a vast literature exists on the subject of promotional discounts, in terms of both discounts to the trade (e.g. Blattberg and Levin 1987) and to the consumer (e.g. Krishna *et al.* 1991). The twin technologies of data from optical scanning of transactors and cheap computer power for analysis have accelerated research on discount (Kalyanam, 1996). Much of this literature has its roots in economic analysis, though other social sciences such as psychology have begun to exert an increasing influence. The interested reader is encouraged to refer to the cited references for a more detailed discussion.

A discourse on the effects of economics on pricing would not be adequate without some coverage on the fundamental concept of price elasticity. Simply put, price elasticity of demand measures the impact that price changes have on demand. Demand is elastic if the ratio of change in demand to change in price is greater than one, meaning demand is responsive to price changes. It is inelastic if the ratio is less than one, signalling that price changes have limited impact on demand. For the marketer, the ability to identify (and market to) segments that are inelastic may pose profitable opportunities. In the area of adoption and diffusion, for example, it has long been posited that early adopters are relatively price inelastic (see e.g. Parker 1992 for a discussion). The influence of advertising on elasticity is also important to the marketer (Mitra and Lynch, 1995). The interested reader is also encouraged to examine the related concepts of income elasticity and cross-price elasticity, which can be found in most economics textbooks. These concepts have significant implications for the marketer (e.g. see Bemmaor and Mouchoux 1991; Walters 1991).

6 Place

> From the point of view of the economic system, the basic role of marketing intermediaries is to transform the heterogeneous supplies found in nature into assortments of goods that people want to buy.
> (Kotler and Turner 1993: 541)

Goods and services in and of themselves are of limited value or meaning. The production of goods, unless somehow channelled into the hands of consumers for consumption, becomes a futile endeavour. Lipsey (1966) indicates that production and consumption are two of the fundamental problems facing economists. There is, of course, an intervening process whereby the goods produced are distributed to those who want the goods. Without a redistribution system, consumers would have to travel to the orchards of the Pacific Northwest to get their apples, to the Charente region of France to get their cognac, and so on. The world of consumption would not be an overly efficient place indeed. As Heilbroner (1971) has observed, the production problem and the distribution problem are two basic issues that society must address to ensure the economic survival of humans. After all, the laws of demand and supply simply would not work unless economic goods were made available (see CHANNELS OF DISTRIBUTION).

The study of marketing, naturally, necessitates an understanding of the construct of market. We may think of a market as a place where people meet to buy and sell their products. In this everyday usage of the term, images of the farmer's market or the stock market come to mind. But market can also be seen as an economic process that facilitates the exchange of goods and services (Samli and Bahn 1992). Exchange, as we have seen, is the fundamental unit of analysis in marketing; the interaction of demand and supply is the basis of the economic process. Thus it is not enough that manufacturers produce and consumers consume. The intermediate process of bringing the two together is also of primary importance. Hence, as Jones and Monieson (1990) point out, the original scholars of marketing were basically concerned with problems of distribution.

Why do firms come together in the formation of a distribution channel? The literature on marketing channels can be divided into the design and management streams. In the design stream, the focus is on the establishment and organization of distribution channels; issues such as structure are important considerations. Should the manufacturer handle its own distribution, for instance? Or should it enlist the services of intermediaries? In this vein, vertical integration is one of those lingering topics that have been subject to much analysis by management researchers. In the management stream, the emphasis is on how best to manage a channel once it is in place; extensive investigation has been made in the topics of conflict resolution, the use of power, and so on (e.g. see Rangan et al. (1992) and Lusch and Brown (1996) for a detailed discussion). The impact of economics theory would appear to be strongest on the design stream, and it is to this aspect of marketing channels that we shall now turn.

The economics idea of specialization, with its manifestation in division of labour, has greatly affected marketing thinking; the impact is particularly obvious in the area of marketing channels. Alderson (1967) suggests that attempts at maximization of productivity leads to specialization, and in turn various marketing agencies work together to form a channel for a given product. This channel, then, facilitates the exchange or flow of resources within an interorganizational network (Ghoshal and Bartlett 1990). It is to the benefit of channel members, in the interest of profit maximization, to act as a unit (Mallen 1973).

To the extent that exchange, or transaction, is the basic unit of analysis, efficient execution of this transaction requires that firms internalize those activities of exchange that they themselves can perform at a lower cost, and rely on other firms for those activities that others can provide more inexpensively. Under the transaction cost approach (TCA (see also the section on Marketing Strategy above)), minimization of transaction costs drives individual firms to participate in a channel of distribution (Williamson 1981). Essentially, TCA suggests that asset specificity and uncertainty are the two main factors guiding the choice between integrated (company-owned) or market (independent) channels. Asset specificity refers to production and distribution, as well as governance, costs. When asset specificity is high, a vertically integrated channel system may be called for. The reverse would be true when asset specificity is low. The relevance of asset specificity increases as the level of uncertainty goes up. At very low levels of uncertainty, vertical integration would not be a reasonable option, thus obviating the need to consider asset specificity at all. As observed by Rangan et al. (1992) and Rindfleisch and Heide (1997), the transaction cost approach is one of the most popular theories applied to the study of marketing channels. It is interesting to note, however, that even though Williamson is an economist by trade, the TCA, despite its basically economics orientation, was conceived because of Williamson's dissatisfaction with the more 'conventional' ability of economics traditions (e.g. microeconomicstheory, IO economics) to address real world problems (see Williamson 1975: 248–53).

We observed earlier that economics takes as its primary interest the efficient allocation of resources (see Table 2). Insofar as the forces of demand and supply purport to lead to economic prosperity for all, questions have been raised as to the social desirability and efficiency of marketing in general, and channels in particular. This efficiency aspect, too, has been under the scrutiny of marketing scholars (e.g. see Moyer and Hutt 1978: 145–54 for a more detailed discussion). Channel 'performance', as a result, has been evaluated primarily on the basis of productivity. Goldman (1992) suggests that the use of productivity measurements as a proxy for channel performance may not be valid in all situations, especially in cross-cultural analyses. Whether this is so is beyond the scope of this entry. Suffice it to say that the economics perspective of efficient allocation has indeed been the dominant paradigm in channel evaluation.

7 Promotion

> The further a man [sic] is removed from physical need the more open he is to persuasion – or management – as to what he buys. This is, perhaps, the most important consequence for economics of increasing affluence.
>
> (Galbraith 1972: 18)

As McCarthy, who originally coined the 'four Ps', explains, promotion is 'concerned with telling the target market about the "right" product' (McCarthy and Shapiro 1983: 43). He also indicates, however, that promotion goes beyond merely presenting information. In fact, the objective of presenting this information is 'to influence attitudes and behavior' (McCarthy and Shapiro 1983: 495). Thus, promotion seeks both to inform and to influence. Marketing researchers have been interested in the effectiveness of advertising and promotions, reach and frequency studies, media selection and scheduling algorithms, and many other aspects of promotion. Lilien and Kotler (1983:

ch. 14) gives a comprehensive coverage of the various decision models affecting this topic. Much of this research, however, takes on a psychology bent. Indeed, as we have noticed earlier, the study of consumer behaviour has shifted away from an economics basis to a more sociological, psychological perspective. It is therefore not surprising that the 'economic man' does not much come into play in promotion decisions.

Nevertheless, this is not to say that economics does not have its impact on the topic. As we shall see, economists have written quite extensively about the efficacy of advertising. (Economists generally group what marketers call promotion under the banner of advertising. Definitions may be slightly different, but the arguments still apply.) It is useful at this point to address how economics and marketing converge on the information and influence functions of promotion (see PROMOTION). Promotion includes all forms of marketing communication. Salesforce control is yet another topic to be influenced by transaction cost analysis (Stathakopoulos 1996).

Promotion as information

Economists, being concerned with the efficient allocation of resources, are understandably anxious as to the potentially wasteful practice of advertising. In Canada alone, advertising expenditure exceeded $10 billion in 1990. That was almost $400 for every woman, man, and child in the country! In the USA and other more populous nations, the figures would be that much more staggering. Defenders of expenditures on promotion (and advertising in general) argue that it serves a vital informational role. By conveying information to the consumer, advertising makes complete the economist's postulate of perfect knowledge (Backman 1968; Mitra and Lynch 1995). Because there is an abundance of products in the marketplace, and since each product is a 'bundle of attributes', consumers cannot reasonably expect to have complete information with which to make purchase decisions. Producers, by promoting their products and services, provide valuable information to the consumers.

Disagreements with this view are mainly of two related varieties. First, while some forms of advertising (e.g. classified ads and department store displays) do primarily serve to convey information, much of it is to manage demand to 'insure that people buy what is produced' (Galbraith 1972: 19). The latter does not add to the economic well-being of the population, and is thus considered economic waste. Second, while acknowledging the information component of advertising, Grabowski (1974) questions the usefulness of this information. He argues that the information which producers offer may not be what is needed for consumers to make their decisions in a 'socially optimal' fashion, because manufacturers are naturally inclined to bias the information in their favour. As such, this information is neither adequate nor complete.

Promotion as influence

Regardless of advertising's effects on society's economic well-being, it plays a key role in a producer's efforts of product differentiation in a monopolistically competitive market. Comanor and Wilson (1974), for instance, report that their analysis of 36 industries shows that advertising has a substantially greater impact on demand than does relative prices, a related issue is whether advertisements carry information or create a perception. The debate is summarized in the *Economist* (1998). Andrews and Franke (1996) in a study of six product categories show that market response to advertising (and price and distribution) change with time and industry maturation. Some leading economists, such as Samuelson and Galbraith, contend that product differentiation is largely a result of advertising, a 'distortion' of consumer demand.

Galbraith (1975) sees advertising as a form of 'want creation'. In economics terms, this involves an attempt 'to shift the demand curve of the individual firm at the expense of others, or to change its shape by increasing the degree of product differentiation' (Galbraith 1975: 30). To the extent that advertisers seek to influence consumers to buy their products instead of their competitors', this is exactly the goal. Again, questions arise as to whether this contributes to the economic well-being of society. Galbraith is perhaps one of the most noted critics of advertising. He suggests that wants that are not inherent in the individual but are created by the production process are inferior, and their satisfaction is not of any economic urgency

45

(Galbraith 1975). Benton (1987) agrees, noting that increased levels of consumption are not accompanied by corresponding increases in consumers' quality of life. In fact, he argues that since 'mass production requires mass consumption for ultimate success' (Benton 1987: 246), industrialization has brought about a culture of consumption that has degraded human life. Advertising, being a major calibre weapon in the producer's arsenal, is thus a leading culprit of this degradation.

8 International marketing

> Effective marketing not only improves the life-style and well-being of people in a specific economy, it also upgrades world markets; after all, a developed country's best customer is another developed country.
> (Cateora 1993: 221)

In reviewing the relationship between economics and marketing in the context of international marketing, it is useful to delineate a macro- and a micro-level of analysis. Some elaboration may be in order here. By macro we mean the ways marketing operates in a macroeconomics sense; how, for instance, marketing contributes to the economic development of a nation. By micro we refer to the more conventional microeconomics issues facing the marketer; how best to meet the needs and wants of consumers, for example. We shall briefly look at each of these levels of analysis.

Macro issues

Cateora's quote (above) points out marketing's contributions from a macroeconomics standpoint. In short, effective marketing facilitates economic growth. Against this backdrop, Heeler et al. (1992) have investigated the state of evolution of the organization of marketing in China. They note that (Heeler et al. 1992: 252) 'a formal bureaucratic approach to marketing exists ... (but) will certainly change as the Chinese economy evolves towards a market orientation'. But overall, while scholars such as Drucker (1958) have championed the important role of marketing in economic development, Douglas and Craig (1992: 296) lament that 'little attention has been devoted to examining the dynamics of market growth and development within different regions or worldwide' (see GLOBAL MARKETING).

Micro issues

Perhaps because of more immediate applications useful to the marketing practitioner, research in international marketing has emphasized a microeconomics orientation. More precisely, research has focused on the options available to the firm. Thus, Douglas and Craig (1992) offer three key phases of global marketing strategy development: market entry, local market expansion and global rationalization. That these phases are evolutionary stages of strategy for the firm brings us back to the theories of supply and demand, and of the law of diminishing marginal utility as a basic element in the mechanism of choice (i.e. microeconomics concerns). The long popular paradigm of resource allocation, standarization versus adaptation has received new empirical attention in Szymanski, et al. (1993, and see also Colvin et al. 1980).

As we have seen (Rindfleish and Heide 1997), transaction cost theory has established increasing potency in shaping marketing thought. It is therefore not surprising when Rugman and Verbeke (1992) offer the transaction cost approach as an effective means of analysing international marketing strategy. They offer three major elements that comprise the transaction cost theory of international enterprise – firm-specific advantages, country-specific advantages and internalization advantages – and demonstrate how an analysis of these elements can help evaluate strategy. For example, a firm facing 'host country-specific advantages' and 'location bound firm-specific advantages' may find the 'multinational' type of firm more appropriate than, say, the 'global' firm.

There are also other ways economics theories have impacted on international marketing thought. Levitt's (1983) argument for globalization is a case in point. According to Levitt, because technology is driving the world to a point of convergence of wants, it behoves the global firm to become standardized in its offerings and marketing practices. By doing so, the firm is able to offer products of an acceptable quality at a much lower cost than competition, on account of greater economies of scale.

As he remarks (Levitt 1983: 102), 'two vectors shape the world – technology and globalization. The first helps determine human preference; the second, economic realities'. Levitt's paper is quoted here only as an example of how economics theory affects thinking in marketing. There are others who dispute Levitt's claims that the world is homogenizing and that standardization is good. For one such counter position, the reader may wish to refer to Douglas and Wind (1987). A trend in the late 1990s is to licensing as a way of solving technology and resource market entry issues (Kotabe *et al.* 1996).

It should be obvious that much of what concerns the domestic marketer also affects the international marketer. The problems of a broader international environment notwithstanding, the fundamental marketing principles of target marketing and the marketing mix remain cornerstones of the discipline. Cateora (1993: 9) puts it well when he writes: 'Marketing concepts, processes, and principles are universally applicable ... (but) the difficulties created by different environments are the international marketer's primary concern'.

9 Summary

> A cross-fertilization of ideas and efforts between economists and marketers will undoubtedly strengthen the scientific foundation of marketing.
> (Horsky and Sen 1980: S8)

Complete volumes can be written on the many subjects that we have covered. For the sake of our limited cognitive abilities, not to say the health of the hard disk on our PCs, we have endeavoured but a superficial level of analysis of the relationship between marketing and economics. The reference list, however, is sufficiently broad and comprehensive that the inquisitive reader may easily explore any of the topics in much greater detail. To the extent that we have raised the reader's level of consciousness as to the important lessons and concepts marketers can learn from economists, and thus enabled the reader, however superficially, to 'return to basics', this entry has served its purpose.

We have explored the economics foundations of our discipline, relating that to the concept of exchange which is so central to the study of marketing. In the area of consumer behaviour, we have seen how the economics perspective has dominated consumer research until relatively recently. The concept of utilities, for example, is still very much a pivotal area of analysis, as is the idea that the consumer is sovereign. Another important way that economics has shaped marketing thinking is illustrated by the theory of monopolistic competition and its impact on the key marketing concepts of segmentation and differentiation. We have also examined how economics theorists have affected research and practice in various elements of the marketing mix. In addition to traditional microeconomics, we have also seen how IO economics have influenced marketing thought, particularly in the area of marketing strategy. Transaction cost theory, moreover, has become a dominant factor in the analysis of marketing channels. We would again refer the reader to Table 2 for a snapshot of some of the important contrasts between economics and marketing.

We have not investigated the impact of economics on industrial marketing. There are also other areas of convergence which we have not reviewed. This is not because we feel the relationship between economics and marketing is any less significant in those areas, but because we will be doing economics theories an even greater disservice if we attempted to be all-encompassing.

ROGER M. HEELER
SCHULICH SCHOOL OF BUSINESS
YORK UNIVERSITY
EDWARD K. CHUNG
NORBERT COLLEGE

Further reading

(References cited in the text marked *)

* Aaker, David (1991) *Managing Brand Equity*, New York: The Free Press.
* Aaker, David (1997) 'Measuring brand equity across products and markets', *California Management Review* 38: 102–20.
* Alderson, Wroe (1967) 'Factors governing the development of marketing channels', in Bruce E. Mallen (ed.) *The Marketing Channel: A Conceptual Viewpoint*, New York: John Wilty & Sons.

The theoretical foundations

* Anderson, Paul A. (1982) 'Marketing, strategic planning, and the theory of the firm', *Journal of Marketing* 46: 15–26.
* Andrews, Rick L. and Franke, George R. (1996) 'Dynamics of aggregate response sensitivities to marketing mix variables', *Journal of Business Research* 36: 145–55.
* Backman, Jules (1968) 'Is advertising wasteful?' *Journal of Marketing* 32: 2–8.
* Bagozzi, Richard P. (1975) 'Marketing as exchange', *Journal of Marketing* 39: 32–9.
* Bartels, Robert (1988) *The History of Marketing Thought*, 3rd edn, Columbus, OH: Publishing Horizons.
* Bemmaor, Albert C. and Mouchoux, Dominique (1991) 'Measuring the short-term effect of in-store promotion and retail advertising on brand sales: a pictorial experiment', *Journal of Marketing Research* 28, May: 202–14.
* Bennett, Peter D. and Kassarjian, Harold H. (1972) *Consumer Behavior*, Englewood Cliffs, NJ: Prentice-Hall.
* Benton, Jr, Raymond (1987) 'Work, consumption, and the joyless consumer', in A. Firat ,Fuat, Dholakia, Nikhilesh and Bagozzi, Richard P. (eds) *Philosophical and Radical Thought in Marketing*, Lexington, MA: Lexington Books.
* Biggadike, E. Ralph (1981) 'The contributions of marketing to strategic management', *Academy of Management Review* 6: 621–32.
* Bitner, Mary J. and Zeithaml, Valarie A. (1987) 'Fundamentals in services marketing', in Sueprenant, Carol (ed.), *Add Value to Your Service*, Chicago: American Marketing Association.
* Blattberg, Robert C. and Levin, Alan (1987) 'Modelling the effectiveness and profitability of trade promotions', *Marketing Science* 6: 124–46.
* Brodie, Roderick J., Bonfrer, Andre and Cutler, Justine (1996) 'Do managers overreact to each others' promotion activity? Further empirical evidence', *International Journal of Research in Marketing* 13: 379–87.
* Bulow, Jeremy and Klemperer, Paul (1996) 'Auctions vs negotiations', *American Economic Review* 86: 180–94.
* Cateora, Philip R. (1993) *International Marketing*, 8th edn, Homewood, IL: Irwin.
* Colvin, Michael, Heeler, Roger and Thorpe, Jim (1980) 'Developing international advertising strategy', *Journal of Marketing* 44: 73–9.
* Comanor, William S. and Wilson, Thomas A. (1974) 'Advertising and the distribution of consumer demand', in Divita, S.F. (ed.), *Advertising and the Public Interest*, Chicago: American Marketing Association.
* Day, George S. and Wensley, Robin (1988) 'Assessing advantage: a framework for diagnosing competitive superiority', *Journal Marketing* 52: 1–20.
* Deligonul, Z. Seyda and Cavusgil, S. Tamer (1997) 'Does comparative advantage theory of competition really replace the neoclassical theory of perfect competition?', *Journal of Marketing* 61: 65–73.
* Dhebar, Anirudh (1994) 'Durable-goods monopolists, rational consumers, and improved products', *Marketing Science* 13: 100–20.
* Dickson, Peter R. (1996) 'The static and dynamic mechanics of competition: A comment on Hunt and Morgan's comparative advantage theory'. *Journal of Marketing* 60: 102–6.
* Dickson, Peter R. and Ginter, James L. (1987) 'Market segmentation, product differentiation, and marketing strategy', *Journal of Marketing* 51: 1–10.
* Douglas, Susan P. and Wind, Yoram (1987) 'The myth of globalization', *Columbia Journal of World Business*, Winter: 19–20.
* Douglas, Susan P. and Craig, C. Samuel (1992) 'Advances in international marketing', *International Journal of Research in Marketing* 9: 291–318.
* Drucker, Peter F. (1958) 'Marketing and economic development', *Journal of Marketing* 22: 252–9.

Drucker, Peter F. (1985) 'Entrepreneurial strategies', *California Management Review* 27: 9–25.

* Drummond, Helga (1992) 'Another fine mess: time for quality in decision-making', *Journal of General Management* 18: 1–14.
* *Economist* (1998) 'The money in the message', 347, 14 February: 78.
* Eliashberg, Jehoshua and Chatterjee, Rabikar (1985) 'Analytical models of competition with implications for marketing: issues, findings, and outlook', *Journal of Marketing Research* 22: 237–61.
* Ferrell, Barbara, Perreca-Smith, Louise and Glascoff, David W. (1991) 'Exchange, expectations, and the definition of marketing', in Childers, T.C., MacKenzie, S.B. Leigh,T.W., Skinner, S., Lynch, J.G. Jr, Heckler,S., Gatignon, Fisk, H.R.P. and Graham, J.L. (eds), *AMA Winter Educators' Conference: Marketing Theory and Applications, Vol.2*, Chicago: American Marketing Association.
* Galbraith, John Kenneth (1972) 'The management of specific demand', in Kangun, Norman (ed.), *Society and Marketing: An Unconventional View*, New York: Harper and Row.

Galbraith, John Kenneth (1975) 'The dependence effect', in Goble, Ross Lawrence and Shaw, Roy T. (eds), *Controversy and Dialog in Marketing*, Englewood Cliffs, NJ: Prentice-Hall.

* Gatignon, Hubert and Robertson, Thomas S. (1989) 'Technology diffusion: an empirical test of competitive effects', *Journal of Marketing* 53: 35–49.
* Ghoshal, Sumantra and Bartlett, Christopher A. (1990) 'The multinational corporation as an

interorganizational network', *Academy of Management Review* 15: 603–25.
* Goldman, Arieh (1992) 'Evaluating the performance of the Japanese distribution system', *Journal of Retailing* 68: 11–39.
* Grabowski, Henry G. (1974) 'Advertising and resource allocation – critique', in Divita, S.F. (ed.), *Advertising and the Public Interest*, Chicago: American Marketing Association.
* Green, Paul E. and Wind, Yoram (1975) 'New way to measure consumers' judgments', *Harvard Business Review* 53: 107–17.
* Halbert, Michael H. (1964) 'The requirements for theory in marketing', in Cox, Reavis, Alderson, Wroe and Shapiro, Stanley J. (eds), *Theory in Marketing*, Homewood, IL: Richard D. Irwin.
* Heeler, Roger M. (1989) 'On quantity discounts and surcharges', in Avlonitis, G., Papavasiliou, N.K. and Kouremenos, A.G. (eds), *Marketing Thought and Practice in the 1990s: XVIII Annual Gnference of the European Marketing Academy, Vol. II*, Athens: The Athens School of Economics and Business Science.
* Heeler, Roger M., Stewart, Sally, Zhi, Chang, Thomas, Huw D. and Lai, Yu (1992) 'Organization for marketing in contemporary China: using the company's creative spirit to serve society with your whole heart', *Advances in Chinese Industrial Studies* 3: 241–53.
* Heilbroner, Robert L. (1971) 'The economic problem', in Wish, John R. and Gamble, Stephen H. (eds), *Marketing and Social Issues: An Action Reader*, New York: John Wiley & Sons.
* Horsky, Dan and Sen, Subrata K. (1980) 'Interfaces between marketing and economics: an overview', *Journal of Business* 53: S5–12.
* Houston, Franklin S. and Gassenheimer, Jule B. (1987) 'Marketing and exchange', *Journal of Marketing* 51: 3–18.
* Howard, John A. (1965) *Marketing Theory*, Boston: Allyn and Bacon.
* Jaworski, Bernard J. and Ajay K. Kohli (1993) 'Market orientation: antecedents and consequents', *Journal of Marketing* 57: 53–70.
* Jedidi, Kamel, Kohli, Rajeev and Desarbo, Wayne S. (1996) 'Consideration sets in conjoint analysis', *Journal of Marketing Research* 33: 364–72.
* Jones, D.G. Brian and Monieson, David D. (1990) 'Early development of the philosophy of marketing thought', *Journal of Marketing* 54: 102–13.
* Kahneman, Daniel and Tversky, Amos (1979) 'Prospect theory: an analysis of decision under risk', *Econometrica* 47: 263–91.
* Kalyanam, Kirthi (1996) 'Pricing decisions under demand uncertainty: A bayesian mixture model approach', *Marketing Science* 15: 207–21.
Kanetkar, Vinay, Weinberg, Charles B. and Weiss, Doyle L. (1992) 'Price sensitivity and television advertising exposures: some empirical findings', *Marketing Science* 11: 359–71.
* Karmarkar, Uday S. and Pitbalddo, Richard C. (1997) 'Quality, class, and competition', *Management Science* 43: 27–39.
* Kerin, Roger A., Varadarajan, P. Rajan and Peterson, Robert A. (1992) 'First-mover advantage: a synthesis, conceptual framework, and research propositions', *Journal of Marketing* 56: 36–52.
Kotabe, Masaaki, Sahay, Arvind and Aulakh, Preet S. (1996) 'Emerging role of technology licensing in the development of global product strategy: Conceptual framework and research propositions', *Journal of Marketing* 60: 73–88.
* Kotler, Philip and Turner, Ronald E. (1993) *Marketing Management: Analysis, Planning, Implementation, and Control*, Canadian 7th edn, Scarborough, ON: Prentice-Hall.
* Krishna, Aradhna, Currim, Imran S. and Shoemaker, Robert W. (1991) 'Consumer perceptions of promotional activity', *Journal of Marketing* 55: 4–16.
* Lambkin, Mary, and Day, George S. (1989) 'Evolutionary processes in competitive markets: beyond the product life cycle', *Journal of Marketing* 53: 4–20.
Lancaster, Kelvin J. (1966) 'A new approach to consumer theory', *Journal of Political Economy* 74: 132–57.
* Lancaster, Kelvin (1979) *Variety, Equity, and Efficiency*, New York: Columbia University Press.
* Lancaster, Kelvin (1980) 'Competition and product variety', *Journal of Business* 53: S79–103.
* Leclerc, France, Schmitt, Bernd H. and Dube, Laurette (1995) 'Waiting time and decision making: Is time like money?', *Journal of Consumer Research* 22: 110–19.
* Levitt, Theodore (1983) 'The globalization of markets', *Harvard Business Review* May–June: 92–102.
Lilien, Gary L. and Kotler, Philip (1983) *Marketing Decision Making: A Model-Building Approach*, New York: Harper and Row.
* Lipsey, Richard G. (1966) *An Introduction to Positive Economics*, 2nd edn, London: Weidenfeld and Nicolson.
* Lusch, Robert F. and Brown, James R. (1996) 'Interdependency, contracting, and relational behavior in marketing channels', *Journal of Marketing* 60: 19–38.
* Mahajan, Vijay, Sharma, Subhash and Buzzell, Robert D. (1993) 'Assessing the impact of competitive entry on market expansion and incumbent sales', *Journal of Marketing* 57: 39–52.
* McAfee, R. Preston and McMillan, John (1996) 'Competition and game theory', *Journal of Marketing Research* 33: 263–7.
* McCarthy, E. Jerome and Shapiro, Stanley J. (1983) *Basic Marketing*, Canadian 3rd edn, Homewood, IL: Richard D. Irwin.

* Mallen, Bruce (1973) 'Conflict and cooperation in marketing channels', in Boone, Louis E. and Johnson, James C. (eds), *Marketing Channels*, Morristown, NJ: General Learning Press.
* Menon, Anil and Varadarajan, P. Rajan (1992) 'A model of marketing knowledge use within firms', *Journal of Marketing* 56: 53–71.
* Mitra, Anusree and Lynch, John G. Jr. (1995) 'Toward a reconciliation of market power and information theories of advertising effects on price elasticity', *Journal of Consumer Research* 21: 644–59.
* Mittelstaedt, Robert A. (1990) 'Economics, psychology, and the literature of the subdiscipline of consumer behavior', *Journal of the Academy of Marketing Science* 18: 303–11.
* Moyer, Reed and Hutt, Michael D. (1978) *Macro Marketing*, 2nd edn, Santa Barbara: Wiley/Hamilton.
* Nagle, Thomas (1984) 'Economic foundations for pricing', *Journal of Business* 57: S3–26.
* Narver, John C. and Slater, Stanley F. (1990) 'The effect of a market orientation on business profitability', *Journal of Marketing* 54: 20–35.
* Park, C. Whan, Jaworski, Bernard J. and MacInnis, Deborah J. (1986) 'Strategic brand concept-image management', *Journal of Marketing* 50: 135–45.
* Parker, Philip M. (1992) 'Price elasticity dynamics over the adoption life cycle', *Journal of Marketing Research* 29: 358–67.
* Porter, Michael E. (1991) 'Towards a dynamic theory of strategy', *Strategic Management Journal* 12: 95–117.
* Rangan, V. Kasturi, Menezes, Melvyn A.J. and Maier, E.P. (1992) 'Channel selection for new industrial products: a framework, method, and application', *Journal of Marketing* 56: 69–82.
* Rao, Ashay R. and Bergen, Mark E. (1992) 'Price premium variations as a consequence of buyers' lack of information', *Journal of Consumer Research* 19: 412–23.
* Rindfleisch, Aric and Heide, Jan B. (1997) 'Transaction cost analysis: Past, present, and future applications', *Journal of Marketing* 61: 30–54.
* Ruekert, Robert W., Walker, Jr, Orville C. and Roering, Kenneth J. (1985) 'The organization of marketing activities: a contingency theory of structure and performance', *Journal of Marketing* 49: 13–25.
* Rugman, Alan M. and Verbeke, Alain (1992) 'A note on the transnational solution and the transaction cost theory of multinational strategic management', *Journal of International Business Studies* (Fourth Quarter): 761–71.
* Samli, A. Coskun and Bahn, Kenneth D. (1992) 'The market phenomenon: an alternative theory and some metatheoretical research considerations', *Journal of the Academy of Marketing Science* 20: 143–53.
* Samuelson, Paul A. (1961) *Economics: An Introductory Analysis*, 5th edn, New York: McGraw-Hill.
* Scitovsky, T. (1944) 'Some consequences of the habit of judging quality by price', *Review of Economic Studies* 12: 100–5.
* Sen, Kabir C. (1997) 'Advertising intensity within the carbonated soft drinks industry', *Journal of Advertising Research* 37: 37–47.
* Shankar, Venkatesh, Carpenter, Gregory S. and Krishnamuthi, Lakshman (1998) 'Late mover advantage: How innovative late entrants outsell pioneers', *Journal of Marketing Research* 35: 54–70.
* Shocker, Allan D. and Hall, William G. (1986) 'Pretest market models: a critical evaluation', *Journal of Product Innovation Management* 3: 86–107.
* Simon, Herbert A. (1976) *Administrative Behavior*, 3rd edn, New York: The Free Press.
* Smith, Gerald E. and Nagle, Thomas T. (1995) 'Frames of reference and buyers' perception of price and value', *California Management Review* 38: 98–116.
* Stathakopoulos, Vlasis (1996) 'Sales force control: A synthesis of three theories', *Journal of Personal Selling and Sales Management* 16: 1–12.
* Szymanski, David M., Bharadwaj, Sundar G. and Varadarajan, Rajan (1993) 'Standardization versus adaptation of international marketing strategy: An empirical investigation', *Journal of Marketing* 57: 1–17.
* Thaler, Richard (1985) 'Mental accounting and consumer choice', *Marketing Science* 4: 199–214.
* Walters, Rockney G. (1991) 'Assessing the impact of retail price promotions on product substitution, complementary purchase, and interstore sales displacement', *Journal of Marketing* 55: 17–28.
* Wansink, Brian and Ray, Michael L. (1996) 'Advertising strategies to increase usage frequency', *Journal of Marketing* 60: 312–46.
* Webster, Frederick E., Jr. (1992) 'The changing role of marketing in the corporation', *Journal of Marketing* 56: 1–17.
* Williamson, Oliver E. (1975) *Markets and Hierarchies: Analysis and Antitrust Implications*, New York: The Free Press.
* Williamson, Oliver E. (1981) 'The economics of organization: the transaction cost approach', *American Journal of Sociology* 87: 548–77.
* Winer, Russell S. (1988) 'Behavioral perspective on pricing: buyers' subjective perceptions of price revisited', in Devinney, T. (ed.), *Issues in Pricing: Theory and Research*, Lexington, MA: Lexington Books.
* Yadav, Manjit S. and Monroe, Kent B. (1993) 'How buyers perceive savings in a bundle price: An ex-

amination of a bundle's transaction value', *Journal of Marketing Research* 30: 350–8.
* Zeithaml, Valarie A., Parasuraman, A. and Berry, Leonard L. (1985) 'Problems and strategies in services marketing', *Journal of Marketing* 49: 33–46.

See also: BRANDING AND BRAND MANAGEMENT; CHANNEL MANAGEMENT; CHANNELS OF DISTRIBUTION; CONSUMER BEHAVIOUR; GLOBAL MARKETING; MARKET SEGMENTATION; MARKETING RESEARCH; MARKETING STRATEGY; NEW PRODUCT DEVELOPMENT; POSITIONING; PRODUCT LIFE-CYCLE MANAGEMENT; PRODUCT POLICY

The psychological basis of marketing

1 Marketing and psychology
2 Understanding marketing management
3 Conclusion

Overview

Marketing is human behaviour. In affluent societies, it is the behaviour of buyers and managers, directed towards the fulfilment of economic objectives through consumption that is satisfying to consumers and profitable for marketers. Psychology is the science of behaviour and its application to marketing is intended to aid understanding of the activities of buyers, users and managers that contributes to the fulfilment of those objectives in more informed ways, as well as increasing academic knowledge. This entry discusses the psychological foundations of marketing, and its implications for both consumer behaviour and marketing management.

1 Marketing and psychology

Marketing psychology has become an immense field of research and teaching in the last two to three decades. There are numerous textbooks on both consumer behaviour and marketing management as well as attempts to integrate what is known about consumer choice with prescriptions for marketing action. Other contributions to this Encyclopedia take these concerns further by discussing the nature of consumer behaviour and the appropriate strategic and tactical managerial decisions (see CONSUMER BEHAVIOUR; MARKETING STRATEGY; MARKETING ORGANIZATION AND MANAGEMENT).

This article is concerned, however, with the fundamentals of both consumer *behaviour* and marketing *response*, with the basic psychological knowledge required to understand the separate activities of consumers and managers and their interactions. This knowledge is basic in the sense that it can be built upon by present and future marketing managers who wish a more elaborate picture of the specific market considerations with which they are engaged. Psychological concepts and frameworks permeate the marketing literature, implicitly and explicitly. Much of the psychology in marketing nevertheless falls short of the needs of students, marketers and researchers: it is either trivial – based on commonsense nostrums dignified with the word 'psychological' – or academically abstruse – useful for an exclusively intellectual audience but of limited applicability. Marketing knowledge requires a sure substructure of basic psychological knowledge if it is to contribute either to academic or managerial goals. This entry summarizes the research programme that is providing that substructure.

Elementary marketing behaviour

There are many ways in which marketing can be approached through psychology. Social psychology, for instance, is a strong contender for special consideration, applicable as it is to the personal interactions of buyers and sellers, the structure and dynamics of groups of consumers each of whom is influenced to buy this or that product, this or that brand, or perhaps nothing at all, by the words and actions of the rest. Dynamic psychology, the work of Freud, Jung, Adler and the other psycho-analysts, might also be proposed for this role. Consumers' suppressed and repressed motives, the formation of such personality structures as id, ego and super-ego in the process of psycho-sexual development might be incorporated in an interpretation of consumer choice based on their supposed unconscious desires.

Cognitive psychology would certainly be an important contender. Indeed, the study of consumer behaviour in the context of marketing is dominated by theories that depict it as information processing, and has been for some forty years, since the farm economists began to view consumer choice as decision making. Nowadays, the consumer behaviour texts are replete with one or other model of the consumer as an

The psychological basis of marketing

information processor, a mechanism which takes in data from the environment and acts upon it to produce the attitudes and intentions that are held to determine purchase and consumption. Physiological psychology could also play a role. Consumers' physical characteristics which stem from genetic endowments may have an immediate effect on choice and consumption; they include body size and build, athletic prowess, some forms of disablement and sexual attractiveness. The importance of these variables is evident from the extent to which they form the basis of marketing programs, notably advertising campaigns and are the subject of consumer research (see ADVERTISING).

All of these theoretical perspectives contribute to the superstructure of marketing psychology. But none provides the psychological *basics* of marketing. For one thing, the overwhelming majority of attempts to incorporate psychology into marketing concentrate on consumer behaviour rather than that of marketing managers. Although the identical cognitive decision models applied to consumers have been used by organizational behaviour specialists to elucidate managerial decision making, what we want is a fundamental discussion of the actions of customers and managers in the same terms, something that links the two while describing them as part of the same system rather than as two apparently separate subsystems (see DIRECT MARKETING).

In seeking the psychological fundament of marketing, we are concerned with what Homans (1974) calls 'elementary social behaviour'. This requires that we focus not on the characteristics of the organizations, even the groups in terms of which marketing is often discussed but on the *behaviour* of the social units involved and the factors that are directly responsible for them. The aim is to emphasize the ways in which consumers and managers actually act as and where they are, rather than to derive stylized or idealized prescriptions that purport to cover every marketing problem or every situation of purchase and consumption. How do customers and managers act in the situations in which they find themselves? The search for elementary marketing behaviour, a task for description rather than prescription, should therefore propose answers to such questions as: What do consumers do – and why? What do marketers do – and why? In fact, by taking this elementary approach, we are re-examining a lot of marketing thought that has been taken for granted for decades. It is not surprising that we arrive at a novel view of why consumers behave as they do and the nature of marketing action and influence on consumer choice.

There is another sense in which the quest for the psychological foundations of marketing is one for *elementary* behaviour. We have argued that, as far as possible, the science and interpretation of marketing behaviour should proceed from direct description of the actions involved. This implies that – at least at a fundamental level – as few theoretical terms as possible should intervene between description and explanation. We should attempt to map out the immediate influences on consumer choice and marketing action, giving as little attention as possible to the hypothetical intervening variables that might account for the behaviour we observe. That is, an account of the psychological fundamentals of marketing should not give major prominence to the notions derived from the very behaviour they are supposed to explain: attitudes and intentions, for example, or personality traits, motives and information processing. All of these unobservables are added by the investigator to explain what has been observed. We do not object to them as such but they tend, in a search for psychological fundamentals, to obscure the simpler determinants of consumer and marketer behaviour with which we are concerned. For now, we can leave them to the textbooks of both consumer behaviour and marketing.

Costs, rewards and exchange

Consumer behaviour brings rewards and costs, almost simultaneously. The rewards are obvious and have been emphasized for decades by the marketing literature. They are the benefits gained from buying, owning and using the product or service in question. The fact that consumer behaviour is also costly is less frequently mentioned. Buyers nevertheless incur the costs of finding a suitable store, product and brand, obtaining information from marketer-dominated sources such as advertising and salespeople, buyer-dominated sources such as friends and neighbours, and neutral sources such as the Consumer

Association's *Which?* magazine. They also incur costs when they make a purchase. Opportunity costs, for instance: surrendering cash means that alternative products have to be forgone. Buying one thing rather than another or rather than saving may attract criticism from people who would have us dispose of our money 'more wisely'; wearing unfashionable or inappropriate clothes may invite ridicule, and so on. We can assume that consumers are constantly balancing the rewards of purchasing an item against the costs of doing so, the rewards and costs of buying one product against those of buying another, the outcomes of patronizing one store against those of shopping at another, and so on (see BRANDING AND BRAND MANAGEMENT; CULTURAL ASPECTS OF MARKETING).

Marketers, also – perhaps more obviously – both reap rewards and incur costs as a result of supplying the market place with products and services that consumers might buy. Their revenues depend directly on the prices customers pay, and their costs derive from their own extraction or purchases of raw materials, production, distribution, advertising, and so on. They, too, have a choice: to sell now (in which case, they are rewarded by the sale) or to retain their produce in the hope that prices will rise (in which case, they must continue to pay inventory and other costs).

The interactions of consumers and marketers, their exchange behaviours, can be summarized by payoff matrices such as those shown in Figure 1. The consumer always has the choice of saving or spending on the product offered by the marketer. The marketer has the choice of selling to the consumer or storing the product for later sale. Figure 1(a) shows the pay-offs available in a simple situation in which the consumer knows the brand on offer, has used and been satisfied with it in the past, and is offered it at (more or less) the prevailing market price. The marketer knows his or her costs and a sale at that price will contribute to profit expectations. If the consumer decides to save, while the marketer decides to retain the product, their gains are not as great as if an exchange takes place. However, if one party to a potential transaction either saves or stores while the other wishes to buy or sell, the former gains (e.g. interest on money that might otherwise be spent, or by holding on to an appreciating asset) while the latter loses out on the desired rewards.

This framework also allows us to speculate what will happen if the behaviours of consumer and marketer change. Figure 1(b) shows the pay-offs on offer when the marketer doubles the price asked for the product. Should a transaction occur, we assume that both parties gain equally, but it is easier now for the consumer to be indifferent between buying and saving. Should he or she not make a purchase, the value of the retained spending power is greater than before. Finally – Figure 1(c) – we assume that the marketer offers a compromise: the price remains twice as high as in the first example but the marketer offers 25% more of the item. If the consumer is now persuaded to buy, the seller still has a better deal than originally but a new equilibrium position is reached and exchange is once again feasible.

Real transactions are more complicated than this hypothetical example conveys. Let us concentrate on the consumer's point of view. The decision to buy or save depends not only on its likely consequence or payoff: it is also a function of the consumer's circumstances and the extent to which the situation is controlled by the consumer or the marketer. Consumer demand is determined in part by the level of satiety the individual has achieved (conversely, by his or her level of deprivation), by such state and personal variables as mood, the availability of credit or other means to pay, and his or her experience of buying and using the product in the past. Most important of all may be the immediate setting in which the transaction or act of consumption takes place. This includes the consumer's physical and social surroundings, and the norms that specify the appropriateness of certain behaviours rather than others. All of these act either to facilitate or inhibit particular acts of purchase and consumption.

At home, to give an example, one generally feels freer to choose certain consumption activities which would incur sanctions if performed elsewhere: entertainment or sleeping are obvious examples but there are doubtless others. Indeed, settings such as the home often encourage consumption: listening to the radio there is more probable than doing so elsewhere simply because it will not be interrupted or disturb anyone else; watching TV or preparing a favourite meal is more probable at home

The psychological basis of marketing

(a) Symmetrical interaction

		Consumer's actions	
		b_1 Save	b_2 Spend
Marketer's actions	Store S_1	1 \ 1	0 \ 1
	Sell S_2	1 \ 0	2 \ 2

(b) Buyer indifference

		Consumer's actions	
		b_1 Save	b_2 Send
Marketer's actions	Store S_1	2 \ 1	2 \ 2
	Sell S_2	\ 2	\

(c) Power equalization

		Consumer's actions	
		b_1 Save	b_2 Send
Marketer's actions	Store S_1	2 \ 1	3 \
	Sell S_2	\ 2	\

Figure 1 Pay-off matrices in a marketing context

because that is where the necessary equipment is. Sometimes, consumption settings are deliberately arranged to encourage purchasing: supermarkets and other retail outlets are arranged to maximize the amount of time the customer spends in them because level of purchase is a function of that time; consumers often buy books on impulse because of the way they are displayed in bookstores; the probability of visiting a speciality store such as a jeweller's is greater if it is situated en route to a departmental store or other 'attractor' which the customer frequently visits; and such determinants of store atmosphere as lighting and crowding are often controlled by retailers to ensure that consumers stay and buy (Foxall and Goldsmith 1994).

Thus in addition to the consequences of behaviour (its outcomes or pay-offs), any understanding of consumer choice must take antecedents such as these into consideration. Doing so allows us to summarize the situation in which consumer behaviour occurs very simply as follows:

$$A : B : C$$

where A = antecedents,
B = behaviour, and
C = consequences.

There is nothing automatic about the ways in which these variables interact. The antecedents which include the nature of the setting, the

The theoretical foundations

consumer and his or her experience of the product and store, and his or her personal, economic and physiological states do not make consumer behaviours such as purchase, saving or consumption inevitable: depending on their precise nature, they make one or other of these responses more likely to occur. Purchase or consumption are more probable when levels of deprivation are high, when the customer is in the right mood, when he or she has the money to make a purchase or the time to consume, when social mores indicate that the act will be approved and when his or her experience of behaving like this in the past was rewarding rather than costly.

The consequences of a particular act of purchase, saving and consumption also make it more or less probable given these antecedents, but they do not make it inevitable in every circumstance. Rewards come broadly in two kinds. Some are intrinsic to the product or service itself and derive directly from its value in use. A lawnmower that cuts the grass with minimum effort and results in a smooth, even lawn that will increase the pleasure of sitting out on sunny days is usually preferred to one that churns up the garden and causes more work. We can call these direct benefits of the product the *instrumental* rewards of purchase and consumption. However, the intrinsic benefits of the product are not the sole reasons they are bought and used. Many items also provide extrinsic or *expressive* rewards.

Being seen to use the latest electronic lawnmower, for instance, one which is known to be expensive, exclusive, highly efficient and incorporating state-of-the-art technology may confer prestige and esteem. It provides a measure of how well one is doing, one's level of performance – not primarily as a gardener, perhaps, but as a consumer, as an earner and as a citizen. The fact that one needs so coiffured a lawn on which to hold garden parties for eminent guests is a signal to others that one is doing well. Consuming such a mower is expressively rewarding as well as instrumentally useful. Of course, the chances that one can buy and use such a machine is also decided by its costs: we have said that it is a highly expensive product; it may also require great skill to operate or entail high maintenance costs. One might have to employ a gardener to use it, though the costs of doing so would be offset to some extent – maybe entirely, depending on our income – by the social esteem this would confer. But we must remember that, in addition to the instrumental and expressive *rewards* of purchase and consumption, there are inevitably *costs*. In particular, the costs of previously buying or using the product in question may inhibit purchase: we might have been embarrassed as a result of asking naive questions in the store last time we tried to make a purchase, we might have been unable to keep up the credit repayments, or we might have been seen by our neighbours as we struggled to learn a new way of cutting the grass.

Figure 2 Consumer interaction
Source: Foxall (1990:79)

The psychological basis of marketing

Marketer–and buyer-dominated communications; corporate image elements; store image elements; brand characteristics; consequences of prior behaviour, market mix variables; level of deprivvtion.	Prepurchase, purchase, and consimption responses Consumer behaviour	Product/service performance, functional and symbolic consequences of purchase and use; reactions of significant others; surrender of spending power.
A ─────────────────▶	B ─────────────────▶	C
C ◀─────────────────	B ◀─────────────────	A
	Market behaviour	
Revenue, profit, and other consequences of sales (social, reputational, legal, etc.). Avoidance of legal complaint; surrender of investment capital.	Product development, marketing action; brand differentiation; design, creation and use of marketing mix(es); product portfolio management; strategic marketing; market research, etc.	Prior marketing action and its consequences; market intelligence; competitor action; patterns of consumer behaviour and their consequences.

Figure 3 Consumer and marketer behaviours
Source: Foxall (1990: 78)

The A:B:C idea can be used to map out consumer behaviour in specific marketing settings as a dynamic process that is influenced by the setting in which it occurs and the consequences it attracts. Figure 2 exemplifies the 'complex lattice of interrelated' A – B – C chains that represent consumer/marketer interactions in a retail setting. John is a consumer who enters a store (B_1), an action which is an antecedent prompt for another customer, Mary, to follow; another antecedent prompt, say an item in the store's window display, also signals the rewards that are available to Mary in the store and makes her entry (B_2) more likely. John's entering the store is also an antecedent for a salesperson, James, to approach him and offer to help (B_3). This action also prompts another customer who is already in the store to approach another salesperson and ask for help.

A great deal of consumer behaviour in interaction with the marketing system can be portrayed in this way. The point is that consumer and marketer behaviours are mutually rewarding, each makes a set of responses on the part of the other more probable. Figure 3 portrays consumer/market interactions in this way. This basic idea indicates that the interactions involved are, in the most fundamental psychological terms, dependent on the setting variables and external rewards that shape them.

The Behavioural Perspective Model

Let's put all of these factors into a model of the consumer and his or her situation. Figure 4 summarizes what has become known as the Behavioural Perspective Model of purchase and consumption (Foxall 1990).

On the basis of the levels of instrumental and expressive rewards provided by various producers, services and retail outlets, we can classify styles of purchase and consumption in several ways. To simplify, note that each class of consumer behaviour can have either a low or a high level of instrumental reward and either a low or a high level of expressive reward. Figure 5 portrays the four broad classes of consumer behaviour that emerge from this analysis.

Consumer behaviours that are absolutely necessary for physical survival and the minimum level of obligation one incurs as a citizen

The theoretical foundations

Figure 4 Simplified diagram of the behavioural perspective model of purchase and consumption personal and state instrumental variables rewards consumer behaviour consumer expressive setting variables behaviour rewards consumer experience costs

include such activities as buying and consuming foods, paying taxes and finding a home. We can sum them up as *maintenance* behaviours because of their essential role in providing the consumer's physical well-being and social standing. These behaviours are shaped by a pattern of reward that includes relatively low levels of both instrumental and expressive reward.

Another class of consumer behaviours includes the accumulation of products or money through saving or by buying a series of linked purchases. What is important in keeping up behaviour of this kind is frequent feedback on how much has been collected or accumulated so far and any bonuses that might have been added. *Accumulation* behaviour is therefore sustained by high levels of expressive reward which informs the consumer about progress to date and relatively low levels of instrumental reward.

A third class of consumer behaviour is *pleasure* which includes the activities involved in being entertained, playing, seeking fun, dining in restaurants. The high levels of instrumental reward that sustain this kind of behaviour are often derived from services rather than products – theatres, videotapes, hotels, etc. By comparison with the instrumental rewards that maintain these activities, the levels of expressive reward provided are relatively low.

Finally, come consumer behaviours that are rewarded by high levels of both instrumental and expressive pay-offs. Such activities as gambling in a casino or shopping for luxury and highly innovative products are included in this class: *accomplishment*. Accomplishment is available to relatively few consumers – those who can afford to pay for the expensive products and services involved and who have been socialized by their previous experiences as consumers to seek such a pattern of reward.

A hierarchy of consumer lifestyles

The model also provides a means of classifying consumer behaviours generally in terms of the scope of the setting in which they occur and the pattern of reward that maintains them (Figure 6).

The four broad classes of consumer behaviour can be seen as a hierarchy of lifestyles which reflect the economic progress of the consumer over all or part of the consumer life-cycle. The consumer life-cycle consists of the sequence of stages through which the typically successful consumer may be expected to pass in the course of his or her economically active years. The cycle is confined to consumer behaviour from early adulthood onwards, when the individual is independently earning as well

The psychological basis of marketing

```
                    Accomplishment  – high expressive reward
                         ↑
  High
  instrumental
  reward
                    Pleasure        – low expressive reward
                         ↑

                    Accumulation    – high expressive reward
                         ↑
  Low
  instrumental
  reward
                    Maintenance     – low expressive reward
```

Figure 5 A hierarchy of consumer behaviours: *accomplishment* – high expressive reward high instrumental reward; *pleasure* – low expressive reward; *accumulation* – high expressive reward low instrumental reward; *maintenance* – low expressive reward

as spending and saving. The general sequence of lifestyles for the individual during these years is *maintenance – accumulation – pleasure – accomplishment*.

Maintenance is fundamental to citizenship of an affluent economic system, and represents the essential level of economic activity to which its members are first socialized. Accumulation, pleasure and accomplishment infer

Closed ←——————————→ Open

Fulfilment	Status goods
Inescapable entertainment	Popular entertainment
Token-based buying	Collecting
Mandatory consumption	Poutine purchase

Figure 6 An integration of consumer behaviour
Source: Foxall (1992: 396)

a rising level of wealth/income. Over the early and middle ranges of the consumer life-cycle, the consumer typically progresses from a lifestyle concerned almost exclusively with maintenance to those devoted in turn to the mounting acquisition of material effects, enjoyment of artistic, cultural and literary pursuits and, finally, the acquisition of status goods, self-development and other forms of fulfilment.

No consumer is ever entirely freed from the necessities of maintenance but his or her lifestyle, given a progressive income and the sequence of obligations implied by the family life-cycle can be portrayed as a series of consumption patterns, each of which is dominated by a specific operant class of consumer behaviours.

We need to bear in mind that each of these four classes of consumer behaviour will also attract a different level of costs; they are not used in the definition of the classes because it is the general pattern of rewards that attracts a customer to each class but we can safely assume that total costs increase as one ascends the hierarchy and a full analysis takes this into explicit consideration (Foxall 1994).

2 Understanding marketing management

We can derive from this account of consumer choice a novel interpretation of how marketing management works. Of course, there are basically only four instruments available to marketers to attempt to control consumer behaviour – product, price, promotion and place, which together form the marketing mix (see THE MARKETING MIX). But the model proposed above suggests that a great deal of marketing activity is concerned with modifying two main variables that influence consumer behaviour. The first involves managing the scope of the consumer behaviour setting with the intention of increasing the attractiveness of the setting for the individual and reducing his or her propensity to avoid or leave it without purchasing or consuming, The second is the management of the ways in which instrumental and expressive rewards are made available to the consumer.

Management of the consumer behaviour setting

A considerable amount of managerial action in marketing can be viewed as attempting to close down the scope of behaviour settings, making the purchase of whatever the marketer offers more likely (whether this refers to spending on buying a product or consuming a service such as depositing money in a savings account) and making other responses (such as leaving the store, buying or consuming an alternative offering) less probable. Obvious examples are the provision of credit facilities for consumers who cannot afford the full cash outlay immediately, changing consumers' moods through in-store music, using advertising to promise desirable rewards contingent upon buying and using the item, and so on. Nor is this strategy of *closure* necessarily manipulative (in the worse sense of the word), especially in a competitive environment. Presenting the consumer with a more pleasant retail environment, for instance, or with clearer way-finding aids and more legible shopping mall designs encourages the potential buyer to stay in the marketing environment and to become an actual consumer (Foxall and Goldsmith 1994). What is the alternative? To allow consumers to find their own way around unpleasant stores where the merchandise is poorly displayed and difficult to find? Failing to compete with other marketers in order to ensure a quiet life for all? There is no doubt what consumers prefer. If closure of the consumer setting – in a competitive environment – is manipulative, it is a matter of manipulation by printed invitation.

The fact that marketing takes place within a competitive context – at least in affluent societies that ensure high levels of discretionary income, an excess of marketing capacity over demand, and thus consumer choice – means that closure strategies are limited by firms' resources. Ecological psychologists have studied the ways in which organizations use what we would call marketing and demarketing in order to respond to their ability to staff their operations. Staffing levels (both qualitative and quantitative) are one source of constraint on firms' resource bases, especially in relation to what the psychologists call overpopulation but which we would recognize as over-demand, but the ability to provide products of the right quality and quantity, to advertise their availability, to price them adequately (for consumers, managers, shareowners and other stakeholders) and to distribute them efficiently also influence the extent to which firms can effect closure of the consumer setting.

Over-demand typically arises because of the density of consumers in a physical setting that interferes with the level of service available to satisfy demand. This service level is relative not only to the size of the public present in the locale but to the level of human and physical resources available to deliver the required service. More significantly, it is relative to the quality of staff and other resources and, particularly, to the implications of the quality and quantity of these resources for the delivery of a demanded level of marketing proficiency. We could suggest many examples of the ways in which marketers respond to over-demand by modifying the scope of the consumer setting in order to increase consumer satisfaction as well as marketing goals. Here are just three examples of the ways in which place has been modified to effect closure.

Control of entrance of consumers into the setting. Consumers are sometimes scheduled

The psychological basis of marketing

through an appointments systems or by active demarketing such as a reduction in the volume or frequency of marketing communications. On occasion the standards required for admission are increased through a price increase or requirement that patrons (e.g. in a restaurant) wear suitable clothing. Customers might also be channelled into a holding area (such as a bar in a restaurant if a table is not immediately available). Some consumer behaviours might be banned (smoking, for instance) so that some potential customers are effectively debarred.

Control of the capacity of the setting. The size of the setting might be increased/decreased – as when airlines fly larger planes. Opening hours may be altered. Staff shortages might be compensated for by the installation of automatic teller machines.

Control of the time consumers spend in the setting. The service/product might be provided more quickly (e.g. a barber might cut hair faster or food operations in a fast-food restaurant might be automated). Motorists may be allowed only 30 minutes' parking and their return prohibited for a further two hours. The flow of consumers through a service area might be controlled to ensure that bottlenecks do not occur: for example, self-service restaurants may require consumers to place orders at one counter, obtain their purchases from another and pay at a third.

Management of rewards

There are three ways in which marketers manage the rewards system: by enhancing the effectiveness of rewards, by controlling the schedules on which rewards are presented, and by increasing the quantity or quality of rewards (Alhadeff 1982). Here are some examples.

Enhancing the effectiveness of rewards. The effectiveness of some rewards can be increased by deliberately delaying their availability to the consumer. This is an ineffective strategy when competitors can quickly step in and supply the product – there is no point in making would-be customers wait for ice-creams on a hot day. But, if the item in question is a service and if the marketer has been successful in closing the consumer setting, there may be some scope for increasing total purchasing or consumption through delay. This is especially relevant to consumer behaviours that can be described as *pleasure*. The consumer who has paid for a cinema or theatre seat, for instance, has entered a relatively closed setting. He or she can get up and leave at any time (though there will be costs such as the forfeiture of the entrance money, the displeasure expressed by other members of the audience who are inconvenienced, and the loss of an opportunity to see the film, play or act). Films and acts in these establishments are often scheduled, however, so that the most popular or most hyped appears last; the audience is, willingly or not, required to consume less highly demanded products such as a minor movie, new short ballets or playlets, advertisements, less well-known acts, and so on. Nevertheless, they usually wait, their expectation of the major film, play or top of the bill act actually increased by the interval of time. The consumer performs a series of responses, chained together so that each rewards its predecessor (watching the minor movie is a reward contingent on sitting through the ads, for example), while each signals the next and makes watching it more probable. The enjoyment of the final act is actually greater because of the anticipation that has been created, the deprivation that has been skilfully managed. Delays are not always deliberately engineered by marketers, of course, Sometimes a wait is inevitable – as when a long-haul air journey will take some hours before customers reach their destination. In the meantime, the airlines often alleviate the demerits of the temporal and physical restrictions imposed by having to sit still in a passenger cabin for along period by offering meals, movies, duty-free products and alcohol.

Another managerial strategy designed to increase the effectiveness of rewards, this time especially relevant to *accumulation*, is the use of token-based marketing in which an ultimate reward (often instrumental) is made dependent upon the purchase or use of a series of other products (which are useful but whose primary reward in this context is expressive since they signal to the consumer how far he or she is advancing towards obtaining the ultimate product). The promotional use of such tokens as trading stamps, the presentation of encyclopaedic works in monthly parts that build into a complete set, the payment of extraordinary rates of interest on long-term savings are all examples. Frequent-flyer programmes in which additional air tickets are available to passengers who accumulate high mileages are another example. Some international hotels also allow customers to accumulate points that are exchangeable for products and services. In each case, the collection of the tokens (stamps, 'air-miles', points) is rewarded by the ultimate prize.

Scheduling of rewards. When a reward is provided every time a particular response is performed, individuals learn the required behaviour quickly – every time the switch is turned, the lights go on – but the response is quickly forgotten or extinguished once the reward ceases. Learning a response is surer when rewards are intermittent – every *n*th response is rewarded or a reward is given every *x* minutes as long as the action has occurred at least once in the period. Behaviours learned under these conditions often take longer to get into the individual's repertoire but they are performed for long periods even when all reward has ceased. Industry has long made use of these effects by making pay contingent on the amount of work done (as in piece-work). They are also apparent in much consumer marketing. An example that comes under the heading of *accomplishment* is gambling in a casino, a fairly closed setting which it may be costly or inconvenient to leave once play has begun. The rewards are both instrumental (money can be won which can then be spent on other things) and expressive (the amount won over time gives accurate feedback on performance). Games of chance are scheduled in such a way that gambling is likely to persist even when nothing has been won for some time. Progressively 'stretching' the schedule of wins to responses has the effect of encouraging long periods of gaming.

Many aspects of *pleasure* are also maintained by scheduled rewards. Take watching the television news, for instance. The 'happy news' format, pioneered in California provides frequent rewards so that even a short period of viewing is reinforced and further viewing is made more probable. The bulletins are meant to entertain as much as they inform, presenting the audience with 'action, pace [and] an almost dizzy attempt to keep the audience from getting bored' (Tunstall and Walker 1981: 123). Stories are chosen for their entertaining and even sensational content and each gets two or three minutes' coverage in a 30-minute broadcast which also contains two three-minute advertising breaks and a five-minute weather forecast which is as exciting as the news items.

Increasing the quality and quantity of rewards

Marketers often increase the quality and quantity of consumers' purchases, the former by engaging in a strategy of continual product improvement, the latter by promotional deals that provide more for the same price or by reducing the price by a given amount or by refunds. Some more elaborate methods involve the creation and scheduling of information to consumers, e.g. when a product paid for now cannot be consumed for some time. Progress reports on expensive furniture that is being hand made over a period of weeks or months, advertisements that remind consumers of the benefits of the exotic vacation they are awaiting, preparatory meetings and detailed instructions pertaining to self-improvement courses are all examples of the use of information to reward a commitment made to *accomplishment* long before the product or service is delivered.

3 Conclusion

This article has shown that a fundamental model derived from the psychology of learning can account not only for consumer behaviour but also for the marketing management that is one of its chief determinants. Some researchers would prefer to include additional terms in the account – to theorize about the possible intervening influence of consumers' attitudes and intentions, their personality traits, and processes of information handling – and to conceptualize managerial behaviour in terms of similar hypothetical constructs. Well and good. As was pointed out at the beginning of the entry, marketing has numerous links with psychological method and theory. But the point of the present account has been to present the *psychological foundations of marketing* and that has meant overcoming the temptation to elaborate.

GORDON R. FOXALL
KEELE UNIVERSITY

Note

Foxall (1996) provides the story to date of the research programme on which this entry is based, including the provenance and development of the theory, and its application to consumer attitudes and behaviour, environmental conservation, the diffusion of innovations. It also provides an extended discussion of the philosophical basis of this approach and the scope for further theoretical and empirical work. The most recent expositions of the Behavioural Perspective Model and its application to understanding the nature of marketing management can be found in Foxall (1997a, 1998a). The philosophical basis of this approach is described in Foxall (1999a). A shorter exposition and a summary of empirical research is available in Foxall, Goldsmith and Brown (1998). Reports of empirical research can be found in Foxall (1997b, 1997c, 1999b), Foxall and Bhate (1998), Foxall and Greenley (1998a, 1998b, 1998c). The application of the behavioral approach to marketing and the firm is covered in Foxall (1998b, 1998c.)

Further reading

(References cited in the text marked *)

* Alhadeff, D.A. (1982) *Microeconomics and Human behaviour: Toward a New Synthesis of Economics and Psychology*, Berkeley, CA: University of California Press.
* Foxall, G.R. (1990) *Consumer Psychology in Behavioural Perspective*, London and New York: Routledge.
* Foxall, G.R. (1996) *Consumers in Context: The BPM Research Program*, London and New York: International Thomson Business Press.
* Foxall, G.R. (1997a) *Marketing Psychology: The Paradigm in the Wings*, London: Macmillan Press.
* Foxall, G.R. (1997b) 'Affective responses to consumer situations', *International Review of Retail, Distribution and Consumer Research* 7: 191–225.
* Foxall, G.R. (1997c) 'The emotional texture of consumer environments: A systematic approach to atmospherics', *Journal of Economic Psychology* 18: 505–23.
* Foxall, G.R. (1998a) 'Radical behaviorist interpretation: generating and evaluating an account of consumer behaviour', *The Behaviour Analyst* 21: 145–78.
* Foxall, G.R. (1998b) 'The marketing firm', *Journal of Strategic Marketing* 6: 1–20.
* Foxall, G.R. (1998c) 'The marketing firm: rejoinder', *Journal of Strategic Marketing* 6.
* Foxall, G.R. (1999a) 'The contextual stance', *Philosophical Psychology* 12.
* Foxall, G.R. (1999b) 'The Behavioural Perspective Model: consensibility and consensuality', *European Journal of Marketing* 33 (9/10).
* Foxall, G.R. and Bhate, S. (1998) 'Computer use-innovativeness: cognition and context', *International Journal of Technology Management* 14.
* Foxall, G.R., Goldsmith, R.E. and Brown, S. (1998) *Consumer Psychology for Marketing*, 2nd edn, London and New York: International Thomson Business Press.
* Foxall, G.R. and Greenley, G.E. (1998a) 'Consumers' emotional responses to service environments', *Journal of Business Research* 43.
* Foxall, G.R. and Greenley, G.E. (1998b) 'The emotional structure of consumer situations', *Environment and Behavior* 30: 779–6.
* Foxall, G.R. and Greenley, G.E. (1998c) Situational Determinants of Consumer Behaviour, Working Paper, Keele Consumer Group.
* Homans, G.C. (1974) *Social Behaviour: Its Elementary Forms*, 2nd edn, New York: Harcourt Brace Javonovich.
* Tunstall, J. and Walker, D. (1981) *Media Made in California: Hollywood, Politics and the News*, New York: Oxford University Press.

See also: ADVERTISING; BRANDING AND BRAND MANAGEMENT; CONSUMER BEHAVIOUR; CULTURAL ASPECTS OF MARKETING; DIRECT MARKETING; MARKETING ORGANIZATION AND MANAGEMENT; MARKETING STRATEGY; THE MARKETING MIX

The sociological basis of marketing

1 Introduction
2 Marketing and sociology
3 Marketing focus and scientific borrowing
4 Concepts and ideas
5 Summary and future outlook

Overview

This article claims that marketing is a basic social activity, and shows how the discipline of marketing has borrowed from and been influenced by sociology.

The similarities between the basic characteristics of marketing and sociology are illustrated and it is demonstrated that marketing is essentially a societal activity which has borrowed significantly from sociology and sociological thinking. Marketing demands that consumers are considered not only as individuals, but also in terms of the groups in which they exist – for example families, social classes and indeed the wider society around them – and taking into account their status, lifestyle, culture and so on. Then marketing must look at relationships within these groups: networking, conflict and power all have a bearing on the marketing approach to be adopted. Furthermore, sociology can be drawn upon to enlighten the marketer on socialization and learned behaviour. Consideration is also given to how a sociological approach might influence the marketing of the future.

1 Introduction

Marketing has long been recognized as a 'borrowing' discipline, in particular from the social sciences (Cox 1964), and is itself claimed to be a social science discipline (Hunt 1991). The historical roots of marketing are embedded in classical economics. Citation analysis to determine the influences of other disciplines on marketing also show extensive borrowing from (among others) sociology (Goldman 1979). An interesting observation is that there has been a considerable mutual influence between economics and sociology as reflected in the sub-discipline of economic sociology (for excellent overviews, see Smelser 1963, Granovetter and Swedberg 1992).The borrowing consists of concepts, theories and models, and methods and techniques for doing research. Particularly important is the conceptual borrowing. Concepts are the building blocks of any theory, model or hypothesis. The concepts and how they are used (and related) guide and direct. They give focus and largely determine what is captured.

As will be demonstrated in the following the borrowing from sociology has had – and still has – a considerable influence on marketing thinking. The emphasis here is primarily on the concepts (and perspectives) borrowed and how they have influenced marketing thinking as reflected in major marketing textbooks. The main reason for using marketing textbooks as a mirror of the sociological influences is that textbooks reflect what is taught and disseminated, and is thus believed to capture important aspects of the (sociological) impact on marketing thinking (and practice). Marketing – as other disciplines – has changed and developed over the years. This is also reflected in the borrowing from other disciplines, e.g. sociology, over time.

The entry proceeds as follows: first, characteristics of marketing and the discipline of sociology are emphasized. In this section it is also demonstrated that marketing is a societal activity. Similarities in marketing and sociological reasoning are also discussed. Then the dominant focus in marketing thinking and practice, and how this has influenced conceptual borrowing and use is discussed. Next, specific concepts and ideas borrowed from sociology are emphasized. A distinction is made between concepts and ideas primarily used to (1) characterize individuals, groups and the larger society, (2) contributions taking relationships between social actors directly into account, and (3) contributions focusing on change. Finally, characteristics of the borrowing from and influences of sociology on marketing are summarized and future influences from this discipline (sociology) on marketing are indicated.

2 Marketing and sociology

Marketing activities have a long history. Through thousands of years man has transacted goods and services to satisfy needs and enhance standards of living. As a scientific discipline, however, marketing is young with its origin at the turn of this century.

Marketing as exchange

Marketing takes place in a societal context. The core of marketing as a scientific discipline relates to exchange between social actors, e.g. individuals, groups or organizations, or as claimed by Hunt (1983): 'marketing (science) is the behavioural science which seeks to explain exchange relationships' (p. 129)

(Social) exchange requires:

- the presence of (at least) two parties,
- that each party has something to offer that might be of value to the other party,
- each party is capable to communicate and deliver;
- each party is free to accept or reject an offer,
- each party believes it is appropriate or desirable to deal with the other party (Kotler 1984: 8).

Exchange as phenomenon is, however, a huge area of inquiry, and has been extensively dealt with in sociology and other disciplines. Exchange theory consists not only of one, but several theories. A distinction is often made between individualistic and collective approaches to the study of exchange. Different modes of exchange have been identified as well, such as the market mode (i.e. exchange through markets), reciprocal exchange mode (which can be thought of as gift exchange between members of a network with reciprocal obligations), and the redistributive mode of exchange (i.e. exchange based on some principle of sharing, e.g. blood donations, (Polanyi 1944)).

For a long time, marketing has primarily been associated with the market mode of exchange, where the market is often thought of, in a neoclassical sense, as a large number of exchange partners, and that market prices yield the necessary information and incentives. The idealized market mode of exchange is considered impersonal (as reflected in neoclassical economics) or, as emphasized by Polanyi, 'it is important to emphasize the abstract and impersonal nature of market exchange' (Polanyi 1944: 5). In modern societies, reciprocal and redistributive exchanges are also taking place. Thirty years ago Codere even claimed that the proportion of market exchanges to all exchanges taking place to be declining (Codere 1968: 57).

Marketers have devoted substantial effort to studying and understanding exchanges. In doing so they have extensively borrowed concepts and perspectives from other disciplines. One of the first marketing scholars to recognize the limitations of 'faceless' transactions (i.e. exchange outcomes) to understand markets and marketing was Wroe Alderson, recognized for his influential contributions on marketing thinking. He introduced the notion of the 'organized behavior system' (Alderson 1958) to capture the fact that the various actors operating in the market are more or less connected (as reflected in the recent emphasis on 'relationship' marketing). Alderson thus recognized the benefit of sociology, and claimed: 'The initial plunge into sociology is only the beginning since the marketing man must go considerably further in examining the functions and structures of organized behaviour systems'.

Sociology

Sociology is one of the major social sciences. The term 'sociology' was invented by Auguste Comte, and first published in the fourth volume of his *Cours de philosophie positive* in 1838, even though the ancient roots of the discipline can be traced back to among others Plato and Aristotle. The term (sociology) has two stems, the Latin *socius* (companion) and the Greek *logos* (study of) – and literally means the study of the processes of companionship. The term 'sociology' can be (and has been) defined in various ways, e.g. as proposed by Giddens 'sociology is the study of human life, groups and societies' (Giddens 1938: 7).

A key point in the sociological perspective is that man does not operate in a vacuum, but is embedded in the surrounding social context. The individual forms and holds expectation about others, and because he or she is assumed to behave purposefully, expectations about others are taken into account. This basic point of departure has a distinct parallel in marketing. Marketing activities take place in a societal context. Exchange requires the presence of and access to others. Since man started transacting goods and services thousands of years ago, the importance of 'others' have been recognized. Sellers have tried to identify potential buyers, their needs and how they evaluate. Buyers learn about sellers and their product offerings. Through word of mouth, own experiences and other sources of information, buyers' expectations towards sellers are shaped and influence their behaviour as well.

The individual-in-context is a human being interacting with her or his social environment. The sociological perspective tries to encompass the acting person and the acting group. The acting person is a specific human being who pursues goals, interprets experiences, responds to opportunities, and confronts difficulties. As an individual-in-action he or she does not necessarily stay within neat boundaries of specialized activity, nor does he or she always conform to conventional expectations. For example, the seller may cheat, the buyer shoplift, and the marketing entrepreneur may 'break the rules', change the 'social game' – and become successful.

Social organization

To capture the social influences, sociologists study how the society is organized. In doing so they often make use of the general term, *social system*, emphasizing the interdependencies and interactions among social actors. The same underlying idea can easily be traced in marketing, e.g. as reflected in 'distribution systems', 'system sales', 'relationships' and 'networks'.

In their study of social organizations sociologists also distinguish between different levels, e.g. micro-level (individual and group) and macro-level or social order. Concepts used and phenomenon focused vary across levels (Collins 1981). There are, however, interactions and interdependencies between the various levels. Changes at the macro-level may influence expectations and behaviour at the micro-level and vice versa. For example the automobile has dramatically changed the mobility of the individual (consumer), which has influenced shopping behaviour – and the structure of the distribution system, as reflected in the dramatic changes in the retail trade. A drop in individual fertility, e.g. influenced by a pessimistic outlook for the future may add up to dramatic changes in demand for specific goods or services. Such demographic changes are (among others) studied by sociologists – and experienced by marketers. Markets have also been an arena for sociological inquiry which has generated substantial insights, and which in turn have also been of importance for the marketing discipline (for a recent overview, see Lie 1997).

Our examples so far, show that there are close parallels between sociology and marketing unrecognized in most contemporary marketing textbooks. In what follows the focus will be on the main concepts borrowed from sociology, how they are used, and why they are used this way.

3 Marketing focus and scientific borrowing

The present writer views the borrowing from other disciplines as purposeful behaviour, i.e. the borrowing is done to obtain something, e.g. to understand the functioning of markets and/or to improve marketing practices. On the other hand what is borrowed, and how the borrowings are used are heavily influenced by the dominant focus of the borrowing discipline, in this case marketing.

The term 'marketing' has been used with at least three different meanings (Arndt 1980):

1 marketing as a management orientation or discipline;
2 marketing as a science;
3 marketing as an ideology.

According to the stated purpose, i.e. to capture the influence of sociology on marketing thinking, as reflected in major textbooks, primarily the first meaning of the term (marketing) will be emphasized.

As a management orientation or discipline marketing can be – and has been until now – primarily considered a *business* discipline. In spite of efforts to apply marketing thinking to the public sector, and in non-business and non-profit settings, there is little doubt that most marketing thinking and activities relate to business firms.

Any business firm specializes and offers a more or less limited set of products (services). The firm is dependent of its surrounding environments, in particular of its market(s), i.e. on actual and potential customers. For the firm to survive and prosper a sufficient number of customers must be willing to buy its products (services) at prices which at least cover costs. Even though a business firm can survive losses, in the long run costs must be covered in order to stay in business. Surplus profit which will create optimism, attract admiration and allow for investments and so on is – of course – considered advantageous.

The number of buyers and sellers varies across markets, and the products and services offered are multiple. Modern marketing as reflected in the majority of (American) textbooks primarily deals with *mass-marketing*. Most textbooks are influenced by the underlying (but implicit) perspective that the market frequently exhibits a situation where a few firms sell their products services to many customers (primarily individuals and households as reflected in cell (c)) in Figure 1.

In such markets with a great many customers, there is little room to pay attention to the individual buyer. This is particularly so for low-priced items, where the contribution from the individual buyer is lowest, and allows for modest individual attention only. In such cases the market is often considered an 'aggregate' of individual customers to which the firm tries to offer its products (services). Deighton, 1996, however shows how advances in modern information technologies allow for the individualization of mass markets. Marketing situations as reflected in the other cells are also taking place. An important point, however, is that the situation as depicted in cell (c) reflects – until now – the dominating perspective on marketing thinking and has influenced the borrowing from other disciplines.

Cell (a) in Figure 1 reflects the prototypical 'small numbers' market. In such markets the numbers of sellers and buyers are few. The actors are highly visible, and each customer really counts. The growing emphasis on relationships and networks primarily relate to small numbers, industrial markets, even though such approaches are highly relevant in consumer markets (see *Journal of the Academy of Marketing Science* 1996). When the focus is on relationships and networks the presence of others are also directly brought into account, and thus the social aspect of marketing. The growing emphasis on relationships and networks has also contributed to a growing emphasis on sociological aspects by marketers.

Marketing is – as noted above – primarily a business discipline. Business firms are headed by managers. In the marketing literature managers are conceived as active individuals (or groups) who, it is assumed, make wise

	Sellers	
	Few	Many
Buyers — Few	(a)	(b)
Buyers — Many	(c)	(d)

Figure 1 Number of sellers and buyers

decisions to reach the goals and influence the destiny of the firms they manage.

Due to the firm's dependence of its market(s) it is of crucial importance for the marketing manager to identify and understand actual and potential customers as the basis for designing and implementing successful marketing strategies. This need to identify, understand, and thus in mass markets to 'profile' customers in order to become effective can be traced in marketing's borrowing from sociology as reflected in most marketing (and consumer behaviour) textbooks.

4 Concepts and ideas

This section focuses on the main concepts and ideas borrowed from sociology. The section is organized as follows: first, concepts and ideas to capture the characteristics of individuals, groups and larger social segments are described. Contributions focusing respectively on relationships between actors, and contributions directed towards change are then discussed.

Individuals, groups and the larger society

Role

An important sociological concept is (social) 'role', which can be conceived as 'the bundles of social defined attributes and expectations associated with social positions' (Abercombie et al. 1988). For example, the role of 'mother' carries with it certain expected behaviours irrespective of the woman's feeling at any one time. Therefore it is possible to generalize about role behaviour regardless of the individual characteristics of the people who occupy these roles. Role is sociologically important because it demonstrates how individual activity is socially influenced and thus follows regular patterns. It should also be noted that sociologists employ roles as 'building blocks' to study various social institutions, e.g. families and organizations (to be discussed later on).

In social life an individual may occupy various roles, e.g. the role of mother or father, university professor or marketing manager. The number of roles occupied may vary considerably between people. The number of roles occupied by an individual need not be static, as the individual may acquire new roles (and leave others). An individual may also perceive two or more roles to be in conflict. For example, a person may perceive his role as employee, e.g. salesperson requiring frequent and lengthy travel being in conflict with his parental role as father associated with expectations of spending time with his child(ren).

The concept of role is a true sociological concept as it implies social relationships. For example, the role as 'husband' is primarily relevant in a household setting, e.g. in the presence of a 'wife'. The role concept has been used and has influenced marketing in various ways. The prototypical expectations associated with various roles, e.g. 'mother' and 'working woman' have been used to identify and profile target groups as the basis for designing appropriate marketing approaches. The frequently quoted roles of 'influencer', 'decider', 'user' and 'gatekeeper' in the organizational (industrial) buying literature have been used in a similar way as the basis for who (and how) to target, as has the focus on 'husband' and 'wife' in the study of family (households). This is a somewhat 'one--eyed' perspective on how the concept of role has been translated into marketing as relationships (e.g. between sellers and buyers) have been also focused on and will be discussed later. However, as noted by Wallendorf (1978), so far only a fraction of the potential of role theory has been exploited in a marketing context.

Status

In any social system (e.g. group, organization or society) one may distinguish between different social positions (compare the discussion of social roles). Such positions can also be rank-ordered, implying that positions may be lower, higher or equal in status. Sociologists have long studied how status is achieved. Often a distinction is made between ascribed (e.g. by heritage) and achieved attributes as a basis for status (e.g. education or sports performance). The concept of status has directly (and indirectly) influenced marketing thinking. For example the observation that things (and behaviours) may symbolize status has been extensively used to develop, introduce and communicate products. In other words, marketers have exploited sociological insights by relating status to consumption alternatives, as reflected in Levy's seminal article, 'Symbols for Sale' (1959).

Norm

The term 'norm' refers to social expectations about correct or proper behaviour. Thus norms imply the presence of legitimacy, consent and prescription. When norms are *internalized* they are learnt and accepted as binding the social values and guidelines of conduct relevant to the individual or her or his group or wider society. Internalized norms are central for social order. Deviations from norms are punished by sanctions.

The sources of norms can be found in established values, law, expectations and accepted behaviours. Often (in most cases) norms are not written, but are learnt through socialization (see below). Norms may also be more or less specific. For example, specific norms may prevail with regard to specific role behaviours.

For marketers it is of importance to know the norms in the marketplace in order to behave adequately. In marketing the concept and knowledge of norms are extensively used as input in market research to get adequate information about target groups. For example, prevailing norms may be barriers to the acceptance of new products. By knowing the norms the marketer may adjust to or even contribute to a change of norms. Mason Haire's well known 'shopping list' study is an example. When instant coffee was introduced several decades ago, the acceptance rate of the new product was modest. The shopping list study exposed a sample of housewives to one of two identical shopping lists. The shopping lists were identical, but for one item, coffee. The one list contained 'instant coffee', while the other contained the brand name of a well-known regular coffee. The respondents were asked to describe the shopping person. Housewives (who were in the majority at that time) tended to describe the shopper behind the list containing instant coffee as 'lazy', 'not a good housewife', while women working outside the home described the shopping person as 'smart', 'modern', 'effective' and so on. Apparently the new product was conceived to be in conflict with existing norms of being a good housewife. This knowledge was successfully used in designing marketing strategies to alter this aspect of the prevailing 'housewife norm'. As norms may vary across societies (and social segments), an understanding of prevailing norms represents a true challenge when expanding internationally. More recently marketers have also studied how norms may influence the governance of seller–buyer relationships.

Groups

Social groups are collectives of individuals who interact and form social relationships. A distinction is often made between *primary* and *secondary* groups. The former are small groups, defined by face-to-face interaction. The household (nuclear family) and the clique may serve as examples. Secondary groups are usually larger in number, and each member does not necessarily directly interact with every other member. Examples are unions and associations where the members (at best) interact only with a subset of other members, and where most of the communication is formalized, e.g. through newsletters. Sociological insights regarding groups have influenced marketing thinking. For example, the family (household) can be conceived as a primary group, and plays an important role in marketing thinking, primarily as a buying and consuming unit. A common observation is that firms' (organizations') buying are usually made by a group, rather than a single individual. This has led to the notion of 'the buying group' or 'buying centre', heavily influenced by sociological group insights. The focus among marketers has been on the role (position) of the buying group, identification (or prediction) of who is included, their tasks and activities, and on their relative influence in purchasing situations, as a basis for designing effective marketing strategies.

A third form of groups is *reference groups*: In forming their attitudes and beliefs, and in performing their actions, people will compare or identify themselves with other people, or other groups of people (reference groups). People can make references both to membership – and non-membership groups. Reference group knowledge has influenced marketing thinking. In particular these insights have been applied to relate products or brands to groups to whom it is assumed they will appear attractive. Research findings have demonstrated that reference group influence can be made both at the product category level (particularly for expensive goods) as well as at the brand level. For example, brands of perfume, clothes and equipment are often associated with (distant) attractive reference groups (e.g. movie stars or sports idols). Specific information about the actual reference group(s) of the target group is needed when designing marketing strategies.

Family (household)

The notion of family (household) is extensively used by marketers. In most cases marketers use the notions of 'family' and 'household' interchangably, indicating the Western perspective that family of kind (i.e. the nuclear family) often coincides with households (i.e the unit of dwelling). The family (household) is often considered as an important primary group. The family (household) can also be considered as an important social *institution*. The term (social institutions) refers to established patterns of behaviour, or as suggested defined by Nicosia and Mayer, 'a set of specific activities performed by specific people in specific places through time' (1976: 67). Sociological insights regarding families (households) have in particular been used by marketers to study the relative influence of spouses (and also children) in buying decisions, but also as a basis for studying buying decision processes, and how households (families) allocate their scarce economic resources and time.

Family life-cycle

The sociological term 'life-cycle' is used primarily to describe the development of a person through childhood, adolescence, midlife, old age and death. The concept does not refer to purely biological processes of maturation, but to the transition of an individual through socially constructed categories of age and to the variations in social experiences of ageing. Even though life-cycle is a dynamic concept, the main focus in marketing has been to classify people according to *stages* in the life-cycle, and – in particular – to characterize buying and consumption at the various stages. Such insights have been used to profile target groups and predict future market developments.

Social class

In most (all?) societies individuals are ranked hierarchically along some dimension of inequality, e.g. wealth, education, prestige, age, or some other characteristics (see discussion of status). Such rank-ordering is the basis of social class, referring to strata of that rank-ordering, e.g. the 'upper', 'upper-middle', 'lower--middle' classes and so on. In Western societies wealth, education and prestige (among others) are important characteristics to determine social class membership. Extensive research has shown that members of the various strata or social classes tend to have common characteristics, e.g. similar consumption patterns and values. For example, research findings demonstrate that the middle classes spend more on housing and the home, they save more, spend substantially more on education, books and art than do the lower classes. (For a detailed description of findings regarding class differences, see Berelson and Steiner 1964). Marketers have primarily used such insights to characterize consumption patterns across social classes in order to identify and characterize target groups and segment markets.

Lifestyle

Consumption patterns and values vary across social strata (and groups). Such differences are *visible* indicators of class position. In sociological research the lifestyle concept has been related to broad classes, e.g. to distinguish between rural and urban, urban and suburban forms of social life. In marketing the lifestyle concept has evolved a more psychological orientation, with an emphasis on identifying specific lifestyles based on detailed mapping of consumption activities, media habits, attitudes and opinions.

Culture

Culture has for long been intensively studied by anthropologists and sociologists. Culture is a multidimensional and complex phenomenon, and for decades there has been an ongoing debate about what is meant by the concept. For example in 1952 Kroeber and Kluckhon reviewed 164 definitions of culture. It is commonly assumed that culture includes patterns of behaviours and values, that culture is learned and shared with other people, and influences not only how one behaves, but also how one expects others to behave. How culture can be best understood and how to explain the functioning of culture, have, however, changed over the years. For example, many anthropologists now prefer the term 'enacted' (instead of learned), which recognizes that people don't just passively accept culture, they actively create it. Swidler (1986) in her penetrating analysis sees culture as shaping a repertoire of a 'tool kit' of habits, skills and styles from which people construct 'strategies of action' (p. 273). The acquisition of a repertoire of skills, habits and styles reflects that how to behave in a deliberately rational (goal-directed) fashion can be learned and that this knowledge is context bound, with the cultural context influencing what is conceived as relevant.

Marketing has for long recognized the importance of culture and has extensively borrowed research findings from anthropology and sociology. For example, culture can be characterized according to its *context of communication*, often dichotomized as 'high' versus 'low' (Hall 1976). Many foreign cultures are characterized as 'high cultural contexts', exhibiting a dependence on non-verbal, 'hidden' insights of communication in contrast to low cultural contexts – relying more on explicit verbal communications and symbols. Such insights have been used to explain market failures and to prepare the marketer when crossing borders. Another finding from cultural research is that the cultural *distance* may vary considerably in importance for marketers when considering new markets to enter. Other aspects from cultural research adopted and used by marketers are differences in media-structure and use, the importance of language and symbols, and variations in specific cultural values. Cultural knowledge has been used to characterize and choose markets, design adequate marketing strategies, and to understand and improve international negotiations.

Sub-culture
This term refers to a system of values, attitudes, behaviours and lifestyles of a social group which is distinct from, but related to the dominant culture of a society. In sociology the concept has been of most use in the study of youth and deviancy. In marketing the concept has primarily been adopted and used to study the buying and consumption activities and lifestyles of specific social groups, e.g. teenagers. Such insights have primarily been used as the basis for target group descriptions and thus to improve marketing activities and performance.

As noted above, many sociological concepts (and elements of theories) have been borrowed primarily as tools to identify and characterize target groups in the effort to improve marketing performance. Thus – even though the concepts are borrowed from a discipline concerned with social relationships, the unit of analysis in the marketing use of these concepts has been the individual acting unit (Zaltman and Wallendorf 1977).

Marketing has also borrowed and applied sociological concepts which in a true sense capture aspects of social relationships. This has in particular been the case in situations other than mass-marketing, e.g. in industrial markets where the numbers of buyers often are limited (cf. cells (a) and (b) in Figure 1). In doing so the unit of analysis is changed from the individual acting unit to the relationship between actors.

Relationships, power and conflict

Relationship
A relationship takes place between (at least) two actors, and the *dyad* is frequently used as the unit of analysis. To be a relationship it has to last (at least for some minimum time). A purposeful relationship assumes some flow of activities. The relationships can be of various kinds and focus on exchange of goods, information, money and so on.

The importance of relationships has for long been recognized in disciplines like sociology and anthropology and business, but has until recently received scant attention in marketing literature. A shift in focus is now apparently taking place, as reflected in the recent focus on and interest in 'relationships marketing' (Webster 1992). An interesting observation is the recent interest in relationships and networks in American marketing thinking in spite of the fact that such ideas have been dealt with by European marketing scholars for more than three decades.

A common observation in industrial marketing is that buyers and sellers tend to enter rather long-term relationships, i.e. they tend to transact not only once, but perform re-occurring transactions. There are several reasons for doing so. For example, it takes time, skill and economic resources to identify, negotiate with and adjust to exchange partners. Such efforts can be conceived as (partly) transaction specific investments easing future transactions. When relationships between exchange partners develop information flows more easily, thereby reducing transaction costs and thus explaining why they (relationships) last. Relationships may, in addition to economics, convey and be influenced by social values and concerns, as reflected in the notion of 'embeddedness' (Granovetter 1985).

Any transaction or relationship is guided by a *contract*, either explicitly or implicitly. There is a vast literature on contracts by researchers from several disciplines. Sociologists have primarily been preoccupied with the importance of 'social contracts', which can deviate from legal contracts (Blau 1964). Understanding social contracts can have important implications for marketing.

Network
The notion of 'network', often used to describe systems of relationships between actors, has a long tradition in sociology and anthropology. More recently there has been an increasing use of the network approach to understand the functioning of markets, and how – through their networking activities – firms may acquire resources, competence, gain access to technologies, and achieve competitive advantages.

Conflict
When social actors exhibit purposeful behaviour, e.g. to gain market share or to make money, the interests of social actors may come into conflict. For example, competition can be seen as conflict over the resources or advantages desired by others. Insights regarding the causes of conflicts, and factors and mechanisms influencing conflict development and solution are important for marketers and have been applied in several ways, e.g. to understand and solve conflicts between marketing and other functions, and conflicts between members of the distribution channel (for an interesting discussion, see Levy and Zaltman 1975).

Power
The study of power has a long tradition in sociology. There are several distinct perspectives of power, and the concept has been defined in many ways, e.g. 'the probability that a person in a social relationship will be able to carry out his or her own will in the pursuit of goals of action, regardless of resistance' (based on M. Weber).

The above definition implies that power is exercised by social actors, and involves agency and choice. Power is exercised over others and may involve resistance and conflict. Insights from sociological studies of power (and conflict) have, for example, been applied to understanding and improving the functioning of distribution systems.

Learning and change

Socialization
This term is used to describe the process whereby people learn to conform to social norms, a process that makes possible an enduring society and the transmission of its culture between generations. This concept has only been modestly used in marketing so far, and has primarily focused on how children are socialized as consumers.

Social change
Sociologists have extensively studied how social systems, e.g. societies, change. This has important implications for marketing. The introduction of marketing thinking and practices to newly developing countries is, for example, assumed to enhance standards of living. A successful introduction of marketing thinking and practice will probably also imply dramatic social changes. Societal characteristics may hamper and/or alter the intended changes as well.

Even though marketing activities are conducted to bring about changes in a societal context, few marketing studies so far have addressed the problem of social change (Levy and Zaltman 1975). As society changes, marketing may change as well. For example, the explosive development in modern information technologies has had dramatic effects on marketing.

Diffusion of innovations relates to how innovations, e.g. new ideas, practices or products, are spread within social systems. This subject has been intensively studied by researchers from many disciplines with great impact from sociology (see Rogers 1995 for overview). The diffusion of innovation literature has had a profound impact on marketing thinking, and researchers from the (marketing) discipline have contributed to this field as well. When studying diffusion of innovations, the innovation (e.g. a new product) represents something new to the potential adopter, but need not be a novelty in an absolute sense. For example, studies have demonstrated that some technologies take decades to be adopted. Diffusion of innovation is a true social phenomenon as it takes the social context directly into account. This becomes clear when looking at the elements in a diffusion process, i.e. (1) the innovation, and (2) its communication (3) from one individual (social actor) to another, (4) within a social system (e.g. a society) (5) over time.

More than 15,000 studies related to diffusion of innovations have been conducted. Research findings show that characteristics of the innovation influence both the extent to which and how fast an innovation is diffused. For example, the perceived relative advantage has been demonstrated to have a profound effect on the propensity to adopt an innovation. This very robust finding is, of course, of prime interest for marketers, and gives direction for marketing activities, e.g. new product development.

A large number of studies demonstrates that the number of adopters over time follow an S-shaped curve. The time dimension for the total adoption process may, however, vary tremendously across innovation. Based on this observed pattern, adopters can be grouped according to when they adopt an innovation. Those adopting at an early point in time, 'innovators' (or 'pioneers'), and 'early adopters' have been found to differ in characteristics and use of information sources compared to later adopters. For example, those adopting at an early stage tend to be more interested in and know more about the actual innovation, and tend to be more willing to try something new compared to later adopters and non-adopters. Such findings are of prime importance for marketers when defining target groups and designing effective marketing strategies. An important finding from diffusion of innovation research is that later adopters tend to seek earlier adopters for advice, and that mass-media information is diffused into the society via personal communication. Those adopting early and/or those who play a key role in personal communication of mass-media information are frequently termed *opinion leaders*.

Findings from research on diffusion of innovation have influenced marketing in many ways, e.g. in marketers' search for, development and evaluation of new products, marketing research and the profiling of target groups, design of marketing communication strategies, positioning of products and the 'stretching' of the product-life-cycles.

5 Summary and future outlook

Marketing has borrowed extensively from sociology. A large proportion of this borrowing has been done in a mass-marketing context with the prime purpose of profiling target groups as a basis for designing more effective (mass-)marketing. Marketing (as other disciplines) changes. More recently the borrowing has changed to encompass the relationships between social actors.

An interesting observation is that almost no borrowing from sociology – with a few exceptions only – has been used to study change. This is surprising as marketing is primarily a dynamic phenomenon taking place in everchanging social contexts; in fact a prime purpose of marketing is to bring about changes.

An additional observation is that the marketing discipline has primarily been preoccupied with transactions and exchanges falling within socially accepted norms, or even more restrictive, visible, socially accepted market transactions (Grønhaug and Dholokia 1987). In most societies many (legal) exchanges are taken out of the visible, legal market, e.g. an exchange of services between neighbours. In addition, illegal exchanges occur. In several countries, the 'black economy' boom, is estimated to constitute something in the range of 20–40 per cent of the gross national product. The distribution and marketing of illegal drugs, and the selling of stolen goods, are examples of deviant behaviours, but so far – in spite of their importance – they have received only scant attention by marketers. As noted by Zaltman and Wallendorf (1977) there are reasons to believe that the study of illegal exchanges can improve our understanding of marketing and its potential influence within legal and accepted social settings.

To summarize, very much of the borrowing from sociology

- has been used as a basis for characterizing and profiling consumers and target groups, i.e. the use of the concepts have been 'one--sided', overlooking their social relational intentions as reflected in the mother discipline. (This 'individualistic' perspective can probably also explain the predominant influence from individual psychology as reflected in any major textbook on consumer behaviour).
- The borrowing from sociology has primarily been applied to legal, visible exchanges, i.e. only a subset of all marketing exchanges taking place. The extensive work in sociology on deviant behaviour has so far almost been neglected.
- The borrowed concepts and ideas have mainly been used as static descriptors and only to a modest extent utlilized to capture the dynamics of and understand societal changes. This is also seen in scholarly empirical marketing research. In spite of the dynamic character of marketing – which involves time – the majority of empirical research is based on cross-sectional research designs, or on experiments which capture only a limited time period between pre- and post-tests.

Recent developments and changes in marketing perspectives indicate that social aspects, emphasizing relationships between social actors will be more focused. This trend is probably only in an early stage, and is believed to continue. The influence of sociology on marketing thinking will very likely increase in the years to come, and probably be manifested in the following ways:

- Previously borrowed concepts, e.g. 'role', 'status' and 'group' will be applied to capture social dimensions as they were created to do, i.e. to capture aspects of relationships.
- Concepts and ideas to understand relationships and networks, their initiation, changes, duration and termination will increase dramatically in the years to come.
- The importance of the social context, and how it influences relationships and exchanges will be emphasized in future marketing thinking and research.

It is also believed that dynamics and change as emphasized in much of sociology will have a greater impact on thinking and research in marketing in the years to come.

KJELL GRØNHAUG
THE NORWEGIAN SCHOOL OF ECONOMICS AND
BUSINESS ADMINISTRATION

Further reading

(References cited in the text marked *)

* Abercombie, N., Hill, S. and Turner, B.S. (eds.) (1988) *Dictionary of Sociology*, London: Penguin Books (2nd ed.).
* Alderson, W. (1958) 'The analytical framework for marketing', in D.J. Duncan (ed.) *Proceedings: Conference of Marketing Teachers from the West*, Berkeley, CA: School of Business Administration., University of California.
* Arndt, J. (1980) 'Perspectives for a theory of marketing', *Journal of Business Research* 8: 389–402.
* Berelson, B. and Steiner, G.A. (1964) *Human Behavior: An Inventory of Scientific Findings*, New York: Harcourt, Brace and World, Inc.
* Blau, P.M. (1964) *Exchange and Power in Social Life*, New York, Wiley. (This books represents a penetrating analysis of various forms of social exchanges and offers important insights to understand marketing phenomena.)
* Codere, H. (1968) 'Social exchange', in D.H. Sills (ed.) *International Encyclopedia of the Social Sciences*, New York: The Macmillan Company and the Free Press, Vol 5, 238–344.

Coleman, J.S. (1988) 'Social capital in the creation of human capital', *American Journal of Sociology* 94: S95–S120. (Penetrating analysis of how relationships between social actors as such represent value and function.)

* Collins, R. (1981) 'On the microfoundations of macrosociology', *American Journal of Sociology* 86: 984–1014.
* Cox, R. (1964) 'Introduction', in R. Cox, W. Anderson and S.J. Shapiro (eds) *Theory in Marketing*, Homewood, IL: Irwin.

Deighton, J. (1996) 'The future of interactive marketing', *Harvard Business Review*, (November–December) 151–62.

Dore, R. (1983) 'Goodwill and the spirit of market capitalism', *British Journal of Sociology* 34: 459–82. (Important contribution to the understanding of relational contracting in embedded markets.)

Emerson, R.M. (1962) 'Power–dependence relations', *American Sociological Review* 27: 31–41. (Important, and very influential article, often quoted by marketers, and deserves to be read.)

Galaskiewicz, J. (1985) 'Interorganizational relations', *Annual Review of Sociology* 11: 281–304. (Penetrating analysis of relationships using a so-

ciological perspective with important marketing implications.)
* Giddens, A. (1993) *Sociology*, 2nd edn, London: Polity Press.
* Goldman, A. (1979) 'Publishing activity in marketing as an indicator of its structure and disciplinary boundaries', *Journal of Marketing Research* 16: 485–94.
* Granovetter, M. (1985) 'Economic action and social structure: the problem embeddedness', *American Journal of Sociology* 91: 481–510. (Important contribution to understanding the importance and disciplining effect of the social context on relationships and transactions.)
* Granovetter, M. and Swedberg, R. (eds) (1992) *The Sociology of Economic Life*, Boulder CO: Westview Press.
* Grønhaug, K. and Dholokia, N. (1987) 'Consumer, markets and supply systems: a perspective on marketization and its effects', in F.A. Fuat, N. Dholokia and R.P. Bagozzi (eds) Philosophical and Radical Thoughts in Marketing, Lexington, MA: Lexington Books.
* Hall, E.T. (1976) *Beyond Culture*, Garden City, New York: Anchor Press/Doubleday.
  Heide, J. and John, G. (1992) 'Do norms matter in marketing relationships?', *Journal of Marketing* 56: 32–44. (One of the few empirical marketing contributions on the importance of norms relationship.)
* Hunt, S.D. (1983) 'General theories and the fundamental explanda of marketing', *Journal of Marketing* 47: 9–17.
* Hunt, S.D. (1991) *Modern Marketing Theory. Critical Issues in the Philosophy of Marketing Science*, Cincinatti, OH: South-Western Publishing Co.
* *Journal of the Academy of Marketing Science* (1995) Special issue on relationship marketing, 23: No 4.
  Katz, E. and Lagarsfeld, P. (1955) *Personal Influence*, New York: Free Press. (An important study which shows the importance of social networks and of personal interactions. Important contribution to the 'two-step-flow of information' hypothesis.)
* Kotler, P. (1984) *Marketing Management, Analysis, Planning and Control*, 4th edn, New Jersey: Prentice-Hall, Inc.
* Kroeber, A.L. and Kluckhon, C. (1952) 'Culture: A critical review of concepts and definitions', *Papers of Peabody Museum* 47: No 1A.
* Levy, S.J. (1959) 'Symbols for sale', *Harvard Business Review* 37: 117–24.
* Levy, S.J. and Zaltman, G. (1975) *Marketing Society, and Conflict*, New Jersey: Prentice-Hall, Inc. (Considers marketing from a social system perspective, and focuses in a useful way on marketing to a cause of consequence of change, and inherent conflict.)
* Lie, J. (1997) 'Sociology of markets', *Annual Review of Sociology* Annual Reviews Inc., 341–60. (Interesting contribution capturing multiple aspects of markets.)
* Nicosia, F.M. and Mayer, R.N. (1976) 'Toward a sociology of consumption', *Journal of Consumer Research* 3: 65–75. (Useful contribution to understanding the importance of consumption and how it is shaped by social forces.)
* Polanyi, K. (1944) *The Great Transformation*, Boston: Beacon Press.
  Polanyi, K. (1957) 'The economy as instituted process', in K. Polanyi, C.M. Arensberg and H.W. Pearson (eds) *Trade Market in Early Empires*, New York: Free Press. (Excellent treatment of exchange and market functioning.)
* Rogers, E.M. (1995) *Diffusion of Innovations*, 4th edn, New York: The Free Press.
* Smelser, N.J. (1963) *The Sociology of Economic Life*, New Jersey: Prentice-Hall, Inc.
* Swidler, A. (1986) 'Culture in action: symbols and strategies', *American Sociological Review* 51: 273–86. (This is a very thought-provoking book on the functioning of culture of its importance to marketers.)
* Wallendorf, M. (1978) 'Social roles in marketing context', *American Behavioral Scientist* 21: 571–82. (Useful contribution regarding the potential of applying the role concept to marketing problems.)
* Webster, F.E. (1992) 'The changing role of marketing in the corporation', *Journal of Marketing* 56: 1–17.
* Zaltman, G. and Wallendorf, M. (1977) 'Sociology: The missing chunk or how we've missed the boat', in B.A. Greenberg and D.N. Bollinger (eds) *Contemporary Marketing Thought 1977 Educators Proceedings*, Chicago: American Marketing Assoc., 235–8. (The paper identifies important topics neglected by marketers, and discusses how sociology can be useful.)

See also: CONSUMER BEHAVIOUR; CULTURAL ASPECTS OF MARKETING; RELATIONSHIPS AND NETWORKS

Cultural aspects of marketing

1. Culture can pose marketing problems
2. Marketing efforts can overcome cultural problems
3. Marketing power should respect culture
4. Marketing campaigns can utilize cultural features
5. Culture and the globalization of markets
6. Dynamic culture and dynamic marketplace
7. Conclusion

Overview

According to Hatch (1985), culture is 'the way of life of a people. It consists of conventional patterns of thought and behaviour, including values, beliefs, rules of conduct, political organization, economic activity, and the like, which are passed on from one generation to the next by learning – and not by biological inheritance'. Also, culture is 'governed by its own principles and not by the raw intellect, and that the differences among peoples do not reflect differences in levels of intelligence'. As such, there are many cultures in the world. In a way, there can be many cultures in a nation (Swanson 1989). It is widely recognized that theories in management and marketing are culture bound (Hofstede 1993; Tse et al. 1988). Marketing in one culture can be very different from marketing in a number of cultures. It becomes important to understand various issues related to launching marketing activities in a different culture.

The heart of the matter in marketing is to form a market and strike a business deal, which will bring benefits to all parties involved in the transaction. 'The marketing concept', the fundamental concept in marketing, refers to a philosophical conviction that customer satisfaction is the key to achieving organizational goals. Whether the customer is an individual or an organization, and whether the customer is nearby or in a foreign country, the challenge to the marketer is the same. Thus, the mission of marketing is to facilitate exchange and form a win–win relationship with other parties. This is no easy task when the marketer and the other parties share the same culture. It becomes even more difficult to accomplish the mission when the marketer and the other parties do not share the same culture.

This entry will specifically examine three related issues on marketing in a different culture. First, can a marketing success in one culture be reproduced in another culture? If not, why not? If so, what are the conditions of success? Second, should a marketing success in one culture be reproduced in another culture? This is a more basic question than the first one. It examines the ethical foundation of marketing activities. Last but not least, will cultures eventually converge? This is even more fundamental than the first two questions. When there is only one culture in the whole world, there is no need to study the cultural aspects of marketing.

1 Culture can pose marketing problems

First, can a marketing success be reproduced in another culture? Marketing people are supposed to be very sensitive to the changing needs of customers. Marketers know that they have to study customers' needs clearly, and deliver products which can meet those needs. When customers have different needs, marketers have to come up with different product offerings. Since customers in different cultures have minds which are programmed quite differently, it becomes important to differentiate their needs and to try to meet those needs differentially. However, even world-class marketers may not be sensitive enough to detect the differences in different cultures all the time.

Procter & Gamble (P&G) is an American giant, a model marketing company widely known to practise the marketing concept. P&G meets basic consumer needs with a strong research commitment to create products that are demonstrably better than the competition when compared in blind tests. P&G uses brand and category management systems and values market research highly, believing that it can enable the company to spot a new trend early and lead in it (see BRANDING AND BRAND MANAGEMENT; POSITIONING). Based on new liquid detergent technology and after extensive blind tests and market tests, P&G launched a new clothing detergent brand named Vizir in the early 1980s in Germany and Europe. Vizir was positioned as a complete main wash product, having superior performance in removing tough, greasy stains even in low temperature washing (Bartlett 1983).

Vizir got off to a good start all over Europe, and quickly became number one in the heavy-duty detergent category. However, in 1983 business began to weaken and the Vizir brand eventually lost about 15 per cent of its sales volume that year. In 1984 there was an additional 15 per cent sales decline. What P&G had failed to take into account was that European washing machines were at that time equipped to accept powder detergents but not liquids. When liquid detergent was added to a powder dispenser, as much as 20 per cent of the liquid was lost to a collecting point at the bottom of the machine. Thus, the product was not meeting consumers' performance expectation.

P&G changed the packages to explain better to consumers how to use Vizir, but research showed that this would not work. Subsequently, P&G managed to convince washing machine manufacturers in Europe to design liquid dispensers, but this had little impact on a market where the average machine was replaced only once every fifteen years. The next P&G attempt was to develop a retrofit system – a plastic device that fitted into existing powder dispensers and kept the liquid from leaking, while dispensing it at the same time. P&G would mail the device to consumers, free of charge, immediately after housewives told them the model number of their washing machines. However, most European machines were bolted to the wall, and the housewives were unable to see the model number; they did not know and they could not tell.

Finally, one technician in a French P&G product development laboratory invented a unique solution – a 'dosing ball' that P&G called a Vizirette. The consumer could fill the porous Vizirette 'dosing ball', place it in the washdrum on top of the clothes, and start the machine. The Vizirette would gradually dispense the detergent, with no waste. Vizir and Vizirette were subsequently introduced as a system (The Editors of Advertising Age 1989).

The story of the Vizir launch sends a strong signal to all marketers. Culture can pose marketing problems. Even when one is dealing with the most established concept in marketing (i.e. satisfying customers' needs), and even when it is implemented by a world-class marketer (i.e. P&G), it is no easy task to claim that one can move freely from one culture to another, and perform consistently well. If the story of the Vizir launch is helpful, the P&G experience in Japan is even more instructive.

2 Marketing efforts can overcome cultural problems

P&G entered the Japanese market first in 1972–73. The consumer mind-set in Japan was quite unique. The primary buyer of packaged goods was the housewife. In Japan at least half the adult women were employed, but almost no Japanese mothers worked outside the home. Child-rearing was the first priority for a Japanese woman. The average family home was fifty square metres. Lack of storage necessitated several shopping trips per week and affected the structure of the distribution outlets, the market information the housewife commanded, and the relationship between shopkeeper and housewife. Thus, the market structure was quite indirect and long. Specialty and small retail stores constituted the bulk of retail outlets, commanding 72.3 per cent in 1982. There was also a close interpersonal relationship between the neighbourhood shopkeeper and the housewife. The typical Japanese customer for branded packaged goods was highly uncompromising, demanding superior quality and defining value more in terms of product performance, quality and reliability, rather than price. This attitude was even more pronounced in the area of personal hygiene. Thus, in Japan virtually all companies manufactured products to a standard of zero defects.

P&G entered Japan through a joint venture with Nippon Sunhome. They picked Cheer laundry detergent powder as a wedge to open the Japanese market for other major brands to follow. P&G followed the 'successful' formula in the USA to position and advertise 'Cheer' as an all-temperature laundry detergent powder in 1973, featured price promotions to support the advertising campaign, and went directly to the major retail chains to promote and distribute it. Cheer gained a substantial market share and managed to capture up to 12.6 per cent in the laundry detergents market in 1979. However, Cheer did not bring in profits. Also, when the featured pricing stopped in 1979 Cheer kept losing market share to different competitive brands (Kao's Wonderful, New Beads, Zab Total and Lion's Top Powder). Upon closer examination, it became clear that the three-temperature washing concept was not relevant to Japanese laundry habits. Women typically washed clothes in tap-water and occasionally the recycled family bath-water in the winter. The aggressive pricing practice only forced all players in the industry to incur substantial losses together. For example, P&G's all-temperature Cheer had been selling at 555 yens for two boxes against a suggested retail price of 800 to 850 yens for one box. Kao's New Beads large box had been selling at 400 yens against a previous resale price of 700 to 750 yens. This aggressive pricing practice antagonized all the competitors. In addition, the distribution policy through the major retail chains antagonized the wholesalers and the small retailers, who were the gatekeepers of mass distribution in Japan.

Practically all other P&G brands either failed in the test market or were preempted by competition due to a competitor's national launch of a copycat prior to the conclusion of P&G's 24-month test market period. The only exception was Pampers, which was launched in 1981 and immediately captured 85 per cent of the disposable diaper market. However, even Pampers was not completely successful. Unicharm, a relatively unknown company in Japan, introduced Moony in 1982, which was sold at a 40 per cent price premium to Pampers and managed to capture 40 per cent of the market share in 1983. In the meantime, Pampers dropped from its 1981 high of 90 per cent to its 1985 low of 6 per cent. It was quite clear that P&G could afford no more illusion. They had underestimated the sophistication level of Japanese consumers. P&G also underestimated the competitive strength of the Japanese companies. The operation in Japan was a total disaster (Yoshino and Stoneham 1990a).

It became clear to P&G in 1983 that what was best in the USA might not be good enough in Japan. This was at least true in the consumer packaged goods industry. P&G could join other well-respected packaged goods companies such as General Foods, General Mills and Colgate, who had all failed in Japan and retreated. However, P&G was convinced that Japan was a leading-edge country in the consumer goods industry, and the world leader had to be successful there. There was no other choice. If P&G could not compete with the Japanese companies in Japan, they would eventually have to compete with them in the USA. This conviction led to P&G's subsequent success in Japan, which managed to show that marketing efforts could overcome cultural problems (Yoshino and Stoneham l990b).

The changing mentality at P&G started with the changing belief in research and development. P&G by that time believed that while American and European trends were helpful, the worldwide centre of innovation should be the Japanese consumer and competition. Thus, the R&D team in Japan was trying to develop products that would meet the needs of Japanese consumers. While there were only 60 people in the P&G R&D group in Osaka, in comparison with Kao's 2000 in Japan, P&G could depend on the unreserved support from the R&D group in Cincinnati. The race in R&D in the diaper product industry was instructive. P&G, Kao and Unicharm took turns to leapfrog one another in product upgrades, rendering the latest generation diaper obsolete within six months. Eventually P&G's R&D groups in Osaka and Cincinnati jointly developed the world's thinnest and most absorbent diaper, which became a clear winner over both Unicharm's Moony and Kao's Merries.

The biggest marketing challenge for P&G was to determine what advertising would work. It became clear to P&G that there was a virtual absence of side-by-side comparisons in Japanese advertising because of the indirectness of communication and the importance of harmony in Japanese culture. The tone of advertising was always friendly and never aggressive. Commercials often used background music and well-known celebrities. This author had a chance to review the P&G commercials used in Japan in the late 1970s and those used in the early 1990s. The improvement was obvious.

For example, previously Pampers commercials featured an unhappy baby in an unhappy situation. Recent commercials featured happy babies in happy situations. To promote Cheer originally, P&G had merely applied the American copy to Japan, although Japanese housewives had no problems with water temperature. Recent commercials focused on the primary product benefit and dirt and odour removal.

There were commensurate changes in the distribution, manufacturing and organization areas. The whole package of changes showed that P&G was willing to take the other culture seriously, and make a commitment to invest resources to meet customers' needs. Where there is a will, there is a way and marketing efforts can overcome cultural problems.

3 Marketing power should respect culture

The examination of the ethical foundation of marketing in a different culture is equally if not more important. Should a marketing success be reproduced in another culture? Although marketing power is formidable, there should also be a limit. Limitation need not come from customers' resistance, which in fact is important in the marketplace to differentiate the capable from the less capable marketers. It will reward the capable and punish the less capable marketers. Such limitation is part of the reality in marketing interaction. However, there is another kind of limitation. It comes from company efforts to restrain the marketing power when it is appropriate for the company to do so. When customers are able to choose what would be best for themselves, consumer sovereignty can be assumed, and companies are free to exercise their marketing power to overcome the resistance and eventually manage to meet the customers' needs and conclude the deals. On the other hand, when customers are not able to choose what would be best for themselves, consumer sovereignty does not exist, and it becomes the responsibility of the company to restrain the marketing power for the sake of the public. One notable example is the case of infant formula selling in the Third World (Lee 1987).

Infant formula was developed by leading food giants in developed countries The product was initially sold in developed countries as a substitute for breast milk. The case for infant formula is that it is available when breast milk is not (a less than 10 per cent chance), and when properly used it is an excellent alternative among all existing alternatives. In the developed and rich countries like the USA, mothers can usually afford to buy infant formula and know how to use it in hygienic conditions. Their education level is high and consumer sovereignty can be assumed. It would be enough to promote breast milk as the best choice while providing mothers a choice of settling with the 'second best' – the infant formula.

However, while infant formula is not defective in itself it is demanding. When risk conditions are present, it can be harmful to users. This became a serious issue in 1970 when the infant formula manufacturers adopted aggressive marketing efforts in developing nations (Post 1986). The problem becomes obvious when infant formula manufacturers promote heavily in a much less developed and poor country like Zambia. There are two real dangers. First, through poverty, compounded by ignorance, mothers tend drastically to overdilute the infant formula in order to make it last. As a result, infants starve and die. Second, poor hygiene causes serious troubles. Nestlé and other companies in the industry repeatedly claimed that they had no desire or intention to see unqualified consumers using their formula products. However, in 1978 at the US Senate hearings, when representatives from these companies were asked whether they had conducted any post-marketing research studies to determine who actually used their products, all representatives answered that their companies did no such research and did not know who actually used the products.

It becomes clear that the companies should be responsible for their marketing efforts. In order to guarantee that the users of infant formula products have proper information on their safe use and can make intelligent consumer choices, the companies may want to withdraw the marketing efforts or even the products from those countries. Mass marketing would certainly not be appropriate in view of the consumers' culture in such countries. If the product supply is meant to be helpful, it may be wise to do the promotion through the medical and health care system. Professionals there can exercise their judgement and make recommendations to the mothers. Nestlé's infant formula should not be regarded as an isolated case. Rather it should be regarded as an illustrative case for all kinds of first world products being sold in the Third World. There should be a similar level of sensitivity in reviewing the situation. It is important for marketing power to respect culture (see MARKETING ETHICS).

4 Marketing campaigns can utilize cultural features

The above discussion may leave readers with the impression that marketing is the conqueror and culture is always trying to defend itself. This need not be the case. As a matter of fact, marketing campaigns can make use of the unique cultural features of the customers and the company to make a lasting impact. When a marketing programme is deeply rooted in a particular culture, the marketing programme can easily enjoy sustainable competitive advantages. In some situations, a company may 'discover' such a 'different' and perfectly compatible culture at home. The turnaround of Harley-Davidson in the American motorcycle industry is one of the most celebrated examples.

Before 1960 the motorcycle market in the USA had been mainly served by the American Harley-Davidson; BSA, Triumph and Norton of the UK; and Moto-Guzzi of Italy. Harley-Davidson was the market leader in 1959. However, in that year Honda and Yamaha entered the American market. Since the Japanese motorcycle industry had expanded rapidly after the First World War to meet the need for cheap transportation in Japan, in 1959 the major Japanese producers, Honda, Yamaha, Suzuki and Kawasaki, together produced some 450,000 motorcycles, which was ten times larger than retail sales in the USA. Honda was already the world's largest motorcycle producer. These Japanese producers approached the American market in a systematic way. They started by penetrating the low end, light-weight market niche. They all placed an emphasis on market share and sales volume. To realize their growth goals, the Japanese producers constantly updated or redesigned products to meet the needs of American customers; set prices at levels designed to achieve market share goals; reduced prices further when necessary; assembled full-time dealers to set up an effective distribution and maintenance network; and launched well-planned and heavy advertising campaigns. Because of scale economy and long-term strategic planning, by 1966 Honda, Yamaha and Suzuki together had 85 per cent of the US market. By 1974 apart from the Japanese producers Harley-Davidson was virtually the only company left in the market, keeping a mere 6 per cent market share (Buzzell and Purkayastha 1978).

The only option left for Harley-Davidson was to adopt niche marketing in a matured market. Harley-Davidson just concentrated on the super-heavyweight motorcycle market. However, because of the aggressive Japanese marketing efforts, even the market share in that niche had fallen from 75 per cent in 1973 to less than 25 per cent in 1980. At that time the parent company AMF was losing interest in Harley-Davidson. Early in 1981 Vaughn Beals and twelve other Harley executives wanted to take over the company through a leveraged buyout arrangement. They thought that they could do a better job and rescue the company. Subsequently, Harley-Davidson made several strategic moves that eventually led to the celebrated turnaround. In April 1983 President Reagan approved a recommendation by the International Trade Commission (ITC), raising the tariff on 'heavyweight' motorcycles (with engine displacements over 700 cc) from 4.4 per cent to 49.4 per cent for four years. The ITC's recommendation was to protect the domestic industry, and essentially the Harley-Davidson operation. Harley-Davidson made tremendous efforts to renovate the production process. They learned just-in-time manufacturing systems from the Japanese companies and adopted measures to encourage employee involvement. Production cost and product reliability were significantly improved. However, the major change and the secret of success was on the marketing side.

Harley-Davidson formed the Harley Owners Group in 1983. The acronym HOG is the affectionate name given by Harley riders to their motorcycles. Since motorcycles are often an impulse purchase, one of Harley's biggest challenges is to hold its new customers after they have bought a bike. HOG gives the new rider instant companionship through organized rides, rallies and charity runs. In 1991, with more than 155,000 members in 700 chapters worldwide, HOG is the motorcycle industry's largest company-sponsored enthusiast organization. Club members enjoy such features as a bi-monthly newsletter (*HOG Tales*), an automobile-club-type travel centre and reimbursement for motorcycle safety courses. The major attraction has been that at state, regional, national and international rallies, thousands of HOG members unite with company employees for a weekend of fun, entertainment, motorcycle demo rides and camaraderie in an atmosphere that clearly defines the 'Harley-Davidson lifestyle experience'. The rallies also give Harley executives a chance to find out what is on customers' minds.

When management celebrated Harley's 85th birthday in 1988, they arranged a party which reflected their unique way of getting close to customers. Motorcyclists were invited to participate in the event. All they had to do was to contribute US$10 to Harley-Davidson's favourite philanthropic organization, the Muscular Dystrophy Association. Starting from as far away as San Francisco and Orlando, Florida, groups of cyclists headed for Milwaukee. Each group was led by a Harley-Davidson executive, including the board chairman Vaughn Heals, and chief executive officer Rich Teerlink. Thousands of Harleys, many flying American flags, rumbled into Milwaukee on 18 June, shaking the air with the sound of their engines. Some riders had dogs, others their children. Riders wore different kinds of clothing, and they were all ages. The celebrants spent the day participating in such activities as slow races. Beals and Teerlink, among other executives, submitted themselves to the celebrity dunk tank, where they were dumped into the water by on-target baseball throwers. Music resounded all the time. At the final ceremonies, 24,000 bikers watched videotapes of their ride to Milwaukee projected on to two giant screens. As riders saw their own groups, they would shout. Thousands of Harley owners rose to their feet and burst into an unrivalled demonstration of product loyalty.

In 1989 Harley-Davidson managed to capture close to 60 per cent of the super-heavyweight motorcycle market in the USA (Rose 1990). The momentum has continued into the 1990s. The charity events and public-spirited programmes such as company reimbursement for Harley owners who took rider education classes, helped a great deal in promoting the company image. The HOG and cross-country motorcycle treks come from the root of American culture. Only Harley-Davidson can utilize these cultural features and promote nationalism in a natural way. Honda tried to form a similar group to HOG, which quite expectedly soon faded away (*Fortune* 1989).

5 Culture and the globalization of markets

It would not be appropriate to discuss the cultural aspects of marketing without mentioning Levitt's widely cited article on the globalization of markets (1983). In this powerful article, Levitt asserted that well-managed companies had moved from an emphasis on customizing items to offering globally standardized products that are advanced, functional, reliable and low priced. Will cultures eventually converge? If so, it will no longer be necessary to examine the cultural aspects of marketing. Levitt's thesis was derived from his observation of a powerful force – technology – which was driving the world toward a converging commonality. High-tech products were standardized. High-touch products like Coca-Cola, Levi jeans and Revlon cosmetics would be the same. According to Levitt, 'everywhere everything gets more and more like everything else as the world's preference structure is relentlessly homogenized'. Levitt predicts that the global corporation will know everything about one great thing. The corporation will know about the absolute need to be competitive on a worldwide basis as well as nationally and seek constantly to drive down prices by standardizing what it sells and how it operates. Its mission is modernity and its mode price competition, even when the corporation sells top-of-the-line, high-end products. What all markets have in common is an overwhelming desire for dependable, world-standard modernity in all things, at aggressively low prices. Later in 1988, in one of the editorials he wrote for *Harvard Business Review*, Levitt created a concept called 'the pluralization of consumption' to supplement his theory of global homogenization. According to his prediction, the whole world is made up of one market segment, which consists of people with plural preferences, the new world of the heteroconsumer.

While this author enjoys reading all Levitt's writings and accepts the points he made in most of his articles, it is only appropriate to reject this contention by Levitt. If world-class marketers like P&G encountered clear cultural problems in Europe and Japan, it is quite obvious that the market is not homogenized even among the most developed countries. The case of Nestlé's infant formula is even more convincing. The economic gap between the North (those who have) and the South (those who have not) is so obvious. It is not possible to assume that people in the Third World should be approached in the same way as people in the first world. If this is still not enough, the case of Harley-Davidson shows us clearly that even in the most developed marketplace in the world, the USA, culture and its consequences play a key role in marketing. Harley-Davidson depends on the cultural features to guard its market niche. No Japanese companies can reproduce the same cultural impact on American consumers. The foundation of Hofstede's (1984) seminal study on culture is the nation. As long as the national boundaries exist, and as long as there are reasons for nations to reinforce the differences between nations, the impact of culture will be here to stay (see GLOBAL MARKETING).

Coca-Cola is probably the best known brand name in the world. If there is a universal standard product in the world, Coca-Cola is very likely to be one of the best, if not the best, contender. However, when the Coca-Cola company began to sell their products aggressively in China, it was clear that the reception there was atypical. Contrary to expectation, Sprite (the number two brand from the Coca-Cola company) was selling much better than Coca-Cola (the flagship) in China. Also, it was quite clear that the universal advertising copy was not at all well received in China. This led to a special advertising production for China. In the new advertising commercial that was launched in 1992, one could see the favourite Chinese images such as family ties, wedding ceremonies, Chinese New Year and the great earth. These cultural themes were clearly unique to China and the Chinese. A pop singer from Taiwan, who was best received in the mainland, was commissioned to compose and sing the theme song for that advertising commercial. This is clear evidence that consumers are not homogenized. The impact of culture is here to stay.

Not only that, when operating in a global environment, executives from a 'strong' business culture should always be sensitive to the opportunity to learn from executives from a seemingly 'weak' business culture. One good example comes from the experience of Sino-US business. After 1993, many more American multinational companies took China business seriously. There was a renewed interest to study the Chinese business negotiating style (e.g. Fang 1997), trying to reexamine what was known in the early days (e.g. Pye 1982). While this whole research area is still quite unclear, American executives already discover that they have at least one important lesson to learn from Chinese executives in negotiating more effectively (Intercultural Training Resources, Inc. 1995). American executives usually arrange negotiation items one by one and prioritize the issues. They would try to negotiate and settle first the most important issue, and then move on to the next one. If there is no settlement for the first issue, they would hesitate to move on. In the meantime, once the first issue is settled, they would hesitate to open up the discussion again when they have already moved on and discussed the second issue. Chinese executives are just the opposite. If they cannot come to an agreement on the most important issue, they are willing to put that aside for the time being and move on to discuss the next issue. In addition, even if they have already reached an agreement on the first issue, they are willing to open up the discussion again on the first issue when they are discussing the second issue. Theoretically, the Chinese executives' approach would enhance significantly the probability for both parties to create more values from the business deal.

6 Dynamic culture and dynamic marketplace

While it is unlikely and undesirable that cultures will converge and form one world culture in the foreseeable future, this does not mean that cultures are stagnant. The impact of culture is here to stay, but culture itself is dynamic and changing. When the culture of a particular economy is changing, more often than not there should be commensurate changes of marketing efforts in order to enable the company and the brand to ride together with the tide. The case of Hong Kong should be instructive since it has gone through significant changes in the past several decades.

Hong Kong had been a British colony for more than ninety years. Culturally, Hong Kong has always been a Chinese society. When the

Communist Party was about to take power in mainland China, many Chinese industrialists in the textile industry came to Hong Kong. They brought with them their best technicians and operators, together with money and their best equipment. In the 1950s and 1960s Hong Kong became a rapidly growing manufacturing centre with a firm base in textiles and clothing. The typical work ethic at that time was diligent and frugal, carried over from the agricultural society. Because of continued growth and prosperity, Hong Kong became quite affluent in the 1970s and well into the 1980s. In the meantime, Hong Kong people began to work more shrewdly rather than harder. They no longer feel that they are poor and even if they actually are they feel that they can become rich if they do it right tomorrow. The issue of the end of colonization in 1997 was much felt in Hong Kong, beginning in late 1982, and remains a part of daily news. Hong Kong people have been forced to reflect on their own identities. Before the issue of 1997 became real, Hong Kong people had refused to think about it, and regarded themselves as Chinese. When the changes in 1997 became a reality, Hong Kong people began to see that there is a difference between the identity of a Hong Kong person and the identity of a Chinese person. Although Hong Kong people are also Chinese, they are not Chinese in the same way as those from the mainland or Taiwan. This development is gradual but real and carries implications for marketing campaigns. It may be instructive to review the development of advertising themes for a popular soft drink in Hong Kong, since the soft drink industry may best reflect the preference of the mass society. It is about the story of Vitasoy, a soya bean milk developed in Hong Kong (Lai 1991).

The Vitasoy story began with a big idea and a little bean. Vitasoy was a milk substitute made from ground soya bean with water and sugar. It was launched as 'the poor people's milk' in the 1940s. The major theme was to deliver adequate nutrition at low cost. They promised that people would become taller, stronger and healthier. Vitasoy had always been sold at about two-thirds of the price level of leading soft drinks such as Coca-Cola. People took Vitasoy because it was thirst quenching and at the same time good for body strength. One bottle of Vitasoy met two kinds of needs. It appealed to people who were poor and frugal. This product position continued to function well in the 1950s and 1960s. However, in the 1970s this advertising theme became ineffective. Hong Kong people no longer thought of themselves as poor and malnourished. In 1974 Vitasoy decided to make a drastic change and reposition the product. They used Tetra Brik Asceptic packaging to present a new image and to make the product available in supermarkets, which had started to become a more important retail outlet than grocery stores. They raised the product price level to the ordinary price level for prestigious soft drinks, since price was no longer a concern among customers. The incremental margin would enable the company to put up more aggressive marketing campaigns. The advertising theme was changed to 'more than a simple soft drink'. The new theme created a 'Fun' image and at the same time preserved the 'nutritious/healthy' image, which was still helpful to differentiate Vitasoy from other soft drinks. This advertising theme went well for more than a decade, and then went off steam. In 1988 they adopted another new theme, 'you must have been a beautiful baby'. This theme reinforced the Hong Kong identity and also enabled Vitasoy to differentiate itself from all other soft drinks which were from different countries. Since Hong Kong people at that time had begun to have confidence in their own identity, this advertising theme was timely and effective. Vitasoy has been continuously successful and the advertising themes adopted over the years have kept pace with the changing culture in Hong Kong. This is strong evidence that culture and marketing go together in a dynamic fashion. There will be no effective marketing if full attention is not paid to its cultural aspects.

7 Conclusion

Marketing theories are culture bound. Marketing success is also culture bound. When a company has developed a successful marketing formula in one culture, it is justified to try to enjoy scale economy and apply it in another culture. However, it is important to take heed and make sure that the conditions exist there to reproduce the same marketing success. Otherwise, the marketing failure can be very costly. The story of the P&G launch of Vizir is very instructive. On the other hand, the eventual success of P&G in

Japan is reassuring. Good marketing efforts, even in a different culture, will pay off.

Marketing is not just profit making. When a company launches a marketing programme in a different culture, the first question that should be asked is whether the company respects the host culture. In some special situations, as demonstrated in Nestlé's infant formula case in the Third World, it may even be appropriate to adopt various demarketing measures at the expense of 'marketing success'. When a company learns to respect culture, the efforts will pay off. When the marketing programme and the culture are glued together, sustainable competitive advantages are guaranteed. The rebirth of Harley-Davidson celebrates this truth.

Although there are merits in Levitt's vision of a convergent world culture (1983, 1988), it is unlikely that this vision will become a reality in the foreseeable future. In view of the fact that people can learn even from a seemingly 'weak' culture, it becomes desirable to preserve cultural diversity so that marketers can learn more effectively. Thus, it will continue to be important to examine the cultural aspects of marketing. Levitt's thesis, in a way, reinforces the conviction that culture is developing and changing. It becomes important for the marketer to continue to study the cultural aspects of marketing even when the company is operating in the same place as before. Since culture is developing and changing, even home culture can become very different in the course of time. It becomes imperative to examine the cultural aspects of marketing whether one is operating at home or abroad.

KAM-HON LEE
THE CHINESE UNIVERSITY OF HONG KONG

Further reading

(References cited in the text marked *)

* Bartlett, Christopher A. (1983) *Procter Gamble Europe: Vizir Launch*, Boston, MA: Harvard Business School.
* Buzzell, Robert D. and Purkayastha, Dev (1978) *Note on the Motorcycle Industry – 1975*, Boston, MA: Harvard Business School.
* The Editors of Advertising Age (1989) *Procter Gamble, How PRIG Became America's Leading Marketer*, Lincolnwood, Illinois: NTC Business Books.
* Fang, Tony (1997) *Chinese Business Negotiating Style*, Linkoping, Sweden: Linkoping University.
* Fortune (1989) 'How Harley beat back the Japanese', *Fortune* 25: 93–6.
* Hatch, Elvin (1985) 'Culture', in Kuper, Adam and Kuper, Jessica (eds), *The Social Science Encyclopedia*, London: Routledge.
* Hofstede, Geert (1984) *Culture's Consequences, International Differences in Work-Related Values*, Beverly Hills, CA: Sage Publications.
* Hofstede, Geert (1993) 'Cultural constraints in management theories', *Academy of Management Executive* 7: 81–94.
* Intercultural Training Resources, Inc. (1995) *Working with China Series*, San Francisco, CA: Intercultural Training Resources, Inc.
* Lai, Linda (1991) 'Fortune built on a bean', *Hong Kong, Inc.* 18: 26–47.
* Lee, Kam-hon (1987) 'The informative and persuasive functions of advertising: a moral appraisal – a further comment', *Journal of Business Ethics* 6: 55–7.
* Levitt, Theodore (1983) 'The globalization of markets', *Harvard Business Review* 61: 92–102.
* Levitt, Theodore (1988) 'The pluralization of consumption', *Harvard Business Review* 66: 7–8.
* Post, James E. (1986) 'Ethical dilemmas of multinational enterprises: an analysis of Nestlé's traumatic experience with the infant formula controversy', in Hoffman, W. Michael, Lange, Ann E. and Fedo, David A. (eds), *Ethics and the Multinational Enterprise*, Lanham, MD: University Press of America, Inc.
* Pye, Lucian W. (1982) *Chinese Commerical Negotiating Style*, Cambridge, UK: Oelgeschlager, Gunn & Hain.
* Rose, Robert L. (1990) 'Harley regains lead in big-bike market', *Asian Wall Street Journal* 7–8 September.
* Swanson, Lauren A. (1989) 'The twelve "nations" of China', *Journal of International Consumer Marketing* 2: 83–105.
* Tse, David K., Lee, Kam-Hon, Vertinsky, Ilan and Wehrung, Donald A. (1988) 'Does culture matter? A cross-cultural study of executives' choice, decisiveness, and risk adjustment in international marketing', *Journal of Marketing* 52: 81–95.
* Yoshino, Michael and Stoneham, Paul H. (1990a) *Procter & Gamble Japan (A)*, Boston, MA: Harvard Business School.
* Yoshino, Michael and Stoneham, Paul H. (1990b) *Procter & Gamble Japan (C)*, Boston, MA: Harvard Business School.

See also: ADVERTISING; BRANDING AND BRAND MANAGEMENT; GLOBAL MARKETING; MARKETING ETHICS; POSITIONING; PRICING; STRATEGIC ALLIANCES AND SUPPLIER PARTNERSHIPS

Quantitative methods in marketing

1 **Marketing modelling**
2 **Validation measures**
3 **Market analysis**
4 **Computer intensive quantitative methods**
5 **Conclusions**

Overview

Quantitative methods take marketing from an art to a science, from conjecture to rigour. They have three main roles:

1 market modelling;
2 validation of research results;
3 market analysis.

Market models represent market behaviour mathematically. For example, an equation can represent the relationship between sales and advertising. Managers can manipulate this on a spreadsheet to ask 'what if' questions, for example: 'What would sales be if advertising was increased by £100,000?' With financial dimensions added it could reveal the profitability of changing advertising levels or show the optimum expenditure.

Validation measures the significance of results. Market researchers often conduct surveys to find how customers respond to different treatments, such as the use of a blue or yellow wrapper on a bar of chocolate. The results could show that 32 per cent of people said they would buy the chocolate in the blue wrapper, compared with 29 per cent for the yellow wrapper. Validation uses statistical methods to measure if the difference between the 32 per cent and 29 per cent is significant. It asks if the results are significantly different or could they have occurred by chance.

Market analysis uses statistical methods to view markets. Sometimes it is a way of viewing mathematically what can be seen manually. A manager could plot sales and price and see the relationship. Alternatively, he or she could use statistical methods to investigate the pattern and so build a marketing model. The great value of quantitative methods in market analysis comes when markets get more complicated and the number of influences increases. There are many influences on a market so plotting sales against price often reveals little since it ignores the intervention of sales promotion, advertising, competitive intervention or economic variables (see ADVERTISING; ENVIRONMENTAL ANALYSIS; POSITIONING; SALES PROMOTION; THE ECONOMICS BASIS OF MARKETING). Quantitative methods can help disentangle this complexity. Techniques can look across thousands of cases where there are many influences and detect patterns that inspection would not reveal.

Market analysis methods can go beyond the automation of manual tasks and the investigation of complex models. Techniques are now available that look at markets in new ways. Their role is like an X-ray or ultrasonic scan in medicine. The doctor could look at a patient from the outside or even cut the patient open to look inside, but X-rays give a new view. The same is true of market analysis models. Markets appear in a way not seen by conventional means.

All three types of quantitative methods in marketing have a huge literature and are developing rapidly. There is also research by different people, who have developed their own traditions. Green *et al.* (1988) and Lilien *et al.* (1992) review the major areas considered here. The remainder of this entry will introduce the elements of the market modelling process, statistical methods of validation, market analysis methods and some of the new computer intensive methods of market data analysis.

1 Marketing modelling

In his influential review Little (1979) showed the main components of a marketing model (Figure 1). Urban (1974) shows how other blocks help build models for managers. Each stage of a full model building and implementation process (Figure 2) is explained.

The theoretical foundations

Figure 1 Managers and models
Source: Little (1979: 12)

Entry

Managers rarely build the models they use. There is, therefore, a relationship between the manager and model builder. The entry stage reflects the importance of the first five seconds, minutes, hours or days of that contact. Unless trust and mutual understanding occur, any model built is likely to fail or be unused. Critical ingredients are for the modellers to understand the needs of managers and for the managers to have ownership of the model. The modeller has to listen and be concerned for the dimensions of successful models identified by Little (1970). A model should be:

1. as simple as possible – contain the necessary detail and no more;
2. robust, be relied upon to give sensible results whatever the manager inputs;
3. easy to use;
4. adaptive, so that it can accommodate new ideas or changes in the way the problem is seen;
5. complete in including all the issues that are important.

Objectives

The objectives set influence a model's design. If the objective is to forecast short-term sales, then a simple time series model will do. These predict future sales based on past sales history (see THE MARKETING AUDIT). More complex models allow managers to see how the

Figure 2 The market model building process

- Entry
- Set objectives
- Subjective specification
- Objective specification
- Data collection
- Estimation
- Validation
- Optimization
- Tracking

marketing mix and their competitors influence sales. The output of a model could still be sales, but that would be dependent on more variables. At a higher level the models can optimize sales or determine strategy. This would influence the inputs and outputs; rather than just looking at sales, a manager may want to view contribution or profitability.

Subjective specification

Subjective specification captures the beliefs of managers and modellers about how markets behave. Table 1 contains a list devised in developing an advertising model for a major retailer (Doyle and Saunders 1990). These are worth explaining because they are generalizations that apply across most marketing variables on most occasions. The first three items express the common belief that the relationship between advertising and sales is a curve showing decreasing returns to scale, like P3 in Figure 3. Advertising effects carry over from one period to the next (Leeflang et al. 1992) (see ADVERTISING). The variability of marketing effects is often surprising. In the margarine market, some brands are more responsive to promotions than others. This may depend on the segments or their advertising. There are also cross-effects between competitors or, in the case of a retailer, between the sales of one merchandise and another (see RETAILING).

Other advertising effects appear in the literature but are less reliable. It is rare to find increasing returns to scale from advertising although some believe that there is a threshold level. Saturation effects may exist at a level of sales beyond which a brand will never sell, but rarely is the dominance of a product such that these points are achievable. The biggest myth of all is super-saturation, where the excessive promotion of a product reduces its sales. After a review of the evidence Simon (1970) declared threshold effects 'to be a monstrous myth'.

This qualitative stage can have a big impact upon the final results given by a marketing model. An extreme case is the difference between the belief in increasing returns to scale (P5 in Figure 3) and decreasing returns to scale (P3 in Figure 3). If a model represents

Table 1 The subjective specification of advertising effects

1	Advertising has a small positive influence on sales
2	It shows diminishing returns to scale
3	Scales are not zero when advertising is zero
4	There are lagged effects
5	Advertsing effects vary across products, brands and campaigns
6	There are cross-effects of advertising – the advertising of one merchandise will influence the sale of others

The theoretical foundations

Figure 3 The shapes of market response

[P1: Through origin; P2: Linear; P3: Decreasing returns (concave); P4: Saturation; P5: Increasing returns (convex); P6: S-Shape; P7: Threshold; P8: Super-saturation]

decreasing returns to scale for three brands, then it will suggest the optimum strategy is to spend evenly across them. In contrast, if there are increasing returns of scale the model will suggest the best strategy is to spend all the money on one brand and neglect the others (see QUALITATIVE RESEARCH IN MARKETING).

Objective specification

Objective specification involves finding a mathematical function that is tractable and comes as close as possible to fitting the subjective specification. It is perhaps surprising to non-modellers to find out how awkward this can be. Table 2 lists some common expressions and Table 3 their relationship to the qualitative specification. The choice made depends on asking a series of questions and parsimony (simplicity):

- How many right features has the expression? No expression has all the desirable features and will always be unable to give a perfect fit to any data. The question then becomes, 'Which are the critical features?' For example, in measuring the impact of shelf space, it may not matter if the log-log expression shows that sales are zero if a product has zero shelf space. This would be quite unacceptable in an advertising model, where sales occur in periods with no advertising.

- How many of the wrong features does the expression have? An expression may have a very good fit in some ways, but be completely wrong in others. A polynomial expression is flexible but it can give ludicrous

Table 2 Common expressions

	Name	Expression
Linear	Simple	$Y = a + bX$
	Squared	$Y = a + bX^2$
	Square root	$Y = a + bX^{0.5}$
	Reciprocal	$Y = a + b^{1/X}$
Log linearizable	Semi-log	$Y = a + b\ln X$
	Exponential	$\ln Y = a + bX$
	Log reciprocal	$\ln Y = a + b/X$
	Log-log	$\ln Y = a + b\ln X$
Not linearizable	Litte	$Y = a + (b - c) \cdot X^d/(e + X^d)$
	Gompertz	$\ln Y = a + b \cdot c^X$
	Logistics	$Y = a/(1 + \exp(b + cX))$
	Modified exponential	$Y = a(1 - \exp(-bX^c))$

results if extrapolated. It will always show sales proceeding towards plus or minus infinity at its extremes.
- Can it be estimated? In some cases the unknown coefficients are easily estimated using regression analysis. In other cases, like the very flexible Gompertz expression, they cannot. This means more computer intensive and less familiar methods have to be used.
- Can it be optimized? The linear expression gives no optimum at all, so is quite hopeless if the aim is to use the model to allocate sales across products or media. It can guide the allocation of resources, but it gives no indication of when to stop. Other expressions, like the semi-log model, give simple allocation rules read direct from the equations. Others, like the non-linearizable expressions, are much harder to optimize. In reality, any expression with diminishing returns can give optima but it is much easier for some than for others.
- Has it worked before? Some expressions have gained credibility by their wide use; others have few applications. The log-log model has some deficiencies but is flexible and so used to represent the marketing mix.

Table 3 Characteristics of specifications

Feature (Proposition)	Threshold (7)	X = Y = 0 (1)	Saturation (4)	Super-saturation (8)	Non-linear	Others
Straight (2)						Linear
Increasing (5)		Log-log				Exponential Squared
Decreasing (3)	Reciprocal Semi-log Log-log	Modified exponential	Reciprocal Semi-log	Quadratic	Modified exponential	Square root
S-shaped (6)		Log reciprocal	Gompertz	Cubic	Logistics Gompertz	
Universal			Little	Polynomial		

The theoretical foundations

The simplicity of the semi-log model makes it popular in allocation problems. Using popular models reduces the chance of a gross misspecification biasing results.

In their advertising budgeting model Doyle and Saunders (1990) used a semi-log model to represent the relationship between sales of recorded music and advertising expenditure:

$$S_t = c + p\ln(P_{t-1}) + v\ln(V_{t-1}) + u_t \qquad (7.1)$$

where:

S_t = sales in week t,
P_{t-1} = press advertising in previous week,
V_{t-1} = TV advertising in previous week,
c = unknown constant,
p, v = unknown elasticities
u_t = error term, and
ln = natural logarithms

Data collection

The data available are limiting. Depending on the problem, the data can be cross-sectional or time series. Time-series models (tracking models) can estimate the effect of advertising or sales promotion on sales or market share. Rarely are annual data usable, since the number of time-series points needed mean the modeller would have to go back too far in order to get enough data (i.e. 24 years). Over time, the relationships between sales and the marketing mix variables must have changed and so the whole exercise is made unreliable. Monthly data are more reasonable because 3 years' data, of which relationships may have been similar, give 36 time points. However, even over that time campaigns can change and there can be discontinuities in the data. There is also seasonality to contend with.

Cross-sectional data exist where data come from several places at the same time. For example, in stores, electronic point-of-sale information means it is possible to look at the relationship between sales and merchandising across a large number of outlets.

Results are biased if the data collected are inaccurate or if some time series are more accurate than others. TVRs that measure television audiences are more accurate than measures of any other media so tend to show stronger results. There will always be bias due to different qualities of data, but where possible the data compared should be similar in quality. This bias suggests the media trade associations would do well to improve the quality of recording their exposure if they hope to improve the measured effectiveness and therefore desirability of using their media.

Estimation

Estimation sometimes seems the easiest of the modelling activities. Anyone with a PC can now input data and use regression analysis to get some results. Results will exist but, if there is poor specification and the methods not understood, expect GIGO (garbage in, garbage out). Estimation is an area in which a little knowledge can do a lot of damage.

Regression analysis is an indirect method because it does not explore the data for a best solution but computes a best fit to data using calculus. Equation 7.1 was estimated using regression analysis to give the following relationship:

$$S_t = 3300 + 323\ln(P_{t-1}) + 359\ln(V_{t-1)} + u_t \qquad (7.2)$$

It shows both press and TV advertising having a similar positive effect on sales. This is an elegant approach but it needs a large number of assumptions to be made. These are embodied in the error term (u_t) in equation 7.1. Very often they are not true. Two examples will explain the situation. It assumes the data are not auto correlated, that means observation 2 does not depend on observation 1, observation 3 does not depend on observation 2, etc. This is certainly not true in much time series data where a sales promotion campaign in one period can mean that none will take place in the next. Another assumption is that of no multicolinearity; that means that the independent variables, say sales promotion and price, vary independently. This is often not true and would be the sign of bad marketing. Defy these rules and the results of regression are unreliable. In some cases artificially high elasticities occur and, in other cases, the significance of one strong variable can drive the significance of a weaker one with which it is multicolinear. These limitations do not mean the regression is unusable but it does mean the user has to understand the limitations and how to test for their presence. This is where validation is important and there is a need to understand the statistics that regression packages produce. All is not lost if the assumptions of ordinary least squared regression, the most common form, are not true. It is sometimes possible to remove the problem by changing the specification by, say, introducing lag effects or combining multicolinear variables. It is also possible to use more advanced forms of regression that relax some of the assumptions of ordinary least squares. Generalized least squares regression, latent root regression and ridge regression are examples (Naert and Leeflang 1977).

In circumstances when expressions are not linearizable, direct methods of estimation are possible. There are many of these search procedures that estimate a model by searching iteratively for a best solution. The methods are usually very computer intensive but the cost of processing is declining so much that it is feasible to use them. They are not one method, but many. Some of these are like trying to climb Mount Everest by starting in the Sahara and looking at the ground immediately beneath one's feet as a way of gauging which direction would lead you to the highest point. Clearly sub-optimization, or climbing a molehill rather than Mount Everest, is a potential problem. There are ways of overcoming these problems. Breightler et al. (1979) review many of the procedures.

Recent years have seen creative leaps in the ways in which we can find a best answer to a problem. Some of these take lessons from nature, like artificial annealing, named after the annealing of metals. Other methods, like neural networks, model the workings of a brain in divining solutions. In the financial markets these methods have proved most impressive. Much development work is still being done and the techniques are far from universally understood or available. For a review of them see Coates et al. (1994).

Validation

There are three stages in the validation of a marketing model. The first stage examines the statistics describing the model. The simplest test is for face validity. This asks does the model look right? If the results show that sales decline with advertising then something is wrong. A second set of validation statistics tests the overall quality of the model. A correlation coefficient, or r-squared, shows how well the model describes the data. If r-squared is 1, then the fit is perfect; if zero, there is no fit at all. An analysis of variance (ANOVA) using the F-test is another way of doing this. It also examines the contribution of parts of a model. Student t-tests are very common and useful because they show whether an independent variable, like sale promotions, has a significant contribution or not.

Providing the first stage validation statistics for equation 7.2 gives:

$$S_t = 3300 + 323\ln(P_{t-1}) + 359\ln(V_{t-1}) + u_t \quad (7.3)$$

$(24.6)^a \quad (3.2)^a \quad (4.5)^a$

$r^2 = 0.93^a \quad\quad F(153,3) = 144^a$

In this equation the numbers in the brackets under the equation are individual t-tests for the constant, press and TV advertising elasticities. The a indicates that the values are all significant at a 0.05 level. That means that there is a less than one chance in twenty of figures occurring by chance. The (r^2) shows how well the equation fits the data used to build it: being close to 1.00, the result is good and 93 per cent of the variation in sales is explained. ANOVA gives the F statistic that compares the variation explained by the constant and the two elasticities (the number 3 in the brackets) against the variation remaining in the other degrees of freedom (153). The degrees of freedom are the difference between the number of estimates in the equation and the total number of observations (155 weeks of weekly data).

Second stage validation usually uses a hold-out sample to see whether the model works in predicting new observations. If the data are a time-series, then six months' data can be kept back and the model used to forecast it; if cross-sectional, a sample of stores not used in the model and then predicted. In second stage validation, equation 7.2 was tested with a 12 weeks holdout sample. This showed a small 1 per cent loss in predictive accuracy compared with the model building sample.

Where data are sparse the U-method can be used. This involves (i) holding out a series of sub-sets of the data; (ii) building a model without that data; and (iii) seeing if that sub-set fits the model. At the extreme case, one observation is held out and the model computed as many

The theoretical foundations

times as there are observations. A benefit of this approach is the realization that the result of estimating this series of different models with subsets of data removed gives average results that approximate to a very large sample. The results from this process are jack-knife estimates.

Optimization

Optimization means using the model to find the best solution, for example, to find the best expenditure across media or allocation of shelf space to merchandise. This may be of no interest if the model is used only to guide decisions. Managers can use spreadsheets to represent and manipulate models easily, so use a model to find their favoured strategy. This works with simple problems but managers quickly hit human limitations. It is hard for people to understand complex interactions or to have the patience to search for a best of many options. There are also cases where there are just too many variables to consider or, in the case of the retailing example, too many stores and too much merchandise to manipulate manually (see RETAILING; WHOLESALING).

If models are simple and conveniently specified, calculus can provide optimum solutions. Often this means introducing a structural equation that adds the cost of action. The model would then represent profitability. Using log-log or semi-log specifications to represent the marketing mix, decreasing returns on expenditure would show. Equation 7.2 can be interpreted very easily, the optimum allocation of advertising expenditure between the media is proportional to their elasticities: £323 on press advertising to each £359 spent on TV.

Iterative processes are an alternative if specifications are too complex for calculus. These could be the old hill-climbing techniques, integer programming – that looks at the marginal effect of spending each individual pound across media – or the more modern artificial annealing.

Nature comes to our aid in optimizing marketing models. Simulations show that, near the best solution, there is a large area where radical changes (in advertising, etc.) have little impact on short-term profitability. This is not because the marketing mix variables have little impact but that at the optimum solution one pound in expenditure is balancing one pound in contributions. This insensitivity of the optimum has two assets and one liability. The assets are that unless the model is grossly misspecified and estimated naively, results tend to be similar. They also give management a great deal of room to manoeuvre since there is a whole range of combinations of variables that give roughly sales or profitability. Viewed in this way, a model provides a ball park in which the manager can play. If the issue is advertising expenditure then, without affecting profitability significantly, the manager can take a low-budget approach and sacrifice sales but keep profits up, or an aggressive approach that tends to give the same profits, but increases market share. The domain in which marketing managers make decisions is fortuitously like a plateau rather than a mountain range, where even significant deviations from the best solution can still give reasonable results. This plateau is also a liability to the optimization process. Although deviation from the best answer does not have a significant impact on profit, so flat is the surface that even slight variations in the estimated effects of the marketing mix variables can have a huge effect on the optimum solution. One year the optimum advertising expenditure may be £2 million and the next £1 million because of a slight change in elasticity. This does not mean that either answer is bad but they are both points on the plateau that, because of local variation, make them look slightly higher at one time.

Tracking

Once started, the need for the market modelling never stops. Each year companies, markets, customers and new campaigns change. This means the marketing mix must also alter. What is the best solution in one year will not be the best in another year. Tracking looks at past solutions to see if they still work. It checks deviations to see if the model needs new information. It feeds back into future model building.

Market modelling summary

Managers need knowledge both to use and to build models. The process leaves traps for the unwary but there is now considerable knowledge about what works. Some convenient conclusions come from experience. Simple methods often give answers that are as good and reliable as much more sophisticated methods. There is a need to understand the basics of the specifications and how to estimate models. Managers need to be able to ask questions and see whether results are reliable.

Market modelling looks rigid and certain but it is not. Experience and judgement play a major role and the results are useful to guide decision making, not make decisions. Mathematics constrain the modeller like nature the engineer. The aeronautical engineer makes do with aluminium with its fatigue problems because that is the best material available for the job. The market modeller faces the same problems. All the dimensions may be understood and all desired characteristics known, but there is just no way of representing them all. A model can guide a manager away from the worst solutions and towards the best ones, but strategic decisions are the managers' own.

2 Validation measures

Validation measures appear in marketing modelling (Coates et al. 1991), but they are also essential to empirical marketing research. They are statistical techniques used to reject or accept a hypothesis. In the tradition of logical positivism a researcher starts by setting out a hypothesis and designing an experiment to test it. Jobber anal Saunders (1988) did this when investigating international questionnaire response rates where they hypothesized that questionnaires between countries would have a lower response rate than questionnaires within countries. As Table 4 shows, there were differences in the response rates within the USA and the UK and between them. It suggests that both the Americans and British are more likely to respond to domestic questionnaires (9 and 13 per cent) than international ones (6 and 5 per cent). Validation measures ask if the difference is sufficient for it not to have occurred by chance. In this case they compared sample proportions using a t-test. This shows that there is a significant difference between the British response rates (5 versus 13) but not between the American ones (6 versus 9). In other words, there is evidence to suggest that the British are more responsive to domestic questionnaires, but there is insufficient evidence to support the hypothesis that Americans have the same bias.

There are similar tests for other situations:

1 If samples are large (over 30), normal distribution tests see if sample scores or proportions are significant. For instance: 'Do salesmen who have gone through a sales training programme make higher commission than those who have not?' or: 'Is the proportion of people responding to a six-page questionnaire significantly less than the proportion responding to a three-page one?'
2 If samples are small (less than 30) then a t-test compares the difference between two small sample means. This is often essential where data gathering costs are high or some sample populations are small, such as industrial markets.
3 It is common to cross-tabulate survey results, say social class versus voting behaviour. A pattern may show but validation measures ask if the results could have occurred by chance.

There are many more tests and each has its role. ANOVA is a powerful tool that evaluates the contribution of several variables. Despite the availability of these statistics in most data analysis packages it is surprising how many researchers still report results without referring to them. To do so is unprofessional and stupid. Unless there is a significant difference between results a researcher has no right to claim any findings.

Validation summary

Validation has traps for the unwary. Computer packages give the statistics but require the user to know whether it is appropriate to use them or

Table 4 Source and destination effects on industrial mail survey resposne rates

	Sent from the UK (200 mailings)	Sent from the USA (200 mailings)
Response rate from UK (%)	13	5
Response rate from USA (%)	6	9

not. All the statistics make assumptions about the structure of the data, the most common one being a normal distribution. If these are not true the statistics are invalid. If this occurs, things become more complicated and less straightforward rules apply. Statistical packages usually give these statistics, but few understand them.

Cross tabulations or contingency tables are particularly prone to problems when samples are not large. The familiar chi-square test is invalid if cells contain less than five items. This problem is overcome by collapsing groups – like combining social classes A and B – so the numbers in each cell increase. This can continue until the matrix is 2×2 where again the assumptions of the chi-square statistic become unreliable. Applying Yate's correction can solve that problem.

Given these problems, the best practice for a researcher is to examine publications in strong journals to see what accepted practices are, understand the methods used there, their limitations and conventions for overcoming them.

3 Market analysis

There are numerous mathematical techniques for market analysis. They can do many things. They vary in their origin and application but are common in being multivariate, that is, manipulating many variables at the same time. This means they can analyse many variables and observations (say people) at the same time. As a result, they can provide insights which managers would be unable to gain by looking at data.

Table 5 gives some of these techniques. Green et al. (1988) and Hooley (1994) review them in more detail. The methods are grouped according to their dominant features, the main group being those that split variables into criterion and predictor variables and those that do not.

Methods with criterion and predictor variables

The early discussion of marketing models was mainly based on a regression analysis. It is also the first method introduced here. Variations in the approach to regression analysis discussed is typical of the variety of options that exists for each of the methods of market analysis.

Whereas regression analysis has a single criterion (or dependent) variable, canonical correlation has two or more. This can be very useful in market research where one needs to know the influences at many stages of buyer behaviour, for instance, attitude of a customer, their willingness to buy and their consumption rate of a brand. The same set of predictor (or independent) variables influences all of these. Canonical correlation examines the impact of the predictor variables on each of the criterion variables simultaneously. It can, therefore, give a much greater insight into buyer behaviour than the single criterion within regression.

Probit and logit analysis are useful when the unconstrained criterion variable of regression analysis is inappropriate. In regression analysis, the criterion variable is metric, meaning it can take up any positive or negative value. Probit and logit are useful when this feature is inappropriate, for instance, when the aim is to predict whether a consumer will buy a product or not. The answer must be either yes or no, or a probability that must lie between 0 and 1. Besides being more realistic, probit and logit's constraints mean the techniques give results that look better than those from regression analysis in similar circumstances. Also, since the results have only a limited set of values, they are more reliable. Jobber and Saunders (1993) provide an example in their modelling response rates depending on questionnaire and survey design. Earlier attempts using regression analysis proved inaccurate and were not robust because they occasionally forecast response rates above 100 per cent. A logit model gave more accurate predictions and believable results are guaranteed.

Although probit and logit models allocate observations to two classes, discriminant analysis predicts the memberships of two or more groups. In marketing this can be particularly useful in understanding the membership of market segments, for instance, the difference between heavy beer drinkers in pubs, heavy beer drinkers at home, heavy wine drinkers or spirit drinkers. For a set of predictor variables, discriminant analysis finds how well they can discriminate between the groups and show which predictor variables associate with what group.

Automatic interaction detection (AID) operates quite differently from other methods of

Table 5 Market analysis methods

Method	Criterion variables	Metric criterion	Metric predictor	Finds groups	Typical uses
Regression analysis	Yes	Yes	Yes and no	No	Predicting sales given the mix or economic factors
Canonical correlation	Yes	Yes	Yes and no	No	Predicting more than one criterion variable
Probit and logit	Yes	No	Yes and no	No	Predicting individual buyer behaviour – will/will not buy
Discriminant analysis	Yes	No	Yes and no	No	Predicting group membership (e.g. segments)
AID[1]	Yes	No	Yes and no	Yes	Splitting items into uniform groups with different usage
Correlation analysis	No	n.a.	Yes	No	Seeing the relationship between individual variables
Factor analysis	No	n.a.	Yes	Can do	Indicating groups of similar variables
Cluster analysis	No	n.a.	Yes (almost always)	Yes	Finding groups of similar observations (e.g. segments)
Conjoint analysis	No	n.a.	No	No	Finding the perceived value of product features
MDS[2]	No	n.a.	Yes and no	Can do	Revealing how customers see markets (e.g. positioning)

Notes: 1 Automatic interaction detection
2 Multi-dimensional scaling

partitioning data. AID starts with a criterion variable – say, response rate to mailshots – and predictor variables search to find those that discriminate most strongly on the criteria. If the issue is response to mailshots, then the strongest predictor variable could be home ownership. If that were so, the data split into two groups; one group of home-owners and one of non-home-owners. AID would then look at homeowners and find out the predictor variable that causes the greatest difference in mailshot response amongst home-owners. This could be gender, and so AID would split the population into three groups, male home-owners, female home-owners and non-home-owners. The method would then look at non-home-owners and find the predictor variable that best works for there. In this case it could be wage earners and non-wage earners. This forms four groups. The process continues until the partitioning makes subgroups too small or no more significant differences. Although a convenient tool, AID has limitations. Its sequential approach can give poor solutions and the series of partitions of data quickly splits large data sets into very small groups. Each of the groups is identical for the predictor variables but may be too small to be managerially useful.

Non-partitioned approaches

The remaining methods of market analysis do not split the variables into criteria and predictor. Instead they view all the variables together and look at the relationship between them. The most simple approach is correlation analysis that looks at the relationship between metric variables. If the correlation coefficient is 0, the variables are unrelated; if 1, they are contiguous. Correlation analysis is rarely used as the sole means of analysis. It is, however, useful before regression and other methods to remove redundant variables that waste time and invalidate the analysis.

Factor analysis, like correlation analysis, is itself often an intermediate method but has many direct and valuable uses. It does not look at the relationships between individual variables but finds sets of variables that are similar. This has very valuable uses. Where a market researcher has measured a large number of variables, they reduce to a smaller set of compound ones, called factor scores. Each of these compound variables has the advantage of being independent of the other ones and therefore ideally suited for use in regression or cluster analysis. Over the last ten years factor analysis has become fundamental to the validation of scales in market research (Churchill and Peter 1984). It is used either in an exploratory way, to find out which variables to combine, or in a confirmatory way, to see whether the expected relationship between variables is true.

Cluster analysis has one major application in marketing: the identification of market segments. Traditional *a priori* segmentation divides a market using a criterion – like age or industry – decided beforehand. In cluster-based segmentation, data on demographic, psychographic or lifestyle characteristics of consumers are used to define similar groups. AID is another way of finding clusters. Whereas AID continually partitions the data in two, then four, then eight, cluster analysis looks at all the variables simultaneously and usually uses a hierarchical progress that starts with all consumers being individuals. Cluster analysis then searches to find a pair of consumers that are most alike and joins them to form a cluster. It then treats those two consumers as one and searches for the next pair that are most alike, then the next, then the next, until a manageable number of clusters remain. Unlike the earlier methods discussed here, cluster analysis is an umbrella name for many techniques that make different assumptions about how to measure the distance between groups, how to combine individuals that are alike or simply what a likeness means. The diversity within cluster analysis can be troublesome since it means that the answer depends on the technique used. Fortunately, there is now a sufficient case history to indicate best practices (Saunders 1994) that give reliable and meaningful results. Nevertheless, such is the openness of cluster analysis that validation of the results is of great importance. This usually means using discriminant analysis to test if the results are replicable.

Conjoint analysis has very a specific but powerful application in markets. Like multidimensional scaling (MDS) it examines perceptions and provides a way of integrating data collection with the mapping of perceptions. In this case it is usually the value of products that features, for instance, the importance of colour to selection of a hi-fi system compared with alternative sizes, prices and power output. Given a set of product features, conjoint analysis explores concepts to find the 'part worth' of each element. The power of conjoint analysis comes in being able to find out this information without resorting to an exhaustive set of permutations and combinations of the product features. Conjoint analysis gives results for each person surveyed. The conjoint results of a sample are cluster analysed to form segments. The result could show that one segment of car buyers is unwilling to pay for extra power but would be quite happy to pay for features that made the product easier to use. In contrast, another segment could be unwilling to pay for looks but happy to pay for advanced features and power.

Multi-dimensional scaling is like cluster analysis in being a range of techniques aimed at one problem, in this case the mapping of how customers perceive markets. Figure 4 shows a typical map produced by this method using information on theme parks and their features. In this figure the space is not the geographical distance between the theme parks, but the psychological space. The map shows how close the customer sees the leisure centres in his or her mind and the dimensions used. Besides visualizing markets, the maps produced by multi-dimensional scaling can also help position

Quantitative methods in marketing

products. By knowing the location of segments, competitors and the underlying dimensions that describe their positions, managers can determine how to position their products.

Market analysis summary

The multivariate methods described here have been called the multivariate jungle (Hooley 1980). Indeed such is the variety and complexity of the methods that they can appear as dark, frightening and mysterious to people who are new to them. Also, like jungles, multivariate methods are a rich source of ideas and inspiration. They can help managers to understand complex situations and draw order from large volumes of information. Few managers are likely to be able to use these methods unaided, but they can understand what the approaches can do and some of their limitations. After being able to visualize markets in the way that multi-dimensional methods allow, viewing them conventionally is like using black and white when true colours are available. There was a time when their computational requirements made them inaccessible to most users, but now all are available in desktop form. The major demands they make are on data collection and understanding, not computation.

4 Computer intensive quantitative methods

The last decade has seen the emergence of new quantitative methods useful in marketing. Many of these depart radically from the traditional statistical approach to model building. Methods like simulated annealing, genetic algorithms and neural networks use inspirations from nature to search for the solutions to problems. The main

Leisure centres (stimuli)
A American Adventure
T Alto Towers
B Belton House
C Chatsworth House
W Warwick Castle
S Woburn Safari Park

Segments (points)
i Mature couples
ii Young families
iii Wild young things

Dimensions (vectors)
1 Big rides
2 Educational
3 Fun and games
4 Sophisticated
5 Noisy/rowdy
6 Pre-teen
7 Theme
8 For all the family
9 Artificial/synthetic
10 Good food

Figure 4 Multi-dimensional scaling map showing dimensions, products and segments
Source: Hooley and Saunders (1993)

Table 6 Computer intensive methods

Method	Key features
Simulated annealing	Neighbourhood structure
	Depends on a cooling schedule (like annealing metals)
	Improvement by random search
Genetic algorithms	Pool of solutions (genes)
	Improvement by cross-over and mutation (like the evolution of species)
Branch-and-bound	Tree structures
	Improvement by selective search of branches of the tree
Tabu search	Neighbourhood structure
	Depends on the length of the tabu list
Neural networks	No underlying model assumed
	Learns from training on a set of data (like the brain)
	Depends on the architecture used

use of these techniques is in the estimation and optimization of marketing models. The basic problems remain the same, but these new techniques can analyse complex problems and find better solutions than before. Although these new methods are computer intensive, computing costs are declining so quickly that they are likely to become common soon. Coates *et al.* (1994) review some of these new methods and their short description is in Table 6.

5 Conclusions

In the coming decade marketing managers will increasingly find themselves in a data-rich environment where the technologies and markets are changing rapidly. Quantitative methods provide a way of ordering and manipulating the large quantities of data that are available. The range is such that they could be an encyclopedia in their own right and their mathematical foundation makes it inaccessible to many of today's managers. Their importance shows in the leading marketing journals that devote as much space to developing these mathematical techniques as to other marketing problems. Without a grasp of them, a marketer is as likely to be able to make good solutions as is a navigator who thinks the world is flat. Mathematical approaches do not provide marketing answers but do give the opportunity for better grounded decision making.

JOHN SAUNDERS
ASTON BUSINESS SCHOOL
BIRMINGHAM

Further reading

(References cited in the text marked *)

* Breightler, C.S., Phillips, D.T. and Wilde, D.J. (1979) *Foundations of Optimization*, Englewood Cliffs, NJ: Prentice-Hall.
* Churchill, G.A. and Peter, J.P. (1984) 'Research design effects on the reliability of rating scales: a meta-analysis', *Journal of Marketing Research* 21: 360–75.
* Coates, D., Doherty, N. and French, A. (1994) 'The multivariate swamp: computer intensive methods in database marketing', *Journal of Marketing Management* 10: 207–22.
* Coates, D., Finlay, P. and Wilson, J. (1991) 'Validation in marketing models', *Journal of the Marketing Research Society* 33: 83–90.
* Doyle, P. and Saunders, J. (1990) 'Multiproduct advertising budgeting', *Marketing Science* 9: 97–113.
* Green, P.E., Tull, D.S. and Albaum, G. (1988) *Research for Marketing Decisions*, Englewood Cliffs, NJ: Prentice-Hall.
* Hooley, G. (1980) 'The multivariate jungle: the academic's playground but the manager's minefield', *European Journal of Marketing* 14: 379–86.
* Hooley, G. (ed.) (1994) 'Quantitative techniques in marketing', *Journal of Marketing Management* (special issues) 10.
* Jobber, D. and Saunders, J. (1988) 'An experimental investigation into cross-national mail survey response rates', *Journal of international Business Studies* 19: 483–90.
* Jobber, D. and Saunders, J. (1993) 'A note on the applicability of the Bruvold-Comer model of mail

survey response rates to commercial populations', *Journal of Business Research* 26: 223–36.
* Leeflang, P., Mijatovic, G. and Saunders, J. (1992) 'The identification and estimation of complex multivariate lag structures: a nesting approach', *Journal of Applied Economics* 24: 273–83.
* Lilien, G.L., Kotler, P. and Moorthy, K.S. (1992) *Marketing Models*, Englewood Cliffs, NJ: Prentice-Hall.
* Little, J.D.C. (1970) 'Models and managers: the concept of a decision calculus', *Management Science* 16: 466–85.
* Little, J.D.C. (1979) 'Decision support systems for marketing managers', *Journal of Marketing* 43: 9–27.
* Naert, P.A. and Leeflang, P. (1977) *Building Implementable Marketing Models*, Leiden: Martinus Nijhoff.
* Saunders, J. (1994) 'Cluster analysis', *Journal of Marketing Management* 10: 13–28.
* Simon, J.L. (1970) *Issues in the Economics of Advertising*, Urban, IL: University of Chicago Press.
* Urban, G. (1974) 'Building models for decision makers', *Interfaces* 4: 1–11.

See also: ADVERTISING; ENVIRONMENTAL ANALYSIS; MARKET SEGMENTATION; POSITIONING; QUALITATIVE RESEARCH IN MARKETING; RETAILING; SALES PROMOTION; THE ECONOMICS BASIS OF MARKETING; THE MARKETING AUDIT; THE MARKETING MIX; WHOLESALING

Channels of distribution

1 Channels of distribution defined
2 Distribution channel structure
3 Determinants of channel structure
4 Flows in marketing channels
5 Distribution channels as social systems
6 Electronic distribution channels
7 Trends in distribution channels

Overview

In virtually any developed country around the world a vast array of products is made readily and conveniently available to millions or even hundreds of millions of consumers as well as to many thousands of industrial firms, institutions and other organizations. Somehow, the myriad different products seem to 'find their way' to the particular buyers who are seeking them at a given time. Whether this involves a consumer walking into a supermarket to buy a can of soup or a giant business corporation purchasing a thousand personal computers, for the most part buyers are able to have the products they want, when they want them – even though the range and diversity of their demands is almost incomprehensible and the products to meet those demands may literally come from all corners of the earth. Yet most buyers have little awareness of the enormity of the task involved in providing such a huge assortment of products. Indeed, most are rather nonchalant about it. The convenient availability of all these products is simply a given – an ordinary fact of everyday life. Yet behind this 'ordinary' process is an extraordinary set of institutions comprising the channels of distribution that have made the vast quantities and varieties of products so conveniently available to millions of consumer and industrial customers.

1 Channels of distribution defined

Channels of distribution have been described in a variety of ways since marketing became a recognized business discipline in the early part of the twentieth century (Shaw 1915). Perhaps the most generally accepted definition of a channel of distribution is that it is the route taken by the title to products from the point of production to point of consumption as it passes through institutions or parties who either take the title or facilitate its transfer (Stanton 1968). Thus, according to this definition, it is the title or ownership rights in products that determines the channel of distribution rather than the physical flow of the products. Take, for example, a product that goes from the manufacturer via rail car to a wholesaler who in turn sends it on to a retailer via a public trucking company before it is finally sold to a consumer. The channel of distribution in this case would not include the rail or truck carriers. Instead, the channel of distribution would consist of the manufacturer, wholesaler, retailer, and consumer. This is portrayed in Figure 1. The reason for this distinction is that a *trading relationship* exists only among the manufacturer, wholesaler, retailer, and consumer but not between any of these parties and the rail and trucking firms. The latter are concerned merely with moving the product from point A to point B and do not take title to the product. Neither do the rail or trucking firms facilitate the transfer of the title to the product even though they, of course, facilitate the transfer of the physical product itself. The same reasoning would also hold for a public warehouse which may be called upon to store the product for a period of time in the event that the manufacturer, wholesaler, or retailer do not have sufficient space to store the product on their own premises during a given period of time.

On the other hand, an agent or broker who does not take title and normally would not take physical possession of the product would be considered part of the marketing channel. This follows because the agent or broker, by helping to bring buyer and seller together to consummate a transaction, facilitates the transfer of the title (Bucklin 1972) and thereby is very much a part of the trading relationship in the channel of distribution.

This distinction is important for gaining an understanding of channels of distribution

Figure 1 Channel of distribution based on flow of title

because it is the trading relationship involving the functions of buying, selling and transferring of title where most of the strategic marketing issues emerge. For example, a consumer goods manufacturer attempting to set up a channel of distribution for a new product would face such marketing strategy issues as identifying and selecting the appropriate kinds of sales representatives, agents, brokers, wholesalers and retailers that might be needed to make the product available to its target market, convincing these intermediaries to take on the product, motivating them to do an effective job of promoting it, setting the terms of the relationship such as credit, payment periods, and inventory levels, as well as numerous other tasks necessary to establish and maintain an effective trading relationship. In contrast, such tasks as providing for transportation, storage, insurance and so forth are essentially tactical or mechanical issues which, while important and challenging, are not strategic marketing issues.

So, although firms that perform solely such functions as transportation, storage and insuring are important participants in the operation of channels of distribution, they are not members of the channel. Only those firms or organizations that are involved in a trading relationship based on the performance of buying, selling or facilitating transfer of title are members of the channel of distribution.

2 Distribution channel structure

The 'form' or 'shape' that a channel of distribution takes to perform the functions or tasks necessary to make products available to final customers is usually referred to as *channel structure* (Rosenbloom 1991). This structure consists of all of the firms and institutions (including the producers or manufacturers and the final customers) who are involved in performing the negotiation functions of buying, selling and transferring title. Firms such as

The theoretical foundations

transportation companies, warehousing firms, insurance companies, and the like are usually referred to as facilitating agencies or sometimes the auxiliary channel structure because they are not involved in buying, selling or transferring title and hence, in the strict sense, are not part of the channel structure. Channel structure has three basic dimensions:

1 length of the channel;
2 intensity at the various levels;
3 the types of intermediaries involved.

Length of channel structure

With regard to length, channels of distribution can range from two stages where the producer or manufacturer sells directly to the final customers (direct distribution) to as many as ten stages where eight intermediary institutions exist between the producer and the final customers. With the exception of Japan, such long channels of distribution are quite rare in industrialized countries. Much more common are channel structure lengths ranging from two stages up to five stages. Figure 2 provides an illustration of typical channel structure lengths for consumer products in developed economies.

Many factors influence the length of the channel structure such as the geographical dispersion of customers, the size of the customer base, and their particular behaviour patterns. The nature of the product such as its bulk and weight, perishability, value and technical complexity can also be very important. For example, technically complex products often require short channels because of the high degree of technical support and liaison needed by customers which may only be available directly from the producer. Moreover, length can also be affected by the size of the manufacturer, its financial capacity and desire for control. In general, larger and more well-financed manufacturers have a greater capability to bypass intermediaries and use shorter channel structures. Manufacturers desiring to exercise a high degree of control over the distribution of their products are also more likely to use shorter

Figure 2 Examples of the length of distribution channel structure for consumer products in developed economies channel structures because the shorter the channel, the higher the degree of control.

Intensity of channel structure

Intensity at the various levels of the channel refers to the number of intermediaries at each level. Intensity is usually described using three terms: *intensive*, *selective* and *exclusive* distribution. Intensive means that all possible intermediaries at the particular level of the channel are used. Selective means that a smaller number of intermediaries are used based on more thorough selection criteria, while exclusive refers to only one intermediary used at the particular level of the channel to cover a defined territory. The intensity dimension of channel structure can be portrayed as a continuum as shown in Figure 3. Although there are significant exceptions, in general, intensive distribution is usually associated with the distribution of convenience goods, selective distribution with shopping goods, and exclusive distribution with speciality goods (Bucklin 1963). Thus, inexpensive ballpoint pens, razor blades or cigarettes (convenience goods) tend to be carried by very large numbers of intermediaries, particularly at the retail level, while home appliances and apparel (shopping goods) by relatively fewer intermediaries, and speciality goods such as Rolex watches or Rolls Royce automobiles by only one dealer in a specified geographical area (territory).

Types of intermediaries in the channel structure

This third dimension of channel structure refers to the various kinds of intermediary institutions that can be used at the various levels of the channel. At the retail level, there may be many possibilities for some products. For example, a candy bar can be sold through many different types of retailers such as candy stores, grocery stores, drugstores, supermarkets, mass merchandisers, discount department stores and many others. For other products, such as automobiles, the choice is far more limited. It should be pointed out, however, that in recent years with the growth of scrambled merchandising, the types of intermediaries that sell various products have broadened considerably. Many hardware items, for instance, are sold not only in hardware stores but in homecentres, department stores, mass merchandisers, supermarkets, and even drugstores. Consequently, manufacturers today need to be broad-minded when considering the types of intermediaries to use in their channel structures. The conventional wisdom of particular products being distributed only through certain types of distributors or dealers may no longer hold.

3 Determinants of channel structure

The structure of distribution channels with regard to their length, intensity and types of intermediary institutions participating is determined essentially by three fundamental factors:

1. The distribution functions that need to be performed.
2. The economics of performing distribution functions.
3. Management's desire for control of distribution.

Distribution functions to be performed

Distribution functions, also often referred to as *marketing functions* or sometimes *channel*

Intensive	Selective	Exclusive
All posible intermediaries	Relatively few intermediaries	Just one intermediary

Figure 3 Intensity of channel structure

functions, have been described in various lists since the inception of marketing as a discipline (Weld 1917). Such functions as buying, selling, risk taking, transportation, storage, order processing, and financing are commonly mentioned. Other more generalized functions such as *concentration*, *equalization* and *dispersion* whereby the main functions of channels of distribution are to bring products together from many manufacturers (concentration), adjust the quantities to balance supply and demand (equalization) and deliver them to final customers (dispersion) have also been used. Other concepts of distribution functions describe them in terms of a sorting process consisting of *accumulating* products from many producers, *sorting* them to correspond to designated target markets and *assorting* or putting products together in conveniently associated groups to ease the shopping burden of target markets (Alderson 1957). Distribution functions have also been described in much more detailed terms whereby very specific activities sometimes unique to the particular industry or trade are presented as distribution functions (Rosenbloom 1987).

Regardless of the particular list of distribution functions one chooses to accept, the underlying rationale is the same for all of them. It can be stated as follows: distribution functions must be performed in order to consummate transactions between buyers and sellers. The reason for this is that discrepancies exist between buyers and sellers that must be overcome through the performance of distribution functions. The channel structure chosen to perform the functions reflects how the functions have been allocated to various marketing institutions such as wholesalers, retailers, agents, brokers or others.

What are the discrepancies that exist between production and consumption that must be bridged through the performance of marketing functions? Four such discrepancies have been discussed in the literature:

1 discrepancy in quantity;
2 discrepancy in assortment;
3 discrepancy in time;
4 discrepancy in space.

Discrepancy in quantity
The quantities in which products are produced to achieve low average total cost are usually too large for any individual customer to use immediately. Thus, institutions in the channel structure such as wholesalers and retailers provide a buffer to absorb the vast output of manufacturers and provide the smaller quantities desired by individual customers.

Discrepancy in assortment
Products are grouped for manufacturing purposes based on efficiencies of production while customers group products based on efficiency of shopping and consuming. In most cases, these production and consumption groupings are not inherently congruent. For example, the thousands of items a consumer finds grouped so conveniently together in a supermarket are not, of course, produced by one manufacturer. Hundreds of relatively specialized manufacturers have made those products. The supermarket retailer and many other intermediary institutions in channels of distribution have performed the functions necessary to regroup this conglomeration of products and thereby overcome the discrepancy in assortment. This enables particular manufacturers to concentrate on producing a relatively limited range of products, that when combined through distribution channels with the products of many other manufacturers, enables final customers to have wide and convenient assortments of products that greatly simplify shopping and consumption.

Discrepancy in time
Most products are not manufactured for immediate consumption or use. Hence, some mechanism must be available to hold products between the time they are produced and needed by final customers. Intermediaries in distribution channels, particularly merchant wholesalers and retailers, who take title to and physically hold goods until they are needed by final customers are crucial in overcoming this discrepancy in time.

Discrepancies in space
The location of manufacturing facilities for products is a function of such factors as raw materials availability, labour supply, expertise, historical considerations and numerous other factors that may have little to do with where the ultimate consumers of those products are located. Thus, the production and consumption of products can literally take place half a world

apart from each other. Channel structures evolve or are consciously designed to connect distant manufacturers and users to reduce or virtually eliminate place or spatial discrepancies.

Economics of distribution function performance

Given that distribution functions must be performed to overcome the four discrepancies discussed above, the channel structure must be organized to perform the functions as efficiently as possible. Two principles underlie the development and organization of efficient channel structure:

- specialization/division of labour (Stigler 1951);
- transaction efficiency (McGarry 1951).

Specialization/division of labour
The principle of specialization/division of labour underlies most modern production processes. Each worker or station in a factory focuses on performing particular manufacturing tasks and thereby develops specialized expertise and skills in the performance of the task. Such specialization/division of labour results in much greater efficiency and higher output than if each worker were to perform all or most of the tasks himself.

This two-hundred-year-old principle applies equally to distribution as it does to production. The various middlemen in channels of distribution are analogous to production workers or stations in a factory but instead of performing production tasks they are performing distribution functions. These middlemen whether they be wholesalers, retailers, agents or brokers develop expertise in distribution that manufacturers would find uneconomical to match. Moreover, many large middlemen such as mass merchandisers have *economies of scale* and *economies of scope* which allow them to spread the cost of performing distribution functions over a large volume and diversity of products which would not be possible for the manufacturer.

Transaction efficiency
This concept, also called *contact efficiency*, refers to the effort to reduce the number of transactions between producers and final users. If many producers attempt to deal directly with large numbers of consumers, the number of transactions can be enormous. Paradoxically, by lengthening the channel structure through the addition of middlemen, the number of transactions can be reduced and hence transaction efficiency increased. This is illustrated in Figure 4. As shown in Figure 4, the number of transactions has been cut in half as a result of the introduction of the retailer into the channel structure. Given that the cost of transactions can be very high, especially if personal face-to-face meetings are necessary to consummate transactions, the reduction in contacts through the use of middlemen in the channel structure is in many cases absolutely vital for the economical distribution of products.

Management's desire for control of distribution

Even though the economics of the performance of distribution functions may imply a particular type of distribution channel structure, management's desire for control of the distribution channel may outweigh the economic considerations. In general, the shorter the channel structure, the higher the degree of control and vice versa. Further, the lower the intensity of distribution, the higher the degree of control and vice versa. For example, suppose an economic analysis based on specialization/division of labour and transaction efficiencies calls for a long distribution channel structure with a fairly high degree of intensity at the various levels. However, management in the manufacturing firm feels the need to protect the image of the product and may also believe it necessary to provide high levels of customer service. To do so, the manufacturer is convinced that it needs a high degree of control and so it may opt for direct distribution or at most one level of middlemen with a very high degree of selectivity in appointing them as channel members based on their willingness to take direction from the manufacturer.

Management might also develop its distribution channel structure so as to avoid *opportunistic behaviour* by channel members. Such behaviour is likely to occur when channel members control major portions of *transaction specific assets* – the unique assets such as

The theoretical foundations

Four manufacturers deal with four consumers directly

[M] [M] [M] [M]

[C] [C] [C] [C]

Number of transactions = 4 x 4 = 16

Four manufacturers use one retailer to deal with four customers

[M] [M] [M] [M]

[R]

[C] [C] [C] [C]

Number of transactions = 4 + 4 = 8

Figure 4 How the introduction of a middleman reduces the number of transactions

facilities and equipment as well as specialized expertise that make them virtually indispensable for performing distribution functions (Williamson 1975). If the channel members recognize the power of their position because of their control of the transaction specific assets, they may act in an extremely self-interested fashion to the detriment of the manufacturer. If the manufacturer wants to avoid such a situation, it may reduce substantially its emphasis on the economic considerations in the use of middlemen in the channel structure. Instead, it may decide to perform all of the distribution function itself via *vertical integration*, even though the cost of doing so could be significantly higher. But by vertically integrating, the manufacturer would keep all of the transaction specific assets 'in-house' and therefore prevent them from falling into the hands of self-serving middlemen.

In contrast to this rather cynical view of channel member behaviour, is the *partnership* or *strategic alliance* approach to the development of channel structure (Anderson and Narus 1990). This approach stresses cooperation and mutually supportive relationships between the manufacturer and channel members rather than the avoidance of opportunistic behaviour. In essence, the manufacturer seeking to develop partnerships or strategic alliances with middlemen believes that allocating significant portions of the distribution functions will enhance its degree of control of the channel because partnerships or strategic alliances require close working relationships and mutual trust between the manufacturer and its channel partners.

4 Flows in marketing channels

Once a channel of distribution has been set up, a series of *flows* evolves which tie all of the institutions in the channel together. Eight flows were originally identified in the literature (Vail et al. 1952), but the following six are the most basic ones that exist in virtually all channels of distribution:

1. title flow;
2. negotiation flow;
3. product flow;
4. finance flow;
5. information flow;
6. promotion flow.

Title flow

As pointed out at the beginning of this entry, it is the movement or flow of the title (ownership rights) in products that is the delineator of the marketing channel. The flow of the title through parties who either take title or facilitate its transfer establishes who is involved in the trading relationship of the channel rather than the mere physical handling, storing, or holding of the products. In essence, the flow of the title is a good surrogate indicator of those parties who *have a stake in the channel* in terms of market and financial risk. For instance, the manufacturer who sells his products through wholesalers and/or retailers is relying on these parties to make its products available to final customers. The wholesalers and retailers are giving up shelf space to the manufacturer and hence bear the *opportunity costs* associated with the space (Rosenbloom 1991). Yet the manufacturer's products may or may not meet the wholesalers' or retailers' sales and profit expectations. Even agents and brokers, who, by bringing manufacturers and wholesalers and/or retailers together, facilitate the transfer of title but do not actually hold the title to products nevertheless have a substantial stake in the channel because they invest time, energy and money. In doing so, they help to establish effective and efficient trading relationships in the channel. If these relationships do not work out, the agents or brokers will not only lose their commissions but their very businesses may also be at risk.

Negotiation flow

The functions of buying and selling within the channel of distribution are carried by the flow of negotiation. For example, a manufacturer selling electronic component parts through selling agents to an industrial distributor who in turn sells those products to a computer manufacturer has initiated a vertical flow of negotiation that runs up and down the channel. A wide array of issues involving specifications, price, terms of sale, delivery schedules, returns policies and many others will need to be negotiated not only initially to establish the trading relationship but also to keep the relationship going on a continuing basis as circumstances change.

Product flow

The flow of the product is, of course, the most obvious flow in the distribution channel. Products can flow down the channel towards the final customer through many different kinds of institutions and several possible modes of transportation before finally reaching their ultimate destinations. In many cases, the product flow may follow closely the title and negotiation flows, but as pointed out earlier, this is not necessarily the case. In fact, when agent middlemen are used and/or *drop shipping* is employed, the flow of title and negotiation will be different from the flow of the product.

Finance flow

The finance flow, sometimes termed payment flow, refers to the financial side of trading relationships in channels of distribution. Because provisions have to be made for financing inventories as products move through channels and for arranging payment for the functions performed by all of the channel members involved, the finance flow is crucial to the title and product flows. Obviously, the flows of title and product could not continue for very long if money were not made available to hold inventories and for providing payment for services rendered to the channel members.

Information flow

The flow of information refers to all of the communication necessary to conduct business through the channel. The flow of information overlaps the negotiation and promotion flows and is usually the prerequisite for the title, product and finance flows because specific information is often required to determine who owns the products, how, where and when products are to be conveyed through the channel, and who will be responsible for holding inventory and making payment. The information flow is also very much a two-way flow both up and down the channel. Final customers communicate with retailers (or in business to business situations, industrial distributors) who, in turn, pass the information up the channel all the way back to the manufacturer. Of course, many types of information flow down the channel through the various middlemen on to final customers.

Promotion flow

Although the promotion flow is at least in concept merely a special case of the information flow, it is presented separately because promotion is such a vital part of channels of distribution. Promotion in the form of such tools as *advertising, personal selling, sales promotion* and *publicity* is vital to the establishment and maintenance of all the other flows. In most cases, negotiating with channel members to carry and enthusiastically sell products and to accept the risk as well as the financial burden of holding them requires strong and effective promotion that starts with the manufacturer. The promotion effort must then be carried via the channel by all of the channel members to assist in both *pulling* and *pushing* products through the channel.

Coordinating the flows

The six flows just discussed do not automatically sequence and synchronize themselves into a coordinated mechanism for linking producers and final customers together. On the contrary, the flows if left untended can be uncoordinated. The communication and promotion flow may herald the arrival of products days or even weeks before they actually become available to customers via the product flow. Negotiation can bog down, stalling the transfer of both products and title. Financing and payments may fail to materialize, which can completely derail the operation of the channel. Thus coordination of the flows requires a conscious effort to manage them by some or all of the members of the distribution channel. Indeed, management of distribution channels can be viewed as the process of analysing, planning, and controlling all the distribution channel flows.

5 Distribution channels as social systems

In recent years the perspective used in the marketing discipline to examine channels of distribution has been broadened considerably. Once viewed only as economic systems, channels of distribution are now seen as *social and political systems* as well (Stern and Brown 1969). Consequently, the rules that govern channel relationships are not solely a matter of economics. In the broader social systems perspective, channels of distribution are subject to the same behavioural processes associated with all social systems. The behavioural processes of most significance in channels of distribution are *power* and *conflict*.

Power in distribution channels

Power refers to the capacity of one channel member to influence the behaviour of another channel member – in other words, to get the channel member to do something that he/she would not have done of his/her own volition. For example, a supermarket chain decides to place a manufacturer's new cereal product in a poor shelf location. Upon hearing of this the manufacturer requests that the supermarket provide more prominent shelf space for the product. If the supermarket responds positively to the request, it can be inferred that the manufacturer exercised power over the supermarket because it got the retailer to do something which it would not otherwise have done on its own. The source of the manufacturer's power in this case might have come from any or all of five *power bases*:

- reward;
- coercion;
- legitimacy;
- reference;
- expertise (French and Raven 1959).

Understanding the dynamics of how these power bases are used in the interorganizational relationships that characterize channels of distribution has become a major area of research in distribution literature. Channel analysts have been discovering that in numerous cases the politics of distribution may be just as important as the economics of distribution in the development and operation of effective and efficient channels of distribution.

Conflict in distribution channels

Since the dawn of recorded history conflict has been an inherent dimension of all social systems. Although the basis for effective and efficient operation of distribution channels is cooperation rather than conflict, because the channel is a social system, conflict is also present in the distribution channel.

Conflict is usually defined in a channels context as *goal impeding behaviour* by one or more channel member so that each becomes the object of the other's frustrations (Stern and Gorman 1969). Therefore it is direct, personal and opponent centred rather than indirect, impersonal and object centred, as is the case with competition. For example, a manufacturer wants a distributor to carry only its particular brand of products and to refrain from selling other manufacturers' brands. But the distributor refuses and continues to carry other manufacturers' brands. A conflict may result from this situation because each party perceives the other to be impeding the attainment of its goals. In the case of the manufacturer, the refusal of the distributor to carry only the particular manufacturer's products reduces its ability to build market share, while from the distributor's point of view, carrying only one brand will hurt its capability for meeting the needs of its customers.

Conflict can affect distribution channel performance and therefore it is a topic of much interest in the literature. The most commonly held belief is that conflict has a *negative effect* on performance, but it might also have *no effect* or even a *positive effect* on performance in some circumstances (Rosenbloom 1973). Unfortunately, empirical research on the effects of conflict is still quite limited.

6 Electronic distribution channels

As the twentieth century comes to a close and we move into the next millennium, the role of Internet-based technologies is expected to grow tremendously. Some observers (Rosenbloom 1999) predict that a substantial portion of this growth will come from *electronic distribution channels*. Such channels may be defined as:

> The use of the Internet to make products and services available so that the target market with access to computers or other enabling technologies can shop and complete the transaction for purchase via electronic means.
>
> (Rosenbloom 1999).

Several points need to be made to clarify this definition.

First, the term *available* as used in the definition does not imply physical availability of the product over the Internet. Although it is true that some products and services such as printed matter and music can be digitized for 'delivery' over the Internet, most products and services cannot be transported over the Internet.

Second, the term *other enabling technologies* is used to leave the door open to other means besides the PC for accessing the Internet which may emerge in the future. One such enabling device which is already here is Web-TV which though a minor factor now may grow dramatically.

Finally, the completion of the transaction through *interactive electronic means* is used to convey the idea of 'stepping over the line' from merely using the Internet as a kind of electronic mail order catalogue. If the sellers do not offer online ordering capabilities for the mechandise they offer and/or customers cannot or will not make use of online ordering (which is still quite common in Internet commerce), little substantive change has occurred. All that has really changed from conventional mail order distribution channels is that the seller's products appear on a computer screen rather than in print and customers scroll through the seller's website rather than turn catalogue, magazine, or newspaper pages before they get on the phone to place an order.

Electronic distribution channels as described above already exist with such well-known firms as Dell Computer Corporation (computer equipment), Amazon.com (books), CDnow (compact musical discs), Peapod (groceries), and Auto-By-Tel (automobiles) being some of the leading firms making extensive use of electronic distribution channels. But development to this point, though substantial, may be just the 'tip of the Iceberg.' By the early part of the twenty-first century, Internet-based electronic distribution channels may change the very 'landscape' of the distribution structure. The brick and mortar of stores and shopping centres and consumer travel to retail stores may be replaced by virtual malls and stores, while shopping in Cyberspace may replace going to the store for millions of consumers (Rosenbloom 1999).

Advantages and disadvantages of electronic distribution channels

Whether or not electronic distribution channels become a major force in distribution channels will depend heavily on how the advantages and disadvantages of this high-tech mode of distribution play out in the marketplace in the near future.

Advantages of electronic distribution channels
Five basic advantages of electronic marketing channels over conventional channels which are often stressed are:

1. global scope and reach;
2. convenience and rapid transaction processing;
3. information processing efficiency and flexibility;
4. databased management and relationship capabilities;
5. lower sales and distribution costs.

Any of these five advantages of electronic distribution channels over conventional channels can be formidable. For example, even a small firm can sell its products all over the world given the global scope and reach of the Internet even as giant firms with millions of customers can tailor their offerings to meet the needs of niche and micro-market segments because of the information processing and databased management capabilities of Internet-based electronic distribution channels. And consumers can literally shop the world without leaving the comfort and convenience of their own homes at substantial savings in cost if the predicted economies in sales and distribution costs of electronic distribution channels are realized.

Disadvantages of electronic distribution channels
Electronic distribution channels also have at least five important disadvantages compared to conventional distribution channels:

1. lack of contact with actual products and delayed possession;
2. fulfillment logistics not at Internet speed or efficiency;
3. clutter, confusion and cumbersomeness of the Internet;
4. non-purchase motives of shopping not addressed;
5. security concerns of customers.

Just as in the case of the advantages of electronic distribution channels, any or all of these disadvantages can be formidable in limiting the growth of Internet-based electronic distribution channels. For example, mail order distribution channels which have existed for over a hundred years account for just a small fraction of retail sales owing to most consumers' desire to have actual contact with products and immediate possession after purchase. Further, while information flows through electronic distribution channels at the speed of light, the physical flow of products moves infinitely more slowly due to the order fulfillment logistics involved in moving products from sellers to buyers. This fact significantly offsets the vaunted speed and efficiency of electronic distribution channels made possible by the Internet. Moreover, aside from worrying about the security of transactions over the Internet, consumers are often motivated to go shopping via conventional distribution channels to get out of the house, have social contact, and experience the fun of shopping which cannot be provided by electronic distribution channels.

7 Trends in distribution channels

Although there are many developments and trends that have affected channels of distribution in recent years, the following five stand out as the most basic:

1. more strategic emphasis by firms on channels of distribution;

2 partnerships and strategic alliances gaining more ground;
3 continued growth of vertical marketing systems;
4 growing power of retailers in distribution channels;
5 greater role for technology in channels of distribution.

Strategic emphasis on distribution channels

Distribution channels had been one of the relatively neglected areas of marketing but they have now come on quite strongly as a focus for strategic marketing emphasis. The main reason for this is that more and more firms are recognizing that superior distribution channels can help the firm to gain a *sustainable competitive advantage* that cannot be easily copied by competitors (Porter 1985). This pattern seems to be occurring in a wide range of industries from automobiles to consumer packaged goods to industrial equipment.

Partnerships and strategic alliances

Although not a new phenomenon, the growth in the use of partnerships and strategic alliances in channels of distribution has been accelerating rapidly. Manufacturers are linking up with wholesalers and/or retailers in mutually supportive and synergistic relationships to achieve far more effective and efficient distribution. The same pattern is occurring in many industrial (business-to-business) channels as well (Fites 1996).

Such partnerships or strategic alliances usually require close cooperative relationships between channel members on a continuing and long-term basis. Hence, they are the antithesis of the 'every man for himself' mentality tradition of more loosely aligned or *ad hoc* channel relationships.

Growth in vertical marketing systems

Vertical marketing systems (VMSs) first described in the mid-1960s (McCammon 1965) have continued their growth through the ensuing decades and are expected to continue to grow into the next millenium, VMSs are divided into three categories:

1 Administrated systems whereby one channel member at the manufacturer, wholesaler or retailer level exercises a high degree of control over the operation of the channel.
2 Contractual systems which consist of retailer cooperatives, wholesaler sponsored voluntary chains and business format franchises.
3 Corporate systems where distribution is vertically integrated by the manufacturer (forward integration) or by a wholesaler or retailer (backward integration).

Such VMS systems create economies of scale and scope and provide a level of managerial and marketing expertise that loosely aligned traditional channels are finding increasingly difficult to match.

Growing power of retailers

Over the past decade retailers have continued to grow in average size in most developed countries. Moreover, the spate of mergers, acquisitions and bankruptcies of retailers in recent years accelerated the growth of large-scale retailers so that now retailers are often larger than all but a handful of the manufacturers who supply them. The growing size of retailers, along with their increased sophistication in the use of technology and modern marketing methods has dramatically increased their power in marketing channels. Consequently, channels of distribution, especially for consumer goods, are increasingly being dominated by giant retailers who have become 'gatekeepers' into the marketplace. As such, they are determining to an increasing extent what products enter distribution channels and in turn what products become available to consumers (McDermott and O'Connor 1995).

Increasing role of technology

Last but certainly not least, the application of technology in channels of distribution, especially – as discussed earlier – the growth of the Internet, has exploded in recent years and is accelerating rapidly. Such use of the Internet for online or Cyberspace shopping enables customers to gain immediate access to a virtually unlimited array of products and services from around the world via the information superhighway (Reilly 1997).

Sophisticated use of point-of-sale terminals, scanning and computerized inventory control systems, which grew so rapidly in the 1990s, are being augmented by greater use of portable and hand-held computers linked to mainframe computers or large networks of personal computers via cellular phone technology. Hence the days of clipboards and pencils to check in inventory and process orders will virtually disappear in the near future.

The use of electronic data interchange (EDI) whereby channel members are linked together in real time is another rapidly growing technology. This enables manufacturers to schedule their production to conform to what products customers are buying as soon as they are being rung up by the retailer because the information is conveyed instantaneously from the retailer's computer to the manufacturer's.

Such technologies have made concepts such as *supply chain management* whereby the entire distribution channel is managed to produce excellent customer service and *efficient consumer response* (ECR) which seeks to provide consumers with better service and more value at lower total costs, practical realities in modern channels of distribution rather than merely slogans (Bowersox and Closs 1996).

A further technological development that is catching on in more and more instances is computerized 'salespeople' and 'consultants' whereby customers interface with the computer at the point of purchase and receive information, advice or even plans and detailed specifications that all but the most knowledgeable human salespeople would be hard-put to match.

Of course, these are just a small sample of the technological developments that are affecting the structure and operation of channels of distribution as we move into the twenty-first century.

BERT ROSENBLOOM
COLLEGE OF BUSINESS AND ADMINISTRATION
DREXEL UNIVERSITY

Further reading

(References cited in the text marked *)

* Alderson, Wroe (1957) *Marketing Behavior and Executive Action*, Homewood, IL: Richard D. Irwin.
* Anderson, James C. and Narus, James A. (1990) 'A model of distributor firm and manufacturer firm working partnerships', *Journal of Marketing* January: 42–58.
* Bowersox, Donald J. and Closs, David J. (1996) *Logistics Management an Integrated Supply Chain Process*, New York: McGraw-Hill.
* Bucklin, Louis P. (1963) 'Retail strategy and the classification of consumer goods', *Journal of Marketing* January: 50–5.
* Bucklin, Louis P. (1972) *Competition and Evolution in the Distributive Trades*, Englewood Cliffs, NJ: Prentice-Hall.
Corey, E. Raymond, Cespedes, Frank V. and Rangan, V. Kasturi (1989) *Going to Market*, Boston, MA: Harvard Business School Press.
Dahstrom, Robert and Dwyer, F. Robert (1992) 'The political economy of distribution systems: A review and prospectus', *Journal of Marketing Channels* 2: 47–86.
Davis, Tom (1993) 'Efficient supply chain management,' *Sloan Management Review* Summer: 35–46.
* Fites, Donald V. (1996) 'Make your dealers your partners,' *Harvard Business Review* March–April: 84–95.
* French, R. P. and Raven, Bertram (1959) 'The bases of social power', in Cartwright, Darwin (ed.), *Studies in Social Power*, Ann Arbor, MI: University of Michigan.
Hunt, Shelby D., Ray, Nini M. and Wood, Van R. (1985) 'Behavioral dimensions of channels of distribution: review and synthesis', *Journal of the Academy of Marketing Science* 13: 1–24.
Journal of Marketing Channels (1991) New York: The Haworth Press.
* McCammon, Bert C. (1965) 'Integrated channels in the American economy', in Bennett, Peter D. (ed.), *Marketing and Economic Development*, Chicago: American Marketing Association.
* McDermott, Christopher M. and O'Connor, Gina C. (1995) 'Managing in the age of the mass merchant,' *Business Horizons* November–December: 74–0.
* McGarry, Edmund D. (1951) 'The contactual function in marketing', *Journal of Business* April: 96–113.
Pellegrini, Luca and Reddy, Srinivas K. (eds) (1989) *Retail and Marketing Channels*, London: Routledge.
* Porter, Michael E. (1985) *Competitive Advantage: Creating and Sustaining Superior Performance*, New York: The Free Press.
* Reilly, Patrick M. (1997) 'Booksellers prepare to do battle in Cyberspace,' *Wall Street Journal* 28 January: B1, D8.
* Rosenbloom, Bert (1973) 'Conflict and channel efficiency: some conceptual models for the decision-maker', *Journal of Marketing* July: 26–30.

* Rosenbloom, Bert (1987) *Marketing Functions and the Wholesaler-Distributor*, Washington, DC: Distribution Research and Education Foundation.
* Rosenbloom, Bert (1991) *Marketing Channels: A Management View*, 4th edn, Chicago: Dryden Press.
  Rosenbloom, Bert (ed.) (1993) *Wholesale Distribution Channels*, New York: The Haworth Press.
* Rosenbloom, Bert (1999) *Marketing Channels: A Management View* 6th edn, Fort Worth, Texas: The Dryden Press.
* Shaw, Arch W. (1915) *Some Problems in Market Distribution*, Cambridge, MA: Harvard University Press.
* Stanton, William J. (1968) *Fundamentals of Marketing*, 2nd edn, New York: McGraw-Hill.
* Stern, Louis W. and Brown, Jay W. (1969) 'Distribution channels: a social systems approach', in Stern ,Louis W. (ed.), *Distribution Channels: Behavioral Dimensions*, New York: Houghton Mifflin.
  Stern, Louis W. and El-Ansary, Adel I. (1992) *Marketing Channels*, 4th edn, Englewood Cliffs, NJ: Prentice-Hall.
* Stern, Louis W. and Gorman, Ronald H. (1969) 'Conflict in distribution channels: an exploration', in Stern, Louis W. (ed.), *Distribution Channels: Behavioral Dimensions*, New York: Houghton Mifflin.
* Stigler, George J. (1951) 'The division of labor is limited by the extent of the market', *Journal of Political Economy* June: 185–93.
* Vail, Roland S., Grether, E. T. and Cox, Revis (1952) *Marketing in the American Economy*, New York: Ronald Press.
* Weld, L. D. H. (1917) 'Marketing functions and mercantile organization', *American Economic Review* June: 306–7.
* Williamson, Oliver E. (1975) *Markets and Hierarchies: Analysis and Antitrust Implications*, New York: The Free Press.

See also: ADVERTISING; CHANNEL MANAGEMENT; DIRECT MARKETING; PERSONAL SELLING AND SALES MANAGEMENT; SALES PROMOTION

Consumer behaviour

1. The development of consumer behaviour research
2. Consumer decision making – the complex approach
3. Differing levels of complexity in consumer decisions
4. 'Purchasing without decisions'
5. Future developments in consumer behaviour

Overview

The fundamental basis of the marketing concept involves the matching of the skills and resources of the organization, profit or non-profit related, to the needs of the customer. Marketing management relies on an understanding of how customers make decisions and their likely reactions to the different elements of the marketing mix. In this context, consumer behaviour not only refers to the physical activity of purchasing but also to related pre-purchase and post-purchase activities. Loudon and Della Bitta (1993) define consumer behaviour as 'the decision process and physical activity individuals engage in when evaluating, acquiring, using, and disposing of goods and services'.

One of the most useful applied distinctions in consumer behaviour is between consumer behaviour studied from a micro perspective and a macro perspective. At the micro-level, the focus is very much on the reaction of the individual consumer with applications that are relevant to advertising managers, salespeople, or product designers of individual firms or organizations. At the macro-level, consumer behaviour involves the study of the influence of consumption on the economic and social conditions within society. The collective behaviour of consumers influences our total quality of life, directing the demand and supply of products and services. The anticipation and forecasting of consumer behaviour at that level can be used for both organizational planning and product development, as well as formulation of public policy to improve the efficiency of the market system.

Research in consumer behaviour allied to the study of marketing basically stems from the 1950s. Prior to that the terminology was essentially confined to the discipline of economics. Economists had a developed series of models explaining consumer choice in terms of changing utilities, or demand preferences, according to variations in price, income and quantity supplied. This approach has been relatively uninfluential within the marketing literature compared with the application of behavioural science concepts taken from psychology and sociology. Detailed reviews of the contribution of all three of these disciplines to marketing are provided elsewhere in this volume. The entries on psychology and sociology show how concepts such as learning, motivation, perception, attitude and social groups have been applied to help our understanding of every element of the marketing mix (see THE PSYCHOLOGICAL BASIS OF MARKETING; THE SOCIOLOGICAL BASIS OF MARKETING; THE MARKETING MIX). This entry primarily seeks to give an overview of consumer decision making and show how those concepts listed above may be integrated to give an understanding of the role they play in explaining decision processes of consumers. However, before considering that material in detail, it is useful to reflect on some aspects of the history of consumer research in marketing in order to appreciate the variety of approaches and the overall complexity of the subject. This historical review is not intended as a comprehensive treatise on the development of consumer behaviour but rather a framework to understand how the subject has arrived at its current status and content. It also helps to provide a platform from which to consider future developments in consumer behaviour later in the entry.

1 The development of consumer behaviour research

Reflecting on the literature in consumer behaviour allied closely to marketing, it is possible to discern three approximate phases of development:

- a segmentation era, primarily associated with work before the mid-1960s;
- a period from the mid-1960s through to the end of the 1970s which was dominated by the development of knowledge on consumer decision making;
- a period of diversification and enrichment in the 1980s and 1990s.

In the 1950s and through to the mid-1960s much of consumer behaviour research involved the evaluation of consumer characteristics for market segmentation. It was at this time that consumer behaviour researchers investigated the application of personality theories and classifications of motives taken from psychology, and the family life-cycle and social class taken from sociology. These were applied with very different degrees of success in cross-sectional studies of markets in order to explain variations in consumer demand for many different classes of products, and also for different choices of brands. Important contributions from this period, which are illustrative of some of the research and are still commonly referred to in the literature and in teaching consumer behaviour, include Koponen (1960), Tucker and Painter (1961), Evans (1959), Haire (1950), Dichter (1964), Martineau (1958), Coleman (1960), Levy (1966), Wells and Gubar (1966), and Barton (1955).

One of the studies from that period which has had a very profound influence on consumer behaviour and marketing is Rogers' work on the diffusion of innovations (1959, 1962). He segmented the potential market for a new product according to the time of adoption and developed a five stage classification within which to describe potential customers – innovators, early adopters, the early majority, the late majority and laggards. Another important facet of Rogers' work was his characterization of the adoption process. During consumers' adoption of innovations, Rogers described the individual as moving through the following series of stages in their decision to purchase:

1 awareness;
2 interest;
3 evaluation;
4 trial;
5 adoption.

This was one of the first attempts to describe a sequential process which illustrated the stages of the consumer decision and, as will be seen in later discussion, the steps described by Rogers are typical of the framework that has been used to underpin models of consumer decision making.

Based upon this emerging theory, the first consumer behaviour textbooks for students were published in the 1960s and the volume produced by Engel, Kollat and Blackwell in 1968 is regarded as especially significant. Their initial edition is regarded as the first complete textbook on consumer behaviour. It helped to define the boundaries of the subject and firmly established the following as integral concepts in the study of consumer behaviour – motivation, perception, learning, attitudes, personality, social groups (especially the family), social class and culture. Further, Engel, Kollat and Blackwell encapsulated the switch from a preponderance of segmentation research towards a focus on decision making, and they provided one of the first, and most enduring, detailed models of the consumer decision process.

The 1968 Engel, Kollat and Blackwell model was one of a series to be developed in the late 1960s and early 1970s. Other particularly important contributions were offered by Howard (1963), Howard and Sheth (1969), Nicosia (1966), and towards the end of the 1970s, Bettman provided another substantial offering with his information processing model of consumer decision making (1979). Taking an historical perspective on this period it is probably difficult to under-emphasize the importance of developments in attitude theory as applied to thinking and research in consumer behaviour. Approaches to the study of attitudes, particularly as represented in the work of Fishbein (1967) and its later extensions (Ajzen and Fishbein 1980), provided marketers with an easily operationalizable way of investigating and modelling consumer preferences and evaluations. If any single concept stands out as being core to the development of consumer behaviour in the 1970s, it is the theory of attitudes.

Two of the other important developments in the 1970s were the emergence of work on the family as a decision-making unit, and the foundation of consumer psychographics and lifestyles as segmentation techniques. Although husband/wife influences had been investigated earlier (e.g. Wolgast 1958), the early 1970s saw major developments in that area, particularly through the work of Davis (e.g. 1976 and Davis and Rigaux 1974). This work placed the investigation of family decision making into a parallel context with individual decision making based around the type of sequence described by Rogers. The recognition of children in the family decision process and the nature of consumer socialization also developed during this period (e.g. Ward 1974 and Ward *et al.* 1977).

In the area of market segmentation, the most important developments of this period were the related concepts of psychographics and lifestyles. Retrospectively it is possible to view their development as an outgrowth of disillusionment with personality and other variables as a good basis for market segmentation. The development of mainframe computers and canned packages of multivariate techniques enabled consumer behaviour researcher and marketers to adopt what has been called a 'backwards' approach to market segmentation. Using huge questionnaires they were able to collect large quantities of data representing the activities, interests and opinions of consumers. Factor and cluster analysis techniques enabled this pot pourri of information to be refined into apparently stable and meaningful portraits of consumer groups (Wells 1974, Mehrotra and Wells 1977).

The latest period of development and enrichment is primarily reflected in the consumer behaviour research of the 1980s and 1990s. Looking back, the dominant paradigm of the 1970s is seen to be one borrowed from cognitive approaches to psychology. Since that time some particularly strong challenges have been made to this approach. For example, Foxall (1990) presents a radical approach to viewing consumer behaviour by drawing on alternative paradigms from behavioural psychology, while in complete contrast other authors have presented consumer research within postmodern contexts (e.g. Hirschman and Holbrook 1992, Holbrook 1995). Research has continued within the decision-making and segmentation frameworks established earlier, but it has also expanded and, as scientific approaches have varied, the subject of consumer behaviour has expanded with significant developments in several concepts. Illustrative of these advancements are new understandings in the role of culture (McCracken 1988), values (Kahle 1985), and language and semiotics (Umiker-Sebeok 1987). The scope of consumer behaviour has also expanded as other social and economic trends have developed that affect marketers. For example, consumer behaviour researchers have expanded their focus to consider phenomena such as shoplifting (Cox *et al.* 1990), the effects of homelessness on consumption (Hill and Stamey 1990) and compulsive buying (Elliott 1993). Perhaps the most comprehensive review of consumer research and social policy is provided by Andreasen (1991).

Also emerging through the 1980s were two major and related contributions to theories of how consumers make decisions. First, there has been the evolution of an alternative 'low involvement' approach to consumer decision making with a different set and sequence of stages to those outlined from Rogers above. Second, consumer behaviour researchers have placed an increased emphasis on the role of affective as opposed to cognitive influences (e.g. Rossiter and Percy 1991). These two changes are outlined in much greater detail in the rest of the entry, which develops the current state of thinking with regard to consumer decision making.

2 Consumer decision making – the complex approach

The complex approach primarily reflects the early cognitively based theories of the subject. Starting with this approach, we can give a general overview of decision making which can be adapted to take more recent variations into account. A good way to appreciate the overall complexities of consumer decision making is to review one of the comprehensive models that have been proposed. One of the most popular and enduring of these models is that offered by Engel, Blackwell and Miniard (1990) (see Figure 1). As indicated above, the basis for this model was first proposed by Engel, Kollat and Blackwell in 1968 and it has been regularly revised and updated to account for new evidence about the behaviour of consumers. It should be noted that evaluations on scientific criteria (e.g. explanation, prediction, generality and heuristic power) have not always been kind to these types of comprehensive models of the

Figure 1 The Engel, Blackwell and Miniard model of consumer decisions
Source: Engel *et al.* (1990).

consumer decision-making process. What the Engel, Blackwell and Miniard model does offer is a comprehensive illustration of the variables influencing consumers and an appreciation of the flexible and dynamic nature of the consumer decision-making process.

As can be seen, the model is arranged in four columns. The essential stages of the decision process are diagrammed in sequence down the third column. Starting from need recognition, the consumer is seen to move through search processes to evaluation of alternatives, purchase and satisfaction or dissatisfaction outcomes. These five stages reflect the same inherent hierarchy underlying Roger's sequence of adoption outlined earlier.

Column one is concerned with the information environment for the decision, and of particular relevance to marketers are the elements of the promotional mix that form the marketer-dominated stimuli and which feed into the information processing part of the model in column two. This second column depicts the processes of perception and learning which govern the acquisition and retention of information and link with the need recognition and information search phases of the decision. Other psychological variables are defined in the alternative evaluation stage, and the model makes the central place of attitudes absolutely explicit since it can be equated to preferences governing behavioural intentions and subsequent purchase. The final column lists the influencing variables which impact on the consumer decision. Understanding how these variables impact on the decision process provides a basic rationale for their importance to market segmentation strategies.

The selection of the Engel, Blackwell and Miniard model for this review does not imply that it is the most superior approach in all situations. For example, Howard has been intensely critical of the model in comparison to his own approach and also that of Bettman's (Howard 1989: 109–21). One problem in operationalizing and actually using the Engel, Blackwell and Miniard model to help in the formulation of marketing strategy is the vagueness of the role of some of the variables. The influencing variables in column four are a good example of this, since the exact nature of their relationship to the decision process is not clearly defined. The variables in both boxes in column four can impact on the decision process directly or indirectly at several stages. However, in terms of the descriptive overview for this entry, it is the inclusion of these very variables that gives the model its appeal and helps to demonstrate the potential complexity of the interrelationships between concepts. The model provides a good starting point from which to refine our understanding of the consumer decision process.

3 Differing levels of complexity in consumer decisions

Since the formulation of early models of buyer behaviour, the most important developments have come in considering variations in the levels of complexity of the decision. Engel, Blackwell and Miniard believe that the same basic model described above can still be used to characterize these different levels of complexity. They argue that intensity, or degree, to which the different stages are used by consumers varies according to the task, but that the essential framework is still appropriate for all situations. However, this claim requires clarification and it is useful to consider alternative theories.

Levels of problem solving

Another of the important early contributions to consumer decision making was made by John Howard in 1963 when he defined consumer behaviour as a problem solving exercise. Howard has retained this approach and his 1989 book *Consumer Behaviour in Marketing Strategy* is still built around this idea. He defines and describes three major types of problem solving. These categories are defined as extended, limited and routine problem solving (EPS, LPS and RPS). They reflect buying situations that essentially vary in the amount of intellectual challenge they offer to the consumer. The main determinant influencing the level of problem solving is the *familiarity* of the task facing the consumer. Howard uses the same basic summary model (Figure 2) for all three situations but adapts the complexity of the cognitive processes involved. Like Engel, Blackwell and Miniard, the overall model is still based on a hierarchy which leads through intentions to purchase. Key differences between the models, as shown in Figures 1 and 2, are Howard's inclusion of a variable to represent consumer

Figure 2 Howard's consumer decision model
Source: Howard (1989)

confidence, and the recognition of direct links between information and attitudes, confidence and intentions. This allows Howard to relax assumptions about the sequence of the stages in the decision process. For example, particularly under RPS, it is possible to have a link directly from information to intention.

EPS is seen as a form of behaviour that is appropriate when the consumer is faced with an innovation, or a first time behaviour, which requires the consumer to form a new product category concept. It is characterized by having two levels of choice, choice between categories and then choice between brands. In this context it would also be logical to extend the definition of EPS so that it is applicable to situations where the consumer faces a choice between non-comparable alternatives such as a holiday or a new car.

LPS is a level of problem solving which Howard believes to be appropriate to situations where the consumer is confronted by an unfamiliar brand in a familiar product class. Consumers take in and process information to produce a cognitive response or image toward the brand, but this is completed within the context of an already existing schema or, in Howard's terminology, product hierarchy.

RPS deals with behaviour for products and brands with which the consumer is very familiar and it is usually characterized by repeat purchasing. The buyer has an evoked set of familiar brands, and choice between brands is made on the basis of very simple heuristics, or decision rules. Typically, a consumer may apply what is known as a conjunctive decision rule. This involves fixing a minimum performance level for relevant product attributes, including price, and the consumer simply buys any brand that passes these criteria subject to availability.

A further important extension of RPS is what Howard refers to as BPS, or Boredom Problem Solving. The argument is quite simple. When a product or brand is too familiar boredom can set in. The result is that higher levels of information search are re-initiated in order to provide some variety in behaviour. This is a notion which fits well with ideas on consumer motivation regarding optimum stimulation levels.

Levels of involvement

Whereas Howard's approach is essentially based on familiarity, a different but related and also more common approach considers different types of choice processes according to levels of involvement. The concept of involvement is first attributed to Krugman (1965) in explaining differences in learning from advertising between magazine and television environments. However, the concept did not make a substantial impact on thinking and teaching in consumer behaviour until the late 1970s. Even now, there exist some differences in interpretation but there is general agreement

The theoretical foundations

```
Antecedents of                  Involvement              Possible results
involvement                     with                     of involvement

Person factors                                           Elicitation of
 - needs                                                 counter arguments
 - importance                                            to ads
 - interest
 - values                       advertisements           Effectiveness of
                                                         advertising
Object stimulus
   factors                                               Relative importance
 - differentiation                                       of product class
   of alternatives
 - source of                    products                 Perceived differences
   communication                                         in product attributes
 - content of
   communication                                         Brand preferences

Situation factors               purchase                 Influence of price
 - purchase/use                 decisions                on brand choice
 - purchase occasion
                                                         Amount of information
                                                         search

                                                         Time spent on
                                                         purchase

                                                         Type of decision
                                                         rule used in choice
```

Figure 3 The nature of consumer involvement

that involvement represents an intensity of interest and is a form of arousal related to a motivational state. Differences in involvement are known to be characterized by differences in overall levels of brain activity and by variations in left and right brain activity. These variations emphasize differences in the type of cognitive activities being pursued under different conditions of involvement (Petty et al. 1983).

Involvement is seen as having three essential dimensions. First, intensity relates to the degree of interest that the consumer experiences. It is usual to talk about high or low involvement situations but, in reality, intensity of involvement is a continuum and this is reflected in the measurement scales that have been developed to assess consumer involvement (Zaichkowsky 1985). The second dimension of involvement is direction or focus. Involvement may be orientated towards the product itself, the advertising, the purchase and purchase decision, or any combination of the three. For example, in a services situation where production and consumption of the service are often simultaneous with the purchase, one may not be able to differentiate between the product and the purchase decision. The final dimension of involvement relates to its persistence. A key distinction is made between enduring involvement and situational involvement. Enduring involvement is long term and represents the ongoing personal interest that people have in particular product areas. The clearest examples of these are the consuming interests developed with pastimes and hobbies such as fishing or stamp collecting. Situational involvement is short term and normally associated only with the purchase decision. Typical examples of products that generate high levels of situational involvement are durables such as dishwashers and washing machines. The consumer may collect a lot of information on the different options and carefully evaluate the best buy for their situation, but once acquired, there is little ongoing interest in the product.

Involvement is related to a consumer's values and self-concept, and varies not only across individuals but also across situations. In itself involvement embraces a number of different properties and, as a determinant of decision mode, it is a much more complex notion than familiarity, or prior knowledge, which underlies variations in Howard's problem solving approach. Figure 3 gives a summary of the major

Table 1: Alternative views of High and Low Involvement Consumers

High Involvement View of an Active Consumer	Low Involvement View of a Passive Consumer
1 Consumers are information processors.	1 Consumers learn information at random.
2 Consumers are information seekers.	2 Consumers are information gatherers.
3 Consumers are an active advertising audience and as a result the effect of advertising on the consumer is *weak*.	3 Consumers represent a passive audience for advertising. As a result the effect of advertising on the consumer is *strong*.
4 Consumers evaluate brands before buying.	4 Consumers buy first. If they evaluate brands it is done after the purchase.
5 Consumers seek to maximize expected satisfaction. Consumers compare brands to see which provide most benefits related to needs and buy based on multi-attribute comparisons.	5 Consumers seek some acceptable level of satisfaction. As a result, consumers buy the brand least likely to give them problems and use few attributes.
6 Personality and lifestyle characteristics are important because the product is closely tied to the consumer's identity and belief system.	6 Personality and life-style characteristics are not important because the product is not closely tied to the consumer's identity and belief system.
7 Reference groups influence consumer behaviour because of the importance of the product to group norms and values.	7 Reference groups exert little influence on product choice because products are unlikely to be related to group norms and values.

Source: Adapted from Assael (1992).

dimensions of involvement. Column one describes its antecedents or influencing factors. Column two refers to the object of the involvement and column three indicates the results where differing levels of involvement have an impact on consumer decision making.

Antecedents of involvement include a variety of variables that interact with each other to generate a degree of involvement at any particular time. Amongst the personal considerations are needs, values, experiences and interests. These interact with different products and services to produce differing levels of involvement for different individuals. The effect of the antecedents on involvement is also moderated by the ability of the consumer to find and process information.

Column two identifies the objects of involvement as discussed above, and column three in Figure 3 gives an extensive list of the results of involvement upon different aspects of consumer behaviour. However, there are two other sets of consequences that should be made clear in addition to those listed. First, in low involvement situations, it is accepted that there may be very little or no evaluation of the product before purchase. Attitudes that are formed are weakly held and are primarily based on experience derived from consumption. This presents a different scenario from the previous models which identify attitude formation as a key concept leading to intentions and purchase. Low involvement is often reflected in consumers proceeding directly from need recognition to purchase with no information search or evaluation of alternatives.

A second important set of consequences relates to post-purchase behaviour and ongoing consumption. Complaints are seen as a high involvement phenomenon, while dissatisfaction with low involvement products is generally seen as resulting in brand switching. Also, brand *loyalty* may be viewed as a high involvement phenomenon. Indeed, the definition of loyalty may be seen to require some degree of emotional attachment which is reflected in enduring involvement. High situational involvement and a positive brand evaluation may result in a high level of brand confidence, but this need not equate to loyalty and may be displaced in a subsequent evaluation. Low involvement situations may be characterized by stable purchasing patterns but these are considered the result of inertia, rather than loyalty. As such it is a form of behaviour which is easily disrupted by situations such as stockouts or sales promotions. The following summary of the alternative high and low involvement approaches to consumer behaviour is adapted from Assael (1992).

4 'Purchasing without decisions'

In 1979 Olshavsky and Granbois published an influential paper entitled 'Consumer decision making – fact or fiction?'. They provided a synthesis of research on the pre-purchase stage of consumer behaviour and concluded that, in very many cases, the pre-purchase stages of information search and evaluation of alternatives were simply not present. Their argument goes far further than simply seeing routine repetitive behaviour as something which has resulted from the earlier application of some more extended process of evaluation. They conclude that at every level of consumption, from general budget allocation down to choice of individual brands, a majority of consumers do not in fact evaluate alternatives and did not therefore make decisions. It is important to realize that the evidence they quote takes into account a wide range of consumer behaviour situations, including strategic consumption decisions relating to the allocation of income across different expenditure categories, choice of retail stores, and a range of products from furnishings and household appliances through to grocery items. 'Purchasing without decision making' is not, therefore, to be regarded as atypical behaviour.

The notion of consumer purchasing without any explicit decision-making process is consistent with several other important contributions to consumer theory in the 1980s. For example, Zajonc and Markus (1982) have emphasized the role of affective, as opposed to cognitive factors, in the formation of consumer preferences. Like Krugman's initial paper on low involvement and passive learning, this is an approach which stresses how people learn through repeated exposure. Familiarity with a product is seen to be sufficient for the formation of preferences without any original cognitive justification. A good illustration of their argument is the way in which Mexican children acquire strong preferences for chilli peppers in their diet despite initial aversive reactions.

The idea of consumers purchasing without decisions is also reflected in what is referred to as the 'experiential' approach to consumer behaviour (e.g. Holbrook and Hirschman 1982). The emphasis in the experiential approach is firmly placed on the symbolic nature of consumption. Consumer behaviour is seen as primarily hedonic and orientated towards aspects of pleasure and emotions rather than being associated with analytical, logical, problem solving.

The consequence of these adaptations in thinking is that consumer behaviour has become more diversified and research has incorporated more studies on consumption as opposed to inquiries solely considering the purchasing process. This has to be a positive move in an applied marketing context. Although the process of acquiring goods and services will always be important for marketers to understand, the long-term matching of products to customer needs has to be based on a thorough understanding of benefits sought by consumers and the way in which products are actually used. A provocative paper by Wells (1993) on the status of current research in consumer behaviour reviews a classification of consumer research developed by Johan Arndt. The classification is based on the five stages of the decision process, from problem recognition through to post-consumption activities, and the importance of the decision. Four categories of importance are considered (see Table 2):

- Acquisition of strategic items. These have a 'life altering' effect and examples include a new home, a new child, or education versus employment.
- Central budget allocation decisions. This refers to allocation of resources among important groups of products or services, for instance the choice between the vacation or the new kitchen.
- Generic product or service decisions, or specific purchases within groups of products and services. An example may be the choice between the built-in oven or the free standing cooker for the new kitchen.
- Variant selection, or choice of individual brands.

Table 2

	Recognition	Search	Purchase	Consumption	Post-consumption
Strategic					
Central					
Generic					
Variant					

Wells emphasizes that consumer researchers have spent most of their time in the bottom left-hand corner of this chart, dealing with the early stages of low level decisions and he makes a strong call to move away from this focus and develop more knowledge in the top right corner which has a strong applied macro focus. The work of Andreasen, Belk, Hirschman, Holbrook, McCracken, and others, has increased our knowledge of the top right-hand corner but a quick appraisal of the contents of the leading journals on consumer behaviour shows that most published material in the 1990s still deals with the lower left corner.

5 Future developments in consumer behaviour

This will be considered first in terms of research and knowledge about the subject area and then in terms of some speculative changes that may take place in the way consumers actually acquire and use goods and services. In 1991 Wind, Rao and Green provided an assessment of recent paradigm shifts in consumer behaviour that, it was suggested, would point the direction for future research. They summarized developments by emphasizing the seven trends listed below.

1. A move to considering more realistic units of analysis; in particular, a greater emphasis on the family buying unit and less attention to the traditional focus on the individual.
2. Consideration of assortments of products rather than individual purchase transactions; realistically, many purchases are related and it is more fruitful to look at sets of behaviours rather than single instances.
3. Examination of situation specific purchase and consumption, rather than general behaviours; recognition of this is seen to increase the validity and value of much consumer research.
4. A move from deterministic to stochastic modelling of consumer behaviour.
5. A lessening of the US focus in consumer research with more cross-cultural studies and recognition of cultural variations in consumer behaviour. In part, this is seen as a response to the interest in globalization that has dominated much business and economic thinking in the last twenty years.
6. A move from a 'low tech' to a 'high tech' consumer environment; advances in computers and telecommunications are fundamentally changing the nature of consumer behaviour. They also have significant implications for methods of consumer research with the potential availability of new databases. This links closely with item four. Retail scanning technology has provided huge improvements in the databases available for modelling patterns of consumer purchases over time.
7. The use of integrated sets of research methods rather than single approaches; enhancement of software for multivariate statistics means that techniques like cluster analysis may be used more effectively with conjoint analysis or multidimensional scaling, offering more complete analyses and a better understanding of behaviour.

In reality several of these have not eventuated. Arguably there has been some move towards the examination of situation specific behaviours in an attempt to increase the validity of much of our knowledge, but this has not been accompanied by efforts to consider assortments of products and services, to move the unit of analysis away from the individual to the examination of more realistic buying groups, or to use integrated sets of research methods. In part this is a comment on the sheer complexity of some of the issues but it is also a comment on traditional university procedures for assessing academic staff. These tend to demand a quantity of published material and it is easier for researchers to stick with the tried and tested methods that are simpler to administer and complete, rather than develop the more complex high risk research strategies demanded by Wind, Rao and Green.

No such excuses can be offered for the failure to make more acknowledgement of stochastic modelling in consumer behaviour. Stochastic models of brand choice have existed since the 1950s (e.g. Ehrenberg 1959) but have had little impact on traditional studies. In recent years there has been some recognition of a stochastic element in consumer behaviour with, for example, the acknowledgement that some brand choice behaviour may be cyclical in nature, but the results of this work in other areas have been consistently ignored. As an illustration, marketers continue to talk about market niches and niche strategies despite the fact that work on double jeopardy highlighted fundamental concerns with the basic concept several years ago (Ehrenberg *et al.* 1990).

The two areas where Wind, Rao and Green were most successful in anticipating changes in consumer behaviour were in anticipating the high technology environment for consumer behaviour and the increase in studies outside North America. Looking further to the future we may expect both of these to continue. Ultimately consumer behaviour is a subsystem of general human behaviour and these changes are both founded on general global trends affecting all aspects of human behaviour. The information technology changes that have affected consumer behaviour in the 1990s are familiar to us all (e.g. retail scanning, eft-pos, and Internet). It is difficult to anticipate what new technologies might affect consumer behaviour in the next century but, at the very least, we must continue to expect rapid and widespread adoption of these technologies by consumers. One fundamental consequence for marketing managers is the continued growth of non-store retailing methods. Though accurate figures on these methods are not available, the indicators that do exist show that they have grown rapidly in popularity in the last few years (Lawson *et al.* 1996). It is not just the buying stage of the process that will be affected by these technologies. Obviously information search is impacted by new alternatives available through the Internet and expert systems are available that can guide consumers through the evaluation of different alternatives (see INFORMATION TECHNOLOGY AND MARKETING).

These developments in information technology may be seen as part of the globalization phenomenon that has been much discussed in the marketing literature. Such technologies and new products are adopted all over the world in rapid time and as such do not become intrinsically bound into individual cultures. Furthermore, along with the large scale movement of people through migration and tourism, these technologies facilitate the sharing of information and different dimensions of culture. Cross-cultural research in consumer behaviour has started to identify many commonalities in the subject. For example, Grunert's work on European food lifestyles shows similar segment patterns across Europe and work on consumer lifestyles in New Zealand shows many similar features to both North American and European work (Faris *et al.* 1996, Lawson *et al.* 1998). One common misconception is that these globalization trends are de-emphasizing the importance of culture as a concept in consumer behaviour. This is not necessarily so. It is the unit of analysis that has changed. The work on lifestyles and values shows large variations within national boundaries as well as common trends between different countries. Nationality is no longer a good approximation of culture and culture becomes a relevant variable for all marketing activity, not just international strategies.

As well as technology and globalization as major forces affecting the future direction of consumer behaviour, the third major trend influencing its future direction is the environment. Much has been made of environmental issues in marketing and 'green marketing' has been advocated not just as desirable but also necessary for long run profit maximization. Many studies in the 1980s identified 'green' consumers who could provide the basis for profitable market segments but in retrospect a degree of cynicism exists about much of this work. First, it is not clear that these segments are enduring. Evidence in New Zealand shows that environmental issues have decreased in importance to consumers in the 1990s (Faris *et al.* 1996). Second, problems with social desirability response bias and a lack of detailed understanding of many environmental issues by consumers suggest that it is really difficult to estimate consumer responses in this area. Relatively few consumers understand what sustainable consumption entails and what type of trade-offs might be required in terms of prices, quality and other product attributes. It is a major challenge for consumer behaviour to understand the consequences of environmental changes and how consumer expectations can realistically be aligned with environmental considerations. Major issues will continue to relate to packaging, energy and water usage, animal exploitation and habitat destruction (see GREEN MARKETING).

Part of the environmental issue is the realization of the externalities involved and the 'true' costs of many human behaviours. Legislation in different countries has already forced marketers to extend their thinking in this respect. For example, the German system places the onus for retrieval and disposal of packaging materials back on the suppliers and in New Zealand the Resource Management Act requires an environmental audit for most new business or product developments. However, the idea of externalities goes into other areas besides the environment. As Hirschman (1991) points out, many other social problems together with their associated costs, that have increased in importance in the last thirty years are due to consumption 'gone wrong'. These range from addictions and abuse of products through to mismanagement of credit and consequent poverty. Hirschman's call was for consumer behaviour researchers to become involved in many of these issues. It is to be expected that marketers will also have to show more responsibility for the unplanned consequences of their actions (see GREEN MARKETING for an extended discussion of these issues).

Overall, the potential changes in patterns of consumer behaviour are enormous. This presents special challenges and opportunities for marketers and for students of consumer behaviour. This review has attempted to give an understanding of three essential aspects – the overall scope and development of the subject; the concentration of much of the work around an information processing and decision-making perspective; and some of the potential changes and problems facing the area. The work on information processing and decision making has had many successes and will continue to be important. In terms of application, it is most relevant to the promotional aspect of the marketing mix and its success is particularly represented by the idea of involvement. Involvement has developed as an accepted theoretical construct from *within* the study of consumer behaviour as opposed to other concepts that have been sometimes integrated into consumer behaviour with little recognition of their place in their parent discipline – the family life-cycle, for example. However, meeting the challenges noted under the last discussion on future trends will demand that marketers develop better understandings of the upper right quadrant of Wells' diagram. To fully understand the changes resulting from technology, environmental pressures or other costs associated with consumer behaviour we must know more about actual use and disposal. Apart from some attempts to model complaining behaviour that are mainly based in the services literature, consumer behaviour analysts have no general theories that deal with the consumption and post-purchase phases that can be described as any way equivalent to the understanding developed on information processing and purchasing. The challenge is to develop similar levels of understanding across the whole subject area.

ROB LAWSON
UNIVERSITY OF OTAGO

Note

Engel, Blackwell and Miniard have produced a slightly revised version of their model in a later edition of their book. However, I have chosen to remain with the 1990 version because it shows more clearly the role that attitudes have traditionally held in models of consumer choice.

Further reading

(References cited in the text marked *)

* Ajzen, I. and Fishbein, M. (1980) *Understanding Attitudes and Predicting Social Behavior*, Englewood Cliffs, NJ: Prentice Hall.
* Andreasen, A.R. (1991) 'Consumer behaviour research and social policy' in T.S. Robertson and H.H. Kassarjian, *Handbook of Consumer Behavior*, Englewood Cliffs, NJ: Prentice Hall.

The theoretical foundations

* Assael, H. (1992) *Consumer Behavior and Marketing Action*, 4th edn, Boston, MA: PWS-Kent.
* Barton, S.G. (1955) 'The life-cycle and buying patterns' in L.H. Clark (ed.), *Consumer Behaviour*, New York: New York University Press.
* Bettman, J.R. (1979) *An Information Processing Theory of Consumer Choice*, Reading, MA: Addison Wesley.
* Coleman, R.P. (1960) 'The Significance of Social Stratification', in M.L. Bell (ed.), *Marketing: A Maturing Discipline*, Chicago: American Marketing Association.
* Cox, D. Cox, A.D. and Moschis, G.P. (1990) 'When consumer behavior goes bad: an investigation of adolescent shoplifting', *Journal of Consumer Research* 17:149–59.
* Davis, H.L. (1976) 'Decision making within the household', *Journal of Consumer Research* 2: 241–60.
* Davis, H.L. and Rigaux, B.P. (1974) 'Perception of marital roles in decision processes', *Journal of Consumer Research* 1: 51–62.
* Dichter, E. (1964) *Handbook of Consumer Motivations*, New York: McGraw Hill.
* Ehrenberg,A.S.C. (1959) 'The pattern of consumer purchases', *Applied Statistics* 8: 26–41.
* Ehrenberg, A.S.C., Goodhardt, G.J. and Barwise, T.B. (1990) 'Double jeopardy revisited' *Journal of Marketing* 54: 82–91.
* Elliott, R. (1993) 'Shopping addiction and mood repair' in M. Davies (ed.), *Emerging Issues in Marketing*, vol 1, Proceedings of the 1993 conference of the marketing Education Group, Loughborough University Business School: 287–96.
* Engel, J.F., Kollat, D.T. and Blackwell, R.D. (1968) *Consumer Behaviour*, New York: Holt, Rinehart and Winston.
* Engel, J.F., Blackwell, R.D. and Miniard, P.W. (1990) *Consumer Behaviour*, Hinsdale, NJ: Dryden Press.
* Evans, F.B. (1959) 'Psychological and objective factors in the prediction of brand choice', *Journal of Business* 32: 340–69.
* Faris, F., Lawson, R.W. and Todd, S.J. (1996) *New Zealand Towards 2000: A Consumer Lifestyles Study*, Dept of Marketing, University of Otago, Dunedin.
* Fishbein, M. (1967) 'A behavior theory approach to the relations between beliefs about an object and the attitude toward an object' in M. Fishbein (ed.), *Readings in Attitude Theory and Measurement*, New York: Wiley.
  Foxall, G.R. (1990) *Consumer Psychology in Behavioural Perspective*, London:Routledge.
  Grunert, K.G., Brunso, K. and Johansen, L. B. (1996) *An Analysis of National and Cross-National Consumer Segments Using the Food Related Lifestyle Instrument in Denmark, France, Germany and the United Kingdom*, Aarhus, Denmark, MAPP, The Aarhus School of Business.
* Haire, M. (1950) 'Projective techniques in marketing research', *Journal of Marketing* 14: 649–56.
* Hill, R.P. and Stamey, M. (1990) 'The homeless in America: an examination of possessions and consumption behaviors', *Journal of Consumer Research* 17: 303–21.
* Hirschman, E.C. (1991) 'Secular mortality and the dark side of consumer behaviour: or how semiotics saved my life', in R.H. Holman and M.R. Solomon (eds), *Advances in Consumer Research*, volume 18, Provo, UT: Association for Consumer Research.
* Hirschman, E.C. and Holbrook, M.B. (1992) *Postmodern Consumer Research*, Newbury Park, CA: Sage Publications.
* Holbrook, M. B. (1995) *Consumer Research*, Thousand Oaks, CA: Sage Publications.
* Holbrook, M. B. and Hirschman, E.C. (1982) 'The experiential aspects of consumption: consumer fantasies, feelings and fun', *Journal of Consumer Research* 9: 132–40.
* Howard, J.A. (1963) *Marketing Management: Analysis and Planning*, Homewood, IL: Richard D. Irwin.
* Howard, J.A. (1989) *Consumer Behavior in Marketing Strategy*, Englewood Cliffs, NJ: Prentice Hall.
* Howard, J.A. and Sheth, J.N. (1969) *The Theory of Buyer Behavior*, New York: John Wiley and Sons.
  Kassarjian, H.H. and Robertson, T.S. (1991) *Perspectives in Consumer Behavior*, Englewood Cliffs, NJ: Prentice Hall.
* Kahle, L.R. (1985) 'Social values in the eighties: a special issue', *Psychology and Marketing* 2.
* Koponen, A. (1960) 'Personality characteristics of purchasers', *Journal of Advertising Research* 1: 6–12.
* Krugman, H.E. (1965) 'The impact of television advertising: learning without involvement', *Public Opinion Quarterly* 29: 349–56.
  Lawson, R.W., Tidwell, P., Rainbird, P., Loudon, D. and Della Bitta, A. (1996) *Consumer Behaviour in Australia and New Zealand*, Sydney: McGraw Hill.
* Lawson, R.W., Thyne, M., Young, T. and Juric, B. (1998) 'Travel lifestyles' in A. Pizam and Y. Mansfeld (eds), *Consumer Behaviour in Tourism*, Haworth Press.
* Levy, S.J. (1966) 'Social class and consumer behaviour', in J.W. Newman (ed.), *On Knowing the Consumer*, New York: Wiley.
* Loudon, D.L. and Della Bitta, A.J. (1993) *Consumer Behaviour: Concepts and Applications*, New York: McGraw Hill.
* Martineau, P. (1958) 'Social classes and spending behaviour', *Journal of Marketing* 23: 121–30.

* McCracken, G. (1988) *Culture and Consumption: New Approaches to the Symbolic Character of Consumer Goods and Activities*, Bloomington, IN: Indiania University Press.
* Mehrotra, S. and Wells, W.D. (1977) 'Psychographics and buyer behaviour: theory and recent empirical findings', in A.G. Woodside, J.N. Sheth and P.D. Bennett (eds), *Consumer and Industrial Buying Behaviour*, New York: Elsevier North Holland.
* Nicosia, F. (1966) *Consumer Decision Processes: Marketing and Advertising Implications*, Englewood Cliffs, NJ: Prentice Hall.
* Olshavsky, R.W. and Granbois, D.H. (1979) 'Consumer decision making – fact or fiction?', *Journal of Consumer Research* 6: 93–100.
* Petty, R.E. Cacioppo, J.T. and Schumann, D. (1983) 'Central and peripheral routes to advertising effectiveness: the moderating role of involvement', *Journal of Consumer Research* 10: 135–46.
* Rogers, E. (1959) *The Adoption of New Products: Process and Influence*, Ann Arbor, MI: Foundation for Research on Human Behaviour.
* Rogers, E. (1962) *Diffusion of Innovations*, New York: Free Press.
* Rossiter, J. R. and Percy, L. (1991) 'Emotions and motivations in advertising', *Advances in Consumer Research*, 18: 100–10.
* Tucker, W.T and Painter, J. (1961) 'Personality and product use', *Journal of Applied Psychology* 45: 325–29.
* Umiker-Sebeok, J. (ed) (1987) *Marketing and Semiotics: New Directions in the Study of Signs for Sale*, Berlin: Mouton de Gruyter.
* Ward, S. (1974) 'Consumer socialisation', *Journal of Consumer Research* 1: 1–16.
* Ward, S. Wackman, D.B. and Wartella, E. (1977) *How Children Learn to Buy: The Development of Consumer Information Processing Skills*, Beverley Hills, CA: Sage.
* Wells, W.D. (ed.) (1974) *Life Style and Psychographics*, Chicago: American Marketing Association.
* Wells, W.D. (1993) 'Discovery-orientated consumer research', *Journal of Consumer Research* 19: 489–504.
* Wells, W.D. and Gubar, G. (1966) 'Life-cycle concept in marketing research', *Journal of Marketing Research* 3: 355–63.
* Wind, J. Rao, V.R. and Green, P.E. (1991) 'Behavioral methods' in T.S. Robertson and H.H. Kassarjian, *Handbook of Consumer Behavior*, Englewood Cliffs, NJ: Prentice Hall.
* Wolgast, E. H. (1958) 'Do husbands or wives make purchasing decisions', *Journal of Marketing*, 22: 151–58.
  Zaichkowsky, J.L. (1985) 'Measuring the involvement construct', *Journal of Consumer Research* 12: 341–52.
* Zaichkowsky, J.L. (1986) 'Conceptualising involvement', *Journal of Advertising* 15: 4–14.
* Zajonc, R.B. and Markus, H. (1982) 'Affective and cognitive factors in preferences', *Journal of Consumer Research* 9: 123–31.

See also: GREEN MARKETING; INFORMATION TECHNOLOGY AND MARKETING; THE MARKETING MIX; MARKETING ORGANIZATION AND MANAGEMENT; THE PSYCHOLOGICAL BASIS OF MARKETING; THE SOCIOLOGICAL BASIS OF MARKETING

Organizational buying behaviour

1 Introduction
2 Historical development of the purchasing function
3 Purchasing behaviour
4 The buying process
5 Influences on the buying process
6 Summary

Overview

Organizations are customers for a wide range of products and services. Understanding how the organizational customer behaves when making purchasing decisions is critically important to effective marketing decisions. The study of how organizations buy (organizational buying behaviour) has evolved to meet this need.

Organizational purchasing decisions are made to meet the objectives of an organization rather than the needs of an individual buyer. There are some problems with this definition since organizational needs and individual needs frequently overlap (for example with the purchase of a company car). However, the rationale for purchase is the distinct characteristic of the organizational buying decision that differentiates it from consumer behaviour. There are two principal determinants of supplier choice. These are the technical suitability of the product or service to meet the customer's needs, and the economic worth or value of the product or service.

This entry begins with a review of the formal tasks of organizational purchasing. The core elements of purchasing are to buy the right product at the right price at the right time. Understanding how buyers handle price, quality and delivery issues is the first stage in analysing organizational buying behaviour. The second part of this entry discusses the nature of organizational buying decisions. It focuses on the nature of the buying process and the range of different influences on that process. This entry has been written from the perspective of an organization wishing to sell to an organizational customer.

1 Introduction

Most of the early focus on organizational buying behaviour stressed the need to understand how customers fixed prices, determined delivery quantities and specified quality. It was assumed that these three elements determined which supplier the customer selected. Failure to meet the buyer's needs on these criteria would lead to loss of the business. These three elements relate to functional aspects of the buyer's role, commonly referred to as purchasing (see PURCHASING MANAGEMENT).

Research from the 1960s onwards has formally confirmed what many practitioners experience throughout their industrial marketing careers. Organizational buying decisions are frequently complex processes that take place over time. Typically there is a sequence of stages in the process, and there are likely to be different influences at each stage. More than one member of the organization is involved in the buying process, and each member of the buying group is likely to have different interests in the outcome. It is not sufficient when making marketing decisions to consider the role of price, quality and delivery alone. Success depends upon developing a complete understanding of how customers make buying decisions.

Organizations buy products and services to enable them, in turn, to supply other customers with products or services. Their demand as potential customers is driven by the demand for their own products or services. Economists term this derived demand. It follows that to sell to an organization it is important to understand the influences on the demand for that customer's own goods and services.

All organizations make purchasing decisions. The scope of organizational buying behaviour includes manufacturing and service industries (see MARKETING OF SERVICES; PRODUCT POLICY). It also includes public sector organizations in sectors such as transport, education and healthcare. Primary sectors such as agriculture and extractive industries are also included. Organizational buying behaviour as a field of study also includes retailing and distribution (see CHANNELS OF DISTRIBUTION; RETAILING; WHOLESALING). The potential scope of an article such as this is considerable. This entry will focus primarily on manufacturing and service sectors. This is a reflection of the extent to which these sectors have been systematically analysed and researched. Although the other parts of the economy are equally important areas of economic activity, they tend to have been neglected in formal analyses of organizational buying decisions.

2 Historical development of the purchasing function

Articles relating to the purchasing function can be traced back to the turn of the century (Fearon 1968). The first two books presenting an analytical view of the function appeared in 1928. However, most of the literature on purchasing has appeared from the 1950s onward. This reflects an increasing interest in the potential contribution of purchasing to organizational performance.

Economic development in many countries has led to increased specialization and therefore interdependence between organizations. When organizations no longer manufacture every part of the end product, and choose to buy components from a third party, they become dependent on the purchasing function to source that component effectively. Current trends suggest that purchasing will become increasingly important as organizations choose to concentrate on developing their core skills and competencies and supplement these with bought-in products or services as required from the most efficient supplier (Hamel and Prahalad 1993).

The traditional role of the purchasing function is to buy the right product or service, to a given specification, at the best possible price. The function is also responsible for making sure that it arrives on time to meet the organization's needs. In this traditional role the specification and delivery requirements are typically set by other functions within the organization. This leaves the purchasing function to concentrate on getting the best possible deal on price, and to ensure that the product or service is delivered on time.

Traditionally purchasing's major role has been seen as restricted to pricing decisions, negotiation and dealing with contracts. This is reflected in the relatively low status given in many organizations to the buying role (Keogh 1993). The major exception to this is in retailing where buyers have historically been recognized as one of the most important functions in the organization (Parkinson and Hogarth-Scott 1993).

Since the 1950s a succession of academics and management consultants have argued that organizations would benefit by giving purchasing a greater strategic role. They consider that bought-in materials and services are a significant proportion of total manufacturing costs in many industries (Reck and Long 1988). In such industries cost management or cost reduction can have a major and direct effect on profitability. Managing costs may be a more effective way of maintaining profitability than maintaining market share. Market share maintenance typically requires marketing expenditure, and cost reduction by definition involves reducing expenditure.

Purchasing's strategic contribution can also include improving the quality of expenditure. Purchasing is responsible for the interface between an organization and its supply markets. A professional purchasing function will identify changes in supply markets that may present opportunities or threats. For example, if a supplier is acquired by one of its major competitors this reduces the sourcing options open to the buyer. Negotiations with an alternative supplier may be more difficult because of the absence of competition. Alternative suppliers may already have contractual relationships with the organization's own competitors. In this situation purchasing may be responsible for monitoring the status of current suppliers. Where problems are anticipated alternative sources of supply may be developed to reduce dependency on a few key suppliers.

Alternatively, a new technology may offer radically improved performance over existing technologies, and give major competitive advantage to those companies which incorporate it in their own products. Purchasing's role is to scan supply markets continuously and identify technological changes that could have major implications for the organization. There is increasing evidence that much significant innovation comes as a result of the purchasing organization stimulating suppliers to develop new products or processes to meet customer requirements.

In some organizations the purchasing function has developed a broader range of supply management responsibilities (Keogh 1993). These include quality management, value engineering, value analysis and material requirements planning. It is becoming increasingly necessary for suppliers to demonstrate to such companies that they are operating to appropriate quality standards. Some purchasing organizations now have a policy of not buying from companies that do not have BS 5750 or ISO 9000 certification (see MARKETING ETHICS). The application of value engineering and value analysis techniques has also provided the purchasing organization with a methodology to identify systematically the specification of a specific product or service and to ensure that the company buys to that specification. Materials requirements planning disciplines have also led to the development of JIT (just-in-time) supply relationships with key suppliers to manage inventory levels.

Each of these professional aspects of the purchasing decision has implications for the marketing behaviour of potential suppliers. Resource management skills are growing in many organizations posing a considerable challenge for conventional marketing decisions. The purchasing organization now increasingly controls the marketplace. Marketing's challenge is to identify the requirements of customers on each of these elements and develop an appropriate response.

3 Purchasing behaviour

While it is important to understand the professional role of the purchasing function it is also important to recognize that purchasing decisions are made by individuals working in an organization. Such individuals are subject to a variety of different influences and use different criteria to make the final choice of supplier. It would be naive to ignore these behavioural influences on the buying decision.

For example, a supplier might assume that a customer will buy if the supplier's product is better than the competition in meeting the customer's technical and economic requirements. This assumption may be invalid if the customer is averse to taking risks. Another customer may be very keen to buy quickly, and be prepared to take the risk of product failure.

These influences on the buying decision are behavioural dimensions. Buyers make decisions for reasons other than economic and technical rationality. Remember the company car example from earlier? The reasons for making a decision in a particular way may be linked to a variety of factors. These include the characteristics of the purchasing company, the buying situation or the individual knowledge and experience of the buyer responsible for the final selection of supplier.

One convenient way of examining the behavioural influences on the organizational buying decision is to distinguish between the buying process and the various influences on this process. By examining the buying process, suppliers can get a feel for the range of decisions that a potential customer makes. This can enable them to anticipate what inputs are required to get the customer to consider their organization favourably.

An awareness of the influences on the buying process guides the supplier towards an understanding of differences in the needs of specific customers. This can be used to differentiate products and services to meet differing requirements. A focus on influences can also be useful in tailoring communications appropriately.

4 The buying process

The organizational buying decision can be seen as a process that takes place over time. There are several key stages in this process. However, each of these stages may not be present in every situation. The process may be extensive in some situations and relatively short in others. A variety of different models have been suggested to reflect the different stages, each with essentially the same elements. These are identification of need, specification of requirements, search for supplier, choice of supplier, purchase order, post-purchase evaluation and supplier management (Moller 1985).

Buying situations have also been classified into three categories, namely straight rebuy, modified rebuy and newbuy situations (Robinson and Faris 1967). The straight rebuy situation involves purchasing the same product or service again from the same supplier. Such a purchase will typically be made quickly and only a few people are likely to be involved in the buying process. A modified rebuy involves a change in the purchase. This could involve a new supplier or a change in specification. More people are likely to become involved in the purchasing process. Finally, a newbuy is a purchase that the organization has not made before. Typical newbuy situations involve more people than the other two purchasing situations and take longer to complete.

The concept of the buygrid has been developed to describe the interaction between the buying process and the buying situation (Robinson and Faris 1967). Each of the different buyclasses (newbuy, modified rebuy and straight rebuy) can be viewed in terms of its associated buying process. This categorization provides a useful way of analysing the organizational buying decision (see Table 1).

Research can be conducted to determine how the supplier's customers identify the need to buy the product or service being offered. Do customers actually recognize the problem in the first place, or does the supplier have to create an awareness of the need? For example, it is obvious when a supply of paper runs out that it must be replaced. Similarly, components are required to keep a production line running, and must be replaced when the supply is exhausted (ideally just before). However for some products it is less obvious that there is a need. A company may be unaware of the need to improve its internal information systems. An audit of communication systems by an external supplier may reveal the extent of the problem.

Specification of requirements involves developing a description of the characteristics and quantity of the product or service that is needed. This may be done by specifying by brand name (for example, a brand of motor fuel). Alternatively, it may involve analysis of the requirement. The specification will be developed from that analysis. This process is termed value engineering. If the vendor can become involved in this process then it is possible to influence the final specification. This could involve sharing knowledge with the customer to assess the technical requirement and build a business case. In some situations the customer may simply indicate what it wants to achieve and invite the suppliers to bid against that specification (usage specification). Here the customer is relying on the expertise of the supplier to solve the problem (Dyer and Ouchi 1993).

Organizations look for suppliers in many different ways. From a supplier's perspective it is important to identify how the customer looks for alternative suppliers. It is also important to determine how many suppliers are likely to be considered. In many situations standard operating procedures specify how many suppliers must be included. This is linked to the value of the contract. The organization may insist that the purchaser obtains quotations from at least three suppliers for purchases placed with a value greater than £2500. This may cause

Table 1 Robinson and Faris's buygrid model of organizational buying behaviour

	Newbuy	Modified rebuy	Straight rebuy
Problem (need recognition)			
Determine characteristics of needed item or service			
Describe characteristics of needed item or service			
Search for supplier			
Acquire proposals			
Evaluate proposals			
Select order routine			
Performance feedback			

Source: Robinson and Faris (1967)

problems if there are only a few competent suppliers.

Evidence from a range of research also suggests that most industrial buyers do not look very far when searching for new suppliers. There is a strong tendency towards inertia. Existing suppliers are favoured over new sources of supply.

It is also important to understand which sources of information are used to find suppliers. Formal media (trade press, exhibitions and direct marketing) typically create awareness. Informal media (face-to-face meetings and personal references from other customers) are used to evaluate and choose suppliers. Some sources of information such as personal contacts are perceived as more reliable than formal contacts. This is particularly the case when considering new products or services from unknown suppliers.

When a customer creates a shortlist of suppliers it is important to understand the criteria that are used in choosing which suppliers to include. Often the shortlist is composed solely of those suppliers of which the customer is currently aware. In the straight rebuy situation the existing supplier is the only company on the shortlist.

In a modified rebuy or a newbuy situation the list of criteria can be extensive. Many government purchasing organizations use a formal list of criteria to shortlist suppliers. The purchasing organization regularly invites companies to register an interest in supplying a specific product or service. Suppliers that are not currently listed are evaluated and if suitable they are included in the list of qualified sources from which bids are subsequently sought. This prequalification process is mandatory for any organization wanting to supply to this sector.

Many other large organizations also adopt this approach (for example, major retailers and the major oil companies). Typical factors considered at this stage could include the financial status of the supplier, the qualifications and previous experience of the supplier, the expertise of specific personnel, location, quality standards (increasingly BS 5750 or ISO 9000 certification), manufacturing skills, design skills and distribution competencies.

In some situations the customer may find that no supplier can meet their prequalification criteria. This may then lead to a process of supplier development. For example, they may assist the supplier to introduce the necessary documented processes to achieve BS 5750 or ISO 9000 certification. Where there is only one approved supplier the customer may choose to develop a second supplier and bring it up to an approved standard to meet its requirements, thereby creating an element of competition (Dyer and Ouchi 1993).

Choice between suppliers will be made against the specification established at an earlier stage in the buying process. The first criterion to be considered is typically the technical match between the supplier's product or service and the buyer's requirements. The quality of the match will depend on how well the customer has specified the requirement and communicated this to potential suppliers. It will also depend on the quality of the supplier's response. Both of these processes depend on the skills of buying and selling organizations. There is therefore considerable potential for misinterpretation of the requirement.

The quality of the technical solution to the customer's problem has to be evaluated against the economic case. Two competing solutions to a customer's problem may have very different technical approaches and different costs. This may require the buyer to trade off additional technical benefits against higher costs. This process may frequently involve several participants from different functional areas in the organization. Each will have his or her own criteria and seek to influence the process in different ways. In the case of straight rebuy situations the choice process will be short and the purchasing function is the only area likely to become involved. Price will be the main area for discussion between buyer and seller.

In modified buy and newbuy situations there are likely to be more people involved in the final decision. The process is likely to take longer and cover a wider range of issues. The skill of the supplier is to identify the needs of each of these members of the buying group (referred to as the 'buying centre' or 'decision-making unit') in the preparation of the business case and proposal to the customer.

The final stages in the process involve placing the order and managing the supplier's subsequent performance. Organizations differ in the extent to which they formally evaluate supplier performance and the criteria which are used. Where supplier performance is formally evaluated this can include monitoring product or service quality and delivery performance. Some purchasing organizations use performance on these criteria to make judgements about future orders.

5 Influences on the buying process

Many factors can influence the organizational buying process. It is important when selling to an organization to be able to identify the influences that might inhibit or facilitate the sale of specific products or services. Understanding the different influences that exist can lead to more effective market segmentation and positioning strategies. These influences have been categorized as environmental, organizational, interpersonal and individual (Webster and Wind 1972) (see ENVIRONMENTAL ANALYSIS; MARKET SEGMENTATION; POSITIONING; PRODUCT POLICY).

Environmental factors

Environmental factors include the full range of PEST factors (political, economic, social and technical). These factors are as important to an evaluation of strategic purchasing decisions as they are to an evaluation of strategic marketing decisions. By understanding the influence of the environment on the customer the supplier is better placed to develop products and services that meet the changing requirements of the customer.

Several elements have made organizations increasingly aware of the impact of environmental factors. These include an increasing dependence on bought-in materials as a percentage of the total value added by the company, increasing shortages and uncertainties in supply markets, and a rapid rate of technical change in many sectors. These factors jointly and severally have made many organizations conscious of the strategic role which purchasing can play.

Purchasing organizations that have recognized that supply market management is an important aspect of their long-term planning, have attempted to integrate purchasing at a strategic level. Suppliers that deal with such organizations are likely to find that the levels of customer contact are senior members of the management team. Time horizons for developing collaboration are also perceived as long run rather than limited to immediate transactions.

The dynamics of the industries in which the organizational customer operates are a crucial aspect of the external environment. Marketing's problem is to assess how the potential customer is influenced by competition from other suppliers, the threat of new entrants, alternative substitute products, and competition from suppliers and its own customers (Porter 1985). This requires an in-depth knowledge of the customer's industries. It also requires an ability to assess how the supplier's product or service can be developed to allow the customer to compete effectively. Analysis of the customer's total business system may be required to identify the areas where the supplier can have most impact on the customer's profitability.

At one level a supplier of telecommunications equipment may offer a telephone management system to customers that allows the customer to track the costs of outgoing messages and introduce budgeting systems to control costs in different parts of the organization. It may also offer training support to improve the quality of management of incoming calls, improving the efficiency of the organization's response to its customers. Both of these services will help the potential customer to respond to its environment. Both may simply maintain the customer's current competitive situation.

In more sophisticated situations the supplier may become involved in joint product or market development activities with the customer. To do this effectively requires close collaboration over a period of time, with joint commitment of resources. To get into the relationship in the first place, the potential supplier needs to understand the end markets of the potential customer and the competitive challenges facing the customer. It is also important to understand how the supplier's product or service can influence the customer's costs or ability to differentiate itself from the competition.

This situation is typical of those facing manufacturers that are seeking to develop new markets (for example in central Europe) where manufacturing and distribution systems are rapidly changing. Recent initiatives in these markets in the retailing sector have included several joint ventures between food manufacturers and specific retail chains.

Organizational factors

Most approaches to the segmentation of organizational markets begin with an analysis of how many potential customers there are, which products they buy, how large each customer is in terms of potential buying power, where each customer is located, and which industries they serve or which services they supply.

These approaches to market segmentation are useful since they help to predict where the opportunities for the supplier are likely to arise. They also help to quantify the value of the market. Sales effort can be directed to those sectors showing greatest potential. New products and services can be developed to meet the needs of new segments. Distribution decisions can be based on an understanding of the location of potential customers and anticipated service levels.

Other aspects of the organization have also been found to be useful in marketing planning. These are essentially 'softer' elements that cannot immediately be observed from the outside, but can have a major impact on buying decisions. Such factors can be considered as aspects of the organization's culture or climate that appear to influence its response to the environment. Organizations present different personalities. Some appear to be more innovative than others. Some will take decisions faster than others. Some have a positive and open attitude to interaction with the external environment. Others do not. Each of these characteristics can have a major influence on the way in which potential customers deal with their suppliers.

Organizational markets can be segmented on these dimensions. Traditional segmentation criteria such as size and location of customer are useful in determining the potential purchasing power of the customer and how to organize the sales team. By contrast an understanding of the culture of the buying organization can indicate why an organization behaves in the way it does and can be useful in developing the sales case for a specific customer.

This can be illustrated by the purchase of new industrial products or processes. This aspect of industrial marketing has been extensively studied over the last 25 years (Baker 1983). Researchers have found that the economic and technical case for purchasing a new product or service is not in itself sufficient reason for many organizations to adopt it. Different organizations will take differing periods of time before they decide to buy when faced with apparently the same technical and economic advantages from buying a new product or service.

Research has established that variations in the rate of adoption of new products can be linked to variations in the structure of the organization, and general management skills, competencies and orientations. Broadly speaking organizations with flatter structures (fewer layers in the hierarchy), more open communication systems (greater lateral channels) and less frequent reporting and control cycles are likely to act faster when faced with a new product or service (to adopt or reject). Organizations with a positive attitude to the recruitment and development of staff will also exhibit greater receptivity.

From a marketing perspective it is important to recognize that different organizations in the same industry may manage their environment in different ways. In the UK offshore oil industry in the late 1970s and early 1980s companies encountered two different types of customer. One type preferred to subcontract its entire requirement to the supplier. A supplier would be commissioned to design and build an element of the offshore platform (for example the subsea production system). It would be responsible for the delivery of the system to the contracted deadline and specification. This type of customer regarded itself as being in the oil extraction and distribution business, rather than in the construction business.

Other operating companies preferred to control the whole operation from design through purchasing and construction to on-site delivery and installation. The supplier became an extension of the customer's business for the period of the contract. These differences in approach reflected the history of the oil company and its preferred way of doing business.

Two segments emerged. Separate strategies were required to meet the needs of each segment. Customers that preferred to have no involvement in the delivery process bought on the basis of a design specification, price and delivery commitment. The supplier's response was typically to keep the customer informed about progress, but not become involved with the client on a day-to-day basis. When the customer took control of the supply and delivery process greater involvement was required. Typically this took the form of joint project teams, secondment of staff to the customer organization and more detailed progress reporting and checking. The supplier became an extension of the customer's organization for the duration of the contract.

Interpersonal factors

Organizational buying decisions are made by individual managers and considerable research attention has been paid in the marketing literature to who those managers are, and what their responsibilities are in the purchase of specific products or services. The marketing rationale is to identify who is likely to influence the final choice of supplier, what their needs are, and how to provide the information that they need in order to make a buying decision. A series of studies has confirmed that the involvement of different managers in the buying decision can vary considerably, almost on a company-by-company basis, even for the same products or service (Woodside 1992).

Researchers have attempted to map the nature of the buying centre for a wide range of different buying decisions. In straight rebuy situations only a limited number of staff appear to be likely to be involved, and they are likely to be relatively junior. Typically the purchasing department plays the major role. In the modified buy and newbuy situation more people become involved and they tend to become increasingly senior within the organization. Design and manufacture have a greater involvement in the specification of the requirement, purchasing takes on the role of supplier search, and general management may ultimately sanction the purchase.

Each of these members of the buying centre is likely to have different needs. The purchasing manager may be most concerned about the cost of the item, seeking to secure a source of supply at the lowest possible cost to the organization. The engineering department may be more concerned about the technical performance of the item. The manufacturing manager may be concerned about the conformance of the delivered item to specification. Finally the marketing function may be concerned about the extent to which the product enhances the appeal of the product to the customer, through cost reduction or enhanced performance.

Given that several members of the organization are likely to be involved in the final choice of supplier, attention has been focused on how choices are made. The economics literature is not particularly helpful in this respect. The theory of the firm implies that organizations make reasoned decisions about the choice of inputs based on full information about alternative consequences. While this is an elegant theory it does not reflect the realities of organizational marketing and purchasing decisions.

There has been considerable research into the criteria that are applied in purchasing decisions (Moller and Laaksonen 1985). A wide range of factors has been identified which influence choice. These include quality in relation to price, technical ability, services, location, reputation, payment terms, previous vendor history on delivery or product quality, and technical quality. An understanding of the factors that influence the final choice of supplier is clearly of immediate relevance to organizational marketing decisions.

Organizational buying decisions are also likely to be a political process with considerable potential for conflict, political persuasion and influence. The relative importance of different criteria is likely to reflect the interaction of individual managers' preferences and perceptions. Decisions are often made in a situation of partial rather than complete knowledge about the organization and its environment. They are often partial rather than complete solutions to the problem. In this situation it is difficult to generalize about the buying decision from one situation to the next.

Some attempts have been made to develop general descriptive models of the buying process that do take account of the way in which decisions are reached (Woodside 1992). In particular researchers have looked at the influence of power and methods of conflict resolution. The impact of opinion leadership within the organization has also been addressed.

Several different classification schemes have been developed to describe the roles which members of the buying centre can play. These include users, influencers, gatekeepers, deciders and buyers (Webster and Wind 1972). Each of these members of the buying centre is likely to play a different role in the purchasing decision. The classification is a useful first reminder to suppliers that there is likely to be a range of people in the organization to influence, typically with differing needs and expectations from the purchase of the product or service.

Some members of the buying centre may be able to exercise power over other members because of their relative status, or because of expertise or access to specialist information or knowledge. For a long time the information services departments of many organizations possessed considerable power and influence over the choice of computer equipment. As managers in the rest of the organization have developed their own understanding of such systems, so this power has been eroded. Today most computer suppliers have realized the importance of targeting the end user to sell computing hardware and software. Many personal computers are now specified and bought by line managers rather than by a central computing services department.

Characteristics of the buyer

Finally, some attention has been paid to the characteristics of individual members of the decision-making unit. The general knowledge and experience of the buyer influence the way in which the buyer deals with suppliers. There has been a considerable increase in the range and quality of training for purchasing management at a functional level that has implications for suppliers. Previous experience with existing suppliers and knowledge of the supply market also has an important mediating effect on the choices made by the buyer. The level of risk perceived in choosing one supplier over another has been shown to be important in understanding the behaviour of individual buyers. Personality traits such as self-confidence and assertiveness appear to be less useful in the prediction of buyer behaviour (Moller 1985).

6 Summary

Organizational buying decisions are made primarily to meet the needs of the organization. Such decisions are therefore strongly influenced by economic and technical considerations. The role of the professional purchasing manager is to make informed choices about the supply of products and services to meet the organization's needs. By taking on an increasingly strategic role professional purchasing managers have begun to exert considerable control over supply markets. Effective marketing depends on developing an understanding of this professional role and responding appropriately.

Organizational buying decisions are also influenced by a range of behavioural factors. These include the characteristics of the buying organization and the buying process. Developing an understanding of these factors can be of use in developing an industrial marketing strategy, particularly in such areas as target marketing and the development of the marketing programme.

STEPHEN PARKINSON
ULSTER BUSINESS SCHOOL
UNIVERSITY OF ULSTER AT JORDANSTOWN

Further reading

(References cited in the text marked *)

* Baker, M.J. (1983) *Market Development*, Harmondsworth: Penguin Books.
  Corey, R. (1983) *Industrial Marketing: Cases and Concepts*, Englewood Cliffs, NJ: Prentice Hall.
  Davies, G. (1993) *Trade Marketing Strategy*, London: Chapman.
* Dyer, J.H. and Ouchi, W.G. (1993) 'Japanese style partnerships: giving companies a competitive edge', *Sloan Management Review* Fall: 51–64.
  Farmer, D. (ed.) (1985) *Purchasing Management Handbook*, Aldershot: Gower.
* Fearon, H.E. (1968) 'Historical evolution of the purchasing function', *Journal of Purchasing and Materials Management*, February.
  Håkansson, H. (ed.) (1982) *International Marketing and Purchasing of Industrial Goods*, New York: Wiley.
* Hamel, G. and Prahalad, C.K. (1993) 'Strategy as stretch and leverage', *Harvard Business Review* March–April: 75–84.
* Keogh, M. (1993) 'Buying your way to the top', *McKinsey Quarterly*: 41–62.
* Moller, K.E.K. (1985) 'Research strategies in analysing the adoption process', *Journal of Business Research* 13, August.
* Moller, K. and Laaksonen, M. (1985) 'Situational dimensions and decision criteria in industrial buying: theoretical and empirical analysis', in

Woodside, A.G.W. (ed.), *Advances in Business Marketing*, vol. I, Greenwich, CN: JAI Press Inc.

Parkinson, S.T. and Baker, M.J. (1986) *Organizational Buying Behaviour*, Basingstoke: Macmillan.

* Parkinson, S.T. and Hogarth-Scott, S. (1993) 'Who does the marketing in retailing', *European Journal of Marketing* 27: 51–62.

* Porter, M.E. (1985) *Competitive Advantage*, New York: The Free Press.

* Reck, R.F. and Long, B. (1988) 'Purchasing: a competitive weapon', *Journal of Purchasing and Materials Management* Fall: 2–8.

* Robinson, P.J. and Faris, C.W. (1967) *Industrial Buying and Creative Marketing*, Boston: Allyn and Bacon.

Taylor, B. and Farmer, D. (1975) *Corporate Planning and Procurement*, London: Heinemann.

* Webster, F.E. and Wind, Y. (1972) *Organizational Buying Behaviour*, Englewood Cliffs, NJ: Prentice Hall Inc.

* Woodside, A.G.W. (ed.) (1992) *Advances in Business Marketing and Purchasing: Mapping How Industry Buys*, vol. 5, Greenwich, CN: JAI Press.

See also: CHANNELS OF DISTRIBUTION; ENVIRONMENTAL ANALYSIS; MARKET SEGMENTATION; MARKETING ETHICS; MARKETING OF SERVICES; POSITIONING; PRICING; PRODUCT POLICY; PURCHASING MANAGEMENT; RETAILING; WHOLESALING

Purchasing management

1. The significance of purchasing
2. Three strategic roles of purchasing
3. Basic conditions affecting purchasing management
4. Strategic issues in purchasing management
5. Make-or-buy
6. The content of supplier relationships
7. Configuration of the supplier base
8. Current issues in purchasing management

Overview

The role of purchasing has evolved over the last three decades from being merely a clerical function to being one of major strategic importance to the economics of the firm. The level of financial resources tied up in purchased goods has led to purchasing departments having an influence on whether to manufacture in-house or to buy from external suppliers (make-or-buy); product design and development; value analysis and the selection of appropriate suppliers; and material flows (just-in-time delivery). The basic forms of purchasing organization are discussed and the key strategic issues are considered in detail. It is suggested that purchasing management is now concerned to a large extent with relationship management, as firms try to find a balance between high and low-involvement approaches to their suppliers. Outsourcing has become another major issue since the 1980s and the increasing development of information technology will continue to shape purchasing in the future.

1 The significance of purchasing

Since 1970, purchasing has undergone major changes both in terms of role and significance. Traditionally, purchasing was considered almost a clerical function with the ultimate objective of buying as cheaply as possible. Today it is regarded as a function of major strategic importance. The main reason for the change is the increasing specialization that characterizes the industrial system as a whole. Companies have gradually concentrated their activities to more and more limited parts of the total value chain in order to enhance efficiency in operations. One consequence of this development is that manufacturing companies have become increasingly dependent on procurement of goods and services from other firms. External suppliers, therefore, have come to play a vital role for most manufacturing companies. Purchased goods often account for more than half of the total costs of a company. This fact has put purchasing in focus, both internally and externally.

Purchasing is a focus of internal interest because an increasing proportion of the resources of a company are handled within the purchasing function. If more than half of the costs of the company are determined by purchasing it must, by definition, be an important strategic function whose activities are decisive to the competitive strength of the firm. Furthermore, owing to increasing specialization, technical resources are also increasingly being made available to companies through their suppliers. Products and components purchased today are more technically sophisticated than before. This has increased complexity and raised the requirements on the purchasing staff. This has also been a reason for improving the status and strategic recognition of purchasing.

From an external point of view, one major consequence is that what goes on in the interface between individual companies has gained in importance. Concepts and techniques such as just-in-time deliveries, quality assurance and the zero-defect principle have more and more impact on company operations. All of this means bringing relations to suppliers into focus. It also means bringing purchasing into focus, as supplier relations are mainly handled and coordinated through the purchasing function. As a whole, therefore, purchasing has become of major strategic importance for companies.

The changing view of purchasing is clearly reflected in the literature. Going back to the 'clerical' time, a representative title of a book for the profession might have been *Handbook of Purchasing*. Such books were mainly concerned with questions regarding purchasing procedures – how much to buy, how to make enquiries, etc. The main objective of this literature was to improve efficiency by developing purchasing routines in the buying company. Around 1970, models of organizational buying behaviour were developed. The aim of these models was to increase the understanding of the decision-making process in the buying company and which factors determined the outcome of this process. One important contribution was the concept of a buying centre. The buying centre is an informal constellation of the people in the organization who are involved in the buying decision process (see ORGANIZATIONAL BUYING BEHAVIOUR). Knowledge of the behaviour and perceptions of buying centre members is an important input for the marketing strategies of selling firms. These models were thus primarily orientated towards enhancing marketing effectiveness of selling firms.

During the 1990s, however, titles like *Handling Supplier Relationships* and *Developing Partnerships* better reflect the prevailing attitudes and views of purchasing and suppliers. This perspective takes the performance of both supplier and customer into consideration. Purchasing management is increasingly about managing supplier relationships (see RELATIONSHIPS AND NETWORKS).

2 Three strategic roles of purchasing

The impact of purchasing operations on company performance can be analysed in terms of three strategic roles of purchasing: the rationalization role, the development role and the structural role. The role of rationalization covers the numerous day-to-day activities undertaken to affect the cost structure. Three types of rationalization can be identified. The first deals with specification of requirements of the item to be purchased. This is a major issue, requiring decisions including whether the item needed should be manufactured in-house or purchased from external suppliers (the make-or-buy decision) as well as the design of the item. Purchasing can contribute greatly to effectiveness in this process through cooperation with internal company functions such as R&D, design and production and a qualified awareness of the capacity and capability of different suppliers. Value analysis is one technique used in this respect, the objective of which is to reduce costs while maintaining the necessary levels of availability and product reliability (see NEW PRODUCT DEVELOPMENT; PRODUCT POLICY).

The second type of rationalization is related to identifying the most appropriate supplier once the specifications have been decided. Traditionally, this has been the same as finding the supplier offering the lowest price. Over time the procedures for supplier evaluation have become more sophisticated, in attempts to identify the total costs associated with using different suppliers. Furthermore, suppliers can affect the revenues of the buying company in different ways, which has also increasingly affected the choice of supplier.

The third type of rationalization, finally, deals with improvements of efficiency in the material flows associated with business transactions. During the 1980s substantial efforts were undertaken to reduce inventories. In the automotive industry just-in-time deliveries and enhanced coordination of manufacturing operations of customer and supplier provided substantial economic benefits. Purchasing plays an important role in such operations because changing delivery frequencies and lot sizes are important prerequisites for gaining the benefits. Material flows are not the only potential source for rationalization. In the same way exchange of information provides considerable potential for improvements. In this respect the development of information technology has made new alternatives available (Figure 1).

Suppliers are important potential resources for the technical development of the customer firm. Often that potential has been used in a rather passive way, i.e. buying companies have waited for suppliers to develop new solutions and then decided whether or not to purchase them. A more active strategy in this respect, however, can turn the purchasing function into a major catalyst for making better use of supplier resources. This can be identified as the development role of purchasing. One reason for activating this role is the increasing specialization of the industrial system. A manufacturing firm, which uses components from a number of

The theoretical foundations

Figure 1 Three strategic roles of purchasing

[Diagram: "Strategic roles of purchasing" connected to three nodes: "Rationalization", "Development", and "Structuring"]

suppliers, needs to coordinate component development undertaken by different suppliers, each with their own R&D activities. The components may even represent different technologies, which makes it difficult for the buying firm to develop and maintain its own knowledge of each specialized technology. A customer relying on suppliers as sources of technical development has to involve them in the R&D process early. This provides another advantage. Early supplier involvement makes it possible to shorten lead times in product development, which has become one of the major competitive factors in most industries.

Purchasing also has a structural role in that the procurement activities will affect the structure of the supplier markets. A company might choose to concentrate its purchases of a certain item to one supplier. The competitiveness of that supplier is then strengthened as compared with the other potential suppliers. Another company might consider the availability of a number of alternative suppliers a major strategic aim. Such a company would probably divide its purchases among several suppliers to maintain an existing supplier structure. The actions undertaken by a firm – whether conscious or unconscious – thus affect the structure of supplier markets in the long run, in terms of the number and location of potential suppliers. It is therefore important for a company to analyse the long-term consequences of its buying behaviour, as well as to identify and predict other trends affecting the supplier markets. A company activating the structural role of purchasing can adjust its own operations towards reinforcing tendencies beneficial to it and counteracting undesirable ones.

3 Basic conditions affecting purchasing management

Buying companies show considerable disparities in purchasing management. Some of these differences are attributable to the fact that companies work under divergent basic conditions. The characteristics of supplier markets will imply certain opportunities for the procurement activities. The technology of the company will also have considerable effects. Purchasing strategies and behaviour have to be very different in mass-producing firms compared with firms manufacturing at customer specification.

In this section two further important conditions affecting purchasing management are discussed. The first is external and related to the characteristics of the item being purchased: it is very different to purchase standardized raw materials and sophisticated complex machinery. The second factor is internal and deals with the way purchasing is organized in the buying company.

The impact of product characteristics

Some of the variability in purchasing management is explained by the characteristics of what is being procured. There are clearly significant differences between major equipment for a big turn-key project and industrial supplies for more or less immediate use. Procurement of major equipment is most often characterized by technical complexity, substantial financial investment and the fact that the products are intended to be used for a long time. Therefore, negotiations preceding a purchasing decision will be extensive, including discussions of alternative designs and functions. One important issue is how the new equipment is related to the existing machinery and facilities. Availability of services, training and spare parts are other important matters. This type of procurement usually involves a large number of people and departments in the buying company. One of the major characteristics is that the choice of equipment may limit the freedom of the purchasing company for a long time. The equipment chosen will largely determine what raw materials and maintenance supplies will be bought.

Procurement of industrial supplies (for maintenance, repair and operations) is very different. Such purchases include a large number of products (fastenings, hand tools, glues and sealants, etc.). These items are purchased frequently, but not completely regularly, as demand fluctuates. The absence of such products when they are needed can pose major problems for the purchasing company. Procurement of industrial supplies, therefore, is characterized by considerable administrative complexity. The major point regarding this type of purchase is to develop well-functioning order and delivery systems. Efficiency is obtained through establishing routines for purchasing as a whole, rather than carrying out each transaction in the most efficient way.

Between the extremes of major equipment and industrial supplies, there are other types of purchasing situations. One concerns raw materials and materials in different stages of processing: this is an important input for many companies. Such items are often more or less standardized. They usually have a global market. Prices fluctuate in relation to the cycles of demand and supply. Expectations of changing prices, therefore, are important determinants of the timing of these purchases. Many companies buy components of various kinds for assembly operations. Procurement of components is characterized by recurring deliveries. This makes it important to take advantage of the repetitive feature to create efficiency. The need to adapt the components to each other and to the production context of the buying company are also important determinants of these purchasing operations.

It is obvious, thus, that the purchasing issues show considerable variation, owing to their specific procurement characteristics. The differences have to do with technical, administrative or supplier market-related considerations. Such variation is typical of purchasing in all companies, as every firm purchases various kinds of items. The major effect of this variation is that it is difficult for a company to find one best solution regarding organization and administrative routines.

Purchasing organization

Purchasing operations can be organized in two fundamentally different ways. Purchasing can be either centralized or decentralized. A centralized purchasing department provides three major advantages. One is economies of scale thanks to larger order quantities than would appear in a decentralized organization structure. The second is that it is possible to coordinate the combined activities from the purchasing company in relation to individual suppliers. The third is that centralization enhances effective allocation of resources. One example is that purchasing staff can specialize in procurement of specific items, which promotes professionalism in purchasing. The major disadvantage of a centralized purchasing organization is that problems may develop with internal communication between purchasing staff and other departments (production, R&D, etc.). Especially in large companies there can be substantial distance – both in physical terms and in attitudes. A sense of 'us-versus-them' between production and purchasing may easily arise.

This kind of problem is more easily dealt with in a decentralized organization. Proponents of decentralized structures claim that purchasing should not be a specialized function, but rather an integral part of a larger context. Since the beginning of the 1980s decentralization of purchasing has become more and more common. One reason is that firms in general have turned towards decentralization. When company divisions and business units are made more and more responsible in economic terms for their own operations, it is not possible to keep their major cost determinant – purchasing – under central control. The most obvious problem with a decentralized purchasing organization is the reduced professionalism of the purchasers. They become more generalists, needing competence and capability for purchasing across an extremely broad product range.

The theoretical foundations

The choice between centralization and decentralization will always require a compromise. Settling for the benefits of one always means sacrificing the potential benefits of the other. For this reason purchasing will always have to put effort into eliminating the disadvantages of the organizational form that has been chosen. A decentralized organization may be supplemented with central purchasing staff, responsible for drawing up group agreements with the purpose of achieving economies of scale. A centralized purchasing organization can be supplemented with shop-floor purchasers who are responsible for acquisition of specific components. This makes it possible to work with a combined approach falling somewhere between the extremes. In a study of large Scandinavian companies such intermediate types were found to be the most common forms (Figure 2).

Traditionally, the purchasing organization of a firm has been determined by internal factors. Over time, external factors have come to play an increasing role. When purchased goods account for almost two-thirds of total costs, it is very obvious that external factors have to be considered more. The purchasing company must be organized in such a way that the exchange with suppliers is facilitated as much as possible.

4 Strategic issues in purchasing management

There seem to be three major strategic issues related to purchasing management:

- the decision of whether to make an item in-house or to buy from external suppliers;
- the development of appropriate relationships with suppliers;
- the managing of the supplier base in terms of size and relations between suppliers.

The first strategic issue is to decide what items to procure. This is defined by the scope of the operations that are undertaken in-house by the buying company. This determines the degree of vertical integration, which in purchasing terms has been addressed as the make-or-buy issue. All companies rely on external suppliers, but to varying extents. For some companies the value added is substantial and the impact of purchasing on the total cost is limited. For other companies, procurement costs account for most of total expenses. The second issue concerns the relationship with suppliers. Buying companies show a wide variety of arrangements adopted in different relationships. Some relationships are characterized by broad contacts among people in the firms, extensive coordination of activities and resource adaptations of various kinds. In

■ Completely centralized.
▨ Centralized purchasing of strategic items, decentralized purchasing of commodities.
☐ Decentralized purchasing combined with a central purchasing department.
▩ Decentralized purchasing combined with voluntary co-operation between various divisions.
▧ Completely decentralized.

Figure 2 Purchasing organization in large Scandinavian firms
(*Source*: Gadde and Håkansson, 1993: 129)

other relationships, however, the amount of coordination and adaptation are limited to a minimum and contacts are consciously kept at 'arm's length'. The third strategic issue, finally, is related to the supplier base. To some extent, the supplier base of a company reflects the choices regarding the extent of outsourcing and the nature of supplier relationships. However, sometimes the outcome of decisions concerning the two first issues might impact on the supplier base in an undesired way. Therefore, the configuration of the supplier base needs to be addressed as a strategic issue of its own (see PRODUCT LIFE-CYCLE MANAGEMENT; PRODUCT POLICY).

5 Make-or-buy

What to produce internally and what to buy from external suppliers has been an issue in manufacturing firms for a very long time, despite the fact that it was apparently not identified as a matter of strategic importance until the 1980s. Before that time the decision of whether to make or to buy tended to be determined on a rather low management level in the buying company. Predominantly, it was based on the expected degree of capacity utilization and historical cost data. Depending on the situation concerning these conditions, the make-or-buy decision could be changed from one year to the next. Such changes caused no major problems because the items subcontracted were either highly standardized or designed by the customer. Over time, the make-or-buy analysis became more sophisticated. Aspects that came to play an increasing role dealt primarily with quality and reliability. Furthermore, the need to protect internal know-how and the opportunities provided by access to the capabilities of other firms became important issues.

It is evident that buying firms over time have come to rely more on 'buy' than on 'make'. This trend has been especially clear since the late 1970s. Outsourcing to external suppliers increased dramatically from that time. For many companies the costs of purchased goods and services came to exceed more than half of the total costs and sometimes the proportion was substantially higher. Traditionally, make-or-buy decisions mainly concerned subcontracting of manufacturing operations. However, to an increasing extent other activities have also become subject to outsourcing, including administrative services, operations in logistics and transportation, market intelligence, process design and even product development.

This means that the degree of vertical integration has decreased substantially. Individual companies concentrate their efforts on a limited part of the total value chain. The major reason causing this development is the benefits provided through specialization efforts. Specialization leads to economies of scale in operations, which means that focused suppliers can contribute to the rationalization role of purchasing. Furthermore, outside suppliers can enhance the development role of purchasing. A first reason is that most firms are affected by multiple technologies, making it difficult to be on the cutting edge of all. One way for a buying firm to cope with this situation is to focus on some of these technologies and rely on specialized suppliers for others. A second reason is that suppliers working with several customers are better at choosing the future direction of technical development than the buying company with its more limited perspective, focusing mainly on its own operations.

The trends on the supply side of companies have changed the nature of the make-or-buy issue. Earlier, this decision could be rather easily modified from one year to the other. The directions taken after the 1980s have made the strategic choices more irreversible. In many cases buying companies concentrating their efforts on what they identify as the core competence will meet severe difficulties if they try to change from buy to make. Often they will find it too resource demanding to return to the frontier of technology once they have left it. Another change is that the attitudes towards resource control have been modified. Ownership is one way of controlling resources. It provides a high degree of autonomy in resource utilization and companies have traditionally shown preference for ownership control. One problem with that approach, however, is that investments in highly specialized resources might lock the firm into a resource structure which may become obsolete through the development of new technologies. Traditionally, therefore, the need for flexibility has been an argument for outsourcing, while control aspirations has favoured vertical integration. Considering the pace of technological development it is not surprising that companies have increasingly come to rely on outsourcing to maintain flexibility. The argument for control has been reconsidered. The prevailing view has been that ownership of resources provides full control while it was supposed that there is no control over resources owned by other firms. Over time, however, a complementary perspective has developed, according to which a buying company, through its supplier relationships, can have some indirect control over resources owned by others. Such a strategy has been identified as quasi-integration and is supposed to provide buying companies with the major benefits of vertical integration without its corresponding disadvantages. This perspective results from – and has contributed to – a changed view of supplier relationships that will be discussed in the following section.

6 The content of supplier relationships

Low-involvement relationships

Traditionally, buying firms were strongly recommended to avoid becoming dependent on individual suppliers. The main reason for this standpoint is that dependency imposes restrictions on purchasing opportunities. Advocates of so called 'arm's-length relationships' have identified three major advantages of such a state of affairs. First, having a number of suppliers can help overcome short-term problems with delivery reliability. Being dependent on a single supplier might cause problems in terms of production capacity and delivery schedules, among other things. Second, too strong a reliance on an individual supplier might give rise to 'lock-in' effects in the long run. By avoiding too much investment in individual vendors, long-term flexibility is supposed to be secured. Third – and maybe most important – being dependent on individual suppliers makes it difficult to make use of market forces. Having suppliers that compete with one another is one way of increasing efficiency in the purchasing operations. A buying company can switch from one supplier to the other and thus influence the vendors towards improving their efforts. The opportunity to play off suppliers against each other in terms of price conditions has been a particularly recommended purchasing strategy. The core of this strategy is to avoid becoming too integrated with suppliers, because integration leads to dependence. Customer relationships based on this logic are characterized by low-involvement from both parties.

The traditional view of efficiency in supplier relationships thus tends to consider suppliers as more or less efficient producers of given inputs. Each procurement situation is evaluated on its own merits. The main task for purchasing is to select the most appropriate vendor for each transaction. One important issue in purchasing management is to encourage competition among suppliers. The 'arm's-length-relationships', following this strategy, often tend to be rather adversarial. The particular buying–selling situation is considered a zero-sum contest; what one stands to gain the other stands to lose. In practice, a low-involvement approach works when the needs of the buyer are well known, well defined and stable. A further prerequisite is the existence of a number of sellers offering a standardized item.

High-involvement relationships

Since 1980 we have seen a shift in the view of the role of supplier relationships based on a complementary view of purchasing efficiency. Partly this is an effect of the changing view of the need for vertical integration. Manufacturing companies rely to an increasing extent on outside suppliers. In many cases outsourcing of operations has provided buying firms with situations where activities undertaken in-house must be coordinated with activities undertaken by a supplier. Coordination may be needed between manufacturing activities or between manufacturing and distribution activities on both sides. Under these circumstances a purchasing strategy aiming at switching suppliers from year to year seems less appropriate. Therefore, the tendency in the overall industrial system towards increasing specialization has called for more coordination between the individual companies. This in turn leads to more adaptation between buyer and seller in terms of activities and resources. These adaptations are made because they improve efficiency and effectiveness. They also create interdependencies between customer and supplier. Such relationships are characterized by a high-involvement approach.

High-involvement relationships typically provide different types of benefits than low-involvement ones, since it is not the individual transaction that is optimized. On the contrary, customers are eager to improve long-term efficiency and effectiveness. Instead of focusing on price in each transaction the efforts are concentrated on affecting long-term total costs. The purchasing behaviour of buying companies affects a number of costs, of which price is sometimes only minor in comparision with other costs (Figure 3). These other costs are often called 'indirect' costs.

Changing indirect costs requires adaptations between buyer and seller – a high-involvement relationship is needed. Benefits provided from such relationships include linking of activities in supply systems (just-in-time deliveries). Such arrangements reduce both transaction costs and capital costs. Joint product development has become increasingly common. Integrating resources with suppliers can reduce lead times in product development and decrease the total R&D spending. Furthermore, the revenues of the buying company might increase owing to enhanced product quality.

A high-involvement approach is always costly. Achieving the benefits of integration requires non-standardized solutions, specific adaptations of resources, and/or coordination of activities and intense contacts among individuals. High-involvement relationships rely on an investment logic. These relationships are costly, but in certain situations the costs are accompanied by benefits from integration. High-involvement relationships are based on a belief that supplier resources are valuable assets. These resources can be used for various purposes, of which only a few can be identified and understood when establishing the relationship – they will be jointly discovered in the interaction between customer and supplier. High-involvement relationships must therefore be managed in quite a different way than low-involvement ones.

High and low-involvement relationships thus provide different kinds of benefits to a buying company. High-involvement relationships are costly, but in certain situations these costs are outweighed by even greater positive economic effects. In other situations, however, a buying company stands to gain more through a low-involvement approach. Sometimes a customer might benefit more from having suppliers compete with each other. In other cases buying firms might prefer to stick to one supplier for long time without making specific adaptations – which is another kind of low-involvement approach.

Every company needs a mix of supplier relationships characterized by variety in the degree of involvement. To make the best use of suppliers requires that high-involvement relationships co-exist with low-involvement relationships. Handling this mix of relationships is a major

Figure 3 Costs affected by purchasing behaviour
(*Source*: Gadde and Håkansson, 1993: 47)

issue in purchasing management. Managing supplier relationships is also a dynamic task. Over time, conditions change – and so must the characteristics of relationships. The extent of involvement needs to be adapted to new situations. Therefore, supplier relationships must be continuously monitored and consciously directed. The activities undertaken in this respect will also have profound effects on the supplier base (see RELATIONSHIPS AND NETWORKS).

7 Configuration of the supplier base

This third strategic issue has become accentuated in the 1990s owing to the new perspectives concerning vertical integration and supplier relationships. Traditionally, the supplier base was not considered an important issue. Low-involvement relationships tend to be accompanied by a multiple sourcing policy resulting in a large supplier base. Over time, however, an increasing awareness of the costs associated with handling suppliers has made buying firms eager to reduce their supplier bases. In some cases customers have supported certain suppliers to increase their undertakings in terms of sub-assemblies of various kinds. Such vendors act as system suppliers bringing together components from a number of sub-suppliers. The development towards high-involvement relationships has also had an impact, not least because attaining the major benefits of integration requires so much interaction that single sourcing is a prerequisite. High-involvement relationships are resource-demanding and a buying company cannot handle too many of them. Thus, the complementary perspective of efficiency in purchasing and the subsequent reconsideration of the role of suppliers has affected the size of the supplier base.

It should be observed, however, that single sourcing/high-involvement relationships and multiple sourcing/low-involvement relationships do not necessarily need to go hand in hand. A buying firm may, for various reasons, prefer to use more than one supplier for an item even if a certain extent of involvement is needed. For example, sometimes customers may prescribe which suppliers to use. The fact that a buying company uses two parallel suppliers for a specific item does not, however, rule out the opportunity to be highly involved with both. Correspondingly, low-involvement with single sources may have its own advantages. If the buyer is a small company the best way to save on costs might be to concentrate procurement on one supplier.

There are numerous examples of improved purchasing efficiency and effectiveness owing to increasing integration of customer and supplier operations. It is most likely, therefore, that even more benefits can be attained if a buying firm is able to promote activity coordination and resource combination among groups of vendors in the supply base. Efforts of this type are known as supply-chain-management. Numerous examples of the substantial advantages that can be obtained when the buying firm can coordinate activities among a large number of suppliers have been reported from the automotive industry, mainly in terms of just-in-time deliveries. Another way of gaining corresponding benefits in the resource dimension is to stimulate exchange of resources with and among suppliers. A good illustration of potential effects of resource integration among supplier relationships is provided by the American footwear producer Nike, which actively tries to transfer capabilities to suppliers. Nike's production system is entirely based on outsourcing. Nike no longer manufactures any shoes in-house, but relies on a variety of suppliers and subcontractors with very different characteristics, illustrated schematically in Figure 4.

Nike's suppliers are classified into three different categories: (i) volume producers, who provide economies of scale in production by supplying a number of footwear producers; (ii) developed partners, who are exclusive Nike suppliers producing the most advanced and latest models; and (iii) developing sources, those suppliers who can produce shoes at a very low cost. Improvements in the performance of this supplier network require that Nike shares its knowledge and resources with suppliers and actively intervenes in their operations. One way of doing this is through an 'expatriate programme' wherein former Nike technicians become permanent staff in supplier factories. Suppliers are also encouraged to participate in joint product development activities (see NEW PRODUCT

Purchasing management

Market
↑
Nike

- Developed partners (Taiwan and South Korea)
- Developing sources (Thailand, China, Indonesia)
- Volume producers (South Korea)

- Locally subcontracted materials and components
- Components, materials, and subassembly from developed partners and Nike
- Internally developed materials and components

- Speciality components (e.g. Nike air soles)

Figure 4 Nike's supplier network
(*Source:* Donaghu and Barff, 1990: 545)

DEVELOPMENT). Some suppliers in low-cost countries have very limited competence. To be able to meet the global standard of Nike, the capabilities of these companies must be continuously improved. Nike asks its more advanced suppliers to actively take part in this process through joint ventures between Nike, one advanced and experienced supplier and a local firm with limited resources and technological competence. The joint venture form is an incentive for the advanced suppliers to transfer technology and knowledge to the less experienced partner.

Nike's way of organizing its production network is an excellent illustration of managing a whole supplier base. It might seem an extreme example, as the entire production process is outsourced, but similar tendencies can be found in other cases. Important elements in this management process are the programmes aiming at developing supplier capabilities, as well as the variety of involvement in different relationships (SEE RELATIONSHIPS AND NETWORKS; STRATEGIC ALLIANCES).

8 Current issues in purchasing management

The changes on the supply side of companies have put supplier relationships into focus. Purchasing management has, to a great extent, become a matter of managing relationships with suppliers. For many buying companies the transition from adversarial relationships to cooperative ones is still a problematic issue. The attitudes and behaviour of people in customer firms need to be modified. Suppliers must be convinced to undertake certain investments in order to reap the potential benefits of more integrated operations. However, the main issue in managing supplier relationships is to find a balance between these high-involvement relationships and those characterized by a low-involvement approach. Currently it seems as if high-involvement relationships and partnerships are advocated as general recommendations. Buying firms, therefore, must carefully analyse what contribution can be attained from a particular partnership before entering into such resource demanding relationships.

The second current issue of significance is related to outsourcing. Since the middle of the 1980s companies have been strongly recommended by consultants and text-books to focus on 'core competence', while activities needing other resources should be outsourced. These prescriptions are characterized by a certain one-sidedness – emphasizing short-term benefits, while long-term consequences are somewhat neglected. The first reflection is that predicting tomorrow's core competence might be an overwhelming task. The second is that buying firms must also consider insourcing as an important issue. In certain situations the customer is not likely to find what is needed in the market, nor will it be possible to push the supplier in the desired direction. If so, the manufacturing company needs to undertake these activities in-house even if they are not considered 'core'.

A third current issue is related to information technology. Communication is a key activity in purchasing. Exchange of information plays a crucial role inside the buying firm as well as in relation to suppliers. The development of information technology, therefore, provides buying firms with great opportunities concerning both the rationalization role and the development role. The main task is to exploit information technology by transferring exchange of standardized information (orders, inquiries, etc.) to electronic media. By doing so, customer and supplier will gain more time to discuss and analyse other problems and opportunities person-to-person. This will be necessary because connections in terms of coordinated activities and integrated resources tend to make high-involvement relationships continue to develop in complexity.

LARS-ERIK GADDE
CHALMERS UNIVERSITY OF TECHNOLOGY
GOTHENBURG

Further readings

(References cited in the text marked *)

Bailey, D. and Farmer, D. (1977) *Purchasing Principles and Techniques*, London: Pitman Publishing.

Blenkhorn, D. and Noori, H. (1990) 'What it takes to supply Japanese OEMs', *Industrial Marketing Management* 19: 21–30.

Blois, K. (1971) 'Vertical quasi-integration', *Journal of Industrial Economics* 20: 33–41.

Burt, D. and Sukoup, W. (1985) 'Purchasing's role in new product development', *Harvard Business Review* September–October, 90-7.

Carlisle, J. and Parker, R. (1989) *Beyond Negotiation. Reedeming Customer–Supplier Relationships*, Chichester: John Wiley & Sons.

* Donaghu, M. and Barff, R. (1990) 'Nike just did it: International subcontracting and flexibility in athletic footwear production', *Regional Studies* 24: 537–52.

Dubois, A. (1998) *Organizing Industrial Activities Across Firm Boundaries*, London: Routledge.

Ford, D., Gadde, L-E, Håkansson, H., Lundgren, A., Snehota, I., Turnbull, P. and Wilson, D. (1998) *Managing Business Relationships*, Chichester: John Wiley & Sons.

Frazier, G., Spekman, R. and O'Neal, C. (1988) 'Just-in-time exchange relationships in industrial markets', *Journal of Marketing* 52: 1127.

* Gadde, L-E and Håkansson, H. (1993) *Professional Purchasing*, London: Routledge.

Helper, S. and Sako, M. (1995) 'Supplier relations in Japan and the United States: Are they converging?', *Sloan Management Review* Spring, 77–84.

Hines, P. (1994) *Creating World Class Suppliers*, London: Pitman Publishing.

Håkansson, H. (ed.) (1982) *International Marketing and Purchasing of Industrial Goods – an Interaction Approach*, Chichester: John Wiley & Sons.

Jauch, L. and Wilson, H. (1979) 'A strategic perspective for make or buy decisions', *Long Range Planning* 12: 56–61.

Kraljic, P. (1982) 'Purchasing must become supply management', *Harvard Business Review* September–October, 109–17.

Krause, D. and Ellram, L. (1997) 'Critical elements of supplier development. the buying firm perspective', *European Journal of Purchasing and Supply Management* 3: 21–32.

Kumpe, T. and Bolwijn, P. (1988) 'Manufacturing: The new case for vertical integration', *Harvard Business Review* March–April, 75–81.

Lamming, R.C., Cousins, P.D. and Notman, D.M. (1996) 'Beyond vendor assessment. Relationship assessment programmes', *European Journal of Purchasing and Supply Management* 2: 173–81.

Miles, R. and Snow, C. (1986) 'Organizations: New concepts for new forms', *California Management Review* XXVIII: 62–73.

Nishiguchi, T. (1994) *Strategic Industrial Sourcing: the Japanese Advantage*. New York: Oxford University Press.

Quinn, J. and Hilmer, F. (1994) 'Strategic outsourcing', *Sloan Management Review* Summer, 43–55.

Webster, F. and Wind, Y. (1972) *Organizational Buying Behaviour*, Englewood Cliffs: Prentice Hall.

See also: ORGANIZATIONAL BUYING BEHAVIOUR; NEW PRODUCT DEVELOPMENT; PRODUCT LIFE-CYCLE MANAGEMENT; PRODUCT POLICY; RELATIONSHIPS AND NETWORKS; STRATEGIC ALLIANCES AND SUPPLIER PARTNERSHIPS

Relationships and networks

1 Marketing mix – a non-relationship approach to exchange
2 Relationships
3 Networks
4 Research on exchange relationships and networks

Overview

Most definitions of marketing relate to the general concept of exchange. To quote a well-known textbook: 'Marketing is a social and managerial process by which individuals and groups obtain what they need and want through creating and *exchanging* products and values with others' (Kotler 1997: 9, emphasis added).

We can distinguish between two, fundamentally different approaches to exchange: the marketing mix approach on the one hand and the relationship approach, with its extended version the markets-as-networks approach, on the other.

In this entry we have primarily industrial, or business-to-business markets in mind, since relationship and network analyses mostly have been concerned with such markets. However, we will also comment on some recent developments as regards marketing research and practice in consumer markets. To make our presentation of the relationship and network approaches clearer we will first compare it with the marketing mix approach in some important dimensions.

In the relationship approach a specific transaction between a seller and a buyer is not an isolated event but takes place within an exchange relationship characterized by mutual dependency and interaction over time between the two parties. An analysis could stop at the individual relationship. However, in the network approach such relationships are seen as interconnected. Thus, the various actors on a market are connected to each other, directly or indirectly. A specific market can then be described and analysed as one or more networks.

There are major differences between the marketing mix approach and the network approach in two respects: one concerns marketing from the firm's point of view, the other the concept of a market as an institution for coordination (or 'governance') of economic systems.

1 Marketing mix – a non-relationship approach to exchange

In the marketing literature one important, even dominating, view is that exchange is an outcome of the seller's marketing activities directed towards the buyer. The seller determines variables such as price, product attributes, advertising, personal selling, distribution channels, etc. Such marketing activities comprise the seller's 'marketing mix' often symbolized by the '4 Ps'. The seller's activities influence the buyer to react by accepting or not accepting the seller's offer. Thus the seller acts and the buyer reacts. How the buyer reacts depends on the attributes of the buyer, e.g. in terms of needs, financial situation, differences between competing offers (see CHANNELS OF DISTRIBUTION; PERSONAL SELLING AND SALES MANAGEMENT; PRICING; PRODUCT POLICY; THE MARKETING MIX).

The marketing mix approach is closely related to the microeconomic theory of monopolistic competition, and to the psychological 'S-O-R' theories that link an individual's response (R) (e.g. to buy a product), to an environmental stimulus (S) (e.g. an advertisement for the product), using the attributes of the individual (O) (e.g. the individual's interests or values) as an intervening variable.

The link between the marketing mix approach and economic theories of market structure are important because they influence how firm behaviour and markets are defined. First, the buyers are analysed and approached in an aggregated way. The buyers may, depending on similarities and dissimilarities in their response to the seller's marketing activities, be divided into market segments but not treated as individuals.

Second, the market is defined from the point of view of substitution. 'A market consists of all the potential customers sharing a particular need or want who might be willing and able to engage in exchange to satisfy that need or want' (Kotler 1997: 13). If we include sellers in the market definition they are thus firms offering substitutes.

Third, the analysis is, in its 'pure form', static. It refers to transactions during one time period and not to the long-term, dynamic nature of market processes. There is however marketing mix related analytical developments where 'delayed responses' and customer learning introduces time in the models.

The link between the marketing mix and the S-O-R approaches is important since it puts the seller in the active role and disregards truly interactive relationships between sellers and individual buyers. The relationship and network approaches are different in all these respects as will be demonstrated below.

2 Relationships

An exchange relationship implies that there is an individual specific dependency between the seller and the buyer. The relationship develops through interaction over time and signifies a mutual orientation of the two parties toward each other. In the interaction the buyer is equally as active as the seller. The interaction consists of social, business and information exchange and an adaptation of products, processes and routines to better reach the economic objectives of the parties involved.

How can we then explain that market transactions are framed within evolving, often long-term relationships, rather than determined by the invisible hand of the market or by the attributes of competing sellers' offers in each time period? The answer to this follows four propositions about the nature of markets.

First, both demand and supply are inherently heterogeneous. Thus the number of sellers that can potentially meet a specific demand from a specific buyer is quite limited. The heterogeneity depends partly on technical interdependencies in products and production systems, partly on how buyers and sellers fit in terms of their resources, organizations and strategies. The heterogeneity is to an important extent acquired through relation specific adaptations between buyers and sellers. The incumbent supplier may have adapted its product and its delivery to make them fit the specific buyer's product and its delivery services to make them fit the specific buyer's product and production process better than offers by competitors.

Second, efficient handling of the flows of goods, services, information and payments between seller and buyer calls for the development of coordination mechanisms other than those provided by anonymous market transactions. Order and delivery systems must be designed to allow for efficient production planning and high service levels. Contemporary emphasis on 'time based competition', 'Just-in-time deliveries', 'customized manufacturing' and the like, signifies a need for mutual development, by seller and buyer, of routines and systems by which individuals transactions can be handled.

Third, resources for effective innovative behaviour as regards products, services and processes are not in the hands of the individual firm but controlled by this firm's suppliers and customers/end-users. Access to communication with customers/end-users helps to identify problems that the firm might solve by product development. Product development by one firm requires complementary inputs of components or know-how from its own suppliers. Innovative behaviour that requires cooperation between firms is more difficult to realize if the parties do not have prior knowledge about each other, acquired over time within exchange relationships (see NEW PRODUCT DEVELPOMENT).

Fourth, both buyers and sellers need to reduce uncertainty about the conditions for acquisition of inputs to, and demand for outputs from, their own production systems. Control through ownership or formal contracts is one way to reduce uncertainty. However, in the exchange relationship approach, social and technical interaction by which both parties can prove their trustworthiness and their mutual commitment to the relationship is considered as a more important control mechanism.

Relationships on consumer markets: distribution channels, service marketing and 'relationship marketing'

In distribution channel research on consumer products and services, relationships between the members of the channel have always been in focus. One of the fundamental issues has been what institutional form the relationships between channel members has or should have. Should firms be linked to each other through ownership, long-term contractual agreements or only through short-term market transactions? Linked to this is the question of how power and dependency influence channel performance, channel conflicts and conflict resolution. It is therefore not surprising that contemporary approaches within institutional economics such as 'transaction cost analysis' (Williamson 1985) and 'relational contracting' (Macneil 1989) have been used to analyse different forms for exchange in distribution channels (see, e.g., Haugland and Reve 1994) (see CHANNEL MANAGEMENT; CHANNELS OF DISTRIBUTION; LOGISTICS AND VALUE CREATION). During the 1970s relationship approaches were developed within the emergent field of consumer services marketing. Researchers found that service transaction often involved close interaction with the buyer during both production and consumption of the services (see MARKETING OF SERVICES). Large parts of the organization of the service provider were involved in the exchange, not only those with direct customer contact. Service marketing researchers argued that planning and implementation of the marketing mix variables by a specialized marketing department could not encompass the essentials of service marketing (e.g. Grönroos 1990).

Since the early 1990s a growing interest in 'relationship marketing' on consumer markets has been evident both in practice and in research. The ability to 'individualize' mass markets, due to modern information, communication and production technology, is an important reason for this development. Databases make information available about individuals; direct marketing and telemarketing makes it possible to get in contact with specified individuals; and customization of products and services are becoming more feasible. Sellers develop and implement marketing programmes aimed to stimulate individual customers to concentrate their purchase to fewer sources and reward them for such 'loyalty' (see INFORMATION TECHNOLOGY AND MARKETING; MARKETING RESEARCH).

The growing body of research and management literature on 'relationship marketing' is quite diverse and is also in several respects different from the managerial and analytical treatment of exchange relationships in the network approach. 'Relationship marketing' in a limited sense is very close to a traditional marketing mix approach since it does not involve interaction in the true sense and no consideration of the network-like nature of the market. There are however also more extended 'relationship marketing' approaches that come closer to a network view of relationships (Mattsson 1997).

3 Networks

Markets-as-networks

Suppose we regard the environment of the individual relationship as consisting of other relationships. Suppose further that the relationships are connected, directly or indirectly, to each other. Then we can envision the market as a network. Following a sociological definition, networks are sets of interconnected exchange relationships between actors (Cook and Emerson 1978). Exchange in one relationship is conditioned by exchange in other relationships. Instead of the concept 'markets-as-networks', also 'industrial networks' and 'business networks' are used, signifying a somewhat different emphasis of the analyses. A relationship between two actors is 'embedded' in a network (Granovetter 1985).

Exchange relationships coordinate activities performed by different actors in a production/distribution system. A network is thus a governance structure for economic activities that can be compared to coordination through a hierarchy, (i.e. through a central plan) or through the invisible hand of a market. Network analyses can focus, first on the individual firm (which we may label the 'focal firm') and second on the network as such. This is equivalent to a focus in the marketing mix approach on the individual selling firm and on the market respectively.

In the network approach, the market includes both complementarities and substitutes, both cooperating and competing firms. This is in contrast to the above mentioned definition according to a marketing mix approach (Kotler 1997) that implies that the market consist of only one level in a value added chain and that a specific market is delimited on the basis of substitutability between offers by competing sellers.

The individual firm has a number of exchange relationships to end-users, distributors, suppliers and other counterparts. Those relationships define that firm's focal network or, as we will label it here, the firm's net. Firms comprising such a net to a large extent carry out complementary activities and control complementary resources. They are predominantly positively connected to each other. Cooperation is the major mode of interaction. The important role of marketing and purchasing is to establish, maintain, develop and also, if needed, terminate relationships in the net. The nets need to have some stability in order to make efficient coordination possible. They need also to have flexibility as exchange relationships develop, new suppliers and customers are added, etc.

Competitors also strive to develop their nets. Such competitive activity is a major force for change in the networks. Competitors are predominantly negatively connected to each other. They might compete for customers, suppliers or other partners. Competing firms also often have customers, distributors or suppliers in common. Sometimes this implies a negative connection but sometimes, competing firms do not have conflicting objectives *vis-à-vis* a common counterpart.

The nets are 'embedded' in a more extended network. Nets may to some degree overlap since firms have common customers, common suppliers, etc. Due to the dynamic features noted above, nets and networks are changing all the time, but the changes are not independent of the network history and present network structure. Most relationships continue over many years and therefore changes in a network structure are based on a considerable overall stability. Thus both stability and change, both cooperation and competition are important aspects of network dynamics.

A firm has a network position. This network position describes to whom a firm is related and the content of the relationships it has with its counterparts. The position of a firm has been influenced by its earlier exchange activities, i.e. by investments in relationships. The position at a specific time reflects the cumulative nature of the firm's marketing and purchasing activities. For example a few years after entry into a new market the firm's efforts to develop a customer base have resulted in a network position that implies both opportunities and restrictions for the firm's future strategic development.

Network boundaries

Since interdependencies between exchange relationships are due to both substitutes and complementarities, to both present and potential future dependencies, it is a rather subjective task to define the boundaries of a network (i.e. the market) that is relevant for a specific analysis. In fact, defining which relationships to include and which to exclude is a creative act by the analyst. The starting point could be one or more specific firms, a specific geographical area, a specific technology, a specific function in a value added chain, a specific project, a specific product or service from the user's point of view or a combination of such criteria. Exchange relationships that imply important present or future interdependencies, given the focus of the analysis, are then included in the network. Network studies have, for example, concerned a firm's entry into a new market, structural change in a service sector, process development in an industry, strategic alliances in two related industries, development of an infrastructural project and evolution of a new technology. Obviously, the definitions of relevant network boundaries vary between such diverse studies.

From relationships to networks

After this introduction to the network approach we can return to the discussion on individual exchange relationships above and ask: What is gained by including the context of the individual relationships, i.e. a number of interconnected relationships, in the analysis if we want to understand marketing and markets? I will use the same four dimensions as in the discussion on relationships.

Heterogeneity is also an important attribute at the network level. There are a great number of different combinations available in the network. However since coordination has to cover more than one relationship, it becomes increasingly difficult to change one relationship without also changing one or more other relationships. There are thus important indirect effects in the network if one of the relationships is changed. For example once a certain technology has become the accepted norm (the 'dominant design'), it is difficult to introduce any major change in one of the activities because other activities coordinated through other relationships must also then be changed.

However, network heterogeneity also opens important opportunities for new, difficult to foresee, combinations of resources that lead to innovations. Firms that belong to the same 'industry', and thus are competitors according to the traditional market model, might not be close substitutes from a buyer's point of view. On the other hand, firms belonging to different industries might, due to heterogeneity between competing technologies, be potential competitors.

A further aspect of heterogeneity is that the allocation of activities among different actors in a specific value added chain differs and is subject to change. Suppliers and buyers might use intermediaries or not, one buyer might decide to 'outsource' a specific component while another makes it in-house, one seller may have a systems selling strategy while another has not. Changes in the allocation of activities among actors is a major aspect of network dynamics.

To handle flows efficiently by adaptation in only one exchange relationship might not be enough. The inter-linked activities that need to be coordinated cover several firms in, for example, a distribution channel or a supply system for an equipment manufacturer's production and spare parts distribution. The coordination not only involves several production and distribution units, but also service organizations such as transportation firms which also have to be included.

The third aspect is innovativeness. The interdependencies between resources between resources and between activities controlled by individual firms in a network make it important to mobilize resources in several firms in order to develop something new. Some of these resources might be accessed through the innovating firm's net and some might require that relations are established in other parts of the network. A major emphasis in the academic network research has been on network interdependencies in technical and organizational innovation processes.

Finally, uncertainty reduction is not only a matter of individual exchange relationships. If coordination can cover several exchange relationships, uncertainty may be reduced. One example of this is when several complementary suppliers join in a systems selling project instead of submitting uncoordinated offers of the separate components. Another example is that a relationship may give access to information about third parties, such as a supplier's supplier or a buyer's customer.

On the other hand, indirect network effects on one specific exchange relationship could well increase uncertainty substantially. Entry of new competitors, development of a new technology, changing demands from other firms in the value added chain exemplify this. Explicit or implicit agreements between competitors, e.g. through trade organizations, strategic alliances involving several exchange relationships, developments of behavioural and legal norms covering a market or an industry, are ways in which uncertainty in networks can be reduced.

Social interaction in networks may also reduce uncertainty by giving actors access to information about the wider network, perhaps also increasing mutual commitment and trust covering several interdependent relationships, for example in a distribution channel. Thus uncertainty about an individual relationship is increased if we also consider it in the context of other relationships, but managerial action in the network may serve to reduce this uncertainty.

Management implications

What are the implications of the relationship and network approaches for marketing management?

First, marketing should be regarded as an investment process that is instrumental for building, developing and maintaining exchange relationships to customers and intermediaries. The firm thereby develops its position in the network. Such relationships should be considered as immaterial assets for the selling firm, since they give the firm access to the resources that buyers are willing to give in exchange for products and services. Marketing should thus have a long-term perspective.

Second, marketing is a strategic activity that is crucial for the firm's development in the market and for its innovative processes. As in all investments a crucial management choice is to decide which customer relationships it wants to establish and develop. Obviously the seller must limit its commitments, both *to whom* it wants to be related to and how *strong* that commitment should be.

The present position in the network is the base for future marketing activities. The position implies both opportunities and restrictions for the future. The relationship to a customer in the home market might, for example, help a supplier to start exporting as the customer internationalizes. Efforts to develop a new strategic alliance might, for example, be constrained by the already existing connections between potential alliance partners and competitors.

Third, marketing must be considered as an organizational problem affecting the whole firm. Interaction with the buyer involves several functions such as manufacturing, logistics, R&D and purchasing. Adaptation processes in the exchange relationships influence all the activities and resources, not just those that traditionally belong to the marketing mix variables. The implementation of marketing activities in an organizational setting is emphasized. The role of marketing is focused on the selection and handling of relationships with individual counterparts. This will also influence the role of salespersons and shows a need for multi-person interaction between the seller and the buyer.

Since the firm has relationships with different types of interdependencies, with different objectives for the development of the relationship, etc., it is important organizationally to differentiate between how different relationships are handled.

Fourth, marketing research, marketing planning and control should focus on individual customers and their relationships to the focal firm and to other actors in the network over time, rather than on aggregates of customers in one specific time period. Most of the market information according to the markets-as-networks view is obtained within exchange relationships and not through separate market research projects outside of the on-going commercial interaction. There is a need to systematize such information about individual relationships to customers. Such types of analyses are probably more frequent in the purchasing function's handling of supplier relationships.

The market analyses must consider how firms are connected to each other and will, depending on the specific objectives of the analysis, cut across traditional market boundaries based on geography, type of industry, or product category.

Marketing planning should start at the relationship level. Interaction with the buyers and potential buyers is an important aspect of the planning process. The planning should include objectives and activities concerning development of the relationships. The objectives should not only be formulated for the business exchange, such as sales volume and type of products, but also for social and information exchange, and for adaptation processes for products, processes and routines. Development of the individual relationships should not be hidden by aggregated data on sales, market shares, customer satisfaction, etc. The investment nature of marketing must be considered both in the planning and in the control processes.

Fifth, marketing activities are much related to technical issues because the exchange relationships relate several firms with technically interdependent resources and activities. Technical change in individual – and indeed in the total economy – are dependent on exchange relationships, and thus also on marketing activities. An important objective of the interaction process between seller and buyer is to identify and solve technical problems as regards both the functioning of the present systems (e.g. 'after sales service') and the development of future products and systems. The parties might want to increase or to decrease their mutual technical interdependency. Often the seller is interested in increasing the buyer's dependence on the seller's specific technical solution by offering a system rather than individual components, a long-term service contract rather than a warranty. The buyer may or may not find such an adaptation to the seller to be in its own interest. The technical competence that is brought by the two parties to the interaction is an important determinant of the outcome.

As we extend the relationship approach to the network approach we broaden our management implications to concern technical interdependencies in production/distribution systems involving many firms. If those interdependencies are strong, marketing of new products and processes that are not adapted to the present interdependencies becomes much more problematic since there is a need to change the network structure in more fundamental ways. On the other hand, a more moderate technical change might serve to strengthen the present network structure.

4 Research on exchange relationships and networks

Important theoretical backgrounds for the network view of exchange relationships and markets are theories on interorganizational behaviour (Pfeffer and Salncik 1978), so called Neo-Institutional Economic theories of social, economic and technical systems (Hodgson 1994; Smelser and Swedberg 1994; Granovetter 1985; Dosi et al. 1988) and basic notions of social exchange (Blau 1964). The growing literature on networks in several social science subdisciplines also provide a background for markets-as-networks studies (Powell and Smith-Doerr 1994; Nohria and Eccles 1992) and the network view, with its dynamic and contextual analytical explanation of institutional form for transactions (Johanson and Mattsson 1987). Inside the academic discipline of marketing, network studies are linked to some interactive schools of marketing, especially to the institutional and functionalist schools (see Sheth et al. 1988).

The long duration and dynamic, complex nature of seller–buyer relationships on industrial markets has been well documented by empirical marketing research (Håkansson 1982; Ford 1997). Normative analyses have also been published to show that it is good marketing policy to strive for long-term relationships with customers.

The markets-as-networks approach is predominantly of a European origin but has, since the initial research in Sweden, Great Britain and some other European countries (see the review by Johanson and Mattsson 1994), grown to a rather globally dispersed undertaking. An annual international research conference on relationships and networks (the IMP conference) has been organized since 1984, in many instances resulting in a book that reports on current research (see, e.g. Gemunden et al. 1997). Other recent books reporting on network research are Axelsson and Easton (1992);
Håkansson and Snehota (1995); Iacobucci (1996) and Ford (1997).

'Relationship marketing' research is also a subject area for international academic conferences. These conferences sometimes result in publications (see, e.g. special issue of *Journal of Marketing Management* 1997).

Network research treats a wide range of subjects in marketing. Early research focused on how the extended role of marketing, implied by the network approach, affected explanations of competitiveness of firms and nations. Research on industrial purchasing, supplier–buyer relationships, systems selling, links between marketing and technical change, internationalization processes, the investment nature of marketing are other examples of network research that in the 1980s laid foundations for later research (Johanson and Mattsson 1994).

Phenomena pursued in network research in the late 1990s continued to focus on dynamics of firms, relationship and networks and several of the above mentioned problem areas were continued. Questions addressed include competitive processes, how do markets evolve after deregulation or after scientific developments change the conditions for technological change; which are the network effects of mergers of formation of strategic alliances; how is international marketing influenced by the internationalization of the markets; how can change in distribution channels be managed; how do firms and industries adapt to new environmental regulation; how are trust and commitment developed between exchange partners. There are continued efforts to link this research in marketing to developments in other areas of the social sciences.

Formal economic and quantitative network analyses in marketing are still rare. It seems to be appreciated by managers that the management implications of the relationship and network approaches give realistic descriptions of markets and marketing behaviour on industrial, business-to-business markets. In fact, the approaches have been developed inductively by researchers in close contact with business. However, there is still much research needed before the network oriented planning and control instruments, that were discussed above, are developed and accepted.

LARS-GUNNAR MATTSSON
STOCKHOLM SCHOOL OF ECONOMICS

Further reading

(References cited in the text marked *)

* Axelsson, B. and Easton, G. (eds) (1992) *Industrial Networks: A New View of Reality*, London: Routledge.
* Blau, P.M. (1964) *Exchange and Power in Social Life*, London: John Wiley and Sons.
* Cook, K.S. and Emerson, R.M. (1978) 'Power, equity and commitment in exchange networks', *American Sociological Review* 43: 712–39.
* Dosi, G., Freeman, C., Nelson, R., Silverberg, G. and Soete, L., (eds) (1988) *Technical Change and Economic Theory*, London: Pintners Publishers.
* Ford, D. (ed) (1997) *Understanding Business Markets: Interaction, Relationships, Networks*, 2nd edn, London: Dryden Press.
* Gemunden, H.G., Ritter, T. and Wlter, A. (eds) (1997) *Relationships and Networks in International Markets*, Oxford: Pergamon.
* Granovetter, M. (1985) 'Economic action and social structure: the problem of embeddedness', *American Journal of Sociology* 91: 481–510.
* Grönroos, C. (1990) 'Relationship approach to the marketing function in service contexts: the marketing and organizational behaviour interface', *Journal of Business Research* 20: 3–12.
* Håkansson, H. (ed.) (1982) *International Marketing and Purchasing of Industrial Goods – An Interaction Approach*, London: John Wiley and Sons.
* Håkansson, H. and Snehota, I. (1995) *Developing Relationships in Business Networks*, London: Routledge.
* Haugland, S. and Reve, T. (1994) 'Price authority and trust in international distribution channel relationships', *Scandinavian Journal of Management* 10: 3.
* Hodgson, G.M. (1994) 'The return to institutional economics', in Smelser, N.J. and Swedberg, R., (eds), *The Handbook of Economic Sociology*, Princeton: Princeton University Press, 58–76.
* Iacobucci, D. (ed) (1996) *Networks in Marketing*, Thousand Oaks: Sage Publications.
* Johanson, J. and Mattsson, L.-G. (1987) 'Interorganizational relations in industrial systems – a network approach compared with the transaction cost approach', *International Studies of Management and Organization* 17: 34–48.
* Johanson, J. and Mattsson, L.-G. (1994) 'The markets-as-networks tradition in Sweden', in Laurent, G., Lilien, G.L. and Pras, B. (eds.), *Research Traditions in Marketing*, Kluwer Academic Publishers, 321–42.
* *Journal of Marketing Management* Special Issue on Relationship Marketing (1997) 13: No. 5.
* Kotler, P. (1997) *Marketing Management*, 9th edn, Englewood Cliffs, NJ: Prentice-Hall.
* Macneil, I.R. (1989) *The New Social Contract. An Inquiry Into Modern Contractual Relations*, New Haven, CT: Yale University Press.
* Mattsson, L-G. (1997) 'Relationship marketing and the markets as networks approach – a comparative analysis of two evolving streams of research', *Journal of Marketing Management* 13: 447–61.
* Nohria, N. and Eccles, R.G. (eds) (1992) *Networks and Organizations. Structure, Form and Action*, Boston: MA: Harvard Business School Press.
* Pfeffer, J. and Salancik, G. (1978) *The External Control of Organizations*, New York: Harper & Row.
* Powell, W.W. and Smith-Doerr, L. (1994) 'Networks and economic life', in Smelser, N.J. and Swedberg, R. (eds), *The Handbook of Economic Sociology*, Princeton: Princeton University Press, 368–402.
* Sheth, J., Gardner, D.M. and Garrett, D.E. (1988) *Marketing Theory: Evolution and Evaluation*, New York: John Wiley and Sons.
* Smelser, N.J. and Swedberg, R. (eds) (1994) *The Handbook of Economic Sociology*, Princeton: Princeton University Press.
* Williamson, O.E. (1985) *The Economic Institutions of Capitalism*, New York: The Free Press.

See also: CHANNEL MANAGEMENT; CHANNELS OF DISTRIBUTION; INFORMATION TECHNOLOGY AND MARKETING; LOGISTICS AND VALUE CREATION; MARKETING OF SERVICES; MARKETING RESEARCH; NEW PRODUCT DEVELPOMENT; PERSONAL SELLING AND SALES MANAGEMENT; PRICING; PRODUCT POLICY; THE MARKETING MIX

Marketing in practice

Marketing strategy

1 The meaning of marketing strategy
2 The basic principles: sustainable competitive advantage
3 The strategic triangle
4 The analysis of history
5 Recent issues
6 Conclusion

Overview

In this entry we will consider the meaning of the term marketing strategy and the basic underlying principle of sustainable competitive advantage. We will then consider the two essential elements within such a principle: the issue of position, particularly with respect to 'space' in the so-called 'strategic triangle' (the customers, competitors and the corporation), and of time, or the analysis of history. We will then consider a number of more recent developments such as the role of intermediaries in the 'enhanced' strategic triangle, the issue of market networks and inter-firm relationships, the resource based view of the firm and, finally, the recent emphasis on business processes. In conclusion, we will consider the likely future development of marketing strategy as both a field of academic study and practice.

1 The meaning of marketing strategy

Marketing strategy is now such a widely used phrase that it is difficult to remember that not long ago it was only to be found in a single chapter or even merely a section of a chapter in any marketing textbook.

Given its rapid adoption in marketing, the term 'strategy' has, not surprisingly, been used rather indiscriminately and this has resulted in a profusion of definitions. Indeed, Abell and Hammond (1979), in the first real textbook on marketing strategy, decided not to define it because of its wide variety of meanings! Other marketers only define marketing strategy implicitly, as what is managed in their definitions of strategic marketing management.

From one perspective, as discussed by Michael Baker, marketing strategy can have a broad impact on the business in terms of instilling a marketing orientation among all those in the firm: the way of thinking or philosophy of the whole organization (see MARKETING – PHILOSOPHY OR FUNCTION?). However, marketing strategy can alternatively be seen as dealing only with the development of competitive advantages directly associated with the marketing function such as customer loyalty and distribution channel control. Hence some definitions of marketing strategy focus on a broad, or philosophical, approach whilst others prefer a narrower, or functional view. In the latter case, the domain is sometimes even further restricted by sole attention to the various elements of the marketing mix rather than the more general issues of customer and channel relationships.

A further part of the confusion concerning the term 'strategy' arises out of its present use in the English language. The word 'strategy' is derived from a Greek term which is translated roughly as the 'art of the general (or commander-in-chief).'(It should be borne in mind that military strategy, and relatively traditional perspectives at that, is only one source of insight into the nature of marketing strategy. Useful analogies can also be found in both sports games and evolutionary ecology as well as in more formal game theory.) Thus, strategy originally referred to the skills and decision-making process of the general (executive), while 'strategem', translated as 'an operation or act of generalship', referred to a specific decision made by the executive. Over time, the term 'strategem' has fallen into disuse and, now, strategy has a dual connotation – it is both the art itself and the result or output of practising the art.

To complicate matters even further, some writers suggest that a 'strategy' implies a formal and explicitly stated logic, whilst others have argued that a strategy can emerge from a set of decisions and need not be explicitly stated. Mintzberg and Walters (1985) even specifically distinguished between 'deliberate' and 'emergent' strategies and, more recently, Henry Mintzberg has been at the forefront of those arguing that it is vital to focus on what might be called issues of strategy implementation rather than formulation (Mintzberg 1994). There is considerable confusion, therefore, about the process and output of strategy as well as its domain. Some authors choose to define strategy more in terms of the explicit nature of the process involved whilst others focus on the content, or at least the form, of the output. Indeed this debate goes back to the distinction made by Herb Simon (1959) about the difference, particularly under conditions of bounded rationality, between substantive rationality and procedural rationality.

2 The basic principles: sustainable competitive advantage

The basic principles of marketing strategy are simply stated: to achieve persistent success in the marketplace over the competition. The firm needs to have the appropriate capabilities (broadly defined), it needs to respond to and indeed anticipate the current and changing nature of customer demand, and finally to do so in a manner which is more effective and efficient than its competitors. The overall notion of Sustainable Competitive Advantage (SCA) is often used to encapsulate this approach.

We will return later to a fundamental theoretical issue in this way of explaining the nature of marketing strategy which has concerned a number of marketing scholars. Broadly the concern is that the notion of SCA only works to explain what has happened but it does not really help develop an understanding of the nature of evolving future advantages in developing and changing competitive markets (Dickinson 1992).

Most marketers are aware of the significant profit potential in products such as premium quality, conveniently prepared, frozen foods; computers for small businesses; robotic and factory automation; and genetically engineered products. However, only firms that have or are able to develop sustainable competitive advantages in these opportunities will realize these potential profits.

Many firms have been early, but unsuccessful entrants, in exciting markets. Some examples of these firms that failed to develop a long-term sustainable advantage are Bowmar in hand-held calculators; Osborne and Sinclair in portable personal computers; Lyons (LEO) in early large commercial computing, Apple in desktop personal computing; Texas Instruments in digital watches; Reynolds in ballpoint pens; Royal Crown in diet and caffeine-free cola drinks; and Advent in large screen television.

Bruce Henderson, the founder of the Boston Consulting Group, emphasized the importance of understanding competition and achieving competitive advantage in product-markets:

> A market can be viewed in many different ways and a product can be used in many different ways. Each time the product-market pairing is varied, the relative competitive strength is varied too. Many businessmen do not recognize that a key element in strategy is choosing the competitor whom you wish to challenge, as well as choosing the market segment and product characteristics with which you will compare.
>
> (Henderson 1980: 8)

Basis for building a competitive advantage

Methods for building a sustainable competitive advantage can be divided into three groups: (i) advantages related to the firm as a whole; (ii) advantages residing in a functional area such as R&D, production, purchasing or marketing; and (iii) advantages based on relationships between the firm and external entities. While this categorization is somewhat arbitrary, it does illustrate how one can differentiate between a statement of business-level strategy and marketing strategy. Business strategy is concerned with the entire arena of potential advantages but the primary focus is on advantages residing in the integration of functional areas within the firm. Marketing strategy concentrates on the bases of competitive advantages associated with the marketing function. In addition, marketers focus on the advantages derived from relationships typically governed by the marketing function – relationships between the firm, its customers, and the distribution channels serving those customers. A more detailed analysis of this approach can be found in the source–position–performance framework developed in Day and Wensley (1988).

The sources of advantages which are associated with marketing often arise from activities performed by a number of functional areas within the firm and therefore cannot be seen as totally independent. However, the marketing function is typically responsible for directing the firm's resources toward satisfying customer needs. The marketing function develops long-term relationships with customers, just as the purchasing function creates competitive advantages through supplier relations. Cost and technology based advantages often interact with market-based advantages. Low production costs can be translated into low prices and high value delivered to customers. Unique technology advantages are translated into developing advantages in terms of cost, quality control and/or flexibility.

Achieving sustainability in the market

Any business activity can in principle be developed into a sustainable competitive advantage. The degree to which a business activity can be used as competitive advantage is a function of the ease with which competitors can overcome the advantage. Some advantages seem to be easier to overcome than others. For example, it is difficult for one well-known firm to develop a sustainable competitive advantage over other well-known firms based on access to low-cost, financial resources, because capital markets are typically very efficient in this situation. Thus, all large firms have relatively equal opportunities to raise needed financial resources. For these firms, the cost of financial resources is based on an accurate appraisal of the risk and return of the strategic investment opportunities facing the firms (Barwise et al. 1989). Thus, a competitive advantage possessed by a firm results in a lower cost of financial resources rather than the cost of financial resources resulting in a competitive advantage. However, businesses engaging in small, little known product-market opportunities may realize a competitive advantage from being able to secure financial resources from a large, cash-rich parent corporation. The parent corporation, based on its unique knowledge of the opportunity, will fund the business; while small, independent competitors may be unable to attract commensurate funding from a less-informed, imperfect, venture capital market.

In a marketing context, it is difficult to secure a sustainable competitive advantage through pricing (Buzzell and Wiersema 1981). Changes in prices are immediately recognized by competition. Competitors can respond easily to these changes, competing away any short-term advantage that might have been created. On the other hand, geographic location frequently results in a sustainable competitive advantage. There are a limited number of high density traffic sites for retail outlets selling convenience goods. Only one outlet can occupy a specific location. Thus, once McDonald's has built fast fast-food restaurants in the best location, Burger King and Wendy's are at a long-term disadvantage when they are located in the second and third best sites. On the other hand, in some cases even the geographic nature of the market can both change and be changed: In the UK, Wimpey's have failed to build on early site choice advantages in comparison with new entrants such as McDonald's.

Two important bases of sustainable advantage related to the marketing function which have received only limited attention from a strategic perspective are customer brand loyalty and channel relationships (see BRANDING AND BRAND MANAGEMENT; CHANNEL MANAGEMENT; CONSUMER BEHAVIOUR). Reibstein outlines the strategic importance of customer loyalty in the context of consumer brands:

> Companies that have built and reinforced brand loyalty can use it as a way to reduce the threat of competition; loyal customers may resist offers from competitors – high levels of brand loyalty serve as a barrier to entry into a market by a competitor.
> (Reibstein 1985)

The economic value of advantages based on brand loyalty is illustrated by the sustainable premium over book value that firms have paid when acquiring brand-name consumer package goods firms. In the UK, this has been illustrated in Nestlé's acquisition of Rowntrees and more recently in the importance attached to brand values in the establishment of Diageo, formed by the merger of Grand Metropolitan and Guinness. In a similar vein, Corey emphasized the

Figure 1 The strategic triangle
Source: Ohmae (1982: 92)

sustainable, long-term nature of channel relationships:

> A distribution system ... is a key external resource. Normally it takes years to build and is not easily changed ... it represents a commitment to a set of polices and practices that constitute the basic fabric on which is woven an extensive set of long-term relationships.
> (Corey 1976: 263)

3 The strategic triangle

The conventional approach to marketing strategy is well summarized by the 'strategic triangle' popularized by Kenichi Ohmae (1982). In this triangle (Figure 1), the firm (corporation) is seen as directly interacting with both customers and competition.

Customers

From a marketing perspective, competition takes place in a market which consists of a number of individual product-markets. Each individual product-market includes a group of potential customers with similar requirements and similar methods (technologies and marketing programs) in providing products(or services) to satisfy those needs. The individual product-market is therefore jointly defined by the specific product/service and the market transaction that is directly involved. In marketing strategy terms it is the most elemental unit of analysis: it is overlayed, for instance, by competitive arenas (a set of product-markets within which a group of competitors 'choose' to compete) and customer clusters (a group of product markets that are used by customers in an integrated fashion).

Market segmentation
Central to the marketing approach to customers has been the notion of market segmentation as a way of characterizing a range of customer requirements without direct recourse to single individuals. The analysis of market segmentation, often defined as one of the most fundamental concepts in marketing has a long and extended history. However, it has, perhaps like the rest of the marketing field, been rather slower to recognize the competitive as well as

Marketing strategy

customer basis for market segmentation (see MARKET SEGMENTATION).

In more recent empirical work the term 'market segmentation' has generally been used to refer to strict customer behaviour based phenomena and the term 'market structure' to incorporate the impact of competitive reactions, but still at the customer level. In the strategic marketing area, however, market segmentation tends to be used with a meaning closer to the notion of 'market structure' and 'market structure' itself to the network of inter-relationships between manufacturers, suppliers, other intermediaries and retailers. Kamakura and Russell (1989) set out to try and clarify this issue by using respectively the terms 'consumer segmentation' and 'elasticity structure' but then, unfortunately, tend to substitute 'consumer' and 'market' segmentation.

There is by now a very large body of empirical work in the general field of market segmentation but even so there remain some critical problems. In particular:

1. We have evidence that the cross-elasticities with respect to different marketing mix elements are likely to be not only of different orders but actually imply different structures of relationship.
2. Competitive behaviour patterns which, after all in a strict sense, determine the nature of the experiment from which the elasticities can be derived, seem to be, to use a term recently coined by, Leeflang and Wittink (1993), 'out of balance' with the cross-elasticity data themselves.

This raises questions about the nature and causes of this imbalance. Leeflang and Wittink, in their original work, were particularly interested in the notion that forms of conjoint analysis could be used to determine the underlying customer trade-off matrix which is, of course, only partly revealed in the empirical customer elasticities (because individual customers can only respond to the actual offerings that are available) and which is 'assumed' (with some degree of bias and error) by individual competitors in determining their competitive actions and reactions. More recently they have also recognized that we may need to consider the impact of management incentive structures and the likelihood that marketing managers rarely get criticized for reacting to competitive moves (Leefland and Wittink 1996)!

The recent empirical evidence also raises severe questions about the commonly accepted notion of customer segmentation itself. Despite various caveats in the textbooks, there is a strong tendency to present segmentation as if:

1. there is little difference between customer segmentation and brand differentiation;
2. 'closeness' of brands in terms of substitution can be represented in a two-dimensional diagram.

As a result of these two simplifying assumptions the notion of positioning has been given considerable emphasis (indeed in some cases, such as Ries and Trout (1985), almost exclusive concern) as a more strategic perspective on brand and product competition. Hence, it is asserted, we can make strategic statements about the positioning of the brand or product within its marketplace and leave more tactical marketing mix decisions to be taken within this strategic context (see THE MARKETING MIX).

Yet attempts to aggregate the specific evidence for cross-elasticities suggest that the patterns of interaction cannot be reduced in this way (or at least such reduction only explains a limited amount of the overall variance). This has lead to the suggested use of overall indicators of competitive 'clout' and 'vulnerabilty' (Cooper and Nakanishi 1988) as a better means of presenting aggregate results. However, we can argue even more radically that the search for any general form of intermediate and hence more 'strategic' representation of the market in these terms is basically flawed and that so-called 'tactical' marketing mix decisions are the very essence of practical strategy.

Competitors

It has been widely commented that marketing as both a discipline and a practice was rather slow to respond to the emergence of increased and sustained competition. Marketing remained defined for a long period primarily in terms of satisfaction of customer needs and the critical strategic role of competition was generally highlighted by economists either within the academic domain, such as Michael Porter, or working in the emerging strategy consultancies, such as Boston Consulting Group.

Nowadays however, the issue of competitor behaviour is seen as central to marketing strategy analysis but it is still important to distinguish between the implications of the two 'generic' forms of competitive behaviour.

Competition by differentiation

The basic principle of competition by differentiation was enunciated as early as the 1930s by both Chamberlain (in terms of his notion of 'monopolistic competition') and Robinson (in terms of 'imperfect competition'). In both cases the principle was that the individual firm or product faced a downward sloping demand curve which was distinctive from the horizontal line at the 'market price' of traditional atomistic and perfect competition. The individual firm was therefore able to make, at least to some degree, its own price-output choices independently of any competitor behaviour. What provided this isolation? The original list provided by Joan Robinson includes a number of items which would now be described as marketing factors such as branding and distribution effects.

There is, of course, a link between this notion of differentiation and the concept of market segmentation, but it is important also to appreciate their differing starting points: market segmentation starts from customers, product or service differentiation from the firm or product itself.

The crucial point in this analysis, however, is that the barriers to direct price competition are both incomplete and, to some degree, temporary. Much of the real, and anecdotal, evidence about individual firms' failure to recognize competition revolves around the extent to which they failed to see the way in which their previously 'protected' position was being eroded either because customer tastes were changing and/or competitors had found new ways of overcoming 'barriers to competition'.

Competition by price

From an economic perspective 'traditional' competition in products or services is through price-levels. With certain adjustments for the nature of accounting systems, this equates with the importance of cost competition. This traditional emphasis received a considerable boost from the popularization of the 'experience curve' effect by Bruce Henderson and others at Boston Consulting Group in the 1960s. Not surprisingly, with a bias towards areas such as electronics, much of this work established the key nature of cost competition in terms of the competitive dynamics of the industry.

Of course, the simple 'experience curve' is only a partial view of the dynamics of cost behaviour in various industries. It became recognized that issues such as 'shared' experience as well as discontinuities in technological changes meant that the simple experience curve model was itself only valid over a limited range: strategies were again needed which whilst striving for greater efficiency within the existing means of doing things also maintained a monitoring of overall effectiveness of the existing means itself.

More recently, the availability of comprehensive industry databases such as that for the disk drive industry has meant researchers have been able to investigate these effects further. Christiansen (1997) for instance noted that in a rather ironic way it was the close link between manufacturers and existing customers that meant that an opportunity developed for new manufacturers in supplying an 'improved' product to new customers in the shift from 5.25 to 3.5 inch hard drives.

Analysis of competitor subgroups

Just as with customers, there are conditions under which, rather than a broad analysis of likely aggregate behaviour, it is more appropriate to consider either subgroups or individual competitors.

It can be argued therefore that we should look at various groups at the sub-industry level which are also apparently making the same conduct choices because they are likely to be in more direct competition with each other than with other industry members. This leads directly to the notion of strategic group analysis which was developed most thoroughly in theoretical terms in Caves and Porter (1977) and Caves (1980) (see THE ASSESSMENT OF MARKETING PERFORMANCE; STRATEGIC ALLIANCES AND SUPPLIER PARTNERSHIPS).

A number of commentators including, in particular, McGee and Thomas (1986), have, however, commented on some of the confusions in the strategic group notion (including the extent to which it is 'rational' for those firms that are, in some sense, most proximate to each other, to follow exactly the same strategy and therefore increase the overall level of effective competition) as well as the problems of identifying such groups in a consistent and stable (over time) manner.

Corporation

Beyond any subgroup analysis, it is also possible to consider an analysis of individual competitors. The analysis of the individual firm or corporation uses a range of techniques. The most common are SWOT (Strengths, Weaknesses, Opportunities and Threats), and Financial Analysis in various forms.

SWOT analysis

SWOT, or sometimes TOWS, analysis attempts to partition the key factors influencing the strategic direction of the firm along two dimensions which are, broadly speaking, internal/external and positive/negative. The implicit assumption in the approach is that for each category there is a strategic response (Threats–Avoid; Opportunities-Exploit; Weaknesses–Compensate; Strengths–Build) and that therefore a 'balanced' strategy can result from a TOWS analysis.

Although a by-now almost traditional way of presenting the initial analysis in an MBA project and similar contexts, there are potentially some major flaws:

1 To a considerable extent the internal–external and positive–negative divisions are reflections of each other so any particular factor can be located in any box within reason (it is merely a question of how it is 'presented').
2 The link between individual factors and proposed strategic action is often naive and merely semantic. In actual practice a more effective approach is to redefine the competitive domain so that negative aspects become marginalized (or indeed even positive).
3 There is a tendency to treat individual factors as distinct and uncorrelated, when they are merely elements in a more general construct such as, say, market position. This applies not only between the boxes (see 1 above) but also within individual boxes.

In summary, the form of analysis often done in SWOT is too trivial to deal with the details of strategy and particularly implementation but also involves too much detail to aid an integrated and synoptic view of higher level strategic choice.

Financial analysis

Most forms of corporate strategic analysis have to include not only a financial evaluation of the current position but also an assessment of the financial impact of future strategic choices.

Such a financial evaluation often relies on the management and financial accounting information systems within the firm but more recently a number of key conceptual issues have been raised. Most important has been the development of so-called 'Activity Based Costing' which, broadly, attempts to shift the focus of cost analysis towards individual elements in the various business activities or processes involved in the development and delivery of products and services. This follows on from earlier developments in management accounting which looked at ways of constructing management accounts so that financial performance could be measured along various dimensions (such as product groups, sales territories, and key customers) as a form of strategic diagnosis.

In interpreting financial data for strategic purposes it is inevitable that two fundamental conceptual issues almost always occur at some stage: the nature of opportunity cost and the distinction between fixed and variable costs. For financial accounting purposes, it is a well established principle that the 'cost' of a particular activity should be based on adjusted, 'real', historic costs. It is also clear that for strategic management accounting purposes, the costs should be an 'opportunity' cost based on alternative possible uses of the assets concerned. This inevitably leads to the difficult position that the cost of any specified activity depends on the cost of other alternatives. Indeed strong advocates of developments in 'Strategic Management Accounting' would argue that even this cost should be compared with one's competitors' costs rather than treated as an absolute figure.

In terms of the variability of costs, the simple principle is that whilst in the short run almost all costs are fixed, strategic analysis with its focus on the longer term tends towards a situation in which, to paraphrase the famous

Keynes Dictum: 'In the long run, all costs are variable'.

The problem with much strategic financial analysis is therefore to ensure that assumptions about what is fixed and what is variable which are built into the financial analysis are consistent with the actual resource choices that the firm or organization faces.

4 The analysis of history

Any analysis related to the longer term implies an appreciation of the time dimension. Hence overlaid on the strategic triangle is the analysis of history. In a marketing strategy context we can consider the analysis of market position as the analysis of advantage alongside the issue of the characteristics of sustainability.

Market position

In terms of explaining strategic performance in marketing terms, the notion of market position is central. Marketing strategies rarely avoid reference to 'premium positioning' or 'maintaining high value added' (see POSITIONING).

In the simplest terms to have (or indeed even talk about) a position, we need to have a map. To talk about market position we need to have a market map. We do however have to be careful about our use of the notion of maps. Weick advises us to distinguish between 'map' and 'territory'. Such maps can vary from, at the simplest, a single dimension designed to represent the price/quality tradeoff to complex multidimensional perceptual maps based on attitude research on customers.

In marketing and market research analysis, the development of such maps is a large field of study in its own right often allied with the use of conjoint analysis to try and relate particular product attributes to expressed purchase behaviour.

From a strategic market perspective the key issues are the extent to which the map is stable through time, and provides a reasonable guide to actual purchase behaviour.

Time stability

Little work has been done on time series rather than cross-sectional attitude data (perhaps because of 'lack' of commercial interest and a lack of public research funds) but we might expect there to be a considerable problem with time stability. This concern is reflected in some of the work on usage segmentation which suggests that the more appropriate unit of analysis is the (product-use situation) rather than just the (product). However since the definition of the (product-use situation) elements itself requires user opinions (on the appropriate use categories) rather than externally defined product categories, there remain obvious dangers of further instability. A rather naive prior hypothesis might be that by introducing two related levels of attitudes – the nature of relevant use-situations and the suitability of particular products/brands within each use situation – we provide more rather than less instability. One is reminded of Frank Bass's useful dictum that forecasts based on larger numbers of input parameters are not necessarily more accurate than those based on a few.

The analysis of sustainability

More recent writers and researchers on SCA have developed rather further the issue of 'sustainability' to which we referred earlier. Williams (1992), for instance has suggested that industries can be viewed as being one of three types in terms of the sustainability of advantages, based on what he calls the cycle speed of 'resource imitation patterns'. His primary distinction is based on the degree to which resources positions are shielded from competitive pressures and he suggests that the long-run trend in real product prices in any particular area is itself a good correlate with the degree of such imitation. Indeed Williams goes further in his analysis to suggest that the common concern with dynamic competition and temporary advantage may be over-played: 'On balance the research suggests that, in spite of the popular perception that markets are generally becoming more competitive, these highly isolated environments, and their strongly isolated resources, are becoming more prevalent and more important to understand'. (Williams 1992: 37). In terms of the our central theme, the key issue is the extent to which significant changes in sustainability are predictable:

shifts in the characteristic rate at which an industry's products are imitated ... precede a new category of market ... such shifts are difficult to predict and tough to adjust to. However, because sustainable resource analysis uses rates of change as benchmarks to competition, many such frame-breaking changes do not have to be unpredictable – early warnings of frame-breaking change can be had by monitoring changes in sustainability.

(Williams 1992: 47)

However, beyond recommending close attention to the present as well as the past it remains unclear how far it is merely an issue of languaging to suggest that it is easier to forecast changes in sustainability if the framework of analysis based on sustainability is used.

Reed and DeFillippi (1990) focus attention on the nature of competencies which simultaneously create both advantage itself and ambiguity (which ensures imitation is difficult and hence the advantage is more sustainable). They suggest that the three key characteristics of such competencies are tacitness, complexity and specificity. Whilst these three elements are clearly important, their particular nature introduces both definitional and measurement problems when it comes to more empirical work.

Ghemawat (1991) and others have focused attention on the nature of commitment as the key element in sustainable advantage. He suggests that analysis of sustainability relates to 'sticky factors' and then proceeds to decompose his analysis into issues of imitation, substitution, holdup (appropriation of economic value by those who are not direct owners of the relevant assets) and slack (failure to realize full economic benefits). Whilst this development in terms of the analytical framework certainly provides for a more refined set of questions, particularly in terms of questions related to the firm and its established market, it is unclear how far the resultant questions related to new entrants become more tractable.

Given all these confusions, it is perhaps not a surprise that two of the key contributors to the earlier debate about the nature of dominant logics in firms (Prahalad and Bettis 1989) have now shifted the attention towards the notion that the most important competitive competence is to be able to adjust the logics themselves (Bettis and Prahalad 1995).

Analysis of investment: the issue of real options

A number of writers, particularly Myers (1984) and, more recently, Kogut and Kulatilaka (1992) have paid more specific attention to the directly related issue of the analysis of major investment decisions. They have recognized that such decisions have important 'optional' consequences in that they provide the base for future actions. Indeed Kogut and Kulatilaka use the term 'platforms' to describe this phenomenon. Again the basis of this insight is clearly sound: the problem lies in how operational the proposed analysis actually is. There are, for instance, severe doubts as to how far the basic framework derived in the Fisher–Black approach for financial options can be sensibly applied to such optional benefits (see Marsh *et al.* 1988) except in the case of rather specialized examples of so-called 'real' options (see Pitts 1994). The list of issues derived by Kogut and Kulatilaka also looks remarkably like the list derived by most sound ex post analysts of competitive advantage.

It could indeed be argued that the major advance represented by these writers is not the development of a new analytical structure but an emphasis towards timing any analysis at the point of a specific and major decision rather than, say, the preparation of a strategic plan. In this sense we are merely rediscovering Drucker's earlier dictum that the key concern should be the 'futurity' of current decisions:

> But even with these improved methods, decisions concerning the future will always remain anticipations: and the odds will always be against them being right. Any management decision must therefore contain provision for change, adaption and salvage ... today's managers must systematically provide for tomorrow's managers. Tomorrow's managers alone can adapt today's decisions to tomorrow's conditions.
>
> (Drucker 1961: 90)

The role of strategic intent

A key assumption in much that is written about strategy is the idea that those organizations that

Figure 2 The 'enhanced' strategic triangle

have maintained a consistent and central purpose or sense of direction have generally shown better performance. The most recent specific form of this behaviour is the espousal of 'strategic intent' as a key element in strategic success.

To some extent this continued emphasis clearly reflects real issues for organizational effectiveness. Any organization depends on sustaining relationships with other individuals and groups, from the sources of key skills and talents amongst its employees to both its suppliers and customers. A crucial element in sustaining such relationships is no doubt some consistency of behaviour as well as the setting of realistic expectations.

At least to this extent therefore, the value of some consistency in strategic intent is clear. More complex is the question of the extent to which public and prior commitment to such intents is of real value. A very active debate in the strategy field remains, particularly influenced, as we discussed earlier by writers such as Mintzberg (1994) over the extent to which such intentions tend to emerge and be revealed much more through a sequence of actions rather than presented as a deliberate and public set of strategy statements. The conflicting contributions surrounding the interpretation of Honda's strategic actions in the US market provides a vivid illustration of these issues. The debate itself is perhaps best summarized by Rumelt's (1996) observation that actually successful strategies in most circumstances require aspects of all three elements: economic logic, organizational adaptability and managerial intention. As he argues, it is advisable to avoid too much emphasis on which element is more important and instead to recognize that each type of explanation is really addressing a different question. The nature of economics is that it inevitably explains the successes and failures after the event but it may give little guidance as to what informed and motivated the prior actions which is much more the domain of intention. Finally some form of adaptive behaviour is inevitably required when the competitive market context is evolving and changing.

5 Recent issues

Inevitably, in a field of study so closely related to the dynamics of the competitive marketplace there are always new developments. In many ways they are individual and *ad hoc* but as we will suggest later they can be seen as part of a more general concern about the longer term value of the basic SCA construct.

Intermediaries: the enhanced strategic triangle

The increased strategic role of intermediaries has been widely recognized in many markets and industries. As such it has become clear that the strategic triangle to which we referred earlier should be enhanced as illustrated in Figure 2.

Intermediaries (or channels given the importance of alliteration in strategy!) are to be seen as independent and self-interested agents in the market; not merely logistical channels to the end-customer.

This leads to an alternative approach in addressing the earlier issue raised of the apparent imbalance between competitive behaviours and customer reactions. Competitive behaviours revealed in the market can be seen as the joint effect of manufacturer and retailer tactics (and possibly strategies). In this sense we could use and extend the concept of 'Cognitive Maps' for various competitors (Porac and Thomas 1990; Hodgkinson and Johnston 1994) to such maps for both key manufacturers and intermediaries such as retailers, which might also help to explain the phenomena of 'over-competition', which we discussed earlier (Leeflang and Wittink 1993; Wensley 1993).

Networks and relationships

A number of researchers and theoreticians in the marketing field, particularly those interested in innovation and industrial buyer behaviour between organizations have started their work with the observation that relationships between firms are relatively stable and complex. This leads to a concern that the basic notion of competitive dynamics may be misleading as a characterization of such relationships. The issue is seen as one of an interacting network rather than a sequence of instantaneous and individual market transactions.

Three main issues do, however, emerge from the current state of the work.

First, there is a danger in confusing a detailed descriptive model with a simple but robust predictive one. The basic micro-economic framework which underlies the SCA approach should not be seen as an adequate description of the analytical and processual complexities in specific situations. It is a framework for predicting the key impacts of a series of market mediated transactions: at the very least outcomes are the joint effect of decisions themselves and the selection process. In this sense the only valid criticisms of the application of such a model is that either the needs of the situation are not met by the inherent nature of the model or that the model fails to perform within its own terms.

Second, it is clear that actual relationships between firms must be seen on a spectrum between outright competition at one end and collusion at the other (Easton *et al.* 1992). At the very least, such a self evident observation raises the issue of the firm (or business unit) as the basic, and often only, unit of analysis: in certain circumstances we might more appropriately consider an informal coalition as the key unit:

Earlier, the border of the company was seen as the dividing line between cooperation and conflict – cooperation within the company and conflict in relation to all external units. The corresponding means for coordination are hierarchy and the market mechanism. The existence of relationships makes this picture much more diffuse. There are great opportunities for cooperation with a lot of external units forming, for example, coalitions. Thus, it is often more fruitful to see the company as a part of a network instead of a free and independent actor in an atomistic market.

(Håkansson 1987: 13)

Third, the recognition that there is a network of relationships is merely the first step. Approaches need to be developed for the analysis of the network. Hakansson has, for instance, suggested that the key elements of any network are actors, activities and resources. He also suggests that the overall network is bound together by a number of forces including functional interdependence, as well as power, knowledge and time-related structure.

Considerable emphasis has also been given to the importance of longer term relationships within the market structure: such a relationship marketing perspective can be seen as similar to the network view or rather different. In particular Mattsson provides an overall comparison between the two perspectives:

My conclusion is that if we take the limited view of relationship marketing, we come close to the first extreme position stated in the beginning of this article: relationship marketing and the network perspective have very little in common. Some relationship marketing aspects are even contradictory to basic views in the network perspective. Relationship marketing in its limited interpretation is just a marketing strategy aimed to increase customer loyalty, customer satisfaction and customer retention. Relationship marketing is aided by modern information technology that makes it possible to individualise communication with customers in a mass market. In that sense relationship marketing is just a basic application of the marketing management thinking.

However, let us consider the extended view that the relationship marketing means true interaction between the parties over time, a relatively high mutual dependency between seller and buyer and a major concern for how individual relationships are interconnected in nets and networks. Then we will come much closer to my second initial position that relationship marketing and the network perspective have much to gain from more research interaction and mutual awareness than what is presently the case. Relationship Marketing Research would benefit from the following aspects of network perspective research: more focus on embeddedness of actors and relationships, more consideration of the buyers point of view, more descriptive studies on interaction and relationships overtime, more concern for the meso and macro levels in the governance structure, more use of longitudinal research methods, including case studies. Obviously, both relationship marketing and the network perspective must become increasingly aware of, and contribute to, research developments in a broader social science framework where the focus is on the function of relationships between economic actors.

(Mattsson 1997)

Core competencies and the resource based view

One set of recent perspectives on the nature of the corporation has been the 'core competencies' approach developed particularly by Hamel and Prahalad (1991).

Hamel and Prahalad chart out a bold and critical role for marketing in the organization: to enable management develop 'the imagination to envision markets that do not yet exist'. Broadly speaking their emphasis is on extensive market research, speedy product development and rapid adjustment to market response. However, most of the examples they quote are also of the 'global' (at least in terms of the developed world) market:

HDTV, CCDs, Flat Screen Displays, Electronic Musical Equipment, Wireless Communications, Electronic Imaging, Medical Diagnosis, Camcorders, Fax Machines, ATMs, Electronic Organizers, Computer Graphics, Video-recorders, Interpreting telephones and, of course, computers themselves and cars,

and it may be that there overall interpretation is only really appropriate for those markets which are technology dominated.

A rather broader view has developed under the general title of the 'resource based' view (RBV) of the firm (Grant 1991). The general RBV perspective was developed by Wernerfeld (1984). In his more recent work, Wernerfeld has suggested that the RBV approach is more and more inevitable but therefore, in a way, almost tautologous: 'basing strategies on the differences between firms should be automatic, rather than noteworthy' (Wernerfeld 1995:173). Overall, however, the general emphasis is to understand the development of firm based strategies as the exploitation of a specific and particular assets to which the individual firm has title. The rather legalistic term 'title' is used here intentionally since given the nature of the relevant markets long-term 'ownership' of assets is too restrictive a notion. Indeed there have been interesting further developments in the view of the firm as itself a bundle of relational and other contracts.

Business processes and the rediscovery of socio-technical systems

There has been, more recently, considerable emphasis on the nature of individual business processes within organizations. In a sense this is no more than an analysis of activities in terms of specified processes rather than forms of work organization, and can be related to both forms of value chain analysis developed by Michael Porter and also the activity based costing framework.

The approach proved to be particularly popular in the context of financial services firms, often under the label 'business process re-engineering'. As a form of analysis it is most evident when considering fairly routine business systems such as customer handling and order processing. It also provides a useful framework for benchmarking activities with other different forms of organization. Its advocates have made strenuous claims for its central importance in the maintenance of competitive performance and there is little doubt that it represents a useful and effective form of analysis for key business processes.

Indeed it can be used to redefine the boundaries of the business by focusing solely on core processes. However, a number of critical issues have been raised, particularly in the extent to which the very approach can negate or ignore the people element in all such activities: indeed some have argued that business process re-engineering can be seen to some considerable degree as the re-discovery of socio-technical systems as developed by Emery and Trist at the Tavistock and elsewhere in the 1950s and early 1960s, but now with no consideration of the 'people' element (Mumford 1994).

6 Conclusion

The central analytical concept in strategic marketing, that of the pursuit of sustainable competitive advantage has remained in place but also evolved substantially since the development of the economic analysis of imperfect competition in the 1930s. The usual forms of analysis of the firm itself alongside both its competitors and its customers still fit comfortably within this overall framework.

Whilst some of the more recent developments, such as the resource based view of the firm can be accommodated reasonably well within this framework, others suggest that we may be approaching a stage at which the range of issues begins to require a reappraisal of the basic concept itself.

In the longer run, it may be that the implications of the 'network-relationship' perspective alongside a more evolutionary and emergent view of the processes of market development and competition (Lambkin and Day 1989) are much more fundamental for the more traditional economic analysis of the firm. The underlying logic of such a theoretical approach would be severely challenged if it appeared not only that the firm is not really an appropriate 'unit of analysis' in explaining micro-economic performance, but also that concepts of both competitors and customers are distinctly fuzzy as key stages in the economic development of particular commercial technologies, and, therefore, that the cognitive frameworks actually applied by managers and executives in making strategic decisions were very different. Finally it could well be that the ways in which market competition evolves cannot be explained solely by the individual intentions of either the firms or their customers.

ROBIN WENSLEY
WARWICK BUSINESS SCHOOL

Further reading

(References cited in the text marked *)

* Abell, D. and Hammond, J. (1979) *Strategic Marketing Planning: Problems and Analytical Approaches*, Englewood Cliffs NJ: Prentice-Hall.
  Barwise, P., Marsh, P. and Wensley, R. (1989) 'Must finance and strategy clash?' *Harvard Business Review* September–October: 85–90.
* Bettis, R.A. and Prahalad, C.K. (1995) 'The dominant logic: retrospective and extension', *Strategic Management Journal* 16: 5–14.
* Buzzell, R.D. and Wiersema, F.D. (1981) 'Successful share-building strategies', *Harvard Business Review* January–February: 135–44.
* Caves, R.E. (1980) 'Industrial organization, corporate strategy and structure', *Journal of Economic Literature* XVIII: 64–92.
* Caves, R.E. and Porter, M.E. (1977) 'From entry barriers to mobility barriers: conjectural decisions & contrived deterrence to new competition', *Quarterly Journal of Economics* May: 242–61.
* Christiansen, Clayton M. (1997) *The Innovator's Dilemma*, Boston: Harvard Business School Press.
* Cooper, L. and Nakanishi, M. (1988) *Market Share Analysis: Evaluating Competitive Marketing Effectiveness*, Boston: Kluwer Academic Press.
.* Corey, R. (1976) *Industrial Marketing* Englewood Cliffs NJ: Prentice-Hall.
* Day, G.S. and Wensley, R. (1988) 'Assessing advantage: a framework for diagnosing competitive superiority', *Journal of Marketing* 52: 1–20.
* Dickinson, P.R. (1992) 'Toward a general theory of competitive rationality', *Journal of Marketing* 56: 68–83.
* Drucker, P.F. (1961) *The Practice of Management*, London: Mercury Books.
* Easton, G. (1990) 'Relationship between competitors', in Day, G.S., Weitz, B. and Wensley, R. (eds), *The Interface of Marketing and Strategy*, Conneticut: JAI Press.
* Easton, G., Burrell, G, Rothschild, D. and Shearman, C. (1992) *Managers and Competition*, Oxford: Basil Blackwell.
* Ghemawat, P. (1991) *Commitment: The Dynamic of Strategy*, New York: Free Press.
* Grant, R. (1991) 'The resource-based theory of competitive advantage', *Californian Management Review* 33:114–34.
* Hakansson, H. (1987) *Industrial Technological Development: A Network Approach*, London: Croom Helm.

* Hamel, G. and Prahalad, C.K. (1991) 'Corporate imagination and expeditionary marketing', *Harvard Business Review* July–August: 81–92.
* Henderson, B. (1980) 'Strategic and Natural Competition', *BCG Perspectives*, 231.
* Hodgkinson, G.P. and Johnston, G. (1994) 'Exploring the mental models of competitive strategists: the case for a processual approach', *Journal of Management Studies* (forthcoming).
* Kamakura, W. and Russel, G.J. (1989) 'A probabilistic choice model for market segmentation', *Journal of Marketing Research* 26: 379–90.
* Kogut, B. and Kulatilaka, N. (1992) 'Options thinking and platform investments: investing in opportunity', Working Paper Wharton School: April.
* Lambkin, M. and Day, G. (1989) 'Evolutionary processes in competitive markets: beyond the product life cycle', Journal of Marketing 53: 4–20.
* Leeflang, P.S.H. and Wittink, D. (1993) 'Diagnosing competition: developments and findings', in Laurent, G., Lillien, G.L. and Pras, B. (eds), *Research Traditions in Marketing*, Norwell MA: Kluwer Academic.
* Leeflang, P.S.H. and Wittink, D.(1996) 'Competitive reation versus consumer response: Do managers overreact?', *International Journal of Research in Marketing*,13: 103–20.
* Marsh, P., Barwise, P., Thomas, K. and Wensley, R. (1988) *Managing Strategic Investment Decisions in Large Diversified Companies*, London: London Business School Centre for Business Strategy.
* Mattsson, L.-G. (1997) '"Relationship marketing" and the "Markets-as-networks approach" – A comparative analysis of two evolving streams of research', *Journal of Marketing Management* 13: 447–61.
* McGee, J. and Thomas, H. (1986) 'Strategic groups: theory, research and taxonomy', *Strategic Management Journal* 7: 141–60.
* Mintzberg, H. and Waters, J.A. (1985) 'Of strategies deliberate and emergent', *Strategic Management Journal* 6: 257–72.
* Mintzberg, H, (1994) *The Rise and Fall of Strategic Planning*, Prentice-Hall
* Mumford, E. (1994) 'Tools for change: modern miracles or dangerous disasters?', Working Paper, Manchester: MBS.
* Myers, S.C. (1984) 'Finance theory and financial strategy', *Interfaces* 14: 126–37.
* Ohmae, K. (1982) *The Mind of the Strategist*, London: McGraw Hill.
* Porac, J. and Thomas, H. (1990) 'Taxonomic mental models in competitor definition', *Academy of Management Review* 15: 224–40.
* Pitts, A. (1994) 'Real options', Working paper Norwich: UEA March.
* Prahalad, C.K. and Bettis, R.A. (1989) 'The dominant logic: A new linkage between diversity and performance', *Strategic Management Journal* 10: 523–52.
* Reed, R. and DeFillippi, R.J. (1990) 'Casual ambiguity, barriers to imitation and sustainable competitive advantage', *Academy of Management Review* 15: 88–102.
* Reibstein, D. (1985) *Marketing: Concepts, Strategies and Decisions*, Englewood Cliffs, NJ: Prentice-Hall.
* Ries, A. and Trout, J. (1985) *Positioning: The battle for your mind*, London: McGraw-Hill.
* Rumelt, R.P (1996), 'The many faces of Honda', *Californian Management Review* 38: 103–11.
* Simon, H.A. (1979) 'Rational decision making in business organizations', *American Economic Review* September.
* Wensley, R (1993) 'On a clear day you can see the market', in Laurent, G., Lillien, G. and Pras, B. (eds), *Research Traditions in Marketing*, Norwell MA: Kluwer Academic, pp. 163–8.
* Wernerfeld, B. (1984) 'A resource-based view of the firm', *Strategic Management Journal* 5: 171–80.
* Wernerfeld, B. (1995) 'The resource-based view of the firm: ten years after', *Strategic Management Journal* 16: 171–4.
* Williams, J.R. (1992) 'How sustainable is your competitive advantage', *Californian Management Review* Spring: 29–51.

See also: THE ASSESSMENT OF MARKETING PERFORMANCE; BRANDING AND BRAND MANAGEMENT; CHANNEL MANAGEMENT; CONSUMER BEHAVIOUR; MARKETING – PHILOSOPHY OR FUNCTION?; MARKET SEGMENTATION; POSITIONING; PRICING; STRATEGIC ALLIANCES AND SUPPLIER APRTNERSHIPS; THE MARKETING MIX

Strategic marketing planning

1 Rationality in planning
2 Strategic marketing planning
3 Setting tentative objectives
4 Historical review and situation analysis
5 Interpretation of the data collected
6 Calculation of the planning gap
7 Problem diagnosis
8 The search for strategies
9 Evaluation of strategies
10 Contingency planning
11 Current issues in strategic marketing planning

Overview

The previous entry dealt with the nature of marketing strategy and its relationships to corporate and business strategy (see MARKETING STRATEGY). This entry centres on the strategic marketing planning process itself. It defines the rationality, role and scope of strategic marketing planning, the planning stages, the decision processes and the search and evaluation of proposed strategies.

1 Rationality in planning

In planning we look ahead to decide what to do. The planning process itself is a systematic way of approaching the following questions:

- Where are we now and how did we get here?
- What is the future?
- Where do we want to go?
- How do we get there?
- How much will it cost?
- How can progress be measured?

Although there is never any certainty about the future, every business or organization will sensibly lean towards a proactive rather than a reactive stance. A proactive stance is one where the organization tries to forecast the future in order to influence it, that is, plan to adapt to it rather than just to surrender to it. This contrasts with a mere reactive stance where action mainly takes place in response to events with no plan to anticipate events and seek to influence them.

One ground for claiming that formal or systematic planning is likely to be more effective than improvisation is because built into the procedure are rules that goals be specified and relevant options be evaluated against the evidence. Lack of thought about goals, insufficient information search to understand problems and alternative solutions, biased evaluation of proposed solutions are the factors that undermine problem solving in business. Formal planning imposes a discipline favouring thought about goals, an extensive search for solutions (options or alternatives) and an unbiased evaluation of the evidence for each option considered.

In spite of what has been said about the need for formal (systematic) planning, there is more to planning than systematic procedure. There is a need to understand the problems of biased thinking and to recognize the political nature of the strategic planning process. In any case following logical procedures and processes is not enough since this is analogous to focusing on the computer program and neglecting the data itself. The focus, it is argued, should be on strategy content.

2 Strategic marketing planning

Organizations that undertake formal planning typically operate a hierarchy of plans. First, there is the planning that occurs at corporate level to guide the whole organization. Strategic marketing planning will get direction from such corporate-level planning, particularly over where the firm will seek its markets, on which strengths or competencies it should build a competitive advantage, and which investment objectives to adopt for what product group, whether growth, hold/defend, harvest, turnabout or whatever.

Marketing is a boundary-spanning activity in that marketing relates the organization to those groups beyond its boundary who use, buy, sell or can influence what is offered and/or sold. Strategic marketing planning (SMP) is planning concerned with the broad conception of how resources are to be deployed to induce those outside groups to respond favourably to the organization's offerings or to overcome resistances from such groups to the organization's marketing efforts. The output of SMP is an integrated system of plans designed to cater to the present or latent wants of some target customer group(s). In the process it addresses some major questions for the business:

- Over what present or future markets or market segments should we deploy our resources to exploit the firm's thrust (distinct functional skills) and core competencies (the firm's demonstrated capabilities in the market)?
- How should we deploy our resources over the marketing mix to position ourselves in the market *vis-à-vis* competition and (hopefully) in the mind of the consumer?
- Why should the target customer group(s) buy from us?
- How are we positioned to do battle with our rivals?

Although being reactive suggests being flexible and having the courage and confidence to be able to defend the current position, being proactive requires the greater courage to take risks in anticipating the future and trying to see what we might become.

Plans in marketing are typically yearly plans with some firms tying the annual plan into some, say, five-year plan: today's annual plan is the detailed plan for the immediate financial year which, if successful, is the first step to achieving the five-year plan that is reviewed and updated to reflect needed changes. What follows considers the process of strategic marketing planning on the assumption that those concerned with corporate-level planning have set objectives, defined the firm's business or businesses, and determined investment objectives. The planning steps to be discussed are:

- setting tentative objectives for the market;
- historical review and situation analysis;
- interpretation of the data collected;
- calculation of the planning gap (if any);
- problem diagnosis;
- search for strategies;
- evaluation of strategies and choice of strategy;
- contingency planning.

Every organization that adopts a formal approach to planning will follow stages somewhat similar to those above. This is not surprising as they mimic the typical steps in problem solving.

Each of the stages in strategic marketing planning will now be discussed while recognizing that systematic planning, rational decision processes, political networking and, last but not least, ideas for strategy content are all essential for strategic marketing planning (SMP) to be effective.

3 Setting tentative objectives

An organization cannot set realistic, realizable objectives until it has the requisite information but, on the basis of experience, marketing management will none the less have tentative goals on sales volume, market share or whatever indicators represent progress towards accomplishing the firm's vision. What exactly these tentative goals are will be influenced by subjective estimates of what is considered reasonable at the time in relation to what resources are likely to be available.

For a manager to be able to direct an activity towards the achievement of some goal, it must be possible to imagine the goal in a way that is meaningful for guiding the activity. This is why goals purely in terms of profit are inadequate; they offer too little guidance.

4 Historical review and situation analysis

To develop a marketing strategy an organization requires information on its past and present position. It needs to analyse information both about its environment and about itself. This is the purpose of doing a historical review and situation analysis.

A 'historical review' records and orders the historical facts about the company, or its products or one of its brands. But understanding how some situation has come about is not identical to understanding the situation as is. There is also a need for a 'situational analysis'. Whereas the historical review is a sort of developmental analysis, the situation analysis is cross-sectional in that it focuses on the current situation, ignoring processes through time. In practice, the historical review and the situation analysis tend to be closely interwoven, the aim of the two of them being to:

- develop a 'reference projection' or a forecast of the future (e.g. in respect to earnings, market share and so on) assuming that current plans and practices remain unchanged;
- identify strengths, weaknesses, opportunities and threats (SWOT);
- determine the historical strengths, capabilities or competencies of the organization and corresponding competitive advantages of the firm.

A strategy is formulated with respect to some business unit or programme and is limited in its scope by what is considered relevant to that business or unit or programme. In the case of marketing planning, the minimum factors considered would be a realistic analysis of the company in terms of its markets, earnings, sales history, innovativeness, strengths and capabilities together with forecasts in respect to factors in the external environment that could affect its success.

Table 1 is a typical checklist of information that is collected. What information is actually collected will depend, as always, on what we believe to be relevant to the analysis. Nothing is relevant that does not relate to some definite question. New techniques for analysing data or new theories are in effect new questions or new ways of asking questions, and until these techniques and theories were introduced, certain facts were not considered relevant. However, as our understanding of marketing grows, there are changes in what we regard as relevant information.

How much information to collect is a constant problem. There is a need for a 'stopping rule' that relates to the cost and benefits of collecting more information. However, no such rule is at present sufficiently operational to be in general use.

External environment

Although a firm is a more self-steering system than a flower in the breeze or a bullet following a predetermined path, it still operates within constraints imposed by the external economy. Every firm thus needs to consider the implications of lifestyle changes, emerging technologies and shifting social and cultural conditions and values. The external environment can affect company performance; factors such as the gross national product (GNP), government legislation, tax changes and interest rates, new technologies and demographics. A growth in national income brings with it a readiness to spend in new directions. An improved level of general education affects consumer tastes and responsiveness to different types of advertising. Shifts in the age distribution of the population make different aggregate demands on industry, and so on. All such trends have a direct impact on markets. Trends need to be identified together with their likely turning-points. Neither is easy. For example, the turn-of-the-century concept of the aeroplane was an elaborate and expensive toy with little commercial future.

Market

Information on market structure reflects Porter's (1980, 1985) five factors (discussed below) of threat of entry; degree of rivalry; substitute inroads from other industries; and the bargaining power of buyers and suppliers. Additionally, information is needed on market growth, seasonality of sales or demand fluctuations, market share trends and industry profitability (see MARKET RESEARCH; POSITIONING).

Customer

Although the 'customer' could be considered under the category of 'market', it deserves to be given visibility as the customer is the major player of interest. A marketing manager would like to know all about buyers and any others who influence the buying decision: who they are, what they seek, where they buy and use the product, when they buy and use the product and how they use the product; and trends among these (see CONSUMER BEHAVIOUR). Just as the successful sculptor in clay must know the behaviour of clay under different conditions, marketing managers must know as much as possible about the behaviour of their buyers. Table 1 lists some of the most important information to collect on the customer.

Marketing management

Table 1 Checklist for strategic marketing planning

1 External environment	*2 Market*
Social environment: • social movements (e.g. the consumer movement) • sociocultural drift (e.g. working wives, lifestyles) • agents for change (e.g. rising educational levels) • demographic changes Add for international markets: • culture (values, beliefs, e.g. religious, social institutions) • language • form of government, ideology and stability • foreign policy Economic environment: • trends in GNP • interest rates • levels of discretionary income • currency fluctuations • inflation rates • unemployment levels • fiscal policies Add for international markets: • balance of payments • wage/price controls Technical environment: • government and industry spending on R&D • technological forecasts • patent protection Legal environment: • government regulation and deregulation • tax legislation • trademark legislation • international trade regulations • employment laws	• barriers to entry (threat of entry) • rivalry • substitutes from other industries • power of buyers • power of suppliers • evolutionary stage • growth rate • demand fluctuations • industry profitability • market share trends *3 Customer* • different choice criteria • shopping habits • attitudes • decision processes • influences *4 Competition* • number of immediate rivals in served markets • identity of and market shares of rivals • strategies of competitors • innovativeness and resourcefulness of competitors • leadership in marketing, manufacture and technology • relative costs • erosion of patent protection/proprietary knowledge *5 Company* • trends in sales, net income and net cash flow • thrust/core competencies • share of served markets • growth path • innovativeness • capacity utilization • cost trends

Competition

The firm is seldom in the position where competition can be ignored. There are usually other companies out there with whom the firm must do battle. A firm needs to know how to evaluate threats from competitors by knowing something about their performance in the market, their capabilities and their likely intentions. Although marketers often talk about how their task is to beat competition, they will not do this just by looking at what the competition is doing (although this is important) but generally by understanding the customer better than the competition do. However, Table 1 shows the key information to collect on market rivals (see POSITIONING).

Company

To know one's own company is to know about its strengths and weaknesses as a basis for considering a vulnerability analysis and in order to develop a competitive advantage based on the firm's core capabilities or competencies. Table 1 lists what needs to be considered on the organization's past and present position.

5 Interpretation of the data collected

Interpretation of the data collected is key since how the situation is interpreted determines what strategies appear most appropriate. All marketing strategies are based on some view of what constitutes the 'reality' or the true position of the firm as strategies are formulated on the manager's representation of that reality. When managers get the picture all wrong, the development of the cleverest of strategies is misdirected. Interpretations that reflect more a brilliance of imagination than any real knowledge of how things work, are likely to be wrong.

No final, absolutely true interpretation can be demonstrated while some conjecture is inevitable as facts are selected, connected and put into a plausible pattern. But interpretations are far from being arbitrary since interpretations must square with the evidence. The better interpretations will be consistent with the agreed facts and account for the facts in a more coherent way: bringing the maximum number of facts into a meaningful relationship with the minimum of conjecture. None the less, disagreements over what the 'facts' mean will occur as they are selected, ordered, weighted and generally interpreted against some perspective or set of presuppositions. Just as those who believe that all dreams reflect secret fears and wishes will interpret dreams in that way, so managers are also in danger of selecting from the data collected only that which suits their presuppositions. But such distortion can be reduced by making clear:

- what is really known? (e.g. actual sales);
- what is unclear? (e.g. competitor intentions);
- what is being presupposed that might be questioned? (e.g. that certain trends will persist)

We all react to the situation as perceived and perceptions can be influenced by wishful thinking. We may seek only confirmatory evidence for what we believe to be the situation and interpret evidence to fit preconceptions. Choosing an interpretation in line with some favoured strategy is particularly common since extremely good or extremely bad experiences with a particular strategy can bias all data interpretation. In fact, if an early examination of data collected supports the preferred strategy, further analysis is apt to cease, while if it does not the analysis is likely to be carried out in much more depth.

What is sought at this stage is an assessment of strengths and weaknesses, opportunities and threats. This is the so-called SWOT analysis. This can be followed by matching strengths against opportunities, weaknesses against opportunities, weaknesses against strengths and strengths against threats. Part of this analysis should include a 'vulnerability analysis', which aims to identify where the firm is vulnerable, such as an overdependence on a few big customers or just one industry, plus also a listing of the 'critical success factors'. Critical success factors are those elements of the business (whether resource inputs, internal organization, processes or whatever) where high performance cannot be taken for granted; yet high performance on these elements, whether singly or in combination, is essential for success. Thus the buying of wool is likely to be a critical success factor in the case of the manufacturer of woolen worsteds; low cost production in the case of ball point pens and a marketing strategy ensuring wide distribution in the case of the gasoline manufacturer.

Another part of the analysis might focus on past decision weaknesses in the organization, namely, failure to anticipate, failure to learn, or failure to adapt when the information at the time suggests such failure was avoidable. It may be that all three failures occur. For example, in the 1980s IBM failed to anticipate that when it gave up leasing its computers to customers, it would lose that continuous relationship with its customers which had previously kept IBM close to its market. Similarly, IBM failed to learn that phasing out old technology slowly, so as not to disrupt sales of its oldest machines, led to a loss in leadership as rivals rushed to fill the gap. Finally, IBM failed to adapt to changes in the market when mainframe computers (the speciality of IBM) were losing their dominance. We need to exmaine past errors and recognize that learning is impeded when the chief concern is to defend past decisions.

Of course, nothing can guarantee that a decision, however well made, will turn out right. It is fallacious to assume that a bad outcome implies the decision was badly made since it may have been the most rationally defensible answer at the time. In any case, past strategies are seldom absolutely wrong or right but have different degrees of imperfection.

The various techniques, like Boston Consulting Group's (BCG's) growth market share matrix, General Electric's (GE's) business screen and Porter's work (mentioned later), plus various quantitative techniques, all help to order and bring out the implications of the data collected. These techniques can be useful in offering frameworks, analogies and models that help structure a problem situation and reduce mental overload as well as being a protection from a complete degeneration into *ad hoc* analysis.

6 Calculation of the planning gap

What do the 'facts' suggest will be the future if the firm takes no action to change current strategies? Such a prediction is known as a 'reference projection'. A reference projection is the future that can be expected in the absence of planned change. The reference projection is compared with some 'target projection' or the set of tentative goals which the firm sets for itself. The planning gap (performance gap) is the difference between the target and the reference projections:

Planning gap (performance gap) =
Target projection less reference projection

The planning gaps identified will depend on which performances are of interest. At the highest level, it could be cash flow projections, economic value added, cash flow return on investment, earnings per share, sales and market share or various financial indices like return on investment (ROI). At the marketing level, it would be in terms of sales, market share, costs, market penetration or various behavioural indices like buyer attitudes.

7 Problem diagnosis

If a firm has a large planning gap, we speak loosely of its being the problem. More accurately, the planning gap is not the problem but the symptom of one. The recognition of a problem situation is not in itself the identification of the actual problem. We do not discover a problem but diagnose one. Problem diagnosis aims at identifying the *type* of solution that applies which is the first step on the road to developing an actual solution, just as diagnosing a failure to start the car as being due to some electrical fault, is the first step towards getting the car started again. Unfortunately, different people will make different diagnoses, depending on their experience, professional expertise and their concerns. Of course, some companies may evade responsibility and define the problem as a problem of persuading the government to increase tariffs on their foreign competitors' products. Here the solution is viewed as increasing the firm's political muscle.

We cannot understand a problem without understanding what would count as a solution, just as we cannot understand an objective without understanding what would count as the achievement of it. The actual problem that is addressed depends somewhat on which individual or group can make the problem, as they see it, count. But all management groups in a company are influenced by credible arguments and so true technical expertise usually wins the day. Hopefully, it must for if the wrong problem is addressed, the wrong decisions are made and this can be more wasteful of resources than solving the right problem in an inefficient way. Although we hesitate to acknowledge it, the fact is that once we move away from some pure deductive system like mathematics, we are in the realm of persuasion where persuasive rhetoric is crucial so that a dramatic description of what is considered to be the problem can emotionally compel attention and often our assent.

8 The search for strategies

The strategic options for closing the planning gap should not only fit the problematic situation and take account of trends and competition but should also exploit the firm's core competencies and strengths. Where the solution is other than a crisis one, there is time for more reflective planning, guided by:

- the situation as revealed by the performance gap;
- the perceived problem;
- the strengths, weaknesses, opportunities and threats identified in the historical review/situation analysis;
- current strategies and policies;
- existing capabilities or competencies.

The strategy search process should always allow for the possibility of inspiration, which may beat anything arrived at by methodical analysis. It is not uncommon for someone to come up with an idea that is instantly recognizable as being the right answer: genius sometimes lies in what appears, once stated, as a truism. The inspired solution is thus accepted, not because it saves time (this would be just to accept a faster way of producing unsatisfactory end results) but because it is perceived to be superior and effective. This said, the identification of appropriate strategies rests on having the requisite experience and the content of the strategy, not procedure, is all important. Where the requisite experience is lacking, the search for strategies becomes opaque.

The mental screening and evaluation of strategies can be demanding. In effect we are mentally rehearsing hypotheses about the relationship between strategies and their likely benefits – but not just benefits since strategies can have side-effects which can constitute dysfunctional consequences. Thus IBM may calculate with some precision the benefits in profitable sales from introducing a personal computer that is competitively priced. More difficult to calculate is the effect on the IBM image and the dilution of that image as very up-market. With many possible strategies and fuzzy endless chains of possible outcomes, it is not surprising that managers are apt to focus on the strategies with which their experience makes them comfortable. Unfortunately, this often means that the cards are stacked against the truly novel and imaginative solution.

Growth strategies entail broadening the firm's technological base, widening its customer base or widening or adding to the functions it serves. Because all growth strategies involve one or a combination of these, the growth option categories are:

- market penetration: same products/same markets;
- market development: same products/new markets;
- product development: new products/same markets;
- diversification and vertical integration: new products/new markets.

(Although vertical integration is typically classified as a form of diversification, in diversification proper the outputs result from activities that are not vertically related to producing the original set of outputs. Vertical integration and diversification can also usually be distinguished by the motives that lie behind their adoption. The motive behind vertical integration is usually the desire to reduce costs and/or to gain greater control over production and/or distribution. It is a move towards self-sufficiency since vertical integration means fewer external dependencies. Diversification, on the other hand, is usually sought to exploit profitable market opportunities and to reduce the risks arising from 'putting all one's eggs in the same basket' though, with regard to the latter, it must be said that much diversification has not proved profitable.)

There are other investment objectives besides growth. There is the hold/defend objective as well as turnaround, harvesting and divesting. The hold/defend is common when firms see no possibility of growth or are satisfied with their current position in the market. The aim is to retain existing customers while attracting enough of the new entrants into the market to replace those that leave. In the most general terms, hold/defend strategies require the firm to keep abreast of competition by upgrading the firm's offering and matching whatever the competition has to offer.

The turnabout or turnaround objective is, as the name suggests, concerned with restructuring the organization or, more simply, 'putting it on its feet' again. A firm in a situation that is ripe for a turnaround strategy typically faces persistent declines in market share, declining profit margins and working capital, increasing debt and probably high voluntary management turnover as managers become aware that the firm is in trouble. A common cause of decline is the result of the firm moving away from its distinctive thrusts (distinctive functional skills) and core competencies (demonstrated capabilities in the market) with a proliferation of products that have nothing distinctive to offer. Sometimes thrusts and core competencies are eroded by cost-cutting, without always knowing such erosion is occurring as organizations often do not know what lies behind their past success. Thus Delta Air Lines in the 1990s dramatically cut costs and, in the process, seemed to forget that service was what gave it an edge (see, for example, the *Economist* 20 April 1996: 69).

'Harvesting' is a way of winding down a business by accepting a continuing decline in market share in exchange for an increase in net cash flow. Many a product that throws off no cash may in fact do so if all promotional support is withdrawn but perhaps not for long as competitors rush in to exploit the absence of support. It is not always possible to harvest a business, however, and some products or businesses continue to be a cash drain regardless of what support expenditure is withdrawn. In such a situation, a firm will try to divest the business. Divestment carries the notion of an orderly approach to leaving the business.

Porter (1980, 1985) argues that it is an industry's competitive structure, as reflected in the strength of just five forces, that determines the state of competition (both the rules of competition and the strategies available for competing) and ultimately the profit potential of the industry. The five forces that give rise to industry profitability are: threat of entry; degree of rivalry; pressure from substitutes; bargaining power of buyers; bargaining power of suppliers. He claims there are just three generic strategies for coping with the five forces. The first strategy is to aim at overall cost leadership to produce a cost advantage. The danger of this strategy is that some technological innovation could wipe out the cost advantage, while an obsessive fixation with cost could result in an insensitivity to changing market wants. The second strategy is that of differentiation whereby something unique is offered to the market. Given some market value in that uniqueness, it is a barrier to entry, shields the firm from rivals and substitutes, increases the dependency of customers and provides the possibility of muting supplier power through the size of its purchases. The risks associated with the strategy are either that differentiation may be imitated (the advantage is not sustainable) or that a rival's cost (price advantage) is too great to be overcome by the benefits of the differentiation. The third strategy is segmentation where overall cost leadership or a differentiated offering is applied but in this case only to a part or segment of the market (see MARKET SEGMENTATION).

It is not clear to many marketers that there are three distinct strategies in that it is difficult to think of product differentiation that does not appeal to just a segment of the market or, if it appeals to the whole market, it is likely to come with a price tag that many in the market are just not willing to pay. In either case differentiation implies segmentation. Porter now refers only to cost leadership and differentiation. Marketers would be tempted to say that both are paths to segmentation in that there can be price segments and there can be segments based on non-price differentiation. We are, of course, talking about *marketing* strategies and arguing that segmentation is inevitable, even if a firm aims its one product at all the market. But Porter may be arguing about strategies in terms of the company's thrust. Thus a firm can focus on cost leadership through its manufacturing efficiency or on differentiation through its marketing or new product development. But these come out as differences in how we segment the market. A recent book by Treacy and Wiersema (1997), which has an echo of Porter, makes this clear in arguing that market leader companies fall into just one of the following three categories and no company they know manages to be world class on more than one of these three dimensions.

- The first category of company focuses on operational excellence, appealing to a broad-based market with products that are competitively priced.
- The second category of company focuses on products being leaders in the field on styling or performance.
- The third category of company focuses on service and being best on service in the product category field.

9 Evaluation of strategies

Management evaluates its strategies before adoption and after implementation. In either case strategies can only be evaluated against some criteria stemming implicitly or explicitly from objectives. Evaluative criteria after strategy implementation revolve around the strategy's effectiveness and reliability. Thus a strategy is effective if it achieves its goals, and it is reliable if it is able to do so consistently.

In evaluating strategies as a basis for adopting one, the criteria selected should help predict a strategy's future effectiveness and reliability after implementation. This is seldom a straightforward process since facts are often uncertain, values and priorities among objectives often in dispute, while the stakes can be high, with the decision urgent and under time pressure. No amount of analysis can ever tell us which is the best possible strategy. It may well be one we have not even considered. All we can do is to pick one which, given the evidence, seems *likely* to be best. Even assembling the relevant evidence and considering it objectively, is never entirely pure since the tradeoffs we make and the weighting of evidence reflect our values and emotional preferences. Given the many uncertainties, strategy choice is not just a matter of logic alone: proposed strategies are not ruled out by logic alone. None the less, every proposed strategy should be evaluated for desirability, practical feasibility and commercial viability.

Desirability

The first step in evaluation is to think in terms of what objectives or goals are being sought. What would count as success? A common error is not to think sufficiently broadly about goals. This is because goals are typically multiple and conflicting so there is a need to establish priorities or, alternatively, set some of the goals as constraints or semi-constraints. A common reason for irreconcilable conflicts among parties to any decision lies in one party having an extremely narrow set of goals. But there will always be some conflict among those involved in SMP because of differential goals; differential perceptions of reality; differential information possessed and differing views about the consequences arising from the adoption of various strategies. This is not to suggest that all conflict over strategy is bad since there can be constructive as well as destructive conflict. Debate can be vigorous and sharp without polarization and this is welcome when the alternative might be 'groupthink'. With groupthink there is a collective sense of not needing outside opinions or ideas, a sense of collective certainty, invulnerability, and an illusion of unanimity. These are just the conditions leading to error arising from an inadequate consideration of goals, of alternative strategies, and the evidence for each. Under the heading of desirability we might ask the following:

1. Does the proposed strategy promote objectives? Any proposed strategy must contribute to the company's mission and goals, cohere with investment objectives and, in the case of the marketing strategy, exploit the firm's thrust (distinctive) and core competencies and be concerned with building customer trust and loyalty.

2. Is the degree of risk acceptable? Risk here is the probability of earning less than what is sought and the magnitude of possible losses. Measuring the degree of risk is generally a matter of judgement. There can never be any certainty of measurement, since the relationship between options (strategies) and outcomes (results) is never entirely clear when long-term consequences are influenced by unpredictable competitive actions while the wants and beliefs of those in the market are often fickle. In the most general terms, it can be said that the more an organization moves away from its existing markets and core competencies, the more risky the strategy.

3. Does the strategy promote portfolio balance? There is a need for a balanced mix in a firm's portfolio of products so that, say, all the firm's offerings are not catering to stagnant markets but the firm is also backing future likely winners.

4. Is the investment required acceptable? The investment requirement has to be estimated. There are the initial entry-level costs and the costs of securing market share. Start-up or entry costs can usually be reasonably estimated but more problematic is the money needed to achieve an acceptable market share.

If a strategy is desirable there must be a strategic fit between the strategy and behaviour in the market, between strategy and internal capabilities and resources and, finally, a fit between the strategy and higher level plans since it is part of the hierarchy of plans. But even if all these 'fits' were in place, it would merely show that means suit ends. This is not enough in itself since there is a need to take account of likely undesirable side effects (dysfunctional consequences).

Practical feasibility

The problem of the feasibility of proposals receives too little attention in discussions on strategy formulation. Although it is accepted that judging feasibility involves judgement and an imaginative recreation of the likely problems encountered in implementing the strategy, the importance of experience is seldom emphasized enough. A strategy on paper is just a thin conceptual creation which has to be fleshed out in detail and this detail needs to be visualized when considering feasibility. There is a good deal of difference between having an intimate acquaintance with the strategy as written and knowing how it will work when implemented. This visualization of how it will perform is closely linked to past analogous experiences. The feasibility of a marketing plan or strategy necessitates knowing about the role of product, price, promotion and distribution; knowing about the likely behaviour of customers and competitors, while knowing a good deal about the specifics of marketing like distribution possibilities.

Commercial viability

Under the heading of commercial viability, we might consider the following:

- Will the strategy yield the profit/cash flow sought? Estimates of potential payoffs can range all the way from what is little more than prophecy to predictions of sales, costs and profits based on hard evidence.
- Does the strategy contribute to minimizing likely competitive retaliation? The selection of any strategy is accompanied by the selection of rivals with whom the firm will do battle. The question arises whether the strategy minimizes the potential for competitive retaliation.
- What are the impediments to achieving commercial goals? This requires us to think about obstacles that may be in the way of success and to plan to get round them.

We make decisions about strategy on the basis of beliefs about the outcomes of each option in relation to our goals. Errors occur when we do not consider the whole set of goals which interest us or we do not examine enough options or do not objectively weigh up the evidence. Weighing up the evidence can be difficult since the process can be so distorted by wishful thinking. Strangely, overconfidence is most common with new projects when caution is needed and people fail to look for evidence that has the potential to reduce faith in their beliefs. Evidence that confirms what we feel to be true is accepted while contrary evidence is dismissed. This suggests the increased need to thoroughly evaluate any proposed strategy for commercial viability. When this is done for several proposed strategies, management will have a good appreciation of the risks involved.

10 Contingency planning

Behind every set of plans is a set of assumptions that needs to be realized if the plans are to be a success. Certain things are assumed to remain constant like government policy or certain trends are assumed to persist like the increasing cost of healthcare. A number of these assumptions have to do with the environment and so are constantly being invalidated by a rapidly changing environment (see ENVIRONMENTAL ANALYSIS). We all know that strategies rarely work out exactly as planned because markets are complex, rivals do not stand still while consumer wants and beliefs are also subject to change. There is a danger in not recognizing this and so exaggerating our ability to control events. It is common to persist with some strategy even though failure and continuing failure is all too obvious to outsiders. This is the 'sunk cost error'.

Where different sets of assumptions are equally tenable, contingency plans are needed. More typically firms allow for certain of the major assumptions being invalid and have alternative plans in reserve. More and more firms see the need to develop contingency plans, just as the military have always done because the need there is so much more pressing. Monitoring the assumptions of a plan as it is put into effect is a major check on the plan's continuing validity. When assumptions are no longer valid, plans need to be revised or previously devised contingency plans put into effect. But plans in practice need to be revised all the time. Moreover, planning must affect today's decisions if it is to be treated seriously by operational managers: long-term planning should be tied to guiding today's decisions.

11 Current issues in strategic marketing planning

Any firm that has adopted a systematic approach to planning will have followed something like the sequence of stages discussed in this entry. But, to repeat, following a sequence of stages is like following some computer program; it does not bring forth a successful strategy in itself as this depends on the data and ideas entering the program. The key to developing an effective strategy lies not in following a sequence of stages, though this does help, but in answering effectively the following questions:

1. What should be the content of our objectives?
2. What is the most relevant information to collect?
3. What is the correct problem diagnosis?
4. What strategies should be considered given our objectives?
5. What evidence is relevant to the evaluation of proposed strategies?

We might also add that, in SMP, logic can only proscribe by identifying inconsistencies and conceptual and logical confusions. But logic cannot prescribe the actual strategy. The selection of any strategy incorporates the values and emotional commitments of the various participants in determining options and tradeoffs and the weighting of the evidence. In such a process there will always be political in-fighting and positions to defend. SMP will never be just a matter of following some formula. Current interest is no longer focused on the sequence of steps in evolving a strategy but on identifying flawed decision processes, tactics for coping with the politics arising from SMP being such a value-laden activity and, last but not least, identifying strategic options and the marketing conditions that suggest when they are most appropriate.

JOHN O'SHAUGHNESSY
UNIVERSITY OF CAMBRIDGE
AND COLUMBIA UNIVERSITY

Further reading

(References cited in the text marked *)

Certo, Samuel C. and Paul, Peter J. (1988) *Strategic Management: Concepts and Applications*, New York: Random House.

Goodstein, Leonard, Nolan, Timothy, and Pfeiffer, J. William (1993) *Applied Strategic Planning: How to develop a plan that really works*, New York: McGraw-Hill Inc.

Hill, Charles W. L. and Jones, Gareth R. (1992) *Strategic Management: An Integrated Approach*, Boston: Houghton Mifflin Co.

Mintzberg, Henry (1994), *The Rise and Fall of Strategic Planning*, Englewood Cliffs, NJ: Prentice-Hall.

* Porter, Michael E. (1980) *Competitive Strategy: Techniques for Analyzing Your Business and Competitors*, New York: The Free Press.

* Porter, Michael E. (1985) *Competitive Advantage*, New York: The Free Press.

Rao, Vithala R. and Steckel, Joel H. (1998) *Analysis for Strategic Marketing*, New York: Addison-Wesley

* Treacy, Michael and Wiersema, Fred (1997) *The Discipline of Market Leaders*, New York: HarperCollins.

Walker, Orville C., Boyd, Harper W. and Larreche, Jean-Claude (1992) *Marketing Strategy: Planning and Implementation*, Homewood, Il: Irwin.

See also: CONSUMER BEHAVIOUR; ENVIRONMENTAL ANALYSIS; LOGISTICS AND VALUE CREATION; MARKET RESEARCH, MARKET SEGMENTATION; POSITIONING; PRICING; PRODUCT POLICY; SALES PROMOTION; THE MARKETING MIX

Marketing organization and management

1 Introduction
2 The organizational dimensions of marketing
3 Organizational forms and marketing
4 Marketing organization and marketing change
5 New organizational forms in marketing
6 The management agenda for the marketing organization

Overview

The goal of this entry is to evaluate the rapidly changing structuring and positioning choices faced by management in locating marketing responsibilities in the organization, but also more broadly in the context of the new organizational forms which are emerging as new ways of going to market, most particularly the alliance-based network organization.

1 Introduction

Issues of marketing organization are attracting a renewed urgency, George Day observes:

> Had we been contemplating the future of marketing a decade ago, organizational issues would have been at the periphery. ... As we approach the millennium, organizational issues are rising to the top of the agenda on the future of marketing.
>
> (Day 1997)

Indeed, in conventional treatments, marketing organization was primarily concerned with the departmentation of marketing (Weigand 1961) and the internal arrangements for the administration of functions within marketing (how to structure sales operations, advertising management, distribution, and so on) (e.g. Bund and Carroll 1957). However, in recent years the marketing organization question has developed far beyond these internal administrative issues. Marketing's role in the organization is articulated as a fundamental customer-driven process, involving the entire organization (McKenna 1991a) and this contemporary view of marketing's scope has important implications for the organizational form of marketing. Marketing organization has become a fundamental strategic issue concerned with intra-organizational relationships and inter-organizational alliances, and the management of critical boundary-spanning environmental interfaces.

The context for 'post-functional marketing' (Hulbert and Pitt 1996) is increasingly seen as part of a new era of market-based strategic management, which takes place in a 're-invented organization' (Cravens et al. 1997). These evolutionary changes in the role and functioning of marketing are dramatic and have major implications for the organization of marketing for the future, and perhaps most particularly the marketing strategy implementation capabilities of organizations (Piercy 1998).

Webster (1997) has recently characterized this evolution of the marketing organization in terms of a number of phases of change:

- First phase – equates marketing with sales and demand generation activities.
- Second phase – bureaucratic and hierarchical organizational forms are developed to plan and control the performance of specialists in areas like marketing research and sales promotion within the sales organization.
- Third phase – marketing becomes a function distinct from sales, pursuing an integrated marketing strategy, often in conflict with sales and weakly integrated with other business functions.
- Fourth phase – marketing competence is integrated with other business functions in team-centred organizational processes focused on the customer.

We will give some consideration to the likely forms and characteristics of such phase 4 marketing organizations in later parts of this article.

This evolution of the marketing organization can be traced to both rapid changes in the marketing environment, and also to the (partly consequent) shifting role of marketing in the modern corporation. For example, Achrol (1991) characterizes the emergent marketing environment in terms of diversity, knowledge-richness, and turbulence, which leads to flatter organizations with 'fuzzier lines of authority, extensive delegation of decision making, and a great emphasis on teamwork'.

Further, Webster (1992) argues that continuing evolution of the marketing discipline, as well as response to environmental change, will demand the adoption of new organizational forms, including strategic partnerships and networks to replace traditional bureaucratic hierarchical organizations. Rapid environmental change and customer diversity will require the marketing organization to respond quickly to new challenges. In this future scenario, increasing attention will focus on the problems of managing strategic partnerships in marketing (see STRATEGIC ALLIANCES AND SUPPLIER PARTNERSHIPS).

This article examines the full range of questions implied by the arguments above. First, we will consider the organizational 'dimensions' of marketing in terms of the impact of structure on the implementation and operation of marketing. We will then discuss briefly the conventional view of the marketing organization and examine some of the empirical evidence collected in this area, as well as views of the future of the marketing organization. Coverage will then broaden to consider the imperatives leading to newer and more innovative perspectives on marketing processes, and hence on marketing organization, leading to a consideration of the new organizational forms which have emerged and are likely to continue to develop in marketing. The article will conclude with a management agenda to be addressed in confronting the organizational dimensions of marketing.

2 The organizational dimensions of marketing

Ames (1968) distinguished the 'trappings' of marketing organization from the 'substance' of marketing. In fact, the pervasiveness and importance of organizational issues in implementing marketing have become increasingly evident in recent years.

Marketing organization and the implementation of marketing strategy

The organizational theorists' theorem that 'structure follows strategy' (e.g. Chandler 1962, Franko 1974) suggests that the implementation of marketing strategies will require the design and adoption of the appropriate administrative and organizational arrangements. For example, at the simplest level, 'going international' might lead to the development of some kind of international marketing organization – whether an export department, an international division, or simply an international sales/distribution office. Many authorities (e.g. Hughes 1980, Bonoma 1985, Cespedes 1991) cite inappropriate and inadequate internal structures and systems as a major source of implementation failures in marketing. Moreover, the unprecedented reforming of many business firms during the last decade documents executives' dissatisfaction with the existing structures of their marketing.

Marketing organization as a determinant of marketing strategy

Importantly, marketing structures may be seen as a *determinant* of marketing strategy, on the grounds that structure influences how organizational members perceive the environment, and represents the source of significant pressures towards maintaining the *status quo* in many organizations (Corey and Star 1971, Baligh and Burton 1979). In this sense, marketing organization may actually shape the strategic choices made, and this may be in unhelpful ways. Pursuing the internationalization example, not having any formal structure for international marketing may lead to the neglect of international issues in marketing strategy.

Marketing organization as part of marketing strategy

Increasingly we see that the organizational arrangements for marketing in a company have significance extending far beyond 'trappings'. The signal sent by the formal organizational arrangements for marketing is underlined by Carl Gustin at Kodak:

> At Kodak, we think marketing matters more than ever; that's why we formed the office of

Chief Marketing Officer over two years ago. ... If you don't do product design, R&D, financial business modeling and everything else in response to customer requirements, sure, you may survive. But you won't grow.

(Gustin 1997, p. 6)

Indeed, it has long been argued that in many situations the way marketing is organized is actually *part* of marketing strategy. For example, Levitt (1980) suggested that if marketing success depends on competitive differentiation, then this differentiation may be based on 'anything' including the structure of the marketing organization. As will be seen below, modern claims for the potency of relationship marketing, service quality, customer care, and the like, rest in part on the ability of the organization to effectively manage the customer/organization interface.

For instance, Doyle (1997) has identified the strategic imperatives and priorities for marketing as:

- *speed* – in reducing 'design to delivery' cycle times;
- *customization* – to meet customer needs in increasingly fragmented markets;
- *quality* – as a basic prerequisite for competitiveness;
- *information* – as a source of competitive advantage;
- *core focus* – on real corporate capabilities;
- *globalization* – to spread risks and costs internationally;
- *software differentiation* – augmenting products with service, and the like;
- *partnerships* – with customers and distributors;
- *innovation* – for constant new products and processes;
- recognizing *multiple stakeholders* in the firm.

The suggestion is that these imperatives can be directly linked to how marketing will best be organized for the future.

The impact of marketing organization design on strategy is illustrated by the successful housewares producer, Rubbermaid Inc. The company uses entrepreneurial teams made up of a product manager, research and manufacturing engineers, and financial, sales, and marketing professionals, to conceive new product ideas and move them from the design stage to the marketplace (Reitman 1992). Many of the products are improvements rather than totally new – such as a new mailbox design with features not available on competitors' units. Rubbermaid's teams introduced 365 new products in 1992 with an amazing success record of 90 per cent. Organization design drives marketing strategy at Rubbermaid.

Marketing organization and market orientation

Commonly a distinction is made between marketing as a philosophy or culture, and marketing as a set of managed activities – strategies, systems, programmes. It is often argued that marketing organization is largely irrelevant to the former, and is concerned only with implementing the latter. New studies of market orientation suggest that for various reasons this argument underestimates the significance of the marketing organization to the culture of marketing in a company.

Kohli and Jaworski (1990) produced a widely-cited conceptualization of market orientation, resting on the notion that market orientation involves the organization-wide dissemination of information and developing appropriate responses related to current and future customer needs and preferences. In fact, as will be seen shortly, one defining variable of the nature, sources and amount of intelligence and information that flows is the structure of the organization.

Parallel work by Narver and Slater (1990, 1992) adopts a view of market orientation as: customer orientation, competition orientation and interfunctional coordination. They recognize the implication that in the market-oriented company marketing specialists and departments may become less necessary. However, they also note that there may be a lengthy transition for many organizations where: 'marketing is likely to be the first function to fully appreciate the benefits of being market oriented and must demonstrate the benefits of market-driven behavior ... marketing may have a key role in the development and maintenance of a market orientation' (Narver and Slater 1992). Indeed, another study links market orientation more explicitly to organizational issues in the following terms: 'organizational actions such as the degree of market orientation are inextricably linked to the organizational structures, systems and processes created to sustain them' (Ruekert 1992). For instance, the Rubbermaid Inc new product planning process, discussed earlier, shows the close relationship between marketing organization and market orientation.

Marketing organization and market structure

A further relationship is between the structure and characteristics of the market (as they are understood in the firm) and the nature of the marketing organization. Howard (1968) argued that managers' perceptions of the characteristics of buyer behaviour shape company structure, while Corey and Star (1971) examined the impact of market segmentation on structuring marketing organization. Others have developed contingency models that examine the impact of market characteristics such as uncertainty, heterogeneity, and interdependence on the marketing organization. Conversely, it has been argued that organization structure may be a major barrier to market segmentation strategy, because structure has an impact on departmental jurisdiction, 'ownership' and commitment, reward and evaluation systems, information gathering and reporting systems, and so on (Piercy and Morgan 1993). It appears that marketing organization provides a critical link between a company and its markets.

Marketing organization and information processing

Underpinning much of this argument is the concept of the marketing organization as an information-processing structure. This view is important for a number of reasons: the collection and reporting of market information is determined in part by the organizational structure, i.e. 'the attentional process is determined largely by the structure of the organization' (Pfeffer and Salancik 1978); the executive's understanding of the marketplace is in turn partly shaped by the way the structure focuses attention on some issues and not others and thus its impact on the process of 'environmental enactment' (Weick 1969); and, the ability of the structure to process market information will directly impact on the success of marketing in fulfilling a significant boundary-spanning role and absorbing market uncertainty for the rest of the organization (Piercy 1985).

There is perhaps no better example of how structure influences the processing of market information than the Western Union Corporation. The firm's sales and marketing executives centred their attention on the company's traditional services (e.g. telegrams), during an era of vast change in telecommunications. Fax technology dealt the final blow in the demise of Western Union. This company never faced the core issue of deciding how to compete in the telecommunications market.

Marketing organization and power

The organization of marketing may be linked to the power and political strength of marketing in a firm: structure represents the control of information, resources, and critical decision-making processes. For example, marketing's power is often gauged by the functional backgrounds of top managers, and the status and influence consequently accorded to the marketing organization. In one highly successful international pharmaceuticals firm, the president, executive vice-president, and divisional vice-presidents all began their careers in sales and marketing. Divisional product management groups exert strong political influence over the strategic direction of the company, and employees comment privately on the power of marketing in the company. Conversely, when popular commentators report that top management considers marketing departments 'a millstone around an organization's neck' (Brady and Davis 1993), and that 'marketing departments are in top management's sights' (Mitchell 1993), then marketing's hidden power in the organization may be on the wane in at least some cases. This has been styled elsewhere as the 'weakening of the marketing paradigm' (Piercy 1998).

The organizational dimensions of marketing underline the fact that marketing organization is a highly significant issue, if often covert, in the operation of corporate marketing. The next section will examine the conventional view of marketing organizational issues, contrasting this with the reality found empirically and the challenges already apparent for the future.

3 Organizational forms and marketing

Webster (1992) points out that the normal conception of marketing organization is part of the large, bureaucratic, hierarchical organization, although he argues that this view is increasingly undermined by the emergence of newer organizational forms. Table 1 represents an attempt to organize these traditional and more innovative issues surrounding marketing organization. By adopting the Hofer and Schendel (1978) model of different levels of organizational strategy, we suggest that there are several levels and associated units of analysis to consider in studying the marketing organization issue. This present section will focus on marketing organization at the functional and business levels.

Functional and business level issues in marketing organization

The units of analysis here are the marketing department and its subsystems. Traditionally, interest has been in the *internal structure* for the marketing department:

- *functional*, to allow the employment of specialists (in advertising, sales, marketing research, and so on) reporting to the head of marketing (e.g. see Bund and Carroll (1957), Piercy (1985));
- *product-based*, to build product or brand specialization (e.g. see Kelly and Hise 1980));
- *market-based*, to reinforce a focus on markets and customer sectors or segments (e.g. see Hanan (1974), Schultz (1993)); or,
- *matrix structures*, with programme leadership (similar to product management) drawing on resource groups (similar to functional management) to achieve both market focus and functional specialization (e.g. see Weitz and Anderson (1981), Corey and Star (1971), Piercy (1985)).

The relative characteristics – advantages and disadvantages – of each of these forms are well-developed in the literature and are not repeated here (e.g. see Piercy (1985) for a review). Perhaps the major developments at the marketing sub-systems level consist of various suggestions for new kinds of specialists to cope with changing market situations: channel managers (Jackson and Walker 1980); marketing information systems specialists (Piercy and Evans 1998); logistics/service systems managers (e.g. Christopher et al. 1980); specialist venture groups and new product departments (Buell 1982); marketing communications managers to integrate communications internally and externally (Schultz 1992); and so on.

The *departmentation of marketing* itself was originally seen as an administrative mechanism to integrate customer-focused functions like advertising and sales (Weigand 1961), and as a logical progression from production-orientation to marketing orientation (e.g. Kotler 1991).

However, there have been many challenges to the continued need for formally organized marketing units: hierarchic bureaucracies will dissolve in favour of networks of buyers and sellers and strategic alliances removing the need for marketing specialists (Webster 1992); market orientation and customer-driven marketing may undermine the conventional position of the marketing department (Narver and Slater 1992, Naumann and Shannon 1992, Kanter 1991); some broader organizational innovations challenge the need for a marketing department, including the development of business sector or segment based structures (e.g. Buell 1982, Gould 1982); the growth in consumer goods firms of trade marketing organizations, where key retailer accounts are managed separately from the conventional marketing operation (e.g. Piercy 1985); the adoption of product/market structures representing different investment priorities (e.g. Hughes 1980); and the growth of new venture and new product departments, e.g. IBM's 'Independent Business Units' (Petre 1983).

Moreover, influenced by the trend toward decentralized management, corporate level marketing units are being eliminated in many US companies, with marketing functions being placed at the business-unit and product-market levels (Hopkins and Bailey 1984). The challenge in this trend is retaining a market-driven orientation at the corporate level. Conversely, in Europe, firms are confronting the tension between the desire for pan-European brand and marketing strategies, and the resulting resentment from executives in national centres when faced with reduced autonomy through the centralization of marketing (Mitchell 1994).

Table 1: Levels and focus of organizational analysis in marketing

Strategic level	Unit of analysis	Examples of major issues	Examples of new organizational forms
FUNCTIONAL	Marketing subsystems	Organizing and coordination sub-functions of marketing such as advertising, marketing research, sales operations.	Channel management. Logistics/services specialists. Information/technology specialists.
BUSINESS	Marketing department	The departmentation of marketing and internal structure of the marketing department. The integration of marketing sub-functions. Relationships with other functions.	Sector/segment management. Trade marketing. Investment specialists. Venture/new product departments.
CORPORATE	Divisional marketing responsibilities and group-wide marketing issues	Centralization/decentralization of marketing decision making and relationships between central and peripheral marketing units.	Marketing exchange and coalition companies. Network organizations.
ENTERPRISE	Strategic alliances and networks	External relationships and boundary-spanning with strategic marketing partners. Marketing 'make-or-buy' choices.	Partnerships. Alliances.

The *status quo* of the marketing organization

There have been various descriptive studies of marketing organization (e.g. Hopkins and Bailey 1984, Schwarz 1990, Hooley *et al.* 1984, Buell 1982), all country-specific, some general and others specific to issues like account management and product/brand management (e.g. Shapiro and Moriarity 1984, Hise and Kelly 1978, Buell 1975, Berthon *et al.* 1997). These studies demonstrate the diversity of organizational forms in marketing departments (Mitchell 1994). We consider two recent studies here as examples of their kind.

Tull *et al.* (1991) examined marketing organization at the corporate level in US companies. Their findings may be summarized:

- in only one-third of the companies studied was there the degree of integration of marketing responsibilities that would be predicted by conventional marketing theories, in the remaining two-thirds, marketing responsibilities were dispersed across other non-marketing organizational units;
- the reasons for this dispersal were: efficiency, span of control limitations, economy, tradition, and personality issues;
- the internal structures used were most commonly functional and product-based;
- organizational choices were related to the environmental factors of market complexity and unpredictability, and product diversity and number (see the discussion of environmental contingencies below).

This may be compared to a UK study of marketing organization in medium and large sized manufacturing companies (Piercy 1986, 1997). This study suggested the following:

- that the formal departmentation of marketing is far rarer than was expected and the integration of marketing functions was very limited in the sample studied;
- chief marketing executive (CME) responsibilities were largely participative and shared.

These CME responsibilities were factor analysed to identify a number of significantly different types of marketing organization, on the basis of CME span and type of responsibility, and the size of the marketing department in headcount (see Figure 1). These may be described in the following terms: the 'integrated/full-service marketing organization', which ranked relatively highly on all responsibility factors; the 'strategy/services marketing organization', with high scores on product policy, corporate strategy and marketing services factors, but relatively low on the others; the 'sales-oriented marketing organization' which ranked high on selling responsibilities, but relatively low on the others; and, the 'limited/staff role marketing organization', which ranked lowest on all responsibility factors. It should be noted that similar classifications have been

Figure 1 Types of marketing department
Source: Piercy 1997: 367.

produced in the retailing sector in the UK (Piercy 1988, Piercy and Alexander 1988) and in the UK financial services sector (Piercy and Morgan 1989).

The implication of such studies is that they undermine certain aspects of the established and conventional model of how marketing operates. The formal organization of marketing assumed implicitly by the traditional literature may be far weaker and the responsibilities of the CME far less than is normally assumed. It should be noted that these stereotypes have proved familiar and accessible to executives in identifying their own marketing organizations and the problems of marketing implementation in these different scenarios (Piercy 1994, 1997).

In addition to empirical works, the speed of change in the organization of marketing is underlined by major change programmes and restructuring in major companies:

- In 1997, IBM announced its global initiative Customer Relationship Management in which most marketing activities are embedded. The goal is to coordinate customer relationships by focusing management on core business processes instead of traditional functions – core processes include market management (to identify key target segments), opportunity management (to find 'owners' for business opportunities), and relationship management (to handle interactions between established customers and the company).
- Proctor and Gamble has moved away from conventional sales organization to its Customer Business Development structure – a mechanism for implementing cooperative relationships with retailers involved in the Efficient Consumer Response programme (i.e. supply chain collaboration).
- In 1993, the Unilever-owned toiletries company Elida Gibbs (now Elida Faberge) abandoned its conventional brand management and marketing management roles by creating Customer Development and Brand Development as centres of expertise, with category management working with retailer customers as part of the sales organization (Piercy 1997).
- A Boston Consulting Group survey of US consumer goods firms reported that 90 per cent had re-structured their marketing departments, with some of the most radical revisions impacting on traditional brand management structures (*Economist* 1994a).
- The dispute as to whether the traditional centralized marketing organization will survive continues (Webster 1992).

Perhaps the most important contribution of such empirical work and observations is to evidence diversity and radical change in organizational practices, and the essential contingencies surrounding organizational choices in marketing.

The future of the marketing organization?

Predictions for the future of the marketing organization are dangerous, given the diversity discussed above. However, an influential Marketing Science Institute essay collection (Lehmann and Jocz 1997) offers a number of interesting insights.

Stephen Greyser described 'migrated marketing' as a 'simultaneous upgrading of orientation and downsizing of formal function' (p. 14), confirming support for the view that the large centralized and specialist marketing organizations of the past are unlikely to survive.

Frederick Webster (pp. 64–5) conjectured that the successful organizations will be those knowing their basic competencies and allowing themselves to be defined by their customers in terms of capabilities and processes required to deliver superior value. Characteristics may be:

- customer-focused not product or technology focused, with a market information competence that links the voice of the market to the firm's value-delivery process;
- customer relationships seen as critical strategic assets, reflected in organizational arrangements with key customers and reseller partners where marketing activities are integrated around the customer;
- business strategies and organizational arrangements linked by flexible customer-driven value-delivery processes that evolve in response to changing environments;
- the organization itself and its capabilities will be the major competitive weapon – customers will increasingly buy the firm's

Figure 2 Evolving marketing organization
Source: Adapted from Day 1997

value-delivery system not products, and the threat will come from competitors who fundamentally redesign their systems for going to market;
- successful marketing organizations will have the skills needed to arrange multiple strategic marketing processes, many of which have traditionally not been regarded as within the domain of marketing.

A similar analysis by George Day described the emergence of hybrid organizations. These marketing organizations combine vertical structures around functions or departments with horizontal or process-oriented structures (e.g. new product development, order fulfillment processes).

Day's scenario for the future organization, though varying in different industries and according to a company's strategic imperatives, is summarized in Figure 2. His model of evolution suggests that traditional hierarchical organization leads to vertical structuring around functions or departments. The vertical functional organization provides functional excellence and technical expertise, but the weakness is likely to be the classic problem of coordination between diverse specialized departments, resulting in slow response times and inflexibility.

On the other hand, a horizontal or process-oriented organization structures the firm around a small number of strategically important processes or work-flows, such as order generation and fulfillment. Each process consists of sets of activities implemented by multidisciplinary teams. New roles emerge for process owners, coaches and leaders.

However, Day notes that most firms are not willing or able to shift to a purely horizontal form – they need also to develop vertical skills and disciplines. Day describes resulting hybrid structures which combine horizontal business processes with integrating and specialist functions. The hybrid form is shown in Figure 2 as a process overlay on a traditional functional structure, and a functional overlay on top of a process structure, as intermediary stages between the traditional hierarchy and the horizontal structure.

Day argues that this hybrid model is a prototype for the future to implement new interactive marketing strategies, which will be driven by dialogue with customers. His view of the future of the marketing organization is a fundamental re-orientation based on four premises:

- Firms will increasingly evolve towards a hybrid organizational form, combining the best features of horizontal process and vertical functional forms, in order to get closer to their customers.
- There will be great variety in these hybrid designs, based on the firm's value strategy and core capabilities, which will dictate the relative importance of staff groups, functional specialists and process teams.
- Advances in information networks will allow internal teams to be linked for better and faster decision making, and to devise more interactive strategies that use information from the customer rather than information about the customer.

- As strategies become more interactive, leading to increasing dialogue and collaboration with customers and channels, there will be a need for greater dispersion of information and decision making throughout the organization.

Such forecasts underline the fundamental changes taking place in the organization of marketing and the urgency for companies to address the issues they face in these new and demanding terms. This entry will continue by tracking in more detail the pressures for change to be considered and the emergence of new forms of organizations.

4 Marketing organization and marketing change

Most conventional pressures for change are associated with the *external* marketing environment, for example:

- Increasingly sophisticated customers place new demands on marketing performance and require new approaches to the delivery of value and hence organizational realignment (Webster 1997; Piercy 1997).
- The power of the marketing channel, particularly in a global marketing context, disrupts many conventional ideas about the location of strategic marketing responsibilities, as between manufacturer and distributor (Piercy and Morgan 1989) and the development of trade marketing structures (Piercy 1985), leading to the development of models of strategic marketing partnerships replacing traditional competitive models (Wortzel and Venkatraman 1991; Jap 1992).
- Competitive and customer imperatives have led increasingly to the demand for the adoption of relationship marketing strategies (e.g. McKenna 1991b; Christopher *et al.* 1992; Gummesson 1994a), as illustrated by the drastic reduction made by Xerox and other large companies in their supplier numbers, accompanied by the formation of collaborative partnerships with their remaining suppliers. Another example is the development of the 'prosumer' – the consumer actively involved in a company's new product development process (Mitchell 1994).
- Webster (1992) describes a range or continuum of marketing relationships leading from transaction-based marketing to the network organization (resulting from multiple strategic alliances between firms producing a confederation or coalition) – which suggests the 'radical transformation' of the marketing organization, in terms of both threats to its existence and changed relationships with other functions in the firm, and the possibility that many marketing functions will be vertically disaggregated to external specialists (Achrol 1991).

However, in parallel, there are many *internal* organizational changes also likely to impact on the traditional role of the marketing organization, for example:

- the advent of Total Quality Management (TQM) raised practical questions in many organizations about the relationship between marketing and operations/production functions, even though the core of the marketing concept is central to the TQM philosophy (e.g. Morgan and Piercy 1992);
- the impact of supply chain management and the powerful 'lean enterprise' model of removing waste and uncertainty from the supply chain has raised many questions about the remaining role for marketing (Piercy 1998);
- new information technology has changed many of the underlying assumptions that have been made about organizational structures, including those in the marketing area (Day 1997);
- there have been many claims that the 'marketing concept' is an outdated paradigm, with consequent implications for the viability of a traditionally conceived marketing organization (e.g. Naumann and Shannon 1992);
- new management approaches place more emphasis on teams, processes and change management than on formal structures, for example Cravens, Shipp and Cravens (1994) discuss the objectives of organizational change as reducing costs, creating more flexibility and building competitive advantage around core competencies.

There have been a variety of attempts to capture such pressures as these in contingency models to explain and prescribe new marketing structures.

For instance, Weitz and Anderson (1981) proposed that the environment be analysed in terms of: *complexity* – the number of elements in the environment relevant to the organization, such as the number of product-markets served; *interconnectedness* – the interdependence of key elements of the environment, for example retail concentration; and, *predictability* – the degree to which variation in the environment is stable and so less uncertain. They proposed an explanatory model of marketing structuring relating these environmental and information attributes to organizational choices in the way shown in Figure 3. Their argument is that environmental complexity pushes marketing structures towards decentralization and matrix or overlay forms, while environmental unpredictability and interconnectedness create a pressure for product or programme-based structures.

A comparable analysis of environmental contingencies based on information theory can be found in Håkansson and Ostberg (1975) and Nonaka and Nicosia (1979). These analyses are particularly apposite in the context of networks and strategic alliances, because of the emphasis placed on social relationships as an environmental contingency which may influence the role and form of marketing structure.

An attempt to integrate the various contingency approaches is provided by Ruekert *et al.* (1985). Their model of archetypical organizational forms is summarized in Figure 4. The concern here is mainly with structural characteristics (centralization, formalization and specialization), and whether activities are organized internally or externally, and they identify four forms: a bureaucratic, an organic, a transactional and a relational.

The *bureaucratic structure* organizes marketing tasks internally, and represents the conventional functional marketing department or salesforce. The *organic structure* relates a pressure to decentralization to higher market uncertainty and leads to specialization by product or market. The *transactional form* represents the outplacement of marketing tasks, where relations with external suppliers are organized with a centralized and formal structure, such as the purchase of logistics services. The *relational form* is associated with conditions of higher uncertainty where the 'spot contract' or transaction approach is replaced by a longer term relationship with an external supplier of an outplaced marketing task. This analysis of archetypes emphasizing partnership and relational

	Environmental unpredictability and interconnectedness	
Environmental complexity	**Low**	**High**
High	Decentralized organization E.g. Product divisions	Matrix organization E.g. Product groups drawing on functional resources
Low	Functional organization E.g. Sales, advertising, etc.	Brand management E.g. Product managers plus functional specialists

Figure 3 Environmental characteristics and marketing organization
Source: Adapted from Weitz and Anderson 1981

Marketing organization and management

Market versus hierarchy

	Internal organization	External organization
Centralized / Formalized / Non-specialized	**Bureaucratic form** • Conditions of low uncertainty, repetitive but specialized tasks • Effective and efficient but less adaptive • Examples: functional marketing organization, company/divisional sales force, corporate research staff	**Transactional form** • Conditions of low environmental uncertainty, with repetitive but non-specialized tasks • Effective but less adaptive • Examples: contracting externally for advertising, transport, market research field work
Decentralized / Non-formalized / Specialized	**Organic form** • Conditions of high environmental uncertainty, with infrequent specialized tasks • Adaptive but less efficient • Examples: product management, specialized salesforce organization, research staffs organized by product groups	**Relation form** • Conditions of high environmental uncertainty with non-routine but non-specialized tasks • Adaptive but less efficient • Examples: retainer contract with advertising agency, continuing relationship with consulting firm

Structure

Figure 4 Archetypal organizational forms for marketing
Source: Adapted from Ruckert *et al.* 1985

choices links to the development of new organizational forms in marketing.

5 New organizational forms in marketing

There is an escalating array of evidence indicating that marketing organization design is evolving into new forms that differ significantly from traditional designs (Alfred *et al.* 1996). Marketing organizations are moving towards network structures as well as more futuristic designs. These organizations present important new challenges to managers and have significant career implications for marketing professionals.

This section is concerned with this evolution of new organizational forms in marketing, both internal to the firm, but also, most particularly, those designed to cope with new forms of environmental relationships: marketing partnerships, strategic alliances, and marketing networks of new kinds. In various ways these, partly speculative, proposals reflect the general phenomenon of disaggregation and the devolution of functions from firms:

> Organizations of the future are likely to be vertically disaggregated: functions typically encompassed within a single organization will instead be performed in independent organizations. the functions of product design and development, manufacturing, and distribution ... will be brought together and held in temporary alignment by a variety of market mechanisms.
>
> (Miles and Snow 1984)

The result of this process of devolution is organizational forms which have been variously characterized as 'confederations of specialists' (Webster 1992); 'networks' (Thorelli 1986); 'value-adding partnerships' (Johnston and Lawrence 1988); 'alliances' (Ohmae 1989); and 'shamrocks' (Handy 1990) – with the suggestion that they are all:

> characterized by flexibility, specialization, and an emphasis on relationship management instead of market transactions .. to re-

197

spond quickly and flexibly to accelerating change in technology, competition and customer preferences.

(Webster 1992)

The full implications of such changes for marketing are likely to be fundamental, but are not well-understood or articulated at present. We can, however, track certain apparent internal organizational implications and more widespread effects as marketing networks develop.

Internal organizational implications

Some of the most significant organizational implications of environmental and strategic change in marketing can be listed as follows:

- *Breaking hierarchies* – speed and flexibility come from reducing organizational levels and numbers of employees, creating smaller business units, and empowering line management to manage key business processes (Quinn 1992, Doyle 1997).
- *Re-engineering* – critical organizational processes will be radically restructured to reduce cost and increase speed and flexibility (see Hammer and Champney 1993) and to improve responsiveness to customers (Quinn 1992).
- *Key organization processes* (e.g. new product planning) comprise the fundamental building blocks for new organizational designs (Porter 1996; Day 1994).
- *Self-managing teams* – critical changes will be managed by groups with complementary skills (see Katzenbach and Smith 1993), in the form of high-performance multifunctional teams to achieve fast precise and flexible execution of programmes (Quinn 1992), possibly organized around market segments (Schultz 1993) and possibly temporary (Doyle 1997) – perhaps in the form of the 'collateral' or 'supplemental' organization like the task force for the major innovation (Huber 1984).
- *Modularity* in product design and production is changing the architectures of organizations (Baldwin and Clark 1997).
- The new *economics of information* is altering the power structures of organizations through the widespread availability of information (Evans and Wurster 1997).

- *Transnational organizations* – competing globally require more complex structures and new skills (see Barlett and Ghoshal 1989).
- *Learning organizations* – organizations will require the continual upgrading of skills and the corporate knowledge-base (Doyle 1997), leading to the adding of value for customers through knowledge feedback to create competitive advantage (Quinn 1992).
- *Customer management* – customer focus may be achieved by structural mechanisms (Schultz 1993; Doyle 1997).

These nine factors all drive organizational change in marketing. Moreover, they are inextricably linked to how the company handles external relationships. Here strategic alliances and network organizations are leading towards the 'virtual corporation' (*Business Week* 1993; *Marketing Business* 1993) – an impermanent set of relationships to exploit a given market opportunity, which then dissolves when its purpose is achieved. These developments merit more detailed consideration.

Inter-organizational relationships

Webster (1992) points to a number of significant changes in the role of marketing in the organization, as the focus moves from transactions to relationships and then increasingly to managing strategic alliances among independent organizations. He suggests that as traditional external boundaries between the firm and its market environment become blurred, so will traditional functional boundaries within the firm become less distinct. His argument leads to the following key conclusions:

- at the corporate level, in the network organization the marketing function will have the unique role – which differs from its traditional role – to help design and negotiate strategic partnerships with vendors and technology partners;
- at the business or strategic business unit (SBU) level, marketing managers will have a new responsibility for deciding which marketing functions and activities are to be purchased in the market, which are to be

performed by strategic partners, and which are to be performed internally;
- at the operating level, the emphasis will be more on relationships with customers and less on customer manipulation and persuasion. Indeed, in the USA, Dickson (1994) predicts that the sales force will become the dominant marketing organization form for companies that continue to perform the sales function internally, and there are some signs of this upgrading of the sales function in European companies also (Mitchell 1994).

The argument is that these new responsibilities and new marketing roles will demand organizational adjustments, although Webster is relatively vague about the form these may take. A more detailed description of the possible impact of networks and alliances on marketing organization is provided by Achrol (1991).

The evolving changes in the role of marketing in the organization have important implications regarding careers, since the evolution of organizational forms drives the ingredients and paths of managerial careers (Alfred *et al.* 1996). A substantial array of evidence strongly suggests that twenty-first-century managerial careers will be based on: (1) a knowledge-based technical specialty; (2) cross-functional and international experience; (3) competence in collaborative leadership; (4) self-management skills; and (5) personal traits of flexibility, integrity, and trustworthiness (Alfred *et al.* 1996: 17). The evolution of network structures and other advanced organizational designs are driving these career changes.

Marketing companies

Achrol has conceptualized two innovative marketing organizational designs as the result of environmental change: the *marketing exchange company* and the *marketing coalition company*. Both organizational forms are seen as 'organizing hubs of complex networks of functionally specialized firms' (Achrol 1991), and both are transorganizational systems where the critical managerial activities are boundary-spanning ones.

The marketing exchange company
The Marketing Exchange Company is compared to a brokerage or marketing information-based clearing-house, where the strategic core is a worldwide network of marketing offices and information centres – the 'marketing information network company'. Prototypes for this organizational form are the 'hollow corporation' (where manufacturing and other operational functions are devolved to external suppliers, and only marketing remains), and the great Japanese trading houses. Indeed, reflection suggests many similarities between Achrol's Marketing Exchange Company, and the powerful wholesalers of the nineteenth century stimulating the entire marketing chain (Shaw 1915)

The marketing coalition company
This organizational form is conceived as the coordinating centre of a network of strategic alliances – whereas the Marketing Exchange Company is a *quasimarket*, the Marketing Coalition Company is a *quasiorganization*. Achrol argues this organization reflects certain key environmental changes: the trend towards smaller in-house manufactured product components; growing recognition of the need for a climate of innovation; and, the rapid growth in strategic alliances.

The critical distinction made by Achrol is that the Marketing Exchange Company is the organizing hub for market information and complex exchanges, while the Marketing Coalition Company is the hub for organizing a division of functions among an alliance of specialist firms. The link is that both are transorganizational entities, and that both have one central function – marketing. It is also argued that the critical managerial focus will shift from organizing internal systems to organizing boundary-spanning processes. Organizational issues will thus be less about internal structure and departmental boundaries, and more about 'alternatives or substitutes for organization' (Achrol 1991): establishing productive norms of behaviour rather than hierarchical control; and, developing a 'quasijudicial system' of management.

Underpinning the logic of Achrol's models is the development of networks of various kinds, to accomplish marketing tasks. Insight into the marketing organization of the future may rely on developing a better and more integrated understanding of the network organization.

Marketing networks

The network form of organization offers an alternative to the traditional hierarchy (Cravens *et al.* 1994). The central concept is that relationships are formed among several corporate units, independent organizations and entrepreneurs. The relationships may be both *vertical* among members of the value-adding system, spanning from suppliers to end-users, and *horizontal* among actual or potential competitors. A key network characteristic is being flexible and adaptable to change. Successful networks are customer-driven – guided by the needs and preferences of buyers. They differ from the traditional command and control hierarchy, displaying a flat organization form and involving interaction between network partners rather than multi-layered functions. The network members are connected via a highly sophisticated information and decision support system, often global in scope. This system performs many of the command and control functions of the traditional organization. As a consequence of the sharing of strategic information, trust among the partners is often a vital success characteristic of strategic alliances and other network relationships.

No one form of network has evolved as the best paradigm. Importantly, networks are not always better than traditional organization forms:

> Like earlier decentralization or SBU concepts, some of these new organization modes have been touted as cures for almost any management ill. They are not. Each form is useful in certain situations, and not in others. But more importantly, each requires a carefully developed infrastructure of culture, measurements, style and rewards to support it. When properly installed, these disaggregated organizations can be awesomely effective in harnessing intellectual resources for certain purposes. When improperly supported or adapted, they can be less effective than old-fashioned hierarchies.
>
> (Quinn 1992: 147)

The motivations to form networks include rapid market and technology change and skills/resources gaps. The conditions that favour adopting a network structure are: fast technological change, shorter product lifecycles, market structures where preferences are segmented, and markets that extend beyond national boundaries (Achrol 1991).

Network formation process

Networks are more likely to be launched by entrepreneurs, since the traditionally vertically integrated, hierarchically organized company faces drastic changes in shifting to a network paradigm (Cravens *et al.* 1994). The older forms of organizational design are changing in major corporations, though more slowly than in the smaller, more agile companies. For example, Sara Lee Corp. (bakery and food products, Coach, Hanes Bali, etc.) announced a strategic shift in 1997 away from capital-intensive manufacturing to a marketing focus. The network means fewer people on the corporate payroll, different management challenges, major cultural changes, and complex collaborative relationships with other organizations.

Some companies are successfully competing by employing more flexible and adaptive organizational forms. For example, Benneton (apparel) and Dell (personal computers) display several network characteristics. The most distinct example of organizational transformation, however, is the 'hollow' or 'virtual' organization, involving a core organization which coordinates relationships with a network of independent specialists.

Network classification

Two useful dimensions of classification for the new organizational forms are: first, the duration of the environmental change, and second, the type of relationships (collaboration versus transaction) among network members (Cravens *et al.* 1996).

The *volatility of environmental change* has an important influence on how the organization is designed to cope with the change (Achrol 1991). In the highly volatile situation, the organization needs a flexible internal structure that can rapidly adjust to new environmental conditions. Similarly, the external relationships that exist between organizations must allow for alteration (and termination) over a short time horizon. When the competitive environment is less volatile, the inter-organizational relationships may be collaborative. The partners must commit a substantial amount of time and resources to developing the relationship, and working towards common strategic objectives.

The modularity paradigm provides a promising framework for designing network organizations in volatile environments. Modularity consists of 'building a complex product or process from smaller subsystems that can be designed independently yet function as a whole' (Baldwin and Clark 1997: 84). Modularity enables linking together several independent organizations, each responsible for a module or subsystem. Modularity may apply to product design, production and other stages in the value added chain. Modularity has its roots in the computer industry and has largely been focused on production processes. None the less, the paradigm has potentially important implications for organizational design, particularly in situations involving networks of organizations.

The second basis for classifying network organizations is *the type of relationship(s) among network members*. The *tie* may range from highly *collaborative* links to *transaction* links. Collaborative links imply an ongoing relationship between the parties, not unlike the highly relational contractual relationships discussed by McNeil (1978). Transactional links are those between parties that do not require collaboration.

The types of links between firms depend on the functions performed by the network members, the rate of environmental change, customer characteristics and requirements, market structure, technological complexity, core competency of the coordinating organization, and core competency of the network members. Though more than one type of link may be found in the network, the dominant relationship can be used in the classification of the network organization. We now examine four illustrative types of network organization (Cravens *et al.* 1996):

- the hollow network;
- the flexible organization;
- the value-added network; and
- the virtual network.

The hollow network

The *hollow network* is a transaction-based organizational form competing in highly volatile environments. It is designed to meet the needs of buyers that can be placed into one or more market segments (Achrol 1991). The hollow corporation is customer-focused, using transactional relationships to link customers with goods and services that meet their needs. The term 'hollow organization' emphasizes that the core organization draws heavily upon other organizations (and individuals) to satisfy customer needs. Organizations competing in this situation are often specialists that coordinate an extensive network of suppliers and buyers (Achrol 1991).

Achrol's (1991) Marketing Exchange Company (see above) is a possible design for the hollow organization paradigm. The hollow organization buffers the frequently changing environment by functioning as a marketing organization that can shift to new opportunities and sources of supply. It does not perform major research and development or production functions internally. Technology is located with network members.

The flexible organization

The *flexible organization* is encountered under conditions of high environmental volatility, but has intra-network links that tend to be collaborative and long term. The network coordinator is likely to be an entrepreneur, or an entrepreneurial unit of an established organization. The network coordinator manages an internal team which identifies customer needs, designs products and establishes sources of supply. The organization generates a stream of new products to satisfy a diversity of customer requirements.

One version of the flexible organization is the 'spider web' company (Quinn 1992). Its characteristics include close communications links between the nodes and the coordinating company, but each node company operates on an independent basis by performing the task(s) agreed with the hub company. The market environment for this paradigm includes fast response times, high value-added, and high risk. The coordinating company is able to leverage its expertise by linking itself with an array of node companies. 'A major driving force is customers who demand increasing flexibility and responsiveness in the supply of ever more complex products and services' (Quinn 1992: 129). Meeting these diverse requirements calls for great knowledge depth, technological competency and response capability.

The value-added network

Companies forming *value-added networks* may compete in markets where preferences are diffused and segments may be difficult to define. This form of organization may utilize a global network of suppliers coupled with substantial internal operations. It differs from the virtual network in that the core organization may perform fewer of the value-added functions. None the less, the core organization in the value-added network is responsible for innovation and product design. Tommy Hilfiger (apparel) displays several characteristics of this organizational form.

The value-added network organization appears to fit product–market situations where complex technologies and customized product offerings are not required. Industries where this network form may be appropriate include apparel manufacturing and marketing, specialty furniture, eye glasses and services.

The virtual network

The *virtual network* is likely to be a reformed design of the traditional organization. It is a version of the 'virtual corporation' (*Business Week* 1993). The 'virtual corporation' is so named because it has a long-term orientation of adapting to meet the needs of segmented market structures, while competing in markets that experience low levels of environmental volatility. Unlike the hollow organization, the virtual network organization utilizes a substantial core competency in product innovation and production efficiency (Achrol 1991). It may perform many of the traditional functions internally, but does so in a different way. This organizational form may be adopted by a traditional organization that has been reformed. It may also be used by an entrepreneur seeking to exploit a long-term growth opportunity, while hedging the risks by networking with other organizations. Low environmental volatility encourages the formation of collaborative relationships with network members and customers. Customer needs are complex and dynamic. Examples of virtual networks include General Electric, Hewlett-Packard and Motorola. Market access and technology are major drivers in these and other collaborative organizations.

Cellular organizations

A new organizational form seems to be emerging. Designated as the 'cellular' organization, it is appearing in a few settings such as professional services. The purpose of the cellular organization is to facilitate the activities of entrepreneurial professionals (Alfred *et al.* 1996). The core function of the cellular organizational form is a facilitating mechanism to assist in the application and enhancement of the knowledge-intensive skills of its membership (cells). It comprises cells (e.g. self-managed teams or units) that could function autonomously, but when interacting with each other are capable of producing more effective outcomes. The cellular organization displays certain characteristics of networks. It may be an evolving new form, or a hybrid form of the hollow or flexible organizational forms.

Multi-firm and multiple industry networks

A broader perspective of network types distinguishes between single-firm and multiple-firm, single-industry and multi-industry and stable or temporary network organizations (Achrol 1997). This view identifies:

- *Internal market networks* – the re-formation of hierarchical, multi-divisional firms into internal enterprise units. General Motors, for example, has reorganized components manufacturing into eight internal market units each specializing in an automotive system area, and able to sell products on the open market as well as within GM.
- *Vertical market networks* – the marketing channel is coordinated by a marketing or technology specialist, For example, IKEA, the Swedish furniture retailer, operates a global sourcing network of 2300 suppliers in 67 countries to get 10,000 products on the shelf at prices 30 per cent lower than traditional rivals (*Economist* 1994b).
- *Intermarket or concentric networks* – in the form of institutionalized affiliations between firms operating in different industries, and the firms linked in vertical exchange relationships with them, characterized by dense interconnections in resource-sharing, strategy, culture and identity. Prototypes are the Japanese and Korean *keiretsu* and *chaebol* enterprise groups. The Virgin group has been

described as a form of *keiretsu* to explain the logic for growth through music, entertainment, transportation, financial services, and diverse consumer goods, linked by the Virgin brand and mainly funded by partner organizations.
- *Opportunity networks* – specialist firms forming temporary alignments around a specific project or problem. Prototypical may be the direct marketing collaborations to offer novel product assortments through the Internet.

These views underline the diversity and potential complexity of network organizations and the role of marketing processes within them. It remains the case that our understanding of these new organizational forms is not yet well-developed:

> network and virtual organizations have been here for a long time, although our ability to define them and communicate their true content is still limited.
>
> (Gummesson 1994a)

Implications of network organizations

In deciding whether or how to develop or gain access to a network organization, several strategy implications should be considered (Cravens *et al.* 1994):

- *Defining core competencies* – A major reason for networking is that each member offers a core competency that the others lack. Thus defining an organization's core competencies is an essential early step in forming networks.
- *Establishing and managing relationships* – Network organizations may employ transaction, collaboration or combination relationships. The network relationship may be vertical with other members of the value-added system (suppliers, producers and marketing intermediaries), or horizontal with competitors. The latter is the most complex of the group and the most different from the experiences of most traditional organizations. These relationships are more equality-based than power-based.
- *Organizational culture and networks* – Establishing networks may impact on existing corporate cultures, particularly in international alliances. The partners must be willing and able to make the necessary concessions to each other.
- *Assessing network effectiveness* – This issue centres on the advantage to the organization in developing a network relationship compared to not pursuing the strategic objective in question. It is useful to compare network results with expectations.
- *Staffing requirements* – Forming and managing the network organization calls for different managerial skills than those required in the hierarchical organization, and there are important managerial career implications. Team-oriented generalists with the ability to manage complex projects should be effective in network situations.

6 The management agenda for the marketing organization

In conclusion, the management agenda to be addressed in considering organizational issues in marketing includes answering the following types of questions:

- Consider the impact of organizational structures and coordination mechanisms on the implementation of marketing strategy and on the formulation of that strategy, and what organizational arrangements imply for the firm in terms of managing the customer/company interface, in achieving market orientation, and in how people in the firm understand the marketplace.
- In addressing the organizational dimensions of marketing, distinguish between those at the functional and business unit level, and those at the corporate and enterprise level. It will be necessary to iterate between these levels because they are inextricably linked, but the issues at each level are somewhat different (see Table 1).
- Recognition should be given to the pressures for change in the marketing organization. This should include both external pressures from market and distribution channel change, and internal pressures from new technology, new management methods, and broader organizational changes.
- The appropriateness of different organizational forms for marketing may be assessed

through the evaluation of different types of market and corporate contingencies.
- At the functional and business unit levels there are questions of the most appropriate internal structure of the marketing function or department, and more broadly the type of marketing department currently operated and that needed to achieve marketing goals.
- The adoption of multifunctional teams in reformed organizations to guide business processes, such as new product planning, creates complex challenges in defining processes, selecting team members, determining incentives, and assessing performance.
- Changing organizational structure from functional to process emphasis will not eliminate functional mind-sets and assure ready adoption of team orientation (Majchrzak and Wang 1996). It will be necessary to change the culture as well.
- At the enterprise and corporate levels the questions to address reflect broad changes in the way large organizations are structured and managed, but also the process of vertical disaggregation and networking. The growing importance of relationship marketing strategies, strategic alliances, and marketing networks should be carefully evaluated in the light of proposals for new organizational forms for marketing to cope with such environmental changes.
- Finally, the trade-off between improving organizational effectiveness and the costs of organizational change must be carefully evaluated. Resigning the marketing organization changes the jobs and responsibilities of personnel. The new design may also require reductions in staff. Such changes are costly and should be compared to the estimated value added by the new organization.

NIGEL F. PIERCY
CARDIFF BUSINESS SCHOOL, CARDIFF UNIVERSITY
DAVID W. CRAVENS
M. J. NEELEY SCHOOL OF BUSINESS, TEXAS CHRISTIAN UNIVERSITY

References

(References cited in the text marked *)

* Achrol, Ravi S. (1991) 'Evolution of the marketing organization: new forms for turbulent environments', *Journal of Marketing* 55: 77–93.
* Achrol, Ravi S. (1997) 'Changes in the theory of interorganizational relations in marketing: toward a network paradigm', *Journal of the Academy of Marketing Science* 55: 77–93.
* Alfred, Brent B., Snow, Charles, C. and Miles, Raymond E. (1996) 'Characteristics of managerial careers in the 21st century', *Academy of Management Executive* 10: 17–27.
* Ames, B.C. (1968) 'Trappings versus substance in industrial marketing', *Harvard Business Review* July/August, 93–102.
* Baldwin, Carliss Y. and Clark, Kim B. (1997) 'Managing in an age of modularity', *Harvard Business Review* September–October, 84–93.
* Baligh, H.H. and Burton, R.M. (1979) 'Marketing in moderation – the marketing concept and the organization's structure', *Long Range Planning* 12: 92–6.
* Barlett, Christopher A. and Ghoshal, Sumantra (1989) *Managing Across Borders: The Transnational Solution*, London: Hutchinson.
* Berthon, Pierre, Hulbert, James M., and Pitt, Leyland F. (1997) *Brands, the Brand Manager, and the Management of Brands: Where To Next?*, MSI Report 97-122, Cambridge, MA.: Marketing Science Institute.
* Brady, John and Davis, Ian (1993) 'Marketing's mid-life crisis', *McKinsey Quarterly* Summer.
* Bonoma, Thomas V. (1985) *The Marketing Edge: Making Strategies Work*, New York: Free Press.
* Buell, Victor P. (1975) 'The changing role of the product manager in consumer goods companies', *Journal of Marketing* 39: 3–11.
* Buell, Victor P. (1982) *Organizing for Marketing/Advertising Success*, New York: National Association of Advertisers.
* Bund, H. and Carroll, J.W. (1957) 'The changing role of the marketing function', *Journal of Marketing* 21: 268–325.
* *Business Week* (1993) 'The virtual corporation', 8 February, 36–41.
* Cespedes, Frank V. (1991) *Organizing and Implementing the Marketing Effort*, Reading, MA: Addison-Wesley.
* Chandler, A.D. (1962) *Strategy and Structure*, Cambridge, MA: MIT Press.
* Child, John (1984) *Organization*, 2nd edn, London: Harper and Row.
* Christopher, Martin, McDonald, Malcolm and Wills, Gordon (1980) *Introducing Marketing*, London: Pan.

* Christopher, Martin, Payne, Adrian and Ballantyne, David (1992) *Relationship Marketing*, Oxford: Butterworth-Heinemann.
* Corey, Edward R. and Star, Steven H. (1971) *Organization Strategy: A Marketing Approach*, Boston, MA: Harvard University Press.
* Cravens, David W., Shipp, Shannon H. and Cravens, Karen S. (1994) 'Reforming the traditional organization: the mandate for developing networks', *Business Horizons* July–August, 19–28.
* Cravens, David W., Piercy, Nigel F. and Shipp, Shannon H. (1996) 'New organizational forms for competing in highly dynamic environments: the network paradigm', *British Journal of Management* 7: 203–18.
  Cravens, David W., Greenley, Gordon, Piercy, Nigel F. and Slater, Stanley F. (1997) 'Integrating contemporary strategic management perspectives', *Long Range Planning*. 30: 493–506.
* Day, George S. (1994) 'The capabilities of market-driven organizations', *Journal of Marketing* October, 37–52.
* Day, George S. (1997) 'Aligning the organization to the market', in Donald R. Lehmann and Katherine E. Jocz (eds) *Reflections on the Futures of Marketing*, Cambridge, MA: Marketing Science Institute, pp. 67–98.
* Dickson, Peter R. (1994) *Marketing Management*, Fort Worth: Dryden Press, pp. 516–17.
  Doyle, Peter (1979) 'Management structures and marketing strategies in UK industry', *European Journal of Marketing* 13: 319–31.
* Doyle, Peter (1997) *Marketing Management and Strategy*, 2nd edn, Hemel Hempstead: Prentice-Hall.
* *Economist* (1994a) 'Death of the brand manager', 9 April, 79–80.
  Economist (1994b) 'Furnishing the world', 19 November, 101.
* Evans, Philip B. and Wurster, Thomas S. (1997) 'Strategy and the new economics of information', *Harvard Business Review* September–October, 70–82.
* Franko, L. (1974) 'The move towards a multidimensional structure in European organizations', *Administrative Science Quarterly* 19: 493–506.
* Gould, P. (1982) 'Kellogg fattens its marketing department', *Marketing* 14 October, 6.
  Gummesson, Evert (1994a) *Relationship Marketing: From 4Ps to 30Rs*, Stockholm: Stockholm University.
* Gummesson, Evert (1994b) 'Service management: an evaluation and the future', *International Journal of Services Industry Management* 5: 77–96.
  Gustin, Carl (1997) 'A conversation with Carl Gustin', *Insights from MSI* Fall, 6–7.
* Håkansson, H. and Ostberg, C. (1975) 'Industrial marketing: an organizational problem?', *Industrial Marketing Management* 4: 113–23.
* Hammer, Michael and Champney, James (1993) *Re-Engineering The Corporation*, London: Brealey.
* Hanan, M. (1974) 'Reorganize your company around its markets', *Harvard Business Review* November/December, 63–74.
* Handy, Charles (1990) *The Age of Unreason*, Boston, MA: Harvard Business School Press.
* Hise, R.T. and Kelley, J.P. (1978) 'Product management on trial', *Journal of Marketing* 42: 28–33.
* Hofer, Charles W. and Schendel, Dan (1978) *Strategy Formulation: Analytical Concepts*, St. Paul: West Publishing.
* Hooley, Graham, West, C.J. and Lynch, James, E. (1984) *Marketing in the UK – A Survey of Current Practice and Performance*, Cookham, Berks: Institute of Marketing.
* Hopkins, David S. and Bailey, Earl L. (1984) *Organizing Corporate Marketing*, New York: Conference Board.
* Howard, John A. (1968) 'Organization structure and its underlying theory of buyer behavior' in S.H. Britt and Harper W. Boyd (eds) *Marketing Management and Administrative Action*, New York: McGraw-Hill.
* Huber, George P. (1984) 'The nature and design of 'post-industrial organizations', *Management Science* 30: 928–51.
* Hughes, G.D. (1980) *Marketing Management: A Planning Approach*, Reading, MA: Addison-Wesley.
  Hulbert, James M. and Pitt, Leyland F. (1996) 'Exit left, centre stage', *European Management Journal* 14: 47–60.
* Jackson, D.W. and Walker, BJ. (1980) 'The channel manager: marketing's newest aide?', *California Management Review* 23: 52–8.
* Jap, Sandy D. (1992) *Evolving Relationships of Retailers and Manufacturers*, Report 92-113, Cambridge, MA: Marketing Science Institute.
* Johnston, Russell and Lawrence, Paul R. (1988) 'Beyond vertical integration – the rise of the value-adding partnership', *Harvard Business Review* 66: 94–101.
* Kanter, Rosabeth Moss (1991) 'Even closer to the customer', *Harvard Business Review* January/February, 9–10.
* Katzenbach, Hon R. and Smith, Douglas, K. (1993) *The Wisdom of Teams: Creating the High-Performance Organization*, Boston, MA: Harvard Business School Press.
* Kelly, J.P. and Hise, R.T. 1980) 'Role conflict, role clarity, job tension and job satisfaction in the brand manager position', *Journal of the Academy of Marketing Science* 8: 120–37.
* Kohli, Ajay K. and Jaworski, Bernard J. (1990) 'Market orientation: the construct, research propositions, and managerial implications', *Journal of Marketing* 54: 1–18.

- Kotler, Philip (1991) *Marketing Management: Analysis, Planning and Control*, London: Prentice-Hall International.
- Lehmann, Donald R. and Jocz, Katherine, E. (eds) (1997) *Reflections on the Futures of Marketing*, Cambridge, MA: Marketing Science Institute.
- Levitt, Theodore (1980) 'Marketing success through differentiation – of anything', *Harvard Business Review* 58: 83–91.
- Majchrzak, Ann and Wang, Qianwei (1996) 'Breaking the functional mind-set in process organizations', *Harvard Business Review* September–October, 93–99.
- *Marketing Business* (1993) 'New marketing vision', January, 12–17.
- McKenna, Regis (1991a) 'Marketing is everything', *Harvard Business Review* January/February.
- McKenna, Regis (1991b) *Relationship Marketing*, Reading, MA: Addison-Wesley.
- McNeil, Ian (1978) 'Contracts: adjustment of long-term economic relations under classical, neoclassical, and relational contract law', *Northwestern University Law Review* 72: 854–902.
- Miles, Raymond E. and Snow, Charles, C. (1984) 'Fit, failure and the hall of fame', *California Management Review* 26: 10–28.
- Mitchell, Alan (1993) 'Transformation of marketing', *Marketing Business* November, 9–14.
- Mitchell, Alan (1994) 'New generation marketing' *Marketing Business* February, 13–16.
- Morgan, Neil A. and Piercy, Nigel F. (1992) 'Market-led quality', *Industrial Marketing Management* 21: 111–18.
- Narver, John C. and Slater, Stanley F. (1990) 'The effect of a market orientation on business profitability', *Journal of Marketing* 54: 20–35.
- Narver, John C. and Slater, Stanley F. (1992) *Market Orientation, Performance and the Moderating Influence of Competitive Environment*, Marketing Science Institute Working Paper 92-118, Cambridge, MA: Marketing Science Institute.
- Naumann, Earl and Shannon, Patrick (1992) 'What is customer-driven marketing?', *Business Horizons* November/December, 44–52.
- Nonaka, I. and Nicosia, F. M. (1979) 'Marketing management, its environment and information processing: a problem of organization design', *Journal of Business Research* 7: 277–301.
- Ohmae, Kenichi (1989) 'The global logic of strategic alliances', *Harvard Business Review*, 67: 143–54.
- Petre, P.E. (1983) 'Meet the lean, mean new IBM', *Fortune* 13 June.
- Pfeffer, Jeffrey and Salancik, G.R. (1978) *The External Control of Organizations*, New York: Harper and Row.
- Piercy, Nigel (1985) *Marketing Organisation: An Analysis of Information Processing, Power and Politics*, London: Allen and Unwin.
- Piercy, Nigel (1986) 'The role and function of the chief marketing executive and the marketing department: a study of medium-sized companies in the UK', *Journal of Marketing Management* 1: 265–89.
- Piercy, Nigel (1988) 'The role of the marketing department in UK retailing organizations', *International Journal of Retailing* 4: 46–65.
- Piercy, Nigel (1994) 'Marketing implementation: analysing structure, process and information' in John Saunders (ed.) *The Marketing Initiative*, London: Prentice-Hall.
- Piercy, Nigel (1997) *Market-Led Strategic Change: Transforming the Process of Going To Market*, Oxford: Butterworth-Heinemann.
- Piercy, Nigel F. (1998) 'Marketing implementation: the implications of marketing paradigm weakness for the strategy execution process', *Journal of the Academy of Marketing Science* 26: 222–36.
- Piercy, Nigel and Alexander, Nicholas (1988) 'The status quo of marketing in UK retailing organizations', *Services Industries Journal* 8: 155–67.
- Piercy, Nigel and Evans, Martin J. (1998) 'Developing marketing information capabilities' in Michael J. Baker (ed.) *The Marketing Book*, 4th edn, Oxford: Butterworth-Heinemann.
- Piercy, Nigel and Morgan, Neil (1989) 'Marketing organization in the UK financial services industry', *International Journal of Bank Marketing* 7: 3–10.
- Piercy, Nigel F. and Morgan, Neil A. (1993) 'Strategic and operational market segmentation: a managerial analysis', *Journal of Strategic Marketing* 1: 123–40.
- Porter, Michael E. (1996) 'What is strategy?', *Harvard Business Review* November–December, 61–78.
- Quinn, J. Brian (1992) *Intelligent Enterprise*, New York: Free Press.
- Reitman, Valerie (1992) 'Rubbermaid turns up plenty of profit in the mundane', *Wall Street Journal* 27 March, B3.
- Ruekert, Robert W. (1992) 'Developing a market orientation: an organizational strategy perspective', *International Journal of Research in Marketing* 9: 225–45.
- Ruekert, Robert W., Walker, Orville C. and Roering, Kenneth J. (1985) 'The organization of marketing activities: a contingency theory of structure and performance', *Journal of Marketing* 49: 13–25.
- Schultz, Don E. (1992) *Integrated Marketing Communications*, Evanston, IL: NTC Business Books.
- Schultz, Don E. (1993) 'Maybe we should start all over with an IMC organization', *Marketing News* 25 October, 8.

* Schwarz, Gordon (1990) *Organizing to Become Market-Driven*, Report 90-123, Cambridge, MA: Marketing Science Institute.
* Shapiro, B.F. and Moriarity, R.T. (1984) *Organizing the National Account Force*, Report 84-101, Cambridge, MA: Marketing Science Institute.
* Shaw, Arch W. (1915) *Some Problems in Market Distribution*, Cambridge, MA: Harvard University Press.
  Staudt, T.A. and Taylor, D.A. (1970) *A Managerial Introduction to Marketing*, Englewood Cliffs, NJ: Prentice-Hall.
* Thorelli, Hans (1986) 'Networks: between markets and hierarchies', *Strategic Management Journal* 7: 37–51.
* Tull, Donald S., Cooley, Bruce E., Phillips, Mark R. and Watkins, Harry S. (1991) *The Organization of Marketing Activities of American Manufacturers*, Report No 91-126, Cambridge, MA: Marketing Science Institute.
* Webster, Frederick E. (1992) 'The changing role of marketing in the corporation', *Journal of Marketing* 56: 1–17.
* Webster, Frederick E. (1997) 'The future role of marketing in the organization', in Donald R. Lehmann and Katherine E. Jocz (eds) *Reflections on the Futures of Marketing*, Cambridge, MA: Marketing Science Institute, pp. 39–66.
* Weick, Karl R, (1969) *The Social Psychology of Organizing*, Reading, MA: Addison-Wesley.
* Weigand, R.E. (1961) 'Changes in the Marketing Organization in Selected Industries, 1950–1959', unpublished Ph.D. dissertation, University of Illinois.
* Weitz, Bart and Anderson, Erin (1981) 'Organizing the marketing function' in *Review of Marketing 1981*, Chicago: American Marketing Association.
* Wortzel, Lawrence H. and Venkatraman, Meera P. (1991) *Manufacturer and Retailer Relationships: Replacing Power with Strategic Marketing Partnerships*, Working Paper 91-129, Cambridge, MA: Marketing Science Institute.

See also: CHANNEL MANAGEMENT; MARKETING COMMUNICATIONS; RELATIONSHIPS AND NETWORKS; STRATEGIC ALLIANCES AND SUPPLIER PARTNERSHIPS

Marketing budgeting and resource allocation

1 **Budgeting: scope and nature**
2 **Locating budgeting**
3 **Establishing a base line**
4 **Developing the master budget**
5 **Some behavioural issues**
6 **Dangers in budgeting**
7 **Other analytical techniques**

Overview

Budgetary control works throughout the organization, dealing with the resources of that organization over a pre-defined period of time. It is involved in more than simply forecasting; it is the planned manipulation of all the variables which impact upon an organization's performance. This entry looks at where budgeting is positioned within the organization, and the various way in which the budget can be drawn up. It also considers how the budget and its effects on company performace should be interpreted with a short discussion of sensitivity analysis. In any resource allocation procedure there are potential pitfalls and these are not ignored.

1 Budgeting: scope and nature

Budgeting (or profit planning) is perhaps the widest ranging planning and control technique in that it covers the entire organization rather than merely sections of it.

A budget is a quantitative plan of action which aids in the coordination and control of the acquisition, allocation and utilization of resources over a defined period of time. The building of the budget may be looked upon as the integration of the varied interests which constitute the organization into a programme that all have agreed is workable in attempting to attain objectives.

Budgetary control works through the formal organization viewing it as a series of responsibility centres, and attempting to isolate the performance measurement of each centre from the effects of the performance of others.

Budgeting involves more than just forecasting since it involves the planned manipulation of all the variables which determine the company's performance in an effort to arrive at some preferred position in the future. The agreed plan must be developed in a coordinated manner if the requirements of each are to be balanced in line with company objectives. Each manager must consider the relationship of his/her responsibility centre (or department) to all others and to the company as a whole in the budgetary planning phase. This tends to reduce departmental bias and empire-building as well as isolating weaknesses in the organizational structure and highlighting problems of communication. Furthermore, it encourages the delegation of authority by a reliance upon the principle of management by exception.

Having determined the plan, this provides the frame of reference for judging subsequent performance. There can be no doubt that *budgeted* performance is a better benchmark than *past* performance on account of the inefficiencies that are usually hidden in the latter and the effect of constantly changing conditions.

There are essentially two types of budgets – the long-term and the short-term. Time obviously distinguishes one from the other, and this raises the point that users of budgets should not be unduly influenced by conventional accounting periods: the budget period which is the most meaningful to the individual company should be adopted. For example, the life-cycle of a product from its development right through to its deletion is in many ways a more natural budgetary period than one an annual cycle because it links marketing, production, distribution and financial planning on a unified basis. The actual choice of a budget's time horizon will tend to depend very much on the company's ability to forecast accurately.

Typically, however, budgets tend to be compiled on an annual basis, with this time-span being broken down into lesser time intervals for reporting, scheduling and control reasons (i.e. half years, quarters, months and even weeks in the case of production and sales activities).

Marketing budgeting and resource allocation

```
═══════════════════▶ ┌─────────────────┐
                     │ Reformulation and│
                     │   relaunch of    │
                     │    Product X     │
                     └─────────────────┘

═══════════════════▶ ┌─────────────────┐
                     │    Continued     │
                     │ market success   │
                     │  with Product Y  │
                     └─────────────────┘

═══════════════════▶ ┌─────────────────┐
                     │  The successful  │
                     │ development and  │
                     │launch of Product Z│
                     └─────────────────┘
```

Figure 1 Programme (or activity budget)

Within this framework of one year the *operating budget* is prepared. This is composed of two parts which each look at the same things in a slightly different way, but which both arrive at the same net profit and return on investment. These two parts are:

1 The programme (or activity) budget which specifies the operations that will be performed during the forthcoming period. The most logical way to present this budget is to show, for each marketing programme, the expected revenues and their associated costs. The result is an impersonal portrayal of the expected future which is useful in ensuring that a balance exists amongst the various activities, profit margins, and volumes – in other words, this is the plan (see Figure 1).

2 The responsibility budget which specifies the annual plan in terms of individual responsibilities. This is primarily a control device which indicates the desired target or level of performance for each manager, but the personalized costs, revenues and profits in this budget must be controllable at the level, of each individual manager, at which they are planned and reported (see Figure 2).

The significance of these two ways of dealing with the operating budget is important since the programme budget is the outcome of the planning phase, whereas the responsibility budget is the starting-point for the control phase. The former need not correspond to the organizational structure, but the latter must. Consequently, the plan must be translated into the

```
┌──────────┐ ┌───────────┐ ┌──────────┐ ┌─────────┐ ┌────────────┐ ┌──────────────┐
│ Research │ │Manufacturing│ │Engineering│ │ Marketing│ │Distribution│ │Administration│
│    &     │ └───────────┘ └──────────┘ └─────────┘ └────────────┘ └──────────────┘
│Development│     │             │            │            │              │
└──────────┘     │             │            │            │              │
     │           ▽             ▽            ▽            ▽              ▽
     ▽
```

Figure 2 Responsibility budget

Marketing management

Figure 3 A simplified output budget format

control prior to the time of execution and communicated to those involved in order that no one will be in any doubt as to precisely what is expected of him/her (see Figure 3).

Given these two complementary aspects of the operating budget, there are two basic ways in which the budget may be prepared:

1 Periodic budgeting in which a plan is prepared for the next financial year with a minimum of revision as the year goes by. Generally the total expected annual expenditure will be spread over the year on a monthly basis on the strength of the behaviour of the elemental costs. Thus 'salaries' will be spread over the months simply as one-twelfth of the expected annual cost per month, but seasonal variations in sales will require a little more attention to be paid to marketing and production costs and their behaviour over time. Revenues should be budgeted in accordance with their anticipated generation.
2 Continuous (or rolling) budgeting in which a tentative annual plan is prepared with, say, the first quarter's inflows and outflows being shown by month in great detail, the second and third quarters' in less detail, and the fourth quarter, in outline only. Every month (or every quarter, as appropriate) the budget can then be revised by adding the required detail to the next month (or quarter), and adding on a new month (or quarter) in such a way that the plan still extends one year ahead. Such a budgeting procedure attempts to accommodate changing conditions and uncertainty, and is highly desirable in that it forces management constantly to think in concrete terms about the forthcoming *year* regardless of where one happens to be in the present *financial* year.

Periodic budgeting will often be satisfactory for companies in stable industries which are able to make relatively accurate forecasts covering the planning period. Conversely, rolling budgeting is of greater value in the more usual cases of somewhat irregular cyclical activity amid the uncertainties of consumer demand.

2 Locating budgeting

It is helpful to consider the role of budgeting in relation to the broad questions contained within the management process as shown in Figure 4.

Stage One raises the question of where the organization is now in terms of its competitive position, product range, market share, financial position and overall effectiveness. In addressing this question we are seeking to establish a baseline from which we can move forward.

Stage Two is concerned with where the organization should go in the future, which requires the specification of ends (or objectives) to be achieved. While top management in the organization will have some discretion over the choice of ends, this is constrained by various vested interests.

Stage Three deals with the question of how desired ends might be achieved, which begs the question of how alternative means to ends might be identified. This strategy formulation stage requires creative inputs which cannot be reduced to mechanical procedures.

Stage Four focuses on the evaluation of alternative means by which the most preferred (or 'best') alternative might be selected. The need to choose may be due to alternatives being mutually exclusive (i.e. all attempting to achieve the same end) or a consequence of limited resources (which means that a rationing mechanism must be invoked).

Stage Five covers the implementation of the chosen means, and the monitoring of its performance in order that any corrective actions might be taken to ensure that the desired results are achieved. Since circumstances both within the organization and in its environment are unlikely to stay constant while a budget is being pursued, it is necessary to adapt to accommodate such changes.

Within these stages are to be found the main managerial activities of:

- planning;
- decision making;
- control.

The entire sequence of Stages One to Five constitutes organizational control, within which the planning activities are to be found in Stages One to Three, decision making in Stage Four and operational control in Stage Five. It is apparent that these managerial activities are closely intertwined. Moreover, their links are spread across three different time dimensions which are not of equal significance: the past, the present and the future. Let us consider these in turn.

The past brought the organization (and its market offering, competitors, etc.) to their present positions. By gaining an understanding of how the organization arrived at its present position the managers of that organization might develop some insights to help them in deciding

Figure 4 The framework

how to proceed into the future. However, there is no way in which the past can be influenced, so the best one can do is to attempt to learn from it instead of being constrained by it. If an organization simply continues on unchanging routes its viability is almost certain to be endangered as the environment changes but it does not (see ENVIRONMENTAL ANALYSIS). Stage One is concerned with establishing the ways in which the past brought the organization to its present position.

The present is transient: it is the fleeting moment between the past and the future when one must take one's understanding of the past and link this to the development of one's aspirations for the future. Decisions are made (with both planning and control consequences) in the present, but their impact is intended to be in the future.

The time dimension which is of major relevance in any planning exercise must be the future rather than the present or the past. There is nothing about an organization that is more important than its future and the spirit of this was aptly summarized by C.F. Kettering: 'I am interested in the future because that is where I intend to live'. The past may help us in deciding how to proceed in the future, but there is no way in which we can influence the past, so there is a limit to the amount of effort that should be applied to it as opposed to planning for the future. Nevertheless, the link between the past and the future is important as the following sequence of steps should make clear:

- We can seek to understand – on the basis of our past experience – the way in which variables of interest to us interact. This enables us to gain insights into, and an understanding of, causal relationships.
- Our understanding of causal relationships in the past gives a basis for making more accurate predictions regarding the future.
- If we are able to make accurate predictions we should be in a better position to control the outcome of events. It is in this context that budgeting can play a valuable role in the management of marketing activities.

We can illustrate some of the roles which budgets play in organizations by reference to the main characteristics of the control process namely: objectives, choice of inputs and outputs, predictive models and the issue of relevant alternative courses of action available to the marketing manager.

Objectives and budgets are related in two main ways. First, a decision maker may face reasonably clear corporate objectives such as:

1. increase the market share for the product range by 20 per cent;
2. expand into the retail/wholesale market;
3. acquire certain related businesses having an asset base of £5–10,000,000.

These general objectives will need to be further specified in the form of detailed operating goals for key decision areas. For instance, the objective of increasing market share by 20 per cent may be translated into a sales target for the next year of £10,000,000 for Division A and £15,000,000 for Division B. In this manner, a budget helps to represent and communicate the broad objectives of top management to middle management and operating personnel.

Budgets also help give form to alternative courses of action by measuring in financial terms the inputs and outputs of a particular strategy. A project or activity may begin as someone's bright idea but this cannot be implemented unless there are clear specifications of the inputs required to implement the idea and the outputs that may be expected to eventuate. A budget is a means whereby the inputs and outputs associated with a future course of action can be expressed with reasonable precision in financial terms.

A budget also enables an organization to express estimated input–output relationships. For instance, sales revenue budgets may be constructed using three alternative sales estimates: £2,000,000, £2,500,000 or £3,000,000. Each of these estimates will give rise to a set of production, cash flow and profit budgets. Having generated these three sets of budgets which, in effect, represent three different scenarios for the organization, decision makers can determine which scenario is both feasible and most acceptable. Note, however, that the quality of the budget (that is, the accuracy of the budget estimates) depends on the knowledge available about the relationship between inputs and outputs. If the level of understanding of the input–output relationship is erroneous then the sets of budgets produced will only be of limited value.

A budget target, like any standard, expresses both a desired and an expected level of performance. For instance, a sales budget of £3,000,000 for a specified time period means the organization expects and desires to achieve £3,000,000 worth of sales revenue during that period. Once this sales budget has been specified and agreed by relevant people within an organization it will be assigned to a particular individual – the sales manager. This manager will then bear overall responsibility for the achievement or non-achievement of this budget. Thus, at the end of the budget period, if the sales budget is not achieved, the sales manager will need to account for this to the marketing director. In this way budgeting enables specific responsibilities to be assigned to particular individuals who are then held accountable for the achievement of their budget targets. This assignment of responsibilities for specific performance is termed *responsibility accounting* and is widely used.

3 Establishing a base line

It is usually found that enterprises – especially smaller ones – do not know what proportion of their resources are devoted to their various activities or segments, or the profit consequences of these allocations. Producing useful computations of segmental costs, revenues and profit contributions can readily be achieved by adopting analytical methods which, while not difficult in principle, are not widely adopted due largely to the preoccupation with manufacturing cost accounting that exists.

The fact that most companies do not know what proportion of their total marketing outlay is spent on each market offering, sales territory or customer group may be due to the absence of a sufficiently refined system of cost analysis, or it may be due to vagueness over the nature of certain costs. For instance, is the cost of packaging a promotional, a production or a distribution expense? Some important marketing costs are hidden in manufacturing costs or in general and administrative costs (including finished goods inventory costs in the former and order processing costs in the latter).

Since few companies are aware of their costs, revenues and profits by segment in relation to sales levels, and since even fewer are able to predict changes in sales volume and profit contribution as a result of changes in marketing effort, the following errors arise:

1 Marketing budgets for individual products are too large, with the result that diminishing returns become evident and benefits would accrue from a reduction in expenditure.
2 Marketing budgets for individual products are too small and increasing returns would result from an increase in expenditure.
3 The marketing mix is inefficient, with an incorrect balance and incorrect amounts being spent on the constituent elements – such as too much on advertising and insufficient on direct selling or customer service activities.
4 Marketing efforts are misallocated among products and changes in these resource allocations (even with a constant level of overall expenditure) could bring improvements.

Similar arguments apply in relation to sales territories or customer groups as well as to products. The need exists, therefore, for control techniques to indicate the level of performance required and achieved as well as the outcome of shifting marketing efforts from one segment to another. As is to be expected, there exists great diversity in the methods by which managers attempt to obtain details of costs (as well as revenue and profits) for segments of their enterprise, but much of the cost data is inaccurate for such reasons as:

1 Marketing costs may be allocated to individual products, sales territories or customer groups on the basis of sales value or sales volume, but this involves circular reasoning. Costs should be allocated in relation to causal factors, and *it is marketing expenditures that cause sales to be made* rather than the other way round: managerial decisions determine marketing costs. Furthermore, despite the fact that success is so often measured in terms of sales value achievements by product line, this basis fails to evaluate the efficiency of the effort (costs) needed to produce the realized sales value (or turnover). Even a seemingly high level of turnover for a specific product may really be a case of misallocated sales effort. (An example should make this clear: if a sales representative concentrates on selling product A which contributes £200 per hour of effort instead of selling product B which would contribute £500 per hour of effort, then it 'costs' the company £300 per hour spent by the

representative in selling product A. This is the *opportunity cost* of doing one thing rather than another and is a measure of the sacrifice involved in selecting only one of several alternative courses of action.)
2. General overheads and administrative costs are arbitrarily (and erroneously) allocated to segments on the basis of sales volume.
3. Many marketing costs are not allocated at all as marketing costs since they are not identified as such but are classified as manufacturing, general or administrative costs instead.

Marketing cost accounting (or analysis) has been developed to help overcome these problems and aims to:

1. Analyse the costs incurred in developing, promoting and distributing products so that when they are combined with production cost data overall net profit can be determined.
2. Analyse the costs of marketing individual products to determine their individual net profit.
3. Analyse the costs involved in serving different classes of customers, different sales territories, etc. to determine their individual net profit.
4. Compute such figures as cost per sales call, cost per order, cost to put a new customer on the books, cost to hold £1's worth of inventory for a year, etc.
5. Evaluate managers according to their actual controllable cost, revenue and profit responsibilities.
6. Evaluate alternative marketing strategies or plans with an awareness of their full costs.

These analyses and evaluations provide senior management with relevant information to help them to decide which classes of customer to cultivate, which products to delete, which products to encourage, and so forth. Such analyses also provide a basis from which estimates can be made of the likely increases in product net profit that a specified increase in marketing effort might create. In the normal course of events it is far more difficult to predict the outcome of decisions that involve changes in marketing outlays in comparison with changes in production expenditure. It is easier, for instance, to estimate the effect of a new machine in the factory than it is to predict the impact of higher advertising outlays. Similarly, the effect on productive output of dropping a production worker is easier to estimate than the effect on the level of sales caused by a reduction in the sales force.

As an example of how productivity analysis can be applied to segments (defined as product lines for this purpose) we might consider Table 1. Table 1 shows, for a hypothetical company, the proportion of each product line's contribution to the net profit of the whole company. Most products make some net profit after their full costs are deducted from the revenues they generate. However, two products (G and H) fail to generate sufficient revenue to cover their full costs.

The segments could equally be sales territories or customer groups, etc., an alternative to product lines and, after the basic profit computation has been carried out, it can be supplemented (as in Table 2) by linking it to an analysis of the effort required to produce the profit outcome. Clearly this is a multivariate situation in which profit depends upon a variety of input factors, but developing valid and reliable multivariate models is both complex and expensive. As a step in the direction of more rigorous analysis one can derive benefits from linking profit outcomes to individual inputs – such as selling time in the case of Table 2.

Table 1 Segmental profits statement

Product	Percentage contribution to total profits
Total for all products	100.0
Profitable products:	
A	43.7
B	35.5
C	16.4
D	9.6
E	6.8
F	4.2
Sub-total	116.2
Unprofitable products:	
G	−7.5
H	−8.7
Sub-total	−16.2

Table 2 Segmental productivity statement

Product	Percentage contribution to total profits	Percentage total selling time
Total for all products	100.0	100.0
Profitable products:		
A	43.7	16.9
B	35.5	18.3
C	16.4	17.4
D	9.6	5.3
E	6.8	10.2
F	4.2	7.1
Sub-total	116.2	75.2
Unprofitable products		
G	−7.5	9.5
H	−8.7	15.3
Sub-total	−16.2	24.8

From Table 2 one can see that product A generates 43.7 per cent of total profits, requiring only 16.9 per cent of available selling time. This is highly productive. By contrast, product E produces only 6.8 per cent of total profits but requires 10.2 per cent of selling effort. Even worse, however, is the 24.8 per cent of selling effort devoted to products G and H which are unprofitable.

A number of obvious questions arise from this type of analysis. Can the productivity of marketing activities be increased by:

1 increasing net profits proportionately more than the corresponding increase in marketing outlays?
2 increasing net profits with no change in marketing outlays?
3 increasing net profits with a decrease in marketing costs?
4 maintaining net profits at a given level but decreasing marketing costs?
5 decreasing net profits but with a proportionately greater decrease in marketing costs?

4 Developing the master budget

Most organizations are too large to permit the detailed planning of all their activities in one budget, so it becomes necessary to use a summary approach which is contained in a *master budget*. Essentially the master budget is a consolidated summary of all the detailed budgets showing their outcomes in terms of their contribution to overall results. Figure 5 gives one possible sequence for developing a master budget.

The sales forecast is the starting point for preparing a budget. Sales revenue, stock levels, production requirements and hence most costs and, more especially, revenue and profit, all follow from a particular level of sales activity. If the sales forecast is grossly inaccurate then the entire budget plan will be wrongly grounded. A sensible approach is to acknowledge that more than one level of sales is possible, so consideration should be given to alternatives.

The sum of sales requirements plus (in a manufacturing setting) changes in stock levels of finished goods gives the production requirements for the period being budgeted. Once it is determined, the level of productive activity becomes the starting-point for the direct materials, direct labour and indirect manufacturing costs budgets. To a large extent the purchasing and manpower budgets follow from these production plans: they also depend to some extent on the purchasing and manpower requirements of other functions within the company.

A budgeted cost of sales schedule can be drawn up on the basis of the manufacturing cost of expected sales units. The marketing activities necessary to achieve the expected level of sales volume will be budgeted in accordance with the resources and actions that are necessary to ensure that the sales forecast (in terms of volume, value and product mix) is achieved. This requires the budgeting of order-getting costs (such as advertising and selling) on the one hand, and orderfilling costs (such as transport and warehousing) on the other.

Closely related to both marketing and production operations are the design and R&D functions which must be budgeted in accordance with policy requirements.

An overall administration budget can be compiled so as to include such cost-incurring items as personnel management, training, secretarial activities, general services and the directorate. Finally, a financial budget can summarize the whole package in the form of five budgeted statements:

1   Budgeted cash statement.
2   Budgeted income statement or profit and loss account.
3   Budgeted balance sheet.
4   Budgeted funds statement.
5   Capital budget.

Once the budget has been developed and implemented any deviations between actual and budgeted results will be of managerial concern for such reasons as the following.

- To highlight errors in budgeting procedures.
- To indicate the need for budget revisions.
- To pinpoint those activities requiring remedial attention.

The principles of management by exception should be applied to this process of comparison, with the focusing of attention on significant variations. However, if the budgeted level of activity differs from the actual level of activity, it will be apparent that variances of an artificial nature arise – such variances are based purely on volume differences rather than efficiency differences. This emphasizes the need for flexibility within the budgeting system: it should be designed to allow for varying circumstances by recognizing and adapting to significant changes in the fundamental operating conditions of the firm. Such adaptability can be achieved by means of a *flexible budget*.

Figure 5 A sequence for budget development

Table 3 Fixed budget analysis

	Budget	Actual	Variance
Sales (units)	10,000	11,000	+1,000
Sales revenue	£15,000	£16,500	+£1,500
Expenditure:			
Direct	10,000	11,000	+1,000
Indirect	4,000	4,200	+200
Profit	£ 1,000	£ 1,300	+£ 300

Flexible budget

In a flexible budgeting system the budget is adjusted in accordance with the level of activity actually experienced in the budget period. For example, a budget which is based on sales of 10,000 units during a particular period is of little value for control purposes if 12,000 units (or 8000 units) were actually sold. The sales manager will be held responsible for the volume variance, but the level of commission, order processing/invoicing, freight and similar cost-incurring activities will tend to depend on the actual level of activity which requires that the budget be adjusted in order to show an efficient budgeted level of expenditure for the achieved level of activity.

A simple way of building a flexible budget is to start with a budget for the most likely level of activity and then to derive budgets for, say, 5 per cent, 10 per cent, 15 per cent above and below this level.

The major advantage of the flexible budget is its ability to specify the budgeted level of costs, revenues and profits without revision when marketing and production programmes are not as expected. It achieves this to a large extent by distinguishing between those costs and revenues that vary with changes in the level of activity and those that do not. In other words, it is based on a thorough knowledge of cost and revenue behaviour patterns.

A static budget (i.e. a fixed budget which relates to a single level of activity) can result in misleading actions. An example should make this clear: Table 3 shows the comparison of a budgeted level of 10,000 units with an actual sales level of 11,000 units. It appears that profit has improved by £300, but not all costs vary in the same way, so a flexible budget analysis is called for. This is shown in Table 4 and indicates clearly that the comparison should be between the actual level of activity and the budgeted costs, revenue and profit for that level. While profit was higher than the budgeted figure, the difference was only £20 rather than £300.

The need to distinguish fixed costs (which remain constant in total during a specific period) from variable costs (which remain relatively constant per unit of output) is of paramount importance. Any costs that are neither one nor the other (i.e. semi-fixed or semi-variable expenses) can usefully be classified as mixed costs. Apart from showing the cost breakdown in some detail, Table 4 also shows the target level of activity (i.e. the fixed budget) as well as the efficiency with which the actual level of activity was attained. This information is vital to effective control since it distinguishes variances due to planning errors on the one hand and those due to operating failings on the other. By identifying variances and ascertaining their causes it is possible to learn.

The procedure for preparing a flexible budget is set out below, but the actual performance of the task is difficult because it must be built on a detailed analysis and understanding of cost behaviour patterns throughout the organization. In addition, there is a major educational obstacle to be overcome when first proposing to introduce flexible budgeting into an organization. All those involved in the operation must be trained to appreciate the purpose of flexible budgeting and to perform the necessary steps in the associated planning and control exercise.

Despite these major difficulties, the procedure to follow is set out in these five steps:

1. Specify the time period that is to be used. This may be, for example, daily, weekly, monthly, or four weekly, depending on the

Marketing management

Table 4 Flexible budget analysis

	Fixed budget	Flexible budget	Actual	Variance
Sales (units)	10,000	11,000	11,000	–
Sales revenue	£15,000	£16,500	£16,500	–
Expenditure:				
Direct	10,000	11,000	11,000	–
Fixed indirect	1,500	1,500	1,450	–50
Variable indirect	2,000	2,200	2,240	+40
Mixed indirect	500	520	510	–10
Profit	£1,000	£1,280	£1,300	+£20

variability of the activities in question: the more variable they are, the shorter the time period should be.

2 Classify all costs into fixed, variable and mixed categories.
3 Determine the types of standards that are to be used.
4 Analyse cost behaviour patterns in response to past levels of activity. From this should come an agreed means by which a total cost figure for a given item can be accumulated at any specified level of business activity. Formulae are commonly used for this purpose: thus freight charges may be expressed as being equivalent to £500 per period plus £1.15 per unit. In this instance the fixed costs of the operation are £500 and the variable costs are £1.15 per unit, so for a sales level of 1000 units during a given period the total freight cost will be:

$$£500 + £1.15 (1,000)$$
$$= £500 + £1,150 = £1,650$$

5 Build up the appropriate flexible budget for specified levels of activity (either actual or anticipated).

5 Some behavioural issues

In many respects budgets help managers either to make sense of or give sense to organizational roles and activities. Some examples will illustrate this point.

1 Making sense of 'facts'. Budgets help managers to make sense of situations by placing particular interpretations on events, happenings and problems. For example, a report may indicate that Division A achieved sales revenue of £500,000 in the period June–December 1999. This is a description of a state of affairs. However, we can use the budget to make another interpretation of this 'fact'. We may use it to point out that this level of sales was 50 per cent below budget which immediately colours our view of the prevailing state of affairs. By using the budget as a benchmark it is possible to assess the adequacy of a sales level of £500,000.

2 Making sense of objectives. Budgets are used to represent the aspirations of top managers within an organization and denote input–output combinations which are 'feasible' and 'desirable'. Through such representation budgets give a sense of the values and goals held by powerful individuals within organizations. In addition, changes in these values and goals will usually be reflected in budgets which play an important communications role (see POSITIONING).

3 Making sense of power and authority. Budgets give a sense of the authority and power networks within an organization by means of the top-down approach, reflecting what senior managers expect from their subordinates with respect to performance on revenue, profits, cost and other dimensions.

4 Making sense of organizational culture. Budgets are also an important means of reflecting the 'culture' or 'climate' of an organization. These concepts refer to the principal values, beliefs and social norms

concerning human interaction within an organization. The culture of an organization is typically reflected in symbols, rituals, ceremonies and distinctive forms of talk, language and dress which permeate organizational life. The budget facilitates many of these characteristics (see CULTURAL ASPECTS OF MARKETING).
5 Making organizations objective and orderly. Budgeted numbers and categories often exude an air of objectivity. However, this objectivity may be only skin deep since both budget numbers and categories can be manipulated to give certain impressions. For example, a sales representative might bias the estimate of next year's sales that he/she uses as a basis for negotiating his/her quota with his/her superior as part of 'playing the system'. Budgets also help to give a sense of order and of rational planning by their formal qualities, but it is not always the case that budgets, once compiled, are used in the control process.

In the light of these points it is possible to make a number of generalizations regarding the relationship between budgets and human behaviour in organizations:

- Budgets affect individuals' work attitudes and their level of performance.
- These individual effects are moderated or influenced by group norms, organizational and societal norms and beliefs.
- Budgets are a Janus-faced social phenomenon: there is a public, rational face and a private, political face both of which are equally real and operative in organizational life.

6 Dangers in budgeting

Budgets drawn up along conventional (i.e. static) lines have certain fundamental drawbacks, such as:

1 They are based on assumed conditions (e.g. stable patterns of demand, unchanging rates of interest) and relationships (e.g. product mix held constant) which are not varied to reflect the actual circumstances that come about.
2 They make allowance for tasks to be performed only in relation to volume rather than time.
3 They compare current costs with estimates based only on historical analyses.
4 Their short-term time horizon limits the perspective, so short-term results may be sought at the expense of longer term stability or success.
5 They have a built-in bias that tends to perpetuate inefficiencies. (For example, next year's budget is determined by increasing last year's by 15 per cent, irrespective of the efficiency factor in last year's.)
6 As with all types of budgets the game of 'beating the system' may take more energy than is being devoted to running the business.
7 The fragile internal logic of static budgets will be destroyed if top management reacts to draft budgets by requiring changes to be made to particular items which are then not reflected through the whole budget.

These typical defects are especially apparent in connection with discretionary costs, such as promotional outlays, which are prominent in a marketing context, and they point strongly to the need for skill and intelligence to be exercised in tailoring a budgeting system to the particular characteristic circumstances and requirements of each individual company.

The business environment is dynamic and a company must not be hindered by its budget from endeavouring to adapt to constantly changing conditions. An unduly rigid framework set up by the budgeting process can interfere with the company's well-being by preventing managers from grasping opportunities which were not predicted when the budget plan was compiled.

Conversely, of course, a budget which fails to give direction (i.e. one which is too loose rather than too rigid) cannot adequately help in coordinating corporate activities in a goal-attaining manner. Under-budgeting, which is the failure to plan ahead in a comprehensive yet flexible way, is as dangerous as over-budgeting, which is exemplified by the rigid situation suggested in points 1–7 above in which an excessive degree of inflexibility causes the budget to become meaningless and unduly expensive.

It should be borne in mind that a budget plan represents a means to an end: it is not an end in itself. The desired end is the attainment of specified objectives. It is dangerous, therefore, to allow the budgeted targets to supersede organizational objectives. This danger can be highlighted by considering a situation in which a budget target is maintained as a major goal, irrespective of changing conditions, instead of being varied (along with other dimensions of the budget plan) in accordance with varying circumstances (subject to whatever constraints have been established) in order that the more important company objective might be achieved.

The practice whereby historical levels of expenditure or revenue are continued into succeeding periods without proper evaluation can hide – and perpetuate – inefficiencies. Past results do not necessarily reflect a desirable level of performance, so future estimates should not be based on them without a reconsideration of standards and other bases of planning by which policies are translated into numerical terms.

Finally, if budgets are used as pressure devices, the result will be resentment and thus a failure in achieving their intended purpose. One highly desirable way of overcoming suspicion and misunderstanding in budgeting is to involve all those who are concerned actively in ensuring that the company reaches its objectives – i.e. to employ the principle of accountability planning as embodied in responsibility accounting.

7 Other analytical techniques

Any marketing model is a simplified representation of a more complex slice of reality. In order to make modelling useful in resource allocation decisions it is appropriate to enquire about the effects (outcomes) that result from changing the inputs (causes) to the model on a 'what if...?' basis. This is known as sensitivity analysis and is one form of experimentation. It indicates the extent to which outcomes are sensitive (i.e. subject to change) in response to variations in particular inputs, and which other inputs can be varied with little impact on outputs. A model's sensitivity should correspond with the sensitivity of the real-world situation and in this sense there is a link between a model's sensitivity and its validity.

In seeking to establish causal relationships by means of experimentation it is necessary to have both 'experimental' and 'control' groups representing, say, two matched samples, two test market locations, two retail outlets, and so on. Selected stimuli (in the form of controllable – i.e. manipulatable – inputs) will initially be identical in both the experimental situation and the control situation, but these stimuli will be selectively and systematically varied in the former while being held constant in the latter. Assuming that the uncontrollable extraneous factors (i.e. environmental inputs) vary in the same way between the experimental and control situations, the differences in observed outcomes can be wholly attributed to the changes which occur in the controllable variables. Let us consider the relationship between sales and advertising for a given product. We could carry out an experiment to determine the nature of this relationship by selecting two matching market situations, one of which would be the control and the other the experimental location. Initially there would be no advertising in either marketplace, but this would be gradually introduced into the experimental location only. Prior to the introduction of advertising, with all other controllable variables being identical in each location, there would have been levels of sales which accorded with existing inputs, so the introduction of a new input should be the main factor in any subsequent variation in the ratio of sales in both locations (subject to the usual tests of statistical significance). In this way it is possible to build up an awareness of the manner in which particular variables (such as sales levels or profit levels) depend on other variables (such as advertising activity or the interaction of cost and revenue functions). Variables of the first type are termed *dependent variables* and those of the second type are termed *independent variables*: the values of independent variables can either be determined by management or emerge from an earlier interaction of variables in which we are not currently interested, and these independent variables then interact to produce the values of the dependent variables in which we are interested.

Diagrammatically, we can portray experimentation in a systems model (see Figure 6).

In an experiment attempts are made to identify all the factors that affect a particular independent variable, and these factors are then manipulated systematically (insofar as it is within the firm's power to do so) in order to

Figure 6 Experimentation

isolate and measure their effects on the performance of the dependent variable.

It is not possible to plan or control all the conditions in which an experiment is conducted; for example, the timing, location and duration of an experiment can be predetermined, but it is necessary to measure such conditions as the weather and eliminate their effects from the results.

The independent variables that are the subject of marketing experimentation may include the demand for one of the company's various products, or one of the environmental factors it faces, and the dependent variable may be one of the company's objectives. Profit is a dependent variable of both the particular marketing strategy adopted and of the external conditions prevailing at the time when that strategy is executed.

Because experiments are concerned with the deliberate manipulation of controllable variables (i.e. such variables as selling prices and advertising effort), a good deal more confidence can be placed in conclusions about the effects of such manipulations than if the effects of these changes are based purely on historical association or vague projections rather than on the basis of experimentation.

Ideas for experiments can result from marketing cost studies. The following questions are fairly representative of those that can be answered as a result of experimentation:

1. By how much (if any) would the net profit contribution of the most profitable product be increased if there were an increase in specific marketing outlays, and how would such a change affect the strategy of competitors in terms of, say, market shares?
2. By how much (if any) would the net losses of unprofitable products be reduced if there were some decrease in specific marketing outlays?
3. By how much (if any) would the profit contribution of profitable products be affected by a change in the marketing effort applied to the unprofitable products, and vice versa, and what would be the effect on the total marketing system?
4. By how much (if any) would the total profit contribution be improved if some marketing effort were diverted to profitable territories or customer groups from unprofitable territorial and customer segments?
5. By how much (if any) would the net profit contribution be increased if there were a change in the method of distributions to small unprofitable accounts or if these accounts were eliminated?

Only by actually carrying out properly designed marketing experiments can management realistically predict with an acceptable degree of certainty the effects of changes in the allocation of marketing effort on the level of sales revenue and profit of each differentiated product, territory or customer segment in the multiproduct company.

Experiments must be conducted under conditions that resemble the real-life conditions of the marketplace insofar as this is possible. It is pointless, for example, to carry out an experiment to prove that the sale of £1's worth of product X in Southampton through medium-sized retailers contributes more to profit than does the sale of £1's worth of product Y through small retailers in Leeds, if the market for product X is saturated and no reallocation of marketing resources can change the situation. This points to the danger of confusing what is happening now with what may happen in the future – ascertaining that product X is more profitable than product Y may be the right answer to the wrong question.

The style of question should be: 'What will happen to the value of dependent variables in the future if the values of specific independent variables are manipulated now?' If the concern is with the allocation of sales effort, the aim of an experiment may be to show how changes in the total costs of each sales team can be related to changes in the level of sales revenue generated. In such a relatively simple case, where only one type of marketing effort is being considered, this effort should be reallocated to those sales segments where an additional unit of effort will yield the highest contribution to profits.

The experiment can be designed to show which sales segment produces the highest value when the following equation is applied to each:

(Additional sales – additional variable costs)/additional expenditure

If an additional budget allocation of £100,000 to the London salesforce results in extra sales of £500,000 with additional variable costs amounting to £200,000, then the index of performance is:

(500,000 – 200,000)/100,000 = 3.

It may happen that the same index computed for the Midlands salesforce has a value of 4, in which case selling effort should be reallocated to the Midlands, *provided* due consideration has been given to the expected level of future demand.

As a result of the high costs involved, experiments must usually be conducted with small samples of the relevant elements. This is generally valid so long as the samples are properly determined and representative. However, it is believed by some that marketing experimentation is not a feasible means by which information can be obtained as a basis for making important decisions.

There are certainly a lot of difficulties to be overcome in planning and executing experiments, and the need to keep special records and make repeated measurements is both expensive and time-consuming. The risk is always present that the results of an experiment will be of limited value because they may not be statistically significant. A further risk is that even temporary and limited experimental variations in the marketing mix may damage sales and customer relationships both during and after the experiment.

Other problems which need to be addressed prior to adopting marketing experimentation include:

1 The measuring of short-term response when long-term response may be of greater relevance.
2 Accurate measurements can be difficult to obtain – despite the high expense involved.
3 It is almost impossible to prevent some contamination of control units by test units since it is difficult to direct variations in the marketing mix solely to individual segments.
4 Making experiments sufficiently realistic to be useful is hindered by such difficulties as the national media being less flexible than may be desired, and the fact that competitors may not react to local experimental action in the same way as they would to a national change in policy.

These problems and difficulties, while discouraging, are insufficient to discount completely the use of experimentation as a valuable means of obtaining information to increase the effectiveness and efficiency of marketing operations. Indeed, it is likely that the use of experimental techniques will become increasingly widespread, as has been the case with test marketing which is the best known form of experimentation in marketing.

Programming

Programming is a form of analytical modelling that is useful in allocation problems. The most widely-used technique is *linear programming*, which aims to determine the optimum allocation of effort in a situation involving many intereacting variables. In other words, it produces that solution which maximizes or minimizes a particular outcome in accordance with given constraints (e.g. How should sales effort be allocated among regions to maximize the level of sales subject to a maximum availability of 10,000 units of product per period, or what product mix should be sold – subject to demand – in order to give the maximum profit?)

In all cases the marketing manager will be interested in making the best use of his/her limited resources and the constraints that exist will set the upper limit to the level of performance that is possible. The company cannot spend more on advertising each product than it has in its advertising appropriation, thus:

$$a_1(W) + a_2(X) + a_3(Y) + a_4(Z) \leq A$$

Where: $\leq$ means 'equal to or less than'
A is the total advertising appropriation
$a_1(W)$ is the amount spent on advertising Product W
$a_2(X)$ is the amount spent on advertising Product X
$a_3(Y)$ is the amount spent on advertising Product Y
$a_4(Z)$ is the amount spent on advertising Product Z

Similarly, a constraint exists in relation to every fixed budget or limited resource such as salesforce time and warehouse space:

$$b_1(W) + b_2(X) + b_3(Y) + b_4(Z) \leq B$$

Where: B is the total available sales force time
$b_1(W)$ is the time devoted to selling product W, etc.

And:

$$c_1(W) + c_2(X) + c_3(Y) + c_4(Z) \leq C$$

Where: C equals the available warehouse space
$c_1(W)$ is the space occupied by the inventory of product W, etc.

The basis on which resources are allocated is the *marginal response*. If the expenditure on advertising of £100,000 produces sales amounting to £500,000 then the *average response* is 5/1; and if an increase in advertising expenditure of £10,000 produces additional sales totalling £100,000 this gives the measure of marginal response, which is equal to 10/1. Marginal response can thus be seen to be a measure of the value of opportunities presented.

If a company's advertising budget is set at £100,000 for a period, the optimal allocation to each of the company's products (A, B and C) is given by equating the marginal responses because this gives the situation where it will not be beneficial to reallocate funds from one product to another. The requirement is to find the best solution to the equation:

$$a_1(A) + a_2(B) + a_3(C) = £100,000$$

where $a_1(A)$ is the advertising budget for product A, $a_2(B)$ for product B, and $a_3(C)$ for product C. This is given when:

$$dYA/dXA = dYB/dXB = dYC/dXC$$

where dYA/dXA is the marginal response for product A measured as change in sales/change in advertising outlay, and so on for products B and C.

Linear programming must be applied in the absence of uncertainty, which means that uncertainty must be eliminated before variables are incorporated into a linear programme. Moreover, all the relationships of problems put into a linear programming format are assumed to be linear, and this may not apply under all possible conditions. For example, costs rarely rise in direct proportion to increases in sales volume. But even with this discrepancy linear programming is able to indicate the best direction for allocating resources to segments. This technique can be used to determine the best (i.e. optimal) solution to allocation decisions in the following circumstances:

1 Where there is a clear, stated objective.
2 Where feasible alternative courses of action are available.
3 Where some inputs are limited (i.e. where constraints exist).
4 Where 1 and 2 can be expressed as a series of linear equations or inequalities.

RICHARD M.S. WILSON
THE BUSINESS SCHOOL, LOUGHBOROUGH UNIVERSITY

Further reading

(References cited in the text marked *)

Duffy, M.F. (1989) 'ZBB, MBO, PPB and their effectiveness within the planning/marketing *process*' Strategic Management Journal 10: 163–73.

Hofstede, G.H. (1968) *The Game of Budget Control*, London: Tavistock.

Mantrala, M.K., Sinha, P. and Zoltners, A.A. (1992) 'Impact of resource allocation rules on marketing investment-level decisions and profitability', *Journal of Marketing Research* 29: 162–75.

Mossman, F.H., Crissy, W.J.E. and Fischer, P.M. (1978) *Financial Dimensions of Marketing Management*, New York: Wiley.

Piercy, N.F. (1986) *Marketing Budgeting*, London: Croom Helm.

Piercy, N.F. (1987) *Budgeting for Marketing – Principles and Practices*, London: Allen & Unwin.
Piercy, N.F. (1988) 'The marketing budgeting process: marketing management implications', *Journal of Marketing* 52: 45–59.
Rayburn, L.G. (1976) *Financial Tools for Marketing Administration*, New York: Amacom.
Schiff, M. and Lewin, A.Y. (1974) *Behavioral Aspects of Accounting*, Englewood Cliffs, NJ: Prentice-Hall.
Sevin, C.H. (1965) *Marketing Productivity Analysis*, New York: McGraw-Hill.
Shapiro, S.J. and Kirpalani, V.H. (1984) *Marketing Effectiveness: Insights from Accounting and Finance*, Boston: Allyn & Bacon.
Stasch, S.F. (1972) *Systems Analysis for Marketing Planning and Control*, Glenview, IL: Scott, Foresman.
Ward, K.R. (1989) *Financial Aspects of Marketing*, Oxford: Heinemann.
Wilson, R.M.S. (1981) *Financial Dimensions of Marketing: A Source Book*, vol. 1 and vol. 2, London: Macmillan.
Wilson, R.M.S. (1999) *Accounting for Marketing*, London: ITBP.
Wilson R.M.S. (1999) *Marketing Controllership*, 9th edn, Aldershort: Ashgate.
Wilson, R.M.S. and Chua, W.F. (1993), *Managerial Accounting: Method and Meaning*, 2nd edn, London: Chapman & Hall.
Wilson, R.M.S. and Gilligan, C.T. (1997) *Strategic Marketing Management: Planning, Implementation and Control*, 2nd edn, Oxford: Butterworth-Heinemann.

See also: CULTURAL ASPECTS OF MARKETING; ENVIRONMENTAL ANALYSIS; MARKETING RESEARCH; POSITIONING; QUALITATIVE RESEARCH IN MARKETING; QUANTITATIVE METHODS IN MARKETING; THE MARKETING AUDIT; THE MARKETING MIX

Information technology and marketing

1 Introduction
2 Information technology and marketing programmes
3 Redesigning marketing processes
4 Information technology and the future of marketing
5 Conclusion

Overview

Recent major developments in information technology (IT) have led to its steadily increasing use in marketing. These changes are affecting each of the major elements of marketing programmes: product design and development, pricing, advertising and sales promotion, salesforce activities, and distribution systems. Within IT marketing decision support systems (MDSS) are currently evolving, assisting managers to make better decisions with respect to these various programme elements.

However, there are prospects for more fundamental modifications in marketing processes via IT – for example supported 'reengineering' of traditional systems. Future prospects for the development of IT-centred applications in marketing and their implications are also considered.

1 Introduction

Throughout history, marketing practices and institutions have been shaped by changes in the technologies available for collecting, storing, communicating and analysing information. To make intelligent decisions, marketing managers need accurate and timely information about sales, customers, competitors' activities and other events in the marketplace. Equally important, in order to make offerings to prospective customers, marketers must communicate with them.

In this article, we describe and evaluate trends in 'information technology' (IT) that are affecting marketing. The evolution of IT has led to especially dramatic changes in marketing since the early 1980s. Among the key developments have been the measurement of retail sales via scanning, outfitting field salesforces with laptop computers, utilization of planning software by product managers, utilization of electronic order-entry systems, and – most recently – the use of the Internet for communications and transactions between suppliers and customers.

Though these and related changes are quite recent, they represent extensions of trends that were becoming evident a generation ago. In a 1965 *Harvard Business Review* article, John Diebold accurately foresaw many of the ways in which IT would transform managers' roles (Diebold 1965). At the same time, articles in *Business Week* and *Sales Management* described applications of computers in marketing, primarily in the areas of inventory control and salesforce reporting (*Business Week* 1965, *Sales Management* 1965), while Kotler (1966) envisioned a 'marketing information and analysis centre' very much like what in the late 1970s came to be termed a '(marketing) management decision support system.'

While some marketing practitioners and scholars anticipated how IT would evolve and transform marketing practice, the changes that have taken place since the 1960s have not been easy or 'automatic'. Enormous effort, creativity and investments have been required to realize the potential that some could envision so long ago. The changes have been cumulative, with each succeeding generation of hardware and software building on its predecessors.

Key developments in information technologies

Increasing use of IT tools in marketing has been driven by continuing improvements in the capabilities and cost effectiveness of information processing and telecommunications systems. In both of these fields, the tools available to managers have become progressively more powerful, less expensive, more portable, and easier to use. In the paragraphs that follow we summarize some of the most important trends.

Marketing management

Processing: more powerful, smaller and less expensive

Computer hardware systems have evolved rapidly from the earlier mainframe-based model toward one based on desktop and portable machines, typically linked in 'client-server' networks within firms and via the Internet and/or private networks to suppliers, customers and others. The development of powerful portable computers has enabled marketers to equip field sales and service personnel with greatly enhanced 'mobile computing' capabilities.

Miniaturization is also enabling manufacturers to incorporate 'computer on a chip' components into a wide variety of products. Office copiers, automobiles, appliances, elevators and other products include microprocessors that diagnose or even anticipate service requirements.

The costs of computer hardware, relative to capabilities, declined dramatically during the 1980s and 1990s. Declining component prices reflected experience-based cost reductions, intense competition and aggressive pricing strategies adopted by producers in order to expand their markets. By 1998 simplified desktop computers were being promoted at prices below $1000 and there was discussion of even less costly machines being introduced with much of their software provided through networks rather than internally.

Data storage: greater capacity, easier access, lower cost

Paralleling the improvements in computer hardware, data storage capabilities are expanding and their costs are declining. Contemporary systems are designed to accommodate video images of ever-higher resolution, along with rapidly growing amounts of alphanumeric data. Digital versatile discs (DVD-ROMs) provide much greater storage capacities than earlier modes, and other technologies are also being developed.

Display: greater resolution, less bulky and less costly

Key developments in display technology include improvements and cost reductions for so-called 'active matrix' colour LCDs (liquid crystal displays) that are used in laptop and notebook computers. Other technologies still in development include new types of flat panel displays and digital high-definition television (HDTV).

Software: easier to use, more versatile

The general adoption of 'graphical user interface' (GUI) systems, pioneered by Apple in its Macintosh machines and later adopted in Windows systems, has made computers much more accessible for inexperienced users. The number and variety of applications programmes, many of them specifically designed for marketing, continues to grow rapidly. The development of applications programmes has been spurred, in part, by the availability of computer-assisted software engineering (CASE) and object-oriented programming tools.

Networks: increased capacities at lower cost

Fibre optics and digital technology are revolutionizing telecommunications networks. Telecommunications companies have already installed large amounts of fibre optic cables in their networks, and plan to extend broadband links to individual households. Concurrently, telecommunications costs have declined, due in part to privatization of state-owned systems and to the entry of new, privately-owned competing carriers. In many countries, cable television companies have started to provide 'cable modems,' which provide much greater bandwidth than traditional telephone connections.

Wireless systems: from voice to data

There has been tremendous growth in the use of wireless voice communications, and similar growth is expected in wireless data communications. Several technologies are emerging in this area, including Cellular Digital Packet Data (CDPD), CDMA and radio-frequency based systems. The rapidly growing popularity of the Internet is fuelling growth in demand for widespread wireless data connectivity.

Client-server systems and groupware

As the use of desktop and portable computers has grown, the 'architecture' of computer systems has evolved toward one in which microcomputers are linked in server-based local networks (LANs) which, in turn, are linked into wide area networks. This structure enables companies to achieve the benefits of both centralized and decentralized computing, as well as providing 'closed-circuit' communications network capabilities.

Within local and wide-area networks, there is increasing use of 'groupware,' which supports collective discussion or decision-making. Teams can be assembled around specific projects, such as the Ford product development task force mentioned in a later section. This approach will undoubtedly be more widely used in the future.

Automated information capture

An important enabling factor for the use of IT in marketing has been the development and widespread adoption of automated data collection systems. Of particular importance are barcode scanners used for measuring and recording retail sales as well as shipments and receipts within production and distribution systems. A related technology is that in which magnetic stripe cards are scanned to approve credit extension and record transactions. Another technology makes use of the US government's Global Positioning System (GPS) satellites to track the movements of trucks, shipping containers and other mobile objects.

Electronic data interchange interchange

A combination of several IT elements is utilized in electronic data interchange (EDI) systems. EDI is the exchange of computer data between organizations in a standard format. Efficient exchange of data requires computer systems, telecommunications networks, and (critically) standards for data format and transmission. EDI is widely used to transmit purchase orders and invoices between buyers and sellers; in some industries, such as automobiles, it has become a required method of doing business. Through 'value-added networks,' EDI is now readily available to virtually all companies. EDI can also be implemented via the Internet, which is discussed next.

The Internet

Without doubt the most dramatic changes in marketing communications during the 1990s have been those related to the explosive growth of the Internet. The predecessor of the Internet, ARPANET, was developed in the 1960s as a network for linking the US Defense Department and key university research institutions working on defence-related projects. The efficient functioning of this network was made possible by the use of 'packet switching' techniques and by the adoption of the TCP/IP protocol, which specifies a standard format for all communications on the system (Cairncross 1997).

What transformed the Internet from a forum of research specialists into a mass communication medium was the development of the World Wide Web around 1990. The web provides access to information throughout the entire worldwide system of computers linked to the Internet, via the use of hypertext and browsers such as Netscape Navigator. These technologies, together with search engines such as Yahoo and Lycos, make locating information within the system easy for virtually anyone.

The number of Internet users and websites has grown very rapidly during the 1990s. By 1997 it was estimated that there were 25–35 million Internet users worldwide, and the number was expected to grow to 200 million by the year 2000.

Both business users and households are using the Internet to obtain information about products and services, to place orders and arrange for payment, and to access customer services. These new capabilities are beginning to have important effects on marketing communications and distribution systems, as discussed in later sections of this article.

According to research firm @plan, 24 per cent of active web users were making purchases online by late 1997. Products and services for which Internet shopping and ordering is becoming popular include computers, books, recorded music, airline reservations and securities trades. The fastest growing categories were airline ticket reservations, stocks and mutual funds, computer hardware, car rental and books. Networking equipment manufacturer Cisco Systems claims to have conducted $3.2 billion in business over the Internet in 1997, while personal computer maker Dell sold $1 billion of PCs over the Internet in 1997.

Consider the case of shopping for cars and groceries using the Internet. J.D. Power estimated that 16 per cent of customers who purchased new cars in 1997 used the Net for research before making a purchasing decision, compared with 10 per cent in 1996. About two per cent (or about $6 billion worth) of the 15 million new cars purchased in 1997 in the US can be directly attributed to the Internet. Specialists foresee as many as 50 per cent of new customers using the Internet for online car purchasing by the year 2000.

Andersen Consulting projects that grocery shopping and the purchase of general household items on the Internet will escalate from a value of $100 million in 1997 to $85 billion in 2007. As many as 20 million people, 15 per cent of households in the US, are expected to favour Internet shopping over going to a store to shop by 2007.

2 Information technology and marketing programmes

The most straightforward applications of IT in marketing are those in which IT tools are used to facilitate or improve analysis and decision making related to the traditional elements of marketing programmes, i.e. the 'four Ps.' In this section we describe how IT is being applied to each of these areas. The changes in practice that we discuss should not be attributed solely to the adoption of IT-supported approaches; other factors, especially intensified global competition, are also influencing marketing during the 1990s.

Product design and development

Competitive pressures have stimulated managers in many companies to seek ways of accelerating and improving the methods they use to conceive, design, develop and test new products and services. Significant applications of IT in this area include uses of computer-assisted design (CAD) systems and utilization of telecommunications among product design groups, users and others.

CAD systems enable designers to create and readily manipulate three-dimensional images of products, which can often replace physical prototypes or patterns that are expensive and time-consuming to make. CAD systems also make it possible for designers to communicate product specifications to manufacturing, as inputs to computer-integrated manufacturing systems.

Improvements in telecommunications enable product designers in different locations to share information and co-ordinate their efforts by transmitting CAD images or other graphics and data. The 1994 Ford Mustang automobile, for example, was designed as a collaborative effort of design teams working in Michigan, England and Italy (Sherman 1993).

IT is making it easier and less expensive to customize products for individual customers. Perhaps the best example of a firm utilizing this capability is that of the Dell Computer Corporation, founded by Michael Dell – an 18-year old college student – in 1985. Dell's computers, marketed primarily to corporate accounts, are built (assembled) to customers' orders. A corporate customer authorizes one or a few combinations of features for laptops, often including pre-loaded software and barcode labelling of the machines for identification purposes. Individual users can then select from these predetermined options. Alternatively, a customer can choose from a menu of components and features at the time he or she places an order.

In the mid-1990s it was generally expected that there would be increasing use of IT to support 'mass customization' of products in many industries. Companies such as Levi Strauss, Dell Computer and others have started to provide customized products to buyers. However, as of mid-1998, mass customization remains a relatively marginal phenomenon in marketing.

Pricing

To the extent that utilization of IT provides managers with more accurate and more detailed marketplace information and more accurate cost data, it enables them to make better-informed pricing decisions. Data provided by scanner systems in supermarkets, for example, give consumer product marketers an improved basis for estimating the effects of a price change or a temporary price reduction, taking into account the other factors affecting sales in a given time period.

A more specific application of IT to pricing that is of strategic importance in certain industries is that of 'yield management' systems. First developed by the major airlines, these systems enable managers to establish and later modify prices on the basis of past history and up-to-date reservations information for each flight. Smith, Leimkuhler, and Darrow (1992) provide a description of American Airlines' 'yield management' system. In this system complex algorithms are utilized, in conjunction with very large-scale databases, to make trade-offs between the opportunity cost of an unsold seat vs. that of being unable to supply a full-fare passenger. The systems are also used for estimating the optimal level of overbooking on a given flight. Similar yield management systems are widely used in the hotel industry as well as by other airlines. In both industries the systems have enabled companies to achieve greater average revenues per unit of capacity.

Another kind of impact of IT on pricing has been a substantial increase in the availability of price information via the Internet. Consumers in the United States, for example, can readily access information about the suggested retail prices and dealer invoice costs of specific automobile models and can 'shop around' to find the lowest offering price. This capability is clearly leading to more competitive pricing among dealers.

Salesforce 'automation'

By the early 1980s companies that rely heavily on field salesforces had begun experimenting with using portable computers and special-purpose terminals to 'automate' salesforce activities. Most of the early efforts in this area were based on special-purpose devices that enabled salespersons to enter orders from a customer location. Later, when high-capacity general-purpose laptop computers became available, most companies adopted them.

In addition to order entry, IT systems are used by field salespersons for such tasks as storing customer information, scheduling, communicating with sales offices, tracking leads and enquiries, and analysing clients' problems. For large firms, equipping salespeople with computers requires a major investment: Frito-Lay, for instance, spent $40 million during 1985–86 on a system for its 10,000 route salespeople (Applegate and Wishart 1987). By the late 1980s hardware costs had declined substantially, user-friendly software was widely available, and it was clear that IT had changed the nature of field selling irrevocably. Among the benefits reported by companies that have adopted the systems are increased sales call capacity per salesperson; improved customer service; ability to roll out promotional programmes more rapidly; and reduced inventories as a result of more accurate, up-to-date information from the field.

Another impact of IT on field selling is in the area of training and product demonstrations. Videos and CDs are now widely used to communicate information about products to salespeople, dealers and users.

Advertising and promotion: micromarketing

Many of the most visible innovations in marketing practice associated with changes in IT are in the area of advertising and sales promotion. Since the 1970s there have been dramatic improvements in the databases available to marketers on individual households, businesses and institutions, and small areas. These databases are used for 'micromarketing', in which marketing programmes—especially advertising and sales promotion—are designed for and delivered to individual customers or small groups of customers. The micromarketing approach may be contrasted with mass marketing, in which standardized products and services are distributed through mass channels and supported by standardized advertising and promotion programmes.

In the paragraphs that follow we discuss briefly three variations on micromarketing approaches to advertising and sales promotion: database marketing, occasion-based marketing and local area marketing.

Database marketing

In database marketing, communications are directed to individuals, households or organizations by name. Cespedes and Smith (1993) suggest that database marketing involves 'three Ts' – *targeting* messages to specific types of customers or prospects (and not others); *tailoring* messages to customer's interests or other characteristics; and the development of *ties* or long-term relationships with preferred customers.

While database marketing methods have long been employed by direct marketers such as catalogue houses and magazine publishers, improvements in IT have made the approach increasingly practical for mass marketers as well since the mid-1980s. Rapp and Collins (1990) describe numerous examples of database marketing programmes carried out by marketers of automobiles, cigarettes, alcoholic beverages, foods, personal care products and services.

Bickert (1992) describes several types of customer databases that are used in marketing. The simplest is one that includes a company's own customers, ideally with their transaction histories. Many kinds of marketers have always had this type of information, although their ability to store and analyse the data was limited until computer systems became sufficiently inexpensive and user-friendly.

External household customer databases include customer or subscriber lists rented from direct marketers or publishers; special-purpose lists derived from public records such as auto registrations or births; and multi-source compiled databases that are derived from a wide variety of sources. Business and institutional customer databases are derived primarily from directories, updated by periodic telephone surveys. Very large-scale databases can be stored on CD-ROMs and utilized on desktop computers or local area networks, making database marketing much easier to implement than in the past (see DIRECT MARKETING).

Occasion-based marketing
Another form of marketing communication made possible by improvements in IT is related to specific 'occasions' such as passing through a supermarket checkout lane or using an automatic teller machine. A system attached to the checkout scanner, for example, can be programmed to issue a coupon based on a shopper's purchase of the sponsor's brand or a competing brand. Other in-store systems have been tested that deliver promotional messages on a video screen attached to a shopping cart, based on the shopper's location in the store.

Local area marketing
The third form of micromarketing involves targeting and tailoring of advertising and sales promotion to small groups of customers, or distribution outlets serving these groups, on the basis of their geographic location. In the United States this approach was first developed after the results of the 1970 Census of Population were provided on computer tapes. Several commercial firms use the Census data, supplemented by other sources, as the basis for so-called 'geodemographic' systems in which the households residing in each of many small areas are assigned to one of 40–50 cluster types, based on demographic indicators of their lifestyles. An individual household in a given area can, then, be 'geocoded' and treated as if its characteristics conformed to the area's averages.

Major uses of geographic customer databases in marketing include retail store location analysis, sales territory and salesperson performance analysis, design of direct mail and telemarketing communications programmes, and design of promotional programmes for individual stores or distributors serving a given area (for examples, see Castle 1993, Baker and Baker 1993).

Privacy issues
Increasing use of micromarketing methods has led to growing concern about privacy issues. A 1992 survey, for example, showed that 78 per cent of US consumers were concerned about threats to personal privacy (Equifax 1992). While marketers were not the only source of these concerns, the growth in consumer databases was clearly a major factor leading to public concern and proposals for additional regulation. In 1990, when computer software producer Lotus Development announced plans to market a CD-ROM containing data on 80 million households derived in part from their credit bureau records, there was a public uproar. Lotus responded by withdrawing the product, and Equifax, the credit rating agency, later discontinued sales of its data to marketers.

For some observers, unwanted telemarketing calls and faxes constituted another form of invasion of privacy; this type of communication was regulated by the Telephone Consumer Protection Act of 1991 and by various state laws.Throughout the 1990s, there have been numerous proposals for additional federal and state legislation to protect consumers' privacy. Most European countries had more stringent regulations on uses of mailing lists and telemarketing than those prevailing in the United States. Bennett (1992) summarizes the common principles of the European countries' laws, including limitations on data collection and use, security requirements and consumer rights to access and correct their records.

Micromarketing outside North America
Most of the IT tools used to implement the various forms of micromarketing in North America were equally available to marketers in other countries. Despite this, micromarketing methods were much less widely used in Europe and Japan as of 1993 (Hughes 1993; Petrison et al. 1993). Among the obstacles to the growth of micromarketing in Japan, for example, were the lack of a standardized address system; the difficulty of coding names in Kanji characters; and regulations limiting the use of directories and lists. Despite these and similar barriers, it was expected that the use of micromarketing programmes would grow in all advanced economies in the future.

Distribution channels

Adoption of new IT-based tools has affected distribution channels in two principal ways: first, by enabling more marketers to distribute their products and services directly to end users; and second, by facilitating the formation of partnerships between vendors and customers in traditional channel systems. The latter is discussed in the section on reengineering marketing processes (see CHANNELS of DISTRIBUTION).

Growth in direct marketing

Advances in IT have greatly expanded the scope of direct marketing, once the almost exclusive province of 'mail order houses,' charities, publishers, and other specialized marketers. Many mainstream marketers in both consumer and business-to-business industries have added direct marketing to their existing distribution methods, while some others rely on it exclusively. Often, but not always, direct distribution is used in conjunction with database marketing programs of the kinds described in the preceding section (see DIRECT MARKETING).

An integral element of many direct marketing systems is the use of toll-free (800 number) long-distance calling facilities, which were first introduced in the USA in 1967. Another key factor has been the rapid spread of credit card ownership, beginning in the 1970s (Sheperdson 1991). Other improvements in telecommunications that facilitate direct marketing include (Deloitte and Touche 1990):

- Growth in automatic number identification (ANI) and telephone channel capacities. ANI allows a telemarketer to match an incoming caller's identity to a customer database.
- Caller-paid (900) services.
- Interactive voice response (IVR) systems, in which callers hear a recorded menu and select from it by entering numbers on their touch-tone telephones.

Major users of direct marketing channels, in addition to traditional direct marketers, include insurance companies, long-distance carriers, major retailers, and microcomputer hardware and software vendors.

No doubt the most far-reaching impact of IT on distribution channels, at least prospectively, will be via the creation of 'electronic marketplaces,' especially home shopping systems. Cable TV-based home shopping networks play this role in a limited way already; eventually, many believe that interactive home systems will become a major form of distribution for a wide variety of goods and services.

In the United States, despite numerous field tests, home shopping systems were still of minor significance in mid-1998. The largest home system, CUC International's 'Shopper's Advantage,' had 3.3 million subscribers by 1993 (Bell 1993). It was generally expected that telephone and cable television companies would continue their efforts to develop home systems in the future, in some cases via strategic alliances and mergers.

By 1998 significant amounts of home shopping and business buying were being carried out via the Internet, as discussed earlier. The trend toward electronic commerce is very strong. Hair and Keep (1997) have summarized the consensus of expectations regarding electronic marketing:

- *Improved market information for sellers*: Better databases will lead to truly customized marketing. Real-time database functions will allow for rapid responses to market trends.
- *Improved market information for buyers*: Buyers will have access to expert systems to help them sift information. They will be able

to view products in 3-D, obtain detailed information on care and usage, ask questions, control and customize their consumption experience.
- *Enhanced interactivity and interconnectivity between buyers and sellers*: Connectivity between buyers and sellers will be broadband, anytime and anyplace. Customers will be able to provide input at every stage, from product idea to launch.
- *Emergence of new market intermediaries*: New intermediaries such as information warehouses will integrate, process and sell data. Intelligent software agents will help customers and sellers optimize exchanges.
- *Expanded technology-based channels of distribution*: 'Digitizable' products such as movies, music, newspapers, magazines, books, tickets and other information will be obtained electronically. There will also be the emergence of new physical delivery channels, which will provide home delivery and pickup from distribution centers.
- *Additional technology-based consumer services*: New technology-enabled services will likely evolve, such as time management services (offering, for example, bill paying and callback reminders), automated routine food purchases, new home security services, etc.
- *More worldwide sourcing*: National boundaries will become increasingly irrelevant as buyers and sellers will be able to find one another easily on the Internet.
- *Increased emphasis on building customer loyalty*: Maintaining customer loyalty will become more difficult but will also become more important. Relationship marketing skills will become extremely important.
- *Safeguards for security and buyer/seller confidentiality*: The privacy and security concerns of buyers will have to be addressed in such a way that they feel empowered and in control. Marketers will have to seek the permission of customers to use their personal information, and will have to emphasize value creation for buyers rather than for themselves.

Marketing decision support systems

The use of computer-supported decision making in marketing started in the 1960s with a focus on simulation models. The use of computers almost exclusively followed the model-building/optimization lines of research (Montgomery and Urban 1969; Kotler 1971). During the 1970s, IT applications dealt primarily with improvements in marketing information systems designed to provide standardized reports to marketing managers within large firms (Choffray and Lilien 1986). Attention also centred on database management systems. The quality and availability of data were key issues in decision making and greater attention was being given to measurement techniques. From these techniques, the focus gradually shifted to managerial problem solving and decision making. There was an emerging trend of support systems for managers in the late 1970s that stressed that a problem-solving technology was emerging that consisted of 'people and knowledge and software and hardware ... successfully woven into the management process' (Keen and Scott-Morton 1978).

Little (1979) suggested the need to shift from status reporting (e.g. sales, market shares) to response analysis (e.g. price and advertising elasticities). This placed greater emphasis on the embedded models and analysis tools rather than on mere reporting of data aggregated in various ways. Little defined a Marketing Decision Support System as: 'a co-ordinated collection of data, systems, tools and techniques with supporting software and hardware by which an organization gathers and interprets relevant information from business and environment and turns it into a basis for marketing action'.

For a detailed treatment of marketing models and decision support systems, see Lilien, Kotler and Moorthy (1992) and Lilien and Rangaswamy (1998).

In the early 1980s, Information Resources Incorporated began to popularize the optical scanner as a data collection device (it had been in use primarily as a means of speeding up store operations). This provided marketers with a large volume of timely, highly accurate data that was complete in most essential respects for the consumer packaged goods industry. This has led, since the mid-1980s, to renewed efforts at data reduction through the greater automation of data analysis. A number of expert systems have been developed which address this need.

Expert systems for marketing

Expert systems are designed to emulate the processes used by human experts to analyse complex problems in relatively narrow domains. Starting in the later 1980s, many companies came to recognize the value of expert systems to improve marketing decision making (see Rangaswamy *et al.* 1987; Sisodia 1992). Some have developed expert systems around small, well-defined problems, using expert system 'shells' (relatively inexpensive and easy-to-use development tools). Other companies have incorporated intelligence into their marketing decision support systems, facilitated by the efforts of major vendors such as Information Resources Incorporated and A.C. Nielsen. The former, for example, provides systems such as PROMOTER (for the evaluation of sales promotions) (Abraham and Lodish 1987) and COVERSTORY (for the automated interpretation of scanner-derived data) (Schmitz *et al.* 1990). The latter sifts through scanner data and performs 'smart exception reporting' in the form of a brief memo giving the marketing manager the 'headlines' it was able to extract from the data.

Many companies (such as DuPont and Digital Equipment Corporation) utilize expert systems to assist in their selling efforts. Often, the expert system can provide detailed product knowledge which a salesperson may lack. Other systems are used to improve the performance of novice salespeople by providing them with the knowledge of expert salespeople. Pricing expert systems are used to generate quotes for custom orders and to assist in bidding for contracts. Expert systems are also being developed to assist in the more creative aspects of marketing, such as advertising development (Burke *et al.* 1990).

Most marketing applications of expert systems thus far have used rule-based approaches. Some companies are beginning to experiment with an alternative approach which utilizes *neural networks,* which are based on pattern recognition and learning. For example, some mail order companies use such systems to identify likely buyers on their mailing lists.

3 Redesigning marketing processes

As business investments in IT grew steadily during the 1980s and early 1990s, many companies began exploring ways to increase the benefits they derived from these investments. Companies came to realize that, rather than using IT to automate existing methods of doing business, they could use the capabilities it provided to create new processes. This realization has impelled the burgeoning 'process reengineering' movement.

The term 'reengineering' was popularized during the late 1980s by Michael Hammer and his collaborators at the CSC Index consulting group (Hammer and Champy 1993). Hammer defines reengineering as 'The fundamental rethinking and radical redesign of business processes to achieve dramatic improvements in critical, contemporary measures of performance such as cost, quality, service, and speed' (Hammer and Champy 1993: 32). Other terms used to designate process analysis and redesign include 'core process redesign' and 'process innovation' (Davenport 1993). All versions of the approach focus on processes, which Davenport defines as 'specific ordering(s) of work activities across time and place, with a beginning, an end, and clearly identified inputs and outputs' (Davenport 1993: 5). Examples of processes include product development and customer acquisition. Most important business processes include activities carried out by two or more functional departments; as a result reengineering can seldom be implemented solely within the marketing component of an organization.

Companies in a variety of industries have reportedly achieved significant performance improvements through process redesign. While process reengineering has thus far had less impact on marketing than on some other business functions, some progress has been made. Two areas in which the reengineering approach has been applied are new product development and distribution channel partnerships.

New product development

In most companies new product development is a process that involves marketing, research and development, and operations management personnel. The process is typically slow, costly and subject to considerable uncertainty. According to Wheelwright and Clark (1992), rapid and effective new product development is increasingly the focal point of competition in many industries. Thus there are strong incentives to improve the new product development process, and some companies have made significant gains in cycle times and development costs via reengineering. One major apparel manufacturer, for instance, was able to reduce the time required for seasonal product line development by a third (Buzzell 1993). Davenport cites similar improvements achieved by manufacturers of automobiles, power tools, pharmaceuticals and photographic equipment. Johansson *et al.* (1993) describe in some detail how AT&T's Power Systems Division simplified the design process for a customized product line. They also provide a step-by-step procedure for process analysis (see NEW PRODUCT DEVELOPMENT).

Channel partnerships

As noted earlier, many buyers and sellers are utilizing electronic data interchange for communication of orders, invoices and other information. In some cases EDI serves as the foundation for 'channel partnerships' between suppliers and retailers or distributors. Buzzell and Ortmeyer (1994) define a channel partnership as 'an ongoing, non-exclusive relationship between a retailer and an independent supplier in which the parties agree on objectives, policies, and procedures for ordering and physical distribution of the supplier's products.'

One of the earliest and most widely-discussed channel partnerships was that established between Wal-Mart and Procter and Gamble in 1985 (CSC Index 1991). Key elements of the partnership, since widely emulated by other retailers and suppliers, included:

- frequent transmission via EDI of point-of-sale sales data, by stockkeeping unit, for the supplier's products in each of the retailer's stores;
- agreement on a 'model stock' of the supplier's products to be displayed in each retail store;
- authorization by the retailer for automatic replenishment of retail stocks by the supplier;
- utilization of advance shipping notice (via EDI) and barcoded shipping container marking to facilitate scheduling and handling of incoming shipments to stores and/or distribution centres.

A primary objective of channel partnerships is to synchronize supplier shipments and, ultimately, production more closely with final customer demand. This is accomplished, first, by providing timely, detailed retail sales data to the supplier and, second, by simplifying the processes used for ordering and physical distribution of products in the channel system. The ordering and physical distribution process is reengineered in several ways:

- IT is used to automate manual activities, including recording of sales, shipments, and receipts via scanning;
- redundant processes, such as entry of order information by both retailer and supplier, are reduced or eliminated;
- some tasks, such as ticketing merchandise, are reassigned from one partner to the other to improve efficiency;
- some control steps, such as checking the content and quality of incoming shipments, are eliminated or reduced to a sampling basis.

Channel partnerships have been widely adopted between retailers and domestic American apparel manufacturers, and between the latter and their upstream textile suppliers. Outside the apparel industry, channel partnerships have also been adopted by suppliers and retailers in such diverse product categories as housewares, personal care products, home furnishings and major appliances. A similar approach, called 'Efficient Consumer Response', has been advocated for the food industry (Kurt Salmon Associates 1993).

The channel partnership approach is not confined to consumer products: similar approaches have been adopted in hospital supply distribution and other business-to-business markets (Index Alliance 1991)(see CHANNEL MANAGEMENT; CHANNELS OF DISTRIBUTION).

4 Information technology and the future of marketing

Several organizational changes have already been observed as a result of the use of advanced information technologies in marketing and its adjacent business functions. Some of these are:

- *Flattening of structures*: As with other functional areas, marketing is being affected by reductions in middle management ranks.
- *Decentralization of marketing activities*: More marketing decisions are now being made by front-line (i.e. customer contact) personnel empowered with information tools. In some companies, regional sales offices are taking over many marketing tasks.
- *Greater use of cross-functional teams*: Some companies have reorganized their marketing divisions into customer-centred teams, which go beyond major account management in that they include personnel from other functional areas.

Looking to the future, two trends are apparent. First, the quality and quantity of marketing data are now such that its mere possession does not confer any competitive advantage. More important today is the quality of a company's knowledge bases, i.e. its ability to utilize its best knowledge and capabilities in every decision-making situation. Knowledge-based systems will thus become more important in the future.

Second, marketing practices will probably be significantly affected by the development of an upgraded computing and communication infrastructure extending into the homes of individual consumers. This system is expected to be interactive (i.e. it will allow for two-way communication) and broadband (it will readily handle video, audio and other forms of information).

Marketing may be profoundly affected by this 'information highway'. Companies will be able to target their advertising, sales promotion and personal selling efforts more precisely. They will be able to ease time and place constraints on consumers by enabling 'anytime, anyplace' access to their offerings, and facilitating the direct delivery of goods and services. The electronic distribution channel represented by the network may be used to deliver a wider range of services.

If these changes come to pass, retailing will be broadly impacted in the process. Some retailers are already planning interactive shopping systems. For a discussion of some of the characteristics of a future information-based 'mall', see Sheth and Sisodia (1993).

Marketing in this environment will involve the 'monocasting' or 'pointcasting' of communications, a high degree of customer involvement, and far greater integration between marketing and operations to deliver more customized products. It will also result in a more efficient use of marketing resources, reduced customer alienation resulting from misapplied marketing stimuli, and increased pressure to deliver greater value.

Advanced technologies allow for the creation of natural user interfaces that are likely to make future systems far more accessible to consumers than videotext systems. For example, virtual reality is a fast-improving technology that enables users to interact with computers in a natural, three-dimensional mode. While enhancing convenience, such systems will also enable buyers to make more informed purchases, since they will get immediate access to a variety of information sources.

5 Conclusion

The marketing function has made rapid strides in making use of IT capabilities. However, the potential exists for many more changes in coming years. More than all other business functions, marketing deals with variables that are intangible and difficult to measure and control. The marketing profession's challenge has been to achieve greater precision in how it manages and measures these variables, and thus more accountability in how it expends resources on them. The use of proven marketing models, better data capture and analysis tools and micromarketing approaches have allowed marketing to make some progress on these fronts.

Notwithstanding, the pressures on marketing remain great. Firms today spend proportionately more on the marketing function than they did in the past, as they have successfully removed many inefficiencies from other areas. Through the judicious use of IT, the marketing function can continue to increase its efficiency and effectiveness.

ROBERT D. BUZZELL
GEORGE MASON UNIVERSITY, FAIRFAX, VIRGINIA
RAJENDRA S. SISODIA
BENTLEY COLLEGE, WALTHAM, MASSACHUSETTS

Further reading

(References cited in the text marked *)

* Abraham, M.M. and Lodish, L.M. (1987) 'PROMOTER: an automated promotion evaluation system', *Marketing Science* 6: 101–23. (Describes an expert system used for a comprehensive evaluation of sales promotions in the consumer packaged goods industry.)
* Applegate, L. and Wishart, N.A. (1987) *Frito-Lay, Inc.: A Strategic Transition (B)*, Boston: Harvard Business School Publishing Division. (One of a three part series of case studies describing Frito-Lay's program to automate salesforce functions.)
* Baker, S. and Baker, K. (1993) *Market Mapping*, New York: McGraw Hill, Inc. (A 'how-to-do-it' manual for using mapping software in marketing.)
* Bell, C.J. (1993) *CVC International: Shoppers Advantage*, Case No. 594-027, Boston: Harvard Business School Publishing Division. (A case study describing CVC's home shopping system.)
* Bennett, C.J. (1992) *Regulating Privacy*, Ithaca, NY: Cornell University Press. (A comparative study of public policies regarding data protection in the United States and Europe.)
* Bickert, J. (1992) 'Database marketing: an overview', in E.L. Nash (ed.) *The Direct Marketing Handbook*, 2nd edn, New York: McGraw-Hill. (A chapter providing a good concise discussion of databases and their uses in marketing.)
  Blattberg, R.C., Glazer, R. and Little, J.D.C. (1994), *The Marketing Information Revolution*, Boston, MA: Harvard Business School Press. (A collection of fifteen contributions on various aspects of information technology impact on marketing.)
  Burke, R.R., Rangaswamy, A., Wind, J. and Eliashberg, J. (1990) 'A knowledge-based system for advertising design', *Marketing Science* 9: 212–29. (A description of 'ADCAD,' an expert system to aid in the design of television commercials.)
* *Business Week* (1965) 'Computers begin to solve the marketing puzzle', Special Report, 7 April. (An early look at the impact of information technology on marketing.)
* Buzzell, R.D. (1993) *Vanity Fair Mills: Market Response System*, Boston: Harvard Business School Publishing Division. (A case study describing Vanity Fair's channel partnership with retailers.)
* Buzzell, R.D. and Ortmeyer, G. (1994) 'Channel partnerships: a new approach to streamlining distribution', Marketing Science Institute Working Paper. (An overview of channel partnerships between retailers and consumer product manufacturers.)
* Cairncross, Frances (1997) *The Death of Distance*, Boston, Harvard Business School Press. (A survey of recent developments and likely future trends in telecommunications.)
* Castle, G.H. (ed.) (1993) *Profiting From a Geographic Information System*, Fort Collins, CO: GIS World, Inc. (A collection of papers on applications of geographic information systems in marketing and other fields.)
* Cespedes, F.V. and Smith, H.J. (1993) 'Database marketing: new rules for policy and practice', *Sloan Management Review* 34: 7–22. (An overview of database marketing with a primary focus on public policy issues.)
* Choffray, J.M. and Lilien, G.L. (1986) 'A decision support system for evaluating sales prospects and launch strategies for new industrial products', *Industrial Marketing Management* 15: 75–85. (Describes marketing information systems for industrial marketing applications.)
* Davenport, T.H. (1993) *Process Innovation: Reengineering Work Through Information Technology*, Boston: Harvard Business School Press. (A practice-oriented textbook on process reengineering.)
* Deloitte and Touche (1990) *A Special Report on the Impact of Technology on Direct Marketing in the 1990s*, New York: Direct Marketing Association. (A consultant's report on potential uses of information technology in direct marketing.)
* Diebold, J. (1965), 'What's ahead in information technology', *Harvard Business Review* 43: September–October. (A highly accurate look ahead at the impact of information technology on managerial roles.)
* Equifax (1992) *Harris-Equifax Consumer Privacy Survey 1992*, Atlanta: Equifax.
* Hair, J.H., and Keep, W.W. (1997) 'Electronic marketing: future possibilities', in R.A. Peterson (ed.) *Electronic Marketing and the Consumer*, Thousand Oaks, CA: Sage Publications. (A compendium of predictions made about the future of electronic marketing by attendees at an academic conference on Electronic Marketing organized by the University of Texas.)
  Hammer, M. (1990) 'Reengineering work: don't automate, obliterate', *Harvard Business Review* 90: 104–12. (A seminal article on process reengineering and its impact on performance.)
* Hammer, M. and Champy, J. (1993) *Reengineering the Corporation*, New York: Harper Business. (A practical guide to process reengineering.)
  Hammond, J. (1993) 'Quick response in retail/manufacturing channels', in S. B. Bradley, J. A. Hausman and R. L. Nolan (eds) *Globalization, Technology and Competition*, Boston: Harvard Business School Press. (A concise summary of the history and impacts of the 'Quick Response' movement in the U.S. textile and apparel industries.)
* Index Alliance (1991) *Channel Partnerships: An Investigation*, Cambridge, MA: CSC Index Inc., pp.

28–31. (Summary of a study of channel partnerships by a leading consulting group in the field.)
* Johansson, H.J., McHugh, P., Pendlebury, A.J. and Wheller, W.A. III (1993) *Business Process Reengineering: Break Point Strategies for Market Dominance*, New York: John Wiley & Sons. (A 'how-to-do-it' primer on process reengineering.)
* Keen, P. and Scott-Morton, M. (1978) *Decision Support Systems: An Organisational Perspective*, Reading, MA: Addison-Wesley. (A textbook on decision support systems with an emphasis on organisational impacts.)
* Kotler, P. (1966), 'A design for the firm's marketing's nerve center', *Business Horizons* 9: 63–74. (An early conceptualization of modern-day marketing decision support systems.)
* Kotler, P. (1971) *Marketing Decision Making: A Model Building Approach*, New York: Holt, Rinehart and Winston. (A comprehensive treatment of how quantitative models can be used to improve marketing decisions.)
* Kurt Salmon Associates (1993) *Efficient Consumer Response: Enhancing Consumer Value in the Grocery Industry*, Washington DC: Food Marketing Institute. (A consultant's report advocating adoption of 'efficient consumer response' programs in the US food distribution system.)
* Lilien, G. and Rangaswamy, A. (1998) *Marketing Engineering*, Prentice Hall. (A 'hands-on' book on the applications of marketing models.)
* Lilien, G., Kotler, P. and Moorthy, S.K. (1992) *Marketing Models*, Englewood Cliffs, NJ: Prentice-Hall. (A thorough source for information on the state-of-the-art in marketing models.)
* Little, J.D.C. (1979) 'Decision support systems for marketing managers', *Journal of Marketing* 43: 9–27. (A seminal article which advocated the development of response-oriented marketing decision support systems.)
  Marchand, M. (1988) *The Minitel Saga*, Paris: Larousse. (A non-technical description and history of the French Minitel system.)
* Montgomery, D.B. and Urban, G.L. (1969) *Management Science in Marketing*, Englewood Cliffs, NJ: Prentice-Hall. (A rigorous and authoritative treatment of analytical approaches in marketing.)
* Petrison, L.A., Blattberg, R.C. and Wang, P. (1993) 'Database marketing: past, present and future', *Journal of Direct Marketing* 7: 27–43. (An excellent overview of the history and status of database marketing.)
* Rangaswamy, A., Burke, R.R., Wind, J. and Eliashberg, J. (1987) 'Expert Systems for Marketing', Working Paper No. 87-107. Cambridge, MA: Marketing Science Institute. (An influential early article on the potential usefulness of expert systems in marketing.)
* Rapp, S. and Collins, T. (1990) *The Great Marketing Turnaround*, Englewood Cliffs, NJ: Prentice-Hall. (A collection of examples of database marketing and related practices.)
* *Sales Management* (1967), 'Some day, I'm going to have a little black box on my desk', 1 May, (33ff). (A surprisingly prescient look ahead at information technology applied to marketing.)
* Schmitz, J.D., Armstrong, G.D. and Little, J.D.C. (1990), 'COVERSTORY: automated news finding in marketing', *Interfaces* 20: 29–38. (Describes how an expert system can be used to automatically extract managerial insights from scanner data.)
* Sheperdson, N. (1991) 'Credit card America', *American Heritage* 125–32. (A brief history of the development and spread of consumer credit cards.)
* Sherman, S. (1993) 'How to bolster the bottom line,' *Fortune* 128: 14–28. (Describes a number of innovative ways in which companies are using information technology.)
* Sheth, J.N. and Sisodia, R.S. (1993) 'The information mall', *Telecommunications Policy* July: 376–89. (A description of the features, benefits and public policy implications of an 'information mall'.)
* Sisodia, R.S. (1992) 'Expert marketing with expert systems,' *Marketing Management* Spring: 32–47. (A detailed description of the state-of-the-art in expert systems for marketing.)
* Smith, B.C., Leimkuhler, J.F. and Darrow, R.M. (1992) 'Yield management at American Airlines', *Interfaces* 22: 8–31. (A description and appraisal of American Airlines' yield management system.)
* Wheelwright, S.C. and Clark, K.B. (1992), 'Creating project plans to focus product development', *Harvard Business Review* 70: 70–82. (Describes the use of 'aggregate project plans' to help companies focus product development efforts.)

See also: CHANNEL MANAGEMENT; CHANNELS OF DISTRIBUTION; DIRECT MARKETING; NEW PRODUCT DEVELOPMENT

Environmental analysis

1 Introduction
2 Information needs
3 The development of environmental scanning
4 Procedures and pitfalls
5 Conclusion

Overview

This entry sets out to show why it is important for organizations to take a formal and systematic approach to environmental analysis. It goes on to describe such an approach and to set out how it can be used by corporate and marketing strategist alike; what benefits it brings to practising firms; what management problems are likely to be encountered; and how possibly to surmount them.

1 Introduction

First considerations

Firms and other commercial organizations owe their existence to the market environment. Like people they are creatures of their environment and they too spend much of their life learning how to cope with the complexity, unforeseen traumas, vagaries and opportunities generated by their environment. Survival and prosperity are conditioned by the demands imposed by this environment. Thus, in the midst of an environment where frequent and major change is becoming the rule, firms must stay at the forefront of trends and issues which will affect their markets and their positions within them.

The market environment consists of the external forces that directly or indirectly influence the firms' goals, structure, plans, procedures, operations, performance, and so on. Environmental analysis is the study of these forces; the relationship between them; and their effects and potential impact on the organization.

The term environmental analysis is often used interchangeably with others such as environmental scanning, competitive intelligence gathering, external search, environmental surveillance and strategic marketing information retrieval. I use the term environmental scanning to encompass the varied information gathering, analysis and dissemination activities that firms pursue in order to keep up-to-date with changes in the market environment. Clearly the purpose of those activities is not merely to keep track of environmental changes. Without environmental analysis and forecasting, there is no basis for strategic planning. Environmental scanning involves activities ranging from highly structured and regularly conducted reviews and forecasts of major trends, issues and events in the business environment, to the irregular 'tip' acquired by means of insider access to a network of private and personal contacts; by reverse engineering competitors' products; by monitoring activity at trade shows and conferences; by obtaining information from employees who used to work for competitors; or even by means of espionage.

Environmental scanning is responsible not only for generating an up-to-date database of information on the changing business scene. It also has the job of alerting management to what is happening in the marketplace, the industry and beyond by disseminating important information and analyses to key strategic decision makers and influencers. However, the conversion of the awareness such dissemination will create into interest, and ultimately to some form of action, is a political process both overt and covert which can emasculate the most penetrating analyses – particularly where vested interests are threatened and top management support absent. It is widely appreciated that the realization of a marketing orientation is, in practice, often inhibited, not by failures of the systems, technology or methodologies of marketing, of which environmental analysis is one, but by disabling management attitudes which often express themselves as resistance to change, conservatism, suspicion and prevarication.

The tasks of gathering, analysing and disseminating information are often organized as discrete activities. The environmental analyst is likely to be a member of the corporate or marketing planning staff, or a top management aid (i.e. a decision influencer), but rarely a strategic decision maker. Strategic decision makers will place their own interpretations on what the expert analyst has to say. In the absence of any other intelligence gathering activity, environmental scanners will, by means of the perceived importance of the information they generate, be in an enviable position to influence strategic decision makers' perceptions of the firm's competitive position and the options available to it. Students of history will recognize that many a bloody political intrigue was spawned by the jealously guarded and often misused privilege of proximity to the seat of power which was conferred on privy counsellors and advisors. Thus, in addition to the analytical skills demanded of environmental scanners, political skills are also important.

Management attitudes have a vital role to play in creating an organizational climate that enables the firm to operate an 'open window of perception' on the past, present and prospective business scene. Readers should understand that the methodology of environmental scanning is no simple panacea for the problems of understanding and coping with the increasingly competitive and turbulent environment of the late 1990s. Methodology alone will not guarantee success and is less important than the thinking it stimulates. Methodologies can be implanted and replicated with much less difficulty than can attitudes or ways of thinking.

The contribution of environmental scanning

Whatever is achieved by environmental scanning will largely depend on the firm's needs and expectations. Small firms may require to be kept up-to-date with local regulatory and economic trends likely to have an immediate impact on day-to-day business prospects. Larger organizations will share the requirements of the small firm, but will also expect information that is broader in scope and with an orientation to the future.

Corporate level environmental scanning is likely to be charged with the responsibility of monitoring, interpreting and forecasting issues, trends and events that go far beyond the customer, market and competitive analyses which most firms perform as a matter of routine. In this context, environmental scanning will be expected to provide a broad but penetrating view of possible future changes in the demographic, social, cultural, political, technological and economic elements of the business environment. The idea is to arm strategic decision makers with the information, analyses and forecasts they consider pertinent to the formulation of the strategies and plans. It should also provide a basis for questioning the assumptions that underpin the firm's strategic thinking and for generating new assumptions. The payoffs from formal environmental scanning can be summarized as follows:

1 Increased awareness by management of environmental changes.
2 More effective strategic planning and decision making.
3 Greater effectiveness in governmental and legislative matters.
4 More informative and insightful industry and market analyses.
5 Improved results in foreign businesses.
6 Improvements in resource allocation.
7 More effective representation of company policies in public fora.

The scope of environmental scanning

The ability to exercise control in the firm's current product markets is derived, at least partly, from a comprehensive and reliable knowledge of customers, suppliers, competitors, regulators and investors. The successful development and upkeep of this knowledge-base is the principal task of formal environmental scanning – one to which the functions of marketing, R&D, purchasing, sales and finance can make a major contribution. However, in the long term it must do more. For instance, as the firm looks away from its existing product markets for future growth opportunities or acquisition candidates within and without its current sphere of operation, knowledge will be required of a new and unfamiliar business environment, having its own unique set of technological, economic, political and social trends. In so doing, greater demands will be made of environmental scanning.

The environment of the firm can be defined as 'those factors which are outside its control but which determine, in part, how the firm performs'. The market environment includes all those factors that exert any influence on the firm, whether directly or indirectly. Given such an unbounded definition you could argue that the rest of the world then constitutes the firm's business environment. Clearly to take such a broad view is of little practical value. The task of environmental scanning is made manageable by taking a selective and carefully considered view of the environment. It will eliminate much of the rest of the world from the firm's immediate attention.

The breadth of the view an organization chooses to take of its business environment has implications for the complexity of the tasks of environmental analysis and forecasting and thus its resource requirements. A broadly defined business mission is associated with a diversified, multiproduct, multi-market firm. It would involve environmental scanning in a very broad arena of operation from which a perspective on international political and economic issues, events and trends may be called for by corporate planning. On the other hand, a narrowly defined business mission may focus the efforts of environmental scanning more on domestic issues concerning immediate events and trends in proximate product markets. Yet the firm's environmental scanning activities should cover as many relevant aspects of the business environment as available resources will permit, particularly those aspects which have an impact on the assumptions being used by the firm in its strategic planning and decision making.

The boundaries of the market environment must be structured in such a way as to enable the analyst to identify important from less important factors and to determine an appropriate time-scale for forecasting changes. One would

Table 1 Framework for analysis of the wider business environment

Cultural	Including the historical background, ideologies, values and norms of the society. Views on authority relationships, leadership patterns, interpersonal relationships, nationalism, science and technology.
Technological	The level of scientific and technological advancement in society. Including the physical base (plant, equipment facilities) and the knowledge base of technology. Degree to which the scientific and technological community is able to develop new knowledge and apply it.
Educational	The general literacy level of the population. The degree of sophistication and specialization in the educational system. The proportion of the people with a high level of professional and/or specialized training.
Political	The general political climate of society. The degree of concentration of political power. The nature of political organization (degrees of decentralization, diversity of functions). The political party system.
Legal	Constitutional considerations, nature of legal system, jurisdictions of various governmental units. Specific laws concerning formation, taxation and control of organizations.
Natural resources	The nature, quantity and availability of natural resources, including climatic and other conditions.
Demographic	The nature of human resources available to the society; their number, distribution, age and sex. Concentration or urbanization of population is a characteristic of industrialized societies.
Sociological	Class structure and mobility. Definition of social roles. Nature of social organization and development of social institutions.
Economic	General economic framework, including the type of economic organization – private versus public ownership; the centralization or decentralization of economic planning; the banking system; and fiscal policies. The level of investment in physical resources and consumption.

Source: Kast and Rosenzweig (1974)

expect there to be factors that deserve to be continuously monitored because of their immediate impact on the industry. These would include users, distributors, suppliers, competitors for customers and suppliers, workforce, government regulators, trade unions, product and process developments. The origin of such factors is known as the 'task environment'. It is defined as 'the more specific forces which are relevant to decision making and change processes of individual organizations'.

The concept of the task environment draws the environmental scanner's eye to the immediate product and supply markets and to those factors which influence the organization's position within them. A wider view casts attention towards the remote areas of community and institutions where developments could be under way which in the longer term would impinge on the firm's position in its current product and supply markets. For instance, substitute products and processes often originate as spin-offs from technological developments that have been made by firms outwith the task environment. Clearly it is important then to look further afield than the task environment. Kast and Rosenweig (1974) divide the wider market environment into nine areas for study and analysis (see Table 1).

Table 2 outlines some of the broad social issues that firms might expect to impinge on their European activities in the late 1990s. Environmental scanning would be expected to follow developments of these issues.

2 Information needs

Organizations subject themselves to the inconvenience and expense of strategic planning in order to acquire more control over the outcome

Table 2 Key international social issues for the 1990s

Issues	Characteristics
Low economic growth	Political instability; rising energy costs; growing unemployment; growth in international capital flows; trends to international protectionism if GATT fails; decline of basic industries; rising inflation; shortages of basic materials; falling productivity; emergence of new market economies of Eastern Europe and Far East trading blocks; increasing national indebtedness and monetary growth; falling investment.
Political uncertainty	Political fragmentation in Europe; expansion of EC; trend towards decentralizing government; growth in terrorism and armed conflict; failure of foreign and international trade policy; rise of nationalism/tribalism; regional convergence on trade and investment policy; decline of liberal democratic values; urban conflict.
Rise of the multi-locals	Large firms decentralize, downsize and form loose federations by devolving responsibility to autonomous units; growth in smaller enterprises; more cross-border networks/partnerships.
Environmentalism	Growing influence of environmentalist lobby; worldwide enactment of legislation on pollution and product liability; closer scrutiny of firms' environmental track record; growth in environmental audit requirements.
Lobby politics	Rising power and influence of lobby groups on issues such as gender, age, consumer protection, health, housing, pollution, materialism, consumer choice, representation, social responsibility, race, poverty, discrimination, access to education.
Growth of government	Closer EC and NAFTA integration and convergence brings with it more bureaucracy and democratic institutions.
Accountability and participation	Demands for greater accountability and transparency in the activities and decisions of government; greater access to local government and participation in it; greater access to information; more disclosure of information and scrutiny of decisions and activities.

of any chosen course of action. Thus, in accordance with Francis Bacon's dictum that 'knowledge itself is power', it could be argued that a knowledge of the business environment must precede the acquisition of any degree of control over it.

The reader is likely to have witnessed the popularization of terms such as espionage, infiltration, moles, security leaks, early warning, electronic surveillance, counter-intelligence, insider dealing, and the like. Although evocative of the anxiety and duplicity of our age, the popularization of the vocabulary of the spy lends some credence to the view that the possession of information is itself a factor endowment, and as such it should be treated as a valuable national asset. It is only one small but logical step to argue that since the gathering of information precedes its possession and dissemination, then this activity also contributes to the generation of wealth.

To the student of military strategy this view follows a familiar line of thought. History offers many examples of battles which could be said to have been fought and won on the basis of 'superior' information. In planning the deployment and employment of their armies' resources, generals rely on the intelligence provided by lines of communications which may have a political origin in their own state, but will certainly infiltrate enemy territory and institutions. By means of the intelligence so provided the general hopes to prepare himself better for the ensuing conflict and to enhance the likelihood of his victory (i.e. to gain some control over the outcome of the conflict).

In the corporate context the tasks of intelligence gathering, surveillance and monitoring are overseen by environmental scanning. The lines of communications are managed to allow a flow of information to be maintained between important elements of the business environment, the environmental scanners and the firm's strategic decision makers. As in the military context, the corporate intelligence service will also provide early warning and careful tracking of possible environmental threats in order that a timely response is conceived and executed. Table 3 indicates corporate sources of information on the business environment. Table 4 comments on their relative importance.

Table 4 also suggests that to enhance the impact of the work of environmental scanning it should seek both the support and involvement of top management in order to implicate or consult all key decision makers and influencers at corporate and divisional level.

In recent years the emergence of information technology has encouraged firms carefully to reexamine the purpose, structure,

Table 3 Sources of information on the business environment

Location	Types	Sources of information on business environment
Inside the company	Written	Internal reports and memos, planning documents, market research, MIS.
	Verbal	Researchers, sales force, marketing, purchasing, advisors, planners, board.
	Combination	Formal and informal meetings (e.g. working parties, advisory committees).
Outside the company	Written	Annual reports, investment reports, trade association publications, institute yearbooks, textbooks, scientific journals, professional journals, technical magazines, unpublished reports, government reports, unpublished papers, abstracts, newspapers, espionage.
	Verbal	Consultants, librarians, government of officials, consumers, suppliers, distributors, competitors, academics, market researchers, industry bodies, journalists, spies, bankers, stockbrokers.
	Combination	Formal and informal meetings, membership of government working parties and advisory boards, industry bodies, trade associations.

Environmental analysis

Table 4 The relative importance of sources of environment information

1	Verbal sources of information are much more important than written sources; 75 per cent of information cited by executives was in verbal form.
2	The higher the executive in the organization, the more important verbal sources became.
3	Of the written sources used, the most important were newspapers (two-thirds), then trade publications, then internal company reports.
4	The major sources of verbal information are subordinates, then friends in the industry, and very infrequently superiors.
5	Information received from outside an organization is usually unsolicited.
6	Information received from inside the organization is usually solicited by the executive.
7	Information received from outside tends to have a greater impact on the decision maker than inside information.
8	The outside sources used varied according to the job of the manager. Thus, marketing managers talked more to customers.
9	The larger the company, the greater the reliance on inside sources of verbal information.

productivity and accessibility of their management information systems, including those governing elements of the business environment. The outcome has often been to reorganize databases and to systematize the tasks of collecting, analysing and disseminating information on the business environment. The demanding task of organizing a database governing elements of the firm's environment is made more so by the difficult nature of environmental information – which often possesses several of the following characteristics:

- poor structure;
- irregular availability;
- provided by unofficial sources;
- qualitative in nature;
- questionable credibility;
- ambiguous definitions;
- opinion-based;
- difficult to quantify;
- insecure methodology;
- likely to change.

3 The development of environmental scanning

Management systems have evolved in response to two trends: the increasing discontinuity, complexity, and novelty of the environmental challenges faced by firms; and the decreasing visibility of the future changes in the business environment. The growing impact of these trends is largely responsible for the widespread following which the strategic planning credo attracted in the wake of the Middle East oil crises of the 1970s. Those events drew attention to environmental scanning as an important element of strategic planning. They also drove developments in environmental scanning techniques and procedures, as well as in the organizational arrangements and systems which support it.

The early evolution of environmental scanning can be traced to the mid 1960s, at which time the market environment was generally being studied only for the purpose of making economic forecasts. In more recent years there has been a wider appreciation of the need to look beyond short-term market conditions to the broad technological, economic, political, social, cultural and demographic elements of the environment.

A pioneering investigation of environmental scanning was conducted by Aquillar in 1967. In this now classic study the process of environmental scanning was originally conceptualized. In his research Aquillar found a lack of a systematic approach to environmental scanning, which is still being reported in more recent research.

Aquillar reported that the firms he had studied collected sixteen types of information about their business environment: he classified them into the five groupings displayed in Table 5. He

Table 5 What information do managers need on the business environment?

Market tidings	
Market potential	Supply and demand consideration for market areas of current or potential interest (e.g. capacity, consumption, imports, exports).
Structural change	Mergers, acquisitions and joint ventures involving competitors, new entries into the industry.
Competitors and industry	General information about a competitor, industry policy, concerted actions in the industry, and so forth.
Pricing	Effective and proposed prices for products of current and potential interest.
Sales negotiations	Information relating to a specific current or potential sale or contract for the firm.
Customers	General information about current or near-potential customers, their markets, their problems.
Acquisition leads	
Leads for mergers, joint ventures, or acquisitions	Information concerning possibilities for the manager's own company.
Technical tidings	
New products, processes, and technology	Technical information relatively new and unknown to the company.
Product problems	Problems involving existing products.
Costs	Costs for processing, operations, and so forth for current and potential competitors, suppliers, and customers, and for proposed company activities.
Licensing and patents	Products and processes.
Broad issues	
General conditions	Events of a general nature: political, demographic, national, and so forth.
Government actions and policies	Governmental decisions affecting the industry.
Other tidings	
Suppliers and raw materials	Purchasing considerations for products of current or potential interest.
Resources available	Persons, land, and other resources possibly available for the company.
Miscellaneous	Items not elsewhere classified.

Source: Aquillar (1967)
Note: Market tidings (52 per cent) was found by far to be the most popular category of environmental information that participants looked for, followed by technical tidings (17 per cent) and broad issues (12 per cent). Aquillar also identified four approaches (i.e. undirected viewing, conditioned viewing, informal search and formal search) to the collection of environmental information and two principal sources of such information. See Tables 3 and 4.

reported that over half the environmental information that was gathered concerned market tidings; very little of the information collected concerned technical tidings and broad issues.

Aquillar identified two principal sources of information on the market environment (i.e. internal and external to the firm). Table 3 classifies sources of information according to Aquillar's scheme. Table 4 summarizes his views on the relative importance of several sources of market information. He found there to be four broad approaches to the collection of this information:

1. Undirected viewing (i.e. exposure to the elements of the business environment without there being a specific purpose in mind).
2. Conditioned viewing (i.e. directed exposure, but without undertaking an active search).
3. Informal search (i.e. collection of purpose-oriented information in an informal manner).
4. Formal search (i.e. a structured process for collecting specific information for a designated purpose).

You will observe that these approaches differ along the following dimensions: the scope of the environment to be analysed; the impetus for the analysis; the degree of active search involved; the formality of the environmental scanning process; and the task orientation of the activity.

Aquillar's study concluded that environmental scanning must be conducted in a systematic fashion. He frequently found the environmental scanning effort to be fragmented and inhibited by the failure of participating managers to gather and disseminate information that users considered important. His proposals called for top management involvement in the definition and execution of analysis activities; for greater coordination and integration of these activities with strategic planning; and for greater support for these activities, not only from top management, but also from line managers.

Three broad models of environment scanning systems are available which represent increasing degrees of systematization, sophistication and resource intensity. *Irregular* systems respond to environmentally generated crises. They are found in firms where the strategic planning culture is not well established. Their emphasis is on finding solutions to short-term problems. Little attention is paid to evaluating future environmental changes.

The *periodic* model is more sophisticated, systematic, proactive and resource intensive. It entails a regular review of the task environment and some elements of the wider environment. A forward view is taken.

The *continuous* model emphasizes the ongoing monitoring of the business environment, rather than specified issues or events. It draws on the expertise of marketing, sales, purchasing, and so on. It operates a clearing-house for environmental information and uses regular information systems for analysis and dissemination. A long-term view of environmental change is taken.

The paradox of environmental scanning is that by the time sufficient information has been collected to enable a well-informed environmental analysis to be made, it may be too late for the firm to respond before the threat strikes, or the opportunity passes. Ansoff (1984) proposes an approach to strategic management that overcomes the paradox by enabling the firm to develop a timely response to partially predictable events which emerge as surprises and develop very quickly. At its heart is the continuous monitoring of the firm's external and internal environment for signals of the evolution of strategic issues which the firm considers able to influence its operations. Ansoff's approach is driven by strategic issues rather than the conventional elements of the business environment. Issue-driven approaches to environmental scanning have also been developed by Nanus (1982) and Murphy (1989).

Ansoff's solution to the paradox is that instead of waiting for sufficient information to accumulate, the firm should determine what progressive steps in planning and action are feasible as strategic information becomes available in the course of the evolution of a threat or opportunity.

4 Procedures and pitfalls

The environmental scanning procedures of an organization will evolve over time as its commitment to them and experience of them change. It is unrealistic for a firm that is about to embrace environmental scanning for the first

Marketing management

Table 6 A typical sequential model of the ideal scanning procedure

1. *Monitor* broad trends, issues and events occurring in the firm's task environment. This can be complemented by means of identifying a core list of relevant publications and assigning them to volunteers who report important articles to environmental scanning for further study. Selected areas of the remote environment should be reviewed from time to time. External consultants may be employed.

2. *Identify* trends which may have significance for the firm. A scanning team of senior executives should determine and implement the criteria by means of which relevance is established. Weak signals may not be amenable to screening in this way.

3. *Evaluate* the impact of significant trends on the firm's operations in its current product markets. Those having a significant impact will either be threats or opportunities. Line managers should participate in the evaluation.

4. *Forecast* the possible future directions of the significant trends and examine the new opportunities and threats they appear likely to generate.

5. *Evaluate* the impact of these threats and opportunities on the firm's long-term strategies.

time to expect to operate a foolproof system from the outset: several technical and managerial constraints will impede the progress of environmental scanning efforts. The provision of top management support throughout the evolutionary period helps to ensure that a viable system emerges from early efforts, which are likely to be directed towards the installation of a system modelled on an ideal scanning procedure such as that shown in Table 6. An established strategic planning culture also helps to expedite matters by providing a receptive organizational climate.

Top management involvement in the commissioning of the environmental scanning system should focus on the definition of the following system parameters:

1. The boundaries of the task and business environment.
2. The appropriate time horizon for future studies.
3. The allocation of responsibility for environmental scanning.
4. The degree of formality circumscribing environmental scanning.
5. The use of environmental analyses in strategy making.

Defining boundaries

To define the boundaries of the firm's environment in terms of concrete measures is a very difficult, open-ended task for all but the smallest of one-product firms servicing a local market. Nevertheless, the environmental scanner needs practical guidelines to enable relevant environmental information to be separated from the irrelevant.

Such guidelines can be developed in consultation with members of the top management team responsible for the formulation of long-term strategies and plans. The user and the analyst can define the terms of reference and objectives of environmental scanning assignments. In this way an operational definition of a target zone of the environment is at least possible, using as a reference point the needs of the strategists for environmental data. Of course the definition will depend on the position and abilities of the members of the environmental analysis team, their past experience in environmental scanning projects and success in the application of the various research and forecasting techniques.

There are no hard and fast rules for making the distinction between relevance and irrelevance. The nub of the problem is one of achieving a balanced view of the scope of the firm's environment. To avoid misdirecting effort to peripheral and irrelevant issues it must not be too wide in scope. Neither should it be a narrow, data-dependent, econometric but relevant, if myopic, view. Clearly the problem will be exacerbated in diversified organizations possessing several relevant environments.

Appropriate time horizon

Given the difficulty experienced by organizations in defining boundaries, it is not surprising that they tend to focus on familiar environments – preferring to study remote environments on an *ad hoc* basis, perhaps with the assistance of consultants. A similarly conservative view is often taken of the appropriate time horizon for future studies to be conducted by environmental scanning. Divisional management tends to prefer shorter time horizons, while corporate management tends to take a longer view.

The time horizon should in theory be determined by the investment cycle of the industry and the nature of the product or service provided. For example: in the oil industry a scanning term of twenty-five years is not unusual; in the fashion industry a period of four years is more appropriate. Therefore the time horizon of environmental scanning should exceed the duration of the firm's strategic plans. If the firm operates a policy of waiting to see what the industry leaders get up to, then environmental scanning activities may be easily resourced. However, there is every chance that they will provide a narrow, reactive view, which is biased towards the short term.

Responsibility for environmental scanning

The responsibility for environmental scanning can be allocated in three different ways. First, line managers in functions such as purchasing, sales and marketing can be asked to undertake environmental scanning in addition to their other duties. These managers are likely to be able to provide information on the business environment and should, therefore, contribute in some way to any environmental scanning system. However, this approach suffers from disadvantages: the demotivating resentment line managers may feel towards this additional imposition on their time, especially when no allowances are made, resources provided or training given; the requirement for specialist analytical, research and forecasting skills which line managers are unlikely to possess; the possibly incompatible mentalities of the roles they are asked to play – creative and far-sighted visionary on one hand and hard-headed operator on the other.

The second approach is for environmental scanning to be made part of the strategic planner's job. This division of labour of strategic planning leads to specialization which may also have some drawbacks, but environmental scanning cannot easily be abdicated to technical specialists. They do not have to answer for the results of business unit performance, and often do not understand the technical requirements of the unit's business. Most importantly, such specialists do not have a system for defining, measuring and interpreting a business's environment more accurately than its own management can. It may then be desirable for both planners and line managers to be involved in environmental scanning.

Ansoff (1984) argues that the need for this involvement is seldom more critical than when making the choice of environmental analysis and forecasting techniques. In his view this choice is too important to be left to the environmental analyst, as is often done in practice. He argues that the user of the output of environmental scanning has an overriding duty to exert influence on the choice of technique, if actionable information and understanding are desired. Knowledge of the applicability of a technique is more important to the strategist than knowledge of the details of the technique's execution. The details of environmental analysis and forecasting techniques can readily be found in a voluminous literature on the subject (see Brownlie and Saren 1983; Brownlie 1994).

The third approach is to establish a separate organizational unit that is responsible for conducting regular and *ad hoc* scanning at all levels, and for channelling the results to those in the firm to whom they may be relevant. General Electric in the USA is known to operate such a unit and to fund its activities by charging recipients for the environmental information provided by scanning. Where large amounts of data are collected and analysed it has proved useful to establish a special team whose task is to make recommendations for action to top management, based on the environmental analysis.

This approach may represent a theoretical ideal. However, combinations of the first two approaches are most popular with all but the very large diversified firms who can afford to underwrite the operation of a separate unit. Combinations often operate by means of a temporary scanning team, set up on an *ad hoc* basis to oversee the study of the impact of a controversial environmental trend issue or event on various areas of the firm's operations.

The team membership may consist of both line (divisional) and general (corporate) management: line managers consider the product market, while top managers scan the wider environment. Line managers may even be temporarily seconded to a staff position for the duration of the study, often as part of on-the-job training for general management. They will often be closely involved in determining the impact of environmental changes on areas of the firm's operations in which they are experienced. Consultants, either internal or external, may be used where the impact of environmental change is likely to threaten the vested interests of line managers in some way.

There is no clear agreement about the best way to assign responsibilities for environmental scanning. Every organization will experience unique circumstances that merit taking a particular approach, which an off-the-shelf environmental scanning system may be incapable of embracing. Attempts to implant an ideal approach to environmental scanning in such a fashion are likely to contribute to inflated and ultimately unfulfilled expectations, and frustration. Researchers agree that firms should involve managers of various levels in environmental scanning activities and that it takes time for those activities, and the system which integrates them, to be assimilated effectively into the corporate culture. However, if environmental scanning is to become an effective contributor to the firm's strategic decision making, then organizational commitment and integration are vital.

Clearly attention should be given to the quality of communications between environmental analysts and managers. Formal management education and training provides ways of forming managers with analytical skills, which may serve as a basis for communication with analysts. Conversely, analysts familiar with the needs of managers will be more able to communicate with strategy makers. Job rotation may also improve communication. The top manager who has previously served as a member of an environmental analysis unit should find it easier to communicate with analysts. For general managers the range of desired skills is too broad, making it virtually impossible for one person to acquire them through job rotation in one lifetime. Intermediary advisors or consultants can also be used to improve communications, particularly in organizations where the career of the strategy maker is very different from that of the analyst – as is the case where a government minister is a politician and the analyst a civil servant.

Whatever the means by which responsibility for environmental analysis is assigned, I argue that those responsible should still undertake the following tasks:

1. Monitoring of trends, issues and events in the business environment and studying their possible impacts on the firm's operations.
2. Development of the forecasts, scenarios and issues analyses that serve as inputs to the firm's strategic decision making.
3. Provision of a destination to which environmental intelligence can be sent for interpretation, analysis and storage.
4. Construction of a means of organizing environmental information so that a library or database on environmental developments can easily be accessed.
5. Provision of an internal consulting resource on long-term environmental affairs.
6. Dissemination of information on the business environment by means of newsletters, reports and lectures.
7. Monitoring the performance of environmental analysis activities and improving it by applying new tools and techniques.

Degree of formality

Who should be responsible for environmental scanning is not the only difficult decision to be made. The degree of formality to be applied is also a matter for top management concern. The view taken by the organization will depend on the extent to which top management feel it necessary to be able to exert some control over the day-to-day activities of environmental scanning. Control may be a problem where responsibility for these activities is devolved to line managers whose own regular responsibilities are likely to take precedence over what they may consider to be marginal 'blue sky' and 'ivory tower' exercises. This problem is likely to be exacerbated where no formal system for collecting, analysing and disseminating environmental information has been agreed. The lack of commitment and scepticism which line managers will often express about environment analysis can only be dealt with by means of

Environmental analysis

Table 7 Attributes of a formal approach to environmental scanning

- Environmental trends, events and issues are regularly and systematically reviewed.
- Explicit criteria have been established that can in turn be used to evaluate the impact of environmental trends.
- Scanning activities are guided by written procedures.
- Responsibility for scanning activities has been clearly assigned.
- Scanning reports, updates, forecasts and analyses are documented in a standardized format.
- Such documentation is generated on a regular basis and disseminated to predetermined personnel according to a timetable.
- The application of formal techniques such as delphi studies and multiple scenarios.

education, training and involvement. They have to understand the need for better informed planning and decision making, and the role that environmental scanning has to play in making this possible. In order to appreciate these requirements they also have to understand the forces acting on the firm in its environment and the strategies it has for dealing with them.

Yet some organizations are content to take an informal approach to environmental scanning, relying on key executives in sales, marketing, purchasing and finance to keep abreast of changes in the business environment through newspapers, trade literature, conferences, exhibitions and personal contacts. Others prefer to organize their efforts into a series of structured and planned activities for which specified staff bear responsibility. The difference is really one of degree. Table 7 indicates the attributes likely to be possessed by a formal approach to environmental scanning.

Larger firms are more likely to take a formal approach to environmental scanning. This is not surprising given that such firms are also more likely to take a broad view of their business environment, competing as they will do in a number of markets with a number of products. The informal approach is not only the prerogative of the small, one-product firm. Diversified companies may prefer to take an informal approach to such scanning activities as long-term forecasting, the generation of alternative scenarios, issues analyses and the management of weak signals. These activities demand a degree of creative thinking that can best be stimulated in an informal environment – even if the output of the process is subjected to a more formal treatment.

Environmental scanning and strategy making

In determining the composition of the environmental scanning unit, top management should also take care to clarify the role of the participating analysts, in order to foster realistic expectations of the contribution they are able to make to strategy formulation. The pursuit of unrealistic expectations can have a debilitating impact on environmental scanning. Such unrealistic expectations are most likely to be held by both analysts and strategists while introducing a formal environmental scanning procedure to a firm for the first time. Fortunately, experience of environmental scanning puts analysts and strategists in a better position to judge each other's contribution realistically, but some unrealistic expectations may still persist. Analysts cannot realistically expect strategy makers always to make full use of their analyses, or to apply their recommendations completely and without question; they should rarely have the power to prescribe strategy. Where analysts tend to have such expectations, the reality of their engagements with strategists may be one of impotence rather than influence. In such circumstances the unfulfilled expectations of the analyst can easily become a source of alienation, misunderstanding and ill-feeling, only serving to weaken communications and impede the impact of environmental analysis on strategy formulation – a position made worse by the lack of any demonstrable, direct effect of such analyses on strategy formulation. Similarly, top management's desire to delegate strategy making to the environmental scanning unit should be treated with caution. The careful deflation of any heroic expectations will contribute to improved communications and understanding.

The data and analyses generated by environmental scanning are only one of several inputs to the strategy-making process. Its major contribution is to identify environmental trends, issues, events or signals that should trigger the reconsideration and, perhaps, revision of the strategic plans. Consequently, there is every chance that environmental scanning will have an important hand in initiating strategy changes. Indeed, where a staff unit for environmental scanning exists, the occurrence of such a trigger is likely to lead to a request from strategists for environmental scanning to conduct a specific study of the related issue or trend.

The indirect use of environmental analyses in strategy making is at least possible, by virtue of the quality of its work. However, its direct use requires an enabling mechanism directed to the translation of the output of environmental analyses into specific recommendations or even a plan for implementing strategy changes. Once again communication difficulties must be surmounted. The problem is not merely that a thorough understanding of environmental analysis demands skills similar to those of the analysts, which strategy makers are unlikely to possess. The vocabulary, assumptions, processes and techniques employed by the analysts will also be alien to them. One answer is not to leave the task of translation only to the environmental analysts. They may also be unfamiliar with the arcane terminology, skills, outlook and expectations of the strategists and their peers. The use of specially convened action teams, staffed by advisers or consultants, is often recommended as a translation mechanism. The best solution is one that brings analysts and strategists closer together as often as possible.

5 Conclusion

Environmental scanning can make an important contribution to the survival and prosperity of the firm. The increasingly turbulent and unpredictable market environment of the late 1990s will convince more and more organizations of the need systematically to scan and analyse their market environment. This is not an easy task. The organization must expect to encounter many technical and managerial problems, particularly in enabling environment scanning to contribute fully to the formulation of business strategy. Reading this entry is no more than a first step.

DOUGLAS BROWNLIE
UNIVERSITY OF STIRLING

Further reading

(References cited in the text marked *)

* Ansoff, H.I. (1984) *Implanting Strategic Management*, New York: Prentice Hall.
* Aquillar, F.S. (1967) *Scanning the Business Environment*, New York: Macmillan.
* Brownlie, D.T. (1994) 'Environmental scanning', in M.J. Baker (ed.), *The Marketing Book*, 3rd edn, Oxford: Butterworth-Heinemann.
* Brownlie, D.T. and Saren, M.A. (1983) 'A review of technology forecasting techniques and their applications', *Management Bibliographies and Reviews* 9 (4).

Diffenbach, J. (1983) 'Corporate environmental analysis in large US corporations', *Long Range Planning* 16: 107–16.

* Kast, F.E. and Rosenweig, J.E. (1974) *Organisation and Management: A System Approach*, 2nd edn, Maidenhead: McGraw-Hill.

Makridakis, S. (1990) *Forecasting, Planning and Strategy for the 21st Century*, New York: Free Press.

* Murphy, J. (1989) 'Identifying strategic issues', *Long Range Planning* 22: 101–5.
* Nanus, B. (1982) 'QUEST – quick environmental scanning technique', *Long Range Planning* 15: 39–45.

Stubbart, C. (1982) 'Are environmental scanning units effective?', *Long Range Planning* June: 139–45.

Taylor, J. (1992) 'Competitive intelligence: a status report on US business practices', *Journal of Marketing Management* 8: 117–25.

West, J. and Olsen, D. (1989) 'Environmental scanning, industry structure and strategy making: concepts and research in the hospitality industry', *International Journal of Hospitality Management* 8: 283–98.

See also: THE ASSESSMENT OF MARKETING PERFORMANCE; EXHIBITIONS; MARKETING ORGANIZATION AND MANAGEMENT; MARKETING RESEARCH; QUALITATIVE RESEARCH IN MARKETING; STRATEGIC MARKETING PLANNING

Marketing and public policy

1. The 'old days': marketing and the law
2. The fork in the road: high-water mark in the 1970s
3. A time of remission
4. Looking ahead
5. Two world views

Overview

This entry treats the marketing and public policy territory of the field of marketing, with particular emphasis on its evolution over the past forty-plus years.

1 The 'old days': marketing and the law

In the period after the Second World War, the operating model of marketing and public policy was generally equated with 'the legal aspects of marketing'. The focus was on anti-trust and issues of competition. The major application areas were market concentration and price discrimination. In addition, false advertising remained an issue, having surfaced as part of the anti-advertising sentiments that had arisen during the Depression.

Reflecting these elements are the major topics treated in the American Marketing Association's *Journal of Marketing* in the post-Second World War period. In the late 1970s, for the book *Marketing Research and Knowledge Development*, a five-yearly content analysis of the major marketing journals was undertaken (Myers *et al.* 1980: 82–3).

In 1947 articles on retail price maintenance (now no longer a meaningful issue) and false advertising were among the major topics in the *Journal of Marketing*, as were the implications of the Robinson–Patman Act in 1952. Not until 1967 (in our quinquennial analysis) did public policy emerge again – in the *Journal of Marketing*'s treatment of government impacts on marketing. Five years later, in 1972, as activism, particularly consumerism, had begun to emerge, articles addressed consumerism and unit pricing.

An analogous trend was found in marketing textbooks. Extensive sections on public policy did not meaningfully appear in textbooks until the mid-1970s onwards. By then the traditional module on marketing and the law had been replaced by a full section – typically termed 'the new environment of marketing' – encompassing law, government, consumerism, and public policy (Myers *et al.* 1980: 91).

2 The fork in the road: high-water mark in the 1970s

In my view the late 1960s and 1970s can be characterized as a period of burgeoning activity and interest in public policy and marketing – by the government itself via a reinvigorated Federal Trade Commission (FTC), by marketers in response (mostly defensive), and by marketing academics as well. The high-water mark of the decade-plus of increased regulation in the wake of Ralph Nader's *Unsafe at Any Speed* (1972) came just prior to the defeat of comprehensive consumer regulation legislation in the late 1970s. By then the cost/benefit-fuelled trend to deregulation was discernible, and the view of the FTC as a 'national nanny' came to transcend its praised role as a consumer protector.

As noted, the late 1960s and 1970s constituted a period of growth in protection-oriented public policy initiatives in a number of new areas of consumer concern. These are detailed elsewhere, notably in several papers from a 1989 Notre Dame conference on marketing and advertising regulation at the FTC (see, notably, Jones 1990). Of all the developments in this decade, perhaps the most significant to marketing academics was the rapid recognition of consumer behaviour specifically, and marketing generally, as relevant disciplines for the public policy community itself. In an early personal conversation with FTC Commissioner Mary Gardiner Jones, she said: 'By my appointment, I am an expert in marketing and consumer behaviour. But in truth, our FTC staff has no one trained in either'. (She hired Murray Silverman for her own staff.)

The 1971 FTC hearings on Modern Advertising Practices represented a major opportunity for the FTC Commissioners and senior staff to absorb much about how marketers and advertisers actually conducted marketing and advertising. The research and literature of the economic and social issues involved in advertising were synthesized in a major Marketing Science Institute monograph (Pearce *et al.* 1971). A coterie of consumer behaviour professors (mostly in annual single file) took up residence as visiting consultants at the FTC. William Wilkie at the Bureau of Consumer Protection was the first resident professor with the FTC staff, followed later by Harold Kassarjian and others (Murphy 1990).

Very quickly, and significantly, the legal basis for what consumers thought shifted from what competing experts thought consumers thought to competing experts interpreting empirical data on what consumers themselves said they thought. Indeed, both consumer research consultants and consumer research professors (sometimes the same person) flourished in an age of empiricism. A new generation of aspiring marketing scholars found a wide range of public policy topics to explore – alas, often using the traditionally readily available students as their subjects, who in turn would render the real-world validity of many of their findings questionable.

By this time the application of behavioural sciences research to marketing, which was in its early stages by 1960, had reached a mature state. This clearly became a very salient dimension of the marketing and public policy arena. In my view, a major – perhaps the major – contributor to the growth in interest in consumer behaviour research was its potential for applicability to public policy issues. Many of today's leading public policy professors are primarily trained in consumer behaviour rather than in economics, as had been their predecessors.

3 A time of remission

If the 1970s constituted a period of almost hyperactivity in the marketing and public policy realm in the USA, the 1980s were largely a time of remission. Government initiatives shrunk. Marketers' interest declined sharply in the absence of 'feeling the pressure', and activism generally waned (at least until it became rather chic to be 'green') (see GREEN MARKETING). Helping to maintain academic interest in the public policy field were the advent of the *Journal of Public Policy and Marketing* and the start of the series of American Marketing Association conferences in the field.

4 Looking ahead

In answer to the question, what of the 1990s? – I see a tremendous potential for growth in the marketing and public policy territory, and have written so long before the 1992 US election of a Democratic administration and its consequent likelihood of a pendulum shift in Federal regulatory activity. We have witnessed regulatory initiatives in food labelling (regarding nutrition information) and in the tobacco industry.

More specifically, consider some key changes that have been taking place in the marketplace itself. We have undergone a technological revolution in communications, on the one hand enabling consumers to gain much more control of their media environment (via the remote button), and at the same time enabling greater audience targeting than marketers have enjoyed via TV in the past.

In the wake of this change in mass communication, we have witnessed a huge increase in direct marketing – via telephone and mail (see ADVANCING FROM DIRECT MARKETING TO INTEGRATED (INTERNET) COMMUNICATIONS). Telephone marketing is arguably more amenable to deceptive selling than is the national advertising that has been the traditional regulatory focus on commercial communication. (Of course consumers themselves can easily control this channel of marketing too – via hanging up the phone and using the wastepaper basket more often.)

We have seen the rapid growth of ethnic populations such as Hispanics and Asians in the USA, for many of whom English is not their first language. One key consequence is increased potential for marketplace fraud.

We have experienced the growth of the services sector – where it is often inherently more difficult to determine what constitutes satisfactory performance for consumers compared to a provider's promise. For example, it is much easier for a consumer to judge that a can-opener opens cans or that a washing machine washes clothes clean than it is for the same consumer to assess his or her satisfaction with a hotel room promising a superior experience or with one's 'personal banking' experience. The potential for services marketers – even when well intentioned – fuelling the promise–performance gap that creates discontent with marketing is much higher in my view than it is for product marketing (see MARKETING OF SERVICES). For the conceptualization and assessment of the 'promise–performance gap', see Greyser (1989) and Greyser and Diamond (1974).

A key dimension of today's public policy scene is that issues appear to be driven much more by consumer problems than by philosophy or ideology. This seems particularly true at the state level in the USA.

One other major change involving marketing in the public arena has occurred over the past twenty years, and actually increased during the 1980s. This change is the great interest in marketing on behalf of not-for-profits and social causes (see STRATEGIC MARKETING FOR NON-PROFIT ORGANIZATIONS). Reflecting broader and deeper interest here is MSI's current research competition, chaired by Paul Bloom, on Using Marketing to Serve Society. The main headings in the competition are instructive as to the breadth of the issues here (MSI 1992):

1 Understanding the social consequences of consumer/buyer behaviour, including responses to risky consumer behaviour, social tradeoffs (e.g. price premiums for perceived socially beneficial attributes), and problems of vulnerable segments.
2 Improving business responses to social needs, including being effective *and* ethical, and evaluation of campaigns encouraging socially beneficial behaviour.
3 Improving public agency responses to social needs, including assessing policy proposals, and improving the marketing knowledge of public agencies.

The increase in both the practice and study of what is called social marketing has broadened the definitions of marketing and its impacts on behalf of society.

5 Two world views

Let me offer some closing thoughts on marketing and public policy. These are not new – but I believe they still pertain in attempting to resolve regulatory issues in marketing. Some 25 years ago my late senior colleague Raymond A. Bauer and I published an article in the *Harvard Business Review*, entitled 'The dialogue that never happens', which posited that two different views of the consumer world – two different conceptions of the marketplace and marketing's role in it – serve to explain the communications gap between business, especially marketers on the one side, and both regulators and critics of marketing on the other (Bauer and Greyser 1967). This is pertinent today because I not only think the gap remains but also believe that research, even well-designed and executed research, can go only part-way to bridge the gap. For example, the two mindsets explain why marketers consider advertising properly to be persuasive while regulators focus on information as advertising's proper role (see ADVERTISING). For further explanation, see Greyser (1983).

Consider five key words or phrases: competition, product, consumer needs, rationality and information. Let me compare the typical regulator's view (recall that the vast majority of marketing regulators are still drawn from the ranks of lawyers and economists) with the typical business view.

The regulator focuses on competition in terms of price (and typically cost-based price), whereas the business view of competition is one of product differentiation (to help escape from price competition) with price based on value for the customer.

Regulators tend to see a product only in terms of its primary function. In contrast the business view of differentiation is dominantly through secondary characteristics, since primary ones are largely generic to a category and often only 'me too' for a given brand.

Consumer needs are seen by regulators as corresponding closely (or directly) with primary function (e.g. a car is for transportation). However, the business view is that consumer needs encompass any desire on which the product can be differentiated, certainly including psychological differentiation (e.g. in terms of self-image).

To the regulator, rationality is the efficient matching of product to consumer needs. Business people, particularly marketers, are more agnostic: any consumer decision that serves the customer's own perceived self-interest constitutes rationality.

Finally, information to the regulator is whatever facilitates the fit of a product's proper function with the customer's needs, already defined rather narrowly as a marketer would see it. Marketers more broadly consider information to be whatever truthfully puts forward the attractiveness of the product in the consumer's eyes. And honest persuasion is a legitimate element of our society.

STEPHEN A. GREYSER
HARVARD UNIVERSITY

Further reading

(References cited in the text marked *)

* Bauer, Raymond A. and Greyser, S.A. (1967) 'The dialogue that never happens', *Harvard Business Review* November–December.
* Greyser, S.A. (1983) 'Advertising as information *and* persuasion in the marketplace', presentation to Federal Trade Commission, May.
* Greyser, S. (1989) 'Services and satisfaction keys to the '90s agenda', *Mobius* Fall.
* Greyser, S.A. and Diamond, S.L. (1974) 'Business is adapting to consumerism', *Harvard Business Review* September–October.
* Jones, Mary Gardiner (1990) 'The Federal Trade Commission in 1968', in Murphy, Patrick E. and Wilkie, W.L. (eds), *Marketing and Advertising Regulation*, Notre Dame, Indiana: University of Notre Dame
* MSI (1992) *MSI Call for Proposals*, Cambridge, MA: Marketing Science Institute.
* Murphy, Patrick E. (1990) 'Past FTC participation by marketing academics', in Murphy, Patrick E. and Wilkie, W.L. (eds), *Marketing and Advertising Regulation*, Notre Dame, IN: University of Notre Dame.
* Myers, J.G., Massy, W.M. and Greyser, S.A. (1980) *Marketing Research and Knowledge Development*, Englewood Cliffs: Prentice-Hall.
* Nader, Ralph (1972) *Unsafe at Any Speed*, New York: Grossman.
* Pearce, M., Cunningham, S.M. and Miller, Avon (1971) (under the supervision of R.D. Buzzell and S.A. Greyser) *Appraising the Economic and Social Effects of Advertising*, Cambridge, MA: Marketing Science Institute.

See also: ADVERTISING; DIRECT MARKETING; GREEN MARKETING; MARKETING COMMUNICATIONS; MARKETING ETHICS; MARKETING OF SERVICES; PRICING; STRATEGIC MARKETING FOR NON-PROFIT ORGANIZATIONS

Marketing research

1. Users of marketing research
2. Information for marketing planning
3. Major research forms
4. Data collection methods
5. The analysis of industrial markets
6. International research
7. Working with research companies
8. Conclusion

Overview

Organizations use many types of resources to function. One of the most valuable, but often the least understood, is their knowledge-base. Management is unable to take informed decisions without knowledge and the quality of that knowledge may be all which distinguishes a successful from an unsuccessful organization. Knowledge, like skills, resides primarily in employees, but the raw material for it can also be collected in databases, reports, patents, plans, budgets, memoranda and a variety of other documents. The knowledge-base covers all aspects of the organization's activities – products, technology, human resources, finance, sales and marketing – and is a wasting asset requiring constant updating, improvement and extension to keep pace with changes in the operating environment.

Nowhere is the need for detailed, accurate and up-to-date knowledge more evident than in the marketing function. Markets have two characteristics which distinguish them from the other environments in which companies operate.

1. They are invariably dynamic and are tending to become more so in response to the increasing pace of technical development, competitive pressure and a continual uplift in customers' expectations.
2. Change is caused by a wide diversity of factors, most of which are beyond the control of any single supplier.

Marketing therefore operates in an inherently unstable environment and it is all too easy for companies to lose touch with conditions in the markets they service. Furthermore, in the quest for growth, or even to defend existing market positions, the problem tends to be exacerbated by the fact that companies continually need to do something new. They develop new strategies, launch new products, target new markets and initiate new service packages – all of which push them into increasingly unfamiliar marketing territory.

The antidote to these conditions is a marketing knowledge-base which is updated and extended in line with the development of the business. Marketing knowledge is created from a number of inputs. Experience and expertise are critical, as are experimentation and analysis, but the key dynamic ingredient is marketing information derived from sources within the marketplace itself, notably customers, competitors and distributors. Marketing research is the marketing service which collects, analyses and interprets marketing information.

1 Users of marketing research

The mainstream users of marketing research are all types of commercial organizations who require information which will assist them to improve the quality of their marketing decisions. Suppliers of raw materials, manufacturers, distributors, suppliers of professional and other services are the main initiators of marketing research surveys. They are sometimes joined by organizations and institutions who participate indirectly in the marketing process or who need to observe what is happening in markets for purposes other than marketing management. Trade associations commission research on behalf of their members. Government agencies with a marketing mandate, such as tourist boards, commission research to obtain the data they require to direct their promotional activity. Television channels, newspapers, the trade press and exhibition organizers commission research to demonstrate the effectiveness of their media as promotional vehicles and, in some instances, to obtain editorial copy.

Some confusion arises from the fact that the survey techniques used by marketing researchers are also used to obtain information which has no marketing application, unless a very liberal definition of marketing is adopted. Opinion polls, which provide a substantial income stream to research companies, are arguably part of the information input required by political parties to market themselves to the electorate; research into attitudes towards government policy forms a basis for government marketing strategies. Investigations into housing conditions, community health or wage and salary levels is in reality social and political research which has little, if any, connection with marketing.

2 Information for marketing planning

Like many sciences, or pseudo-sciences, market research is plagued with impenetrable terminology. Terms such as perceptual mapping, psychographics and behavioural research, while all worthy in their own right, disguise the fact that most market research is devoted to providing information which will solve the most basic marketing problems – what should I sell, how much of it can I sell, what do I have to do to sell it, where do I sell it and what prices can I achieve? There is a host of more esoteric problems which research can tackle, but it tends to concentrate on the provision of three broad groups of information:

1   market measurement;
2   customer research;
3   competitor analysis.

Even within this relatively simple framework, research can help to solve a wide diversity of marketing problems and the following paragraphs outline only the most common research applications.

Market measurement

A primary requirement for business planners is to set achievable sales targets and to show how these can be achieved. The quantitative element of a basic marketing plan for a product or service will show the planned sales progression (in volume or value), the customer groups that are to be targeted and the distribution channels that are to be used. To do this it is essential to know the total volume of sales that the market is absorbing (or is capable of absorbing) and the structure of the market. Sales data need to be broken down by product type or product category and the structural data need to show the channels through which products are distributed and the relationship between channels and customer groups. Sales targeting also requires detailed information on the customer base – who are the purchasers of the product or service, how large is each purchasing group and what relationships exist between the products purchased and the types of purchasers (see CHANNELS OF DISTRIBUTION; CONSUMER BEHAVIOUR; THE ASSESSMENT OF MARKETING PERFORMANCE; QUANTITATIVE METHODS IN MARKETING).

Tracking data, which monitor the progress of sales, in total, by customer group, by brand and by supplier, permit planners to assess the impact of their marketing and promotional strategies on a continuous basis.

Forecasts are essential for planning future business. Information on how markets are expected to develop in the future enables planners to assess the attraction of the market, set forward budgets and allocate marketing promotional resources in the light of the yield they could be expected to achieve. Surveys of buyers' intentions can provide a strong, though far from infallible, indication of short-term market performance. Longer term projections rely on an analysis of trend data and the relationship between demand and general economic variables such as consumer expenditure and industrial investment (see MARKETING BUDGETING AND RESOURCE ALLOCATION; SALES FORECASTING).

Customer research

Customer strategies that will achieve the sales targets which have been set are a core component of marketing and promotional activity. Detailed analysis of the customer, be it an individual or an organization, therefore represents a major task for marketing research. If, in essence, marketing is devoted to providing what the customer wants, market research is there to define what that is. Customer research is designed to provide marketers with an understanding of product and service requirements, customer behaviour, attitudes, purchasing preferences and purchasing procedures.

Market research is at its most valuable when assessing the potential demand for new products since this is where the unknowns are greatest and risk is high. The use of research for conceptual evaluations of customer needs and the testing of prototype designs replace gut feel with more tangible evidence of what will sell. This process extends to modifications to existing products to take account of changing customer requirements and to the definition of the services which customers require in support of their product purchases.

The analysis of customer behaviour is most concerned with the factors that determine customer choice of product and supplier. Understanding the interaction between price, product quality, product features and a host of service considerations such as delivery, installation and customer advisory services is critical to success in any marketplace. The weighting of product and supplier selection criteria shows how product and service packages should be constructed and also supplies a key input to the definition of promotional messages.

It is also essential to know the extent to which suppliers are meeting customers' expectations and this has given rise to customer satisfaction research to provide a numerical measurement of supplier performance. Image research is closely allied in that it shows customers' perceptions of suppliers. Perceptions can be equally as powerful as reality in determining supplier acceptance and research can highlight changes in image which need to be engineered in order to improve the chances of success.

Customer research is commonly used to define discrete segments of a market which lend themselves to separate marketing approaches. It is rarely easy to be all things to all men and marketing effectiveness can be improved by targeting specific market segments with the products, services and marketing messages they find most acceptable. Segments can be defined by parameters such as geography, demographics, taste, attitudes and buying practices, but research is required to show whether the segments are sufficiently different and homogeneous to support separate marketing approaches (see MARKET SEGMENTATION).

Research into customers' purchasing intentions is used to compute short-term forecasts of demand for products and to predict the success of new products. The accuracy of the results tends to be higher in industrial and professional markets where there is a close correlation between stated purchasing intentions and actual behaviour, but surveys of consumer purchasing intentions can also provide a valuable input to short-term forecasting models.

The study of the effectiveness of individual marketing communication and promotional techniques provides planners with guidelines for the allocation of their marketing expenditure. The effect of advertising, direct marketing, sales promotion, exhibitions and public relations is usually studied indirectly by testing recall and customers' reaction to content such as copy, images and venues. The real effectiveness of advertising, namely the effect on income, is difficult to establish, though a number of models are available to compute the relationship between advertising expenditure and sales. The effectiveness of below-the-line expenditure is normally apparent in the form of response and take-up rates and does not need to be established by research (see ADVERTISING; EXHIBITIONS; SALES PROMOTION).

Media research is an important component of communications research, which is devoted to analysing newspaper and journal readership and radio and television audiences, poster viewing and cinema audiences. To be fully effective media research should be allied with research into purchasing decision making, so that the relationship between those responsible for purchase decisions and media audiences can be demonstrated.

Other aspects of marketing activity which can be pre- and post-tested by studying customer reactions include the use and effectiveness of distribution channels, packaging, merchandising and perhaps, most importantly, pricing. Pricing decisions are critical to the success of all marketing strategies and customer research can provide valuable insight into the acceptability of pricing proposals before they are activated in the marketplace (see PACKAGING AND DESIGN; PRICING).

Competitor analysis

The widespread adoption of customer research by suppliers of consumer and industrial products and suppliers of professional services has resulted in noticeable similarities in product and service strategies. Reductions in differentiation in customer strategies has heightened interest in competitor strategies, which tend to be aimed at improving market share.

In order to compete it is essential not only to identify the competition but also to understand their resources, their strategies, their strengths and weaknesses as perceived by customers, the threat they pose to other suppliers and their vulnerabilities to attack. Detailed knowledge of competitors has never been easy to acquire and marketing history is littered with examples of successful businesses that have been brought down by competition which was either unknown or known but undervalued. There are also countless examples of opportunities missed through failures to capitalize on competitors' weaknesses.

Keeping abreast of competition is becoming increasingly difficult as the pace of change in markets accelerates. Competitive tension is being heightened by powerful forces which are driving existing competitors to be more aggressive and at the same time attracting new competitors. Deregulation, reductions in trade barriers, radical political realignments and the increasing globalization of supply all create new opportunities but at the same time threaten those who fail to appreciate that the competitive environment is changing and that previous competitive boundaries have been blurred.

The most basic information requirement is a map which plots the competitive environment and shows who the competitors are, where they are, where they have come from and the resources they deploy. A typical competitor information profile will cover:

- ownership and organizational structure;
- financial history;
- financial resources;
- key decision makers and their track records;
- staff resources;
- production resources and locations;
- product lines and portfolios;
- patents, licences and other unique assets;
- markets and segments serviced;
- distribution channels used;
- export activity and countries supplied;
- sales and marketing activities.

The profile can be extended by probing each competitor's image, reputation, strengths and weaknesses among customers.

3 Major research forms

The market research industry has responded to the information requirements of its clients in a variety of ways, each reflecting the difficulty and cost of acquiring the information and the extent to which clients require information which is proprietary to themselves and not shared with others. The main research forms are:

- continuous consumer panels;
- retail audits;
- *ad hoc* surveys;
- omnibus surveys;
- syndicated surveys.

Continuous consumer panels

Continuous consumer panels are used to collect information regularly, normally month by month, from standing panels of customers selected to be representative of households or specific groups of individuals. They are best suited to the collection of information on purchases that are made regularly and record simple data, such as products or services purchased, brands purchased, the source of purchase, prices paid and the receipt of any incentives or special offers with the purchase.

Retail audits

Retail audits collect similar data to that recorded on consumer panels but the source of the data is a sample of retail outlets rather than customers. Electronic data collection techniques are moving retail research more towards censuses than samples, though far from all retailers are prepared to cooperate with agencies on this research. Clearly what passes through retail outlets should agree with purchases made by customers and the main differences between consumer panel and retail audit data lie in the ways in which the data can be structured and analysed.

Retail audits and consumer panels are both used to provide quantitative information which tracks purchasing trends. Neither seeks information that explains the trends which are observed. Both obtain high degrees of accuracy and produce detailed information by covering large samples of respondents. They are costly to mount and are viable only because the resultant data are sold to large numbers of clients.

Ad hoc surveys

Ad hoc surveys cope with research requirements which arise sporadically. Each survey is custom designed to meet specific information needs or to solve one of a wide variety of marketing problems. The main advantage of *ad hoc* surveys is that the client obtains the precise information that is required and retains proprietary control over it. Panel and retail audit data can be customized by means of special analysis, which is also the proprietary property of the client who commissions it, but the amount of tailoring that can be achieved is limited by the type and structure of the initial data that are collected.

Ad hoc surveys fall into two groups, which also reflect two major divisions in the research business. These are quantitative and qualitative research. As the name implies, quantitative research records what is happening by quantifying requirements and the patterns that arise in the market. Qualitative research seeks to understand why consumers behave the way they do and to describe the alternative patterns of behaviour that can exist (see QUALITATIVE RESEARCH MARKETING; QUANTITATIVE METHODS IN MARKETING).

Omnibus surveys

Omnibus surveys are regular research exercises carried out weekly, monthly or quarterly with defined samples of respondents such as motorists, mothers with young children or a general sample representative of the population as a whole. Clients use omnibus surveys as a vehicle for carrying questions they want answered, but which do not justify the cost of a specially mounted *ad hoc* survey. An omnibus questionnaire can carry two to three questions from ten to fifteen separate clients. Each client receives an analysis of the responses to the questions he or she has placed and pays a fee for each question asked.

Syndicated surveys

Syndicated surveys are *ad hoc* research programmes with the cost shared by a group of clients who wish to participate. Shared cost means that clients gain the benefit of research programmes many times larger than they could afford on their own. The disadvantage is that competitors have access to the same data. Syndicates can either be 'closed', meaning that a predetermined group of clients buys the research and no further sale is permitted, or 'open' meaning that anyone can buy the research.

4 Data collection methods

Quantitative and qualitative survey techniques are well defined and are common to all branches of market research. The essence of all surveys is the collection of information:

- from existing published (or secondary) sources;
- directly from participants in a market.

Secondary research

The information age has been characterized by an ever-growing corpus of published information on industries and markets of all types. The sources of information are as diverse as the industries they cover though there is a growing tendency to collect data into computerized databases (such as Textline, Dialog, Infoline and Nexis) which are available online for efficient and rapid searching.

Secondary (or desk) research is still an undervalued research technique, often relegated to the role of providing clues which will verify data collected by primary research techniques. However, if used properly desk research can make a significant contribution to the basic information required for market analysis. The depth and quality of information available varies considerably from market sector to market sector and from country to country but a diligent search can be expected to yield data on:

- population size, structure into geodemographic groups and growth;
- the structure of distribution and the importance of various channels;
- total sales, imports and exports of products;

- imports and exports by origin and destination;
- products available and their specifications;
- new product launches;
- sources of supply;
- new contracts and successful bidders for outstanding contracts;
- list prices;
- advertising expenditure by product, industry sector and supplier;
- new market entrants;
- staff movements;
- financial performance of suppliers.

The sources of published information are too numerous to list in their entirety and the process of source identification is a skill which takes time to acquire. Researchers are assisted by the existence of a number of 'sources on sources', such as Marketsearch, Findex, Predicasts, the Research Index and Reports Index, which collectively list most of the data that are available.

Much published information is available free of charge or at very low cost. The main disadvantage is that the sources can be highly fragmented and the data collection process can be time consuming. There is, however, an increasing trend to publish research reports on specific products, industries or activities which bring together the data available from secondary sources and are designed to provide researchers with comprehensive overviews of markets. These reports, also available at relatively low cost, provide the useful function of predigesting and harmonizing information and commonly add an element of primary research to support the data obtained from secondary sources.

Primary research

Primary research techniques are used to collect original data from participants in markets. They can be directed at all types of respondents who possess information that has value to those designing and running marketing strategies. The targets include:

- customers;
- distributors – retail, wholesale and specialist;
- specifiers and advisors;
- designers;
- suppliers.

The most frequent target for survey research is the customer – the person buying for his or her own consumption or on behalf of the organizations that employ them. The major primary research techniques currently in use for marketing research are:

- personal (face-to-face) interviews;
- telephone interviews;
- group discussions (focus groups);
- mail/fax questionnaires:
- diaries;
- electronic data collection techniques;
- hall tests;
- observation techniques.

All of these involve direct contact with respondents using a questionnaire or an interview guide and sometimes requiring display material or samples of the product being researched.

The interview

Whether carried out face-to-face or by telephone the interview is the most common market research technique. It seeks information on respondents' actions, reactions, preferences, perceptions or requirements. It can be carried out in a variety of locations of which the most common are the street, the home, the place of work or a specific venue associated with the research topic, such as a shop or an airport. The live contact between the interviewer and the respondent permits not only data collection but also the verification of responses and the introduction of supplementary questions to probe the unusual or unexpected. An advantage of face-to-face interviews is that they can be set up to permit subjects to be explored in-depth – in which case they are called 'depth personal interviews'.

As telephone ownership has become universal, telephone research has tended to displace personal interviewing, largely because it is quicker, can be controlled better and is less expensive. The telephone is ideally suited to the collection of small amounts of highly structured information from samples that are scattered over a wide geographical area. It is unsuitable for individuals who are unlikely to respond well on the telephone, such as children, or those that are difficult to reach by telephone, such as residents in old people's homes or farmers; nor can it be used when material needs to be displayed to the respondents. The telephone can be less intrusive than personal interviews but can also be unwelcome during the evenings when respondents are most likely to be at home. For business research the telephone can be the most acceptable method of data collection because it requires the least time commitment by respondents. The main disadvantages of telephone research are the lack of visual contact, which means that respondents' reactions cannot be observed, and the relative ease with which respondents can refuse to cooperate.

Group discussions

Group discussions are face-to-face interviews carried out with a collected group of respondents. Though difficult and expensive to organize, they yield massive amounts of qualitative information enhanced by the fact that participants argue and debate between themselves. The moderation of such events is a skilled process but, done well, a few groups of six to eight participants can reveal far more about customers' requirements or attitudes than the equivalent twelve to sixteen interviews. Groups can only be used with respondents who can be brought together physically, commonly in specialist facilities with video, sound recording and viewing capability. This is rarely a problem with consumer groups where there are usually enough qualifying respondents living in the catchment area of the facility, but it can become more problematical for specialist respondents such as purchasing of officers or surgeons. Part of the added cost of group discussion research arises from the fact that participants are commonly remunerated for the time they have devoted to take part in the group.

Mail questionnaire

The mail questionnaire, which is either posted or handed out to respondents for completion and returned to the researcher, is a low-cost research technique still used in social research but of declining importance in market research. They have a value in extracting information from respondents who are difficult to contact by other methods, such as executives constantly on the move, or in situations where respondents can be identified but where an interview on the spot is not feasible, as in traffic surveys for example. The main problem with mail surveys is the lack of control over the response. Response rates tend to be low and it is difficult if not impossible to demonstrate that those who choose to reply are typical of the universe as a whole. The most extreme example is the guest questionnaire placed in hotel bedrooms which is invariably completed only if the guest has experienced a problem. In business research, faxing questionnaires injects an element of urgency which can be missing in postal surveys. Faxed questionnaires are also as effective as the telephone in their ability to reach the targeted respondent (a major weakness in mail surveys which too often end in the post-room wastebin along with 'junk mail'). Unfortunately, domestic fax ownership is too low for this technique to be effective for consumer surveys.

Diaries

Diaries are used in surveys that seek to track respondents' actions over a period of time. The diary is in effect a questionnaire on which the respondent records his or her purchases daily, weekly or monthly, depending on the nature of the survey. Diaries are placed with respondents at the commencement of the survey and collected once the diary period is completed. Diaries can run for a fixed calendar period or can be completed once a target number of transactions or events are recorded.

Electronic data collection

Electronic data collection has come into its own with the spread of computers and information technology. The most basic form of automation in research is the computerization of questionnaires for administration by telephone (computer aided telephone interviewing – CATI) or face-to-face (computer aided personal interviewing – CAPI) or by respondents themselves (computer aided self competion interviewing – CASI). These sophisticated programmes display the questionnaire on a screen, capture the responses via the keyboard, verify each response (to ensure that it is compatible with other responses given), insert the correct skip patterns and prepare the data for analysis. The associated management system holds a file of potential respondents and ensures that the quotas of different respondent types are maintained. The set-up costs of CATI, CAPI and

CASI surveys are relatively high, which generally means that they are employed only in large-scale surveys. They are also less effective for surveys in which a high proportion of the questions are open ended, requiring the entry of large numbers of verbatim comments.

At a higher level, electronic point-of-sale (EPOS) and stock control systems which collect point-of-sale and stock information have proved to be of considerable value in tracking the flow of products through distributors. The analysis of tapes obtained from retailers and wholesalers has replaced physical store checks for many product groups.

Electronic meters are widely used in television audience research to collect viewing statistics. Current versions record the times a representative sample of sets are switched on and off, the channels tuned and, via a sensor system, the number of individuals watching the set. These data are collected automatically through a telephone link to a central computer for overnight analysis. The use of meters for other measurements which lend themselves to mechanical analysis, such as the use of vehicles, have been explored but not as yet implemented.

Hall tests
Hall tests are employed largely in new product development programmes when samples of the products need to be shown or tested on a large sample of potential buyers. They comprise a physical set-up in a hall located in or near a shopping precinct. Respondents are recruited to visit the hall, test the product and record their reactions.

Observation techniques
Observation techniques encompass a wide range of research approaches ranging from measured reactions to products or advertising material to recording the ways in which customers shop, handle products or behave. Observation is a physical, as opposed to a reported, record of customer actions and can therefore be more accurate. Unfortunately the situations in which customers can be observed are often artificial and their actions may differ from those occurring in real life.

Internet research
The Internet is, in principle, the answer to a market analyst's prayer. Many of the tasks that can be carried out on the Internet could almost have been designed with market research in mind. As a massive showcase of data and as an effective and low cost mechanism for collecting information on any topic and from any point of the globe, the Internet represents a resource with which no traditional library counld conceivably compete. As a method of sending and receiving text, images and voice messages to and from any individual, commercial organization, government body or institution that is connected, the Internet has the potential to displace many of the traditional primary data collection techniques. The process has already begun but the Internet still suffers from serious flaws which limit the applications it can be used for in market research. These will be solved over time and the research industry will certainly adopt the Internet as an important tool in its armoury of research techniques.

The Internet features which are of most value to market researchers are:

- e-mail
- discussion forums
- File Transfer Protocol (FTP)
- newsgroups
- online service providers
- the World Wide Web

The first four of these are offered by the organizations providing Internet access, using the Internet itself as a means of communication. The last is the vast and ever expanding network of web sites that can be accessed from the Internet.

The reasons that researchers will be drawn inexorably towards the Internet for survey research are that it has the potential to reduce research costs and speed up the data collection process whilst also improving research quality. The Internet cannot, as yet, meet all research needs but it nevertheless offers researchers a number of advantages, some of which are unique. In summary they are:

- global coverage
- cost savings
- low entry costs
- interactivity

- speed
- access to a massive range of sources
- the ability to include sound and still and moving pictures in presentations such as questionnaires
- convenience

At present the Internet is being used for secondary research and a limited amount of primary research in the form of e-mail questionnaires, Internet questionnaires written in HTML and Internet focus groups. The main disadvantage of the Internet as a research tool is that good sampling can be carried out only among groups in which there are high levels of Internet connections. Whilst this certainly applies to research amongst Internet users and certain business sectors such as information technology, it will be some time before connections amongst the consumer population will be sufficiently common to accommodate all research needs.

Questionnaires

The questionnaire, however applied, is the general workhorse of all market research activity. The use of a questionnaire ensures that the research is carried out consistently and that the results are collected in a format which facilitates analysis. The format of the questionnaire to be used depends on the type of data to be collected, the number of interviews to be completed and the method of analysis. Large quantitative surveys generally deploy short, highly structured questionnaires which are suitable for machine analysis. Qualitative surveys are normally based on small numbers of interviews using a long, unstructured questionnaire which is likely to be analysed by hand. Questionnaires generally incorporate one or more of the following types of question:

- dichotomous questions (yes/no);
- multiple choice questions (giving a list of possible responses);
- semantic scales (scales based on words such as excellent, average, poor);
- scaling questions (numerical importance or rating scales or Likert scales);
- open-ended responses.

Questionnaires can be either unstructured (in which all the questions are open-ended checklists), fully structured (in which all questions are multiple choice or scaling questions), or semi-structured (a mixture of the two). Fully structured questionnaires assume that the full range of responses is known in advance and to achieve this may require preliminary, unstructured research. There is nothing worse than to design a questionnaire with multiple options only to find that a high proportion of respondents opt for the 'others' category.

Sampling

All forms of survey research rely on the fact that the activities, requirements or attitudes of any given universe can be described by analysing a small sample of that universe. This in turn requires that the sample be representative of the universe and is structured to reflect the various types of individuals or units that make up the universe. The prime determinants of the size of sample required depends on the homogeneity of the universe and the level of detail required in the final analysis. Samples of several thousand, structured by income group, lifestyle or region are regularly used to represent national populations of tens of millions, but if the analysis is required by fine breakdowns of consumer type the numbers can increase dramatically. Sample numbers are also affected by the characteristic of the product being surveyed. Products or services purchased frequently by a high proportion of individuals, such as food and drink, can be researched using relatively small samples. Products or services purchased infrequently, such as automobiles or consumer durables, may require large samples simply to identify customers that have made a purchase within the recent past.

Sampling is an exact science but in market research it is usually practised pragmatically. The true random sample, in which all units of the universe have an equal chance of appearing in the sample, is rarely practised – mainly because it is too costly to implement. The most common approach is the quota sample in which quotas are set for respondents fulfilling certain criteria. Individuals are then screened to determine whether they fit one of the quotas and interviewing proceeds until the quotas are filled. Geographically random samples are feasible using telephone interviews but are commonly abandoned in favour of random locations, which concentrate interviewing in specific parts of the territory.

A major concern of researchers is to ensure that the sample contains no bias which might make the results of the survey unrepresentative. Bias can occur from the way in which the sample is structured or the way in which it is selected, either of which can favour particular members of the population. The over-representation of some groups of the population and the under-representation of others will lead to results which do not represent the population as a whole. The sample design strategy must seek to eliminate or at least minimize these problems.

Geodemographic and lifestyle data

Knowledge of the structure of the consumer universe, and therefore the types of sample that need to be drawn, has been considerably enhanced by the development of geodemographic and lifestyle information. Traditionally, the primary segmentation of consumers was by socioeconomic group implying that the requirements and expenditure patterns of high income, managerial grades and other key groups were reasonably homogeneous. This system worked reasonably well for years, though the category into which a respondent fell could not normally be determined until they were interviewed. It was then shown that the type of residence and its location, as defined by postcode, was not only a more effective predictor of purchases but was also more accessible. Thus, geodemographic group has become more widely used as a basic structure for sampling. Similarly, lifestyle research has shown that definitions such as age, marital status and size of family can be replaced by descriptors which take account of the aspirations and perceptions of individual consumers. 'Yuppies' and 'Empty nesters' have distinct expenditure patterns which are unique to them and enable suppliers to apply a more relevant segmentation approach to their marketing.

Analysis

The final stage in the research process is the analysis of findings and recommendations. In large-scale quantitative surveys this is normally undertaken mechanically using survey analysis packages. Qualitative surveys, for which the samples are smaller, are generally analysed by hand. The output, be it tables or qualitative description, is reported to the research user in a report which interprets the findings and draws conclusions. The report is the prime record of what has been done and the outcome from the research.

5 The analysis of industrial markets

By far the highest proportion of research expenditure is spent on the analysis of consumer markets. However, there are important applications for market research in the analysis of industrial markets where the risks attached to poor decision making are as high if not greater than in consumer goods marketing. Outside certain specialist sectors such as pharmaceuticals, marketers of industrial goods and services have rarely been consistent users of market research. This is partly because of the size and structure of the market environments in which they operate and partly because the marketing process tends to be more direct, giving the vendor substantially higher exposure to his customers than is normally the case in consumer markets (see ORGANIZATIONAL BUYING BEHAVIOUR).

Industrial markets are considerably more complex than consumer markets. The main causes of complexity lie in the fact that specifying and purchasing are rarely in the hands of a single individual and that the criteria by which suppliers are selected and evaluated take into account a wide range of technical and commercial considerations as well as the emotional factors that operate so powerfully in consumer markets. Buyers of industrial products have a heightened need to be seen to have made a good decision, as their jobs are at stake as well as their professional esteem. All of this points to an increased need for market analysis to provide marketing and sales staff with a firm foundation for decisions. However, in most industrial markets the number of potential customers is a fraction of the customer base for consumer products. There are exceptions such as office equipment and telecommunications which are sold into very large industrial universes, but the norm is small customer universes in which it is theoretically easier to gain in-depth knowledge of practices and requirements. An industrial salesforce calling regularly on clients can easily be persuaded that it understands the market in which it is operating. This is rarely true, since purchasers of industrial goods and services have a number of good reasons to bias the information provided to suppliers and any sense of complete understanding is usually misplaced.

Despite their added complexity, industrial markets are researched in much the same way as consumer markets. The key differences lie in sampling procedure, which is substantially more complex, and in the need to employ research staff who can understand the technicalities of the businesses being researched. The research techniques are virtually identical, though there is a tendency to use more qualitative approaches to provide a deeper understanding of customer requirements, buying procedures, supplier evaluation criteria and the performance of suppliers.

6 International research

As markets develop globally there is a growing requirement for global information. Research can be carried out in most, if not all countries and research services are available on a global scale either through multinational research groups or independent local research companies. Whereas, some years ago, market research would have been an alien concept in certain cultures, increasing use has made it acceptable everywhere (see GLOBAL MARKETING).

Given the enormous differences in culture, lifestyle and the patterns of purchases, research surveys are surprisingly similar in approach and structure worldwide. When defining international surveys the problems are more of adaptation to suit local conditions in each country than the adoption of completely different approaches. Some of the more obvious differences in research in different countries are:

1. In many countries the demand for continuous research programmes is insufficient to justify their establishment and this type of data is therefore unavailable.
2. The quality of secondary information sources can vary considerably from country to country; as a general rule they are good in the industrialized countries but weak in the developing world.
3. The quality and recency of demographic information on individual consumers and industry varies substantially from country to country.
4. The usefulness of telephone research is obviously dependent on the quality of the telephone service and the incidence of telephone ownership. There are also cultural barriers to collecting information by telephone – in Japan for example (see CULTURAL ASPECTS OF MARKETING).
5. Data which are willingly given in some countries are regarded as strictly confidential in others.
6. In many countries products are not purchased in standard packages, which may make it difficult to track the volumes of purchases.
7. Structures of distribution can vary significantly from country to country and this must be reflected in the research approach.

National surveys that examine markets in a single country are rarely problematical. However, multinational surveys seeking comparable results in two or more countries do generate problems. Such surveys need to be planned with considerable care to ensure that recorded differences in attitude and approach reflect market conditions and not differences in survey approach. There is an increasing trend towards international surveys which are set up, analysed and reported centrally but with fieldwork carried out separately in each market. These have the major advantage of a common approach and harmonized analysis and are generally less costly than a series of individual country surveys. There has also been some use of centralized telephone interviewing into a number of national markets regarded as suitable for a telephone approach. To be effective this demands a supply of linguists and an ability to work round the clock to take account of time differences.

7 Working with research companies

Over the last decade there has been a continual trend amongst research users to outsource their research requirements from professional agencies rather than undertake studies themselves.

This has brought advantages such as anonymity, objectivity and cross-fertilization as well as cost savings, but it also means that in order to get the most from their budgets clients require skills in working with outside agencies. The three elements of the research programme that are key to ensuring a successful outcome are:

1. the research brief;
2. the agency proposal;
3. liaison during the research.

These are most applicable to *ad hoc* research. Where data are being purchased off the shelf, as is commonly the case with continuous or syndicated surveys, there is less interaction with the research agency and the findings can be viewed in advance to ensure that they are what is required. Even then, if special analysis of the data is required, the following guidelines may prove important.

The research brief

A survey is only as good as the initial brief. If users fail to set out what they require it is unlikely that the right result will be obtained. A good briefing document flows naturally from the planning process which results in the need for a survey being defined and should contain at the very least:

- background information (the company, its record, its association with the business to be considered in the survey);
- the nature of the problem to be tackled by the research;
- the product or service to be researched;
- relevant internally available information on the market;
- thoughts on the best research approach;
- time and budgetary constraints.

This document should be sent to a shortlist of companies thought to be capable of carrying out the project, together with an invitation to quote and a time-scale within which the quotation is required. If requested the client should agree to a meeting in which the research requirement is explained in more depth.

The proposal

Those invited to quote should respond with a proposal which will be the basis for selection of the research agency to be used. At its simplest, in situations where the client has provided a very precise specification of what is required (number of interviews, interview type, interview length, sample methodology and analysis routines), the proposal will contain the agency's credentials, a response to any questions raised in the brief, suggestions for improving the project or reducing costs and a fee. Where the brief does little more than outline the problem the proposal needs to be much fuller and should contain:

- the objectives of the research;
- the information to be sought;
- the research approach, the types of research techniques to be deployed and the numbers of interviews and group discussions;
- the cost;
- the time the survey will take to complete;
- the research team and their qualifications;
- any related experience the agency has.

It should be borne in mind that some agencies write better proposals than research documents, but the content, format, presentation and amount of thought provided in the proposal should give a reasonable guide to the ability of the agency.

Controlling the research process

Once the agency has been chosen there are some simple ground rules for ensuring that the survey runs smoothly. The client should follow the following procedures.

1. Meet the research team and brief them personally to ensure that they all understand what is required.
2. Pass over all information that is relevant and non-confidential; there is no point in asking research staff to regenerate what is already in existence.
3. Obtain frequent progress reports.
4. Do not change the research specification midway through the research project.
5. Receive an oral presentation of the findings once the data have been analysed, but prior to a report being written.
6. Ensure that the research team interpret their findings and specify what they see as the solution to the client's problem.

8 Conclusion

Research is a complex, time-consuming and costly process which must be used effectively. It is essential to recognize when additional data can enhance the quality of decision making, but it is equally essential to know when research is an expensive luxury, the cost of which cannot be justified. The results of too many research projects have languished unused on marketing managers' shelves, acting as a discouragement for further expenditure. The application of simple specification rules will help to ensure that expensive mistakes are avoided and that research will make its rightful contribution to the efficiency and effectiveness of the marketing process.

CHRISTOPHER WEST
MARKETING INTELLIGENCE SERVICES LTD

Further reading

(References cited in the text marked *)

Baker, M. (1991) *Research for Marketing*, London: Macmillan.
Birn, R., Hague, P. and Vangelder, P. (eds) (1991) *A Handbook of Market Research Techniques*, London: Kogan Page.
Bradley, U. (1987) *Applied Marketing and Social Research*, London: John Wiley.
Chisnall, P. (1991) *Marketing Research*, London: McGraw-Hill.
Dutka, A. (1993) *AMA Handbook for Customer Satisfaction*, Lincolnwood IL.: NTC Business Books.
Hague, P. (1990) *The Industrial Marketing Research Handbook*, London: Kogan Page.
Malhotra, N. K. (1993) *Marketing Research: An Application Orientation*, Englewood Cliffs, NJ: Prentice Hall.
Moroney, M. (1992) *Facts From Figures*, London: Penguin.
Sutherland, K. (ed.) (1991) *Researching Business Markets*, London: Kogan Page.
Worcester, R. and Downam, J. (eds) (1986) *Consumer Market Research Handbook*, Netherlands: Elsevier.
West, C. (1998) *Marketing Research*, London: Macmillan.

See also: ADVERTISING; THE ASSESSMENT OF MARKETING PERFORMANCE; CHANNELS OF DISTRIBUTION; CONSUMER BEHAVIOUR; CULTURAL ASPECTS OF MARKETING; EXHIBITIONS; GLOBAL MARKETING; MARKETING BUDGETING AND RESOURCE ALLOCATION; MARKET SEGMENTATION; ORGANIZATIONAL BUYING BEHAVIOUR; PACKAGING AND DESIGN; PRICING; SALES FORECASTING; QUALITATIVE RESEARCH IN MARKETING; QUANTITATIVE METHODS IN MARKETING; SALES PROMOTION

The marketing audit

1 Technique
2 Identifying respondents
3 A checklist approach
4 Obtaining the information
5 Mechanics
6 Who should do the audit?
7 The report

Overview

Every company, without exception, has locked within its operations resources that are either unused, underused or wrongly used. These resources could take many forms – physical, administrative, know-how, image, customers, skills, markets, brands, R&D are just a few. They have in common that their potential in terms of their contribution to marketing is not known or not always fully appreciated by their owners.

The marketing audit is a relatively simple, low-cost technique that enables a company to identify and exploit these possessions – thereby yielding usually low-cost, often no-cost, techniques, which when released into the marketing activity will materially improve the company's position. Lack of timely and detailed knowledge is caused partly by familiarity with the organization and its markets, but above all because the pressure of everyday events prevents standing back and taking an objective look at the company.

The marketing audit should not be confused with the market audit. The market audit is, as implied in its title, a quantification and qualification of markets (i.e. size, structure, trends, shares). The marketing audit is an analytical tool for identification, evaluation, measurement, motivation and action for improved performance. It gives a marketing profile for the audited company and it provides a method of assessing marketing effectiveness in a number of functions. The results of such examinations indicate where action is required to improve marketing. Properly conducted, the marketing audit highlights clearly where an organization stands along a scale ranging from no marketing to total sophistication. However, the major purpose is to give clear guidelines to top management on how to respond to a low or mediocre position or to improve further a satisfactory performance by introducing better marketing motivation and action.

Audits, which are commonplace in business, are almost invariably after-the-fact studies. The marketing audit provides evaluation and analysis before the actions are decided upon and is designed to ensure that all resources, even those with no apparent contribution to make to marketing but nevertheless impacting on it, are fully employed to release their maximum potential. The audit technique, as applied to marketing, provides a simple, logical, coherent and structured approach to a business activity to which objective scrutiny is not normally applied.

Conventionally, audits tend to be introduced when a company's marketing activities are perceived as not wholly effective. This is usually demonstrated by the firm losing market shares or by declining profit or a loss. Recently, however, the audit is being adopted for regular periodic use – in fact as a benchmarking technique rather than as a damage limitation exercise.

It should be clear that the marketing audit is as much concerned with the overall marketing strategy of the company as with tactical considerations. It can investigate the successes, failures and potential of the three main components of strategy – segmentation, marketing and product mix – and the variables which the strategy influences or controls. See Figure 1.

1 Technique

The audit method is based on extracting and interpreting information already in the company. It does not seek original external facts and therefore no market or other research, which can be expensive and time consuming, is involved. Any lack of data identified does or can lead to appropriate action for obtaining recent, detailed and better information.

The marketing audit

Figure 1 The marketing audit

The audit commences with the collection and study of the company's documentation. This usually comprises the following, but for the individual organization there may also be specific items:

- organization chart (official and informal);
- corporate/market/profit plan/budgets;
- sales analyses;
- job specifications of marketing and sales personnel including the sales or order office;
- catalogues and brochures (own and competitors');
- press releases;
- salesforce costs analyses;
- media advertising and direct mail material (including schedules and appropriations (own and competitors');
- other marketing costs analyses;
- salesforce reporting formats;
- customer database formats;
- enquiry records;
- pricing forms including discount structure;
- sales analyses (home and export);
- salesforce's, agents' and distributors' performance assessment forms;
- new product search reports and evaluations;
- list of journals and publications received;
- list of external statistics regularly received;
- guarantee claim record;
- credit note analyses;
- complaints analyses;
- service record formats;
- agency contracts;
- terms of business;
- costing and pricing formats;
- training programmes for sales and/or marketing people – content and frequency;
- details on any market research and customer satisfaction undertaken or bought in during the last one or two years.

Even at this early stage of the process, recommendations can arise. The lack of up-to-date competitor literature is a frequent omission that is easily rectified. Indeed, a recommendation would be to create a dossier for all important competitors comprising their literature, every reference found in trade and other press (there are commercial services which will undertake this task), annual reports, relevant extracts from salesmen's reports and all other contacts and sources. Within a very short space of time a picture emerges of the competition and, indeed, of competitive scenarios.

Another example of how the collection of documentation can lead to early recommendations is whether 'terms of business', often devised many years ago, are appropriate for today's conditions. For example, a clause stating the contract shall be read under English law may not be acceptable to European Union customers. Statements such as: 'Goods manufactured by us and which are shown to our satisfaction to be defective' no longer fit today's ethos of customer care.

As can be appreciated, the key aspects of documentation collection are: identification of what is not as well as what is available; whether the documentation yields useable information; whether those who provide it are acknowledged; whether it is demonstrated to them how that information is to be used. Those who provide input, most particularly the salesforce, can be greatly demotivated if they perceive the documentation to be pure bureaucracy, with no practical application or benefit to the person involved in input.

2 Identifying respondents

The first step in the audit proper is to identify who within the organization will be able to provide information. The company's structure schematic, as well as any informal networks which can be traced, will give an indication of who should be consulted. This can be amended as the programme proceeds. The personnel needed are those who can provide information because of their knowledge, experience and activities. Substantially, the lists will be drawn from marketing and sales functions, but it is not unusual for other departments to be included such as servicing, R&D, production, personnel and finance.

Typically, respondents will include a stratum of top and middle management and, where appropriate, 'sharp end' personnel such as field sales, servicing engineers, order office staff, and even reception and telephone operators. An example of the value of the contribution of this last, apparently unlikely, group can be found in a professional service firm where a conversation with the telephonist revealed a problem with strong negative image connotations. She complained that in a large and rambling building it was difficult to locate professional staff who lacked the discipline to notify her when they were away from their offices and where they could be contacted. This caused clients to be forced to wait while a search was made and the aggravation caused often led to irritation being directed against the operator as well as the missing member of staff. Apart from the obvious effect on clients the problem also inflamed interpersonnel relations which in turn led to a further deterioration in service. The resolution of the problem was simple. Given that discipline could not be imposed an internal paging system was introduced. The interesting aspect of the situation was the total unawareness of top management that any problem existed.

3 A checklist approach

The most efficient way to conduct an audit is to develop a specially designed checklist, or to adopt or adapt any of those which are available in published form. The Further Reading list gives details of some published checklists. Apart from imparting discipline into the information gathering process, the checklist ensures that the same ground is covered in the same way if the audit is used for benchmarking each time a check is taken.

Since the essential tool of the auditor is the checklist, the questions must be structured while also being free-ranging. They should cover every significant aspect of a company's marketing activities. Conventionally, but not exclusively, they will embrace some twenty-eight subjects (see Appendix). However, as with documentation, individual companies may have areas which are specific to them.

The core of the technique, indeed one of the principal skills required, is to select the subjects to be investigated and the questions to be posed and to devise supplementary questions which will yield the information (or conversely any lack of important information) required.

In using a typical pre-prepared checklist, the first stage is to eliminate all sections which are irrelevant. A company manufacturing advanced technical products would have no interest in non-differentiated (commodity) marketing (Appendix, item 26). Companies which do not export could ignore an export list (Appendix, item 5). Service companies are not concerned with physical distribution (Appendix, item 21). Of the list in the Appendix, typically some ten to fifteen subjects could be abandoned at once.

It is now necessary to study each of the remaining lists and remove any irrelevant questions. Asking questions about 'brand' visibility for a company that does not have branded products is obviously unnecessary (although in parenthesis it should be said that a question as to whether they should have brands will need to be asked). Similarly probing appropriations for direct response campaigns when this particular marketing tool is not part of the 'mix' of course eliminates this and other enquiries related to direct mail. Typically 30–40 per cent of the questions in any one list will be abandoned, making the final selection far less daunting and more manageable.

The supplementary questions

As important as the basic questions are, the supplementary questions which the original answer engenders will be critical. The following conversations are a precis of actual interviews.

The marketing audit

Q 'Which directories, yearbooks and buyers' guides do we appear in?'
A '*Kompass, Printers Year Book, Printing Trades Directory, Printing Portfolio* and about six Yellow Pages.'
Q 'What do these entries cost us?'
A 'Without checking I would say in the region of £50,000 a year.'
Supplementary question 'Can you trace any business directly to these insertions?'
A 'No.'
Supplementary question 'How do you justify continued use of these media?'
A 'All our competitors appear in them and if we don't it could affect us badly.'
Supplementary question 'Have any of your competitors dropped out?'
A 'I'm not sure. We don't monitor this and we don't keep out-of-date copies.'

From this exchange the recommendations are clear, namely to substantiate the statement which implied non-appearance would lead to loss of business and to establish the level of new and discontinued competitor entries and their market performance over, say, the past five years and then take the appropriate decisions.

Another example leading to a recommendation was:

Q 'How many days in the working year do the salesmen actually spend visiting customers?'
A 'Average (taken after reference to records) 152.'
Supplementary question 'Taking 222 days as a typical year of available days, what happens in the missing 70 days?'
A 'Administration matters, making appointments, order progress chasing in the plant.'
Supplementary question 'Which of these activities could someone with equal but different skills undertake for them?'
A 'Perhaps appointment making and progress chasing, possibly some administration.'
Supplementary question 'What would one extra call per sales person per week increase the annual call rate to?'
A 'Across the whole salesforce about 650 per annum.'
Supplementary question 'On the basis of current conversion of calls to orders can you give me a feel for how many extra orders 650 calls would produce?'
A 'Assuming the quality of calls remained the same, about 125 orders.'
Supplementary question 'What is the average value of an order?'
A 'There is a big variation, but at a guess, about £500.'
Supplementary question 'If the extra orders then represent perhaps over half a million of additional business would this offset the cost of having someone else lift part of the non-selling burden?'

The recommendation would be to analyse the average daily/weekly order intake and values to see if extra days gained at the cost of having someone else take over non-selling work would justify such a policy.

A last example relating to demonstrations can be given.

Q 'What is the conversion rate of enquiries to orders?'
A 'About 1: 6.5.'
Supplementary question 'Can you break that down to show the conversion rate between enquiries to orders and enquiries to demonstrations to orders?'
A (after consulting records) 'Demonstration to order is about 1:3.'
Supplementary question 'If you were to increase the number of demonstrations would that ratio be maintained?'
A 'Probably drop slightly.'
Supplementary question 'Given improved conversion would it not be a better sales platform to "sell" demonstrations instead of machines?'

The recommendation was to change the sales platform to seek to obtain demonstrations. Since it is more difficult to get prospects to the factory it was recommended that a demonstration caravan should be fitted out to take on to customer sites.

A critical supplementary question to every response must always be 'how do you know?' The answer must be interpreted in terms of validity of the source and its timeliness.

4 Obtaining the information

The above sequences occurred in a one-to-one personal interview but there are other ways, none so satisfactory, but worthy of consideration, which can be adopted.

Table 1 Advantages and disadvantages of self-analysis

Advantages	Disadvantages
The method can be quick and is cheap	The wrong respondents may be chosen or be self-selected.
It forces the consideration of key issues in a logical sequence.	It is difficult for respondents to be totally objective.
Self-analysis is generally more acceptable where criticism of the marketing operation is inherent.	Some of the answers are on a semantic scale and it is not always possible to place a real meaning on the chosen answers or on the scale interval.
It does not imply an imposed solution.	The respondents may attempt to answer questions where their knowledge is inadequate, lacking or out of date.

Self-analysis

The self-analysis or self-completed questionnaire technique calls upon the chosen personnel to answer a series of questions. While a narrative response is always preferable and should be encouraged, most busy respondents prefer a structured response where they only have to tick, eliminate or score. When scoring is invoked each question should be weighted to arrive at a final score. A weighting and rating system relating to ease of entry to new markets and which can be adapted for any subject will be found in Wilson (1991) *New Directions in Marketing*, chapter 3. A simple rating of each issue does not give an accurate result unless the importance of the questions in relationship to each other is allowed for. That is, scoring high on an issue such as 'accessibility of the marketing department' and scoring high on 'punctual delivery' does not make them of equal importance. Similarly, and unfortunately, scoring high on an unimportant (to the customer) issue does not cancel out scoring badly on an important issue. Thus, it is very necessary to weight each question to enable the grossed-up score to have immediate relevance to the issues involved and to influence the final score.

The auditor has to make a trade-off between the advantages and disadvantages of the self-analysis approach before making a decision to adopt it (see Table 1).

Self-analysis plus independent evaluation of the analysis

This technique follows the self-analysis method and the resulting questionnaire is then used for discussion between the respondents and the analyst. Each answer is discussed and probed. In particular, facts are called for to support the opinions expressed. In order to avoid the suspicion of a predetermined and/or imposed solution, possible courses of action arising out of the point in question are sought from the respondent. This is essentially an iterative process in which values and actions are examined, but without comment by the analyst (see Table 2). The final appraisal is drawn up by

Table 2 Self-analysis plus independent evaluation

Advantages	Disadvantages
Inherent biases and ambiguities in the self-completed questionnaire can be probed.	The interrogation technique can create hostility unless handled with sensitivity.
It is a process of forcing 'second thoughts' or reconsideration of the original answers, particularly those which are given impulsively or without cross-reference.	Under questioning the respondent may feel, particularly where the evaluation is showing a fairly low level of marketing effectiveness, that they are being subjected to unfair or even prejudiced criticism.
It challenges conventional wisdom, folklore or unsubstantiated statements.	The interrogation itself may imply lack of belief in the original self-completed questionnaire.

Table 3 Mail interrogation

Advantages	Disadvantages
Relatively cheap and total coverage in that all departments or companies in the group can be dealt with at the same time.	For the process to be completed rapidly it is necessary that the respondent should in fact reply quickly, which may not be particularly easy to achieve when people are pressed with other work, travelling, or resent the work involved.
Question formulation, reply and evaluation can receive careful consideration.	Communication by mail tends to be less clear, whereas in a personal interview questions can be explained more fully.
The respondent feels in control of the situation.	—

the analyst, which can (but does not have to) be submitted to the respondent for further comment and perhaps correction or change. Such corrections and changes are themselves part of the evaluation process.

Mail interrogation

Mail interrogation can be undertaken on the self-analysis basis, but with the questioning recycled via correspondence so that the respondents have time to think about what is required of them and do not feel pressured. The process not only gives the respondents time to consult and to prepare replies, but the interviewer also has time to reflect on the formulation of the questions as each cycle of the enquiry is developed (see Table 3).

Visits and interviews

This approach is for the analyst to undertake the audit by straight interviewing techniques using semi-structured or unstructured methods. The respondent has no prior knowledge of the questions to be asked and therefore the replies tend to be more spontaneous, but at the same time it is possible for the analyst to ask for validation of views given. Moreover, by visiting the respondent it is possible to examine and observe some types of marketing activity and to arrive at a view on attitudes and activities. Visits and interviews can either be single interviews with a designated respondent whose job specification and activity can be checked at the interview for his or her ability and authority to deal with all the points to be raised. Alternatively, the visit can be for multiple interviews, with all the personnel involved. This enables the entire questionnaire to be covered in one meeting and also ensures that comments made are within the knowledge of everyone involved in the marketing process (see Table 4).

Table 4 Visits and interviews

Advantages	Disadvantages
Cross-evaluations and checks can made.	Respondents may answer with more consideration for their colleagues' attitudes and reactions than the interviewer or the purpose of the interview.
Taken in groups, respondents, far from feeling at a disadvantage, feel at an advantage over the interviewer, and therefore are more inclined to cooperate.	Answers may be withheld or given defensively where respondents feel they may be criticized by their colleagues.
Group dynamics apply and modification of views (not simply consensus) will occur, which is of considerable value.	There may be resentment at inclusion/exclusion in the group chosen.

Method choice

The final choice of method(s) will depend upon the structure of the company and the units to be audited and to some extent on the numbers and types of personnel to be involved in the process. There can be no one approach which will work in all circumstances. Experience indicates that the personal interview, either one-to-one, or as a group, has many advantages in terms of time and yield. Working in groups enables a Delphi approach to be adopted when each member can hear the advocacy for and against a particular opinion and as a consequence and if needs be to modify his or her views. However, while suggestions for actions should be welcomed, care must be taken not to get into the stultifying position of arguing about them. It is the job of the auditor to decide what are the implications of the information. An action plan created by a committee is going to be the antithesis of quick movement and decisiveness.

An important psychological point must be considered. The audit and questioning process can well disturb respondents who may regard the whole process as a personal performance assessment leading perhaps to some disadvantage. Before any meeting takes place, or at the very beginning of a meeting, the purpose of the audit must be explained to respondents – that it is the contribution of their knowledge, experience and ideas which is sought and that the interview is not a performance review. It is vital to obtain their enthusiastic cooperation. Thus, the purpose and outcome of the audit need to be completely understood by respondents.

5 Mechanics

Once the questioning is complete the auditor must then evaluate the yield in terms of the actions which are required. The examples given above are indicative of the types of recommendations which can emerge. A typical audit for a company with say a £12 million turnover should generate about 70–80 action points most of which, as has been indicated, could be introduced at low cost.

In terms of mechanics of the information-gathering stage it has been found that the best way to administer the questionnaire is to note responses in three different coloured pens or using three different symbols. Replies are noted using one colour. Any responses which would lead to a recommendation should be circled in another colour or marked with the appropriate symbol. Those replies which require further investigation, perhaps later during the interview, carry the third identification. As with all good interviewing, respondents should not be interrupted when they are providing relevant information, but only when discrepancies or contradictions that occur or the answers themselves raise new points. These are better dealt with separately, probably at a different part of the interview or at the end when any clarification can be sought. By adopting this method when the interview notes are interpreted the recommendations will stand out for transfer to the report, using the notes as a justification for the recommendation.

It is recognized that not all the recommendations can be implemented within the resources and time span available, so it may be necessary to place an order of priority on the introduction of changes or activities that are deemed necessary. To this end it is advisable to extract all action points for categorization into priority groups with an indication of, at the very least, the time implied by such terms as 'at once', 'short-term'. Without this and, on their own, time designations of this type have no real meaning. It is also useful to classify recommendations by likely cost implications, so that no-cost and low-cost measures can be initiated without budget changes or authorization. This alone should ensure the removal of one possible blockage to progress. It is well worth stating that any recommendation that can be adopted without cost or disturbance becomes a priority and has a high implementative value.

6 Who should do the audit?

It is essential that whoever conducts an audit should be totally unbiased and neutral. It is asking too much of a person to expect them to remain objective when reporting on a situation that may reflect on themselves or on their department or activity. There is certainly no technical reason why a member of the firm should not conduct the audit provided the desiderata can be met. The use of internal personnel carries the great advantage that they know a great deal about the company, its organization, personnel, markets, systems, opportunities and threats, thus learning-curve costs are not incurred. This very knowledge can unwittingly produce its own biases, which is something to be resisted, however difficult that may be.

Using an external consultant for the most part avoids the problem of lack of objectivity, but the advantage of familiarity with the organization is lost. However, while these factors might balance themselves out the one advantage the external consultant brings is the cross-fertilization of ideas and solutions which can occur between widely different industries. A recommendation successfully adopted by a travel agency was found, with modifications, to be applicable to a leading-edge electronics designer.

It is not possible to designate which is the best solution – both have their advantages and disadvantages. One feasible compromise is to have internal staff trained by an experienced external consultant using a hands-on approach. Hence, the first audit is conducted by the consultant, using the internal staff member as assistant and explaining the thinking behind the questions and how the recommendation emerges. On a second audit the consultant and staff member act as a partnership, undertaking some sections together and other parts alone. The consultant checks, amends and expands the internal staff member's sections, again explaining any changes. On a third audit the staff member leads with the consultant acting as assistant, with an occasional touch on the tiller. The consultant also edits the final report and again, as before, always explains any changes introduced.

Such a sequence will give the internal auditor confidence, help him or her identify their own biases and subjectivities and clearly demonstrate both technique and the wide-ranging thinking necessary to produce really creative recommendations.

7 The report

The report will tend to be quite daunting in size but must be capable of being handled easily and quickly. The format should follow the headings of the subjects audited and each item should comprise:

- Situation analysis – the auditor's understanding of the activities and performance.
- Recommendation for a course of action.
- Justification for the recommendation made.

In order to assist rapid implementation it is always advisable to extract the recommendations alone and restate them in the briefest form in a separate document or as an appendix. They must be cross-referenced to the body of the report, so that it is possible to consider the situation and justifications without allowing them to obscure the recommendation itself.

The last action of the audit is to place a date for initiation and completion of each activity, to decide who is responsible for carrying it through and who is to monitor progress and satisfactory completion. This point requires extra emphasis. Completing an audit does not automatically imply that the appropriate actions will be taken. To be certain that the marketing resources will be fully realized it is important to ensure that every action decided upon is allocated to an individual or group, that the time for its completion is scheduled and promulgated and that someone monitors that the task is satisfactorily completed by the due date. Allocate, schedule and monitor are the key words for guaranteeing action.

There are some basic rules which apply:

1. Peer pressure is better than instruction. If everyone knows what everyone is supposed to be doing and by when, the activity is more likely to get completed.
2. Volunteers are better than conscripts. In making recommendations, although not the task of the auditor to carry them out, it is helpful if he or she can weld together a team to implement the suggestions. However enthusiastic volunteers may be, it is obvious that they must have the skill to undertake the task.
3. While time recommendations are important relative to starting and completing, the likelihood of enthusiastic cooperation is greater if those who have accepted the tasks can set their own schedule. This way there can be no question that the requirements were unreasonable.

A format (see Figure 2) circulated to all those involved ensures that the whole action plan is known to everyone.

The marketing audit is not a substitute for action, nor should it be permitted to delay decision taking. The auditor should keep this thought foremost in mind when undertaking the work. The audit process can be summarized as follows:

Figure 2 Format for an action plan.

- collect documentation;
- decide the subjects for investigation;
- devise or adopt a question checklist;
- delete all non-relevant questions;
- auditor answers all questions within his or her capability and recommends courses of action;
- list others who need to be consulted to complete audit;
- decide whether to take individual replies or operate as a group;
- identify which questions will be asked of which persons (for individual responses);
- decide how response will be taken (i.e. personal interview, advance notice of questions and personal interview, written request and written response) (for individual responses);
- conduct interviews;
- analyse yield;
- suggest courses of action with justification arising from the responses;
- extract all action points and categorize according to urgency, likely cost, ease of implementation;
- allocate each task by name, schedule it by date or elapsed time, agree monitoring procedure.

Appendix

Subjects for consideration

1. Marketing strategy and planning.
2. Product/service range.
3. The service element in marketing.
4. Company performance.
5. Export marketing.
6. Marketing information: systems and use.
7. Market size and structure.
8. Future market.
9. The salesforce and its management.
10. Support staff's role in marketing.
11. Cross-selling and internal marketing.
12. The agency system.
13. Non-personal promotion: methods and media.
14. The distributive system.
15. The buying process.
16. Analysing lost business.
17. Introducing new products/services.
18. User industries.
19. Key customer marketing.
20. Competitive climate.
21. Physical distribution and packaging.
22. Industry contacts.
23. Pricing.
24. Images and perceptions.
25. Quality in marketing.
26. Non-differentiated products and commodities.
27. Service businesses.
28. Product/service financial information.

AUBREY WILSON
AUBREY WILSON ASSOCIATES

Further reading

(References cited in the text marked *)

These titles all contain checklists.

Alles, Alfred (1988) *Exhibitions – Key to Effective Marketing*, London: Cassell.
Anderson, A.G. (1986) *Marketing Your Practice*, Chicago: American Bar Association.
Davidson, J.P. (1990) *Essential Management Check Lists*, London: Kogan Page.
Godferoy, G.H. and Robert, C. (1993) *The Outstanding Negotiator*, London: Piatkus.
Hitchcock, E.B. (1981) *How To Sell Effectively Through Manufacturers' Agents*, New York: Frost & Sullivan.
Kotler, P. and Scheff, J. (1997) *Standing Room Only – Strategies for Marketing the Performing Arts*, Boston: Harvard Business School Press.
McDonald, M. (n/d) *Handbook of Marketing Planning*, Bradford: MCB Publications.
Maister, David (1993) *Managing the Professional Service Firm*, New York: Free Press.
Martin, W.B. (1991) *Managing Quality Customer Service*, London: Kogan Page.
Mendelsohn, Martin (1980) *How To Evaluate A Franchise*, London: Franchise Publication.
Stapleton, J. (1989) *How To Prepare A Marketing Plan*, Farnborough: Gower.
Walmsley, John (1989) *The Development of International Markets*, London: Graham & Trotman.
* Wilson, Aubrey (1991) *New Directions in Marketing*, London: Kogan Page.
Wilson, Aubrey (1992) *Marketing Audit Check Lists*, Maidenhead, London: McGraw-Hill.
Wilson, Aubrey (1993) *The Industrial Marketing Researchers Check List*, London: Department of Trade and Industry.
Wilson, Aubrey (1994) *Emancipating of the Professions*, Chichester: Wiley.
Winkler, J. (1989) *Winning Sales and Marketing Tactics*, London: Heinemann.

Sales forecasting

1 Forecasting methods: an overview
2 Direct extrapolation of sales
3 Causal approaches to sales forecasting
4 New product forecasting
5 Evaluating and selecting methods
6 Estimating prediction intervals
7 Implementation
8 Conclusions

Overview

Interesting and difficult sales forecasting problems are common. Will the 1998 Volkswagen Beetle be a success? Will the Philadelphia Convention Hall be profitable? How will our major competitors respond if we raise the price of our product by 10 per cent? What if we cut advertising by 20 per cent?

Sales forecasting involves predicting the amount people will purchase, given the product features and the conditions of the sale. Sales forecasts help investors make decisions about investments in new ventures. They are vital to the efficient operation of the firm and can aid managers on such decisions as the size of a plant to build, the amount of inventory to carry, the number of workers to hire, the amount of advertising to place, the proper price to charge, and the salaries to pay salespeople. Profitability depends on (1) having a relatively accurate forecast of sales and costs; (2) assessing the confidence one can place in the forecast; and (3) properly using the forecast in the plan.

Marketing practitioners believe that sales forecasting is important. In Dalrymple's (1975) survey of marketing executives in US companies, 93 per cent said that sales forecasting was 'one of the most critical' or 'a very important aspect of their company's success.' Furthermore, formal marketing plans are often supported by forecasts (Dalrymple 1987). Given its importance to the profitability of the firm, it is surprising that basic marketing texts devote so little space to the topic. Armstrong, Brodie and McIntyre (1987), in a content analysis of 53 marketing textbooks, found that forecasting was mentioned on less than 1 per cent of the pages.

Research on forecasting has produced useful findings. These findings are summarized in the Forecasting Principles Project, which is described on the website http://www-marketing.wharton.upenn.edu/forecast. This entry draws upon that project in summarizing guidelines for sales forecasting. These forecasting guidelines should be of particular interest because few firms use them. I also describe some commonly used approaches that are *detrimental* to sales forecasting.

After a brief overview of forecasting methods, I discuss the direct extrapolation of sales data, either through statistical data or simply judgemental. Next, I describe causal approaches to sales forecasting. Attention is then given to new product forecasting. This is followed by a discussion of how to select appropriate methods and by a description of methods to assess uncertainty. I conclude with suggestions for gaining acceptance of forecasting methods and of forecasts.

1 Forecasting methods: an overview

Forecasting involves methods that derive primarily from judgemental sources versus those from statistical sources. These methods and their relationships are shown in the flow chart in Figure 1. Judgement and statistical procedures are often used together, and since 1985, much research has examined the integration of statistical and judgemental forecasts (Armstrong and Collopy 1998b). Going down the figure, there is an increasing amount of integration between judgemental and statistical procedures. A brief description of the methods is provided here. Makridakis, Wheelwright and Hyndman (1998) provide details on how to apply many of these methods.

Intentions studies ask people to predict how they would behave in various situations. This method is widely used and it is especially

Figure 1 Characteristics of forecasting methods and their relationships

important where one does not have sales data, such as for new product forecasts.

A person's role may be a dominant factor in some situations, such as in predicting how someone would behave in a job related situation. Role-playing is useful for making forecasts of the behavior of individuals who are interacting with others, and especially in situations involving conflict (see CONSUMER BEHAVIOUR).

Another way to make forecasts is to ask experts to predict how others will behave in given situations. The accuracy of expert forecasts can be improved through the use of structured methods, such as the Delphi procedure. Delphi is an iterative survey procedure in which experts provide forecasts for a problem, receive anonymous feedback on the forecasts made by other experts, and then make another forecast. For a summary of the evidence on the accuracy of Delphi versus unstructured judgement, see Rowe and Wright (1999). One principle is that experts' forecasts should generally be independent of one another. Focus groups *always* violate this principle. As a result, they should not be used in forecasting.

Intentions can be explained by relating the 'predictions' to various factors that describe the situation. By asking consumers to state their intentions to purchase for a variety of different situations, it is possible to infer how the factors relate to intended sales. This is often done by regressing their intentions against the factors, a procedure known as 'conjoint analysis'.

As with conjoint analysis, one can develop a model of the expert. This approach, judgemental bootstrapping, converts subjective judgements into objective procedures. Experts are asked to make a series of predictions. For example, they could make forecasts for the next year's sales in geographical regions. This process is then converted to a set of rules by regressing the forecasts against the information used by the forecaster. Once developed, judgemental bootstrapping models offer a low-cost procedure for making forecasts. They almost always provide an improvement in accuracy in comparison to judgemental forecasts, although these improvements are typically modest (Armstrong 1999).

Extrapolation methods use only historical data on the series of interest. The most popular and cost effective of these methods are based on exponential smoothing, which implements the useful principle that the more recent data are weighted more heavily. Another principle for extrapolation is to use long time-series when developing a forecasting model. Yet, Focus Forecasting, one of the most widely-used time-series methods in business firms, does not do this. As a result, its forecasts are inaccurate (Gardner and Anderson 1997).

Still another principle for extrapolation is to use reliable data. The existence of retail scanner data means that reliable data can be obtained for existing products. Scanner data are detailed, accurate, timely and inexpensive. As a result, the accuracy of the forecasts should improve, especially because of the reduction in the error of assessing the current status. Not knowing where you are starting from has often been a major source of error in predicting where you will wind up. Scanner data are also expected to provide early identification of trends.

Empirical studies have led to the conclusion that relatively simple extrapolation methods perform as well as more complex methods. For example, the Box-Jenkins procedure, one of the more complex approaches, has produced no measurable gains in forecast accuracy relative to simpler procedures (Makridakis *et al.* 1984; Armstrong 1985). Although distressing to statisticians, this finding should be welcome to managers.

Quantitative extrapolation methods make no use of managements' knowledge of the series. They assume that the causal forces that have affected a historical series will continue over the forecast horizon. The latter assumption is sometimes false. When the causal forces are contrary to the trend in the historical series, forecast errors tend to be large (Armstrong and Collopy 1993). While such problems may occur only in a small minority of cases in sales forecasting, their effects can be disastrous. One useful guideline is that trends should be extrapolated only when they coincide with managements' prior expectations.

Judgemental extrapolations are preferable to quantitative extrapolations when there have been large *recent* changes in the sales level and where there is relevant knowledge about the item to be forecast (Armstrong and Collopy 1998b). Quantitative extrapolations have an advantage over judgemental methods when the data are ample and changes are expected to be large (Armstrong 1985: 393–401). More important than these small gains in accuracy, however, is that the quantitative methods are often less expensive. When one has thousands of forecasts to make every month, the use of judgement is seldom cost effective.

Experts can identify analogous situations. Extrapolation of results from these situations can be used to predict for the situation that is of interest. For example, to assess the loss in sales when the patent protection for a drug is removed, one might examine the results for previous drugs. Incidently, the first year loss is substantial.

Rule-based forecasting integrates judgemental knowledge about the domain. Rule-based forecasting is a type of expert system that is limited to statistical time-series. Its primary advantage is that it incorporates the manger's knowledge in an inexpensive way.

Expert systems use the rules of experts. In addition, they typically draw upon empirical studies of relationships that come from econometric models. Expert opinion, conjoint analysis, bootstrapping and econometric models can aid in the development of expert systems.

Despite an immense amount of research effort, there is little evidence that multivariate time-series provide any benefits to forecasting. As a result, these methods are not discussed here.

Econometric models use data to estimate the parameters of a model given various constraints. When possible. Which is nearly always in management problems, one can draw upon prior research to determine the direction, functional form, and magnitude of relationships. In addition, they can integrate expert opinion, such as that from a judgemental bootstrapping model. Estimates of relationships can then be updated by using time-series or cross-sectional data. Here again, reliable data are needed. Scanner data can provide data from low-cost field experiments where key features such as advertising or price are varied to assess how they affect sales. The outcomes of such experiments can contribute to the estimation of relationships. Econometric models can also use inputs from conjoint models. Econometric models allow for extensive integration of judgemental and statistical sources.

Econometric methods can relate directly to planning and decision making. They can incorporate the effects of marketing mix variables as well as variables representing key aspects of the market and the environment. Econometric methods are appropriate when one needs to forecast what will happen using different assumptions about the environment or different strategies. Econometric methods are most useful when (1) strong causal relationships with sales are expected; (2) these causal relationships can be estimated; (3) large changes are expected to occur in the causal variables over the forecast horizon; and (4) these changes in the causal variables can be forecast or controlled, especially with respect to their direction. If any of these conditions does not hold (which is typical for short-range sales forecasts), then econometric methods should not be expected to improve accuracy.

2 Direct extrapolation of sales

If one does not have substantial amounts of sales data, it may be preferable to make judgemental extrapolations. This assumes that the person has good knowledge about the product. For example, the characteristics of the product and market and future plans are all well-known.

When one has ample sales data, it is often sufficient merely to extrapolate the trend. Extrapolation of the historical sales trend is common in firms (Mentzer and Kahn 1995). Extrapolation methods are used for short-term forecasts of demand for inventory and production decisions.

When the data are for time intervals shorter than a year, it is generally advisable to use seasonal adjustments, given sufficient data. Seasonal adjustments typically represent the most important way to improve the accuracy of extrapolation. Dalrymple's (1987) survey results were consistent with the principle that the use of seasonal factors reduces the forecast error. Seasonal adjustments which also led to substantial improvements in accuracy were found in the large-scale study of time series by Makridakis et al. (1984).

If the historical series involve much uncertainty, the forecaster should use relatively simple models. Uncertainty in this case can be assessed by examining the variability about the long-term trend line. Schnaars (1984) presented evidence that the naive forecast was one of the most accurate procedures for industry sales forecasts. Uncertainty also calls for conservative forecasts. Being conservative means to stay near the historical average. Thus, it often helps to dampen the trend as the horizon increases (see Gardner and McKenzie 1985 for a description of one such procedure and for evidence of its effectiveness).

One of the key issues in the extrapolation of sales is whether to use top-down or bottom-up approaches. By starting at the top (say the market for automobiles), and then allocating the forecast among the elements (e.g. sales of luxury cars or sales of the BMW 3-series) one typically benefits from having more reliable data, but the data are less relevant. In contrast, the bottom-up approach is more relevant and less reliable. (For a more complete discussion on these issues, see Armstrong, 1985: 250–66 and MacGregor 1998.) Research on this topic has been done under the heading of 'decomposition' or 'segmentation'. Additive breakdowns tend to be fairly safe. Seldom do they harm forecast accuracy, and often they provide substantial improvements (Dangerfield and Morris 1992).

3 Causal approaches to sales forecasting

Instead of extrapolating sales directly, one can forecast the factors that cause sales to vary. This begins with environmental factors such as population, gross national product (GNP) and the legal system. These affect the behaviour of customers, competitors, suppliers, distributors and complementors (those organizations with whom you cooperate). Their actions lead to a market forecast. Their actions also provide inputs for the market share forecast. The product of the market forecast and the market share forecast yields the sales forecast.

The breakdown of the problems into the elements of Figure 2 may aid one's thinking about the sales forecasts. It is expected to improve accuracy (versus the extrapolation of sales) only if one has good information about each of the components and if there is a good understanding about how each relates to sales. If there is high uncertainty about any of the elements, it might be more accurate to extrapolate sales directly.

Marketing management

Figure 2 Causal approach to sales forecasting

The primary advantage of the indirect approach is that it can be more directly related to decision making. Adjustments can be made in the marketing mix to see how this would affect the forecast. Also, forecasts can be prepared to assess possible changes by other decision makers such as competitors or complementors. These forecasts can allow the firm to develop contingency plans, and these effects on sales can also be forecast. On the negative side, the causal approach is more expensive than sales extrapolation.

Environment
It is sometimes possible to obtain published forecasts of environmental factors from Tablebase, which is available on the Internet through various subscribing business research libraries. These forecasts may be adequate for many purposes. However, sometimes it is difficult to determine what methods were used to create the forecasts. In such cases, econometric models can improve the accuracy of environmental forecasts. They provide more accurate forecasts than those provided by extrapolation or by judgement when large changes are involved. Allen (1999) summarizes evidence on this. Important findings that aid econometric methods are to: (1) base the selection of causal variables upon forecasting theory and knowledge about the situation, rather than upon the statistical fit to historical data (also, tests of statistical significance play no role here); (2) use relatively simple models (e.g. do not use simultaneous equations; do not use models that cannot be specified as linear in the parameters); and (3) use variables only if the estimated relationship to sales is in the same direction as specified *a priori*. The last point is consistent with the principle of using causal not statistical reasoning. Consistent with this viewpoint, leading indicators, a non-

causal approach to forecasting that has been widely accepted for decades, does not seem to improve the accuracy of forecasts (Diebold and Rudebusch 1991).

Interestingly, there exists little evidence that more accurate forecasts of the environment (e.g. population, the economy, social trends, technological change) lead to better sales forecasts. This, of course, seems preposterous. I expect that the results have been obtained for studies where the conditions were not ideal for econometric methods. For example, if things continue to change as they have in the past, there is little reason to expect an econometric model to help with the forecast. However, improved environmental forecasts are expected when large changes are likely, such as the adoption of free trade policies, reductions in tariffs, economic depressions, natural disasters, and wars.

Customers

One should know the size of the potential market for the given product category (e.g. how many people in region X might be able to purchase an automobile), the ability of the potential market to purchase (e.g. income per capita and the price of the product), and the needs of the potential customers. Examination of each of these factors can help in forecasting demand for the category.

Company

The company sets its own marketing mix so there is typically little need to forecast these actions. However, sometimes the policies are not implemented according to plan because of changes in the market, actions by competitors or by retailers, or a lack of cooperation by those in the firm. Thus, it may be useful to forecast the actions that will actually be taken (e.g. if we provide a trade discount, how will this affect the average price paid by final consumers?)

Intermediaries

What actions will be taken by suppliers, distributors and complementors? One useful prediction model is to assume that their future decisions will be similar to those in the past, that is, the naive model. For existing markets, this model is often difficult to improve upon. When large changes are expected, however, the naive model is not appropriate. In such cases one can use structured judgement, extrapolate from analogous situations, or use econometric models.

Structure typically improves the accuracy of judgement, especially if it can realistically mirror the actual situation. Role playing is one such structured technique. It is useful when the outcome depends on the interaction among different parties and especially when the interaction involves conflict. Armstrong and Hutcherson (1989) asked subjects to role play the interactions between producers and distributors. In this disguised situation, Philco was trying to convince supermarkets to sell its appliances through a scheme whereby customers received discounts based on the volume of purchases at selected supermarkets. Short (less than one hour) role plays of the situation led to correct predictions of the supermarket managers' responses for 75 per cent of the 12 groups. In contrast, only one of 37 groups was correct when groups made predictions without benefit of formal techniques. (As it turned out, the decision itself was poor, but that is another story.)

Econometric models offer an alternative, although much more expensive approach to forecasting the actions by intermediaries. This approach requires a substantial amount of information. For example, Montgomery (1975) described a model to predict whether a supermarket buying committee would put a new product on its shelves. This model, which used information about advertising, suppliers' reputation, margin and retail price, provided reasonable predictions for a hold-out sample.

Competitors

Can we improve upon the simple, 'naive', forecast that competitors will continue to act as they have in the past? These forecasts are difficult because of the interaction that occurs among the key actors in the market. Because competitors have conflicting interests, they are unlikely to respond truthfully to an intentions survey.

A small survey of marketing experts suggested that the most popular approach to forecasting competitors' actions is unaided expert opinion (Armstrong *et al.* 1987). Because the 'experts' are usually those in the company, however, this may introduce biases related to their desired outcomes. For example, brand managers are generally too optimistic about their brands. Here again, role playing would appear to be relevant. Although no direct experimental evidence is available on its value in forecasting competitor's actions, role playing has proven to be accurate in forecasting the decision made in conflict situations (Armstrong 1999).

Market share

Can we do better than the naive model of no change? For existing markets that are not undergoing major change, the naive model is reasonably accrate (Brodie *et al.* 1999). This is true even when one has excellent data about the competitors (Alsem *et al.* 1989). However, causal models should improve forecasts when large changes are made, such as when price reductions are advertised. Causal models should also help when a firm's sales have been artificially limited due to production capacity, tariffs, or quotas. Furthermore, contingent forecasts are important. Firms can benefit by obtaining good forecasts of how its policies (e.g. a major price reduction) would affect its market share.

4 New product forecasting

New product forecasting is of particular interest in view of its importance to decision making. In addition, large errors are typically made in such forecasts. Tull (1967) estimated the mean absolute percentage error for new product sales to be about 65 per cent. Not surprisingly then, pretest market models have gained wide acceptance among business firms; Shocker and Hall (1986) provide an evaluation of some of these models.

The choice of a forecasting model to estimate customer response depends on the stage of the product life-cycle (see PRODUCT LIFE-CYCLE MANAGEMENT). As one moves through the concept phase to the prototype, test market, introductory, growth, maturation and declining stages, the relative value of the alternative forecasting methods changes. In general, the movement is from purely judgemental approaches to quantitative models that use judgement as inputs. For example, intentions and expert opinions are vital in the concept and prototype stages. Later, expert judgement is useful as an input to quantitative models. Extrapolation methods may be useful in the early stages if it is possible to find analogous products (Claycamp and Liddy 1969). In later stages, extrapolation methods become more useful and less expensive as one can work directly with time-series data on sales or orders. Econometric and segmentation methods become more useful after a sufficient amount of actual sales data are obtained.

When the new product is in the concept phase, a heavy reliance is usually placed on intentions surveys. Intentions to purchase new products are complicated because potential customers may not be sufficiently familiar with the proposed product and because the various features of the product affect one another (e.g. price, quality, and distribution channel). This suggests the need to prepare a good description of the proposed product. This often involves expensive prototypes, visual aids, product clinics or laboratory tests. However, brief descriptions are sometimes as accurate as elaborate descriptions as found in Armstrong and Overton's (1970) study of a new form of urban mass transportation (see CHANNELS OF DISTRIBUTION; NEW PRODUCT DEVELOPMENT).

In the typical intentions study, potential consumers are provided with a description of the product and the conditions of sale, and then are asked about their intentions to purchase. Eleven-point rating scales are recommended. The scale should have verbal designations such as 0 = 'No chance, almost no chance (1 in 100)' to '10 = Certain, practically certain (99 in 100)'. It is best to state the question broadly about one's 'expectations' or 'probabilities' to purchase, rather than the narrower question of intentions. This distinction was raised early on by Juster (1966) and its importance has been shown in empirical studies by Day *et al.* (1991).

Intentions surveys are useful when all of the following conditions hold: (1) the event is important; (2) responses can be obtained; (3) the respondent has a plan; (4) the respondent reports correctly; (5) the respondent can fulfil the plan; and (6) events are unlikely to change the plan. These conditions imply that intentions are more useful for short-term forecasts of business-to-business sales.

The technology of intentions surveys has improved greatly over the past half century. Useful methods have been developed for selecting samples, compensating for nonresponse bias, and reducing response error. Dillman (1978) provides excellent advice that can be used for designing intentions surveys. Improvements in this technology have been demonstrated by studies on voter intentions (Perry 1979). Response error is probably the most important component of total error (Sudman and Bradburn 1982). Still, the correspondence between intentions and sales is often not close. Morwitz (1999) provides a review of the evidence on intentions to purchase.

As an alternative to asking potential customers about their intentions to purchase, one can ask *experts* to predict how consumers will respond. For example, Wotruba and Thurlow (1976) discuss how opinions from members of the sales force can be used to forecast sales. One could ask distributors or marketing executives to make sales forecasts. Expert opinions studies differ from intentions surveys. When an expert is asked to predict the behaviour of a market, there is no need to claim that this is a representative expert. Quite the contrary, the expert may be exceptional. When using experts to forecast, one needs few experts, typically only between five and twenty (Hogarth 1978; Ashton 1985).

Experts are especially useful at diagnosing the current situation, which we might call 'nowcasting'. Surprisingly, however, when the task involves forecasting change, experts with modest domain expertise (about the item to be forecast) are just as accurate as those with high expertise (Armstrong 1985: 91–6 reviews the evidence). This means that it is not necessary to purchase expensive expert advice.

Unfortunately, experts are often subject to biases. Salespeople may try to forecast on the low side if the forecasts will be used to set quotas. Marketing executives may forecast high in their belief that this will motivate the sales force. If possible, avoid experts who would have obvious reasons to be biased (Tyebjee 1987). Another strategy is to include a heterogeneous group of experts in the hopes that their differing biases may cancel one another.

Little is known about the relative accuracy of expert opinions versus consumer intentions. However, Sewall (1981) found that each approach contributes useful information such that a combined forecast is more accurate than either one alone.

Producers often consider several alternative designs for the new product. In such cases, potential customers can be presented with a series of perhaps twenty or so alternative offerings. For example, various features of a personal computer, such as price, weight, battery life, screen clarity and memory might vary according to rules for experimental design (the basic ideas being that each feature should vary substantially and that the variations among the features should not correlate with one another). The customer is forced to make trade-offs among various features. This is called 'conjoint analysis' because the *con*sumers consider the product features *joint*ly. This procedure is widely used by firms (Wittink and Bergestuen 1998). An example of a successful application is the design of a new Marriott hotel chain (Wind *et al.* 1989). The use of conjoint analysis to forecast new product demand can be expensive because it requires large samples of potential buyers, the potential buyers may be difficult to locate, and the questionnaires are not easy to complete. Respondents must, of course, understand the concepts that they are being asked to evaluate. Although conjoint analysis rests on good theoretical foundations, little validation research exists in which its accuracy is compared with the accuracy of alternative techniques such as Delphi or judgemental forecasting procedures.

Expert judgements can be used in a manner analogous to the use of consumers' intentions for conjoint analysis. That is, the experts could be asked to make predictions about situations involving alternative product design and alternative marketing plans. These predictions would then be related to the situations by regression analysis. Following the philosophy for naming conjoint analysis, this could be called *exjoint analysis*. It is advantageous to conjoint analysis in that few experts are needed (probably between five and twenty). In addition, it can incorporate policy variables that might be difficult for consumers to assess.

Once a new product is on the market, it is possible to use extrapolation methods. Much attention has been given to the selection of the proper functional form to extrapolate early sales. The diffusion literature uses an S-shaped curve to predict new product sales. That is, growth builds up slowly at first, becomes rapid as word-of-mouth and observation of use spread, then slows again as it approaches a saturation level. A substantial literature exists on diffusion models. Despite this, the number of comparative validation studies is small and the benefits of choosing the best functional form seem to be modest (research on this is reviewed by Meade 1999).

5 Evaluating and selecting methods

Assume that you were asked to predict annual sales of consumer products such as stoves, refrigerators, fans and wine for the next five years. What forecasting method would you use? As indicated above, the selection should be guided by the stage in the product life-cycle and by the availability of data. But general guidelines cannot provide a complete answer. Because each situation differs, you should consider more than one method.

Given that you use more than one method to forecast, how should you pick the best method? One of the most widely used approaches suggests that you select the one that has performed best in the recent past. This raises the issue of what criteria should be used to identify the best method. Statisticians have relied upon sophisticated procedures for analysing how well models fit historical data. However, this has been of little value for the selection of forecasting methods. Forecasters should ignore measures of fit (such as R^2 or the standard error of the estimate of the model) because they have little relationship to forecast accuracy. Instead, one should rely on *ex ante* forecasts from realistic simulations of the actual situation faced by the forecaster. By *ex ante*, we mean that the forecaster has only that information that would be available at the time of an actual forecast.

Traditional error measures, such as mean square error, do not provide a reliable basis for comparison of methods (for empirical evidence on this, see Armstrong and Collopy 1992). The Median Absolute Percentage Error (MdAPE) is more appropriate because it is invariant to scale and is not overly influenced by outliers. For comparisons using a small set of series, it is desirable, also, to control for degree of difficulty in forecasting. One measure that does this is the Median Relative Absolute Error (MdRAE), which compares the error for a given model against errors for the naive, no change forecast (Armstrong and Collopy 1992).

One can avoid the complexities of selection by simply combining forecasts. Considerable research suggests that, lacking well-structured domain knowledge, equally-weighted averages are as accurate as any other weighting scheme (Clemen 1989). This produces consistent, though modest improvements in accuracy, and it reduces the likelihood of large errors. Combining seems to be especially useful when the methods are substantially different. For example, Blattberg and Hoch (1990) obtained improved sales forecasts by equally weighting managers' judgemental forecasts and forecasts from a quantitative model.

The selection and weighting of forecasting methods can be improved by using domain knowledge (about the item to be forecast) as shown in research on rule-based forecasting (Collopy and Armstrong 1992). Domain knowledge can be structured, especially with respect to trend expectations. These, along with a consideration of the features of the data (e.g. discontinuities), enable improvements in the weightings assigned to various extrapolations.

6 Estimating prediction intervals

In addition to improving accuracy, forecasting is also concerned with assessing uncertainty. Although statisticians have given much attention to this problem, their efforts generally rely upon fits to historical data to infer forecast uncertainty. Here also, you should simulate the actual forecasting procedure as closely as possible, and use the distribution of the resulting *ex ante* forecasts to assess uncertainty. So, if you need to make two-year-ahead forecasts, save enough data to be able to have a number of two-year ahead *ex ante* forecasts.

The prediction intervals from quantitative forecasts tend to be too narrow. Some empirical studies have shown that the percentage of actual values that fall outside the 95 per cent prediction intervals is substantially greater than 5 per cent, and sometimes greater than 50 per cent (Makridakis *et al.* 1987). This occurs because the estimates ignore various sources of uncertainty. For example, discontinuities might occur over the forecast horizon. In addition, forecast errors in time series are usually asymmetric, so this makes it difficult to estimate prediction intervals. The most sensible procedure is to transform the forecast and actual values to logs, then calculate the prediction intervals using logged differences. Interestingly, researchers and practitioners do not follow this advice except where the original forecasting model has been formulated in logs.

When the trend extrapolation is contrary to the managers' expectations, the errors are asymmetrical in logs. Evidence on the issue of asymmetrical errors is provided in Armstrong and Collopy (1998a). In such cases, one might use asymmetrical prediction intervals. Notice that this discussion takes no account of asymmetric economic loss functions. For example, the cost of a forecast that is too low by 50 units (lost sales) may differ from the cost if it is too high by 50 units (excess inventory). But this is a problem for the planner, not the forecaster.

Judgemental forecasts are also too narrow. That is, experts are typically overconfident (Arkes 1999). To a large extent, this is because forecasters do not get good feedback on their predictions. When they do, such as happens for weather forecasters, they can be well calibrated. When forecasters say that there is a 60 per cent chance of rain, it rains 60 per cent of the time. This suggests that marketing forecasters should try to ensure that they receive feedback on the accuracy of their forecasts. The feedback should be relatively frequent and it should summarize accuracy in a meaningful fashion. Another procedure that helps to avoid overconfidence is for the forecaster to make a written list of all of the reasons why the forecast might be wrong.

7 Implementation

There are two key implementation problems. First, how can you gain acceptance of new forecasting methods, and second, how can you gain acceptance of the forecasts, themselves?

Acceptance of forecasting methods

The diffusion rate for new methods is slow. Exponential smoothing, one of the major developments for production and inventory control forecasting, was developed in the late 1950s, yet it is only recently that the adoption rate has been substantial (Mentzer and Kahn 1995). Adoption is probably slow because there are many steps involved in the diffusion of the method. Here is the traditional procedure. Techniques are first developed. Some time later they are tested. At each stage they are reported in the literature. They are later passed along via courses, textbooks, and consultants, eventually reaching the manager who can use them. Even then they may be resisted, perhaps because the procedures are too complex for the users.

The future is promising, however. The latest methods can be fully disclosed on websites and they can be incorporated into expert systems and software packages. For example, the complete set of rules for rule-based forecasting is kept available and up-to-date and can be accessed through the forecasting principles site (www-marketing.wharton.upenn.edu/ forecast).

Acceptance of forecasts

Forecasts are especially useful for situations that are subject to significant changes. Often, these involve bad news. For example, Griffith and Wellman (1979), in a follow-up study on the demand for hospital beds, found that the forecasts from consultants were typically ignored when they indicated a need that was less than that desired by the hospital administrators.

Firms often confuse forecasting with planning, and they may use the forecast as a tool to motivate people. That is, they use a 'forecast' to drive behaviour, rather than making a forecast conditional on behaviour. (One wonders if they also change their thermometers in order to influence the weather.) One way to avoid this problem is to gain agreement on what forecasting procedures to use prior to presenting the forecasts.

Another way to gain acceptance of forecasts is to ask decision makers to decide in advance what decisions they will make given different possible forecasts. Do the decisions differ? These prior agreements on process and on decisions can greatly enhance the value of the forecasts, but they are difficult to achieve in many organizations. The use of scenarios offers an aid to this process. Scenarios involve writing detailed stories of how decision makers would handle situations that involve alternative states of the future. Decision makers project themselves into the situation and they write the stories in the past tense. (More detailed instructions for writing scenarios are summarized in Gregory 1999.) Scenarios are effective in getting forecasters to accept the possibility that certain events might occur.

8 Conclusions

Extrapolations of sales are inexpensive and often adequate for the decisions that need to be made. In situations where large changes are expected or where one would like to examine alternative strategies, causal approaches are recommended.

Some of the more important findings about sales forecasting methods can be summarized as follows:

- Methods should be selected on the basis of empirically-tested theories, not statistically-based theories.
- Domain knowledge should be used.
- When possible, forecasting methods should use behavioural data, rather than judgements or intentions to predict behaviour.
- When using judgement, a heavy reliance should be placed on structured procedures such as Delphi, role playing, and conjoint analysis.
- Overconfidence occurs with quantitative and judgemental methods. In addition to ensuring good feedback, forecasters should explicitly list all the things that might be wrong about their forecast.
- When making forecasts in highly uncertain situations, be conservative. For example, the trend should be dampened over the forecast horizon.
- Complex models have not proven to be more accurate than relatively simple models. Given their added cost and the reduced understanding among users, highly complex procedures cannot be justified at the present time.

The sales forecast should be free of political considerations in a firm. To help ensure this, emphasis should be on agreeing about the forecasting *methods*, rather than the *forecasts*. Also, for important forecasts, decisions on their use should be made before the forecasts are provided. Scenarios are helpful in guiding this process.

J. SCOTT ARMSTRONG
THE WHARTON SCHOOL, UNIVERSITY OF PENNSYLVANIA

Further reading

(References cited in the text marked *)

* Allen, G.P. (1999) 'Econometric forecasting strategies and techniques', in J.S. Armstrong (ed.) *Principles of Forecasting: Handbook for Researchers and Practitioners*, Norwell, MA: Kluwer Academic Publishers.
* Alsem, K.J., Leeflang, P.S.H. and Reuyl, J.C. (1989) 'The forecasting accuracy of market share models using predicted values of competitive marketing behavior', *International Journal of Research in Marketing* 6: 183–98.
* Arkes, H. (1999) 'Overconfidence in judgemental forecasting', in J.S. Armstrong (ed.) *Principles of Forecasting: Handbook for Researchers and Practitioners*, Norwell, MA: Kluwer Academic Publishers.
* Armstrong, J.S. (1985) *Long-Range Forecasting: From Crystal Ball to Computer*, New York: John Wiley.
  Armstrong, J.S. (1999) 'Role playing: A method to forecast decisions', in J. S. Armstrong (ed.) *Principles of Forecasting: Handbook for Researchers and Practitioners*, Norwell, MA: Kluwer Academic Publishers.
* Armstrong, J.S. (1999) 'Judgemental bootstrapping: Inferring experts' rules for forecasting', in J.S. Armstrong (ed.) *Principles of Forecasting: Handbook for Researchers and Practitioners*, Norwell, MA: Kluwer Academic Publishers.
* Armstrong, J.S. and Collopy, F. (1998a) 'Prediction intervals for extrapolation of annual economic data: Evidence on asymmetry corrections', Working paper.
* Armstrong, J.S. and Collopy, F. (1998b) 'Integration of statistical methods and judgement for time series forecasting: principles from empirical research', in G. Wright and P. Goodwin (eds.) *Forecasting with Judgement*. Chichester: John Wiley.
* Armstrong, J.S. and Collopy, F. (1993) 'Causal forces: Structuring knowledge for time series extrapolation', *Journal of Forecasting* 12: 103–15.
* Armstrong, J.S. and Collopy, F. (1992) 'Error measures for generalizing about forecasting methods: Empirical comparisons', *International Journal of Forecasting* 8: 69–80.
* Armstrong, J.S. and Hutcherson, P. (1989) 'Predicting the outcome of marketing negotiations: Role-playing versus unaided opinions', *International Journal of Research in Marketing* 6: 227–39.
* Armstrong, J.S. and T. Overton (1970) 'Brief vs. comprehensive descriptions in measuring intentions to purchase', *Journal of Marketing Research* 8: 114–17.

* Armstrong, J.S., Brodie, R. and McIntyre, S. (1987) 'Forecasting methods for marketing', *International Journal of Forecasting* 3: 355–76.
* Ashton, A.H. (1985) 'Aggregating subjective forecasts: Some empirical results', *Management Science* 31: 1499–508.
* Blattberg, R.C. and Hoch, S.J. (1990) 'Database models and managerial intuition: 50 per cent model + 50 per cent manager', *Management Science* 36: 887–99.
* Brodie, R. J., Danaher, P., Kumar, V. and Leeflang, P. (1999) 'Market share forecasting', in J. S. Armstrong (ed.) *Principles of Forecasting: Handbook for Researchers and Practitioners*, Norwell, MA: Kluwer Academic Publishers.
* Claycamp, H.J. and Liddy, L.E. (1969) 'Prediction of new-product performance: An analytical approach', *Journal of Marketing Research* 6: 414–20.
* Clemen, R.T. (1989) 'Combining forecasts: A review and annotated bibliography', *International Journal of Forecasting* 5: 559–83.
* Collopy, F. and Armstrong, J.S. (1992) 'Rule-based forecasting: Development and validation of an expert systems approach to combining time-series extrapolations', *Management Science* 39: 1394–414.
* Dalrymple, D.J. (1975) 'Sales forecasting: Methods and accuracy', *Business Horizons* 18: 69–73.
* Dalrymple, D.J. (1987) 'Sales forecasting practices: Results from a U.S. survey', *International Journal of Forecasting* 3: 379–91.
* Dangerfield, B.J. and Morris, J.S. (1992), 'Top-down or bottom-up: Aggregate versus disaggregate extrapolations', *International Journal of Forecasting* 8: 233–41.
Day, D.B., Gan, B, Gendall,P. and Esslemont, D. (1991) 'Predicting purchase behavior', *Marketing Bulletin* 2: 18–30. Full text available at http://marketing-bulletin.massey.ac.nz/bulletin/index.html.
* Diebold, F.X. and Rudebusch, G.D. (1991) 'Forecasting output with the composite leading index: A real time analysis', *Journal of the American Statistical Association* 86: 603–10.
* Dillman, D.A. (1978) *Mail and Telephone Surveys*, New York: John Wiley.
* Gardner, E.S. Jr. (1985) 'Exponential smoothing: The state of the art', *Journal of Forecasting* 4: 1–28.
* Gardner, E.S. and Anderson, E.A. (1997) 'Focus forecasting reconsidered', *International Journal of Forecasting*, 13: 501–08.
Gardner, E.S. Jr. and McKenzie, E. (1985) 'Forecasting trends in time series', *Management Science* 31: 1237–46.
* Gregory, L. (1999) 'Scenarios as a strategy for the presentation of forecasts', in J. S. Armstrong (ed.) *Principles of Forecasting: Handbook for Researchers and Practitioners*, Norwell, MA: Kluwer Academic Publishers.
* Griffith, J.R. and Wellman, B.T. (1979) 'Forecasting bed needs and recommending facilities plans for community hospitals: A review of past performance', *Medical Care* 17: 293–303.
* Hogarth, R.M. (1978) 'A note on aggregating opinions', *Organizational Behavior and Human Performance* 21: 40–6.
* Juster, F.T. (1966) 'Consumer buying intentions and purchase probability: An experiment in survey design', *Journal of the American Statistical Association*, 61: 658–96.
* MacGregor, D. (1998) 'Decomposition for judgemental forecasting and estimation', in J. S. Armstrong (ed.) *Principles of Forecasting: Handbook for Researchers and Practitioner*, Norwell, MA: Kluwer Academic Publishers.
Makridakis, S. and Wheelwright, S.C. (1989) *Forecasting Methods for Management*, New York: John Wiley.
* Makridakis, S., et al. (1984) *The Forecasting Accuracy of Major Time Series Methods*, New York: John Wiley.
* Makridakis, S., Hibon, M., Lusk, E. and Belhadjali, M. (1987) 'Confidence intervals: An empirical investigation of the series in the M-competition', *International Journal of Forecasting* 3: 489–508.
* Meade, N. (1999) 'Forecasting the diffusion of innovations: Implications for time series extrapolation', in J. S. Armstrong (ed.) *Principles of Forecasting: Handbook for Researchers and Practitioners*, Norwell, MA: Kluwer Academic Publishers.
* Mentzer, J.T. and Kahn, K.B. (1995) 'Forecasting technique familiarity, satisfaction, usage, and application', *Journal of Forecasting*, 14: 465–76.
* Montgomery, D.B. (1975) 'New product distribution: An analysis of supermarket buyer decisions', *Journal of Marketing Research,* 12: 255–64.
* Morwitz, V. (1999) 'Methods for forecasting from intentions and probability data', in J. S. Armstrong (ed.) *Principles of Forecasting: Handbook for Researchers and Practitioners*. Norwell, MA: Kluwer Academic Publishers.
* Perry, P. (1979) 'Certain problems in election survey methodology', *Public Opinion Quarterly* 43: 312–25.
* Rowe, G. and Wright, G. (1999) 'The Delphi technique as a forecasting tool', in J. S. Armstrong (ed.) *Principles of Forecasting: Handbook for Researchers and Practitioners*, Norwell, MA: Kluwer Academic Publishers.
Sanders, N.R. and Ritzman, L.P. (1992) 'The need for contextual and technical knowledge in judgemental forecasting', *Journal of Behavioral Decision Making* 5:39–52.

* Schnaars, S.P. (1984) 'Situational factors affecting forecast accuracy', *Journal of Marketing Research,* 21: 290–7.
* Sewall, M.A. (1981) 'Relative information contributions of consumer purchase intentions and management judgement as explanators of sales', *Journal of Marketing Research* 18: 249–53.
* Shocker, A.D. and Hall, W.G. (1986) 'Pretest market models: A critical evaluation', *Journal of Product Innovation Management* 3: 86–107.
* Sudman, S. and Bradburn, N.R. (1982) *Asking Questions: A Practical Guide to Questionnaire Design,* San Francisco: Jossey-Bass.
* Tull, D.S. (1967) 'The relationship of actual and predicted sales and profits in new-product introductions', *Journal of Business* 40: 233–50.
* Tyebjee, T.T. (1987) 'Behavioral biases in new product forecasting', *International Journal of Forecasting* 3: 393–404.
* Wind, J., Green, P.E., Shifflet, D. and Scarbrough, M. (1989) 'Courtyard by Marriott: Designing a hotel facility with consumer-based marketing', *Interfaces,* 19: 25–47.
* Wotruba, T.R. and Thurlow, M.L. (1976) 'Sales force participation in quota setting and sales forecasting', *Journal of Consumer Research* 8: 162–71.

See also: CHANNELS OF DISTRIBUTION; CONSUMER BEHAVIOUR; MARKETING RESEARCH; NEW PRODUCT DEVELOPMENT; PRODUCT LIFE-CYCLE MANAGEMENT

Market segmentation

1 Use of segmentation in marketing and business strategy
2 Decisions required in implementing a segmentation strategy
3 Advances in segmentation research
4 Segmentation in the global information age
5 Extending the segmentation concept
6 Issues and associated research agenda

Overview

All markets are heterogeneous. This is quite evident from the proliferation of popular books describing the heterogeneity of the US market. Consider, for example, *The Nine Nations of North America* (Garreau 1982), *The Nine American Lifestyles* (Mitchell 1983) and *Latitudes and Attitudes: An Atlas of American Tastes, Trends, Politics and Passions* (Weiss 1994). When reflecting on the nature of markets, consumer behaviour and competitive activities, it is obvious that no product or service appeals to all consumers and even those who purchase the same product may do so for diverse reasons. Effective marketing and business strategy therefore requires a segmentation of the market into homogeneous segments, understanding of the needs and wants of these segments, design of products and services that meet those needs and development of marketing strategies to effectively reach the target segments. Thus focusing on segments is at the core of organizations' efforts to become customer driven; it is also the key to effective resource allocation and deployment. Following such a market segmentation strategy would allow the firm to increase its profitability, as suggested by the classic price discrimination model which provides the theoretical rationale for segmentation.

Since the early 1960s segmentation has been viewed as a key marketing concept and has been the focus of a significant part of the marketing research literature. Until recently the concept of segmentation (as articulated, for example, in Frank *et al.* 1972) has not been altered. Similarly, the fundamental approaches to segmentation research have not changed greatly (Wind 1978), despite the publication of a number of increasingly sophisticated research and modelling approaches for segmenting heterogeneous markets.

Yet the recent advances in information technology and the trend towards globalization are introducing a discontinuous change to the segmentation area. The revolution in information technology and strategy makes possible the creation of databases on the entire universe and enormous advances in database marketing and innovative distribution approaches. It has also facilitated much of the development in flexible manufacturing with the consequent emergence of mass customization. These changes are leading to the creation of 'one-on-one marketing' or segments of one. The globalization of business expands the scope of operations across tens of countries and requires a new approach to local, regional and global segments.

These changes require not only an appraisal of what we know about segmentation, what works and what does not work, but also a review of the segmentation area as part of an entirely new marketing and management paradigm.

Therefore the purpose of this article is to introduce the reader to both the 'best practice in the segmentation area and the likely new developments in this critical field. These observations are based on advances in marketing concepts, marketing science research and modelling tools, generalizations from empirical studies, successful practices of leading firms and the conceptual implications of operating in the global information age. This discussion of the best segmentation practices and likely advances encompasses five areas:

1 Use of segmentation in marketing and business strategy.
2 Decisions required for the implementation of a segmentation strategy.
3 Advances in segmentation research.

4 Impact of operating in the global information age on segmentation theory, practice and research.
5 Expansion of segmentation to other stakeholders.

The article concludes with a set of critical issues that provide the guidelines for a research agenda in this area.

1 Use of segmentation in marketing and business strategy

Conceptually any market and business strategy should be based on understanding, meeting and even exceeding the needs of target segments. Figure 1 clearly illustrates the centrality of segmentation by suggesting that at the core of any strategy is the understanding of the needs of target segments. This provides the guidelines for the development of products and services and their associated positioning which could meet the need of the target segments. These products and services as positioned to meet the needs of the target segments provide the foundation for the rest of the marketing strategy and the processes, resources and other activities of the firm.

In support of the value of segmentation, there are numerous published and unpublished case studies. For example, Gensch *et al.* (1990) provide compelling evidence of the positive consequences of segmentation of electrical equipment buyers. In a one-year test segmentation applied in two of three geographic districts resulted in sales increases of 18 per cent and 12 per cent – while sales declined 10 per cent in the district in which segmentation was not applied and 15 per cent for the industry. The firm reports continuous market share increases from the segmentation approach. This is not an isolated case. The popular business press and the conference circuit are full of anecdotal cases in which creative segmentation has paid off. In fact a growing number of firms do use segmentation as the basis of their marketing strategy.

Yet despite the general acceptability of segmentation and its value, too many firms are not segmenting their markets effectively and are not basing their strategies on the needs of target segments. The experience of the more successful firms in consumer and industrial markets alike suggests, however, that effective

1. Who are the customers and what are their needs and wants?

2. What product/service offerings will meet the target segments' needs and offer us a substainable competitive advantage?

3. What strategies and processes are required to capabilities, and processes are required to develop and implement effectively the product/service solutions?

Figure 1 Customer-driven strategy questions

Table 1 A segmentation audit

Practice	Completely describes us	Somewhat describes us	Does not describe us at all	Do not know
1 Our business strategies recognize the need to prioritize target segments				
2 Our marketing plans include specific plans for each of the selected segments				
3 We have specific product offerings for each target segment				
4 We have a process for updating the information on our segments on an ongoing basis				
5 Our segments are unique to the USA, and are not developed across countries				
6 We have an effective process for implementing segmentation research				
7 We have an effective process for implementing segmentation strategies				
8 We have P&L reports and accountability by segment				
9 We have detailed information about segments, including: • current size of segment • potential size of segment • key business needs of the segment • information system needs of the segment • their prioritized needs/benefits sought • their prioritized preference for product and service features • demographic characteristics of the segments • product/system ownership and usage • competition's strength in each segment • perceived positioning of each competitior by the members of the segment				
10 Information about the target market segments are incorporated effectively into the followiing strategies: • positioning • product and service offerings • pricing • promotion • advertising • distribution • salesforce				

segmentation is a must. The likelihood of a positive response to the firm's offerings is increased, the cost of reaching customers and chances of new product and service failure are reduced.

In order to determine whether a firm uses an effective segmentation strategy, it may help if a segmentation audit is undertaken. Table 1 presents such an audit, which was developed for a large computer manufacturer. In scoring the audit it is important to note that effective segmentation requires a positive answer to each question. Any lower score on any of these dimensions requires correction.

2 Decisions required in implementing a segmentation strategy

An effective segmentation strategy requires answers to five sets of questions:

1. How to segment the market.
2. What research procedure to use to develop a segmentation strategy.
3. What segment(s) to target.
4. How to allocate resources among the segments.
5. How to implement the segmentation strategy.

Segment identification decision

This decision involves the determination of which set of variables – basis – to use for segmentation of the market. Should we segment on product usage patterns (e.g. users versus non-users or heavy versus light users)? Should we segment based on benefits sought (e.g. product performance versus convenience versus price sensitivity)? Should we use some other measure of consumer response to marketing variables (e.g. likelihood of buying a new product concept, response to price promotion, participation in a loyalty programme)? The 'best practice' in this area suggests three propositions:

1. An effective basis for segmentation should allow one to differentiate among segments based on their response to marketing variables. Thus buyers versus non-buyers or price sensitive versus non-price sensitive are possible bases for segmentation. Age, sex, marital status, psychographic characteristics or other general characteristics of the consumer are not good bases for segmentation since they do not assure differential response to marketing variables.
2. The selected basis for segmentation should be directly related to the strategic purpose of the segmentation effort. In general, there are two reasons for segmentation:
   - A general segmentation of the market which allows the organization to organize itself around the selected target segments. As increasing numbers of companies shift from a product management organization to a market-driven organization or a matrix organization of product by market, it is critical to identify relatively stable and large segments which could serve as strategic business units. Examples of such segments, in the case of a financial service firm, are the delegators – consumers who prefer to have a money manager take complete control over the management of their financial affairs, and the electronic DIY – who prefer to do it themselves using direct computer trading. To reach these two segments effectively the firm needs quite distinctly different strategies. Members of each of these strategic segments share some common financial/investment needs. Yet each of these segments may still be quite heterogeneous with respect to other needs and, thus, could benefit from further sub-segmentation into more homogeneous groups.
   - Specific segments for specific marketing and business decisions. For example, in the introduction of a new product, a focus on the segment that has the highest likelihood of buying the product. In the launch of a new online electronic shopping service, a focus on those with access to computers and who are likely to use an electronic shopping service. Other specific segments can be developed for each of the marketing mix decisions. Consider, for example:
   - For positioning:
     product usage
     product preference
     benefits sought
     a hybrid of the variables above
   - For new product concepts (and new product introduction):
     reaction to new concepts (intention to buy, preference over current brand, etc.)
     benefits sought
   - For pricing decisions:
     price sensitivity
     deal proneness
     price sensitivity by purchase/usage patterns
   - For advertising decisions:
     benefits sought
     media usage

Market segmentation

Table 2 Variables commonly used as basis for segmentation and as descriptors of segments

Basis for segmentation (or descriptors)	Descriptors of segments
Organizational	**External**
• share	• socioeconomic, political environment
• trial	• (culture, technology, economic,
• purchase/adoption	• political, regulatory, legal)
• source loyalty	• behaviour towards competitiors
• price sensitivity	• etc.
• customers of key competitors	**Organizational**
• etc.	• industry type (e.g. SIC)
Buying centre	• size
• buying process	• degree of centralization
• information search	• capabilities (technical, financial, etc.)
• criteria/benefits sought	• geographic location (country, region,city, etc.)
• negotiation style	• etc.
• application	**Buying centre**
• decision	• size
• post-purchase evaluation	• composition
• etc.	• buying situation
Individual	• influence
• awareness	• consensus among the members
• knowledge	• buying process
• perceptions, preferences, attitudes	• buying organization and policies
• towards the brand	• relations with suppliers
• preference	• etc.
• recommendation	**Individual**
• purchase	• demographic (age, sex, family life-cycle, income, education, socialclass, etc.)
• US age	• psychographics (personality, lifestyle, activities, interest opinions, etc.)
• loyalty	• etc.
• etc.	

psychographic/lifestyle
a hybrid (of the variables above with or
without purchase/usage patterns)
• For distribution decisions:
store loyalty and patronage
benefits sought in store selection
• For general understanding of a market:
benefits sought (in industrial markets, the
criterion used is purchase decision)
product purchase and usage patterns
needs
brand loyalty and switching pattern
a hybrid of the above variables

3 To gain a better understanding of the various segments and their characteristics, it is critical to profile the segment's key discriminating characteristics. These include the complete segment profile on demographic, psychographic, product usage, perceptions and preferences, attitudes and the like. In the case of industrial (business-to-business) segmentation, these variables should include both the characteristics of the organization and each of the key members of the relevant buying centre. Table 2 identifies a list of variables commonly used as a basis for segmentation and as segment

descriptors. It is important to note that variables not used as a basis for segmentation can become descriptors of segments that are developed based on other bases.

Selecting a research programme

The quality of a segmentation programme depends largely on the quality of information (see INFORMATION TECHNOLOGY AND MARKETING; MARKETING RESEARCH). Segmenting any market requires information on the characteristics of the market including:

- The size and growth of the market.
- The criteria buying centres use in making their buying decisions (including the benefits they seek and problems they try to solve).
- The perceptions of preference for, attitudes towards and usage of the products and services of the firm and its competitors.
- The demographic characteristics of the members of the buying centre and the organization in the case of business-to-business markets.
- The psychographic (lifstyle, personality and other psychological and attitudinal) characteristics.
- Reaction and sensitivity to the marketing actions of the firm and its competitors.

To collect data on these variables and to analyse and interpret them requires a research programme; historically, segmentation research centred on customer surveys. Yet there are a number of additional approaches that should be considered.

Figure 2 outlines the range of options. Formal primary research and especially surveys on a sample of customers and prospects have been the most common approach to segmentation research. Recent developments of databases on the entire universe have changed the nature of segmentation research. Consider, for example, the pharmaceutical industry in which a number of firms are developing databases on the entire industry – 400,000-plus physicians, 7000 hospitals and thousands of managed care organizations.

A second type of formal research includes secondary data analysis using geodemographic data which can be used both for segmentation research as well as for experimentation.

Adaptive experimentation is another approach which could yield insights into the characteristics of various market segments and their response to marketing activities.

The third approach is input from ongoing business activities. In this case, we include both data on the market response to various strategies and insights gained from strategic alliances with customers. This latter approach is

Figure 2 Selecting a segmentation research programme

especially critical in the new product development area when the firm works closely with its customers on the development of new products and service.

Best research practice would include using a number of these approaches, integrating the resulting data in a database, continuously updating the database and having it as part of a decision support system (DSS).

Selecting target segments

Having segmented a market it is often not desirable to pursue all segments.

Thus, a critical decision is the selection of target market segments. All segments have to meet four conditions: measurability (ability to measure the size and characteristics of the segment); substantiality (having a minimum profitable size); accessibility (ability to reach and serve the segments); actionability (ability to implement strategies to serve the segments) (Kotler 1991). Beyond these requirements, the selection of target market segments requires answers to the following questions:

- What is the likely response to the firm's offering, including response to the positioning of the firm's products and services?
- What is the size of the segment in terms of the revenues and profits it is likely to generate?
- Can the segment be reached (via controlled media and distribution or via a self-selection strategy)?
- What are the current and likely competitive activities directed at the target segment?
- What are the likely costs of reaching effectively the target segment?
- What is the likely impact of changes in relevant environmental conditions (e.g. economic conditions, lifestyle, legal regulations, etc.) on the potential response of the target market segment?
- Do we have the required offerings and competencies effectively to develop, reach and serve the selected segments?
- How many segments can you manage effectively?

These and related criteria often require information that is not always available from market research. Consequently, a decision support framework is needed to aid managerial decision making. This framework should utilize both managerial experience and available data. At the minimum it should include: identifying

Figure 3 An illustrative output of an analytic hierarchy process (AHP) designed to select a portfolio of market segments relevant criteria; evaluating the segments on the selected criteria.

Following the logic of product and business portfolio analysis, a portfolio of current and potential market segments can be constructed (Wind and Robertson 1983). Figure 3 illustrates a portfolio of segments in which each segment is evaluated on its attractiveness, on the firm's expected strength in the segment and on synergy. The first two criteria are the same dimensions used in the GE/McKinsey portfolio matrix. These dimensions can be based on a single criterion or represent a composite of multiple criteria. For example, segment attractiveness could include such factors as the segment's size and growth, risk factors and the cost of reaching the segment. Segment strength could include such factors as current and expected share in the segment and expected profitability. The specific criteria and their relative weights can be determined by management judgement and marketing research input.

The segment selective process illustrated in Figure 3 utilized the analytic hierarchy process (AHP). The AHP (Wind and Saaty 1980; Saaty 1992) is a measurement approach and process that helps quantify management subjective judgements. The essential steps in implementing an AHP include: setting up the decision problem by the relevant management group as a hierarchy of interrelated decision elements; evaluating the various elements of the hierarchy by pairwise comparisons and using a mathematical method to estimate the relative weights of decision elements. The *Expert Choice* software greatly facilitates the implementation of an AHP.

The application of AHP to segment selection involves bringing together the key executives and presenting to them all available marketing research information. This provides input to the deliberation and evaluation of the various segments, in a pairwise comparison, against each of the chosen criteria. The results in the prioritization of the segments are illustrated in Figure 3. An examination of this illustrative hierarchy suggests a number of segmentation related conclusions:

- Management established three criteria (segment attractiveness, strength in segment and synergy) which vary in their importance with respect to the firm's ability to achieve their four objectives (profit, profit growth, sales growth and downside risk). The objectives, in turn, vary in their importance under short- or long-term conditions (not shown in the figure). The overall importance of the four objectives, assuming an 80/20 weight for short versus long term is presented in Figure 3. The seven current segments when evaluated against the three criteria (segment attractiveness, strength and synergy), which in turn are weighted by their importance to the accomplishment of the four objectives (weighted by their importance for the short- and long-term well-being of the firm), suggest that three of the segments – D, E and G – are not very attractive and should be considered as candidates for deletion, or at least destined to receive no incremental resources.

- Five new segments were identified. When evaluated on the three criteria, two of the segments – H and I – were viewed as candidates for inclusion in the portfolio and three – J, K and L – as candidates for deletion.

- As a result of the process, a new portfolio of segments was established with segments A, B, C, F, H and I.

- The outcome also suggests how much resources to allocate to each segment. Since the dimensions included in the hierarchy encompass both the expected benefits from each segment as well as the cost of reaching them and risk, the priorities can be used as a rough guide for resource allocation. This would lead to the following allocation: A = 11 per cent, B = 24 per cent, C = 13 per cent, F = 21 per cent, H = 11 per cent and I = 20 per cent.

Another example for a portfolio of segments pursued by a firm is a recent advertisement by Citibank which identified products and services for six segments. These segments were:

- Planning for retirement: tax deferred investments make more sense than ever.
- Retirees: don't ignore the new tax law.
- When leaving a job: be certain to protect your retirement fund.
- Paying for college: start a fund early and invest regularly.
- Home equity/borrowing: a great strategy for a host of reasons.

- Small business owners: a long-term strategy is crucial.

Allocating resources among segments

The selection of target segments and the allocation of resources among segments are interrelated and iterative decisions. For example, in the preceding section, AHP was utilized to select a portfolio of segments. It also provided guidelines for resource allocation among the segments. Allocation of resources typically involves not only the allocation among segments, but also the allocation of resources to the various marketing mix variables – products, price, distribution, promotion and advertising.

The basic problem of resource allocation is to decide on the mix of resources that generates optimal response (sales, profitability, etc.). How, for example, should sales persons currently covering a market be allocated across segments to optimize their return? Estimating and modelling the sales response of each segment to the various marketing resources is critical. The more innovative resource allocation models have been developed in the context of designing optimal product lines. These approaches, which are typically based on conjoint analysis studies among current and potential customers, have been applied to a wide range of situations including computers, telecommunications products and services, pharmaceuticals, etc. (Green and Krieger 1985). In the cases in which empirically based market response functions are not available, management's subjective judgement, using either decision calculus methods (Little 1979) or the AHP (Wind and Saaty 1980), can be employed.

The disguised AHP example outlined in Figure 3 included, in its original application, a lower level focusing on various marketing strategy options. This allowed management to generate the marketing programmes best suited for reaching the selected segments. A similar application, but for a consumer service, was reported by Dunn and Wind in 1983. The complexity and importance of the resource allocation decision suggests the advisability of employing a methodology such as the AHP that incorporates managerial judgement, empirical data derived from both econometric market response models and experiments, consumer studies and decisions models.

Implementing a segmentation strategy

The most difficult aspect of any segmentation project is the translation of the study results into a marketing strategy and programme. No rules can be offered to assure a successful translation and, in fact, little is known (in the published literature) on how this translation occurs.

Informal discussions with executives and observations of 'successful' and 'unsuccessful' 'translations' suggest a few generalizable conclusions on the conditions likely to increase successful implementation (see STRATEGIC MARKETING PLANNING).

1. Involving all relevant decision-makers (e.g. product managers, new product developers, advertising agency, sales management, etc.) in the problem definition, research design, strategy generation and evaluation.
2. The segment characteristics should be rich enough to provide the basis for innovative product positioning and product, pricing, communication and distribution decisions.
3. The segment characteristics should also provide guidelines for the generation of creative executions of the selected strategy.
4. Recognizing the non-marketing orientation of product management, it is desirable to shift the responsibilities for segmentation strategy to segment-driven managers and teams.
5. Since information on media and distribution reach is rarely linked to market response functions, it is critical to develop data that link market response to media and distribution systems and use 'self-selection' strategies. (Members of a target segment self-select the message which is designed to appeal to them from a general media.)

3 Advances in segmentation research

Many of the papers published in *Marketing Science* and the *Journal of Marketing Research* offer advances in segmentation research and modelling. Yet the key segmentation research and modelling centre around six sets of 'tools'.

Classification

The classification of methods for segmenting the market is especially critical for clustering-based segmentation approaches and for hybrid designs. A clustering-based segmentation design involves determining the number, size and characteristics of the segments based on the results of clustering of respondents on a set of 'relevant' variables. Benefit, need, and attitude segmentation are examples of this type of approach. Significant advances have been made in the clustering area.

Hybrid segmentation design includes those cases in which *a priori* segmentation design such as product purchase or usage, loyalty or customer type is augmented by some cluster-based segmentation on variables such as benefits sought. Hybrid designs are especially common in business-to-business segmentation.

Approaches such as macro- and micro-segmentation (Wind and Cardozo 1974) and sequential clustering (Peterson 1974) are often used in practice. Sequential clustering, for example, clusters on some market-based demographics followed by attitude (or benefit) clustering within each demographic segment. In both cluster-based design and hybrid design, the size and other characteristics (demographics, socioeconomic, purchase, etc.) of the segments are estimated.

Discrimination
Discrimination methods employed to establish the profile of the segments commonly use multiple discriminant analyses or regression analysis. Such statistical methods are often augmented with graphics packages that graphically display the profile of the segments.

Simultaneous evaluation of number of segments, profile and desired positioning for a set of product and service offerings
This is one of the areas receiving the attention of academic researchers and typically involves sophisticated multi-dimensional scaling and multivariate statistical analyses. Consider, for example, the work on simultaneous determination of the size of the segment and the segment's preferences for various products and their positioning. Such studies often result in joint space maps and the output of logit and nested logit models to the simultaneous estimation of segment size, choice and incidence probabilities which apply simultaneously to segmentation and market structuring. See, for example, Bucklin and Gupta (1992) and other approaches such as Grover and Srinivasan (1987).

One of the most interesting developments in this area is the componential segmentation approach. This model was proposed by Green and De Sarbo (1979) and shifts the emphasis of the segmentation model from the partitioning of a market to a prediction of which person type (described by a particular set of demographic and other psychographic attribute levels) will be most responsive to what type of product feature. The componential segmentation model is an extension of conjoint analysis and orthogonal arrays to cover not only product features but also person characteristics. In componential segmentation the researcher is interested in developing, in addition to parameter values for the product stimuli, parameter values for various respondent characteristics (demographic, product usage, etc.).

In a typical conjoint analysis approach to market segmentation, a matrix of subjects by utilities is developed. This matrix can serve as the input to the determination of the profile of some *a priori* segments (e.g. product users versus non-users) or alternatively as the input to a clustering programme which would result in a number of benefit segments. In componential segmentation, the same design principles which guide the selection of (product) stimuli are applied also to the selection of respondents. For example, in a study for a new health insurance product, four sets of respondent characteristics were identified on the basis of previous experience and management judgement: age, sex, marital status and current insurance status. Employing an orthogonal array design, one screens respondents to select those who meet the specific profiles specified by the design. Each respondent is then interviewed and administered the conjoint analysis task for the evaluation of a set of hypothetical health insurance products (also selected following an orthogonal array design).

Having completed the data collection phase, the researcher would have a matrix of averaged profile evaluations of the product stimuli by the groups of respondents. This data matrix is then submitted to any number of componential segmentation models, which decompose the matrix into separate parameter values (utilities) for each of the levels of the product feature factors (comprising the stimulus cards) and separate parameter values (saliences) for each of the levels of the customer profile characteristics (describing the respondents) which indicate how much each profile characteristic contributes to variation in the evaluative responses.

Given these two sets of parameters, the researcher can make predictions about the relative evaluation of any of the possible product features by any of the respondent types. The results are used with a simulation to estimate: for each respondent segment the frequency of first choices for each of the considered new product combinations; for each new product combination the frequency of first choices across segments.

Componential segmentation offers a new conceptualization of market segmentation in that it focuses on the building blocks of segments and offers simultaneously an analysis of the market segment for any given product offering and an evaluation of the most desirable product offering (or positioning) for any given segment. The concept and algorithm of componential segmentation can be extended to cover not only two data sets (product feature and respondent characteristics) but three or more data sets by adding, for example, the components of usage situations and distribution options.

Database management

Database management involves the creation, management and access to databases and its incorporation in a decision support system. The interest in this area is increasing especially from management, yet the field is still in its infancy.

Simulation and optimization

Simulation and optimization are at the core of models for selection of a target portfolio of segments. These models are typically based on conjoint analysis studies. Among the most powerful of these approaches is flexible segmentation. In contrast to *a priori* segmentation in which the segments are determined at the outset of the study and clustering-based segmentation in which the selected segments are based on the results of the clustering analysis, the flexible segmentation model offers a dynamic approach to the problem. Using this approach one can develop and examine a large number of alternative segments, each composed of those consumers or organizations exhibiting a similar pattern of responses to new 'test' products (defined as a specific product feature configuration). The flexible segmentation approach is based on the integration of the results of a conjoint analysis study and a computer simulation of consumer choice behaviour.

The simulation model in a flexible segmentation approach uses three data sets:
1 utilities for the various factors and levels for each respondent;
2 perceptual ranking or rating of the current brands on the same set of attributes;
3 a set of demographics and other background characteristics.

The active participation of management is also requisite to design a set of 'new product offerings' (each defined as a unique combination of product features – specific levels on each factor included in the conjoint analysis study). Management participation can be on a real-time basis in which managers interact directly with the computer simulation. Alternatively, management can specify in advance a number of plausible new product concepts or react to a number of 'best' product combinations.

The consumer choice simulator is based on the assumption that consumers choose the offering (new product or existing brand) with the highest utility. The simulator is designed to establish: the consumer's share of choices among the existing brands, which can be validated against current market share data if available; the consumer's likely switching behaviour upon the introduction of any new product. This phase provides a series of brand-switching matrices. Within each matrix management can select any cell or combination of cells as a possible market segment (e.g. those consumers remaining with brand *i* versus those who switched to new brand *j*, etc.). Once the desired segments (cell or cell combination) have been selected, the demographic, lifestyle, product purchase and usage and other relevant segment characteristics can be determined by a series of multiple discriminant analyses which can be incorporated in the simulation.

Some of the more significant developments in the segmentation area in the last decade have been the advances in simulation and optimization procedures and associated user-friendly software. The developments by Green and Krieger (1991, 1994) greatly facilitate the task of selecting an optimal (or close to optimal) set of segments.

Linking segmentation findings with management subjective judgements
Given the complexity of the decisions which a portfolio of segments has to target, it is helpful to use a framework and methodology that captures management's subjective judgement while allowing the incorporation of findings from various segmentation studies. The analytic hierarchy process (AHP), as illustrated in Figure 3, is ideally suited for this task.

Addressing the problems

In addition to methodological advances in these six areas, some of the more interesting advances in segmentation research and modelling are those developed to address three of the criticisms of segmentation research – that it has too narrow a focus, that it is static and deterministic and that it is poorly integrated with strategy. The advances in addressing these problems are briefly discussed below.

Too narrow a focus
This criticism encompasses five areas that can be addressed using specific advances in research and modelling.

1 The traditional focus on 'one segment per customer': the assignment of individuals to mutually exclusive and collectively exhaustive segments is too narrow. This problem can be overcome by the use of overlapping clustering – a relatively new clustering procedure that allows for an individual to belong to more than one segment. For a discussion of this method, see Arabie *et al.* (1981) and Chaturvedi *et al.* (1994).
2 One segmentation scheme fits all: this problem of trying to fit one segmentation scheme for all marketing decisions can be solved by employing the flexible segmentation approaches or by developing a number of segmentation schemes and linking them.
3 Neglect of sub-segments: with the exception of segments of one, most segments are heterogeneous. It is important to recognize this and augment the basic segmentation with additional sub-segmentation. This is the concept underlying hybrid segmentation models and is increasing in its popularity. In this context it is also helpful to develop a hierarchy of segments. A byproduct of this research is the development of measures on the segmentability of each market (and the degree of homogeneity of selected segments).
4 Individual as the unit of analysis: most segmentation studies use data on individuals. However, few decisions are made by a single individual. Most households and industrial (business-to-business) decisions are made by a buying centre (see ORGANIZATIONAL BUYING BEHAVIOUR). An important advance in segmentation research is the shift in the unit of analysis from individuals to buying centres. Recognizing the heterogeneity within a buying centre, the use of key informants as representative of the buying centre is often not appropriate. A better approach would be to identify all the members of the buying centre and collect the information on a subset of the buying centre members. This allows an assessment of the level of consensus among members of the buying centres. The level of consensus as well as the composition of the buying centres can be used as a basis for, or descriptors of, segments. Choffray and Lilien (1978) demonstrate critical differences in decision criteria among members of buying centres for industrial heating and cooling equipment. In addition, Wilson *et al.* (1991) describe and test the best ways to combine the preferences of individuals and buying centre members when trying to determine how the buying centre is most likely to act.
5 The segmentation of the month: the segmentation area has not escaped other management fads and has had its share of 'segment of the month' promise and advocates. To avoid this trap, there has been some progress in theory-driven segmentation. Also it helps to keep the focus on market response variation as bases for segmentation and to include all other variables as segment descriptors.

Static and deterministic perspective
A major limitation of many of the segmentation studies is their neglect of the dynamic aspects of segmentation. Static/deterministic segmentation tends to ignore segment change and market dynamics; ignoring such changes often has several consequences. (See Johnson and Lilien

(1994) for a conceptualization and model-based approach to deal with segment dynamics). To address this issue one can do the following:

- Define bases for segmentation that focus on change.
- Monitor changes in segment composition over time.
- Focus on strategies that will change segment membership (from non-users to users, light to heavy users).
- Incorporate competitive actions and reactions, since the desirability of a segment depends not only on the segment's characteristics and our own strategies but also on competitive actions and reactions.

A second major weakness of much of the segmentation research is the missing stochastic component. To solve this problem there have been a number of efforts to introduce stochastic components to estimates of segment size and characteristics. Some attention has also been given in the academic world to fuzzy clustering (see, for example, Wedel and Steenkamp 1991).

Poor integration with strategy
To address the problem that segmentation studies are often not reflected in the resulting strategy, a number of actions can be taken. These include:

1. Analyse the results of all studies such as copy, concept, product, distribution and other marketing studies at the segment level.
2. Avoid infrequent and expensive large baseline segmentation studies and instead include in all marketing and business studies a segmentation analysis.
3. Link the segmentation to positioning and its associated marketing mix strategies. Specifically recognize the interdependence between the two. Given a positioning, what is the best segment(s)? Given a segment, what is the best positioning(s)? Having fixed on a segment/positioning, it is critical to develop a marketing strategy that will meet the needs of the selected segment and reflect the target positioning.
4. Carry the segmentation efforts to the salesforce level by encouraging each salesperson to segment his/her market. In addition, segmentation can also be very helpful in segmenting the salesforce.
5. Carry through the segmentation strategies to the business and corporate level by focusing on a portfolio of segments and by using the portfolio of segments as the core of the business and corporate strategy.

4 Segmentation in the global information age

The information revolution, which has been receiving enormous coverage in the business and popular media and has been the subject of an increasing number of scholarly studies, has captivated the imagination of scholars, managers and the population at large. This revolution is greatly affecting the ways in which firms are managing their operations and is likely to change dramatically the way in which business is conducted. Information strategy is at the heart of most recent efforts to reengineer and reinvent the corporation and is leading to the creation of a new management and associated marketing paradigm (see INFORMATION TECHNOLOGY AND MARKETING).

In the new management and marketing paradigm (Wind 1994), information is having a profound effect on: (i) the nature and quality of management decisions; (ii) the nature of business strategies; (iii) the creation of innovative communication and distribution systems.

Management decisions
Management decisions are affected by the advances in the development and management of databases (on the entire population) and their linkage to decision (and executive) support systems (DSS/ESS), which in turn can include expert/knowledge based systems. In this context, many advances in segmentation research and modelling can be incorporated in the DSS and much of our knowledge of segmentation can be developed as rules for a knowledge-based system that could help management to select target segments.

Some of the advances in this area include the ability to have 'live' databases in which one can update on an ongoing basis the customer database. Consider, for example, Citibank, which is developing an interactive intelligent decision-support system to guide all interactions with the customer; for example, the delivery of a direct mail or telephone sales message will be targeted by the system which will also coordinate a number of customer interactions to create a 'dialogue' to follow the consumer with the appropriate interaction at each point of contact of the consumer with Citibank such as subsequent telephone enquiry, while using an ATM, when meeting with a bank teller, when receiving the statement. This system is based on a new relationship model with household and not only on the traditional banking focus on accounts.

Data mining

Other interesting developments are in data mining (Lewinson 1994). This term refers to a number of pattern recognition models using either neural nets or fractal technology to discover patterns in the data. These methods have been employed commercially to identify segments of customers most likely to buy a given product (in banking, for example) and to discover the identity of customers most likely to leave (cellular telephones, for example). These approaches, although intriguing, are still in their infancy and require further validation.

Whereas the Citibank example illustrates future development, much of the work today relies more on the traditional geodemographic segmentation based on consensus and other data. An example of this type of effort is the Claritas Prizm lifestyle segmentation. This segmentation divides the USA into 62 clusters. These clusters are further divided into 15 groups that vary with respect to the type of location – rural, town, suburb or urban – and with respect to level of affluence. The Prizm lifestyle clusters can be related to any target group of interest.

Information strategies

Information strategies are relatively recent additions to the traditional set of marketing strategies. One of the early and most effective information-based strategies was the 'capture the client' strategy of America Hospital Supply's direct link between hospital computers and AHS computers, eliminating the need for human interaction in the straight rebuy case. 'Capture the clients' strategies such as the direct computer link between PEG and Walmart are increasing in popularity.

New communication and distribution options

Information technology is also changing dramatically the nature of the communication and distribution options. Electronic shopping via kiosks, CD-ROM or online are being developed at a much faster pace than was ever expected (see, for example, Rangaswamy and Wind 1994). For a more general discussion of impact of information technology on marketing see Blattberg et al. (1994) (see INFORMATION TECHNOLOGY AND MARKETING).

These changes affect all aspects of our lives and are altering the concept of segmentation. In the new marketing paradigm the traditional mass market is being replaced with segments including, at the extreme, segments of one. In a breakthrough book, *The One to One Future*, Peppers and Rogers (1993) present a vision of their one-to-one paradigm which includes and focuses on:

- share of customers not share of market;
- collaborating with customers to create products and relationships;
- customizing products, services and promotional efforts for each customer;
- economics of scope;
- engaging the customers in dialogues – the interactive individualization of media is here.

The shift to segments of one requires both a rethinking of the segmentation concept as well as the development and utilization of sophisticated databases, marketing analysis, modelling and strategy. The trend towards such developments is inevitable and is accompanied by another discontinuous trend – the globalization of business.

Globalization

Increasing numbers of industries are global. To succeed in this environment firms have to shift from a domestic perspective to considering the world as the arena of operations both with respect to the consumer markets for products and services as well as for the resources markets for raw material, R&D, manufacturing, human and capital resources (see GLOBAL MARKETING).

The globalization of industries is also accompanied by trends towards regional economic integration – the European Union,

NAFTA and the various other efforts for regional integration in Asia and Latin America. The implication of these developments for segmentation is that management has to consider portfolios of segments that include:

- global segments;
- regional segments;
- segments within specific countries.

Added to this complexity is the need to consider as the unit of analysis not just countries but countries by mode of entry, since the risk and attractiveness of a country depend on the mode of entry. The selection and implementation of a portfolio of segments which includes global segments, regional segments and segments within countries (by mode of entry) requires a significant amount of information on all relevant markets around the world. The creation and maintenance of such a data/knowledge base is not a trivial undertaking and is one of the major obstacles to the development of global segmentation strategies. Creation of processes for the development and maintenance of country, regional and world databases is a high priority undertaking for all global firms. Yet the development of effective segmentation can take place even without such databases if the firm will proceed in an iterative bottom-up and top-down segmentation. This process involves three bottom-up steps:

1. Segmentation of the market in each country (by mode of entry).
2. Examination of the resulting segments in all the selected countries to identify common segments across countries – clustering of country segments.
3. The creation of a global portfolio based on various clusters of segments.

The resulting portfolio of segments should be compared to a desired (top-down) conceptual portfolio of segments. The comparison and contrast of the two portfolios should be driven by the concept of global operation which balances the need to develop strategies that best meet the needs of the local markets (given the idiosyncratic market, competitive and environmental conditions), while at the same time trying to achieve economies of scale and scope by focusing on cross-country segments in a number of markets. The AHP framework and methodology can and has been used in this context to help make such decisions, even in the absence of the needed 'hard' market data. As data become available, both from the firm's own experience and from other sources, the data can be integrated in a database and used as input to the AHP process.

The segmentation of global markets offers enormous opportunities but is still one of the neglected areas of segmentation. It does offer intellectual and methodological challenges and is critical from a management point of view. The literature presents scattered examples of global segmentation. See, for example, the proposed segmentation based on multinational diffusion patterns (Helsen et al. 1993). However, the opportunities for breakthrough research in this area and especially as it relates to the information revolution are staggering.

5 Extending the segmentation concept

In the marketing literature, in practice and in the discussion so far, segmentation has been limited to 'customer' markets. Yet the concept applies to all heterogeneous populations and can and should be extended to the other stakeholders in the firm – all those who have a 'stake' in its survival and growth.

Consider, for example, the firm's own salesforce. Most large firms employ thousands of sales people who vary considerably in their performance. The 20/80 rule often applies to them as it does to the customers (i.e. 20 per cent of the salesforce often accounts for 80 per cent of the profits). In multiproduct firms, different salespeople often tend to sell different mixes of products. They differ in their family life-cycle stages and hence have different financial and time needs (some are still worried about college education for their kids while others are single, etc.). These and other differences among the salespersons of any firm suggest that the traditional approach, in which a single sales strategy and compensation is employed, is suboptimal. To benefit fully from one's salesforce, it is critical to segment it.

The segmentation of the salesforce based on needs, benefits sought, expertise, perceptions and preference or any other relevant characteristics could lead to the identification of homogeneous segments and the design of separate strategies towards them. In fact in any situation where management relies heavily on a salesforce a dual marketing strategy should be developed – one for the (target segments on customers and a corresponding one for the (segments of the) salesforce. Obviously these two strategies should be coordinated and integrated. Furthermore, a segmented strategy towards compensation is also desirable. To implement it while avoiding discriminatory practices requires the use of a compensation system with a number of options relying on a self-selection strategy in which the various salespeople could select the option most appropriate for their needs. While the segmentation of the salesforce and the resulting segmented strategies are likely to meet with considerable resistance, future research needs to address whether the benefits outweigh the difficulties and cost involved.

Similarly, a segmentation strategy can benefit the firm's dealings with its other stakeholders. Wind (1978) described a segmentation of security analysts and portfolio managers that led to better understanding by a firm of the criteria used in the evaluation of firms in their industry and the perceptions of the given firm and its competitors. Following a segmentation/positioning study, a strategy was developed to meet the needs of a target segment of security analysts that resulted in a spectacular increase in the P/E ratio of the given firm.

Other stakeholders such as suppliers, customer service personnel, competitors, government agencies and the firm's own shareholders are often heterogeneous. In all of these cases, understanding the key segments and selecting desired target segment(s) can greatly enhance the firm's effectiveness. In fact, as the cost of doing business in today's environment increases, a segmented strategy may be essential for any organization concerned with the return of their marketing investments.

6 Issues and associated research agenda

In the author's introduction to the *Journal of Marketing Research* special issue on segmentation research (Wind 1978) the following conclusions were presented:

> Market segmentation has served as the focal point for many of the major marketing research developments and the marketing activities of most firms. Yet, too many segmentation researchers have settled on a fixed way of conducting segmentation studies. This tendency for standardization of procedures is premature and undesirable. Innovative approaches to segmentation have been offered in the past few years, and further work on the new conceptual and methodological aspects of segmentation should be undertaken.

Of particular importance seems to be research on the following areas:

1. New conceptualizations of the segmentation problem.
2. Reevaluation and operationalization of the normative theory of segmentation with emphasis on the question of how to allocate resources among markets and products over time.
3. The discovery and implementation of new variables for use as bases for segmentation (i.e. new attitudinal and behavioural constructs such as consumption-based personality inventories and variables which focus on likely change in attitude and behavioural responses to the marketing variables) of the markets for products, services and concepts.
4. The development of new research designs and parallel data collection and analysis techniques which place fewer demands on the respondents (i.e. data collection which is simpler for the respondent and data analysis procedures capable of handling missing data and incomplete block designs).
5. The development of simple and flexible analytical approaches to data analysis capable of handling discrete and continuous variables and selected interaction at a point in time and over time.
6. Evaluation of the conditions under which various data analytical techniques are most appropriate.
7. The accumulation of knowledge on successful bases for segmentation across studies (products, situations and markets).
8. Undertaking external validation studies to determine the performance of segmentation strategies which were based on findings of segmentation studies.
9. Designing and implementing multi-trait, multi-method approaches to segmentation

research aimed at both the generation of more generalizable (reliable) and valid data.
10 Integration of segmentation research with the marketing information system of the firm.
11 Exploring alternative approaches to the translation of segmentation findings into marketing strategies.
12 Studies of the organizational design of firms which were successful and unsuccessful in implementing segmentation strategies.

Review of some of the issues and current advances in segmentation research indicates that despite the great advances in the management of and research practice of segmentation, numerous frontiers still require creative and systematic study.

(Wind 1978)

The basic conclusions and their related research agenda are still valid. Despite the advances in academic research during the past sixteen years, we still do not have satisfactory solutions to the issues raised in the 1978 research agenda. The changes in the business environment and especially the implications of operating in a global information age do suggest, however, the need to add a few additional items to the research agenda. These include:

1 Reconceptualization of segmentation problems in light of the impact of operating in the global information age.
2 Development of expert system/knowledge-based systems to help management to select and manage the portfolio of segments. Such systems would ideally be incorporated in an effective decision support system. Key to this is the development of a set of rules summarizing our current understanding of market segmentation. These rules can reflect the empirical generalizations in this area and can be aided by appropriate meta-analyses.
3 Development of the processes and organizational architecture required to assure effective adaptation and management of segmentation. This includes adoption of the segmentation concept as the foundation of all marketing and business decisions (as outlined in Figure 1) as well as the development of guidelines for effective management of segmentation.

Addressing these newer challenges and continuing building our knowledge concerning the items identified in the 1978 research agenda would be critical to our ability to increase the value of segmentation. Continuous innovation and improvement in segmentation research and modelling for generating and evaluating segmentation strategies is essential. However, real progress in this area requires rethinking the role of segmentation in the global information age and concentrated efforts by management to develop and implement innovative and effective segmentation strategies.

The obstacles to effective segmentation are not methodological, nor even the lack of data, but rather the ability and willingness of management to undertake a segmentation strategy and establish the processes and resources required for successful implementation. The concept of segmentation, once adjusted to reflect the impact of the information revolution and the globalization of business, is sound and valid. It is the practice of segmentation that is fraught with problems. These problems are solvable but the solutions require revision and alteration to most of the current approaches used to segment markets. If we have the conviction and courage to reexamine the traditional segmentation concept and approaches, we shall be able to increase significantly the worth of our segmentation efforts in creating value to our customers and other stakeholders.

YORAM (JERRY) WIND
THE WHARTON SCHOOL
UNIVERSITY OF PENNSYLVANIA

Further reading

(References cited in the text marked *)

* Arable, Phipps, Carroll, J. Douglas, DeSarbo, Wayne S. and Wind, Jerry (1981) 'Overlapping clustering: a new method for product positioning', *Journal of Marketing Research* 18: 310–17.
* Blattberg, Robert, Glazer, Robert and Little, John (1994) *The Marketing Information Revolution*, Harvard: Harvard Business School Press.
* Bucklin, Randolph E. and Gupta, Sunil (1992) 'Brand choice, purchase incidence, and segmentation: an integrated modeling approach', *Journal of Marketing Research* XXIX: 201–15.
* Chaturvedi, Anil, Carroll, J. Douglas and Green, Paul E. (1994) 'Market segmentation via overlapping K-centroids clustering', Working paper,

Pennsylvania: Wharton School, University of Pennsylvania, May: 1–21.
* Choffray, Jean-Marie and Lilien, Gary L. (1978) 'A new approach to industrial market segmentation', *Sloan Management Review* 19: 17–30.
* Frank, Ronald, Massy, William and Wind, Jerry (1972) *Market Segmentation*, Englewood Cliffs, NJ: Prentice Hall.
* Garreau, Joel (1982) *The Nine Nations of North America*, Boston: Houghton Mifflin.
* Gensch, Dennis, Aversa, N. and Moore, S. (1990) 'A choice modeling market information system that enabled ABB Electric to expand its market share', *Interfaces* 20: 6–25.
Green, Paul E. (1977) 'A new approach to market segmentation', *Business Horizons* 20: 61–73.
* Green, Paul E. and DeSarbo, Wayne S. (1979) 'Componential marketing in the analysis of consumer trade-offs', *Journal of Marketing* 43: 83–91.
* Green, Paul E. and Krieger, Abba M. (1985) 'Models and heuristics for product line selection', *Marketing Science* 4: 1–19.
* Green, Paul E. and Krieger, Abba M. (1991) 'Segmenting marketing with conjoint analysis', *Journal of Marketing* 55: 20–31.
* Green, Paul E. and Krieger, Abba M. (1994) 'An evaluation of alternative approaches to cluster-based market segmentation', Working paper, Pennsylvania: Wharton School, University of Pennsylvania.
* Grover, Rajiv and Srinivasan, V. (1987) 'A simultaneous approach to market segmentation and market structuring', *Journal of Marketing Research* 24: 139–53.
* Helsen, Kristiaan, Jedidi, Kamel and DeSarbo, Wayne S. (1993) 'A new approach to country segmentation utilising multinational diffusion patterns', *Journal of Marketing* 57: 60–71.
* Johnson, Brent and Lilien, Gary L. (1994) 'A framework and procedure for assessing market segment change', Penn State ISBM working paper, Penn State University, University Park, PA.
* Kotler, Philip (1991) *Marketing Management*, Englewood Cliffs, NJ: Prentice-Hall.
* Lewinson, Lisa (1994) 'Data mining: tapping into the mother code', *Database Programming and Design*, February: 50–6.
* Mitchell, A. (1983) *The Nine American Lifestyles*, New York: Macmillan.
* Peppers, Don and Rogers, Martha (1993) *The One to One Future*, New York: Doubleday.

* Peterson, Robert A. (1974) 'Market structuring by sequential cluster analysis', *Journal of Business Research* 2: 249–64.
* Rangaswamy, Arvind and Wind, Yoram (1994) 'Don't walk in, just log in! Electronic commerce on the information highway', Wharton School Working Paper, February.
* Saaty, Thomas L. (1992) *Decision Marketing for Leaders*, Pittsburgh: RWS Pittsburgh Publications.
* Wedel, Michel and Steenkamp, Jan-Benedict E.M. (1991) 'A clusterwise regression method for simultaneous fuzzy market structuring and benefit segmentation', *Journal of Marketing Research* XXVIII: 385–96.
* Weiss, Michael (1994) *Latitudes of Attitudes: An Atlas of American Tastes, Trends, Politics and Passions*, Boston: Little Brown and Company.
* Wilson, Elizabeth J., Lilien, Gary L. and Wilson, David T. (1991) 'Developing and testing a contingency paradigm of group choice in organizational buying', *Journal of Marketing Research* 28: 452–66.
* Wind, Yoram (1978) 'Issue and advances in segmentation research', *Journal of Marketing Research* XV: 317–37.
* Wind, Yoram and Cardozo, Richard N. (1974) 'Industrial marketing segmentation', *Industrial Marketing Management* March: 153–65.
Wind, Yoram and Dunn, Elizabeth (1987) 'Analytic hierarchy process for generation and evaluation of marketing mix strategies', in Frazier, Gary and Sheth, Jagdish (eds), *Contemporary Views on Marketing Practice*, Boston: Lexington Books: 111–31.
* Wind, Yoram and Robertson, Thomas (1983) 'Marketing strategy: new directions for theory and research', *Journal of Marketing* Spring: 12–25.
* Wind, Yoram and Saaty, Thomas L. (1980) 'Marketing applications of the analytic hierarchy process', *Management Science* 26: 641–58.

See also: ADVERTISING; CHANNELS OF DISTRIBUTION; GLOBAL MARKETING; INFORMATION TECHNOLOGY AND MARKETING; MARKETING RESEARCH; ORGANIZATIONAL BUYING BEHAVIOUR; POSITIONING; PRICING; PRODUCT POLICY; SALES PROMOTION; STRATEGIC MARKETING PLANNING; THE MARKETING AUDIT

Positioning

1. Key concepts and ideas
2. Effective positioning strategy
3. Current issues in the development of a positioning strategy
4. Future directions for positioning

Overview

Positioning refers to the place in the market that a company, product or service occupies relative to others in that same marketplace. It is defined in terms of the target customer groups the offerings are aimed at and the differential advantage or uniqueness created and offered to that target. There are two types of positioning: company competitive positioning; and product or brand positioning.

A company's competitive position relates to how it attempts to build its overall competitive advantage in the marketplace. Competitive position is the totality of offer and image of the company relative to competing companies. In UK food retailing, for example, Marks and Spencer (M&S) occupy an 'up-market' position competing on the basis of quality and gourmet appeal while Aldi competes primarily on the basis of low price. Both have a clear (but different) view of their target customers and both have a clear (but different) basis on which they attempt to create their uniqueness.

Company positioning is generally based on the combination of price, quality and, increasingly, service positioning. Low price positions are clearly targeted at the most price conscious customer groups. 'Bargain', 'budget', 'economy' and 'super economy' positionings typically, but not always, signal lower quality products at lowest prices. Higher quality positions are, again typically but not always, associated with higher prices at the 'luxury' or 'premium' end of the market. Higher price can be used as a quality signal to indicate a high-quality product. Service positionings concentrate on the less tangible aspects of product, on service in choice, delivery, use and after sales care as a means of differentiation for service demanding customers.

Where company position is well developed the full range of the company's offerings benefit, or suffer, from that positioning. For example, new products or extended product ranges offered with the St Michael (Marks and Spencer) brand benefit from the good-quality positioning enjoyed by M&S. Similarly customers shopping for food items in Aldi can be confident that the prices charged will be, if not the lowest, very close to the lowest available in any major food shop.

Product or brand positioning is more concerned with a particular offering and how that is received by customers and potential customers relative to other, competing, brand offerings. In cases where company positioning is strong (well-defined) such as in food retailing the brand positioning might be affected by it. When the H.J. Heinz company purchased the Weight Watchers brand in 1978 it was to exploit the strong weight control association's position in the minds of consumers. Within a decade Heinz had 60 frozen food items and 150 non-frozen food items on the market under the Weight Watchers brand (see Aaker 1991).

Positioning is closely related to two key concepts in marketing: market targeting (see MARKET SEGMENTATION); and product differentiation (see BRANDING AND BRAND MANAGEMENT). Decisions on these two aspects of marketing are at the heart of competitive strategy development. Without a clear idea of the position aimed for, it is difficult if not impossible to take coordinated decisions on the rest of the marketing mix. Indeed, defining the competitive positioning aimed for often dictates the most effective combination of other elements of the marketing mix (see THE MARKETING MIX).

1 Key concepts and ideas

There are a number of central ideas and issues in positioning. First, positioning is concerned with long-term strategy rather than short-run tactics (see MARKETING STRATEGY). Positions take time to create and are not just produced by short-term advertising campaigns. They offer a sustainable means of differentiation and creation of a competitive advantage. Well-crafted positions are sustainable, defensible and further exploitable. That said, positions may be managed to evolve and change over time as markets develop, mature and die.

Second, positioning is in the mind of the customer (see Ries and Trout 1981). It is what the customer believes about the company, product or service. This is generally brought about by a combination of reality (the tangible features of the product, its pricing, the distribution channels and the type and levels of service built into the product) and image (created through advertising, PR, promotions and so on). Therefore it is crucial that position be defined from the customer, rather than the company, perspective. Note that some of the 'tangible' features, such as price and the channels chosen for distributing the product, may also serve to reinforce (or clash with) the image created through promotion (see ADVERTISING; CHANNELS OF DISTRIBUTION; PACKAGING AND DESIGN; PRODUCT POLICY).

Third, positioning is essentially benefit based. Strong positions translate features of the company or product (such as an ability to produce at low cost) into benefits of value to the target customers (such as low relative price). Effective positions not only convey a clear image to the customer but also offer clear reasons (benefits) for buying what the company has to offer.

Fourth, because positioning is benefit based, and because different customers are often seeking different benefits in buying and using essentially the same products and services, the position a particular product occupies in the mind of one customer may be different from the position it occupies in the mind of a different customer. In segmented markets it is clearly important to understand the position the company and its offerings occupy in the minds of all relevant market segments.

Finally, positioning is a relative concept. Products and brands only occupy positions relative to competing products and brands. A price level in isolation from competition is neither 'bargain' nor 'premium'. Similarly quality and service levels can only be judged relative to what is offered by the competition.

A number of alternative bases for establishing product and brand positions have been suggested (Wind 1982). These include product features (e.g. notebook-size computers), the benefits those features convey (portability), specific use occasions (when travelling away from home or office), particular user groups (professionals who work in a variety of locations) or directly against alternatives (more versatile).

2 Effective positioning strategy

For positioning to be effective four main conditions need to be met (see Arnold 1992; Hooley et al.1998):

1. There must be a clear view of the target market and customers aimed for. Given that the same position in a market may be viewed differently by different customers, it is essential that the impact of the positioning on all the key targets be understood and also that the impact on non-target segments be anticipated.
2. Similarly, the benefits on which the positioning is built must be important to the target customers aimed at. Clearly a low-price positioning when aiming for a segment that is not price sensitive does not make sense. The benefits or features built into the positioning must be ones which are attractive to the target customers.
3. The positioning should build on real strengths of the company and/or its brands. Ideally, these strengths or the combination of core competencies used to create the strengths should be unique to the company. This 'asset-based' approach (see Davidson 1997), using the company's assets to best effect to create competitive positions, ensures that they are both defensible and sustainable in the face of competitive attack.
4. Finally, positions should be communicable. They should be capable of being communicated to the target market. This often means that they should be simple and uncomplicated, amenable to translation into attractive and creative advertising or other communication means.

3 Current issues in the development of a positioning strategy

Positioning strategy involves three main phases:

1 identify where you are currently positioned;
2 decide where you wish to be positioned;
3 implement the strategy to get you there.

Each are discussed in turn below.

Identifying current product positions

A starting-point for developing a positioning strategy is to understand the position the product currently occupies in the minds of the customer and potential customer. Whether this has been pursued overtly or not, the product will occupy some current place in the market. There have been a great many research approaches over the years to identify product positions. There are typically, however, several stages in a positioning study.

1 *Identification of the competitive set.* The first step involves identifying which other offerings are considered as alternatives (see Lehmann and Winer 1991). This may be product form competition (e.g. for Diet Pepsi that would include other diet colas such as Diet Coke); product category competition (other soft drinks including non-diet forms, 7-Up, Ir'n Bru); generic competition (other beverages including beer, milk, tea, coffee); or budget/need priority competition (other foods such as a hamburger or even entertainment such as a visit to the cinema). Identifying the competitive set can be done from a company perspective by looking for substitute products that can serve the same function or, and more usefully, by directly asking customers what alternatives they consider when making a purchase. Note that the competitive set could be scenario specific. It may depend on the purchase or usage context. Thus for one use (e.g. thirst quenching) one competitive set may be important, while for another (e.g. socializing with friends) a different set might be appropriate.

2 *Identification of relevant product dimensions.* Once the competitive set has been defined the next issue is to identify the bases on which customers select between the various alternatives open to them. Central to this is identifying what product benefits are important to them. This information is best obtained through the use of qualitative research techniques such as group discussions (see QUALITATIVE RESEARCH). Projective techniques such as Kelly's Repertory Grid, brand personality research, free association and picture interpretation can also be useful. The result should be a comprehensive listing of product benefits and/or features used by customers to compare the alternatives in the competitive set. Again it should be noted that benefits sought are likely to be dependent on the usage context or scenario. When purchasing a pen as a gift for someone else different factors might be important than when buying for one's own use.

3 *Estimation of relative importance of attributes.* Not all features will be equally important to all customers. Step three seeks to identify what is important and how important it is to each customer/group (see MARKETING RESEARCH). This is best done through quantitative research, ranking or rating attribute importance on importance scales or by points allocation methods (e.g. 'divide 100 points across the features giving most points to the features you consider most important') (see QUANTITATIVE METHODS IN MARKETING). Note that at this stage it is important to segment the market if differences in importances arise. Indeed, this is a very powerful way of segmenting markets (benefit segmentation).

4 *Identify positions of competing products on the important attributes.* The fourth step attempts to find where the competitors sit on the various dimensions important to the segments under study. Again, quantitative research using a representative sample is the most appropriate approach. Techniques such as semantic differential scales or Likert scales can be used to elicit brand attribute data. It is important to identify differences in perceptions between various respondents. In addition to differences in importances, noted above, within importance (benefit) segments there may be different views of the market and competing offerings.

5 *Identify customer requirements.* On the same dimensions customer requirements can be identified. This may be achieved by asking customers to rate their 'ideal' brand. Alternatively ideals may be inferred by asking respondents to rank in preference order the alternatives available (a technique known as 'unfolding'; see Green *et al.* 1989). Again, at

311

Marketing management

Figure 1 A hypothetical brand map

this stage it is possible that there will be differences in requirements (despite possible similarity in importances and in perceptions found previously). Hence it is important to look for market segments based on different requirements and preferences.
6 *Putting it all together.* Finally, there is a need to put all the above data together in a way that encapsulates the data and facilitates an understanding of the results. This can be accomplished through the use of multidimensional scaling techniques (see Green et al. 1989) to produce brand maps (see QUANTITATIVE METHODS IN MARKETING). The maps summarize the dimensions that are important to customers, the current positions of competing offerings on those dimensions and the location of customer requirements on those dimensions. This can form the basis for deciding on the positioning strategy to adopt (see Figure 1).

In Figure 1, six competing brands were identified in the competitive set (Brand 1 to Brand 6 on the diagram). Two dimensions were found to be important to customers when selecting between alternative brands (price and durability) Three distinct market segments were identified requiring different combinations of the price/durability features (Segment 1 to Segment 3).

Brands 5 and 6 compete directly with each other for sales in Segment 1. Both brands offer the combination of durability at a low price required by the segment. Segment 3, on the other hand, prefers a non-durable brand, but again at a low price. Brands 1 and 2 both serve this segment but neither offer exactly what the segment requires (Brand 1 is too non-durable, while Brand 2 is not low enough in price). Brand 3 appeals to Segment 2 offering a durable product at an average to high price. Finally, Brand 4 appeals directly to no segment being seen as high price and non-durable, a combination no segment is looking for.

Deciding where you wish to be positioned

Once the current positions of the various competitors and the locations of customer ideal requirements have been identified the company is ready to decide which positioning to aim for. The decision encapsulates two key decisions:

1 The selection of target market (and hence of target competitors).

		Market segment attractiveness		
		Unattractive	Average	Attractive
Current and potential company strengths in serving the segment	Weak	Avoid	Avoid	Avoid
	Average	Avoid	Avoid	Lesser targets
	Strong	Lesser targets	Secondary targets	Prime targets

Figure 2 Target market selection

2 The definition of competitive advantage, or points of difference with the competitors (see Hooley *et al.* 1998).

The decisions are made on the basis of market segment attractiveness and current or potential strength in serving the market segment (see Figure 2).

A number of factors affect the attractiveness of alternative-target market segments. Market factors include the size and growth rate of the segment, the stage of industry evolution (stage of PLC (see PRODUCT LIFE-CYCLE MANAGEMENT), predictability of the market (see SALES FORECASTING), price elasticity, cyclicality and seasonality of demand and the bargaining power of customers. Economic and technological factors include barriers to entry and exit, bargaining power of suppliers, level of technology utilization, investment required and margins available. Competitive factors include competitive intensity, quality of competition, threat of entry, threat of substitution and degree of current differentiation. Wider (macro-) environmental factors include exposure to national and international economic fluctuations, exposure to political and legal factors, degree of market and industry regulation, social acceptability and physical environment impact (see ENVIRONMENTAL ANALYSIS).

Other factors affect current and potential company strengths in serving a particular target market. Current market position is indicated by relative share of the market, rate of change of share of market, existence of exploitable marketing assets and the existence of unique and valued products and services. Economic and technological position concerns cost structure relative to competitors, capacity utilization and technological capability. The wider capability profile includes management strength and depth, marketing strength and degree of forward, backward and horizontal integration.

The most attractive market positions are therefore those which combine attractive market segments with strong current or potential company strengths Where these combinations do not exist positionings are selected that trade-off on one or other factor. The strong evidence from the literature on competitive success (see Saunders 1993) is that companies are well advised to pursue less attractive markets where they still enjoy clear strengths over competitors in preference to possibly more attractive markets where their strength or potential strength is only average. Markets where the company is at a competitive disadvantage (weak) should be avoided.

Implementing the positioning strategy

Positioning strategy depends on the selection of a target market and the creation of a complete offering to attract and satisfy that target better than the competition. Having identified current position and decided on the position to be aimed for there are several main strategy alternatives.

Reinforce existing position

Where the existing position is a favourable one (i.e. the position is close to what the target market wants and is distinct from competing offerings) the strategy may be one of reinforcing that position. In the example shown in Figure 1, this strategy could be appropriate for Brand 3 if it sought to serve Segment 2. This strategy may be achieved by continuing with similar product configurations and similar communications.

The position to be reinforced may not necessarily be a leadership one. In car rental Avis successfully positioned as number two in the market behind Hertz with the slogan 'because we're number two we try harder', appealing to the customer on the basis of the plucky underdog, striving to give a higher level of service than a complacent market leader. When Hertz eventually retaliated, however, the positioning backfired to some extent. The retaliation was 'for years Avis have been telling you we're number one. Here's why'.

Incremental repositioning

Where customer wants are changing or expected to change, or the technology for delivering customer satisfaction is developing, movement from current positions may become inevitable. Such changes may be incremental or radical. An example of incremental repositioning is the washing powder Persil. For half a century Persil has been a market leader in the UK, continuously being adapted to meet changes in washing habits and customer requirements. Product reformulations and communications modifications have attended customer usage changes from hand to machine washing, top-loading to front-loading washing machines, and more recently lower temperature washing. This incremental repositioning has enabled Persil to retain its market leadership position in the face of strong competitive attacks.

Where the physical product is close to what customers want there may be a need for image re-engineering to change the image to draw that closer to what target customers want. Brand 1, for example, may be equally as durable as Brand 2 but past communications have failed to convey that to target customers. A promotional campaign using advertising, PR and other communications tools (see ADVERTISING; MARKETING COMMUNICATIONS) may help to change the image and make Brand 1 closer to what Segment 3 is looking for.

Radical repositioning

Where the position is not favourable (too far from target customers – Brand 4), or too indistinct from competitors (Brands 5 and 6) then more drastic repositioning may be required. This could mean physical re-engineering of the product to make the offer closer to what customers want. In the case of Brand 4 there is an obvious need to improve on the durability of the brand if it is to appeal to Segment 2, or a dramatic reduction in price (together, presumably, with a commensurate reduction in costs) if it is to appeal to Segment 3.

Radical repositioning may mean attacking a completely new market segment. Lucozade, the carbonated glucose drink, was originally positioned as an energy provider to children when ill. Parents administered it almost as a medicine. More recently, however, in an attempt to enter more attractive segments of the market, the drink has been repositioned as an energy source for fit and healthy adults. The advertising campaign featuring superfit athletes such as decathlon gold medallist Daley Thomson signalled this repositioning most effectively. The comparison between Thomson (arguably at the time of the advertisements the fittest man in the world) and sick children could hardly be more stark.

Repositioning may appeal to new values not currently addressed in the market. Hellmann's mayonnaise was sold in the UK primarily as an accompaniment to salad dishes. The market was highly seasonal (summer period dominant) and the product competed with salad cream and other salad dressings. A strong advertising campaign in the mid-1990s attempted to reposition the brand as a suitable accompaniment to a variety of dishes that could be served throughout the year including high recall advertisments promoting use at Christmas as an accompaniment to turkey dishes.

Competitor depositioning

Where position is a favourable one but competitors are encroaching and gaining ground the strategy may be one of attempting to displace the competition. By the early 1990s the traditional dominance of butter as a 'yellow fat' for spreading on bread had been seriously eroded by margarine brands. The launch of buttergrade margarines such as 'I Can't Believe it's not Butter' and 'Utterly Butterly' were so successful that major attempts were made by butter marketers to convince the public that margarine was no real substitute ('no buts – it's got to be butter').

4 Future directions for positioning

A number of trends in marketing can be identified and their impact on positioning predicted. First, in most markets both domestic and international competition is increasing apace (see GLOBAL MARKETING). That means that positioning will need to be sharper to help differentiate one offer from another and ensure that the various offerings are more closely targeted at specific market segments.

The customers of the future will be more highly educated and have far greater choice due to the increased levels of competition. Consequently, they are less likely to be influenced by image-based positionings where products do not live up to their promises. Customers will demand increased levels of service and quality at ever more competitive prices. Positionings for the future will be based more on reality than image.

At the same time advances in manufacturing technology, and the continued take up of Total Quality Management (TQM) (see TOTAL QUALITY MANAGEMENT) techniques are leading to a degree of quality convergence in the physical aspects of many product offerings. This makes it increasingly difficult to differentiate on the basis of the physical, or core product (see Levitt 1986). Differentiation, and hence positioning, is likely to depend increasingly on the augmentations and additional services of value that can be built into product offerings.

Finally, we should note that the tools and techniques available to the marketer are becoming ever more sophisticated. Through direct mail marketing (see DIRECT MARKETING), for example, it is now possible to target highly focused campaigns at more tightly defined customer groups. Mail order marketers in particular now maintain sophisticated databases detailing prior purchases and relating them to socioeconomic, demographic and other data. This again will lead to more closely targeted positioning. Ries and Trout (1981) announced two decades ago that 'the positioning era cometh'. It is still here and will be even more pronounced in the fragmented markets of the twenty-first century.

GRAHAM J. HOOLEY
ASTON BUSINESS SCHOOL, ASTON UNIVERSITY

Further reading

(References cited in the text marked *)

* Aaker, D.A. (1991) *Managing Brand Equity: Capitalising on the Value of a Brand Name*, New York: The Free Press.
* Arnold, D. (1992) *The Handbook of Brand Management*, London: Economist Books Ltd.
* Davidson, H. (1997) *Even More Offensive Marketing*, Harmondsworth: Penguin Books.
* Green, P.E., Carmone, F.J., Jnr and Smith, S.M. (1989) *Multidimensional Scaling: Concepts and Applications*, Boston: Allyn and Bacon.
* Hooley, G.J., Saunders, J.A. and Piercy, N.F. (1998) *Marketing Strategy and Competitive Positioning*, Hemel Hempstead: Prentice Hall Europe
* Lehmann, D.R. and Winer, R.S. (1991) *Analysis for Marketing Planning*, 2nd edn, Boston: Irwin.
* Levitt, T. (1986) *The Marketing Imagination*, New York: The Free Press.
* Ries, A. and Trout, J. (1981) *Positioning: The Battle for your Mind*, Maidenhead: McGraw-Hill.
* Saunders, J. (ed.) (1993) *The Marketing Initiative*, London: Prentice Hall International.
* Wind, Y.J. (1982) *Product Policy: Concepts, Methods and Strategy*, Reading, MA: Addison-Wesley Publishing Co.

See also: ADVERTISING; BRANDING AND BRAND MANAGEMENT; CHANNELS OF DISTRIBUTION; DIRECT MARKETING; ENVIRONMENTAL ANALYSIS; GLOBAL MARKETING; MARKETING COMMUNICATIONS; MARKETING RESEARCH; MARKETING STRATEGY; MARKET SEGMENTATION; PACKAGING AND DESIGN; PRICING; PRODUCT LIFE-CYCLE MANAGEMENT; PRODUCT POLICY; QUALITATIVE RESEARCH IN MARKETING; QUANTITATIVE METHODS IN MARKETING; SALES FORECASTING; THE MARKETING MIX; TOTAL QUALITY MANAGEMENT

The marketing mix

The marketing mix

1. Nature and scope
2. Four generic functions
3. The multiple functions of mix instruments
4. The Four P classification
5. The peculiar nature of promotion instruments
6. The Four P classification revisited
7. Explications and extensions
8. Criticism of the marketing mix concept
9. Conclusion

Overview

In 1953 Neil Borden coined the term 'marketing mix' in his presidential address to the American Marketing Association. Borden had been inspired by James Culliton who, in the preceding decade, had pictured the marketing executive as somebody combining different ingredients. The term 'marketing mix' referred to the mixture of elements useful in pursuing a certain market response. The metaphor not only suggested the availability of a wide range of possible ingredients, as well as the numerous ways in which these elements could be combined, but also the fact that different amalgamations produce different results, with some preferable to others. The expression reminds one of many other types of combination with similar characteristics – not every mixed grill is as delicious as another and not every drink can be combined successfully with another.

Since the 1960s the use and interpretation of the concept of the marketing mix has evolved and developed, not least through the classification of the Four Ps by McCarthy (1960). This classification, although it quickly became a standard, has not remained static. Later researchers have sought to expand the classification; others still have sought to criticize it.

1 Nature and scope

The concept of the marketing mix refers to the set of 'controllable demand-impinging instruments that can be combined into a marketing programme used by a firm (or any other organization) to achieve a certain level and type of response from its target market' (van Waterschoot and Van den Bulte 1992: 88). By definition instruments are concerned that more or less directly influence demand to a greater or lesser extent, like the price of a product or the way in which it is advertised. The price of a product will exert a greater or lesser immediate impact on demand, depending, among other things, on the type of product and on the type of market. Private demand for basic telephone services offered by a state monopolist will not be very much influenced by the price charged. Industry demand by car manufacturers for exhaust pipes, delivered by one specific supplier out of a greater number, will be rather price sensitive. Advertising may hardly be able to raise demand in either case. If a supermarket chain uses television advertising to announce a temporary discount on a major brand of beer during a particular week, its sales may rise very markedly that same week. Advertising may also influence demand to a great extent indirectly by creating and sustaining a brand image, as in the case of many Coca-Cola advertisements.

However, not all marketing instruments are also marketing mix instruments. For example, marketing research – if carried out properly and if its information value exceeds its costs – is often a useful marketing instrument, without belonging to the marketing mix (see MARKETING RESEARCH). The reason is that marketing research does not directly influence demand in any way or to any extent. Customers will not start buying more of a brand for the mere reason that its producer or distributor increases his marketing research budget or employs more competent research personnel or hires a more skilled research agency or starts using more appropriate research techniques. Adequate marketing research will only influence demand indirectly (e.g. by helping to (re-)specify product characteristics better to match customer needs and desires). Such improved product characteristics make up part of the marketing mix, since they may more or less directly influence demand to a greater or lesser extent depending on the case. The marketing research efforts that gave rise to the ameliorated product characteristics have only affected demand in an intermediate or indirect way and therefore by definition do not belong to the marketing mix.

Next to exerting a more or less direct effect of a greater or smaller magnitude sooner or later, the demand impinging element should also be controllable to be a marketing mix instrument. Fine weather fosters coastal tourism, but is not a marketing mix instrument. However, the distinction between controllable and non-controllable elements, is not always obvious and lack of control does not necessarily imply lack of influence. Controlling over a variable means being able to establish its value. Influence over a variable means having some but not complete control of it (Ackoff 1981: 174). A country's birth rate, for example, is an important but uncontrollable demand impinging element for a manufacturer of baby clothes. If, however, government measures such as birth premiums can significantly raise demand and if government measures are highly dependent on company lobbying, then the birth rate can be called susceptible to influence. As the example suggests, controllable (marketing mix) variables may be used to influence crucial, but uncontrollable environmental elements (see ENVIRONMENTAL ANALYSIS).

The traditional target groups at which the marketing mix is directed consist of an organization's intermediate and ultimate buyers. (For a description of the typical behaviour of these groups and the way they interact with the marketer see CHANNELS OF DISTRIBUTION; CONSUMER BEHAVIOUR; ORGANIZATIONAL BUYING BEHAVIOUR.) Conceptually, however, the marketing mix need not limit itself to these groups, but may and often should also serve to relate an organization to any of its so-called 'transactional publics', consisting of 'those individuals, organizations and institutions with which the corporation interacts directly' (Ackoff 1981: 90). Examples are suppliers, investors, creditors, government and regulatory agencies, competitors and the press.

Like the marketing concept itself, the mix idea applies not only beyond mere consumer publics, but also beyond business organizations (see STRATEGIC MARKETING FOR NON-PROFIT ORGANIZATIONS). To realize some of its manifold aims such as heightening environmental awareness and provoking environmentally favourable behaviour, as well as to gain financial support from ecologically minded individuals, an environmentalist organization like Greenpeace has a set of instruments at its disposal that – notwithstanding its own peculiarities – is similar to strictly commercial marketing mixes. Greenpeace mainly and successfully tries to generate free advertising or publicity. Their daring and imaginative non-violent actions – like steering a small inflatable craft between the harpoon guns of whalers and their prey – yields them spectacularly wide media exposure. Their marketing programme towards the general public further relies on personal mailings and sales of Greenpeace merchandise via mail order as well as via a small set of specialized shops in major cities (see GREEN MARKETING).

Marketing mix instruments are typically combined in order to provoke a certain type and level of demand, which an organization deems worthwhile in pursuing its ultimate objectives. In the realization of these ultimate objectives, demand creation constitutes an intermediate goal. An organization may, for instance, try to maximize its long-term profits. It might therefore stimulate demand by developing a high-quality product with unique features, which focuses on a segment of affluent buyers willing to pay a high price, preferably buying in specialized upper-class boutiques and probably reading advertisements in exclusive magazines. Mix instruments, however, are not only apt to encourage demand but also to discourage it – an approach called 'demarketing' (Kotler and Levy 1971). In the 1990s – due to a continuous oversupply of practitioners – organizations of Belgian doctors visited secondary schools in order to discourage school-leavers, or at least some of them, from studying medicine.

2 Four generic functions

For exchange to come about, it is essential that there are at least two parties believing that it is appropriate or desirable to deal with one another and being free to make, accept or reject an offer. Moreover, each of these parties must possess something that might be of value to the other and each must be capable of communication and delivery (Kotler 1972). The latter condition summarizes the four fundamental or generic functions that marketing mix instruments have to fulfil.

Obviously, exchange or demand creation is not possible if one does not have any object or service at one's disposal that might be of value to the other party. So a primary function of the marketing mix consists of configuring something that is valued by the prospective exchange party. (see MARKET SEGMENTATION) Since the idea behind a potential exchange is to gain from it in some way or another, a second function consists of determining the offers and sacrifices that need to be made by the prospective exchange party. The previous two functions would not allow any exchange if no communication could take place. The respective parties need to be informed about one another's intentions and requirements and perhaps be persuaded about the attractiveness of the other party's offering, or even about entering into such an exchange relationship. This third fundamental function consists of bringing the offer to the attention of the prospective exchange party and influencing its feelings and preferences about it. Even now no exchange would come about if the respective parties were unable actually to deliver the object or service that is exchanged for some higher valued object or service. Here arises a fourth fundamental function of placing the offer at the disposal of the prospective exchange party.

The marketing discipline considers these four mix functions as generic, in the sense that they have to be fulfilled, for exchange to come about (see Table 1, lefthand column). This necessity follows from the marketing discipline's realistic market assumptions, which would be called impure by economists because of the supposed lack of instantaneous transactions and perfect knowledge (Houston and Gassenheimer 1987: 15) (see THE ECONOMICS BASIS OF MARKETING). Consequently, poor execution of any of these functions will bring about poor exchange results or worse results than those that could potentially have taken place. However, if any of these functions is not carried out, no exchange can take place, no demand can be created, fulfilled or maintained.

3 The multiple functions of mix instruments

In practice, numerous marketing mix instruments exist. Out of an endless theoretical list of mix instruments a specific actual combination has to be chosen, taking into consideration its expected effects. A fundamental observation is the fact that any instrument predominantly serves one of the four generic functions mentioned previously, but at the same time it also contributes – be it to a lesser extent – to the fulfillment of the three other functions (see Table 1). Take, for example, the choice of the type of retail outlet. If a certain brand is exclusively for sale in upper-end shops, then this choice predominantly takes part in the availability function. At the same time, however, the first generic function is also affected, since shopping in a highly esteemed outlet fills needs such as prestige and dominance. Due to the relatively low density of such shops, however, transportation costs will be higher in terms of monetary expenses, time and effort and as such act upon the price function. Finally, the communication function is influenced, since the choice of the particular type of sales outlet strengthens or weakens the image of the product itself. A brand that is only for sale in a very limited set of exclusive shops will be perceived differently from a brand that is available in any mass distribution outlet, even if the objective product characteristics were identical.

To the previous example numerous others can be added. Any specific marketing mix instrument affects all four generic marketing mix functions, but predominantly one of them. Vice versa, any generic marketing mix function is served by any specific marketing mix instrument or hampered by it. Since in actual applications several specific instruments contribute to the fulfillment of all four generic functions, coordination becomes of the utmost importance. The instrumental choices should be made in such a way that the different elements not only reinforce one another's positive effects and neutralize one another's negative effects with regard to one generic function, but also with regard to all four such functions simultaneously. Moreover, each generic function actually consists of a set of specific subfunctions that require specific instrumental goals. Communication, for example, presumes

Table 1 Relative importance of diverse marketing mix instruments in the fulfillment of generic marketing functions

Generic function	Product instruments	Price instruments	Distribution instruments	Communication instruments
Configuration of something valued by the prospective exchange party	xxxxx	x	x	x
Determination of the compensation and sacrifices to be brought by the prospective exchange party	x	xxxxx	x	x
Placing the offer at the disposal of the prospective exchange party	x	x	xxxxx	x
Bringing the offer to the attention of the prospective exchange party and influencing its feelings and preferences about it	x	x	x	xxxxx

Source: van Waterschoot and Van den Bulte (1992: 89)

amongst other things the creation of awareness, knowledge, preference and conviction (see DIRECT MARKETING)

4 The Four P classification

In the development of a new body of thought, such as marketing throughout the twentieth century, the making of listings and taxonomies is one of the primary tasks. Typically, early taxonomies are not developed in *a de*ductive way on strictly logical grounds as a derivation from existing theory (Hunt 1991). Rather they are made in *an in*ductive way. Known elements, supposedly belonging to the investigated population, are inventoried and grouped into classes on the basis of their similarity. In this way early writers on the marketing mix tried to itemize the large number of controllable demand impinging instruments. Frey (1956) and Borden (1964) adopted a checklist approach. Other authors developed more succinct and convenient classifications that could be easily memorized (Frey 1956; Howard 1957; McCarthy 1960; Lazer and Kelly 1962). Of the many developed schemata, only McCarthy's has survived and has become the 'dominant design' or 'received view'.

The McCarthy typology has become known as the Four P classification of the marketing mix, since it distinguishes four classes of items under four headings beginning with the letter P: Product, Price, Place and Promotion. Although McCarthy only named these classes without defining them, they roughly correspond to the four previously mentioned generic marketing mix functions.

The first class contains instruments that mainly – although not exclusively – aim at the satisfaction of the prospective exchange party's needs such as product variety, product quality, design, features, brand name, packaging, sizes, services, warranties and return.

The second class comprises instruments that mainly – although not exclusively – fix the size and the means of payment exchanged for the goods or services. Examples are the list price, discounts, allowances, the payment period and credit terms.

The third class holds instruments that mainly – although not exclusively – determine the intensity and manner of how the goods or services will be made available. Examples are the choice of distribution channels, the coverage of existing outlets and location of outlets.

The fourth class of instruments in the McCarthy typology is a hybrid one. Whereas the three previous classes nicely correspond to the three cited generic functions, McCarthy's fourth P only roughly corresponds to the fourth generic function. Indeed this fourth P is typically subdivided into four classes, of which only the first three exclusively encompass instruments that mainly aim to bring the offer to the attention of the prospective exchange party and to influence feelings and preferences about it. These three subclasses are Advertising, Personal Selling and Publicity. Traditional definitions are the following:

> Advertising: any paid form of nonpersonal presentation and promotion of ideas, goods, or services by an identified sponsor.
>
> Personal Selling: oral presentation in a conversation with one or more prospective purchasers for the purpose of making sales.
>
> Publicity: nonpersonal stimulation of demand for a product, service, or business unit by planting commercially significant news about it in a published medium or obtaining favorable presentation of it upon radio, television, or stage that is not paid for by the sponsor.
>
> (Alexander 1960)

The fourth P of the McCarthy typology, however, also encompasses a residual fourth subcategory, which serves as a catch-all to host all marketing mix instruments that do not find a place in any other category. In contrast with the three previously mentioned typical communication subclasses, only the fourth subcategory of McCarthy's fourth P consists of promotion instruments in the strict sense of the word. A traditional description of this (sales) promotion category is the following:

> Those marketing activities, other than personal selling, advertising and publicity, that stimulate consumer purchasing and dealer effectiveness, such as displays, shows and exhibitions, demonstrations, and various nonrecurrent selling efforts not in the ordinary routine.
>
> (Alexander 1960)

5 The peculiar nature of promotion instruments

A fundamental drawback to the traditional promotion concept, however, is its negative definition. Instead of defining promotion in a residual way it should be defined positively. More recent marketing literature contains sufficient elements to compose such a definition. One important view is that promotion concerns activities directed at inducing potential exchange partners to consummate immediate exchange. For example, a price reduction may cause a customer to take immediate action, whereas the same customer may hesitate or postpone his or her purchase in its absence. Another important view concerns the non-routine, short-duration element of promotion instruments. It stresses that a price reduction can be considered as promotional to the extent that this reduction is of a temporary nature. In fact, the first view is structurally linked to the second. If people are not convinced of the exceptionality of a price reduction it becomes unlikely that it will provoke an immediate purchase.

Interpreting promotion instruments as inducements implies that they are not identical to the communication category of the marketing mix. Communication creates awareness, provides knowledge and motivates use desires, whereas promotion amplifies and accelerates the decision to buy. Persuasive communication is used to overcome a lack of awareness or appreciation (information barriers), or a lack of credibility (credibility barriers), or even to change the preference structure of prospects (Beem and Shaffer 1981). In contrast to these three 'barriers to wanting', promotion tackles 'barriers to acting' such as physical and psychological inertia barriers, risk barriers, or competitive barriers from close substitutes (Beem and Shaffer 1981: 16, 18).

Notwithstanding the previous observation, some communication instruments also possess a genuinely promotional nature, such as supermarket advertisements which announce a temporary price discount. In other words, there is a typical overlap between some promotional tools and some communication instruments. A similar overlap occurs between other promotional tools and the rest of the marketing mix. Whereas trade shows and exhibitions are clearly of a communicative nature, other typical promotions are not. Coupons, for instance, essentially represent a specific form of price reduction. Economy packs form another promotion example where communication is not the most important issue, but rather where the product aspect is, since economy packs offer a larger quantity of the product at the original price. In the same vein trade promotions typically

Table 2 An improved classification of the marketing mix

Marketing mix	Product mix	Price mix	Distribution mix	Communication mix		
				Mass communication promotion mix	Personal communication mix	Publicity mix
Basic mix	Basic product mix Instruments that mainly aim at the satisfaction of the prospective exchange party's needs.	Basic price mix Instruments that mainly fix the size and the way of payment exchanged for the goods or services.	Basic distribution mix Instruments that mainly determine the intensity and manner of how the goods or services will be made available.	Basic mass communication mix Non-personal communication efforts that mainly aim at announcing the offer or maintaining the awareness and knowledge about it: evoking or maintaining favourable feelings and removing barriers to wanting.	Basic personal communication mix Personal communication efforts that mainly aim at announcing the offer or maintaining awareness and knowledge about it; evoking or maintaining favourable feelings and removing barriers to wanting.	Basic publicity mix Efforts that aim at inciting a third party (persons and authorities) to favourable communication about the offer.
	e.g. product characteristics options, assortment, brand name, packaging, quantity, factory guarantee.	e.g. list price, usual terms of payment, usual discounts, terms of credit, long-term savings campaigns.	e.g. different types of distribution channels, density of the distribution system, trade relation mix (policy of margins, terms of delivery, etc.), merchandising advice.	e.g. theme advertising in various media, permanent exhibitions, certain forms of sponsorship.	e.g. amount and type of selling, personal remunerations.	e.g. press bulletins, press conferences, tours by journalists.

Source: Van Watershoot and Van den Bulte (1992: 90)

Table 2 cotinued An improved classification of the marketing mix

Promotion mix	Product promotion mix	Price promotion mix	Distribution promotion mix	Mass communication promotion mix	Personal communication promotion mix	Publicity promotion mix
	Supplementary group of instruments that mainly aim at inducing immediate overt behaviour by strengthening the basic product mix during relatively short periods of time.	Supplementary group of instruments that mainly aim at inducing immediate overt behaviour by strengthening the basic price mix during relatively short periods of time.	Supplementary group of instruments that mainly aim at inducing immediate overt behaviour by strengthening the basic distribution mix during relatively short periods of time.	Supplementary group of instruments that mainly aim at inducing immediate overt behaviour by strengthening the basic mass communication mix during relatively short periods of time.	Supplementary group of instruments that mainly aim at inducing immediate overt behaviour by strengthening the basic personal communication mix during relatively short periods of time.	Supplementary group of instruments that mainly aim at inducing immediate overt behaviour by strengthening the basic publicity mix during relatively short periods of time.
	e.g. economy packs, 3-for-the-price-of-2 deals; temporary luxury options on a car at the price of its standard model.	e.g. exceptionally favourable price, end-of-season sales, exceptionally favourable terms of payment and credit, short-term savings campaigns, temporary discounts, coupons.	e.g. extra point of purchase material, trade promotions such as buying allowances, sales contests; temporary increase of the number of distribution points.	e.g. action advertising, contests, sweepstakes, samples, premiums, trade shows or exhibitions.	e.g. temporary demonstrations, salesforce promotions such as salesforce contests.	e.g. all measures to stimulate positive publicity about a sales promotion action.

Source: Van Watershoot and Van den Bulte (1992: 90)

intensify the distribution effort, without communication being the major aspect (see SALES PROMOTION).

6 The Four P classification revisited

The very existence of promotion instruments indicates that the list of four generic mix functions described earlier is incomplete. Direct inducement or provocation is in some situations a necessary condition for the exchange to take place. Hence, promotion represents a 'situational' or 'complementary' marketing function (van Waterschoot and Van den Bulte 1992: 88). As a result, McCarthy's Four P classification is improved by systematically and explicitly combining the idea of four generic marketing mix functions, with a 'situational' or 'complementary' marketing mix function (see Table 2).

The columns of Table 2 represent a classification of the marketing mix variables on the basis of the generic function they primarily fulfil. Vertically, the marketing mix variables are subdivided according to the criterion of whether the instruments are basic to the consummation of an offer or whether those instruments are more complementary. This supplementary mix actually contains the elements fulfilling the previously mentioned 'situational' function that is usually found in the promotion mix. However, this mix is now defined in a positive and not in a residual manner and not limited to the narrow domain of communication instruments, but spread out over all the major classes of marketing instruments. The promotional mix can be positively defined as follows:

> [The promotional mix] contains demand-impinging instruments that have no power of themselves but can, during relatively short periods of time, complement and sustain the basic instruments of the marketing mix (namely product, price, distribution, and communication) for the purpose of stimulating prospective exchange partners (commonly referred to as target market(s)) to a significant degree of desirable forms of immediate, overt behaviour.

(van Waterschoot and Van den Bulte 1992: 89)

Desirable forms of immediate, overt behaviour usually consist of straight buying. However, other forms of overt – or visible – behaviour also exist, such as information gathering. Many promotional activities and actions in consumer goods marketing in general and in direct marketing in particular (see DIRECT MARKETING) are aimed not at stimulating immediate purchase, but at moving the prospect one step forward in the buying process. Free sampling, clearly a promotional activity, is used to induce trial use, not buying (see sales promotion).

7 Explications and extensions

Throughout the years a number of alternative marketing mix classifications have been formulated, often to reflect the peculiarities of a specific field of application. In most instances this adaptation was realized by adding one or more Ps to McCarthy's mnemonic Four P list. In instances where an explication of a subcategory of instruments is concerned, such an addition – although conceptually not strictly necessary – is defensible on pedagogical grounds. In instances where an extension outside the boundaries of the marketing mix is concerned, no conceptual justification exists. Despite the indisputable relevance of the managerial issues behind the added Ps, the extension of the mnemonic list mainly serves as an eyecatcher. In further instances, the proposed names of the new categories are not appropriate as a result of the obligatory P. The subsequent paragraphs summarize the main examples of such explications and extensions.

Occasionally, a separate fifth P is added to denote People, Personnel or Personal selling. In this way a collective noun is provided to stress the importance of all types of selling and servicing efforts which are being carried out by any person within the organization (see PERSONAL SELLING AND SALES MANAGEMENT). In applications where sales efforts are of a typically high strategic value – as for example in the case of service marketing – no fundamental objection can be made to this explication, although there is no conceptual necessity since the provision of services belongs to the P of the (service) Product, and sales efforts form part of the 'P' of Communication. In retail marketing, as well as the supplementary P of People a further P is often added to denote the Presentation of merchandise as well as the store layout. Again an explication is involved that is defensible on pedagogical grounds, but which is not necessary from a conceptual or classificatory point of view, since the generically rooted Four Ps also hold these elements.

In service marketing Ps have also been added to represent Participants, Physical evidence and Process (Booms and Bitner 1981)(see MARKETING OF SERVICES). The Participants in a service marketing situation can significantly improve or harm the quality of the execution of service. However, the activities of the personnel carrying out the service conceptually belong to the first P of Product, encompassing all instruments which aim primarily at want fulfillment. Insofar as the clients are meant by Participants, the addition becomes conceptually incorrect, since the marketing mix groups demand impinging elements and not the actual demand constituting elements. The Physical environment where the service is provided, together with tangible elements which are used to support the service, obviously influences demand. Where these elements are under the control of the marketer, they form part of the Product or Place instruments. If these elements cannot be controlled by the manager, they are by definition not marketing mix variables. The same remark also holds for the procedural elements of servicing, meaning that a separate P for Process is not really necessary.

With regard to the persuasion of the public outside the most typical target groups, Kotler (1986) has introduced the concept of 'megamarketing', denoting the art of supplying benefits to parties other than target consumers and intermediaries like agents, distributors and dealers – parties such as governments, labour unions and other interest groups that can block profitable entry into a market. Specific instruments in this context are Public Relations and Power. Public relations try to influence public opinion, mainly by means of masscommunication techniques (see PUBLIC RELATIONS). Power on the other hand addresses itself to 'influential industry officials, legislators, and government bureaucrats to enter and operate in the target market, using sophisticated lobbying and negotiating skills in order to achieve the desired response from the other party without giving away the house' (Kotler 1986: 120). The term power is not appropriate in this instance. Power refers to the ability of the marketer to get some other party (consumer, distributor, government) to do what the latter would not otherwise have done (buy, search for information, give a permit) (Stern and El-Ansary 1992: 268). Marketing mix instruments – if properly combined – are capable of developing a certain amount of power. Calling one instrument category, applied in a specific context, Power, implies a linguistic distortion to make the instrument fit a mnemonic row.

8 Criticism of the marketing mix concept

In spite of the immediate and widespread acceptance of the marketing mix concept, it has been criticized in several respects. Van den Bulte (1991) summarized these criticisms under nine headings. The following reflects Van den Bulte's inventory, together with our personal assessment.

The marketing mix concept is accused of applying to micro issues only, because it takes the stance of only one exchange party, namely the seller or the 'cake mixer' or the 'channel captain' rather than the consumer or society at large. Indeed, the channel captain perspective typifies the marketing discipline as a whole, except for those fields where social goals dominate from the outset, as in the case of true charity marketing. The marketing mix concept cannot be criticized in this respect, since the usefulness of a known and classified set of demand impinging instruments – even if suggested by the specific metaphoric expression – is not by its own nature limited to channel captain applications, but applies to any exchange situation.

A second criticism concerns the concept's limited managerial use in an organizational context, because of its attributed 'lack of attention to the internal tasks of the marketing function, like disseminating information to all people involved in or affected by marketing activities, human resources management, and developing incentive and control systems' (Van den Bulte 1991: 11). Also this point of criticism results from unrealistic expectations about a basic and powerful but at the same time limited concept. The marketing mix concept has not been developed to encompass guidelines for internal organization and communication. On the other hand, a clearly defined and classified set of demand impinging instruments contributes to a sound organization of commercial efforts. The existence of the concept and the corresponding classification should be seen as a necessary, but at the same time insufficient, condition for theoretical and practical development.

Valuable research has been conducted regarding interactions and interdependencies between mix variables. The mix concept is criticized because the hypotheses cannot be derived from the metaphor itself. This criticism can again be countered quite easily: the mere inventory of a set of instruments cannot be supposed to encompass a theory about the interactions amongst them. The classification of these instruments, however, to some extent, can. Empirical investigation and theory building rely heavily on the way such instruments are classified. The classification itself, however, cannot be anything more than a solid tool for theory building and empirical investigation, which it cannot replace.

A fourth point of criticism accuses the marketing mix concept of a mechanistic view on markets. The market is often described in terms of response curves, depending on a certain 'parameter' or 'marketing decision variable' or on the entire mix. In this way the optimization problem upon which the concept of the marketing mix focuses is solved. Modelling the relationship between commercial instruments and market response serves analytical and forecasting purposes. Forgetting the limitations and assumptions of the model or technique represents an undeniable risk, which cannot be attributed to the marketing mix as a concept. Models – whether they are of a stimulus-response or of an interactive type – suppose a sound marketing mix concept and classification, but the characteristics of the former should not be attributed to the latter and vice versa.

A fifth point of criticism comes very close to the previous one. The concept is accused of having a one-way (stimulus–response) character, which impedes marketing from shifting its focus from exchange as an isolated act towards the richer concept of exchange relationships (see RELATIONSHIPS AND NETWORKS). The marketing mix concept in no way conflicts with an idea of interaction. Indeed, its instruments and their categorization perfectly fit such approaches, as they also fit the idea of an exchange relationship. An exchange relationship supposes, for example, a more pronounced quality and service accent than a mere one-time exchange.

The concept's poor market orientation also follows from the suggested view of the customer as someone to whom something is done – by the cake mixer – and not as someone for whom something is done. The stimulus–response approach that is attributed to the marketing mix is at the same time criticized for proposing to lump individuals into a market of homogeneous respondents. Presence or absence, as well as degree of market orientation, depends on factors like market structure, power balance between parties, organizational structures and procedures, personal attitudes, corporate culture, business mission and business goals. However, to blame the mix concept for causing a lack of market orientation is intellectually not correct. This basic, but by its very nature limited, concept is a factual device in any market approach.

The mix concept is also criticized for implying a view of the firm (or any exchange-seeking party in general) – perhaps suggested to some people by the picture of the independent cake mixer – as being a rather self-sufficient social unit having access to a considerable resource base (see STRATEGIC ALLIANCES AND SUPPLIER PARTNERSHIPS). Except for manufacturer–distributor links, the concept would remove resource dependency between social units. As a result the different bridging strategies – such as bargaining contracting, cooption, joint programmes, licensing, integration, trade associations and government action – are issues that would not be taken into consideration. Once again this is an example of unjustified criticism, resulting from unrealistic expectations. Also here the argument can be turned round. Interorganizational 'bridges' will influence the specific marketing mix choice. As such an argument is given not against but in favour of a clear concept and classification.

A further point of criticism concerns the concept's supposed reactive attitude towards the environment.

> Traditionally, marketing mix proponents have myopically considered the transactional environment to be composed of customers and dealers only, putting all other social units into the category 'contextual',

hence lumping them together into faceless environmental forces. Thus blinding themselves, they have not taken into consideration the fact that the links with some transaction-environmental units and the activities these deploy can be changed through lobbying, legal action, public relations, issue advertising, strategic partnering and so on. Finding a way to control or influence variables that were previously considered to be beyond discretion, is often the cornerstone of great marketing creativity and the gateway to superior profitability.

(Van den Bulte 1991: 18)

This citation contains a major and well-expressed lesson in marketing management. Marketing practice and marketing theory have been putting too much emphasis on their traditional public, but there is no logic in blaming the mix concept for it.

Finally, critics accuse the mix concept of possessing a mechanistic and rational-economic neoclassical view of markets and firms, and stripping out the institutional and social supports to market processes such as attraction, trust, friendship, power and interdependency. As a result the marketing mix would be 'rendered impotent before many strategic management problems' (Van den Bulte 1991: 20). In this case the criticism also concerns actual marketing practice as well as the conceptual development that has taken place at an instrumental, tactical and strategic level; the criticism does not hit the mix concept itself.

9 Conclusion

The mix metaphor has gained usage spectacularly quickly as a result of its expressiveness, liveliness, compactness and therefore memorability. Equally imaginative has been McCarthy's pragmatic grouping of the instruments. His Four P classification also received acceptance speedily and easily, presumably as a result of its strong mnemonic appeal. The Four Ps have even become synonymous with the marketing mix. The mnemonic row, however, has too often been used as a means of explication of submixes or in order to draw the attention to marketing aspects that were not always mix issues. Over the years the limitations of the original mnemonic approach have become apparent, amongst other things as a result of the increased importance of promotion instruments in marketing practice. Consequently, the Four P classification, with its inherent negatively defined Promotion category within the communication family, has been contested by many authors. Its adaptation, based on modern insight into promotion, significantly improves the original scheme.

The marketing mix concept itself is as elementary, powerful, and at the same time limited in marketing thinking as the alphabet is in the use and development of language. It is therefore unjustifiable to blame the mix concept for the peculiarities of the overall discipline. In the same way the concept cannot be blamed for the limitations of the metaphor, which contributed so significantly to its popularity and understanding. The marketing mix concept forms a fundamental building block in theory and practice. A clearly defined, named and classified concept is a necessary, but at the same time insufficient, condition for successful theory building and practical implementation. Marketing theory should concentrate its attention on measuring, explaining and predicting the isolated as well as the combined effects of the mix instruments, as a solid basis for actual practice in diverse fields and circumstances.

WALTER VAN WATERSCHOOT
UFSIA UNIVERSITY OF ANTWERP

Further reading

(References cited in the text marked *)

* Ackoff, R.L. (1981) *Creating the Corporate Future: Plan or Be Planned For*, New York: John Wiley.
* Alexander, R.S. (1960) *Marketing Definitions: A Glossary of Marketing Terms*, Chicago: American Marketing Association.
* Beem, E.R. and Shaffer, H.J. (1981) *Triggers to Action – Some Elements in a Theory of Promotional Inducement* (Report 81–106), Cambridge, MA: Marketing Science Institute.
* Booms, B.H. and Bitner, M.J. (1981) 'Marketing strategies and organization structures for service firms', in Donnelly, J.H. and George, W.R. (eds), *Marketing of Services*, Chicago: American Marketing Association proceedings.
* Borden, N. (1964) 'The concept of the marketing mix', *Journal of Advertising Research* 4: 2–7.
* Frey, A.W. (1956) *The Effective Marketing Mix: Programming for Optimum Results*, Hanover,

NH: The Amos Tuck School of Business Administration, Dartmouth College.
* Houston, F.S. and Gassenheimer, J.B. (1987) 'Marketing and exchange', *Journal of Marketing* 51: 3–18.
* Howard, J.A. (1957) *Marketing Management: Analysis and Decisions*, Homewood, IL: Richard D. Irwin, Inc.
* Hunt, S.D. (1991) *Modern Marketing Theory: Critical Issues in the Philosophy of Marketing Science*, Cincinnati, OH: South-Western Publishing Company.
* Kotler, P. (1972) 'A generic concept of marketing', *Journal of Marketing* 36: 46–54.
* Kotler, P. (1986) 'Megamarketing', *Harvard Business Review* 64: 117–24.
* Kotler, P. and Levy, S.L. (1971) 'Demarketing, yes, demarketing', *Harvard Business Review* 49: 71–80.
* Lazer, W. and Kelly, E.J. (1962) *Managerial Marketing: Perspectives and Viewpoints*, rev edn, Homewood, IL: Richard D. Irwin, Inc.
* McCarthy, E.J. (1960) *Basic Marketing: A Managerial Approach*, Homewood, IL: Richard D. Irwin, Inc.
  Mason, J.B., Mayer, M.L. and Wilkinson, J.B. (1993) *Modern Retailing: Theory and Practice*, 6th edn, Homewood, IL: Richard D. Irwin, Inc.

Payne, A. (1993) *The Essence of Services Marketing*, London: Prentice-Hall International
* Stern, L. and El-Ansary, A. (1992) *Marketing Channels*, London: Prentice-Hall International.
* Van den Bulte, C. (1991) *The Concept of the Marketing Mix Revisited: A Case Analysis of Metaphor in Marketing Theory and Management*, Ghent, Belgium: The Vlerick School of Management, University of Ghent.
* van Waterschoot, W. and Van den Bulte, C. (1992) 'The 4P classification of the marketing mix revisited', *Journal of Marketing* 56: 83–93.

See also: CHANNELS OF DISTRIBUTION; CONSUMER BEHAVIOUR; DIRECT MARKETING; ENVIRONMENTAL ANALYSIS; GREEN MARKETING; MARKETING RESEARCH; MARKET SEGMENTATION; ORGANIZATIONAL BUYING BEHAVIOUR; PERSONAL SELLING AND SALES MANAGEMENT; PUBLIC RELATIONS; RELATIONSHIPS AND NETWORKS; SALES PROMOTION; STRATEGIC ALLIANCES; STRATEGIC MARKETING FOR NON-PROFIT ORGANIZATIONS; THE ECONOMICS BASIS OF MARKETING

Product policy

1. **What is a product?**
2. **The product life-cycle**
3. **The growth vector**

Overview

Central to the marketing concept is the notion of an exchange between two parties which delivers satisfaction to both. The media through which this theoretical, mutual satisfaction is derived are those products and services offered by the supplier to the customer. Thus, products and services must be seen as central to marketing strategy if they are to deliver satisfaction to the customer and profit to the supplier. However, two factors affect this issue: the need to manage the exchange relationships over time and the nature of customer satisfaction. These two factors are inter-related in that the needs and wants of customers are themselves dynamic, not static. As customers and markets become familiar with the array of products and services available in a given product-market, their needs evolve, become more sophisticated and discerning. It follows, therefore, that the nature of the exchange (product and/or service in return for money) will also have to change. This changing complexion of products and services offered is the core of 'product policy'. If no change occurs, the product or service offered will quickly become out of tune with customer requirements and will meet with less success. This contention reveals the link between product policy and marketing strategy since the adaptation of the products and services offered by companies to customers to effect long-term growth and profitability is what is understood to be the essence of marketing strategy. Consequently, marketing strategy and product policy are intimately related, and address the central question of managing the firm's future.

While the optimal approach to product policy may well be to start with customer needs and then to develop products and services as 'bundles of satisfaction', few companies, apart from business start-ups are faced with such a *carte blanche* on which to design their offerings. The reality is that of having to manage existing products for maximum profits which can then be invested into the design and development of products and services of the future. In other words, firms must begin with their current resource base – current manufacturing capabilities and technologies, current management skills, current products and customers.

Accordingly, the objective of this chapter is to explore the key issues involved in constructing a product policy which delivers 'bundles of satisfaction' to customers and delivers profits for reinvestment and renewal for the future.

1 What is a product?

Formal definitions of what a product is tend to agree that a product is the focus of an exchange process wherein customers exchange cash for satisfaction. In order to explicate the levels on which this satisfaction may or may not be delivered, Kotler uses a five-level product concept comprising:

- *core benefit*: the fundamental service or benefit being purchased.
- *generic product*: the material properties which deliver the core benefit.
- *the augmented product*: the 'package' which includes additional services and benefits that distinguish the company's offering from competitors.
- *the potential product*: the augmentations and transformations that the product might endure in the future. (Kotler 1989).

Viewed this way, a complete specification of a product should cover at least the first four of these levels. Saren and Tzokas (1994,1998) have questioned the utility of this view of the product in a way which is particularly relevant for our discussion of the link between user needs and product concepts. The basic criticism is that conceptualizations of the product, such as Kotler's, attempt to define the product in isolation from the customer-supplier context.

It regards the product as an autonomous unit which can be de-constructed and understood in its basic elements. But this is fundamentally wrong since the mere understanding of the existence of a product for consumption is realized, not by its material nature (which sometimes need not be there at all), but by its symbolic meaning that the society and individual consumers and producers have ascribed to it by means of culture, use or experience and their interaction with each other.

(Saren and Tzokas 1994: 904)

Instead, the authors propose that a product is the outcome of a 'continuous tri-partite signification process' between buyers, suppliers and the object. This outcome is the pluri-signified product shown in Figure 1.

Such a conceptualization offers potential for re-defining the role of the product in competitive marketing strategy by encouraging firms to seek competitive advantage within the 'dynamic process of interaction among the buyer, supplier and the object' (Saren and Tzokas 1998: 458). Focused more towards the nature of relationships firms establish and maintain, the pluri-signified conceptualization of the product has much to offer within the evolving paradigm of relationship marketing.

Another way of understanding the concept of the product is through the medium of product classification schemes.

Melvin T Copeland (1923) made one of the earliest contributions to the classification of consumer goods. He proposed that consumer goods could be classified as shopping goods, convenience goods and speciality goods. These were defined formally by the American Marketing Association's Committee on Definition (1948) as follows.

- *Convenience goods*: Those consumer goods which the customer purchases frequently, immediately, and with the minimum of effort. (e.g. snacks, bus journey, newspapers).
- *Shopping goods*: Those consumer goods which the customer, in the process of selection and purchase, characteristically compares on such bases as suitability, quality, price and style (e.g. cosmetics, PCs, health club).
- *Speciality goods*: Those consumer goods on which a significant group of buyers are habitually willing to make a special purchasing effort (e.g. house, car, holiday).

Copeland's Schemata has been subject to much comment and criticism since it first appeared but it remains a remarkably robust conceptualization which has been found to be operationally useful. Bucklin (1963) seeks to synthesize some of the criticisms of Copeland by introducing the notion that consumer buying is a form of problem solving which enables one to distinguish two broad categories, shopping goods and non-shopping goods. 'Shopping goods are

Figure 1 The pluri-signified product
Source: Saren, M.A.J. and Tzokas, N. (1994) *Proceedings of the Annual Conference of the European Marketing Academy*: 911.

those for which the consumer *regularly* formulates a new solution to his need each time it is aroused. They are goods whose suitability is determined through search before the consumer commits himself to each purchase'. By contrast non-shopping goods are those 'products for which the consumer is both willing and able to use stored solutions to the problem of finding a product to answer a need ... non-shopping goods have purchase determinants which do not change, or are perceived as changing inconsequentially, between purchases.'

Bucklin emphasizes that the underlying objective of the attempt to classify goods in terms of consumer buying is the development of marketing strategies, with specific advice as to which strategy should be used under what circumstances. However, Bucklin also points to 'manifold barriers that lie in the way of attempting to validate any classification of goods theory' which probably accounts for the limited attention the theory has received in marketing literature. Despite the lack of theoretical validation, and in common with many other current marketing ideas and techniques, the theory is widely referred to in writings intended 'to instruct practitioners in the profession', providing, as it does, a framework for the analysis of marketing problems, at least at rudimentary level, and suggesting where students might look to devise answers to marketing strategy problems. On the other hand, classifications do little to explain the ways in which products might contribute to competitive success, which is central to understanding marketing strategy.

At the heart of competitive marketing strategy are products.

The strategic choices expounded by Porter (1980) to achieve competitive advantage are cost leadership and differentiation. The former is to offer a comparable product to the marketplace at a price which is lower than, or near to that of the competition, based on lowest costs in an industry. On the other hand, a strategy of differentiation aims to offer a superior product to the customer. It follows that a necessary condition for competitive success is that one's own product is better than that of one's competitors. Overall, 'better' reflects a combination of both objective and subjective factors as implied by Rogers' (1960) definition of 'relative advantage'. In most cases the objective characteristics of a product are a *sine qua non* of the intending consumers' willingness even to consider it. However, the value attached to particular objective features of a product will vary significantly according to the intending users' attitudes, knowledge, discretionary purchasing power, etc. In other words, they are *situation specific*. They also *change over time*.' Central to the differentiation strategy, therefore, is a continuous understanding of the factors influencing the intending user's choice among products on offer, both now and in the future.

Each of these two basic competitive strategies have products at their centre. The cost leadership strategy depends on offering standardized (usually no-frill) products to customers who have a *need* for a particular type of product. The differentiated strategy depends on the existence of groups of customers who have different *needs* of the product for which they are prepared to pay. A third competitve strategy involves choosing one major market segment and concentrating efforts in order to tailor the company's offering closely to its particular needs, which may be for low-cost or differentiated products. This element of strategy really defines the scope of the company's market definition.

Virtually all product categories contain examples of these two strategies, where, basic low-cost functionality versions of product co-exist with others displaying varying degrees of added-value. Personal organizers range from simple diaries which cost around £10 to palm-top computer-like models, featuring modem links, print facilities, diary, word-processing and so on, retailing at over £300. Base products are stripped of added value and are sold purely on the basis of price and often the past performance of the company.

It would, however, be misleading to portray all product strategy as the choice between differentiation and low-cost. Developments in production technology have led to the possibility of 'mass customization', where a low-cost strategy for production does not exclude very detailed levels of customization, even in mass consumer markets.

The question of the relative success rates of these strategies ultimately depends on whether the target markets perceive the extras supplied by some companies as real benefits which deliver satisfaction or prefer the low-price-no-extras option. Thus the task is to define

The marketing mix

products in terms of customer benefits. Manufacturing companies can choose among a battery of product characteristics in order to define their product range. These characteristics are specific in terms of the raw materials and technologies used in their production. Yet management has to understand which of these characteristics are considered most important by the customer if it is to produce a competitive range of products or run the risk of devoting time to the creation differences between competitive products through service and promotional effort on the assumption that small differentiating features will be considered of value to customers.

The home laundry market in major developed economies serves as a prime example of this. Washing powders are produced in 'traditional' and 'concentrated' form. There are detergent- and soap-based powders as well as both biological and enzyme-free brands. There are 'environmentally friendly' and more harmful products, as well as original and replacement packaging. In addition, there are powders developed to preserve brightness of colour in washed clothes. There are, on top of this diversity, liquid versions of most of the major brands, sold complete with their dispensing systems which are independent of the design of washing machines. Some liquids and powders have built-in fabric softeners, while an entire range of independent fabric softeners is also marketed by the industry's main players – in both standard and concentrated form. In addition, one manufacturer also markets a fabric softener for use in tumble driers.

How much control can be exerted over this range and how easy or profitable it is to develop or sustain these differences are important questions. If differences can be created through developing user-relevant product characteristics, then the constant need to invent producer-defined differences will be reduced. In other words, product policy is an activity which must focus beyond the invention of differences in products which merely leads to product proliferation of the kind described as applying to the home laundry market, above. Product policy ignores changing markets and technologies at its peril (Bennet and Cooper 1981; Hayes and Abernethy 1980). Furthermore, it is equally important that companies review their product offerings to remove products which interfere with the task of delivering products attuned to user needs. This requires attention to the job of deleting products – or replacing them – and has become an important element in the competitive strategies of Procter and Gamble, in both the skincare and babycare categories, and Unilever in the liquid detergent category.

Having established that product policy is at the heart of dynamic competitive strategy, the remainder of this entry is devoted to describing tools used to aid the business of managing a firm's product strategy.

2 The product life-cycle

The concept of the product life-cycle is depicted in Figure 2, where the four phases of introduction, growth, maturity and decline in terms of sales over time can be seen.

One of the earliest exponents of this concept was Theodore Levitt, whose 1960 article 'Marketing myopia' in the *Harvard Business Review* describes the way in which product life is limited by the emergence of new ways of delivering satisfaction of market need(s) provided by

Figure 2 The product life-cycle

alternative products and technologies. The classic product histories he cites are the American railroad, superseded by road and air transport and the Hollywood film industry, threatened by television. The underlying point is that while market needs remain stable, the way in which those needs are satisfied is changed by the development in technologies. Other examples include the replacement of vinyl records with compact discs, minicomputers with PCs, film recording with digital video recording, to name but a few.

The value of the concept of the product life-cycle (PLC) rests in the way it emphasizes that while underlying needs may not change (transportation, communication, entertainment, for example), current products will not always satisfy customers' needs. Therefore, although precise specification of where a product is situated on a PLC curve may not be possible, it is a certainty that at some point, the product will penetrate the market, up to the point where a competing product satisfies the need better or more cheaply, or until a new technology renders its mode of need satisfaction obsolete.

In addition, different stages of the life-cycle demand different approaches to both products and their marketing, as described below.

At the *introduction stage*, a product will require heavy investment, largely in the form of the new product launch and promotional campaign. In addition, despite the fact that the launch of the new product may be confined to one or two variations, design and development will continue in order to keep the advantages of the new product ahead of the competition, demanding more investment.

During the *growth stage* the drive for improvement will increase quality and technical performance differentiation of competitive products. Promotion costs are still high, but as sales are growing quickly at this stage, the volume sold, combined with the improvements to manufacturing, marketing and distribution that accompany the growing experience of the product, the profitability of the product continues to increase.

At the *maturity stage*, a company may market several product variations, which are differentiated in superficial, rather than fundamental ways. With the product type now well diffused through the market, many customers have tried the early versions of a product, and, learning from this what improvements are required, are ready to trade up to enhanced versions. Although the manufacturing cost base for mature products is likely to be based on efficiency, overall product profitability may begin to get squeezed as the market, familiar with the product, begins to seek out, not only improved products, but ones at a lower price. Manufacturer experience, coupled with incipient overcapacity in a given industry make the lower price achievable.

At the *decline stage* product sales begin to fall away. Decreasing values make larger capital investment in the product hard to sustain. The result is that companies de-invest, in terms of manufacturing plant and product variants. Finally, they will begin to withdraw marketing support, leaving a basic product variation to sell at its own pace to only the most loyal of customers.

The profit curve that accompanies the PLC is shown in Figure 3.

These phases describe the cycle of a product within an industry that is experiencing the same cycle at an aggregate, for example, the 'personal hi-fi' market can be seen to have passed

Figure 3 The profit curve that accompanies the product life-cycle through three of the stages: introduction, growth and maturity, the current phase. The earliest models, were produced by a limited number of suppliers – Sony being the chief developer – and commanded high prices to recoup development costs and capitalize on novelty in the marketplace. Within three to four years, several competitors had entered the market, prices were beginning to fall, while the first companies strove to introduce improvements and extend their first-mover advantages to customers ready to trade up. Thus personal hi-fis that could *record* were launched, versions for use underwater were introduced. In the current mature stage, a host of manufacturers compete, the product's price is a fraction of that of the original models and the early entrants have moved on to new endeavours, such as the Discman, a portable CD-player. This last idea is an important element of the PLC concept as a strategic tool, as it highlights the need to have products each at different stages in their PLC trajectories in order to achieve a balance between the cash-rich and the cash-hungry products. The PLC knowledge of the likely competitive situation of products over time gives clues as to the likely profitability of these products. Thus, managers can see the financial risks of having too many products at any one stage of the life-cycle. The PLC is not without its critics, however.

During the 1960s the product life-cycle (PLC) concept was the subject of considerable research especially at the Harvard Business School and, through it, at the Marketing Science Institute. Among the leading researchers in the field was Robert D Buzzell whose definition of the product life-cycle is still widely cited: 'a generalized model of the sales trend for a product class or category over a period of time, and of related changes in competitive behaviour'. This definition underpins the use of the PLC concept as the organizing principle for the present book as it is believed that the basic model provides a sound foundation for the development of a normative theory of product policy and management.

In adopting this definition and the basic model which describes it (see below) the authors are conscious that PLC, concept and theory, have been widely challenged by many and rejected by some. If we look back to the 1960s it is possible to see how this disparity has arisen. Fundamentally, of course, it is symptomatic of a much larger division within the academic marketing community between those who regard marketing as a social process of great dynamism and complexity and, therefore, unlikely to be amenable to much more than broad generalizations, and those who believe, like Lord Kelvin and the generations of scientists who have followed him, that, if you can't measure it, it doesn't exist. This polarization is evident everywhere and epitomized by the differences between the *Journal of Marketing Research*, which often requires advanced mathematical skills to become intelligible (though still not particularly meaningful for everyone), and the *Harvard Business Review* which is accessible to anyone who can read and highly meaningful for many practitioners.

In the particular case of the PLC, once the generalized model had been articulated, the search began for more refined versions, especially where they could be used predictively. Among the researchers who took up this challenge were Victor Cook and Rolando Polli with the assistance of the Marketing Science Institute (MSI). Scheuing refers to their work in suggesting that while Buzzell's definition 'is principally correct, a few qualifications are in order.' (19XX: 269). Two main qualifications are proposed. First, there are extraneous influences which may distort the picture and Scheuing cites the three singled out by Cook and Polli – population growth (one assumes a declining population would also affect demand), change in the level of personal consumption, and price changes. Second, it is necessary to be clear on the level of aggregation with which one is concerned – product, product line or product category. Unfortunately, there are no universally agreed definitions to ensure these descriptors are used consistently.

In essence the product is the lowest common denominator and may be distinguished in some way from other very similar products. Thus, a number 8, 1 inch screw may be made of steel, stainless steel, brass or plated, have a countersunk or round head with a straight, Phillips or Pozidrive slot and may be self-tapping or not: 48 product permutations for number 8 alone. In the case of consumer goods (and some industrial products too) otherwise near perfect substitute products will be distinguished by their brand name – Coke and Pepsi, Camel and Marlboro, Daz and Surf, M&Ms and Smarties, etc.

A product line consists of a number of related products which are close substitutes for one another but sufficiently distinctive to form a subgroup within the product category which defines all those objects satisfying the same basic needs. Thus, within the product category 'carbonated beverages' the major producers have a variety of flavours – cola, orange, lemon, etc. – which compete head-on with each other at the brand or product level and less directly at the product line level which includes all the different brands.

For predictive and tactical purposes the major interest is at the brand or product level where the action is. But, for strategic and planning purposes, it is the product category which is important. Product categories are based upon distinctive technologies and manufacturing operations and frequently develop specialized channels of distribution and after-sales service. Producers of goods within a product category compete directly with one another and constitute what is commonly referred to as an 'industry'.

In the view of Dhalla and Yupseh (1976) the major limitations of the PLC are both conceptual and pragmatic. The conceptual limitations are: as products are not living, a biological metaphor is inappropriate, since products can be managed to confound any inevitable demise; it is a misplaced concept for brands whose purpose is to extend a product's life by creating consumer loyalty and preference, within which managers can introduce and delete many product varieties; the whole business of fitting sales to a predetermined curve are merely 'sterile exercises in taxonomy'. In short, argue Dhalla and Yupseh (1976) it is a *dependent* variable determined by marketing actions, not an *independent* variable to which marketing plans should be adapted. The practical limitations relate to the fact that there are no clear definitions of the four stages, thwarting the determination of a product's position in its PLC. Hence, the PLC cannot be used as a planning tool. In addition to these criticisms, the PLC ignores the important variables of markets and technologies, both of which have the power to upset a predictable sales pattern. A new technology can wipe out the 'satisfaction' delivered by a previous technology, while markets can quickly turn away from established and preferred products, as in the case of CFC-aerosol sprays where environmental damage caused by CFCs has caused manufacturers across many product markets to develop aerosols without CFCs.

A final shortcoming is the extent to which the PLC is fore-shortened in some industries, leaving no time for either a high-price strategy in the early months or perfecting product quality. In electronics industries, for example, new products have to be introduced at optimal quality and at a price consistent with current applications and solutions. This apparent contradiction is the result of extremely short PLCs, due to the high levels of technological competition.

In view of this criticism, the PLC is a weakened concept. As it underlines the notion that sales growth and profits are finite for any particular product a company offers, the PLC concept remains a valuable indicator of the need for companies constantly to redevelop their products and services in order to ensure a range which contains different products at different stages of their life-cycles.

In providing these perspectives, however, the PLC still has to be considered product-by-product. In reality, all but single-product companies have to consider their products as a collection or portfolio of products within their respective markets. This notion of ranges of products each at different stages in their life-cycles and each requiring different or contributing different amounts of cash does not explicitly recognize the levels of demand in the market, which leads to an incomplete picture of the product's potential. The development of analytical frameworks to take account of these dimensions is epitomized by the Business Portfolio, developed by the Boston Consulting Group.

The Business Portfolio

The idea of the product portfolio is, of course, borrowed from that of investment management, where the investor seeks to acquire a selection of stocks and shares which will meet his needs. Usually these needs will embrace a desire for current income balanced by a desire for capital growth. In turn, investment management theory is derived from the broader field of economics in which the portfolio may

The marketing mix

comprise any kind of asset and the purpose of portfolio analysis is to determine the composition of the ideal or optimum portfolio taking into account basic preferences for fixed or variable yields, short- or long-term returns, etc. It follows that the construction of a product portfolio will depend very much upon the overall objectives of an organization and its attitude towards the basic trade-off between risk and return. Once these have been established it becomes possible to determine what kinds of product are needed to achieve the desired balance.

One of the earlier contributions to the idea of developing a portfolio of products was Peter Drucker's *Harvard Business Review* article 'Managing for Business Effectiveness' in which he proposed that products could be classified as falling into one of six categories:

- 'bread winners' – today's, tomorrow's and yesterday's;
- also-rans;
- failure;
- in-betweens (i.e. capable of becoming successful given appropriate action).

Drucker's classification was based on the contribution of the product to overall profitability. Once diagnosed, the prescription was simple – support today's and tomorrow's breadwinners, 'milk' yesterday's breadwinners, make up your mind on the in-betweens and drop the also-rans and failures. Given that one is able to measure the criterion value (others use profitability, growth, market share, etc. as criteria) then classification is relatively simple.

The business portfolio is reproduced in Figure 4.

Four types of product are identified requiring four different types of marketing strategy. Products experiencing high market share in growth markets are stars: these are competitively attractive products achieving high sales in expanding markets. While they require high investment, both for marketing and redevelopment, they are largely profitable, due to buoyant market conditions. If investment is appropriately managed, these products will become cash cows in the future; if not, they will become dogs when the market is no longer growing. The cash cow is the established product, with a high market share in a market that is no longer growing. Volumes are high in a large market, contributing healthy profits, hence the label. Where market growth is high, but market share is low, considerable investment would be required to turn the product into a star. This is a difficult situation because the low market share does not return much profit for such investment. If improving the competitive position is deemed inappropriate, deletion of the product would be advised. Dogs have weak competitive positions in low-growth markets. They have little chance of increasing market share and are not very profitable. This said, where a dog has a relatively strong position in a *segment* of the market, there may be enough cash return on the product to warrant its classification as a *cash dog* which can be sustained until such time as

	Star	Question mark
Market growth High		
Low	Cash cow	Dog
	High	Low
	Market share	

Figure 4 The business portfolio

returns become unacceptable. The value of using a diagnostic tool such as this is in deciding upon the strategic use of resources. As can be seen, the market share, indicative of competitive position, indicates the amount of investment required and the amount of revenue returned by each type of product in the portfolio. Thus it gives theoretical insights into cash flow. It follows then, that, whatever the strategic orientation the company takes in relation to product policy in terms of differentiation, there must be a balance of cash generating and cash absorbing products in the firm's portfolio.

Like many models designed to facilitate marketing management, the business portfolio has been criticized on a number of counts. First, it ignores many factors in the external environment which have a bearing on product decisions. Technological change, legal requirements, social trends and political pressures all have a bearing on current product performance and new product potential. In addition, there will be instances where, despite high market share and growth, price competition may erode profits. Alternatively, the benefits of scale production that are supposed to accumulate with the 'cash cow' product can be obliterated by production–technology innovations which reduce the costs of short production runs.

As with most management models, it is necessary to treat them, not as prescriptions for strategy and outcome, but as aids to decisions which further understanding of the company's present position and future options.

The Business Portfolio is one of several analytical frameworks that have been developed, in some cases by major companies. For example Shell's 'Directional Policy Matrix' (Figure 5) is based on the company's competitive capabilities and prospects for sector profitability.

Similarly, the Business Assessment Survey, developed with General Electric, uses 'industry attractiveness' and 'business strengths' to develop another three-by-three matrix. These models offer similar ways to structure management's thinking about its current and future products. Ultimately every company could tailor the concept of portfolio analysis to suit their particular industries, products and markets; paying special attention to the dimensions used and their measurement. Further reading on how to design portfolios can be found in Wind and Mahajan (1981).

3 The growth vector

The desirability of a portfolio or range of different products is implicit in the concept of the product life-cycle which emphasizes that, ultimately, all products and the technologies which underlie them will change. It follows that as a result of technological innovation even the most successful of products will become obsolescent and displaced by new and better ways of serving a particular need.

Indeed, as we have seen earlier in this chapter, given that both generic strategies of cost leadership and differentiation depend on innovation, new product and process development

Prospects for sector profitability

		Unattractive	Average	Attractive
Company's competitive capabilities	Weak	Disinvest 9	Phased withdrawal 6 Custodial	Double or quit 3
	Average	Phased withdrawal 8	Custodial 5 Growth	Try harder 2
	Strong	Cash generation 7	Growth 4 Leader	Leader 1

Figure 5 Directional Policy Matrix

have become the basis for competitive activity in all kinds of markets. In turn this has led to an acceleration in the substitution of new products for old and a shortening of product life-cycles.

Faced with such a scenario it is clear that the firm must take active steps to ensure that it does not become a victim of market myopia and continues to grow. Ansoff's Growth Vector Matrix (see below) is a simple summary statement of the strategic options available. In order to survive, let alone grow, the firm needs to pursue simultaneously the strategies of market penetration, (selling more of the existing product to existing users) market development, (finding new customers in new geographic regions with similar needs to one's existing customers) and product development (improving and changing the product both to keep up with the changing wants of one's existing customers and to attract new customers whose needs were not satisfied by the original product).

The growth vector matrix is based upon the consideration of the implications of change in both the product (technology) and the product market.

Table 1 Growth vector matrix

Product market	Present	New
Present	Market penetration	Product development
New	Market development	Diversification

- *Market penetration*: the company increases sales for its present products through aggressive selling, promotion and distribution.
- *Market development*: the company increases sales by taking its present products into new markets.
- *Product development*: the company increases sales by developing improved products for its current markets.
- *Diversification*: the company increases sales by developing new products for new markets.

The first three strategies capitalize on at least one of the current core strategic variables, building upon the common thread of the business. The common thread is composed of:

1. The product-market scope – a specification of the industries where the company consolidates its position.
2. The growth vector – an indication of the direction the company takes in relation to its current product market position.
3. The competitive advantage, an identification of properties of the product-market that will yield strong competitive position.

Of vital importance here is that maintaining a common thread is not a straight choice set against breaking with tradition. Product penetration is the least risky option, while diversification is the most risky. However, as is intimated by portfolio analyses, companies should not regard these as discrete directions but rather as options from which an appropriate mix should be chosen, in order to supply the company with a product portfolio which yields enough profits for future investment in products.

Future perspectives of product policy

Product policy is at the centre of marketing, at both strategic and operational levels. It is intimately related to strategic planning, competitive strategy and positioning. Several concepts useful for managerial guidance in product policy matters have been explained in this chapter, all of which emphasize that in order to survive, firms need to be looking constantly for new products and markets. However, there is a working rule of thumb in marketing which states that it costs five to six times as much money to create a customer as it does to keep one. It is for this reason that in recent years the emphasis in marketing has moved away from the transaction to the relationship. The tendency for customers – individual and organizational – to prefer to repeat purchase from a known and proven source of supply may amount to satisficing behaviour but that is the way most of us behave. In the absence of any compelling evidence to the contrary why would one want to change one's behaviour provided it yields satisfactory results? It is also a well-known fact that many of the best ideas for new products are generated by customers who identify means of improving or changing existing products so that they will perform better. Therefore, the future of product policy must take into consideration the 'shrinking' global market, increased competition and the extent to which new conceptualizations of marketing – and with it – the product might yield new relational frameworks in which to make decisions.

This follows on from the questioning of the extent to which traditional product policy tools as discussed above suffocate the entrepreneurial spirit in management which is so essential to create and maintain vibrant businesses (Hayes and Abernethy 1980). In addition, it has been argued that traditional analytical methods do not focus enough on how to gain competitive advantage (Wensley 1983). In the last analysis there are two essential options to product policy based on the transactional view of products in marketing: make products of a comparable quality to competitors more cheaply and offer them at a lower price, or, make a better product for which a higher price can be demanded. The future of product policy must consider the relationship context of customer–supplier transactions, and, whilst products may still be at the centre, a focal point, they are no longer viewed as discrete objects, but rather like the nucleus surrounded by a series of elements defined in a relational mode. The challenge for those involved in the construction of product policies is therefore to integrate these newer perspectives which are changing the arena of marketing.

SUSAN J. HART
UNIVERSITY OF STRATHCLYDE

Further reading

(References cited in the text marked *)

Ansoff, H.I. (1965) *Corporate Strategy: An Analytical Approach to Busines Policy for Growth and Expansion*, Maidenhead: McGraw-Hill.

Baker, M.J. (1992) *Marketing – An Introductory Text*, 5th edn, Basingstoke: Macmillan.

* Bucklin (1963) 'Retail strategy and the classification of consumer goods', *Journal of Marketing*.

* Copeland MT (1923) 'Relation of consumer's buying habits to marketing methods', *Harvard Business Review* 1: 282–9.

Day, G.S. (1986) *Analysis for Strategic Market Decisions*, West Publishing Co. (General Electric Business Screen).

* Dhalla, G.S. and Yuspeh, S. (1976) 'Forget the product life-cycle concept', *Harvard Business Review* January–Feruary, 102–12.

* Drucker, P. (1963) 'Managing for business effectiveness', *Harvard Business Review* 42.

Garvin, D. (1984) 'What does product quality really mean?', *Sloan Management Review* 26.

* Hayes, R. and Abernethy, W. (1980) 'Managing our way to economic decline', *Harvard Business Review* July–August.

Hedley, B. (1977) 'Boston Consulting Group approach to business portfolio', *Long Range Planning* 10.

King, R. (1987) *Better Designs in Half the Time: Implementing QFD in America*, Methven, MA: GOAL 1 QPC.

* Porter, M.E. (1980) *Competitive Strategy: Techniques for Analysing Industries and Competitiors*, New York: The Free Press.

Rothwell, R., Schott, K., Gardiner, P. and Pick, K. (1983) *Design and the Economy*, London: The Design Council.

* Wensley, R. (1981) 'Strategic marketing: betons, boxes or basics', *Journal of Marketing* 45: 173–82.

* Wind, Y. and Mahajan, V. (1981) 'Desiging product and business portfolios', *Harvard Business Review* 59.

New product development

1. New products: the key to corporate prosperity
2. High odds of failure
3. What are 'new products'?
4. The new product process
5. Go/kill decision points
6. Why new products fail
7. New product success factors
8. Cycle time reduction in product innovation

Overview

Developing new products is frequently vital to a firm's future stability and to maintaining or improving its position in the market. However, it also involves huge risks. The success rate of new products is far from good. This entry considers why there is such a high failure rate and looks at length at the new product development process to discover whether and how the success rate might be improved. It is demonstrated that bringing a new product to market and having it reap financial rewards from it is a combined company effort and not the work of a single department.

1 New products: the key to corporate prosperity

New product development (or product innovations) is one of the riskiest yet most important endeavours of the modern corporation. Countess companies owe their success today to successful new products: Glaxo in the UK with its anti-ulcer pharmaceutical, Zantac; Apple in the USA with its Macintosh computer; Lego in Denmark with its plastic blocks, to name a few. Today new products account for a staggering 40–50 per cent of company sales or turnover. (Here a product is defined as 'new' if it has been on the market by that firm for five years or less.) The figure has been going up dramatically (see Table 1).

New products have a similar impact on corporate profits. In the period 1976–81 new products contributed 22 per cent of corporate profits. This had grown to 33 per cent for the next five-year period (1981–6). By 1995, it was estimated, the figure would rise to 46 per cent. That is, profits from new products accounted for almost half of corporate profits (Page 1991).

R&D expenditures are also impressive: the USA is the largest spender with R&D expenditures amounting to $138 billion annually, or about 2.9 per cent of GDP (in the USA, however, 49 per cent has been for military work) (*R&T Mgmt* 1991). In Japan and Germany R&D spending is also about 2.8 to 2.9 per cent of GDP (but much less is military – private industry finances 71 per cent of Japanese and 64 per cent of German R&D spending).

Certain industries, noted for their growth and profitability in recent decades, spend heavily on R&D. For example, office products and services, including computers, business machines and software averages 7.9 per cent of sales on R&D in the USA; and electrical and electronics products (which includes instruments and semiconductors) averages 5.5 per cent of sales on R&D (*Business Week* 1991). This quickening pace of new prorluct development has a number of drivers (Booz-Allen and Hamilton 1982):

Table 1 Percentage of company sales by new products

Year	Company sales by new products (%)	Source
1976–81	33	Booz-Allen and Hamilton (1982)
1981–6	40	Booz-Allen and Hamilton (1982)
1985–90	42	Page (1991)
1995	52	Page (1991)

1. *Technology advances*: the world's base of technology and know-how increases at an exponential rate, making possible products not even dreamt of a decade or so ago.
2. *Changing customer needs*: marketplaces are also in turmoil, with market needs and wants and customer preferences changing regularly (see MARKETING RESEARCH).
3. *Shortening product life-cycles*: within a few years of launch, sometimes even months, the new product is superseded by a competitive entry (see PRODUCT LIFE-CYCLE MANAGEMENT). A study by A.D. Little shows that product life-cycles have been cut by a factor of about four over the last 50 years (von Braun 1997).
4. *Increased world competition*: globalization of markets has created significant opportunities for the product innovator: the world product targeted at global markets (see GLOBAL MARKETING). It has also intensified competition in every domestic market. Both factors have speeded up the pace of product innovation.

All four drivers are likely to remain, perhaps intensify, in the next decade or two, meaning that product innovation will be even more critical to corporate prosperity in the years ahead.

2 High odds of failure

While product innovation is critical to long-term success, the hard realities are that the great majority of new products are failures: most never make it to market; and those that do face a failure rate on launch somewhere between 25 and 45 per cent. These figures vary, depending on what industry and how one defines a 'new product' and a 'failure'. Some sources cite the failure rate at launch to be as high as 90 per cent. But these figures tend to be unsubstantiated, and are likely to be wildly overstated. According to one thorough review, the true failure rate at launch is about 35 per cent (Crawford 1979).

Note that these failure rate figures only describe new products that were launched, but do not include the majority of new product projects that are killed along the way and long before launch, yet had considerable time and money spent on them. The attrition curve of new products tells the whole story. A recent investigation reveals that for every 11 new product concepts, 3 enter the development phase, 1.3 are launched and only 1 is a commercial success in the marketplace (Page 1991). Further, an estimated 46 per cent of all the resources allocated to product development and commercialization by US firms are spent on products that are cancelled or fail to yield an adequate financial return (Booz-Allen and Hamilton 1982).

3 What are 'new products'?

How does one define a 'new product', 'innovativeness' or 'newness'? There are many different types of new products. Newness or new products can be defined on at least two dimensions:

1. New to the company, in the sense that the firm has never made or sold this type of product before, but other firms might have.
2. New to the market or 'innovative': the product is the first of its kind on the market.

Viewed on a two-dimensional map, six different types or classes of new products have been identified (Booz-Allen and Hamilton 1982):

1. *New-to-the-world products*: these new products are the first of their kind and create an entirely new market. This category represents only 10 per cent of all new products. Well-known examples include the Sony Walkman, the first home VCR (developed by Philips) and 3M's yellow Post-It Notes.
2. *New product lines*: these products, although not new to the marketplace, none the less are quite new to the particular firm. Reckitt & Colman's UK launch of an adult soft drink line, Robinsons Aquiesse, is a new product line to the firm, but in a well-established market with many competitors. About 20 per cent of all new products fit into this category.
3. *Additions to existing product lines*: these are new items to the firm, but fit within an existing product line the firm makes. They may also represent a fairly new product to the marketplace. Hewlett Packard introduced its LaserJet 6, a more advanced version of its laser printers (more features, scalable fonts) within the LaserJet line; its added performance made it somewhat novel or 'new to the market'. Such new items constitute about 26 per cent of all new product launches.

4 *Improvements and revisions to existing products*: these 'not-so-new' products are essentially replacements of existing products in a firm's product line. They offer improved performance or greater perceived value over the 'old' product. These 'new and improved' products also make up 26 per cent of new product launches.
5 *Repositionings*: these are essentially new applications for existing products, and often involve retargeting an old product to a new segment or for a different application (e.g. the repositioning of aspirin or ASA from a headache/fever reliever to a blood clot, stroke and heart attack preventer). Repositionings account for about 7 per cent of all new products.
6 *Cost reductions*: these are the least 'new' of all new product categories. They are new products designed to replace existing products in the line, but yield similar benefits and performance but at lower cost. They represent 11 per cent of all new product launches.

Most firms feature a mixed portfolio of new products. The two most popular types, additions to the line and product improvements or revisions, are common to almost all firms. By contrast, the 'step-out' products – new-to-the-world and new-to-the-firm product lines – constitute only 30 per cent of all new product launches, but represent 60 per cent of the products viewed as 'most successful'. Many firms stay clear of these two more innovative categories: 50 per cent of firms introduce no new-to-the-world products, and another 25 per cent develop no new product lines. This aversion to 'step-out' and higher risk products varies somewhat by industry, with higher technology industries launching proportionately more products that are innovative (Kleinschmidt and Cooper 1991).

4 The new product process

The conception, development and launch of a new product is a process. This new product process begins with an idea and, all going well, culminates with a commercially successful new product in the marketplace.

Figure 1 The five-stage new product process with expenditure breakdown
Source: Booz-Allen and Hamilton (1982: 12)
Notes: 1 14.7 % of all the monies that firms spend on product innovation go to this first stage, idea generation.
2 Of all the money spent on this idea generation, only 34.7% goes to successful new products.
3 In a typical project, only 7.3% of project costs go to this first stage.

The new product process, like most processes in companies, can be flowcharted and described schematically. Although models differ, there are essentially five main stages or phases (see Figure 1). Here is a simplified, somewhat normative, description of the new product process (Booz-Allen and Hamilton 1982; Cooper and Kleinschmidt 1986), complete with a resource allocation breakdown (Cooper 1993).

Idea generation, exploration and screening

This first stage generates the idea and performs an initial culling (screening out) of the poor ideas. Ideas can arrive from many sources, both inside and outside the firm. Common external sources of ideas include: customers and lead users; competitors; trade shows and conferences; trade publications; universities, consultants and private inventors. Internal sources of ideas include company employees, most often in technical positions (R&D, engineering) and marketing/sales positions. Idea generation may be proactive (for example, the result of activities such as holding brainstorming groups with customers or employees, or undertaking preliminary or exploratory technical research in new fields) or simply reactive (ideas are sent in by employees or requests are made by customers). Ideas can also be 'technology push', where a technical discovery (for example in a laboratory) opens up new possibilities: Post-It Notes involved the serendipitous discovery of a glue that would not stick; or 'market pull', where a customer need or an unfilled demand is identified and technical solutions are sought.

The source of new product ideas does not seem to have a major or consistent impact on the new product process or new product success. There are some tendencies however:

- The great majority of all successful new products are market derived (a figure of 75 per cent is often quoted). But then just about 75 per cent of all failures are also market derived!
- Lead users are an excellent source of new product ideas (Von Hippel 1988). Lead users are particularly innovative customers, who often experiment with or redesign existing products to meet their needs better. Ideas derived from customers of all types also seem to do better than internally generated ones, on average (Cooper and Kleinschmidt 1993a).
- There are mixed views on technology push ideas. The greatest innovations have been technology push, even technological breakthroughs. Nylon, the laser, radar, early computers and others were largely technology-driven projects, often with little idea of ultimate market demand or market requirements. Against this is the fact that success rates tend to be much lower here, perhaps because technology push projects fail adequately to build in the needs of the customer (Cooper and Kleinschmidt 1993a).

Stage one also sees initial attempts to qualify and screen projects. Some companies have developed rigorous screening, selection and prioritization tools to help choose new product projects, barely at the idea stage, on which to focus resources.

The typical company spends about 15 per cent of its total product innovation expenditures on this first stage (Booz-Allen and Hamilton 1982). Note from Figure 1 that 65 per cent of this expenditure goes towards unsuccessful projects, the message being that much exploration must be done to uncover a few worthwhile projects. On a per project basis, this first stage accounts for about 7 per cent of the total project costs.

Business analysis – build the business case

This second stage – the critical homework phase – ideally defines the product: it determines the target market and positioning strategy, benefits to be delivered, product requirements and perhaps even detailed product specifications. This stage also provides justification for the project, most often in the form of financial analysis.

Activities that might occur in stage two include a variety of marketing, technical, production and financial tasks (see MARKET SEGMENTATION; MARKETING RESEARCH; MARKETING STRATEGY; POSITIONING). Marketing tasks can involve:

- desk research or secondary research – accessing published information, library

(key word) searches, a search through company materials (e.g. existing market studies, competitive analysis files) and inputs from company salespeople and technical service people.
- focus groups with potential customers or users to scope out the product requirements and determine level of market interest.
- detailed market research (for example, personal interviews or discussions with customers) to determine exactly customer needs, wants and requirement as input to the final design of the product. Positioning studies, to identify possible positioning strategies, may also be undertaken.
- concept tests with customers, where a representation of the product is presented to potential customers (e.g. a concept statement, a drawing, a storyboard, a dummy spec sheet) and potential customers' reactions – interest, liking, preference and purchase intent – are gauged. Concept tests help to assess likely market acceptance and possible positioning strategies.
- competitive analysis, involving a thorough review of competitive products, competitive strategy (and pricing), and competitive results (e.g. share and profits).

Technical activities also occur during stage two, usually designed to assess (and sometimes prove) technical feasibility (that the product can indeed be developed) and manufacturing feasibility. Such technical work varies by industry but could include: library research and a thorough technical literature search; conceptual work to identify possible technical routes or solutions; very preliminary development work (e.g. some lab work; computer modelling; initial design work) to probe feasibility and identify technical risks; development of an R&D plan (complete with a schedule and spending estimates); and legal (patent), environmental, health and safety assessments.

Manufacturability is also an issue in stage two, where a detailed manufacturing appraisal may be undertaken: this determines the likely production route, possible manufacturing costs and throughputs and capital equipment and expenditures needed.

Given the results of these marketing, technical and manufacturing analyses, a financial analysis is conducted during stage two to help justify the project prior to opening the door to a full-scale development project (stage three).

Given all these vital activities in stage two, one might expect it to be quite expensive. Quite the contrary, this stage receives the least resources, typically only 6.1 per cent of total expenditures and 3.7 per cent of the total project cost. This low level of spending on this homework phase may explain why the remainder of the new product process is problematic for too many projects, and why so many new products fail. Indeed, there is considerable evidence that firms which spend more time and money on these stage two homework (or pre-development) activities have much higher success rates (Cooper and Kleinschmidt 1988).

Development

The development and initial testing of a prototype product is the major objective of stage three. This phase tends to be dominated by technical work, as scientists, engineers, software writers or other technical professionals translate the product as defined in stage two into reality. This stage is most costly, accounting for 36.9 per cent of company spending, and 27.7 per cent of spending on a per project basis. This is also a hit-and-miss stage, with almost half (47.9 per cent) of development expenditures going to unsuccessful projects, perhaps the result of a rather weak and underfunded business analysis stage (stage two).

Marketing work also continues during stage three, as the product should be constantly checked by the marketplace to ensure that the evolving product satisfies the customer. Progressive companies make the customer an integral facet of this development phase by building rapid prototypes and seeking immediate customer reaction, and by including a number of customer checks throughout the development phase as the new product takes shape. This iterative rapid-prototype-and-test approach stands in marked contrast to traditional schemes, which see the R&D department develop the product, and only much later (following development) is it exposed to the customer via customer tests.

Testing and validation

Phase four is where the product, its production and its marketing are tested and validated.

Although some in-house or alpha testing usually takes place as part of development (stage three), much more extensive in-house testing remains to ensure that the product meets its specifications and requirements, and performs as expected. These in-house tests are typically technical ones, and are undertaken in controlled or laboratory settings.

Customer tests of the product come next. These are designed to prove that the product really does work under live (or real world) conditions, and in some cases, to establish purchase intent – that the product does delight the customer. These tests, called field trials, customer tests, beta tests or user preference tests, are often conducted at selected and representative users' premises (home, office or factory) and can extend over a long period of time.

The production process can be tested during phase four. Here trial, pilot or test production methods are used to prove (and debug) the manufacturing process and to confirm costs and throughputs.

Some companies also include test market activities in phase four. Test markets can be conducted for both industrial and consumer goods and services. Here, the product is sold to a limited number of test customers: for example, in a limited geographic area; or through a limited number of stores, distributors or sales offices. A test market is an experiment to determine market acceptance of the new product (e.g. expected sales or market share). Test markets can also be used to test alternate strategies: for example, two different pricing or positioning strategies. Unlike customer tests or trials (above), which test only the product, the test market tests the entire strategy: the product, positioning, price, promotion and sometimes the distribution (see CHANNELS OF DISTRIBUTION; LOGISTICS AND VALUE CREATION; POSITIONING; PRICING; SALES PROMOTION).

Frequently repurchased consumer goods can be subjected to another customer test, called a simulated (or pre-) test market. Various market research firms have developed novel methodologies which provide a simulated shopping experience: the potential customer is exposed to the product (e.g. via an advertisement) and is then allowed to 'shop' for the product in a simulated shopping environment. The consumer decision (whether they buy the new product or not) together with their reaction to the product after several weeks of use enables the research firm to make very predictive estimates of trial and repurchase rates, hence market share. These pre-test market techniques have proven to be considerably less expensive, much faster, more controlled and almost as predictive as a full test market (see MARKETING RESEARCH).

Phase four, testing, is a moderately expensive stage, accounting for 16.7 per cent of company expenditures on product innovation, and 18.6 per cent of expenditures on a per project basis. By this point in the process, many of the would-be losers have been culled out, so that for the first time in this process, the majority of expenditures goes to winners (58.8 per cent of spending is spent on successful projects by this stage).

Commercialization

The final stage witnesses the commercialization of the product. This includes the start-up of full-scale production (or the transfer of production from batch or limited production to the plant).

Market launch or roll-out occurs concurrently, and the various elements of the launch plan are implemented: advertising, promotion, the salesforce effort.

On a per project basis, commercialization is by far the most expensive of all stages, amounting to 42.7 per cent of project spending. But most projects do not reach this stage, so as a percentage of all company spending on innovation, commercialization accounts for only 25.6 per cent.

This high figure (42.7 per cent of project costs) is a reflection of the substantial market launch costs for many products, especially consumer goods (Procter & Gamble spends about $100 million to roll out a new brand in the USA). Additionally, capital costs can be substantial, especially if a new plant or new production equipment are required.

5 Go/kill decision points

Throughout the new product process are a set of go/kill decision points which follow or precede each stage. These are the culling points, where poor projects are weeded out of the process. Several important decisions points include:

- Initial screening, which follows the generation of the idea and precedes the business analysis. It marks the decision to spend significant resources on the project.
- The 'Go to Development' decision, which precedes stage three and signals a full-fledged development project. It is often based on a full financial and business analysis, the result of efforts in stage two.
- The launch decision, which precedes the last stage, commercialization, and opens the door for a full launch and production start-up.

Additionally, some companies build in a final point following launch, which signals the end of the project and where a retrospective analysis is undertaken: 'what happened and what can we learn?'

Having tough go/kill decisions is strongly correlated with the profitabilities of businesses' new product efforts. Sadly, this ingredient – tough go/kill decision points – is *the weakest ingredient* of all process ingredients studied in a recent benchmarking study (Cooper 1998). Another study revealed that formal evaluations do not take place, especially from the development phase onward (Cooper and Kleinschmidt 1988). When undertaken, these go/kill decision points are plagued by vague, inconsistent and sometimes no criteria. Often the wrong decision makers are involved (e.g. marketing makes the decision without the involvement of R&D or production).

To correct these deficiencies and to ensure that resources are devoted to the right new product projects, some companies have developed a formal set of decision points or 'gates', complete with required deliverables, 'criteria for Go', and a multifunctional group of decision makers to ensure that only the best projects proceed to the next stage.

The three main formal approaches to project evaluation or making go/kill decisions are (Cooper 1993):

1. Benefit measurement techniques, which capture qualitative facets of projects, and include methods such as checklists, scoring models and sorting techniques.
2. Economic models, which include a variety of financial methods.
3. Portfolio approaches, which consider the totality of projects underway and attempt to allocate resources to the most appropriate subset of projects.

Economic models are the best known, and include a variety of standard methods such as payback period and discounted cash flow (internal rate of return and net present value). Today's computer-based spreadsheets enable DCF methods to be easily combined with sensitivity analysis in order to identify key risks and possible downside losses. While popular for new product evaluation, note that financial/economic methods are often very unpredictive: financial data are both limited and unreliable, especially in the earlier (pre-development) stages of the project (see THE ECONOMICS BASIS OF MARKETING).

Checklists are simply lists of qualitative criteria thought to be important in project selection (see QUALITATIVE RESEARCH IN MARKETING). Criteria often include mandatory items such as strategic alignment, technical feasibility, existence of a customer need and meeting company legal, safety and environmental standards. Such mandatory items are called 'must meet' criteria and are used as 'knock out' or initial culling criteria. Highly desirable characteristics (or 'should meet' items) can be handled via a scoring model, where the project is rated on a number of characteristics (for example, using 0–10 scales), which are then added to yield a project score. Desirable characteristics that enhance the attractiveness of a project include various elements of product or competitive advantage, synergies with the firm's resource base, market attractiveness, and the existence of a project champion. Often, weights are applied to the criteria to reflect the fact that some scoring criteria (such as product advantage) may be more important than others (such as synergy with the plant). Checklists and scoring models have proven to be particularly effective for making gross distinctions between good and poor projects, especially for the first few gates, that is, near the beginning of the project where financial methods are unreliable.

Portfolio management is the newest challenge in product innovation management. Here, management treats new product or R&D projects as investments, and applies concepts of investment or financial portfolio management. The goal is to seek a portfolio of projects that maximizes the value of the portfolio, achieves the right balance or projects, and also mirrors the business's strategy (Cooper et al. 1998). Bubble diagrams have emerged as popular visual techniques for displaying a portfolio of projects. In one popular method, a four quadrant risk-reward plot of all new product projects is developed with 'probability of success' plotted versus 'value to the company' (Evans 1996, Roussel et al. 1991).

6 Why new products fail

The new product process described above provides an idealized view of product innovation. Reality is very different: new products fail at an alarming rate; and new product management is often deficient. As a result, many studies have probed the causes of failure so that management can then take corrective action (Hopkins 1980; Cooper 1993). Here are some major reasons for new product failure:

A lack of a market orientation
Inadequate market analysis, a failure to understand customer needs and wants and insufficient attention to the marketplace are consistently cited as major reasons for new product failure. Managers confess to a serious misreading of customer needs, too little field testing or overly optimistic forecasts of market need and acceptance. Management often falls into the trap of deciding in advance what the marketplace wants without asking that market what its priorities are. Another common mistake is to assume that because a product may be adequate in the eyes of the designers or R&D department, the customers will see it the same way.

Many firms omit critical marketing tasks, especially those in the early phases of a project. Detailed market studies (to determine customer needs and wants and to assess likely market acceptance) and test markets (to test the launch plan and determine market penetration) are most often omitted – in about three-quarters of projects, according to some studies (Cooper and Kleinschmidt 1986). Moreover, preliminary market assessment and detailed market studies are poorly executed. Finally, marketing actions receive a disproportionately small share of the total resources spent on projects: 32 per cent of funding (most of which goes to the market launch); and only 16 per cent of the effort (measured in person-days) (Cooper and Kleinschmidt 1988).

Moving too quickly or too slowly
The penalties of moving too slowly, or too fast, stem both from technical problems and also from flawed planning, organization or control (Hopkins 1980). Numerous new product failures result from not moving quickly enough, given a limited window of opportunity. In some cases there is a shift in customer preferences during the development cycle; in others the competitor moves more quickly with a new product, and seizes the market opportunity.

The need to move quickly to market – the fast-paced company – has created yet another set of timing problems: rushing a product through the process, and cutting corners to do so. Shortcuts are taken with the best intentions, but too often result in disaster. Key steps and stages are often skipped (or handled too quickly), such as market studies, prototype testing and field trials, with inevitable results: serious quality problems; the need for product redesign once into production; and marketing and sales weaknesses.

Poor quality of execution
Errors of omission and of commission abound in the new product process, and reveal a process very much in trouble. Key actions, often considered central to success, are arbitrarily omitted, so that the typical new product process is very much a truncated or incomplete one (Cooper and Kleinschmidt 1986). Certain pivotal activities are noticeable more for their absence than presence: detailed market studies, test markets and pre-commercialization business analysis are left out of the majority of projects. Quality of execution is rated as 'mediocre' across a broad spectrum of actions, some of the weakest areas being initial screening, preliminary market assessment, detailed market studies, business/financial analysis, pre-commercialization business analysis, production start-up and market launch.

Not enough homework
Three themes above – inadequate market analysis, moving too quickly, and poor quality of execution – all point to weaknesses in the homework or business analysis phase, specifically those actions that precede the

development phase. The homework simply does not get done: typically the project moves from idea through a rather superficial definitional and homework phase right into a full-scale development: a 'ready, fire, then aim' approach. The pre-development activities receive a relatively small proportion of the total resources – 7 per cent of the money and 16 per cent of the effort for a typical project – and are also plagued by serious omissions and poor quality of execution (Cooper and Kleinschmidt 1986, 1988).

A lack of differentiation
Too many new products are reactive efforts – a 'me too' product which lacks differentiation, fails to provide superior benefits or to deliver customer value, and meets a competitive brick wall. The failure to do one's homework, responding to competitive moves, a lack of willingness to seek customer input, and the desire to move quickly too often leads to a reactive, 'copy-cat' product as the easy solution. Such 'me too' products provide the firm with no competitive advantage and are one of the most popular ways of failing.

Technical problems
A common cause of new product failure is technical problems in design and production (Hopkins 1980). Difficulties in trying to convert from laboratory or pilot plant scale to full-scale production are common, while manufacturing glitches and product quality problems frequently arise. In many cases, it is a failure to conduct the earlier phases more thoroughly – technical research, design, engineering – before moving to the commercialization phase. At other times, the technical problems stem from a lack of understanding of the customer's requirements – for example, trying to develop the 'perfect product' – one that is simply over-engineered (and too costly) when compared to what the customer wanted.

No focus, too many projects and a lack of resources
A lack of resources, particularly from certain functions in the company (e.g. marketing) and for specific activities in a project (e.g. the upfront or pre-development stages) plagues too many new product projects. This lack of time, money and people is the root cause of many errors of omission and poor quality of execution, which in turn have such serious consequences for new product results. Why this lack of resources? In some firms senior management has simply starved product innovation: management has grossly underestimated the resource requirements for an effective new product programme. In most firms, however, it boils down to not enough focus and hence too many projects for the available resources. The result is that scarce resources are dissipated across many fronts and that the truly deserving projects are under-resourced.

7 New product success factors

The quest for new product success has led to numerous studies into what makes winners and what distinguishes successful new products from unsuccessful ones. Here are the more important success factors and/or lessons uncovered by these success/failure studies (Montoya-Weiss and Calantone 1994):

1. A differentiated product that delivers unique benefits and superior value to the customer is a key success factor. Product superiority separates winners from losers more often than any other single factor, according to many studies (Maidique and Zirger 1984; Cooper and Kleinschmidt 1987; Cooper 1993). Note that product superiority is defined in the eyes of the customer, not in the eyes of the R&D, engineering or even marketing departments. Product superiority is based on an in-depth understanding of customer needs and wants as well as competitive product weaknesses.

2. A strong market orientation – a market-driven and customer-focused new product process – is critical to success. This finding is supported in virtually every study of product success factors: a thorough understanding of customers' needs and wants, the competitive situation and the nature of the market is an essential component of new product success. To be successful, a market orientation must prevail throughout the entire new product project:
   - idea generation – seeking ideas from customers; understanding customers' problems;

- the design of the product – using market research, not just to check for market acceptance, but to determine users' needs, wants and preferences;
- during the development phase of the project, constant and continuing customer contact via frequent rapid-prototype-and-test iterations;
- as part of testing – building in customer tests and test markets;
- the launch – based on a solid marketing plan.

3. More pre-development work – the homework – must be done before product development gets underway. Studies show that the quality of execution of the pre-development steps – initial screening, preliminary market and technical studies, market research and business analysis – is closely tied to the product's financial performance. Successful projects have over 1.75 times as many person days spent on pre-development steps as do failures. These initial screening, analyses and definitional stages are critical to success, so managers must resist the temptation to skip over the up-front stages of a project, moving an ill-defined and poorly investigated project into the development phase (Cooper 1988).

4. Sharp and early product definition is one of the key differences between winning and losing at new products. How well the project is defined prior to entering the development phase is increasingly cited as a key success factor (Cooper and Kleinschmidt 1990). This definition includes:
   - specification of the target market: exactly who the intended users are;
   - description of the product concept and the benefits to be delivered;
   - delineation of the positioning strategy;
   - a list of the product's features, attributes, requirements and specifications (prioritized: 'must have' and 'would like to have').

5. Successful new products feature the right organizational structure, design and climate. Product innovation is not a one-department show. A cross-functional project team, with core team members drawn from various functions in the firm and led by an empowered, committed champion is a fundamental key to success (Larson and Gobeli 1988). Similarly, organizational climate – one that supports and rewards entrepreneurial behaviour – facilitates successful innovation.

6. Top management support is a necessary ingredient for getting the product to market. Top management can muster the resources and cut through the organizational bureaucracy to get the project done. In successful firms, top management's main role is to set the stage for product innovation to occur, to be a 'behind the scenes' facilitator, and not so much to be an actor, front and centre. Top management commits to internal product development as a source of growth; they develop a vision, objectives and strategy for product innovation that is driven by corporate objectives and strategies (Booz-Allen and Hamilton 1982). They make available the necessary resources and ensure that these resources are not diverted to more immediate needs in times of shortage. They commit to a disciplined game plan to drive products to market. Senior management empowers project teams, and supports committed champions by acting as mentors, facilitators, 'godfathers' or sponsors to project leaders and teams – acting as 'executive champions'.

7. Market attractiveness and synergies with the firm are two important success drivers. New products aimed at attractive markets – high growth, high need markets, high margin markets and markets which lack strong, dominant competitors – fare better. Synergies are also important to success: marketing synergies, where the product sells to the firm's existing customer base, via the firm's existing salesforce and channel system; and technological synergies, where the product can leverage in-house technical and production skills and resources. Both elements – market attractiveness and synergies – can be used as project selection criteria in order to make sharper project selection decisions and yield better focus.

8. A well-conceived, properly executed launch is central to new product success. The best products in the world will not sell themselves, hence the need for a strong marketing effort, a well targeted selling approach and effective after sales service. A well integrated and properly targeted launch does not occur by accident; it is the result of a fine-

tuned marketing plan, properly backed and resourced and proficiently executed.

9. Completeness, consistency and quality of execution make the difference between winning and losing. Certain key activities – how well they are executed, and whether they are done at all – are strongly tied to success (Cooper and Kleinschmidt 1990). These activities include undertaking preliminary market and technical assessments early in the project, carrying out a detailed market study or marketing research prior to product design, performing a detailed business and financial analysis and executing the test market and market launch in a quality fashion.

One solution is to treat product innovation as a process. Design a formal new product process and engineer into this process quality assurance approaches: for example, introduce check points in the process that focus on quality of execution, ensuring that every action in this process is executed in a quality fashion; and design quality into the process by making mandatory certain key activities that are often omitted, yet are central to success.

10. Companies that follow a multi-stage, disciplined new product process fare better. A number of companies have implemented formal new product processes or disciplined 'stage-gate' systems (Cooper and Kleinschmidt 1991) and have reaped the benefits. According to the PDMA's latest best practices study, 'nearly 60% of the firms surveyed use some form of Stage-Gate©tm process (Cooper 1990). Over half of the firms which have adopted Stage-Gate©tm process have moved from a basic process to more sophisticated versions with formal process ownership and facilitation (18.5% of the total) or third generation processes with more flexible gates and stage structures (Cooper 1993). Third generation processes match the complexity and difficulty of the project.'

A stage-gate system is a conceptual and operational model for moving new product projects from idea through to launch (Cooper and Kleinschmidt 1993b; Cooper 1994). It is a blueprint or road map for managing the new product process to improve efficiency and effectiveness. Operationally the scheme breaks the new product process into a series of multi-functional stages comprising multiple, parallel activities; each stage is preceded by a gate or decision point. This stage-gate process is not unlike the idealized process described above, except that it is more rigorous, formal and disciplined. The stage and gate format leads to names such as 'gating' or 'stage-gate' or 'toll-gate' systems.

8 Cycle time reduction in product innovation

Speed has become the new competitive weapon. Speed yields competitive advantage; it means less likelihood that the market or competitive situation might change; and it means a quicker realization of profits. But speed is only an interim objective – a means to an end; the ultimate goal is profitability. Often attempts to reduce cycle time end up costing the firm both time and money. Here are some ways that progressive firms use to reduce cycle time in product innovation:

- Instead of developing 'one-off' products, develop platforms, which then spawn a number of new product projects. A platform is the design and components that are *shared* by a set of products in a product family (e.g. an electric motor from which many power tools can be built); it also includes *technological capabilities* (e.g. a catalyst which yields many new polymers). Thus, from a single investment, a number of products can be developed relatively quickly and at lower cost.

- Do it right the first time: build in quality of execution at every stage of the project. The best way to save time is by avoiding having to recycle back and do it a second time. Quality of execution pays off not only in terms of better results, but via reducing delays (see item 9 above).

- Homework and definition: doing the up-front homework and getting clear project definition, based on fact rather than hearsay and speculation, saves time downstream: less recycling back to get the facts or redefine the product requirements; and sharper targets to work towards (see items 3 and 4 above).

- Organize around a multi-functional team with empowerment: multi-functional teams are essential for timely development: 'Rip apart a badly developed project and you will unfailingly find 75 percent of slippage attributable to 'siloing' or sending memos up and down vertical organizational 'silos' or 'stovepipes' for decisions, and sequential problem solving', according to Peters (1988). Sadly, the typical project resembles a relay race, with each function or department carrying the baton for its portion of the race, and then handing off to the next runner or department (see item 5 above).
- Parallel processing: the relay race, sequential or series approach to product development is antiquated and inappropriate for the 1990s. Given the time pressures of projects coupled with the need for a complete and quality process, a more appropriate scheme is a rugby game or parallel processing. Here, activities are undertaken concurrently (rather than sequentially) so that more activities are undertaken in an elapsed period of time. Parallel processing demands the use of a cross-functional team approach.
- Prioritize and focus: the best way to slow projects down is to dissipate the firm's limited resources and people across too many projects. By concentrating resources on the truly meritorious projects, not only will the work be done better, it will be done faster. But focus means tough choices: it means killing other and perhaps worthwhile projects. And that requires good decision-making and the right criteria for making go/kill decisions (see item 7 above).
- Keep it simple: find opportunities for unbundling products and projects. For example, instead of a project where three inventions are required, break it into three separate new product projects: introduce three successively better generations of products. The experience here is: project complexity doubles and triples the cycle time; so work to reduce the complexity of projects.
- Use flowcharting: that is, map out each and every activity in a project (or in your NPP), and remove the time-wasters. Any NPP can be accelerated by shortening each stage (Rosenau 1988). Sensible shortcuts (omitting the unrequited) are obvious timesavers.
- Use planning tools: utilize critical path planning and project management software (e.g. Microsoft Project). Look for opportunities for undertaking tasks concurrently, or for beginning one task before another ends.
- Add flexibility to the process to ensure greater speed. Overlap stages; bring long lead-time activities forward into an earlier stage; for lower risk projects, collapse stages and combine gates; and allow 'fuzzy' or conditional gate approvals (Cooper 1994).
- Deadlines must be regarded as sacred if speed is the objective. Time-based innovation is impossible without a discipline adherence to deadlines. Delays are dealt with via extra input of effort and resources, not by postponement.
- Have flexible funding: that is, set aside envelopes of money (or resources) so that one does not have to wait for a new budget year for money to start a promising project.

ROBERT G. COOPER
MCMASTER UNIVERSITY

Note

This entry focuses on physical or tangible products as opposed to new service products. Although obvious differences exist, there are also many similarities between the two, and indeed many of the concepts and methods explained in this entry also apply to new service products.

Further reading

(References cited in the text marked *)

* Booz-Allen and Hamilton (1982) *New Product Management for the 1980s*, New York: Booz-Allen and Hamilton Inc.
Boznack, R.G. and Decker, A.K. (1993) *Competitive Product Development: A Quality Approach to Succeeding in the 90s and Beyond*, Burr Ridge, IL: Irwin.
* *Business Week* (1991) 'R&D statistics', *Business Week*, Special 1991 Issue 25 October: 173–208.
Cooper, R.G. (1988) 'The new product process: a decision guide for managers', *Journal of Marketing Management* 3: 238–55.
Cooper, R.G. (1990) 'Stage-gate systems: a new tool for managing new products', *Business Horizons* 33 May–June.

* Cooper, R.G. (1993) *Winning at New Products: Accelerating the Process from Idea to Launch*, 2nd edn, Reading, MA: Addison-Wesley.
* Cooper, R.G. (1994) 'Third-generation new product processes', *Journal of Product Innovation Management* 11: 3–14.
* Cooper, R.G. (1998) 'Benchmarking new product performance: results of the best practices study', *European Management Journal* 16: 1–17.
  Cooper, R.G. (1998) *Product Leadership: Creating and Launching Superior New Products*, Reading, MA: Addison-Wesley.
* Cooper, R.G. and Kleinschmidt, E.J. (1986) 'An investigation into the new product process: steps, deficiencies and impact', *Journal of Product Innovation Management* 3: 71–85.
* Cooper, R.G. and Kleinschmidt, E.J. (1987) 'New products: what separates winners from losers', *Journal of Product Innovation Management* 4: 169–84.
* Cooper, R.G. and Kleinschmidt, E.J. (1988) 'Resource allocation in the new product process', *Industrial Marketing Management* 17: 249–62.
* Cooper, R.G. and Kleinschmidt, E.J. (1990) *New Products: The Key Factors in Success*, Chicago: American Marketing Association.
* Cooper, R.G. and Kleinschmidt, E.J. (1991) 'New product processes at leading industrial firms', *Industrial Marketing Management* 10: 137–47.
* Cooper, R.G. and Kleinschmidt, E.J. (1993a) 'New product success in the chemical industry', *Industrial Marketing Management* 22: 85–99.
* Cooper, R.G. and Kleinschmidt, E. (1993b) 'Stage gate systems for new product success', *Marketing Management* 1: 20–9.
* Cooper, R.G., Edgett, S.J. and Kleinschmidt, E.J. (1998) *Portfolio Management for New Products* Reading, MA: Addison-Wesley.
* Crawford, C.M. (1979) 'New product failure rates – facts and fallacies', *Research Management* September: 9–13.
  Crawford, C.M. (1993) *New Products Management*, 4th edn, Homewood, IL: Dow Jones Irwin.
* Evans, P. (1996) 'Streamlining formal portfolio management', *Scrip Magazine*, February.
  Griffin, A. (1997) *Drivers of NPD Success: The 1997 PDMA Report*, Chicago, Product Development & Management Association.
  Gruenwald, G. (1993) *New Product Development: Responding to Market Demand*, 2nd edn, Lincolnwood, IL: NTC Business Books.
* Hopkins, D.S. (1980) *New Product Winners and Losers*, Conference Board Report, number 773, New York: The Conference Board.
  Katz, R. (ed.) (1997) *The Human Side of Managing Technological Innovation*, New York, London: Oxford University Press,.
* Kleinschmidt, E.J. and Cooper, R.G. (1991) 'The impact of product innovativeness on performance', *Journal of Product Innovation Management* 8: 240–51.
* Larson, E.W. and Gobeli, D.H. (1988) 'Organizing for product development projects', *Journal of Product Innovation Management* 5: 180–90.
* Maidique, M.A. and Zirger, B.J. (1984) 'A study of success and failure in product innovation: the case of the U.S. electronics industry', *IEEE Trans. in Engineering Management* EM–31, November: 192–203.
* Montoya-Weiss, M.M. and Calantone, R.J. (1994) 'Determinants of new product performance: a review and meta analysis', *Journal of Product Innovation Management* 11: 397–417.
  Moore, W.L. and Pessemier, E.A. (1993) *Product Planning and Management: Designing and Delivering Value*, New York: McGraw-Hill.
  Myer, M.H. and Lehnerd, A.P. (1997) *The Power of Product Platford*, New York: Free Press.
* Page, A.L. (1991) *PDMA New Product Development Survey: Performance and Best Practices*, Chicago: PDMA Conference, Chicago, 13 November.
* Peters, Tom (1988) *Thriving on Chaos*, New York: Harper & Row.
* R&T Mgmt (1991) 'Year end R&D numbers', *Research & Technology Management* 34: 6.
* Rosenau, M.D. Jr. (1988) 'Phased approach speeds up new product development', *Research and Development* 30: 52–5.
  Rosenau, M.D., Jr (ed) (1996) *Handbook for New Product Development*, New York, NY: John Wiley & Sons Inc.
  Rosenau, M.D., Jr. (1993) *Faster New Product Development: Getting the Right Product to Market Quickly*, New York: Amacom.
  Rosenthal, S.R. (1992) *Effective Product Design and Development: How to Cut Lead Time and Increase Customer Satisfaction*, Burr Ridge, IL: Irwin.
  Rothwell, R. (1972) 'Factors for success in industrial innovations', in *Project SAPPHO – A Comparative Study of Success and Failure in Industrial Innovation*, Brighton: SPRU, University of Sussex.
  Rothwell, R. (1976) 'Innovation in textile machinery: some significant factors in success and failure', *SPRU Occasional Paper Series* (2), Brighton: SPRU, University of Sussex.
  Rothwell, R. (1976) 'The "Hungarian SAPPHO": some comments and comparison', *Research Policy* (3): 30–8.
  Rothwell, R., Freeman, C., Horseley, A., Jervis, V.T.P., Robertson, A.B. and Townsend, J. (1974) 'SAPPHO updated – project SAPPHO phase II', *Research Policy* (3): 258–91.
  Roussel, P., Saad, K.N. and Erickson, T.J. (1991) *Third Generation R&D, Managing the Link to Corporate Strategy*, Cambridge, MA: Harvard Business School Press.

Scheuing, E.E. (1989) *New Products Management*, Columbus, OH: Merrill Publishing Co.

Souder, W.E. (1987) *Managing New Product Innovations*, New York: Lexington Books.

Urban, G.L. and Hauser, J.R. (1993) *Design and Marketing of New Products*, 2nd edn, Englewood Cliffs, NJ: Prentice Hall.

* von Braun, C. F. (1997) *The Innovation War*, Upper Saddle River, NJ: Prentice-Hall PTR.

* Von Hippel, E.A. (1988) *The Sources of Innovation*, New York: Oxford University Press.

Wheelwright, S.C. and Clark, K.B. (1992) *Revolutionizing Product Development: Quantum Leaps in Speed, Efficiency and Quality*, New York: The Free Press.

Zangwill, W.I. (1992) *Lightning Strategies for Innovation: How the World's Best Firms Create New Products*, New York: The Free Press.

See also: CHANNELS OF DISTRIBUTION; GLOBAL MARKETING; LOGISTICS AND VALUE CREATION; MARKET SEGMENTATION; MARKETING RESEARCH; MARKETING STRATEGY; POSITIONING; PRICING; PRODUCT LIFE-CYCLE MANAGEMENT; QUALITATIVE RESEARCH IN MARKETING; SALES PROMOTION; THE ECONOMICS BASIS OF MARKETING

ND management

1 Cycles of confusion
2 Weaknesses of the product life-cycle
3 Market dynamics
4 The evolution of markets
5 Formulating marketing strategies
6 Summary

Overview

This entry explores two related issues essential to developing marketing strategies. First, it examines how markets evolve over time – how they start, grow, reach maturity and eventually decline. This involves reviewing the concept of the product life-cycle and examining the broader underlying market dynamics which shape the behaviour of both customers and competitors. While we show that there is no standard product or market 'life-cycle', there are common evolutionary processes which influence markets over time.

Second, the entry describes how an understanding of this process of change in a market should influence marketing strategy. By anticipating developments in buyer behaviour, competitive activities and emerging technologies, managers can reposition their businesses and proactively change products and marketing policies to strengthen their competitiveness and improve their financial performance. Finally, the entry explores the strategic issues facing businesses in different competitive positions. It looks at the forces which should determine the different marketing strategies of the pioneers of the industry, those seeking to challenge the market leader, and those companies aiming at niche positions within the larger market.

1 Cycles of confusion

The concept of a product life-cycle has had a major impact on the marketing literature. Every textbook has a chapter on the subject and numerous articles have appeared on it. It has also influenced many of the popular management techniques such as the Boston Consulting Group matrix and the McKinsey portfolio.

Figure 1 shows the popular representation of the theory. The theory postulates that a product has a life-cycle (usually described by an S-shaped sales curve), which can be divided into four stages: introduction, growth, maturity and decline. The slow introductory phase reflects the difficulty of overcoming buyer inertia and stimulating trial of a new product. Rapid growth then occurs as many new buyers are attracted once the product is perceived as successful. Saturation of the product's potential buyers is eventually reached, causing the rapid growth to level out to the underlying rate of growth of the relevant target market. Finally, decline will set in as new substitute products appear

From this product life-cycle theory it has then been common to draw implications for marketing strategy, the marketing mix and the organization of marketing (e.g. Levitt 1965) (see MARKETING ORGANIZATION AND MANAGEMENT; MARKETING STRATEGY; THE MARKETING MIX). The main recommendations are summarized in Table 1. It is argued that in the introduction stage the strategic objective should be to aggressively develop the market, focusing on the most innovative customers and seeking to preempt competition. As the product moves into the growth stage new competitors enter, the initial product has to be enhanced with features and line extensions, prices have to be cut and distribution intensified as a mass market is emerging. As the market for the product matures, profit margins fall, competition is intense and the organization has to shift from a focus on marketing to one of efficiency and cost control. Finally, in the decline stage, the future is bleak and the business should seek to milk the product for cash. This cash is then pushed into new products and the product life-cycle is repeated.

Despite the popularity of the product life-cycle, there is unfortunately no evidence that most products follow such a four-stage cycle. Nor is there any evidence that the turning-points of the different stages are in any way predictable. On the contrary, the shapes of the sales curves appear to be completely idiosyncratic. One review of life-cycles identified sixteen different

Product life-cycle management

Figure 1 The product life-cycle

patterns in addition to the S-curve. Some of the more common curves found in empirical studies are illustrated in Figure 2. Similarly, the turning-point from maturity to decline can occur after a few months (e.g. the hula hoop) or not be evident after several generations (e.g. Scotch whisky). If the shape and length of the product life-cycle are so irregular and unpredictable, the concept would appear to have little utility for market planning and decision-making.

Table 1 Product life-cycle: implications for marketing

	Introduction	*Growth*	*Maturity*	*Decline*
Characteristics				
Sales	Low	Fast growth	Slow growth	Decline
Profit	Negative	Rapid rise	Falling margins	Declining
Cash flow	Negative	Moderate	High	Moderate
Strategy				
Objective	Aggressive entry	Maximize share	Boost profits	Milk product
Focus	Non-users	New segments	Defend share	Cut costs
Customer targets	Innovators	Early adopters	Majority	Laggards
Competitor targets	Few, preempt	Growing number	Many	Declining
Differential advantage	Product performance	Brand image	Price and service	Price
Marketing mix				
Product	Basic	Extensions and enhancements	Differentiation, variety	Rationalize range
Price	High	Lower	Low	Stabilizing
Promotion	High	High	Falling	Low
Advertising forms	Awareness	Brand performance	Loyalty	Selective
Distribution	Selective	Intensive	Intensive	Rationalize
Organization				
Structure	Team	Market focus	Functional	Lean
Focus	Innovation	Marketing	Efficiency	Cost reduction
Culture	Freewheeling	Marketing led	Professional	Pressured

The marketing mix

Figure 2 Alternative product life-cycle patterns

Part of the problem with the product life-cycle concept is that it has never been properly defined. What does 'product' mean? Some studies use the total industry sales (e.g. computers); others use product forms (e.g. notebook computers); still others use brands (e.g. Apple Mac). Each 'product' has quite a different life-cycle: one can be in long-term decline while another exhibits rapid growth.

To see the managerial implications of these differences it is useful to show how they relate to one another (Table 2). Market analysis starts not with the product but with the needs of customers. A need is a basic requirement of customers. For example, customers have needs for transportation, calculating power or energy. Such needs may persist and grow over centuries and indeed may never have a decline stage.

Table 2 Alternative product life-cycle concepts

Concept	Definition	Typical length	Examples
Need	Basic underlying requirement	Indefinite	Transportation, calculating
Demand	Specific solution to a need	Very long	Car, computer
Technology	Current state-of-the-art	Short	Composite engine, 32-bit computer
Product	Product with specific technology	Shorter	4-wheel drive car, 32-bit PC
Product form	Variant of product	Very short	Open-top, 4-wheel drive, 32-bit notepad PC
Brand	Manufacturer's offer	Long	Honda Civic, IBM PC, Coca-Cola

Next, at one level of disaggregation, we have a *demand* for a specific solution to the need. This is sometimes called a demand-technology life-cycle. For example, the demand for transportation was once met by a coach and horses, now it is met by a car. The electronic computer has replaced the mechanical comptometer. The life-cycle of these broad product solutions, while shorter than the need curve, can be extremely long.

Next is the *current technology* curve. While the demand curve represents a broad technological solution (e.g. internal combustion engine, electronics) beneath this curve are a whole series of incremental technological changes which obsolete previous processes. For example, 32-bit technology replaces 16-bit; ceramic filters replace copper; fibre optic cables replace wire. Technology curves can be quite short and are certainly getting shorter.

At the next level of disaggregation managers make choices. A *product* curve is a category of offer incorporating current technology. For example, companies offer four-wheel drive cars or a 32-bit personal computer.

Next, line extensions or alternative *product forms* normally appear such as open-top four-wheel drive cars or 32-bit notepad computers. Both product and product forms may exhibit short life-cycles due to changing tastes and technology.

Finally, there is the *brand* product life-cycle. This is the distinctive offer of a specific business. The brand life-cycle can be long or short depending upon the marketing strategy. Unilever believes that, by incorporating the latest technology and adapting the product and product form to changing market conditions, the brand can have an indefinite life. Brands such as Persil, Coca-Cola, Range Rover and many others last for generations because they change the technological, design and service content of the offer while still retaining the brand values.

For managers to talk of a product being at the declining stage can therefore be highly misleading. First, sales are often resuscitated by new uses and new markets. Second, for every declining product there are almost invariably rapidly growing technologies, product forms and brands. For example, total sales of tea have been declining for generations, but within this, total sales of some product forms such as herbal and instant teas have been showing explosive growth in recent years.

2 Weaknesses of the product life-cycle

To summarize, for the following reasons, the product life-cycle is not of much use for marketing strategy.

Undefined concept
There is no agreement about the level of aggregation to which the concept is supposed to refer. Needs, demands, technologies, product categories, forms and brands have quite different driving forces.

No common shape
However products are defined there appears to be no standard curve. An S-shaped curve appears to describe only a minority of products. The actual sales development is shaped by both outside events and by the strategies of competitors.

Unpredictable turning-points
While most products and brands do peak eventually, there is no way of predicting when the turning-point will occur. For some it is a matter of months, for others it may be generations.

Unclear implications
Even where a life-cycle pattern can be identified the implications are not clear. For example, the growth phase may or may not be associated with high profit margins. If barriers to entry are low and industry competition is fierce (e.g. as in some areas of electronics), rapid growth can be accompanied by very low profits. By contrast, if there are low exit barriers and little competition, the decline stage can be exceptionally profitable (e.g. the foundry supplies business).

Not exogenous
The product life-cycle is often the result of management actions rather than being caused by outside events. Many managers have been taught to think that the product life-cycle is inevitable. When sales have plateaued, rather than looking to upgrade the technology and search for new opportunities, management have defined the business as a cash cow and sought to 'diversify' into other businesses. In

The marketing mix

these situations the product life-cycle becomes a self-fulfilling concept.

For example, Foseco was the leader in supplying linings to steel refractories around the world – a £300m-a-year business. The linings were fibrous boards installed inside the furnaces. A small competitor entered with a cheaper spraybased alternative. Foseco, with its strong reputation and marketing capability, could easily have responded to this threat by adopting the technology. In fact, they were given the opportunity to acquire the competitor. Instead management had identified their business as a 'cash cow' end so declined to invest. The result was that the competitors rapidly took over the market. Spray linings became a high-growth business as the steel companies substituted from board. Foseco refractory profits collapsed. A few years later an ailing Foseco was acquired by Burmah Castrol.

Product oriented

The core concept of marketing is that the business should seek to meet the needs of customers rather than focus on selling its products. The product life-cycle is a production rather than a marketing orientated concept. By focusing on the product, managers fail to understand those factors which shape the business's ability to satisfy the needs of its customers in competitive markets. The fortunes of the company are not tied to its products but to five other primary forces which determine its ability to maintain a competitive advantage. These forces are:

- the changing requirements of customers;
- the objectives and strategies of competitors;
- the attractiveness of the market to new competitors;
- the emergence of new technologies which can replace existing solutions;
- the performance and power of those companies supplying resources, raw materials and components to the business.

These are the drivers which obsolete the product. A product will die if the needs of its customers change, if competitors come up with better offers, if new technologies permit cheaper or superior solutions, or if suppliers to the firm choke off its ability to satisfy the market profitably. Therefore it is better to tune managers into concentrating on the causes of change rather than the consequences of it. In this way they can more effectively anticipate developments in the market and create product strategies which adapt to these opportunities.

3 Market dynamics

Just as there is no uniform, predictable product life-cycle, so there is no standard pattern of market evolution. However, there are common processes which shape markets. By analysing these processes managers can anticipate how markets and competition will develop. From this analysis they can develop strategies both to capitalize on these changes and to influence these forces of change. Such processes affect each of the following five 'actors' in the industry (see Figure 3).

Customers

As a market evolves certain changes can be anticipated among customers. First, the level of demand changes. Sales are a function of the number of buyers and the frequency with which they buy. In the initial stages, growth can be extremely rapid because of the number of new buyers being attracted to the market. Eventually this pool of available non-users diminishes, the market becomes saturated and sales slow as

Figure 3 Market dynamics

they become largely a function of repeat purchasing. A second change to be anticipated is that customers' expectations will progress. The primary function of the product comes to be accepted as the 'norm' offered by all competitors. Customers look for additional attributes which add new benefits to the product.

For example, in the early 1980s doctors hailed Squibb's revolutionary new hypertensive drug, Capoten, which eventually sold over £1 billion a year. Subsequently, twenty competitors entered the market. The new products were not superior in the primary function of lowering blood pressure but they began to offer additional desirable attributes such as lower dosage and fewer side effects. Today the market leader is Merck's Vasotec which has the attribute that a patient needs to take it only once a day rather than the two or three times daily required by Capoten.

Finally, three factors cause customers to become increasingly price sensitive. First, customers become more knowledgeable and are willing to shop around. Second, there are more competitors to choose from. Third, as the market develops, more price sensitive customer segments have to be penetrated to maintain growth. Innovative customers tend to be less price sensitive because they attach a high value to the new product, later customers have to be attracted by lower prices.

While evolutionary processes in the market push towards slower growth and falling prices, both can be postponed or forestalled by firms making product or market innovations. By innovative repositioning, the firm can meet new needs, offer new attributes or create new markets. Such innovations have fuelled resurgent growth and maintained high prices in many markets such as those for bicycles, ice-cream, alkaline batteries and industrial lubricants.

Competition

Evolutionary processes also lead to certain expected changes in the behaviour of current competitors in the market. First, the intensity of competition will initially be low because the rapid rate of growth makes competition a non-zero sum game – all can grow. But later, as the market slows and firms have added to capacity, competition for customers becomes increasingly intense. Second, during the latter part of the growth phase, the more aggressive competitors begin to pursue repositioning strategies that put them into direct competition with firms which were previously in different strategic groups.

For example, up to the mid-1980s, IBM and Apple did not compete head-on. IBM dominated the mainframe market, Apple the emerging PC market. Then in 1984 IBM, concerned about the slowing growth in the mainframe market and the expanding purchases of PCs by its customers, launched its own PC. With this new direct clash between the two leaders competition was massively increased, producing a rapid shake-out of the weaker players.

A third change is that during the growth stage winning strategies begin to emerge and industry leadership tends to become established. The winners are those that have aggressively built market share in the early stages, moved down the experience curve and built economies of scale into operations and marketing. As the industry matures they have lower unit costs and powerful marketing and distribution systems. The leaders are then hard to dislodge unless a competitor can introduce radically innovative products or marketing strategies.

New entrants

A market is pioneered by one or two companies. However, a rapidly growing market automatically attracts new competitors – often in large numbers. Sometimes there is an interval in which patents, lack of technical expertise and uncertainty about the market's potential, act as barriers to entry. But this interval is now very short in most industries. Less than one year after Apple launched the first personal computer, it had ten competitors; eight years later it had five hundred. Speciality chemical companies expect their new products to be copied within six months.

Today all well-managed companies are scouring the environment for growth markets that might utilize their capabilities. As the market's potential becomes less uncertain, large firms will seek to enter the market. Sometimes they will establish their own businesses, more often they will acquire one or more of the pioneers. Existing competitors have to compete not only with local entrants but global competition increasingly becomes the pattern.

As the market enters its mature phase, the number of new entrants sharply reduces and companies begin to exit. Slow growth normally triggers a shakeout and the number of competitors declines. The survivors are increasingly those who have pursued the winning strategies of achieving high market shares, broad product lines and global markets. Consequently, managers in innovative businesses must appreciate that their lead time is always short and that soon they will be challenged both by small, nimble followers and large, resource-rich giants. If they are to survive, their technological edge must be matched by strategy to build share rapidly and create a viable brand.

Substitute product and technologies

Over time managers should expect substitute products and technologies to threaten their position in the market. A substitute is anything that meets the same customer need. Concrete can be a substitute for steel in building a bridge, high fructose corn syrup can substitute for sugar, acrylic for nylon. Several factors increase the threat from substitutes as the market evolves.

First, competitors in adjacent industries are attracted by the growth and profit to be made in the market. For example, commercial banks once dominated the financial markets, but in the last decade they have lost share. On the commercial side the banks have lost share to securities firms. On the retail side they have lost share to building societies and non-banks such as ATT and Marks & Spencer who now offer services such as credit cards and investment funds.

Second, needs in the market change, making old technologies less appropriate. For example, today's customers find making a special trip to a bank for a routine transaction a chore. A new bank, First Direct, attracted nearly half a million customers by offering telephone banking. Unlike old rivals, First Direct has no branches, all the functions and transactions are available through a 7-day, 24-hour telephone service.

Third, progress in adjacent technologies is likely to eventually threaten current solutions. For example, new plastics which are light and strong increasingly substitute for steel in car manufacturing. Finally, the government can influence the position of substitutes through regulations, quotas and subsidies. For example, environmental regulations are forcing the wind-down of many packaging and chemical products and stimulating the creation of new substitutes.

In these situations management have to decide whether to beat the emerging substitutes or to modify their strategies and incorporate the new products and technologies. The answer will depend upon an analysis of which alternative best meets the needs of customers and of the trend in the relative price–performance ratios.

Supply relationships

Entrepreneurial firms depend upon suppliers and subcontractors to facilitate growth. During the initial stages of the market obtaining suitable supplies may be a constraint on growth. Those early competitors that can access efficient suppliers or have the resources to integrate backwards can lever important competitive advantages.

Suppliers can limit the potential of a company to exploit its capacity for innovation. Porter (1980: 27–8) suggests a supplying group is powerful where the following conditions apply in the market.

- It is dominated by a few suppliers and is more concentrated than the industry to which it sells.
- It is not obliged to compete with other substitute products for sales to the industry.
- The industry is not an important customer of the supplier group.
- The supplier's product is an important input to the buyer's business.
- There are high switching costs in moving away from the products of the supplier group.
- The supplier group poses a credible threat of forward integration.

In general supplier power diminishes as the market grows. Nevertheless control and power over suppliers can offer a sustainable competitor advantage. For example, Marks & Spencer's long-term relationship with its suppliers, its skill in influencing their design and processes, and its ability to negotiate strongly with them have been central to the company's sustained position as Europe's leading retail firm.

4 The evolution of markets

These five key components are affected by evolutionary forces. For convenience, these developments can be divided into four phases.

The emerging market

A new market is triggered by an innovation. This innovation may be a new product that is superior to earlier ones; a new marketing concept that creates a new set of customers; or a process innovation that dramatically cuts costs or increases the availability of a product.

For an innovation to succeed it has to offer benefits that customers perceive as superior to current solutions. The customers who perceive this benefit first and who can act on this perception are called innovators. Innovators are normally not price sensitive because they value the benefit highly and do not want to wait for competition to bring prices down. The central marketing task at this stage is to segment the market with the aim of identifying those buyers most likely to benefit from the performance or the promise of the new product. Typically some potential customers will benefit hugely, others perceive very little benefit at all. The former are the ones to target.

For example, when Rolm (now part of Siemens) invented the electronic PABX (the telephone switching system used by an office or company), the primary benefit was that it allowed companies to economize on long-distance call costs. For the top two per cent of companies with very large long-distance call bills, the savings averaged over £100,000 a year. On the other hand, for most companies, with more modest long-distance bills, the savings were minimal. Rolm's initial strategy was therefore to identify and target the former segment.

At the beginning sales growth is normally slow, buyers have to be informed about the innovation and to be persuaded of its benefits. Uncertainty, high switching costs and the lack of established distribution and service infrastructures also restrain buyers. Barriers to adoption are more easily broken down when the new product has the following characteristics:

- a major performance advantage which is easily demonstrated;
- the cost of switching into it is low;
- the cost of product failures is limited;
- support requirements are small;
- buyers in the segment have the resources to change.

Once the innovators begin to adopt the product, the market may grow very fast, fuelled by the penetration of the large non-user group.

Competition is initally weak. The pioneer's main competition comes from the older technology. New entry is temporarily forestalled by barriers which include:

- patents;
- lack of technical know-how;
- uncertainty about what customers want;
- lack of expertise in sourcing supplies and parts;
- shortage of risk capital.

Unfortunately for the innovator, such barriers to entry tend to crumble very rapidly. Movements of personnel, the spread of knowledge and the adaptability of aggressive, fast followers soon erode the leader's temporary monopoly. Within a year there are likely to be several new entrants in the market.

The high growth phase

The high growth phase is characterized by the expansion of the market to new customer segments and new uses. These are stimulated by the spread of knowledge about the product beyond the innovator group, the reduction of uncertainty about standards and switching costs and the inevitable decline in prices. As prices fall, the new product becomes increasingly attractive to customers who only perceive a modest advantage in it.

The number of competitors often grows to strikingly high numbers. For example, in the motor cycle industry, at its peak, there were 136 manufacturers in the UK alone and an estimated 700 worldwide. They were attracted by the rapid growth and profitability of the market. In addition, the development of a strong infrastructure of subcontractors and distributors facilitates entry. Prices generally fall rapidly as experience and scale economies lower unit costs and competition increasingly forces most of these gains to be passed on to the customer.

In the later stages, as the growth rate begins to slow, competition for market share intensifies. The leading players begin to develop global ambitions and to broaden their product lines, pushing them into markets and segments occupied by other strong competitors. Companies which have not developed strong market positioning strategies or achieved low cost structures begin to see their profit margins falling and more are forced to exit the market.

The mature phase of the market

Market maturity occurs when the number of new users and new uses dry up. The marketing focus then has to switch from attracting non-users and creating new uses to maintaining or gaining market share. Since current users are more experienced, price and service become more important. Difficulties in finding new uses for the product and additional attributes to differentiate it at this stage of the market, heightens the drift towards commodity status.

Competition has normally become fierce. There will be excess capacity, the market has become zero-sum and the inroads of international competitors all tend to increase the pressures on companies. Two other factors amplify these pressures on margins. First, dealers become more powerful. They can play off alternative suppliers and may introduce their own brands. Second, it is harder for competitors to reduce costs because most of the scale economies and experience curve effects have already been obtained. The shake-out of marginal competitors then usually proceeds rapidly through amalgamations, takeovers and bankruptcies.

At the late stage of maturity the market may consolidate around a handful of large competitors who effectively create barriers to entry. These barriers centre around the scale economies they possess, the high capital requirements, the advantage of established brand names and the implicit threat of sharp retaliation newcomers may face. Markets that have matured into this oligopolistic pattern include the oil industry, the supermarket sector and the detergents business.

While internal competition in the industry may become more constrained, competition from substitute technologies is likely to grow over time. For example, continual improvements in plastics and composites add to the problems of steel producers seeking to maintain volume. Such companies then face the dilemma of a vain attempt to fight off the threat or a substantial investment in acquiring and adapting to the substitute technologies.

The decline phase

A new stage is reached when the market enters a period where volume looks set for permanent decline. This occurs when the pool of potential new users and new uses has dried up, when substitute products have demonstrated clear superiority or when buyers' needs change.

Characterizing the market as 'in decline' can be a dangerous mistake. Many markets have developed new sources of growth after entering what appeared to be the decline phase. Resurgent growth can be created by new products, new users and new uses. The motorcycle market declined by 50 per cent in the 1960s, then exhibited explosive growth as new, younger customers bought it as a fun product rather than as a cheap form of transport. Nylon has been written off many times, but instead, as Figure 4 illustrates, new uses have continually fuelled resurgent growth.

Even if the decline phase looks certain, the strategic implications are not clear. The usual recommendation from advocates of product life-cycle theory or portfolio concepts such as the Boston Consulting Group's matrix, is to divest from the market. But, in practice, such a view can be a costly oversimplification. Many markets in decline can be highly profitable and substantial cash generators for a very long period if managed properly (e.g. the cigarette market). Further, today there are many more declining markets than in the past. Slower world economic growth, rapid technological change and a fast-changing environment make the management of declining industries an important issue for most firms. The appropriate strategy depends upon how the evolutionary process affects the pattern of declining demand and the intensity of competition.

A market does not decline in a homogeneous pattern, rather the more innovative segments leave the market for new alternatives leaving behind customer groups who are reluctant or unable to change. Often these remaining customer groups are conservative and price inelastic. This occurs where, perhaps because of habit, the product is perceived as important to

Product life-cycle management

Figure 4 Extending the market: the case of Nylon
Source: Yale (1964: 33)

them. Other factors may be a lack of acceptable alternatives, if it is not seen as a major cost element in the budget, or if past long-term advertising has built up strong brand loyalties. In these situations, the remaining competitors may be able to push up prices to offset the decline in volume.

Whether this is possible depends upon the intensity of competition. Factors which may damp down competition allowing the survivors to earn reasonable returns are:

- when there are only a small number of large, evenly-balanced competitors remaining in the market;
- if general agreement exists that the market will continue to decline so that costly battles to win market share look unattractive;
- if significant non-price differences exist between competitive products so that they are not perceived as commodities;
- if exit barriers are low so that it is not too costly for competitors to leave the market as prospects decline;
- if fixed costs are relatively low so that total costs decline in line with volume.

In some markets (e.g. heavy chemicals) these conditions are clearly not present. Here fixed costs are high, there are major international competitors pursuing varying strategies, plants are highly specific and buyers regard the product as a commodity. In such markets the decline stage is often characterized by intensive competition, ruinous price wars and large losses.

Porter (1980: 267–73) identified four strategic options available to the business in the decline phase.

1 *Leadership*. The firm invests in acquisitions and other market share building strategies to rationalize and dominate the market. This is a high-risk strategy only justifiable if management are convinced that the resulting market structure will allow the firm to recover its late investment.

2 *Niche*. The firm focuses on a segment which is more robust and price insensitive than the mass of the market. Again this may be a difficult strategy since the remaining competitors are likely to target such a segment.

3 *Harvest*. Here the firm seeks to optimize cash flow rather than market share. Harvesting strategies involve cutting costs, raising prices and rationalizing the range of products, customers and channels. This strategy is most attractive if the firm has been a strong player in the market. If it has not been recognized as an industry leader, the harvesting strategy will normally lead to a rapid collapse of volume thereby eliminating any gains to be obtained from the strategy.

4 *Divest*. Here the business is sold off to maximize its net investment recovery This strategy is only likely to be profitable if a decision is made early in the decline phase. If left until later, or after the business has been harvested, it is not likely to find much interest in an acquisition.

Choosing the right strategy depends upon analysing the strength of the firm's competitive position and assessing the evolutionary processes affecting the market. If the firm has a strong position and the decline phase is expected to be steady and without bruising price wars, the attractiveness of a leadership or niche strategy is enhanced. On the other hand, if the company has no marked advantage, if no robust niches are apparent, and if the products are seen as commodities, rapid exit may be the best alternative. The earlier the oncoming decline phase is recognized and the better the evolutionary characteristics are understood, the more options are available to management.

5 Formulating marketing strategies

The marketing strategy that management should adopt depends upon three factors. First, what is its competitive position – is it a market leader or a challenger? Second, what is its strategic objective? Is it seeking market dominance or merely to carve out a profitable niche? Third, at what stage is the market? Is it in its early growth stage or does it look to be in late maturity?

If the company is the one to create the market through a significant innovation, it has the opportunity to gain first mover advantages. These include image advantages, customer loyalty, higher margins and economies of scale and experience. But these advantages are far from assured. There are numerous examples of the pioneer being quickly caught up and disappearing from the scene. The evidence suggests that to exploit an innovation the pioneer has to move both quickly and substantially to push into the main markets and to capture a significant market share. Such requirements are costly and difficult problems for the smaller company.

As the market moves from growth to maturity the strategy has to change from aggression to defence. Recently marketing academics have found the writings of the military strategists such as Clausewitz (1908) and Liddel-Hart (1967) illuminating for discussing the defensive options open to companies seeking to maintain the leadership positions they have built up. Such options include offensive defence, position defence, flanking defence, mobile defence, etc. Kotler and Singh (1981) have written the best known summaries of these military analogies applied to marketing.

If the company is not the innovator but a later entrant seeking to challenge the pioneer, different strategies will apply. Attacking a leader is easier when it is pursued at the early stage of a market's evolution. This is particularly the case when the pioneer has not aggressively expanded the market beyond the small innovatory niche. At the early stage of the market the two most effective strategies for the challenger are to seek new market segments or new attributes.

If the challenger is attacking at the maturity stage of the market, there are again military analogies to draw on. Kotler and Singh (1981) describe frontal, flank, encirclement, guerrilla and by-pass attack strategies.

6 Summary

Managers have to understand that markets are highly dynamic. Today customer requirements, competitive activity and technological solutions are impermanent and in constant flux. The product life-cycle is too simple a model for predicting the nature of these changes. Instead management have to assess the six underlying evolutionary forces which shape the behaviour of markets.

Successful competitive strategies are based on anticipating these evolutionary forces and using them to advantage. Most pioneers need to appreciate that their advantage is shortlived and that the strategic window they create must be rapidly and decisively exploited and then vigilantly defended. Newcomers find the odds stacked against them when they attack an effective market leader. A successful leader is rarely overtaken by a head-on strategy. Instead success usually depends upon further innovation in identifying new market segments and additional attributes not yet identified or exploited by the leader.

Market evolution is characterized by competitors crossing into each other's strongholds. Competition increases both in intensity and scope. This makes it difficult for companies pursuing single-niche strategies. Over time, high value niches become attractive to larger companies searching for new avenues of growth.

PETER DOYLE
WARWICK BUSINESS SCHOOL

Further reading

(References cited in the text marked *)

Buzzell, R.D. and Gale, B.T. (1987) *The PIMS Principles: Linking Strategy to Performance*, New York: The Free Press.
* Clausewitz, C. Von (1908) *On War*, London: Routledge.
Doyle, P. (1994) *Marketing Management and Strategy*, 2nd edn, Hemel Hempstead: Prentice-Hall International.
* Kotler, P. and Singh, R.A. (1981) 'Marketing warfare in the 1980s', *Journal of Business Strategy* Winter: 30–41.
* Levitt, T. (1965) 'Exploit the product life-cycle', *Harvard Business Review* November: 81–94.
* Liddell-Hart, D.H. (1967) *Strategy*, New York: Praeger.
* Porter, Michael E. (1980) *Competitive Strategy: Techniques for Analyzing Your Business Competitors*, New York: The Free Press.
Yale, Jordan, P. (1964) 'The strategy of Nylon's growth', *Modern Textiles Magazine* February: 33.

See also: MARKETING ORGANIZATION AND MANAGEMENT; MARKETING STRATEGY; THE MARKETING MIX

Packaging and design

1. Packaging provides one of the most fertile areas in the marketing mix for adding more value than cost
2. Packaging and design provide an excellent mechanism for changing category rules
3. Innovation in marketing as a whole often finds its basis in packaging
4. Brand positioning is key: understand positioning before you identify the role of packaging and design
5. Understand your brand's packaging and design equities and ensure they are protected
6. See the environment as an opportunity not a constraint
7. It is not enough to be individually effective: packaging also has to work at the point-of-sale
8. Effective packaging is one of the most difficult parts of the mix to progress in companies: it concerns almost every discipline
9. Use suppliers and outside advisers for new ideas and industry experience
10. An international point; the world is getting smaller and brands need to harmonize cross-country boundaries
11. Summary

Overview

Marketing is about the process of adding value. The more successful one brand is over the competition in adding value provides flexibility and leverage – either to make more profit from a price premium or to make more profit by selling more at a lower relative price, or, in the most successful cases, to do both (i.e. sell more than the competition at a higher price).

There are many constituents that go towards 'added value': the reputation of a brand – how long it has been around, its heritage; its performance and effectivity; its image, caused mostly, but not solely, by advertising and other forms of communication. By image we mean how the brand feels to the users personally, together with what the users think it will say about themselves as viewed by other people.

In this entry about packaging it is asserted that as media get more difficult, more fragmented and more expensive, the role that packaging can play in adding value to a brand has increased significantly. The trick, of course, is to add more packaging value than cost, and hence be able to charge a price premium and make an increased profit. This entry is about practical advice, not theory, and it has been organized under the following ten key themes.

1 Packaging provides one of the most fertile areas in the marketing mix for adding more value than cost

The easiest area to consider regarding 'adding value' is surface design, in the sense that if a label or pack has to be printed with something, the ink may as well show something excellent; the best it can possibly be. The corollary is also true: if the surface design is ineffective then it is a constant dampener on the brand's rate of sale; a lead weight that prevents the brand from flying high. The cost is only the once-off cost of developing a superb design; the variable on-cost of such a design can be zero or thereabouts – and so value is added.

Trade brands, especially in the UK, have certainly recognized the importance of design in recent years. A glance through the 1994 edition of *British Packaging NOW* reveals that around a third of the 250 or so examples chosen are 'brands' of UK retailers. They have recognized the mechanism of added value through design, albeit that they normally want to get increased volume at a lower price as their competitive position versus traditional brands.

Traditional brands have therefore not only got to get the most effective possible surface designs, they have also got to look for other ways to add value, and this can only come from structural innovation, a topic considered below (see 'Innovation in marketing as a whole often finds its basis in packaging').

The key point to recognize is that most categories are now looking at how to add more structural value: whether it is an easy-opening lid on a tin can, an easy to open and close 'stopper' on a cardboard liquid package, a tear-tape to get into a packet of biscuits more easily, or ice-cream packaging that actually keeps the product cold out of the freezer.

What's more, if most companies are moving into more functional packaging innovation, there are a number of consequences: first, better do it faster than the rest of the category to gain competitive advantage; and second, better be sure that it really will be possible to earn a return via a higher price or an increased volume, or both. Otherwise moves like 'easy-open' cans, while giving instant and excellent added value for the consumer, if not charged for, and copied across the category, simply lead to erosion of category profitability.

2 Packaging and design provide an excellent mechanism for changing category rules

Marketing is about creating brand norms that provide safe, secure and shorthand mechanisms for consumers to make quick, confident choices. Brand leaders try to own the high ground in a market, appealing to most people most of the time and trying to capture the combination of the most important needs/benefits in the market: 'Ivory liquid is gentle on your hands and it washes more plates per penny'. 'Lever 2000 is a family deodorant soap that's gentle on your skin'.

Just as the biggest brands are trying to control their category and continually judging a carefully planned evolutionary approach to brand development and range extensions, the new challengers in the category want to make their presence felt in no uncertain terms. They have something new to offer and therefore have to say it in a new way as well, to gain attention and to be convincing about their new idea.

Packaging offers a superb vehicle for expressing newness and changing the 'rules' of the category. In several markets, most ice-cream was sold in rather large plastic tubs until Haagen Däzs came along with a much smaller tub which was cardboard not plastic. Admittedly the product was excellent – but the nature of the packaging caused a fundamental reappraisal of the premium ice-cream market. And the well-judged size and shape made it extremely tempting to eat individually.

Pet food is sold in tin cans or paper sacks. Several years ago Pedigree Petfoods introduced some new super-premium brands of petfood in small flexible aluminium trays. They changed the category rules and created a new subcategory at a price/feed premium of over 200 per cent.

In Germany, as in most countries in Europe, there is a large edible fats (butter and margarine) market, where for years brands like Rama dominated and created the design rules of the category. Lätta was a healthy half-fat spread (that tasted excellent) and launched a new (more dairy-like) design into the market (it had originally been launched into the Swedish market). It was a credit to Unilever that they marketed both the brand that created the category norms, Rama, and the brand that challenged them, Lätta.

In France the Personal Products Division of Unilever noticed in the late 1970s that men were becoming far more confident in personal grooming and that they demanded a new generation of more sophisticated products to meet their needs. Current brands of aftershave and deodorant lacked the spirit of their newfound confidence. Axe (Lynx in the UK) changed the rules of the male deodorant market and created a new subcategory of male body spray. The key ingredients were the shape of the can, the colour (black), the contrast in finish between can and cap and the surface graphics.

So in conclusion, packaging and design play vital roles in both creating and challenging the category rules, as new generations of consumers and new competitors fight to gain and regain the initiative.

3 Innovation in marketing as a whole often finds its basis in packaging

Apart from 'adding value', one of the other buzz words in marketing today is innovation. Or in other words introducing new and creative ideas that better satisfy consumer needs. Today it is not only legitimate, it is essential to consider such consumer parameters as novelty, fun, secondary uses and user interaction. We have moved on from a world where we are satisfied by the traditional basics of products. It is not enough to wipe on a liquid window cleaner with a cloth: today we expect it in a trigger pump spray with refill docking mechanism to save money longer term. It is not enough to have a plain bar of soap in the shower: today we expect something that opens, closes, dispenses, hangs conveniently and does not expel its contents if the nozzle is inadvertently left open.

Innovation is many different things. Most often it translates itself as a representation of already existing or known parameters. One of the richest sources of innovative inspiration is to combine seemingly uncombinable things. In fact, they can seem so uncombinable that the opportunity may have been dismissed as impossible. For decades dentists in the USA have been telling their patients that the two best substances to clean their teeth were baking soda and peroxide (bleach). And these two ingredients could not possibly live together (they were too reactive). So, end of story.

Unilever persevered, however, with a packaging-led solution to the problem (opportunity). They invented a two-cavity bottle with a pump mechanism that combined the two ingredients at the point of dispensing. Terribly easy in hindsight, but it took a lot of internal energy and some considerable packaging innovation skill to invent exactly the right container.

For years hospitals and medical institutions have been using very small plastic capsules to hold just a few millilitres of a drug or other vital medical substance. This packaging form provided the starting point for Elizabeth Arden to launch its time capsules containing the new generation of anti-ageing ceramides. The packaging form presented the ceramides in exactly the right way: scientific, almost medical, precious, expensive, measured dosage, and with good branding and other balance points to add the necessary degree of cosmetic attractiveness. Other brands have now copied the Arden initiative. Packaging has created a whole new sector.

Packaging has given birth to many other highly innovative ideas in recent years. Müller Yoghurt redefined the meaning of yoghurt and how to eat it with its famous duo-cavity pack. A more expensive, more space inefficient, more factory complex, more trade unfriendly, more wasteful pack – but one that was entirely new and relevant to consumers who were keen to buy a new way of thinking about and individualizing their consumption of yoghurt.

Refills, systems, secondary usage containers, easier to open, easier to store, directable, concentrated, dilute, beer that comes out with a head (as if from draught), pumps, air sprays, microwavable, small portions, big portions – the world is exploding with packaging innovation. And as the pace hots up consumers are demanding more, better, faster than ever before.

4 Brand positioning is key: understand positioning before you identify the role of packaging and design

One of the most crucial tasks for any brand's manager is to be clear (and right) about a brand's positioning (see BRANDING AND BRAND MANAGEMENT):

- Is the brand differentiated?
- Is there a clear reason why consumers should buy it?
- Does it satisfy functional and emotional needs?
- Does the brand deliver its promise consistently?

These are some of the most basic marketing questions – and yet they are the ones most frequently ignored by marketers. Successful brands have (or at least once had) clear positionings (see POSITIONING).

In many cases the packaging will replicate or emphasize the brand's overall positioning, and this is the most frequently occurring relationship. A clear view about positioning means a clear brief to the designer and in turn a creative solution that fits the brand. Body Shop packaging underlines the positioning as earth friendly, straightforward, 'under-marketed', reusable, not wasteful. Sheba petfood comes in small flexible trays that look valuable and almost humanistic and the graphic design looks indulgent and special. The packaging clearly and correctly encapsulates the brand positioning.

Some categories are much more complicated and it will be necessary to understand the packaging as a constituent part of a total communication mix. In these situations it is vital to analyse other communication media such as television advertising in coming to a conclusion about the exact role of packaging. In the beer/lager market, for instance, whereas television will often be used to give a brand a distinctive identity and personality (satisfying the emotional part of the positioning), packaging will communicate authenticity, product values, origins, heritage (satisfying the more functional part). Similarly compare the packaging/advertising mix for Campari and Malibu.

In some brands of cosmetics, the role of television and packaging are complementary with their own distinctive roles. Take Chanel, for instance. The equilibrium achieved by advertising and packaging allows both media to push their individual role to the limit.

All too frequently these complementary roles are not discussed sufficiently, with the respective talents of packaging design and advertising not being combined at an early enough stage. It is, after all, a crucial decision whether the packaging should attempt to 'be the total brand' or, alternatively, play a clearly defined role of emphasis of just one or two specific aspects.

5 Understand your brand's packaging and design equities and ensure they are protected

Branding was invented to communicate something specific to a potential purchaser. Early producers of pottery would invent their own special mark to single out their pottery from that of the competition. Over 100 years ago pioneers of modern branding such as William Hesketh Lever 'branded' various different types of soap with names such as Sunlight and Lifebuoy. Not only were the names deliberately unusual, but the way in which they were written was also unique.

The crucial point is that such a name, styled in such an individualistic way, would allow the brand to be protected by law. In other words there was a solid foundation on which to build the credibility and goodwill of the brand.

Looking around the world today, it is remarkable how companies differ in the importance they place on registering and protecting their brand names and associated 'get-up' (distinctive features). Some have centralized departments that monitor and control the use of brand names and, through ensuring total consistency, make it as difficult as possible to be imitated (especially by trade brands).

Other companies appear to have lost sight of the fact that a consistent use of a brand name, logo style and associated marques or features is the most important legal protection that they can have to ensure their ownership. There are few controls and brand managers around the world appear to have considerable freedom to add their own personal preferences to the brand's basic identity. It is not surprising that the imitators have had such a field day.

There is another crucial point here, beyond the legal one, which has to do with consumers and how they recognize the brands to which they have become loyal or semi-loyal. We know that in the supermarket consumers do not have time to consider every purchase from a fundamental point-of-view. Most often, with limited time, they pick the brands they know. The recognition is produced by a familiar combination of brand name, logo style, colouring and other symbols or features that have come to equal the brand. So it is essential to review whether the heartland 'brand' design is as strong as it should be. Dove cleansing bar does a great job of communicating a name, a unique style, a colour and a symbol clearly and effectively. Pedigree dogfood uses a distinctive typeface, with a 'rosette' symbol in red, on a yellow-gold background. McDonald's uses its famous M symbol, together with a red and yellow colour scheme.

Some brands can be recognized by a symbol alone, although not all great brands have great symbols (Coca-Cola has a famous typeface but not a famous symbol) and not all great symbols are attached to great brands. It is important to note that symbols do not need language to communicate and so they travel around the world. For example, in China the Woolmark is a widely understood and valued symbol.

Finally, it is important to be aware of what the consumer sees as the equities of a brand. This is often completely different from what the brand manager believes that the consumer sees. Change what is important to the consumer at your peril. On the other hand why hold on to design 'clutter' if it has no consumer value?

A checklist of possible packaging and design equities would include the following:

- the shape of the container (e.g. Toilet Duck);
- a distinctive opening device (e.g. Grolsch);

- the packaging material (e.g. Ferrero Rocher);
- the packaging material finish (e.g. Absolut vodka);
- any other distinctive physical features (e.g. the shape of the capsules in Elizabeth Arden time capsules, ceramides);
- the colour of the packaging (e.g. Marlboro);
- the logo style (e.g. Coca-Cola);
- the use of a symbol (e.g. Woolmark);
- the use of a personality (e.g. Colonel Saunders);
- any other surface design feature, possibly more abstract (e.g. the simplicity and elegance of Chanel).

6 See the environment as an opportunity not a constraint

There is no doubt that there is a clear trend in most of the world today towards more environmentally friendly packaging. There are many manifestations:

- Less bulk: simply using less material.
- Removal of secondary packaging: why sell toothpaste in two containers when it is perfectly OK sold in one?
- Concentration: concentrated detergents now use less than half the packaging material compared to before.
- Reusable: many products are now sold in a 'first time' box/tin/jar, which can then be replenished via a 'refill' pack.
- Secondary usage (especially important in developing markets): design the packaging for its original purpose and for a secondary purpose (e.g. a storage jar).
- Recyclable: design the material and its construction so that it can be collected back in and either reused directly or reprocessed.
- Bulk or home delivery: the ultimate non-use of packaging, but not yet commonplace.

There are other manifestations which involve clever new materials, more space-efficient shapes and so on – and in some markets, in some countries, there is a certain competitive advantage to be had in being rated as 'environmentally friendly' (see GREEN MARKETING).

There is no point in the marketer ignoring these environmental trends. They should not be viewed as constraints but rather as challenges and opportunities. The new rules and new sensitivities will apply to everyone, so the race is still on to do it better, cheaper and more effectively than the competition. Innovation in environmentally sensitive packaging will be a key area in which to gain competitive advantage in the future.

7 It is not enough to be individually effective: packaging also has to work at the point-of-sale

The point has already been made that packaging has a vital role to play at the point of purchase. Far too much emphasis is given to the design process as to how a pack looks and feels individually, and not nearly enough emphasis to the need to stand out and communicate in store. These objectives are not alternatives: they are both crucial. Consideration must be given to impact and display value, as well as the detailed and more subtle features of the individual pack. There are a number of points that should be taken into account:

- How will the packaging look in a mass display? Will the colour form a 'block' of colour to stand out effectively (e.g. Kodak film)?
- Will the design structure work in a mass display? The OXO logo works well on a box and in combination where all the letters join up: OXOXOXOXO.
- Will the mass effect stand out from the competition? If everyone else is coloured, then is it better to be white? If the category language for cooking oil is yellow, what will consumers think of red (a real example from Italy)?
- Will the packs stack neatly and be space efficient for the shop? Some cans fit one into the other – they are far more easy to stack than ones that do not have this feature.
- Will the brand name and/or sub-brand and/or variety be clearly and unmistakably recognizable, not only from a couple of centimetres but also a metre or so? This is especially true about brands that offer a wide range of varieties.

There are two golden rules: truly understand the trade/selling arena first, before the packaging is designed or changed. Second, judge and test the new designs in a selling arena as well as individually.

8 Effective packaging is one of the most difficult parts of the mix to progress in companies: it concerns almost every discipline

Most of the headings considered in this entry make points about the substance of packaging itself. In large corporations, however, the key to developing great packaging lies in how the resources of the organization are utilized. This is because, unlike, say, advertising, packaging development can impinge on almost every department, especially if it involves physical structure. There are a number of key process requirements:

- Understand the role and expertise of all the various disciplines involved (e.g. production, packaging development, distribution, supply chain, customer marketing, consumer marketing, PR).
- Ensure senior manager sponsorship for the changes or developments that are proposed.
- Involve everyone at an early stage and establish a 'teamwork' *modus operandi*.
- Be clear about objectives, responsibilities, time scales, costs and record them regularly in writing.
- Establish clear leadership of the team so that the pace and direction of activities can be judged.

The more organized and systematic the process, the easier it will be to be innovative and creative. When all the key players are involved and confident about proposed changes, then it is far easier to take more adventurous and courageous decisions.

9 Use suppliers and outside advisers for new ideas and industry experience

The experts are often involved far too late in the process. The world is changing very fast. Artwork can now be sent around the world at the touch of a button. The top design companies working with the best clients have computerized interaction so that design can be appraised simultaneously and amended by agency and client in collaboration.

New materials such as polymers and laminates are appearing faster and faster; new ways of opening and closing; longer-life storage; more efficient distribution; more cost-effective use of materials; more environmentally friendly materials: 'Should I move away from steel and into aluminium? Or vice versa? Is paper better than plastic? If plastic is better, can I make it look like paper? Should I have a budget for a widget or a gadget?'

There are three broad streams of expertise: the suppliers of the packaging (sometimes including the suppliers of the packaging production equipment); the agencies and consultants who develop the physical packaging and the surface graphics; and the agencies and consultants who research and help clients judge whether new ideas are more effective from a consumer and customer point-of-view.

The suppliers have a perspective across a broad range of industries and will be able to offer guidance on trends and preferences. They have their own innovation processes and are often on the lookout for breakthrough ideas themselves. They can sometimes be persuaded to channel their new ideas into an exclusivity deal with a top customer.

The packaging/design agencies form an extensive industry around the world, with over a thousand separate companies in operation. Again it is important to do one's homework before deciding on exactly who to work with. A possible list of questions could be:

- Do I need physical development or surface graphics, or both?
- Do I need a high level of creativity and design flair?
- Do I need purely packaging advice, or marketing as well?
- Do I need international expertise, with the ability to translate languages and work cross-border?
- Do I need specific expertise in one particular category (e.g. food, ice-cream, cosmetics)?

- Do I need an agency with full digital capability that can send me artwork, in colour, instantly?
- Is a high level of confidentiality/security important?
- Is this a job to try out someone new, or do I need the confidence of one of my regular suppliers?

The marketing and research agencies who will help a client to evaluate both current packaging and future ideas is the other crucial outside source of expertise. Some experts in the industry have stated that research is unnecessary. However, the writer of this entry has the opposite view with the usual caveat that research should not dictate a decision – rather research informs and shapes a decision. Many sensitive and reliable techniques have been developed using audit, qualitative and quantitative research. The best processes are often when packaging/design agency, marketing/research agency, other suppliers and client all work together as a team (see QUALITATIVE RESEARCH IN MARKETING; QUANTITATIVE METHODS IN MARKETING; THE MARKETING AUDIT).

10 An international point; the world is getting smaller and brands need to harmonize cross-country boundaries

Some of the most successful designs are managed on a global basis, both from a legal and a consumer point-of-view. Kodak is the same colour yellow throughout the world. McDonald's M can be recognized in Tokyo and Tahiti. The Woolmark stands for pure new wool in China and Barlaston, where Wedgwood make china, and are famous for their Wedgwood blue, which is extremely popular in Tokyo. Satellite television, global sponsorship, increasing trans-global production, an increasingly mobile and knowledgeable consumer, and the need to produce goods more cost effectively are some of the influences upon multinational companies to work towards global harmonization (see GLOBAL MARKETING).

The problem of a global image has been less difficult for companies in sectors such as cosmetics and luxury goods (where such an image has been part of the brand's prestige from the very beginning), than in more mundane sectors such as food, detergents, functional personal products or paper products. Here, multinational companies were often organized on a country-by-country basis, with each local unit arguing the case for why they should be different from everyone else. This led to a massive proliferation in packaging and design, making it virtually impossible to centralize sales, production or communication.

For most sectors the key objective should be 'glocalization'. This means adopting a global approach, a global vision and global harmonization wherever it is common sense so to do, but at the same time being sensitive to the local culture in such areas as (obviously) language, recipe fine tuning (e.g. sweetness, strength of flavour), perfume note/strength and cultural insensitivities.

Achievement of localized packaging needs strong global leadership with the ability and power to direct the global process, while being sensitive and aware of local needs. The key is that the former precedes the latter, and not the other way round.

11 Summary

Most fast-moving consumer goods (FMCG) companies spend considerable sums of money in variable packaging costs, sometimes many times more than the amount spent on theme advertising. As marketing becomes more competitive, it is imperative that companies renew their focus and commitment.

PETER DART
ADDED VALUE GROUP

Further reading

(References cited in the text marked *)

Booth-Clibborn, E. (1993) *British Packaging Now*, Internos Books Ltd.
Coleman, Lipuma, Segal & Morrill, Inc (1994) *Package Design and Brand Identity*, Rockport Publishers.
Added Value Group (unpublished) *Effective Packaging*, available from Added Value Group, Surrey, UK.
Harckham, A.W. (1989) *Packaging Strategy – Meeting the Challenge of Changing Times*, Technomic Publishing Company.
Olins, W. (1989) *Corporate Identity*, London: Thames and Hudson.

Paine, F.A. (1981) *Fundamentals of Packaging*, Leicester: Brookside Press Ltd.

Pynor, R. and Booth-Clibborn, E. (1991) *Typography Now: the next wave*, Internos Books.

Upshaw, Lynn B. (1995) *Building Brand Identity*, John Wiley & Sons Inc.

Wozencroft, I. (1992) *The Graphic Language of Neville Brody*, London: Thames and Hudson.

See also: ADVERTISING, BRANDING AND BRAND MANAGEMENT; GLOBAL MARKETING; GREEN MARKETING; MARKETING COMMUNICATIONS; POSITIONING; QUALITATIVE RESEARCH IN MARKETING; QUANTITATIVE METHODS IN MARKETING; THE MARKETING AUDIT

Branding and brand management

1. The value of brands
2. The features of great brands
3. Hierarchy of brand information
4. Brand range
5. Branding in service industries
6. Brand management
7. The future of brands

Overview

Marketing has come to be seen as the central business discipline. The marketing function acts as a sort of 'gearbox', making a profitable connection between a company's core competencies and the needs of the market. For most marketers brands are the cogs in the gearbox. Brands and brand marketing lie at the heart of business and many of the world's best known companies, Unilever, Procter & Gamble, Mars, are structured around their brands.

Companies become attractive takeover targets and the value of their stock rises because of the strength of their brands. Some have even gone as far as putting a balance sheet value on their brands to reflect this. Branding is most commonly associated with consumer goods companies, but in fact the notion of branding has now gone well beyond this narrow view. Service industries have discovered and exploited the power of branding. Where previously they relied on their corporate name to differentiate themselves in the market they have now developed brands and sub-brands. Indeed, in every industry the importance of the corporate brand itself has been recognized and much of the theory of branding in consumer goods and services has been applied to corporations and many other organizations, even charities. If one understands brands one understands that Oxfam is as much a brand as Coca-Cola.

So what is a brand, what are the features of great brands and what is their value to companies and consumers? Let us take consumers as our starting-point, as any good marketer would do, and look at the history of brands.

1 The value of brands

The value of brands to consumers – an historical perspective

The act of marking a product with a device that signifies its origins is branding and the value to consumers is that it assists and simplifies choice. When in Roman times artisans signed or in some other way identified their produce they branded it and in so doing they helped consumers to pick out their products if they had been given a recommendation by a friend (the most powerful form of advertising), or find them again if they had tried them, appreciated them and wished to repeat the experience. Branding for consumers represents the mark of a given level of quality and value that helps them choose between one product and another. Even in Roman times consumers were required to make so many purchase decisions and, like any sensible consumer, did not want to risk a bad experience (a poor quality chariot?); branding had real utility for them as a simplifier of choice.

In more recent times Lord Lever branded his soap in order to provide his target consumers with a way of recognizing it from the many, poorer quality alternatives. He even advertised the soap to gain widespread acclaim for it, using the advertising to imply values that went beyond the mere cleansing characteristics. He implied that a certain type of person used Sunlight Soap which made you feel a certain way, thereby endowing it with outer directed and inner directed emotional values to add to the established functional cleaning values. Unfortunately, this was no help to him if the shopkeeper, upon whom many customers relied for advice, recommended a competitive brand, and while the retail trade operated in this way the power of brands was restricted (see RETAILING). The advent of the self-service supermarket signalled the start of the golden age of brands since the consumer had to rely on them more and more to guide their choice.

Thus, the fundamental driving force behind brands is that they have utility for consumers. Life would not only be duller, it would be a good deal more complicated without brands. Imagine how long the weekly grocery shop would take if everything came in unmarked brown packages.

The value of brands to companies

Brands also have utility for the company. Consumers' loyalty to a brand based on their experience of it gives the brand protection against new rivals. This loyalty will decay if in reality the brand is no better than its competitors, but that may take some time during which the company can rebuild its competitive advantage.

The other advantage of brands is that they allow companies to target different groups of consumers, or segments of the market, with different branded offerings (see MARKET SEGMENTATION). Not everyone has the same needs, outlook on life or budgets. In every market, even water, particular groups of consumers can be persuaded to pay more if they believe they will get more. Developing more than one brand enables a company to segment a market and target different consumers. As long as they add more value than cost for these new segments, they will increase their overall profitability. It also enables the company to defend itself from competitors seeking to do the same. This use of different brands to segment and dominate markets is very evident in areas such as detergents, confectionery and petfoods, where companies like Unilever and Mars have a large portfolio of brands competing in the same product category but aimed at different groups of consumers.

The development of a portfolio of discrete brands has further advantages for the company. It enables them to insulate the problems of one product from the rest of the range (as Johnson & Johnson were able to do during the Tylenol product tampering scare in the USA) and it can allow them to sell off brands (as SmithKline Beecham were able to do with Marmite). However, there is a limit to the number of brands a company will want to have since each brand has a fixed cost in terms of the investment needed to differentiate it and communicate its uniqueness. Heinz has predominantly gone down the road of developing one 'umbrella' house brand, while companies such as Ford and Kellogg have a house brand with various sub-brands. The advantages and disadvantages of different approaches to brand structures is returned to below.

By developing a range of brands to cover different consumer segments a company can be well positioned to benefit from changing consumer needs. Silk Cut was a small part of Gallagher's portfolio for many years before concerns over smoking generally, and tar content in particular, made it one of the company's major profit earners. This leads on to a consideration of brands as a means of resource allocation within a company. Competing companies are themselves the mechanism whereby scarce resources are allocated to the best performing areas in a capitalist economy. Brands perform the same function within a company. Resources can be taken from an underperforming brand and directed at a growth brand to achieve higher returns. The Boston Consulting Group developed a model that enables a company to group sectors or brands into four quadrants ranging from 'Star' to 'Dog' as a way of deciding strategic investment priorities.

The value of brands – a summary

- Brands have value to consumers as a way of identifying a given and consistent level of quality that simplifies choice.
- This builds consumer loyalty, which provides a company with a degree of profit protection over time.
- Developing a portfolio of brands can enable a company to target different consumer segments, thereby increasing share and profit, and providing a defence against competition.
- Some companies will seek to dominate their market through one house brand and a range of products or sub-brands. This gives economies of scale but carries risks if an individual product fails.
- Brands are a means whereby finite investment resources are allocated within a company.

2 The features of great brands

Value performance

Behind every great brand is a great product. So much has now been written about the clever use of advertising to hype marginal benefits and develop brand personalities that will inflate consumer demand that the real product

The marketing mix

performance is often neglected. Every great, durable brand either has or has had for a significant part of its history a demonstrable and well-recognized product advantage. Mercedes may now sell many cars on the basis of what they say about the purchaser, but the fact is that for many years they were a better engineered car compared to any of an equivalent price, and it is this reputation, jealously maintained through successive product improvements, that provides the foundation for customer loyalty. As noted above, this loyalty will decay over time if Japanese cars continue to erode or even overtake the product lead Mercedes have enjoyed, but it is this well-earned reputation that sustains sales in the face of tough competition, and all other values are based on it.

To go further, Mercedes are excellent value for money, which shows the foolishness of those who talk about 'value brands' when they mean lower value. All brands are bought because their consumers believe them to be best value. Consumers have different hierarchies of needs and different budgets, which allow for different brands in a market. However, consumers have also learnt that market competition usually ensures you get what you pay for. There are of course many subtleties of positioning but in essence there is a value curve in any market and to be a great brand you have to be on it or at least in the 'combat zone'. A simple example for the car market is given in Figure 1, showing how Ford, BMW and Mercedes are positioned on the value curve.

As shown in Figure 1 each brand is successful, each offers great value (i.e. for a given price each gives the best value performance where performance is the summary of all the characteristics a consumer looks for in a car). Based on past reputation a brand may, for a limited period, operate below the line, but only because at some point in its history the brand operated above the line, which is to say that for a given price it gave the customer more. It is upon this competitive advantage, current or past, real or perceived, that its brand credentials have been built.

Highest common factors

For the purpose of explaining the value curve, the idea of performance being an aggregate of what people look for in a car was used, the implication being that consumers then have the choice to buy different amounts. In reality consumers are often asked to make tradeoffs between possible benefits. One can either have the personal service of a small airline company at a higher price or the convenience of a large airline carrier at a lower price. These tradeoffs are what allow brands to adopt different positioning targeted at different consumers with different needs, attitudes and budgets. However, the big durable brands stay big by keeping most of the people happy most of the time. In other words, they offer consumers a higher common factor between two or more conflicting benefits. To use the airline example, British Airways tries to convey the convenience of the big airline with the

Figure 1 The value curve ('You get what you pay for!')

service one would expect only from a smaller carrier, the overall proposition being 'The world's favourite airline'. Apple computers offer leading-edge technology that is easy and fun to use. Many detergent brands including Persil and Fairy offer tough cleaning yet with care for the item they are used upon.

In this way the big brands will try to dominate the high ground of the market. Smaller brands will then position themselves on one of the dimensions (e.g. the best efficiency but at the expense of care, or the most care but at the expense of efficiency). The new entrant will try and change the rules by introducing a new dimension (e.g. a deodorizing perfume, or care for the environment). Big brands react to this by relaunching to include the new benefit. However, if, in functional terms, there is a real tradeoff between existing benefits and the new one (better care for the environment can only be delivered at the expense of cleaning efficiency, to take the example above) then the new brand can successfully defend its new positioning in the market and the market ground rules will have changed.

Spiritual reward

Life is not all about rationality and functionality. People seek experiences that make them feel better about themselves, and outward expressions that communicate their self-worth to others. In a way not to be overly exaggerated brands help us in this. A mother will reassure herself that she is doing the best for her family by buying brands that reinforce this (OXO or Persil) and will want that brand to communicate this to her family and friends. The successful businessman will want to reward himself and communicate his success to his peers through the purchase of a Rolex watch. These are the so-called inner directed and outer directed values that brands can deliver. In their own small way they nourish the soul.

As already outlined, these values spring from, and work symbiotically with, the product values. Persil's caring values originally came from its soap-based formula, which made the clothes not just clean but nicer to wear. Mercedes' status values came from the fact that the company did indeed offer better engineering and more comfort for those with the means to afford it. These non-functional values, like the functional ones, are intrinsic to the brand and are reinforced by the other people that use the brand and what they say about it. They can of course be amplified by advertising and other forms of promotion.

The brand value, its distinctive competitive advantage, is referred to as its positioning (see POSITIONING). There are many different ways to express this, such as the way you would expect a consumer to describe the brand to a friend. Figure 2 demonstrates another useful approach. The centre circle contains the summary of the brand proposition; the next layer shows the various things in the brand that substantiate the proposition at a functional level; the outer layer contains the non-functional values that come from the substantiation (i.e. what the brand says about the purchasers and how it makes them feel).

Distinctive added value

The essence of a great brand is therefore its ability to target this rounded package of functional and non-functional values at particular groups of consumers. At the heart of the brand is a core set of beliefs that represent its distinctive proposition to its target consumers, which is supported by the tangible things that substantiate the proposition, and the intangible, that is inner- and outer-directed values.

What distinguishes the brand from the commodity is that it has added values. In functional terms these values add cost, since extra performance adds manufacturing cost. However, the skilful manufacturer, by focusing on and understanding the needs of the target customers better than the competition, can create functional advantages so unique that they command a price premium. In other words, more value than cost is added. This value is further increased through the unique non-functional attributes that the brand offers.

This added value must be communicated to consumers in a distinctive way. How do you know that the unique properties of a Rolex watch are relevant to you, that its expensive craftsmanship and style will reward you and signify your success to your friends, if you and they cannot recognize it from any other watch? The basis of this recognition lies in the product itself – its visual identity. Experiments show that consumers only have to be able to see the smallest fraction of a famous brand's logo or

The marketing mix

Figure 2 Volvo brand proposition

some other aspect of its design to be able to recognize it. Just the combination of colours in thin stripes will tell you that the computer is an Apple; just the glimpse of the 'd' in Dunhill will tell you that the belt or tie is made by Dunhill. Marlboro have invested a huge amount of advertising and sponsorship money to ensure that the colour red will conjure up the brand in your mind. Great brands have evolved very distinctive liveries to ensure that the added value they offer is instantly recognized (see PACKAGING AND DESIGN; PRODUCT POLICY).

Coherent brand mix

With real product performance plus the intangible values that come from this, and distinctive packaging design as the foundation blocks, brands can also use the other elements of what is called the 'brand mix' to communicate the total proposition. Two have already been touched on.

First, price is part of the brand mix since it works in conjunction with the other elements to determine the value equation. Second, there is promotion which covers all aspects of paid-for advertising as well as free support from opinion formers such as the press, and sales promotion – although not so much the tactical money-off sort but rather promotional schemes that make a statement about the brand (e.g. the chance to win tickets to a rock concert from Pepsi) (see PRICING; SALES PROMOTION).

The place you see a brand and indeed the people you see using it also communicate the proposition. This explains why Rodeo Drive in Hollywood, St Honoré in Paris and Bond Street in London command such high rent premiums from the luxury goods brands which have shops there, and also why marketers will 'seed' the brand with aspirational figures to gain acceptance from the masses. These Six Ps of the brand mix – product, packaging, price, promotion, place, people – are all employed consistently and coherently by the great brands to communicate and reinforce their competitive advantage.

Branding and brand management

Summary

- Great brands are based on performance and value. Even if over time their performance advantage has been competed away, a great brand will have residual consumer loyalty based on perceptions of superior product performance and value. This reputation is durable but not everlasting.
- Brands attempt to dominate the high ground of a market by offering the highest common factor between conflicting benefit areas (e.g. hi-tech but easy to use, efficient but caring).
- Based on functional advantages brands develop inner- and outer-directed values (how they make you feel and what they say about you). These added values, both functional and non-functional, separate brands from commodities.
- It follows therefore that strong brands can command a price premium or at the very least a higher volume for an equivalent price.
- Great brands develop very distinctive visual identities that act as the summary of their brand proposition (i.e. their added values).
- Brands use all aspects of the brand mix consistently and coherently to communicate their proposition.

This summary can also be expressed as a very practical checklist for a brand.

1. Does the brand have performance that is recognized as superior by its target consumers in blind (unbranded) product trials?
2. Are those performance advantages closely aligned to what consumers say are the key parameters upon which they make purchase decisions?
3. Does the brand have a personality which the consumer sees as motivating in the context of the product category (a loving mother for a range of baby products, a successful sportsperson for a high performance car)? Note that in small research groups this can be tested by asking consumers to describe the brand as a person if it came to life.
4. Does the consumer believe the brand is purchased by other consumers that they regard as aspirational?
5. Does the brand charge a price premium and/or have a significant volume share lead over other brands in its market segment (at least a 2 to 1 sales advantage)?
6. Does it have a significantly higher loyalty profile (e.g. a greater proportion of its consumers who chose it in more than three out of their last five purchases in the case of grocery category, or a higher propensity to repurchase in the case of a consumer durable)?
7. Is the brand instantly recognizable among its target consumers through just small portions of its visual identity?
8. Is every aspect of its brand mix communicating all or at least a significant part of its proposition? Note that brands can use different aspects of the mix, even different media, to emphasize certain values.

If the answer to any of these questions is negative then the brand may still continue to deliver profit but it is living on borrowed time.

3 Hierarchy of brand information

It has been established that a brand is a bundle of values that makes it distinctive and this distinction is communicated through a bundle of elements known as the brand mix. Within the values there is a hierarchy that will vary with each brand (the intangible or non-functional elements are more important for a perfume, and the tangible or functional elements are more important for a parachute). So it is with the elements within the brand mix. Figure 3 sets out a fuller list of elements (but by no means comprehensive) that in total communicate the brand. Examples are given that expand on the product related, 'from where', part of the brand information.

In the case of the car the specific descriptor or sub-brand (see Brand structures, below) Gti is more important than Golf, which is in turn more important than VW. The country of origin also plays a role, since other brands of cars have established a reputation for Germany as a source of reliable, well-engineered cars. German origin is part of what distinguishes the Golf Gti from other rivals made in, say, Japan or Italy, since for cars, as for many other product categories, the countries themselves have brand identities.

In the case of the paint the primary focus is on Dulux. That it is 'Gloss finish' and for indoor/outdoor use is quite important information

381

The marketing mix

	Examples		
Country of origin	Germany	UK	France
Manufacturer/ corporate brand	VW	ICI	LMVH
Brand	Golf	Dulux	Moët & Chandon
Sub-brand description	Gti	Gloss finish	Medium-bodied
Product	5-door small car	Indoor and outdoor paint	Champagne

Product → Packaging → Price → Promotion → Place (distribution) → People (users)

Figure 3 Hierarchy of information

but probably only after the brand choice has already been made. The corporate brand, ICI, has a role in the hierarchy of information but the country of origin, the UK, is not important at all.

For the wine, its French origins are vital, as is the fact that it is a champagne. However, its parent brand LMVH is not really relevant at all and Moët & Chandon is not as important a part of the brand proposition for this wine as Gti is for the car, or Dulux is for the paint.

Thus, there is a hierarchy of brand information that must be understood through research and reflected through other elements of the mix such as packaging design and advertising. Over time the hierarchy can be changed through the actions of the brand owner and the attitudes of consumers. Australia has been made a feature of some beers, but Germany is no longer relevant to cameras because consumers have become more interested in electronic rather than optical features.

4 Brand range

Brand range extension

A variant of a brand is the provision of extra choice within the same product category that essentially leaves the core brand proposition untouched, for example the addition of a new peach flavour to an ice-cream brand. The intrinsic values of the ice-cream remain the same but you can now enjoy a new peach flavour if you happen to like peaches. Where the new product within the brand range is addressing different needs, and in so doing changes the way people see the brand, this is a range extension. The addition to the ice-cream brand of a new line of flavours based on alcoholic drinks for eating on special occasions and called 'After Hours' would make quite a difference to the way one would view the 'parent' brand which had been originally positioned as, for example, the most fun ice-cream for children (Figure 4).

Range extensions can therefore be aimed quite close to the original or parent brand, perhaps just to a new segment within the same product category, or can carry the brand into a new category altogether. The two golden rules are that the brand must have values that in part or whole are relevant to the new segment or market, and that the new range extension enhances or adds back to the core brand. Since brands are now regarded as valuable assets for a company, financial analogies in branding are often used. The core brand values, carefully nurtured over many years, are often referred to as the 'brand equity' and represent a sort of 'capital account'. As well as ensuring that the parent brand core equity has relevance for the new segment, the new range extension should repay the capital account and build the total brand equity. Good examples of range extensions or 'equity stretch' that obeyed the golden rules are Marks & Spencer foods and Mars ice-cream; bad examples are Cadbury's Smash (instant potatoes) and Levi suits.

The decision to range extend an existing brand rather than exploit a new opportunity through launching a different brand is a cost–benefit analysis. Studies have shown that

Figure 4 Brand range extension

[Diagram: The virtuous circle — Existing brand → Range extended → New brand repays by reinforcing existing values and adding new ones → Existing brand; Existing brand confers relevant values]

significant savings can be made in launching a range extension compared to a new brand since the extension needs less advertising to establish its credentials. Success rates too can be higher for the range extension as consumers are less resistant to try a new product from a name they trust. However, this line of thinking can be dangerous. Companies can be tempted into underestimating the investment needed and overestimating the relevance of the parent brand values to the new market. Despite the risks and costs it can still be better to launch a new brand. Unilever have been able to develop a very profitable global shampoo brand, Timotei, based on care, where they might have been tempted to try and seize the same opportunity with their Pears brand, which had similar credentials but was seen as old-fashioned in a sector that demanded modernity. Procter & Gamble, on the other hand, were able to do the reverse by using the Vidal Sassoon brand and its salon credentials to establish 'Wash 'n' Go', where new brands from competitors had failed to overcome consumer scepticism that just one product could successfully clean and condition hair.

Brand stretch and limits to range extension

Warning notes have been sounded about range extensions that fail to live up to the core brand values and thereby risk killing the original brand. In reality there are few examples of this because most range extension has occurred on well-established brands which can withstand even quite big failures (witness the disastrous Coca-Cola relaunch which resulted in consumers demanding the return of the original). On the positive side range extensions can revitalize tired brands by clearly demonstrating the core values of the brand and establishing new ones. Dunhill, having started as a range of tobacco products including a well-crafted lighter, has developed into a global luxury goods brand for men covering clothing, watches and even a successful fragrance. In research the technique of asking consumers to react to the use of a brand on many different types of products is used to disclose what consumers really think about the brand. One study revealed that crunch was the core property of a potato crisp rather than its potato taste since consumers were able to relate to it as a biscuit more easily than they could as a new oven chip.

As well as revealing the core values, these types of study also show the degree of stretch in a brand. In principle any brand can extend into any market if one has the time, commitment and money to invest, but its inherent elasticity will tell you how long, how hard and how much it will take, and can help show the steps on the way. (See Figure 5.) The Dunhill brand moved from lighters to accessories such as pens and cufflinks, then to belts and ties, a blazer and eventually a full range of menswear. Through range extension Dunhill was able to find a higher order of brand values, such as British craftsmanship and style, on which to build its brand, rather than remain locked into smoking requisites. Lucozade was able to develop energy from a health drink to launch a new range of isotonic sports drinks. However, where a

The marketing mix

Figure 5 As a brand moves further from its current market segment it stretches its equity. Brand elasticity varies and can be enhanced over time with successive moves

brand becomes so closely associated with the product characteristics of its category its elasticity can be low. It is harder to see Ford as a range of consumer electronics than it is, for example, to see Sony as a car.

Brand structures

When range extending a brand the issue of brand structure needs to be carefully considered. There are two questions that must be addressed. The first is what to call the new range extension. Should it just be given a descriptor, e.g. 'Heinz Baked Beans', where 'Baked Beans' is the descriptor, or a sub-brand, e.g. 'Ford Scorpio', where 'Scorpio' is a sub-brand. 'Scorpio' is a sub-brand because it is a new name that means nothing in the context of cars, although it may start to suggest certain things, and so gives the opportunity to add new values, in this case values relevant to the luxury executive car market. There is an option in between, the 'ownable descriptor' (e.g. 'Heinz Big Soup'). 'Big Soup' is semi-descriptive of what it is but still offers the vehicle whereby Heinz can segment the market and offer new values, in this case a more male-orientated soup that can be a meal in itself. By dint of the fact that different companies have successfully employed different approaches (Heinz, Kellogg, Unilever and others have employed all three), each route is viable but each has different implications.

The descriptor does not allow for much that is new to be said about the brand. Heinz Baked Beans conjures up nothing new about Heinz. On the other hand, if one's experience of the product is good it translates instantly into an enhanced view of Heinz. Ford needed to say something different to make the brand appropriate to a successful business executive wanting to trade up to a more prestigious car such as a Mercedes or BMW. Scorpio afforded Ford the opportunity to position a new car for these consumers. However, a good experience of a Scorpio does not instantly transfer back into an enhanced view of Ford as a brand. The consumers, by having a sub-brand to refer to, can tell their friends that while the Scorpio is a great car they are still not sold on Ford generally (Figure 6).

The test of the relationship between the range extension and the parent brand is whether the name of the range extension is sufficient in itself to allow consumers to get what they want. Ask for baked beans and you may or may not get Heinz; ask for a Scorpio and you will get only the Ford Scorpio. The ownable descriptor operates somewhere in the middle. Leaving aside retail copies, 'Frosties' will get you Kellogg's Frosties. The experience of it will also feed directly back into Kellogg and add to the core equity of the child values which the range extension embodies. The consumer will say 'Frosties' but will visualize 'Kellogg's Frosties'.

Branding and brand management

```
                        Parent
                        brand
                    ┌───────────┐
                    └───────────┘
          ↗                              ↖
Ability to develop new      The         Ability to feed back new
values will be less for a  virtuous     value will be stronger for
descriptor and greater for  circle      a descriptor and weaker
a sub-brand                              for a sub-brand
          ↘                              ↗
                        Range
                     extension
                    ┌───────────┐
                    └───────────┘
                          ↓
                    ┌───────────┐
                    │ Naming options │
                    └───────────┘
```

Descriptor   e.g. Heinz Baked Beans

Ownable
Descriptor   e.g. Heinz Big Soup

Sub-brand   e.g. Ford Scorpio

Figure 6 Range extension

The decision of which option to take (and it must be noted that there are 'shades of grey' between the three options outlined) will therefore depend on how appropriate are the values of the parent brand to the new segment or market, whether the range extension needs to be able to express new values on the one hand, and the degree to which one wants those new values to feed back into the parent brand on the other.

The second question to be addressed in brand structures follows from the analysis used to determine the name for the range extension. What weight in communication and especially the packaging should be given to the parent brand and the range extension? This refers back to the idea of a hierarchy of information. The options range from full endorsement where the parent brand is most prominent (e.g. 'Kodak Gold'), to recessive endorsement (e.g. 'Lexus, the Luxury Car from Toyota') where the sub-brand is most prominent, with options in between. The key factor is the relevance of the parent brand values. Where they are wholly appropriate, as in the case of Kodak, the manufacturer is only too keen to see positive product experience feed directly back into the parent brand (and make savings in marketing costs since sub-brands need more support than descriptors). Where the parent values are not wholly relevant the manufacturer will allow the parent brand to take a back seat and the sub-brand to develop new values which will slowly enhance the parent brand.

Corporate branding adds another dimension to the issue of brand structures. There are many examples where the brand structure falls into several tiers, the corporate brand, parent brand, sub-brand, with possibly even product descriptors and country of origin. The principles are the same in arriving at the hierarchy of brand information. To a certain extent the decisions rest on consumer attitudes but the brand owner can make choices about how to manage these attitudes through use of the brand mix which will in total communicate the overall brand proposition.

Range extension and brand structures – a summary

- A range extension is where the new addition to the range changes the core values of the parent brand.

385

The marketing mix

- The values of the parent brand should be relevant in part or whole to the new segment or market and the range extension should reinforce and enhance the parent brand's core values or 'equity'.
- Range extending rather than launching a new brand offers cost savings and a lower risk of failure but, while riskier, a new brand can give higher returns if the parent brand values do not fully stretch to the new market opportunity.
- Different brands have different elasticities, that is the ability to stretch their core values to exploit new segments or markets. The elasticity can be changed and improved over time depending on commitment, investment and the sequence of moves made.
- Choosing whether to give the range extension a descriptive name or a sub-brand name depends on the appropriateness of the core brand values and the degree to which the extension is required to feed new values back to the parent. This also determines the weight to put behind the parent versus the range extension in the information hierarchy.

5 Branding in service industries

Quite deliberately the emphasis up to this point has been on consumer goods brands since the theory of branding has largely been developed in this area. In service industries the historical approach has been to rely on the corporate brand with simple descriptions of services beneath it. However, the acquisition of a range of service brands by companies such as BET in the area of industrial services or Sears in retail, has required the brand owners to address the branding issues more seriously. Sears has a number of retail brands (including four in the UK just in the area of womenswear) which need to be positioned and developed. Furthermore, sub-brands have been used within service brands just as in consumer goods brands to target particular consumer groups, for example McDonald's 'Happy Meals' or 'McPizza'.

There are two key differences about branding in service sectors. First, the brand mix is significantly more complex. Consider retail where the brand proposition is conveyed by a very wide range of factors such as store ambience, range stocked, display, returns policy, opening hours and many more. Second, the importance of the various elements and the hierarchy of information, is often very different. Advertising is an important part of consumer goods branding as a means to communicate brand values and generate trial, but in retail it is relatively less important since consumers can experience the total offering just by walking into the store. Probably the most important element in the brand mix in any service industry is staff. In most cases they are the brand for consumers and are therefore the single most important means by which brand values are communicated. Interestingly, Marks & Spencer have built one of the most successful retail brands in the world with no advertising but they do have a widely admired staff loyalty.

Thus, in many ways brand development is more complex in service companies than in consumer goods companies. The difficulty of this task is often increased by the fact that the marketing department has a more limited role, with its remit being in the 'marketing services' of research and promotions, while product development, the key part of marketing, is made the responsibility of other functions.

6 Brand management

Returning to consumer goods, the brand management system that most companies employ was developed by Procter & Gamble in the USA. A typical organizational structure is illustrated in Figure 7.

Each brand will have a brand manager who will get involved with every aspect of the company's operation which has a bearing on the brand. This is virtually every other area since, as has been outlined above, the brand mix incorporates everything from product development to sales and distribution. The brand manager has been likened to the managing director of their particular brand, responsible for everything from strategic development to bottom-line profitability. Thus the brand manager will look at the organization as depicted in Figure 8.

The analogy of marketing as the gearbox of the business holds true for the brand manager who will work with the full range of the business functions and will employ a wide range of

Branding and brand management

```
                          Chief Executive
                                |
                         Managing Director
                                |
   ┌──────────┬──────────┬──────┴──────┬──────────┬──────────┐
Personnel  Finance     R&D         Technical   Sales      Marketing
                                                              |
                    ┌─────────────────────────────────────────┼──────────────────┐
                Marketing                                  Marketing        Market services
                Manager                                    Manager          and research
                    |                                          |
            ┌───────┼───────┐                          ┌───────┼───────┐
         Brand   Brand   Brand                      Brand   Brand   Brand
        Manager Manager Manager                    Manager Manager Manager
```

Figure 7 A typical organizational structure

external help and information to create forward energy behind the brand.

In truth this model of brand management is breaking down and was never appropriate for one-brand companies. As noted above, this includes many service companies, where a matrix structure is used with more than one function owning the decisions that affect the development of the brand. However, even for the multi-brand consumer goods companies the traditional role of the brand manager is changing. In the first place the brand is too important to be left to brand managers alone. Their role is one of advocacy, using their intimate knowledge of all aspects of the brand to make business cases for the allocation of finite resources that are decided by the board against competing cases being made by other brand teams. In the

```
                        Market
                        research
                           ↑
   Planning and            |           Advertising
   accounts                |           agency
         ↖                 |              ↗
              ┌────────────────────────┐
              │                        │
   R&D    ←→  │      Brand             │  ←→   Design and
   department │      Manager           │       promotions
              │                        │       agencies
              └────────────────────────┘
         ↙                 |              ↘
                           |            External
       Factory             |            research
                           ↓            agencies
                        Salesforce
```

Figure 8 Brand manager's role within an organization

387

second place, many brands are now international, global even, and brand management has become another type of matrix involving multinational as well as multi-functional teams. In common with most aspects of business the new order in brand management is one of continually forming and reforming project teams geared to innovation events through which the business and the brands attempt to fulfil agreed strategies. To ensure that there is still good stewardship of the brand in these more complex international business structures many companies have appointed very senior franchise or brand group managers to be responsible for formulating strategy that is then implemented by local brand teams across several geographic markets.

Nevertheless, brand management is increasingly the prime responsibility of the chief executives, since it is they who are ultimately responsible to shareholders for maximizing the return on assets employed and the brand(s) are one of the company's most important assets, second only to its people.

7 The future of brands

Brands probably reached their zenith in terms of prominence and numbers in the 1980s. Since then there has been a 'market correction' and the 1990s began with some sections of the business press announcing, almost certainly prematurely, the death of brands. A number of factors lie behind this swing of the pendulum.

First, in the 1980s bull market many brands were guilty of adding more cost than value. They have been found out by consumers who, in more recessionary times, have shown themselves less willing to pay the premiums demanded. The addition of some gold to the label, and 'Gold' to the brand name, did not mean that the value equation had genuinely been improved for consumers. Behind every great brand is a great product and behind every declining brand is a product which no longer offers real competitive advantage.

Second, the retail trade in many areas has been growing in strength and sophistication and developing 'own label' products. These retail branded products have been promoted at the expense of the weaker brands, which in many cases have been delisted from the major stores altogether. This trend will almost certainly continue but it is of course merely the replacement of one brand, the manufacturer's brand, with another, the retailer's. The fundamental value of brands to consumers and the principles of brand management remain the same.

Third, the emphasis has switched to global brands and bigger umbrella brands. The latter reflects the trend towards range extension of existing brands rather than the development of new brands for the reasons, largely to do with cost saving, outlined above. The world is probably 'over-branded' and there will be continued consolidation behind fewer global brands with wider product ranges (Macrae 1991).

Against this trend is the emergence of new brands in many sectors such as financial services and indeed well beyond the traditional business world. For to understand brands is to understand that anything is a brand which is distinctive, well differentiated, and has competitive advantage in that it meets consumer needs, both functional and non-functional, better than alternatives. Charities are brands, the Louvre in Paris or the British Museum in London are brands, even the Pope is a brand. In the world of business, the structure and ownership of brands may change but brands will remain for one basic reason – consumers want them and value them as simplifiers of choice. Back in Roman times when the artisans branded their products they were effectively saying 'I made this, I'm proud of it, you can trust it and I will stake my reputation on it'. This is useful information if you are a consumer.

MARK SHERRINGTON
ADDED VALUE GROUP

Further reading

(References cited in the text marked *)

Cowley, D. (1991) *Understanding Brands By 10 People Who Do*, London: Kogan Page Ltd.
Interbrand (1990) *Brands: an International Review*, London: Gold Arrow Publications with Interbrand Group plc.
Jones, J. P. (1986) *What's in a Name? Advertising and the Concept of Brands*, Aldershot: Gower.
King, S. (1984) *Developing New Brands*, Letchworth: Garden City Press.

Levitt, T. (1986) *The Marketing Imagination*, London: Collier Macmillan.
* Macrae, C. (1991) *World Class Brands*, Reading, MA: Addison-Wesley Publishing Co. Inc.
Nilson, T.H. (1992) *Value-Added Marketing, Marketing Management for Superior Results*, Maidenhead: McGraw-Hill.

See also: ADVERTISING; CONSUMER BEHAVIOUR; CORPORATE IDENTITY; MARKET SEGMENTATION; PACKAGING AND DESIGN; POSITIONING; PRICING; PRODUCT POLICY; RETAILING; SALES PROMOTION; STRATEGIC MARKETING FOR NON-PROFIT ORGANIZATIONS

Pricing

1. Pricing: concepts and issues
2. Analysis of the pricing environment
3. Pricing objectives
4. Pricing strategy
5. Implementation of pricing strategies: price determination and adjustment
6. Pricing tactics
7. Conclusions

Overview

Pricing is not a single concept, but a multidimensional one with different meanings and implications for the manufacturer, the retailer and the consumer. Pricing strategy is of great importance because it affects both revenue and buyer behaviour. The whole pricing environment is therefore considered, first from the point of view of the company and its strategies and then from the aspect of the consumer. However, it must not be forgotten that there are other, external influences on pricing – not just a firm's competitiors but also from government and legislation. Once these factors have been taken into account, various pricing strategies are reviewed and some attention is given to how best to implement those strategies; how pricing levels can be adjusted and how such tactics do affect buyer behaviour and company revenue.

1 Pricing: concepts and issues

Price is traditionally defined as 'the number of monetary units a customer has to pay to receive one unit of that product or service' (Simon 1989). Many marketers now advocate the use of a broadened price definition that reflects the complexity and multifaceted character of the price concept (e.g. Zeithaml 1988).

For the consumer, price is more than the objective monetary value charged by the manufacturer or retailer. It also comprises non-monetary components (e.g. time) and risk (see Zeithaml 1988); and not only the objective price but in particular the price perceptions guide consumer behaviour. Perceptions may deviate substantially from objective prices and can have a negative and a positive component (price as a sacrifice or loss, and price as a quality indicator, see below). For the manufacturer or retailer, price performs several (conflicting) functions as well: it is an important component of the marketing mix and in this sense an instrument to boost demand or respond to competitive threats, but also a major determinant of profit margins.

The multidimensional character of price should be taken into account for the pricing of products and services. Pricing involves the determination (and adjustment) of a price structure and price levels, as well as decisions on short-term price changes. According to Rao (1984) and Nagle and Holden (1995), pricing is one of the most important marketing mix decisions, price being the only marketing mix variable that generates revenues, and that has an immediate and direct effect on buyer behaviour. In practice however, pricing decisions are often made arbitrarily or merely on the basis of cost-related criteria, with no or limited pricing research to guide them. As a result, prices often fail to capture the value realized by other marketing mix instruments (Nagle and Holden 1995).

A more effective, goal-oriented approach to pricing is needed, that explicitly takes into account the role of price as a marketing mix instrument and as a profit generator. The purpose of this text is to provide a framework for effective, goal-oriented pricing, and to highlight the major aspects and factors of the pricing decision. Additional information can be found in Monroe (1990) and Nagle and Holden (1995), and in review articles on the topic (Monroe and Della Bitta 1978, Rao 1984, Gijsbrechts 1993). Figure 1 provides a schematic overview of the steps involved in effective price decisions.

Obviously, thorough analysis of the environment is a prerequisite for proper strategy selection. Company goals and costs, buyer behaviour, characteristics of competitors and of other publics may strongly affect relevant pricing options and are discussed in Section 2.

Environmental analysis is a building block for the specification of pricing objectives,

```
                    ENVIRONMENT
         COMPANY BUYER COMPETITORS PUBLICS
                          │
                          ▼
                 PRICING OBJECTIVES
                          │
                          ▼
                  PRICING STRATEGY
                          │
                          ▼
  LONG           PRICE DETERMINATION
  TERM
  -----------------------------------------
  SHORT
  TERM                    ▼
                   PRICING TACTICS
```

Figure 1 Effective pricing
Source: Adapted from Nagle and Holden (1995) and Morris and Calantone (1990)

which must – on top of being consistent with the environment – be attainable and operational. Section 3 gives a summary of the most important pricing objectives.

The next step is to specify which pricing strategies enable achievement of the objectives, and to select the alternative most appropriate for the pricing environment. The major types of strategies are discussed in Section 4.

To implement the selected strategy, a price structure and price level(s) have to be determined. Section 5 summarizes the different approaches and techniques that can be used for price determination and strategic price changes. The impact of short-term price adjustments is the subject of Section 6. The discussion concentrates mainly on price promotions, the most important class of price tactics.

It goes without saying that the process just described is not a purely chronological one. As the dotted lines in Figure 1 indicate, environmental characteristics influence each subsequent step, also feedback loops within one decision period and over time are bound to occur.

2 Analysis of the pricing environment

To be effective, pricing objectives and strategies must be in line with the characteristics of the environment. Four important characteristics are discussed here: company characteristics, buyer behaviour, competitive conditions and the influence of other publics.

Company goals, strategies and costs

Pricing objectives and strategies have to be consistent with company goals and overall marketing strategy (see MARKETING STRATEGY).

Company goals are 'general aspirations toward which all activities in the firm, not only pricing, are directed' (Nagle and Holden 1995). For a discussion of the different types of company objectives we refer to Kotler (1997) and Nagle and Holden (1995), and to Levy and Weitz (1995) for retailers. The impact of company goals on pricing objectives and strategies will be discussed in Sections 3 and 4 respectively.

To obtain the selected goals, a global strategy has to be developed. Since price is an important component of a firm's marketing mix, the pricing strategy must be part of an overall market strategy, and take interrelationships with other marketing instruments into account (see THE MARKETING MIX). First, the pricing strategy must be adjusted to the product's (perceived) value and cost characteristics (e.g. dynamic effects), and its relation to other products in the line (demand, costs). Other relevant characteristics (especially for the planning of pricing tactics) are the perishability and purchase frequency of the product (durable versus consumer goods; see Simon 1989). Advertising also affects customers' reactions to prices. While non-price advertising decreases price sensitivity (Kaul and Wittink 1995), feature ads increase the impact of price deals (Blattberg *et al.* 1995). Finally, the products' distribution influences consumer price perceptions as well as the practicability of segmented pricing strategies (see Nagle and Holden, 1995, for a more detailed discussion). A number of these issues will be taken up below.

Price is not only an important marketing mix instrument, it is also a major determinant of a firm's profits and cash flows. To analyse the profit implications of a pricing decision, cost information is indispensable. Not all costs are relevant however: according to Nagle and Holden (1995) only forward-looking, incremental and avoidable costs must be taken into account for pricing. At the same time, the company should look beyond costs associated with production activities. Costs incurred as a result of transportation, maintenance, and assistance in product use, equally come into play, and often constitute an important part of the total cost (see, e.g. Keegan 1995). Monroe (1990) gives a detailed discussion of the different cost types, and the ways in which they can be measured and forecasted. Traditional methods for profit evaluation on the basis of cost and price information are break-even and contribution margin analysis.

Break-even analysis determines the sales volume that is needed to cover variable and fixed costs at a given price level. To be profitable, the price must at least generate the break-even sales volume. The *contribution margin* consists of the difference between price and unit variable costs: if negative, selling the product at the given price level would lead to a loss; if positive, at least some of the fixed costs can be covered. Consequently, costs set a price floor: to be profitable, price must be equal to or greater than unit variable cost in the short term, and equal to or greater than unit total cost in the long term.

Important in this respect is the fact that unit (variable) costs are not static, but often decline as accumulated production volume increases (see below), and that the profitability analysis is more complicated in the case of product line pricing because of shared costs and interrelated demand.

A fourth group of company characteristics that influence the pricing decision are the type of company and type of buyer.

With respect to company type, a distinction should be made between manufacturers and retailers, because they may face substantially different pricing problems. Manufacturers often have to take two prices into account: the selling price to the wholesaler or retailer, and the resale price to the ultimate consumer. The resale or final consumer price determines final demand, but is not under direct control of the manufacturer (see below). Retailers only have to set final consumer prices, but often face very complex pricing problems because of huge assortments, cross-product effects, and difficulties in assessing the impact of individual prices on the store's overall price image. The following discussion concentrates mainly on the manufacturer's pricing decision. Important differences for retailer pricing will be indicated where needed.

In addition, a distinction should be made between two types of buyers: consumers and businesses. The corresponding pricing decisions are termed consumer pricing and industrial or business-to-business pricing. Specifics of industrial pricing will not be treated here. For more information we refer to Monroe (1990), Akintoye and Skitmore (1992), and Hutt and Speh (1992).

Buyer behaviour

Price–volume relationship
Price is an important determinant of demand and sales volume. According to the economic theory of buyer behaviour the price volume relationship is generally negative: higher prices will generate lower demand. The magnitude of the sales reduction (increase) for a given price increase (reduction) reflects the price sensitivity of the consumers. In economics, price sensitivity is measured by price elasticity: the percentage change in sales due to a one percent price change.

The price sensitivity of consumers varies considerably among products, and may change over time. In a meta-analysis relating changes in a product's regular price to changes in demand, Tellis found elasticities for a diversity of consumer products to range between approximately −10 and +2.5, with an average value of −1.76 (Tellis 1988).

Product related factors that reduce price sensitivity are believed to be: the unique value of a brand, the difficulty of comparing substitutes, the use of price to signal quality, payment of costs by someone else (wholly or partly) and sunk investments in assets for which the product is used (Nagle and Holden 1995). Conversely, price sensitivity tends to be stronger for products that have high prices, are easy to stock, are used in combination with other products to produce a single benefit, or for which many substitutes are widely available.

For most products, price sensitivity increases over the product life-cycle (PLC) as competitive offers become more standardized, are perceived as closer substitutes, and as consumers become better informed. Empirical investigations have demonstrated however, that this is only true for the decline stage of the PLC (see PRODUCT LIFE-CYCLE MANAGEMENT). More information on the factors that affect price elasticity dynamics can be found in Nagle and Holden (1995) and Parker and Neelamegham (1997).

Price perceptions

Estimated price–volume relationships provide a direct link between actual price levels charged, and company results; as such, they seem a practical and valuable basis for decision making. By treating the consumer as a black box, however, they ignore the complexity of the role of price in the potential buyer's decision process. Closer attention to the variety of phenomena and reactions on the part of consumers uncovers important implications for strategic and tactical pricing.

A first point of interest is the distinction between real prices and perceptions: rather than exclusively concentrating on 'objective' or factual prices, decision makers should be concerned with how these prices are perceived and evaluated.

To start with, recent studies on consumer price knowledge unequivocally point at low awareness levels for specific item prices of frequently purchased consumer goods (Dickson and Sawyer 1990, McGoldrick and Marks 1987, Krishna *et al.* 1991). This lack of price knowledge concerns regular as well as promotional prices. Many reasons may account for the incompleteness of price information, such as the complexity of the offer (variety of brands and package sizes, at different prices in different stores); the time pressure during a shopping trip, and the limited absolute (differences between) prices in many consumer goods' product classes. In any case, these findings suggest that managers cannot take consumer awareness of actual prices for granted.

Numerous sources further suggest that 'customers' response to prices are based on much more than rational calculations' (Nagle and Holden 1995), and that price perception/evaluation relies on convenient and simple decision processes. It is widely believed that consumers build up an 'acceptable price range' for a given product or product class, characterized by an upper and a lower price limit (see, e.g. Rao and Sieben 1992). The upper bound (reservation price) identifies the price above which a product is considered 'too expensive' and stems from the negative role of price in the decision process (monetary loss). The lower bound specifies a price level below which consumers are suspicious of quality, or worry about the (lack of) social status signalled by the product. This lower bound illustrates that price can be viewed as an asset, and thus play a positive role in the buying process.

Considerable research has investigated the relationship between price and product quality. Studies analysing the link between actual prices and objective quality have come up with mixed results; on average, the relationship is positive but fairly weak, it is also highly variable among product classes (see e.g. Rao and Monroe 1989, and Tellis 1987). As to the link between price and perceived quality, evidence suggests that consumers sometimes use price as a quality indicator. Whether such inferences are made depends on the availability of other cues (e.g. brand name), and on the degree of prior knowledge (on true product characteristics and price).

It is further believed that consumers, in evaluating specific observed prices, confront the actual price of an item with a 'reference price', and that the distance between the two affects the probability of purchase of the particular item. The notion of a reference price is widely accepted now, and a variety of conceptual and operational definitions have been put forward. An important distinction is that between external and internal reference prices. External reference prices, as the term suggests, are provided by 'observed stimuli in the purchase environment' (Mayhew and Winer 1992). Internal reference prices, in contrast, are standards or benchmarks stored in consumer memory. A variety of such internal standards may be used. A common view is that the internal reference price(s) reflect(s) the consumer's perception of a 'normal', 'fair' or 'appropriate' price for an item under the circumstances considered.

The formation of internal reference prices is shown to be based not only on past prices and currently observed price levels, but also on expectations concerning future price evolutions, and is strongly influenced by the purchasing context (see e.g. Nagle and Holden 1995).

For retailers, it is not only important how consumers perceive prices of individual items and brands, but also how the store as a whole is viewed (expensive versus cheap). Though store price images have been shown to strongly affect store traffic and performance, fairly little is known about how they are formed. Recent evidence suggests that store price images are based on prices of a subset of 'exemplar' products (typically categories with large dollar volume, high visibility, and low differentiation), but also heavily depend on non-price cues like store atmosphere and design (Grewal and Baker 1994).

Psychological aspects of pricing
It has become clear by now that consumers can encode and evaluate price information in different ways. The extent to which potential buyers are aware of prices; as well as the way they perceive them, evaluate them, and use them to 'update' reference prices, depends on many factors, and exhibits 'rational' as well as seemingly 'irrational' features.

Consumers can 'encode' information on actual item prices in absolute terms (amount to be paid), but also in relative terms. Consumers' awareness of absolute versus relative prices is found to be closely linked to their 'processing goals' (for choice set formation or choice: Bronnenberg and Vanhonacker 1996; for direct or later use: Mazumdar and Monroe 1990; for brand choice or purchase quantity: Krishnamurthi and Raj 1988 and 1991).

Psychological 'peculiarities' further affect how item prices are not only recorded, but also perceived. Price endings may significantly affect price perceptions (odd prices, see e.g. Stiving and Winer 1997, and Gendall *et al.* 1997). Another phenomenon that decision makers should bear in mind is the 'relative' evaluation of price cuts: the same absolute price discount is perceived as less important when it constitutes a smaller percentage of the item's normal price; and the further a brand's price is from the average price level in the category (in either direction), the less sensitive consumers tend to be to price changes to that item (Monroe 1990).

The formation and dynamic adjustment of reference prices is also subject to 'specific' psychological processes: e.g. a minimum price change (threshold) is needed for a reference price adaptation to occur (Lattin and Bucklin 1989, Monroe 1990), and the presentation order of observed prices affects the presence and magnitude of the adjustment.

In the context of price discounts, the impact of externally provided reference prices on a consumer's internal price standard is shown to depend on whether this external reference is seen as plausible or implausible (Gupta and Cooper 1992, Bobinski *et al.* 1996).

Finally, the evaluation of a price offer will strongly depend on its 'mental framing', that is, on whether they are presented as 'gains' or as 'losses' (see e.g. Diamond and Sanyal 1990). In a similar vein, it is found that price increases tend to entail a stronger (negative) reaction than discounts of the same magnitude (positive immediate sales effect).

Consumer heterogeneity
So far, we have emphasized the complexity of consumer reactions toward prices, and the psychological factors affecting the role of price in the decision process. An even more important observation is the enormous heterogeneity in price reactions among potential buyers. This heterogeneity is already apparent at the level of price awareness and knowledge. In addition, consumers may evaluate prices differently, because they are more or less informed about prevailing prices and product characteristics (they have different search costs, see Urbany *et al.* 1996); or because they attach more or less importance to the negative role of price (they have different reservation prices). Also,

transaction costs (e.g. costs of shopping) strongly vary among consumers, causing differences in their willingness to pay for specific items on given purchase occasions (Tellis 1986). Decision makers should recognize these differences, and positively 'exploit' consumer heterogeneity in the development of pricing strategies and tactics.

Competition

The results of the pricing strategy will not only depend on consumer response, but also on the reaction of competitors. Competitive behaviour varies considerably with market structure, intensity of competition, and the existence and nature of significant competitive advantages.

Market structures can be classified according to the number of sellers and the degree of product differentiation (see Kotler 1997; alternative classifications can be found in Simon 1989). These characteristics affect the pricing decision in two ways.

First, the number of sellers (available substitutes) and the degree of product differentiation influence the price sensitivity of consumers. Second, the intensity of competition depends on the number of competitors, and the threat of substitute products (see Porter 1980 for other factors), and determines the likelihood of competitive reactions to pricing decisions. Competitors' prices are therefore more directive for own pricing decisions in markets with many undifferentiated competitors.

Market structure and intensity of competition change over the product life-cycle (PLC) as new competitors enter the market and products become more homogeneous. Competition intensifies in most cases, and becomes especially severe in the maturity and decline stage, because sales growth can now only be accomplished at the expense of the competitors' sales volume.

Intense competition implies an increased likelihood of competitive reactions to pricing decisions (adjustments in price and/or other marketing mix variables). Besides market structure, the distribution of market shares, the sources and types of competitive advantages and the marketing goals and strategies of competitors affect the likelihood and nature of competitive reactions (Porter 1980). Competitive retaliation may attenuate pricing effects, and sometimes provoke real price wars (prices are continually reduced, even to unprofitable levels). The analysis of competitive behaviour is therefore a prerequisite for effective pricing. On the one hand, *potential* competition warrants attention; the use of non-myopic, entry deterring strategies turns out to be particularly rewarding in new product settings (see below). On the other hand, insight into reaction patterns of *current* market players is indispensable. As emphasized by Guiltinan and Gundlach (1996), competitors respond to actions of other market players by using those marketing variables that are their 'best weapons', such that price as well as non-price reactions should be monitored. Competitive response behaviour can be investigated in several ways, e.g. by means of competitive response profiles (Porter 1980), reaction matrices (Lambin, Naert and Bultez 1975), or game theory (Moorthy 1985).

Substantial deviations from competitors' price levels are only feasible through significant competitive advantages.

Information on the different types of competitive advantages, their sources, measurement, and associated market strategies can be found in Aaker (1992) and Day and Wensley (1988). The most important competitive advantages for pricing relate to costs and unique product values.

Cost advantages exist when the product can be produced and/or distributed at a lower unit cost than competitors; they result from superior skills or resources (e.g. location: see Stern 1986), or from learning. The learning effect is usually represented by the experience curve, which implies that 'each time cumulative production volume of a product doubles, unit costs fall by a constant percentage, the learning rate' (Simon 1989: 125). A pricing strategy that exploits these cost dynamics is experience curve pricing (see Section 4).

Unique product value results from (tangible or intangible) product characteristics that are valued by consumers and differentiate the product from its substitutes (Nagle and Holden 1995). Unique product value reduces the price sensitivity of consumers, thereby enabling the firm to set prices above the competitors' level without experiencing a considerable decrease in demand.

Retailers may find it especially hard to obtain sustainable competitive advantages, because costs cannot easily be reduced, competitive stores often sell the same or highly similar products, and many other differentiating characteristics can easily be copied (Berman and Evans 1986).

Other publics

In addition to buyers and competitors, a number of other publics influence pricing decisions. The most important are government (legal constraints), distribution channels and suppliers. Other individuals, groups or institutions may have an impact on the pricing decision (e.g. financial institutions, workforce) but are not discussed here.

A number of government laws set legal constraints to competitive pricing behaviour, consumer pricing, international pricing and (the control over) retailer pricing.

Prohibited or restricted competitive pricing practices are price fixing, price discrimination, and predatory pricing. Important legal constraints on consumer pricing are regulations against deceptive pricing and consumer price discrimination. Moreover, in specific product categories like pharmaceuticals, or bread, governments exert direct price controls and establish ranges of legally acceptable consumer prices. More detailed information is provided in Nagle and Holden (1995), Kaufman et al. (1994), and Monroe (1990). In an international setting, firms must comply with transfer pricing rules, and anti-dumping regulations (see e.g. Keegan 1995). Finally, control over retailer pricing by the manufacturer is severely restricted by regulations concerning Resale Price Maintenance (see Sheffet and Scammon 1985; Fabricant 1990). These regulations prohibit agreements by which a manufacturer can enforce a minimum resale price to the retailer. Information on other laws that restrict retailer pricing can be found in Berman and Evans (1986; e.g. minimum-price laws, unit pricing legislation, bait-and-switch advertising) and Levy and Weitz (1995).

In addition to legal constraints, manufacturers have to account for the impact of the distribution channel on their pricing decisions (see LOGISTICS AND PHYSICAL DISTRIBUTION). The structure of the distribution channel (number of levels, number of players at each level), its degree of vertical integration, and the allocation of power within the channel, strongly influence the nature of the price decision and the appropriateness of alternative strategies. Channel conflicts and interdependencies have received widespread interest in the recent marketing literature, and contributions on how they affect pricing are gaining way (see Gerstner and Hess 1995; Lal et al. 1996; Agrawal and Lal 1995; Ingene and Parry 1995; Chan Choi 1996).

3 Pricing objectives

Environmental analysis provides crucial inputs for the specification of operational and attainable pricing objectives, which are in line with company goals and strategies, and exploit the possibilities offered by the marketplace. Many pricing objectives can be pursued and these can be classified as: (i) profit-oriented objectives (e.g. profit maximization, profit satisfaction, target return on investment); (ii) cost-oriented objectives (e.g. recover investment costs over a particular time period, generate volume so as to drive down costs); (iii) demand/sales-oriented objectives (e.g. sales growth or maintenance, market share growth or maintenance, use price of one product to sell other products in the line, build traffic); or (iv) competition-oriented objectives (e.g. be the price leader, discourage entry by new competitors, discourage others from lowering prices).

Companies may pursue more than one pricing objective: in that case, pricing objectives should be mutually consistent, and priorities (or interrelationships) clearly defined (Monroe 1990). Managers (especially retailers) often concentrate on cost-oriented pricing objectives, because these can easily be translated into rules of thumb that simplify the pricing problem (see Section 5). In doing so, however, they disregard opportunities for profitable pricing based on factors other than cost (see Section 4).

Other examples of pricing objectives and their classifications can be found in Morris and Calantone (1990) and Ansari et al. (1996); and Levy and Weitz (1995) and Karande and Kumar (1995) for retailers. Of particular relevance to us is the typology suggested by Tellis (1986). Tellis distinguishes three major pricing objectives: companies can (i) exploit consumer heterogeneity and the presence of various market segments; (ii) they can take competitive position as a basic asset for the pricing strategy; or

(iii) they may concentrate on opportunities offered by product line pricing. Although these different objectives are not mutually exclusive, they indicate 'key' points of interest in pricing, and provide a basic framework for positioning the variety of pricing strategies described in literature and practice.

4 Pricing strategy

A myriad pricing strategies have been put forward by marketing academics and practitioners. Which of these are feasible in a given problem situation depends on two main factors (Tellis 1986, Nagle and Holden 1995): the characteristics of the environment (in particular: those of the target market), and the objectives of the company (e.g. following Tellis: segment, competition, or product line oriented priorities). Some typical pricing strategies are highlighted below.

Segmented or differential pricing strategies charge different prices to alternative consumer segments to take advantage of their differences. Because 'straight' price discrimination may cause legal problems and consumer segments are not always easy to identify, many of these strategies rely on self-selection. In *peak-load pricing*, lower prices are charged in off-season periods, an example would be off-season sales for fashion goods. *Price skimming* refers to a strategy of introducing new products at a high price level, which is gradually reduced in later periods. Both strategies have a time-based pricing scheme that exploits consumer differences in willingness to pay. In *random discounting*, a product's regular price is maintained at a high level, but temporary price cuts are offered at random points in time. The idea behind this strategy is to make consumers with low levels of price knowledge pay the full price, while allowing price sensitive consumers, who will 'search' for bargains, to profit from the price cut. In some situations, more *direct price discrimination* schemes can be used; based on consumer identity or market membership. Examples are the use of different price rates for children, students, adults and new members; or price dumping. A strategy that has gained increased attention is the use of *price-quantity discounts*, where the consumer is offered more advantageous purchase conditions if he buys larger product quantities (see e.g. Dolan 1987).

So far, we have looked at cases where the pricing regime is primarily linked to consumer characteristics. Other strategies crucially rely on competitive differences in order to be successful. In *price signalling*, a company offers its low quality product at a high price; hoping that non-knowledgeable consumers will take this elevated price level as a quality indicator. Obviously, this strategy only works if at least some competitors follow an 'honest' strategy (low quality and price, or high quality and price). *Geographic pricing* becomes an issue when the company serves geographically distant markets, and transportation constitutes an important component of transaction costs. Depending on the competitive conditions in those markets and on the threat of entry, it may be more profitable to charge *uniform delivered prices* in all markets; to adopt an *FOB* strategy (customer pays for transportation cost); or to settle for an in-between strategy (*zone pricing*). *Experience curve pricing* as well as *penetration pricing* refer to the introduction of new products at low prices to preempt competition, gain economies of experience more rapidly (in the case of experience curve pricing), or stay in business in the price sensitive segment (in case of penetration pricing).

A number of strategies are relevant for multi-product companies, offering a line of products. *Premium pricing* implies that lower quality versions in a line of substitute products are priced below cost, but that this 'loss' is made up for by the premium charged for superior versions. This strategy is particularly useful when demand is heterogeneous (consumers differ in their quality requirements and willingness to pay), and when joint economies of scale exist for products in the line. In *image pricing*, the same product is marketed under a different name (with a different positioning strategy) and at a different price level, so that consumers who attach a lot of importance to the positive role of price (quality or status signal) would buy the higher priced version. *Price bundling* refers to a situation where two or more products are marketed in a single package for a special price. This strategy may be used for 'imperfect substitutes' (for instance: season tickets for a theatre) as well as for complementary items (e.g. packages of options on automobiles); it may be pure (products only available in bundle) or mixed (separate item purchase is still possible). A rationale for price bundling is demand asymmetry: consumers vary in their preferences and reservation prices for different items. *Complementary pricing* is adopted when, in a line of complementary products, some are sold at a very low price, while a premium is charged on other items. Typical variants are 'loss leadership selling' by retailers, 'captive pricing', and 'two-part pricing' for services (see Tellis 1986).

A variety of other strategies are described in the literature that are all more or less related to the ones discussed here. As pointed out, each of those strategies will be more or less appropriate depending on specific environmental conditions, company type (for a discussion on retailer pricing strategies, see Levy and Weitz 1995) and company objectives. Also, a number of Tellis' 'generic' strategies may be combined. Ultimately, the success of a pricing strategy will strongly depend on how it is carried out; that is; on the cost and accuracy of implementation, and on the exact price levels charged within the framework of the suggested strategy. It is this issue of price determination that is taken up next.

5 Implementation of pricing strategies: price determination and adjustment

To implement the pricing strategy, a (general) price structure and specific price level(s) have to be determined. In addition, effective pricing is a dynamic process, responding to significant changes in the environment, and to the threat of competitive reactions.

Price structure

A pricing strategy outlines the basic 'principles' to be adopted. Within the confines of these principles, a price structure specifies how the characteristics of a product will be priced, and lays the foundation on which price levels will be set (Stern 1986). It determines (i) which aspects of each product or service will be priced; (ii) how prices will vary for different customers in the case of differential pricing strategies, and for different products or services in the case of product line pricing; and (iii) time and conditions of payment. More information on these issues can be found in Nagle and Holden (1995), Dada and Srikanth (1987), Day and Ryans (1988), Monroe (1990), Morris and Calantone (1990), and Lal (1990).

Price structure is an important component of an effective price policy: it provides for the pricing flexibility that is needed for a successful implementation of differential and product line pricing strategies, and for a quick and effective instrument to respond to competitive threats (Stern 1986). Guidelines for the development of a strategic price structure can be found in Morris and Calantone (1990) and Monroe (1990).

Methods and techniques for setting price levels

Numerous methods and techniques have been developed for determining price levels. Rather than enumerating all the available techniques, we will indicate the major approaches and illustrate each approach by one or more specific techniques.

Optimization methods
Optimization methods attempt to derive the optimal price level analytically or numerically. In general, the derivation of optimal prices involves: (i) the specification and estimation of demand and cost functions (recent contributions also include competitive response functions in the optimization approach); (ii) the selection of a pricing objective (in most cases profit maximization); and (iii) derivation of optimal prices by means of mathematical optimization techniques.

Typical of this class of pricing methods is the traditional microeconomic pricing model (see e.g. Monroe 1990; Simon 1989). Examples of price optimization for manufacturers can be found in Bultez *et al.* (1995), and for retailers in Feichtinger *et al.* (1988).

Some important limitations of the optimization approach are the use of simplifying assumptions to keep models tractable, the focus on profit maximization, and difficulties to obtain the necessary information to calculate optimal prices. To solve these problems more complex models and alternative pricing methods have been developed. A review of extensions to the traditional economic pricing model can be found in Nagle and Holden (1995). A class of pricing techniques that tries to avoid or reduce measurement problems are the rules of thumb that will be discussed next. Simulation and perceived value pricing techniques attempt to limit the use of simplifying assumptions and to derive prices on the basis of more realistic relationships (e.g. taking psychological pricing effects into account).

Rules of thumb

In many cases, optimization methods cannot be applied because the necessary information is not available or is too costly to obtain. To solve this problem, a number of rules of thumb have been developed. Most of these rules are cost-based, because cost information is more readily available for most companies.

Mark-up or cost-plus pricing is one of the most widely practised pricing heuristics, especially by retailers (Levy and Weitz 1995). A second cost-based pricing rule is target return pricing (see Kotler 1997 for examples). Both techniques are easy to apply and require only cost information, but they ignore price–volume relationships, dynamic cost effects and competitive reactions.

A third rule of thumb that is more competition-oriented is going-rate pricing. In this case the firm bases its price largely on competitors' price levels. Going-rate pricing mainly attempts to maintain competitive (price) position, and is not based on a thorough analysis of competitive conditions and behaviour. Demand relationships and cost differences are also being ignored.

The main advantages of these pricing rules consist, therefore, in their ease of use and low information requirements. They are not likely to yield optimal or near-optimal price decisions, since important pricing determinants are ignored.

Simulation techniques

Like optimization methods, simulation techniques first specify and estimate demand (and cost) relationships, subsequently select pricing objectives, and finally determine the price(s) that best meet the objectives. Both methods differ, however, in the way 'optimal' prices are derived. Whereas optimization methods make use of mathematical optimization techniques to calculate the optimal price, simulation methods estimate and compare results for various pricing scenarios. The scenario that gives the best results provides the (near-optimal) price.

Simulation is often used in combination with conjoint analysis, a technique for estimating utility functions for existing or new products (see Goldberg *et al.* 1984 for an example). The estimated utility functions can be used to simulate choice behaviour of consumers, and to estimate the market share or sales volume at different price levels. To evaluate profit implications, the demand relationship must be combined with a cost function (see e.g. Kohli and Mahajan 1991). Simulation and conjoint analysis can also be applied to more complex pricing problems, such as product line pricing (Dobson and Kalish 1993).

Limitations of conjoint analysis for preference modelling are discussed by Green *et al.* (1981).

Perceived value pricing

Perceived value pricing sets price level(s) in relation to the product's value as judged by consumers. Like simulation, this pricing technique concentrates mainly on the demand side of the pricing problem, but can take cost and profit implications into account.

The first step of the procedure consists of the estimation of perceived value. Monroe (1990) defines perceived value as the weighted sum of acquisition and transaction value. Acquisition value consists of the ratio of perceived benefits to perceived sacrifice, and the transaction value is the difference between the reference and the actual price. In this way, the perceived value reflects the multifaceted character of price, and the buyers' perceptions.

The next step consists of the determination of the price level. Price can be set above, below or equal to perceived value, depending on costs, pricing objectives and strategy (see Nagle and Holden 1995). Various methods can be used to determine specific price levels (see e.g. Nagle and Holden 1995; Monroe 1990; Kijewski and Yoon 1990; Kortge and Okonkwo 1993).

Important advantages of perceived value pricing are that psychological pricing effects can be incorporated into the pricing decision, and that the method can be used for different pricing objectives and strategies. Disadvantages are that 'the' perceived value is difficult to estimate, especially for new products. Moreover, value perceptions may vary considerably among consumers, and even over usage situations.

Limitations of price setting methods
In addition to the disadvantages indicated in the previous paragraphs, the price setting methods of the above paragraph all share some common limitations. First, they implicitly assume that the manufacturer has direct control over final consumer prices while, in reality, control over consumer prices is restricted by Retail Price Maintenance regulations. Manufacturers can only suggest resale prices, base selling prices on retailer's pricing policy and the target consumer price, or try to obtain dealer/retailer cooperation (e.g. by means of trade discounts, special promotions or trade deals: see Monroe 1990; Lal 1990; Lal *et al.* 1996). Second, most methods do not explicitly take cross product effects into account. This severely limits their usefulness for product line pricing and retailer pricing. In recent years, efforts have been undertaken to incorporate cross-product effects in the traditional pricing methods. Examples are optimization models for product lines (see e.g. Oren *et.al.* 1984, Reibstein and Gatignon 1984, and Dobson and Kalish 1988), simulation models for product lines (e.g. Dobson and Kalish 1993), and perceived value of product bundles (e.g. Yadav and Monroe 1993; and Venkatesh and Mahajan 1993). Third, most methods cannot be used for planning short-term price changes. Approaches specifically tailored to the problem of sales promotion planning are, e.g. Tellis and Zufryden (1995), and Kopalle, Rao and Assunçao (1996); tactical price decisions are further discussed in Section 6. Finally, the previous methods are myopic in the sense that they rely on stable cost and demand functions, and largely ignore competitive reactions.

Dynamic pricing models

The methods for setting price levels, discussed above, determine an optimal or satisfying price level at a given point in time.

In reality, though, several price determinants are not static, but change in a more or less predictable and uniform way (e.g. experience curve and product life-cycle phenomena). Some of the strategies discussed in Section 4 make use of these dynamic effects to increase profits (e.g. skimming strategy), obtain competitive advantages (e.g. experience curve pricing) or preempt competition (e.g. penetration pricing).

Dynamic pricing models explicitly take cost and/or demand evolutions into account, and determine an (optimal) price path, rather than one (optimal) price level. Examples are the models of Kalyanam (1996), and Kopalle and Winer (1996).

Models including cost dynamics predominantly concentrate on experience curve effects. Most dynamic demand models are based on the diffusion model developed by Bass (1980). A review of diffusion models is given in Parker (1992) and Horsky (1990); dynamic pricing models are further discussed in Simon (1989) and Gijsbrechts (1993).

For the determination of the optimal price path, analytical solutions can be derived by means of optimal control theory. Because of the complexity of such derivations, simplifying assumptions are usually needed to keep the models tractable.

Another limitation is that the pricing methods above do not explicitly take competitors' reactions to price decisions into account, although their impact, especially in mature and declining markets, may be considerable. To incorporate competitive dynamics into the pricing model, demand and cost relationships have to be supplemented with a competitive response model. The dominant approach to modelling competitive behaviour is based on game theory (see Moorthy 1985 for the basic concepts and applications to price competition).

A distinction can be made between models that determine competitive reactions to (i) general changes in competitive conditions (e.g. entry of new competitors: see Eliashberg and Jeuland 1986; threat of entry or copying: see Nascimento and Vanhonacker 1988) and (ii) price information or price decisions, in particular. In the latter case, the reaction models used may be simple response functions (competitors react to price actions with a change in their own price), or multiple reaction functions (all marketing mix instruments could be used to retaliate). Also, available models differ in their assumptions on the amount of price information available to companies. A comprehensive review of analytical models of competition is given by Eliashberg and Chatterjee (1985). More recent references can be found in Griffith and Rust (1993). Examples of models that combine dynamic and competitive effects are Dockner and Jorgensen (1988) and Coughlan and Mantrala (1992).

Finally, as indicated earlier, reactions of other channel members affect the impact of price decisions. Examples of studies incorporating the impact of manufacturer–retailer interactions on pricing are Lal *et al.* (1996) and Gerstner and Hess (1995).

6 Pricing tactics

Pricing strategy versus pricing tactics

Some confusion exists in the pricing literature on the distinction between pricing strategies and pricing tactics. In this text, we adhere to the viewpoint of Van Waterschoot and Van Den Bulte (1992) and Morris and Calantone (1990), who state that *pricing strategies* determine long-term price structure and price levels, and their evolution over time in response to long-term changes in the environment; while *pricing tactics* consist of short-term price decisions (mostly price reductions from the normal or long-term level) to induce immediate sales increases or to respond to short-term changes in the environment.

Part of the confusion stems from the fact that the same set of instruments and actions can serve both strategic and tactical purposes. This is, for instance, true for the use of price deals. From a strategic point of view, temporary price cuts can be used as a legal way of price discrimination, e.g. in a random discounting strategy. The aim of this strategy is clearly to increase long-term sales. At the same time, price deals, and sales promotions in general, can be used to temporarily support various pricing strategies (e.g. to eliminate stocks), and thus serve as a tactical instrument.

Price promotions

The measurement of sales promotion effects has generated a great deal of interest in recent years. While a variety of promotional activities is available, the bulk of sales promotion actions take the form of either a straight price cut, or a more indirect price reduction (e.g. in the form of a coupon or extra quantity). Typical of such price promotions is their temporary character; nevertheless, they may generate effects that extend over a longer period of time. In this section, we summarize findings on the immediate as well as long-term effects of promotional actions.

Concerning the short-term effects of promotional price cuts, the literature is fairly unanimous: sales promotions, and in particular price deals, create a dramatic boost in the sales of a brand (see Blattberg *et al.* 1995). Promotional elasticities are certainly more pronounced than immediate advertising impacts (Sethuraman and Tellis 1991) and, depending on category characteristics, may be much larger (in absolute value) than regular price effects (see Bolton 1989; Bemmaor and Mouchoux 1991 for examples). A large portion of the observed sales increase stems from brand switching. These switching effects appear to be asymmetric: recent findings suggest that dominant, manufacturer, higher priced (and often higher quality) brands attract a large portion of other brands' buyers during promotional periods, but that the reverse is not true (Blattberg *et al.* 1995). Price promotions may induce product class sales effects, mainly as a result of sales displacement (e.g. purchase acceleration, or purchase postponement when a deal is anticipated). If observed, however, the magnitude of such effects is generally low.

Blattberg and Neslin (1989) emphasize the importance of interaction effects between price promotions and other marketing mix activities. Experimental studies point to a considerable increase in the impact of a price cut when supported by point of purchase promotional signals or advertising announcements (see e.g. Inman *et al.* 1990; Bemmaor and Mouchoux 1991). Also, the form of the advertisement or display is deemed important: presenting advertised prices as a reduction from regular prices tends to increase the impact of the discount (Cox and Cox 1990). Apparently, insight into the psychological aspects of the consumers' decision process *vis-à-vis* prices (cfr. supra) pays off.

While the immediate impact of price cuts on sales of the promoted brand is clearly positive, long run implications are more complex. In general, sales promotion activities could enhance repeat sales and build consumer franchise. Yet, evidence of such effects is scarce (see, e.g. Lal and Padmanabhan 1995 for an empirical investigation of long term-effects).

According to Jones (1990), temporary price reductions have about the weakest positive long-term effects of any below the line activity since they appeal to rational (financial) arguments rather than building brand image or franchise. While the evidence on positive long run implications on brand sales is limited, there are indications that price deals lead to purchase acceleration and stockbuilding, followed by sales dips in the post-promotion period. In other words, sales promotions may partly 'borrow sales from the future'. More importantly, frequent price cuts may reduce the consumer's willingness to buy the product at the regular price (perhaps as a result of a downward reference price adaptation, see Folkes and Wheat 1995), and eventually damage product image (to the extent that a price–quality inference is made). Several authors emphasize that these negative effects jeopardize the long run profitability of price deals from the point of view of the individual brand (Hardy 1986; Jones 1990).

So far, we have concentrated on price deal implications for the promoted brand. For multiproduct manufacturers, and especially for retailers, additional impacts are worth noting. First, the switching effects towards the promoted brand may cause (unwanted) cannibalization of more profitable non-promoted items. On the other hand, some studies reveal significant positive effects of price promotions on the sales of complementary items (e.g. Walters 1988; 1991). From the retailer's point of view, the profitability of price promotions strongly depends on their ability to attract new customers to the store (see, e.g. Mulhern and Leone 1990; Mulhern and Padgett 1995). Evidence on the traffic building capacity of price cuts is still inconclusive; so far, interstore brand substitution seems to be limited.

In the long run, retail promotions may be useful in creating barriers to entry (Walters 1988), and in increasing store competitiveness. Closely related to this is the impact of sales promotions on the store's price image, which, as mentioned in Section 2, is a major determinant of store patronage. To date, however, only fragmented insights are available on how store price images are formed, and more research is needed in this area.

Overall, the impact of price promotions on brand sales, product line sales, and store performance seems to be a multifaceted and tricky issue. The nature and impact of promotional effects varies widely from case to case. The recent literature, however, has succeeded in providing (i) more theoretical insights into the economic rationale behind price cuts and their behavioral underpinnings, (ii) empirical evidence on factors affecting the magnitude of promotional elasticities. Consumer characteristics (e.g. loyals versus variety seekers), product type (e.g. perishability), promotional activity in the product class or in the retail environment, all seem important determinants that interact in a complex way (see, e.g. Blattberg et al. 1995; Campo 1997; Dhar and Hoch 1996). The lesson to draw is that managers interested in profit should not engage in promotional tactics too hastily, but should carefully analyse the characteristics of the market setting in which they operate.

So far, the discussion has implicitly concentrated on the impact of promotions directed at consumers. Manufacturers spend increasingly large budgets on trade promotions, i.e. temporary price cuts towards retailers. While the impact of trade promotions bears similarities to that of consumer promotions, their (long-run) implications are even more complex. For a more detailed discussion, see Blattberg and Neslin (1989) and Lal et al. (1996).

7 Conclusions

In recent years, marketing scholars as well as practitioners have increasingly recognized the importance and the complexity of the pricing decision. To be effective, pricing must be the outcome of a systematic and goal-oriented process, in which characteristics of the internal and external environment are carefully researched; and pricing strategies, structures, regular price levels and temporary deviations are set to fully exploit the possibilities offered by this environment.

Recent marketing publications contribute to effective pricing by shedding more light on the intricacies of consumer and competitor reactions, by describing a range of possible pricing strategies and the rationale behind them, and by offering measurement instruments and methods for assessing price impacts and levels. Yet, a lot remains to be done. Future contributions should continue to evaluate empirically the consumer's price sensitivity and competitor's reactions in a variety of (dynamic) settings. Also, the role of the retailer, and the issue of multiproduct pricing, seem to be undervalued to date. Above all, there appears to be a need for the development of managerial guidelines, such that the 'state of the art' in pricing finds its way to practice.

KATIA CAMPO
UNIVERSITY OF ANTWERP UFSIA
ELS GIJSBRECHTS
UNIVERSITY OF ANTWERP UFSIA

Further reading

(References cited in the text marked *)

Aaker, D.A. (1992) *Strategic Market Management*, New York: John Wiley.
* Agrawal, D. and R. Lal (1995), 'Contractual arrangments in franchising: an empirical investigation', *Journal of Marketing Research* 32: 213–21.
* Akintoye, A. and Skitmore, M. (1992) 'Pricing approaches in the construction industry', *Industrial Marketing Management* 21: 311–8.
* Ansari, A., Siddarth, S. and Weinberg, C.B. (1996) 'Pricing a bundle of products or services: the case of nonprofits', *Journal of Marketing Research* 33: 86–93.
* Bass, F.M. (1980) 'The relationship between diffusion rates, experience curves, and demand elasticities for consumer durable technological innovations', *Journal of Business* 53: s51–s67.
* Berman, B. and Evans, J. (1986) *Retail Management: a Strategic Approach*, New York, Macmillan.
* Bemmaor, A.C. and Mouchoux, D. (1991) 'Measuring the short term effect of in-store promotion and retail advertising on brand sales: a factorial experiment', *Journal of Marketing Research* 28 202–14.
* Blattberg, R. and Neslin, S. (1989) 'Sales promotion: the long and the short of it', *Marketing Letters* 1: 81–100.
Blattberg, R. and Wisniewski, K. (1989) 'Price induced patterns of competition', *Marketing Science* 8: 291–309.
* Blattberg, R., Briesch, R. and Fox, E. (1995) 'How promotions work', *Marketing Science* 14: G122–G132.
* Bobinski, G.S., Cox, D.and Cox, A. (1996) 'Retail sale advertising, perceived retailer credibility, and price rationale', *Journal of Retailing* 72: 291–306.
* Bolton, R. (1989) 'The relationship between market characteristics and promotional price elasticities', *Marketing Science* 8: 153–69.
* Bronnenberg, B.J. and Vanhonacker, W.R. (1996) 'Limited choice sets, local price response, and implied measures of price competition', *Journal of Marketing Research* 33: 163–73.
* Bultez, A., Gijsbrechts, E. and Naert, Ph. (1995) 'A theormen on the optimal margin mix', *Zeitschrift für Betriebswirtschaftswissenschaft* 4: 151–73.
* Campo, K. (1997) 'Variety seeking and the sensitivity to in-store promotions', unpublished doctoral dissertation, UFSIA, University of Antwerp, May.
* Chan Choi, S. (1996) 'Price competition in a duopoly common retailer channel', *Journal of Retailing* 72: 117–34.
* Coughlan, A. and Mantrala, M. (1992) 'Dynamic competitive pricing strategies', *International Journal of Research in Marketing* 9: 91–108.
* Cox, A.D. and Cox, D. (1990) 'Competing on price: the role of retail price advertisements in shaping store price image', *Journal of Retailing* 66: 428–45.
* Dada, M. and Srikanth, K.N. (1987) 'Pricing policies for quantity discounts', *Management Science* 33: 1247–52.
* Day, G.S. and Ryans, A.B. (1988) 'Using price discounts for a competitive advantage', *Industrial Marketing Management* 17: 1–14.
Day, G.S. and Wensley, R. (1988) 'Assessing advantage: a framework for diagnosing competitive superiority', *Journal of Marketing* 52: 1–20.
* Dhar, S.K. and Hoch, S.J. (1996) 'Pice discrimination using in-store merchandising', *Journal of Marketing* 60: 17–30.
* Diamond, W.D. and Sanyal, A. (1990) 'The effect of framing on the choice of supermarket coupons', *Advances in Consumer Research* 17: 488–93.
* Dickson, P. and Sawyer, A.G. (1990) 'The price knowledge and search of supermarket shoppers', *Journal of Marketing* 54: 42–53.
* Dobson, G. and Kalish, S. (1988) 'Positioning and pricing a product line', *Marketing Science* 7: 107–25.
* Dobson, G. and Kalish, S. (1993) 'Heuristics for pricing and positioning a product-line using conjoint and cost data', *Management Science* 39: 160–75.
* Dockner, E. and Jorgensen, S. (1988) 'Optimal pricing strategies for new products in dynamic oligopolies', *Marketing Science* 7: 315–34.
* Dolan, R.J. (1987) 'Quantity discounts: managerial issues and research opportunities', *Marketing Science* 6: 1–23.
* Eliashberg, J. and Chatterjee, R. (1985) 'Analytical models of competition with implications for marketing: issues, findings, and outlook', *Journal of Marketing Research* 22: 237–61.
* Eliashberg, J. and Jeuland, A.P. (1986) 'The impact of competitive entry in a developing market upon

dynamic pricing strategies', *Marketing Science* 5: 20–36.
* Fabricant, R.A. (1990) 'Special retail services and resale price maintenance', *Journal of Retailing* 66: 101–18.
* Feichtinger, G., Luhmer, A. and Sorger, G. (1988) 'Optimal price and advertising policy for a convenience goods retailer', *Marketing Science* 7: 187–201.
* Folkes, V. and Wheat, R.D. (1995) 'Consumers' price perceptions of promoted products', *Journal of Retailing* 71: 317–28.
* Gendall, Ph., Fox, M.F. and Wilton, P. (1997) 'Estimating the effect of odd pricing', *Proceedings of the Emac Conference* 4: 1684–97.
* Gerstner, E. and Hess, J. (1995) 'Pull promotions and channel coordination', *Marketing Science* 14: 82–104.
* Gijsbrechts, E. (1993) 'Prices and pricing research in consumer marketing: some recent developments', *International Journal of Research in Marketing* 10: 115–51.
* Goldberg, S.M., Green, P.E. and Wind, Y. (1984) 'Conjoint analysis of price premiums for hotel amenities' *Journal of Business* 57: s111–s132.
* Green, P.E., Carroll, J.D. and Goldberg, S.M. (1981) 'A general approach to product design optimization via conjoint analysis', *Journal of Marketing* 45: 17–37.
* Grewal, D. and Baker, J. (1994) 'Do retail store environmental factors affect consumers' price acceptability? An empirical examination', *International Journal of Research in Marketing* 11: 107–15.
* Griffith, D.E. and Rust, R.T. (1993) 'Effectiveness of some simple pricing strategies under varying expectations of competitor behavior', *Marketing Letters* 4: 113–26.
* Guiltinan, J.P. and Gundlach, G.T. (1996) 'Aggressive and predatory pricing: a framework for analysis', *Journal of Marketing* 60: 87–102.
* Gupta, S. and Cooper, L.G. (1992) 'The discounting of discounts and promotion thresholds', *Journal of Consumer Research* 19: 401–11.
* Hardy, K. (1986) 'Key succes factors for manufacturers' sales promotions in package goods', *Journal of Marketing* 50: 13–23.
* Horsky, D. (1990) 'A diffusion model incorporating product benefits, price, income and information', *Marketing Science* 9: 342–65.
* Hutt, M.D. and Speh, T.W. (1992) *Business Marketing Management*, The Dryden Press, Fort Worth.
* Ingene, C.A. and Parry, M.E. (1995) 'Coordination and manufacturer profit maximization: the multiple retailer channel', *Journal of Retailing.* 71: 129–51.
* Inman, J.J., Mc Alister, L. and Hoyer, W.D. (1990) 'Promotion signal: proxy for a price cut?', *Journal of Consumer Research* 17: 74–81.

* Jones, J.P. (1990) 'The double jeopardy of sales promotions', *Harvard Business Review* 68: 145–52.
* Kalyanam, K. (1996), 'Pricing decisions under demand uncertainty: a bayesian mixture model approach', *Marketing Science* 15: 207–21.
* Karande, K.W. and Kumar, V. (1995) 'The effect of brand characteristics and retailer policies on response to retail price promotions: implications for retailers', *Journal of Retailing.* 71: 249–78.
* Kaufman, P.J., Smith, N.C. and Ortmeyer, G.K. (1994) 'Deception in retailer high-low pricing', *Journal of Retailing* 70: 115–38.
* Kaul, A. and Wittink, D.R. (1995),'Empirical generalizations about the impact of advertising on price sensitivity and price', *Marketing Science* 14: G151–G160.
* Keegan, W. (1995) *Global Marketing Management*, Prentice Hall, Englewood Cliffs, New Jersey.
* Kijewski, V. and Yoon, E. (1990) 'Market based pricing: beyond price performance curves', *Industrial Marketing Management* 19: 11–9.
* Kohli, R. and Mahajan, V. (1991) 'A reservation price model for optimal pricing of multiattribute products in conjoint analysis', *Journal of Marketing Research* 28: 347–54.
* Kopalle, P.K. and Winer, R.S. (1996) 'A dynamic model of reference price and expected quality', *Marketing Letters* 7: 41–52.
* Kopalle, P.K., Rao, A.G.and Assunçao, J.L. (1996) 'Asymmetric reference price effects and dynamic pricing policies', *Marketing Science* 15: 60–85.
* Kortge, G.D. and Okonkwo, P.A. (1993) 'Perceived value approach to pricing', *Industrial Marketing Management* 22: 133–40.
* Kotler, P. (1997) *Marketing Management: Analysis, Planning, Implementation, and Control*, 9th edn, London: Prentice-Hall.
* Krishna, A., Currim, I.S. and Shoemaker, R.W. (1991) 'Consumer perceptions of promotional activity', *Journal of Marketing* 55: 4–16.
* Krishnamurthi, L. and Raj, S.P. (1988) 'A model of brand choice and purchase quantity price sensitivities', *Marketing Science* 7: 1–20.
* Krishnamurthi, L. and Raj, S.P. (1991) 'An empirical analysis of the relationship between brand loyalty and consumer price elasticity', *Marketing Science* 10: 172–83.
* Lal, R. (1990) 'Manufacturer trade deals and retail price promotions', *Journal of Marketing Research* 27: 428–44.
* Lal, R. and Padmanabhan, V. (1995) 'Competitive response and equilibria', *Marketing Science* 14: G101–G108.
* Lal, R., Little, J.D.C. and Villas-Boas, J.M. (1996) 'A theory of forward buying, merchandising, and trade deals', *Marketing Science* 15: 21–37.
Lambin, J.J., Naert, P.A. and Bultez, A.V. (1975) 'Optimal marketing behavior in oligopoly', *European Economic Review* 6: 105–28.

* Lattin, J.M. and Bucklin, R.E. (1989) 'Reference effects of price and promotion on brand choice behavior', *Journal of Marketing Research* 26: 299–310.
* Levy, M. and Weitz, B. (1995) *Retailing Management*, Chicago: Irwin.
* Mayhew, G.E. and Winer, R.S. (1992) 'An empirical analysis of internal and external reference prices using scanner data', *Journal of Consumer Research* 19: 62–70.
* Mazumdar, T. and Monroe, K.B. (1990) 'The effects of buyers intentions to learn price information on price encoding', *Journal of Retailing* 66: 15–32.
* McGoldrick, P.J. and Marks, H. (1987) 'Shoppers' awareness of retail grocery prices', *European Journal of Marketing* 21: 63–76.
* Monroe, K. (1990) *Pricing: Making Profitable Decisions*, New York: McGraw Hill International Editions.
* Monroe, K.B. and Della Bitta, A.J. (1978) 'Models for pricing decisions', *Journal of Marketing Research* 15: 413–28.
* Moorthy, K.S. (1985) 'Using game theory to model competition', *Journal of Marketing Research* 22: 262–82.
* Morris, M.H. and Calantone, R.J. (1990) 'Four components of effective pricing', *Industrial Marketing Management* 19: 321–9.
* Mulhern, F.J. and Leone, R.P. (1990) 'Retail promotional advertising', *Journal of Business Research* 21: 179–94.
* Mulhern, F.J. and Padgett, D.T. (1995) 'The relationship between retail price promotions and regular price purchases', *Journal of Marketing* 59: 83–90.

Murphy, P. and Enis, B.M. (1986) 'Classifying products strategically', *Journal of Marketing* 50: 24–42.

* Nagle, T.T. (1984) 'Economic foundations for pricing', *Journal of Business* 57: s23–s26.
* Nagle, T.T. and Holden, R.K. (1995) *The Strategy and Tactics of Pricing: A Guide to Profitable Decision Making*, Englewood Clifs, NJ: Prentice-Hall.
* Nascimento, F. and Vanhonacker, W. (1988) 'Optimal strategic pricing of reproducable consumer products', *Management Science* 34: 921–37.
* Oren, S., Smith, S. and Wilson, R. (1984) 'Pricing a product line', *Journal of Business* 57: s73–s99.

Parker, Ph.M. and Neelamegham, R. (1997) 'Price elasticity dynamics over the product life cycle: a study of consumer durables', *Marketing Letters* 8: 205–16.

Porter, M.E. (1980) *Competitive Strategy*, New York: The Free Press.

Rao, V.R. (1984) 'Pricing research in marketing: the state of the art', *Journal of Business* 57: S39–S60.

Rao, A. and Monroe, K.B. (1989) 'The effect of price, brand name and store name on buyers' perceptions of product quality: an integrative review', *Journal of Marketing Research* 26: 351–7.

* Rao, A.R. and Sieben, W.A. (1992) 'The effect of prior knowledge on price acceptability and the type of information examined', *Journal of Consumer Research* 19: 256–70.
* Reibstein, D.J. and Gatignon, H. (1984) 'Optimal product line pricing: the influence of elasticities and cross-elasticities', *Journal of Marketing Research* 21: 259–67.
* Sethuraman, R. and Tellis, G.J. (1991) 'An analysis of the tradeoff between advertising and price discounting', *Journal of Marketing Research* 28: 160–74.
* Sheffet, M.J. and Scammon, D.L. (1985) 'Resale price maintenance: is it safe to suggest retail prices?', *Journal of Marketing* 49: 82–91.

Simon, H. (1979) 'Dynamics of price elasticity and brand life cycles: an empirical study', *Journal of Marketing Research* 16: 439–52.

* Simon, H. (1989) *Price Management*, Amsterdam: Elsevier.
* Stern, A. (1986) 'The strategic value of price structure', *Journal of Business Strategy* 7: 22–31.
* Stiving, M. and Winer, R.S. (1997) 'An empirical analysis of price endings with scanner data', *Journal of Consumer Research* 24: p.57–67.
* Tellis, G.J. (1986) 'Beyond the many faces of price: an integration of pricing strategies', *Journal of Marketing* 50: 146–60.
* Tellis, G. (1987) 'Consumer purchasing strategies and the information in retail prices', *Journal of Retailing* 63: 279–97.
* Tellis, G.J. (1988) 'The price elasticity of selective demand: a meta analysis of econometric models of sale', *Journal of Marketing Research* 25: 331–41.
* Tellis, G.J. and Zufryden, F.S. (1995) 'Tackling the retailer decision maze: which brands to discount, how much, when and why?', *Marketing Science* 14: 271–99.
* Urbany, J.E., Dickson, P.R. and Kalapurakal, R. (1996) 'Price search in the retail grocery market', *Journal of Marketing* 60: 91–104.
* Van Waterschoot, W. and Van Den Bulte, C. (1992) 'The 4 P classification of the marketing mix revisited', *Journal of Marketing* 56: 83–93.
* Venkatesh, R. and Mahajan, V. (1993) 'A probabilistic approach to pricing a bundle of products or services', *Journal of Marketing Research* 30: 494–508.
* Walters, R. (1988) 'Retail promotions and retail store performance: a test of some key hypotheses', *Journal of Retailing* 64: 153–81.
* Walters, R. (1991) 'Assessing the impact of retail price promotions on product substitution, Complementary purchase, and interstore sales displacement', *Journal of Marketing* 55: 17–28.

* Walters, R.G. and McKenzie, S.B. (1988) 'A structural equations analysis of the impact of price promotions on store performance', *Journal of Marketing Research* 25: 51–63.
* Yadav, M.S. and Monroe, K.B. (1993) 'How buyers perceive savings in a bundle price: an examination of a bundle's transaction value', *Journal of Marketing Research* 30: 350–8.
* Zeithaml, V. (1988) 'Consumer perceptions of price, quality and value: a means-end model and synthesis of evidence', *Journal of Marketing* 52: 2–22.

See also: ADVERTISING; CONSUMER BEHAVIOUR; LOGISTICS AND VALUE CREATION; MARKET SEGMENTATION; MARKETING STRATEGY; ORGANIZATIONAL BUYING BEHAVIOUR; POSITIONING; PRODUCT LIFE-CYCLE MANAGEMENT; RETAILING; THE MARKETING MIX

Channel management

1 Introduction
2 Perspectives for channel management
3 Basic areas of channel management
4 Trends in channel management

Overview

Channels of distribution are vital to a firm's objectives, but they must be effectively managed if the objectives are to be successfully achieved. Although channel management can be considered from the perspective of the retailer, back towards the manufacturer, it is much more common for analysis and research on the topic – and therefore this entry – to be approached from the perspective of the producer or manufacturer, looking down the channel towards the market.

There are six areas in which channel management should focus its decision making: formulating channel strategy; designing the channel structure; selecting the channel members; motivating the channel members; coordinating channel strategy with the marketing mix; and evaluating channel member performance. Each of these areas is discussed in turn, before a number of recent developments in the field are considered: an increasing emphasis on developing channel strategy; growth of partnerships and strategic alliances; a heavy emphasis on managing to reduce costs of distribution; more and more emphasis on technology; and broadened behavioural perspectives used in managing channels.

1 Introduction

No less of a management guru than Peter Drucker has said that channels of distribution should be 'a major concern to every business and industry'. He goes on to say that:

> To be able to anticipate changes in distribution channels and in where customers buy (and how, which is equally important), one has to be in the marketplace, has to watch customers, and non-customers.
>
> (Drucker 1990)

What Drucker is saying, in effect, is that channels of distribution cannot be ignored or left to their own devices if firms expect them to serve their target markets effectively and efficiently. Rather, channels of distribution need to be managed if they are to achieve the firm's distribution, marketing, and corporate objectives (Cespedes 1988). If channels are not managed the distribution of goods and services will be left largely to the competitive forces of the marketplace, as each firm in the channel attempts to maximize its own returns. Although this may result in effective and efficient distribution channels in some cases, for the most part this is not a good state of affairs for firms that want to exercise some influence over how, when and where their products and services are distributed.

Yet channel management, the analysis, planning, organizing and controlling of the firm's channels of distribution, can be a complex and challenging undertaking (Rosenbloom 1999). Not only are there many elements or issues to consider, but there are also the problems stemming from the interorganizational setting of channel structure. That is, channels of distribution by their nature consist of independent business organizations such as manufacturers, wholesalers and retailers as well as agents and brokers who, although 'linked' together in a trading relationship to form channels of distribution, are nevertheless still independent businesses. As such, each has its own objectives, policies, strategies and operating procedures, which may or may not be congruent with those of the other members of the channel (McVey 1960). Moreover, in most cases, in a channel of distribution there are no clear organization structures, superior/subordinate relationships, or lines of authority so typical of management in single-firm intraorganizational settings. Hence, managing a channel of distribution, and especially gaining a high degree of control of the channel, is frequently more challenging than managing within the intraorganizational setting of a single firm (Cespedes and Corey 1990).

2 Perspectives for channel management

Channel management can be viewed from two basic vantage points:

1. From the producer or manufacturer looking 'down the channel' towards the market.
2. From the retailer (or other final reseller) 'up the channel' back to the producer or manufacturer.

Although either of these perspectives is a valid one for examining the subject of channel management, the first one (from the producer or manufacturer looking down the channel towards the market) is by far the most commonly used perspective in the literature of channel management. Indeed, virtually all modern analysis and research on the subject is from this vantage point. This is probably because channel management is generally regarded as a subset of the larger field of marketing management, which has almost universally been treated from the perspective of the producer or manufacturer (Kotler 1988). Consequently, our discussion of channel management will be from the producer/manufacturer perspective.

3 Basic areas of channel management

Channel management viewed from the perspective of the producer or manufacturer looking down the channel towards the market can be divided into six basic decision areas (Rosenbloom 1999):

1. formulating channel strategy;
2. designing the channel structure;
3. selecting the channel members;
4. motivating the channel members;
5. coordinating channel strategy with the marketing mix;
6. evaluating channel member performance.

```
┌──────────────────────────────────────┐
│          Decision area 1             │
│   Formulating channel strategy       │
└──────────────────────────────────────┘
                  ↓
┌──────────────────────────────────────┐
│          Decision area 2             │
│   Designing the channel structure    │
└──────────────────────────────────────┘
                  ↓
┌──────────────────────────────────────┐
│          Decision area 3             │
│   Selecting the channel members      │
└──────────────────────────────────────┘
                  ↓
┌──────────────────────────────────────┐
│          Decision area 4             │
│   Motivating the channel members     │
└──────────────────────────────────────┘
                  ↓
┌──────────────────────────────────────┐
│          Decision area 5             │
│ Coordinating channel strategy with   │
│         the marketing mix            │
└──────────────────────────────────────┘
                  ↓
┌──────────────────────────────────────┐
│          Decision area 6             │
│ Evaluating channel member performance│
└──────────────────────────────────────┘
```

Figure 1 Major decision areas in channel management

This entry is organized around a discussion of each of these areas of channel management. Figure 1 provides a schematic overview of these decision areas.

Formulating channel strategy

Channel strategy refers to the broad principles through which the firm seeks to achieve its distribution objectives. Distribution objectives are usually set in terms of how, when and where the firm plans to have its products made available to its target markets. If the firm places heavy emphasis on distribution for gaining a competitive advantage, then the achievement of distribution objectives and hence the formulation of channel strategy can become a key strategic tool for the firm (Abell and Hammond 1979). For example, an automobile manufacturer who wants to improve on the experience that customers have when shopping for cars may set a distribution objective in terms of improving the customer service level provided by its independent dealerships. This may involve a substantial investment by the manufacturer in dealer education and training programmes aimed at changing the culture and operating procedures of its dealers towards a more customer-oriented focus. Indeed, the manufacturer may believe that superior customer service by its independent dealers is crucial to its long-term profitability or even its very survival. In this case, channel strategy that seeks to effect such an improvement in dealer service would unquestionably be seen as a key strategic issue for the manufacturer.

Distribution objectives that seek to help differentiate products through very selective or exclusive distribution (often the case with prestige or luxury products); or that provide a novel means of making products available (such as selling via the Internet) not available from competitive manufacturers; or that seek to offer much faster response times for customers through superior systems and technology, are all examples of methods which raise channel strategy to a level of strategic importance (Benjamin and Wigand 1995). In short, if the firm looks to channel strategy as a major means for gaining a sustainable competitive advantage (Porter 1985) by achieving higher levels of target market satisfaction via distribution, then it will be of strategic importance in helping the firm to achieve its long-term goals and objectives.

On the other hand, many distribution objectives, while important, may not be of strategic significance. For example, distribution objectives relating to the availability of products at a level consistent with competitors, those involving terms of sale, and geographical coverage of territory, for the most part would probably not be of strategic concern. Of course, there may be exceptions to this. For instance if the geographical coverage objective involved setting up distribution channels in new foreign markets, then indeed this distribution objective could be of strategic importance.

In any case, channel strategy, whether involving the pursuit of distribution objectives at the strategic level or at a lower operational level, is still an area that needs to be given high priority if any of the following four conditions exist:

1 target markets (customers) demand a strong emphasis on distribution;
2 competitive parity exists in other marketing mix variables;
3 competitive vulnerability exists because of distribution neglect;
4 opportunities for synergy exist through distribution strategy.

Target market demand and channel strategy
Modern marketing management is, of course, based fundamentally on customer orientation. Marketing managers therefore need to focus on the demands of their target markets and attempt to develop the best marketing mix of product, price, promotion and distribution variables to satisfy those demands more effectively than the competition (see PRICING; PRODUCT POLICY; PROMOTION; THE MARKETING MIX). Channel strategy (along with logistics) comprises the distribution variable of the marketing mix (see CHANNELS OF DISTRIBUTION). If customers in the target market have needs and wants that can best be addressed via channel strategy, management must adapt to meet these requirements. Such responses can range from making products more widely available to customers (e.g. Woolite tripled its sales by selling the product through supermarkets as well as department stores), to creating an entirely new dealer organization (as Honda motors did in the

USA to establish a luxury car identity for its new Acura division) or even to creating an entirely new mode of distribution as Amazon.com did in pioneering retailing of books on the Internet (Reilly 1997). In short, if customers can be served better through changes in channel strategy, then marketing managers must remain as alert to this need as they would be to the need for changing strategies in the other marketing mix variables.

Competitive parity and channel strategy
From a competitive standpoint, it is becoming increasingly common for competitive parity to exist among firms in the products they offer, the prices they charge and the promotional messages they convey (Cravens 1988). Such competitive parity in the product, price and promotional variables of the marketing mix has grown even more pronounced with the growth of global competition in recent years. Faced with this situation, more and more firms are focusing on the distribution variable in the marketing mix, and particularly the channel strategy component, as a means for standing out from the competition. What these firms have discovered is that channel strategies that serve target markets effectively and efficiently are not easily copied by competitors. This is because channel strategies and decisions are long term in nature and require substantial planning, development and investment to create a combination of organizational and human resources that result in superior channels. The superb worldwide dealer organization developed by Caterpillar Tractor Corporation which provides unmatched customer service in literally all corners of the earth is an outstanding example of a long-term competitive advantage provided through superior channel strategy and management (Fites 1996).

Distribution neglect and channel strategy
Of the four variables of the marketing mix, distribution, particularly channel strategy, has been neglected in relation to product, price and promotion strategies. With the exception of the logistical aspects of distribution, relatively little systematic attention has been given to the strategic questions of how, when and where, products and services should be made available to target markets. Instead, conventional thinking and evolutionary developments have characterized changes in channel structures rather than carefully formulated channel strategies. In fact, bold and innovative approaches to distribution are rather rare. However, when they do occur they tend to stand out. Timex watches, the first watchmaker to sell watches through mass market channels, Haynes, with its L'eggs pantyhose, the first firm to sell hose through supermarkets and drug stores, and Dell Computers, the first to sell personal computers via mail order, and more recently on the Internet are some of the best known examples of bold and innovative channel strategies that had apparently been overlooked by competitors.

Synergy through channel strategy
In recent years the terms partnership and strategic alliance have been heard with increasing frequency in connection with channel strategy (Anderson and Nanus 1990). The reason for this is that firms at various levels of the channel are seeking synergies by linking themselves more closely with other channel members (see RELATIONSHIPS AND NETWORKS; STRATEGIC ALLIANCES). Manufacturers of consumer products such as Procter & Gamble are developing strategic alliances with giant retailers such as Wal-Mart. Manufacturers of industrial products are forming partnerships with industrial distributors in an effort to meld their distinctive capabilities into a more effective and efficient *supply chain* than would be possible with traditional, more loosely aligned or 'arm's length' channel relationships. By working closely together and with mutual commitment to each other spelled out, opportunities to create synergy are enhanced because each firm is more aware of the other's strengths and weaknesses while dysfunctional tendencies or working at cross purposes are reduced. Thus, as more manufacturers learn that synergistic relationships can be built by developing partnerships or strategic alliances with their channel members, an emphasis on the channel strategies needed to create such relationships will increase. The term *supply chain management* has often been used in recent years to describe this more cooperative, coordinated, and intensely managed approach to channel management (Davis 1993).

```
                    ┌─────────────────────────┐
                    │        Stage 1          │
                    │ Setting distribution    │
                    │      objectives         │
                    └───────────┬─────────────┘
                                ▼
                    ┌─────────────────────────┐
                    │        Stage 2          │
                    │ Specifying the functions│
                    │   that need to be       │
                    │  performed by the       │
                    │       channel           │
                    └───────────┬─────────────┘
                                ▼
                    ┌─────────────────────────┐
                    │        Stage 3          │
                    │ Considering alternative │
                    │   channel structures    │
                    └───────────┬─────────────┘
                                ▼
                    ┌─────────────────────────┐
                    │        Stage 4          │
                    │  Choosing an 'optimal'  │
                    │    channel structure    │
                    └─────────────────────────┘
```

Figure 2 Stages in the channel decision process

Designing the channel structure

Having considered the overall strategic role of channel strategy in the firm, management then needs to turn its attention to the task of designing the firm's channels of distribution (see CHANNELS OF DISTRIBUTION). *Channel design* is the process of developing new channels where none had existed before, or making significant modifications to existing channels (Rosenbloom 1999). The process of channel design can be broken down into four basic stages or phases:

1 setting distribution objectives;
2 specifying the functions that need to be performed by the channel;
3 considering alternative channel structures;
4 choosing an 'optimal' channel structure.

These stages are depicted in Figure 2.

Setting distribution objectives

As alluded to in the previous section on channel strategy, distribution objectives refer to what the firm would like its channel strategy to accomplish in terms of how, when and where its products and services are provided to its target markets.

At the stage of channel design, distribution objectives need to be stated explicitly so that they can be made operational. Usually this means expressing the distribution objectives in quantifiable terms such as the following: within eighteen months we would like to have XYZ cereal available in 90 per cent of the supermarkets in which consumers of this product are likely to shop.

Distribution objectives must also take into account the firm's broader marketing and corporate objectives so that there are no inconsistencies. A manufacturer of a prestigious product, for example, would have to pay close attention to whether distribution objectives which seek to broaden the availability of its products would detract from the exclusive image of the goods.

Specifying the functions

Making products and services available to final customers how, when and where they want them can involve a great deal of work. The various activities, tasks or functions needed to perform this objective have to be specified at this point. Such tasks can range from providing 'simple' transportation for products all the way to the development of sophisticated electronic data interchange (EDI) systems for linking the manufacturer's and channel member's computers together for instantaneous information transmittal (Rosenbloom 1987) (see INFORMATION TECHNOLOGY AND MARKETING; MARKETING COMMUNICATIONS). Management must therefore try to be as comprehensive and precise as possible in spelling out just what functions need to be performed to attain the distribution objectives.

Alternative channel structures

The form or shape that the channel of distribution takes to perform the distribution functions is the channel structure. Unless a direct channel structure from manufacturer to final customer is used, the structure will include some combination of independent intermediaries such as wholesalers, retailers, agents and brokers (see RETAILING; WHOLESALING).

Management needs to be concerned with three dimensions of channel structure:

1 length of the channels;
2 intensity at the various levels;
3 the types of intermediaries involved.

With regard to length, in developed countries management usually has only three or four options for the distribution of consumer goods ranging from direct up to possibly three levels of intermediaries. In channels for industrial products, the range of choice for levels in the channel is usually even less.

The intensity dimension, which refers to the number of intermediaries to be used at each level of the channel, is usually characterized as:

- *intensive distribution* – where as many intermediaries as possible are used;
- *selective distribution* – where the number of intermediaries to be used is limited through more careful selection;
- *exclusive distribution* – where only one intermediary is used in a given geographical territory.

With regard to the types of intermediaries to be used at each level in the channel structure, this can vary quite widely depending upon the industry in question.

Decisions involving any of the dimensions of channel structure, particularly those of intensity and type of intermediary, should be guided by channel strategy and the distribution objective being pursued to avoid channel structures that are inappropriate to the strategy and objective. For instance, if a firm's objectives and strategy stress high levels of attention and service for final customers, this would generally be far more difficult to attain with an intensive distribution structure than with a more selective one because the very large numbers of channel members involved in intensive distribution would be harder to monitor and control than a small group of carefully chosen ones.

Choosing an optimal structure

In practice it is not possible to choose an optimal channel structure in the strictest sense of that term. However, it is possible to choose an effective and efficient channel structure that can meet the firm's distribution objectives.

Many different approaches have been suggested over the years for choosing such a channel structure. Very formal management science approaches, financial capital budgeting methods, distribution cost analysis techniques, and relatively recently, transactions cost analysis (Dwyer and Oh 1988) have all been offered as means for choosing channel structure. For the most part, these methods have not found much use in practice. Much more common are *judgemental and heuristic approaches* that rely on managerial judgement augmented by some data on distribution costs and profit potentials. Sometimes these judgemental, heuristic-type approaches are made more formal, through explicit identification of criteria to be used in choosing a channel, along with weighting and scaling techniques for ascertaining the relative importance of criteria and to provide a general scheme for scoring various channel structure alternatives (Rosenbloom 1999).

Of course, in the process of applying its best judgement, management also needs to takes into consideration a number of key variables that are usually relevant when choosing channel structure. The most basic of these are:

- market variables;
- product variables;

- firm variables;
- intermediary variables;
- behavioural variables;
- external environmental variables.

The location of final customers, the numbers of customers and their density, together with their patterns of buying behaviour, would all be key market variables.

Such factors as bulk and weight, unit value, newness, technical versus non-technical and perishability are product variables that are frequently important.

The financial capacity of the firm, its size, expertise and desire for managerial control are some of the most important firm variables.

Cost, availability and services provided are indicative of significant intermediary variables which management needs to consider.

Factors such as the potential of particular channel structures to reduce conflict, while maximizing power and communications effectiveness are critical behavioural variables for management to consider.

Finally, variables such as economic conditions, socio-cultural changes, competitive structure, technology, and government regulations can all be important environmental variables to consider when choosing channel structure.

Selecting the channel members

The *selection of intermediaries* who will become channel members can be viewed as the last phase of channel design (choosing the channel structure), or as an independent channel management area if selection is not undertaken as part of an overall channel design decision. In any case, the selection of channel members essentially consists of four steps:

1. developing selection criteria;
2. finding prospective channel members;
3. evaluating the prospective channel members against the criteria;
4. convincing prospective channel members to become actual channel members.

Developing selection criteria
Each firm should develop a set of criteria for selecting channel members that is consistent with its own distribution objectives and strategies. Obviously then, there is no universal list of selection criteria which would be applicable for all firms under all conditions. As a general rule, however, there is a basic guiding principle or heuristic that most firms can use which can be stated as follows: the more selective the firm's distribution policy, the more numerous and stringent the criteria used for selection should be and vice versa (Pegram 1965).

Thus, the list of criteria for a firm practising highly selective distribution might include such factors as the prospective channel member's reputation, competing product lines carried and management succession. A firm using very intensive distribution might use little more than one criterion consisting of the ability of the prospective channel members to pay the manufacturer for the products it ships to them.

Finding prospective channel members
The search for prospective channel members can utilize a number of sources. If the manufacturer has its own outside field salesforce, this is generally regarded as the best source because of the salesforce's knowledge of prospective channel members in their territories.

Other useful sources include final customers, trade sources, advertising and trade shows. Usually, a combination of several of these sources is used to find prospective channel members whether they be at the wholesale or retail levels.

Assessment against criteria
Once the group of prospective channel members has been identified, they need to be assessed against the criteria to determine those who will actually be selected. This can be done by an individual manager (such as the sales manager) or by a committee. Depending upon the importance of the selection decision, such a committee might well include top management even up to and including the chairman of the board if the selection decision is of great strategic importance. For example, when Goodyear Tyre and Rubber Company selected Sears Roebuck and Company to sell its tyres, Goodyear's board chairman was heavily involved in the decision because it would have long-term strategic implications for Goodyear.

Converting prospects to actual channel members
The key issue of concern here is to recognize that the selection process is a 'two way street'. Not only do producers and manufacturers select

retailers, wholesalers or various agents and brokers, but these intermediaries also select producers and manufacturers. Indeed, quite often it is the intermediaries, especially large and powerful retailers and wholesalers who are in the 'driver's seat' when it comes to selection. Consequently, the manufacturer seeking to secure the services of quality channel members has to make a convincing case that carrying its products will be profitable for the channel members. Given the sophistication of today's retailers and wholesalers, owing to the excellent computerized information systems they use, manufacturers must make their case very carefully and thoroughly to win the acceptance of such channel members.

Motivating the channel members

Motivation in the context of channel management refers to the actions taken by the manufacturer to secure channel member cooperation in implementing the manufacturer's channel strategies and achieving its distribution objectives (Rosenbloom 1990). Because the manufacturer's efforts to motivate channel members take place in the interorganizational setting of the marketing channel, the process is often more difficult and certainly less direct than would be the case for motivation in the intraorganizational setting of one firm.

Motivation management in the marketing channel can be viewed as a sequence of three steps:

1 learning about the needs and problems of channel members;
2 offering support for channel members to help meet their needs and solve their problems;
3 providing ongoing leadership.

Although the stages in the motivation process are sequential, the process is also iterative because of the continuous feedback from stages two and three. This is shown in Figure 3.

Learning about channel members' needs and problems

As mentioned earlier, channel members as independent businesses have their own objectives, strategies and operating procedures. But also as independent businesses they have their own needs and problems, which might be quite different from those of the manufacturer (Wittreich 1962). Hence, if the manufacturer seeks strong cooperation from the channel members, it is incumbent on that manufacturer to discover the key needs and problems of channel members in order to be able to help meet those needs and solve those problems. This is not a simple or straightforward task for the manufacturer because the range of needs and problems of channel members can be legion. Small retail channel members may

Figure 3 The motivation process in channels of distribution be overburdened with inventory, lack modern information systems, need better managerial skills and newer ideas for competing against giant retailers. On the other hand, giant retailers may face problems of how to reduce costs to operate profitably on razor-thin gross margins while being forced to carry larger and larger inventories as wholesalers disappear from the channel and new products proliferate. At the same time, wholesale channel members may be in desperate need of finding ways of competing successfully against power-buying retailers and customers who seek direct sales from the manufacturers. This list could go on and on for different channel members in particular industries, times and circumstances.

How does the manufacturer discover the particular needs and problems of channel members that need addressing? Basically, by taking a proactive rather than a reactive approach where the manufacturer merely waits for the information about channel members to somehow flow in through the 'grapevine'. Effective proactive methods include:

- in-house research on channel members;
- outside research;
- channel member advisory committees.

In-house research of channel members consists of the manufacturer applying the same research capabilities used to gather information about final customers to channel members in order to learn about their needs and problems.

Outside research of channel members can be used by firms who do not have an in-house research capability, or by those firms that do but want to avoid the possibility of bias that can creep into in-house research.

A channel member advisory committee consists of representatives from wholesale and/or retail level channel members and key executives from the manufacturer meeting on a regular basis (such as twice a year) in some neutral location. This type of close interaction between the manufacturer and channel members can foster the kind of candid dialogue needed to uncover channel member needs and problems which may not emerge in the normal course of business.

Offering support for channel members
Offering support to channel members to help meet their needs and solve their problems can be done in a variety of ways, from an informal 'hit or miss', *ad hoc* approach through to formal and carefully planned partnerships and strategic alliances.

The *ad hoc* approaches, also called cooperative support, are the most common in loosely aligned traditional channels. Basically, advertising dollars, promotional support, incentives, contests and a host of other *ad hoc* activities are offered by the manufacturer to 'jump start' the channel member's efforts to push the manufacturer's products or to 'firelight' a particular need or problem.

Partnerships and strategic alliances, in contrast, represent a more substantial and continuous commitment between the manufacturer and channel members. Support provided by the manufacturer is based on extensive knowledge of the needs and problems of the channel members and tends to be carried out on a longer term basis, with specific performance expectations that have been carefully worked out by the manufacturer in conjunction with channel members (see STRATEGIC ALLIANCES).

Providing continuing leadership
Even a well-conceived motivation effort, based on a thorough attempt to understand channel member needs and problems, together with a carefully articulated support programme still requires leadership on a continuing basis to achieve effective motivation of channel members. In other words, someone has to be in charge to deal with the inevitable changes and unforeseen problems that arise such as new forms of competition, technological developments and government regulations. While the manufacturer cannot always assume the leadership role and immediately deal with any problems, it is important that support should be available to provide direction and input over the long term instead of only while a new motivation programme is being developed and then quickly left to the channel members to deal with on a day-in-day-out basis (Mehta *et al.* 1996).

Coordinating channel strategy with the marketing mix

Channel management does not, of course, take place in a vacuum. All the other variables of the marketing mix are also in operation: hence, channel strategy needs to be coordinated with the marketing mix. Such coordination should help reduce strategies and actions in the four areas of marketing mix that work at cross purposes. Ideally, good coordination should enhance the effectiveness of the firm's overall marketing mix strategy by creating synergies among the marketing mix variables rather than the debilitating incongruencies that can result from neglecting this important issue.

To achieve such coordination, management needs to be aware of and sensitive to the many possible interfaces and relationships of channel strategy with product, price and promotional strategies. A few of these are discussed below (see STRATEGIC MARKETING PLANNING).

Product strategy and channel management
Product strategy is often dependent on channel strategy because some key product strategies interface with channel strategies in ways that can spell the difference between success or failure for both (Rao and McLaughlin 1989). For example, the successful introduction of new products relies heavily on strong channel member support in stocking, displaying and promoting the product. Product strategies implemented during the various stages of the product life-cycle have significant implications for channel management. In the maturity stage, for instance, when competitive products fight especially fiercely for shelf space, the right channel strategy is critical in helping to keep the manufacturer's products on the channel members' shelves. Other major product strategies such as *product differentiation, product positioning, product line extension* and *brand strategies* are also dependent on channel strategy for their implementation.

Pricing strategy and channel management
Pricing strategy is related to channel management because pricing decisions need to take into account channel factors if the manufacturer expects strong cooperation from the channel members (see PRICING). Although costs, market demand and competitive factors are obviously crucial in developing pricing strategy, so too are channel factors. In other words, most manufacturers do not have the luxury of being able to ignore the views of channel members when formulating pricing strategies. Clearly, such factors as the profit margins available to channel members, the different prices charged to various classes of channel members, prices of competitive products carried by channel members, special pricing deals, meeting various price points, changing pricing policies, the use of price incentives and 'grey market' pricing are all factors of major concern to many channel members. Thus, the manufacturer needs to make sure that it knows something about the expectations of channel members for these and other relevant pricing factors before embarking on any pricing strategy. What should not be forgotten is that when it comes to securing the services of channel members, the manufacturer must 'buy' those services from them (Warshaw 1962). The margins on the sale of its products are, in effect, the price charged by the channel members. If the manufacturer does not meet the price being sought by the channel members, in the long run they will not continue to offer their services.

Promotion strategy and channel management
Promotion in the form of both *push and pull promotion strategies* interfaces extensively with channel management (see PROMOTION). This is because many promotions undertaken by the manufacturer require strong channel member support and follow-through to work successfully. For example, major advertising campaigns frequently require point-of-purchase displays in the store, special deals and merchandising campaigns require channel members to stock up on extra inventory; contests and incentives call for participation from retailers and wholesalers.

Gaining channel members' cooperation and follow-through in promotion is not something that happens as a matter of course. On the contrary, very substantial effort is needed to sell the channel members on the value of any promotional campaign from their perspective before they will enthusiastically participate in presenting it to final customers. Moreover, a growing body of research shows that manufacturers need to develop carefully planned promotional programmes that are sensitive to the channel members' concerns to gain their continuous and long-term cooperation in promotional programmes (Curhan and Kopp 1988). *Ad hoc*, quick fix type promotions that are not part of a carefully planned channel strategy for gaining channel member cooperation in promotion programmes tend to be ineffective and costly relative to the results achieved.

Channel management

Evaluating channel member performance

The evaluation of channel member performance is necessary to assess how successful the channel members have been in implementing the manufacturers' channel strategies and achieving distribution objectives.

Evaluations require the manufacturer to gather information on the channel members. The manufacturer's ability to do this will be affected by:

- degree of control of channel members;
- importance of the channel members;
- number of channel members.

Usually, the higher the degree of control, the more information the manufacturer can gather and vice versa.

With regard to the importance of channel members, if the manufacturer relies heavily on them for the distribution of its products, it will tend to put more effort into evaluation than those who do not rely heavily on independent channel members.

Finally, when large numbers of channel members are used such as in intensive distribution, evaluation tends to be much more cursory than when smaller, more carefully selected channel members are used. The actual performance evaluation essentially consists of three steps:

1. developing performance criteria;
2. evaluating channel members against the performance criteria;
3. taking corrective actions if necessary.

Developing performance criteria

Although a wide variety of performance criteria can be used to evaluate channel members, by far the most commonly used ones are:

1. sales performance;
2. inventory maintenance;
3. selling capabilities;
4. attitudes;
5. competitive products handled;
6. growth prospects.

Of course, this list can be supplemented to fit the particular circumstances of the manufacturer. The relative importance of each criterion may also vary considerably based on the policies of a particular manufacturer.

Evaluating channel members against criteria

The use of a list of criteria to evaluate channel members can be done in an informal, judgemental fashion or by using a more formal quantitative approach (see QUALITATIVE RESEARCH IN MARKETING; QUANTITATIVE METHODS IN MARKETING).

In the former approach, criteria are used as a general benchmark of what the manufacturer is seeking. Channel members are then assessed against this list based on qualitative managerial judgements.

In the latter approach, formal weighting schemes can be developed to specify precisely the importance of criteria relative to each other. Formal scoring systems such as a scale of one to ten can then be used to rate each channel member against each criterion. It is then possible to arrive at an overall quantitative performance index for each channel member by multiplying the criteria weights by the scores and adding up the results.

Taking corrective actions

The management purpose behind evaluation is not only to monitor performance but also to take the necessary actions to improve the performance of those channel members who are below the standards. Thus, an integral part of the evaluation process is to have a set of preplanned steps to be taken to help channel members to meet or exceed performance expectations. Termination of the relationship with the channel member should be the very last step in this preplanned corrective process.

4 Trends in channel management

In recent years some significant developments in channel management have occurred. Perhaps the most basic and important ones are:

1. an increasing emphasis on developing channel strategy;
2. growth of partnerships and strategic alliances;
3. heavy emphasis on managing to reduce costs of distribution;
4. more and more emphasis on technology;
5. broadened behavioural perspectives used in managing channels.

Emphasis on channel strategy

More and more companies are 'discovering' channel strategy as an important area of focus for gaining long-term competitive advantages. At both the corporate and marketing levels, firms are finding it increasingly difficult to sustain competitive advantages through product, pricing, or promotional strategies and so they are looking to channel strategy as a viable alternative. In short, distribution channel strategy has become a valuable strategic competitive tool.

Growth in partnerships and strategic alliances

Partnership or strategic alliances in the context of channel management refer to the establishment of close working relationships between the manufacturer and key channel members to create mutual advantages and synergy. In contrast to traditional, loosely aligned channels, partnerships and alliances link the manufacturer and channel members more formally and closely and explicitly spell out the mutual expectations of all parties. In other words, the channel operates as a team instead of a collection of independent businesses. As a consequence of this trend, much more stress on channel management will be needed to create and nurture these partnerships and alliances. Supply chain management which implies careful and thorough management of relationships in the entire channel is therefore rapidly becoming the norm for effective channel management.

Cost reduction emphasis

Over the past decade there has been a tremendous emphasis in many industries on cost reduction through mergers and acquisitions to create economies of scale, re-engineering to develop more rational organizations, flattening out of organizations to reduce layers of management and downsizing to increase productivity. While not exactly parallel, the same type of thinking has begun to permeate channel management because a much greater emphasis is being placed on finding ways to reduce the costs of distribution through superior management of distribution channels.

Increased emphasis on technology

Closely related to the distribution cost reduction trend is the greatly increased focus on technology for enhancing distribution effectiveness and efficiency. Telecommunications and computer technology (especially the growing role of the Internet) have, of course, been at the forefront of this technological emphasis. From a channel management standpoint, this growing role for technology means that executives involved in channel management will need more in-depth knowledge of technology and, even more importantly, insight into how it can be gainfully applied to improve the effectiveness and efficiency of distribution channels.

Broadened behavioural perspective

Until the last quarter of the twentieth century, distribution channels were viewed only as economic systems and virtually devoid of social interactions and processes. Over the last two decades, the behavioural approach, which takes a broader perspective of channels by viewing them as social systems as well as economic systems, has grown substantially (Stern 1969). Thus, such basic issues as the use of power and the management of conflict in channels of distribution are approached from a behavioural perspective using the concepts and methods of the behavioural sciences instead of just economic analysis. Those involved in channel management need to be aware of this broadened perspective on social systems because it provides an enhanced set of tools for channel management.

BERT ROSENBLOOM
DREXEL UNIVERSITY

Further reading

(References cited in the text marked *)

* Abell, Derek F. and Hammond, John S. (1979) *Strategic Market Planning Problems and Analytical Approaches*, Englewood Cliffs, N.J.: Prentice Hall.
* Anderson, James C. and Nanus, James A. (1990) 'A model of distributor firm and manufacturer firm working partnerships', *Journal of Marketing* January: 42–58.
* Benjamin, Robert and Wigand, Rolf (1995) 'Electronic markets and virtual value chains on the Information Superhighway,' *Sloan Management Review* Winter: 62–72.
Boedecker, Karl A. and Morgan, Fred W. (1980) 'The channel implications of product liability developments', *Journal of Retailing* Winter: 59–72.
Butanay, Gul and Wortzel, Lawrence H. (1988) 'Distribution power versus manufacturer power: the customer role', *Journal of Marketing* January: 52–63.
Calantone, Roger J. and Gassenheiner, J.B. (1991) 'Overcoming basic problems between manufac-

turers and distributors', *Industrial Marketing Management* Winter: 215–21.
* Cespedes, Frank V. (1988) 'Channel management is general management', *California Management Review* 98–120.
  Cespedes, Frank V. (1992) 'Channel power: suggestions for a broadened perspective', *Journal of Marketing Channels* Spring: 2–37.
  Cespedes, Frank V. and Corey, E. Raymond (1990) 'Managing multiple channels', *Business Horizons* July–August: 67–77.
* Cravens, David W. (1988) 'Gaining strategic marketing advantage', *Business Horizons* September–October: 44–54.
* Curhan, Ronald C. and Kopp, Robert S. (1988) 'Obtaining retailers' support for trade deals: key success factors', *Journal of Advertising Research* January: 51–60.
  Dahlstrom, Robert and Dwyer, F. Robert (1992) 'The political economy of distribution systems: a review and prospectus', *Journal of Marketing Channels* Fall: 47–86.
* Davis, Tom (1993) 'Efficient supply chain management,' *Sloan Management Review* Summer: 35–46.
* Drucker, Peter (1990) 'Manage by walking around – outside', *Wall Street Journal* 11 May: A12.
* Dwyer, F. Robert and Sejo Oh (1988) 'Transaction cost perspective on vertical contractual structure and interchannel competitive strategies', *Journal of Marketing* April: 21–34.
* Fites, Donald V. (1996) 'Make your dealers your partners,' *Harvard Business Review* March–April: 84–95.
  Hardy, Kenneth G. (1986) 'Key success factors for manufacturer's sales promotions', *Journal of Marketing* July: 13–23.
* Kotler, Phillip (1988) *Marketing Management Analysis, Planning, Implementation and Control*, 6th edn, Englewood Cliffs, NJ: Prentice Hall.
* McVey, Phillip (1960) 'Are channels of distribution what the textbooks say?', *Journal of Marketing* January: 61–5.
* Mehta, Rajiv, Larsen, Trina and Rosenbloom, Bert (1996) 'The influence of leadership style on co-operation in channels and distribution,' *International Journal of Physical Distribution and Logistics Management* 26.
  Nanus, James A. and Anderson, James C. (1986) 'Turn your industrial distributors into partners', *Harvard Business Review* March–April: 66–71.
* Pegram, Roger (1965) *Selecting and Evaluation of Distributors*, New York: The Conference Board.
* Porter, Michael E. (1985) *Competitive Advantage Creating and Sustaining Superior Performance*, New York: The Free Press.

* Rao, Vithala R. and McLaughlin, Edward W. (1989) 'Modeling the decision to add new products by channel intermediaries', *Journal of Marketing* January: 80–8.
* Reilly, Patrick M. (1997) 'Booksellers prepare to do battle in Cyberspace,' *Wall Street Journal* 28 January: B1, D8.
* Rosenbloom, Bert (1987) *Marketing Functions and the Wholesaler-Distributor: Achieving Excellence in Distribution*, Washington. DC: Distribution Research and Education Foundation.
* Rosenbloom, Bert (1990) 'Motivating your international channel partners', *Business Horizons* March–April: 53–7.
  Rosenbloom, Bert (1995) *Marketing Channels: A Management View*, 5th edn, Fort Worth, Texas: Dryden Press, Harcourt Brace Jovanovich.
* Rosenbloom, Bert (1999) *Marketing Channels: A Management View*, 6th edn, Fort Worth, Texas: Dryden Press, Harcourt Brace Jovanovich.
  Rosenbloom, Bert and Anderson, Rolph (1985) 'Channel management and sales management: some key interfaces,' *Journal of the Academy of Marketing Science* Summer: 97–106.
  Shipley, David D. (1984) 'Selection and motivation of distribution intermediaries', *Industrial Marketing Management* October: 249–56.
* Stern, Louis W. (1969) *Distribution Channels: Behavioral Dimensions*, New York: Houghton Mifffin.
  Stern, Louis W. and El-Ansary, Adel I. (1992) *Marketing Channels*, 4th edn, Englewood Cliffs, New Jersey: Prentice-Hall.
  Sutton, Howard (1986) *Rethinking the Company's Selling and Distribution Channels*, New York: The Conference Board.
* Warshaw, Martin R. (1962) 'Pricing to gain wholesalers' selling support', *Journal of Marketing* July: 50–6.
* Wittreich, Warren J. (1962) 'Misunderstanding the retailer', *Harvard Business Review* May–June: 147–59.

See also: CHANNELS OF DISTRIBUTION; INFORMATION TECHNOLOGY AND MARKETING; MARKETING COMMUNICATIONS; PRICING; PRODUCT POLICY; PROMOTION; QUALITATIVE RESEARCH IN MARKETING; QUANTITATIVE METHODS IN MARKETING; RELATIONSHIPS AND NETWORKS; RETAILING; STRATEGIC ALLIANCES AND SUPPLIER PARTNERSHIPS; STRATEGIC MARKETING PLANNING; THE MARKETING MIX; WHOLESALING

Logistics and value creation

1. A closer look at logistics and what it does
2. Logistics value chain
3. Logistics of value chain
4. Value chain operating objectives
5. Logistics activities
6. A competency model of world class logistics
7. Conclusion

Overview

Logistics involves all activities required to plan and move items from a material or manufacturing source to the point of consumption. Historically, logistics referred to military support activities that provided food, clothing, supplies and equipment to troops. Generals understand well the importance of sound logistics in effective military operations. These activities include transportation and storage of supplies and equipment as well as personnel transport.

While the role of logistics has not always been visible and well defined in commercial enterprises, transportation, inventory storage and customer service have always been performed. However, top management did not always fully understand the strategic importance and competitive impact of integrated logistics. Wide acceptance of enterprise operating philosophies such as just-in-time, total quality management, customer satisfaction and customer responsiveness served to enhance the role of logistics in achieving competitive advantage. A well-planned and executed logistics effort can achieve timely shipment arrival, undamaged product and satisfied customers at the lowest attainable total cost. Both the professional and popular press recognize logistics' role in serving customers effectively.

Simply stated, customers expect nine rights in any transaction:

1. the right product;
2. the right quantity;
3. the right quality;
4. the right location;
5. the right time;
6. the right form;
7. the right price;
8. the right packaging;
9. the right information.

Logistics plays a major role in achieving each of these customer expectations.

This entry describes logistics and its role in achieving value creation through customer satisfaction for an enterprise. The discussion describes activities required to achieve the logistics mission and logistics' role in firm strategy. The first section offers a formal definition of logistics and discusses its contribution to the marketing mix. The second section describes logistics value creation. The value chain constitutes the institutions, inventory, information and financial flows required to serve customers effectively and efficiently. The third section describes capabilities associated with world class logistical competency. Strategies used by leading edge logistics firms to achieve their mission and sustain competitive advantage are illustrated. The entry concludes with a summary and suggestions for further study.

1 A closer look at logistics and what it does

This section defines logistics and elaborates on some of the managerial activities involved in the logistical process. The alignment of logistics relative to the other elements of the marketing mix is also discussed.

The Council of Logistics Management, the major logistics professional organization, defines logistics as 'the process of planning, implementing and controlling the efficient, effective flow and storage of goods, services and related information from the point of origin to the point of consumption for the purpose of conforming to customer requirements'. A few comments regarding this definition are appropriate.

First, logistics includes the actions required to design (plan), manage (implement) and measure (control) the movement of materials or finished products to customers. The design or planning activities include the selection of distribution participants. The participants involved in logistical process management include wholesalers, distributors, retailers and third party service providers necessary to provide warehousing, transportation and a wide range of other value added services. The transportation service decision includes selection of transport modes and providers. The managerial aspect of logistics includes scheduling and execution of activities to respond to customers and facilitate shipments. Management or execution activities include order processing, selection and shipment. Measurement includes monitoring activities to ensure performance both satisfies customers and deploys firm resources effectively. Typical measures include customer service level, cost, productivity, asset utilization and quality (see CUSTOMER CARE AND SATISFACTION; TOTAL QUALITY MANAGEMENT).

Second, while logistics has historically focused on goods movement, current definitions broaden the scope to include services and information since customers typically require that goods, services and related information arrive concurrently. Examples of product-related services and information include order and shipment documentation, manuals, warranty information, invoices, and reverse movement.

Third, logistics includes product movement and storage from point of origin to point of consumption. This scope specifically encompasses the movement of raw material and components from suppliers to manufacturing sites and movement of finished product to distribution facilities and ultimately to customers. Although not specifically stated, the discipline also includes activities related to recycling, returns handling and product recalls. (see CHANNEL MANAGEMENT; CHANNELS OF DISTRIBUTION).

While logistics has been defined as a discipline of its own, it is important to note that logistics is also a critical component of the firm's marketing capability. The contribution of logistics to the firm's marketing efforts is discussed below.

A firm's marketing mix is defined as the combination of product, price, promotion and place that combine to provide superior value to customers (see THE MARKETING MIX). The product is the physical good or service desired by the customer. In general, logistics offers timely delivery or positioning of the rights specified earlier. A firm must make many positioning decisions when developing a marketing strategy. Some such decisions include:

- Which wholesalers or distributors to include in the channel structure.
- How large a geographic area to serve.
- Method of end-consumer sale (retail or direct).
- Inventory strategy regarding make to stock or to order.

Make to stock means inventory is produced to forecast or plan, in anticipation of customer demand. Make to order implies custom production and demand driven distribution. The right product, price and promotional mix is useless without dependable and timely product availability (place). Timely availability creates value by allowing customers to purchase products or services where desired and if appropriate arrange delivery when and where desired. For a customer, availability or timely availability is equally as important as price and assortment (see SALES FORECASTING).

2 Logistics value chain

The logistics value chain links all activities required to support profitable transactions as a single process linking business with customers. In some situations the value chain is owned by a vertically integrated firm which controls all activities from raw material procurement to retail sales. Such vertical integration is found in the petroleum industry where firms control product value added from the drill to retail sales.

The more common value chain involves a number of independent firms such as material suppliers, manufacturers, wholesalers, retailers and logistics service firms. Due to the potential efficiency and effectiveness benefits, most firms linked together in a value chain seek to integrate some behaviours. Such collaboration is what distinguishes a traditional channel of distribution from a value chain. Figure 1 presents a traditional channel of distribution is in comparison to an integrated value chain. As illustrated, a traditional channel of distribution comprises of multiple chain members each attempting to optimize their individual performance. For example, each channel member may seek to minimize inventory investment rather than coordinating activities to reduce overall value chain inventory. The integrated value chain perspective attempts to coordinate value chain activities in an effort to reduce redundancy and duplication. It is the degree of collaboration in joint planning and coordinated operations that differentiates a traditional channel of distribution and an integrated value chain (see CHANNELS OF DISTRIBUTION).

Value chains facilitate a combination of value added flows. The primary three are inventory, information and financial flows. Information flow consists of sales activity, forecasts, plans and orders that must be refined into deployment, manufacturing and procurement plans. As products and materials are procured, an inventory flow is initiated which ultimately creates the product and transfers ownership of finished product to customers under the terms and conditions of sale. The financial flow from the end-consumer to the supplier provides the profit for coordinating and conducting the overall value added effort. Thus, the value added process is not viewed in the context of traditional functions such as order processing, transportation, inventory deployment and warehousing but rather in terms of three interrelated flows that create end-consumer value.

Two observations are in order prior to discussing each flow in detail. First, the value added process illustrated in Figure 1 is not limited to manufacturing firms. Retailers and wholesalers typically link physical distribution and procurement activities even though no change in product form typically occurs. Nevertheless, wholesalers and retailers are key contributors to the value added process. Wholesalers develop assortments of products from multiple manufacturers allowing retailers to purchase desired end-combinations in smaller quantities. Retailers make a broad range of products conveniently available to customers. Such sorting and positioning is an essential element of the value added process.

A second observation is that normal inventory flow toward end-customers must at times be reversed. Product recall capability is a critical competency to accommodate increasingly rigid safety standards, product expiration, and responsibility for hazardous material. Reverse logistics is also necessary due to the increasing number of laws prohibiting disposal and encouraging recycling of containers and packaging materials. Reverse logistics does not usually enjoy the scale economies characteristic of outbound movement. However, reverse movement capability is a social responsibility that must be accommodated in logistical system design. A significant reverse logistics requirement is the need for maximum control when a potential health or liability exists (e.g. spoiled or tainted product). In this sense, a recall programme is similar to a maximum customer service strategy that must be executed on a zero defect basis without concern for cost. Johnson

Figure 1 Traditional channel and integrated value chain

& Johnson's response during the Tylenol crisis is a classic example of maximum control capability. Thus, operational requirements of reverse logistics range from lowest total cost, as in returning bottles for recycling, to maximum control for critical recalls. The important point is that sound logistics strategy cannot be developed without careful evaluation of reverse logistics requirements.

3 Logistics of value chain

As previously discussed, the value chain includes inventory, information and cash flows. The participants, components and activities involved in each flow are discussed in greater detail.

Inventory flow

Logistics operations are concerned with movement and storage of materials and finished products. Logistics operations begin with the initial shipment of materials or component parts from a supplier and finalize when manufactured or processed product is delivered to end-customers. From the initial material or component purchase, logistics establishes value by moving inventory closer to the market and making it available in assortments and quantities end-consumers desire. Material absorbs costs and ideally gains value as it is transformed into finished product or moves closer to the market. For firms using assembly processes, work-in-process inventory must also be positioned to facilitate manufacturing operations. The cost of each component and its transportation becomes part of the value added process. The final and only meaningful value occurs when ownership is conveyed to end-customers when and where specified.

For large manufacturers logistical operations may include thousands of movements, which ultimately culminate in the delivery of assembled products to an industrial user, retailer, wholesaler, dealer or other customer. For large retailers logistical operations may commence with the procurement of products for resale and terminate with consumer purchase, for take away or home delivery. For hospitals, logistics begins with procurement and ends with full support of patient surgery and recovery. Logistics also includes return and appropriate disposal of post-consumption material as well. The significant point is that regardless of the size and type of enterprise, logistics is essential and requires continuous management attention. For better understanding, it is useful to divide logistical operations into three operating areas: physical distribution, manufacturing support and procurement.

Physical distribution involves product movement to end-consumers. Physical distribution links a value chain with its customers by providing the time and place component of the marketing mix. All physical distribution systems have the common characteristics of linking manufacturers, wholesalers and retailers into processes that make product available throughout the marketing channel.

Manufacturing support concentrates on managing work in progress inventory as it moves between manufacturing stages. The primary manufacturing related logistics responsibility is facilitating a master production schedule and arranging timely material and component availability. Thus, the overall logistics concern is not how production is performed, but ensuring that materials and components are positioned in a timely manner and that finished goods are as scheduled to physical distribution. The difference between manufacturing support and physical distribution is that the former serves customers and therefore must be designed to identify and accommodate market uncertainty. Manufacturing support generally involves moving materials under enterprise control. The uncertainties introduced by random customer ordering and erratic demand characterizing physical distribution are not typical of manufacturing support.

Procurement involves the purchasing and arranging for inbound movement of materials, parts and/or finished inventory from suppliers to manufacturing or assembly plants, warehouses or retail stores. Depending on the situation the acquisition process is commonly identified by different names. In manufacturing, acquisition is typically called purchasing; government acquisition has traditionally been termed procurement; retailers and wholesalers often use the term buying to describe the work involved; in many circles the total process is referred to as inbound logistics. Acknowledging that differences do exist concerning acquisition requirements, procurement is used here to include all types of purchasing. Procurement is concerned with availability of the desired material assortments where and when required. Whereas physical distribution is concerned with product shipments, procurement is concerned with inbound materials timing, sorting and assembly. Under most marketing situations involving consumer products, such as a grocery manufacturer who ships to a retail food chain, a manufacturer's physical distribution directly interfaces with the retailer's procurement. Although similar or even identical transportation requirements may be involved, the degree of managerial control and risk relative to the implications of performance failure vary substantially between those responsible for physical distribution and procurement.

Within a single enterprise, the three logistical operations overlap. Viewing each as an integral part of the value adding process creates opportunities to capitalize on unique characteristics of each while facilitating efficiency of the overall process. The prime concern of integrated logistics is to coordinate overall value added inventory movement to reduce redundancy and waste. A total logistics perspective must provide integrated management of materials, semi-finished components and finished products moving between suppliers, manufacturers, wholesalers and customers of the enterprise. In this sense, logistics is concerned with strategic management of total movement and storage.

Information flow

Information comprises the second key flow in the value added process. Information communicates forecasts, plans customer and replenishment requirements, provides order status updates and initiates physical activities to process orders. Replenishment orders resupply wholesalers and distributors from suppliers or manufacturing plants. Lower cost information technology and demand for reduced operating uncertainty have focused attention on enhanced information flow as a primary means to increase efficiencies. Value creation is enhanced through information accuracy, timelines and appropriateness, thus reducing the personnel, capital and inventory resources required to accomplish the logistics mission.

There are two primary information flows that drive logistics operations: (i) planning and coordination requirements and (ii) operational requirements. Planning and coordination requirements information drives capacity, logistics, manufacturing and procurement requirements planning. Based on business and product forecasts, planning and coordination requirements systems time phase which products are needed where and when. Such requirement plans are used to plan facility and manufacturing capacity requirements and subsequent product replenishment schedules. Accurate and timely planning and coordination reduces uncertainty, thus reducing the need for anticipatory inventory deployment and safety stock positioning. Safety stocks are extra inventories positioned to accommodate excessive demand or extended delivery times. Planning and coordination serves to reduce the occurrence of such accommodations.

Operational fulfilment systems initiate and control customer and replenishment orders. While planning and coordination requirements focus on anticipatory product demands, operational fulfillment systems coordinate realized demand fulfilment. The operating activities included in operational fulfilment are order entry and management, warehouse operations, inventory control, transportation and invoicing. These activities represent the day-to-day work of logistics. The operational fulfilment system is the backbone of most firm information systems.

The combination of the two systems constitutes logistics information flow. Planning and coordination fulfilment systems manage the firm's production and inventory capacity while operational fulfilment systems serve to accommodate customer demand. When the firm operates in a make-to-order environment, the systems coincide since it is not necessary to maintain anticipatory inventory. When the firm operates under a make-to-stock strategy, the logistics information system must rationalize conflicts between facility and operating capacities, inventory levels and customer demands.

Financial flow

Financial flow includes the processing of receivables and payment of value chain participants for the activities performed by each.

Characteristics of supply chain financial flow include electronic funds transfer and other Electronic Data Interchange (EDI) that serves to reduce duplication, facilitate transfer, reduce delays, and eliminate errors. Speed of financial transfer is an essential aspect of efficiency since it serves to reduce assets deployed in the value creation process (see INFORMATION TECHNOLOGY AND MARKETING).

4 Value chain operating objectives

When designing and administering the logistics process, each firm and its value chain collaborators must simultaneously strive to balance six somewhat conflicting operational objectives. These objectives are the primary determinants of value added performance and include:

1 rapid response;
2 minimum variance;
3 minimum inventory deployment;
4 movement consolidation;
5 total quality;
6 life-cycle support.

Rapid response

Rapid response concerns the value chain's ability to satisfy customer requirements in a timely manner. Demands may be in the form of special product requirements, quick delivery or product status information. Information technology increases the potential to postpone logistical decisions to the last possible moment and then helps facilitate rapid delivery of expected requirements. Examples of such information technology applications include using point-of-sale (POS) data to drive replenishment of retail inventory. In the past, retail inventory deployment was based on forecasts, which included substantial uncertainty resulting in significant safety stock. The ability to track daily retail sales and rapidly respond with the exact replenishment assortment reduces safety stock requirements (see INFORMATION TECHNOLOGY AND MARKETING). Rapid response introduces the capability to shift operational emphasis from anticipatory planning based on forecast to a response-based operation based on actual sales. Such shift from a push to a pull operating position can significantly reduce overall inventory investment in a value chain.

Since inventory in a response-based system is typically not positioned until customer requirements are known, limited tolerance exists for operational failure. Rapid response eliminates safety inventories required to satisfy anticipated customer requirements.

Minimum variance

Minimum variance is the second objective. Variance constitutes any unexpected disruption of logistics system operations. For example, order receipt delays, manufacturing disruptions, damaged goods or demand surges all result in operating variances that must be resolved. Logistics variance can result in stockouts and excess inventory is typically required to avoid such disruption. Variance can be both internal and external to an enterprise. An example of internal variance is the inconsistency in order processing time due to delays correcting or validating order information. External variance is the more difficult to identify and typically the most costly to resolve. A major form of external variance is deviations in transit time as trucks are delayed by traffic, weather or equipment breakdowns.

All aspects of logistics system operations have variance potential. The traditional way to eliminate the impact of variance was to maintain costly safety stocks or use high-cost premium transportation. Reliance on such costly practices is being replaced by exacting forms of logistics process control. Rather than maintaining safety stock just in case of disruption, a preferred solution is to identify and eliminate the source of the uncertainty. To the extent that variances can be minimized, logistics productivity is improved. Thus, the second logistics process performance objective is to minimize such variance.

Minimum inventory

The third objective, minimum inventory, focuses on asset commitment level and related velocity. Asset commitment level is the value of inventory deployed throughout the value chain. Turn velocity refers to the rate of inventory usage over time. For an average retail food item, the distribution channel maintains about fifteen weeks of supply, which includes inventory located at the manufacturer through finished items on the retail shelf. This implies the total value chain inventory 'turnover' is approximately 3.5 times per year (52 weeks/15 weeks). High turnover rates mean that assets devoted to inventory are being effectively utilized. Conversely, low turnover rates suggest that excessive inventory is being maintained by manufacturers, wholesalers and retailers. The goal is to reduce inventory as low as possible while simultaneously meeting desired customer service goals and achieving the lowest total logistics cost. Concepts like zero inventory have become increasingly popular as managers seek to reduce inventory risk. Operational deficiencies in a value chain are often not visible until inventory is reduced to the lowest possible level. For example, high inventory may mask operating problems caused by variances in manufacturing or transportation cycle time. A goal of eliminating all inventory is not practical, and could even cause efficiency problems. It is important to remember that inventory can and does provide some important logistics benefits including decoupling demand and supply. Inventory can also provide improved return on investment through manufacturing or procurement economies of scale. To achieve the minimum inventory objective, a logistics system achieves inventory commitment and turnover velocity for the entire value chain as contrasted to each enterprise. The extension of inventory management to a total value chain requires cross-organizational planning and collaboration. Managing inventory deployment for the total value chain reduces duplication and wasted effort caused by poor communication between partners.

Maximum movement consolidation

The fourth logistics objective is to achieve maximum movement consolidation. Transportation expenditures are the largest single logistics cost representing nearly 58 per cent of total cost. In general, transportation cost increases with distance, size of shipment, and product susceptibility to damage. Transportation cost per unit of weight decreases as shipment size and length of haul increases. Many logistical systems are designed to use high-speed, dependable transportation to achieve premium service at a high cost. Maximum movement consolidation can help to reduce transportation expense. Consolidation can be achieved by aggregating multiple smaller shipments into one large quantity for linehaul (i.e. long distance) movement. The linehaul shipment is then split for delivery to customer destinations. Although there is usually some expense for local distribution, there is substantial cost saving from the consolidated linehaul move. Maximum consolidation requires cooperation to group small shipments for movement. Such cooperation must transcend the overall value chain.

Total quality

The fifth logistics objective is to seek continuous total quality improvement. Total quality management (TQM) is a major commitment throughout industry. A defective product or poor service detracts from value added potential. Once a product is moved closer to an end-customer, logistics expenses for storage and transportation cannot be recovered if the product is damaged. In fact, when product or service quality fails either prior to or within the logistics system, the logistical process typically needs to be reversed and then repeated. Logistics itself must perform to demanding quality standards. The management challenge of achieving zero defect logistical performance is magnified by the fact that logistics activities are performed across a geographic area at all times of the day and night. The quality challenge is further magnified by the fact that most logistical work is performed without direct or on-the-spot supervision. Repeating a shipment as a result of incorrect content or in-transit damage is far more costly than performing logistics requirements correctly the first time. Logistics is a prime component in achieving continuous TQM improvement (see TOTAL QUALITY MANAGEMENT).

Life-cycle support

A final logistics objective is life-cycle support. Few items are sold without some guarantee that the product will perform as advertised over a specified time period. In fact, some products, such as copying equipment, derive the majority of their profits from after market sales and service of supplies and parts. The importance of life-cycle support varies directly between products and customers. For firms marketing consumer durable or industrial equipment, the commitment to life-cycle support constitutes a demanding operational requirement as well as one of the largest costs of logistical operations. The life-cycle support capabilities of a logistical system must be carefully designed. As noted earlier, reverse logistical competency, given worldwide attention to environmental concerns, requires the ability to recycle ingredients and packaging materials.

5 Logistics activities

While it is appropriate to consider the logistics process across an integrated value chain, it is also useful to identify the major work required to accomplish the logistics mission. Traditional organizations incorporate four areas of logistics functionality:

1. customer service;
2. transportation;
3. inventory management; and
4. distribution operations.

Even though many firms have integrated the logistics process with other internal units and externally with suppliers and customers, these work areas remain the heart of the logistics value chain. Each work area is described.

Customer service manages the primary interface between a firm and its customers from an order fulfilment perspective. Customer service includes order taking and modification, order status inquiry and customer problem resolution. While the historic customer service focus has been order taking and change, other customer service considerations are receiving increasing attention. Order taking excellence reflects a normal customer expectation. However, a key service determinant is often a firm's ability to offer responsive and flexible service tailored to meet each customer's needs at the lowest possible total cost. For example, customers expect the firm's customer service activity to be capable of providing accurate information regarding product availability, delivery time, product substitution, pricing and product customization options.

Transportation controls product movement from manufacturing sites to distribution facilities and from distribution facilities to customers. The responsibilities include selecting the type of carrier, scheduling, routing and freight payment. In addition to managing the firm's shipping activities, transportation is responsible for monitoring carrier performance. Logistics is responsible for improving transportation service levels while simultaneously decreasing overall cost. The transportation management objective is to minimize total cost associated with all movements from suppliers to the final customer. When speed and service reliability are taken into consideration, the lowest total cost of logistics may result from the same decisions yielding the lowest cost of transportation. While there have not been many fundamental advances in transportation technology, carriers offer customized services that can provide value to customers. Examples of such value added services include electronic scheduling, billing and invoicing, consolidation with other shippers, merging components in transit, cross-docking and product storage. Transportation is responsible for monitoring the service offerings of carrier (or other third-party service providers) and evaluating effective ways to incorporate new services into the overall value chain.

Inventory management consists of monitoring inventory levels and requirements at manufacturing plants and distribution facilities. The objective is to maintain enough inventory to satisfy customer demands while minimizing total asset deployment. Historically, inventory management has focused on establishing the necessary safety stock to meet desired service level. The focus today is to identify information technology applications that reduce operating uncertainty and thus reduce safety stock requirements. Leading edge firms gather knowledge regarding sales, customer demand, customer promotion plans, delivery times and replenishment cycles so that inventory can be synchronized with demand.

Distribution operations have responsibility for the physical facilities and activities that take place at the distribution facilities used by a firm. The facilities include the buildings, offices, communications equipment, storage racks and material handling equipment. The activities include product receipt, storage, order selection and shipment. The distribution operations objective is to minimize expenses for receiving, storing and shipping product from a distribution facility. The historical operations focus has been to minimize the variable cost associated with handling or moving a product through a distribution facility. However, minimum variable cost is not the only objective. A more comprehensive focus is to reduce assets required to support logistics while simultaneously increasing operating flexibility. Reduced assets removes distribution facilities and handling equipment from a company's books. Operating flexibility is necessary to accommodate both larger, time-critical orders and smaller, less service-sensitive orders. While some firms attempt to service both types of orders through the same facility, others improve flexibility while using fewer assets through the employment of third-party service providers such as public or contract warehouse operators.

While management of each of the above activities must focus on cost reduction, the major objective is minimization of total cost for providing coordinated logistics services that satisfy customer service. In this sense, the cost-to-cost tradeoff between each activity must be evaluated to identify unified performance improvements. For example, use of air freight as the transport mode may increase transportation expense but may also decrease total logistics cost by reducing inventory management and distribution operating expenses. Logistics management is responsible for identifying the tradeoff that can provide comparable or enhanced customer value added while reducing total logistics expense.

6 A competency model of world class logistics

What characteristics define world class logistics? The key to a better understanding of what demonstrates logistical excellence is found in the relationships among practices, drivers and capabilities. A practice is a job-related work action. A driver is a collection of practices aimed at achieving a capability. A capability is the knowledge and achievement essential to developing logistical competency.

In the world class logistics research reported by Michigan State University, seventeen universal logistical capabilities were identified. Each capability is the composite of multiple best practices, each of which is highly relevant to specific work situations. Whereas the practices and their grouping into drivers are highly business and situation specific, the capabilities they inspire are universally observable across business situations.

Both survey and interview research overwhelmingly support the conclusion that the seventeen capabilities of world class logistics are universal. These capabilities transcend channel position, being observable among manufacturers, wholesalers and across the full range of retail formats. The capabilities also transcend industries, nations and even cultural boundaries. The capabilities can also be observed and measured among firms of all sizes. Specific capabilities will at times be more visible or prominent because economic, social and competitive situations are different. However, some presence of all seventeen universal capabilities can be observed in all situations. Simply stated, world class logistics firms have a higher total level of capability achievement than their less accomplished competitors.

The importance of identifying and measuring capabilities results from the fact that they combine to create logistical competencies. The term competency describes a state of 'being sufficient to gain and maintain selected customers'. Competencies result from a fusing of capabilities. Competencies are about being superior to competition in terms of satisfying customer expectations and requirements.

World class logistics results from high level achievement and fusing of four competencies: (i) positioning; (ii) integration; (iii) agility; and (iv) measurement. In the sense used here, a competency serves to synthesize capabilities into a logically coherent and manageable end state. At the competency level the dimensions of a discipline begin to blur into the whole of business. It is at the competency level that all disciplines begin to merge to create a sum of the business or holistic enterprise.

Positioning is concerned with strategy and structure. Positioning is about envisioning strategic and structural approaches to guide logistical operations. Strategy establishes objectives and the way they are to be achieved. Structure is concerned with how human and physical resources are organized and allocated to implement strategy.

Integration deals with what to do and how to do it to create logistical operating excellence. To be integrated means that a firm undertakes specific initiatives following formalized rules and procedures designed to facilitate successful attainment of desired goals. Logistical integration facilitates excellence in day-to-day operations and execution. The essence of logistical performance rests upon overall integration. It is internal and external integration that allow world class firms to effectively perform logistics and participate in supply chain relationships.

Agility relates to a firm's competitiveness. Agility captures the combined capabilities of relevancy, accommodation and flexibility. These capabilities that result in agility engender customer loyalty.

Measurement relates to a firm's achievement level. Effective measurement calibrates a firm's achievement in terms of functional assessment, process assessment and benchmarking. It is essential that managers have a clear and continuous understanding of their relative achievement if they are to be successful in initiating effective change.

A generalized logistical competency model is illustrated in Figure 2. Illustration in the format of interlocking circles was selected to convey the strength inherent in simultaneously achieving a high state of the four essential competencies. The interlocking circles are placed within a box to reflect the ever-changing competitive technological, economic, social and legal environments. Within each competency, specific capabilities are essential. The capabilities combine to create the competency. No firms participating in the research achieved a perfect score with respect to all four competencies. World class firms have one thing clearly in common: they continually seek to improve capabilities related to all four competencies and generally do it better than key competitors.

Table 1 provides definitions of world class competencies and related capabilities. The capabilities that result in world class logistical competencies have their foundation in learning. Those related to positioning involve learning about the external world of consumers, competitors and market dynamics. The capabilities that achieve integration deal with learning and adapting best practices to logistical operations. The learning that results in agility is characterized by shared experience. Finally, the learning that relates to measurement is all about the calibration of specific work, achievement level and cross organizational integration. It is the combined accumulation of knowledge and skill related to these four competencies within a specific environment that is difficult for competitors to duplicate. (For a more detailed discussion and capability examples, see the *World Class Logistics* research monograph listed in the references.)

7 Conclusion

This review of logistics and its contribution to value creation suggests three conclusions. First, logistics is a significant component in the engine driving economic development. Logistical management plans, performs and monitors the movement of product from the suppliers through value-chain ultimately to consumers. On average logistics consumes about 11 per cent of the gross domestic product and employs approximately 20 per cent of a nation's

Figure 2 World class competency model

The marketing mix

Table 1 World class logistics model definitions

Competency – Positioning: The selection of strategic and structural approaches to guide operations.

Capability

- Strategy: The establishment of financial, channel and customer objectives and the means to achieve them.
- Supply chain: The alignment of logistics resources through channel alliances.
- Network: The structure and deployment of physical resources.
- Organization: The structure and deployment of human resources.

Competency – Integration: The establishment of what to do and how to do it creatively.

Capability

- Supply chain unification: Relative intensity across the distribution channel.
- Information technology: The hardware, software and network investment and design to facilitate processing and exchange.
- Information sharing: The willingness to exchange key technical, financial, operational and strategic data.
- Connectivity: The capability to exchange data in a timely, responsive and useable format.
- Standardization: Establishment of common policies and procedures to facilitate logistics operations.
- Simplification: Designing routines and work to improve efficiency and effectiveness.
- Discipline: Adherence to common operational policies and procedures.

Competency – Agility: The achievement and retention of competitiveness and customer success.

Capability

- Relevancy: The ability to maintain focus on the changing needs of customers.
- Accommodation: The ability to respond to unique customer requests.
- Flexibility: The ability to adapt to unexpected circumstances.

Competency – Measurement: The internal and external monitoring of operations.

Capability

- Functional assessment: the development of comprehensive functional performance measurement capability.
- Process assessment: The extension of performance measurement systems across internal and external logistical processes.
- Benchmarking: The comparison of metrics and process with best practice performance.

workforce. While the cost and magnitude of logistics operations is significant, the level of logistics performance in most developed countries is even more impressive. While there are occasional out-of-stocks, it is rare that customers cannot be satisfied through product substitution or alternative sourcing. On the other hand, inadequate logistics systems in underdeveloped economies significantly contribute to a low quality of life.

Second, increased demand and globalization will continue significantly to challenge logistics operations and management. Customers demand more specialized products and services from a wider range of sources resulting in a need for logistics capabilities that can handle more product variations in alternative formats. Such demand increases logistics system complexity since customers are increasingly less willing to purchase standardized products.

Logistics capability must provide assortments in a number of different package configurations. In an increasing number of situations, actual finalization of product form and packaging may be postponed until the product is within the physical distribution system. Such innovation reduces inventory but it also dramatically increases logistics operating complexity. Global logistics must support global procurement and marketing across diverse geographical areas. This support increases product diversity, distance and documentation requirements, all of which increase the complexity of logistics.

Third, logistics expertise can contribute to a substantial competitive advantage for high performance firms. Strategies such as value chain integration, performance enhancement, information collaboration and time-based competition can position firms to provide more time or service value performance across the supply chain at lower total cost. Since these strategies cannot be duplicated readily by competitors, logistics can provide a sustainable source of competitive advantage.

DONALD J. BOWERSOX AND DAVID J. CLOSS
MICHIGAN STATE UNIVERSITY

Note

This material is adapted from the text Bowersox, D.J. and Closs, D.J. (1996) *Logistical Management: The Integrated Supply Chain Process*, New York: McGraw-Hill Publishing.

Further reading

Bowersox, D.J. (1990) 'The strategic benefits of logistics alliances', *Harvard Business Review* 68: 3–5.

Bowersox, D.J. and Closs, D.J. (1996) *Logistical Management: The Integrated Supply Chain Process*, New York: McGraw-Hill.

Bowersox, D.J., Daugherty, P.J., Droge, C.L., Germain, R.N. and Rogers, D.S. (1992) *Logistical Excellence: It's not Business as Usual*, Burlington, MA: Digital Press.

Global Logistics Research Team (1995) *World Class Logistics: The Challenge of Managing Continuous Change*, Chicago, IL: Council of Logistics Management.

Stalk, G., Evans, P. and Shulman, L. (1992) 'Competing on capabilities: the new rules of corporate strategy', *Harvard Business Review* 70: 57–70.

See also: CHANNELS OF DISTRIBUTION; CHANNEL MANAGEMENT; CUSTOMER CARE AND SATISFACTION; INFORMATION TECHNOLOGY AND MARKETING; MARKETING ORGANIZATION AND MANAGEMENT; SALES FORECASTING; THE MARKETING MIX; TOTAL QUALITY MANAGEMENT; WHOLESALING

Wholesaling: the role of marketing intermediaries

1 Rationale for the emergence of modern wholesalers
2 The structure of wholesaling
3 Selecting and using wholesalers
4 A hard-nosed assessment
5 Conclusion

Overview

The focus of this entry is on the functions of specialist markets and intermediaries between producers and organizational buyers (i.e. wholesaling). Wholesaling is concerned with the activities of those persons or establishments which sell to retailers and other merchants, and/or to industrial, institutional and commercial users, but which do not sell in significant amounts to ultimate consumers.

Of course, accepting this definition as the gospel truth means that every sale made by every organization to anyone but an ultimate consumer is a 'wholesale transaction'. This would include every manufacturing firm (with the exception of the small amount of sales made through factory outlets to household consumers) as well as sales made by such diverse organizations as hotels, insurance companies and accounting firms when they deal with 'industrial, institutional and commercial' users in booking rooms, arranging pension plans, or preparing annual reports. Therefore, almost all organizations (except those dealing with ultimate consumers) are engaged in wholesaling and their transactions are classified as wholesale transactions.

1 Rationale for the emergence of modern wholesalers

The wholesaler's functions are shaped by the vast economic task of coordinating production and consumption, or, in Alderson's words (1971: 20), of matching heterogeneous demands for assortments at various levels within distribution (see CHANNELS OF DISTRIBUTION). Thus, wholesalers aid in bridging the gap between periods and places in which goods are produced and those in which they are consumed or used.

The sorting process of wholesalers is the key to their economic viability. It frequently happens that the quantities in which goods are produced or the characteristics with which they are endowed by nature do not match either the quantities in which they are demanded or the characteristics desired by those who use or consume them. Channel intermediaries (e.g. wholesalers and retailers) essentially solve the problem of the discrepancy between the various assortments of goods and services required by industrial and household consumers and the assortments available directly from individual producers (see CHANNEL MANAGEMENT; RETAILING). In other words, manufacturers usually produce a large quantity of a limited number of products, whereas consumers purchase only a few items of a large number of diverse products. Middlemen reduce this discrepancy of assortments, thereby enabling consumers to avoid dealing directly with individual manufacturers in order to satisfy their needs.

Wholesalers may participate in the performance of any or all of the marketing flows (i.e. ownership, physical possession, information, financing, risk taking, negotiating, ordering and payment). However, the rationale for a wholesaler's existence boils down to the 'value adding' functions he performs for the suppliers and customers he serves as illustrated in Figure 1. His economic justification is based on just what it is that he can do for his clientele, whether they are retailers, institutions (e.g. hospitals, schools, restaurants), manufacturers, or any other type of business enterprise. For example, in the case of industrial goods needed in the assembly of a given product (e.g. transistors for radios), it may be less costly for the purchasing organization to place the burden of handling, owning, storing, delivering and ordering the goods on a wholesaler rather than having to order in very large

```
                Marketing functions                    Marketing functions
                performed for                          performed for
                manufacturers                          customers
        ┌─────────────────────────┐            ┌─────────────────────────┐
        │    Market coverage      │            │   Product availability  │
        ├─────────────────────────┤            ├─────────────────────────┤
        │    Sales contact        │  ╱Wholesaler-╲     │ Assortment convenience │
        ├─────────────────────────┤ │ distributors │   ├─────────────────────────┤
        │    Inventory holding    │◄┤  perform     ├──►│    Bulk-breaking        │
        ├─────────────────────────┤ │ all of these │   ├─────────────────────────┤
        │    Order processing     │  ╲ functions ╱     │  Credit and finance     │
        ├─────────────────────────┤            ├─────────────────────────┤
        │    Market information   │            │    Customer service     │
        ├─────────────────────────┤            ├─────────────────────────┤
        │    Customer support     │            │ Advice and technical    │
        └─────────────────────────┘            │        support          │
                                               └─────────────────────────┘
                                  ◇ Result? ◇
                                       │
                                       ▼
                         ┌─────────────────────────────┐
                         │       Value added           │
                         │ (reflected in margins earned│
                         │  by wholesaler-distributors)│
                         └─────────────────────────────┘
```

Figure 1 Value added by wholesaler/distributors through the performance of marketing functions
Source: Rosenbloom (1987: 26)

lots directly from the manufacturer, especially if the goods will have to be held for a considerable period before they are used up in the production process.

2 The structure of wholesaling

Wholesaling may be characterized as a sector of the economy in which the degree of specialization has constantly increased. In fact, as depicted in Table 1, the institutional variety in wholesaling is almost overwhelming. Such a variety offers buyers and sellers many channel choices, as dictated by such considerations as size, market segmentation, financial strength, services offered and chosen method of operation. It also makes possible a high degree of marketing flow or functional shiftability, whereby any of the functions performed at the wholesale level of distribution may be shifted from one type of agency to another.

From a channel analysis perspective, it is important to understand what specific roles the various wholesaling institutions and agencies assume, so that when a channel is designed or adjusted the appropriate kind of organization can be included. An essential piece of information in this regard is whether a wholesaler participates in all or only a few of the marketing flows (physical possession, ownership, promotion, negotiation, financing, risking, ordering and payment). That is, assuming a manufacturer's or a retailer's perspective for the moment, what is it that one could expect to receive from a wholesaler in the way of services performed? Clearly, the more services performed, the higher the wholesaler's compensation will have to be from the channel as a whole. Table 2 produces a summary of the flows participated in by the variety of wholesaling enterprises.

An examination of Table 2 indicates that full-function merchant wholesalers participate in all the flows while brokers and manufacturers' agents participate in only a few of them. Therefore, if a manufacturer were to 'employ' full-function merchant wholesalers, the functional discount granted to them would have to be considerably more than the commission he or she would have to pay to manufacturers' agents or brokers for selling his or her products to end-users. But when a manufacturer does not use a full-function wholesaler the discount is not 'saved', because he or she must assume all of the services the wholesaler would have provided. This is why the discount is called 'functional'. It is granted for these wholesalers to compensate them for the cost incurred in the performance of these functions.

3 Selecting and using wholesalers

It is an old axiom of marketing that it is possible to eliminate wholesalers (or any middlemen, for that matter) but impossible to eliminate their functions. The major question facing a manufacturer is whether, by vertically integrating (that is, by establishing his or her own sales branches and warehouse facilities), he or she can perform the functions more efficiently and effectively than a wholesaler. This question is a cause of considerable controversy in formulating marketing channel strategy (see MARKETING STRATEGY; CHANNEL MANAGEMENT).

The likelihood is that the cost of marketing through wholesalers is not going to be vastly different from the funds a firm would have to expend on its own to obtain the same services. If this is so, then what accounts for the large amount of direct selling that goes on? Why is vertical integration of wholesaling functions so popular, especially among large manufacturing and retailing firms?

The answer lies not only in efficiency considerations but mainly in effectiveness considerations. The fact that a given type of wholesaling firm participates in a number of marketing flows gives some idea about the potential for a division of labour in the channel. But the crucial question from a management perspective is to what extent (i.e. how heavily) and with what level of quality does the firm participate? To answer this question, we must first examine what it is that wholesalers can, ideally, provide. Then, we will juxtapose this description against a hard-nosed assessment of the orientation of many wholesalers.

How can wholesalers serve suppliers?

Ideally, wholesalers have a great deal of potential as channel partners for suppliers. From an operational perspective, suppliers of both industrial and consumer goods may rely on wholesalers for several key reasons. (Many of these points have been made in more detail by

Table 1 Types of operation, wholesale trade

Merchant wholesaler
Wholesale merchants or jobbers
Industrial distributors
Voluntary group wholesalers
Importers
Exporters
Cash-and-carry wholesalers
Retailer cooperative warehouses
Terminal and country grain elevators
Farm products assemblers
Wholesale cooperative associations
Petroleum bulk plants and terminals
Manufacturers' sales branches and offices
Sales branches (with stocks)
Sales offices (without stocks)
Agents, brokers and commission merchants
Auction companies
Import agents
Export agents
Selling agents
Merchandise brokers
Commission merchants
Manufacturers' agents

Source: US Dept of Commerce, Bureau of Census (1990: A–10 A–11)

Table 2 Summary of wholesalers' participation in the marketing flows

	Physical possession	Ownership	Promotion	Negotiation	Financing	Risk	Ordering	Payment
Merchant wholesalers								
Full-function or service wholesalers	High	High	High	High	High	High	High	High
Limited-function wholesalers								
Drop shipper (desk jobber)	None	High	Low	High	High	High	High	High
Cash-carry wholesalers	High	High	Low	High	None	Low	High	High
Wagon (truck) jobbing	Low	Low	Low	High	Low	Low	High	High
Rack jobbers (service merchandise)	High	High	High	High	High	High	High	High
Converters	Low	High	Low	High	High	High	High	High
Wholesaler-sponsored (voluntary)chains	High	High	High	High	High	High	High	High
Retailer-sponsored cooperatives	High	High	High	High	High	High	High	High
Functional middlemen (agents and brokers)								
Brokers	None	None	High	Low	None	None	High	Low
Manufacturers' agents	None	None	High	None	None	None	High	Low
Selling agents	None	None	High	High	None	None	High	Low
Commission merchants	High	None	High	High	High	High	High	High

The marketing mix

Ideally, wholesalers have a great deal of potential as channel partners for suppliers. From an operational perspective, suppliers of both industrial and consumer goods may rely on wholesalers for several key reasons. (Many of these points have been made in more detail by Hill (1963: 10–14); see also Webster (1984: 194–204)).

1. Wholesalers have continuity in and intimacy with local markets. Being close to customers, they are in a position to take the initial steps in the sale of any products – identifying prospective users and determining the extent of their needs.
2. Wholesalers make possible local availability of stocks and thereby relieve suppliers of small-order business, which the latter can seldom conduct on a profitable basis. Also, they tend to have an acute understanding of the costs of holding and handling inventory in which they have made major commitments.
3. Within their territories, wholesalers can produce suppliers with a salesforce that is in close touch with the needs of customers and prospects. Also, because a wholesaler represents a number of customers, prospects and suppliers, he can often cover a given territory at a lower cost than the manufacturer's own sales representative.
4. Wholesalers perform financial services for suppliers by providing volume cash markets through which they can recover capital that would otherwise be invested in inventories.

The economic role of the distributor (or wholesaler) is to transfer marketing costs from the manufacturer into his own business. This is achieved through the performance of critical marketing functions by the wholesalers on behalf of the manufacturers they represent.

From the point of view of the manufacturer, the performance of these functions shown in Table 3 by wholesalers must be evaluated in determining the type of wholesaling establishment to use. Such evaluation must always be conditioned by the nature of the ultimate market for the goods in question. Therefore, manufacturers must equally examine how well does each wholesaler–distributor perform functions viewed as critical by their customers as shown in Table 4.

How can wholesalers serve retailers?

Manufacturers are interested in getting retailers to promote and sell their own brands in the lines of products they produce. On the other hand, wholesalers have a strong vested interest in building up their retail customers as merchants of assortments of multiple brands in multiple lines of products. Hence, it is quite likely that, particularly in the case of smaller retail establishments, an individual wholesaler will be able to supply a large part of the retailer's requirements for merchandise. It is in the wholesaler's interest to spend considerable effort and resources on training, stimulating and helping retailers to become better merchandisers. Therefore, high-performance wholesalers become highly knowledgeable in retail merchandise management. In this respect, the benefits to the retailer derived from relying on wholesalers may be described as follows:

1. Wholesalers can give their retail customers a great deal of direct selling aid in the form of price concessions of featured items, point-of-sale material and cooperative advertising, all of which are frequently generated by specific suppliers for wholesalers to pass along to retailers.
2. Wholesalers can often provide assistance in planning store layout, building design and material specifications.
3. Wholesalers can offer retailers guidance and counsel in public relations, housekeeping and accounting methods, administrative procedures and the like.

In the toy industry, for instance, many retailers prefer to make a significant proportion of their total annual toy purchases from wholesalers rather than from manufacturers for the following reasons:

1. In many instances reorders are filled more quickly.
2. Wholesalers guarantee the sale (any items not sold can be returned for full credit).
3. Defective products are replaced promptly.
4. The wholesaler extends long-term credit.
5. The percentage of mark-up by working through a wholesaler is more than offset by decreased inventory costs and improved service.

Obviously, the foremost advantage for many retailers in relying on wholesalers is the fact

Table 3 Marketing functions performed by wholesaler–distributors for manufacturers

Market coverage function
Markets for the products of most manufacturers consist of many customers spread over large geographical areas. To have good market coverage so that their products are readily available to customers when needed, manufacturers can call on wholesaler–distributors to secure the necessary market coverage at reasonable cost.

Order processing function
Many customers buy in very small quantities. Yet manufacturers both large and small receive a number of small orders from thousands of customers. By carrying the products of many manufacturers, wholesaler–distributors' order processing costs can be absorbed by the sale of a broader array of products than that of the typical manufacturer.

Sales contact function
The cost to manufacturers of maintaining outside salesforces is quite high. If manufacturers' products are sold to a large number of customers spread out over a large geographical area, the cost to manufacturers of covering all customers with their own salesforce can be prohibitive. By using wholesaler–distributors to cover all or a substantial portion of their customers, manufacturers may be able to reduce significantly the costs of outside sales contacts because their salesforces would be calling on a relatively small number of wholesaler–distributors rather than the much larger number of customers.

Market information function
Wholesaler–distributors are usually quite close to their customers geographically and in many cases have continual contact through frequent sales calls on their customers. Hence, they are in a good position to learn about customer product and service requirements. Such information if passed on to manufacturers can be valuable for product planning, pricing, and the development of competitive marketing strategy.

Inventory holding function
Wholesaler–distributors take title to and usually stock the products of the manufacturers whom they represent. By so doing, they can reduce the manufacturers' financial burden and reduce some of the manufacturers' risk associated with holding large inventories. Moreover, by providing a ready outlet for manufacturers' products, wholesaler–distributors can help manufacturers to better plan their production schedules.

Customer support function
Besides buying products, customers need many types of service support. Products may need to be exchanged or returned, set up and adjustment may be required, as well as repairs and technical assistance. For manufacturers to provide all such service directly to large numbers of accounts can be very costly and ineffective. Instead, wholesaler–distributors can be used by manufacturers to assist them in providing these services to customers.

Source: Rosenbloom (1987: 73)

that the latter buy in large quantities, break bulk to suit the convenience of their customers, and then pass along the savings effected both in cost and transportation. These savings are frequently very favourable when compared with the costs of obtaining merchandise directly in small lots from distant points. Thus, by using wholesalers, independent retailers can avoid diluting the energies of their often overtaxed executive staffs. Furthermore, these retailers obtain access through wholesalers to a large group of products of small manufacturers that might not otherwise be available to them. Even for large establishments, reliance on wholesalers allows conversion of deadweight store space, formerly devoted to merchandise storage, into profit-making selling or customer service space. For example, although supermarket and discount chains can buy at the same price as a rack jobber or service merchandiser, the latter's hold on the market comes from knowing precisely what to buy and minimizing the handling and inventory costs of a variety of non-food products, such as health and beauty aids, tapes and records, hardware and sporting goods. Even for the more mainstream grocery items, managers of large chains operating in widely scattered areas have found it beneficial to get some of their supplies from wholesalers.

Table 4 Functions performed by wholesaler–distributors for customers

Product availability function
Probably the most basic marketing function offered by wholesaler–distributors to their customers is providing for the ready availability of products. Sometimes this even includes fabricating operations, assembly and set-up of products. Because of the closeness of wholesaler–distributors to their customers and/or their sensitivity to their customers' needs, they can provide a level of product availability that many manufacturers would be hard put to match.

Assortment convenience function
Closely related to the previous function is the wholesaler–distributors' ability to bring together from a variety of manufacturers an assortment of products that can greatly simplify their customers' ordering tasks. So customers, instead of having to order from dozens or even hundreds of manufacturers, can turn to one or a few general line or specialty wholesaler–distributors who can provide them with all or most of the products they need.

Bulk-breaking function
Quite often customers do not need large quantities, or even if they do at times they may need only small quantities of products in a given order. Many manufacturers find it uneconomical to sell directly to small order customers and so they establish minimum order requirements to discourage small orders. By buying from manufacturers in large quantities and breaking these bulk orders down into the smaller quantities desired by customers, wholesaler–distributors provide customers with the ability to buy only in the quantities they need.

Credit and finance function
Wholesaler–distributors provide their customers with financial assistance in two ways. First, by extending open account credit on products sold, their customers have time to use products in their businesses before having to pay for them. Second, by stocking and providing ready availability for many of the items needed by their customers, wholesaler–distributors significantly reduce the financial inventory burden their customers would bear if they had to stock all of the products themselves.

Customer service function
Customers often require many types of services such as delivery, repairs, warranty work. By making these services available to their customers, wholesaler–distributors can save their customers considerable effort and expense.

Advice and technical support function
Many products, even those that are not considered technical, may still require a certain amount of technical advice and assistance for proper use, as well as advice on how they should be sold. Wholesaler–distributors, often through the use of trained outside salesforces, are able to provide this kind of technical and business assistance to customers.

Source: Rosenbloom (1987: 74)

How can wholesalers serve the business user?

Although many of the advantages to the business user from relying on wholesalers are exactly the same as those mentioned for retailers, some additional factors are briefly discussed here. The short lead times on deliveries made available through wholesalers are especially important to industrial users. Flexibility in production scheduling can generally be achieved if production planners know that speedy local deliveries can be forthcoming. This factor is especially important for just-in-time (JIT) inventory scheduling. Just-in-time is requiring industrial distributors to work more closely with manufacturing customers in planning inventory needs. The manufacturers are paring the number of distributors from which they buy in order to make closer planning more workable. The introduction of just-in-time is requiring distributors to hold larger inventories, thus pressuring profit margins. However, just-in-time represents a great opportunity for many distributors who are capable of capitalizing on it.

Demands by customers for rapid delivery are expected to increase in the 1990s. A study of future trends in wholesaling reports that 'the durable wholesaler–distributors' customers are expected to place a greater value on the frequency and speed of delivery, principally because of the increased focus on just-in-time inventory requirements and the manufacturers' increased attention to productivity' (Arthur Andersen 1987: 35).

In addition, many types of wholesalers provide unique forms of technical assistance that are relatively costly to duplicate elsewhere, except in situations where a buyer can purchase in very large quantities. For example, machine tool and accessories wholesalers often have specialists on their staff who are available to help customers with problems pertaining to the selection and use of tools and parts. It is not unusual to find such technically trained persons as metallurgists, chemists, craftsmen and mechanical and civil engineers employed by wholesalers for this purpose. In data processing, wholesalers called value added resellers (VAR) have emerged who package computer software with computing equipment to solve specific problems for specific industries (e.g. inventory control for autoparts dealers). Even managerial assistance is being increasingly provided to business users by wholesalers. For example, one electronics distributor analyses the stockkeeping methods of one of his industrial customers and recommends revised delivery schedules, prearranged items, packs suitable for assembly line use and standardized item identification. The customer was able to reduce the possession costs on his stock by 15 per cent of its value.

Business users and retailers alike must be concerned with the overall or ultimate cost of the goods they purchase, handle and store – not merely with the price at which such goods are obtained. When adequate accounting is made, it can often be found that the ultimate cost of dealing with wholesalers is less than the ultimate cost of dealing directly with manufacturers, even though the quantity discounts made available by the latter are not generally available when wholesalers are used as suppliers. This ultimate cost concept can justify the use of wholesalers in situations where they might not otherwise appear to be economical.

Recognition of the ultimate cost concept by both wholesalers and their customers has led to a phenomenon called systems selling.

Systems selling is a broad, inconclusive term that may be used to describe any form of cooperative contracting relationship between an industrial distributor and his customer for the ordering and distribution of low-value, repetitively used items for maintenance, repair, or operating (MRO) purposes, or for use in manufacturing original equipment.

(Hannaford 1976: 139)

Wholesalers offer such purchasing systems in order to alleviate the high cost and paperwork facing firms seeking to acquire a wide variety of items, ranging from power tools and welding supplies to lamps, electronic equipment and hardware. The major means employed by wholesalers' system selling arrangements to solve these problems include:

1 Shifting the bulk of customer's on-premises MRO inventory back to the stocking wholesaler.
2 Providing for automatic and semiautomatic ordering of these items on an as-needed basis.
3 Providing one-day delivery of the ordered items (Hannaford 1976: 139).

4 A hard-nosed assessment

Most of the preceding description of what a wholesaler can do for suppliers, retailers and business users provides optimistic pictures. However, the channel analyst should approach the selection of wholesalers as channel partners with a great deal of caution.

Over the past forty years, the position of wholesalers has been significantly threatened with regard to the marketing of consumer goods. Relatively few wholesalers have been successful in meeting the challenges head on. Although there have also been changes in the marketing of industrial goods, it appears that wholesalers have, from a managerial perspective, shown greater adaptability and innovativeness in their approaches to industrial goods suppliers and markets than they have in their approach to consumer goods. To obtain a realistic perspective of wholesaling, it is important to delve briefly into developments in both sectors of the economy as they have affected wholesalers.

The marketing mix

Consumer goods

Retailers have been particularly active in revolutionizing physical distribution practices. They have taken advantage of large-volume purchasing, warehousing and delivery operations by forming mass merchandising chain organizations. To a large extent, as the chains grew and prospered, wholesalers were quickly relegated to meeting the needs of small businesses. Because there are still tens of thousands of small manufacturers and retailers in existence, many wholesalers of consumer goods have continued to serve an economic purpose, but to a shrinking portion of the market.

On the other hand, those wholesalers who saw the writing on the wall and tried to secure the marketing and physical distribution advantages of large-scale retail chain operations while permitting local ownership of individual retail units have succeeded handsomely. They formed voluntary (wholesaler-sponsored) chains, franchised systems and administered systems in order to gain efficiencies in purchasing, advertising, warehousing, accounting, inventory control and virtually every other business function. They also permitted themselves to become part of retailer-sponsored co-operatives (see RELATIONSHIPS AND NETWORKS).

Beyond those consumer goods wholesalers who have formed vertical marketing systems, there are those who have been successful without changing their corporate organization. Some have restricted their activities to a limited range of products and have sought market niches that do not require high sales volume to be competitive. In groceries, drugs, hardware and jewellery, specialty wholesalers have been able to develop a substantial volume of business. For example, in the grocery trade, such firms supply products like frozen foods, dairy products, fancy or gourmet foods, bread and baked goods and beverages.

A good example is service merchandisers or rack jobbers. They have been particularly effective because they focus on supplying value added services listed in Table 5. The more successful specialty wholesalers, like rack jobbers, have been able to serve both large suppliers and

Table 5 Services offered by service merchansiders (rack jobbers)

Merchandising services
Recommend type, brand and amount of merchandise to stock.
Design a plan for the rotation of goods, especially high-risk seasonal items.
Develop merchandise 'planograms' for stores.
Prepare ad mats that customers can use in local newspapers.

Computer services
Track customers' sales and gross profit by category.
Print price labels and conduct other paperwork.
Provide tailor-made information upon request.

Salesperson's services
Check merchandise at the back of the store after it arrives from the warehouse to ensure that the customer receives exactly what has been ordered.
Serve as a store consultant by helping managers plan and execute promotions.
Plan the rotation of merchandise.
Advise on in-store display techniques.
Conduct in-store order writing.
Stock shelves and keep them orderly.

Warehouse and delivery services
Receive shipments from manufacturers.
Separate and warehouse shipments.
Select, label and box merchandise for individual stores.
Deliver merchandise to stores.

Source: Takeuchi (1980: 12). Adapted and reprinted by permission.

large buyers, thus severing the wholesalers' traditional dependence on small-scale retailing.

On the other hand, there have also been a number of general- or full-line consumer goods wholesalers who have achieved viability. Their route to success has been to improve their management and marketing practices, particularly by creatively utilizing advanced information processing technology. Excellent examples are formed in the wholesale distribution of pharmaceuticals (i.e. wholesaler distributors who sell pharmaceuticals, over-the-counter drugs and toiletries to small, independently owned drugstores). Leading wholesalers have adopted innovative electronic data-processing procedures that have brought efficiencies to pharmacists' handling of inventories. For example, a clerk in a drugstore can alert a hand-held computer to a product's identity simply by waving a small wand across a code on a shelf label. Then the clerk can feed the computer an order from that particular item, and the machine relays it over telephone lines directly to the wholesaler distributor's warehouses. Electronic systems have helped drugstores not only eliminate errors and reduce clerical expenses but also keep inventories down because the wholesaler can deliver within twenty-four hours. The wholesalers also sell customized shelf labels and stickers for each product, priced to the druggist's specifications. They can pack items in the order in which the merchandise will be placed on shelves. The wholesalers also provide retailers with management information reports, which measure sales and mark-ups for groups of products in each store.

The wholesalers have set up computerized accounts-receivable programs that enable pharmacists to offer charge accounts to preferred customers – something most small businesses cannot handle without investing in processing equipment of their own. The pharmacists can also check a patient's drug allergies or provide customers with records of drug purchases for submission with their tax returns (see Corey 1985: 29–51).

Industrial goods

Manufacturers of many types of industrial goods tend to be more engineering oriented than marketing oriented. They prefer to allocate resources to research and production rather than to distribution, which they know has historically delivered a much lower return on investment. Given this orientation, it is not surprising that they frequently turn 'troublesome' marketing problems over to distribution specialists. This is one of the reasons that industrial distribution, in contrast with consumer goods, has been a particularly viable sector of wholesaling over the years.

The situation involving industrial distribution is particularly intriguing because in some respects it is generally a microcosm of the dynamics of distribution. Industrial distributors are frequently viewed as a special class of merchant wholesaler.

An industrial distributor sells primarily to manufacturers. He stocks the products he sells, has at least one outside salesperson as well as an inside telephone and/or counter salesperson, and performs a broad variety of marketing channel functions. The products stocked include: maintenance, repair and operating supplies (MRO items); original equipment (OEM) supplies, such as fasteners, power transmission components, fluid power equipment and small rubber parts, which become part of the manufacturer's finished product; equipment used in the operation of a business, such as hand tools, power tools and conveyors; machinery used to make raw materials and semi-finished goods into finished products.

On average, industrial distributors are as small as the wholesalers serving retailers, but the median size is increasing as the number of distributors declines and as the market expands. The increase in size means that more firms are able to adopt electronic data processing for inventory control, order processing and other administrative matters.

The distributor's importance in the marketing channel for industrial goods is growing for a variety of reasons:

1. The desire of manufacturers to shift more physical distribution responsibilities to distributors as a result of inflationary cost pressures.
2. The tendency of a number of products (e.g. bearings) to become commodities, which permits distributors more control over the relationship with the customer because of the diminishing importance of brand names for such products.

3 The increased value that distributors are adding to products by performing special services, such as assembly and submanufacturing, for their customers (Webster 1984: 198).

From the supplier's perspective, industrial distributors have become more capable in fulfilling their major responsibility in the channel. That is, their job has been primarily to contact present and potential customers and to make the product available – with the necessary supporting services, such as delivery, credit and technical advice – as quickly as is economically feasible. In this respect, they may have discouraged the kind of integration of wholesaling functions so prevalent in consumer goods channels. In fact, it is much easier for the industrial goods manufacturer to go 'direct' than it is for the consumer goods manufacturer. In consumer goods the major problem for wholesalers is the backward vertical integration of retailers into wholesaling. In industrial goods, the problem is one of manufacturers integrating forward. While such integration is occurring, the problem for wholesalers appears to be more acute relative to consumer goods.

One of the ways in which industrial distributors have maintained and even increased their importance in the marketing channel is by doing something some of their counterparts selling consumer goods have also done (i.e. they have specialized their operations).

Another way in which industrial distributors have enhanced their role in the marketing channel is the formation of distributor chains. Individual entrepreneurs have either acquired or established multiple outlets. As a result, they have been able to secure significant economies of scale by establishing one highly sophisticated inventory, purchasing and distribution system.

The formation of distribution chains is critical for serving national accounts in the hospitality, health care, and fast food industries. Some of the advantages that distributor chains have over small, privately owned, single-warehouse firms are as follows:

1 Inventory power. Chain inventories are not only deeper and cheaper but also broader and more diversified.
2 Large, linked warehouses. Such warehouses permit adding highly sophisticated computerized systems, purchasing in quantity, and stocking in depth which result in lower warehousing costs per outlet.
3 Quantity discounts.
4 Multiple brand coverage.
5 Private labelling. This movement is particularly strong for such product lines as bearings, electrical motors and equipment, and MRO supplies.

From a potential customer's perspective, the chains incorporate many of the attributes that are important to industrial customers in choosing a source of supply. They are able to keep delivery promises, offer a better discount structure, maintain an efficient phone order system, provide stock breadth and depth, offer technical services, enact appropriate sales procedures (e.g. regular sales calls), maintain a strong assortment of brand names, offer quick delivery time and provide quality assurance. Indeed, because of their capabilities, they have created serious policy questions for manufacturers seeking to employ both independent and chain distributors in their channels. Some of these questions are as follows:

1 Can we afford to offer exclusives to independents? to chains? If we offer them to independents, is there any way to protect existing exclusives and still sell to chains?
2 How do we sell to chains? De we need separate salesforces, one for chains and one for independents?
3 Is our volume to chains large enough to permit us to withdraw our branch warehousing support to independents?
4 Should we help independents to pool?
5 How large a reduction in price are we willing to grant chains for assuming the entire warehousing burden?
6 Do we want to provide private labels?
7 What kind of discounting structure should we employ?

5 Conclusion

The significance of the wholesaler's role in a channel of distribution is defined by the efficiency of his or her sorting function, whereby he or she helps match the heterogeneous output of suppliers on the one hand with the diverse needs of retailers and industrial and business users on the other. There have been increased pressures on wholesalers to prove their economic viability in this respect.

The wholesaler–distributor continues to face market, technological, financial and organizational forces of change. In order to remain a viable force in the distribution channel in the twenty-first century, wholesalers must devise strategies to deal with forces of change projected well into the future. These include:

- Competitive threats from relatively newer forms of competition such as catalogue and warehouse chains.
- Dramatic rise in mergers and acquisitions to achieve diversification, increase market share, enter new territories and achieve economies of scale.
- Continued decline in gross margins accompanied with rising customer service standards including order fill rates, electronic order entry and just-in-time inventory management.
- Doubling of technology expenditures with emphasis on the use of new supplier and customer communication techniques such as videotext and electronic data interchange.
- Rising need for externally generated capital necessary to compensate for the decline in internally generated funds and to finance capital expenditures for new technology investment in information systems, marketing and logistics.
- Transitioning from family-owned and managed corporation to professionally managed, publicly held, and perhaps foreign-owned corporation (Arthur Andersen 1987: 12–16).

ADEL I. EL-ANSARY
UNIVERSITY OF NORTH FLORIDA
LOUIS W. STERN
NORTHWESTERN UNIVERSITY

Note

This chapter is based in its entirety on Louis W. Stern and Adel I. El-Ansary (1992) *Marketing Channels*, 4th edn, Englewood Cliffs, New Jersey: Prentice Hall: 106–48.

For more information about EDI systems, see Stern and Kaufmann 1985: 52–73.

Further reading

(References cited in the text marked *)

* Alderson, Wroe (1971) 'Factors governing the development of marketing channels', in Moller, William G., Jr. and Wilemon, David L. (eds), *Marketing Channels: A Systems Viewpoint*, Homewood, Ill.: Richard D. Irwin.
* Arthur Andersen and Company (1987) *Facing the Forces of Change: Beyond Future Trends in Wholesale Distribution*, Washington DC: Distribution Research and Education Foundation.
* Corey, Raymond (1985) 'The role of information and communications technology in industrial distribution', in Buzzell, Robert D. (ed.), *Marketing in an Electronic Age*, Boston, MA: Harvard Business School Press.
* Hannaford, William J. (1976) 'Systems selling: problems and benefits for buyers and seller', *Industrial Marketing Management* 5: 139.
* Hill, Richard M. (1963) *Wholesaling Management*, Homewood, IL: Richard D. Irwin.
* Rosenbloom, Bert (1987) *Marketing Functions and the Wholesaler-Distributor: Achieving Excellence in Distribution*, Washington, DC: Distribution Research and Education Foundation.
* Stern, Louis W. and Kaufmann, Patrick J. (1985) 'Electronic data interchange in selected consumer goods industries: an interorganizational perspective', in Buzzell, Robert D. (ed.), *Marketing in an Electronic Age*, Boston, MA: Harvard Business School Press.
* Takeuchi, Hirotaka (1980) *A Note on Wholesale Institutions*, Boston, MA: Harvard Business School: 9–581–011.
  US Department of Commerce, Bureau of Census (1990) *1987 Census of Wholesale Trade*, Subject Series, Report WC87-5-1, Washington, DC: US Government Printing Office.
* Webster, Frederick E. Jr. (1984) *Industrial Marketing Strategy*, 2nd edn. New York: John Wiley and Sons, Inc.

See also: CHANNEL MANAGEMENT; CHANNELS OF DISTRIBUTION; MARKET SEGMENTATION; MARKETING STRATEGY; RELATIONSHIPS AND NETWORKS; RETAILING; ORGANIZATIONAL BUYING BEHAVIOUR;

Retailing

1 Retailing: definition and scope
2 Evolution of retailing
3 Types of retail organization
4 Major retail formats
5 Retail functions
6 Internationalization of retailing
7 Non-store retailing

Overview

Retailing is a wide concept, with the popular definition of the word evolving over time. This entry considers retailing as supply to end-consumers rather than to industrial buyers, and the supply of goods rather than of services. Retailing has grown from serving a manufacturer-led industry, to being a leading player in its own right, and the concepts of the wheel of retailing and the retail life-cycle are considered to help explain this change of focus. The growth of retailer power and influence is largely due to the concentration of trade into the hands of fewer, larger enterprises. This process of concentration is discussed and consideration given to symbol retailing, franchises and cooperatives.

The format of the retail outlet can vary considerably. Shopping centres, retail parks, superstores, hypermarkets, department stores and variety stores are all examined briefly. There are a wide range of activities that comprise retailing, but each major function is discussed, giving consideration to its contribution to the marketing of goods and its significance for the marketing mix and the value chain.

The entry then goes on to examine the potential for retailing concepts and methods to be expanded into the global marketplace before concluding with a look at non-store retailing and the potential and growing impact of technology on retailing.

1 Retailing: definition and scope

Originally defined as 'the sale of goods in small quantities', a better working definition of retailing is: 'the sale of goods and services to consumers for their own use'. This distinguishes retailing from the supply of goods, in quantities large or small, to industrial buyers. It also recognizes the adoption of retailing terms and concepts by a wide range of services providers. For example, banks and other financial services providers use the term 'retail' to differentiate their consumer and their corporate activities (McGoldrick and Greenland 1994).

As the marketing of services is considered in another entry (see MARKETING OF SERVICES), the focus of this entry is upon the sale of goods to consumers. The principal types of institution involved in retailing are examined, as are the major functions of retailing. Attention is given to the trends in retail internationalization and to the threats/opportunities of non-store retailing. First, we will consider how retailing has evolved, and the key role it now plays within the 'marketing channel'.

2 Evolution of retailing

The growth of power

Retailing has always been a major component of economic activity. In Great Britain alone, there are 196,653 retail businesses, with a total turnover of £148,743 million, employing 2.3 million people (NatWest Markets 1998). On a wider scale, there were 3.3 million retail enterprises in the European Union (EU) employing 14 million people (Eurostat 1997; European Retail Digest 1997). Within Western Europe as a whole, there were over 4 million retail outlets, capturing 39.5 per cent of consumer expenditure, compared with 61.5 per cent in Eastern Europe, 31.3 per cent in North America (Euromonitor 1995). Such expressions of scale alone cannot capture the major changes that have taken place, as retailing has switched from a more passive to a highly proactive role within the overall marketing process.

Many of the revered concepts of marketing, including the marketing mix, originated in a period when the manufacturer was truly 'king'. Post-war product shortages focused attention upon production, which gave way to an emphasis upon branding as shortages diminished. Inevitably, retailing tended to be depicted as just part of the marketing channels, largely controlled by manufacturers. The last two decades have seen retailers grow in size and sophistication, often exceeding that of their largest suppliers (see THE MARKETING MIX; WHOLESALING).

Figure 1 depicts in outline the growth cycle of powerful retailers. Growth enhances bargaining power and helps in the achievement of other economies of scale. The improved margins thus gained may be used to achieve further growth, through competitive pricing and/or a product–service mix which offers superior value to customers. As the growth cycle continues, major retailers have invested in better management and superior information systems. Their power has been increased further by the development of retailer brands, extensive advertising and sophisticated trading environments (see ADVERTISING; BRANDING AND BRAND MANAGEMENT).

Many large retailers have subsumed the roles traditionally ascribed to wholesalers, increasing further their dominance of the marketing channel. It is now equally appropriate to present a view of consumer goods marketing that is retailer driven (McGoldrick 1990). Within this alternative view, manufacturers may be depicted as part of the 'channels of supply', with only limited power to influence the marketing strategies of major retailers. Large scale retailers have truly evolved from shopkeeping to strategic marketing (see CHANNEL MANAGEMENT).

Theories of retail change

Given the dynamic nature of retailing, several theories have developed to explain aspects of evolution and change. Two of the most influential are the 'wheel of retailing' and the 'retail life-cycle'. These and other theories of retail change are discussed in detail by Brown (1987).

The wheel of retailing suggests that new types of retailers tend to enter as low-price, low-margin, low-status operators. Over time, they acquire more elaborate facilities, incur higher operating costs and cease to be as price competitive. Eventually, they mature as higher-cost, higher-price retailers, vulnerable to newer types who enter at the first phase of 'the wheel'. Many examples can be found of retail types and individual companies that have evolved in this way, including department stores and supermarkets. The process has been ascribed to various influences, including a shift away from the aggressive management style of the founders, the attraction of the up-market segments, a preference amongst leading

Figure 1 The retail growth cycle

Figure 2 Retail life-cycles in EU countries
Source: Eurostat (1993: 20)

Table 1 Concentration in grocery trade

	Percentage of outlets		Percentage of turnover	
	1995	*1997*	*1995*	*1997*
Top 7 multiples	7.5	8.0	65.6	69.2
Other multiples	6.9	9.2	16.1	16.4
Cooperatives	6.0	6.1	8.6	7.0
Independents	79.6	76.7	9.7	7.4

Derived from: Nielsen (1998)

retailers for non-price forms of competition, and possible 'misguidance' by suppliers of elaborate equipment and fitments. It is also possible that the boom–recession cycles within most advanced economies contribute to the process, encouraging trading-up during the boom years and encouraging new forms of price competition during recessions.

The retail life-cycle concept derives from the better known product life-cycle, elaborated on in a previous entry (see PRODUCT LIFE-CYCLE MANAGEMENT). Retail institutions and formats appear to be moving from innovation to maturity with increasing speed. Davidson *et al.* (1976) estimated that the city centre department store took some 80 years to mature, whereas the home improvement centre in the USA took only 15 years. Figure 2 shows the four main phases of the retail life cycle, illustrating that the life-cycle phase for any given retail format may differ greatly between the countries of Europe.

3 Types of retail organization

The growth of retailer power and influence has stemmed largely from the concentration of trade into the hands of fewer, larger enterprises. This section looks first at this process of concentration, involving the shift of trade from independent to multiple retailers. Consideration is then given to symbol retailing, franchises and cooperatives.

Independents and multiples

The term 'multiple' signifies more than one outlet but different data sources use different definitions, e.g. at least two, five or 10 outlets. In Great Britain, nearly 70 per cent of retail trade is accounted for by multiples with 10 or more outlets. The concentration of trade is especially marked in the grocery sector and, as Table 1 illustrates, it is still growing rapidly. The top seven multiples ran just 8 per cent of all grocery outlets in 1997, yet took nearly 70 per cent of grocery turnover. Concentration levels are also growing in other retail sectors. Multiples account for 69 per cent of menswear trade, 74.2 per cent of ladieswear, 76.9 per cent of electrical appliances and 70.4 per cent of DIY (do-it-yourself) (NatWest Markets 1998).

Retail structures contrast markedly across different countries, and different continents. In Western Europe as a whole, there were 135 inhabitants per outlet, similar to the ratios in Asia (130) and Oceania (134), but contrasting with North America (324) (Euromonitor 1995). Table 2 expresses two measures of 'retail density'. By Western European standards, Austria, U.K., Germany, Finland and Switzerland show high levels of outlet concentration, whereas Greece, Portugal, Spain and Italy still have more outlets, relative to population levels. Employees per outlet provide another comparison of structure, ranging from 7.24 in the U.K. to 1.90 in Greece.

Not all small stores are independently owned; the convenience store or 'c-store' format has been developed by multiples, voluntary groups and franchisers. For example, Alldays operates over 500 such outlets, an increasing proportion of their stores being franchises (see below; see FRANCHISING). Definitions of the convenience store vary somewhat but Nielsen (1998) suggests the following criteria:

- self service;
- 1000 – 3000 sq.ft selling area;
- parking facilities;
- open seven days a week for long hours;
- wide range but limited brand choice, including groceries, toiletries, some medicines,

447

The marketing mix

Table 2 Contrasting retail structures

Country	No. of outlets	Outlets per 1000 inhabitants	No. of persons employed per outlets
Greece	175,000	17.40	1.90
Italy	888,330	15.65	2.69
Portugal	132,094	13.36	2.76
Spain	511,927	13.08	3.00
Belgium	121,912	12.07	1.94
Denmark	47,597	9.19	4.17
Norway	38,401	8.91	3.21
Luxembourg	3,587	8.95	5.45
Ireland	29,337	8.29	4.48
France	451,800	7.84	4.48
Netherlands	102,900	6.69	6.19
Sweden	54,549	6.23	5.29
Switzerland	41,935	6.13	7.65
United Kingdom	330,491	5.76	6.66
Finland	28,309	5.57	4.66
Germany	435,471	5.37	6.58
Austria	40,040	4.99	7.24

Source: Eurostat (1997)

alcohol and stationery; some also offer video hire, take-away foods and petrol.

It was estimated in 1998 that there were 6500 c-stores in the UK, including those developed on petrol forecourts.

Voluntary groups

One response of independent retailers and wholesalers to the growth of the multiples has been the formation of 'voluntary', 'symbol' or 'affiliation' groups. Within this form of contractual chain, a group name is utilized and the retailers are normally required to buy a given proportion of their merchandise through the group. The organization typically provides buying and other marketing services, including special promotions, advertising and frequently own brands. The group is therefore able to achieve some of the buying power and economies of scale characteristic of major multiples.

Table 3 gives examples of voluntary groups in four sectors. In that restrictions apply to the opening of pharmacies in the UK, in order to protect the network of outlets, this sector has been protected somewhat from the full effects of multiple completion. The voluntary groups hold over 50 per cent of this sector, Vantage and Numark being the major groups. In the grocery sector, the leading player is Spar, which also operates in 17 of the 19 European countries within Nielsen's analysis (Nielsen 1998). This international presence gives Spar a European grocery share of 2.2 per cent, close to the shares of Aldi and Carrefour.

Euromonitor estimates for 1995 showed a great diversity in percentage penetration within the total retail trade of other European markets:

Belgium	13
Denmark	36
Finland	42
Netherlands	30
Norway	20
Spain	4
Sweden	39
Germany	35

Table 3 Examples of voluntary groups

Sector	Group	UK Outlets
Grocery	Spar	2700
	Happy Shopper	2000
Chemists	Vantage	2500
	Numark	1030
Department Stores	Associated independent stores	540
Hardware	Fair & Square	485

Derived from: Nielsen (1998)

This type of affiliation appears well suited to areas of low population densities but the voluntary groups are under pressure from the multiples in most countries.

Franchises

Franchising, in various forms, has a long history both in Europe and in the USA Its fastest growth as an element of retail structure occurred through the 1980s. From 2600 franchised units in the UK in 1980, the number grew to 21,500 by 1996, of which 4500 could truly be classified as retail outlets (Key Note 1997). Franchising can take many different forms, notably the following.

1. The manufacturer–retailer franchise: common in the sale of cars and petrol.
2. The manufacturer–wholesaler franchise: e.g. franchises to bottle Coca-Cola or Pepsi-Cola.
3. The wholesaler–retailer franchise: includes some voluntary groups, discussed above.
4. The business format franchise: typical in fast food or car hire.

The benefits of franchising can flow from achieving the best of both worlds in business, combining the power, sophistication and reputation of a large organization with the energy, motivation and commitment of the independent owner-manager. For well conceived and well managed business formats, franchising has proved to be a powerful vehicle for expansion, as in the cases of Body Shop, Benetton and Seven-Eleven Japan (Sparks, in McGoldrick 1994) (see FRANCHISING).

Cooperative societies

There is essentially one cooperative movement in the UK but its retail activities have been fragmented into a large number of relatively autonomous societies. This fragmentation has been a major reason for the decline in the share of retail trade held by the cooperatives, in spite of the potential for buying power and economies of scale within the movement as a whole. The Co-op share of UK retail sales fell from 5.6 per cent in 1982 to 4.2 in 1992. Table 1 illustrated that their grocery share declined from 8.6 per cent to 7.0 per cent between 1995 and 1997.

Whereas 231 individual societies existed in 1977, this had fallen to 52 by 1997; significant mergers have occurred since then. Rationalization of outlets has continued and the societies have developed strength in discounting and neighbourhood retailing.

In some countries of Europe, the cooperatives hold a far higher share of retail sales. In Switzerland, the two major cooperatives, Migros and Coop Schweiz, held 27 per cent of all retail sales in 1988, 38 per cent of the food trade. The cooperatives also held over 20 per cent of the food trade in the Scandinavian countries. If the cooperative societies had combined both nationally and internationally, they could well have been Europe's largest retail organization.

4 Major retail formats

The type of organization that owns or manages a store is not always obvious to the consumer. Other, more striking characteristics of shops serve to differentiate one format from another in the minds of shoppers. A retail format can be defined along a number of different dimensions, including:

The marketing mix

single store	– group of stores
in-town	– out-of-town
large	– small
innovative	– mature
food	– non-food
specialized	– generalized
niche	– commodity
high added value	– discounter

This section examines briefly shopping centres, retail parks, superstores, hypermarkets, department stores, variety stores and a number of formats that use the term 'discounter'.

Shopping centres and retail parks

The term 'shopping centre' is normally applied to a coherent, planned and controlled group of retail establishments, as distinct from the more random grouping of a 'shopping district'. In Europe, the most typical location for shopping centres is still within existing town centres; the out-of-town centre is a relatively recent phenomenon. Whereas out-of-town centres developed from the 1920s in the USA, some 50 years elapsed before they started to make an impact in Europe.

The differences between the USA and European development patterns can be ascribed in part to differences of economics, geography and demography. Most of all, the more restrictive planning regulations within most European countries have served to restrict developments out-of-town. The planning debates revolve around a range of economic, environmental and social issues, summarized in McGoldrick and Thompson (1992).

The move out-of-town has been described as three 'waves' of development (Schiller, in McGoldrick and Thompson 1992). The first comprised the superstores, selling mostly food and limited ranges of non-food items. The second wave of decentralization involved bulky goods, such as DIY, carpets, furniture, large electrical items and garden centres. The third wave involved clothing and other comparison shopping, representing the most direct threat to existing town centres. The decision by Marks & Spencer to develop out of town, both within major new centres and in freestanding schemes with food superstore partners, was a major element of this third wave. The late 1980s and early 1990s saw the opening of four especially large out-of-town centres in the UK, each in excess of one million square feet. Situated in Tyneside, South Yorkshire, West Midlands and Essex, each represented a full alternative to the traditional town centre.

Table 4 illustrates a further contrast between the form of retailing in different European countries. Both the UK and France have a relatively high level of shopping centre provision, compared with that of Germany. However, changes in planning regulations and trading restrictions are already serving to reduce these differences.

Retail parks are more utilitarian groupings of 'retail sheds' and are also termed 'retail warehouse parks'. They offer convenient access and car parking arrangements but lack the indoor malls and many of the other comforts of the new, out-of-town shopping centres. The first such scheme opened in the UK in 1982; by 1997, there were 474 in operation (NatWest Markets 1998). They involve far lower development costs than the major, full service shopping centres, which typically include extensive leisure and catering facilities. The trading format of the retail park has proved fairly resilient

Table 4 Shopping centres in five countries

Country	Centres (no.)	Retail space (m.sq. ft)	Sq. ft per person
United Kingdom	768	142.1	280
France	611	134.6	258
Netherlands	139	20.5	137
Spain	262	39.8	87
Germany	102	45.2	27

Derived from: NatWest Markets (1998)
Note: Many UK sources measure space in square feet: one square metre is equal to 10.76 sq. ft.

to adverse economic conditions and their development has continued, shifting the balance away from traditional town centres.

Factory Outlet Centres made their appearance in the UK in 1992. By 2000, some 23 such centres will be trading. They comprise groupings of mainly designer outlets, selling below the normal price for these brands. One of the largest, Cheshire Oaks, includes 300,000 sq.ft of retail area and 120 factory outlets (NatWest Markets 1998).

Department and variety stores

In most new shopping centres, developers seek to ensure that they attract key 'anchor tenants' in the form of major department and variety stores. Ironically, the market shares of both these retail formats have tended towards decline in most European countries.

According to the International Association of Department Stores, a department store must have at least 2500 sq.metres of space (26,900 sq.ft.). Furthermore, it must offer a product range that is both wide and deep in several product categories. The Association estimates that there were around 960 such stores in the EU in 1990, a slight decline from 1112 in 1980. Table 5 summarizes the changes in market share, showing decline in France, Germany and the UK. Spain is one of the few countries within which this format is growing, the leading operator being El Corte Inglés. In the UK, the leading department store retailers are John Lewis and Debenhams, each with around 20 per cent of the sector share. John Lewis is the more productive in terms of space utilization, achieving £453 per year per sq.ft, compared with £200 at Debenhams (Retail Review 1998).

Many European variety stores were founded in the 1930s by department store operators, in order to offer a lower priced, lower service and lower assortment format. Examples include Prisunic by Printemps and Priminime by Bon Marche. In the UK, there are few such links between the department and variety store sectors and variety stores hold a relatively strong 6.2 per cent of retail trade, compared with 2.1 per cent in France and 1.1 per cent in Germany.

Marks & Spencer, the leading variety store in the UK, holds a 15.1 per cent share of the clothing market and 3.3 per cent share in food retailing (Retail Review 1998). As many variety stores have traded up and diversified; on the other hand, department stores have tended to withdraw from some product ranges in the face of specialist, lower priced competition. Accordingly, the distinction between the department and variety formats has become blurred.

Superstores and hypermarkets

Whereas the supermarket format has reached maturity in most countries (Figure 2), the superstore and hypermarket formats have been claiming increased share in most countries. Being situated mostly outside traditional shopping centres, they tend to enjoy greater accessibility by car, greater economies of scale and the benefits of being purpose built. Superstores form the 'anchor stores' of retail warehouse parks and of many partnership schemes, such as the Marks & Spencer–Tesco partnership at Handforth, Cheshire.

In Britain, a superstore is defined as having at least 25,000 sq.ft of selling space; a hypermarket has at least 50,000 sq.ft. (Some sources use the near equivalent metric measures of 2500m^2 and 5000m^2 respectively.) Comparisons between countries encounter great difficulties as these thresholds vary considerably. In some cases, the terms imply large stores selling primarily groceries; in others, the terms are used with more flexibility to describe any large

Table 5 Department store shares

	Percentage of share of retail trade		
	1970	*1980*	*1990*
France	3.4	2.9	1.9
Germany	11.0	7.2	5.6
UK	5.5	4.7	4.0

Source: Tordjman (1993).

The marketing mix

Table 6 Hypermarkets and superstores of 2500 m.sq and over

	1990/91 (no.)	1995/96 (no.)
France	914	1089
Netherlands	31	40
Spain	151	221
United Kingdom	733	1053
Sweden	63	77

Derived from: Institute of Grocery Distribution (1997)

scale, specialist format, offering a strong depth of assortment, trading on one level and providing ample car parking. Having noted these caveats, Table 6 offers an indication of growth within five countries of Europe. There are however new regulations upon large store and centre developments, introduced by the governments of France, Germany, Italy, the Netherlands and Spain (NatWest Securities 1997)

Discounters

Like so many of the descriptive terms in retailing, 'discounter' is regrettably imprecise. As the wheel of retailing concept suggests, many new concepts have entered by offering prices at levels below the existing competition, i.e. by discounting. Accordingly, the term 'hard discounter' has been adopted in some countries to distinguish between new, deep discount formats and other, more mild manifestations of price competition.

In the context of food retailing, Tordjman (1993) distinguished between the key financial and operational characteristics of discounters and hypermarkets, as shown in Table 7. This demonstrates the ability of the format to produce reasonable net margins through the strict control of operating costs. As Figure 2 depicted, the discount food format is in growth within most countries but has reached maturity in Germany. Table 8 summarizes the shares held by food discounters in 14 European countries, showing also the expected growth in outlet numbers.

The concept of the warehouse club represented an addition to hard discounting in Europe in the 1990s. These clubs started to

Table 7 Discounters and hypermarkets compared

Typical key indices	Discount supermarket	Hypermarket
Store size: m^2	600	6,000
Number of lines	1,000	35,000
Stockturns per year	40	22
Gross margin percentage of sales	14.5	16.0
As percentage of sales:		
Labour	5	7
Distribution	2	3
Property	1	2
Other costs	3	2
Net margin as percentage of sales	3.5	2.0
Asset turnover (times)	7	9
Return on investment (per cent)	24.5	18.0

Derived from Tordjman (1993)

Table 8 Food discounters in Europe

Country	Number of stores 1996	Number of stores 2000 (f)	Percentage share of turnover 1996
Austria	395	414	17
Belgium	628	634	25
Denmark	648	654	20
Finland	782	793	12
France	1,656	2,080	7
Germany	8,910	8,930	30
Italy	745	1,195	10
Netherlands	584	615	13
Norway	890	895	37
Portugal	135	350	9
Spain	1,275	1,435	9
Sweden	238	240	11
Switzerland	615	625	8
United Kingdom	1,832	2,122	11

Derived from: Nielsen (1998); Institute of Grocery Distribution (1997)

develop from 1982 in the USA; the first such unit opened in the UK in 1993, after strong opposition from major supermarket chains. Warehouse clubs charge a membership fee to customers, which ensures selectivity and generally greater loyalty. A wide range of mostly packaged foods and non-foods is offered, usually in large or multiple packs, in sparse surroundings of 100,000 sq.ft or over.

5 Retail functions

Given the enormous breadth of activities that comprise retailing, it is possible here to provide only a glimpse of its major functions. A more comprehensive treatment is provided in the chapters of McGoldrick (1990) and the case studies of McGoldrick (1994). The emphasis here is to:

1 indicate the role of each function within the overall process of marketing consumer goods;
2 outline the significance of each function within the strategic mix and within the value chain of retailers.

Each element of the value chain can serve to increase value, real or perceived. Most elements incur costs but can contribute to the process of differentiation. For comprehensive discussions of strategic planning in retailing, see Johnson (1987). Strategies for change and renewal in retailing are suggested in the *McKinsey Quarterly* (1997).

Location

Store location decisions are probably the single most crucial elements of retail marketing strategy. They represent long-term investment decisions which, if incorrect, are very difficult to change. While good locations cannot alone compensate for a weak overall strategy, a poor location is a very difficult deficit to overcome. Bad location decisions also undermine the asset value of the retail organization – such stores are difficult to sell.

The retail location decisions must address both macro and micro issues and they are often depicted in three stages (Brown 1992).

1 Search – identifying geographical areas that may have market potential.

The marketing mix

2 Viability – evaluating the turnover potential of the best available sites.
3 Micro – examining the detailed features of the shortlisted sites.

Clearly, not all location decisions pass through this sequence, and a great deal of intuition and executive judgement is still applied. A number of more systematic techniques are available to assist decision makers.

1 Checklists – very detailed lists of factors relevant to location evaluations have been evolved and are widely used. The factors include many aspects of the population within the catchment area, competition (existing and potential), accessibility by car and by foot, and the specific costs of developing a store on that site.
2 Geographic information systems – can provide detailed analysis of many checklist factors, such as income, employment and expenditure profiles within specified localities.
3 Analogue methods – extrapolate the performance of a site under consideration, based upon analogous sites already in operation.
4 Regression models – help to forecast turnover by modelling the influence of location factors which contribute to, or detract from, the turnover of existing stores.

Product selection and buying

The buying function represents the main interface between retailers and other members of the supply chain. Accordingly, many suppliers create specialist sales teams to serve key retail accounts, developing a close knowledge of the organization and the individuals involved. In some retail organizations, individual buyers have extensive autonomy within their specific product category; in others, the buying team is the norm, which typically includes selectors, merchandisers, technologists and quality controllers.

Numerous criteria must be considered by retail buyers, not least of which are the projections of sales and profitability. Product selection is also a key element of differentiation and buyers are becoming increasingly proactive in sourcing items that will help to provide a competitive edge. Buyers must also consider the capabilities of the supplier, in terms of volume, flexibility and reliability.

In the USA, the Robinson Patman Act limits the scope of major retail buyers to obtain better terms, purely on account of their buying power. Such legislation has been considered but not implemented in the UK Accordingly, large

Table 9 Retailer brand shares in Europe

Country	Percentage of grocery trade	
	1991	1993
Switzerland	40	41
United Kingdom	30	31
Germany	23	24
Belgium	19	20
France	18	19
Denmark	18	19
Netherlands	16	17
Austria	11	12
Spain	5	8
Italy	5	7
Portugal	1	3

Derived from: Samways (1996)

retailers can demand a wide range of additional benefits, analysed by the Office of Fair Trading (1985).

Retail brands

A significant manifestation of retailer power has been the ability of major retailers to develop their own brand product ranges. These are defined as: products sold under a retail organization's house brand name, which are sold exclusively through that retail organization's outlets. The name may be that of the retailer, for example Tesco, or a name closely linked with the company, such as Marks & Spencer's St Michael brand. From time to time, grocery retailers have also launched ranges of 'generics', a low priced, plain label variant upon the own brand concept.

Retailer brands have been especially important within grocery retailing. The three leading grocers in the UK, Tesco, J. Sainsbury and Safeway, derived 45, 56 and 45 per cent of their turnover respectively from their own brands in 1997 (Retail Review 1998). Table 9 summarizes own brands across Europe. Such brands are not restricted to grocery sectors; with 100 per cent own brands, Marks & Spencer has been described as 'a manufacturer without factories'. This company is totally involved in the specification, design and quality control processes (see BRANDING AND BRAND MANAGEMENT).

Motives for developing retailer brands vary, as does the positioning of the ranges. Generally, retailers are seeking to reinforce their images, generate better margins and improve competitiveness, in terms of price and/or differentiation.

Pricing

Since the abolition of resale price maintenance in most areas, the control of retail prices has shifted largely from manufacturers to retailers. This now represents one of the most complex elements of retail management. Whereas 100 products could represent a fairly wide assortment for a manufacturer, a retailer may be responsible for pricing 10,000 or more items. Compounding upon this complexity is the fact that many multiples differentiate prices between branches. As each store serves a different market, why not differentiate in response to local market conditions?

Retailers conduct or obtain audits of competitors' prices in order to help determine their own price levels. In the retailing of wide product assortments, such as groceries, it is consumers' perceptions of price levels that are of crucial importance. Retailers are able to determine which products are 'known value items', items for which shoppers have high levels of price awareness, and ensure that these items are priced very competitively. In other areas of retailing, notably clothing and footwear, extensive use is made of prices such as £49.95, which

Table 10 Retail advertising expenditures

	1993 (£m.)	1996 (£m.)
Dixons Group	37.7	98.4
J. Sainsbury	24.9	31.7
Safeway	19.2	29.2
Comet	23.9	25.8
MFI	20.2	25.3
B&Q	22.9	25.2
Homebase	28.9	24.1
Asda	15.3	21.4
Boots	13.5	21.0
Woolworths	19.8	20.5

Derived from: Nielsen (1998)

are thought to create a lower price perception. Conversely, if the price is intended to signal a prestige purchase, round numbers such as £220 tend to be preferred.

Pricing is also used widely as a promotional tool, usually in conjunction with advertising and in-store support. Short-term special offers, often subsidized heavily by manufacturers, are a feature of many retail sectors. 'Seasonal sales' are also used extensively to clear lines, to generate additional turnover and as a response to the promotional activities of others. A number of countries have legislation that restricts the use of 'loss leader' or below cost pricing. From 1997, the Loi Galland prevented French retailers from using 'excessively low' prices. Similar restrictions were imposed from 1996 in Spain, plus a limit of only two 'seasonal sales' per annum, (NatWest Securities 1997) (see PRICING).

Advertising

In that advertising is the theme of another entry (see ADVERTISING), here it will suffice to emphasize the financial and strategic importance of advertising to retailers. Expenditure by UK retailers grew from £285 million in 1985 to £1079 million in 1996 (Nielsen 1998). Table 10 shows a few of the major spenders, although it should be recognized that some of this expenditure is subsidized by manufacturers, in the form of 'cooperative advertising' deals.

Retailers have many ways of communicating with their own regular customers, both in-store and by mailings sent to account or loyalty/store card holders. Major objectives of media advertising are therefore to attract new customers, or to increase the visit frequency/expenditure of more marginal customers. Some retailers also make use of sponsorship as a promotional vehicle, which can avoid much of the 'clutter' in conventional media advertising.

The selling environment

The in-store environment offers retailers numerous opportunities to influence the purchasing patterns of shoppers. The overall design and atmosphere of a store creates/ reinforces an image, as well as affecting mood states and shopping behaviour. 'Atmospherics' has been defined as: 'the conscious designing of space to create certain effects in buyers' (Kotler 1973). An atmosphere includes the many visual aspects of a store, the sounds, scents and textures. Experiments have shown how various colours or different types of music can affect customer behaviour. The smell of fresh bread is commonly used by supermarkets; some retailers are now experimenting with the use of more subtle aromas.

In that most retailing environments invite self-service, the detailed allocation of selling space has become an important science. Major retailers tend to use computer models both to optimize and to visualize space allocation. They aim to achieve a balance between the desire to maximize impulse purchasing, the need to offer a wide range, the need to hold adequate stock and the need to offer a convenient and pleasant shopping environment.

Human resources

With around 14 million people employed in retailing in Europe (Eurostat 1997) – 2.3 million in Great Britain – it is clear that retailing is a 'people business'. Retailers also face the challenge that their lowest paid staff interface directly with their customers. Imagine how images of cars or chocolates would change if customers dealt directly with assembly line workers, rather than receiving these images through carefully crafted advertisements.

In retailing, the shelf packers, cleaners and checkout operators all represent key components of the service experience. This highlights the need for careful selection and training; overall, the need for an effective human resource function (see Marchington, in McGoldrick 1994). Large retail chains also have the challenge of communicating their mission, values and expectations to a large and geographically dispersed staff.

There are of course some retail contexts within which staff hold highly creative selling roles. In the retailing of fashion goods, cars or other major durables, the sales staff are expected to combine extensive product knowledge with the skills of personal selling (see PERSONAL SELLING AND SALES MANAGEMENT).

Information and logistics

A summary of key retail functions would be incomplete without the component of logistics (see LOGISTICS AND VALUE CREATION). The logistics role is largely unseen by most customers, becoming more apparent when it fails to maintain stock levels. Out-of-stock conditions may cause not only the immediate loss of item sales, they also undermine customer loyalty by increasing the need to shop elsewhere. The efficient management of the supply chain is therefore a key strategic function.

The benefits of checkout scanning equipment to supply chain management are starting to be fully realized. 'Efficient consumer response' developments include the sharing of live data with some major suppliers, with the effect of increasing stock availability, improving choice for customers, reducing stock levels and improving stockturns. At Asda, for example, the average rate of stockturn improved from 15 in 1992 to 23 in 1997.

Such systems require a high proportion of scanner equipped stores. By 1996, 7580 grocery stores in the UK used scanners, representing 88.6 per cent of grocery turnover (Nielsen 1998). Scanning also offers direct benefits to customers in terms of faster service and itemized receipts. Further service enhancement is provided by the integration of electronics payment systems, accepting credit or debit payments and, in the latter case, offering customers the facility to request cash back. The same systems also capture individual customer purchase data, via the 50 million loyalty cards estimated to be in use in the UK by 1998.

6 Internationalization of retailing

In spite of the power and sophistication of large scale retailers, the process of internationalization has been slow and painful. In addition to the legal, linguistic and logistical problems, it is difficult to export even the most successful of retail concepts into other markets (see GLOBAL MARKETING). As noted earlier, competitive structures differ greatly and there are still major differences in consumer tastes and preferences. (McGoldrick and Davies 1995).

Difficult or not, the internationalization of retailing is gaining pace. Figure 3 summarizes the major facets of this process, including the arrival of foreign competition and entries into foreign markets. A view of internationalization should also recognize the flow of know-how and the import/export of retail concepts. International product sourcing has a long history in some companies but is becoming more widespread; for some retailers, it has facilitated the development of branches abroad. Table 11

Figure 3 Facets of retail internationalization

summarizes the international activities of certain European retailers that derive a relatively large proportion of turnover from operations outside their home market.

Motives for internationalization

The pressures towards/reasons for internationalization are diverse, but may be summarized as 'push', 'pull' or 'facilitating' factors.

1. 'Push' factors, including the maturity or saturation of home markets, domestic trading restrictions, unfavourable economic conditions, rising costs, adverse demographic changes and imitation of trading styles.
2. 'Pull' factors, including more enlightened corporate philosophies, perceptions of growth opportunities abroad (niche or underdeveloped markets), established bridgeheads in other countries and imitative 'bandwagon' effects'.
3. 'Facilitating' factors, including the lowering of political, economic and perceived barriers between countries, the broader vision of senior management, an accumulation of expertise, the ability to assess other retailers' international moves and the improvement of communication technologies (see INFORMATION TECHNOLOGY AND MARKETING).

The particular mix of these factors often determines the most appropriate route to internationalization. Also relevant is the availability of capital, the level of understanding of market needs within other countries, and the compatibility of the domestic trading format(s) with those needs. It is clear that retailers have sometimes adopted the wrong approach to internationalization. There are several examples of leading retailers in domestic markets running into difficulties abroad.

Entry strategies

A number of alternative approaches are available, including the following (Table 11).

1. Self-start entry, the chain being built up from scratch, or developed through organic growth from a very modest initial acquisition. Examples include Woolworths development in the UK and Laura Ashley in the USA.
2. Acquisition, providing a quick entry route but at cost, not least because companies available for acquisition may well be in financial difficulty. This approach has been used by many UK retailers, including the acquisition of Kings supermarkets and Brooks Brothers menswear in the USA by Marks & Spencer.
3. Franchising, avoiding much risk and demands upon capital; especially appropriate where a retailing concept can be readily exported. Notable examples include Italian manufacturer/franchiser Benetton, with over 6000 outlets in over 80 countries.
4. Joint venture, reducing time, cost and risk of entry by working with a partner already familiar with the market. In spite of their benefits at the outset, many joint ventures/partnerships have been terminated, having not met expectations.
5. Concessions, (shops in shops), a relatively low cost/risk approach to exploring new markets, used for example by Burton in Spain and elsewhere.

Cross-border alliances have become a major element of international retail cooperation and expansion in recent years. There are four main types, namely, purchasing led alliances, development alliances, skills based alliances and multi-function alliances. Within this last category may be included the development of the European Retail Alliance (ERA) and Associated Marketing Services (AMS), linking retailers across Europe and opening opportunities for many forms of cooperation, including purchasing, sourcing, logistics, product development, promotion and political lobbying (see GLOBAL MARKETING).

The internationalization of retailing has produced very diverse styles of operation, ranging from global to multinational. Global retailers such as Benetton vary their format very little across national boundaries, achieving the greatest economies of scale but showing the least local responsiveness. Multinationals, on the other hand, tend to develop or acquire a diversity of formats internationally, usually achieving rather lower benefits from integration. A middle course may be termed 'transnational' retailing, whereby the company seeks to achieve global efficiency while responding to national needs, opportunities and constraints. Some of

Table 11 Examples of international retailing in the Europe

Company	Country of origin	International turnover (M.U ECU)	Percentage of total turnover	Main activity
Ikea	S	2,138	76.2	Furniture
Delhaize le Lion	B	5,283	72.4	Food
Tengelmann	D	12,656	55.7	Food
Ahold	NL	4,548	50.6	Food
Otto Versand	D	3,602	45.9	Mail order
Vendex	NL	2,808	35.3	Department store/food
La Redoute	F	879	35.0	Mail order
Metro	D	6,036	35.0	Department store/food
Promodes	F	5,506	34.4	Food
Carrefour	F	3,414	31.1	Food
Dixons	UK	726	30.6	Electrical

Source: Eurostat (1993).

the more recent developments by Marks & Spencer could best be described as transnational, recognizing that even the most successful retail formats within the domestic market may require adaptation to suit markets aboard.

7 Non-store retailing

In conclusion to this entry, it is appropriate to mention potential and existing forms of nonstore retailing. This category includes itinerant traders, a category for which little information is available, traditional 'home shopping' and various forms of electronic shopping.

Home shopping

In that telephone ordering has largely replaced the posting of orders, the term 'mail order' is giving way to 'home shopping'. In spite of numerous predictions that home shopping would take over a large share of retail trade, its role in Europe is still fairly modest. In Germany it holds the largest share, around 4.8 per cent of retail trade, the sector being dominated by Otto Versand and Quelle. This compares with 3.4 and 2.7 per cent in the UK and France respectively, as Table 12 illustrates. Further afield, home shopping accounts for 2.9 per cent of retail sales in the USA., 3.4 per cent in Canada and 3.2 per cent in Australia (Redler 1995).

The structure of home shopping in the UK is highly concentrated. Great Universal Stores (GUS) alone holds 24.5 per cent of the market, followed by Littlewoods at 15.5 per cent. At the European level too, the home shopping industry is highly concentrated. The top four companies, Otto Versand, Quelle, La Redoute and GUS control around 47 per cent of the market (Redler 1995). The sector has been the target of international acquisition, Grattan being sold to Otto Versand and Empire being acquired by La Redoute. Although holding a relatively modest share, the Next Directory represented a significant departure from traditional catalogues in the UK. Its style and design illustrated that home shopping could be targeted towards younger, more affluent shoppers. In response, major operators introduced 'specialogues', designed for specific needs and groups.

Catalogues are not of course the exclusive domain of non-store retailers. Many retailers send or make available seasonal or specialist catalogues to their customers, to encourage pre-selection at home and to generate more store visits. The catalogue showroom

The marketing mix

represents a hybrid retail format, allowing selection at home from an extensive catalogue but usually requiring collection from a store. The advantage over conventional home shopping is that the item can be obtained without delay. Catalogue showrooms also display some of the seasonal or higher value items, allowing inspection before purchase. The format is well developed in the UK – the largest operators being Argos and Index (Littlewoods) – and in the Netherlands.

Electronic shopping

Although logically a sub-set of home shopping, forms of electronic or teleshopping merit special attention, representing an area of future development in retailing. Existing systems include the following:

1. Videotex Services – a combination of telephone transmission and television screen display of 'pages' of information. Experimental systems have used the Prestel system but with little commercial success; that technology is old and not especially user friendly. Major advances are however being made in the quality of images that can be transmitted down telephone lines.

2. Shopping channels – delivered by satellite or cable, thus providing high quality picture and sound, but usually requiring telephone ordering. Many such channels have failed in the USA but the QVC channel grew to a customer base of over four million by 1995; it started satellite broadcasting in Europe in 1993.

3. Interactive cable television systems – which allow the customer to access more detailed information about specific products. J.C. Penney's 'Teleaction' claimed to be the first commercial system of this type in the USA.

4. Internet based sites – providing both information and ordering facilities. Some companies also use their sites to encourage feedback from customers. In 1995, Barclays Bank launched Barclaysquare, which included J. Sainsbury, Toys R Us, Blackwells, Argos and Innovations (http://www, iti-net/barclaysquare).

Table 12 Home shopping in Europe

Country	Leading provider	Overall percentage of retail sales
Germany	Quelle Otto Versand (OV) Neckermann	4.8
United Kingdom	GUS Littlewoods Grattan (OV)	3.4
France	La Redoute Trois Suisses (OV)	2.7
Switzerland	Heine (OV) Quelle Vedia (GUS)	2.7
Belgium	Trois Suisses (OV) Quelle	1.5
Netherlands	Otto Versand La Redoute Wehkamp (GUS)	1.5
Portugal	La Redoute	0.8
Spain	Catalogo (OV) Quelle	0.4

Derived from: Redler (1995)

Projections for the future of home shopping include many possibilities, including videophones, compact disc and multimedia. It is also possible that the technology of virtual reality, currently used to visualize kitchen layouts by some retailers, could be used at home to simulate the experience of browsing a store and touching the goods. With the history of failures and withdrawals from teleshopping, it is not surprising that most retailers are waiting for more widespread adoption of the relevant, home based technologies. Estimates vary enormously but even a conservative forecast expects home shopping to more than double by 2010 (Corporate Intelligence 1997). Only one thing is certain, technological developments, both in-store and out of store, will continue to be a major driving force for change in this dynamic sector called retailing (see INFORMATION TECHNOLOGY AND MARKETING).

PETER J. MCGOLDRICK
MANCHESTER SCHOOL OF MANAGEMENT

Further reading

* Brown, S. (1987) 'Institutional change in retailing: a review and synthesis', *European Journal of Marketing* 21: 5–36. (An incisive review of retail change theories; an extensive bibliography.)
* Brown, S. (1992) *Retail Location: a Micro-Scale Perspective*, Aldershot: Avebury. (Examination and critique of retail location theory; many examples, maps and references.)
* Corporate Intelligence (1997) 'Cyberlogues – the next generation of mail order?', *Retail Report* 97: 87–92.
* Corporate Intelligence (1998) *The European Retail Handbook*, London: Corporate Intelligence.
* Davidson, W.R., Bates, A.D. and Bass, S.J. (1976) 'The retail life cycle', *Harvard Business Review* 54: 89–96. (Classic article, relating the life-cycle concept to retailing, with examples.)
* Euromonitor (1995) *Retail Trade International*, London: Euromonitor.
* European Retail Digest (1997) 'Employment in retailing: trends and issues', *European Retail Digest* 14: 14–16.
* Eurostat (1993) *Retailing in the Single European Market*, Brussels: Statistical Office of the European Community.
* Eutostat (1997) *Retailing in the European Economic Area 1996*, Brussels: Statistical Office of the European Communities.
* Institute of Grocery Distribution (1997) *The European Food Industry*, Watford: IGD.
* Johnson, G. (1987) *Business Strategy and Retailing*, Chichester: John Wiley.
* Key Note (1997) *Franchising*, London: Key Note.
* Kotler, P. (1973) 'Atmospherics as a marketing tool', *Journal of Retailing* 49: 48–64.
* McGoldrick, P.J. (1990) *Retail Marketing*, London: McGraw-Hill.
* McGoldrick, P.J. (1994) *Retail Management Cases*, London
* McGoldrick,.P.J. and G. Davies (1995) *International Retailing: Trends and Strategies*, London: Pitman.
* McGoldrick, P.J. and Greenland, S.J. (1994) *The Retailing of Financial Services*, London: McGraw-Hill.
* McGoldrick, P.J. and Thompson, M.G. (1992) *Regional Shopping Centres*, Aldershot: Avebury.
* NatWest Securities (1997) 'Relevant legislation', *European Food Retailing* (February): 5–9.
* NatWest Markets (1998) *Store Wars* London: NatWest Markets.
* Nielsen (1998) *Retail Pocket Book*, Oxford: NTC Publications.
* Office of Fair Trading (1985) *Competition and Retailing*, London: OFT.
* Redler, E. (1995) *Mail Order in Europe*, London: Pearson Professional.
* Retail Review (1998) *Retail Review*, Manchester: Cooperative Wholesaler Society.
* Samways, A (1996) *Private Label in Europe*, London: Pearson Professional.
* Tordjman, A. (1993) *Evolution of Retailing Formats in the E.C.* Jouy-en-Josas: Groupe HEC.

See also: ADVERTISING; BRANDING AND BRAND MANAGEMENT; CHANNEL MANAGEMENT; FRANCHISING; GLOBAL MARKETING; INFORMATION TECHNOLOGY AND MARKETING; LOGISTICS AND VALUE CREATION; MARKETING OF SERVICES; PERSONAL SELLING AND SALES MANAGEMENT; PRICING; PRODUCT LIFE-CYCLE MANAGEMENT; THE MARKETING MIX; WHOLESALING

Direct marketing: advancing to integrated (Internet) communications

1 Introduction
2 The major opportunities/benefits and problems with direct marketing strategies and IMC programmes
3 Modelling customer/marketer information search and relationships in integrative marketing communications
4 Direct marketing implications for designing and implementing effective IMC programmes

Overview

The Direct Marketing Association defines direct marketing as 'an interactive system of marketing that uses one or more advertising media to effect a measurable response and/or transaction at any location, with this activity stored on database.' The good news about this definition in the minds of senior corporate executives is that direct marketing includes hard measures of advertising and marketing performance: in generating customer inquiries, sales leads, and sales. The bad news: most direct marketing strategies fail; they fail most often because most senior executives and advertisers do not design an effective integrated marketing communications (IMC) programme for building long-term relationships with prospects/customers. The proposition is examined here that modeling what actually happens in customer/marketer information search and two-way responses in direct marketing strategies may be helpful for designing effective IMC programmes. An 18-step, customer-marketer, direct marketing model is described with implications offered for designing effective IMC programmes. This article also provides specific strategy steps for using the Internet as a medium for marketers to form close relationships with customers.

1 Introduction

According to the Direct Marketing Association (*Direct Marketing* 1993) 'Direct marketing is an integrative system of marketing that uses one or more advertising media to effect a measurable response and/or transaction at any location, with this activity stored on database.' About two-thirds of all advertising in the USA, Canada, the UK, and other developed nations include one or more ways for viewers, listeners or readers to respond directly to receive additional information or to buy the product/service being promoted. In the USA, this two-thirds amounts to $142 billion in 1991 (*Direct Marketing* 1993). Direct response mechanisms include telephone numbers, coupons, reader service (bingo) cards, free-standing-insert coupons and fax numbers.

Most direct marketing strategies include combinations of three or more advertising vehicles to achieve a measurable response from prospects. For example, a television commercial might include the offer of a free brochure if the viewer will telephone the toll-free number on the screen, or complete and mail a postcard. Thus, a communication process, usually involving more than three media, needs to designed to complete an effective exchange: *television* to make the offer; the *telephone* and *postcard-mailing* response media; the *brochure*; the *computer* to create/store/retrieve the customer–product–firm database; the *marketer reply medium* to send the brochure (often via mail) to the customer; *people* to process responses, stuff envelopes, and/or talk on the telephone; and the *products/services* in the brochure (a product is always a communication medium as well as combination of attributes that provides benefits).

Given the impact of combining, that is, integrating multiple media, to make direct marketing strategies effective, it should not be surprising that direct mail expenditures represent less than 20 per cent of the total direct marketing expenditure. However, to say that direct marketing is much more than direct mail misses the really important point: the use of multiple media needs to be integrated well to make direct marketing work.

Integrated marketing communication (IMC) programmes include designing and implementing a dynamic, interactive, marketer-customer system that incorporate multiple media, measured customer responses, and immediate access and use of customer databases. Many details of why IMC programmes are needed and how to design them are described in Roman's (1988) *Integrated Direct Marketing*, Rapp and Collins' (1987) *Maxi-marketing*, Schultz et al.'s (1993) *Integrated Marketing Communications*, and Shepard's (1990) *The New Direct Marketing*. Thus, several advocates have made compelling cases for IMC programmes.

In this article, the major opportunities and problems with direct marketing and IMC programmes are reviewed briefly. Next, a model of the early stages in customer–marketer information search and responses in integrative marketing communications is described; some research findings related to the model are reviewed. Finally, based on the discussion of the model, direct marketing implications for designing and implementing effective IMC programmes are offered. The aim here is to start to detail all the important small, and big, behavioural steps that need to be integrated and assessed in interactive systems known as direct marketing.

2 The major opportunities/benefits and problems with direct marketing strategies and IMC programmes

Both opportunities/benefits and problems are associated with designing and implementing effective direct marketing strategies and IMC programmes. Substantial increases in marketing effectiveness and efficiency have been documented in case studies of IMC programmes (see monthly issues of *Direct Marketing Magazine*, the industry trade publication in the USA). Unfortunately, the problems that always occur with starting and running IMC programmes receive little attention in the literature. Three major opportunities and benefits gained from an effective IMC programme are described; two major problems that almost always occur with designing/implementing IMC programmes are then discussed.

Opportunities/benefits

Building close, long-term relationships with customers

Effective direct marketing and IMC programmes permit the building of long-term, close relationships linking the marketer and customer; this feature of direct marketing is the most important benefit of effective IMC programmes. The marketer is able to respond to customers individually through the marketer's IMC programme; thus, the first of Tom Peters and Nancy Austin's (1985) two sustainable strategic advantages can be achieved via effective IMC programmes: creating and maintaining an obsession with customers (the second is to constantly innovate). Individual service designed to meet the personal needs of *a* customer who the marketer communicates with *by name*, is a useful description of relationship marketing. Relationship marketing is achieved by effective direct marketing and IMC programmes.

A well-designed and implemented IMC programme prevents relationships from going stale. Levitt (1983) points out that relationships tend to grow stale without continual attention:

> The sale merely consummates the courtship, then the marriage begins. How good the marriage is depends on how well the relationship is managed by the seller. ...The natural tendency of relationships, whether in marriage or in business, is entropy – the erosion or deterioration of sensitivity and attentiveness. ... A healthy relationship requires a conscious and constant fight against the forces of entropy.
> (Quoted in Peters and Austin 1985: 82)

The argument might be offered here that dramatic increases in marketing costs will occur from designing and implementing an IMC programme. Contrary to this conventional wisdom, *decreases* in total marketing expenditures often occur from effective IMC programmes for two reasons. First, because of technological advances in using computers and databases, data handling and customer contact costs continue to fall. Second, with an effective IMC programme, marketers start spending substantially less money on trying to reach prospects who will never buy or who become unprofitable customers. Also, such improved allocations of marketing funds result in higher net returns per dollar spent because specific marketing actions can be targeted to reach the customers most likely to buy. Thomas Roger, a US producer of software for direct marketing, offers the following example, 'We tell people, "you can mail 1,000 letters, or you can use one of these [IMC database] systems and mail 100 letters and get the same results"' (quoted from Bulkeley 1993). Thus, contrary to conventional wisdom, embracing direct marketing and an IMC system need not – should not – increase marketing costs substantially.

Using 'frequency-marketing' to increase sales to best customers

We know that all customers are not alike: for both consumer and industrial firms, 5 per cent of a firm's customers often provide more than 20 per cent of total sales and more than 30 per cent of net profits (Dubinsky and Ingram 1984; Dwyer 1989. This knowledge is leading more firms to create and maintain 'frequency marketing' (FM) programmes.

Frequency marketing is 'to identify, maintain, and increase the yield from best customers, through long-term, interactive, value-added relationships' (Colloquy 1991). A firm's best customers (e.g. the customers above the 90 per centile in total purchases among all customers in a firm's customer base) usually are the most sensitive to the firm's new product offerings, special promotional offerings of the firm, and tend to buy products from the firm that provide the highest contribution to overhead and profits (for a detailed example see Woodside and Soni 1991). Even though very few customers are loyal 100 per cent of the time, an enterprise can often capture a larger share of the available business among its best customers by creating frequency-marketing programmes. Frequent traveller membership programmes among airlines are early examples of such FM programmes.

Often, it is much cheaper and more profitable to persuade established customers (especially best customers) to respond to a specific marketing action than it is to bring in new customers. James Pisz, the national direct response manager for Toyota Motor Corporation in the USA, estimates that it is 'three-to-five times more expensive to attract a new customer than a repeat customer' (in Bulkeley 1993). Pisz uses a computer workstation to locate best customers among a seven million US customer database. When Toyota dealers plan 'tent sales', Pisz provides mailings to local area residents who have bought new Toyotas three years before.

Certainly an enterprise needs to design/implement marketing strategies to attract new customers. The point here: most firms do not have explicit strategies directed toward their best customers; FM programmes are made possible by well-developed direct marketing and IMC programmes.

A Mighty Dog Example

A pre-emptive competitive strategy by Mighty Dog provides a packaged-product example of initial steps toward an FM strategy (from 'Trend Setters' 1992). In 1992 Mighty Dog wanted to defend its brand and market share against a larger competitor about to launch a national campaign for a new dogfood entry (Heinz's Reward). The problem was that Reward's spending levels could not be matched. The strategy was to use a targeted mailing to pull known Mighty Dog households out of the market prior to Reward's roll out. Mighty Dog wanted dog owners to stock up on their product before Reward's campaign hit.

Mighty Dog sent a direct mail piece to 526,291 households, the majority of which came from Mighty Dog's own database of names generated from previous promotions. Tactics included timing the mailing to be in consumer's homes two weeks prior to the Reward launch and deliver 10 time-sensitive, computer personalized, sequentially dated coupons to the user households. The direct mail package included $5 worth of Mighty Dog coupons and the chance for consumers to purchase a dog's personalized bowl and blanket once they sent in the appropriate number of UPC symbols from Mighty Dog Products.

A total of 6.7 per cent of the coupons distributed were redeemed. Premium redemption was 13 per cent: 71,000 households redeemed the UPS symbols for either the bowl or blanket. The Mighty Dog used coupon values forcing high-purchase commitment (saving $1 on 10

December 19, 1991

Dr and Dr Jerome D. Wilson
North Hills Court
Rural Route 2, Box 467-C
Hodges, South Carolina 29653

Dear Dr and Dr Wilson,

Well it's a shame you couldn't make it down for the coonhunt this year, because we sure had a good time. And like I said in my note to you, we didn't hurt your property much at all since the dogs went off in the other direction and never did circle back to your place. When they finally did tree a coon, it was the only one we saw the whole hunt. There was quite a discussion as to who's dog actually did the treeing, since the commotion was so loud and two or three of the dogs sound just about alike.

Well I finally settled the question by declaring everybody's dog a winner, which seemed to satisfy everybody except Roger, but he calmed down after a spell. And after a little Black Label.

It was a clear night, but a bit chilly and we were glad we had our long handles on. There were a few out-of-towner Tennessee Squires along this year, and I tried to take a picture of the whole group. Unfortunately I had some camera trouble. By the time I got it working most everybody had gotten tired and left, including the dogs, and the few that were still hanging around weren't very cooperative as you can see.

What with these hunts getting bigger every year, Dr. and Dr. Wilson, I sure hope you can figure a way to join us one of these times. Just drop me a line if your plans look hopeful, and I'll be glad to add your name to the list.

Cordially yours,

Bill Weaver

Figure 1 Tennessee Squires letter

cans) and attracted *known customers* to complete a programme of having enough UPC symbols to redeem for a personalized bowl or blanket. Mighty Dog's market share increased 0.5 per cent during the first two weeks of the promotion. The promotion minimized Mighty Dog's market share loss (only 0.2 per cent) to Reward, in the first eight weeks.

The Jack Daniel's Tennessee Squires example

The 'Tennessee Squires' is an FM customer association, 'club,' founded by Jack Daniel's to create brand loyalty among the firm's best customers. Each member of the club receives a deed to a small plot of land owned by the distiller, invitations to local raccoon hunts, updates on 'municipal' business, a Squire card, and a certificate of membership. The letter shown as Figure 1 helps create and maintain a strong sense of being a Tennessee Squire, 'belonging' to the club, and probably helps maintain top-of-mind-awareness and preference for Jack Daniel's whiskey among club members.

Note the informal, very enjoyable, reading in the letter, for example, 'we didn't hurt your property much at all since the dogs went off in the other direction and never did circle back to your place.' Accompanying the letter was an out-of-focus, color photograph showing 24 club members, one child, and four coon-hunting dogs. The photo explains the sentence in Figure 1, 'Unfortunately I had some camera trouble.' (The club members are posed with no rifles in the photograph, a thoughtful tactic given the negative connotations that might come to mind with drinking alcohol and guns.)

Note that the letter ends with a personal reference to the Wilson's in the last paragraph. This illustrates the individual, personalizing, feature of effective FM programmes and direct marketing.

Jack Daniel's started the Tennessee Squires in 1957; the club pre-dates all airline frequent traveller programmes. By 1993 80,000 US households include one or more Tennessee Squires. In other mailings, members of the Tennessee Squires receive new product information and how-to-consume product information (e.g. brief, lovely poems to offer as toasts when 'sipping' Gentleman Jack Rare Tennessee Whiskey).

Assessing performance and building forecasting models

Advertising budgets and other marketing expenditures are much easier to justify to senior management when sales can be linked directly, and accurately, to money spent. This is the beauty of direct marketing: a performance tracking system can be created to continually monitor relationships with customers, including how customers respond to specific advertising executions. Thus, the term, *measurable response*, in the DMA definition of direct marketing is particularly noteworthy.

A particularly strong case for designing-in a measurable response in *all* advertising executions, including image ads, appears in *Maximarketing*:

> Most advertisers of products, services, and establishments who devote their advertising to building their favorable awareness can, at the very least, incorporate a direct-response element as an index of performance. Inviting a direct response of some sort can measure comparative creative impact, comparative positioning effectiveness, and comparative media performance.
>
> (Rapp and Collins 1988)

Performance tracking systems can be developed at different levels of sophistication, for example, from low (say, Stage 1) to high (Stage 5):

- Stage 1: one-time, conversion studies;
- Stage 2: one-time, true experiments;
- Stage 3: continual monitoring and relationship building;
- Stage 4: continual monitoring/relationship-building with true experiments;
- Stage 5: continual monitoring/relationship-building, true experiments, with forecasting models of consumer response functions.

Stage 1: One time, conversion studies

In Stage 1, the performance of ads and ad placements in competing media vehicles in delivering inquirers (prospects) is measured for an ad campaign. The conversion power of ad and ad placements is measured; conversion is the proportion of inquirers who convert into buyers. Also, revenues and the net profits associated with each ad and ad placement can be monitored. Conversion rates can be tracked by surveying inquirers to learn if they purchased the brand or service for which they requested information.

CPI, RPI, and ROI are index values of performance used often to compare impact in direct marketing campaigns. CPI is cost per inquiry, calculated by dividing all costs assignable to a particular ad placed in a given media vehicle (e.g. ad space cost and expenses in fulfilling the prospect's inquiry, including fulfilment literature expenses) by the total number of inquiries generated by this ad placement. RPI is the revenue per inquiry, calculated by dividing the revenues to the advertiser from the ad placement by the total number of inquiries generated by this ad placement. ROI is return on investment, calculated by dividing revenue net of assignable costs by assignable costs.

A tracking system developed by the State of Louisiana for assessing advertising performance for attracting tourist visitors provides details of such a Stage 1 tracking system (Woodside and Soni 1990). In the Woodside and Soni (1990) report, the conversion proportion of visitors-divided-by-inquirers for ads placed in 1987 ads in *Southern Living* magazine was very high (0.46) compared to the conversion proportion from ads in *Bon Appetit* (0.11).

Table 1 Revenue and cost analysis of advertising in competing magazine vehicles

Category	Magazine	Revenue per inquiry (RPI) $	Cost per inquiry (CPI) $	CPI as a percentage of RPI
Life-cycle	Magazine X	240	$49.51	20.6
	Magazine Y	35	15.16	43.3
Food	Gourmet	256	14.28	5.6
	Bon Appetit	89	6.60	7.4
Women's service	Family Circle	159	7.60	4.8
	Ladies Home Journal	105	4.18	4.0
Regional focus	Southern Living	237	5.99	2.5
	Texas Monthly	227	18.15	8.0
Travel related	Travel & Leisure	446	12.27	2.8
	N.G. Traveler	180	7.59	4.2

Source: Woodside and Soni (1990: 63).

However, conversion rates are only one measure of performance. Similar to a medical doctor examining a patient, multiple-method measurements should be included to assess well-being, that is, ad performance. Tables 1 and 2 are examples of RPI, CPI, and profit measures of performance for the 1987 Louisiana ad campaign (Tables 7 and 8 in Woodside and Soni 1990). Note in Table 2 that profits associated with the *Bon Appetit* ads are positive; thus, the Louisiana ad 1987 performance associated with *Bon Appetit* might be judged to be pretty-good, even with the low conversion rate.

(Magazines X and Y are not named in Tables 1 and 2 because of their poor profit performance for the advertiser.)

Data evaluation is a critical issue in Stage 1, and other stages, in performance monitoring. Managers looking at the study, and evaluating the evaluation, should ask how the data variables are defined in the study. What are the details of the procedures with which the data were collected? What factors were controlled and not controlled in obtaining the data? What are the statistical properties of the data? In what direction will data problems bias the results? (Clarke 1993: 41).

Table 2 Profitability analysis of advertising by magazine vehicles

Category	Magazine	Advertising total cost $	Total tax revenue* $	Net profit to state and local governments $
Life-cycle	Magazine X	28,856	10,843	−14,013
	Magazine Y	12,524	2,602	−9,922
Food	Gourmet	26,616	42,947	16,331
	Bon Appetit	29,934	36,293	6,359
Women's service	Family Circle	91,480	172,292	80,812
	Ladies Home Journal	30,108	68,059	37,951
Regional focus	Southern Living	46,968	166,564	119,596
	Texas Monthly	21,581	24,184	2,603
Travel related	Travel & Leisure	38,516	125,994	87,483
	N.G. Traveler	32,396	69,158	36,762
Total		$354,979	$718,936	$363,957

*Estimated using 9 per cent of total revenue.
Source: Woodside and Soni (1990: 63).

In several respects, data evaluation of the 1987 Louisiana study lead to the conclusion that data look pretty-good. The study was designed to achieve a high response rate (52 per cent) for the questionnaire sent to inquirers; the data included questions on buying competing brands (i.e. visiting other states); and the questionnaire and cover letter did not reveal the sponsor of the study (to reduce sponsor-identity biases in responding to the questions). Most tourism conversion research studies report very high, overall, conversion rates, for example, above 45 per cent. Such reports make the advertising expenditures look very good, even if the estimates are unrealistic (i.e. invalid estimates of reality). One reason such high conversion rates are estimated is often that multiple attempts are not made to reach non-respondents in sampled households. Non-respondents are usually different from respondents in surveys – not in their demographic profiles but in their product use profiles (Woodside and Ronkainen 1994).

Stage 1 performance evaluations have two major shortcomings: (i) relationship marketing is not done and (ii) the basic issue of advertising effectiveness (does advertising cause sales) is not answered adequately. A major shortcoming with Stage 1 performance tracking is that no long-term relationships are developed with inquirers. After the inquiry is 'fulfilled' by sending some literature, possibly a brochure or an information kit that might include a video or offers for additional information, that is the end to the relationship. No additional contacts with the customer by the marketer are attempted; the marketer discards the names, addresses, and other information provided by the inquirers. Hard to believe, isn't it? Yet, many marketers using direct marketing do only Stage 1 performance evaluation; they do not attempt additional 'sales calls' by telephone, personal visits or through the mail other than a one-time response to the customer inquiry. Almost all state travel offices in the US and Canadian Provincial tourism agencies do Stage 1 type performance evaluations of their advertising programmes, even though they are marketing a high-ticket service (*average* expenditures in a state by overnight, visiting travel parties are typically above $1000).

Stage 1 tracking does not answer the basic question: how many sales (how much revenue was gained) because of the advertising. As a research tool, Stage 1 research is an unscientific way to gain valid answers to cause-and-effect relationships, even if customers respond favourably when asked whether seeing the advertising and receiving the literature they requested influence them to buy (would they accept a medical report that a new drug works well because patients report that they felt better after taking the pill containing the new drug?). Scientific research to learn cause-and-effect influence requires a direct comparison of results between two equal groups, one exposed to a treatment (say, advertising) and one not exposed. Such comparisons are know as 'true experiments' (Banks 1965).

Stage 2: True experiments
Doing true experiments to estimate cause-and-effect relationships between advertising and sales are more sophisticated than conversion research studies. While Stage 1, conversion studies, may provide useful information of the relative performance of alternative ad executions and media vehicles, they cannot answer the more basic questions, did the advertising cause sales beyond what would have occurred without the advertising? *or* did the sales performance of the new ad beat the sales performance of the old ad?

Stage 2, true experiments, provides useful answers to the question, does advertising cause sales. *True experiments* are creating two, three or more equal groups of subjects (e.g. prospects) and exposing one group to treatment A and a second group to treatment B and other groups to other treatments. Treatment A might be a new ad and treatment B might be the standard ad often used by a firm; the executives in the firm want to know if the new ad performs better than the standard ad in generating inquiries, new customers, sales and profits. Equal groups are created by randomly assigning a sample of subjects (say, 20,000) from a representative population to each group (10,000 to group A and 10,000 to group B) in the study; demographic and buying behaviour characteristics of the groups can be checked to insure that the random assignment worked to create two or more groups which do not differ (see Banks 1965 for details).

Treatment A might be tested against treatment B, where treatment B is no advertising, that is, one group of subjects is assigned randomly to be exposed to ad A and the second group is exposed to no advertising. This test is designed to examine how much impact is caused by advertising exposure versus no exposure: thus, how much, if any, does advertising cause sales?

True experiments are used in medical research to test the effectiveness of new drugs versus a placebo (sugar pills) in double-blind designs, that is, the administrators of the drug and the patients receiving either treatment A versus treatment B do not know which of the treatments is being administered. Thus, care is taken to avoid false reports of impact often made because subjects know they are being tested.

True experiments are known as *split-run tests* in advertising and direct marketing. A 'split-run' is an old newspaper term referring to splitting a publication run by removing an ad, or newspaper section, and adding a second ad, or newspaper section.

Split-run testing and other forms of true experiments can be used in testing the cause-and-effect influence of advertising versus no advertising, newspapers versus television, station A versus station B, magazine X versus Y, appeal M versus R, headline T versus U. Here is one example (from Caples 1974: 279) of split-run testing two headlines, the copy and illustrations were identical in both ads except for a change in headline wording:

- Headline of Ad A: Save one gallon of gas in every ten.
- Headline of Ad B: Car Owners! Save one gallon of gas in every ten.

Ad B pulled 20 per cent more inquirers (while the sales results were not in this test, most likely ad B pulled more total sales orders than ad A).

John Caples' (1974) book continues to be the best on true experiments, and wisdom, in advertising. It contains the following, now well-known, quote:

> I have seen one mail order advertisement actually sell, not twice as much, not three times as much, but nineteen and a half times as much goods as another. Both advertisements occupied the same space. Both were run in the same publication. Both had [the same] photographic illustrations. Both had carefully written copy. The difference was that one used the right appeal and the other used the wrong appeal.
>
> (Caples 1974: 11)

David Ogilvy makes a telling observation about direct marketing in the Forward to Caples' (1974) book:

> Experience has convinced me that the factors that work in mail order advertising work equally well in *all* advertising. But the vast majority of people working in [advertising] agencies, and almost all their clients, have never heard of these factors. That is why they skid helplessly about on the greasy surface of irrelevant brilliance. They waste millions on bad advertising, when good advertising could be selling nineteen and a half times as much.

In 1993 Don Schultz's report stated that most advertising agencies are still unable to embrace direct marketing and IMC programmes; unfortunately Oglivy's observations about advertising agencies still holds true as we enter the mid 1990s (see Schultz 1993). Schultz (1993) reports two problems many ad agencies perceive about direct marketing: it's a bit tacky and less profitable (for the ad agency) compared to placing image advertising on television.

Workable solutions to transforming advertising from image communicating to integrated marketing communications have to start in client firms – not with their advertising agencies. Advertising and marketing managers need to insist on creating relationship marketing strategies with customers (i.e. IMC programmes) because: (i) IMC programmes are more effective than image advertising; (ii) IMC programmes provide the hard evidence demanded by senior management as *to what extent* advertising and marketing cause sales; (iii) most advertising agencies will not do it unless they are forced to do it. The real problem is that many advertising and marketing managers lack the knowledge/ability (they do not know how to do it) and conviction (they do not really believe in it) needed to create IMC programmes; we return to this issue in the next section of the article.

The single-best, technical reading on true experiments in marketing continues to be Banks' 1965 book. Banks offers detailed numerical examples of simple true experiments,

The marketing mix

as well as sophisticated research designs to test cause-and-effect relationships. The book is out of print but well worth finding because it is readable and provides the technical training needed by advertising and marketing managers.

Stage 3: Continual monitoring and relationship-building

Two important features of relationship marketing are: (i) creating unique products/services for distinct groups of customers in a firm's customer database, and (ii) communicating the offer only to these distinct groups. For example, Cindy Lay used her personal computer to find 1400 Southern women who buy Anne Klein dresses only on sale. Evaluating their past purchases, she discovered that when they waited until the second markdown, they 'cost me an additional $75 per person.' So before the first markdown period ended, she spent $850 to notify these customers of a 'special sale' on the clothes they wanted. The two-day event increased volume on the dresses by 97 per cent in a normally slow period (Bulkeley 1993). Ms Lay is the director of market research for Proffitt's Inc., an Alcoa, Tennessee, department store chain that has recently created an IMC programme.

All firms in some industries have transformed themselves into relationship marketers by creating such IMC programmes: direct marketing, financial investment firms, for example, Fidelity Investments; credit card companies, for example American Express; airlines for customers in their frequent flyer programmes, for example Delta Airlines; direct marketing, clothing companies, for example, L. L. Bean; mail order seed companies, for example, Burpee. Some firms, and whole industries, have yet to start IMC programmes, for example, marketing departments in state and Canadian provincial governments; most banks; many department stores.

With an IMC programme, most marketers are able to keep and use a customer database of the complete buying history of each customer. Customer demographic and lifestyle information can often be included in such databases. Individual customer account databases frequently begin by including the following information:

- how many years the customer has been buying from the company;
- what items were purchased each year;
- how the customer responded to each marketing communication to reach this customer;
- customers' complaints and how the firm responded;
- the total dollar amount purchased by the customer per year;
- how frequently the customer buys each year.

The 'SALES' model developed by Pareto, a Cincinnati-based database marketing company, is an example of a database system to provide department store marketers with the capability to target customers having unique buying histories to receive marketing communications especially designed for them. The SALES model is based on five key indicators of customer activity and value. Sales data are processed through the SALES model and customer/department summary entries are created. For each unique relationship between a customer and a department in the store, a numeric indicator value is computed ('A Database...' 1991). The indicators are:

S Sales history (sales volume for this customer, in this particular department);
A Across departments (cross buying in other departments);
L Last purchase (last purchase in days in this department);
E Extent of the relationship (how long a customer);
S Shopping frequency (frequency of buying in this department).

Here is an example of using the SALES model. If a retailer decides to invite 1000 of its best customers to a special preview of the men's fall suit selections, customers can be selected by criteria based upon the entries in the SALES model for the menswear department. A typical selection criteria might include:

- select all customers:
  1 in the top 20 per cent for sales history in menswear (S);
  2 in the top quartile for buying across departments (A);
- in the top 20 per cent for last menswear purchase in days (L);

Table 3 Sales system womenswear

Name	Account Number	S	A	L	E	S
Joe Smith	1434528	8	2	7	3	7
Melanie Jones	1417076	4	1	4	9	3
Carrie Loftus	1381154	6	4	8	6	6

Note: The example above illustrates three partial database entries from the SALES system for a particular department. Melanie Jones has a 4 under the first S (Sales history) which indicates that she falls somewhere between the 40th and 49th percentile in 'sales history' (year to date spending in this department). The 1 under A indicates that she falls into the lowest of four equal sized groups in terms of 'tendency to buy across departments.' The 4 under L indicates that she falls somewhere between the 40th and 49th percentile in terms of 'days since the last purchase in this department.' She falls at or above the 90th percentile in terms of 'extent of relationship' with the womenswear department. And finally, the 3 under the second S indicates that she falls somewhere between the 30th and 39th percentile in terms of 'frequency of purchase' in this department.

- in the top 30 per cent for extent of relationship (E);
- in the top 40 per cent for menswear shopping frequency (S).

The first criterion (the first S requirement) selects the biggest spenders in the department for the year. If the count turns up less than 1000 customers, the criteria for an indicator may be revised, and the selection computer run made a second time. Table 3 is a summary of entries in the customer database in the SALES model.

The biggest problem in creating the customer database needed for relationship marketing is that firms' management information systems (MIS) are programmed only to meet the needs of the finance and accounting departments. For example, banks generally have customer account databases for each product: mortgages, car loans, savings and credit cards, savings accounts. The databases may even identify the same customer differently – without a middle-initial, for example, or last name first. Marketers want one customer database that includes all details of the firm's relationship with each customer.

The most workable solution to this problem is *not* in trying to transform a firm's existing MIS to a complete customer database; given the substantial decreases in costs of customer database software programmes and computer workstations, the faster and most workable solution is to create a customer database from scratch – by selecting from several high-quality, available, spreadsheet software programmes and using a workstation or personal computer with the necessary hard drive memory. A critical point related to this approach: now is the time for the marketer to develop finger-tip computer capability to mine her own customer database on her own personal computer.

For years, marketing gurus have been preaching the merits of 'mining' corporate databases. But the databases used for billings, deposit records and installment-plan payments usually have been inaccessible except to the programmers who maintain them. Marketers designing direct-mail campaigns have had to stand in line to ask programmers to search for particular types of customers. Now the marketing experts themselves (programmers not needed) can get at the data. High-end PCs with two-gigabyte hard drives – 20 times larger than the 100 megabyte drives most home users buy now – can hold several million customer names on hardware that costs about $10,000 now. The software to manage such data starts as low as $15,000.

(Bulkeley 1993)

Thus, given that the marketer is willing to invest some time, she (and he) is now able to personally have the technical capability and wisdom to create and handle a customer database to fulfil the two major benefits of direct marketing: (i) relationship marketing including forecasting net profit contributions of marketing tactics using customer response functions and financial data; and (ii) hard-evidence measuring of how much advertising and marketing influences sales. Before the 1990s, low cost approaches for high-quality relationship marketing (IMC) programmes were not widely available. The situation has finally changed. The best technical introduction to customer database management and relationship marketing is likely to be Clarke's (1993, 2nd edition) of *Marketing Analysis and Decision Making*. Reading Clarke (1993) provides the marketer with basic training and wisdom of handling databases to make better marketing decisions.

Stage 4: Continual monitoring/relationship-building with true experiments

Stage 4 is including true experiments (Stage 2) in relationship marketing programmes (Stage 3). Thus, Park Seed, a mail-order seed company, might test a special high-price bulb offer designed to be purchased by the firm's best customers (identified using a SALES-type software programme) by randomly assigning a randomly selected sample of best customer to two groups: one group receiving the special offer (treatment A) and the second group not receiving the special offer (treatment B). Note that two types of randomization are used: (i) random selection to achieve representativeness of the sample to the population of best customers, and (ii) random assignment to achieve equality between the two groups on all variables so that only the marketing offer (treatment A versus B) is available to explain any difference in sales response.

Quasi-experiments can also be performed in Stage 4 IMC programmes. Quasi-experiments are looking at changes in customer responses to the presence and absence of marketing offers through time, without equivalent test and control treatment groups. Quasi-experiments do not meet the two requirements of true experiments for testing cause-and-effect relationships, but examining database relationships between marketing actions and customer responses through time provides useful information, even when true experiments are not planned. Customer response models can be considered and tested to learn which models, if any, are useful for explaining customer responses among some groups of customers to particular marketing actions. The best, advanced, reading on quasi-experimentation is the book by Cook and Campbell (1979); reading Banks (1965) is helpful preparation for reading Cook and Campbell (1979).

Stage 5: Continual monitoring/relationship-building, true experiments with forecasting models of customer response functions

Stage 5 relationship marketing is what David Shepard (1990) means by the phrase, 'The *New Direct Marketing*'. In Stage 5, the marketer uses the customer database, develops and tests customer response functions, and does financial, payback ('what if') sensitivity analysis of different marketing strategies and tactics. For example, with useful customer response models developed from insight and tested using the database, a catalogue company might examine what if its business was built on the assumption of three catalogue mailings to customers per year instead of two? Instead of using a third catalogue mailing, what would be the net contribution to profit if the firm spent the available marketing funds on attracting new customers? A life time value analysis of new customer marketing can forecast useful answers to this question, based on the valid customer response functions. Shepard (1990) is a very useful introduction to Stage 5 relationship marketing.

Equation 1 is an illustration of a customer response model. In this model, unit sales for product X are influenced by four variables: price of the product, advertising, customer annual household income, and age of household head. The two marketing variables are advertising and price. The model was developed, and tested against other possible models from data in the firm's customer database.

Equation 1:

$$\text{unit sales} = 320\,[1 + ((1/250{,}000)(\text{advertising})^{1.5})((1/12)(\text{price})^{-0.9})] + (.065)(\text{income}) + (.86)(\text{age}).$$

This hypothetical model indicates that increasing advertising has a positive influence on unit sales; increasing price has a negative influence; increases in income has a positive effect; and increases in age have a positive effect. Unit sales forecasted from Equation 1 can be used with revenue and cost of goods sold equations to forecast net contribution for different prices and advertising combinations.

Equation 2: revenue = (unit sales) (price).
Equation 3: COGS = ($8.00) (unit sales).

If the firm wants to consider the impact on net contribution of four prices at each of three levels of advertising, then twelve (4 prices by 3 advertising) combinations of specific prices and advertising expenditures can be included in Equation 1 in a computer spreadsheet programme to forecast sales for each combination. Equations 2 and 3 can then be used to estimate the net contribution for each pricing–advertising mix.

Airlines, mail-order seed companies, credit card companies, and many firms in several industries are now using such customer response functions to provide specific forecasts of results of specific marketing actions.

Problems with direct marketing strategies and IMC programmes

Two major problems almost always occur in designing and implementing IMC programmes: (i) not planning and coordinating deeply, not enough even to accomplish Stage 1 direct marketing. This problem includes: (a) marketing team members refusing to contact new customers (i.e. not responding to inquiring prospects who reply to an advertising offer); (b) no follow-up to learn if prospects have received the information they requested and to prompt purchase; and (ii) the advertiser's and marketer's lack of knowledge, technical ability, in modelling customer/marketer information search and relationships in IMC programmes.

Not planning and coordinating deeply enough

Two independent studies confirm that about 20–40 per cent of customer requests for product/service information offers in direct response advertising go unanswered. The conclusion would be reasonable that some (more than a few) marketers refuse to fulfil customer requests for the information offered in the marketer's own advertising.

In one five-year study, Performark researchers, pretending to be potential customers, mailed in thousands of reader-response cards, the kind found in business and trade publications with offers of more information on goods and services. They responded to solicitations from hundreds of companies selling industrial products costing at least $5000.

> What happened? It took an average of 58 days for the requested pamphlets or brochures to arrive. Nearly one out of four inquiries went unanswered. Only one in eight generated a follow-up call by a sales representative, and those contacts came an average of 89 days after Performark's initial indication of interest.
>
> (Gibson 1993)

The President of Performark, Joseph Lethert, reports, 'The problem is sales and marketing aren't working together. No one has responsibility for making sure prospects are converted to customers.' Too often marketing people blame the sales force for not pursuing leads, while salespeople are loath to share information about their customers (Gibson 1993).

Similar findings are reported in a second study of business-to-business and consumer marketers responses to inquiries (Woodside *et al.* 1991). Acting as customers, inquiries were sent to 90 direct marketers (47 business and 43 consumer firms). After eight weeks, 25 per cent of the business marketers and 28 per cent of the consumer marketers had yet to respond in any manner. However, the proportion of responses did vary according to the media used to make the inquiry: overall, 80 per cent of the marketers responded to telephone inquiries; 80 per cent to direct mail inquiries, but only 60 per cent responded to reader-response inquiries. Follow-up calls after responding to the inquiries were made by only 34 per cent of the business marketers and 25 per cent of the consumer marketers.

Thus, besides many advertising agencies not supporting direct marketing and IMC programmes (see Schultz 1993) many advertising and marketing team members within firms with active IMC programmes fail to implement the programme and/or fail to design in IMC steps for effective relationship marketing. One specific example serves to illustrate the problem: in 1984 the sales manager of an office furniture distributor in Greenville, South Carolina, did *not* want area customers (recently buying furniture) interviewed for the company's customer newsletter (photographs of the customer executives using the product were always run with the news stories and the newsletter is direct response advertising for the company); the sales manager's reasoning was that too many persons in companies who would not be buying might call him and tie him up on the phone; this problem was not occurring in the other four company sales territories participating in the programme. The Greenville sales manager also reported, 'I know all customers in the Greenville-Spartanburg area and they know me, there's no reason for sending them a newsletter or advertising to them.'

Part of this first problem is not creating a database to store each marketing contact-attempt and customer response within each customer's file record. Unfortunately, most companies in Stage 1 direct marketing are probably *not* operating an online, customer database that includes marketing contacts (including second, follow-up contacts to learn if prospects received the information requested and whether or not they would like help in their buying decisions) and customer responses.

Part of the solution to this serious problem is creating and continual (daily) use of an online, customer/marketer computer database to help create and maintain relationships with new and established customers. Given the continuing lowering of software and data handling and storage costs, this solution is feasible in the 1990s. Given that relationship marketing includes knowing the customer by name and the nature/quality of your current contacts and responses with this customer, storing such information in the heads of a few persons and on paper is inadequate for designing active marketing strategies and building valid marketing response models. Monitoring the execution of planned marketing contacts with customers (including follow-up calls) and customer responses can occur systematically with an online customer/marketer database.

To make online entries and analysis of such databases, and to achieve widespread acceptance and enthusiasm for IMC programmes, requires senior executives (including the CEO) to be technically competent in personally handling the database, and in understanding customer response functions and what-if, sensitivity analyses of marketing moves. Thus, the time has come to put away the old solution to the problems on failing to deliver the literature offered and not following-up on inquiries by 'educating sales people on the importance of direct marketing'. The new solution is in leading by behavioural example from the CEO and other executives in contacting customers and in a hands-on ability to handle a computer based, customer/marketer database.

Lack of knowledge and skills for modelling customer/marketer IMC relationships

Up until the mid-1980s, creating and running an effective and efficient IMC programme (and achieving Stage 5) was very difficult to accomplish for three reasons. First, low-cost help was unavailable for managers to develop and test explicit, and useful, market response models for estimating how much marketing actions affect customer responses; there were no low-price computer software programmes and inexpensive personal computers. As discussed, this problem now has been eliminated.

Second, skill-building books and manuals have not been available widely for combining useful marketing response models and financial spreadsheet analysis into decision models (for forecasting net contribution impacts of alternative marketing actions). With the availability of skill-training books such as Clarke (1993) and Shepard (1990) this problem has now been eliminated. The unique moment of the mid-1990s is captured well by Clarke:

> Developments in the fields of statistics, mathematical marketing models, and marketing research have advanced by slow increments over the years to provide finally a meaningful, critical mass of useful knowledge. Parallel developments in computer technology, computer software, and commercially available software, which have advanced at a fantastically rapid rate, have converged to provide an analytical capability for marketing managers that could only have been dreamed of ten years ago. In terms of both power and accessibility, these developments have the potential to greatly expand the manager's knowledge of how the marketplace works, as well as to explode old myths and increase the manager's ability to exploit his or her knowledge.
>
> (Clarke 1993: 5)

This second problem includes not fully describing, understanding and modelling the search and choice processes involved in customer/marketer IMC programmes. For example, the substantial possibilities are usually not included in such models that customer requests for information offered in ads may *not* be fulfilled and customers may *not* receive or notice they have received the information requested and sent to them. This issue is discussed more fully in the next section.

Third, illusion of knowledge may be the last major obstacle for advertisers and marketing managers to overcome. All successful marketing managers have an intuitively insightful model (of customer responses) for making decisions and implementing actions. 'The result is that most marketing managers base their decisions on conceptual models of the marketplace that are part fact and part imagination. Like Christopher Columbus, who died believing that the island of Cuba was the east coast of Asia, the misconceptions of marketing managers will never be corrected by monitoring the same data in the same way as they have in the past' (Clarke 1993: 6). The goal is not to replace marketing imagination with database decision models but to combine them to achieve better decisions.

3 Modelling customer/marketer information search and relationships in integrative marketing communications

Effective IMC programmes require deep understanding, and database entries, of the multiple give-and-take responses between the customer and marketer. Figure 2 is an overview of two-way responses that may occur in using direct marketing for starting an IMC programme with customers. Figure 2 is intended to be a model of the sequence of steps that often occur in direct marketing and to emphasize the many possibilities for re-occurring communication breakdowns/failures. The model is intended to be relevant for both business and consumer marketing. The steps in the model and some research findings related to these steps are summarized in this section.

In Figure 2, this direct marketing model begins with asking whether or not the customer is exposed to an advertisement that includes a direct response offer. Prior media steps, such as vehicle distribution and customer exposure to the vehicle, are described in the Advertising Research Foundation's (ARF) model for evaluating media (see ARF 1961; Phelps 1993).

Mere exposure effects of advertising

Given that customer exposure to an advertisement containing a direct response occurs (box 1) the advertisement may have an influence even if the customer does not notice the ad (boxes 2 to 3). Thus, including box 3 in the model is to include the hypothesis supported by empirical evidence that mere exposure can influence attitude and purchase choices (see Krugman 1965; Zajonc 1968; Fazio *et al.* 1989; Petty *et al.* 1991). Thus, the sequence of moving through boxes 1–2–3–5–7–15 is to indicate the peripheral route to persuasion described by Petty and Cacioppo (1986) and the possible impact of perception without awareness (see Bornstein and Pittman 1992).

The central route to persuasion

The central route to persuasion described (ee Petty and Cacioppo 1986; Petty *et al.* 1991) applied to direct marketing is reflected in the customer noticing and being motivated to request the direct response offer (linking of boxes 4 and 6) or increases in customer awareness of the advertising affecting a favourable attitude toward the brand (linking of boxes 4 and 5).

TOMA$_a$ and TOMA$_b$ linkage: to Box 5 and beyond

Image advertising effects are accounted for in the model by linkage between boxes 4 and 5, as well as the mere exposure effect. TOMA$_a$ is the customer's top-of-mind-awareness for an ad in a product category. Shares of TOMA$_a$ for different brands in different product categories are reported in one issue each month in *Advertising Age* from monthly US household surveys sponsored by Gallup and *Advertising Age*. Unaided TOMA$_a$ by brand is measured by asking sample members, to name the advertising that first comes to mind from all they have seen, heard, or read in the previous 30 days. The hypotheses are supported empirically that: increasing TOMA$_a$ is associated with increasing TOMA$_b$, top-of-mind-awareness toward the brand; and TOMA$_b$ is associated positively with building preference (box 5) intentions (box 7) and sales (box 15); see Woodside and Wilson (1985).

The marketing mix

Figure 2 Model of customer-marketing initial communications and relationships
Source: Woodside 1994: 25.

The customer direct-response-route to persuasion

Rapp and Collins (1988) emphasize that advertisements can (should) 'do double-duty by inviting a [direct] response from 'your best prospects while increasing general awareness of your product or service.' Rapp and Collins (1988) then advocate that, 'Advertising a high-price, high-involvement product should focus first on getting a response from prime prospects rather than on creating an image. Then, convert that response to a sale by providing powerful linkage [the fulfilment literature].'

Actively noticing a direct response offer is a central route to persuasion that may lead to deciding to request the offer in the ad, for example, requesting a free catalogue or brochure offered in a television commercial, or magazine or newspaper ad (linking boxes 4 and 6). Note that in Figure 2 a delay is indicated between boxes 6 and 8: customers may decide to request the direct response offer but never get around to doing so. Advertisers sometimes attempt to reduce the delay by reducing the effort and time necessary for the customer to respond; such attempts include placing a telephone number in

476

the ad, sometimes toll-free, using free-standing-inserts (FSIs) and suggesting in a magazine ad that a number be circled on the reader-service card to respond. Systematic differences in buying behaviour vary according to the mode customers use to request information (see Manville 1987; Woodside and Soni 1988). For example, when advertising a high-involving service, vacation destination travel, the proportions buying the service (visiting the destination) varied from a low of .26 for reader-service card inquirers, to .36 for direct-response coupon inquirers, to .43 for toll-free telephone inquirers.

Marketers' responses to customer inquiries
According to the DMA, direct marketing is 'an interactive system'. Thus, two-way customer/marketer communications are planned for implementation. However, as described earlier, substantial numbers of marketers do not fulfil requests made by customers to offers included in the marketers' ads. Thus, the marketing activity of getting back to the customer (boxes 8 to 9 to 10) is not a given; it has to be built-in and actively monitored in the IMC programme. This first fulfilment step is often subcontracted out by the advertiser or the advertising agency to a 'fulfilment house.' Such a marketing strategy has the advantage of bringing in the expertise of fulfilment experts, but also increases the need for careful coordination and attention to customer requests.

Unfortunately, in most directing programmes, little attempt to gain information and to build a relationship (i.e. bonding) are designed into the initial linkage of customer-response and marketer-fulfilment. As a test of this proposition, make ten telephone calls in response to television commercials and magazine ads and record the number of questions asked by the person fulfilling your request beyond asking for your address. Also record persuasive attempts to encourage readership included in the fulfilment package. Also record whether or not the advertiser calls you back to learn if you received the fulfilment linkage and to ask for your order. The proposition is that most marketers are missing the opportunity to build relationships with new customers at the first moment-of-truth, even for high-price products and services.

Customer use of fulfilment materials
What happens after customers receive the fulfilment literature they request? Customers vary considerably in how they process fulfilment literature; some are not aware of receiving it; some do not report ever asking for it when later asked; and some do use the materials extensively for making buying decisions.

In a study, 45 per cent of inquirers, who were sent the literature they requested, did not report either asking for nor receiving the literature (see Woodside and Soni 1991). Thus, customers may not process (notice, look at, or read thoroughly) information they request and receive: reaching box 11 in Figure 2 is not a certainty; monitoring this step in the direct marketing process is necessary to insure customer usage of fulfilment literature. 'Great, creative advertising work that results in high inquiry rates is not good enough; the direct-response offer may have to be even better to get through the second level of clutter – all the competing advertising brochures and catalogues being received by the inquirer' (Woodside and Soni 1991).

Customer information processing of the fulfilment materials may often be helpful in convincing the customer to buy (box 13) and her/his purchase choices (box 15). Note that a delay is shown in Figure 2 between boxes 13 and 15 to indicate the effects of direct-marketing fulfilment on buying behaviour may be long-term and not immediately visible in one advertising campaign. Monitoring the impact of direct marketing on sales should include assessing the effects over several time periods beyond the immediate advertising-and-buying time frame. The term 'enhanced purchase consumption experience' is used in Box 17 to express the proposition that the customers' experiences in using the product or service are affected by processing the fulfilment literature before purchase versus not requesting, receiving or processing such literature.

In some industries, customers may refer to the fulfilment materials while using the product or service (box 18). For example, consumers buying seeds and plants using mail-order may refer to their catalogues for planting information and recipes for preparing vegetables grown; vacation travellers may refer to destination 'visitor guides' dying to learn about places to visit, things to do, and products to buy during their visit. In one tourism advertising study of visitors to Prince Edward Island in Canada (Woodside *et al.* 1993) total dollar purchases more than doubled among customers using fulfilment literature while on their visit compared to expenditures using the literature only before visiting Prince Edward Island (comparing sales results between box 17 and 18).

Limitations

For many customer–marketing interactions, the model summarized in Figure 2 is a simplification of the first stages in an IMC programme. Multiple two-way contacts may occur between the customer and marketer before the first purchase-sale. In the US office furniture industry for example, customer response to a direct mail or to a newspaper ad is often followed by several telephone conversations and four to seven personal sales calls and customer visits to the marketer's showrooms, all before the first purchase! The recent and long-term history of interactions with many established customers may be exist only in the long-term memories of one or two persons in the marketing firm, no computer database may yet be developed for such relationships in many firms.

However, some firms (including some office furniture marketers) and entire industries have accomplished IMC programmes with long-term customers that meet the DMA definition of direct marketing. Handling a database built on such long-term interactive systems, and estimating customer response functions to marketing actions in such systems, are more than a possibility. Such interactive systems and the use of decision models for sensitivity analysis is now more than the future promise of direct marketing. However, building and using computer databases for forecasting net contribution effects of marketing decisions is still time-consuming, not inexpensive, and requires management and science expertise. The good news is that the high-performing, low-price, computer software and hardware tools, and modelling skill-training, have become available in the 1990s.

4 Direct marketing implications for designing and implementing effective IMC programmes

In 1986 Stan Rapp predicted, 'When the light of a new day dawns on January 1, 1990, I believe that all service companies and many product manufacturers will be spending as much time and money maximizing their relationships with known customers as they now do on their brand-image advertising to the world at large' (Rapp and Collins 1990: 57). The review here of some of the empirical studies in direct marketing indicates that this prediction has not come to pass. However, substantial strides have been made in achieving the opportunities and benefits of direct marketing by some marketers.

The transformation from the illusion of knowledge into marketing wisdom is now occurring in many IMC programmes because of: (i) advances in computer software/hardware tools in creating and handling databases and (ii) marketers' use of customer response functions in decision models for 'what if' analyses. The model and empirical findings described here of the initial stages in customer–marketer, direct-marketing, interactions indicate that monitoring of each of multiple points-of-contact needs to occur for an IMC programme to be useful.

Transforming marketing away from image-advertising towards relationship marketing, that is, an effective, working IMC programme, requires technical computer software, skill-training by marketers, including the CEO and CMO (chief marketing officer). Those tools and skill-learning materials are now available. Creating and using decision models from such IMC programmes will enable marketers to justify their marketing strategies and tactics with hard evidence; senior management continues to demand nothing less. Recommendation: let each of us make the transformation before 2000.

Direct marketing: the Internet cometh

As recently as July 1997, President Clinton stated, 'In the 21st century, we can build much of our prosperity on innovation in cyber-space, in ways most of us cannot even imagine.' (*Brand Strategy* 1997) True to his words, the Internet is becoming an important channel of commerce and more quickly than most imagined. Witness the success of Dell computers, which has revenues of over $5 million a day or Amazon.com, the Internet bookseller with revenues of $203 million in the first six months this year. However, the Internet poses a challenge for most large established businesses. Faced with a new business paradigm of marketing and forced to challenge convention they stand to lose out to the new stars.

This section presents the opportunities offered by the Internet, followed by a discussion of the role of the Internet in the communications mix. Next, some challenges that the Internet faces and closing comments.

Opportunities on the Internet

Traditional marketing options, such as direct mail and telemarketing are becoming more expensive and less successful. The Internet offers an attractive alternative with important advantages.

A global audience
Almost overnight, the Internet audience has mushroomed into mass proportions (*Direct marketing* 1998). Last November, an Intelliquest survey estimated that the total US online audience had grown to 55–60 million users. Compare this to a Louis Harris/*Business Week* survey in spring 1997, which estimated that about 40 million Americans were online. Within eight months, the US Internet audience grew by nearly 50 per cent.

Even though the numbers indicate a market slowly approaching 'mass proportions', Internet users remain a demographically attractive group. Users are in prime spending years (median age 38); about half have children living at home; they are moderately upscale (median household income around $66,000); and well educated (50 per cent are college graduates). 40 per cent of the user base is female.

Paralleling the growth in numbers is a positive shift in attitudes. Find/SVP's 'American Internet User Survey' in 1997 demonstrated how the Internet is going mainstream: 28 per cent of users consider the Internet 'very indispensable', and another 45 per cent call it 'somewhat indispensable'.

Overseas, growth rates are even higher; although nearly two-thirds of the world's Internet users are in the US, high growth elsewhere (Western Europe, Japan, etc.) is slowly making the distribution more even. In the USA, almost two-thirds of Internet users access it from home. It is estimated that Internet usage could reach over 150 million by the year 2000.

Once giant multinationals with established brands were the only ones capable of reaching global consumers. Under the old model, a company sold its products locally and expanded gradually. A global company was synonymous with being huge. No longer! With the Internet constantly expanding its reach, the smallest start-up can aspire to a global market. Aussie Lures, a tiny business run from a garage in Sydney, sells fishing lures to customers across the globe via the Internet.

As mentioned above, Internet users are already demographically attractive. What's more, companies searching for an attractive audience are increasingly likely to strike gold as the number of consumers earning more than $10,000/year at purchasing power parity swells from 800 million today to almost 2.4 billion by 2025, aided by the growing economies in India, China and Indonesia (*McKinsey Quarterly* 1997).

The success of pioneers is also speeding up the development of the Internet as a sophisticated marketing medium. Last year was a breakthrough year for Internet commerce. In 1996, Internet commerce was in its infancy, comprising barely half a billion dollars in total sales. In 1997, sales jumped to a record $2.4 billion, an increase of nearly 400 per cent. This does not include business-to-business commerce, which also grew at a spectacular rate (*Direct Marketing* 1998).

The new dynamics of consumer relationships
The information rich medium of the Internet will reduce market imperfections on which intermediaries thrive. The near perfect market conditions and consequent low switching costs have set in motion a quiet revolution – a shift in power from vendors of goods and services to the customers who buy them. Companies who understand this transfer of power and choose to capitalize on it will be richly rewarded with both peerless consumer loyalty and impressive returns. To do this, companies have to learn to put the consumer in the driver's seat and treat the Internet as a personal medium.

First, the Internet allows companies to personalize interactions and empower their customers to get the information they seek. Dell Computers, for example, has nearly 40 country specific versions of its site, each using the appropriate currency and language. The site distinguishes between first time and repeat visitors and offers them the ability to design their own system. Once the system is designed, the potential customer may not actually buy it right away. Dell stores these profiles for up to two weeks, which provides an opportunity for potential customers to gather more information or shop around. Once an order is placed, customers can check its status online. Says Scott Eckert, Director of Dell Online, 'What is good for the customers is good for us. A year ago we received 1 web visit for every phone call. Today, we're getting more than 3.5 visits for every phone call. Even when web customers call to close a sale, they are a lot closer to a purchase decision by the time they get to the phone. That's the Holy Grail of this business.' (quoted in *Fast Company* 1998).

On Time Warner's Pathfinder site, which contains over 25 of the company's publications, customers can register themselves and select their preferences. When they return, the site provides a customized view of the content. A personalized version of *TIME* magazine is now available online to subscribers in Australia, for example. It costs only a few cents and is delivered instantaneously; back in 1987 it cost $5 and took 4 days. (*McKinsey Quarterly* 1997).

Second, companies can offer new and narrowly targeted products and services very easily. Consumers have rarely seen the value for providing personal information. As companies offer personalized service and consumers see immediate value, companies will have access to better quality and timeliness of information. This data can be mined inexpensively to target customers more precisely and to pursue small groups and even individuals profitably. Customer transaction data obtained on the web can be supplemented by third party lifestyle data for better results.

Consider the case of Prudential Securities, which has an extensive website that allows customers to check account balances, manage their portfolio and e-mail their adviser. This clearly promotes loyalty among its customers and erects a formidable barrier for competitors. Meanwhile, the extensive use of its website allows it to gather detailed information about its customers and use that information to manage one-to-one relationships. It can help better serve the most profitable customers and move others to premium products.

At Amazon.com, providing information will prompt suggestions of book titles. Over time, as I buy more books and provide more information, the suggestions get more relevant for me, but also provide more valuable information for the company. It's a win–win situation! Best of all consumer information is available real-time when it is often of greatest significance. Let's say a potential customer configures a PC system at Dell's site but does not buy. This provides a real-time indication that can promptly be met with a discount.

Not all Internet marketing involves consumer 'pull' and visits to appealing, customized websites. Marketers can also use e-mail 'push' to supplement an online presence. Though not as glamorous as a website, customized e-mail can go a long way towards building relationships. It means guaranteed distribution and can provide enough information for potential customers to determine whether to visit a website. Often the best way is to let visitors to your website sign-up to receive it and have the ability to get off the mailing list.

Third, the Internet offers new ways to providing customers with added value. American Airlines offers last minute Internet auctions of its seats which not only increases its own load balancing factor but provides incredible value to customers with a flexible schedule.

Smart companies recognize that like any other communications network, the Internet is all about establishing and reinforcing connections between people. The rise of online communities is a great example. Witness the developing online community of book-lovers at Amazon.com. When you go to select a book, you can read the reviews of peers who have already read the book. Who would you rather go with – the experience of real managers like yourself or the publisher's words on the cover? Buy a book on advertising, for example, and you can see what people who shared your interests also bought. Suddenly, consumers directly benefit from the value their demographic histories and transaction histories represent. They can take control of their own value as potential purchasers of goods and services.

What sells! Convenience is key
Convenience is the biggest reason, people shop online, which makes it perfect for certain kinds of products. Fragmented markets, where

Direct marketing

```
                                          Insurance/Financial Services
                                          Computer Software/Hardware
                                          Travel
High                                      Books
                                          Magazines
                                          Music/Video

                                Flowers/gifts

                                Automobiles

Selection and
information is
key


Low                Home furnishings


           Cigars


    Low         Internet Business Opportunity         High
```

Figure 3 Immediate opportunities on the Internet

selection, information and convenience are critical lend themselves especially well to online purchase. Insurance, financial services, travel, books are therefore some of the most successful online efforts thus far. Interestingly, prices are not the reason to shop on the Internet. In a recent article in *Business Week*, authors Ira Sager and Heather Green point out that with very few exceptions (like books and CDs) few retailers are price focused. 'What really locks the consumer in' says Steve Johnson, a co-director of Andersen Consulting's electronic-commerce practice is the convenience and the satisfaction of knowing the price is in the ballpark.'

Direct marketers should ask the question – How can the information I gather about customers make it easier for them to do business with me? What help can I give customers by providing them the experience of other customers?

The Internet offers the potential for dramatic cost savings

In the case of credit cards, for example, marketing costs have grown 46 per cent since 1992, representing approximately 30 per cent of issuer's operating expense today. In acquiring new cardholders, savings over direct mail can range from $12.50 to $97 per approved application. (Depending on mail volume, processing costs, credit bureau unit costs and response rates). Savings over Telemarketing can range from $2.50 to $77 (depending on response rates, staff, processing and credit bureau unit costs) (*Strategy & Business* 1997). In addition to reaching an attractive audience, the Internet can improve application processing through greater efficiency. Internet-processed applications save data entry costs and are more likely to be error free, because applicants enter their own data and applications are not entered until complete.

In catalogue or direct mail marketing, printing hundreds, thousands or even millions of custom catalogues, personalized using database information, like transaction or demographic data, would be prohibitively expensive. The Internet, through customized websites can easily exploit the capabilities of database marketing.

Making the Internet work: an integrated approach

The Internet is not yet a true brand-building medium, lacking the emotive appeal and imagery of TV. However, it is terrific at providing detailed information about brands recognize already from other media, the way Ford Motor does with its automobiles, or for selling things directly, as Amazon.com does with books.

Let's say you are in the market for a car. Now every company has a website, but which company's site has the ability to convert your need for a car into the desire for a certain car?

The Ford site for instance, has a feature that allows you to come up with an affordable

The marketing mix

Table 4 The role of the Internet (personalize the information and the transaction)

	Getting attention	More informaion	Making the transaction
Objective	Branding	Information	The sale
Tactics	TV advertising Print	Internet Brochures Sales people	Internet Store Telephone

monthly lease amount based on income and expenses. This could be very helpful to know as you shop around. Based on other options you may select, it can help you decide on a model and could allow you to custom configure it. You may then be able to print out an invoice and take it to the dealer nearest you. Another site may do it based on lifestyle. Are you a single guy and prefer a sports car versus.a sedan, then perhaps a Dodge Viper might be the choice you are offered.

In the case of Prudential Securities mentioned before, it has an extensive website that allows customers to check their account balances and manage their portfolio. Prudential will obviously continue their use of mass media to manage the Prudential brand. This combination of traditional media with the web is what works best. Use traditional media for exposure, and the web for managing relationships and results.

Getting customers to the Internet
Having realized the role of the Internet in providing information and closing the transaction, the next question is how do you get your target audience to your website.

First, you can mention in it all your traditional communications from TV and print to mailings, promotional materials etc. This is the case for Fidelity Investments where it places its URL (Internet address) on every marketing communication in every medium. It is obviously simple to do with very little incremental cost.

Secondly, the Internet allows for creating links to your site from other sites, often without any cost. The more popular your site is, the more likely that other sites have created links to it. The drawback of course is that you are not in control of where these links exist and they may do more harm than good. An interesting case is Amazon.com, the Internet bookseller that has introduced an Internet version of digital franchising to attract users to its site. Amazon.com selects sites with content that may match book selections on Amazon.com and create custom links from it to Amazon.com, based on the subject of the content on that site. Every time, someone referred from those sites makes a purchase, the referring site gets a percentage of the sale. For example, on the movie site, imdb.com, most searches for movies also create a link to Amazon.com for buying a book on the movie where available. If the offer is accepted and a sale made, imdb.com collects a small percentage.

Finally, there is the option to buy 'banner' ads (strips of advertising) on the most popular sites to entice users to click and get transferred to your site. After the initial novelty, the 'click-through' rate (percentage of users who are exposed to the ad and actually click on it to get to your site) has universally gone down from around 4 per cent to 1 per cent (*Business Week* 1998). There are challenges of non-standardized measures across sites and services that place these banners as well as limited capability of what these banners can do. At best, these are a minimal increment to other efforts to boost visits to your site.

It is not just the case of brands that exist in the real world that are making the transition to the Internet. Even brands that exist only on the Internet, from AOL to Yahoo! have learned the value of using other media effectively. On the increasingly cluttered Internet the only way to succeed is through an integrated communications programme that maximizes the value of each part of the mix.

Challenges and moving forward

Though the Internet has undeniably great potential, there are several challenges that have yet to be overcome.

Privacy and the control of virtual Information
The greater the reach of online environments, the more robust the information capture

technology platform, and the broader the scope of information capture by individual companies, the more privacy is likely to rise as a significant issue.

In dealing with concern over privacy, it is important to remember a key distinction. When consumers are asked about concerns over privacy, they invariably express a high degree of concern. However, when the question is reframed to test willingness to accept something of value in return for access to detailed information, respondents seem to become much more favourable to providing that information. What seems to upset consumers most is when the information is captured without their knowledge and when they appear to receive nothing in return for that information.

Now marketers are taking notice. As mentioned before, some of the best sites encourage users to provide information in a manner that treats them at a peer-to-peer level and provides immediate value; more specific offerings and individualized service.

However, how this will play out over the longer term is still uncertain. Who will control online information? Aside from the current scenario where any one company has only a fragmented view of the consumer, two likely scenarios emerge; the consumer as the keeper of his or her information or the emergence of a new kind of intermediary, one who owns customer profiles on behalf of the customer.

Consumers could store information on their own PCs releasing it to vendors when desired. In the case of the information intermediaries, success will depend on their ability to build strong bonds of trust with customers whose information they protect. While trust has always been important in business, it will become even more so in the online world with its expanding choices and declining switching barriers. Strong brands will be crucial to developing emotional bonds that engender high levels of trust. Only firms that have substantial brand equity; whom customers view as reliable and trustworthy will be provided with sensitive financial information.

Internet as a communications medium
The Internet is still to mature as a medium for communications and questions exist as to its eventual role *vis-à-vis* traditional media.

As recounted earlier, the prevalent 'banner' advertising on the Internet needs to change to perhaps more persuasive advertising formats. Can these advertisements or other online vehicles ever achieve the emotional resonance of a little boy in a Crest TV commercial bounding up to say 'Look Ma!, No cavities!'. It never may, but given the current dissatisfaction over their effectiveness, there are certain to be changes in size, function of these banner advertisements, etc., as technology and our understanding of this medium expand.

Perhaps within the next few years, the blending of conventional TV, the computer and easily available bandwidth (much faster than slow modems that most people use today) will create a new rich interactive medium and bring the image building and branding objective online.

There will also be better systems for measuring advertising effectiveness and online audiences. Traditionally, advertisers compare the cost of buying print pages and broadcast time based on the amount of money it takes to reach a thousand consumers (CPM). A typical network show might have a CPM of $5, while a typical newspaper or magazine may have a CPM of $40–60 since they provide a smaller but more targeted geographic or demographic segment. In the early days, websites arbitrarily charged $75–100 CPM on the theory that a website can provide an even more targeted audience. However lacking complete knowledge of whether they were indeed attracting the right audience, advertisers were reluctant to pay up and these rates kept falling and few sites get these rates today. The Internet is not about impressions but about time spent. While interruptions were the basis of the traditional model (programmes interspersed or 'interrupted' by commercials) interactions will be the basis for the new model on the Internet.

At a recently concluded Procter & Gamble organized Fast Summit (Future for Advertising Stakeholders Summit) four industry groups, advertisers, online media sellers, ad agencies and researchers agreed to work together to draft standards for measuring online audiences as well as advertising types before the end of the year. Also on the agenda, was the development of a way to reconcile contradictory data provided by various online services and develop the web as a true advertising medium (*Wall Street Journal* 1998).

The Internet has the potential to revolutionize global commerce at a scale never witnessed before. At the same time it poses interesting challenges. Understandably, risk results from the uncertainty concerning how Internet-based business models will arise over time, where value creation will concentrate, and what technologies will emerge that will enhance and/or transform commercial activity on the Internet. In the near future, the most successful marketers will be those who follow leveraged strategies, incorporating the Internet as an integral part of their mix and use a medium like TV for imagery and branding and creating the need and Internet to fulfil it.

ARCH G. WOODSIDE
TULANE UNIVERSITY, NEW ORLEANS
RAHUL ROSHA
DMB&B, NEW YORK CITY

Further reading

(References cited in the text marked *)

'A Database Designed Especially for Department Stores' (1991)' *Colloquy*, October: 12–13.
* ARF (1961) *Toward Better Media Comparisons*, New York: Advertising Research Foundation.
* Banks, Seymour (1965) *Experimentation in Marketing*, New York: McGraw-Hill.
Beatty, Sally (1998) 'P&G, Rivals & Agencies…', *The Wall Street Journal* 24 August: B2
* Bornstein, Robert F., and Pittman, Thane S. (eds) (1992) *Perception Without Awareness*, New York: Guilford Press.
Branigan, Lynn (1998) 'The Internet: the emerging premier direct marketing channel', *Direct Marketing Magazine* 46.
* Bulkeley, William M. (1993) 'Marketers mine their corporate databases,' *The Wall Street Journal* 14 June; B6.
Butler, Patrick, Hall, Ted W. *et al.* (1997) 'A revolution in interaction', *McKinsey Quarterly*, 5.
* Caples, John (1974) *Tested Advertising Methods*, Englewood Cliffs, NJ: Prentice-Hall.
Chadderdon, Lisa (1998) 'How Dell sells on the web', *Fast Company Magazine* 58.
* Clarke, Darral G. (1993) *Marketing Analysis and Decision Making*, South San Francisco, CA: The Scientific Press.
* *Colloquy* (1991) 'Calling All Tennessee Squires,' *Colloquy*, Milford, OH: Frequency Marketing, Inc., October, 3. (*Colloquy* is a free quarterly newsletter published by Frequency Marketing Inc., P. O. Box 3920, Milford, Ohio 45150; fax: 513-248-9084.)
* Cook, Thomas D., and Campbell, Donald T. (1979) *Quasi-Experimentation*, Chicago: Rand McNally.
* *Direct Marketing* (1993) 'Direct marketing…an aspect of total marketing,' *Direct Marketing Magazine* April: 2.
* Dubinsky, Alan J., and Ingram, Thomas N. (1984) 'A portfolio approach to account profitability,' *Industrial Marketing Management* 13: 57–62.
* Dwyer, Robert F. (1980) 'Customer lifetime valuations to support marketing decision making,' *Journal of Direct Marketing* 3: 8–15.
* Fazio, R. H., Powell, M. C. and Williams, C. J. (1989) 'The role of attitude accessibility in the attitude-to-behavior process,' *Journal of Consumer Research* 16: 280–8.
Gibson, Richard (1993) 'Poor handling turns leads into no-sales,' *The Wall Street Journal* 31 March: B1.
Hansell, Saul (1998) 'The media business: advertising – selling…', *The New York Times* 24 August: 1.
Howe, David E. and Ranasinghe, Samal P. (1997) 'Credit cards on the Internet', *Strategy & Business* Fourth Quarter
IAC (1997) 'The rise of cyberbrands – are they the future of marketing?', *Brand Strategy*.
* Krugman, Herbert (1965) 'The impact of television advertising: learning without involvement,' *Public Opinion Quarterly* 29: 349–56.
* Levitt, Theodore (1983) *The Marketing Imagination*, New York: Free Press.
* Manville, Richard (1987) 'Does advertising–or product 'publicity'–pull more inquiries? which ones are more valuable?' *BPAA Communicator*, New York: Business and Professional Advertising Association.
* Peters, Tom, and Austin, Nancy (1985) *A Passion for Excellence*, New York: Warner Books.
* Petty, Richard E., and Cacioppo, J. T. (1986) *Communication and Persuasion: Central and Peripheral Routes to Attitude Change*, New York: Springer/Verlag.
* Petty, Richard E., Unnava, Rao and Strathman, Alan J. (1991) 'Theories of Attitude Change,' in Robertson, Thomas S. and Kassarjian, Harold H. (eds), *Handbook of Consumer Behavior*, Englewood Cliffs, NJ: Prentice-Hall, 241–80.
* Phelps, Stephen P. (1993) 'A media evaluation model for the 21st century,' in Esther Thorson (ed.), *Proceedings of the 1993 Conference of the American Academy of Advertising*, Columbia, MO: School of Journalism, University of Missouri-Columbia, 60–72.
* Rapp, Stan, and Collins, Tom (1988) *Maximarketing*, New York: McGraw-Hill.
* Rapp, Stan, and Collins, Tom (1990) 'Special report: the great marketing turnaround,' *Direct Marketing Magazine* October: 57–60.

* Roman, Ernan (1988) *Integrated Direct Marketing*, New York: McGraw-Hill.

Sager, Ira and Green, Heather (1998) 'Cyberprices: So where are all the bargains ...', *Business Week* June: 162.

* Schultz, Don E. (1993) 'Why ad agencies are having so much trouble with IMC,' *Marketing News* 26 April: 12.

* Schultz, Don E., Tannenbaum, Stanley I. and Lauterborn, Robert E. (1993) *Integrated Marketing Communications*, Chicago: NTC Business Books.

* Shepard, David (1990) *The New Direct Marketing*, Homewood, IL: Business One Irwin.

Weidlich, Thom (1998) 'Casting the net', *Direct Magazine* August; 1.

* 'Trend Setters' (1992) *Direct Marketing Magazine* November: 41.

* Woodside, Arch G., and Ronkainen, Ilkka A. (1994) 'Improving conversion research studies,' in Brent Ritchie ,J. R. and Goeldner,Charles R. (eds) *Travel, Tourism, and Hospitality Research*, 2nd edn, New York: Wiley, forthcoming.

* Woodside, Arch G., and Soni, Praveen K. (1988) 'Assessing the quality of advertising inquiries by mode of response,' *Journal of Advertising Research* 28: 31–7.

* Woodside, Arch G., and Soni, Praveen K. (1990) 'Performance analysis of advertising in competing media vehicles,' *Journal of Advertising Research* 30: 53–66.

* Woodside, Arch G., and Soni, Praveen K. (1991) 'Direct-response advertising information: profiling heavy, light, and nonusers,' *Journal of Advertising Research* 31: 26–36.

* Woodside, Arch G., and Wilson, Elizabeth J. (1985) 'Effects of consumer awareness of brand advertising on preference,' *Journal of Advertising Research* 25: 41–8.

Woodside, Arch G., Brose, Frederick C. and Trappey, Randolph J., III (1991) 'Assessing performance of business-to-business and consumer direct marketing fulfillment strategies,' working paper, New Orleans: Freeman School of Business, Tulane University.

Woodside, Arch G., MacDonald, Roberta and Trappey, Randolph J., III (1993) 'Effects of knowledge and experience on purchasing behavior and consumption experiences', Working Paper, New Orleans: Freeman School of Business, Tulane University.

Marketing communications

1. What is 'marketing communications'?
2. What is known about how marketing communication works?
3. Planning the marketing communications campaign
4. Deploying the marketing communications mix
5. Delegating campaign management

Overview

Marketing communication is often seen to be synonymous with promotion. However, promotion itself is a complex entity and the right mix of elements is required for a marketing communications plan to achieve its objectives successfully. Seven activities are proposed as the main ingredients: advertising; publicity; packaging; personal selling; direct marketing; sponsorship; and sales promotion. The effectiveness of the marketing communications mix must be assessed, and the AIDA model is considered.

The entry goes on to suggest a framework for constructing a marketing communications plan, breaking the process down into six areas: raw materials; constraints; objectives; strategy; timetable ; and implementation. Whether and how these areas might be delegated within or without the organization is considered. Delegation may involve a loss of control, and the importance is stressed of the right brief being drawn up at the outset.

1 What is 'marketing communications'?

The familiar 'Four Ps' mnemonic reminds us that products (or services) need to be made available in the right place, offered at the right price and backed by the right kind of promotion, if they are to be successful in today's crowded and noisy marketplace.

Here, we are concerned with the last of those four variables in the marketing equation, for 'promotion' and 'marketing communications' are in practice virtually interchangeable terms.

The task of promoting a product or service is essentially a matter of selecting, deploying and controlling a marketing communications mix within the broader framework set by the marketing mix (see THE MARKETING MIX). Since experts disagree about the number of ingredients it contains and how those should be defined, the working definitions which follow have been formulated specifically to emphasize both the close family similarities and the strategically important differences among seven varieties of marketing communication activity.

1. *Advertising* communicates via a recognizable advertisement placed in a definable advertising medium, guaranteeing exposure to a target audience in return for a published rate for the time or space used (see ADVERTISING).
2. *Publicity* communicates via a news release to definable news media in the hope of secondary exposure to a target audience through an editorial mention earned by the newsworthiness of the subject matter.
3. *Packaging* communicates via display, guaranteeing exposure to a potential customer at the point of sale but not normally to a wider target audience (see PACKAGING AND DESIGN).
4. *Personal selling* communicates person to person via a sales pitch by a sales representative to a prospect, or by a sales assistant to a customer, guaranteeing exposure to a selected individual within a target market (see PERSONAL SELLING AND SALES MANAGEMENT).
5. *Direct marketing* communicates person to person but through an intervening channel, such as the post (a mailshot or mailing), door-to-door delivery (a mail drop), the telephone (telemarketing) or a fax line (no specific description yet), guaranteeing exposure to a selected individual within a target market. For many years, the only form of direct marketing in use was direct mail (see DIRECT MARKETING).
6. *Sponsorship* communicates via explicit association of a product or service with an entity, event or activity, in the expectation of secondary exposure to a target audience

through identification during associated media coverage.
7. *Sales promotion* communicates via a variety of promotions not encompassed by any of the definitions above, each aiming for exposure to a target audience and some furthermore offering an incentive to respond actively (see SALES PROMOTION).

Several of these activities may be prefixed by the description direct-response if reply facilities are incorporated, to collect data for mailing-list building or to win an order immediately (see INFORMATION TECHNOLOGY AND MARKETING). The term 'mail order' may be used to describe initiatives with the second of those two objectives. Typical examples of direct-response marketing communications are advertisements specifying free-call or local-charge telephone numbers, or mailshots including pre-paid reply coupons, but there are many other possibilities.

Two of our seven working definitions are subject to a certain amount of misuse in practice. Sales promotion initiatives are often described loosely as 'promotions', inviting confusion with other elements of the broader 'promotion' within the Four Ps. Publicity can be used to describe what is actually advertising, though there is a fundamental and obvious strategic difference between the two. Unfortunately, in three major languages, the word for advertising is in fact a version of 'publicity'. It is therefore wise to make sure that vocabulary is being accurately used if a key decision is going to be made.

Some readers may be surprised not to find *public relations* in this version of the marketing communications mix. It is deliberately excluded because it is an expression of corporate strategy rather than marketing strategy and hence belongs outside the marketing discipline, let alone within marketing communications. Indeed, it is itself a prolific user of three ingredients of the latter mix: advertising, publicity and sponsorship.

Likewise, younger readers will be equally surprised to find no reference to the Internet or the World Wide Web. The reason is that these 'new media' have not yet quite come of age. It is unhelpful to think of them as a radically new addition to the existing marketing communications mix, but rather as modern varieties of *advertising* and *direct marketing*, which employ different delivery channels. Internet messages and banners or pages on the World Wide Web are undoubtedly a potentially powerful business-to-business marketing communications medium already. The *Financial Times* reported that almost 30 per cent of British businesses were connected to the net in 1996, and that all but 5 per cent of the laggards were expected to have joined them within a year. The potential for effective cyber-communication with consumer audiences will take longer to develop. BMRB, a prominent British market research organization, estimated that the net had achived a 'household penetration' of only 2 per cent in Britain in 1995. That translates to no more than 400,000 home computers hooked up. Its survey further showed that almost two-thirds of current Internet users were under thirty-five, exactly a third between twenty-five and thirty-four. Campaign reported that 95 per cent were male. As for the World Wide Web, research figures from the Georgia Institute of Technology in the USA show that it is predominantly an American phenomenon, and that the British are Europe's heaviest users, probably because the dominance of the English language is no obstacle for them. Making a few reasonable assumptions, one can extrapolate their data to produce an estimate of no more than 220,000 households in the UK paying periodic visits to websites. These facts point to the conclusion that, despite its undoubted eventual potential, 'new media' are not *yet* a mass-market rival to any of the established major media.

2 What is known about how marketing communication works?

The seven definitions above all beg the crucial question how the activities described actually 'communicate' with the target audiences, and the answer is by no means straightforward.

Practitioners around the world are liable to respond with one member or another of a family of hierarchical models of marketing communications effect. The progenitor first appeared in an American textbook on the psychology of selling published in 1925. It has since been widely adopted as an explanation of advertising effect, and can just as logically be applied to the other elements of the marketing communications mix. It is the famous 'AIDA', a mnemonic to remind us that sales pitches, advertisements and the rest are forces that can move a target audience sequentially through states of Awareness, Interest and Desire to eventual Action. Successors, the best known of which are DAGMAR and the Hierarchy of Effects, both published in 1961, increased the number of steps and used different labels to describe them but did not increase the sophistication of the original in any other way. The problem is that such so-called 'models' provide an intuitively reasonable explanation of what may happen in certain stereotypical situations, but no explanation at all of how or why it does. Though their conceptual shortcomings were eloquently summed up by an influential academic critic more than thirty years ago, they are as frequently encountered today as they were then.

Fairly thorough discussions of this unduly influential paradigm and some theoretically superior alternatives have been published by Crosier (1998a) and McDonald (1992) but no single text can be recommended as a complete synopsis of current thinking. Notably absent from typical marketing textbooks is any serious analysis of the contribution that might be made by information processing theory or by the discipline of semiotics, which approaches the subject from the direction of the audience's decoding rather than the originator's encoding. Readers wishing to discover the state of the art with respect to the mechanism of persuasive marketing communication will need to consult the collection of papers on a 'How Advertising Works Project' published by the American Advertising Research Foundation (1991) and screen recent issues of the American *Journal of Advertising Research* and the British *Admap* and *International Journal of Advertising*. Despite strong traditions of relevant empirical research in France and the Netherlands, no correspondingly influential journals seem to exist in either language. Little has been written on the subject in the context of marketing communications mix elements other than advertising.

A crucial but concealed drawback of the popular hierarchical model is the powerful influence it exerts in practice on the way campaign effectiveness is assessed. In an ideal world, this process would consist of comparing results recorded by appropriate measures of performance with specific criteria derived from explicit objectives. However, only in the obviously special case of direct-response initiatives is the process generally so controlled. Otherwise, inspection of case histories shows that both objectives and measures are very often based on the unsatisfactory hierarchical model in one guise or another, though seldom overtly. This point is elaborated in Crosier (1998b).

Four surrogate criteria are especially common: awareness, recall, attitude and sales. Ready-to-use measures are widely available in each case. Established tests of unprompted and prompted awareness are used to demonstrate that attention has been gained, sometimes offered as evidence that the campaign was 'effective' regardless of other, unstated objectives it may have been meant to achieve. Likewise, equally common measures of recall may be used to test for a somewhat higher-level response, on the grounds that memory indicates a degree of interest in the proposition. A variety of tried and tested attitude scales borrowed from psychology are used to measure desire to engage more actively with the communicator in some way, on the grounds that one common definition of attitude is a 'predisposition to act'. Lastly, measurement of *posthoc* sales movements correspond to the highest level hierarchical response, action or the lack of it. Of course, it may in truth be virtually impossible to separate the effect of communications initiatives from many other controllable and uncontrollable variables in the cause–effect equation, and there may be a considerable time lag in practice before lower level responses are converted to action, but the assertion is regularly heard that this particular surrogate variable is the only 'real' test of effectiveness.

While it is perfectly logical that a model of effect should be used as the basis for measurement of effectiveness, the point is that AIDA and its derivatives are inadequate for the purpose. Readers interested in pursuing this vital issue further could begin with the comprehensive review of European and American empirical research by Franzen (1994).

3 Planning the marketing communications campaign

Given the degree of uncertainty about effect and effectiveness just noted, it is obviously

Marketing communications

Table 1 The format of a marketing communications plan

1 RAW MATERIALS
What are we offering to whom?

1.1 Product or service profile

Specification:	what can it do?
Benefits:	what can it offer?

1.2 Company or organization profile

Specification:	what do we do?
Identity:	how do we present ourselves?
Image:	how are we seen?

1.3 Audience Profile

Socio-demographics:	– who are they, and where?
Psychographics:	who do they want to be?

1.4 Market profile

Structure:	what does it look like?
Competition:	who is there with us?
Dynamics:	what's coming?

2 CONSTRAINTS
What is beyond our control?

2.1 Marketing mix

Product policy:	what effect on advertising strategy?
Pricing policy:	what effect on advertising strategy?
'Place' policy:	what effect on advertising strategy?

2.2 Givens

Precedents:	what is traditional?
Mandatories:	what is compulsory?

2.3 Budget

Appropriation:	what funds are available?
Allocations:	how and where are they to be spent?
Control:	how will cost-effectiveness be monitored?

3 OBJECTIVES
What do we need to achieve?

3.1 *Goals*	what are our overall, long-term aims?
3.2 *Targets*	what are the intermediate aims of this plan?
3.3 *Criteria*	how will communication effectiveness be measured?

4 STRATEGY
How will we achieve our objectives?

4.1 *Communication*:	what do we want to say?
4.2 *Creative*:	how do we want to say it?
4.3 *Media*:	how will we deliver the message to the audience?

5 TIMETABLE
How will our strategy become a campaign?

5.1 *Timescale*:	how soon must the objectives be met?
5.2 *Schedule*:	what needs to happen when?

6 IMPLEMENTATION
How will the campaign be managed?

6.1 *Authority*:	who can say yes or no?
6.2 *Responsibility*:	who will co-ordinate it?
6.3 *Delegation*:	what will be sub-contracted?
6.4 *Procedures*:	how will we keep track of progress?
6.5 *Evaluation*:	how will we measure results?

---

essential that practitioners plan their actions methodically, at the very least.

The outcome, a formal marketing communications plan, is a document for the guidance of those charged with the responsibility for converting general objectives into an operational campaign. Whether the recipient is an in-house specialist or one of the many intermediaries specializing in a particular ingredient of the marketing communications mix, it is important to notice that the purpose is to provide guidance about implementation by explaining the predetermined broad strategic framework, not to present a ready-made prescription. Accordingly, the template shown in Table 1 provides for transmission of the essential background information needed for that second-phase decision making (see DEVELOPING AND IMPLEMENTING A MARKETING PLAN; MARKETING STRATEGY; THE MARKETING AUDIT).

Context

With reference to Table 1, it is vital that the profile of the product or service in section 1 specifies the benefits that can be delivered to potential customers. Narrow-minded concentration on the technical specifications of the offering runs counter to the very principle of marketing orientation, but happens all too often in practice. Likewise, the description of the target audience needs to provide a 'psychographic' profile, if it is to realize its full potential as a key factor in the development of the communication strategy. It should explain what is known about the audience's lifestyles, aspirations, reference group affiliations and so on. An example of such psychographic profiling in practical use, in Britain, is the commercially available ACORN Lifestyles system for segmenting target markets.

When considering the marketing mix, the strategically crucial fact that all four of the Four Ps have the potential to transmit messages about the organization and its offering, not just the one labelled 'promotion', should always be kept in mind. The practical issue raised concerning imperatives is that the execution of a marketing communications plan can in practice be constrained by precedents set in previous campaigns and by non-negotiable requirements set at a higher level in the organization.

Objectives

Part 2 of the plan is perhaps even more crucial. In practice, objectives are all too often so vague as to be quite unhelpful for the development of a marketing communications strategy. This problem is discussed in Crosier (1998c), where guidelines for the formulation of usable objectives are offered. While it is self-evidently useful to set goals and targets, such potential performance indicators too frequently remain implicit in practice and the process of measurement becomes, as we have already seen, a questionable process of 'testing' effectiveness by reference to surrogate criteria.

Budget

Without a clear answer to the question posed about the 'appropriation' available, the rest of the plan will become somewhat academic. Many textbooks cite a potentially bewildering variety of procedures for deciding how much should be spent on advertising, the general principles of which can be transferred to other elements of the marketing mix. The fact is, however, that most are fairly unsophisticated and suffer from critical weaknesses if applied on their own. Research surveys have repeatedly shown over the years that marketing managers typically rely on one method, or two at most, and that the least sophisticated options dominate practice. Space does not permit further elaboration here, but interested readers can find a full account in two textbooks by the internationally acknowledged expert on the subject, one written for American practitioners (Broadbent 1988) and the other from a British perspective (Broadbent 1989). Alternatively, there is a brief review in Crosier (1998b).

Strategy

The content of part 4 of the plan will vary considerably according to the particular pattern of deployment of the marketing communications mix, which will in turn directly affect the budgetary allocations required in part 3. It is therefore important to identify the criteria which should guide decisions among the available options.

Space does not permit discussion of more than the five most crucial of those, which are considered in the next section. The delegation decision to be made in part 6 is also sufficiently crucial to demand a section to itself, which follows thereafter.

Deploying the marketing communications mix

This decision is essentially a matter of striking a balance among target, message, cost, measurement and control.

Some target audiences are more effectively reached by one kind of marketing communications initiative than by another. For instance, business executives might be relatively easily reached by a well-constructed advertisement in an appropriate magazine or newspaper but would probably miss positive publicity in a daytime radio discussion programme. Prudent marketing managers will therefore base their choices on reliable target audience research data, perhaps drawing upon the accumulated experience of the professional consultancies that have proliferated in all branches of the marketing communications discipline over the past decade.

Sometimes the nature of the message will have more influence than the specification of the target audience. A simple, brash claim would lend itself to poster advertising, for example, while the communication of a complex argument could best be accomplished by a well-constructed mailing to a carefully chosen list.

Thus, reaching a target audience of business executives might come down to a choice between direct mail and press advertising, in which case the decision maker will want to know about the relative cost of the two options. The facts are straightforwardly accessible in practice, but susceptible to change over time and variable from country to country to the extent that it would be rash to offer even broad generalizations here.

Cost is only half of the cost-effectiveness equation, of course, and prudent decision makers will make sure to compare the availability and reliability of procedures for the measurement of effectiveness, as discussed in an earlier section. A few options offer the prospect of clear cut and very direct assessment of results, direct-response press advertising being an obvious example. In the case of some others, such as television advertising, long-established and well-understood tests are available, but there can be heated debate among experts about the interpretation of the results obtained. In yet other cases, a total absence of accepted measurement techniques demands a virtual act of faith, sponsorship being at present the most obvious case in point.

A quite separate consideration is the degree of control a user can exert over the outcome. The definitions offered earlier are careful to speak in terms of 'exposure' to target audiences, which is fairly routinely achieved by all the ingredients of the marketing communications mix. If the initiative is well designed, active attention may be engaged but the key strategic issue is the extent to which the outcome is the intended one.

This kind of control is high in the case of advertising, for instance. Users buy the right to fill blocks of space or time with messages and graphics exactly to their own specification, within the law and various codes of practice, and the advertising media have a duty to ensure that no distorting influences occur. However, the price of that control varies from high to very high. The situation is exactly reversed in the case of publicity. It costs comparatively little to disseminate a news release, but those who choose that option are repeatedly frustrated by outright rejection or significant distortion. The perfect right of editors to use information to suit their own purposes rather than the supplier's is the potentially high penalty of low cost.

It is clear, then, that strategic decisions concerning deployment of the marketing communications mix demand careful trading-off among these five key criteria, and many less crucial ones besides.

Explicit identification of one of the Four Ps with strategies for communication tends to divert attention from the fact that the other three also have the potential to transmit a message about the organization and its product or service.

It is not hard to imagine a situation in which, for instance, the visibly basic features of a product are at odds with the up-market claims being made for it in an advertising campaign. Similarly, it is easy to picture the damage done to a quality offering by an ill-judged sales promotion initiative. Marketing managers repeatedly ignore the fundamental truth that the 'positioning' of a product or service in the audience's mind is decided by the audience itself, on all the available evidence. Even if these two of the Four Ps are in harmony, the product or service still needs to be offered to its potential customers in a location which is in keeping with the perceived and promoted image. Otherwise, the audience may come to its own conclusions about an apparently up-market product on the shelves of an unarguably down-market discount store. Even if three out of four deliver a consistent message, the remaining one, price, can destroy the whole position.

The issue is synergy, of course. If all four elements of the marketing mix are pulling the marketing communications cart in the same direction, the outcome will potentially add up to more than the sum total of the parts. If they are all pulling in different directions, the outcome is all too easy to predict: counter-synergy. In between, luck will have a dangerous role to play. It is clearly in the best interests of managers with responsibility for marketing communications to pay close attention to the messages sent out by the activities of others in the organization and, if possible, to make sure that they can exercise some degree of influence over marketing mix decisions.

5 Delegating campaign management

Part 6 of the marketing communications plan directs attention to decisions about the subcontracting of campaign development and execution.

In the particular case of advertising, the responsibility for development and execution of the campaign strategy outlined in the marketing communications plan is routinely delegated to advertising agencies in Britain, for example, less than a quarter of total annual advertising expenditure is not transacted in this way. Until the 1980s it was also normal to entrust the management of campaigns involving other elements of the marketing communications mix to so-called 'full service advertising agencies'. Since then, specialist intermediaries in sales promotion, direct marketing, sponsorship and packaging have proliferated. There is no reason to suppose that marketing managers are less willing to use their services, in which case responsibility for strategy implementation will nowadays not only be delegated but also shared among several intermediaries.

A breed of generalist 'integrated marketing communications agencies' has recently developed, threatening to reduce the traditional full-service advertising agency's role to provider of one specialist service among many and starting a reversal of the trend towards multiple delegation. For reasons too complicated to explain here, those newcomers are sometimes described as 'through-the-line' operators.

Responsibility is delegated because the implementation of marketing communications strategy has become a far more complicated process than it once was. For instance, advertising media options have been both increasing in number and changing in nature in every decade in the second half of the century, while developments in direct marketing are currently happening at a frenetic pace. Even the most sophisticated marketing managements would find it virtually impossible to keep abreast of prices and availability across the marketing communications mix, month-by-month, let alone maintain quality control and verify that every initiative had been executed as planned.

Even if an organization prepared to recruit a marketing communications staff large enough to contend with such a challenge, there are three more reasons for delegation. First, the salaries commanded by many of the experts in the typical disciplines would be an excessive operating overhead. Second, because marketing communications campaigns are normally discrete events rather than continuously developing activities, it is unlikely that a single marketing division would be able to keep a variety of costly specialists fully employed throughout the year. In engineering terms, it would be paying for significant periods of machine downtime. Third, few organizations could provide the atmosphere, stimulation and motivation enjoyed by specialists working in an agency on projects for several clients. These facts explain why it has become normal to buy a share in the collective skills of established expert service providers, rather than to try providing the required expertise in-house.

The penalty of delegation is, of course, loss of control. The client provides the agency with a brief; the agency provides the solution. The client may require the agency to justify its particular campaign proposals but will in the end have to concede that it has delegated responsibility to what it accepted in the first place as the expert. Therefore, it is vitally important that the client exercises as much control as is practically possible. This can be achieved in two main ways: by taking great care over the selection of collaborators and by delivering the right kind of guidance in the briefs given to them. Unfortunately, neither process is typically carried out efficiently in practice.

There is no great practical difficulty in setting up a systematic procedure for the selection of an expert collaborator, which makes the many case histories of ineptitude and disappointment all the harder to understand. Space does not permit us to go through one in detail here, but a specimen framework is offered by Crosier (1998c).

As for the brief, the structure of a marketing communications plan (Table 1) provides a usable framework. Constructing one will be a relatively simple matter of deciding which components are properly part of the brief and which are more internal concerns. However, it is important to recognize that the process of briefing is a matter of offering guidance, not giving orders; clients must beware of dogmatism, which can only have a stultifying effect on their agency's response to the brief.

Furthermore, the amount of detail to be provided is an issue: too little will leave too much room for inference and interpretation, perhaps counter-productively; too much will obscure the wood with trees. Striking the right balance is not straightforward. The professional association representing the clients of advertising agencies in Britain has suggested that 'a good brief will be as short as possible but as long as is necessary', implying that brevity should be the main aim. The recipient can always ask follow-up questions, after all.

KEITH CROSIER
UNIVERSITY OF STRATHCLYDE

Further reading

(References cited in the text marked *)

* Advertising Research Foundation (1991) *ARF Seminar: Breakthrough Marketplace Research for Bottom Line Results*, New York: Advertising Research Foundation.
Baker, M. J. (ed.) (1998) *The Macmillan Dictionary of Marketing and Advertising*, 3rd edn, London: Macmillan.
Brierley, S. (1995) *The Advertising Handbook*, London: Routledge.
* Broadbent, S. (1988) *The Advertiser's Handbook for Budget Determination*, New York: Lexington Books.
* Broadbent, S. (1989) *The Advertising Budget: The Advertiser's Guide to Budget Determination*, Henley-on-Thames, England: NTC Publications for the Institute of Practitioners in Advertising.
Broadbent, S. (1995) *Best Practice in Campaign Evaluation*, London: Institute of Practitioners in Advertising.
Broadbent, S. (1997) *Accountable Advertising*, Henley-on-Thames: Admap Publications.
Bullmore, J. (1991) *Behind the Scenes in Advertising*, Henley-on-Thames: NTC Publications.
Butterfield, L. (ed.) (1997) *Excellence in Advertising: The IPA Guide to Best Practice*, Oxford: Butterworth-Heinemann.
Cooper, A. (ed.) (1997) *How to Plan Advertising*, 2nd edn, London: Cassell.
Crosier, K. (1994) 'Promotion', in Baker, M.J. (ed.), *The Marketing Book*, 3rd edn, Oxford: Butterworth-Heinemann.
Crosier, K. (1995) 'Marketing communications', in Baker, M.J. (ed.), *Marketing: Theory & Practice*, 3rd edn, London: Macmillan.
* Crosier, K. (1998a) 'How advertising works', in Kitchen, P.J. (ed.), *Marketing Communications: Principles and Practice*, London: International Thomson.
* Crosier, K. (1998b) 'Does advertising work?', in Kitchen, P.J. (ed.), *Marketing Communications: Principles and Practice*, London: International Thomson.
* Crosier, K. (1998c) 'What advertising can and can't do', in Kitchen, P.J. (ed.), *Marketing Communications: Principles and Practice*, London: International Thomson.
Crosier, K. (1998d) 'How much to spend?' in Kitchen, P.J. (ed.), *Marketing Communications: Principles and Practice*, London: International Thomson.
Crosier, K. (1998e) 'Selecting an advertising agency', in Kitchen, P.J. (ed.), *Marketing Communications: Principles and Practice*, London: International Thomson.
DeMooij, M. (1994) *Advertising Worldwide: Concepts, Theories & Practice of International, Multinational & Global Advertising*, 2nd edn, Hemel Hempstead, England: Prentice-Hall.
Fill, C. (1995) *Marketing Communications: Frameworks, Theories and Applications*, London: Prentice-Hall.
Fletcher, W. (1992) *A Glittering Haze: Strategic Advertising in the 1990s*, Henley-on-Thames: NTC Publications.
* Franzen, G. (1994) *Advertising Effectiveness: Findings from Empirical Research*, Henley-on-Thames, England: NTC Publications for the Advertising Association.
Griffin, T. (1993) *International Marketing Communications*, Oxford: Butterworth-Heinemann.
Institute of Practitioners in Advertising (1981–1997) *Advertising Works*, vols. 1–9, Henley-on-Thames: NTC Publications.
Mayle, P. (1990) *Up the Agency*, London: Pan Books.
* McDonald, C. (1992) *How Advertising Works: A Review of Current Thinking*, Henley-on-Thames: NTC Publications.
Rijkens, R. (1992) *European Advertising Strategies*, London: Cassell.
Smith, P.R. (1993) *Marketing Communications: An Integrated Approach*, London: Kogan Page.
White, R. (1993) *Advertising: What is and how to do it*, 3rd edn, McGraw-Hill.
Wilmshurst, J. (1993) *Below-the-Line Promotion*, Oxford: Butterworth-Heinemann.

See also: ADVERTISING; DEVELOPING AND IMPLEMENTING A MARKETING PLAN; DIRECT MARKETING; INFORMATION TECHNOLOGY AND MARKETING; MARKETING STRATEGY; PERSONAL SELLING AND SALES MANAGEMENT; PACKAGING AND DESIGN; SALES PROMOTION; THE MARKETING AUDIT; THE MARKETING MIX

Advertising

1 **Advertising statistics**
2 **People involved**
3 **The advertising process**
4 **Advertising and society**
5 **Next steps**

Overview

Advertising is paid-for communication to more than one person, intended to inform or to change behaviour.

This article is about 'traditional' media advertising (i.e. in television, newspapers and magazines, radio and outdoor). It is part of 'integrated communications', which also include direct and database marketing, consumer sales promotions such as coupons, trade promotions, public relations, sponsorship and events. These are discussed elsewhere; they also use media advertising and share many of the procedures described below. The distinction between the different sorts of communication is becoming increasingly hard to make and in practice it is hardly necessary to do so.

Whether small or substantial sums of money are involved, an individual advertisement – or certainly its underlying idea – is basically the work of a very small team, often only one or two people. The fact that an idea can affect the fortunes of a large company, but could have been a bath-time inspiration, is one of the romantic appeals of advertising.

We have already started discussing 'advertising' as though it were a uniform commodity. For simplicity the word will continue to be used and other generalizations will be made, but the variety of advertisements is one of the most striking aspects of the subject. The product, service or cause advertised may only just be launched – or we may have grown up with it. The advertiser may be a person, a company or a government. An appeal in your local newspaper for a lost puppy, the announcement in your national newspaper of a bank's interest rate, and a multi-million expenditure on a television campaign for a household-name grocery brand – all of these are advertisements.

Planning and buying advertisements can be methodical; indeed it should be. This does not mean it has been automated – far from it. Advertising was defined, before television, as 'salesmanship in print'. Salespeople can be trained but must have hunger, flair and good judgement. So it is with advertising people.

1 Advertising statistics

Data

The reason for advertising is usually to defend or to increase sales volume and profit. Total spend on advertising is of course the sum of many separate decisions, but broadly varies with business and consumer confidence, with consumers' expenditure and with the level of profits which businesses are making.

Data for your country are collected by your local organizations. Table 1 shows as an example some UK expenditure.

Table 1 Total advertising expenditure in the UK including production costs and agency commission

	At curent prices £m	At 1985 prices by RPI £m	Percentage of GNP
1985	4608	4608	1.50
1986	5321	5145	1.63
1987	6055	5622	1.69
1988	7044	6235	1.77
1989	7827	6426	1.79
1990	7885	5914	1.65
1991	7577	5368	1.53

Source: Advertising Association, London

Table 2 UK expenditure on display advertising 1991

Sector	Percentage
Consumables (drink, household goods, pharmaceuticals, food, toiletries and cosmetics, tobacco)	36.9
Durables (leisure equipment, auotmobiles, household appliances and equipment, wearing apparel)	19.6
Retail	14.4
Services (entertainment, vacations, travel, transport, publishing)	11.2
Financial	9.1
Industrial (institutional, agricultural, office equipment)	6.5
Government	33.2

A lot of advertising is 'classified', often placed by individuals or small businesses; it appears in directories or on classified advertisement pages in newspapers. The rest is called 'display'. Display expenditure in 1991 came from the broad sectors shown in Table 2.

Such numbers are available in much more detail, on the assumption that full rate-card costs were paid, which is rarely the case for large advertisers. They indicate the sizes of several important sectors not fully dealt with here, for example business-to-business, corporate, recruitment, political and charity advertising (see STRATEGIC MARKETING FOR NON-PROFIT ORGANIZATIONS). Manufacturing categories are also reported separately: in 1991, £332 million on new motor cars, £10 million on training shoes, £1.6 million on disinfectants and so on. Spend by individual campaign and by the media used are similarly estimated.

The largest UK advertising company in 1991 was Procter and Gamble; the Rover Group was twenty-fifth; International Distillers and Vintners was fiftieth. Tesco Stores was the largest brand; W.H. Smith was twenty-fifth; *TV Quick* magazine came in fiftieth.

The money spent by the advertiser mostly goes to media owners, who provide the time (on television and radio) and space (in newspapers, magazines and outdoor sites). In 1991 advertising contributed 62 per cent of total newspaper revenue and 50 per cent for periodicals, as well as nearly all television income.

A smaller part of the advertiser's money goes to those employed to plan and make the advertisements. The numbers shown in Table 1 are gross (i.e. they estimate the total spend by manufacturers, including commission paid to agencies and production costs, although they exclude other overheads). The way advertisers pay their agencies is in flux. Once it was normal for agencies to keep the commission paid by media owners, at 15 per cent of the gross, but other arrangements now exist, for example different commission rates or fees.

In 1991 the largest advertising agencies each handled over £100 million in 'billings' (i.e. what their clients spent in the media at rate card). For an agency around twenty-fifth in size, £20 to £30 million is typical. The last ten of the top fifty agencies each had about £15 million billings. There are many smaller agencies,

Table 3 Division of total UK 1991 advertising expenditure between the media

Medium	£m	Percentage
Newspapers and magazines		
Display	2893	38.2
Classified	1923	25.4
TV	2303	30.4
Outdoor and transport	267	3.5
Radio	149	2.0
Cinema	42	0.6

each billing a few million. Table 3 demonstrates how total UK expenditure in 1991 was divided between the media.

International comparisons

As a percentage of gross domestic product (GDP), expenditure on advertising in the UK is relatively high: 1.20 per cent in 1990. This compares with 1.36 per cent in the USA; 1.56 per cent in Spain; 0.89 per cent in Japan; 0.85 per cent in Germany; 0.78 per cent in France; and 0.62 per cent in Italy.

The business is truly international, with very similar practices across the developed world. Staff move with little difficulty from country to country, though intimate knowledge of the local language and customs are necessary for fine-tuning.

Some campaigns are also international, since big ideas cross borders easily. Deliberately aiming at international campaigns provides the advertiser with central control and some economies. If it is clumsily done, it may result in mid-Atlantic advertisements, written by committee and truly satisfying no one.

2 People involved

The following description sounds complicated only because it covers several possible organizations of the work. It is a disadvantage if the particular route followed is actually complex. Decisions should be taken by the smallest number of people possible – both on the advertiser's side and by his partners. Tiers of executives may exist in large companies, some of whom can say 'no' but cannot give final approval. This dilutes the work and adds time and cost.

You may be the only person responsible. You can plan and write your own small advertisement, send it to the paper with your cheque, and sit back. But for companies this is rarely sensible.

There is a wide choice open to advertisers, not only concerning who to employ, but how to organize the choice. The simplest decision is to pass all the work to a single company, a full-service advertising agency. At the most complex, the advertiser can mix and match, doing part in-house and using *à-la-carte* several agencies or suppliers as well. This is practical only if the advertiser has sufficient experience and time, both to brief out and to coordinate, and in addition to keep standards up to the best available. Otherwise what looks like clever buying may ultimately add expense.

Whatever the organization, advertisers need to maintain a good level of advertising skills. They may not have to master all the detail of how the process works, but they need to know enough not to be blinded by suppliers. They are responsible for spending millions of their companies' money and should be professional about it, neither overtrustful and naive, nor oversuspicious and self-contained.

Appointing an agency is a costly business – on both sides. It is sensible for an advertiser to keep himself informed about what is available (i.e. to meet other advertising agencies than the one employed, to consider other media buying arrangements and to talk to consultants about all sides of his business). But continuity has considerable value and frequent changes of partner spell trouble. This is not only because of the time spent in getting new suppliers up to speed, but because of the way advertisements work on consumers: some novelty helps but constant change is inefficient.

The advertiser

There are no willing advertisers, only marketers who know no better tool. Advertising is usually controlled by the marketing director, but in a company where it is a major expense, the CEO and board may pay particular attention to it. The finance director or budget committee may also be directly involved though their grasp of the subject is sometimes tenuous.

The advertiser orchestrates the range of communications touched on above. These work more efficiently if they are seamless. The structure to ensure this, which also balances the spend between the different activities, is the subject of current debate.

Day-to-day matters may be under a brand manager, but in mature companies it is understood that advertising will have long-term effects; it is argued that it is unwise to alter strategy as fast as personnel change. So a brand manager may have little influence, much as he wants to make a mark.

The advertising agency

The norm was once the 'full-service' advertising agency and this is still the most usual supplier. It is a business in its own right, with its own version of a factory, a salesforce, research and development and so on. It handles all the necessary jobs, though parts may be sub-contracted. It is legally responsible for the financial commitments to media for carrying the advertisements.

The full-service agency has two essential functions: creative and media. The creative department includes 'writers' or copywriters, and 'art directors'. Put simply, writers write copy (the words in a newspaper or magazine advertisement or outdoor) and scripts (the words and directions in a television or radio commercial). Art directors look after the appearance of the advertisement. Normally, the two work as a team; what people are going to do and say in the advertisement, and how it is directed or laid out are hard to separate.

The media department includes 'media planners' and 'media buyers'. Again the two work together as a team or may be the same person. The two main jobs are to recommend which media to use and to deal with media owners about price – remember that rate cards are complex and often negotiable.

There are two other functions of the agency which concern the advertiser. The first is account management. The advertiser works directly with an account director or manager who adds his own experience and ideas, and may be an allrounder who does a lot of the work himself. He also coordinates all the work in the agency, represents the advertiser to the agency and vice versa.

The second function in a large agency is account planning or, sometimes, research. The agency which handles a number of advertisers builds up expertise in understanding consumers. Part of the input into an advertising idea are insights into what consumers think and feel; it is important to have a general understanding of how they react to advertising. The planners represent these consumer views and contribute to advertising strategy. They take part in briefing creatives and work with them in advertisement development. A researcher in an agency may also function as the advertiser's research department: designing, buying (or carrying out) and interpreting consumer research.

Naturally the advertiser and agency employ others who administer the business, keep accounts, control the production of advertisements, coordinate with distribution partners, manage client consumer databases, ensure advertisements meet legal and industry codes, program computers and make coffee, but they are not further described here.

Media

The media services just outlined have in some cases shifted outside the full-service agency. Some advertisers have decided to give the work to specialist firms, called 'media independents' (i.e. independent of the other functions). In turn, some of these now also offer creative services which they have in-house or buy from creative specialists or 'boutiques'. Advertisers, and even agencies, may also make use of these services. This decision depends largely on how media recommendations are evaluated: is media a commodity, bought by the yard, and cost is all that matters? Alternatively, there are advantages in having media under the same roof as planning and creative departments. There are qualitative aspects of the advertisement-target-medium interaction of which advantage can be taken and which may outweigh crude cost considerations (see QUALITATIVE RESEARCH IN MARKETING).

Media departments and independents are serviced by the representatives of media owners, who compete for the business. Large advertisers will also meet these salesmen, who try directly to influence them. They may also have in-house media coordinators.

Research

Advertisers usually buy directly their own research into marketing and advertising. In addition to data used for several marketing purposes (sales audits, panels and surveys), they may purchase tracking studies, or usage and attitude surveys, in which there is a major advertising component. They or the agency often commission creative development research or pre-tests specifically about advertisements. An evaluation of media performance may also be bought, usually into the prices paid by the media buyer, but also about media planning (see MARKETING RESEARCH).

3 The advertising process

In this section is an outline of how an advertising campaign is put together. The alternative organizations outlined above are not dwelt upon. Whoever is responsible, the work has to be done. Also a brief may be queried or modified, mistakes may have to be put right, this may be the first time the team tackles the job or it may be a routine; such comments are not repeated below.

The job begins when the advertiser approaches the agency. This starts a two-way process: the advertiser knows the marketing objectives but is usually not ready to write or to sign off a creative brief. It is a dialogue between advertiser and agency which produces the best advertising brief.

Strategy

There are three essential inputs to the marketing strategy which are also used in planning advertising. First is information about the product – its content, performance, price, distribution, comparison with competition and so on (see LOGISTICS AND PHYSICAL DISTRIBUTION; POSITIONING; PRICING).

Second, who are the purchasers and consumers – both existing and others targeted? What is their behaviour, their understanding of the product and of competitors, their attitudes, beliefs and so on? These facts and decisions are used in some ways more intensively in planning advertising than in planning product improvements, distribution policies and other marketing decisions. Because advertisements are so public, and can be so effective, advertising decisions can lead other parts of the marketing mix. After all, marketing begins by deciding what the consumer will buy, which depends on how you sell. Deciding what to say about yourself is a good discipline in setting priorities (see MARKET SEGMENTATION; THE MARKETING MIX).

The final introductory comment is the most important. We have to decide what job the advertisements have to do. Exactly how is exposing an advertisement going to change or reinforce a person's behaviour or beliefs?

Further, we have to decide why the investment in advertising is likely to be worthwhile. What is the economic value of the activity? Is the return looked for in the short term, and do we want clear evidence? Or, are we mainly contributing to branding, so facilitating other marketing activities, and expecting indirect and long-term effects which may be hard to identify? (see BRANDING AND BRAND MANAGEMENT)

Not only do we need objectives in the marketing sense, we need a theory to connect communication with action. This is a tall order. 'How advertising works' has been the subject of hundreds of books and papers. There is no general theory, though much effort has been spent in searching for one. There are as many ways as there are campaign strategies, individual brand situations and of course advertisements (see MARKETING COMMUNICATIONS).

It matters whether sales are already increasing naturally, are static or are falling. It is not always practical to aim at increasing or 'conquest' sales; often it is more realistic to reinforce existing behaviour, to defend the territory. It matters whether or not we have 'news' to announce. It matters whether our product has real, discernible advantages over competitors or whether we are selling what is virtually a commodity.

As examples, here are a few common ways in which advertisements may work. Often the most important is to 'add value' which helps to turn a 'product' into a 'brand'. There are many kinds of added value: explaining the consumer benefit of a property of the product, giving it a personality, and so on. This is a slow job, in contrast to expectations for some advertising effects. A brand is worth more than a product because of all the associations attached to it. The reader will not need to be reminded of the very large sums paid for some companies, well above the value of their fixed assets, because of the brands they own. Advertisements are not all that create brand equity, but they are often a major part.

As well as this usually fundamental job, advertising often brings a brand to the front of the minds of consumers who buy among a repertoire. Such reminders typically create 'blips' in the plot of sales over time, just after a burst of advertising.

Straightforward communication is often the purpose of advertising, when we have news about the product to put across or coupons to distribute.

By reassuring retailers about the rate of sale of the brand, advertising often helps salespeople in getting and holding distribution in today's competitive retail environment. Display,

Advertising

shelf footage, other aids at the point of sale may similarly be assisted. We do not see as frequently as we used to 'As seen on TV' but the message is still relevant.

It is often overlooked that advertising can encourage the manufacturer's own employees, for example by setting standards for counter staff and others in touch with the public.

The last two points are examples of the apparent target – the purchaser – being no more important than another target – retailers, our salesforce, shareholders, the financial community, opinion leaders and so on.

Budget setting

Deciding whether to advertise at all is hard. The question should be approached methodically, as set out in the rest of this section. The answer will be yes only if communication to a reasonably large target is desirable. Advertising agencies are sometimes criticized for not advertising themselves enough. But if their target (or yours) is only a few hundred people then an advertisement may be an inefficient way to reach them.

This point is illuminated by the famous postcard comparison. You can hardly pay less than 30p each to print and send a postcard to 1000 people, at a total cost of £300. Though the media cost of a 30-second television spot is large, it may work out at only £5 per 1000 (to which you may add 10–20 per cent production cost). If you buy 20 cms by 3 columns in the *Daily Mail* you will pay around £6000 media cost plus production, but there are over 4,000,000 adult readers so for 1000 readers you pay £1.50 or so. Thus, in one sense television and newspapers are cheap: you pay only about £6 or less than £2 per thousand people reached. In another sense they are expensive: a sizeable investment is needed.

This example makes two other points. You will have to judge (or decide after an experiment) how to compare the effect of reading a postcard with the effect of seeing an advertisement. Second, your cash flow restrictions, and the actual amount you need to spend, matter as much as calculated efficiencies.

Deciding how much to spend behind a brand, for example for the coming year, is also not an easy decision. No formula is adequate, though rules of thumb are much used. Most advice on the subject consists of methods which suggest a budget; but these should not determine it. No method takes into account every one of the factors which should properly be considered. This is done by a procedure which is recommended below.

There are cases where the decision is not worth much trouble – when the budget is a very small part of overall costs or a small sum in itself. Then common sense will do, plus perhaps one of the following methods.

It is advisable to consider separately three parts of the overall spend on advertising. First, on media, including agency commission, usually the largest part and which is the subject of the rest of this section. Second, on production, which has its own section below. Finally, there are other costs, which will vary according to the conventions of the firm (e.g. overheads, staff directly attributable to the advertising function, related research and so on).

The budget is not decided by a detached, abstract procedure. It depends on the task to be done, the effects expected, the creative idea and even production costs. The process below will lead to a suggested expenditure. This may well change as creative development proceeds, or as other circumstances alter.

Reviews

The process is preceded by four reviews. This sounds onerous, but in fact the information should already have been collected. First, what are the brand's objectives, including the advertising objectives? Often these are summed up as the task we have to do, but as well as immediate jobs the objective should include the company's vision, or long-term goals. Second, what have your budgets been in recent years and how were they decided and modified? Third, a history and forecast of the category in which we compete is required. Thus, we review what competitors spent, how they fared and how they are likely to affect us next year. Fourth, what have we learned, and what do we estimate, about the effects of our advertisements? It is because this last item is usually so uncertain that the overall job is hard.

After the reviews, one or more of the methods below should be used to give suggestions about what to spend. The following is not a complete list of ways of indicating a sum of money. Nor will they normally agree, though they will bracket a range.

The marketing mix

Task method

Many companies say they use the task method. That is, an amount of advertising exposure to the target is first decided, deemed to be sufficient to achieve the task. The cost of this exposure is then worked out. For example: 'We need six opportunities to see a 30-second commercial in order to create awareness of our product improvement; this costs X'. It is not always clear that the immediately defined task is all that our communications are needed for, nor that six exposures will work and four are not enough, but the method is understandable and with experience and common sense works reasonably well.

Ratio to sales

Another common method is to set a ratio to sales. This means that the spend on advertising is in a fixed ratio to sales revenue, or to sales volume, often based on a category average. For example, '2 per cent of gross revenue'.

It is of course necessary to define precisely the terms used, and also to decide on the ratio (the problem has not been solved, only restated). You must not compare your actual spend and factory-gate revenue with a competitor's spend reported at rate card and his sales at retail level. Because of economies of scale for large brands, and because the desire to grow small brands leads to investment and aggressive marketing spends, the ratios for large brands are usually less than for small ones.

Brand history review

You will discover how this works in your own category if you use the third recommended method: brand history review. This may be part of one of the initial reviews you should start with; it pays particular attention to what you and competitors have spent, how well or badly you have done, and what connections there may be between spend and copy on the one hand, sales volume on the other (allowing for other factors which affect sales).

After the initial reviews, and with one or more suggested budgets, you finally choose how much to spend. Decide whether the suggestion is too much – in the light of your financial targets. Decide whether it is enough – given your view of its effects and your volume targets. If the answers are incompatible, decide what has to give way: your cash limits, your volume (which has a financial effect, of course), your long-term goals. Compromise is normal, as in all budgeting.

Creativity and the creative brief

This article will not teach you to write advertising copy, draw storyboards or lay out press advertisements. Part of the work should be methodical; craft skills can be learned. But making effective advertisements depends on being noticed, fresh, believable, motivating – and many other words which are summed up as 'creative'. Although the aim – to be effective – is simply stated, someone has to decide how.

There is plenty of dubious advice, and there are even more offputting recipes, about being salient, involving, credible, memorable, linked to the brand and so on. It is still a job which some people are consistently better at than others.

The work has also to be doubly relevant. That is, both meaningful to the viewer or reader in the target, and also meeting the advertising objectives which have been agreed as part of the marketing strategy. The latter is ensured at the beginning by the way the creatives are briefed; during development by creative research; after exposure by evaluative work.

The brief may consist of a document, but is normally expanded by discussion. It may be summed up by two questions: Where are we? Where do we want to be? That is, a description of the product or service; its competitors; its purchasers and users and what they think and feel. Then, the role for advertising and what it is we want to communicate, which may be facts and emotions, with an explanation of why these are believable and desirable, plus how the recipients will be different after exposure. There may be a summary: the advertising proposition, with its supporting evidence. There will also be an indication of the possible budget and perhaps of the media likely to be used. If the work is not a totally new project, there may also be guidelines about details in the advertisement, learned from experience.

Developing and pre-testing

After writers and art directors have some work to show, initially in rough form, their ideas go through internal screening, by peers, department heads, account managers, planners and so on.

It has been reasonably estimated that the difference in value between an ordinary and a great advertisement is higher than most media budgets, and much more than anything spent in pre-testing (as research at this stage is often and intimidatingly called). Hence it has been argued that methodical estimation of likely effects deserves serious time and money. On the other hand, it has also been shown that such estimates are dubious – for the reasons given below. Advertisers may well like to have, but should not expect, over-literal or precise forecasts of how a campaign will perform in the field after an assessment of a crude exposure of one advertisement.

Because of the expense, finished work is not normally used in development research, and this is only one of the reasons why it requires judgement and involves risk, particularly when the finished work will look very different from the rough. In addition, the exposure of the rough advertisement is necessarily in circumstances unlike natural viewing and reading. Finally, its effect is usually judged by the answers to questions, rather than by the way it influences behaviour.

Too often, pre-testing is seen as a simple pass-or-fail technique. It has even been presented as a sales forecast. Because of the weaknesses of the techniques, neither of these views is recommended. Nevertheless, early work is often seen by representatives of the target group. Research is carried out, directed by the advertiser or by the planner, among small groups of target consumers. This may be done at the 'concept stage', that is, when the stimuli are strategic statements written to be explained to consumers, without any 'added values'; or they may be actual advertisements (i.e. 'executions' or 'treatments') though in rough form. Several different and well-publicized systems are available (see MARKETING RESEARCH; SALES FORECASTING).

Pre-testing is controversial. There is a lot of money riding on decisions at this stage, not to mention egos and careers. The technical decisions crystallize some of the key questions about advertising. Who is it aimed at (who is in the sample)? How does it work (what is the idea or model behind the particular measurements made)? Can it be judged in the short term (is one exposure enough – if not, how many)? Can what consumers say be taken literally (how rational and verbal are the true responses to advertising)?

Here some well-worn controversies may flare up: 'Trust me: I'm an Art Director', versus a businessman's need for reassurance and often for quantification; 'Small works of art at someone else's expense' versus the need for marketplace effectiveness. Undoubtedly some very successful campaigns have gone ahead despite apparently damning findings at this stage (less publicized, vice-versa). Although conflicts occur, they are not necessary. After all, creativity and effectiveness are not antonyms: one is the means and the other is the end. One is stimulus, the other is response. When the partners (advertiser, agency, research) respect and trust each other, mutual understanding and compromise will determine the outcome.

More importantly, guidance can improve some work. Research should be seen more in its diagnostic role. That is, not 'this ad is good, that is bad', but 'this ad seems to work because …, that one has these problems which might be solved if…'.

Advertisements at an early stage of development can often be improved by sensitive, usually qualitative, research. We most want to know about communication – do consumers take out what we think we have put in? Sensitivity is exercised not only in the interpretation of respondents' answers; it also has to be used in working with the writer of the advertisement. Creatives should want to understand how people will react, and should see the consumer's interpreter as a partner in the creative act.

Production

Once rough advertisements or advertising ideas have been agreed, they must be turned into the form from which the media will reproduce them. A television or cinema script and storyboard are shot on film or videotape and edited. A radio script is recorded, and also edited. A magazine or newspaper rough is typeset and illustrated.

These are not mechanical procedures, though a lot of technology is involved. The quality which can be added in the process can be critical to the effectiveness of many advertisements. Financial prudence here does not

The marketing mix

consist of saving as much money as possible, but of spending only what is needed to get the job properly done.

Making a television or cinema commercial has a lot in common with making any film. In cost per second, the commercial often exceeds the feature film. This is partly because of the diseconomies of the small scale, partly because extreme care is taken to get this fragile vehicle in shape for its precious cargo, the impressions which may be costing hundreds of thousands of pounds to communicate.

Specialists in film production are required to plan and direct the film, often a producer from the advertising agency as well as independent people hired by the day. Production often takes months from start to finish though actual shooting may last only a day or two. Pre-planning, as well as talent, is vital. It is at the early stage (as well as when the writer starts with the words 'Open on a cast of thousands lining a Pacific beach') that costs are best explained and determined. The shooting schedule is planned, the cast, location and props are selected.

When the film has been shot, time is needed to produce cuts of the right length, to record voice and music tracks, to add special effects and so on. Copies are supplied to the TV stations on broadcast-quality tape.

Producing a radio commercial is much less complicated, and less costly. Voices, music and sound effects are recorded in a studio on individual tracks, then edited and mixed to make the finished commercial.

Equally careful technical work and judgement are required to lay out and set press advertisements. Generally illustrations are required, which means that a photographer or illustrator is briefed to produce the artwork. Typesetting is done separately and then the two elements – pictures and words – are combined in a 'mechanical', which is the final definition of how the advertisement should look. Colour film separations of the finished work are made, and sent to the various media for printing.

The media brief, media planning and buying

An essential part of the advertising plan is how the message will reach the target. Wise expenditure requires decisions about effectiveness as well as cost negotiation and much practical detail.

A full description of the media available, their costs and what they can do is not given here. Changes are frequent, in ownership of the media, their content and the audiences they reach. The number of different media is increasing, but the time people choose to give to reading and viewing changes little. Hence individual audiences fragment into smaller numbers. Expert and up-to-date advice is essential. Forecasting is part of the skill.

The currency at this stage is media research – the syndicated data about how people are exposed to the different media. Because there are many different users of these data, both buyers and sellers, the design of this research is often shared through joint decision taking and the specification is then put out to tender.

The advertiser is not really buying the transmission of a commercial or the printing of millions of newspapers. He is buying people in his target seeing the screen during the transmission, or reading his advertisement in the paper. Only careful interpretation of media research can estimate these numbers. They vary, of course, by channel, by TV programme, by time of day, by time of year, by individual publication, by position and size of advertisement, and so on. A medium can deliver only people with open eyes and ears in front of the advertisement. After that we are back to creative skills.

Evaluating the campaign

This step naturally comes at the end. However, for most brands it is also the beginning of another cycle. Knowing what advertisements have done – or not done – has already been stressed as an aid in planning and budgeting. Although we can hardly ever know exactly what our work has achieved, we always learn from trying to find out.

First, we need to have agreed how our advertisements are expected to have their effect. The advertiser and agency must work on common ground: what it is they look for and how it will be measured. The variety of possible effects was indicated above in the section on strategy.

Many of the comments made about controversy in development research apply at this stage also. When we carry out consumer research, whether qualitative or quantitative, we again have to take care in the interpretation of how respondents answer, which usually needs specialist skills. For example, high awareness of the advertisements themselves tells us little about the relevance or persuasiveness of their content.

As well as such 'soft' data, there is now the possibility of 'hard' data: sales or other behaviour, either observed as it fell, or in some planned test. Unfortunately, sales data, even in an experiment, usually fail to give unequivocal answers. Sales are always influenced by factors other than our advertisements, and these have to be allowed for statistically. Worse, the effect of advertising is a construct: what we observe less what would have happened without advertising, or different advertisements, or more or less spent. Time also enters disturbingly: we have to ask ourselves whether enough time has passed to predict effects over several years, which may include the larger part of the results we hope for.

An objective of advertising research is to measure the brand equity which, as stated above, is often the most important reason for investment in advertising. There is as yet no agreed way to do this; some methods at least indicate lower estimates for this value (see QUALITATIVE RESEARCH IN MARKETING; QUANTITATIVE METHODS IN MARKETING).

4 Advertising and society

Advertising, public opinion and the economy

We are all exposed to hundreds of advertisements each day. Most of them are for products and services we are not at that moment interested in. We filter many of them out as not worth conscious thought; others we look to for entertainment. Only a very small proportion get real attention.

From these facts it follows, first, that advertisements are part of Western 'culture' in the broad sense. We grew up with them, most of us take them for granted, we have learned to cope with them and to use them for our own purposes. Second, we are genuinely unaffected by most of them, and the advertiser accepts this: the nature of mass media is such that much is apparently 'wasted'. Most people say 'Advertising does not affect me', and they are broadly correct. This is quite consistent with advertising's efficiency as a means of communicating with specific target audiences.

The pervasiveness and blatantly commercial nature of advertisements is distasteful to some. There are also those who exaggerate what they see as manipulation and the advertisers' misuse of this power. Thus, as well as 'never making me buy anything', it is claimed that advertisements 'create unnecessary wants and discontent' and 'force people to buy products' of which the critic disapproves.

In the latest UK Advertising Association survey of attitudes to advertising, it comes low on the list of 'things in most need of immediate attention and change', scoring 4 per cent. This compares with education at 32 per cent, the government at 30 per cent, bringing up children at 12 per cent, and so on.

There is a small arena, in politics and economics, where the general effects and desirability of advertising is debated. Reference to facts in such debates is less frequent than it should be. In a free society, advertising is an important tool in the competition which is the invisible hand guiding production. It is a shop window, displaying what is freely available. It speeds up innovation and encourages mass production and competitiveness which lower prices.

People are well aware that they are being sold to and they make up their own minds; they use advertising both for information and entertainment. Advertising provides massive subsidies for television and for nearly all publications, themselves valued products and sources of information.

Advertising controls

Marketers should be aware that their liberties are under threat. This is no exaggeration. The industry argues that freedom of speech must apply to commercial communication, subject to no more laws than other messages (about libel, for example). The Trade Descriptions Act and other legislation apply to advertising as well as to business generally.

Advertising is largely self-regulated. Despite the theoretical weaknesses of self-policing, its advantages over government rulings are agreed by a majority. The UK Advertising Standards Authority, the Independent Television Commission and the Radio

Authority operate clearance systems so that advertisements under development can be discussed in advance of production. The press is less formal.

The Advertising Standards Authority also deals with complaints by the public about print and cinema advertising. In 1991 it received 10,610 complaints, of which it pursued 4203; 67 per cent of these complaints were upheld (i.e. it was held that the advertisements were not 'legal, decent, honest, truthful' and therefore they were changed or dropped). In addition, the Authority carries out its own monitoring. It may check whether claims can be substantiated or whether particular parts of the Code of Advertising Practice were violated, such as for cars, tobacco products, alcohol and products for children. These findings are also reported.

5 Next steps

Associations

Each country has equivalents of the following UK trade associations, which can be contacted for information and reading lists. The Advertising Association deals with matters common to the two following bodies, and to media owner groups, which all belong to it but also have their own interests.

The Advertising Association, Abford House, 15 Wilton Road, London SWlV INJ. Tel: 0171–828 2771.

The Incorporated Society of British Advertisers, 44 Hertford Street, London W1Y 8AE. Tel: 0171–499 7502.

The Institute of Practitioners in Advertising, 44 Belgrave Square, London SWlX 8QS. Tel: 0171–235 7020.

SIMON BROADBENT
THE BRAND CONSULTANCY

Further reading

(References cited in the text marked *)

Broadbent, Simon (1989) *The Advertising Budget*, Henley-on-Thames: NTC Publications Ltd for the Institute of Practitioners in Advertising.

Bullmore, Jeremy (1992) *Behind the Scenes in Advertising*, Henley-on-Thames: NTC Publications Ltd.

Cowley, Don (ed.) (1989) *How To Plan Advertising*, London: Cassell/APG.

Hedges, Alan (1988) *Testing To Destruction*, London: Institute of Practitioners in Advertising.

Jones, John Philip (1986) *What's In A Name?*, Lexington, MA: Lexington Books.

McDonald, Colin (1992) *How Advertising Works*, Henley-on-Thames: The Advertising Association in association with NTC Publications Ltd.

White, Roderick (1988) *Advertising, What it Is and How To Do it*, 2nd edn, Maidenhead: McGraw-Hill in association with the Advertising Association.

See also: BRANDING AND BRAND MANAGEMENT; DIRECT MARKETING; EXHIBITIONS; INFORMATION TECHNOLOGY AND MARKETING; LOGISTICS AND VALUE CREATION; MARKET SEGMENTATION; MARKETING COMMUNICATIONS; MARKETING RESEARCH; POSITIONING; PRICING; PUBLIC RELATIONS; QUALITATIVE RESEARCH IN MARKETING; QUANTITATIVE METHODS IN MARKETING; SALES FORECASTING; SALES PROMOTIONS; STRATEGIC MARKETING FOR NON-PROFIT ORGANIZATIONS; THE MARKETING MIX

Sales promotion

1 The role of sales promotion
2 The development of sales promotion
3 Types of sales promotion
4 Promotions and the rest of the marketing mix
5 Promotions as a means of communication
6 Tactical and strategic dimensions of promotions
7 Sales promotion pitfalls
8 Managing and planning sales promotions
9 Selecting an appropriate promotion
10 A focus on trade promotions
11 Evaluating the effectiveness of sales promotions
12 The future for sales promotion

Overview

Within the field of marketing communications the term 'sales promotion' is frequently used as a 'catch all' term encompassing all those elements which cannot be classified as advertising, selling or public relations (PR). Sales promotion can be defined as:

> marketing activities usually specific to a time period, place or customer group, which encourage a direct response from consumers or marketing intermediaries, through the offer of additional benefits.
> (Peattie and Peattie 1994: 534)

Sales promotions are often referred to as being 'below-the-line'. The line in question originally denoted whether or not communications efforts were channelled through advertising agencies. The line has become something of an anachronism with the trend towards integrated marketing communications agencies, and with an increasing tendency for sales and PR to be treated as separate functions. Advertising is still referred to as being 'above-the-line', and 'below-the-line' has now become synonymous with sales promotion.

The everyday vocabulary relating to promotion in marketing is full of inconsistencies. For simplicity and brevity, the word 'promotion' will be used here to refer to a sales promotion, rather than its broader context of marketing promotion.

1 The role of sales promotion

Sales promotions are all around us. If you pick any form of breakfast cereal from the supermarket shelf the chances are that the box will contain an extra product, a free gift, or will have printed on it a recipe, puzzle, competition entry form or a token to collect. Coupons and free samples tumble through our letter boxes, or are tucked inside the periodicals that we buy, and it is difficult to walk through a retail district and avoid seeing the word 'Sale' somewhere.

People commonly associate sales promotions with 'special offers' which provide customers with an additional incentive to purchase, usually by a reduction in price or an increase in the quantity of product offered. Such offers are an important part of sales promotion, but our definition takes a wider perspective in terms of the parties that promotions can be targeted at, the responses that can be sought and the benefits that can be offered.

Promotions can be targeted at three distinct groups:

1 *Consumers*. Most promotions targeted at consumers are designed to provide them with an incentive to purchase, and to provide a reason for buying the promoted brand rather than its competitors. These are known as 'pull' promotions. Consumers vary in terms of their responsiveness to a promotion for a particular product. Some consumers will remain brand loyal regardless of promotional activities; others will allow usual brand loyalties to be overridden by attractive promotions; while others will frequently switch among brands to take advantage of different promotions. As well as influencing brand choice, promotions can affect the timing and volume of consumers' purchasing (McAllister and Totten 1985). Brand-loyal consumers may stockpile while their

preferred brand offers a promotion, and brand switchers may stockpile while any brand is being promoted. Responsiveness to promotions can form a basis for market segmentation, and it can be valuable for marketers thinking of running promotions to understand what proportion of the market is likely to change its purchasing behaviour in response to a promotion, and whether that response will involve brand-switching, stockpiling or both.

2 *Retailers and other external marketing intermediaries*. Trade or 'push' promotions involve offering intermediaries incentives such as special discounts (known as allowances), gifts, contests, marketing information or extra product to gain their enthusiasm and shelf space. Other trade promotions involve providing management training and assistance, point-of-sale displays, trade shows and inventory control assistance.

3 *The salesforce*. The salesforce of a company are frequently the targets of promotional contests aimed at improving their performance and adding a 'fun' motivational challenge into their work. Around three-quarters of companies use such contests which are usually linked to the achievement of sales goals.

It would be unwise for a marketer to plan a 'pull' promotion, without first considering what must be done to encourage intermediaries and the salesforce to provide the necessary support. Therefore one promotional campaign may have elements aimed at each of the three parties.

A common, and quite logical assumption, is that the response that any sales promotion seeks from its target will be an increase in sales. Despite the fact that most promotions are sales-orientated, this is a rather narrow and potentially misleading view. Promotions, like all marketing activity, ultimately aim to generate profitable sales to satisfied customers, but the direct responses that they may aim for are many and varied. A promotion might seek to get a customer to consume a free product sample, to visit a retail outlet, to fill in an enquiry coupon or to explain why they like a product in twelve words or less.

The benefits which different promotions offer to their targets also vary widely. A fundamental distinction can be made between value increasing, and value adding promotions (see PRICING). Value increasing promotions alter the basic 'deal' (the relationship between the product and the price) by increasing the quantity or quality of the product on offer, or by lowering its price. The price can be altered directly, through a sale or discount, or indirectly through the use of a coupon or a refund offer. Such promotions emphasize a rational economic view of consumers and assume that they are relatively aware of prices, and are willing and able to change their consumption behaviour in search of a better deal.

Value adding promotions leave the product/price relationship intact, and instead add something extra into the total product offering. This 'something' could be a premium, an entry into a competition or an extended guarantee. Value adding promotions can offer their targets benefits which are less tangibly economic than the extra value that comes from getting more product for less money. Some promotions provide the customer with benefits in terms of simplifying the buying process or reducing the risks associated with purchase. The distribution of product catalogues, or allowing a product to be tested provides customers with information which can help them make their purchase decisions with confidence. Another increasingly popular form of promotion involves a proportion of the purchase price of a product being donated to charity by the manufacturer. While this provides no direct material advantage to the consumer, it provides them with the psychological benefits that come from knowing that one payoff of their consumption has been a contribution to a worthy cause.

2 The development of sales promotion

The traditional stronghold of promotions is among fast moving consumer goods (FMCG) markets, and packaged foods in particular. In recent years promotions have become a major feature in a more diverse range of markets including financial services, consumer durables and the marketing of charities. The 1980s witnessed widespread growth in expenditure on promotions. Although estimates concerning the costs of promotions vary widely, reflecting the different definitions of sales promotions used, it is fair to say that in a wide range of markets sales promotion expenditure comfortably exceeds that on classic brand image advertising. A number of factors are behind the growth in promotions:

1 Growing doubts about the cost effectiveness of advertising, in the face of rising prices and increased advertising 'clutter': a lack of conclusive evidence to directly link advertising to consumer preference and buying behaviour, and apparent consumer hostility towards advertising have fuelled these doubts. The advent of videos and remote controls which allow adverts to be 'zapped' has also eroded television advertisers' confidence in their ability to reach their target audience (see ADVERTISING; CONSUMER BEHAVIOUR).
2 Sales promotions' new found 'respectability', through greater use by market leaders and increasing professionalism among sales promotion agencies.
3 Increased impulse purchasing; particularly for FMCG products. In key markets such as confectionery and snack foods around two thirds of all purchase decisions are made in-store, and can therefore be influenced by in-store promotions.
4 Planning time horizons have been foreshortened; reflecting increasing market volatility and rivalry, and accelerating product life-cycles. The development of advertising campaigns which build and nurture the desired image for a brand is a slow and painstaking process. The more immediate boost offered by promotions is attractive to marketers under pressure to improve market share and sales volume in the short term (see PRODUCT LIFE-CYCLE MANAGEMENT).
5 Micro-marketing approaches: in response to fragmenting markets, where promotions can provide more tailored and targeted communication than mass media.
6 Declining brand loyalty: caused by widening choice, narrowing perceived differences between brands and, in FMCG markets, retailers' own brands becoming increasingly credible (see BRANDING AND BRAND MANAGEMENT).
7 A 'snowball' effect in some markets, with companies feeling obliged to match rivals' sales promotion activity, or risk losing market share and competitive position.
8 Affordability: national mass media have become prohibitively expensive for many companies, particularly during recessionary squeezes on marketing budgets. Promotions allow national coverage at a lower cost, cost sharing with co-promoters and can even be self-funding.

3 Types of sales promotion

There is a very wide range of marketing activities which seek to gain response from consumers and marketing intermediaries by providing them with additional benefits, and which therefore could be classified as a form of promotion. The most common forms of promotions can be categorized as follows.

Price-based value increasing promotions

Discount pricing and sales
Discounting is a widely used form of promotion in a range of markets. It is only effective where the additional sales volume will compensate for the lost revenue, and in markets where a reduction in price will not be interpreted as a reduction in quality. Discounts are a relatively expensive form of promotion in that they provide a price reduction for all consumers, regardless of their price and promotion sensitivity. Discounting also carries with it the danger that it will undermine the consumer's expected reference price, so that they come to expect discounting and will resist a return to 'normal' prices (Lattin and Bucklin 1989).

Money-off coupons
Coupons are a very popular form of promotion, particularly in FMCG markets. Coupons can be delivered by direct mail, in stores, as inserts in publications or on packages. The traditional disadvantages of couponing are in the logistical effort of the redemption handling process, losses due to misredemption and consumer resistance to the need to physically clip and carry coupons. New technology may overcome all of these problems with innovations such as barcode scanning for coupons, and 'smart cards' for consumers which store information about coupon entitlements (see INFORMATION TECHNOLOGY AND MARKETING).

The marketing mix

Refunds
'Cashback' offers have become an increasingly popular way of reducing the cost to consumers of relatively expensive items, without eroding the reference price in consumers' minds. Consumers receive a refund by mailing in their proof of purchase and, unlike discounting, this will only benefit those consumers who are price-sensitive enough to follow through the refund application process.

Improved payment terms
Interest free credit and 'buy now, pay later' offers make purchase easier for consumers, and may reduce the real cost of purchase, while allowing the price to stay constant. Special payment terms are popular for relatively expensive consumer durables such as cars and domestic appliances.

Product-based value increasing promotions

Product samples
Samples are frequently used to encourage product trial for products such as foods, drinks and toiletries. There are a variety of methods of delivering samples including direct mail, inserts within publications or packages, or sampling points inside stores. Sampling is a relatively expensive form of promotion, which often involves a high degree of wastage. It can also be difficult to assess its effectiveness, since there is no way to establish whether those who receive samples later go on to purchase (unless the sample is accompanied by a coupon).

Multipacks and multibuys
Offers of 'three for the price of two' are a useful means of getting consumers to stock up on a particular brand. Banding multiple product units, or complementary products together can now be accomplished electronically through the use of electronic point-of-sale (EPOS) systems, rather than physically.

Increased product quantity
Goods such as packaged foods and bottled drinks can offer so many per cent extra for free. The marginal cost of the extra product is usually relatively small for the producer, as long as their packaging processes are easily customized. There is a danger of a 'reference quantity' effect in markets such as canned beers where extra product is so frequently offered that it can become expected by consumers.

Improved product quality or features
Major consumer durables such as cars or new homes are often marketed with additional free features such as a car stereo or a free fitted kitchen.

Tangible value adding promotions

Valued packaging
This is a relatively unusual type of promotion, used in food and drink markets and occasionally for other forms of product that need to be contained in use. Typical valued packaging offers involve selling audio cassettes in storage boxes, tea bags in tea caddies or cookies in cookie jars.

Premiums
Premiums are free gifts which can be supplied in or on packages, or in the mail. Self-liquidating premiums require the consumer to mail in money to cover the cost of providing the item. A typical in-pack premium might involve a free mug packaged up with two jars of coffee.

Gift coupons
Collecting gift coupons is a relatively unfashionable occupation, but petrol companies and cigarette manufacturers still make extensive use of them.

Opportunity-based value adding promotions

Competitions
Competitions are a very versatile promotional tool that can be aimed at consumers, intermediaries or the salesforce. Selecting the right prize can help to reinforce the brand's image. The limited number of winners and known cost of prizes generally make competitions a very cost effective form of promotion, and one which can appeal to a wide range of consumers (Peattie and Peattie 1993).

Promotional information
A great deal of promotional activity involves providing prospective customers with information which assists their purchasing process. The information provided can also be put into an

entertaining and informative format which reinforces the image of the brand and its advertising. Some companies issue information with little direct 'selling' message, which aims to educate consumers and hopefully make them likely to discern in the company's favour. Examples include financial service providers issuing a beginner's guide to investment videos, and hi-fi manufacturers issuing guides to hi-fi and music.

Guarantees
Extended guarantees for major consumer durable purchases are a useful way of reducing the perceived risk associated with purchase.

Product buyback and exchange schemes
Buyback and exchange schemes are an alternative means of reducing the perceived purchase risk used in a range of consumer durable markets such as cars, televisions and audio products.

Clubs
Clubs are a good method of developing a long-term relationship with a customer and are useful for encouraging customer loyalty. These have proved popular in service industries such as air travel and hotels, and in the marketing of products to children.

4 Promotions and the rest of the marketing mix

Although promotions are often referred to as a subset of marketing communications, it would be more accurate to consider them as a customization of other mix elements (see THE MARKETING MIX). Each mix element offers different benefits to customers (see Figure 1). To increase the desirability of the total product offering, sales promotions can provide additional benefits which:

- enhance the product offering's utility by enhancing quality, or adding extra tangible benefits;
- improve affordability by increasing the quantity offered, decreasing the price or easing the payment terms;
- improve accessibility by gaining access to distribution channels and through extras such as free delivery;
- support the advertising, sales and PR effort to boost the product's visibility and credibility through eye-catching and newsworthy promotional materials, and by creating subjects for advertising campaigns or discussions with customers.

Promotions are usually temporary customizations of the marketing mix, but some promotions can become annual events or permanent features. Airline frequent flier schemes were originally envisaged as temporary promotions, but have gone on to become a significant and lucrative (through the sale of related services) component of the travel business. Some would argue that such permanence turns a marketing activity from a promotion into a different element of the marketing mix. This is rather a moot point, but it illustrates the difficulties of

Figure 1 Satisfaction chain

drawing clear and consistent boundaries around the whole field of sales promotion. Exactly where the borderline is between promotional pricing and ordinary pricing, or between promotional events and public relations is impossible to say.

Figure 2 illustrates how sales promotions interface with the other mix elements, represented as an expanded 'Nine Ps'. The emphasis placed on value increasing promotions means that it is the relationship with the product and with pricing that attracts the most attention. However, promotions offer considerable opportunities for integration with other forms of marketing communication (see MARKETING COMMUNICATIONS).

Promotions and advertising
Promotions and advertising have frequently been portrayed as rivals methods of marketing communications. This rivalry represented the competition between the agencies that serviced the different types of campaign rather than any form of marketing logic. In fact advertising which features promotions has been proven to be particularly effective in communicating to consumers and to enhance a company's image. Promotions have also been proven to be most effective when supported by advertising.

Promotions and selling
Promotions targeted at distributors and retailers are very important in FMCG markets to support the efforts of the salesforce to introduce new products, to gain shelf space and encourage intermediaries to 'push' products. Temporary auxiliary sales staff may also be necessary to support a particular promotion, such as a trade fair or a seasonal sale. Promotions can play an important part in supporting the sales efforts of industrial, as well as consumer, marketers. The negotiation of special deals for key customers, participation at trade fairs, product samples and the provision of product information all play a vital part in reducing the buyers' perception of risk and helping to win contracts. Promotional gifts as humble as calendars, pens and mugs all play a part in communicating, and in keeping the promoter's name at the potential purchaser's fingertips.

Promotions and PR
Promotional events such as trade fairs and product launches form a major area of crossover between sales promotion and PR. Such events will provide potential customers with extra benefits such as entertainment, refreshment, promotional gifts, information and may provide opportunities for product trial or participation in a competition (see PUBLIC RELATIONS).

Promotions and the place of purchase
Manufacturers are very aware that the visibility and location of their products within a retail outlet can be crucial to their success. This makes them keen to develop posters, special dispensers and shelf cards to be used by the retailer at the point of sale (POS). However, only some 25 per cent of POS display materials that are sent to retailers are eventually used (Shultz 1987). This relatively low success rate is caused by a tendency among marketers to overlook the retailer's needs when planning POS materials. The result is displays that are unsuitable for the particular retail environment, that are too bulky, or which are too difficult for the retailer to set up correctly (see RETAILING).

5 Promotions as a means of communication

Although it would be misleading to think of promotions simply as a form of marketing communications, promotions do have an important role to play in communicating with the marketplace. Communicating effectively requires the marketer to develop the right message, select an appropriate media, and accurately target the campaign. When it comes to targeting, promotions are more flexible than advertising, which essentially presents one message at a time to the entire audience (a 'shotgun' approach). Promotions have the ability to communicate different messages to different customer groups, perhaps through the offer of a variety of prizes in a competition or through customized electronic catalogues held on computer disc being sent to different types of customer.

In terms of persuasion, promotions' direct response orientation has focused attention on the 'action' phase of Strong's classic AIDA model (1925) when discussing their communications capabilities. In fact, promotions work

Figure 2 Promotions and the marketing mix: an integrated model effectively during each phase of this communication process:

1 *Attention*: promotions are undoubtedly attention grabbing. Words such as 'Extra', 'Free', 'Win' and 'Special' all help promoted products to stand out on supermarket shelves which can contain over 35,000 different products jostling for the consumer's attention.
2 *Interest*: promotions can inject novelty and even fun into the most familiar or mundane of products, and the most habitual of purchases.
3 *Desire*: encouraged by the offer of additional benefits, and by promotions which reinforce the desirability of a product, for example by offering it as a desirable competition prize.
4 *Action*: promotions differ from advertising (with the exception of direct response advertising) in seeking a direct response. The responses which a promotion might try to generate, include encouraging consumers to:

- accelerate their purchase timing of a brand;
- select a brand for their initial purchase;
- stay loyal to a brand;
- switch brands;
- replace a consumer durable;
- overcome their previous objections to a brand and sample it;
- gather information about a brand.

6 Tactical and strategic dimensions of promotions

The majority of promotions are of the value increasing type, with coupons and discounting being particularly popular. Such price-orientated promotions will clearly only be effective while they are on offer. Their popularity has led to an overemphasis on the rational economic dimensions of promotions, and the emergence of a conventional wisdom that regards them as tactical weapons whose results are short-term in nature. Any longer term effect of promotions was generally held to be negative in terms of potentially devaluing a brand in the minds of consumers, or creating post-deal resistance to the 'normal' selling price (Jones 1990).

As a tactical weapon, promotions can be an effective and swift response to competitors' advertising campaigns or new product introductions. Responding with a new product or advertising campaign may take months or even years. Promotions can be put into place in a matter of weeks, particularly since previous successful promotions can often be taken 'off the shelf', given a fresh theme and relaunched. This can allow a company to regain the initiative in the short term, while more strategic responses are developed. Promotions can also be a very effective remedy for situations which otherwise appear disastrous. Following a 55-day strike, company executives at United Airlines feared that it would take seven months for lost market share to be regained. Instead, an offer of half-price flight coupons devised by their marketers restored their market share in only eleven days.

During the 1980s many companies began to take a much less tactical and more strategic approach to the management of sales promotions. This was partly a response to the growing proportion of the marketing budget being invested in promotions, and partly a result of the development of integrated marketing communications strategies which used each form of communications in a co-ordinated, and hopefully synergistic, way. Companies became aware that promotions which are managed effectively, and avoid simple price cutting can contribute to the strategically important tasks of building up the image of a brand, nurturing brand loyalty and building market share (Davies and Saunders 1992, Peattie and Peattie 1997).

7 Sales promotion pitfalls

Although careful investment in sales promotions has been proven to be a flexible and effective way of generating competitive advantage, the use of promotions is not without potential risks and drawbacks. Sales promotion as a marketing activity has often drawn criticism from marketing commentators. Some critics have suggested that overuse is training customers to buy products only on promotion, while others claim that promotional overkill is desensitizing consumers to their benefits. It is certainly the case that any promotional tool must be used with care, since overuse tends to blunt effectiveness. There is also the concern that emphasizing promotions leads marketers to focus on short-term tactical issues instead of longer term strategy. The question of whether the growing importance of promotions is a symptom or a cause of waning brand loyalty and shortening marketing planning time horizons is very difficult to answer. However, it is clear that many of the promotions that are growing in popularity, such as on-pack coupons, clubs, or those which require the collection of purchase proofs, are aimed at producing rather than overcoming brand loyalty.

Promotions have definite limitations. They will neither compensate for fundamental weaknesses in the rest of the marketing mix, nor revive the fortunes of an outdated brand, and overuse can be counterproductive. Unless carefully managed, promotions can also present serious risks to the marketing strategy and the business as a whole. Advertising, with its fixed upfront costs, is often considered as riskier than promotions, whose costs are generally more spread out and related to sales volume. However, while misconceived advertising dents credibility and wastes communications budgets, a bungled promotion can also incur significant 'clean-up' costs. This was vividly demonstrated by the fallout from a mismanaged competition run by Pepsi-Cola in the Philippines which cost the company an initial £8 million, led to them facing over 22,000 lawsuits, and provoked riots, death threats against company executives and grenade attacks on Pepsi lorries.

Since discounting and couponing are the dominant forms of sales promotion, the key problems associated with promotions are the danger of sparking price wars, the effects of discounting on consumers' reference prices, and the costs of coupon fraud. However, each different form of promotion brings its own particular potential pitfalls which must be carefully avoided. Competitions involving gamecard promotions require careful attention to printing accuracy and security to prevent the problems of excessive prize awards that have befallen the likes of Esso and Beatrice Foods. Coupons, giveaways and buyback schemes all require accurate estimates of the potential response. If such promotions are unexpectedly successful in attracting customers, they can result in significant financial losses. Misjudging the extent or timing of consumer response can also lead to stock-outs and subsequent customer dissatisfaction (see SALES FORECASTING). The mechanics of returning mail-in premiums are usually dealt with by specialist handling houses. Although this arrangement is usually very effective, there have been instances where handling house fulfilment delays and failures have occurred. These cause consumer dissatisfaction and reflect badly on the promoter.

Promotions generally encounter problems for one of four reasons (Strang 1976; Quelch 1989):

1. A failure to apply the type of rigorous planning and control processes afforded to advertising campaigns.
2. Time pressure leading to poor decision making and mistakes.
3. A tendency for the implementation and evaluation of promotions to be delegated too far down the organization.
4. A failure to integrate the promotion with other elements of the marketing strategy and mix.

8 Managing and planning sales promotions

Although tactical promotions may have to be organized almost immediately, promotions benefit greatly from thorough planning. Any plan for a sales promotion should be drawn up with reference to the overall marketing strategy, which in turn will reflect the environmental opportunities and threats facing the business and the internal organizational realities of corporate strategy, resources and politics. An ideal situation is to have a specific corporate communications strategy which seeks to divide the marketing communications tasks and resources between the different forms of marketing communications in a cost effective and co-ordinated way. This slightly idealized situation is reflected in the model summarizing the sales promotion planning process shown in Figure 3.

Once the overall sales promotion objectives and budgets have been set, the sales promotion plan will usually be divided into a series of campaigns. Each campaign will aim to fulfil specific objectives, and will use one or more type

The marketing mix

Figure 3 The sales promotion planning process

of promotion, each with its particular underlying concept, marketing message and means of reaching its target.

In addition to the obvious objectives of increasing sales or encouraging product trial, promotions can pursue a wide range of strategic and tactical objectives (Peattie and Peattie 1997) including:

- creating awareness of, or interest in, the product;
- overshadowing a competitor's promotional or other activities;
- deflecting attention away from price competition;
- reinforcing advertising themes;
- developing a relationship with customers or intermediaries;
- gathering marketing information.

To develop a promotion which will meet its objectives, it is important for the marketer to select the appropriate form of promotion, to apply it correctly in terms of geographic area and product variants (sizes or models), to offer benefits which appeal to the target in both nature and scale, and finally to time the launch and duration of the promotion to maximum effect.

The planning and implementation of a promotion will frequently be supported by a sales promotions agency. Such agencies resemble advertising agencies in many respects. They operate on a fee basis for their creative input, with 'account handlers' representing the interests of each client. Agencies provide clients with impartial advice about which form of promotion will best suit their needs. They will also be able to supply or arrange all the artwork, design, prizes and premiums that are needed to bring a promotion to fruition. The tactical origins of promotions has been reflected in a tendency for promotions to be sought and supplied on an *ad hoc* basis. The increasing trend towards strategic promotions has led to more sales promotions agencies working with clients on a retainer basis. It has also led to the emergence of an increasing number of agencies supplying integrated marketing communications services instead of just advertising, sales promotions or direct mail.

9 Selecting an appropriate promotion

With the bewildering array of different types of promotions available, selecting an appropriate type can be a daunting task. The choice of promotional tool will be influenced by a number of factors:

1 *Marketing problem to be addressed*. A free sample is an excellent way of stimulating product trial; a money-off coupon is useful for prompting past customers to repurchase; a sale can help to smooth seasonal demand fluctuations; while a competition can help to generate a database of customers to whom future promotions can be targetted.
2 *Stage in product life-cycle*. The marketing challenges faced by a particular product will frequently reflect its life-cycle stage. Products being introduced will require consumer promotions aimed at gaining product trial, such as sampling programmes, and trade promotions aimed at getting channels to stock and display the product. More mature products may need to rely more on price promotions and on trade promotions aimed at generating salesforce and retailer enthusiasm for a familiar product and ensuring that channels are protected.
3 *Nature of the product*. Different promotions suit different types of product. An offer of 10 per cent extra free is a logical choice for packaged goods, but would look very strange in a hairdressing salon.
4 *Target consumer groups*. Different types of promotion appeal to different types of people. The likely success of any form of promotion will be influenced by the profile of the target market in terms of factors such as age, sex, nationality, socioeconomic grouping and ethnic origin.
5 *Geography*. The cultural acceptability of, and legal restrictions on, different forms of promotion vary between different countries. Such differences need to be taken into account when attempting to plan a promotion for an international brand, on an international scale.

10 A focus on trade promotions

A key choice in planning sales promotion strategy is whether to target consumers to stimulate demand, or whether to invest in trade promotions aimed at intermediaries. During the last decade retailer mergers, increasingly centralized buying and the retailer access to marketing information from electronic-point-of-sale (EPOS) systems have all shifted power away from producers towards retailers. Many products now rely heavily on retailer support, and increasing trade promotions reflects their importance in maintaining good channel relationships (see CHANNEL MANAGEMENT; RETAILING).

Trade promotions need to offer retailers or other marketing intermediaries benefits in terms of direct financial incentives or some means of improving their own performance. Retailers will tend to favour those promotions which aim to increase the volume of a product sold overall, as opposed to those which will encourage the switching of purchases from one brand to another. They will only be interested in supporting brand-switching promotions which are likely to encourage switching away from brands that they do not carry, or which offer them improved margins on the promoted brand.

Trade promotions can aim to:

- encourage or reward sales efforts from intermediaries;
- support the introduction of new or revised products;
- increase or maintain floor or shelf space for products;
- encourage stocking up by intermediaries;
- gain acceptance for special displays outside normal shelf locations;

- gain access to new sales outlets;
- insulate intermediaries from temporary sales downturns or pressure on margins;
- reduce excess inventories and increase revenue;
- create a basis for joint retailer/producer advertising;
- reinforce communication to, or education of, intermediaries.

Many products such as cars, hi-fi, cosmetics, jewellery and domestic appliances need to be actively 'sold' to consumers by retailers or dealers, and the skills and knowledge of their salespeople will be a key determinant of marketing success. It is clearly in the interests of both manufacturers and intermediaries to ensure that the staff selling the products are knowledgeable and well trained. This has led to an increasing emphasis on sales training by manufacturers. Such training can be provided by the manufacturer's sales representatives or, as is increasingly popular, through the use of training video-tapes.

Trade shows are another form of promotion which, usually on an annual basis, allow manufacturers to display and demonstrate their products to current and potential future buyers. Trade shows are a popular forum for introducing new products. In a short space of time they can provide access to most major customers or channels, and allow feedback on products and potential sales leads to be gathered. The marketing effort at such shows is usually backed up by a range of other promotions including free gifts, catalogue distribution and competitions open to those who visit a given stand.

11 Evaluating the effectiveness of sales promotions

An important final step in the management of promotions is to monitor and evaluate their effectiveness. In terms of measurability the direct nature of the consumer response makes their short-term effect on sales easier to measure accurately than for advertising, particularly with the advent of information from EPOS systems.

The monitoring of the effect of promotions on sales can be attempted by a number of techniques:

1. *Monitoring sales data by time periods.* Breakdowns of sales, possibly on a weekly basis, covering before, during and after the promotion can help to identify its effect on sales.
2. *Monitoring sales data by matched markets.* For promotions run on a geographic basis it can be useful to compare sales for areas where the promotion ran against comparable areas in which it did not.
3. *Comparison with sales forecast.* Where sales trends for a market can be made quite accurately by using historical sales data, it is possible to project the likely sales pattern for the brand and compare this with the actual pattern produced by the promotion.
4. *Comparisons by channel.* Where a promotion was run through specific channels, results can be compared to those for channels in which it was not.

Longer term, or non-purchasing responses can be more difficult to evaluate and are unfortunately often ignored as a result. As well as measuring the impact on sales, it is quite possible to measure other dimensions of consumers' response to a promotion. This can be done through personal interviews, telephone surveys, postal questionnaires or 'scratch' response cards.

12 The future for sales promotion

Despite the criticisms aimed at sales promotion by many within the field of marketing, as the new millennium approaches, there is every indication that promotions will continue to grow in importance. Consumers today are faced with an ever increasing range of products and brands from which to choose. In many markets the differences between brands are also becoming increasingly slim, with any innovations which yield competitive advantage being rapidly imitated by the pack of brands chasing the market leaders. It is therefore not surprising that many consumers are abandoning previous brand loyalties to experiment and to take advantage of brands which differentiate themselves through the offer of additional benefits.

A number of trends bode well for the future growth of sales promotion. Technological advances in packaging and information processing are making it possible to target additional benefits at consumers and the trade more accurately and cost effectively than ever before. The increasing trend towards the sharing of promotions with retailers and other manufacturers has opened up whole new worlds of opportunity for companies to target new customers and to offer new benefits to entice previous purchasers back towards the brand.

The view of sales promotion is also maturing to recognize their effectiveness, flexibility, brand-building potential and strategic importance. Instead of being viewed as a tactical 'bolt-on extra' which is added into the marketing mix as a defensive move in times of difficulty, promotions are being viewed increasingly as an integral part of the marketing mix. In the future, effective use of sales promotion will be an increasingly important factor in determining the competitive success of a wide range of brands.

KEN PEATTIE
CARDIFF BUSINESS SCHOOL
UNIVERSITY OF WALES

Further reading

(References cited in the text marked *)

Chandon, P. (1995) 'Consumer research on sales promotion: a state-of-the-art literature review', *Journal of Marketing Management* 11: 419–41.
Cummins, J. (1989) *Sales Promotion: How to Create and Implement Campaigns that Really Work*, London: Kogan Page.
* Davies, M. and Saunders, J. (1992) 'The double delight of sales promotion', in Whitelock *et al.* (eds) *Marketing in The New Europe and Beyond, Proceedings of the 1992 MEG Conference*, Salford, pp. 371–81.
Fraser, C. and Hite, R. (1990) 'Varied consumer responses to promotions: a case for response based decision making', *Journal of the Market Research Society* 32: 349–75.
* Jones, J.P. (1990) 'The double jeopardy of sales promotion', *Harvard Business Review* 68: 145–52.
* Lattin, J.M. and Bucklin, R.E. (1989) 'Reference effects of price and promotion on brand choice behaviour', *Journal of Marketing Research* 26: 299–310.
* McAllister, L. and Totten, J. (1985) 'Decomposing the promotional bump: switching, stockpiling and consumption increase', paper presented at ORSA/TIMS 1985 Joint Meeting.
* Peattie, K. and Peattie, S. (1993) 'Sales promotion: playing to win?', *Journal of Marketing Management* 9: 255–70.
* Peattie, K. and Peattie, S. (1997) 'Promotional competitions as a strategic marketing weapon', *Journal of Marketing Management* 13: 777–89.
* Peattie, S. and Peattie, K. (1994) 'Sales promotion', in Baker, M.J. *The Marketing Book* (2nd edn), London: Butterworth-Heinemann, pp. 534–54.
* Quelch, J.A. (1989) *Sales Promotion Management*, Englewood Cliffs, NJ: Prentice-Hall.
Robinson, W.A. Schultz, D.E. (1982) *Sales Promotion Management*, Chicago: Crain Books.
Shimp, T.A. *Promotion Management and Marketing Communications*, (2nd edn), Fort Worth: The Dryden Press.
* Shultz, D.E. (1987) 'Above or below the line ? growth of sales promotion in the United States', *International Journal of Advertising* 6: 17–27.
* Strang, R.A. (1976) 'Sales promotion: fast growth, faulty management', *Harvard Business Review* 54: 115–24.
Tellis, G.J. (1998), *Advertising and Sales Promotion Strategy*, Reading MA: Addison Wesley.
Toop, A. (1992) *European Sales Promotion: Great Campaigns in Action*, London: Kogan Page.

See also: ADVERTISING; BRANDING AND BRAND MANAGEMENT; CHANNEL MANAGEMENT; CONSUMER BEHAVIOUR; CUSTOMER CARE AND SATISFACTION; INFORMATION TECHNOLOGY AND MARKETING; MARKETING COMMUNICATIONS; PRICING; PRODUCT LIFE-CYCLE MANAGEMENT; PUBLIC RELATIONS; RETAILING; SALES FORECASTING; THE MARKETING MIX

Personal selling and sales management

1 The importance of personal selling
2 Organization and deployment of salespeople
3 Recruitment
4 Training
5 Motivation of salespeople
6 Evaluation of salesforce performance
7 Summary

Overview

One of the conflicts in marketing management which presents difficulties for both academics and practitioners is the problem of resolving the conceptual nature of strategic decisions with the reality of day-to-day operations. Nowhere is this conflict more apparent than with issues in personal selling and sales management. While it is necessary to focus on what the business is and where it should be, vital to target markets and match resources to fulfil customers' expectations and essential to be customer oriented, businesses must sell today's output to survive. The frontline of revenue generation is the salesforce. This entry will briefly review the traditional role of personal selling and sales management and focus on the changes in this important area concerned with the organization, motivation and evaluation of the salesforce. This is a wide-ranging subject and could conceivably involve types of selling, characteristics of salespeople, interaction and behavioural theory, time and territory management with issues of recruitment, selection, training, leadership, motivation and many more aspects of what constitutes managing the sales function. The content is, by necessity, limited to a few of these important issues and the extensive reading list is intended to give the interested reader more comprehensive coverage of the subject.

1 The importance of personal selling

Personal selling is the personal contact with one or more purchasers for the purpose of making a sale. To be effective, marketing management needs to integrate personal selling with other promotional elements, with other organizational functions such as distribution and production and with the customer and competitive structures prevailing in the market. The importance of personal selling is such that expenditure on the salesforce usually exceeds the budget for all other marketing activities added together, with the possible exception of promotion in fast-moving consumer goods companies. The role of personal selling has three interrelated functions – providing information, persuading and creating, building and sustaining relationships. The information role is part of a two-way process whereby information about the company's product or offer needs to be communicated to existing and potential customers and, in the reverse direction, customers' needs are correctly interpreted and understood by management. Salespeople impart knowledge about the product or service which provides benefits to customers and also a range of information on promotional support, finance, technical advice, service and other elements which contribute to customer satisfaction. Salespeople are also the face-to-face contact between purchasers and the company and for good reason are referred to as 'the eyes and ears of the organization' since senior management's customer contact may be limited.

A second role that salespeople must fulfil is persuasion. The importance of correctly identifying customers' needs and market opportunities can never be overstated. Nevertheless, in competitive markets prospective customers are usually faced with an abundance of choice. As a result, adoption of the marketing concept can be no guarantee of competitive advantage. Purchasers will have to be convinced that their needs have been correctly identified by the company and that the offer provides benefit over any other firm. Salespeople are part of this process through persuasion and service.

Today, the salesperson's most vital role is creating, building and sustaining profitable relationships. Relationship marketing predicates an intimacy between the firm and its customers (Morgan and Hunt 1994; Sheth and Parvatiyar 1995). Owing to their boundary-spanning role, the field salesforce of a company has traditionally been a vital link between the firm and its customers (Cravens *et al.* 1992) and a prime platform for communicating the firm's marketing message to its customers and the voice of the customer to the firm. However salespeople and sales manager, although the emissaries of the firm's marketing message have, in the past been orientated towards '*closing the sale*' as the main driving force behind the sales management efforts of the firm. Relationship marketing has shifted attention from 'closing' the singular sale to creating the necessary conditions for a long-term relationship between the firm and its customers that breeds successful sales encountered in the long run. This shift necessitates a reappraisal of existing sales management practices and the sales philosophy and culture that has driven the development of the sales management field in the past. The role of the salesperson is continuing to move away from the traditional aggressive and persuasive selling, to a new role of 'relationship manager'. Also, in practice, we are witnessing a tendency to change the sales lexicon from salesforce to sales counsellors, professional representatives or sales consultants. This change in title is designed to facilitate the transition of the salesforce's tasks from selling to advising and counselling; from talking to listening, and from pushing to helping as suggested by Pettijohn *et al.* (1995). The new reality of relationship marketing directs salespeople and sales managers to develop long lasting relationships with their customers based on mutual trust and commitment. Each selling occasion is an opportunity to strenghten the relationship between them and their customer, and increase the loyalty of the customer to the firm.

The most significant difference between selling and other elements in the marketing effort is the personal contact. The need for this personal contact will vary depending on such factors as the scale of risk, size of investment, type of customer, frequency of purchase, newness of product and many other factors. In some situations the information or persuasion role can be achieved by impersonal means of communication, particularly advertising. Advertising is impersonal, indirect and aimed at a mass audience, whereas selling is individual, direct and much more adaptable. With advertising the message is more limited, cheaper per contact but unidirectional, relying on a pull approach rather than personal selling which is two-way, but employs a push strategy and is relatively expensive per contact. Database marketing, covered earlier, offers an alternative combining the advantages of low cost per contact with a more personalized appeal (see INFORMATION TECHNOLOGY AND MARKETING).

Types of personal selling

In most exchanges, except direct response campaigns, it is unlikely that a sale can be made without first establishing a personal contact. This is the primary role of personal selling. While selling skills are always important, it is worthwhile to distinguish between different types of selling such as transaction and relationship selling and between new business and service selling. In the case of one-off transactions, salesmanship is often the reason a sale is made or not and therefore gives rise to hard-sell techniques. In some cases these techniques seem to be the opposite of marketing, as characterized by double glazing, timeshare and second-hand car salespeople where customer dissatisfaction and post-cognitive dissonance levels are unacceptably high. In these direct selling situations the task of the salesperson is to provide prospective buyers with information and other benefits, motivating or persuading them to make buying decisions in favour of the seller's product or service. In other situations, salespeople are involved with regular rather than one-off customers where repeat business is both the aim and the norm and it is more appropriate to think of exchange as a continuing relationship, not merely that of making a sale. This form of exchange is characterized by buyer and seller being known to each other, by business being lost rather than won and by forms of joint cooperation in the exchange relationship.

It is also important to distinguish between new business selling and maintenance selling. In a new business situation the salesperson has to identify worthwhile prospects, identify the influences and decision makers within the buying unit and, by establishing a relationship based on identification of customer needs, problem solving and shared values, build up a rapport with prospects and customers. This type of salesperson has to match their offer to the buyers' real needs and motivate the prospect to change. Further, this change has to materialize into an initial order and, finally, the salesperson has to convert the initial purchase into repeat ordering behaviour. This is a time-consuming, difficult job. Most salespeople are employed to sell existing products to existing customers. This type of selling, service selling, requires different skills and a different approach to that of the new business or development salesperson. Here the task is to consolidate existing customers, to preserve and expand the volume of business these customers do and maintain inertia in the buyer-seller exchange relationship. Service salespersons know their customers very well, know their customers' business, have access to a number of personnel in the buying organization and seek to maintain the status quo and continue the favoured buyer-supplier relationship. A salesperson's tasks might include taking orders, product display, advice to distributors, advice to users and specifiers, after-sales service, complaint handling, collecting payment, stock management, training customers' staff and many other activities. A priority for management is to be clear on which tasks have to be performed and the most effective and efficient ways in which this can be done.

The role of sales management

Sales management is the management process of directing strategy, organizing tactics and implementing policies which fulfil the firm's sales, marketing and corporate objectives. This is achieved by means of influencing subordinates to be more efficient and effective. The job of the sales manager is not to sell but to achieve sales through subordinates. Managing a salesforce is different to selling. Put simply, sales managers need to establish the role salespeople can be expected to perform, the tasks to be accomplished and the means to achieve their sales objectives.

Three problems hamper sales managers. First, there is the high cost of personal selling. In 1997 the average cost of a salesperson in the UK was £49,499 per annum (Rewards Group/CIM, 1997). Secondly, only about 20-30 per cent of a salesperson's time is spent face to face with customers (other time is spent in driving, administration, call preparation, merchandising). Thirdly, customer buying is changing, becoming more professional, efficient and increasingly automated and centralized. These issues are emphasized in a later entry on strategic alliances and supplier partnerships (see STRATEGIC ALLIANCES AND SUPPLIER PARTNERSHIPS). There may be a danger that with the passage of time and maturity in product markets the salesforce may become courtesy callers rather than salespeople and this is an expensive resource for this purpose. An amusing way to describe salespeople is to refer to them as inter-organizational boundary spanners, but this is exactly what they are and what makes their management both challenging and difficult. As a result, increasing the productivity of salespeople is a necessary and important managerial activity.

2 Organization and deployment of salespeople

Having decided on the role salespeople will play, management must select and organize individuals into an effective salesforce by deciding first on the type and structure of organization, second, on how best to recruit and train salespeople and third, how to lead and motivate their sales team.

Direct salespeople versus independent agents

The high proportion of marketing expense accounted for by direct sales costs, the relatively fixed nature of these costs and the low face-to-face selling time has encouraged a reappraisal of how salesforces operate. One important decision is whether to use manufacturers' representatives (agents) or to employ a direct salesforce. Management have traditionally been wary of acknowledging this choice, instead preferring to alter training and remuneration or to change deployment or other features when problems arise. There is some evidence that contracting out the sales function, similar to the trend to subcontract many non-core activities, may be a viable alternative to the high cost of a national direct salesforce. Traditionally, agents have been used where the market is new (such as exporting), where the company has lacked adequate resources or where tradition has encouraged this practice (e.g. printing and publishing). However, a salesforce of service callers has become something of a luxury item and serious consideration should be given to using highly motivated independent agents. The independent agent whose survival and prosperity depends on sales performance may be a realistic alternative. Such people can be used where a number of complementary products are sold to the same customer as with computer software, the food broker or financial services. The agent requires less training, will already have established a relationship with customers and prospects and is only paid when sales are made. Supervision, recruitment and training costs will be much less and turnover in personnel will be significantly lower. They are also unlikely to transfer to the competition. As markets extend yet fragment the local knowledge of an agent may be a significant advantage if it brings continuity and greater customer knowledge.

Generally, a direct salesforce would be preferred where there is high investment, specialized products and a need to control the selling situation because of uncertainty in the market or environment in which the company operates. If sales performance is difficult to evaluate and non-selling activities such as technical advice and goodwill are likely to be important then a direct salesforce is more likely.

Structure of the salesforce

A second management task is to decide how to deploy salespeople to achieve the best, most productive result. There are six concepts to be borne in mind when designing an organizational structure:

1 Organizational structure should be marketing oriented.
2 Organizations should be designed for activities not people.
3 Clearly defined responsibility and maximum possible delegation of authority to subordinates.
4 A reasonable span of control.
5 Organizations should be stable yet flexible.
6 Organizations should be balanced and coordinated in the activities to be performed.

Inevitably there will be some conflict between organizational and sales objectives and between management and individuals as to the best way to organize selling effort. The salesforce organization will achieve best results where duplication of effort is eliminated, where internal conflicts are minimized and where cooperation is maximized. This is not easy. The sales manager must:

- set clearly defined objectives;
- specify the role of salespeople and the tasks to be performed;
- group activities into specific jobs with clear authority and responsibility;
- assign personnel to these jobs;
- provide effective coordination and control.

Geographical specialization

This is the traditional and most widely used type of sales organization. In this type of structure each salesperson is responsible for all tasks, all products and all existing and prospective customers within a geographical area. It is most appropriate in larger rather than smaller organizations, where there is a widely spread customer base rather than only a few, where regional variations are more important than national standards and where personal contact between buyer and seller is frequent rather than occasional. The advantages of a geographical split are likely to be that travel time and expense is lower. Each salesperson can build good customer and area knowledge, which itself is a motivating factor in that salespeople manage their territory. There is less confusion since multiple calling on a single customer is avoided, customers know who is the point of contact. Additionally, management control and evaluation is more easily administered. These advantages are important but the complexity of today's selling job and the dynamics of the business environment may require specialization. The need to specialize in product or customer, the need to use experts to meet customers' needs and the problem of using low-level personnel for key management decisions does exist. Further, while control is straightforward, overhead costs may rise as more layers of management evolve.

Product specialization

A company with product lines which differ in technical complexity, end users and profitability would benefit from product specialization, with each salesperson attaining the necessary expertise in product knowledge to handle different customer requirements more effectively. Companies who take over or merge with others sometimes continue to operate separate salesforces. Also, the case for expertise with a new product may require specialist development salespeople. With this type of organization problems do arise concerning duplication of effort and multiple calling on one customer. This requires management to promote cooperation between salespeople with minimum conflict and confusion as to who does what job.

Market specialization
This type of sales organization is not yet popular in UK industry but there has been a trend for some industries to organize by customer or prospect. Implementation of the marketing concept would suggest that the most appropriate form of specialization is that based on the customer. Where market segmentation policies can be applied it is sensible to operate the salesforce specializing on the respective segments. Grouping of customers into suitable classifications means salespeople can develop customer expertise and implement marketing policy and programmes. In dynamic, innovative markets the information exchange process may require this form of specialism. In other cases, too much specialization will result in excessively high selling costs.

Combined methods
The advantages and disadvantages of the three previous methods encourage many firms to seek systems of organization which combine the benefits of specialization with reduced selling costs. The increasing complexity of the selling job in dynamic, changing markets gives impetus to this organizational dilemma. The problem still remains of how to deploy salespeople to achieve sales objectives. Several more recent developments in salesforce organizational structure must be considered:

Key account selling
A newer form of market-based organization may split customers into key accounts, different channel members or by industry type. In several markets, particularly food, DIY and household goods, there is no doubt that the disproportionate effect of major customers' control on the market necessitates specialist sales treatment. This in turn affects the job to be done by salespeople on the ground at branch level. A separate merchandising salesforce may be used to call on branches rather than to sell to buyers. In some markets such as office equipment a junior salesforce establishes contact and evaluates prospects. In 1991–2 Kraft General Foods PLC reduced their UK salesforce from just under 300 to a mere 24. The traditional sales role of calling on individual supermarket accounts at local level was replaced in favour of a small number of account managers dealing with the head offices of the major supermarkets and the major wholesale chains. This combination of key account selling and boosting inside sales and customer service was considered to be the most appropriate organization for the company throughout the 1990s.

Telesales
The application of the 80/20 rule can also mean that large numbers of customers account for a relatively small proportion of sales. An inside salesforce or telemarketing operation may be used to complement the outside salesforce for specific tasks. The most obvious advantage of telemarketing is the ability to target specific contacts quickly at much lower cost than a personal sales call. These issues are addressed in the entry on database marketing (see INFORMATION TECHNOLOGY AND MARKETING).

Team selling
Based on successful implementation in 'high tech' selling and 'big ticket' items, a recent development has been the emergence of team selling whereby the salesperson is supported in negotiations by technical, operations and financial specialists, or others, as appropriate. This approach has extended to other markets as the advantages of relationship building between supplier and buyer, or intermediary, become apparent. For example, Procter and Gamble, recognizing that 80 per cent of sales come from a number of key accounts, have developed business teams whose sole responsibility is to sell the whole product range for one key customer. In some cases this team has offices within their customer's head office. The role of the salesperson has changed to customer account manager or category manager and this change is more than cosmetic. These key people have one of the most vital tasks of anyone in their

organization, namely solving their customer's problems and increasing the amount of business that their existing customers do with their firm.

Information technology (IT)
A related but separate issue has been the impact of IT on sales operations. The ability to obtain, store, analyse and retrieve large amounts of information quickly and cheaply has given innovative sales organizations a competitive edge. It enables the firm to collect data from dispersed and diverse sources such as prospects, customers, distribution channels, company sources and salespeople themselves. If relevant information can be drawn together, formatted, stored, retrieved and manipulated into meaningful sales support information that is relevant, timely and cheap then salesforce productivity will improve. This applies not only in administration and reporting but in assisting in routing, call scheduling and other forms of time management.

Salesforce size

It should now be accepted that problems in sales management are complex and solutions seldom permanent. In determining salesforce size the temptation to look for a simple, universal formula should be avoided. The type of sales organization will affect the size of the salesforce, particularly the degree of specialization considered appropriate. The nature of the selling task between development and service selling will be fundamental. Other aspects of the selling task will be affected by the time required to be spent on activities such as:

- demonstration/presentation;
- negotiating on price;
- explaining company policy;
- providing information on competitors and customers;
- dealer support programmes;
- stock checking;
- display work;
- complaint handling;
- credit problems;
- prospecting for new business;
- report writing.

These activities should be part of the salesperson's job description, being included to reflect their importance to the firm. This importance will in turn affect whether six or sixteen calls per day are possible. Questions about salesforce size will also depend on company objectives, company resources and on competitive or other environmental factors. Neither can issues of salesforce size be divorced from the form of organization, the method of specializing and territory allocation.

The traditional approach to determining salesforce size was based on one of three methods. The workload method is a composite figure made up from the total work time available, the allocation of this time to sales tasks and the time spent with each customer or prospect, usually on the basis of size of sales revenue per account. This is the most commonly used technique in UK sales management. With this approach each salesperson should have a similar workload in terms of size of accounts, number of calls and travel time. It is rarely the case that accounts can be distributed evenly so that travel time in some areas will eventually be much greater than in others. Other weaknesses in this approach may be that larger accounts are not necessarily those with the highest future potential. If potential is used these may not be the most profitable if costs of servicing the account are higher or a less profitable product mix is taken. The most serious problem is the simplistic assumption that quantity equals quality. Each account and each salesperson will be different in quality, a factor not incorporated in this method. Put simply different call frequencies (and time per call) may yield higher sales and profits.

A second method is to base size on an estimate of sales potential for the company's products (sales forecast) based on management objectives and a desirable market share. If each salesperson performs to their job description an average productivity level per person can be calculated. Some allowances should be made for the loss of someone leaving, say 10 per cent per annum. Part of the problem with this method is the accuracy in estimating each variable, particularly average productivity. The accuracy of such an average is influenced by the effects of someone leaving, the lead time for a replacement to become established and the effects of cross-selling between salespeople in

The marketing mix

different areas. It assumes a rather static market position when most companies will experience growing or declining sales productivity and perhaps regional variations within an overall sales forecast.

In order to overcome weaknesses in both previous methods, the incremental method is suggested. Intuitively this makes good business sense since the salesforce should be expanded as long as additional sales revenue exceeds additional costs. The difficulty of estimating incremental revenues and costs can be quite daunting. This formula oversimplifies the economics of selling by assuming the product mix is uniform, that extraneous factors can be correctly assessed in advance in each area, that the costs of selecting, recruiting and dismissing salespeople can be accurately predicted and that other forms of promotion such as advertising have an equal effect on all prospects. It is unlikely these assumptions will prevail. The simplicity of sales responding to personal selling effort where all other factors are constant is simply not tenable. The dynamic nature of markets coupled with economic growth or decline patterns, distort the calculations of the effectiveness of salespeople in terms of a sales response function. Seasonal, cyclical and competitive fluctuations create market uncertainty with a possible danger of overstaffing leading to cost inefficiencies. Companies may compound these problems by adding salespeople as long as profits are positive. The important weakness here is that salespeople become the result of sales rather than the creators of sales. Further, it fails to take account, or alternatively dismisses the effects of differing abilities, knowledge, skills and aptitude of salespeople.

As a result of weaknesses in these traditional approaches, management should consider methods which combine good organizational practice with sound territory planning and which incorporate flexible management and lean organizational structures. These are considered next.

Territory management

One aspect of sales management and a key determinant of organization, performance and control is territory management. It would be wrong to isolate organization, especially salesforce size, from territory management or to suggest that suitable territories can be determined and evaluated without studying other determinants of performance such as salesperson ability, distribution, economic conditions or marketing effectiveness. Nevertheless, sales territories are established to facilitate effective salesforce operations. This is achieved by allocating a number of present and potential customers within a given area to a particular salesperson. The benefits of sales territories are:

- more thorough coverage of the market;
- clearer definition of an individual's responsibilities;
- more specific performance evaluation;
- reduced selling expense;
- better fit between sales resources and customer's needs;
- improved job clarity for the salesperson.

To establish sales territories management must decide on the basic unit, evaluate the number of accounts and sales potential, analyse salesperson workload, design the basic territories and assign salespeople to these territories. The optimal territory design is achieved where:

- territories are easy to administer;
- sales potential is relatively easy to estimate;
- travel time and expense are minimized;
- equal sales opportunity is provided across customers and prospects;
- workload is equalized.

The aim of good territory design is to make more effective use of salespersons' time. The most significant improvements can be achieved through salespeople being more disciplined and professional, by better planning of work, less calling on unqualified or unimportant prospects, more use of the telephone, including making appointments, and more systematic paperwork. Various attempts have been made to model the territory allocation problem. CALLPLAN (Lodish 1971), was the original computerized sales call model and most packages today refine this basic idea. Computer software packages, for example Tracker or Unitrac, can assist in the more efficient allocation of salespeople's time and effort. This helps management to focus resources, set realistic targets and better monitor customer response and sales performance. Whatever model or package is used, research confirms that the most significant factor in territory sales performance is to put the effort where sales potential is greatest. Territory design on the basis of anything other than potential (e.g. workload, historical rule of thumb) will be less efficient (Ryans and Weinberg 1979; Hurley and Moutinho 1997).

3 Recruitment

Many sales management problems could be eliminated or at least mitigated if a successful sales type could be found. This would imply that successful salespeople are born, have acquired the necessary skills or possibly have been self-taught by experience. The sales manager's task is to find such people. Some of the best books on selling show that many are still searching for this formula. Other books on personal selling present formal lists of attributes that people should or must have while others suggest that the mysteries of the super salesperson are to be found in personality and psychological characteristics (Lamont and Lundstrom 1977).

Sales situations are often unique or, at the very least, vary by type as outlined above. The various roles, complex tasks and variety of situations which can occur require some adaptability by individuals to any list of principles of selling which may be put forward. Not least, the problem of the measurement of personality and psychological traits is complex. The nature of the job (new business versus service calling) may mean that entirely different characteristics are needed to be effective in different situations (Greenberg and Greenberg 1980). A unidimensional approach will be inadequate and better explanations have yet to be found between the fit of certain jobs and the personality of individuals and vice versa. The evidence on the characteristics of successful salespeople is inconclusive and contradictory. Indeed the basic premise that there is an ideal sales personality may be unsound. Should not the characteristics of buyers rather than salespeople be examined for a better explanation of sales performance?

Sales managers, like marketing managers, must respond to changes in supply, demand, or the framework in which business is conducted. People operating at the interface or boundary between different units in a dynamic environment need a wide range of skills from strategic problem solving and profit orientation to highly developed communication capabilities. The modern salesperson has had to acquire more qualities, more skills and a more flexible approach. Unfortunately for sales recruiters, people who have these skills may consider selling as low in status and unable to provide them with the necessary levels of job satisfaction.

In a marketing context, personal selling facilitates the matching of product offerings with buyer requirements. An important dimension of selling ability is the individual's competence in matching and influencing the variety of needs and behavioural complexities of the buyer. The factors that determine job success are not necessarily the intellectual dimensions which most selection devices are designed to measure. Instead, the result reflects a match between the prospect's and the salesperson's personalities and the knowledge, judgement and persuasive powers of both parties. Salespeople are 'made' rather than 'born'. This does not mean that personality and physical characteristics are no longer important in the type of salesperson employed but that such characteristics need to be cultivated and channelled by training, leadership and other forms of motivation.

Training

Traditionally salespeople have been trained in simplified sales processes usually seen as a series of sequential steps beginning with making the initial contact, arousing interest, creating preference, presenting a specific proposal, closing the sale and retaining business. It is seldom the case that this form of stylized process operates in reality and, while useful as a pedagogical tool, the process does not relate to the reality of most exchange situations. Further, salespeople rarely conform to the popular stereotype. Today salespeople are better trained and qualified, professional sales teams are used and there is increasing use of technology. There are fewer, larger customers, more tasks to be performed such as merchandising and service support, improved purchasing and supply management and increasing levels of competition across industries, especially internationally. To respond to these changes requires enlightened sales management. Increased sales, reduced costs and achieving a more profitable product and customer mix are the three ways to improve salesforce performance. At the individual salesperson level, performance can be improved by first increasing the number of calls. While such improvement, by definition, is finite, various studies in the USA and the UK show that higher call rates equate with higher performance. Second, most salespeople are also aware of the importance of controlling costs and try to improve on this dimension but again the improvement is limited and finite. Third, the allocation of effort between products and customers can be changed. Training can contribute to all three of these areas but it is in the third area that the main differences in performance can be found. It is interesting to note that sales managers estimate that on average the difference between an average salesperson and the top salesperson is about 20 per cent – so quality matters (Ingram *et al.* 1992). Training should aim to get salespeople to work smarter, not just harder. Basically, quality improvement in sales performance can be achieved in one of three ways. These are by improving message content, by more effective communication and by development of interpersonal relationships (see RELATIONSHIPS AND NETWORKS).

5 Motivation of salespeople

At any one time ability and technique may make the difference as to whether a sale is won or lost but the key factor in sales performance over time is motivation. The motivation problem is how to get salespeople who operate on their own, away from head office, in a hostile environment, geographically distant, at a relatively high cost, to do their job well in the way management wants it to be done. Motivation is the amount of effort a salesperson expends on each of the activities or tasks associated with their job. Salespeople respond to stimulus and sales managers can influence this process. Various theories of motivation are suggested as relevant to salesforce problems: Maslow's Hierarchy of Needs (Maslow 1970); Herzberg's Motivator-Hygiene theory (Herzberg 1966); and Vroom's Expectancy theory (Vroom 1964). Space does not permit coverage here and the interested reader is recommended to consult the selected references for this entry, in particular Churchill *et al.* (1996).

The motivation of salespeople is neither easy nor straightforward but there is no doubt that it has great significance on sales performance. Part of the complexity of this problem is the multiplicative nature of the variables which impact on performance such as aptitude, role perception and the components of motivation itself. The problem is compounded by the individuality of the selling job since the nature of the task, the individual's perception of each element and the prospect's reaction to sales stimulii are all variable. The problem of industry-specific contexts, the type of selling and the characteristics of individuals all hamper the search for definitive solutions and create unique problems. To prescribe a management solution requires a selection of factors or influences to be considered which can then be adapted to the particular circumstances. Some of the factors that affect motivation include:

1. *The job itself*: If a salesperson does not find the job challenging or interesting there will be a motivation problem. Compared with many jobs this problem will be less for salespeople than, for example, an assembly-line worker. Sales managers should be careful that excessive routines, job simplification or too strict a discipline do not demotivate staff. Part of the attraction of the job is the freedom of action which is permitted. This autonomy combines with a variety of tasks and their perceived importance.

2. *Accuracy and feedback*. A problem already identified is that sales tasks and sales effort have an indirect rather than a direct effect on sales performance. Missionary selling is particularly prone to this difficulty. For others, organizational complexity or dual effort may confuse the sales process and its effect on performance. Nevertheless accurate and timely feedback for salespeople has a positive effect on job performance and job satisfaction.

3. *Motivated people*. Salespeople who have drive and a need for achievement will have higher sales performance. Motivation can be expressed as a function of a salesperson's economic needs, social needs and self-actualizing needs.

4. *Participation*. There is a greater commitment and involvement when salespeople take an active part in decision making. The

use of management by objectives or similar schemes can have a positive effect on salesforce motivation.

5 *Being part of the company*. As with participation, so involvement is increased by salespeople who are committed to their company, colleagues and supervisors. This belief extends to the products being sold (task importance) and that sales effort will make a contribution to the company's prosperity and the prosperity of other employees.
6 *Morale*. Motivation is affected by morale. Morale is difficult to define but is a mix or sum of a person's feelings towards their job, pay, other employees, conditions of work, competitors and other factors. Good morale by itself is not sufficient to motivate but poor morale can be a demotivating factor.
7 *Discipline*. Views on the correct amount and type of discipline vary but it is a factor to be considered. Too strict a discipline can discourage people but little or weak discipline can lead to a situation of anarchy. A fair code of actions not allowed (e.g. dishonesty), of areas requiring improvement (e.g. late reports, poor appearance) and areas of freedom (e.g. call patterns) should be established. Generally negative factors are weak motivators.
8 *Monetary rewards*. Remuneration is the most important reward used to motivate salespeople. The variety of payment plans in operation, even within similar industry and sales situations, suggests that management do not understand the effect of payment on their employees' motivation.
9 *Good management*. Although management practices are a difficult concept to measure with the necessary degree of precision to make conclusions on sales motivation and performance, it should be recognized that they do have a combined impact. Factors such as goal setting, evaluation, control, coaching, understanding and know-how contribute to individual salespeople's motivation.

The importance and complexity of motivation and its effect on performance has led to the idea of the motivational mix which represents the combination of factors to be considered, including remuneration, financial incentives, non-financial incentives, leadership, management controls and the salesperson's personality (Donaldson 1998). These factors, individually and collectively, influence an individual's motivation to work and, ultimately, their job performance. The individual may respond, positively or negatively, to the different factors which management can deploy to motivate the salesforce. The quest for understanding the components of motivation and its impact on performance should at least lead to some tentative formula for improving salesforce motivation. Before doing this, it is first necessary to restate and highlight the problems created by a lack of motivation. One problem is that sales will be lower. Enthusiasm, drive and hours worked will be less if individuals are not fully motivated. These factors directly affect sales performance. A related problem is that sales staff turnover will be higher, especially among better performing salespeople who are more able (and motivated) to find work elsewhere. A lack of motivation not only results in less hours being worked but often higher expense claims, more give-aways to customers and higher mileage. Lower motivation often coincides with indiscipline or 'bad mouthing' to other colleagues or customers. As in most occupations the importance of minor complaints becomes magnified, diverting management time to peripheral issues. Conditions to avoid which may exacerbate the problem include poor working environment, poor reporting procedures, unfairness in rewards, lack of promotion opportunity, lack of individual involvement and participation, no incentives, a disproportionate number of older salespeople and poor communication between subordinates, supervisors and top management.

1 *Status enhancement*. Acknowledgement of a job well done, a more prestigious title, a management training course, an above average pay increase are not only important in themselves but as recognition of effort and a stimulus to greater effort.
2 *Positive communication*. People are less motivated if they have negative views about the job, the company or their performance. If these views are accurate the cause of dissatisfaction must be corrected via product, price, distribution policies or organizational and managerial changes. If the views are inaccurate then management must improve

their communication message. This can be done by measuring existing levels of satisfaction through a complaint procedure, suggestion box, formal survey, exit interviews (leavers) or by keeping close to employees. Whatever the technique or approach, good two-way communication is vital for effective management of the salesforce.

3 *Individual recognition.* Salespeople exist in an environment of relative isolation. It follows that they will be sensitive to the distance between themselves and control of the operation. They require not only rewards for work done but frequent and positive acknowledgement of their performance.

4 *Ability to handle rejection.* In the course of doing the job salespeople will inevitably get many rejections, rebuffs and lost sales. To overcome these negatives, especially in newer recruits, management must train salespeople to handle and expect rejection. These problems relate to an individual's role perceptions and, in particular, role conflict and ambiguity.

5 *Group involvement.* Since salespeople operate on their own, fostering team spirit, camaraderie and group involvement is part of the management task.

6 *Availability and understanding.* As with any employee individuality is important. At any one time salespeople may face personal problems such as health, finance, marital difficulties and so on. These can only be treated on an individual basis.

The formula for the management of motivation is, first, give status rewards. Second, pay particular attention to role problems and rejection handling, especially for new recruits. Third, arrange frequent communication, both individually and via regional or team meetings. Fourth, provide coaching and training for sales staff, including special assignments for older, more experienced staff. Finally, stay close to subordinates – be available and understanding.

6 Evaluation of salesforce performance

At one level evaluation of salespeople is easy – they either make target or they do not. The problem with the link between sales effort and sales response is that it is neither simple nor direct. Most companies do conduct some form of evaluation but few do this in a formal way which assesses the causes as well as the outcomes. Part of the problem with evaluation is that it is far from easy and if done properly it is time-consuming, costly and downright difficult. At the individual salesperson level evaluation is necessary to identify above and below average performers, to identify possible candidates for promotion or dismissal, to identify areas of weakness in the meeting of sales objectives. For management, evaluation is necessary to assess the efficacy of sales management practices such as territory deployment, recruitment, training, remuneration and so on. Finally, evaluation is necessary to modify the sales tasks in line with customer and company needs so that sales plans, and assessment of these plans, are against the most appropriate criteria for improved sales performance. A good salesforce evaluation programme should be realistic and fair. It should be positive and contribute to motivation and improved job performance. It should be objective, involve salespeople themselves and be economic in cost and time to administer. These aims inevitably conflict. Accountants, operational researchers, behaviourists, management scientists, economists and many other disciplines have tried to find better and more accurate measures of sales performance with varying degrees of success. It appears that evaluating salespeople is still something of an art struggling to be a science. Before commenting further on evaluation it is worthwhile to reconsider the unique problems of the selling job.

- Salespeople have inadequate or incomplete information about their job, especially concerning the needs and preferences of customers and customer organization.
- Salespeople usually work alone and independently without direct supervision. Although considered by many to be an advantage this independence creates other problems of role clarity.
- Salespeople operate in an inter-organizational boundary position which creates role conflicts.
- The sales job is demanding in terms of the degree of innovation and creativity required. There is no one right approach.

- The job requires adaptability and sensitivity from salespeople to the needs of customers, frequently met by different degrees of antagonism, hostility and aggression.
- Sales decisions may have to be made quickly requiring decisiveness and mental alertness.
- Individual sales performance evaluation lacks direct observation of inputs – only outcomes are assessed.
- Evaluation is often inferred and subjective, people biased.
- Salespeople have little control over the conditions in which they operate.

As a result of these peculiarities traditional systems of evaluation fail to measure the complete job. Evaluation has relied on inadequate definition of the necessary inputs to achieve the desired outputs. That is, the use of sales, call rates or other easily assessed measures are preferred to the more difficult quality dimensions of the job. The quality measures are often the most important. Further, most sales managers place an over-reliance on subjective factors. Seemingly contrary to the first point, many managers evaluate salespeople on selected personality traits or qualities. These characteristics are seldom proven measures of quality in sales performance. More likely they are factors considered by managers to have made themselves successful when they were selling. Evaluation will be a greater motivation if used in a positive rather than a negative way. It is incumbent upon sales managers to improve their evaluation procedures. Ways in which this can be done include the systems approach (Henry 1975); the sales management audit (Dubinsky and Hansen 1981); and the company-focused approach (Ryans and Weinberg 1981).

In the review by Churchill et al. (1985) of the many studies which have been conducted on the evaluation of salesperson performance, they uncovered 116 separate studies, listing 1653 possible associations. The only certain conclusion of this meta-analysis is that there is no one variable which has a significant influence on salesperson performance. In these studies, with few exceptions, on average only 4 per cent of variation in salesperson performance could be explained by a single predictor variable. The answer must therefore be sought from multiple predictor relationships and causes. Although these studies are only partial explanations of salesforce performance they do provide some help for the bemused but enlightened sales manager. First, solutions must be sought within the relevant context of the sales job. Service calling and development selling, organizational and individual customers, industrial, consumer or service selling can be so varied as to require separate, perhaps unique, analysis. In the complex trading situations now encountered, the use of sales volume or value is itself incomplete if not inadequate. Further, the mix of hard and soft data, quantitative and subjective, cause real assessment problems. The search goes on. Multiple determinants of sales performance are a better explanation but no single factor, or single set of factors, provides an adequate and satisfying explanation of salesperson performance. Personal characteristics, aptitude and skill will be important but sales managers need to concentrate not only on improving these attributes via training but also on relating them to the buyers and needs of the market. The right people, experience, skill and role clarity do matter but only when matched to the prospect. This confirms what successful salespeople and sales managers already know but few seem able to achieve.

7 Summary

The importance of personal selling to the achievement of company marketing objectives, and to the efficiency of the exchange process, must not be underestimated. Salespeople provide information on their products and services, use persuasion and salesmanship to obtain and sustain a competitive advantage and are responsible for building a relationship between a supplier and its customers. These activities are fundamental to both customer satisfaction and the competitiveness of the firm. Sales managers should be clear as to whether salespeople are employed to win new business or service existing customers. While these tasks are not mutually exclusive, they do require different skills and perhaps separate organizational solutions. The job of the sales manager is to achieve sales targets through subordinates. This involves decisions on whether to employ direct salespeople, use independent agents, or a combination of both. They must decide and manage a suitable sales structure on the basis of geographic, product or customer specialization, or by a combination of these methods. The use of key account salespeople, telesales, team selling and information technology should be used in an efficient combination to ensure that the productivity of the salesforce is maximized. Various ways of determining salesforce size can be recommended but by recruiting the most suitable people, training them effectively and, most of all, motivating them to work to their full potential, salesforce performance and company prosperity will be enhanced.

BILL DONALDSON
UNIVERSITY OF STRATHCLYDE

Further reading

(References cited in the text marked *)

Buzzotta, V.R., Lefton, R.E. and Sherberg, G.M. (1982) *Effective Selling Through Psychology*, Cambridge, MA: Ballinger.

Carlisle, J.A. and Parker, R.C. (1989) *Beyond Negotiation: Redeeming Customer-Supplier Relationships*, Chichester: Wiley.

* Churchill, G.A., Ford, N.M., Hartley, S.W. and Walker, O.C. (1985) 'The determinants of salesperson performance: a meta analysis', *Journal of Marketing Research* XXII: 103–18.

* Churchill, G.A., Ford, N.M. and Walker, O.C. (1996) *Sales Force Management*, 5th edn, Homewood, IL: Irwin.

* Cravens, D., Grant, K., Ingram, T., LaForge, R. and Young, C. (1992) 'In search of excellent sales organisations', *European Journal of Marketing* 26: 6–23.

* Donaldson, Bill (1998) *Sales Management: Theory and Practice*, 2nd edn, Basingstoke: Macmillan.

* Dubinsky, A.J. and Hansen, R.W. (1981) 'The sales force management audit', *California Management Review* XXIV: 86–95.

Forsyth, P. (ed.) (1988) *Sales Management Handbook*, Aldershot: Gower.

* Greenberg, H.M. and Greenberg, J. (1980) 'Job matching for better sales performance', *Harvard Business Review* September–October: 128–31.

Hartley, B. and Starkey, M.W. (eds) (1996) *The Management of Sales and Customer Relations*, London: International Thomson Business Press.

* Henry, P. (1975) 'Manage your sales force as a system', *Harvard Business Review*, March–April.

* Herzberg, F. (1966) *Work and the Nature of Man*, Cleveland: World.

* Hurley, S. and Moutinho, L. (1997) 'A simulated annealing algorithm for sales territory alignment – Part II', *Journal of Targeting, Measurement and Analysis* 5: 319–26.

* Ingram, T.N., Schwepker, C.H. and Hutson, D. (1992) 'Why salespeople fail', *Industrial Marketing Management* 21: 225–30.

Jobber, D. (ed.) (1997) *The CIM Handbook of Selling and Sales Strategy*, Oxford: Butterworth-Heinemann.

Kotler, P. (1988) *Marketing Management Analysis, Planning, Implementation and Control*, 6th edn, Englewood Cliffs: Prentice Hall.

* Lamont, L.M. and Lundstrom, W.J. (1977) 'Identifying successful industrial salesmen by personality and personal characteristics', *Journal of Marketing Research* XIV: 517–29.

Lidstone, J. (1986) *Training Salesmen on the Job*, Aldershot: Gower.

* Lodish, L.M. (1971) 'CALLPLAN: an interactive salesman's call planning system', *Management Science* 18 Part II: 4–11.

* Maslow, A.H. (1970) *Motivation and Personality*, 2nd edn, New York: Harper & Brothers.

* Morgan, R.M. and Hunt, S.D. (1994) 'The commitment-trust theory of relationship marketing', *Journal of Marketing* 58: 20–38.

* Pettijohn, C., Pettijohn, L. and Taylor, A. (1995) 'The relationship between effective counselling and effective behaviors'. *Journal of Consumer Marketing* 12: 5–15.

Rackham, N. (1995) *Spin Selling*, Aldershot: Gower.

* Reward Group (1997) *Sales and Marketing Rewards 1997*, Stone, Staffs: Rewards Group/CIM.

* Ryans, A.B. and Weinberg, C.B. (1979) 'Territory sales response', *Journal of Marketing Research* XIV: 453–65.

* Ryans, A.B. and Weinberg, C.B. (1981) 'Sales management: integrating research advances', *California Management Review* 24: 75–89.

* Sheth, J.N. and Parvatiyar, A. (1995) 'The evolution of relationship marketing', *International Business Review* 4: 397–418.

* Vroom, V. (1964) *Work and Motivation*, New York: Wiley.

Weitz, B.A. (1981) 'Effectiveness in sales interactions: a contingency framework', *Journal of Marketing* 45: 85–103.

See also: INFORMATION TECHNOLOGY AND MARKETING; RELATIONSHIPS AND NETWORKS; STRATEGIC ALLIANCES AND SUPPLIER PARTNERSHIPS

Public relations

1. What is this public relations business?
2. How does public relations work within the organization?
3. Companies gain the support they deserve
4. Effective marketing demands effective public relations
5. Develop public relations strengths as insurance

Overview

Public relations as a management function is a relatively recent phenomenon, but it is now seen as a vital function. This entry concentrates on public relations in commercial organizations, and begins by considering what exactly constitutes public relations and how it is manifested within organizations: how it differs from marketing and how it affects decision making and commerical success. Public relations must be an attitude which permeates the entire organization, starting at the topmost levels and being maintained consistently throughout the company. Public relations policy will help to shape the company image and reputation and therefore the rewards of a strong policy are public support and loyalty. One of the roles of marketing should be to build on the public relations policy and encourage a strong public image. In this way a company can achieve a value far in excess of its asset value. The entry considers how the various activities of marketing, such as advertising, communications and promotion, can be integrated to achieve the optimum business environment.

1 What is this public relations business?

Virtually every one of the Fortune 500 and *The Times* Top 1000 companies utilizes formalized public relations in its operations – defined as having a senior executive with public relations responsibilities, according to studies by such bodies as the Public Relations Society of America and the Institute of Public Relations of the UK. Yet this management function barely existed, outside some Western governments and their military forces, before the 1950s.

This entry explores the role of public relations within organizations – particularly commercial companies, though the principles apply to any body (or individual) with relations with various groups of people. For example, trade unions, charities, government departments and professional bodies all use public relations techniques to improve communications. This section also looks at the inter-relationship of public relations with marketing, finance, human resources and other company operations.

However, it is helpful to appreciate the relatively short history of public relations as a formalized business discipline. For example, it has not always been universally understood. It continues to evolve. It has often been practised with an informal or unstructured approach – in much the same way as marketing was some decades earlier in its development.

All this has been changing. Public relations has been developing its own body of theory and case experience. Both practical and learned books have been published on the craft. Professional bodies have become well established. In the USA public relations has been offered as an academic course in many universities. The same development, though coming from a later start, has been noted in countries such as Australia Canada, Germany, India, the Netherlands and the UK.

How did public relations achieve such universal acceptance, certainly within sophisticated commercial operations? This was probably part of the growing education of the consumer: this led to the consequent demand for better information; the desire for choice; the need to understand products and services offered; indeed, the desire to approve the organization behind the commercial offer. Public relations became the organized link between the company and its publics. Both marketing and public relations have grown as a result of what could be described as commercial democracy operating in the court of public opinion.

Not corporate 'image' but personality that counts

Public relations helps both to define and project the 'personality' of the organization to the audiences that it depends on for success.

One view of public relations describes the craft as the projection of the personality of the organization. The corporate personality is what the organization is, reflects what it believes in, determines where it is heading. But, above all, the personality can be developed and controlled by the management, to become the central factor in the building of the corporate reputation. Perhaps, the most satisfactory practical description of public relations is that it is the management of corporate reputation.

Just as we can anticipate how someone with a developed and balanced personality will behave, we should be able to predict how high profile corporations will handle themselves.

A useful working definition of public relations is those efforts used by management to identify and close any gap between how the organization is seen by its key publics and how it would like to be seen.

Of course, there are many other factors that are essential to success, above all, marketing itself. The best public relations will not compensate for weaknesses in production, quality, service or personnel and many other important business areas. Indeed it is likely that an active public relations policy will expose rather than hide such weakness.

The official definition of the craft by the Institute of Public Relations (1994) describes it as the planned and sustained effort to establish and maintain goodwill and mutual understanding between an organization and its publics.

Some definitions of public relations only cover 'mutual understanding'. This is not satisfactory for they focus on the knowledge of the publics but not necessarily their opinions and attitudes. Clearly, information is only part of communications, as communications is only part of public relations. For what the company does is as important as what it says.

Marketing is defined by the Chartered Institute of Marketing (1994) as the management process responsible for identifying, anticipating and satisfying customer requirements profitably. Implicit in this definition is the need to create the best business environment within which these products or services can be sold and supported. It is not unreasonable to extend this to the creation of goodwill between the organization offering the products and services and the purchasers of these – this is the normal situation within an information democracy.

2 How does public relations work within the organization?

Organizations can win the reputation they wish; whatever they do, they will get the one they deserve. Current public relations practitioners do not see themselves as publicists but as custodians of the public reputation of the organizations they represent. Their craft may involve publicity functions but it should also include the responsibility for advising on and helping develop the stance the organization takes towards issues – strategic policy making. Public relations professionals are concerned with the relations between the organization and the diverse publics (sometimes called audiences) that can affect any aspect of its operations.

If the organization is to win the goodwill and support of those publics upon whom it depends for success, then what it does matters as much as what it says. Its attitude to these publics will shape their attitudes to the organization and its products and services. Therefore, true public relations starts before communications and should be all about company policy – and not just the brands.

This might seem to be true for marketing overall, but it has not always been the case. In Europe, for example, until well into the 1990s, Unilever believed the corporate reputation should be carried almost entirely by the brands. The company felt it could afford to remain virtually anonymous to the public. More recently, as with many major corporations, it has realized that the organization behind the brands is important – marketing presents and develops the brands and their values while, in a sense, the corporate public relations is 'marketing the company'.

This was brought to the forefront by the detergent wars when claims and counterclaims on product performance and damage to clothes as well as worries about dermatological hazards made the public deeply concerned about the corporate philosophies behind those famous brands. A similar shift in public focus towards the men and women in grey suits that ran the corporations happened when IBM ran into trouble; when Pepsi-Cola challenged Coca-Cola; when Ford and General Motors faced major legal challenges over product safety that brought their corporate policies under scrutiny.

Marketing and public relations have different responsibilities

'Marketing public relations' can be one of the most powerful and effective influences within the broader craft of marketing. It should work in harmony not only with other marketing communications disciplines such as advertising and sales promotion but with other elements of public relations targeted at those audiences that are not always considered part of the marketing responsibility – for example, employees, shareholders, suppliers, factory neighbours and government.

Is public relations part of marketing, as might be suggested by such phrases as 'public relations and other marketing disciplines'? Yes and no. Yes, because marketing is concerned about relations with important publics such as customers, potential customers, wholesalers, distributors, retailers. No, because marketing is focused on marketing audiences and public relations has the broadest responsibilities across all the activities of the corporation. The exception to this is in those rare companies where marketing is made responsible for all relations with all corporate audiences.

The chairman or the CEO/chief executive are not always happy to delegate relations with groups that they view as their personal responsibility – such as shareholders – to the marketing discipline.

Companies like American Express and Boeing have developed effective methods to ensure the coordination of the public relations and the marketing efforts, while keeping each separate with its own performance and reporting responsibilities. Of particular importance is to ensure that the marketing-support public relations truly supports marketing, while being integrated into the larger public relations programme.

The quality of corporate reputation affects commercial success

However these responsibilities may be allocated, the success of all business activities – including marketing, sales and, therefore, profit – are dependent on how the company is regarded. Corporate reputation can be the most valuable asset. To quote George Washington, a little out of context: 'With public opinion you can do anything – without it, nothing.'

The principles involved in building good relations with the public the company serves and private relations are the same, believed Lord Forte, founder of the major international hotels, catering and leisure group: 'Reputation and respect can only be built on foundations of honesty and trust. Honesty can conceivably get you into trouble but it remains the best policy. Anything less can destroy in a day what may have taken years to achieve.'

Attitude is a vital factor in most decisions

Attitude is a critical factor in virtually every decision. In business there is an understandable pressure to focus only on the tangible factors that make business sense – for example, is the price competitive; are the working conditions acceptable; will this earn the right return for the shareholders; might the factory neighbours accept this planning application?

Most of the audiences upon which every company depends for business success are not in business with the company. They may have a very different agenda; employees may be looking at security or career options; shareholders comparing investments for their pensions; local politicians seeking a votewinning business/community alliance.

One aim in many public relations programmes will be to win the hearts and not just the minds of these key audiences. Sometimes managers rely too much on logic and believe all decisions are made on a rational basis alone. The factor they may overlook is that decisions can be influenced by opinions and attitudes. One of the prime functions of public relations is to manage company policies and associated communications to build the regard in which the organization is held.

When Exxon ran a tanker aground in Alaska and failed to react decisively, one of the first measures of the impact was a collapsing share price. Why? This was long before any real damage to the trading position could be calculated. It was simply that the public liked neither pollution nor cynicism.

When British Airways explained to its staff that customers were number one – and trained them in how to make their travellers feel that they were number one – sales soared. Customers liked being treated as if they mattered. In many cases, this approach proved to be more important to flyers than the ticket price.

The attitudes of the key publics to any organization are shaped largely by the attitudes of the organization towards them. It is easy to test such attitudes. Would the public expect Ford knowingly to sell a dangerous vehicle? Or Shell to compromise marine safety by cutting down on crew training, or Dow to put the health of employees at risk through poor environmental health policies? Or Forte deliberately to mislead its shareholders? Positive or negative, the feelings such possibilities arouse indicate an appraisal of these companies' attitudes to the audiences concerned. Public relations should be the central function in presenting corporate attitudes to important publics.

Policy must be decided – and supported – from the top

Public relations is an essential top management responsibility – not an optional extra, nor a mechanical function that can be delegated to administrators.

International businessman, Lord Hanson, built one of the world's largest and most diversified corporations over the course of his career, starting from virtually nothing. Effective public relations was central to this; indeed, many journalists rated him as a great personal practitioner. He has commented that the basis of good public relations, as he saw it, was to do it yourself:

> Do not delegate the key elements. Let advisers set up the procedures – but never let them become the spokesman for your organisation. That is the job that senior executives must undertake themselves. Creative people may be able to develop great advertising for you, but this principle should not be applied to public relations. This is essentially a personal skill and a senior responsibility.

(Lord Hanson quoted in Haywood 1994: 7)

Public relations must be a two-way activity – listening to what the public thinks, as well as projecting the organization's messages. It follows that public relations efforts can only be effective where the aims of the organization are compatible with the aims of the public. The concept of the hidden persuader in public relations is nonsense.

Sir Denys Henderson, when chairman of ICI, one of the largest chemical manufacturing companies in the world, oversaw a dramatic reorganization of its operations when the bioscience activities were successfully separated out as Zeneca; this bold move created two distinct and buoyant companies able to concentrate in their different markets. Public relations was an essential element in smoothly and efficiently completing the complex and far-reaching changes that had an impact on all stakeholders in the company. Integrity in communications, he believed, was central as was the basic need to be honest. As Sir Denys Henderson explained:

> The most skilful use of 'smoke and mirrors' can disguise fundamental problems for no more than a limited period. In the end, there must be substance behind the promise – truth will undoubtedly out, regardless of any camouflage efforts by the most expert 'spin doctor'. Management has to accept responsibility not only for the success or otherwise of the message but also for the facts behind it. It is for this reason that I view the professional management of communication as an essential tool for business success.
>
> The ability to communicate key messages, with fluency and integrity, is a vital skill which managers must acquire if they are to succeed in today's complex, everchanging business world. The audiences to be addressed may well cover employees, customers, shareholders, politicians, local communities and the general public, often, both at home and across the world. The different concerns of each group must be met sensitively. The relevant messages, whether good or bad news, must be communicated with consistency, clarity and honesty. An evasive, inarticulate introvert is unlikely to be successful.

(Sir Denys Henderson quoted in Haywood 1994: 8)

Any failure of the directors to be on top of communications could be most damaging. Should the company experience difficult times, it is likely that shareholders or statutory bodies might become interested in how the public relations aspects of key issues were being considered at board level, as they unfolded.

Critical questions on public relations can have been asked when problems arise; companies that do not review their corporate communications at board level are taking a risk. Yet with proper planning, the review of a responsibly run programme takes little time. Indeed, the fact that the board signs off policy may be one vital element in ensuring that the programme is responsibly run.

When Sir Adrian Cadbury, chairman of the UK Committee on the Financial Aspects of Corporate Governance, was gathering evidence, he confirmed that communications, particularly investor public relations, was an essential and integral element within proper corporate governance, as was well appreciated by the City of London.

When it was subsequently published in 1993, the *Code of Best Practice on the Financial Aspects of Corporate Governance* specifically required that the board should have a formal schedule of matters for decision to ensure that control of the company was firmly in its hands. This referred, of course, to financial matters where communications were central. In addition, the Code also said that it was the board's duty to present a balanced and understandable assessment of the company's position. Again this focused on financial communications.

Mobil, the US oil and petroleum corporation, ran a very successful word-of-mouth campaign to change public attitudes – supported by some skilful media relations. The CEO and other senior executives projected their philosophies through a planned series of public speeches to key audiences across the USA, often business leaders but also including political and community groups judged to be opinion leaders.

The responsibilities of directors are extending steadily to encompass all aspects of corporate communications. However, few companies have written communications policies and fewer publish these. Such policies can be an invaluable way to help define the responsibilities of the board and senior executives.

3 Companies gain the support they deserve

The ideal reputation for the organization will not be earned by accident. It will be won through application, direction and commitment. Therefore, managers should ensure that the public relations implications of all company operations are considered in all appropriate policies and plans.

Ideally, the mission statement (or the corporate objectives) will include an appropriate commitment to the development of the corporate reputation. This will also need to be reflected in all business and marketing plans. As an illustration, marketing may be all about satisfying customer needs profitably, but it also has a responsibility to develop and reinforce the reputation of the organization. A suitable statement in the marketing plan about the reputation objective will help avoid the adoption of unacceptable sales techniques or promotional activities – for example, those that may be better for short-term results than they are for the longer-term perceptions among those who matter.

Despite fluctuating fortunes, IBM, as an illustration, follows policies that reflect its belief in behaving properly. People relate to such decent values. Being well regarded by the public creates a good reputation. People like to buy from and work for those that have good reputations. Companies that people like to deal with have an advantage over those who are not popular. If IBM products and prices are as good as its promised services and proven values, it will have a competitive edge. Companies with shorter-term horizons may risk being more cavalier with customers, but those with long-term aims need the goodwill of those who can make or break them – as IBM proved when they traded through the difficult times.

Make the policy shape company behaviour

Many companies are choosing to define and publish their mission. They make a formal commitment against which individual managers and employees can measure their own performance or, indeed, direct their staff, peers or even their bosses when standards appear to be in conflict with some of the points in the mission statement. One of the weaknesses of some corporate mission statements is that companies

The marketing mix

will tend to write them to be broad enough to cover most eventualities; this means they do not have quite enough focus.

One helpful recommendation might be to start with a general mission statement but to refine it over a period of time. Certainly no company should be publishing the identical mission statement year after year in, for example, the annual report unless they are convinced that this is the definitive version. It can always be improved and the sharper the focus of the mission statement, theoretically, the sharper the focus of the organization. Similarly, corporate aims can be shaped over time to become measurable objectives.

Appraisal of reputation should be on the board agenda

The only satisfactory reporting method must be for public relations to be a regular and routine board item. Directors should not just be concerning themselves with communications when there is a problem. Perhaps winning a good company reputation is a little like building a good marriage – it requires constant work, through the good times and the bad. When problems strike, it may be too late to apply remedial treatment. Effective relations between the organization and its various publics require constant attention.

It may not be necessary for the board to become involved in the detail but each director must be comfortable that he has a good overview. Public relations strategy might be reviewed once or twice a year with brief progress reports in between. A strategy review paper presented to the board might cover the following areas:

1. *Objectives*. What is to be achieved over the coming period to support the mission statement or corporate objectives? Aims for the communications efforts may be acceptable. However, could these be quantified, to identify a specific point that should be reached over an agreed period of time?
2. *Strategy*. What tone of voice is being adopted to achieve these objectives? Do all the elements support this and how do they combine into an overall plan? Is each activity complementary? Can any be extended to reach broader audiences and improve cost effectiveness?
3. *Perceptions*. How is the company seen? What are the attitudes of those whose goodwill the company needs for success? (Every so often these must be identified by research, but interim reviews should note the observations of public relations, marketing, sales, personnel and other professionals in contact with prime audiences.)
4. *Messages*. How do directors wish the company to be seen? What gaps are there between reality and perception? Is the company communicating in the way that will win support – and behaving in the way that will win support? Are all the communications activities reinforcing these agreed messages?
5. *Tactics*. What communications methods are to be used? How will these relate to other corporate activities? Who is directing and implementing the programme? What are the company contingency plans, proposed to deal with the unexpected?
6. *Initiatives*. Are there special events of which directors should be aware – such as the preview of the new corporate video, the launch of the new sponsorship? Are these on strategy and, if so, how can these be best tied in to the broader company business timetable?
7. *Calendar*. What are the major activities in the corporate calendar that have public relations implications? What are the plans to support these? Is the programme scheduled realistically to coordinate such events with any new communications initiatives?
8. *Concerns*. What issues might the communications professionals wish to discuss? Are there areas of policy where the directors' views and support are essential? Will members of the board be expected to participate in functions? If not, might these be enhanced if they did?
9. *Competition*. Are there public relations activities by competitors that should be discussed? How is their public relations effectiveness, say in the tone of media coverage, in comparison with yours? Is this competitive position improving?
10. *Appraisal*. How effective is the programme overall? What performance criteria are set so that the effectiveness can be appraised and the direction fine tuned? What are the achievements to date, ideally measured against the objectives that were set?

11 *Management.* How is the competence of those charged with managing the function? Do directors have any commendations or concerns that should be voiced? How are consultants or other advisers performing? Any changes that need considering?

12 *Resources.* What is the total cost of the activity proposed – including staff time? Does anything require additional company resources – such as regional seminars, factory open days, wholesaler briefings? How well prepared are the communications team to handle any crisis that may arise?

4 Effective marketing demands effective public relations

Public relations as a marketing support technique is well understood. Indeed, the craft has come of age over recent years. This success has sometimes overshadowed other important areas of influence. For example, public relations is less often seen as a strategic approach to undertaking business – in effect, creating the environment within which the marketing efforts can be most successful.

Major business successes have been built on the strength of effective public relations. Brand awareness and loyalty can be more credibly developed through communications channels. For example, McDonald's identified public relations as central to the business strategy originally developed by the founder of the company, the late Ray Kroc. His policy, continued by the company, was to make a significant commitment to local community relations, consistently year after year, market by market, to build a deep consumer trust in the business. For McDonald's, public relations is not an option. As senior executives have commented, the payback is there for all to see.

Get the corporate projection right and the company will have the business environment in which to thrive with the right products, service, prices and people. Get it wrong and, whatever the quality of the rest, the company may not survive. So, where does public relations fit in and how does it relate to marketing?

A central aim of marketing must be to build reputation

Public relations is an essential element in the building of goodwill. Any marketing plan that does not consider public relations is likely to be dangerously deficient. One MORI survey confirmed that goodwill towards the company is closely linked to public perceptions of product quality – a central element in marketing. Some 70 per cent of a sample of the general public believed that reputable companies do not sell poor quality products.

Also, shoppers are more likely to try something new from a trusted name. Such an advantage, built through marketing techniques (including relevant public relations and advertising), can be very significant in sales and market share terms.

Other studies have demonstrated the direct relationship between familiarity and high regard. All such evidence confirms the importance of the brands as well as the company behind the brands. The credibility of public relations as a communications technique which tends to be trusted by consumers can be important in the marketing mix – and certainly able to justify its own significant proportion of the spend.

However, does that mean that public relations is part of marketing? Certainly not. Is finance part of personnel? Or production part of sales? However closely they need to relate, each has separate responsibilities. Of course, public relations has a crucial role to play in supporting (and sometimes leading) marketing, but these are different disciplines with distinct responsibilities. The critical decision that management must make is where should public relations report?

Use marketing public relations to build tangible asset value

The goodwill of a company may well be its largest single asset. With consumer goods companies, this goodwill is often represented as the value of the brands. In recent years there has been much debate about whether these should be shown on the balance sheet.

The Accounting Standards Committee in the UK suggested that a brand value should be written off against profits over an agreed period of twenty or more years. Of course, this makes no sense as major brands like Buick, Burberry, Marlboro, Stella Artois or Tide may be of vastly increased value and some of these have been around for fifty or more years. Of course, in some cases it becomes difficult to separate the brand value from the company – particularly where the same name is in use, such as BMW, Campbells, Electrolux, Firestone, Hoover or Olivetti.

Consider the commercial value that brands can have and, therefore, the potential return on the marketing effort that can build those brands. Nestlé bought Rowntree Macintosh for a sum in excess of £2.5 billion in 1988 when the physical assets represented only 20 per cent of this price. The balance was to pay for marketing expertise, distribution capability and the range of brands. In other words, Nestlé were prepared to pay five times as much as the assets to acquire these brands and the mechanics that had been perfected for delivering the brands to the market. Similar deals carried out in the late 1980s valued companies at four or five times the asset value.

Separate marketing promotion from corporate projection

Whatever company policy, it is still important that public relations keeps the brand statements separate from the values of the company. Ideally there should be two public relations programmes, promoting the products and projecting the corporation – separate but coordinated.

The marketing approach to the corporation can put a fresh perspective on the management of this important asset, the company name. Sometimes companies can create a whole aura around an organization. The statement that 'We try harder' was credible and worked hard for Avis around the world

In the business-to-business sector, European agrochemicals leader Scheering created an interesting example. The company recognized that many of its products were seen as damaging to the environment. Through a skilful mix of public relations, technology, new products, customer service and marketing the company repositioned itself under a theme, Green Science. The result was better credibility, an enhanced reputation and an award for excellence from the Chartered Institute of Marketing in the UK. Even more important Scheering won for itself a stronger commercial competitive position.

Integrate customer relations and consumer public relations

Good public relations can not only build brand loyalty, it can reinforce customer relations efforts, backing both the salesforce and customer services operations.

In the car rental industry, Hertz built a world brand using marketing and public relations policies that were consistent around the world, even where local management were resistant to global branding. Public relations was used to promote the customer experience.

The thinking was that a Coca-Cola-type brand spelled consistency wherever it was developed. Business travellers and holidaymakers alike were more reassured at the prospect of hiring a car which would be prepared to conform to the same high standard – and provided on comparable terms through identical payment methods. Above all, the customers' relationship with the company would be recognized, even if this was the first time they had visited Manhattan, Madras or Madrid. Local variations may be attractive in food fashion or shopping but not in car rental.

Avis later fought this challenge through similar harmonizing of operations, plus an appealing, impertinent challenge to the leader – effectively, 'we're number two so we have to try harder'. A decade later number three in the Europe market merged some ten or so operations – one owned by Volkswagen and one by Renault – to form Europcar. Various old brands were dropped, such as Inter-rent and Godfrey Davis. Coordinated public relations, working within a clear marketing framework, across all operating markets helped project the new offer and establish the new brand with customers.

5 Develop public relations strengths as insurance

The best laid marketing plans can sometimes be devastated by factors that are outside the control of marketing management. Confidence in products has been shaken by health, safety or pollution scares which often attract wide news coverage. A couple of angry shareholders at an annual general meeting have been known to attract more attention than the announcement of a massive new production facility. A few neighbours have been influential in stopping planning permission for extensions to factories.

Public relations for the company, its values and aims will be important, but this will be most effective if it is consistent with the messages projected through marketing.

An historical problem with mercury pollution at one site created poor local media coverage for international chemical giant, Rhône-Poulenc. Under an enlightened management, the company developed possibly some of the finest environmental policies in the industry and called in professional public relations resources to improve community relations. These joint initiatives were so successful that, with the full cooperation of local communities, the company has since invested over £50 million on that site in new research and manufacturing facilities. Community relations was essential to enable the products to be properly marketed; a poor community reputation is equally damaging to sales.

A chicken production facility jointly owned by a leading feed company and a large retailer had such a smell problem that local residents successfully blocked planning permissions for extensions which would have created many new jobs. The problems could not be solved by technical improvements alone. The goodwill and support of the local people had to be won through a public relations programme to show the company listened and acted vigorously to end the nuisance and become a good neighbour.

Cargill corn milling plants have been threatened with closure through complaints from neighbours over smells. When Union Carbide suffered the tragic accident at Bhopal in India, planning permissions for many factory developments at locations around the world were blocked, even where the processes were unrelated to the chemicals involved in the Bhopal incident. With both companies, technical improvements were successfully introduced in parallel with effective communications to win community support.

In all these cases the product marketing could not solve the problem and sales were threatened by issues remote from the normal responsibilities of the marketing function.

Consider leading marketing communications with public relations

Some marketing campaigns will be led by advertising. Everyday products of limited news value and which are frequently bought may need the strength of advertising to lift them above the competition, stress their special features and benefits, remind the purchaser of their brand values. Examples might include soft drinks, coffee and most grocery products. Public relations may be used in support to reach both trade and consumer audiences. Coca-Cola has an active involvement in soccer, for example.

Yet many products and services can best be supported with public relations, with this discipline taking the lead. This will be particularly relevant where the product or service has a broad interest because it is new or affects the quality of our lives, for example.

Philips, the Netherlands-based electronics company, used public relations to launch a sophisticated energy management system for business premises. The Canadian mushroom industry developed a public relations approach into which the advertising was designed to fit. First Direct, Europe's first telephone home banking service established its position of strength almost entirely through public relations.

Marketing professionals will be making the decisions on which discipline will play which role. However, a useful exercise is to ensure that the advertising, sales, promotion and public relations professionals identify the balance and the priorities for each craft. Of course, advertising and public relations should not be viewed as competitive but should be run as complementary, reinforcing communications techniques. Therefore, liaison between the advertising and public relations must be close and effective.

Ensure that public relations and advertising work together

Coordination will only be possible if marketing management brings the advertising and public relations people together and establishes mutual understanding and trust. It is essential to get all elements in the marketing mix working together. This puts a special onus on the client for there are usually quite powerful personalities at work heading up the advertising agency, public relations consultancy, marketing, research house design company, sales promotion specialists and so on. The loudest or most powerful should not dominate the others.

Once the budgets have been agreed, there should be no competition for expenditure between advertising and public relations. The effective coordination of advertising and public relations could be assisted by following these ten simple suggestions:

1. Involve both disciplines in the marketing planning.
2. Define complementary public relations and advertising objectives.
3. Allocate separate and firm budgets to each.
4. Agree responsibilities and planned activities.
5. Establish practical routines for coordination.
6. Have regular joint liaison sessions.
7. Get public relations/advertising to present their campaigns to each other.
8. Arrange for them to make a joint presentation to the organization's management.
9. Ensure regular exchange of all documents/information.
10. Insist that all parties work together this year – or they might not get the chance next.

Good public relations creates the right business environment

Public relations alone cannot win orders, generate profit or reduce costs. However, used skilfully, public relations can substantially enhance the effectiveness of marketing, helping to develop the goodwill of the key corporate audiences. In essence, along with other communications disciplines, it can create the business environment within which the marketing offer can be presented.

To paraphrase the famous McGraw-Hill advertisement: I know your company, you have a good reputation, your products and services are well regarded. What is the proposition you wish to put to me?

ROGER HAYWOOD
KESTREL COMMUNICATIONS

Further reading

(References cited in the text marked *)

Bell, Quentin (1991) *The PR Business*, London: Kogan Page.
Bernstein, David (1986) *Company Image and Reality: A Critique of Corporate Communications*, London: Cassell.
Bing, Richard and Bowman, Pat (1993) *Financial Public Relations*, 2nd edn, Sevenoaks: Butterworth Heinemann.
Black, Sam (1989) *Introduction to Public Relations*, London: Modino.
Black, Sam (1989) *Exhibitions and Conferences from A to Z*, London: Modino.
Bowman, P. (1989) *Handbook of Financial Public Relations*, Sevenoaks: Butterworth-Heinemann.
Cadbury, Sir Adrian (ed.) (1993) *Code of Best Practice on the Financial Aspects of Corporate Governance*, London: Gee & Co.
Connelly, John (1992) *Dealing with Whitehall*, London: Century Business.
Ellis, N. (1988) *Parliamentary Lobbying*, Oxford: Heinemann.
Haywood, Roger (1991) *All About Public Relations*, 3rd edn, Maidenhead: McGraw-Hill.
* Haywood, Roger (1994) *Managing Your Reputation*, Maidenhead: McGraw-Hill.
Howard, Wilfred (ed.) *The Practice of Public Relations*, 3rd edn, Sevenoaks: Butterworth Heinemann.
* Institute of Public Relations (1994) *Professionalism in Practice*, London: Institute of Public Relations.
Jefkins, Frank (1992) *Public Relations*, 4th edn, London: Pitman.
Olins, Wally (1990) *The Corporate Identity*, London: Thames and Hudson.
Patterson, B. (1992) *Lobbying: an Introduction*.
Phillips, David (1992) *Evaluating Press Coverage*, London: Kogan Page.
Ross, Dina (1990) *Surviving the Media Jungle*, London: Pitman.
Stone, Norman (1991) *How to Manage Public Relations*, Maidenhead: McGraw-Hill.
White, Jon (1991) *How to Understand and Manage Public Relations*, London: Century Business.

See also: ADVERTISING; BRANDING AND BRAND MANAGEMENT; CORPORATE IDENTITY; DEVELOPING AND IMPLEMENTING A MARKETING PLAN; POSITIONING; PRODUCT POLICY; SALES PROMOTION; STRATEGIC MARKETING

Exhibitions

1 Types of exhibitions
2 Role of exhibitions in marketing strategy
3 Exhibitions as marketing tools
4 Developing an exhibition strategy
5 Current issues and potential future developments

Overview

Exhibitions come in a variety of sizes and formats, but they are all a marketing opportunity intended to bring products or services to the direct attention of consumers. They may be classified by their geographical range, their intended market coverage and whether they are market or trade oriented. Exhibitions have three major roles: selling, relationship building and marketing research. Organizations can use exhibitions as markting tools in a number of ways: to communicate with their customers; build networks; demonstrate products; etc. This may be particularly useful for firms entering new or expanded markets, especially outside of their existing boundaries.

It is vital that a firm has a well-thought out exhibition strategy with clearly-defined objectives. Such a strategy will address issues of which exhibitions to attend, budgeting, staffing, display design, how to attract visitors and whether to stage any supplemtentary activity. The strategy should include procedures for pre-show invitations and post-show evaluation. This last aspect – evaluating the worth of exhibition attendance in general or attendance at a particular exhibition – is one of the thorniest issues for management. The entry discusses the problems of evaluation and also considers the likely future impact of technology and globalization.

1 Types of exhibitions

Exhibitions are important arenas where marketing opportunities occur. An exhibition is defined as:

a facilitating marketing event in the form of an exposition, fair, exhibition or mart .|.|. whose primary objective is to disseminate information about, and display the goods and services of competing and complementary sellers who have rented specifically allocated and demarcated areas or 'booths', clustered within a particular building(s), or bounded grounds; and whose audience is a selected concentration of customers, potential buyers, decision influencers, and middlemen.

(Banting and Blenkhorn 1974)

Exhibitions, expositions, trade fairs or trade shows (all terms are used interchangeably) are a form of direct marketing. Most exhibitions are regularly occurring events lasting between one day and several weeks. A particular industry's trade show often brings together most of that industry's buyers and buying influences under one roof for the express purpose of shopping. There are also permanent exhibits or marts. Here, potential customers and distributors can view new displays at any time or make appointments with an exhibitor. Examples are the Merchandise Mart in Chicago which displays household and office furniture and the InfoMart in Dallas which focuses on computer and communication equipment.

There are several types of exhibition which need to be evaluated by the prospective user. Exhibitions can be classified according to geographical reach, market coverage and whether or not they are consumer or trade oriented.

Geographical reach

Exhibitions are held at the local, regional, national and international levels. Local exhibitions are relatively small-scale events intended to attract participants from the immediate vicinity. Some local events are mobile exhibitions that firms organize to travel around the country. The participants (usually preselected and invited) are from an immediate local area for each stop of the mobile exhibit. Regional exhibitions are often regional offshoots of national shows and are defined in the USA as drawing a minimum of 40 per cent of their attendance from within 200 miles of the show site. Examples are the Nepcon shows. Nepcon West, one of the largest of the electronic component shows occurs several times a year in different geographic regions of the USA. The Machine Tool Builders Association also sponsors a series of regional exhibitions each year. International exhibitions such as the Frankfurt Book Fair and the Paris Air Show have as their exhibitors and visitors firms from many countries. The American Textile Machinery Association operates two shows worldwide: the European show is held every four years in different cities and the US show is held every two years in Greensville, South Carolina.

Historically, exhibitions have been a major marketing medium for the dominant exporting countries. Germany, for example, has utilized international trade fairs to build its position as one of the world's leading exporters. More than half the world's major exhibitions are held in Europe. Brussels, Barcelona and the National Exhibition Centre in Birmingham, England, which are medium-sized European exhibition sites, have larger international audiences and exhibitors than even the largest American centres.

Market coverage

There are both specialized (vertical) shows and shows which have broad appeal (horizontal shows). Vertical shows promote a single or related industry category to a specialized professional clientele, sometimes by invitation only. Examples are the fire prevention equipment fair in Ostrava and Interpack, the world's largest packaging exhibition. There are many examples of vertical shows serving the computer, information handling and communications industries: computer shows for the medical industry, for the legal profession, for the financial community and so on. Trade fairs have become increasingly specialized and certain centres have achieved international status as the focal point of a particular industry.

In contrast to vertical shows, 'horizontal' shows have many product categories with broad appeal. Examples include trade fairs held in Hannover and Milan. The annual Hannover Fair attracts about half a million visitors and over 5000 exhibitors from more than 40 nations. Other fairs which are not restricted to particular industry categories include the Poznan International Fair in Poland, the Bucharest International Fair and the Cairo International Fair.

Customer orientation

Some exhibitions are intended for business customers (manufacturers, wholesalers, retailers) whereas others are consumer exhibitions open to the general public. The latter often feature products and services associated with specific themes or activities. Manufacturers and retailers showcase their newest merchandise to consumers by creatively displaying products in booths designed to inform and persuade (Barczak et al. 1992). Most medium and large cities offer an array of highly targeted consumer events such as camping shows, pet shows and home improvement shows. As well as these vertical shows, there are horizontal consumer shows such as the annual Canadian National Exhibition in Toronto.

2 Role of exhibitions in marketing strategy

Exhibitions are used in various aspects of marketing strategy. They have three major roles: selling, relationship building and marketing research.

Selling

Exhibition activities related directly to selling include identifying new prospects, selling to new and current customers, servicing current customers at the show as well as developing exhibition-related strategies that will encourage follow-up sales after the show. A visit to a booth by a prospect is comparable to a sales call. Yet an exhibition has the following advantages for selling products and services (Dudley 1991):

1 sales staff meet a large number of customers in a short time;
2 these customers are in a buying frame of mind;
3 it is a cost-effective way of meeting a large number of responsive buyers.

Relationship building

Exhibitions are events where firms can develop a network, maintain relationships and establish a presence in the market. At international shows firms can find local agents, distributors and joint venture partners. In some market contexts it is also important to meet with government officials. Trade shows are microcosms of the industries they represent, with a multitude of buyers and sellers, service providers, partners, industry and regulatory bodies all gathered in one place to do business so that for the duration of the show, the show almost becomes the market (Rosson and Seringhaus 1995). Trade shows are therefore ideal places to network with others in the industry.

Market research

Like relationship building, marketing research is an activity indirectly related to selling. At exhibitions firms can learn about the latest technologies. Through observation, surveys and focus groups conducted during the show, information can be gathered about competitors, distributors, existing customers and potential customers. A firm can build a mailing list, test new products and find new applications for existing products.

3 Exhibitions as marketing tools

Exhibitions as communication tools

The first two roles of selling and relationship building are ways of communicating with customers. A firm's complete marketing communications programme consists of advertising, personal selling, public relations and sales promotion (see ADVERTISING; MARKETING COMMUNICATIONS; PERSONAL SELLING AND SALES MANAGEMENT; PUBLIC RELATIONS; SALES PROMOTION). Dudley (1991) explains how exhibitions share common attributes with each of these programme components. As an advertising tool, exhibiting uses specific media (shows) to convey messages to target audiences. Exhibiting has the added advantage of being a form of direct marketing and can generate an immediate response from the audience. As a sales promotion tool, exhibiting is versatile and provides excitement and urgency. Exhibiting is also often exploited as a public relations activity to enhance corporate image (see CORPORATE IDENTITY; POSITIONING; PUBLIC RELATIONS).

Trade shows efficiently deliver integrated messages about products and services because the exhibition format utilizes a variety of coordinated personal and non-personal information sources (Barczak *et al.* 1992). Personal sources are staff members in the booth, special show events like seminars and receptions, and live demonstrations. The trade show environment is action oriented, ideal for demonstrations by exhibitors. Seeing products in action attracts the attention of show visitors and spurs them to ask questions. Providing visitors with hands-on experiences of product usage enhances their learning and the probability of them remembering the exhibit. Non-personal information sources include booth signage and pictures, product displays and samples, film and videos, and sales literature.

Importance of exhibitions for different types of firms

The relative importance of exhibitions as a marketing tool differs for different types of firms. Research by Lilien (1983) and Faria and Dickinson (1986) shows that exhibitions are of greatest importance to firms with the following characteristics: relatively high amount of sales and market share; a moderate number of product lines, selling through middlemen; and technically complex products for which many people are involved in the purchase. Consumer product manufacturers that sell to retailers participate in shows because of the large and geographically dispersed audience they must reach. However, industrial firms tend to have high field expense ratios and generally allocate proportionately more funds to trade shows than do consumer goods firms (Browning and Adams 1988). Trade shows are especially important in industrial markets because the products are often more complex and have high purchase value (see POSITIONING; PRICING; PRODUCT POLICY). These characteristics contribute to high levels of perceived risk and investment. Also, it is common for firms to use flexible and modular manufacturing strategies, constantly update products, and tailor them to customer demands. Trade shows are useful in helping managers to position their products and learn more about customers' delivery, service and price criteria. In particular, a firm can reach specifiers and influencers in the decision process who are not regularly seen by the salesforce.

Exhibitions as a tool for exporting

The efficiency of exhibitions in delivering a high quality target audience is particularly important in an overseas context where it is even more expensive to communicate with a customer or a potential customer and where other forms of promotion may be restricted. Participation in trade shows is likely to vary according to the firm's commitment to international business. For example, a passive exporter may take advantage of unsolicited orders obtained from overseas buyers attending shows in the exporter's country. Active exporters will travel to participate in trade shows in foreign countries, in search of potential customers and to learn about competition on a global scale. Research suggests that the impact of attending trade shows overseas may be greater for new exporters. After trade fair participation 60 per cent of new exporters and 42 per cent of experienced exporters increased their marketing efforts (Rosson and Seringhaus 1991) (see EXPORTING; GLOBAL MARKETING).

4 Developing an exhibition strategy

When carefully planned, exhibitions can be one of the most cost-effective components of the marketing programme (see MARKETING BUDGETING AND RESOURCE ALLOCATION). Developing an exhibition strategy involves setting objectives, choosing an exhibition, setting a budget, pre-show activity, booth design and location, staffing, special in-booth promotions and specific activities for attracting and holding the attention of visitors, post-show activity, and evaluation of the strategy's effectiveness. The following highlights certain aspects of strategy development.

Setting objectives

Objectives need to be targeted and measurable and should be put in the context of the firm's overall marketing strategy. These written objectives should be used to define the exhibition strategy.

Managers should segment the market according to the requirements of customers and be adaptable to these varying needs when developing strategy. Selling and relationship building strategies for different customer segments (potential customers, new customers and established customers) can be planned in advance. For example, the objectives and strategy pursued with respect to potential customers may be quite different from the objectives sought when furthering relationships with long-term customers.

Selecting an exhibition

For the choice of an exhibition, decisions include geographic location (local, regional, national, international) and market coverage (horizontal or vertical) as well as customer orientation. A good decision requires knowledge of market targets and understanding of the special features, benefits, costs and opportunities at particular shows. The decision needs to be made at least a year in advance in order to accomplish the necessary arrangements.

Exhibition audiences tend to be heterogeneous at large-scale horizontal and international events. Research studies imply that firms that participate in vertical shows are more successful and are more satisfied with their performance (Gopalakrishna and Williams 1992; Kerin and Cron 1987). Because a vertical show attracts visitors from a specific industry, almost all visitors can be potential leads. In contrast, a horizontal show, like Comdex in the USA, attracts visitors from several industries having an interest in computer technology and equipment. Exhibits are thus more likely to attract a larger number of 'window shoppers' rasher than serious potential leads.

Managers should make decisions concerning government or industry association assistance, that is, whether to participate in the show by having a booth or being part of a sponsored pavilion. This decision will depend on the firm's resources and prior trade show experience. Governments and business organizations, like trade associations, promote trade shows extensively. All twelve developed countries in a study by Seringhaus (1987) offered trade fair programmes as part of their export promotion programmes. For example, the US Department of Commerce promotes American firms' attendance at overseas trade shows. In addition, state, county and municipal authorities also help firms to attend international fairs and often organize group exhibits. Governmental assistance to firms participating in trade shows can ease the burden facing many new or expanding exporters by helping them to overcome operational and resource-based barriers to exporting (Rosson and Seringhaus 1991). For example, at the huge international fair at Nuremburg, as well as other overseas shows, many British toy firms go under the auspices of a joint venture scheme between the British Toy and Hobby Manufacturers' Association (BTHMA) and the British Overseas Trade Board.

Trade shows have their own promotional organizations. For example, at all Hannover fairs, US pavilions (which include booths for many US exhibitors) are organized and managed by Hannover Fairs USA, the marketing and communications office for Hannover fairs. The office provides exhibitors with extensive assistance, including training workshops and promotional activities (Tesar 1988).

Staffing the booth

It is often the quality of the staff that determines the success or failure of a trade show exhibit. Salespeople working the booth must establish personal contact with visitors and screen out 'casual' visitors so as to generate good leads. Body language and dialogue as well as knowledge are important to a salesperson's success (Wiesendanger 1990).

Bello (1989) found that personal in-exhibit sources are a much more utilized source of information than are personal out-of-exhibit and non-personal sources. His research also suggested that show audience members were more interested in gaining technical information than in getting transactional information. Studies by the Trade Show Bureau in the USA emphasize that the salesperson's knowledge is most often the critical issue of importance for visitors. A survey of computer industry decision-makers revealed that at trade shows they prefer to speak to technical and engineering personnel (Gibson 1991). This preference is particularly strong when the primary interest of visitors is to learn about new products or when complex products are involved. In order to be effective, a booth must be staffed by personnel trained to deliver the firm's technical message.

The location of the exhibition also has an impact on staffing. For cultural reasons, use of female executives may be unwise in some situations. In shows outside of the USA it is often the norm for top managers to participate in the show, in contrast to the American practice of having middle managers at the booth. A European multinational firm is likely to have the heads of its own foreign subsidiaries in the USA, Asia or South America on hand to speak directly to potential buyers coming from their parts of the world. The intercultural, interpersonal contact that upper-level managerial peers form at trade fairs can have implications for long-term business relationships. Since trade shows are especially important to the marketing strategies of European firms, the calibre of a firm's staffing as well as of its display, reflects its position in the industry. Firms that are not represented, or appear in limited capacity, risk losing market share. In the USA, while it has not been traditional to send upper-level management to trade shows, a survey of 100 chief executive officers from 500 major US corporations found that 82 per cent had visited at least one company exhibit in 1989 (Konopacki 1990).

Pre-exhibition activity

This includes public relations activity as well as identifying prospects in advance and sending them special invitations. Such an invitation can be the most influential factor in a prospect's decision to attend the exhibition.

Special in-booth promotions

For subsequent interaction between visitors and booth personnel to be successful, that is resulting in qualified sales leads, certain information must be gathered by both suppliers and customers at the show. Relationship development is a dynamic process and opportunities for follow-up by the exhibitor are crucial. The busy, complex nature of the exhibition environment may necessitate special strategies to ensure the information is obtained. For example, Everett (1989) described how one company offered a customized monogrammed pen to everyone who completed a detailed questionnaire about projected product requirements. Delivery of the pen occurred after two weeks. If the questionnaire revealed that the person was 'qualified', delivery of the pen was done by a company salesperson, thus giving the company an additional contact with a potential customer. Non-qualified visitors received their pens by mail.

Trade show participation is too expensive to be left to the formal exhibit alone. The real value of shows often lies in 'behind the scenes' negotiations. The atmosphere at European shows is designed to encourage people to spend significant amounts of time in the booths they visit, thus lengthening interactions. Most stands (the European term for booths) have their own seminar rooms, conference rooms and lounges; drinks, snacks and even entire meals may be served to visitors.

Seminars and lectures arranged by a firm at a trade show can enhance the relationship development process between suppliers and customers. Many potential benefits hinge on a company's ability to develop a strong relationship with customers in the course of educating them. At the CeBIT fair in Hannover, the world's leading fair for office, information and telecommunications technology, lectures have two purposes: as a forum for the exchange of information between professionals and as a vehicle for the presentation of product information aimed at a particular target group, such as systems packages for lawyers, architects and retailers.

Post-show activity

Information collected at an exhibition should be consolidated into the exhibiting firm's marketing information system. Leads uncovered must be pursued while the exhibit and any exhibition discussions are still fresh in the visitor's mind.

Evaluating exhibitions

There is a lack of useful and meaningful measures of the effectiveness of trade show performance. Often, managers cannot easily identify the return on their investment nor can they relate performance to their specific trade show objectives.

Exhibitors' purposes vary and therefore firms use different evaluation techniques. There is probably no single criterion against which the effectiveness of all kinds of exhibitions can be measured precisely, because exhibitions are not homogeneous with respect to objectives and strategies. Another complicating factor is that some objectives for participation are qualitative and some are quantitative.

Bonoma (1983) has thus described trade shows as an inherently 'sloppy' marketing problem.

To aid exhibitors in show evaluation, exhibition organizers provide statistical information on show attendance. In the USA the Business Publications Audit of Circulation Inc. audits registered attendance at trade shows. It provides detailed statistical information which enables measures such as 'audience quality', 'audience activity', and 'exhibit effectiveness' to be calculated. Exhibit effectiveness includes the total number of visitors attracted by a display and the cost per visitor reached (Bellizi and Lipps 1984). Research is also conducted by the exhibition industry itself on various shows and on the memorability of individual exhibits.

Research studies on exhibition effectiveness suggest ways to conduct the evaluation task. For example, Kerin and Cron (1987) use subjective measures of managers' satisfaction with exhibition performance. A model tested by Dekimpe et al. (1997) captures differences in exhibition effectiveness across industries, companies and two countries: the USA and the UK. Independent variables included are the amount of pre-show promotion, booth size, staff density, firm prominence, exhibition type and size, and industry. The dependent variable is booth-attraction effectiveness. Gopalakrishna and Williams (1992) focus on an objective measure: the generation of leads at the show (in particular, lead efficiency), as a basis to assess trade show performance. It is important to recognize, however, that genertging leads is not the ultimate objective of most firms' participation in exhibitions; rather the conversion of leads into profitable sales is what counts. As the authors emphasize, evaluating exhibition effectiveness is further complicated by the fact that sales are not necessarily a direct consequence of the show alone. Thus, the evaluation task for exhibitions is very similar to that for evaluating the effectiveness of advertising (for more details, see ADVERTISING, in particular the discussion of 'Evaluating the campaign').

To improve the evaluation of trade show sales, developing a good lead tracking system is essential. An important study by Gopalakrishna and Lilien (1995) is a step in this direction. They estimated a model involving three measures of exhibition effectiveness: attraction (the percentage of a firm's audience attracted to the booth), contact (the percentage of those attracted from the target and that were actually contacted by the salespeople at the booth, and conversion (the percentage of those contacted that turned into sales leads). The data for this study were gathered from a single US show, however, and the results cannot be generalized to other exhibition situations. Also, the study is limited because it does not measure the percentage of leads that resulted in sales.

Rosson and Seringhaus (1991) note that exhibiting has results which cannot be captured solely through leads and sales measures. These results include a learning experience which influences a firm's future marketing efforts. They demonstrate both subjective and objective measures of exhibition effectiveness. These include sales (achieved on site, within twelve months and committed future sales) as well as the extent to which an exhibition helped a firm to achieve its stated objective. The extended period for measurement of sales is particularly appropriate for situations in which buyers and sellers interact over a period of time. Although results can occur quickly, they are more likely to occur after some extended time. The majority of sales may occur not at the show but several months after exhibiting. The trade show environment itself, lasts for only a short time.

5 Current issues and potential future developments

The most prominent issues in the further development of exhibitions as a valuable element of marketing strategy concern the difficulties of evaluating exhibitions, the impact of technological change and globalization on exhibitions and the need for more information about the worth of exhibitions.

Evaluation difficulties

While exhibitions are believed to be cost effective and have many marketing communications benefits, there is an important issue yet to be resolved by industry specialists, managers or researchers. This issue concerns the method of measuring the effectiveness of an exhibition. As participation costs for exhibitions increase, this issue gains in importance. The emphasis on effectiveness measures such as the number of leads/contacts made, cost per lead/contact, amount of literature distributed and sales achieved suggests that most managers view trade shows as merely an extension of personal selling done in mass fashion (Bonoma 1983). The evaluation of exhibitions should also acknowledge their additional roles as tools for relationship building and marketing research.

Impact of technological change

Technologies such as video and computers have for some considerable time enhanced presentations and product demonstrations at exhibitions. Questions can be raised concerning the impact on exhibitions of the merging of technologies along with the continuing development of the information industry. For example, what changes will occur in:

1 The decision to use exhibitions rather than some other communications media?
2 How exhibitions will be used (booth design, activities at the exhibition and so on) in response to developments in technologies such as telecommunications, robotics and virtual reality?

The results of a survey of US exhibit attendees and salespeople (Konopacki 1996) suggested that the use of modern communications technology does not make exhibitions less useful as a marketing tool. In contrast, the value of exhibitions has increased as a place for essential face-to-face meetings. Konopacki suggests that the emphasis of the marketing approach, however, is better placed on consultation and negotiation rather than presentation of new products and services. The use of faxes and e-mail and the Internet means that many attendees have already learned about new developments.

To extend the reach of the CeBIT show, its promoters began to provide video coverage beamed via satellite to North America and Australia. Video is also used to promote the show to prospective foreign exhibitors (Bovet 1995).

Impact of globalization

Along with the increasing globalization of business in general (see GLOBAL MARKETING), globalization of the exhibition business is expected to continue. National shows are more likely to be international events, attended by exhibitors and customers from around the world.

The 1980s was a period of extensive growth in the exhibition business. This growth occurred in terms of the number of exhibitions held in the USA, the Far East, Asia, Africa and Latin America. China and Singapore, in particular, saw substantial growth in their exhibition industries during the period. International exhibitions are important to developing countries where such events are viewed as valuable economic development tools.

Economic reforms in Eastern Europe spawned a proliferation of smaller, provincial fairs in outlying cities to supplement the well-known international trade fairs. Leipzig was traditionally a significant centre for East–West trade. It is now one of the exhibition centres in unified Germany and is attempting to strengthen its competitiveness by offering a series of specialized fairs, focusing on industries such as construction and tourism.

Wherever exhibitions are located, they are used by participating firms in the same way for the same purpose. Yet logistical issues and the idiosyncrasies of individual markets and regions necessitate special attention to international exhibitions (Dudley 1991). For example, at the huge shows in Europe, higher level personnel are involved and many visitors arrive at shows ready to order products. European firms also allocate a significantly greater percentage of their annual marketing budgets to trade shows than do American firms (Schafer 1987).

The environment of international shows is different; since these are attended by exhibitors and visitors from many countries, opportunities exist for social interaction to take place in a multicultural environment. With respect to purchasing behaviour (by consumers or businesses), culture makes a difference in problem identification, in the objectives motivating choice and in negotiation of terms. At an exhibition, understanding different cultures and the likely purchasing strategies of the various visitors to a booth is essential for success. Staffing should include salespeople responsible for territories from the countries of the foreign buyers attending the exhibition. Language capabilities of staff are important, as well as having literature and audio-visual displays in appropriate languages.

Many of the US results of Dekimpe *et al.*'s (1997) cross-national exhibition effectiveness study are generalizable to UK-based exhibitions. Attendees in the two countries, however, appear to behave differently with respect to 'browsing' or 'wandering around' the exhibition and with respect to their stage in the buying decision process (see ORGANIZATIONAL BUYING BEHAVIOUR). Dekimpe *et al.* therefore recommend that different performance benchmarks should be used when a firm is participating in exhibitions in different countries.

Need for information

There is a dearth of impartial and publicly available information on how firms manage the exhibiting process and how this process might be improved. Many studies have been conducted by industry specialists working for organizations like the Trade Show Bureau and the International Exhibitors Association, but these bodies are in the business of promoting the exhibition industry. As an area of academic research, exhibitions suffer from a distinct lack of attention, even though the importance of exhibiting is widely acknowledged. The emphasis in the 1990s on networks and relationship marketing, however, encouraged more study of exhibitions and their role in firms' marketing strategies.

GILLIAN RICE
THUNDERBIRD
AMERICAN GRADUATE SCHOOL OF
INTERNATIONAL MANAGMENT

Further reading

(References cited in the text marked *)

* Banting, P.M. and Blenkhorn, D.L. (1974) 'The role of industrial trade shows', *Industrial Marketing Management* 3: 285–95.
* Barczak, G.J., Bello, D.C. and Wallace, E.S. (1992) 'The role of consumer shows in new product adoption', *The Journal of Consumer Marketing* 9: 55–67.
* Bellizi, Joseph A. and Lipps, Delilah J. (1984) 'Managerial guidelines for trade show effectiveness', *Industrial Marketing Management* 13: 49–52.
* Bello, D.C. (1989) 'Buyer-based management of a major promotion medium: trade shows', in Bloom, P. *et al.* (eds), *AMA Educators' Proceedings Enhancing Knowledge Development in Marketing*, Chicago: American Marketing Association.
  Bello, D.C. and Barczak, G.J. (1990) 'Using industrial trade shows to improve new product development', *The Journal of Business and Industrial Marketing* 5: 43–56.
  Bello, D.C. and Barksdale, H.C. (1986) 'Exporting at industrial trade shows', *Industrial Marketing Management* 15: 97–206.

Bello, D.C. and Lohtia, R. (1993) 'Improving trade show effectiveness by analyzing attendees', *Industrial Marketing Management* 22: 311–18.
* Bonoma, T.V. (1983) 'Get more out of your trade shows', *Harvard Business Review* January–February: 75–83.
* Bovet, S. (1995) 'VNR promotes European expo to other continents', *The Public Relations Journal* 51: 12.
* Browning, J.M. and Adams, R.J. (1988) 'Trade shows: an effective promotional tool for the small industrial business', *Journal of Small Business Management* October: 31–6.
Chapman, E. (1995) *Exhibit Marketing*, 2nd edn, New York: McGraw-Hill.
Deaton, W.R. (1994) *Exhibiting in Mexico*, Proteus Publishing.
* Dekimpe, M.G., Francois, P., Gopalakrishna, S., Lilien, G.L. and Van den Bulte, C. (1997) 'Generalizing about trade show effectiveness: a cross-national comparison', *Journal of Marketing* 61: 55–64.
* Dudley, J.W. (1991) *Successful Exhibiting*, Holbrook, MA: Bob Adams, Inc.
* Everett, M. (1989) 'Using a carrot to qualify your prospects', *Sales Marketing Management*, June: 91.
Exhibitions Round the World 1992–3 (1992) Dallas, TX: Trade Winds, Inc.
* Faria, A.J. and Dickinson, J.R. (1986) 'What kinds of companies use trade shows most – and why', *Business Marketing*, June: 150–5.
* Gibson, M.M. (1991) 'Who do you want to talk to in a trade show booth?' *Business Marketing* February: T8.
* Gopalakrishna, S. and Lilien, G.L. (1995) 'A three-stage model of industrial trade show performance', *Marketing Science* 14: 22–33.
* Gopalakrishna, S. and Williams, J.D. (1992) 'Planning and performance assessment of industrial trade shows: an exploratory study', *International Journal of Research in Marketing* 9: 207–24.
Gopalakrishna, S., Lilien, G.L., Williams, J. and Sequira, I. (1995) 'Do trade shows pay off?', *Journal of Marketing* 59: 75–84.
* Kerin, R. and Cron, W.L. (1987) 'Assessing trade show functions and performance: an exploratory study', *Journal of Marketing* 51: 87–94.
Kijewski, V., Yoon, E. and Young, G. (1993) 'How exhibitors select trade shows', *Industrial Marketing Management* 22: 287–98.
* Konopacki, A. (1990) 'CEOs attend trade shows to grab "power buyers"', *Marketing News* 15 October: 5–18.
* Konopacki, A. (1996) *How and Why Exhibitions Have Changed in 1995,* Bethesda, MD: Center for Exhibition Industry Research.
Lilien, G. (1983) 'A descriptive model of the tradeshow budgeting decision process', *Industrial Marketing Management* 12: 25–9.

Motwani, J., Rice, G. and Mahmoud, E. (1992) 'International trade shows as export promotion tools: macro and micro perspectives', *Review of Business* 13: 38–42.
Ponzurick, T. (1996) 'International buyers' perspective toward trade shows and other promotional methods', *Journal of Marketing Theory and Practice* 4: 9–20.
Rice, G. (1992) 'Using the interaction approach to understand international trade shows', *International Marketing Review* 9: 32–45.
* Rosson, P.J. and Seringhaus, F.H.R. (1991) 'International trade fairs: firms and government exhibits', in Seringhaus, F.H.R. and Rosson, P.J. (eds), *Export Development and Promotion: The Role of Public Organizations*, Boston: Kluwer Academic Publishers.
* Rosson, P.J. and Seringhaus, F.H.R. (1995) 'Visitor and exhibitor interaction at industrial trade fairs', *Journal of Business Research* 32: 81–90.
* Schafer, J. (1987) 'German trade fairs open foreign markets for US products', *Marketing News*, 8 May: B.
* Seringhaus, F.H.R. (1987) 'Export promotion: the role and impact of government services', *Irish Marketing Review* 2: 106–16.
Seringhaus, F.H.R. and Rosson, P.J. (1994) 'International trade fairs and foreign market involvement: review and research directions', *International Business Review* 3 (1).
* Tesar, J. (1988) *Trade Shows: Opportunities to Sell. A Case Study of Hannover Fair CeBIT*, Denver: Trade Show Bureau.
Tradeshow Week Data Book International Edition (1993) New Providence, NJ: R.R. Bowker.
Webster, V.J. (1993) *Trade Shows Worldwide*, 7th edn, Detroit, MI: Gale Research, Inc.
* Wiesendanger, B. (199()) 'Are your salespeople trade show duds?' *Sales & Marketing Management* August: 40–6.
www.ceir.org Center for Exhibition Industry Research
www.exponet.com Trade Show Marketing Resource Network
www.tsea.org Trade Show Exhibitors Association (formerly the International Exhibitors Association)

See also: ADVERTISING; CORPORATE IDENTITY; EXPORTING; GLOBAL MARKETING; MARKETING BUDGETING AND RESOURCE ALLOCATION; MARKETING COMMUNICATIONS; ORGANIZATIONAL BUYING BEHAVIOUR; PERSONAL SELLING AND SALES MANAGEMENT; POSITIONING; PRICING; PRODUCT POLICY; PUBLIC RELATIONS; RELATIONSHIPS AND NETWORKS; SALES PROMOTION

Customer care and satisfaction

1 Origins
2 Scope of customer care
3 Marketing activity
4 Customer care and the organization
5 Future perspectives of customer care
6 Summary

Overview

Customer care and satisfaction are often overused and abused terms in marketing. Many aspects of marketing activity appear to give priority to the philosophy of customer care and satisfaction but in fact often pay little more than lip-service to it. Why should customer care and satisfaction have such high profiles and why should there be such an apparent deficiency in performing to promises and achieving expectations? In answering these questions it is useful to consider customer care and satisfaction in the broader context of marketing as a whole.

Marketing can be considered as having a fundamental philosophy which is based around the customer/consumer – indeed this philosophy is the essence of marketing. In meeting the requirements of the customer the management of marketing activity must be organized in such a way that it is customer oriented as well as organizationally efficient. On the bases of these two concepts – a customer-oriented philosophy and efficient management organization – marketing activity itself will be performed.

This article will consider the scope and nature, body of knowledge, and current issues and future development of customer care and satisfaction in relation to its origins; the organization and management of marketing activity, and the relevant aspects of marketing activity. The article will conclude with a comment about future development in customer care, by describing a fully integrated concept of customer care based on contemporary marketing management thought.

1 Origins

Customer care and satisfaction have their foundations in the fundamental concepts of marketing. As already stated, the philosophy of marketing is essentially that of customer orientation.

This marketing orientation puts the customer at the core of thinking and activity. In many organizations the philosophy is manifested in terms such as: 'everything an organization does is with the customer in mind'; 'the customer is the focus of everything we do'; 'what the customer wants is paramount'. In striving to achieve this philosophy marketing practitioners seek to satisfy every whim of their customers. Indeed, some writers suggest that many companies have developed a 'marketing mania' whereby they have become obsessively responsive to such customer whims.

Today more enlightened companies encompass the philosophy of marketing orientation by concentrating on 'looking after' their customers and 'maximizing' their satisfaction. Thus it is easy to see the essential foundation of a sub-philosophy centred around the concepts of customer care and satisfaction. The overall purpose of this essential foundation is to gain long-term commitment from customers. Such commitment will undoubtedly be built upon positive relationships, between a company and its customers, which will be served by customer care and satisfaction programmes.

The origins of customer care and satisfaction stem from attempts by marketers to enhance the dimensions of after sales service. Originally, after sales service was provided primarily, if not solely, as a necessity to support certain products. These were products that required regular maintenance or occasional repair. This after sales service was largely seen as a necessary and integral part of the product itself. Companies did not sell certain types of machinery or equipment without the recognition that such products automatically required servicing. Similarly, the sale of spare parts and process equipment often came under the umbrella of after sales service.

As marketing decision makers became increasingly aware of the advantages of providing good after sales service, so the concept of incorporating such service into the total product package began. In order to gain maximum impact from such incorporation this concept was marketed as 'added value'. That is, the product benefited from the added value of a range of things over and above after sales service. Also, since added value could literally mean add-one to 'basic' products, the concept of added value spread to a wide range of products and marketing variables in a variety of marketing circumstances. In the early stages of the development of this concept the enhancement of a product through added value was viewed as providing something beyond the minimum or standard version of a product. Later this was to lead to the concept of 'core' and 'peripheral' dimensions of customer care. An additional benefit provided by added value, from a company perspective, was the enhancement of brand image.

The advantages to be gained from providing and marketing added value products soon led to marketers incorporating the total package into a fully integrated sales programme. Such programmes offered a multiplicity of variations for product purchase.

Of course, most of this development of after sales service towards customer service, and thereby greater customer satisfaction, did not occur in isolation from market changes and trends. Throughout this development the marketing environment was subjected to increased competitive activity. Such competition occurred because of a variety of factors. From a consumer perspective there was a general increase in demand stoked by greater affluence and higher disposable income. Such affluence required greater variety and choice and as consumers became more confident in making discernible decisions, consumer sophistication demanded more custom-made variations to products.

In responding to these consumer requirements marketers were in effect behaving in the enlightened way of the marketing orientated firm. Thus began the emergence of the customer-led firm which placed an emphasis on customer care and satisfaction rather than simply perfecting a stand-alone product for sale. There is a general recognition that consumers who are striving for satisfaction do not simply look for the end product or service but also draw satisfaction from the completeness of the service interaction and transaction.

An obvious area of development of customer care has been in the arena of services. Because of the intangible characteristics of services it is obvious that aspects of customer care that focus on these will greatly enhance the impact of a service. A similar circumstance prevails with the widening of the marketing concept beyond the confines of commercial transaction and into non-profit sectors.

Currently, much of the development of customer care activity is closely linked with improvements in 'quality', both throughout an organization and also in terms of the total marketing package across all of an organization's marketing variables. Manifestation of this can be seen in the many 'loyalty' programmes devised by companies operating in competitive consumer markets.

Today the guiding concept of customer care and satisfaction, indeed of marketing, is 'value', incorporating the ideal package in the ideal use – that is, a 'complete' package in use.

The importance of customer care and satisfaction is underlined by the fact that most major texts in marketing now contain chapters specifically on the topic, or at least frequent references to the concepts in relation to customer service, consumer behaviour and aspects of marketing activity such as the areas of communications and selling.

2 Scope of customer care

What are the significant variables of customer care? Indeed, what is the scope of customer care activities? Chaston (1990) outlines the variables of customer care as:

1 The product knowledge and interpersonal skills of the employees who interact with the customers.
2 The type of service required by the customers and their perception of how the organization fulfils their expectations on quality.
3 The organizational structure of the company, which determines the efficiency with which services (products) are delivered at all phases from the point of initial contact through to the customer's post-purchase evaluation of the service [product] received.
(Chaston 1990: 145)

Customer care and satisfaction transgress all aspects of marketing, whether it be in consumer markets or industrial markets, inter- or intra-industry. However, it is in the area of services marketing that most progress and attention has been given to customer care and satisfaction. Much of this attention began with the notion of perceiving service as a product and also the notion of the 'service package' and 'value added' services. These issues will be explored later in this entry.

Many authors have volunteered a variety of definitions of customer care. One of the most current and comprehensive descriptions is provided by Clutterbuck (1988): 'Customer care is a fundamental approach to standards of service quality. It covers every aspect of a company's operations, from the design of a product or service to how it is packaged, delivered and serviced.' This emphasizes the importance of attention being given to every element of the exchange process from design and production through to delivery and service back-up. Indeed, Christopher (1986), when discussing the dimensions of logistics and marketing processes argues that:

> Customer service is the thread that links the logistics and marketing processes, because in the end, the output of the logistics system IS customer service. The skill lies in managing the twin arms of marketing and logistics in such a way as to maximize the value added through customer service whilst still seeking a cost advantage.

Essentially, as Peters and Austin (1985) state, customer care 'all boils down to perceived and appreciated and consistently delivered service and quality to customers'.

These statements serve to assist appreciation of the 'concept' of customer care, but what are the actual parameters of its scope of activity? Many terms have been used both by authors and companies to label customer care activity, such as customer service, product quality, service quality and after sales service. These terms appear to have different meanings in different companies and different situations. To clarify these terms for the purpose of this discussion and to emphasize the complete definition of customer care as an all-encompassing term, these four aspects are explained as follows:

1 *Customer service.* Generally includes advice and information for customers regarding the technical specifications of a product or service and after sales back-up arrangements and procedures. To emphasize this point Christopher (1986) writes that 'ultimately customer service is determined by the interaction of all those factors that affect the process of making products and services available to the buyer'.
2 *Product quality.* Relates to standards and measures set to ensure a product conforms to specifications and is therefore fit for its purpose and safe to use.
3 *Service quality.* Refers to the company/customer interface and relationship, focusing on the customer's experience during the process of the transaction.
4 *After sales service.* Covers after sales enquiries and complaints, together with repair and maintenance procedures.

All of these aspects form part of the total customer care package which is about adopting a caring attitude through being helpful, friendly, concerned and reassuring. The aim is continuously to satisfy customer requirements and comply with expectations. In this context customer care applies to all aspects of marketing.

Customer care can incorporate anything that an organization does for and on behalf of its customers. What form this takes will depend on a multiplicity of factors, such as the nature of the product or service, the industry, the competition and the expectation of consumers. Consequently, customer care may be found somewhere between a whole range of general parameters. For example, minimum aspects of care may be sufficient to satisfy customers, or alternatively, maximum levels of care may be necessary in order to be competitive. Customer care may be deemed poor but the differentiation of the product may more than compensate for this. Alternatively, excellent care may be a core requirement for some products or services. Equally, simple care may be all that is necessary for some situations, while sophisticated care may have been developed as a significant marketing differentiation. Whatever the scope and nature of customer care, two things are likely to be constant: it is determined by management and judged by customers and consumers in terms of expectations.

Customer expectations and satisfaction

The scope of customer care marketing activity will encompass customer experience from the pre-purchase, through the purchase period and end with post-purchase follow-up. A company's pre-purchase activity will consist of building customer awareness and desire through attractive and efficient information flow and distribution. It will strive to balance changing customer expectations and requirements while ensuring ease and flexibility of enquiry and diminution of anxiety. Pre-purchase customer care establishes the first bridge-head in organization/customer relationships and serves as a 'draw' in encouraging and enticing the customer towards purchase. The purchase period of customer care is most obviously linked with the core product or service in an integral way. In addition to the product aspects of customer care there is considerable requirement for efficiency in processing orders and in the overall order management cycle, paying attention to small details and meeting customer demands in ways which are entirely compatible with the customers' expectations and requirements both in terms of function and time. It is here that organization/customer interface and relationship is bonded by the mutually beneficial negotiations. The post-purchase customer care activity will focus upon efficient follow-up and full completion of the product or service transaction. In the longer term this follow-up will concentrate either on reliable continuous servicing or on persistent maintenance of awareness. The eventual object will be to entice the customer back for further purchases.

In the marketing of customer care it is important to position the term 'satisfaction' in terms of a company's experience and previous trading activity in its marketplace. Thus, it is important to distinguish between customer expectations that relate first to satisfaction and are seen as predictors or probabilities of what is likely to happen during a transaction and, second, expectations viewed as desires or wants based on what will actually be offered (Lewis 1993). It is the latter part of this distinction to which the term satisfaction most relates in this discussion.

How can customer care fully encompass customers' expectations that stretch across the whole scope of customer experience as outlined above? Swan and Combs (1976) argue that there are two dimensions to customer expectations, 'instrumental' expectations and 'psychological' expectations about a product or service performance. These expectations relate both to quantifiable factors which can be measured using 'herd' data and to qualitative factors which can be measured using 'soft' data. Hard data are those which relate to quantifiable issues such as performance and reliability. Such issues are tangible and therefore relatively easy to measure by both the company and the customer. However, it is more difficult to measure customer care in relation to the qualitative elements of customer relations. These 'soft' issues can be described as those concerned with descriptions of and knowledge about customer feelings, perceptions, expectations and requirements. These are more difficult to measure because they are intangible (Carson and Gilmore 1989).

Dimensions of customer care

The interrelationships between quantitative hard standards and qualitative soft standards can be seen in Figure 1. This model illustrates the range of factors that can be included in the complete definition of customer care. These elements range from the hard, tangible aspects such as packaging, to the soft, intangible aspects such as the degree of courtesy and consideration experienced by the customer.

Many of these aspects of customer care are difficult to measure and evaluate by both customers and companies. An examination of the nature of the characteristics upon which they can be evaluated allows classification of goods or services into three categories (Derby and Karni 1973; Nelson 1974). These classifications are 'search' properties, 'experience' properties and 'credence' properties. Search properties are those which a consumer can determine prior to purchasing a product, for example, packaging, price, and so on. Experience properties are those such as courtesy, ease of contact, dependability, and as such can be discerned only after purchase or during consumption. Credence properties are those qualities or attributes which consumers may find impossible to evaluate even after purchase and/or consumption, perhaps because they do not have the knowledge or skill to do so and therefore have to rely on the professional credence of the supplier.

The marketing mix

Figure 1 Dimensions of customer care.
Source: Carson and Gilmore (1989: 52)

TANGIBLE ELEMENTS (Relatively easy to measure) — Instrumental qualitative standards:
- Physical facilities
- Product and packaging
- Speed of delivery
- Credit facilities
- Repair service
- Technical support
- Appearance of staff
- Image

INTANGIBLE ELEMENTS (Relatively difficult to measure) — Psychological qualitative standards:
- Individual responsibility for customer care
- Accessibility/courtesy
- Responsiveness
- Willingness to help
- Congenial atmosphere
- Good communication
- Competence of staff
- Information/advice
- Security/confidentiality
- Trustworthiness

In the dimensions model shown in Figure 1, there are relatively few elements which can be described as having search qualities. Those which may contain search properties are those which are part of the instrumental 'hard' dimension of customer care. In fact, it can be argued that the majority of elements listed in Figure 1 contain more experience and credence properties than search properties. Indeed, experience and credence qualities have been described as those which are less absolute, more conditional, less concrete and more intangible than search qualities. Consequently, this makes the evaluation of experience and credence qualities more difficult for consumers and for companies.

It is argued that the variables in the dimensions model which primarily have experience and credence properties are also those which are part of the psychological 'soft' dimension of customer care. For example, courtesy and responsiveness of staff can be evaluated only through experiencing these dimensions. Similarly, security and confidentiality must have an inherent credence to be accepted. Where there are more search qualities in evidence not only is it easier for the customer to evaluate the quality, but also it is easier for the producer to determine, offer and standardize those qualities. This is manifested in dimensions such as credit facilities, product and packaging, speed of delivery, and comparisons between competitive offerings. Thus, there is a tendency by management to concentrate on the instrumental standards and a corresponding difficulty in defining and measuring psychological standards. In the case of 'hard' instrumental standards, which are primarily tangible, management can identify customer expectations by various quantitative methods and can therefore set appropriate specifications, rules or procedures to allow for those requirements. In this respect, many companies will have data on aspects such as the time period customers perceive to be reasonable in waiting for delivery of the product just purchased, or how long they would be prepared to wait for it to be repaired after a breakdown. Similarly, management can set standards relating to a product's fitness for use, performance, safety and reliability. Further, it can set procedures for what the company should do if the product breaks down.

Measuring customer care

When quantitative measures have been applied to determine less definite areas such as the number of staff required at any point on a shop floor, or in any service situation, they have been less successful. In this case quantitative measures alone are not sufficient because they fail to take into account the inherent psychological dimensions which relate to the customer's expectation evaluation in terms of experience and credence qualities. It is acknowledged that some companies, such as airlines and hotel chains, have used quantitative techniques in measuring relatively intangible service dimensions – for example, in check-in waiting time, baggage labelling, toilet cleaning and telephone answering. These are all duties which may have relied on intuitive behaviour on the part of service personnel in executing the tasks. However, by stipulating rigid procedures and minimum performance standards, these companies have considerably improved their service offerings. Thus, for example, telephones are required to be answered within a given time period, or waiting at check-ins reduced to stated efficiency levels.

Total customer care should also attempt to take account of customers' feelings, perceptions and requirements in respect of a product or service. This is particularly important where the qualitative psychological dimensions are dominant in the transaction and where customers rely heavily on experience and credence qualities. However, where such qualities are difficult to define, customers will be influenced strongly by the customer contact personnel and to a lesser extent the environment in which the contact takes place. To summarize, consideration of the elements illustrated in the Figure 1 model suggests that the instrumental 'hard' dimensions can be implemented mainly through suitable rules and procedures, whereas the psychological 'soft' dimensions of customer care are determined by an emphasis on perceptions, attitudes and behaviour of customer contact staff.

Balanced customer care

A good customer care package will benefit from consistency in performing the tasks and balancing the performance across all the dimensions. Consistency is crucial in maintaining standards of performance. This is particularly so with regard to the soft intangible dimension of customer care. Because of the 'personal touch' aspect it is easy to have high variances in standards of performance if due care and attention to consistency are neglected. Concentration on the instrumental dimensions may improve the customer care offering, but much of the improvement will be negated by the neglect of the psychological dimensions. Companies can provide better 'balanced' customer care in two ways. First, they can improve the environment where the transaction takes place and, second, apply marketing concepts internally, particularly amongst customer contact staff.

One of the initial steps is to ensure that management pay sufficient and continuing attention to the processes of meeting customer needs. This attention should extend to the environment within which the product or service is transacted. Indeed, as Bitner (1992) stresses, 'Research in organisational behaviour suggests that the physical setting can influence employee satisfaction, productivity, and motivation.' The same physical settings will have a similar impact on customers' satisfaction with the product or service. The environment lends itself to highlighting the instrumental and largely tangible elements of customer care illustrated in Figure 1, for example physical facilities, such as modern efficient equipment, appearance of staff, and so on. Similarly, many companies go to considerable effort to show tangible evidence of some or more of the tangible variables. For example, companies in financial services may provide secluded booths for private interviews, thus giving the impression of confidentiality. Indeed, equally or alternatively, they may design their customer interaction points as 'retail shops' which create an ambience of convenience and serviceability. Also in retailing the introduction of new technology has speeded up transactions and redesigned stores have improved the customers' shopping environment by implying more responsiveness and a calmer atmosphere. However, it is not enough to focus only on an efficient environment, it is also important to balance this with the personal touch dimensions.

One way of achieving a balance between the personal touch and modern efficiency is to focus on the 'soft' psychological dimensions of customer care. Obviously, because of the characteristics of face-to-face interaction, front-line company staff can have a major influence upon the perceived service quality and customer care in general.

3 Marketing activity

Core and peripheral product

What are the key component parts of customer care? What is the scope of customer care marketing activity? Much of the explicit focus of customer care and satisfaction lies outside the 'core' of marketing activity. Obviously there is an implicit dimension of customer care and satisfaction in all aspects of marketing activity. As a consequence, the 'tangible' aspects of marketing, primarily the core product, represent the broader aspects of customer care in terms of meeting customer needs, perceptions and expectations. The 'core' aspects of customer care focus on the customer/organization interactions and as a consequence are primarily people related and 'intangible' in nature. It is this dimension which sometimes leads to the perception that the concepts are primarily about the customer service package' (Shostack 1977; Grönroos 1990; Normann 1991).

This service aspect is easily accepted in the wide area of service marketing. It is in service industries that most concentrations of customer care improvement and development can be found. Indeed, some might argue that customer care represents the core of service marketing activity. It is in services marketing that concepts such as 'total service offering' and 'quality of services' can be found.

In addition to the core customer care will have a 'peripheral' dimension. This peripheral aspect can be substantial and can consist of a wide range of factors and activities. It is here that the little added extras and attention to detail can be provided that will complete a good customer care programme. Peripheral aspects can often be provided by other marketing variables other than people dimensions.

It is an established view that peripheral aspects of the customer care package will eventually evolve into meaningful core aspects in themselves. Therefore, as a company enlarges and expands the level of customer care around added peripheral aspects these will be viewed by customers as integral and standard to the customer care package. Thus, after a period of time a company would actually disappoint customers by withdrawing these aspects which had become part of the actual core of customer care.

Other marketing variables

In all marketing variables customer care will require attention to be given to interaction points at various stages of the transaction. Customer care at these interaction points will be efficient, friendly and stimulating, designed to avoid or at least solve problems, to prevent passive customer periods and to encourage active customer involvement. In its entirety a customer care programme will create a unique ambience, appearance and atmosphere surrounding an organization and its customers.

The four actual marketing variables of most significance to customer care in creating this ambience are as follows:

1. *Product or service.* This will obviously be the core of customer care activity in terms of its range, choice and variety, and provide scope for customization and personalization to suit the individual customer.
2. *Communication materials.* These will include any literature which is designed to create and stimulate awareness through customer orientated information flows. This information will focus on customer care dimensions of product use, availability and delivery, and price/value perceptions.
3. *Sales incentives.* These will play an important role in customer care. They may be tangible, covering such things as samples and trials or tests, price discounts and give aways, and intangible, such as extra service or extended service.
4. *Positive public relations.* This will play a significant role in customer care, both in terms of its scope and spread and the degree of activity. Public relations will enable customers to be informed and to feel they belong to an organization.

In marketing activity in general, customer care and satisfaction will be of a prime concern in all aspects of marketing communications, sales incentives and motivations, quality improvements and value added dimensions. Each individual in a company, irrespective of level or function, has an important role to play in the customer's perceptions of the product or service. Many writers refer to this as the 'people factor'.

4 Customer care and the organization

Internal customers

If management does indeed determine customer care then what procedures will management address in maintaining and developing aspects of customer care? The core essence of management-determined customer care is that of genuine and comprehensive marketing orientation incorporating both internal and external dimensions.

In an attempt to improve perceptions of staff towards customer care, some companies have tried schemes which involve treating their employees as customers, that is internal marketing training. Berry (1981) describes this as 'viewing employees as internal customers, viewing jobs as internal products and then endeavouring to offer internal products that satisfy the needs and wants of these internal customers while addressing the objectives of the organisation'. Internal marketing is important in that it recognizes that customer service is not just the responsibility of front-line staff. The concept of internal marketing involves the application of marketing principles to 'selling the staff' on their role in providing customer satisfaction.

TQM and total systems

Much of the internal marketing concept has been superseded by new and wider approaches, such as total systems and total quality management (TQM) (see TOTAL QUALITY MANAGEMENT). A total systems approach requires an organization to incorporate what it does as a cohesive whole. That is, all departments and functions must be viewed as a coordinated grouping of activities whereby the sum of the whole operation is greater than the sum of the individual component parts. Total quality management adds another dimension by evaluating and improving the quality of all operations within an organization in a cohesive and coordinated fashion. The effect of these types of 'systems' upon an organization's customer care performance is obvious, since they will contribute significantly towards the overall marketing orientation of the organization. By improving the quality of an organization's performance the efficiency and end products of a firm's offerings will be passed on directly and indirectly to its customers. But the external dimensions of customer care must be addressed in a way which is compatible with internal improvements.

Relationship marketing

The external management of customer care must focus upon building stronger links and cementing closer relationships between an organization and its customers (see MARKETING COMMUNICATION). The essence of this focus is on communication. Good customer care communication signals efficiency and flexibility from a customer perspective and is manifested in the quality and ease of contacts with an organization. Thus, consistent customer care will be provided at all stages and all areas of contact. An organization will not only be aware of its core contact personnel, but also its peripheral contact points, as well as its first and last contact points. A weakness in any one of these contact points may result in damaging the expected customer care performance. The concentration of any customer care contact point should be on establishing sound one-to-one interactions between company personnel and the individual customer at a personal level. Customers must feel that they are not only known but are individually important to an organization.

Implementation of customer care

How can management improve customer care through internal marketing orientation? Internally, organizations will strive to engender a culture of customer orientation. Such an orientation will be wide ranging in its approaches to doing business and measures of performance which are designed to motivate and stimulate good customer relations. Thus systems of management procedure and administration are structured in such a way as to be customer friendly, efficient and flexible, from the beginning to the end of transactions. Key aspects of good performance competence are measured through accountability and responsibility for satisfying customers and establishing and maintaining good customer/organization relationships. Performance at key management positions within an organization will be crucial in internal marketing activity – by applying the principles of marketing in terms of appreciating the requirements of other departments and servicing them to their satisfaction, while at the same time marketing themselves to other departments in terms of their own performance requirements. Any commitments undertaken by staff must be followed through. Guarantees and promises must be met. Tasks must be completed. In other words good customer care relies as much upon the implementation performance of an organization as it does upon stated objectives and plans.

Equally, the success of a customer care programme will be determined by the efficiency of staff performance in their tasks. Thus, good customer care programmes will place much credence upon accountability and responsibility of staff towards the task performance. The level and range of accountability and responsibility will be dependent upon the overall staff competencies and skills. Customer care cannot be left in the hands of incompetent or inefficient staff. There is a clear implication therefore that successful customer care programmes are highly dependent upon the personnel required to perform and implement them. Like any other management function customer care may require sound training and staff development if the function itself is to be maintained at a satisfactory level and if it is to be developed.

5 Future perspectives of customer care

Customer care will continue to evolve along with marketing developments, which in turn will be heavily influenced by environmental changes and pressures. Future perspectives in customer care will reflect new perspectives in marketing. These new perspectives are important enough to warrant an entry in this text on the future of marketing (see THE FUTURE OF MARKETING), on a wider scale, they are increasingly gaining the attention of large marketing representative bodies such as the American Marketing Association and the Academy of Marketing and Chartered Institute of Marketing in the United Kingdom. Some of these new perspectives have already been alluded to, principally relationship marketing. Sheth (1993) includes relationship marketing as one of ten emerging marketing strategies. Two others that may have most impact upon customer care and satisfaction are network marketing and customer focused quality. Relationship marketing and networking are debated elsewhere in this text (see RELATIONSHIPS AND NETWORKS). However, it is useful to consider both together with the dimension of quality from the specific perspective of customer care. Relationship marketing is implicit to network marketing and also to the notion of marketing competencies.

Marketing competencies

There is an increasing recognition of the fact that managers should have competence in their relevant functional area. It is also widely recognized that developed management competencies are the key to improved management performance. These issues are no less relevant in the context of customer care. Management and staff must have appropriate competencies for successfully implementing customer care packages. What is meant by management competencies and which are appropriate for customer care?

Boyatzis (1982) suggests that a competence is an underlying characteristic of a person which consists of an effective mix of motives, traits, skills, aspects of one's self-image or social role, or body of knowledge used by an individual. From a management perspective it can be considered that competence is the ability to use knowledge and skills effectively in the performance of a specific task. Competencies may embrace a more tangible set of attributes: ability to make sound judgements, creativity, willingness to take risks, decisiveness, high energy level, ability to take initiative, results orientation, tenacity, integrity, adaptability, resilience, ability to deal with detailed information and lateral thinking. The list can be inexhaustible in terms of human traits. When applied to the marketing concept and, in particular, to customer care the focus is upon those competencies which are most appropriate to performing effective customer care. Assuming that customer care personnel have a 'common sense' knowledge of the marketing concept, then it is a matter of concentrating on enhancing appropriate competencies for the task. There are two competencies which can be deemed most appropriate for customer care – knowledge and communication.

Any manager or member of staff must possess and develop knowledge of the company's products or services in the context of the total customer care package. In addition, customer care requires a sound knowledge of customer expectations, desires and satisfactions and a knowledge of how to translate these to the transaction and interaction processes of customer care. Clearly, this requires considerable and compatible competency in communication in order to maintain a mutual understanding between company and customer. In addition, experience and judgement can be added as key factors towards effective customer care. Sound judgement in decision making is essential, but this will only be achieved by the effective mix of knowledge and communication and these will be immensely enhanced by meaningful experience competency. By focusing upon these aspects of competency, management can enhance and develop its overall customer care performance.

Networking

As well as developing competencies, management must take full cognizance of good networking. These competencies will be naturally enhanced by good networks, since they revolve around meaningful 'personal contacts'. The personal contact network defines any relationship, either direct, in terms of a particular impact upon the company/customer interface, or indirect in that it may lead to further contact through and with other people. The density, reachability and diversity of a personal contact network will have considerable bearing on the impact it has on customer care.

The network most appropriate for customer care is one that reflects aspects of marketing. Thus, people who are involved in the company/customer interface represent the richest sources of personal contact, for example, buyers, gatekeepers, store managers, office administrators, and so on. These are important people from both the perspective of the company and of its customer. By proactively nurturing and enhancing the relationship network with all of these individuals a person with customer care responsibility will perform more effectively.

Quality

Quality is a much abused term in all aspects of business and in marketing particularly. When marketers talk of improving quality the focus has traditionally been on improving the features of the product or service. While this is a wholly acceptable objective, it displays a myopic view of the total marketing effort (Gilmore and Carson 1993). Marketing is not just concerned with the product dimension, it must also maintain a balance with decisions on price, promotion, distribution, and not least customer care. Thus, fundamental to the consideration of quality improvement in customer care is the wider consideration of improving, in a balanced way, the same aspects of quality across the whole spectrum of customer care related activities. This article alluded earlier to aspects of quality in total quality management and total marketing systems. Quality consistency was also considered across the full range of customer experience in relation to a company, from pre-purchase through to post-purchase and everything in between. Clearly, dimensions of quality are integral to the whole concept of customer care. Therefore how can management hope to perform and improve effective customer care across such a wide range of activities?

Fully integrated customer care

The ultimate answer to effective customer care is a fully integrated package of activities and decision-making functions. This means focusing on key factors and linking these together into such an integrated package. The key factors drawn from this overview of customer care are:

1 Wide consideration of all marketing functional variables – variables which include product or service, advertising, promotion, personal selling, delivery, order processing.
2 Identification and enhancement of key marketing competencies and personal contact networks – concentration upon knowledge, communication, experience, and judgement; in addition, the nurturing and development of personal contacts at all aspects of customer care influence.
3 Consistent and balanced delivery of key customer care activities – consideration across the whole spectrum of customer care activities (outlined in Figure 1).
4 A consistent and balanced perspective on the customer/company interface – acknowledgement of all aspects of the interrelationships between customers and a company,

particularly in relation to hard instrumental and soft psychological dimensions.

By combining all four of these factors under clear and precise customer care objectives and policies an organization will perform customer care with an impact which will have a lasting effect on its customers and provide maximum satisfaction.

6 Summary

This article has attempted to outline the important factors of customer care and satisfaction. It has considered these from the perspective of organizations providing customer care and at the interface between companies and their customers. There are many important issues not debated here which specifically influence customer care. Most significantly are customer satisfaction from the perspective of consumer and buyer behaviour; sociological and psychological aspects of marketing; relationship marketing and networking; and the total marketing environment. All of these aspects are covered elsewhere in this volume and should be taken into account when reading and understanding this entry (see CONSUMER BEHAVIOUR; ENVIRONMENTAL ANALYSIS; PSYCHOLOGICAL BASIS OF MARKETING; RELATIONSHIPS AND NETWORKS; SOCIOLOGICAL BASIS OF MARKETING).

This article has focused upon the key issues of customer care to provide the reader with an appreciation and understanding of the scope and activities of this function, its importance in modern marketing and its growing influence. This importance is growing as markets and consumers become more demanding and sophisticated. As expectations rise, so to must customer care and satisfaction grow to match them. Increasingly, companies are recognizing this importance and investing heavily in a myriad customer care and satisfaction initiatives. These initiatives require many additional, well-trained personnel whose sole focus is on the customer and providing and achieving customer care and satisfaction. As a consequence of this it can be expected that an emphasis on future employee requirements will be on customer care and satisfaction staff.

DAVID CARSON
UNIVERSITY OF ULSTER AT JORDANSTOWN

Further reading

(References cited in the text marked *)

Bateson, J.E. (1989) *Managing Services Marketing. Texts and Cases*, Chicago: The Dryden Press.
Berry, L.L. (1981) 'The employee as customer', *Journal of Retail Banking* 3: 33–40.
Bitner, M.J. (1992) 'Servicescapes: The impact of physical surroundings on customers and employees', *Journal of Marketing* 56: 57–71.
Boyatzis, R.E. (1982) *The Competent Manager: A Model for Effective Performance*, New York: J. Wiley.
Carson, D. and Gilmore, A. (1989) 'Customer care: the neglected domain', *Irish Marketing Review* 4: 49–61.
Chaston, I. (1990) *Managing for Marketing Excellence*, Maidenhead: McGraw-Hill.
Christopher, M. (1986) 'Reaching the customer: strategies for marketing and customer service', *Journal of Marketing Management* 2: 63–71.
Christopher, M., Payne, A. and Ballantyne, D. (1991) *Relationship Marketing: Bring Quality, Customer Service and Marketing Together*, Oxford: Butterworth Heinemann.
Clutterbuck, D. (1988) 'Developing customer care training programmes', *Industrial and Commercial Training* November–December: 11–14.
Darby, M.R. and Karni, E. (1973) 'Free competition and the optimal amount of fraud', *Journal of Law and Economics* 16: 67–86 in Parasuraman, A., Zeithaml, V. A. and Berry, L.L. (1985) 'A conceptual model of service quality and its implications for future research', *Journal of Marketing* 49: 41–50.
Gilmore, A. and Carson, D. (1993) 'Enhancing service quality: A case study', *Irish Marketing Review* 6: 64 73.
Griffin, J. (1996) Customer Loyalty: How to Earn It, How to Keep it, New York, Lexington Books.
Grönroos, C. (1990) *Service Management and Marketing. Managing the Moments for Truth*, Massachusetts: Lexington Books.
Lewis, B.R. (1993) 'Service quality measurement', *Marketing Intelligence and Planning* 11:4–12.
Murley, P. (ed.) (1996) *Gower Handbook of Customer Service*, Aldershot, Gower.
Nelson, P. (1974) 'Advertising as information', *Journal of Political Economy* 81, July–August: 729–54 in Parasuraman, A., Zeithaml, V.A. and Berry, L.L. (1985) 'A conceptual model of service quality and its implicatons for future research', *Journal of Marketing* 49: 41–50.
Normann, R. (1991) *Service Management and Marketing*, Chichester: J. Wiley and Sons.
Peters, T.J. and Austin, N. (1985) *A Passion for Excellence: The Leadership Difference*, New York: Random House.

Sheth, J.N. (1993) 'Emerging marketing strategies in a changing macroeconomic environment', *Journal of International Marketing* 1: 9–14.

Shostack, G.L. (1977) 'Breaking free from product marketing', *Journal of Marketing* 41: 73–80.

Swan, J. E. and Combs, L.J. (1976) 'Product performance and customer satisfaction', *Journal of Marketing* 40: 25–33.

Zeithaml, V.A., Parasuraman, A. and Berry, L.L. (1990) *Delivering Quality Service. Balancing Customer Perceptions and Expectations*, New York: The Free Press.

See also: CONSUMER BEHAVIOUR; ENVIRONMENTAL ANALYSIS; MARKETING COMMUNICATION; PSYCHOLOGICAL BASIS OF MARKETING; RELATIONSHIPS AND NETWORKS; SOCIOLOGICAL BASIS OF MARKETING; THE FUTURE OF MARKETING; TOTAL QUALITY MANAGEMENT

Developing and implementing a marketing plan

1. Modes of strategic decision making
2. The importance of marketing planning
3. What marketing planning is
4. Marketing strategies
5. The marketing planning process
6. Key account planning
7. Marketing planning systems

Overview

The overall purpose of marketing planning and its principal focus is the identification and creation of sustainable competitive advantage.

It is a logical sequence and a series of activities leading to the setting of marketing objectives and the formulation of strategies and tactics for achieving them, together with the associated financial consequences.

It is necessary because of the complexity caused by the many external and internal factors that interact to affect an organization's ability to achieve its objectives. There are two outputs from the process of marketing planning:

1. the strategic marketing plan, which covers a period of between three and five years.
2. the tactical marketing plan, which is the detailed scheduling and costing out of the specific actions necessary to achieve the first year's objectives in the strategic marketing plan.

The strategic marketing plan is a model of a unit's position in its market relative to competitors and contains a definition of market needs, the objectives to be achieved, the strategies to achieve the objectives and the resources required to achieve the desired results.

The marketing planning process starts with financial objectives, moves on to the marketing audit stage, then to the setting of draft marketing objectives and strategies for a three to five year period. At this stage, other functional managers get involved, to ensure that the organization is capable of resourcing the market's requirements. Strategic marketing plans are then finalized and tactical marketing plans are prepared. Headquarters will often consolidate all of these into corporate plans. At the start of the organization's fiscal year, the tactical marketing plan is implemented and measured, until the whole process starts again. Thus, it can be seen that the process is continuous.

The degree of formalization of the process depends on an organization's size and complexity, but the process is universally applicable, irrespective of circumstances.

1 Modes of strategic decision making

Strategic decisions are concerned with:

- The long-term direction of the organization, as opposed to day-to-day management issues.
- Defining the scope of the organization's activities in terms of what it will and will not do.
- Matching the activities of the organization to the environment in which it operates, so that it optimizes opportunities and minimizes threats.
- Matching the organization's activities to its resource capacity, be it finance, manpower, technology or skill levels.

Strategic management is characteristically dealing with an uncertain future and new initiatives. As a result of this, it is often the harbinger of change. Organizations build their business strategies in a number of different ways. There are six accepted strategy forming models (Bailey and Johnson 1994).

1. A *planning model*. Here strategic decisions are reached by using a sequential planned search for optimum solutions to defined problems. This process is highly rational and is fuelled by concrete data.
2. An *interpretative model*. Here, the organization is regarded as a collection of associations, sharing similar values, beliefs and perceptions. These 'frames of reference' enable the stakeholders to interpret the

organization and the environment in which it operates. Information which does not fit with the dominant reference system is actively ignored or downgraded. The same could be said of people. In this way, a particular culture emerges which encourages individuals to lend themselves to self-fulfilling organizational prophesies, uncontaminated by deviant behaviour or information. Strategy thus becomes the product, not of defined aims and objectives, but of the prevailing values, attitudes and ideas in the organization.

3 A *political model*. Here strategy is not chosen directly, but emerges through compromise, conflict and consensus seeking among interested stakeholders. Since the strategy is the outcome of negotiation, bargaining and confrontation, those with the most power have the greatest influence.

4 A *logical incremental model*. Here, strategies emerge from 'strategic subsystems', each concerned with a different type of strategic issue. Strategic goals are based on an awareness of needs, rather than the highly structured analytical process of the planning model. Often, due to a lack of necessary information, such goals can be vague, general and non-rigid in nature until such a time when events unfold and more information becomes known.

5 An *ecological model*. In this perspective, the environment impinges on the organization in such a way that strategies are virtually prescribed and there is little or no free choice. In this model, the organization which adapts most successfully to its environment will survive in a way which mirrors Darwin's natural selection.

6 A *visionary leadership model*. Strategy emerges as the result of the leader's vision, enforced by his/her commitment to it, his/her personal credibility, and how he/she articulates it to others.

It is unlikely that an organization will use a pure version of any of these models. In all probability, its strategic decision-making model will be a hybrid of some of them. However, it is possible that one or two of these will predominate and thereby give strategic decision making a distinct 'flavour'.

While these various models help to explain the different flavours of strategic decision making, at first sight they appear to have little in common. Closer examination shows that this is not the case. All of them see the organization and the environment as inseparable, even though the point at which the balance is struck varies from model to model. For instance, in the ecological model, the environment looms large, whereas in the incremental model, the organization appears to receive most consideration.

Another common theme is that strategies are perceived as necessary to help the organization to cope with changes in the environment.

Whilst academics cannot seem to agree on a single, best approach, company executives have to get on with planning as best they can, using a combination of experience, intuition and hope. The formality of this process will be a function of the degree of product/market complexity, organizational size and the degree of environmental turbulence. In other words, the degree of formality will be driven in part by the dominant decision-making model in the organization.

Strategic marketing planning obviously cannot be discussed in isolation from the above strategic planning modes and it is likely that the way in which an organization's marketing planning is carried out will be a microcosm of the principal mode of the total process.

2 The importance of marketing planning

All organizations operate in a complex environment, in which hundreds of external and internal factors interact to affect their ability to achieve their objectives. Managers need some understanding, or view, about how all these variables interact and they must try to be rational about their decisions, no matter how important intuition, feel and experience are as contributory factors in this process of rationality.

Most managers accept that some kind of formalized procedure for planning the organization's marketing helps sharpen this rationality so as to reduce the complexity of business operations and add a dimension of realism to the organization's hopes for the future.

This is born out by research into the efficacy of marketing planning, which has shown that the main effects within organizations are:

- the systematic identification of emerging opportunities and threats;
- a preparedness to meet change;
- the specification of sustainable competitive advantage;
- improved communication among executives;
- a reduction of conflicts between individuals and departments;
- the involvement of all levels of management in the process;
- a more appropriate allocation of scarce resources;
- consistency of approach across the organization;
- a more market-focused orientation across the organization.

These effects have made a major contribution to commercial success, according to the research of: Thompson (1962); Leighton (1966); Thune and House (1970); Kollatt (1972); Ansoff (1977); McDonald (1984) and Greenley (1987)

3 What marketing planning is

The contribution of marketing to business success in manufacturing, distribution or merchanting activities lies in its commitment to detailed analysis of future opportunities to meet customer needs and a wholly professional approach to selling to well-defined market segments those products or services that deliver the sought-after benefits. While prices and discounts are important, as are advertising and promotion, the link with engineering through the products is paramount. But such a commitment and activities must not be mistaken for budgets and forecasts, which have always been a commercial necessity. The process of marketing planning is concerned with identifying what and to whom sales are going to be made in the longer term to give revenue budgets and sales forecasts any chance of achievement. Furthermore, the chances of achievement are a function of how good an organization's intelligence services are; and how well suited their strategies are in relation to the identified market opportunities.

Marketing planning is a logical sequence and a series of activities leading to the setting of marketing objectives and the formulation of plans for achieving them. It is a management process. Conceptually, the process is very simple. Marketing planning by means of a planning system is, *per se*, little more than a structured way of identifying a range of options, for the company, of making them explicit in writing, of formulating marketing objectives which are consistent with the company's overall objectives and of scheduling and costing out the specific activities most likely to bring about the achievement of the objectives. It is the systematization of this process which lies at the heart of the theory of marketing planning.

Marketing planning, then, is a managerial process, the output of which is a marketing plan. There are two principal kinds of marketing plan:

- the strategic marketing plan;
- the tactical marketing plan.

The strategic marketing plan

The strategic marketing plan is a plan for three or more years. It is the written document which outlines how managers perceive their own position in their markets relative to their competitors (with competitive advantage accurately defined), what objectives they want to achieve, how they intend to achieve them (strategies), what resources are required, and with what results (budget).

Three years is the most frequent planning period for the strategic marketing plan. Five years is the longest period and this is becoming less common due to the speed of technological and environmental change.

The tactical/operational marketing plan

The tactical marketing plan is the detailed scheduling and costing out of the specific actions necessary for the achievement of the first year of the strategic marketing plan. The tactical plan is usually for one year.

Research by McDonald (1984) into the marketing planning practices of organizations, shows that successful ones complete the strategic plan before the tactical plan. Unsuccessful organizations frequently did not bother with a strategic marketing plan at all, relying largely on sales forecasts and the associated budgets. The problem with this approach is that many managers sell the products and services they find easiest to sell, to those customers who offer the least line of resistance. By developing short-term, tactical marketing plans first and then extrapolating them, managers merely succeed in extrapolating their own shortcomings. Preoccupation with preparing a detailed marketing plan first is typical of those companies that confused sales forecasting and budgeting with strategic marketing planning.

The contents of a strategic marketing plan

The contents of a strategic marketing plan are listed below:

1. Mission statement
2. Financial summary
3. Market overview
   - market structure
   - market trends
   - key market segments
   - gap analysis
4. Opportunities/threats
   - by product
   - by segment
   - overall
5. Strengths/weaknesses
   - by product
   - by segment
   - overall
6. Issues to be addressed
   - by product
   - by segment
   - overall
7. Portfolio summary
8. Assumptions
9. Marketing objectives
   - strategic focus
   - product mix
   - product development
   - product deletion
   - market extension
   - target customer groups
10. Marketing strategies (4 × Ps Positioning/branding)
    - product
    - price
    - promotion
    - place
11. Resource requirements
    - budget

Explanations of the terminology used in this contents list follow.

The contents of a tactical marketing plan

The contents of a tactical marketing plan are as follows:

1. Overall view:
   - Overall objectives these should cover the following:

     | Volume or value | Last Year |
     | Current year estimate | Budget next year |

     | Gross margins | Last year |
     | Current year estimate | Budget next year |

     Against each there should be a few words of commentary/explanation.
   - Overall strategies – e.g. new customers, new products, advertising, sales promotion, selling, customer service, pricing.
2. A more detailed view:
   - Sub-objectives – more detailed objectives should be provided for products or markets or segments or major customers, as appropriate.
   - Strategies – the means by which sub-objectives will be achieved should be stated.
   - Action/tactics – the details, timing, responsibility and cost should also be stated.
3. Summary of marketing activities and costs.
4. Contingency plan – it is important to include a contingency plan, which should address the following questions:
   - What are the critical assumptions on which the one year plan is based?
   - What would the financial consequences be (i.e. the effect on the operating income) if these assumptions did not come true? For example, if a forecast of revenue is based on the assumption that a decision will be made to buy new

The marketing mix

Table 1

	Three years ago	Two years ago	Last year
Volume/turnover			
Gross profit (%)			
Gross margin (£000)			

plant by a major customer, what would the effect be if that customer did not go ahead?
- How will these assumptions be managed?
- What action will be taken to ensure that the adverse financial effects of an unfulfilled assumption are mitigated, so that the same forecast profit results at the end of the year?

To measure the risk, assess the negative or downside, asking what can go wrong with each assumption that would change the outcome. For example, if a market growth rate of 5 per cent is a key assumption, what lower growth rate would have to occur before a substantially different management decision would be taken? For a capital project, this would be the point at which the project would cease to be economical.

5 Operating result and financial ration, to include:
   - net revenue
   - gross margin
   - adjustments
   - marketing costs
   - administration costs
   - interest
   - operating result
   - return on sales (ROS)
   - return on investment (ROI)
6 Key activity planner – finally, there should be a summary of the key activities, indicating the start and finish. This should help considerably with monitoring the progress of the annual plan.
7 Other – there may be other information, such as sales call plans, that might usefully appear in the one year marketing plan.

Mission statement

This is the first item to appear in the strategic marketing plan. The purpose of the mission statement is to ensure that the *raison d'être* of the unit preparing the plan is clearly stated. Brief statements should be made which cover the following points:

1 Role or contribution of the unit – for example, profit generator, service department, opportunity seeker.
2 Definition of business – for example, the needs the unit satisfies or the benefits provided. Do not be too specific (e.g. 'we sell milking machinery') or too general (e.g. 'we are in the engineering business').
3 Distinctive competence – this should be a brief statement that applies only to the unit preparing the plan. A statement that could equally apply to any competitor is unsatisfactory.
4 Indications for future direction – a brief statement of the principal things the unit would give serious considerations to (e.g. moving into a new segment.)

Financial summary

This section is designed to give a bird's eye view of the unit's total marketing activities. There should be a quantitative summary of performance (Table 1).

Unit managers should give a summary of reasons for good or bad performance. They should use constant revenue (*t*–1) in order that the comparisons are meaningful. Make sure the same base year values are used for any projections provided in later sections of this system.

Next, there should be a summary of the financial projections. Its purpose is to summarize for the person reading the plan, the financial implications over the full three-year planning period. It should be presented as a simple diagram along the lines shown in Figure 1. This should be accompanied by a brief commentary.

Market overview

This section is intended to provide a brief picture of the market before descending to the

Figure 1 Summary of financial projections over three-year planning period

particular details of individual market segments, which form the heart of the marketing plan.

This system is based upon the segmentation of markets, dividing these into homogeneous groups of customers, each having characteristics which can be exploited in marketing terms. This approach is taken because it is the one which is often the most useful for unit managers to be able to develop their markets. The alternative, product-orientated approach, is rarely appropriate, given the variation between different customer groups in the markets in which most organizations compete. The market segmentation approach is more useful in revealing both the weaknesses and the development opportunities than is an exclusively product orientation.

While it is difficult to give precise instructions on how to present this section of the marketing plan, it should be possible to present a market overview which summarizes what managers consider to be the key changes in their markets. In completing this section, unit managers should consider the following:

1. What are the major products, markets (or segments) which are likely to be able to provide the kind of business opportunities suitable for the organization.
2. How are these changing? i.e. which are growing and which are declining?

This section should be brief and there should be some commentary by the unit manager about what seems to be happening in their market. It is very helpful if unit managers can present as much of this information as possible visually (i.e. bar charts or pie charts, product life-cycles, etc.)

Opportunities and threats, strengths and weaknesses, issues to be addressed

To decide on marketing objectives and future strategy, it is first necessary to summarize the unit's present position in its market(s). In respect of the major products, markets (segments) highlighted in the previous section, the position must now be summarized in the form of a number of SWOT analyses. The word SWOT derives from the initial letters of the words *strengths, weaknesses, opportunities* and *threats*. In simple terms:

- What are the opportunities?
- What are the present and future threats to the unit's business in each of the segments which have been identified as being of important?
- What are the unit's differential strengths and weaknesses *vis-à-vis* competitors? In other words, why should potential customers in the target markets prefer to deal with the unit preparing the plan rather than with its competitors?

Finally, there should be a summary, by major segments, of the key issues that have to be addressed in the planning period. These key issues will be clear from the SWOT analyses.

The marketing mix

Figure 2 Portfolio summary – four-box matrix (directional policy matrix)

Portfolio summary
This is a summary of the previous SWOT analyses that makes it easy to see at a glance the overall competitive position and relative importance of each of the segments to the unit preparing the marketing plan. This is best done by drawing a diagram in the form of a four box matrix which shows each of the important product/market segments described earlier. An example is shown in Figure 2.

From Figure 2 it can be seen that the horizontal axis reflects the scores in the strengths and weaknesses analysis and that the vertical axis quantifies the attractiveness to the organization of each of the important segments contained in the plan. The circle sizes are relative to the current turnover in each. The dotted circles indicate sales in three years' time.

Thus, some segments are becoming less attractive, some more so, whilst in some the unit is becoming stronger against competitors, in others, less.

In the bottom left box, strengths are high, but the markets are less attractive, probably because of a lack of growth. The unit should probably seek to maintain these and manage them for sustained earnings.

In the top left box, strengths are high and the markets are attractive, probably because they are growing fast. The unit should probably invest heavily in these markets and seek to increase market share.

In the top right box, we have low strengths, but the markets are attractive. Here, the unit should probably invest selectively in order to improve its competitive position.

Finally, in the bottom right box, the unit has low strengths and the markets are not attractive. In such cases, it should probably manage these markets for profits.

This matrix, which is sometimes known as the directional policy matrix, gives a clear indication of the kind of marketing objectives and strategies that should be set for each segment shown.

Assumptions
The unit should now highlight the assumptions which are critical to the fulfilment of the planned marketing objectives and strategies.

Key planning assumptions deal in the main with outside features and anticipated changes which would have a significant influence on the achievement of marketing objectives. These might include such things as market growth rate, the organization's costs, capital investment and so on.

Assumptions should be few in number and relate only to key issues such as those identified in the SWOT analyses. If it is possible for a plan to be implemented irrespective of the assumptions made, those assumptions are not necessary and should be removed.

Marketing objectives
Following the identification and statement of key strengths, weaknesses, opportunities and threats, and the explicit statement of assumptions about conditions affecting the business, the process of setting marketing objectives is made easier, since they will be a realistic statement of what the unit desires to achieve as a result of market-centred analysis.

As in the case of objective setting for other functional areas of the business, this is the most important step in the whole process, as it is a commitment on a unit-wide basis to a particular course of action which will determine the scheduling and costing out of subsequent actions.

An objective is what the unit wants to achieve. A strategy is how it plans to achieve it. Thus there are objectives and strategies at all levels in marketing. For example, there can be advertising objectives and strategies, pricing objectives and strategies, and so on.

However, the important point about marketing objectives is that they should be about products and markets only, since it is only by selling something to someone that the unit's financial goals can be achieved. Advertising, pricing and other elements of the marketing mix are the means (the strategies) by which the unit can succeed in doing this. Thus, pricing objectives, sales promotion objectives, advertising objectives and so on should not be confused with marketing objectives.

If profits and cash flows are to be maximized, each unit should consider carefully how its current customer needs are changing and how the products it offers need to be changed accordingly. Since change is inevitable, it is necessary for units to consider the two main dimensions of commercial growth, i.e. product development and market development. Marketing objectives are concerned with the following:

- selling existing products to existing segments;
- developing new products for existing segments;
- extending existing products to new segments;
- developing new products for new segments.

Marketing objectives should be quantitative, and should be expressed where possible in terms of values, volumes and market shares. General directional terms such as 'maximize', 'penetrate' should be avoided unless quantification is included (see QUANTITATIVE METHODS IN MARKETING).

The marketing objectives should cover the full three-year planning horizon and should be accompanied by broad strategies (discussed in the following section) and broad revenue and cost projections for the full three-year period.

The one-year marketing plan should contain specific objectives for the first year of the three-year planning cycle and the corresponding strategies which will be used to achieve these objectives. At this point, it is worth stressing that the key document in the annual planning round is the three-year strategic plan. The one-year plan represents the specific actions that should be undertaken in the first year of the strategic plan.

4 Marketing strategies

Marketing strategies should state in broad terms how the marketing objectives are to be achieved, as follows:

- The specific product policies (the range, technical specifications, additions, deletions, etc.).
- The pricing policies to be followed for product groups in particular market segments.
- The customer service levels to be provided for specific market segments (such as maintenance support).
- The policies for communicating with customers under each of the main heading such as salesforce, advertising, sales promotion, etc. as appropriate.

The following summarizes some of the marketing objectives and strategies that are available to managers.

Objectives

1 Market penetration.
2 Introduce new products to existing markets.

3 Introduce existing products to new markets (domestic).
4 Introduce existing products to new markets (international).
5 Introduce new products to new markets.

Strategies

1 Change product design, performance, quality or features.
2 Change advertising or promotion.
3 Change unit price.
4 Change delivery or distribution.
5 Change service levels.
6 Improve marketing productivity (e.g. improve the sales mix).
7 Improve marketing administrative productivity.
8 Consolidate product line.
9 Withdraw from markets.
10 Consolidate distribution.
11 Standardize design.
12 Acquire markets, products, facilities.

Resource requirements

Finally, units preparing the plan should provide financial projections for the full planning period under all the standard revenue and cost headings as specified by the organization. It will be obvious from all the foregoing, that the setting of budgets becomes not only much easier, but the resulting budgets are more likely to be realistic and related to what the whole company wants to achieve rather than just one functional department.

The most satisfactory approach would be for marketing directors to justify all their marketing expenditure from a zero base each year against the tasks they wish to accomplish. This is possible if the procedures described above are followed, as a hierarchy of objectives is built up in such a way that every item of budgeted expenditure can be related directly back to the initial corporate financial objectives. For example, if sales promotion is a major means of achieving an objective in a particular market, when sales promotional items appear in the programme, each one has a specific purpose which can be related back to a major objective.

Doing it this way not only ensures that every item of expenditure is fully accounted for as part of a rational, objective and task approach, but also that when changes have to be made during the period to which the plan relates, such changes can be made in such a way that the least damage is caused to the company's long-term objectives.

The incremental marketing expense can be considered to be all costs that are incurred after the product leaves the factory, other than costs involved in physical distribution, the costs of which usually represent a discrete subset.

There is no textbook answer to problems relating to questions such as whether packaging should be a marketing or a production expense, and whether some distribution costs could be considered to be marketing costs. For example, insistence on high service levels results in high inventory carrying costs. Only common sense will reveal workable solutions to issues such as these.

Under price, however, any form of discounting that reduces the expected gross income, such as promotional discounts, quantity discounts, royalty rebates, and so on, as well as sales commission and unpaid invoices, should be given the most careful attention as incremental marketing expenses.

Most obvious incremental marketing expenses will occur, however, under the heading 'promotion', in the form of advertising, sales salaries and expenses, sales promotional expenditure, direct mail costs, and so on.

The important point about the measurable effects of marketing activity is that anticipated levels should be the result of the most careful analysis of what is required to take the company towards its goals, while the most careful attention should be paid to gathering all items of expenditure under appropriate headings. The healthiest way of treating these issues is a zero-based budgeting approach.

5 The marketing planning process

Figure 3a depicts the relationship between the marketing planning process and the output of that process – the strategic and tactical marketing plans.

Figure 3b shows the same process in a circular form, as this indicates more realistically the on-going nature of the marketing planning process and the link between strategic and tactical marketing plans.

Developing and implementing a marketing plan

This is the marketing planning process. It must not be confused with what appears in the plan itself, which is described on the right

This is what Unit managers must present in their strategic marketing plans

March
Planning team 'kick-off' Meetings with unit managers to discuss overall guidelines for the three-year planning period

Between March and May
Unit managers carry out marketing audits

May — Stage 1 meetings
Planning team discuss three-year business plans with unit managers and amend as necessary

May
1. Unit mission statement
2. Summary of Unit's performance last year
3. Summary of financial projections for the next three years
4. A market overviev
5. SWOT analyses (of major products/markets)
6. Portfolio sunnary
7. Major assumptions
8. Marketing objectives and strategies for next three years
9. Financial projections for next three years

Between September and October
Prepare detailed one-year operational plan with forecasts and budgets

November — Stage 2 meetings
Present amended three-year plan and detailed one-year plans to planning team

December
HQ consolidation of one-and three-year plans

Figure 3a The marketing planning process

The marketing audit

It will be seen that a marketing audit appears as a step in the marketing planning process. An audit is the means by which a company can understand how it relates to the environment in which it operates. It is the means by which a company can identify its own strengths and weaknesses as they relate to external opportunities and threats. It is thus a way of helping management to select a position in that environment based on known factors.

Expressed in its simplest form, if the purpose of a corporate plan is to answer three central questions:

1. Where is the company now?
2. Where does the company want to go?

571

The marketing mix

Figure 3b Strategic and operational planning cycle

3 How should the company organize its resources to get there?

The audit is the means by which the first of these questions is answered. An audit is a systematic, critical and unbiased review and appraisal of the environment and of the company's operations. A marketing audit is part of the larger management audit and is concerned with the marketing environment and marketing operations.

Any company carrying out an audit will be faced with two kinds of variables. First, there are variables over which the company has no direct control. These usually take the form of what can be described as environmental, market and competitive variables. Secondly, there are variables over which the company has complete control. These are known as operational variables.

This indicates how an audit should be structured. That is to say, in two parts:

1 external audit;
2 internal audit.

The external audit is concerned with the uncontrollable variables, while the internal audit is concerned with the controllable variables. The external audit starts with an examination of information on the general economy and then moves on to the outlook for the health and growth of the markets served by the company and competitor activities in those markets.

The purpose of the internal audit is to assess the organization's resources as they relate to the environment and *vis-à-vis* the resources of competitors.

6 Key account planning

Due to the maturity and internationalization of many American and Western European markets, customer power has increased, leading in turn to the growing importance of strategic planning for major accounts.

There is much debate about this, but it will be clear from looking at the planning cycle in Figure 3b that key account planning must take place at the same time as, or even before, draft plans are prepared for a strategic business unit.

If this is not clear, let us give an example of a supplies company servicing the needs of a national health service.

It will be seen there are four 'markets' within hospitals to be served. These are:

1 medical;
2 administration;
3 catering;
4 energy.

There will be a number of key accounts, or hospital groups, referred to here as Hospital Groups A, B, C, D, etc. Each of these hospital

Figure 3c Key accounts

groups may well have their own key account manager who has to plan for them. Figure 3c illustrates this.

Thus, for example, the Key Account Manager for Hospital A has to prepare a draft plan across all four 'markets' and this would clearly be a key input to the planning process shown in Figure 3d.

The position of key account planning in strategic marketing planning

It is clear that planning should start in the market where the customers are. Indeed, in anything other than small organizations, it is clearly absurd to think that any kind of meaningful planning can take place without the committed inputs of those who operate where the customers are.

Figure 3d shows a hierarchy of planning starting with key account planning. Every principle outlined in this article applies right down to the individual key account. Thus, the planning process shown in Figure 3a would start with key accounts. The content of the strategic plans for key accounts will be more or less the same as for a strategic marketing plan.

7 Marketing planning systems

The degree to which organizations need formalized systems for marketing planning depends on size and complexity. In small companies, top management tends to have an in-depth knowledge of both the technology and the market, hence they have a clear view of their comparative strengths and weaknesses. There is often also a shared understanding between top and middle management of the logical framework of ideas within which they are all working.

In large organizations and in those operating in complex product and market situations, a more formalized approach via operating manuals, procedures and processes is more necessary, because of the sheer size and complexity.

In all cases, however, research has shown that the process is universally applicable. All that varies is the degree of formality in its systematization.

The relationship between marketing planning, business planning and corporate planning

Marketing planning is based on markets, customers and products. Business planning involves the other corporate resources that must

Figure 3d Hierarchy of planning

The marketing mix

be brought to bear on the identified markets. Corporate planning usually involves applying business planning to several different units of the business aggregate.

Table 2 depicts marketing planning and its place in the corporate planning cycle. If marketing is a major activity in an organization, as in the case of consumer goods companies and many service organizations, it is usual to have a separate strategic and tactical marketing plan. In other cases, the marketing elements are incorporated into business plans for all the other organizational functions at the same time as marketing objectives and strategies are set. Often, these business plans get incorporated into a corporate plan, which will contain long-range corporate objectives, strategies, plans, profit and loss accounts, and balance sheets.

One of the main purposes of a corporate plan is to provide a long-term vision of what the company is or is striving to become, taking account of shareholder expectations, environmental trends, resource market trends, consumption market trends, and the distinctive competence of the company as revealed by the management audit. What this means in practice is that the corporate plan will contain the following elements:

1 desired level of profitability;
2 business boundaries:
   - what kinds of products will be sold to what kinds of markets (marketing),
   - what kinds of facilities will be developed (production and distribution),

Table 2 Marketing planning and its place in the corporate planning cycle

Step 1	Step 2 Management audit	Step 3 Objective and strategy setting	Step 4 Plans	Step 5 Corporate plans
	Marketing audit Marketing	Marketing objectives, strategies	Marketing plan	
	Distribution audit Stocks & control, transportation, warehousing	Distribution objectives, strategies	Distribution plan	Issue of corporate plan, to include corporate objectives and strategies; production objectives and strategies; long-range profit and loss accounts; balance sheet
Corporate financial objectives	**Production analysis** Value analysis; engineering development; work study; quality control; labour; material, plant and space utilization; production planning; factories	Production objectives, strategies	Production plan	
	Financial audit Credit, debit, cash flow and budgetary control; resource allocation; capital expenditure; long-term finance	Financial objectives, strategies	Financial plan	
	Personnel audit Management, technical and administrative ability, etc.	Personnel objectives, strategies		

- the size and character of the labour force (personnel),
- funding (finance);
3. other corporate objectives, such as social responsibility, corporate image, stock market image, employer image, etc.

Such a corporate plan, containing projected profit and loss accounts and balance sheets, being the result of the process described above, is more likely to provide long-term stability for a company than plans based on a more intuitive process and containing forecasts which tend to be little more than extrapolations of previous trends.

In contrast, the headquarters of one major multinational company with a sophisticated budgeting system used to receive 'plans' from all over the world and coordinate them in quantitative and cross-functional terms such as numbers of employees, units of sales, items of plant, square feet of production area, and so on, together with the associated financial implications. The trouble was that the whole complicated edifice was built on the initial sales forecasts, which were themselves little more than a time-consuming numbers game. The really key strategic issues relating to products and markets were lost in all the financial activity, which eventually resulted in grave operational and profitability problems.

In summary, strategic and tactical marketing planning has been shown to make a vital contribution to an organization's long-term financial health.

MALCOLM H. B. MCDONALD
CRANFIELD INSTITUTE OF TECHNOLOGY

Further reading

(References cited in the text marked *)

* Ansoff, H.I. (1977) 'The state and practice of planning systems', *Sloan Management Review* 18 (2).
* Bailey, A. and Johnson, G. (1994) 'The process of strategy development', Cranfield School of Management Research Paper.
* Greenley, G. (1987) 'An exposition into empirical research into marketing planning', *Journal of Marketing Management* 3 (1). (This paper reviews all recent empirical research into the process of marketing planning and concludes that it remains one of the most difficult domains in the whole field of marketing.)
* Kollatt, D.J. et al. (1972) *Strategic Marketing*, Holt, New York: Reinhart and Winston.
* Leighton, D.S.R. (1966) *International Marketing Text and Cases*, New York: McGraw-Hill.

Leppard J. and McDonald, M.H.B. (1987) 'A reappraisal of the role of marketing planning', *Journal of Marketing Management* 3 (2). (This paper throws quite a considerable amount of light on to why marketing planning is rarely done. It examines the organization context in which marketing planning takes place and gives a fascinating insight into how corporate culture and politics often prevents the marketing concept from taking hold.)

* McDonald, M.H.B. (1984) 'The theory and practice of marketing planning for industrial goods in international markets', PhD, Cranfield Institute of Technology.

McDonald, M.H.B. (1989) *Marketing Plans: how to prepare them; how to use them*, Oxford: Butterworth-Heinemann. (This books is the standard text on marketing planning in universities and organizations around the world. It is practical, as well as being based on sound theoretical concepts.)

McDonald, M.H.B. and Wilson, H. 'State-of-the-art developments in expert systems and strategic marketing planning', *British Journal of Management* 1 (3). (This paper explores a number of key planning techniques, looks at the interrelationships between them and shows how they can be intelligently combined into an Expert System. In particular, Exmar, an expert system in strategic marketing planning is described.)

* Thompson, S. (1962) *How Companies Plan*, AMA Research Study, no. 54, AMA.
* Thune, S. and House, R. (1970) 'Where long-range planning pays off', *Business Horizons* 7 (4).

See also: ADVERTISING; BRANDING AND BRAND MANAGEMENT; MARKET SEGMENTATION; POSITIONING; PRICING; PRODUCT LIFE-CYCLE MANAGEMENT; PRODUCT POLICY; QUANTITATIVE METHODS IN MARKETING; SALES FORECASTING; SALES PROMOTION; STRATEGIC MARKETING PLANNING; THE MARKETING MIX

Marketing management

Commodity marketing

1 What are commodities?
2 The development of commodity marketing
3 Trading in commodities
4 Marketing of commodities
5 The futures market
6 Marketing information
7 Organization for marketing commodities
8 Promotion of commodities in the market
9 Current and future developments in commodity marketing

Overview

Trade in commodities is probably the world's largest business and each year it continues to grow. Fully 70 per cent of the world's 125 largest economies depend on primary commodities for more than half their export earnings. Constant change, progressively fiercer competition and the rise in the number of large transnational companies is changing the nature of world commodity markets increasing the marketing role as an element of the business. Schorsch (1994) states that mix-based competition and skimpy promotional budgets have been major constraints of marketing in the commodity environment in the past. This entry examines the past, current and future roles of marketing in relation to world trade in commodities or undifferentiated world products.

1 What are commodities?

A commodity can be broadly defined as 'an item suitable for trade' which can assume many different forms and characteristics which render it suitable to be bought and sold for commercial purposes (Gordon-Ashworth 1984). Kiel (1997) defines commodities marketing as first having to distinguish between commodity goods and services and commodity markets. A commodity good or service is one for which the core benefit is largely undifferentiated. A large number of goods and services fit this definition including energy, telecommunications and banking. A commodity market, however is a different concept having the following features:

- the product sold in the commodity market is a commodity good;
- the product is an industrial product;
- there are relatively few buyers and sellers;
- there is widely disseminated price information
- price movements are broadly related to changes in demand and supply.

Commodity markets occur in areas such as minerals, agriculture, chemicals and finance. Primary commodities can be described as goods in or near to their first stage of transformation (Gordon-Ashworth 1984). However Brown (1975) offers an alternative definition as commodities being all products of the land – whether they are extracted from, grown on or raised on – which can be considered primary commodities while they remain in an unprocessed or partially processed state. Products that are harvested or fished from bodies of water are also primary commodities until they have undergone substantial transformation. If the product has undergone some processing, but with only minor inputs which do not change its essential characteristics, it can still be considered a primary commodity. Many commodities do undergo some processing before they are first exchanged internationally, e.g. rubber in its unprocessed state straight from the tree has to undergo a transformation process to make it solid rubber, the final commodity which is bought and sold.

One criterion of a commodity is the relative lack of differentiation among producers. Differentiation should be considered in the continuum as shown in Figure 1. Some commodities have absolutely no differentiation in their physical characteristics.

For example a currency or equity is totally homogenous and for gold and silver strict physical specifications exist. However, other commodities, such as coal, have considerable

Marketing in practice

```
                    Physical characteristic of a product
    Perfectly                                                      Each supplier
    identical                                                         different

    ←─────────────────────────────────────────────────────────────────────→
        Currency    Gold       Copper                         Wool      Coal
                    Silver      Lead
                                Zinc
```

Figure 1 The commodity continuum

differentiation depending on the mine they are from and the resulting different physical and chemical characteristics. Some of the characteristics will be more highly prized by one or more buyers of the product. Nevertheless coal, for example, can still be considered a commodity as the level of buyer differentiation is small – there are relatively few buyers and sellers and spot prices are available daily for coal.

In more recent times many new innovative products in various industries such as chemicals, plastics, electronic products, semiconductors, salmon and financial instruments were differentiated products. With economies of scale, learning by doing, oligopolistic exploitation of these advantages, low cost mass producers and international competition, these products have been rendered essentially manufactured commodities in world markets (Furash 1996). As Rangan and Bowman (1992) state, even though such products are loosely characterized as commodities, in reality it is the product market combination that one usually refers to in making such a characterization. Regardless of whether the product is corn or computers it is the market dynamics that distinguish a commodity. Most managers recognize the early warning signs of commoditization – increasing competition, availability of 'me too' products, the customer's reluctance to pay for features and services accompanying the product, and pressure on prices and margins in general. Steadily and deliberately as the market transforms into a commodity, many buyers begin to perceive the product and its suppliers to be homogenous, and price becomes the predominant buying criterion. Additionally with a diminishing base of modern, distinctive suppliers, more large manufacturers are encouraged to treat all purchased inputs as commodities (Luria 1996).

A commodity market is thus one where the company has minimum advantages in terms of differentiation and cost. Commodity products are those where the customer has no particular requirement to buy from a particular supplier, and will readily purchase other origin products almost entirely on the basis of comparative pricing.

When a product is in a commodity situation, the conventional market theory is to differentiate the product by adding value in packaging, convenience, or in the delivery system. This is not possible with many commodity products such as metals, crude petroleum product, financial product and agricultural products such as grains. However, traditional commodities of the past, such as chicken have been successfully moved from a commodity position to a differentiated product, to the extent that chicken is now a branded product with the marketing opportunities that affords (Thomas and Koonce 1989; Jereski 1985).

Commodity products thus cover a wide range of product options from raw materials through partially processed products to manufactured goods. For the purpose of this chapter manufactured commodities will only be considered where they add to the understanding of the marketing of primary commodities. Commodities will be treated as basically primary commodities, which are traded in a relatively standardized state with minor if any differentiating features. Consideration will be given to the immense marketing pushes occurring today to differentiate traditional commodities.

2 The development of commodity marketing

The trading of commodities involves huge, worldwide markets. All countries produce some primary products, in particular primary commodities are the single most important contributor to trade in 75 per cent of developing countries if mineral fuels are excluded. Some commodities are traded widely but others because of high transportation costs, are largely traded regionally compared with internationally e.g. quarry products that are bulky and of low margin return.

The development of the marketing of commodities requires a brief consideration of the history of commodity trading. The importance and value of commodities reflects marketing developments in the past, current activities today and developments underway for the future.

In 1938 the top three commodities traded were cotton, coal and crude petroleum. Cotton was the commodity with the highest value of $600 million annually in 1938. By 1977 the situation had changed dramatically and the three most traded commodities were crude petroleum, petroleum products, and coffee, with cotton having fallen to twentieth place – a situation that has continued through the 1980s and into the 1990s. Agricultural commodities are the major primary commodities produced though not traded internationally. In more recent years many services and products have become tradable commodities, such as financial instruments (Furash 1996) and environmental commodities (McCann 1996). Additionally the first tentative steps are being taken in the commoditization of electricity promising the emergence of a paper market for power (Krapels and Stagliano 1996).

The role and importance of nations has also changed a lot since the turn of the century. In the 1930s the United Kingdom and colonies were the most important traders accounting for over 50 per cent of world trade of wool, rubber, tea and tin, and over 30 per cent of wheat, butter, beef, lamb, mutton, rice, wheat and flour. However, following the outbreak of the Second World War primary commodity trade changed. The severe foreign exchange regulations radically changed the ways in which primary commodities were distributed and marketed. In the UK and the USA governments bought in bulk from producer organizations and distributed to the final consumer. Exporters were faced with one or two large buyers and the effect on marketing was the replacement of private merchandizing with almost complete government control. It was not until 1956 that the private merchandizing system was fully in place and commodity marketing developed.

The greatest trend since the Second World War has been the decline in real prices of commodity goods compared with manufactured goods. The long-term decline is mainly the outcome of falling long-term production costs as a result of intensified competition in the world economy, including competition generated by more advanced country exporters.

Price decline is continuing to be a dominant trend but primary commodity exports still account for the bulk of foreign exchange earnings for many less developed countries (LDCs). For the majority of LDCs most export earnings come from sales of three or less primary commodities. For example, in 1994, Burundi, Ghana and Zambia received 65 per cent of their export earning from one primary commodity. The fall in primary export earnings in real terms has greatly added to the indebtedness of LDCs. The problem for these countries is further exacerbated by import barriers from developed countries that make it harder for LDCs to sell their primary commodities and therefore reduce their debt.

The high volatility of prices is also contributed to by the rigidities of supply caused by the very nature of the commodities such as dependence on weather conditions or long gestation periods of investments e.g. a coffee tree has to grow for five years before a crop can be harvested. These supply rigidities are very often reinforced by inappropriate domestic policies which insulate domestic from international price movements (Fischer 1991).

From a demand perspective, technological progress, low population growth and the increasing availability of substitutes more desired by consumers has impacted significantly the demand for some commodities. Demand for coffee is nearly saturated in terms of per capita consumption; artificial substitutes for sugar have taken increasing shares of the markets as consumers demand diet products; demand for oil has decreased as nations have exploited their own alternative fuels such as oil or gas; and demand for raw materials like copper or cotton is sensitive to growth of industrial output.

Agricultural policies, most notably in the USA, EU (European Community) and East Asia (including Japan and South Korea), have impacted significantly on trade in agricultural commodities. Subsidies for agricultural production and export have contributed to increased world supply and lower prices. Protectionism has reduced demand and contributed to price volatility and to the need to differentiate products to circumvent non-tariff trade barriers. These have all distorted international commodity markets to varying extents. Marketing monopolies in both producer and consumer countries have also markedly distorted trade.

In the 1990s there have been three principal consuming markets for commodities. The USA was the biggest importer of coffee, sisal, sugar and lead; the UK imports the most meat, dairy products, tea and zinc and Western Europe was the largest importer of petroleum, wheat, cotton, vegetable oils and seeds, wool, rubber, copper, tobacco, cocoa, jute and maize.

3 Trading in commodities

Although the trading of primary commodities is essential to the functioning of the world economy, there are a number of problems that must be addressed in order for the system to operate efficiently. Four of these important problems will be discussed here. First, the perceived declining terms of developing countries trade has a negative influence on international commodity policy. Second, the high dependence of developing countries' economies on primary commodities means they are greatly affected by price reductions. Therefore the developing countries are much more vulnerable as their export portfolios are highly concentrated on primary commodities. For example, in 1987 twelve developing countries relied on one primary commodity for 90 per cent of their income and 23 developing countries relied upon crude petroleum and petroleum products for 50 per cent or more of their export earning. In comparison, only one developed country (Iceland) relied on one primary commodity (fish) for more than 50 per cent of its export earnings. Another problem is that manufactured goods have caused particular problems for the economies of developing countries. Hence, price stabilization has formed a recurrent objective of international commodity controls. The fourth problem is that without careful planning and control the supply of some primary commodities may be depleted if demand increases.

To overcome some of these problems a number of world commodity controls have been developed with some form of control being applied to most commodities impacting on the marketing of them. Two main types of commodity control exist. The first are international commodity agreements between governments and producer organizations. The most clearly defined of these have been applied to tin, wheat, sugar, rubber, coffee, cocoa and tea. The principal aim of international commodity agreements has the main emphasis on balancing supply with demand resulting in an increase in export earnings to the producers. The most common form of control mechanism has been some form of quantitative restriction on exports, used in conjunction with either international or national stock control policies (Gordon-Ashworth 1984). The second type is international cartels described as 'arrangements between producers or traders with the aim to control production and distribution to their common advantage'. Crude petroleum (OPEC – Organization of Petroleum Exporting Countries), copper, mercury, bauxite, uranium and iron ore are notable cartels that have varied in strength over the years with increasing disintegration in more recent times.

These controls, while they have their advantages, do bring up several issues for debate. Agricultural protectionism policies, especially in Europe, cause problems for other overseas exporters. The Common Agricultural Policy (CAP) of the EU is a significant obstacle as the EU represents the largest world market for agricultural goods. This policy effectively excludes competition from more cost-efficient nations. The EU also creates instability in world markets by dumping surplus products as subsidized exports and through variable import levies. For example, levies rise when world prices fall, thus restricting demand when world supplies are plentiful. The effect of these protectionism policies is damaging to the protecting nations (higher consumer prices) and to developed agricultural exporters and to developing nations. The tariff escalation policies aim to deter exporters from attempting to differentiate or add value to their products thus maintaining them as commodities. These policies dictate that the tariff increases, as further processing is done. Thus, the tariff varies inversely with value added resulting in exceptionally high rates of protection. This denies countries the opportunity to effectively increase their income by adding value where they have a comparative advantage in growing or processing.

Primary commodity producers in LDCs have particular problems in that they have limited bargaining power in relation to large transnational companies and therefore find it difficult to improve their share of the final price. There are two alternative strategies to overcome this problem. The first strategy attempts to reduce the concentration in trade and increase marketing. This requires producers to increase their marketing efforts with the aim of increasing the number of buyers or to stimulate competition between existing buyers. An alternative strategy is to endeavour to increase the price elasticity of supply. This could be achieved by establishing a single marketing board for each commodity in each country and this would mean the producers are acting as a monopoly to counterbalance the power of transnational companies. However, the ability to increase price is still limited in many country cases due to relatively weak market positions. Their power ultimately depends on their ability to market directly to the final consumer. LDC producers are at a great disadvantage with transnational corporations in processing and marketing products because these organizations have certain monopolistic advantages which make it difficult for the LDCs to independently develop their own effective marketing strategies. The major problems facing the LDCs is that they have limited access to relevant market information, they don't have cheap transport and they face many obstacles from the intra-firm agreements of transnational companies.

Several world organizations have attempted to aid LDCs in the marketing of commodities. For example, the United Nations Conference on Trade and Development (UNCTAD) established the Integrated Programme for Commodities (IPC) which aimed 'to establish within the context of the IPC a framework of international co-operation in the field of marketing and distribution of LDCs' commodity exports, with the objective of increasing their export earnings'. Only a few producer associations were formed and they had limited success. They resulted in improved information sharing, promoted the harmonization of marketing policies and established co-operative marketing but did not succeed in raising prices.

4 Marketing of commodities

An integral part of the process of selling commodities is the marketing process. It has been suggested (Kiel 1997) from a marketing mix paradigm, that commodity markets should be treated as a specific type of industrial marketing to which industrial buyer behaviour models and marketing mix based decision making can apply (see ORGANIZATIONAL BUYING BEHAVIOUR; THE MARKETING MIX). However Rowe (1965) defines the marketing process as 'the process of transferring supplies of the commodity from the producing units, whether these be individuals or small or large corporations, to the processors or manufacturers in consuming countries. Marketing involves the physical processes of collection from the actual producers, transport within the producing country to the ports, ocean shipment, stockholding, and distribution within the consuming countries'. This process is often aided by a commodity exchange defined as 'an organization usually owned by member traders, which provides facilities for bringing buyers and sellers of specified commodities or their agents, for promoting trades in these commodities' (AMA Committee on Definitions 1963). The marketing of commodities is an intricate process with the main structure and principles of marketing being much the same for all commodities, though varying in detail for specific commodities. Ownership of the goods is transferred many times during the process and the price must be determined for each exchange allowing considerable flexibility for producers to put together a 'marketing mix' for the commodity. Buyers usually satisfy their requirements through issuing tenders or through placing 'spot' orders with commodity merchants or brokers. Most transactions take place directly between commodity manufacturers and food or non-food manufacturers, but merchant traders sometimes act as agents or commission brokers. Some countries have government controlled marketing boards that act as the sole buyers and sellers of the commodity. For example, the Cocoa Marketing Board in Nigeria guarantees minimum prices for the growers and aims to reduce exploitation.

Buyers choose suppliers that are product differentiated on the basis of the products being within different ranges of specification and delivered at specified times. Buyers who are exposed to the open world commodity market are particularly sensitive to variations in commodity prices and wish to avoid the risk of holding higher-priced stocks on a falling market.

Manufacturers who have the option of procuring commodities by tender or spot purchase sometimes derive higher value from direct contractual linkages with producers. There is evidence of relationship marketing in many commodity markets. As in forms of industrial marketing, it is often the basis of these relationships that result in contracts being renegotiated year after year for varying quantities, depending on customer needs and the market situation. Contracts provide assurances of reliable supply, consistent quality and service. They also enable buyers to make requests for limited special features, such as delivery schedules. Premiums of up to 5 per cent over free market prices can be obtained for some commodities under such contractual arrangements. Government buyers are particularly prevalent in this increasingly used type of exchange for commodity purchase.

Price determination is critical for commodity buying and selling. Prices in all markets for commodities tend to be relatively uniform once allowances are made for differences in quality and in transport and distribution costs. The world market price reflects the demand and supply conditions over the world as a whole, both immediately and in the foreseeable future. Rivalry in tendering and spot commodity markets is based largely on price competition.

Price fluctuation is a problem with the marketing of primary commodities. The prices of all primary commodities, without an organized control scheme, would fluctuate dramatically. With most commodities supply and demand are continually changing and this can greatly affect prices. In general, in the short term, final consumer demand is inelastic due to slow changes in consumers' tastes and supply is inelastic since producers cannot rapidly increase or decrease their output. The effect of this is that prices tend to fall very considerably if supply is even slightly larger than demand, and rise sharply if it is even slightly smaller. In the long term, prices are affected by changes in final consumption, demand and current production. In the long term, final demand is inelastic for small price changes but may alter if the price change is sufficiently large. The commodities most affected by price changes are those which have competitive substitutes. For example, during the Second World War tin shortages dramatically raised the price and therefore the demand for substitute metals increased. However, after the war when tin supplies increased and it became a moderately low priced commodity demand for tin did not increase as consumers were used to substitutes. Generally a continued low price is needed to prevent the development of artificial substitutes. A sustained price change can lead to large changes in production capacity, but usually only in response to large and prolonged price changes. One problem is that short-term price fluctuations often mask long-term trends. Thus production is likely to be increased or decreased too much causing further oscillations in price. These price changes greatly affect the economies of exporting countries hence the desire to move out of the commodity pricing trap.

5 The futures market

Commodities face sharp fluctuating prices depending on the output, exports, political and climatic conditions and the world economy (Boonekamp and Cathelinaud 1996). Many producers and users in the marketing system attempt to minimize these swings in value because of the lack of financial ability to withstand these price and earning risks. The market mechanism established to stabilize commodity prices or earnings uses the futures market as the market instrument to protect against price fluctuation beyond one's control. This is done by trading some of the output in advance of its actual production at prices known at the moment of trade. By choosing the quantity agreed to be delivered at a fixed price, the producer is able to alter the price and earnings distribution in a desirable way, but leave the price and earnings distribution for the rest of the market unchanged.

Futures exchanges exist throughout the world. The most notable are the Chicago Board of Trade operating principally in agricultural products; the Coffee, Sugar, and Cocoa Exchange in New York; the New York Cotton Exchange and the London Metal Exchange which is the world's premier exchange for commodity metals such as aluminium, copper, zinc, lead, nickel and silver.

Futures contracts can be exchanged through traders or brokers in an extremely wide range of commodities based on agricultural, metallurgical and petroleum products in exchanges based all over the world with those listed above tending to be price setters. Delivery of the commodity is possible on many futures markets but is optional and seldom occurs in practice. The usefulness of the futures market in protecting traders against adverse price changes depends on the convergence of cash and futures prices as the contract approaches maturity.

Futures markets can protect both producers and processors alike from price changes. Increasingly producers are managing costs through a smoothing out of the purchase price by buying on the futures exchange (Dwyer 1997) or gaining some assurance of what price they will pay for the commodities they need (Shuldiner and Norkus 1996). Futures markets also have a role in price determination in that the market takes account of information about the conditions of supply and demand and provides estimates of future prices based on this information.

To assist trading, transactions in various commodities are standardized. For wool the standard contract is 2500 kilograms, for live cattle 10,000 kilograms liveweight, copper 25 tonnes, gold 250 grams, cocoa 25 tonnes, EU wheat 100 tonnes, fuel oil 100 tonnes, etc.

The disadvantages of a futures market is that it is possible for people who have no direct interest in a particular commodity to operate in the relevant futures market; however their presence is considered to made a more efficient market (Campbell and Fisher 1991).

The futures market, while not engendering any loyalty to a particular product or producer, plays a valuable role in risk transfer, equity financing, market intelligence, price discovery and forward pricing. In theory at least a futures market should result in more stable prices. There are, however, other ways to organize these functions and activities in particular in food commodities. Today, many commodities appear to be marketed efficiently without the benefit of futures trading. Kohls and Uhl (1990) conclude that marketing costs are reduced by the costs of risk for a net increase in operational efficiency for the food industry. Whether this is true of the metals commodity market is open to debate. The commodities futures markets are much criticized, but play a necessary and important role in price determination and price stabilization in the marketplace. It is, however, extremely difficult to look at a pricing strategy for commodities in such a marketplace.

6 Marketing information

Marketing information is critical for success in exporting commodities. Accurate information is particularly important when predicting future demand and supply and future prices. The amount and quality of information readily available varies among commodities largely because of differences in trading practices. For example, if the commodity is sold at an auction (as is tea) or on an exchange (such as used for sugar and coffee) then information on sales is generally available daily. However, if the commodity is sold on a long-term contract or intrafirm (e.g. bauxite and jute) information on sales is not easily obtainable by outsiders. There are a number of secondary sources of published information which provide useful information. These include information from government departments, international commodity study groups and major trading firms' publications of marketing information and forecasts, information from the Food and Agricultural Organization and the World Bank, and material from specific trade journals. However, this type of information is not really detailed enough to serve as an effective aid to decision making, compounding the problems of marketing commodities.

Marketing intelligence and economic analysis are critical in the futures market with constant monitoring of long-term demand trends, long-term resource availability, process trends as well as investment trends required to build new production capacity. New tools for commodity producers are being developed to assist in price determination but tools for forecasting future demand (Pohl 1996) and assessing risk tools available to producers of commodities are limited (Blank et al. 1997).

7 Organization for marketing commodities

Commodity marketing of agricultural products, in particular, is characterized by marketing by producer co-operatives or by marketing boards. Marketing boards are potent marketing agencies with the combined powers of co-operatives, marketing orders and bargaining associations. They are common worldwide such as the New Zealand Dairy Board (New Zealand); the Australian Wheat Board (Australia) and also operate in Canada, France, the UK and Africa.

Marketing boards are essentially producer-controlled organizations with government monopoly powers over a broad range of farm production and marketing activities. The chief functions of these operating boards have been outlined by Kohls and Uhl (1990) as

1. collective bargaining and price negotiation, acting as a single agent for all producers of the commodity;
2. sole marketing agent for the commodity, with broad controls over all aspects of marketing, including the ownership of storage facilities;
3. sponsorship of market-intelligence activities and market research;
4. producer pooling arrangements to divide receipts among farmers;
5. settling production and marketing controls and quotas.

The argument in support of such boards is that marketing regulation is very important in commodity trading to exploit market power, thus maximizing producer returns. References to orderly marketing, weak selling, destructive competition, market premiums and the need to extract the most from the market, are the arguments for those advocating regulations to achieve co-ordinated and disciplined marketing of agricultural commodities.

The marketing power most readily exploited by these boards is that arising through preferred access to a restricted and higher priced market under quota and access restrictions. Such quotas exist for commodities in many markets such as agricultural quotas into the EU, cheese and beef quotas into the USA, and the butter quota into the UK. The entitlement or quota to sell, usually a maximum quantity, in a market where trade and domestic policies maintains prices above international levels is valuable. These quotas exist widely in the commodity trade and distort the traditional marketing process of a product.

With global changes and increasingly open access of some markets, calls have been made for the abolition of such marketing boards in that the regulations and marketing structures emphasize a marketing objective of maximizing farm gate prices rather than profit maximization in the marketplace through allowing a series of suppliers to compete in a marketplace (Hussey 1992).

Commodity markets are shrinking relative to consumer products. A new era in food demand and marketing has already commenced. There are no longer principally generic markets for products such as dairy products, meat or wool. Instead there is an increasing diversity of markets for products derived from these raw materials with product form, packaging, and methods of retailing differing between markets. While there has been a trend from commodity to consumer products in some country's agricultural marketing it is questionable whether it has matched the rate of market change. The tendency of monopoly sellers or marketing regulations to restrict product range and to innovate more slowly than competitive sellers is being used as the argument for changing marketing boards monopoly selling status (Hussey 1992).

8 Promotion of commodities in the market

As commodity markets reach saturation and competing products develop, the role of market boards is in promotion of the product. These operate domestically in many countries and play a significant role in promoting commodity products. Organizations such as the National Livestock and Meat Board of the USA, the Ontario Milk Marketing Board of Canada and the Danish Dairy Board of Denmark widely promote sales of their products domestically and internationally.

International commodity producers have bonded together as competition from alternative products or declining consumer demand is evident. These 'commodity' groups funded by producers generically promote the product. Notable examples of these are the International Wool Secretariat (IWS) and the International Coffee Organization both based in Australia and the UK respectively. (The IWS was based in the UK until 1996.) The argument of effectiveness of generic promotion can be considered in contrasting these two products.

The International Wool Secretariat conducts wool promotion on behalf of the growers of its member countries (Australia and South Africa with Uruguay an associate member) using the 'Woolmark' symbol. It promotes wool in the major wool consuming markets around the world principally in Western Europe, the USA and Japan. An important distinction between wool and other commodities subject to generic promotion is that, for the most part, wool is not directly the object of consumer choice. Promotion is typically directed at increasing the demand for final products in which wool is an attribute. Dewbre and Beare (1992), in a study on the effectiveness of such generic promotion, showed that wool promotion, prices and household income were all statistically significant variables in household level wool-in-apparel demand. The conclusions of this study were that such expenditures were profitable and stimulated demand for wool but the question remains as to whether there is an increasing or decreasing response to further promotional expenditure.

In a review of the role of promotion of the International Coffee Agreement (Greer and Chattalas 1989) it was concluded that despite the many advertising themes and campaigns the critical areas of theme appropriateness, setting of objectives, continuity, potential for synergy between generic and brand campaigns, and evaluation have received inadequate attention. The Promotion Fund had ignored many opportunities such as decaffeinated coffee, had not developed cooperation between the commodity producing nations and largely capitalist consuming countries and had the misconception that promotion is mainly a capitalist-colonialist tool used for the exploitation of their national markets.

Generic promotion of a commodity has the unique potential to help smooth out the devastating effects that demand instability can have on commodity industries. Promotion would tend to stabilize Third World economies since price alone has not proved to be a sufficient stabilizer of demand and revenue. Promotion would make demand more predictable and consequently more dependable for market development than price stabilization alone.

The effectiveness of generic advertising from a commodity perspective has come under increasing scrutiny recently. Collectively generic commodity advertisers spend significant amounts, with the likelihood that as new mandatory check off programmes such as for beef, pork and milk in the USA become mandated, the total value will increase significantly. Despite the large sums spent and the apparent willingness of producers to support the programmes, little is known about the economic impacts of generic advertising. The impacts of generic advertising on middlemen and producers either are not addressed or are inferred from retail impacts. Inferences about producer level impacts based on measurement at the retail level may be misleading especially if middlemen possess the market power (Wohlgenant 1991).

Commodity groups are, through their advertising initiatives, attempting to promote the marketing of their product. Conventional marketing wisdom advocates getting a product to market first hence there is a belief that generic advertising is not a prudent way to spend money. It is generally agreed that new evaluation techniques are needed to evaluate generic advertising and its effectiveness (MacDonald and Gould 1992). Success cannot be measured by profit and loss, as is the case for private companies.

Results of a major study on the catfish industry in the USA (Zidack *et al.* 1992) suggest that the generic advertising programme increased producer returns both at the wholesale and farm levels of the market. It was concluded that despite industry concentration at the wholesale level, it appears that farmers could benefit from promotional programmes aimed at shifting retail demand. Results suggested that commodity promotion programmes did not have to be big to be effective, even limited-budget programmes could increase demand and be profitable, especially if supply is inelastic. Recent developments have seen some of the greatest opportunities for branding being taken up in working in tandem with commodity boards, in

Marketing in practice

Figure 2 A traditional view of competitiveness focusing on the production sector

order, for example, to promote a specific agricultural product, meat, seafood, or other basic foodstuff. The Idaho Potato Commission has done this very successfully with the Great Escape Restaurant Chain, as has Denny's with the National Pork Producers Council in the USA (Anon 1997).

In contrast with food industry based commodities the major efforts in promotion of mineral based commodities tend to be in the area of personal selling, largely of a relationship building nature. Little is undertaken in terms of the traditional elements of the communication mix but with the explosion of the World Wide Web some industry organizations are now offering web sites e.g. http://www.copper.org.

The results of international and domestic studies highlight the critical need for carefully allocating funds to ensure they are used in the most efficient manner possible. In particular with commodities because markets are dynamic, subject to rapid change due to changes in relative prices, income, new products and other factors, advertising programmes must be routinely assessed to determine their effectiveness and to provide guidance for future funding decisions.

9 Current and future developments in commodity marketing

As commodity markets change, producers are attempting to differentiate their product. Traditionally firms operating in the commodity sector have tended to focus their efforts on a specific segment of the sector. The implicit demarcation according to Hudson (1990) between the production and processing subsectors has been commodity processing, i.e. the killing of livestock, the milling of grain. Firms involved in activities, which impact the commodity prior to processing, are in the production subsector and firms involved after processing in the processing subsector. Firms in the production subsector view commodity producers as the primary consumers of the goods and services they provide, while firms in the processing subsector focus on the final consumers.

Hudson (1990) depicts the view of competitiveness in the agribusiness industry focusing on the production sector.

As depicted in Figure 2 the producer is the central focus of the firm and the emphasis is on surrounding the producer with goods and services which are either inputs associated with commodity production: (feed, seed and fertilizer; machinery and equipment; financing; and production information) or outputs associated with commodity marketing and distribution (marketing services; commodity processing; market information; and transportation).

Commodity firms with a view to competitiveness strive to surround the commodity producer using vertical coordination to control the various spokes of the wheel in Figure 2. Hudson (1990) cites numerous examples, which illustrate the application of this perspective.

This perspective is changing with firms aggressively pursuing contractual arrangements for the production and procurement of commodities. The common thread Hudson (1990) identifies is the merging of the production and processing sectors towards a strategy of vertical coordination. Strong evidence of this is seen in the USA and increasing evidence in New Zealand, Australia and Denmark.

Advances in technology, increasing concern by consumers over diet, and an expanded demand for convenience, have created a two-tier processing sector; commodity processing and further processing. With this two-tiered structure we have commodity firms and value added firms. Some firms specialize in either commodity or value added processing and other firms in both activities. Commodity marketers are likely to consider the perspective shown in Figure 2 and utilize a generic strategy of cost leadership to survive. Such firms will differ largely by their geographic location and the services which they offer producers. An approach being increasingly utilized is one of a cost leadership strategy augmented by a move to achieve differentiation through service to customers.

However Hudson (1990) predicts that as the focus on consumers continues to characterize the food and agribusiness sectors, new relationships within the vertical production–marketing channel will evolve. Both commodity processors and value added processors will seek increased control of the activities between production of commodities and the final consumer product and an increasing blurring of the commodity and value added sector will occur. These changes will likely become increasingly important in shaping the future of commodity marketing. Goldberg (1985) suggested that 'a systems approach to each major commodity system has to be developed in order to position a firm or a nation in its global food setting'. To survive as a commodity marketer in the future will require a close evaluation of your position and involvement in the food chain.

Commodity bundling, involving grouping products and services such that when they are combined a unique marketing offering is formed, has potential for the marketing of traditional commodities. It is a familiar approach in many industries, yet the strategic and structural implications are not well developed. Lawless (1991) discusses the potential advantages of commodity bundling resulting in lower costs or increased benefits at a higher cost based on products that could be loosely defined as manufactured commodities. Such as strategy has the potential to be increasingly used by commodity marketers to differentiate their product. For example the New Zealand Dairy Board offers strong technical support, pilot scale facilities and training with sales of milk proteins in the USA. It also tailors commodity production to meet tight customer specifications. The vulnerability of commodity trading has led producers to differentiate their commodity offerings by reducing buyer's risk. They do this by guaranteeing delivery schedules, volumes and product specifications.

Commodities have been successfully differentiated. Poultry products traditionally were considered relatively homogenous and undifferentiated products at both farm and retail level Branding and brand advertising is now relatively common for eggs and usual for chickens. The success of branded chickens such as Perdue, Tysons and Holly Farms attests to the ability to differentiate a commodity. Adverse market conditions, unique among food processors, of slim profit margins, feed prices that are variable on an hourly basis and the distribution problems of a fresh product – all that conspire against the creation of a brand – were overcome. Tysons succeeded in dispelling the commodity image of the industry by marketing and distributing a wide variety of new processed products in what the industry called value enhanced products. A non-agricultural product which has been successfully branded is ice. WLR Foods packaged ice under the Cassco label for retail distribution with a strong marketing mix resulting in it being the largest ice retailer in the USA (Cassco 1997). These value enhanced products allow processors to differentiate their offerings from those of their competitors as well as making profits less susceptible to fluctuation in raw material costs, improving profit stability (Thomas and Koonce 1989).

Strategies of differentiating through value enhancement are being made, for example, by the New Zealand Dairy Board for milk powder in new forms of convenient packaging for industrial users or in reducing dust problems through the use of new powder forming technologies. Branding strategies have been developed, for example, for the ENZA brand of the New Zealand Apple and Pear Marketing Board allowing it to sell apples of equivalent quality sourced worldwide, rather than simply from New Zealand and similarly the Zespri brand for kiwifruit. Branded merino wool in its commodity state is being sold as Merino Gold out of Australia. With time branding and differentiation strategies will move many commodities into differentiated product markets changing commodity marketing in some products, as we know them. Developments in the meat, many fruit and vegetable and some parts of the cereal sectors are clearly directed towards a differentiation strategy.

The future will see increasing differentiation of commodity products, a shrinking of the commodity markets for many products, increasing vertical integration of the commodity processing and value added sectors of the food industry reducing the need for commodity marketing, and increasing competition in what remains of the traditional commodity markets. The commodity market will remain distorted through marketing control, protectionism, and the particular nature of trading of commodities on the futures market or using commodity brokers. The results of the Uruguay GATT round may in years to come change commodity marketing significantly, in particular from the perspective of trade in agricultural commodities, but the implications of the Caribbean Basin Initiative of the USA, NAFTA and Asia Pacific Economic Council agreements may countervail the opening up of a freer commodity trade. The challenge is to look for and take opportunities to use marketing concepts to differentiate and stimulate markets for commodity products in an often very distorted marketplace.

DAVID H. BUISSON
UNIVERSITY OF OTAGO

Further reading

(References cited in the text marked *)

* AMA Committee on Definitions (1963) *Marketing Definitions: A Glossary of Marketing Terms*, American Marketing Association, Chicago, p. 15.
* Anon (1997) 'Branding commodities', *Restaurant Business* Brand Power Supplement, 16–19.
  Araim, A.S. (1991) *Intergovernmental Commodity Organisations and the New International Economic Order*, New York: Praeger
* Blank S.C., Carter, C.A. and McDonald, J, (1997) 'Is the market failing agricultural processors who wish to manage risk?', *Contemporary Economic Policy* 15: 103–112.
* Boonekamp, L. and Cathelinaud Y. (1996) 'Agricultural markets from now to 2000', *OECD Observer* 199: 19–23.
  Breyer, R.F. (1931) *Commodity Marketing*, New York: McGraw Hill
* Brown, C.P. (1975) *Primary Commodity Control*, London: Oxford University Press.
* Campbell K.O. and Fisher B.S. (1991) *Agricultural Marketing and Prices*, Melbourne: Longman Cheshire
* Cassco (1997) Http://www.wlrfoods.com/cassco.htm and http://www.wlrfoods.com/
* Dewbre, J. and Beare, S. (1992) 'Measuring wool promotion response with household survey data', in H.W. Kinnucan, S.R. Thompson and H.S. Chang (eds) *Commodity Advertising and Promotion*, Ames: Iowa State University Press.
* Dwyer, S. (1997) 'What do the futures hold', *Prepared Foods* March, 17–18, 20.
* Fischer, B. (1991) 'From commodity dependency to development', *OECD Observer* 169: 24–7.
* Furash, E.E. (1996) 'Commoditization', *Journal of Lending and Credit Risk Management* 79: 9–14.
* Goldberg, R.A. (1985) 'A concept of a global food system and its use by private and public managers', *Agribusiness* 1: 5–23.
* Gordon-Ashworth, Fiona (1984) *International Commodity Control*, New York: St Martins Press.
* Greer, T.V. and Chattalas, M.J. (1989) 'The role of the promotion fund of the International Coffee Agreement', *International Marketing Review* 6: 47–61.
* Hudson, M.A. (1990) 'Toward a framework for examining agribusiness competitiveness', *Agribusiness* 6: 181–9.
  Hughes Hallett, A.J. and Ramanujam, P. (1990) 'The role of futures markets as stabilisers of commodity earnings', in L.A. Winters and D. Sapsford (eds) *Primary Commodity Prices: Economic Models and Policy*, Cambridge: Cambridge University Press.

* Hussey, D. (1992) *Agricultural Marketing Regulation: Reality versus Doctrine*, Report prepared for the New Zealand Business Roundtable, Wellington, New Zealand Business Roundtable.
* Jereski, L.K. (1985) 'The wishbone offense : branding a commodity', *Marketing and Media Decisions* May: 80–4, 176.
* Kiel, G. (1997) 'Toward a normative theory of commodity marketing'. Paper presented to the British Academy of Management Annual Conference, London, 8–10 September
* Kohls, R.L. and Uhl, J.N. (1990) *Marketing of Agricultural Products*, New York: Macmillan Publishing Company.

  Kolb, R.W. and Hamada, R.S. (1988) *Understanding Futures Markets*, Glenview: Scott Foresman and Company.
* Krapels, E. and Stagliano, V. (1996) 'A milestone year: Power in the commodity markets', *Public Utilities Fortnightly* 134: 32–6.
* Lawless, M.W. (1991) 'Commodity bundling for competitive advantage: strategic implications', *Journal of Management Studies* 28: 267–80.
* Luria, D. (1996) 'Why markets tolerate mediocre manufacturing', *Challenge* 39: 11–16.
* MacDonald, A. and Gould, P. (1992) 'Generic advertising: a commodity perspective', in H.W. Kinnucan, S.R. Thompson and H.S. Chang (eds) *Commodity Advertising and Promotion*, Ames: Iowa State University Press.
* McCann, R.J. (1996) 'Environmental commodities markets: 'Messy' versus 'ideal' worlds', *Contemporary Economic Policy* 14: 85–97

  Nappi C. (1979) *Commodity Market Controls*, Lexington: Lexington Books

* Pohl, F. (1996) 'Thinking about the future', *The Futurist* Sept/Oct, 8–12.

  Pope, J., Cullwick, D. and Kennelly, J. (1997) 'Commodity branding' in Hart, S. and Murphy, J.M. (eds) *Brands: The New Wealth Creators*, London, Macmillan Press.
* Rangan, V.K. and Bowman, G.T. (1992) 'Beating the commodity magnet', *Industrial Marketing Management*, 21: 215–24.
* Rowe, J.W.F. (1965) *Primary Commodities in International Trade*, Cambridge University Press, London, p. 32.
* Schorsch, L.L. (1994) 'You can market steel', *McKinsey Quarterly* 1: 111–20.
* Shuldiner, A. and Norkus, G.X., (1996) 'Buying prices on the commodity futures market', *Cornell Hotel and Restaurant Administration Quarterly* 37: 30–5.
* Thomas, J.G. and Koonce, J.M. (1989) 'Differentiating a commodity: Lessons for Tyson Foods', *Planning Review* Sept/Oct: 24–9.
* Wohlgenant, M.K. (1991) 'Distribution of gains from research and promotion in multistage production systems: the case of the US beef and pork industries'. Unpublished manuscript cited in Zidack *et al.* 1992.
* Zidack, W., Kinnucan, H. and Hatch, U. (1992) 'Wholesale and farm level impacts of generic advertising: the case of catfish', *Applied Economics* 24: 959–68.

See also: ADVERTISING; BRANDING AND BRAND MANAGEMENT; ORGANIZATIONAL BUYING BEHAVIOUR; THE MARKETING MIX

Business marketing

1 Characteristics of business markets
2 Market offering and competitive target marketing
3 Management of customer portfolio

Overview

Business marketing includes the development and marketing of products and services to business markets. Business markets are local and international markets for products and services purchased by businesses, government and institutions (like hospitals), for consumption (e.g. production materials, office supplies, consulting services), for use (e.g. machinery, office equipment), or for resale.

There are important distinctions to be drawn between business marketing and consumer marketing. The customers of business marketers are organizations buying with different motivations than customers purchasing for their own or family needs. The organizational buyer is acting for many others in the organization and is governed by a set of purchasing policies that define the rules of buying whereas the consumer buyer in most cases acts alone and is not governed by any formal procedure.

Organizational buying behaviour (see ORGANIZATIONAL BUYING BEHAVIOUR) forms a key requisite for both the understanding and managing of business marketing. An important aspect of business marketing is doing business through long-term customer–supplier relationships (see RELATIONSHIPS AND NETWORKS). An increasing part of the contemporary business marketing scene draws its sources and marketing strategies from international markets and firms (see GLOBAL MARKETING).

We describe business marketing through the following key phenomena and concepts:

1 types and characteristics of business markets illustrated through products, services, and customers;
2 describing the interplay of competitive and cooperative relationships;
3 a discussion of segmentation and positioning a product in a competitive business market;
4 the management of a portfolio of different types of customers;
5 looking into the future: value creating networks and electronic commerce

1 Characteristics of business markets

Business markets occur when one organization sells goods or services to another organization. We envisage a broad view of industrial or business markets including all markets except the transactions between an organization and the final consumer. When Procter and Gamble (P&G) sells products to channel members such as distributors and chain stores or when they sell to the government, they are acting as business marketers but when P&G sells to consumers they act as consumer marketers. Our broad definition is narrowed for the purposes of this chapter to describe the marketing of goods and services between 'for-profit' organizations.

What defines business markets?

Business markets include the industries that are in the value chain from producer to consumer ranging from the agriculture, forestry, mining and fisheries to construction and manufacturing and includes services such as transportation, communication, banking, finance, insurance and public utilities. In order to place a can of tuna in the hands of a consumer, the value chain would include catching and processing the tuna, making cans for the processor, paper for labels, distributors, advertising and trucking the brand to market. Figure 1 describes a simplified value chain linking some of the many key elements that must be accomplished to bring a can of tuna to a consumer.

Consumer and industrial markets differ along a number of major dimensions. Buyers tend to be fewer in number than in consumer markets and a few buyers may control a large proportion of the volume in the industry.

Figure 1 A simplified value chain to deliver a can of tuna to a customer

Industrial markets tend to be geographically concentrated, for example more than 50 per cent of the USA industrial buyers are concentrated in seven states.

From an economic perspective industrial markets tend to be derived demand markets. The sale of tyres to automobile producers is dependent upon the number of cars that consumers buy. At the market level, industrial demand is inelastic as the total demand for goods and services is not greatly affected by price changes. A drop in the industry price for tyres will not increase the demand for tyres because the lower tyre cost to the car producer will not change the final price of the vehicle to the consumer enough to stimulate consumer demand.

A major difference between consumers and industrial buyers is size. An individual consumer usually represents a small portion of any seller's total sales whereas, frequently, an industrial buyer is a large portion of a seller's total sales. If the consumer is unhappy or dissatisfied they have limited direct power to pursue their grievance but an unhappy industrial buyer has a great deal of power to force the seller to rectify the situation. Business markets are characterized by much greater interdependence between the suppliers and customers.

Another aspect influencing business marketing is the simplicity–complexity continuum of products or services in question. At one end of the spectrum are the consumer-like products such as fax machines and small copiers where there is a large dispersed market. The marketing programme for these consumer-like products approaches a consumer marketing programme in concept (segmentation, targeting and positioning, and applying the marketing mix tools; see MARKET SEGMENTATION; POSITIONING; THE MARKETING MIX) and execution. At the other extreme there is a market with very few buyers such as the commercial aircraft market or the telecommunications network which require a

Table 1 Types of marketing relationships

Marketing relationships	Influencing forces	Characteristics
Transactions and repeated transactions	Market forces Competition	Sellers' market Buyers' market
Short-term and long-term relationships	Competition Interdependence Mutual goals	Balanced command
Partnerships (J-I-T, R&D, market entry, channels)	Interdependence Mutual goals Competition	Balanced Unbalanced

Adapted from Webster (1992) and Möller and Wilson (1995).

highly targeted and tailored marketing programme.

Increasing product complexity means that more functional experts will be involved in the buying process as different functions have a stake in the purchase. A business marketer will often have to deal with a buying centre (see ORGANIZATIONAL BUYING BEHAVIOUR) when selling a product or service. For example, the buying of a packaging machine may involve not only the interest of production engineers concerned with machine maintenance, running and productivity but also marketing people who are concerned about the quality and variation potential of the packages, and management who may be additionally concerned about the machine's impact on the workers and the environmental safety of both the machine and the packages.

The traditional assumption in industrial markets has been that an adversarial relationship generates the lowest price purchases. Today most firms are moving to a cooperative model that assumes cooperating with a single source of supply results in a lower total cost of acquiring the goods or services results. This lower total comes from containing other costs in the manufacturing process such as inventory costs being offset by just-in-time (JIT) delivery and by developing tailored components through supplier partnerships. Buyer–seller relationships are dramatically reducing the number of suppliers any one firm uses. This outsourcing has been most evident in the automotive industry. Ford in the USA reduced its supplier base from 3200 to 2100 in six years. Chrysler decreased the number of its suppliers from more than 3000 to just over 1000 in the first half of the 1990s. This trend is also evident in all other industries. Rank Xerox is a good example, reducing its supplier-base from almost 5000 to little more than 300 (Ford et al. 1998, ch.6).

Types of business marketing relationships

Classification of the different forms of relationships helps to reduce the complexity of business markets into a few basic types. In Table 1 a distinction is made between market based transactions, short and long-term relationships, and buyer–seller partnerships. Transactions refer to business marketing exchanges where the competitive market forces (number of buyers and sellers and homogeneity vs differentiation of products/services) determine not only the price level and terms of delivery, but also the success of competing business marketers. The above situation can be called traditional or competitive marketing. It relies on identifying the target markets through segmentation and then positioning the product according to the competitors' offerings. These practices form the platform for planning and executing a marketing programme based on the marketing mix approach. (see MARKETING SEGMENTATION; POSITIONING; SALES FORECASTING).

Short-term and long-term buyer–seller relationships are characterized by more complex interaction between the marketer and customers. These interactions can be composed of social, economic, legal, technical, informational and procedural relationships. In the implementation phase, considerable effort to gain a contract needs to be given – for example, establishing an annual supply contract for important components such as different memory chips in PCs or a large maintenance order contract of mining machinery. Through established relationships, companies become interdependent; consequently, changing a supplier might involve considerable switching costs.

In short-term relationships the goal is to win a contract. In addition to competitive marketing practices the emphasis is on negotiations and bargaining behaviour. In this area, salespeople are the prime influence on the outcome. The organization of marketing and purchasing is often based on group interaction. Marketing or selling centres, as well as buying centres represent inter-functional forms of managing the dyadic marketing and purchasing relationship. Creating the customer relationship demands skills and activities that we refer to as relationship marketing.

In long-term business relationships (which we define as relationships ranging from several to tens of years) the focus shifts from establishing a dyadic contract to developing and managing the customer relationship (see RELATIONSHIPS AND NETWORKS). Long-term relationships create many new issues such as how to make the relationship effective and efficient, how to maximize benefits while minimizing risk, how to solve the inevitable conflicts which may occur. These issues form the content of relationship management. Market forces still influence the relationship. Depending on the balance of the interdependence a customer relationship can be dominated either by the seller or the buyer or it can be more balanced.

The distinction between long-term business relationships and partnerships is often blurred. A key characteristic in marketer–customer partnerships is their intentional character. Both parties seek mutual benefits by cooperating and sharing information and resources. Examples of these business partnerships are J-I-T supply relationships, joint market operations, sharing distribution networks, and R&D cooperation (see STRATEGIC ALLIANCES AND SUPPLIER PARTNERSHIPS).

In partnerships each party approaches total dependence on the other. Trust and cooperative management replaces market control. Management of the relationship generally includes multiple level interaction between the participants involving representatives from several functions. Task forces and joint management groups are often employed for establishing the partnership and for monitoring the performance of activities. Relationship marketing has expanded into relationship management. In the next section we discuss competitive business marketing and conclude with a discussion of relationship marketing and the management of a portfolio of customer relationships.

2 Market offering and competitive target marketing

The unique features of business markets that are described above makes the developing of global competitive advantage a challenge for business marketing managers. The customer and the selling organization are linked together through the market offering of the selling firm. The challenge is to create a market offering that provides differentiated value to the buyer that cannot be readily copied by competitors resulting in the selling firm having a sustainable competitive advantage.

The market offering of a firm may be conceptualized as having four components. The physical component is the actual physical representation of the product or service. For example, a mobile phone can be described by a set of electronic and engineering specifications that can be translated into a physical entity. A service company such as Federal Express creates the physical aspects of its service through the distinctive dress of its uniforms, trucks, airplanes and tracking software.

Technology is an increasingly important part of the market offering. Interactive technology represents the technology with which we interact with the product. We may interact with a computer to use a word processing program through the strokes of a keyboard or we can give directions to the program using a mouse and a windows program. Facilitating technologies are playing an increasingly important part in the market offering, including also electronic data exchange between the manufacturers, logistics companies and distributors.

People represent all of the individuals with whom the buyer's firm interacts in acquiring the product or service. People from such diverse groups as sales, order entry, service, installation and accounting all impact the performance level on the attributes the customer seeks. People with whom the customer interacts are an important part of the business firm's market offering.

Company attributes are the fourth part of the market offering. These attributes go across all of the products or services that the firm offers. In a broad sense they represent the reputation of the firm in the marketplace.

The market offering connects the firm to the customer. The customer can be conceptualized as having a hierarchy of expectations that are based in needs and expressed in the benefits expected from the market offering. A marketing offering that matches the customer's needs leads to satisfaction and to the ultimate goal of creating customer value. Value is the provision of superior benefits at a price that the customer considers to be less than the benefit package is worth. Value is usually seen within the context of competitive marketing offerings.

Sellers use resources such as technology, plant, capital and people to create capabilities, which in turn create a superior market offering. The firm's market position determines the ease with which it can manage the market offering in a market. A strong market position enhances the likelihood of success for a new market offering from the firm. A weak market position will require considerable resources to gain a market position and achieve success.

Both buyers' and sellers' interactions are coloured by their experiences and perceptions of the marketplace. The market offering is the connection that joins buyers and sellers and a business marketer needs to focus on markets that will be most receptive to the market offering.

In order to make the best match of market offerings to customer needs we begin by structuring the market. The goal of business market segmentation is to get beyond the basic segmentation criteria that divide markets on such mundane divisions as SIC code or size of firm. These are good fundamental criteria but we need to go beyond the basic criteria to find ways of segmenting the market that provide a richer insight into the customers and their needs. Bonoma and Shapiro (1983) suggest a nested set of factors for segmenting business markets. Figure 2 presents their variables and a brief description of the each variable.

Demographics
Basic demographic factors such as industry, firm size and location

Operating variables
Factors such as which technologies to focus on heavy versus light users and non-users of the product

Purchasing approach
Softer factors such as how the company buys, strength of our existing relationships with the buyer and influence structures within the buying organization

Situation factors
Are there markets where size of order or the needs for high levels of service or rush orders define segments?

Personal characteristics
Individual characteristics of the buying centre such as risk taking, personality and buyer loyalty

Figure 2 Important segmentation variables for business markets
Source: Bonoma and Shapiro (1983)

The segment structure is matched with groups of products to create a product/market matrix. Product in this instance means your market offering. The objective is to prioritize the cells in the matrix and develop a unique marketing programme for the top priority cells (see DEVELOPING AND IMPLEMENTING A MARKETING PLAN).

Because of the special characteristic of business markets, marketing programmes tend to focus on the sales and channel decisions more than mass media issues. Although price is important it is not usually the most critical attribute in supplier selection. More detailed discussion of the marketing mix variables is available in other sections of this book.

The segmentation becomes more micro the further one goes into the nested segmentation criteria. Demographic descriptors allow us to broadly segment markets at a macro level. We enrich the segmentation by considering operating variables such as the rate of usage. When we segment on the basis of personal characteristics such as innovativeness and risk taking we are operating at a micro level. In selecting marketing targets we generally define these targets using segmentation criteria at several levels in the nest hierarchy. Cheron and Kleinschmidt (1985) offer a more detailed discussion.

We target markets that offer us the best set of opportunities available within the possible set of markets available to us. The selection of the target markets is a function of fit with our market offer and capabilities and resource base that constrains the size of the set of markets in which we can effectively compete.

3 Management of customer portfolio

Business marketers can have a very diversified customer base. For example, personal computer manufacturers like COMPAQ, IBM and ICL have business end-users who vary from small one-person businesses to large scale customers who can place orders and service contracts for thousands of PCs. These different customers purchase through a mix of distribution channels: direct company sales, computer stores, direct mail order operations, and various general retailers. Customers can vary in their purchasing expertise, buying strategy, supplier loyalty, and potential profitability. To be successful a business marketer has to resolve two key issues:

1 How to manage a portfolio of different customers.
2 How to manage a particular customer relationship.

The number and type of customers that a firm has can be viewed as assets as they influence directly sales volume, cost structure and margins that in turn influence profits. The efficient management of a customer portfolio refers to the development and maintenance of such customer relationships to ensure stable long-term profitability. Management time and other scarce resources need to be allocated carefully between potential and current customers to ensure both current and future cash flows.

Customer portfolio (CP) management involves two basic levels: strategic level portfolio management which focuses on the allocation and acquisition of strategic resources and concerns key customer types; and operational management of major customer types. Strategic CP management is discussed by Campbell and Cunningham (1983, 1985), Turnbull (1990) and Olsen and Ellram (1997); the essence is depicted in Table 2 which shows a classification system for customers based on their present and future importance to the firm.

Tomorrow's customers represent firms that the marketer is especially trying to gain. They may be customers with a high reference value or access to distributors in new export markets or customers in new product application areas that have been opened up as a result of technical development. Technological leaders generally make important potential customers because supplying them offers a vehicle for developing the marketer's own product technology. Today's special customers are firms that either buy an important share of products or have become a partner with the business marketer. Examples of these special customer relationships are just-in-time supply partnerships, product or process development relationships, marketing and distribution oriented cooperation. Because the development and maintenance of special relationships may require considerable resources, the direct revenue from this kind of customer can be low or even negative. Successful relationships return the investment in developing the relationship through increment revenue

Marketing in practice

Table 2 Life-cycle classification of customer relationships

Criteria for classification of customers	Customer categories			
	Tomorrow's customers	Today's special customers	Today's regular customers	Yesterday's customers
Sales volume	Low	High	Average	Low
Use of strategic resources*	High	High	Average	Low
Age of relationship	New	Old	Average	Old
Supplier's share of customer purchases	Low	High	Average	Low
Profitability of customer to supplier	Low	High	Average	Low

* The technical, marketing and production resources devoted to developing future business rather than maintaining existing business.
Source: Campbell and Cunningham (1983)

gained from improved production technology, customer know-how, distribution capability or gaining market access.

Today's regular customers represent the established 'mainstream' customers of the producer. They are an important source of revenue but do not generally request special services or attention. They can generally be nurtured through the marketing system. Yesterday's customers refer to customers whose demand is decreasing or small, who do not possess any special resources of interest for the marketer and who represent declining sectors.

By classifying its customers into the four life-cycle categories the business marketer can respond to the essential issues of customer portfolio management. Each firm needs to develop its own portfolio to fit its customer base. Do today's customers, both special and ordinary, provide enough profit for developing tomorrow's products and customers? Are yesterday's customers taking an unwarranted share of resources compared to their contribution? Do we have enough of tomorrow's developmental customers in the relationship creating process to ensure future competitive advantage and profits?

A key issue in successful management of customer portfolio is the assessment of a customer's potential value and the costs involved in achieving and serving a customer; in essence this means being able to evaluate our value to the customer and vice versa. In the case of the existing customer base this can be approached through monitoring the customer specific costs and revenues, see Shapiro et al. (1987) and Turnbull and Zolkiewski (1997). When evaluating the value of major potential customers/partners the task is much more problematic involving the assessment of not only direct benefits and costs but also such indirect benefits as the value of new technology, market access, etc. The potential opportunity costs of being linked to the particular customer/supplier needs to be assessed. Also, network effects should be considered, as being engaged with a particular customer often brings linkages with customers/suppliers which may prevent potential relationships with other potential customers/suppliers (cf. Wilson and Jantria 1995; Ford et al. 1998).

Another aspect constraining the marketer's ability to manage its customer portfolio is the active role of buyers. In business markets the buyers have often led the drive to create longer-term supplier relationships. A current major trend is for buyers to reduce the number of suppliers they use, which limits the marketer's ability to make choices about firms who may be in their portfolio.

At a more operational level the portfolio approach can be employed for analysing and managing the relationships with various types of regular customers. This is relevant when the regular customer base, being fairly large and diverse, can be classified according to criteria relevant to their buying responses. For example, one group might be served through special distributors, another with independent sales representatives and a third might prefer closer contacts with the sales persons and technical service people. When these customers are large enough they can be serviced through a key account management system (Peck 1997). Sometimes customers can simply be dichotomized into the ones preferring 'hands off' competitive supply relationship and those opting for a more interactive based relationship requiring means of relationship marketing.

Managing a customer relationship

Relationship management has been depicted as a five-stage process involving the pre-relationship stage, initiation, development, maintenance and closure of a business relationship (Ford 1990, Ford et al. 1998, see also Dwyer et al. 1987; Halinen 1997). The basis of the management of a relationship lies in understanding its dynamics.

1 In the *pre-relationship stage*, the actors evaluate each other's business potential with the help of available internal and external information. The seller's marketing activities or the buyer's problems with its current suppliers often trigger the purchaser's interest in the new supplier. If a large gap between the partners exists because of cultural or technological distance, the relationship may terminate despite the partners holding common views in other areas.

2 In the *early stage* the supplier or marketer begins negotiations, which may take the form of trial, small orders but may also involve large investment projects, major equipment purchases or systems sales. Parties begin building interactive opinions about business practices, the products and services in question, as well as the representatives of the counter organization. If the buyer perceives problems or feels that the cultural distance is too wide, the process may be aborted. The development of the exchange relationship is also very much dependent on the availability of other customers/suppliers and on their relative attractiveness.

3 Trust and commitment increase in the *development stage* of the relationship, as the interaction becomes strong due to an increased volume of business or expansion of the relationship to other projects. Generally both parties have to adapt or change their products, procedures and organizations in order to maximize the relationship potential. Because these changes are costly, the partners refrain from making adaptations unless they see the potential for long-term profits.

4 Commitment between parties characterizes the *long-term stage* of the relationship. In complex relationships (e.g. JIT) commitment may lead to extensive adaptations to business processes resulting in considerable switching costs. Conversely, parties that trust each other generall take the benefits of the relationship for granted. The management of a routine relationship becomes an institution, demanding fewer resources than in the development phase. The potential lack of interest in the management of the relationship may cause the marketer to ignore the buyer's new demands, creating dissatisfaction and making the relationship vulnerable to competitive entries.

5 The *final stage* describes these rare yet stable institutionalized relationships. Only in industries or markets where competition is low and both parties are complacent do these relationships flourish. This situation is, however, vulnerable to the opening of new competition in the market.

These five stages cover the full life-cycle of a customer relationship and portray a complex and deep relation. Obviously many business relations are not so complex and can also end at any stage.

Relationship management presumes skills beyond mastering the ordinary competitive marketing programme (a combination of product, price, distribution, and marketing communications solutions) but does not make them in any way obsolete. Relationship management is based on close scrutiny of the potential new customers, investigating their demands, their preferred management techniques, previous and existing supplier history, and the key persons or buying centre responsible for the target business. This knowledge guides the development of a marketing strategy that offers to do business in the way in which the potential customer prefers. The marketing team or key account manager relates to the buying centre and is able to understand its needs. Partners need to learn each other's business culture.

Managing the development of a relationship presumes communication and negotiations skills and a strong motivation to understand the customer. Expertise in problem solving helps to prevent conflicts. Clearly defined goals, conflict resolution techniques, incentive and monitoring practices which are related to the defined objectives, and especially mutually agreed upon ways of handling setbacks and financial losses are powerful means of successful relationship management.

A marketer should be able to evaluate both the revenue potential and the level of involvement needed to retain a customer, along with investments necessary to generate the potential revenue. The expected net profits should be compared to other alternatives. In practice this is difficult as future revenues depend on how both parties manage the relationship. However, this basic economic goal of the relationship should be a strong guiding factor of relationship management.

Future directions in business marketing

Business marketing is going through a rapid development period, with several issues needing our attention as marketers. The management of customer portfolios needs better tools. Database management concerning the development of such databases that allow the integration of customer characteristics (their purchase histories, buying policies and practices, buying centre membership, evaluation criteria) and management information system data (revenue per customer types and per major accounts, sales objectives, development type objectives) is rapidly developing. Management needs to develop business processes and organizational solutions that facilitate the strategic management of the customer – and supplier – portfolio, the operational management of customer segments and individual major customers. More advanced measurement of customer value and a working monitoring system of customer commitment are essential (see Vavra 1995; Peck, 1997).

Integrating and using customer resources is a management issue. First, many large manufacturers are utilizing a growing number of marketing channels to deal with different customer types. National account management, own sales representatives, telemarketing, direct mail, retail stores, distributors, dealers and value-added resellers, and also electronic communication systems are employed jointly. To avoid conflicts, coordinating these 'hybrid marketing systems' to achieve efficiency must be the goal of business marketing in this time of change (see Moriarty and Moran 1990).

A second level of coordination concerns the various activities that form the customer relationship. Generally several functions (marketing and sales, R&D, quality management, technical service, etc.) are involved in the development of a complex business relationship. Coordinating business activities, personnel and communications targeted to a major customer is a challenge for the marketer. Integrated use of marketing communication channels forms another challenge for business marketers. The rapid development of telecommunications and forms of electronic data interchange (EDI) combined with database customer management is rapidly changing how buyers and sellers communicate and interact (see INFORMATION TECHNOLOGY AND MARKETING; MARKETING COMMUNICATIONS).

Value creating networks

An important development, facilitated by the discussed technological innovations, is the emergence of strategic value creating networks of firms. Value creating networks or value chains are emerging as a major shift in how business firms compete. No longer do they compete on a firm-to-firm basis but rather they compete as a network or value chain against a rival network or value chain. Value networks describe all of the activities necessary to build and deliver a product. For example, a value network for a computer can start at the very basic level of combining copper and plastic to form a circuit board that goes into a computer or the value network may begin with a printed circuit board as the first step. The value chain is described from printed circuit board to the retail store selling computers. How a firm conceptualizes their value chain or network structures describes how they will compete in the industry. A full understanding of every player's value chain and their position within that chain is important for strategy development. Those firms who purposely form cooperating supplier and dealer networks may gain an advantage over competing firms or networks, as they are able to reduce the non-value adding activities on the boundaries of the firms.

Value chains/networks are built upon creating value for the ultimate customer by combing the core capabilities of the firms that form the network. Relationships or strategic alliances create cooperative business interactions so that the whole is greater than the sum of the parts. Value networks are extensions of the firm-to-firm relationships we discussed above into a network of firms that work together to deliver value to the consumer. The placing of the consumer as the target for value creation by the network is a major difference with current thinking, which focuses on the next level customer and supplier.

Calyx and Corolla is an example of how a firm can combine core capabilities to fully exploit opportunities in the market with a value-creating network. The channels for delivering flowers to the ultimate consumer were long and complex taking up to nine days for flowers to reach the consumer. The entrepreneur, Ruth Owades, saw an opportunity to create value by delivering flowers from the field to consumer in three to four days resulting in fresher flowers for the customer. To do this she designed a value chain/network that would link the grower and the customer through a catalogue of floral arrangements. She had the core capabilities of catalogue list management and catalogue creation but needed partners to develop her concept. She approached a number of growers who were wholesalers of flowers but did not sell anything at retail. She taught her partners how to package the flowers so that they arrive at the customer looking like the flowers described in the catalogue. This became a core capability of the growers.

The ability to quickly deliver flowers to the customer is an important part of the concept. Ruth Owades approached Federal Express, who has a strong reputation for reliability in delivering packages to customers, to be Calyx and Corolla's delivery system. Convincing Federal Express was not an easy task because the growers are generally located in rural areas, not in high-density areas. However, when Owades approached Federal Express, they were looking for new ways to grow their business and were willing to become a partner in her enterprise. Their core capability of moving things overnight and delivering them the next day was an essential ingredient in speeding the flowers to the customer. The concept was predicated upon the belief that a significant proportion of the market would find value in having flowers several days fresher than they could obtain through local florists. Calyx and Corolla has been successful in developing and selling their product, based on an integrated value-network.

Many business marketers are a long way up the network from the ultimate consumer and do not know how they contribute to consumer value. Since a firm's ability to extract benefits is in proportion to its contribution to the total value created, it is important to understand one's role in the value chain/network. Individual trends of value creation, core capability development, and the movement to a cooperative partnering environment in many firms is taking us into an era where competition is going to be defined by networks of firms rather than at the individual level. For example, Nokia Mobile Phones, a major operator in the portable or mobile phones business has developed a global supplier network which supply nearly all its components on a customized basis; there is no room for market-based purchases of standard components any more.

Electronic commerce

As value networks emerge, one of the great forces shaping them is electronic commerce. The Dell Corporation is now selling computers worth $6 million a day or over a billion dollars a year over the network. The cost of Web sales is significantly lower than the cost of sales that are made through either the direct sales force calling on large organizations or through individuals talking to other individuals on the telephone. Low cost Web sales add significantly to overall profitability. The ultimate force in redefining value networks will be electronic commerce that has the potential to redefine marketplaces.

The benefits of electronic commerce are many, beginning with the ability to broaden the reach of the firm and offer a larger potential customer base. Geographic boundaries no longer exist and the e-commerce site, depending upon the software and hardware behind the Website can operate 24 hours a day, 365 days per year. The Web opens a new channel to service current customers and build sales with new customers. Business-to-business marketers should be natural users of e-commerce as they have a customer base who have computers and are likely to be connected to the Web. Payment systems and delivery systems are in place and management control can be established through control of who is authorized to buy and where the product may be shipped.

Electronic commerce makes it possible to reduce the costs associated with holding large physical inventories as the time gained in order processing reduces the need for holding inventories in branch locations.

The value network can be connected electronically; improving the responsiveness of the system and reducing inventory. The costs of serving a customer who specifies their needs and places an order over the Web is significantly less than a sales call or telephone sales system. Faster customer response is accomplished with 24-hour access. Customers with questions are able to directly access centrally maintained current information. Customers can see the status of their orders and shipment information. It is possible to have a 'hot' button that will connect the customer to a 24-hour sales operation.

In some circumstances, new products can be developed working with lead users over the Internet as they respond to prototypes. Launching a new or revised product is fast as product, specifications and prices can be quickly added to the Web server and made available to the customer base.

Customer relationships exist at a different level than traditional relationships. Since, electronic commerce may offer the buyer a choice of how they connect with the company either through a sales person, over the Web or a combinatio, each customer will be able to build the type of relationship that they prefer. A customer visit and requirement profile can be developed for each customer by running a data collection program in the background. This data can be used as input to new product development, target marketing and gaining better understanding of the customer.

The Web delivers images, text; voice and video organized on hyperlinked HTML pages. Interesting multimedia presentations can make the shopping experience an educational and compelling buying experience.

Looking into the future, it is possible to visualize a Web-based customer system that would elicit customer needs from a technology buyer and then create a product to meet those needs.

The buyer would then be able to manipulate the product and make a trade-off between different levels of engineering performance and price. The system could even provide comparisons in performance and price between off-the-shelf products and the custom product. The buyer could be informed as to when the product could be manufactured and the delivery date. The hardware and software is currently available to build such a system.

Redefining value chains or networks through using the Web to sell and manage customer relationships is a powerful force for change in a channel system (Alba *et al.* 1997; Benjamin and Wigand 1995). Firms who have strong channel structures may have problems adopting to direct selling via the Web, as their channel partners will resist the change. Firms without the constraint of channel partners will not be inhibited from using the Web to sell direct, as threats from the channel members are meaningless, as they do not have anything to lose. There may be some turmoil in industry channels as economic forces push firms to use the Web and channel members who may be by-passed through direct sales will resist the changes (see CHANNEL MANAGEMENT).

An increasing number of firms are beginning to develop value network or value chain analysis, including the Web-possibilities, as a critical step in their strategic positioning. Creating and managing these value-integrating organizations is the emerging challenge of strategic business marketing.

KRISTIAN MÖLLER
HELSINKI SCHOOL OF ECONOMICS AND BUSINESS ADMINSITRATION

DAVID WILSON
UNIVERSITY OF OTAGO

Further reading

(References cited in the text marked *)

* Alba, J.W., Lynch J., Janiszewski, C., Lutz, R.; Sawyer, A. and Wood, S. (1997) 'Interactive home shopping: consumer, retailer, and manufacturer incentives to participate electronic marketplaces', *Journal of Marketing* 61: 38–53.
* Benjamin, R. and Wigand, R. (1995) 'Electronic markets and virtual value chains on information superhighway', *Sloan Management Review* Winter: 62–72.

* Bonoma, T.V. and Shapiro, B.P. (1983), *Segmenting the Industrial Market*, Lexington, Mass: Lexington Books.
* Campbell, N.C.G. and Cunningham, M.T. (1983) 'Customer analysis for strategy development in industrial markets', *Strategic Management Journal* 4: 369–80.
* Campbell, N.C.G. and Cunningham, M.T. (1985) 'Managing customer relationships. The challenge of deploying scarce managerial resources', *International Journal of Research in Marketing* 2: 255–62.
* Cheron, E.J. and Kleinschmidt, E.J. (1985) 'A review of industrial market segmentation research and a proposal for an integrated segmentation framework', *International Journal of Research in Marketing* 2: 101–15.
* Dwyer, F.R., Schurr, P.H. and Oh, S. (1987) 'Developing buyer–seller relationships', *Journal of Marketing* 51: 11–27.
* Ford, D. *et al.* (1998) 'Managing relationships with suppliers', in Ford, D., Gadde, L-H., Håkansson, H., Lunders, A., Snehota, I., Turnbull, P. and Wilson, D. (eds) *Managing Business Relationships*, Chichester: Wiley.
* Ford, D.I. (1990) 'The development of buyer–seller relationships in industrial markets', in Ford, D.I. (ed.) *Understanding Business Relationships*, Chichester: Wiley.

Ford, D.I. (ed.) (1998) *Understanding Business Relationships*, 2nd edn, Chichester: Wiley.

Håkansson, H. and Snehota, I. (eds.) (1995) *Developing Business Relationships in Business Networks*, London: Routledge.

* Halinen, A. (1997) *Relationship Marketing in Professional Services*, London: Routledge

Hutt, M.D. and Speh, T.W. (1998) *Business Marketing Management: A Strategic View of Industrial and Organization Markets*, 6th edn, Orlando: The Dryden Press.

Iacobucci, D. (ed.) (1996) *Networks in Marketing*, Thousand Oaks:Sage Publications.

Möller, K. and Wilson, D.T. (1995) 'Introduction: Interaction and Network Perspective' in Möller, K. and Wilson, D.T. (eds) *Business Marketing: Interaction and Network Approach*, Boston: Kluwer Academic Publishers.

Möller, K. and Wilson, D.T. (eds) (1995) *Business Marketing: Interaction and Network Approach*, Boston: Kluwer Academic Publishers.

* Moriarty, R.T. and Moran, U. (1990) 'Managing hybrid marketing systems', *Harvard Business Review* 68: 146–55.
* Olson, R.F. and Ellram, L.M. (1997) 'A portfolio approach to supplier relationships', *Industrial Marketing Management* 26: 101–13.
* Peck, M.E. (1997) *Integrated Account Management*, New York: AMACOM.
* Shapiro, B.P., Rangan, V.K., Moriarty, R.T. and Ross, E.B. (1987) 'Managing customers for profits (not just sales)', *Harward Business Review* September–October: 101–8.
* Turnbull, P.W. (1990) 'A review of portfolio planning models for industrial marketing and purchasing management', *European Journal of Marketing* 24: 7–22.
* Turnbull, P.W. and Zolkiewski, J. (1997) 'Profitability in customer portfolio planning', in Ford, D.I. (ed.) *Understanding Business Markets*, Chichester: Wiley.
* Vavra, T.G. (1995) *After Marketing. How to Keep Customers for Life through Relationship Marketing*, Chicago: Irwin.

Webster, F. (1992) 'The changing role of marketing in the corporation', *Journal of Marketing* October.

* Wilson, D.T. and Jantria, S. (1995) 'Understanding the value of relationships', *Asia-Australia Marketing Journal* 2: 55–66.

See also: CHANNEL MANAGEMENT; DEVELOPING AND IMPLEMENTING A MARKETING PLAN; GLOBAL MARKETING; INFORMATION TECHNOLOGY AND MARKETING; MARKETING COMMUNICATIONS; MARKET SEGMENTATION; ORGANIZATIONAL BUYING BEHAVIOUR; POSITIONING; RELATIONSHIPS AND NETWORKS; SALES FORECASTING; STRATEGIC ALLIANCES AND SUPPLIER PARTNERSHIPS; THE MARKETING MIX

Marketing of services

1. The emergence of services marketing
2. Unique characteristics of services
3. Types of services and the service perspective
4. Expanded marketing mix versus relationship marketing
5. The service production and delivery process
6. Service development and design
7. Service quality and service productivity
8. Marketing organization in service firms
9. Service infrastructure
10. The future of services marketing

Overview

This article deals with the unique characteristics of services and their consequences for marketing. However, all companies depend on both goods and services, and many of the lessons learnt in goods marketing are also applicable to services and vice versa. The article does not deal with issues that are accepted as generally applicable to all types of marketing, for example segmentation or market research techniques.

The presentation is structured around the following themes: the emergence of services marketing; unique characteristics of services; different types of services and the service perspective; the expanded marketing mix approach versus the relationship marketing approach; the role of marketing and the customer in the service production and delivery process; the significance of service development, service design and re-engineering for marketing; service quality and service productivity as a basis for marketing; the organization of services marketing; the importance of infrastructure for services marketing; and, finally, thoughts on the future of services marketing.

1 The emergence of services marketing

Since the mid-1970s the interest in services marketing has grown and it continues to grow. Its emergence has also met with resistance, 'There is no such thing as services marketing,' said one American professor to his Ph.D. students in the late 1960s. There are still people who advocate that services marketing is the same as goods marketing and that services are just peripheral to goods. 'We can't live on cutting each others' hair,' is such a statement. No, but we cannot live better on selling scissors to each other. Haircuts and scissors are complementary; both create value for the customer but they provide their services differently. Services and goods are sometimes substitutes. Products can be designed in such a way as to diminish the need for services. For example, modern maintenance-free small copiers, which are bought off-the-shelf, are little dependent on services.

'Goods are wanted because they are able to perform services,' stated Norris (1941) quoted in Abbot (1955). Levitt (1972) has claimed that everybody is in service. A long-term trend in management thinking goes in the direction of these statements. Services are gradually replacing goods as the vantage point for the customer offering. At the beginning of the 1990s private and public sector services constituted approximately two thirds of the gross national product in the industrialized world. At the turn of the millennium it will account for 70–90 per cent of employment (size depending on which definition is used). It is a matter of providing an offering which is characterized by benefits and value to the customer customer satisfaction and customer perceived quality.

The development of services marketing is the outcome of contributions from scholars and practitioners in many countries. They represent different schools of thought, but due to international cooperation, services marketing thinking has converged towards certain issues which will be dealt with in this article. Particularly influential contributions have come from the UK, France, Scandinavia (The Nordic School of Services) and the USA. Among the earliest adopters of the new service thinking were Scandinavian Airlines (SAS) and British Airways (BA).

2 Unique characteristics of services

Certain unique traits are ascribed to services, and to some extent these require different marketing practices from those used in goods marketing. Four characteristics of services are usually given. The first three characteristics are *intangibility* (as opposed to the tangibility of goods); *perishability* (cannot be stored); and *heterogeneity* (difficult to standardize).

Although these give some guidance to the marketing of services, the fourth characteristic – *inseparability* (or *simultaneity*) – more distinctly captures the essence of services. It states that services are partly produced and marketed at the same time and by the same people, that the customer is partly involved in the production and delivery process, and that the customer partly consumes the service during its production. In conclusion, services marketing cannot be dealt with in isolation from other functions of the firm or in isolation from the personal contact with the customer. Services marketing has to be approached as an integral part of a total management process.

3 Types of services and the service perspective

Goods marketing and services marketing – rather than being two clearly delimited types of marketing – could be approached as two perspectives on the marketing of the same offering. At the same time we have more products than ever before. From a marketing point of view, however, it is not a matter of goods or services.

The traditional classification into service companies (hotels, airlines, hospitals, banking, insurance) and manufacturing companies is gradually losing importance. If more than 50 per cent of a company's output is services, official statistics usually refer it to the service sector; if it is the other way around it is classified as a manufacturing company. This classification is not operational from the point of view of marketing. Marketers have to understand the total offering and treat both the goods part and the service part on their own unique terms and not let one suppress the other. Manufacturing companies are also heavily involved in services such as installation, maintenance, transportation, consulting and finance. Even if the services do not necessarily account for the major share of a manufacturer's revenue, they may be a strategic necessity. They are used to differentiate a company from the competition and may thus constitute its marketing edge. Service companies need products to perform their services (e.g. aircraft) and to make them more attractive (e.g. a selection of wines during a transatlantic flight).

Within services, different marketing practices may be required, depending on the characteristics of a specific service and its target customers. Some services are primarily consumer services whereas others are producer services (i.e. they are sold to other organizations).

Services can be mass produced or customized. Some services are simple to perform, while others require unique skills and long training. The latter are referred to as professional services, rendered by individual specialists in knowledge-based organizations, such as hospitals or management consulting firms.

Moreover, work inside an organization – traditionally labelled administrative routines, office work or white-collar work – is gradually being treated as internal services, delivered to internal customers. Computer support, property maintenance and internal mail are examples of internal services that are often assigned to profit centres, sometimes to incorporated subsidiaries. These have to sell their services on the internal market and the internal customers have the option of outsourcing the service. The internal suppliers enter into a competitive situation and have to develop their marketing skills.

The public sector is primarily a service sector. Deregulation (or more realistically, re-regulation) and privatization of public services have become internationally accepted policies since the 1980s. In many service areas private alternatives are offered in competition with previous government monopolies. This requires a dramatic change in government agencies having to learn how to deal with the citizen as a customer with a choice.

Public services are largely non-profit services. This creates a unique situation in the relationship with the customer/citizen; for example, the connection between payment and delivery is not direct as 'payment' is handled via the tax system. There are also other types of non-profit organizations such as voluntary organizations and educational institutions for whom fund raising becomes an important part of their marketing (see STRATEGIC MARKETING FOR NON-PROFIT ORGANIZATIONS).

Other classifications have also been proposed, based on generic features, for example high and low contact services. Without further elaboration, it is obvious that such diversity within services needs a contingency marketing solution in each specific instance. Knowledge of the conditions of a particular service industry and its markets is necessary in order to design a proper marketing plan and marketing organization.

4 Expanded marketing mix versus relationship marketing

To explain differences in the approach to services marketing, two vantage points will be used. They are partly overlapping but are also different.

The reigning approach to marketing management is the marketing mix theory, mostly described as the Four Ps: *product*, *price*, *promotion* and *place*. In a service context, *product* refers to the service and its design and production. *Pricing* of services can be different from pricing of goods which has to do with the difference in the delivery system, industry tradition, etc. *Promotion* partly occurs during the service production process, partly through traditional promotion channels such as personal selling and advertising. *Place* represents the distribution and availability of the service (see THE MARKETING MIX). For many services, for example telecom services and certain financial services, it is a matter of applying information technology in the distribution; for others, the physical proximity of a service-producing unit to the local market is an absolute necessity.

The marketing mix approach has been criticized for being incomplete and manipulative, not properly considering the needs of the customer. The marketing concept postulates that once you know your customers, through market research or otherwise, you can design, price, promote and distribute a product that matches these needs and become a success in the marketplace. The seller is considered the active party and the customer has to be persuaded to buy. The empirical base of the marketing mix theory is mass manufacturing of standardized consumer goods. It has never become particularly successful for services as it disregards their unique features. In order to overcome some of its deficiencies, the Four Ps have been expanded into Seven Ps, adding the following three '*service* Ps' (Booms and Bitner 1992): *participants* (the service provider's employees and the customers who participate in the service delivery and thus influence its quality and the present and future purchases); *physical evidence* (the environment of the service organization – its servicescape – and all the physical products and symbols used in the communication and production process); and *process* (procedures, mechanisms, flows of activities and interaction that form the service production and the contact with the customer).

Kotler (1986) has suggested two additional and general Ps, *political power* and *public opinion formation*. He further refers to them as megamarketing, thereby implying that marketing takes place above the market proper. For example, services are often produced in heavily regulated markets and there might be a need to change regulations in order to open up a market. Lobbying becomes an important marketing activity.

As an alternative to the marketing mix approach, the core of services marketing can be seen as relationships, networks and interaction. This approach is referred to as relationship marketing, a term that has gained rapid acceptance during the 1990s (Gummesson 1994b). Although the addition of the 'service Ps' incorporates relationships and interaction into the marketing mix theory to some extent, relationship marketing provides a new paradigm. Relationship marketing emphasizes a long-term interactive relationship between the service provider and the customer and long-term profitability. It recognizes that both the customer and the seller can be active parties. They should see each other as equal partners and both must find the relationship rewarding; it is a win–win relationship. Ritz-Carlton Hotels express this approach in their motto: 'We Are Ladies and Gentlemen Serving Ladies and Gentlemen'.

It is particularly obvious in the relationship approach that services marketing cannot be isolated from the service management process. It is more appropriate to speak of marketing-oriented management than of marketing management. The following four sections will show how marketing is embedded in the management process.

5 The service production and delivery process

Service production and delivery are most often a simultaneous process and the terms production and delivery are therefore used as synonyms. Four aspects of the generic service production process and its significance for marketing will be described below.

1. *Interaction between the service provider's contact person (the front-line) and the customer* (for example between doctor and patient, advertising agency and product manager, passenger and flight attendant). The customer is a co-producer. The quality of the service is enhanced if both the customer and the service provider are knowledgeable. The contact is sometimes extremely intense and intimate and includes enormous stakes for the customer (such as in surgery or counsel in a divorce case). The shared experience can cement or prevent long-lasting relationships. Other service encounters can be trivial but regular, such as taxi and postal services, but because of the repeated need for these services, they are assessed as important by the customer. All such contacts provide face-to-face marketing opportunities.
2. *Interaction among customers*. Customers partly produce the service between themselves if the seller provides a service arena: the right systems, the right environment, and the right staff. An obvious example is a dance restaurant. If the customers refuse to dance with each other, no service will be produced. The choice of segmentation variables therefore becomes important. The interaction among customers is sometimes non-existent, for example when services such as cleaning are performed on the customer's premises. The waiting time for a service may be dependent upon other customers who want the service at the same moment; queues can be viewed as other customers blocking access to a service.
3. *Interaction between the customer and the provider's physical environment, equipment and products*. The marketing director of a hamburger chain stated that his most important marketing staff were a group of architects who design the restaurants. They influence the visibility of the restaurant through the architecture of the building and the signs, attract the desired customer segments through the right interior decoration, affect the number of customers that can be seated. The physical access is important; the service operation must be conveniently located for the customer. Information technology reshapes services and replaces human activity with machines. The physical environment is also perceived as evidence of the price class and of the professionalism of the service provider.
4. *Interaction between the customer and the provider's system*. The first three types of interaction constitute the part of the service production system which is visible to the customer. From a marketing point of view, systems should be customer friendly. Aspects of access to the system are important, such as location and opening hours. Systems sometimes scare away customers (for example, the withdrawal of money from an automated teller machine may be difficult for old people). One strategy is to create seamless services (i.e. services which consist of a well integrated flow of events rather than a set of loosely connected discrete events). A number of systems-related questions that affect the marketing of services can be raised, such as: What should the customer do and what should the service provider's employees do? What should the 'high-tech, high-touch' ratio be (i.e. what should be automated and robotized, and what should be carried out by human beings)? How does the replacement of employees with information technology affect the marketing and the customer relationships?

The description above is based on situations where the customer interacts with the service provider during part of the production and consumption phase. This interaction is referred to as the service encounter or moment of truth. Due to the customer's involvement in the process, these encounters are an essential part of the service organization's marketing. They provide natural opportunities for the provider to influence the customer and for the customer to assess the provider.

There are exceptions to the interactive production of services, for example, the courts, military defence and road maintenance. We only interact with these service providers in rare cases, but they provide ongoing services to all citizens.

6 Service development and design

As marketing is an integral part of the service delivery, it must be designed into the service from its very conception. This is often not done properly and marketing and sales are assigned the task of promoting impossible services, which are neither in demand nor offer opportunities for profits. Services must be designed in minute detail. It takes an average of twelve years from the conception of a pharmaceutical substance to the actual launch on the market. During this period the future medication goes through a rigorous design process. The major portion of this process consists of tests on human beings. Only one in four thousand compounds will be approved for sale. Although this may be an extreme, pharmaceutical companies are accustomed to the fact that lead time from idea to market is considerable. Cutting down time to market, however, is an essential competitive strategy.

A major problem with services is that they are often launched without having been properly tested and properly designed. There is no general methodology for designing services; there is no profession called service designers. During the 1980s efforts began to be made to find generally applicable service design methods. As the service part of an offering may be interactive with customers, a different type of design methodology is needed than is used for designing buildings, engines or drugs. The drawings and specifications must show activities and processes; they become 'dynamic drawings', a special type of flowchart. Such methodologies have gradually emerged, the best known being service blueprinting – or service mapping (Kingman-Brundage et al. 1995).

The novelty of the service flowchart is that it shows the service delivery process not only from the perspective of the provider, but also from the perspective of the customer. It shows the interaction between the provider and the customer as well as interactions inside the organization; the latter being behind the customer's line of visibility. Weak links – fail points – can be revealed in the service process. In doing these drawings the service designer must understand customer logic as well as provider logic. Unfortunately, service design is often governed by provider logic where computer programming, legal considerations and bureaucratic rigidity may rule. Moreover, service design needs to be integrated with the design of physical products such as buildings, motor vehicles or computer keyboards.

Adjusting existing services to changing preferences among consumers, changing competition, new segments or new needs and lifestyles – is part of the quality strategy *kaizen*, meaning continuous improvements involving all staff. If the design of a service is inadequate, the provider's personnel as well as the customers have to live with this every day. It creates frustration, low quality and low productivity, and consequently the design does not support long-term customer relationships. The feedback process from the front-line to management is most essential, but is often hampered by departmental and hierarchical boundaries.

7 Service quality and service productivity

The field of service quality was developed during the 1980s and most contributions came from services marketers. Within this quality tradition marketing becomes a matter of influencing customer perceived quality through designing and managing the services operations in such a way that the services are favourably perceived. Quality is often used synonymously with customer satisfaction.

The perceived service quality is usually explained by means of the 'disconfirmation model' according to which a customer compares his or her experience of a service with his or her expectations, thus getting the expectations confirmed or disconfirmed (Oliver 1997). Two partially different aspects of the outcome are identified. One is process quality (also called relational quality or functional quality) which refers to how a service is delivered, for example with a smile. The other is outcome quality (technical quality) stressing what is delivered, for example punctuality of a train arrival. Perceived quality can be influenced by managing expectations, experiences and image, areas where marketing is engaged.

Even if the market represents a customer-oriented perspective, the internal management of service quality – the sources of quality – must not be neglected. In a model of service quality Grönroos and Gummesson (Grönroos 1990) have added two sources, *design quality*, and *production and delivery quality*. Design quality refers to how well the offering is designed, with the support of drawings, specifications, flow charts or whatever means are used. Production and delivery quality refers to how well the offering is produced as compared to the design. Low production and delivery quality results in delays, the need to correct errors, missed sales opportunities and disruptions in customer relations.

There is not necessarily a match between quality in fact and quality in perception (Townsend 1990). For example, waiting time on a telephone may be one minute but is perceived by the customer as five minutes.

Among the active proponents for quality as a basis for services marketing are Zeithaml et al. (1990). They are best known for Servqual, which includes five quality dimensions, the gaps model and a technique for measuring customer-perceived quality. The five customer-related quality dimensions are as follows:

1 *Tangibles*. Special mention is made of equipment, consumer goods, people and communication materials. Including people is logical but, at the same time, people are very much the carriers of the quality dimensions below. Personal appearance and clothes are important aspects in the perception of quality.
2 *Reliability*. The provider's ability to keep promises and perform the service dependably and accurately. Studies suggest that customers consider reliability the most important dimension; it is also closely linked to the core service.
3 *Responsiveness*. Refers to the provider's willingness to help the customer and deliver prompt service. It includes recovery, the ability of the provider to correct errors and to do so with a minimum of inconvenience to the customer.
4 *Assurance*. This includes the knowledge, courtesy and credibility of the service provider's personnel. Pleasant behaviour is often promoted as the key to customer relationships but has sometimes been turned into artificial smiling and superficial quality, thus failing to deal with the root causes of a problem.
5 *Empathy*. The ability to put oneself in the position of others, to adopt their perspectives and give caring, individualized attention. It includes availability, language that communicates and the avoidance of internal industry jargon.

Even if lists such as this can act as a guide, each company needs to define those dimensions that are specific to their current situation. For example, for a railway company security and punctuality are keys to 'reliability'. In the dimension 'tangibles', one could specify quality features used in evaluating goods which emanate from quality management in manufacturing, such as performance, durability and aesthetics. Moreover, computer software, which is at the heart of many services, has its own quality management systems and dimensions. Caution should be used in ranking the dimensions as they are supportive of each other and all contribute to the quality of the total offering.

The gaps model defines gaps between the customers' expectations and management's perception of their expectations; between management's perception of the customers' expectations and the design of the service; between the design and the actual service that is produced; between the actual service produced and the communication directed towards the customer; and finally between the expected service and the perceived service. Expectations, though, are not precise; there is a tolerance zone between the desired service and the adequate service, within which the customer remains satisfied.

International and national quality awards are becoming increasingly frequent and they also include services. The model for most of these prizes is the Malcolm Baldrige National Quality Award, which was established in the USA in 1988. It excludes non-profit and government services. The focus of the Baldrige Award is both on internal, production-oriented processes and external, customer-oriented processes. Service companies that have won the award include Federal Express (postal services), AT&T (telephone card services), and Ritz-Carlton (hotel services).

ISO9000 certification becomes a necessity for services marketing if organizational buyers require it in order to include a company in its list of suppliers. ISO9000 was not originally a quality system but a tool for standardization of contract provisions in order to facilitate purchasing. A special instruction on services has been added to the original documents.

While service quality established itself during the 1980s, service productivity is still in its infancy. Service quality improvements are assumed to influence favourably the profitability of the service firm. There is a lack of empirical evidence to justify this assumption, which also assumes a favourable influence on service productivity. Service productivity is to some extent inherent in service quality, for example in the strategy of 'doing it right the first time'. The rework of services that have gone wrong not only disturbs the customer's perception of quality, but also lowers productivity, thus increasing the costs of the provider and reducing its competitiveness.

8 Marketing organization in service firms

In the section on service production and delivery, two roles of the marketing organization were identified: the customers and the contact (front-line) personnel. An original contribution of services marketing is to see customers as part of the organization; they are sometimes even called part-time employees. The other two generic roles of the service organization are support functions and management. Support functions – sometimes referred to as the back office or backstage – are, for example, the kitchen of the restaurant, repair of the car rental company's vehicles and maintenance of the computer systems.

The task of management is to provide a platform for the front-line and the support functions. Managers may also assume the roles of both support and contact personnel; for example, the hotel manager who fills in on reception when there is a queue. They may want to be visible to the customers part of the time; for example, to chat with regular guests in the restaurant, thus reinforcing the relationship with them. Management should delegate authority and make sure that operating conditions are known throughout the organization. The behaviour of contact personnel, interaction between customers, physical environment and systems can only partly be improved by the front-line and support functions. An important task for management is to contribute to continuous improvements by initiating major systems and resource changes.

The marketing and sales departments – which are populated by full-time marketers – are unable to handle more than a limited portion of services marketing. Staff cannot always be in the right place at the right time with the right customer contact. As a consequence of the embeddedness of marketing in all functions of the service operation, everyone else becomes part-time marketers. A company should identify where the full-time marketers would be superior in fulfilling the marketing tasks and where the part-time marketers would be superior; organize one or several marketing and sales departments; recruit, train and motivate part-time marketers; and design the service production system to support marketing activities.

Empowerment of front-line employees to deal with customers without delay is becoming an increasingly important marketing strategy. For example, the employee who can correct mistakes and handle claims quickly and smoothly without having to refer the issue back to a manager reinforces the positive relationship with the customer and also improves productivity. Empowerment requires enabling employees to take responsibility and work more independently.

Internal marketing is a means to empower and enable employees. The concept has emerged from services marketing, but is now used in all types of organization. Internal marketing is based on the notion that in service firms, where so many people have direct customer contact, it is essential that all employees represent the company well. As part-time marketers, they should understand the company mission, the organization, the services that can be provided. They should behave in a way that creates positive rapport with customers and a long-term relationship. In internal marketing, know-how from external marketing is applied to the 'employees market'. The purpose is to communicate new information in order to enhance knowledge, influence attitudes and motivate employees.

Large service companies are often heavily decentralized because of the need for local presence, for example, a retail chain or a firm of accountants. Growth is a matter of multiplying a well-defined business concept to more sites. Franchising has proved to be a viable concept for rapid growth. It unites the best of two worlds: large-scale strategic strength and small-scale closeness to the customer. Examples of large franchise operations are The Body Shop and McDonald's.

9 Service infrastructure

A well-developed service infrastructure provides an environment amenable to service delivery and marketing. Traditionally, infrastructure is focused on manufacturing with many basic services, such as goods transportation and postal services, being ancillary to goods. The public service sector is in itself an infrastructure that caters for basic needs such as defence, education and health care.

The infrastructure of a nation is largely a network or cluster of services. Some service networks are well established, such as railways, mail services and telecom services. Global reservation systems for airlines, railways, car rentals and hotels have been around for decades. During the 1990s, telecom and computer services have taken a quantum leap through mobile phones, the Internet and e-mail.

The regulations between countries, prohibiting free movement of labour and capital over borders, have limited internationalization of services. The current trend of deregulation and privatization as well as transnational alliances such as the European Union (EU) and the North American Free Trade Agreement (NAFTA; with USA, Canada and Mexico) will dissolve some of these restrictions.

General changes in society as well as private initiatives can change the service infrastructure for whole countries, regions or towns. Examples are the Eurotunnel between England and the European continent and the bridge between Denmark and Sweden.

Disneyland Paris is large enough to become an infrastructure in itself with its theme park, hotels and convention centres. It attracts other theme parks and hotels to the area as well as retailing and taxi services. Simultaneously, a transportation infrastructure is necessary for Disneyland to attract visitors. Thus, it has its own station which is connected both with a local Paris train and the high-speed services to Brussels and London; it has a bus service to Charles de Gaulles airport. Destination marketing is emerging as a special type of marketing, closely connected with services and infrastructural developments.

10 The future of services marketing

During the 1980s services marketing established its own identity. Moreover, it has become a driving force in the development of marketing thinking in general. Going back to the early 1800s the gross national product and employment were dominated by agriculture. Gradually manufacturing took over. Services were referred to as residuals, and later as intangibles and invisibles. Beginning in the 1960s, we have slowly entered into a service society, where services constitute the major portion of economic activity. Consequently, it is natural that services should have become the focal point for the new marketing, just as agricultural marketing was surpassed by the marketing of manufactured goods.

Services marketing has contributed with new approaches and concepts. The interactive production and marketing of services with customer involvement has become better understood. Relationship marketing, in part inspired by service thinking, is gradually establishing itself as a new general framework for marketing. Service quality has developed its own approach to marketing while service productivity is still not well established. The interaction and causal connections between service quality, service productivity and profitability need to be further understood. Systematic service design is yet little understood and little applied, but may be the most important area for future development. The concept of the part-time marketer has emerged in services and shows that marketing is deeply embedded in the whole service management process. Internal marketing has become a household word in marketing in general, although the concept was generated within services marketing. The deregulation and privatization of government monopolies will continue. Information technology will provide new services and new ways of performing traditional services.

Some of the tenets of services marketing may have face validity but lack depth. The understanding of the real nature of services and their relationship with goods is still limited. Although services marketing has come a long way, there is need both for basic research and further development of hands-on techniques (Gummesson 1994a).

EVERT GUMMESSON
STOCKHOLM UNIVERSITY

Further reading

(References cited in the text marked *)

* Abbott, Lawrence (1955) *Quality and Competition*, New York: Columbia University Press.

  Berry, Leonard L. and Parsuraman, A. (1993) 'Building a new academic field – the case of services marketing', *Journal of Retailing* 69: 13–60.

* Booms, Bernhard H. and Bitner, Mary J. (1992) 'Marketing strategies and organisation structures for service firms', in Donnelly, James and George, William R. (eds), *Marketing of Services*, Chicago: American Marketing Association.

  Congram, Carole A. and Friedman, Margaret L. (eds) (1991) *Marketing for the Service Industries*, New York: American Management Association, Amacom.

  Glynn, William J. and Barnes, James G. (eds) (1995) *Understanding Service Management*, Dublin/London: Oak Tree Press/Wiley.

* Grönroos, Christian (1990) *Service Management and Marketing*, New York: Macmillan/Lexington Books.
* Gummesson, E. (1994a) 'Service management: an evaluation and the future', *International Journal of Service Industry Management* 5: 77–96.
* Gummesson, E. (1994b) 'Making relationship marketing operational', *International Journal of Service Industry Management* 5: 5–20.
* Kingman-Brundage, Jane, George, William, R. and Bowen, David E. (1995) 'Service logic: achieving service system integration', *International Journal of Service Industry Management* 6: 20–39.
* Kotler, Philip (1986) 'Megamarketing', *Harvard Business Review* March–April: 117–24.
* Levitt, Theodore (1972) 'Production line approach to service', *Harvard Business Review* September–October.

  McDonald, Malcolm (1996) *Marketing Planning for Services*, Oxford: Butterworth-Heinemann.

  Normann, Richard (1992) *Service Management*, London: Wiley.

* Oliver, Richard L. (1997) *Satisfaction*, New York: Irwin/McGraw-Hill.
* Townsend, Patrick L. (with Gebhardt, Joan E.) (1990) *Commit to Quality*, New York: Wiley.

  Vandermerwe, Sandra (1993) *From Tin Soldiers to Russian Dolls. Creating Added Value through Services*, Oxford: Butterworth-Heinemann.

  Woodruffe, Helen (1995) *Services Marketing*, London: Pitman.

  Zeithaml, Valerie A., and Bitner, Mary Jo (1996) *Services Marketing*, New York: McGraw-Hill.

* Zeithaml, Valerie A., Parasuraman, A. and Berry, Leonard L. (1990) *Delivering Quality Service*, New York: The Free Press.

See also: MARKET SEGMENTATION; MARKETING RESEARCH; STRATEGIC MARKETING FOR NON-PROFIT ORGANIZATIONS; THE MARKETING MIX; TOTAL QUALITY MANAGEMENT

Franchising

1. What is franchising?
2. Why franchising has developed
3. What makes a business franchisable?
4. Components of a franchise system
5. Franchisor/franchisee relationship
6. Recent franchise trends
7. The future

Overview

Having taken a brief look at what franchising is and how it has developed historically, the entry considers the benefits of franchising from the point of view of both the franchisee and the franchisor. However, franchising has not evolved simply because it benefits the participants – there have also been strong socioeconomic influences, especially in the 1970s and 1980s, when high unemployment made the manpower available and often supplied capital in the form of redundancy settlements. However, the franchise format is not without disadvantages, and these are usually found to lie in the management sphere.

Not all businesses are appropriate for franchise operations, and the reasons for this are discussed. Consideration is given to the necessary components of a successful franchise system, including the selection of suitable franchisees. A crucial factor in any franchise is the relationship which is built up between the franchisor and franchisee. In the UK at the present time – although this is not the case in several other countries – there is no legislation specifically aimed at the protection of franchisees. The arguments for and against specific franchise legislation are considered.

The entry goes on to consider recent and likely future trends in franchising. One development which is already occurring is franchisees who have a personal wish to expand and therefore are starting to seek multi-unit franchises. While this may obviate a loss of ambition and drive in previously successful franchisees who find they have fulfilled their original ambitions, it may cause problems for the franchisor.

1 What is franchising?

The term franchising encompasses a wide variety of business relationships and is often used interchangeably with the term licensing. However, the distinguishing feature of *business format franchising*, with which this entry is concerned, is that it entails a more integrated relationship between the parties involved compared to other forms of licensing. As a business format it has been increasingly utilized as an alternative method of distribution and of business expansion over the last forty years.

In business format franchising (hereafter simply referred to as franchising) the licensor (i.e. the franchisor) does not only grant permission for the licensee (i.e. the franchisee) to sell the franchisor's branded products or services. The franchisor should also provide a proven method of operating, support and advice on the setting up of the franchisee's business and ongoing support to the franchisee. The franchisee has invariably to pay an initial fee to the franchisor, some type of ongoing fee, and a marketing/advertising levy. Although the two parties work together, and combine their efforts with the aim of creating a successful business formula, the franchisor and the franchisee remain legally distinct.

The history and development of franchising

Business arrangements similar to franchising, as we know it now, seem to have been in existence as far back as the Middle Ages. The more modern origins of franchising began in the USA and specifically with the establishment of the Singer Sewing Machine Company in the latter half of the nineteenth century. The relationship between Singer and the outlet owners of its network which sold sewing machine spare parts and undertook repairs bore certain resemblances to modern day franchising, including branding the outlets with Singer signage (see BRANDING AND BRAND MANAGEMENT).

Second generation franchising, which is a term used interchangeably with business format franchising, began in the USA in the late 1940s and early 1950s. For the first time franchising was applied as a distinct way of starting a new business as opposed to merely a way of distributing an existing product.

Franchising expanded rapidly in the USA during the 1950s and early 1960s. From the few franchisors who could be identified in 1946, by 1960 there were over 700. During that period many businesses which have since become household names were established, such as McDonald's, Holiday Inn, Budget Rent-a-Car. In the late 1960s the US economy began to slow down which adversely affected the development of franchising. This led many American franchisors to consider moving into foreign markets. For example, franchising was first established in the UK in 1955 when J. Lyons & Co. Ltd. purchased the master franchise rights for the UK from the American Wimpy hamburger restaurants. Since that time franchising has spread throughout the world where it is present in varying stages of development in some 140 countries, many of which have mature franchise communities (Mendelsohn 1992b).

In the UK, during the 1970s and 1980s franchising grew rapidly and gained acceptance. The main impetus to the development of franchising has been from newly-emerging businesses which have utilized this method of marketing goods and services as a means of financial expansion with less risk. Furthermore, in recent years a growing number of large well-established companies have entered franchising as a means of developing their businesses. These firms have had varying degrees of success, because the decentralized organization and operating methods implicit in the franchising concept and its implementation is usually alien to or difficult to reconcile with the centralized decision making, management and culture of a corporate concern.

Although franchising is found mainly in the retail and service sectors, it is also utilized by manufacturers in order to secure outlets for their products, and by wholesalers not only to obtain outlets for products but also to enable them to make more economic use of storage and distribution facilities. In addition, some established retail chains have introduced franchising as a means of achieving specific strategic objectives alongside their managed outlets. Such objectives have included: the need to achieve a more rapid rate of market penetration than would have been possible through their company-owned operations alone; in order to raise capital by converting existing branches and, finally, to improve the performance of some of their marginally profitable outlets by converting them to franchising (see CHANNELS OF DISTRIBUTION; MARKETING OF SERVICES; POSITIONING; RETAILING).

The main source of statistics on franchising in the UK are the annual surveys commissioned by the British Franchise Association (BFA) since 1984 and sponsored by NatWest Bank. These surveys are valuable to the understanding of the scope and growth of franchising. On the other hand, they have certain limitations. For example, the response rates are low, and a much higher proportion of respondents are BFA members, who tend to be the more long-established franchises, than non-members.

According to these trade statistics the overall turnover of the franchise industry rose between 1984–90 from £0.84 billion to £5.2 billion The average *annual* percentage increase during these years was 36 per cent, admittedly from a low base. In comparison in the following five years of reduced economic activity from 1990 to 1995 the average *annual* increase in turnover of the franchise industry was 3 per cent which encompasses changes of –8 per cent (1990–91) and 11 per cent (1992–93).

The number of franchise systems increased between 1987 and 1991 from 253 to 432. Then from 1992 – and employing a stricter definition – the number of systems increased from 373 to 474 by 1995, the latter showing a 14 per cent increase over 1994 (BFA 1996).

It is unfortunately not possible to compare accurately the scope of franchising in the UK with that of the USA. American franchise statistics, for instance, include the sales turnover from the company owned outlets within a franchise system, and also the turnover of automobile dealers and petrol retailers, whereas UK figures do not include any of these categories. Similarly, although franchising in the UK does not seem to be as developed as in France where it is estimated to generate £10 billion turnover annually, and there are some estimated 675 franchise formats, it is difficult to make a meaningful comparison with that country – and indeed any other countries – due to differences in definitions and the varying methods of data collection.

In which business sectors is franchising found?

In the USA where franchising is further developed than elsewhere at least 65 categories of franchised business sectors have been identified, several with numerous subclassifications. These range from the ubiquitous fast food operations, car rentals, printing and duplicating services, hotel and motel chains, employment and temporary help services to travel agents, vending operations, and sales training. In the USA franchising has also penetrated into such professional and financial services as pharmacists, opticians, accountants and insurance brokers. In the UK the BFA's membership covers 46 business classifications, with an additional 38 subclassifications. Many of these business sectors are the same as those which have been successfully franchised in the USA but also include parcel delivery services, driving schools, many forms of home improvements, playgroups and milk delivery.

2 Why franchising has developed

Franchising has expanded over the past forty years as a preferred marketing and distribution channel option over alternative business formats due to: the advantages it offers both franchisor and franchisee; developments in the socioeconomic environment; and the role of interested third parties.

Franchisor perspective

The prime motivation for franchising is usually lack of capital or, alternatively, unwillingness to take on the risk of borrowing. Since franchisees provide the capital which is invested in the outlet, expansion should be achieved with a lower capital input from the firm; some of the business risks are passed from the firm to the franchisee; there is the potential for more rapid growth than would otherwise be possible; the franchisor needs fewer staff than if the outlets were all company-owned; and the relatively lower capital investment of the franchisor should lead to high returns on capital employed. Moreover, franchising should enable firms to acquire some of the characteristics of a small business operation at outlet level, e.g. local knowledge, extended opening hours, flexibility. And, since franchisees who have invested their own wealth in the business are generally highly motivated individuals the performance of outlets should be superior to those of outlets operated by company managers. Finally, and by no means least importantly, it should also prove easier to attract quality franchisees than quality managers because of the benefits connected to owning your own business so that, where a firm may have found itself unable to afford the required calibre – or specific expertise – of an outlet manager, franchising may help to solve its staffing problems.

Franchisee perspective

A person may choose to become a franchisee rather than an independent small business person because they wish to gain the beneficial combination of a large and small business.

Although franchisees have to be prepared to relinquish some independence, in return they receive 'opportunity and support' which considerably reduces the risk inherent in establishing a new business. This is because the small firm has the freedom to operate in a controlled, assisted and supported environment, while at the same time gaining the benefits of a brand name, professional management, and the economies of scale of a larger organization. Finally, the franchisee has a business which, hopefully, can be sold on at a profit.

Impact of socioeconomic influences and third parties

Several environmental factors have facilitated the expansion of franchising. In particular, the shift in the economy towards the service sector – where franchising is concentrated – has been a stimulus because the input of a committed and highly motivated franchisee should encourage a high quality of service.

The prevalence of an 'entrepreneurial culture' since the 1980s also gave a further impetus to franchising, because it represents an easier and less risky entry into business. A high incidence of unemployment during that period also made redundancy money available for the purchase of franchises. Moreover, franchising has benefited from the increased interest in the expansion of small firms by central government.

The European Union (EU) has also acknowledged the value of franchising for the survival and health of the small business sector, and as a means of stimulating the creation of small businesses in less well commercially developed areas of the EU. As a consequence, in 1988 franchise agreements were exempted from the normal EU competition legislation (Mendelsohn and Harris 1992).

British banks also take a very positive view of franchising because the failure rate amongst franchisees is lower than among other small businesses and hence represents a lower risk. As a result franchisees receive preferential funding treatment. Those UK banks involved in franchising are prepared to lend up to 70 per cent of the investment requirements of prospective franchisees, and sometimes a lower rate of interest than that offered to an independent small business. Furthermore, in order to lessen the risk still further of lending to franchisees, in the 1980s the banks established dedicated Franchise Departments/Units. Their prime task is to scrutinize and evaluate the financial position, organization, and operation of a franchise network. On the basis of this investigation *inter alia* the Franchise Department decides whether it is prepared to extend finance for franchisees of that franchise.

Lastly, the efforts of the British Franchise Association (BFA), the trade assocation of franchisors, has helped to raise the profile and image of franchising, and to improve standards.

The downside of franchising

Franchising has many advantages for the franchisor and the franchisee, but it is not an easy concept to manage. Although the franchisee may bring motivation, commitment and initiative, together with an input of capital to a business, these assets may be offset somewhat by the expense and difficulty of ensuring, in such a decentralized operation, the maintenance of uniform standards of service and a consistent public image across the network. Franchisees can be highly motivated but can also be very demanding of senior management time and effort. To some degree this is due to the fact that the business of the franchisee is legally separate from that of the franchisor. As a consequence, compared to managed outlets, the scope for issuing commands is limited. Essentially, a franchise is a partnership – albeit an unequal one – and it has been the difficulties experienced in coping with the complexities of this arrangement, and the potential for conflict that may ensue, that has sometimes led to the failure of franchised operations. In addition, the fact that it is necessary to 'persuade' franchisees compared with the ability to 'tell' company managers has led some observers (Williamson 1991) to conclude that franchised firms are less capable of adapting to change than fully-integrated companies.

For the franchisor the biggest challenge is to manage successfully the relationship with the franchisee in all its aspects. For the franchisee the most important concerns are the quality of the franchisor, how well the business concept has been tested, and how well the franchisor will fulfil its ongoing responsibilities to its franchisees.

3 What makes a business franchisable?

By no means all businesses are suitable for the introduction of the franchise format. There are some specific criteria which require to be taken into consideration in order to establish whether the basic ingredients for franchising a business exist. These comprise the following.

- That the products and/or services offered should already have been proven in practice. This is to ensure that franchisees are confident they are buying into a viable business.
- That the product/service is distinctive, and backed by a brand name or trade mark, already well-known in the business sector of the potential franchisor. This enables franchisees to be offered a valuable commercial asset they would otherwise have difficulty in acquiring.
- That the processes and systems the franchisor needs to pass on to the franchisees must be simple, easy to learn and capable of being put into operation within a short time. This is to ensure successful replication and the projection of a consistent image across all the outlets.
- That the margin must be adequate to provide both the franchisor and the franchisee with an acceptable level of income and return on investment.

In addition the following criteria are essential.

- A mechanism must have been built up to provide the franchised network with ongoing support and assistance, and the development of the business.
- An adequate supply of franchisees must be available, and be consistent with the business plans of the potential franchisor.

4 Components of a franchise system

The major components of a franchise system comprise: the pilot operation, the franchise contract, franchise manual, franchisee selection, and ongoing support. Since franchise systems are more heterogenous that might be first thought, it will be appreciated that there will be some variations in these components. It is also necessary to point out the intensive input which is required at the very early stages of developing a system, particularly with regard to time, manpower and other resources.

The 'pilot'

At least one pilot operation is an essential component in the development of a franchise before beginning to sell franchises. As in any test marketing exercise, its purpose is to emulate the proposed franchised outlets as closely as possible to gain an accurate indication of their likely performance; to identify problems in order to take the necessary steps to overcome them; and, not least, to determine whether it is worthwhile to continue with the development of the franchise system. Although 'pilots' do provide valuable information they are unlikely to test two of the most significant factors in a franchised business, namely, the aptitude and commitment of the franchisee and the franchisor/franchisee relationship, because they are usually operated by company employees.

Franchise documents

The two key franchise documents are the manual and the contract. The manual contains detailed advice and guidelines to the franchisee on how the business should be operated. The contract defines the formal relationship between the franchisor and the franchisee, and is comprehensive and specific in terms of the obligations of franchisees (see below for the effect of the contract on the franchisor/franchisee relationship). The contract specifies, for example, the three financial charges which the franchisee pays to the franchisor: the 'initial fee' which is mainly to cover the costs of the franchisor in setting the franchisee up in business; the ongoing 'management service fee', and the 'levy' contribution towards advertising and marketing. Both the latter are calculated as a percentage of the franchisees' sales turnover. The management service fee varies widely from 5.5 per cent (catering and hotels) to 9.6 per cent (vehicle services) depending on the degree of support provided, and profit margins. Franchisors may also, or alternatively, place a mark-up on goods supplied to franchisees. Some franchisors use this as their main source of income and charge a very low management service fee. On average the various ongoing charges collected by franchisors in 1996 accounted for an estimated 8.9 per cent of franchisees' turnover (BFA 1997).

Franchisee selection

The selection procedures employed to recruit the first franchisees is especially important to the subsequent success of a franchise operation. In order to overcome their initial lack of experience of franchisee selection franchisors are recommended to draw up a profile of 'ideal' franchisees. In practice this is difficult to accomplish in the early stages of a franchise, but as time goes on franchisors tend to learn from experience which attributes they are looking for in a franchisee. Other aspects of franchisee recruitment which require to be considered include if, and where, to advertise for franchise applicants and the screening procedures to be used.

Ongoing support

The final ingredient of a franchise is to determine the type and quantity of ongoing support required by the franchise network. Support may encompass many different aspects of the operation such as the provision of assistance by the franchisor's field staff, a continuous training programme for franchisees, the development of new products and systems, and the updating of manuals. Not least, support includes the continuous monitoring of the marketplace for the benefit of the franchisees and the franchise.

5 Franchisor/franchisee relationship

The major topics which are the subject of debate in franchising revolve around the franchisor/franchisee relationship since this is one of the key determining factors in the success or otherwise of the business. Aspects of the relationship include: the relative independence of franchisees when compared to other small business men or women; how far conflict is inherent in the contract; and the extent and type of regulatory framework in which franchising should operate.

The contract is often considered the pivotal factor in inhibiting the independence of franchisees and in leading to conflicts. It has been argued that its bias in favour of the franchisor enables the latter to hold the balance of power in the relationship (Felstead 1993). It is pointed out, for example, that the contract obliges the franchisee to put into operation any changes made to the operating manual over the period of the franchise, and that the franchisee signs the franchise contract before they see the franchise manual in detail.

Nevertheless, there is an opposing view to the above which maintains that the specific nature of the contract is unavoidable if uniformity is to be achieved across the system. Such homogeneity is seen as an advantage not only for the franchisor, but as beneficial to all franchisees, because it diminishes the likelihood of wide variations in service and offering which may well lead to dissatisfied customers, and penalize all franchisees not only those who breach the rules. Termination clauses are also sometimes regarded as unfair to franchisees. There is again, however, a third view that such clauses may be necessary to ensure uniformity of standards and service across the network and thereby the success of the franchise (Mendelsohn 1992a).

In practice, the contract may not be a reliable guide to the extent of the franchisees' independence, because there appears to be a difference between formal independence (as expressed in the contract) and operational independence (as experienced in the course of the relationship). It is not only franchisees who relinquish some of their independence, franchisors do so as well. This is because they are dependent upon their franchisees to operate as stipulated, to implement changes in the operation, and not to bring the franchisor's name into disrepute. With a company-owned network this dependence on a person who is not an employee would not exist. Due to the interdependence, therefore, of the franchisor and the franchisee both parties have to accept some trade-off in terms of loss of independence in return for the advantages they receive.

Conflict and the contract?

The extent to which the contract inevitably leads to conflict in the franchisor/franchisee relationship has also been closely examined. While there is always likely to be some degree of conflict in such a complex relationship compared with that of a company-owned network this does not emanate from the clauses of the contract alone. It is also neither necessarily destructive nor unwelcome. Some franchisors actively welcome the continual dialogue that is the essential feature of a franchise, and the forthright and critical comments of their franchisees.

In practice most franchisees seem prepared to renew their contracts, and express little desire to change the content of the contract. There is also some evidence that franchisees are able to negotiate certain clauses with their franchisor prior to signing. That most franchisees do not seem to hold the view that the contract is detrimental to them may be because few have been threatened by franchisors with contract clauses. In reality, the contract appears to have little bearing on the relationship, because experience has shown that management by persuasion and example, rather than by threat, seems more likely to lead to channel co-operation. The franchisor's non-coercive sources of power include the training programme which – if formal, authoritative, and detailed – will influence the franchisee to operate in line with the franchisor's guidelines. However, as some empirical findings have demonstrated, perhaps the most important factor which leads to the reluctance of either party to exercise power is the recognition that it is in their mutual interest to keep disagreements to a minimum by making the necessary commitment and compromises which will enable the network to operate successfully (Manaresi and Uncles 1995).

Franchisee protection: self-regulation or legislation?

Although franchising is generally acknowledged as being beneficial to the creation of small businesses and employment, nevertheless concern has been expressed that franchisees are insufficiently protected both in the negotiations leading up to the signing of the franchise contract and during the ensuing relationship.

At present in the UK – unlike in the USA and several other countries – there is no legislation specifically aimed at the protection of franchisees. Although the EU block exemption regulation governs the structure of franchises this is to allow a franchise to operate in ways which would otherwise infringe EU competition legislation. Apart from the BFA's voluntary Code of Ethics, which in any case is only applicable to its members, the franchisor/franchisee relationship in this country is governed by general business legislation. The issue has, therefore, arisen whether self-regulation is sufficient to protect franchisees, or whether there is a case for legislation.

Those who believe that self-regulation provides insufficient protection propose the introduction of specific franchise legislation to ensure that before signing the contract franchisees are provided with adequate and comprehensive information on which to base their decision. The second area where there is a demand for legislation is to curtail the ability of franchisors to include and enforce 'unfair' contract clauses, particularly in terms of renewal, termination, assignment, goodwill and conflict resolution.

The purpose of regulation whether through self-regulation or by legislation is to encourage franchisors to behave in a manner which is not 'unfair' to franchisees. Legislation tends to be favoured by those who view the franchisee as being significantly disadvantaged *vis-à-vis* the franchisor (Terry 1991). On the other hand, supporters of self-regulation regard voluntary Codes of Ethics as an equally efficient means of 'policing' franchising with the added advantage of avoiding the additional costs and barriers to entry which legislation may cause. They also point out that the small occurrence of unscrupulous actions by *bona fide* franchisors does not warrant legislation, and that dissatisfied franchisees have existing avenues of seeking redress.

Legislation aimed at inducing appropriate disclosure of information prior to the signing of the franchise contract is prevalent in the USA. France has also introduced trade mark licensing disclosure laws which include franchising and seek to achieve this aim. In the USA there are two methods of attempting to ensure that the contents of the disclosure document are appropriate. The first requires a franchisor to register their disclosure document with the state authorities for approval on a continuous basis. The second, included in American Federal legislation, lays down guidelines on the information which should be included in a disclosure document, but no registration of the document is necessary.

Those who oppose the introduction in the UK of widespread legislation fear that it will lead to some of the undesirable consequences which have followed legislation in the USA. These have included: higher costs; in many instances the disclosure of less information rather than more as intended; and some evidence that it has acted as a barrier to entry and helped to slow down the rate of expansion of franchising. In order, therefore, to avoid these possible hindrances to the growth of franchising, the opponents of legislation maintain that the UK should retain self-regulation, and continually strive to improve it. They also argue that prospective franchisees have an obligation to thoroughly investigate any business proposition before entering the relationship.

In Australia the establishment of a 'mandatory' Code of Practice may herald a practical answer to the self-regulation versus legislation dilemma. This 'mandatory' Code was introduced after Australia had experimented with, and had experience of operating franchising systems over two decades under a variety of legislative, quasi-legislative and non-legislative regimes, and was the proposal of a 'Task Force' which had been set up to investigate how franchisees could be protected without inhibiting the growth of ethical franchising. The successful implementation of a 'mandatory' franchising Code of Practice may offer a compromise solution that satisfies both the proponents and opponents of legislation as it is possible that it will provide franchisees with an adequate degree of protection without hindering the expansion of franchising.

6 Recent franchise trends

Over the past decade, some notable developments have occurred in franchising in the UK. First, the growing maturity of many franchise systems has led to an increase in the number of so-called 'comfort level' franchisees (those whose lifestyle expectations have been fulfilled), and also in the number of multi-unit franchisees. Secondly, the economic downturn of the early 1990s accelerated the growth of franchisee associations. At the same time it exposed a more long-term and deep-seated problem, i.e. the difficulty experienced by many franchisors in recruiting franchisees of sufficiently high calibre and with the necessary funds to invest.

'Comfort level' franchisees

Over the past decade an increasing number of franchisees have been reaching their so-called 'comfort level' (those whose life-style expectations have been fulfilled). The attainment of this goal can lead to a diminution of drive, ambition and entrepreneurship to the detriment of all the franchisees in the network. Franchise organizations most likely – but by no means exclusively – to encounter this problem are those which have been in operation for 10 or more years. In order to stimulate and remotivate such franchisees so that they rekindle their former enthusiasm franchisors have found it necessary to employ a variety of carrot and stick measures. These have included: regular competitions with neighbouring franchisees, negotiating away some of the franchisee's territory, and arranging for early retirement.

Given that the 'comfort level' syndrome is likely to become more widespread in the future how to maintain the enthusiasm of franchisees may well become the most difficult part of the franchise operation. On the other hand, research findings (Fulop 1996) indicate that few franchisors intend to overcome this syndrome by switching to a higher proportion of company-owned outlets. They still consider that franchised outlets are more beneficial than managed outlets for their business.

Multi-unit franchisees

Evidence from the USA suggests that as a franchise becomes more mature there is a tendency for the number of multi-unit franchisees within that network to grow. This development has already happened in the fast-food trade in the UK and it seems inevitable that successful franchisees in other trade sectors will also seek to expand by seeking additional outlets with the same franchisor.

Nevertheless, multi-unit franchisees who may be operating mini-chains within a network pose power problems which may impact adversely on a franchise. Moreover, their operational efficiency has also been questioned. As a result many franchisors impose severe restrictions on the number of outlets any one franchisee is allowed to own. On the other hand, a minority of franchisors regard them as a valuable means of generating growth from within if the franchisee is of sufficiently high calibre and managerial ability.

Despite the undoubted misgivings of franchisors regarding the potential for conflict with multi-unit franchisees within a network, it seems to be generally recognized that successful franchisees could become frustrated if they are not able to generate more than one outlet, and that might equally lead to conflict!

Franchisee associations/councils

The rate of increase in the number and influence of franchisee associations accelerated in the UK during the economic downturn of the 1990s mainly due to pressure/lobbying from franchisees who were dissatisfied with the performance of the franchise. In the USA it has been estimated that 74 per cent of franchises have a franchisee association/franchise council, most of which date from the 1980s. The major objectives of these associations are, first, to reduce conflict by better and more regular communication and, secondly, to harness franchisees' innovation and entrepreneurship for the benefit of the franchise. In the USA the widespread introduction of franchise associations has enhanced the power of franchisees. Since there is a similar trend in progress in franchise networks in the UK, the power of franchisees will be strengthened when potential areas of disagreement arise regarding changes in products, operating methods and territory.

Recruitment/funding criteria

To a greater or lesser extent, UK franchisors have been experiencing growing difficulty in attracting franchisees of high enough calibre and with enough money to invest. This problem was accentuated in the early 1990s when it became evident that many of the franchisees who failed to survive the downturn in economic activity had sometimes been accepted simply because they had sufficient finance, or because the firm wanted to get the franchise network up and running quickly, or through overeagerness to recoup the costs incurred in developing the system. As a result of this experience, many franchisors have introduced more rigorous franchisee selection criteria to try and ensure that in future their franchisees will be able to cope even under adverse trading conditions.

Similarly, many franchisors have become increasingly aware that their projected rate of expansion may be hindered unless alternative sources of funding can be made available to potential recruits without the required finances. To date *two* sources of funding exist:

1. First, a minority of franchisors are prepared to offer 'easy entry' financial schemes to suitable potential franchisees. In effect, the franchisor finances the start-up costs of the franchisee with the loan being repaid at a later date from the profits of the business.
2. Second, at least one bank offers funding to suitable prospective franchisees – who may not have the security normally required – in exchange for equity in the business. Such an arrangement is usually restricted to a franchise network which requires franchisee funding of more than £50,000.

7 The future

There are a number of conflicting trends which are likely to affect the future prospects of the franchise industry. Some of these influences are external to franchising; others are factors which are internal to the operation and organization of the franchise itself.

External influences

Undoubtedly the two most important external factors which will determine the development of franchising are the buoyancy or otherwise of the economy, and the continuing shift towards the service sector in which franchising tends to be concentrated.

The expansion of the tertiary sector is a long-term trend which in 1996 in the UK accounted for an estimated 63 per cent of the output of the economy. There is scope for franchising, for example, to penetrate further in the UK – as has already occurred in the USA – into such professional and financial services as opticians, accountants, insurance brokers, pharmacists and estate agents. To a large extent, the expansion plans of the growing number of multiples in these sectors will depend on the recruitment of highly-qualified staff to operate their outlets. Conversely, the increasingly competitive environment in many of these sectors may make many professionally qualified people who would formerly have set up in business by themselves consider franchising as an alternative option which provides them with the opportunity to gain the benefits of working under the umbrella of a large organization, while still operating as a small business.

Another favourable external factor is the willingness by an increasing number of mature organizations to develop their businesses through franchising as a means of assisting them in the implementation of their diversification and/or market penetration strategies, the need of some of them to recruit qualified and skilled staff, and the need of other such firms to maximize the potential output of the outlet.

Lastly, the movement by franchisors into foreign markets is likely to accelerate as an increasing number of franchise systems reach maturity in their domestic markets. In particular, US franchise systems will increasingly seek out other markets, of which the UK will probably continue to appear the most attractive because of the widespread belief that we share a common language(!), but with the intention of then moving into the rest of Europe. Thus while British franchisors will be seeking to develop abroad, particularly to Eire, France, Germany and Spain, they will also face the potential threat of foreign competition.

International franchising is also likely to benefit from the increasing number of retailers – who do not operate franchising in their domestic market – but who utilize this marketing technique as a mode of entry into overseas markets where population size or per capita expenditure may be insufficient to support a major programme of expansion. Some retail organizations also employ the franchise format as a means of test-marketing in foreign countries prior to establishing a full-scale operation, and thus helping to lessen the financial risk of moving abroad (see GLOBAL MARKETING).

Internal influences

Several internal organizational and operational developments in franchising are likely to influence its future. These include two factors which may well constrain the rate of expansion of franchising. Growth, for instance, may well depend on the extent to which franchisors are prepared/able to offer alternative funding arrangements to suitable potential franchisees with insufficient money to invest. Expansion will also be affected by the extent to which franchisors who have adopted more stringent selection criteria will continue to maintain them even if they experience difficulties in attracting appropriate recruits. Although the implementation of more rigorous recruitment criteria appears to lead to a diminution in sources of friction within the network, this may only be achievable at the expense of a slowdown in growth.

Other internal developments which have taken place in UK franchising are affecting the power distribution within the franchisor/franchisee relationship in favour of the franchisee. First, as a network matures the number of multi-unit franchisees tends to grow. As a result, franchisors will have to learn to contend with the enhanced power of larger multi-unit franchisees. Secondly, the number and influence of franchisee associations in the UK expanded rapidly throughout the 1990s and this trend will continue as happened in the 1980s in the USA. These associations/councils tend to strengthen the power of franchisees, and shift the balance of power within a franchise towards the franchisee. Thus both a higher proportion of multi-unit franchisees within a network and the growing importance of franchisee associations may make franchising an even more complex organization to manage in the future.

CHRISTINA FULOP
CITY UNIVERSITY BUSINESS SCHOOL

Further reading

(References cited in the text marked *)

Beddall, D. (1991) *Franchising Task Force*, Final Report to the Australian Minister for Small Business and Customs, December.
* BFA (1984–97) *The NatWest-Franchise Survey*, Henley-on-Thames: British Franchise Association.
Burt, S. (1994) 'Temporal trends in retailer internationalisation', in P.J. McGoldrick (ed.) *International Retailing: Trends and Strategies*, London: Prentice-Hall.
Commission of the European Community (1991) *Towards a Single Market in Distribution*, Com (91) Brussels.
Department of Trade and Industry (1995) *An Introduction to Franchising*, London: DTI Small Firms and Business Link Division.
Felstead, A. (1993) *Franchising at Work: The Corporate Paradox*, London: Routledge.
Forward, J. and Fulop, C. (1993) 'Elements of a franchise: the experiences of established firms', *Service Industries Journal*, 13: 159–78.
Forward, J. and Fulop, C. (1996) 'Large established firms entry into franchising: an exploratory investigation of strategic and operational issues', *International Review of Retail, Distribution and Consumer Research* 6: 34–52.
* Fulop, C. (1996) *Overview of the Franchise Marketplace 1990–1995*. London: City University Business School.
Fulop, C. (1997) 'Insights into franchising: a review of empirical and theoretical perspectives', *Service Industries Journal* 17: 603–25.
Fulop, C. and Warren, K. (1992) 'The marketing of a professional service: opticians', *International Journal of Advertising* 11: 287–305
* Mendelsohn, M. (1992a) *The Guide to Franchising*, 5th edn, London: Cassell.
* Mendelsohn, M. (ed). (1992b) *Franchising in Europe*, London: Cassell.
Mendelsohn, M. (1995) *The Ethics of Franchising*, 2nd edn, Henley on Thames: British Franchise Association.
* Mendelsohn, M. and Harris, B. (1992) *Franchising and the Block Exemption Regulation*, Harlow: Longman.
Roddick, A. (1991) *Body and Soul*, London: Ebury Press.

Sanghavi, N. (1991) 'Retail franchising as a growth strategy for the 1990s', *International Journal of Retail and Distribution Management* 19: 4–9.

Sibley, S.D. and Michie D.A. (1982) 'An exploratory investigation of co-operation in a franchise channel', *Journal of Retailing* 58: 23–45.

Stanworth, J. (1991) 'Franchising and the franchise relationship', *The International Review of Retail, Distribution and Consumer Research* 1: 175–99.

Stern, L.W. and El-Ansary, A. (1992) *Marketing Channels*, 4th edn, New Jersey: Prentice-Hall.

Stern, P. and Stanworth, J. (1988) 'The development of franchising in Britain', *NatWest Bank Quarterly Review* May: 34–48.

* Terry, A. (1991) 'Policy issues in franchise regulation: the Australian experience', *International Journal of Franchising and Distribution Law* 6: 77–90.

* Williamson, O.E. (1991) 'Comparative economic organisation: the analysis of discrete structural alternatives', *Administrative Science Quarterly* 36: 269–96.

Zeidman, P.F. and Loewinger, A.P. (1993) 'Pre-sale franchise disclosure: a review and comparison of disclosure requirements in France, the United States and Canada', *Journal of International Franchising and Distribution Law* 7: 21–36.

See also: BRANDING AND BRAND MANAGEMENT; CHANNELS OF DISTRIBUTION; GLOBAL MARKETING; MARKETING OF SERVICES; POSITIONING; RETAILING

Exporting

1 Introduction
2 Involvement in exporting
3 Company export decisions
4 Role of government
5 Special exporting topics
6 Summary

Overview

This article provides an overview of the important activity of exporting which can be considered a strategy for business expansion. As with any business strategy, it is not without risk. Exporting involves the sale of products or services in any country other than the country of origin. In most countries, only a minority of companies are involved in exporting. The barriers to exporting are therefore considered, as are the reasons why companies do enter export markets.

Once taken, the decision to export necessarily involves a number of other managerial decisions, e.g. how to undertake the internationalization, which exports markets to target; how to enter those markets; and how to sustain progress over time. Each of these issues is considered in turn. Exporting is frequently important to the economics of nations, and, therefore, there tends to be greater governmental involvement in exporting than in domestic trade. This aspect of exporting is considered in some detail.

The article continues with a number of short discussions of special exporting topics – trading companies; consortia; countertrade; capital projects; and franchising – before looking at how successful exporting can be achieved.

1 Introduction

Companies around the world are increasingly engaged in marketing to foreign customers as well as those at home. As a result, exports grew from $200 billion to $5 trillion in the three decades to 1995. This article provides an overview of the important activity of exporting. The focus is largely on manufactured products, since the international trade in commodities is dealt with in a previous entry (see COMMODITY MARKETING). Although the marketing of services is covered elsewhere (see MARKETING OF SERVICES), some mention of services exporting is made here.

Exporting is a strategy for business expansion. Any strategy that takes a company into a new area is demanding and risky, and exporting is no exception. The extant literature is largely concerned with company readiness for export involvement; market selection, entry and penetration activities; and the process of internationalization.

Exporting defined

Exporting is defined here as: where a company located in country A makes sales of its products and/or services in other countries, supplied from its operations in country A. Two facets of exporting which distinguish it from domestic marketing are implied in this definition: first that exported products/services move across national borders and second that exporters deal with foreign customers at some distance. When companies move their products or services across national borders, a variety of new issues are encountered. Documentation is one example. Movement across a border and into the market will be halted unless the correct documents accompany the export product/service. A second example is selling prices: will these be quoted in the currency of the exporter, the importer, or in the currency of some third nation? (see PRICING). Since the risk of non-payment is often higher overseas than at home, another issue concerns the terms of sale that should apply. These are some of the more important matters that companies must deal with from the very first export order. The early literature on exporting tended to concentrate on such issues. Fortunately, the development of an operational capability in these and other areas is not too difficult. A variety of service companies such as freight forwarders, banks and customs brokers can provide assistance to the exporter. The literature in this area is largely descriptive and experiential, with few studies of company practices.

Since exporters supply overseas customers with products/services from their home location, they are usually several steps removed from foreign customers. A sales and supply 'separation' results and provides a major challenge for exporters. Although some sales separation may exist between suppliers and customers at home, because of greater proximity and cultural similarity, these are less acute than those experienced in exporting. Intermediaries, partners and/or sales subsidiaries located in the foreign market help to reduce the sales and supply separations but add another managerial complication for the exporter. These questions are more strategic in focus and have attracted research attention. This strand of the literature is more conceptual and empirical than the former, with considerable attention paid to company practices, especially as these relate to export performance (see MARKETING BUDGETING AND RESOURCE ALLOCATION; MARKETING ORGANIZATION AND MANAGEMENT; RELATIONSHIPS AND NETWORKING; STRATEGIC MARKETING PLANNING).

A further distinctive feature of exporting which is not apparent from the definition above, is that government usually plays a more direct role in exporting than in domestic marketing activities. Given the importance of exports to the economic well-being of most nations, governments are very active in the promotion of exporting and in the development of an increased capability among companies.

Exporting research

Exporting (and the more general activity of international marketing (see GLOBAL MARKETING)) has attracted more limited attention from researchers than might be expected given the contribution of exports to gross national product in many nations. This situation prompted the editor of a leading marketing journal to state that international marketing has a 'stepchild' status in the marketing literature (Wind 1979). Although the level of activity has increased in recent years, the complexity and cost involved in exporting research constrains the amount of empirical work undertaken. The body of knowledge that currently exists is dominated by results from North American and European studies. Although Japan is a leading export nation and one from which many lessons might arguably be learned, relatively little empirical research at the company level has been published in English. This is not the case for Hong Kong, Korea, Singapore and Taiwan, where an increasing number of export studies are being undertaken. This is also true for Latin America. As far as other regions are concerned – Africa, the Middle East, Asia, Eastern and Central Europe – with notable exceptions, little is known about company export behaviour.

2 Involvement in exporting

Four generic strategies exist through which companies can expand their operations (Ansoff 1988). Market penetration is often the easiest to accomplish, since expansion involves no new products or markets. Where existing products are introduced to new markets, a market development strategy is pursued. A product development strategy seeks growth through offering new products to existing markets. A diversification strategy involves both new products and markets and is therefore a riskier expansion strategy. Exporting should be seen as a particular type of market development strategy, where products/services that have proven themselves at home are subsequently sold in markets located overseas. Although this pattern of development characterizes a majority of companies, for others exporting is a factor from establishment. Some specialist products/services face such restricted demand that they must be exported from the very start. Still other companies are established explicitly to export, because knowledge of, and contacts in a foreign market provide the company's competitive advantage. For the majority of companies however, exporting is a way to develop incremental sales for proven products/services.

Two streams of research have investigated the involvement of companies in exporting. Some researchers have examined the barriers that prevent companies from exporting while others have studied the factors that motivate companies to begin exporting. A second group has sought to understand export involvement by contrasting exporters with non-exporters.

Export barriers and motivators

In most countries, a minority of companies are involved in exporting. Numerous factors that inhibit greater export participation have been identified. One classification identifies motivational, informational and operational/resource-based barriers (Cavusgil 1983). Motivational barriers deter serious investigation of foreign markets by many companies and include: a buoyant or large home market; the perceived higher costs and risks of transacting business overseas; and the burden of documentation requirements. A lack of adequate information on foreign markets is a second barrier for companies, which seldom possess data on the demand for their products overseas and/or fail to understand how these data might be accessed. Operational factors also deter many companies. Exporting requires additional resources – whether for working capital or additional staff – and marshalling these is another barrier to export involvement by companies. Moini (1997) provides empirical evidence of the most important barriers faced by Wisconsin manufacturers, as well as those that are most difficult to overcome.

Factors motivating companies to begin exporting have also been examined. The reasons companies provide to explain initial exporting are many but fall into either 'proactive' or 'reactive' categories (Czinkota 1982). Examples of the former include: unique products, exclusive market information, economies of scale, and profit advantage. Reactive reasons for exporting include: unsold inventories, saturated domestic markets and excess capacity. Studies suggest that companies more often begin exporting for reactive rather than proactive reasons. The initial foray into exporting is frequently serendipitous (an unsolicited enquiry/order arrives from a foreign buyer or intermediary) or a way of dealing with unfavourable conditions (production capacity is seriously underutilized). A minority of companies start exporting because it is suggested by a corporate strategic planning exercise.

Exporters and non-exporters

Another substantial stream of enquiry has examined whether there are discernible differences between exporters and non-exporters. This research has practical implications for both companies and government, for if it were demonstrated that exporters do have 'different' characteristics, such information could:

1. help companies decide whether they should venture overseas;
2. permit government export promotion programmes to be targeted on appropriate companies.

This stream of research began with a study of Wisconsin manufacturing companies (Bilkey and Tesar 1977; Cavusgil et al. 1979) and has been carried forward by its originators (e.g. Cavusgil and Naor 1987) and many others (e.g. Dichtl et al. 1990; Reid 1981). The studies typically examine relevant industry, company and management factors and have generated profiles that are often markedly different for exporters and non-exporters. For example, exporters have been found to be in more technology-intense industries, to be larger, to spend more on R&D, and to have younger, better educated and more cosmopolitan managers. Unfortunately, these findings are not consistent across studies, making it difficult to generalize and to use such information for diagnostic purposes. Some researchers attribute the inconsistent findings to the differing study approaches and methods employed. Others argue that the findings reflect reality. A good illustration is provided by Bonaccorsi (1992) who demonstrates that, in contrast to the results of many US studies, company size does not explain the export involvement of Italian companies and theorizes why this should be so.

3 Company export decisions

Once a decision has been made to expand into international markets, companies face several issues. These are reviewed below, following discussion of the overriding matter of the company internationalization process.

The company internationalization process

A prevailing view in the literature is that companies internationalize their operations in a logical and incremental manner. Thus, expansion first takes place in nearby (geographic, cultural or psychic) markets, through the low-cost, low-involvement method of exporting. Over time, as knowledge and experience is developed, more distant markets are entered. Further, as sales grow to a sufficient level, exporting is replaced by more direct and local operations such as sales subsidiaries and foreign direct investment. The genesis of this view developed from research conducted at Uppsala University into the internationalization of four Swedish industrial companies (Johanson and Wiedersheim-Paul 1975), and was reinforced by later empirical (Luostarinen 1980) and conceptual work (Johanson and Vahlne 1977). A merit of the theory is that it treats export decisions in a systemic fashion, through its consideration of the linkages between company resources, export markets, entry methods and operations.

Although this view of international development is widely held, the theory was based on limited empirical research and has come under increasing challenge as the results of more studies have been reported. For example, the notion that managers' experiential knowledge leads them to enter more and distant foreign markets is not supported by research on European forest products companies (Sullivan and Bauerschmidt 1990). Turnbull's (1987) study of market operating methods found that British companies used a combination of methods to serve single European markets, rather than the dichotomous structures implied by the stages theory. These and other studies (Andersen 1993) suggest that the widely accepted Uppsala theory of internationalization should be treated with caution. A comprehensive review is provided by Leonidou and Katsikeas (1996).

Rather than seeking out such general theories to explain company export behaviour, emphasis is increasingly focused on 'middle-range' theories. Reid (1983b), for example, has argued that company- and market-specific factors explain the arrangements that are made to handle exports. This view is echoed by others and approaches of this kind are reflected in the discussion of market selection and entry methods below.

Which export market?

The choice of foreign market is the first major decision for the company that is expanding internationally. For a number of reasons, this decision tends not to be handled well. It was noted earlier that many companies begin exporting in response to an unsolicited order or enquiry. When this is so, the choice of market is made for rather than by the exporter. Although this saves time and the expense of market analysis, the exporter might forgo much better market opportunities. The position can be more serious since filling an unsolicited order might commit the company to a foreign intermediary as well as a market. In some cases then, the separate decisions – first, to export; second, to a given market; and third, through a given intermediary – are collapsed into one. A further influence can also mean that optimum market choices are not made. Government export support programmes (see below) often encourage companies to take part in trade missions or trade fairs to specific countries or regions. Participation in such activities again leads the company to markets that have been chosen by others. While government trade departments target the best markets for given industry sectors, there is no guarantee that individual companies will be well served. Thus, export orders might be filled as a result of participation in an event of this kind, but better markets may be overlooked in the process.

Even when smaller companies make their own market choices, their behaviour is at variance with textbook models. Despite a surfeit of data on most markets and a variety of analytical methods, most companies consider only a few markets (see QUANTITATIVE METHODS IN MARKETING). This stems from their inadequacies and preferences. Knowledge of, and access to information is one problem, as is the fact that most companies are ill-equipped to undertake or interpret quantitative market analysis. Company practices are also heavily influenced by a preference to enter markets which are geographically, culturally and psychically close. As a result of these factors, a restricted and fairly obvious list of markets is usually considered by management (i.e. the process is non-systematic; Papadopoulos and Denis 1988). Recognizing this situation, simpler but systematic foreign market selection procedures have been proposed (Walvoord 1980; Papadopoulos 1987).

Which market entry method?

Figure 1 shows the major alternatives that exist for foreign market entry and operations. Emphasis is placed here on the more common

Marketing in practice

Figure 1 Foreign market entry and operating methods

methods, with the special cases of trading companies, consortia and franchising described separately below.

With a market chosen, the new exporter must decide how entry will be effected. This is an important matter since it determines how the company's products/services will be marketed abroad. Key questions for companies include the resources available for market entry and development, the amount of control required over foreign marketing, and the degree of risk that can be tolerated. Studies in a number of countries indicate that new exporters of products most frequently choose one of the following methods: commission-based foreign agents/brokers/representatives, foreign distributors and company sales visits. These methods do not require much investment of money or managerial time, and involve limited risk. Exporters give up some control when they employ agents and distributors to represent their interests in foreign markets. This is not the case when markets are developed through company sales visits. However, this approach can be expensive if frequent and distant travel is required. In contrast, agent and distributor usage involves limited expense beyond start-up, communication and visit costs. If a suitable agent or distributor is appointed, the exporter benefits from immediate access to prospective customers in the market in question (see CHANNELS OF DISTRIBUTION; RELATIONSHIPS AND NETWORKS). Direct selling through company sales visits is often employed when there are relatively few customers for their products/services in the foreign market and these are easily identified (e.g. rail cars).

Because of a very limited literature, the foreign market entry practices of service companies is less clear. One difference in services is that foreign agents and partners are sometimes employed to deal with non-tariff barriers that favour local service businesses. Another difference involves the use of local partners to produce and deliver the service, the former function not needed for product exports. At the same time, many of the same principles guide the choice of entry method for services as products. For example, the greater knowledge, lower uncertainty and less risk faced by service companies which followed clients into foreign markets led them to use higher involvement entry methods than companies going it alone overseas (Erramilli and Rao 1990). Further service company insights are offered by Arvidson (1997).

Choice of foreign market entry method often involves selection of a company to carry out the marketing task. The limited literature suggests that this is another area of weakness, with exporters carrying out only the most rudimentary of checks on prospective partners prior to their appointment.

Managing exporting operations over time

Following the first move into foreign markets, a variety of fresh challenges face management. With success, thoughts inevitably turn to further development; whether this involves entry into additional markets or adaptation of marketing in the existing market.

An issue that has attracted attention concerns the number of foreign markets that should be entered and the speed of entry. A market concentration strategy is said to be pursued when a company enters the most promising market(s) first, followed by others only when success has been achieved and resources are available. In contrast, a market spreading strategy involves simultaneous entry into as many markets as possible, followed by later emphasis on the most profitable markets. Factors favouring one approach over the other have been identified by Hirsch and Lev (1973), and expanded on by Ayal and Zif (1979) and Piercy (1982). The former authors' findings show that both strategies are pursued by companies, for different reasons and with varying results. The concentration strategy is more suitable for risk-averse companies; it requires smaller initial investment in marketing, and subsequently leads to more diversified and stabilized exports than the spreading strategy.

Another issue faced by companies that have achieved a level of success in a market is whether marketing adaptations should be made. A company's initial export operations are usually based on its domestic market experience, with only essential changes made to the product/service, promotion, distribution and price (Cavusgil and Kirpalani 1993). Over time, as the company seeks to strengthen its position in the foreign market through satisfying more fully customer needs and preferences, these aspects of foreign marketing are likely to see greater change. Indeed, companies sometimes develop new products/services for particular foreign markets. An important element in the process of adaptation is change in the method of market operation. Okoroafo (1990) argues that changes in operating method can be either incremental or non-incremental, and identifies factors that explain company substitution patterns. A study of 139 changes in international operating methods led Calof (1993) to conclude that no one theory explained the behaviour of the companies involved.

The emphasis of the exporting literature is almost exclusively on growth. The Uppsala theory of internationalization, for example, only considers expansion of foreign activities. However, not all companies are able to develop their foreign operations along these lines; many withdraw from export markets, while others continue less than successfully. Few studies focus on negative export experiences but those that exist are instructive. Companies are vulnerable in the initial stage of exporting, with internal (preparation, commitment) and external (exchange rate shifts, competition) factors often leading to failure (Welch and Wiedersheim-Paul 1980). Other research indicates that a substantial proportion of companies discontinue exporting, and that attitudes are more important than economics in explaining their decisions (Roy and Simpson 1981). Even among experienced exporters, success is often elusive, forcing management to think more in terms of experimentation or consolidation rather than expansion and/or greater involvement (Rosson 1987).

4 Role of government

Three types of export barrier have already been referred to. Programmes and initiatives have been established by government to help companies to overcome these barriers, including:

Marketing in practice

Table 1 Export assistance: providing organizations and approaches

Providing organization(s)	Loose coordination	Integrated, strategic
Government	Coordination attempted between different federal and other levels of government. No strategic view of overall export promotion effort (e.g. Australia, Canada).	Industry sector and company export plans are developed, monitored and evaluated (e.g. France).
Government/private sector	Restricted government involvement. Chambers of commerce, industry associations and export councils cooperate in offering assistance (e.g. The Netherlands, Italy).	Partnership approach to achieve trade policy and/or jointly developed objectives. Sharing of resources to promote exporting and achieve goals (e.g. Sweden, UK)
Private sector	Chambers of commerce and industry associations provide export assistance to member companies (e.g. Germany)	Ties to chamber of commerce and industry associations are obligatory. Exporting subjected to strategic planning approach (e.g. Austria).

- *motivation* – advertising and local seminars highlighting the benefits of export involvement;
- *information* – market reviews and overseas visits that enable the assembly of timely and inexpensive foreign market data;
- *operational/resource* – export financing and trade fair participation on a cost-shared basis.

Although governments recognize that companies need assistance to compete in world markets, the level and nature of export support varies quite markedly. Canada, for example, spends proportionately more than the UK, while Sweden supports marketing activities in contrast to South Korea's emphasis on financing and guarantees. Despite the fact that national governments make large expenditures in this area, the impact of such export support is seldom well-documented. Assistance programmes are clearly useful, but precisely how useful is difficult to determine. Programme evaluations usually reveal positive benefit/cost ratios. However, studies at the company level produce equivocal results, export programmes being viewed positively in some quarters and critically in others.

In the developed world, export assistance programmes reveal certain common elements. These programmes: focus on small and medium-sized companies; offer forms of assistance that vary by export stage; provide support across the full spectrum of foreign market involvement. Because of these common elements, there are many similarities in the assistance that is extended to companies in the industrialized world. However, these same services are executed in quite a different manner from country to country. Export assistance is provided by government in some countries, the private sector in others, and a mixture of the two in still others. There are other differences too: assistance to companies is loosely coordinated in some countries whereas a more integrated and strategic approach is employed elsewhere. Table 1 describes six 'models' of assistance.

Although some developing countries have become important exporters of manufactured products, many more have similar aspirations. Accordingly, export promotion organizations have been formed in many countries and charged with the responsibility for developing and diversifying exports. Many of these organizations have been established with the assistance of the International Trade Centre (ITC) of the United Nations Committee on Trade and Development/General Agreement on Tariffs and Trade (UNCTAD/GATT). In 1994, GATT metamorphosed into the World Trade Organization (WTO). Created in 1968, the ITC is the focal point in the UN organization for assisting developing countries with trade promotion. ITC works with these countries to develop more effective trade institutions, strategies and operations. As in the developed world, a variety of organizational export promotion arrangements and approaches exist. Although export promotion has been studied from a macro standpoint in the developing world, the effectiveness of the programmes delivered to companies – the micro standpoint – is generally not well-documented (Keesing and Singer 1992; Seringhaus 1993). Exceptions are found in Brazilian (Christensen et al. 1987; Haar and Ortiz-Buonafina 1995) and Turkish research (Kumcu et al. 1995).

Export promotion has evolved into a comprehensive instrument for trade stimulation in the developed and developing world. The following types of government export promotion are generally considered acceptable under the GATT:

1. Provision of market research information.
2. Support for participation in international trade missions and trade fairs.
3. Establishment of trade promotion offices overseas.
4. Investment in R&D leading to exportable products.
5. Provision of exporting financing and insurance.
6. Rebate of indirect taxes on exports.
7. The establishment of free-trade zones.

Other methods for stimulating exports – direct government monies to support exports, for example – are viewed as subsidies and are in contravention of the GATT. Three books provide a perspective on this subject area: Cavusgil and Czinkota (1990) principally focus on developments in the USA, whereas Seringhaus and Rosson (1990, 1991) are more international in their coverage. Some developed nations have encouraged imports from developing countries through the establishment of import promotion offices (Gripsrud and Benito 1995).

5 Special exporting topics

In this section, a number of special exporting topics are addressed.

Trading companies

Trading companies have a long history of involvement in international commerce. The earliest trading companies were European, date back to the thirteenth century and include such organizations as the Hanse, the British East India Company and the Compagnie Français de l'Afrique Occidentale. Trading companies such as Mitsui and C. Itoh (*sogo shosha*) were established in the 1870s when Japan decided to end its dependence on foreign traders. Socialist countries have historically used state trading companies to channel exports to foreign markets. Trading companies have also played a critical role in the internationalization of domestic industries in other countries, including Brazil and South Korea (Cho 1987). Given the success of trading companies in developing exports for smaller companies in many countries, it was hoped that passage of the 1982 Export Trading Company Act would produce similar results in the USA. For a variety of reasons, however, this has not transpired (Terpstra and Yu 1992).

Trading companies vary in their ownership, purpose and functions. In most countries, they are privately owned while in other countries they are seen as important to trade development and are publicly owned. Some trading companies have existed for many years as major players in specific commodity trades, whereas others have been founded by multinationals as an adjunct to normal operations. A majority of trading companies focus on export and import functions and have an industry sector and/or geographic region focus. Some, however, are involved in more complex international business forms, such as countertrade, mega-project development and joint ventures (Amine 1987). For the beginning exporter, however, it is the foreign marketing capability that is of greatest interest. Either on a commission or merchant basis, trading companies develop export sales for companies and deal with the associated risks and uncertainties. This is attractive to many companies since they are able to expand their market coverage internationally while engaging only in domestic transactions.

Consortia

For companies that are new to exporting, an alternative to the use of a trading company is participation in an export consortium. Export consortia (groups or cooperatives) come into being when companies voluntarily decide to combine and centralize their export activities so as to achieve greater strength. The main benefits result from better and more extensive selling and promotion, lower costs and more professional management (Organization for Economic Cooperation and Development 1964). Other benefits include greater visibility, enhanced attractiveness to foreign partners, skill and resource sharing, economies from joint use of export facilities at home and abroad, and risk and cost spreading. Export consortia help overcome the resource deficiencies and risk concerns associated with exporting and, in so doing, create stronger and more viable entities. However, the fact that consortia are collaborative organizations means that questions surface. Who will lead/manage the consortium? How will decisions be made? How will sales be allocated and profits shared?

Research indicates that the job of the consortium manager is a challenging one, involving not only the development of group trust and cohesion, but also the execution of a strategy for successful foreign market penetration (Welch and Joynt 1987). As well as the choice of consortium manager, critical to operational success are organizational factors such as: the size of the group, the extent of product diversification, complementarity among members, and legal and financial provisions (Lanzara et al. 1991).

In overall terms, consortia account for a small portion of total export sales. Although holding out great potential, relatively few smaller companies have embraced this form of exporting. In large measure this stems from the preference most companies have for autonomy. Companies only cooperate if there is some compelling reason that outweighs all other factors or if an outside change agent, such as government or a private sector organization with a vested interest, forces the issue.

Countertrade

Countertrade is a form of trade where the buyer pays for those products/services received either wholly or partly with products rather than money. Buyers principally use countertrade when they lack the cash to pay for their purchases or where the cash is non-convertible. Sellers principally become involved in countertrade activities as a means of exporting to countries that face foreign exchange shortages.

Increased demands for countertrade have been experienced since the global debt crisis in the mid-1970s. Due to a lack of reliable data, estimates of the importance of countertrade to world trade vary widely. However, countertrade is generally held to account for 10 per cent of world trade. The main forms of countertrade are barter, counterpurchase, buy-back, switch trading, and offsets. Counterpurchase deals are most frequently used, involving the signing of two separate contracts which specify the products/services to be exchanged. Offsets are also very important and frequently employed in defence and other high value sales. For example, where one country purchases aircraft from another, a condition of the contract may require that part of the aircraft be built in the buying country.

Specialized intermediaries are frequently used by companies in countertrade contracts and these are often located in neutral, strategic cities such as Vienna and Zurich. Some trading companies have expertise in this area. Governments in the developed world officially frown on countertrade but recognize that it is an inevitable feature of modern trade. Similarly, most companies would prefer to sell on a cash basis but many have been forced to deal on a non-cash or part-cash basis. Okoroafo (1993) provides a review of this method of exporting from both a country and company perspective. Fletcher et al. (1997) report on Australian companies' attitudes towards and involvement in countertrade.

Capital projects

Depending on its level of economic development, 20–30 per cent of a country's gross domestic product is accounted for by fixed capital investment (e.g. power generating plants, transportation systems). In developed countries, such investment is primarily financed by national governments and private businesses and, for a number of reasons, it is difficult for foreign companies (i.e. exporters) to supply goods and services to the resulting projects. In developing countries the situation is different. The local supply of engineering, construction and project management services and industrial equipment is generally poor in relation to demand, and funding – usually provided through aid or loan programmes – requires a call for tenders. Consequently, it is estimated that 60–75 per cent of the market for international capital projects is concentrated in developing countries (The World Bank 1990).

The market for international capital projects can be segmented according to the nature of the project, its size and the execution structure. These criteria help companies to focus their efforts, for skill, experience and capability in a given project field must be demonstrated to be seriously considered, as must the staff and resources to undertake a project of a specific size. As in other areas, the capital project exporter will most often be seeking foreign business based on its domestic market experience. The large scale of much capital project work means that a relatively small number of companies will be seen as capable of executing the contract. Small companies interested in such contracts must form a consortium or joint venture to be viewed as credible competitors. Whichever approach is taken, very large contracts frequently require home government political and financial support as well as concerted marketing effort by the bidding company. A variety of execution structures exist, including the following contracts:

1 government-controlled;
2 project management;
3 turnkey;
4 product-in-hand;
5 market-in-hand;
6 build, operate, transfer (or BOT).

These execution structures involve a different allocation of tasks and responsibilities between the buyer and the seller. Specifically, the supplier's responsibility and the supply of goods and services increases, whereas the managerial and technical capability required of the buyer decreases, from (1) to (6).

Exporting in the capital project field – often of services – is essentially the same as elsewhere. A company must assess its capabilities, match these to potential markets and search out projects, promote the company overseas, secure local agents/partners, position itself to bid, submit a winning proposal and execute the contract well. For smaller companies, the development of databases of planned projects and suppliers by agencies such as the World Bank, has made the market search and promotion functions somewhat more easily managed than in the past. In several respects, however, the capital projects field is still particularly demanding of exporters, requiring an understanding of the capital project cycle, sources of bilateral or multilateral project funding, an ability to work with government agencies at home and abroad, and, perhaps, a greater willingness to collaborate with other companies through consortia or other arrangements (Dhawan and Kryzanowski 1978).

Franchising

Franchising has been a major engine of economic growth in recent decades. Although product and tradename franchising still dominates, business format franchising is growing the most quickly. Under the latter arrangement, a franchiser provides a proven business format to a franchisee, in return for initial fees and continuing royalties (see FRANCHISING). Franchising involves the export of know-how or services rather than products. In a sense, franchising is a special form of licensing. Before 1970 very few franchise organizations had developed their networks internationally. Levels of international involvement were low, even among those US companies which are most often associated with franchising. Considerable development took place in the 1980s and the 'exporting' of franchising continues at a fast pace, led by but not restricted to US companies.

Two factors have fuelled franchise exports. First, foreign customer receptiveness to franchise products and services, and second, foreign business person interest in the franchise method. Competition is growing more intense in some markets where local franchise systems have arisen to challenge well-known 'imported' franchises. In some cases, these local franchise systems have themselves become strong enough to internationalize. Marketing know-how to foreign markets through franchising essentially involves the same steps and considerations as product exporting. Markets have to be selected, entered and decisions about standardization of the marketing programme made (Preble 1992). One difference stems from the nature of franchise channels which are contractual and characterized by overt power/dependence relations. This contrasts to the situation in channels for most exported products/services, characterized by more conventional 'buy and sell' relationships and diffused power. In the USA franchisees seem increasingly prepared to bring legal actions against abusive franchisers. Whether similar events will unfold as franchising grows internationally remains to be seen (Welch 1992).

Success in exporting

Numerous attempts have been made to discern the reasons for export success. Two main approaches have been employed, the most common of which has been to examine levels of export performance across a broad sample of companies. Researchers pursuing this approach typically attempt to explain variations in performance in terms of company characteristics and export strategies. The second approach is more focused. Rather than working with a random sample of companies, several researchers have examined only high-performance exporters. These are companies that have been recognized by governments for their export achievement and are cited as exemplars for others.

Irrespective of research approach, a fundamental question concerns how 'success' or 'high performance' should be defined. Most studies use measures for which data are relatively easy to collect, such as the export portion of total sales (or 'export intensity'), export sales volume or growth rate over a defined period. Government has employed similar success criteria in export award schemes, supplemented sometimes by others, such as entry into a difficult market or above average exports for a given industry. While convenient, these measures are not entirely satisfactory (Kirpalani and Balcome 1987).

A review of 17 field studies of export performance is provided by Madsen (1987), who, based on the research examined, provides managerial guidelines on pre-export activity; market selection; market entry; and market operations. Recent studies have addressed methodological shortcomings — particularly direction of causality, specification error and interaction effects — identified by Madsen, as well as examining other determinants of export success. Three studies exemplify new research thrusts in this area. First, Axinn and Thach (1990) examine the link between export commitment, distribution and promotion activities, and performance in the US and Canadian machine tool industries. Second, Dominguez and Sequeira (1993) identify export performance/strategy clusters for Central American companies. Third, Cavusgil and Zou (1994) conduct a wide-ranging study of strategy-performance linkages in over 200 US export ventures.

Studies of export award winning companies have been undertaken in a number of countries, including Australia, Canada, the UK and the USA. These have employed either survey or clinical case methods and find consistent patterns in the export success of companies, as well as elements that vary depending on the situation faced, such as company size (Cunningham and Spigel 1971), industry sector and geographic market (Brooks et al. 1990).

6 Summary

Exporting is one of several avenues for company expansion. Although the essentials of marketing are the same overseas as at home, exporting is a challenging activity for management. This is particularly so in the initial phase of exporting activity, when numerous barriers may have to be overcome in order to realize market opportunities abroad. Over time, management develops greater familiarity and experience with foreign customers and business practices, and export resources usually grow to support the exporting function. Beyond the initial export phase, the key tasks frequently involve managing the transition from one international business method to another, and coordinating operations in several (to many) markets.

The exporting literature has matured over the years. A good level of basic knowledge exists about export practice, although there are gaps and areas that, compared to other areas of marketing, are backward. More attention will be paid to theory development and testing, with more realistic conceptions of exporting and increasingly sophisticated methods being employed. Thus, whereas in the past it was treated as a stand-alone function, a growing number of researchers now see exporting as being inseparable from the other activities of companies (Reid 1983a). Another stream of research with potential employs the network paradigm to examine exporting (and other marketing) activity in companies (Håkansson 1982; Ford 1990). One linkage of increasing interest and study is that to the importer. Liang and Parkhe (1997) argue that importers are seldom the passive party to trade that the export literature often assumes. Export performance studies are increasingly emphasized, building on the pioneering work of authors such as Bilkey (1982). These and other research initiatives will help improve exporting knowledge and practice.

PHILIP ROSSON
DALHOUSIE UNIVERSITY

Further reading

(References cited in the text marked *)

Albaum, G., Strandskov, J., Duerr, E. and Dowd, L. (1994) *International Marketing and Export Management*, 2nd edn, Wokingham, UK: Addison-Welsey.
* Amine, L.S. (1987) 'Toward a conceptualization of export trading companies in world markets', in Cavusgil, S.T. (ed.), *Advances in International Marketing*, volume 2, Greenwich, CT: JAI Press.
* Andersen, O. (1993) 'On the internationalization process of firms: a critical analysis', *Journal of International Business Studies* 24: 209–31.
Anderson, P.H. and Strandskov, J. (1998) 'International market selection: a cognitive mapping perspective', *Journal of Global Marketing* 11: 65–84.
* Ansoff, I. (1988) *The New Corporate Strategy*, New York: John Wiley.
* Arvidsson, N. (1997) 'Internationalisation of service firms: strategic considerations', in Chryssochoidis,G., Millar, C. and Clegg, J. (eds.), *Internationalisation Strategies*, New York: St. Martin's Press.
Axinn, C.N. (ed) (1994*) Export Marketing: International Perspectives, Advances in International Marketing*, Vol. 6, Greenwich, CT: JAI Press.
* Axinn, C.N. and Thach, S.V. (1990) 'Linking export performance to the marketing practices of machine tool exporters', in Cavusgil, S.T. (ed.), *Advances in International Marketing*, volume 4, Greenwich, CT: JAI Press.
* Ayal, I. and Zif, J. (1979) 'Market expansion strategies in multinational marketing', *Journal of Marketing* 43: 84–94.
Belch, T.J. and Dubinsky, A.J. (1995) 'Factors related to information acquisition in exporting organizations', *Journal of Business Research* 33: 1–11.
Bello, D.C. and Lohtia, R. (1995) 'Export channel design: the use of foreign distributors and agents', *Journal of the Academy of Marketing Science* 23: 83–93.

Bilkey, W.J. (1978) 'An attempted integration of the literature on the export behaviour of firms', *Journal of International Business Studies* 9: 34–46.
* Bilkey, W.J. (1982) 'Variables associated with export profitability', *Journal of International Business Studies* 13: 39–55.
* Bilkey, W.J. and Tesar, G. (1977) 'The export behavior of smaller-sized Wisconsin manufacturing firms', *Journal of International Business Studies* 8: 93–8.
* Bonaccorsi, A. (1992) 'On the relationship between firm size and export intensity', *Journal of International Business Studies* 23: 605–36.
* Brooks, M.R., Patton, D.J. and Rosson, P.J. (1990) *The Export Edge: Advice from Successful Canadian Companies*, Ottawa: External Affairs and International Trade Canada.
Buckley, P.J., Pass, C.L. and Prescott, K. (1992) *Servicing International Markets: Competitive Strategies of Firms*, Oxford: Blackwell.
* Calof, J. (1993) 'Shifting market internationalization strategies – understanding mode change', in *Proceedings*, International Marketing Division, Administrative Sciences Association of Canada.
* Cavusgil, S.T. (1983) 'Public policy implications of research on the export behavior of firms', *Akron Business and Economic Journal* 14: 16–22.
* Cavusgil, S.T. and Czinkota, M.R. (eds) (1990) *International Perspectives on Trade Promotion and Assistance*, New York: Quorum Press.
* Cavusgil, S.T. and Kirpalani, V.H. (1993) 'Introducing products into export markets: success factors', *Journal of Business Research* 27: 1–15.
* Cavusgil, S.T. and Naor, J. (1987) 'Firm and management characteristics as discriminators of export marketing activity', *Journal of Business Research* 15: 221–35.
* Cavusgil, S.T. and Zou, S. (1994) 'Marketing strategy-performance relationship: an investigation of the empirical link in export market ventures', *Journal of Marketing* 58: 1–21.
* Cavusgil, S.T., Bilkey, W.J. and Tesar, G. (1979) 'A note on the export behavior of firms: exporter profiles', *Journal of International Business Studies* 10: 91–7.
Chang, T.-L. and Grub, P.D. (1992) 'Competitive strategies of Taiwanese PC firms in their internationalization process', *Journal of Global Marketing* 6: 5–28.
* Cho, D.-S. (1987) *The General Trading Company*, Lexington, MA: Lexington Press.
* Christensen, C.H., da Rocha, A. and Gertner, R.K. (1987) 'An empirical investigation of the factors influencing exporting success of Brazilian firms', *Journal of International Business Studies* 18: 61–77.
Chryssochoidis, G., Millar, C. and Clegg, J. (eds) (1997) *Internationalisation Strategies*, New York: St. Martin's Press.

Marketing in practice

* Cunningham, M. and Spigel, R. (1971) 'A study in successful exporting', *British Journal of Marketing* Spring: 2–12.
* Czinkota, M.R. (1982) *Export Development Strategies: U.S. Promotion Policy*, New York: Praeger.

Czinkota, M.R. (ed.) (1983) *Export Promotion: The Public and Private Sector Interaction*, New York: Praeger.

Czinkota, M.R. and Johnston, W.J. (1981) 'Segmenting U.S. firms for export development', *Journal of Business Research* 9: 353–65.

Czinkota, M.R. and Ronkainen, I.A. (1998) *International Marketing*, 5th edn, Forth Worth: The Dryden Press.

Czinkota, M.R. and Tesar, G. (eds) (1982) *Export Management: An International Context*, New York: Praeger.

Dalli, D. (1995) 'The organization of exporting activities: relationships between internal and external arrangements', *Journal of Business Research* 34: 107–115.

Denis, J.-E. (1983) 'Promoting export trade through trading houses', in Kirpalani, V.H. (ed.), *International Marketing: Managerial Issues, Research and Opportunities*, Chicago: American Marketing Association.

Denis, J.-E. and Depelteau, D. (1985) 'Market knowledge, diversification and export expansion', *Journal of International Business Studies* 16: 77–89.

* Dhawan, K.C. and Kryzanowski, L. (1978) *Export Consortia: A Canadian Study*, Montreal: DEKEMCO Ltd.
* Dichtl, E., Liebold, M., Koglmayr, H.-G and Mueller, S. (1990) 'International orientation as a precondition for export success', *Journal of International Business Studies* 21: 23–41.
* Dominguez, L.V. and Sequeira, C.G. (1993) 'Determinants of LDC exporters' performance', *Journal of International Business Studies* 24: 19–40.
* Erramilli, M.K. and Rao, C.P. (1990) 'Choice of foreign market entry modes by service firms: role of market knowledge', *Management International Review* 30: 135–50.
* Fletcher, R., Barrett, N.J. and Wilkinson, I.F. (1997) 'Countertrade and internationalisation – an Australian perspective', *Journal of Global Marketing* 10: 5–23.
* Ford, D. (ed.) (1990) *Understanding Business Markets: Interaction, Relationships, Networks*, London: Academic Press.

Ford, D. (1997) *Understanding Business Markets: Interaction, Relationships and Networks*, 2nd edn, London: The Dryden Press.

Gray, B. (1997) 'Profiling managers to improve export promotion targeting', *Journal of International Business Studies* 28: 387–420.

Gripsrud, G. (1990) 'The determinants of export decisions and attitudes to a distant market: Norwegian fishery exports to Japan', *Journal of International Business Studies* 21: 469–85.

* Gripsrud, G. and Benito, G.R.G. (1995) 'Promoting imports from developing countries: a marketing perspective', *Journal of Business Research* 32: 141–8.
* Haar, J. and Ortiz-Buonafina, M. (1995) 'The internationalization process and marketing activities: the case of Brazilian export firms', *Journal of Business Research* 32: 175–81.
* Håkansson, H. (1982) *International Marketing and Purchasing of Industrial Goods: An Interaction Approach*, Chichester: Wiley.
* Hirsch, S. and Lev, B. (1973) 'Foreign marketing strategies – a note', *Management International Review* 6: 81–8.
* Johanson, J. and Vahlne, J.-E. (1977) 'The internationalization process of the firm – a model of knowledge development and increasing foreign market commitment', *Journal of International Business Studies* 8: 23–32.

Johanson, J. and Vahlne, J.-E. (1992) 'Management of foreign market entry', *Scandinavian International Business Review* 1: 9–27.

* Johanson, J. and Wiedersheim-Paul, F. (1975) 'The internationalization process of the firm: four Swedish cases', *Journal of Management Studies* 12: 305–22.

Johansson, J.K. (1997) *Global Marketing: Foreign Entry, Local Marketing and Global Management*, Chicago: Irwin.

* Keesing, D.S. and Singer, A. (1992) 'Why official export promotion fails', *Finance & Development* March: 52–3.
* Kirpalani, V.H. and Balcome, D. (1987) 'International marketing success: on conducting more relevant research', in Rosson, P.J. and Reid, S.D. (eds), *Managing Export Entry and Expansion: Concepts and Practice*, New York: Praeger.
* Kumcu, E., Halcar, T. and Kumcu, M.E. (1995) 'Managerial perceptions of the adequacy of export incentive programs: implications for export-led economic development policy', *Journal of Business Research* 32: 163–74.

Lanzara, R., Varaldo, R. and Zagnoli, P. (1991) 'Public support to export consortia: the Italian case', in Seringhaus, F.H.R. and Rosson, P.J. (eds), *Export Development and Promotion: The Role of Public Organizations*, Boston: Kluwer Academic Publishers.

Lee, W.-Y. and Brasch, J.J. (1978) 'The adoption of export as an innovative strategy', *Journal of International Business Studies* 9: 85–93.

* Leonidou, L.C. and Katsikeas, C.S. (1996) 'The export development process: an integrative review of empirical models', *Journal of International Business Studies* 27: 517–51.

- Liang, N. and Parkhe, A. (1997) 'Importer behaviour: the neglected counterpart of international exchange', *Journal of International Business Studies* 28: 495–530.
- Luostarinen, R. (1980) *Internationalization of the Firm*, Helsinki: Helsinki School of Economics.
* Madsen, T.K. (1987) 'Empirical export performance studies: a review of conceptualizations and finding', in Cavusgil, S.T. (ed.), *Advances in International Marketing*, volume 2, Greenwich, CT: JAI Press.
- Mattson, J. (1986) 'Initial penetration of European continental markets by small and medium-sized firms', in Cavusgil, S.T. (ed.), *Advances in International Marketing*, volume 1, Greenwich, CT: JAI Press.
* Moini, A.H. (1997) 'Barriers inhibiting export performance of small and medium-sized manufacturing firms', *Journal of Global Marketing* 10: 67–93.
- Naidu, G.M. and Prasad, V.K. (19494 'Predictors of export strategy and performance of small and medium-sized firms', *Journal of Business Research* 31: 107–15.
* Okoroafo, S.C. (1990) 'An assessment of critical factors affecting modes of entry substitution patterns in foreign product markets', *Journal of Global Marketing* 3: 87–103.
* Okoroafo, S.C. (1993) 'An integration of countertrade research and practice', *Journal of Global Marketing* 6: 113–27.
* Organization for Economic Cooperation and Development (1964) *Export Marketing Groups for Small and Medium-Sized Firms*, Paris: OECD.
- Paliwoda, S.J. (1993) *International Marketing*, Oxford: Butterworth Heinemann.
* Papadopoulos, N. (1987) 'Approaches to international market selection for small- and medium-sized enterprises', in Rosson, P.J. and Reid, S.D. (eds), *Managing Export Entry and Expansion: Concepts and Practice*, New York: Praeger.
* Papadopoulos, N. and Denis, J.-E. (1988) 'Inventory, taxonomy and assessment of methods for international market selection', *International Marketing Review* Autumn: 47–60.
- Patterson, P.G. Cicic, M. and Shoham, A. (1997) 'A temporal sequence model of satisfaction and export intentions of service firms', *Journal of Global Marketing* 10: 23–43.
* Piercy, N. (1982) *Export Strategy: Markets and Competition*, London: George Allen & Unwin.
* Preble, J.F. (1992) 'Global expansion: the case of U.S. fast-food franchisers', *Journal of Global Marketing* 6: 185–205.
* Reid, S.D. (1981) 'The decision-maker and export entry and expansion', *Journal of International Business Studies* 12: 101–12.
* Reid, S.D. (1983a) 'Export research in a crisis', in Czinkota, M.R. (ed.), *Export Promotion: The Public and Private Sector Interaction*, New York: Praeger.
* Reid, S.D. (1983b) 'Firm internationalization, transaction costs and strategic choice', *International Marketing Review* 2: 45–56.
- Reid, S.D. (1983c) 'Managerial and firm influences on export behaviour', *Journal of the Academy of Marketing Science* 11: 323–32.
- Reid, S.D. and Burlingame, L. (1982) 'Documentation and logistics issues in exporting firms', in Kothari, V. (ed.), *Proceedings*, Academy of Marketing Science Conference.
* Rosson, P.J. (1987) 'The overseas distributor method: performance and change in a harsh environment', in Rosson, P.J. and Reid, S.D. (eds), *Managing Export Entry and Expansion: Concepts and Practice*, New York: Praeger.
- Rosson, P.J. and Ford, I.D. (1982) 'Manufacturer-overseas distributor relations and export performance', *Journal of International Business Studies* 13: 57–72.
- Rosson, P.J. and Reid, S.D. (eds) (1987) *Managing Export Entry and Expansion: Concepts and Practice*, New York: Praeger.
* Roy, D.A. and Simpson, C.L. (1981) 'The decision to discontinue exporting: the experience of the smaller manufacturing firm in the southeastern United States', in Bellur, V. (ed.), *Proceedings*, Academy of Marketing Science Conference.
- Samiee, S. and Walters, P.G.P. (1990) 'Rectifying strategic gaps in export management', *Journal of Global Marketing* 4: 7–37.
* Seringhaus, F.H.R. (1993) 'Export promotion in developing countries: status and prospects', *Journal of Global Marketing* 6: 7–31.
* Seringhaus, F.H.R. and Rosson, P.J. (1990) *Government Export Promotion: A Global Perspective*, London: Routledge.
* Seringhaus, F.H.R. and Rosson, P.J. (eds) (1991) *Export Development and Promotion: The Role of Public Organizations*, Boston: Kluwer Academic Publishers.
* Sullivan, D. and Bauerschmidt, A. (1990) 'Incremental internationalization: a test of Johanson and Vahlne's thesis', *Management International Review* 30: 19–30.
- Terpstra, V. and Sarathy, R. (1998) *International Marketing*, 7th edn, Forth Worth: The Dryden Press.
* Terpstra, V. and Yu, C.-M.J. (1992) 'Export trading companies: an American trade failure?' *Journal of Global Marketing* 6: 29–54.
* Turnbull, P.W. (1987) 'A challenge to the stages theory of the internationalization process', in Rosson, P.J. and Reid, S.D. (eds), *Managing Export Entry and Expansion: Concepts and Practice*, New York: Praeger.
* Walvoord, R.W. (1980) 'Export market research', *Global Trade Magazine* May: 83.

* Welch, L.S. (1992) 'Developments in international franchising', *Journal of Global Marketing* 6: 81–96.
* Welch, L.S. and Joynt, P. (1987) 'Grouping for export: an effective solution', in Rosson, P.J. and Reid, S.D. (eds), *Managing Export Entry and Expansion: Concepts and Practice*, New York: Praeger.
* Welch, L.S. and Weidersheim-Paul, F. (1980) 'Initial exports – a marketing failure?', *Journal of Management Studies* 17: 333–44.
* Wind, Y. (1979) 'From the editor', *Journal of Marketing* 43: 9–12
* World Bank (1990) *Guide to International Business Opportunities*, Washington: The World Bank.

Wortzel, L.W. and Wortzel, H.V. (1981) 'Export marketing strategies for NIC & LDC based firms', *Columbia Journal of World Business*, Spring: 51–9.

Yang, S.Y., Leone, R.P. and Alden, D.L. (1992) 'A market expansion ability approach to identify potential exporters', *Journal of Marketing* 56: 84–96.

Yaprak, A. (1985) 'An empirical study of the differences between small exporting and non-exporting U.S. firms', *International Marketing Review*, 2: 72–8.

See also: CHANNELS OF DISTRIBUTION; COMMODITY MARKETING; FRANCHISING; GLOBAL MARKETING; MARKETING BUDGETING AND RESOURCE ALLOCATION; MARKETING ORGANIZATION AND MANAGEMENT; MARKETING OF SERVICES; PRICING, QUANTITATIVE METHODS IN MARKETING; RELATIONSHIPS AND NETWORKING; STRATEGIC MARKETING PLANNING

Global marketing

1. Introduction
2. Global strategy parameters
3. Defining the global strategic thrust
4. Establishing the marketing mix
5. Configuring the global portfolio
6. Summary

Overview

For many industries, whether manufacturing or service-based, business is no longer carried on simply in the national marketplace. Improved communications and technological developments have created a worldwide marketplace. the implications of this are huge and cover finance, manufacturing, personnel, logistics and marketing. There are now global brands, global services, global customer profiles and global company images – and, of course, global marketing strategies. Firms must consider whether to enter the global marketplace; how they should do so; what aspects of the firm should be globally standardized; and the implications of all these decisions for the future growth and prosperity of the firm.

1 Introduction

The globalization of markets is one of the most significant developments in business today. Its consequences are profound and far-reaching both for strategy development as well as for policies in all areas of business activity including marketing, manufacturing, finance and personnel. Evidence of the impact is widespread, ranging from the growing proliferation of global products and brands, to the increasingly complex systems of production logistics being developed in the automobile, electronics and computer industries, and the growing number of cooperative agreements and joint ventures among firms of different national origins (see STRATEGIC ALLIANCES AND SUPPLIER PARTNERSHIPS).

Increased communication and interchange of people, ideas and experience between countries has stimulated the identification and targeting of global market segments. Customers such as upscale consumers, teenagers or environmentally concerned individuals with similar tastes and interests in different countries are identified, and products, brands or services targeted to these customers worldwide. For example, Rolex and Cartier watches, Hermes scarves and leather goods and Waterman pens, are targeted to the affluent worldwide, while Bodyshop targets the environmentally concerned. McDonald's, Coca-Cola and Levi-Strauss have also been highly successful in creating strong global brands – symbols of a modern Western lifestyle in markets worldwide (see MARKET SEGMENTATION; POSITIONING).

Parallel to this trend, is the development of global sourcing and production logistics, facilitated by increased awareness of differential labour, production and raw material costs in different countries as well as the growing efficiency of international transportation and communication networks (see LOGISTICS AND PHYSICAL DISTRIBUTION; MARKETING COMMUNICATIONS). Adidas and Nike source many of their products, including their running sports shoes, in Asia. Similarly, Ford has developed a Year 2000 initiative, to consolidate manufacturing and sourcing operations in Europe and North America, with a view to cutting costs and streamlining the organization. A common vehicle platform is used to produce the Ford Mondeo for the European market and the Contour and Mystique for the US market. This reduces duplication of design, and dramatically reduces the number of parts suppliers.

Such developments imply that in many industries competition is taking place on a global, rather than a national or even regional scale. As a result, in order to compete effectively companies must globalize their marketing strategy. This entry develops a framework for viewing global marketing strategy. It begins by identifying the key parameters of strategy: business definition, identification of the company's driving force, and determination of its global strategic thrust.

This provides the basis for formulating global marketing strategy. First, the choice of

Marketing in practice

```
┌─────────────────────────┐         ┌─────────────────────────────┐
│   Business definition   │         │      Driving force          │
│   • Product market      │◄───────►│   • Product offering        │
│   • Geographic scope    │         │   • Marketing skills        │
│                         │         │   • Technology              │
│                         │         │   • Production capability   │
│                         │         │   • Method of distribution  │
│                         │         │   • Raw materials           │
└─────────────────────────┘         └─────────────────────────────┘
             │                                   │
             ▼                                   ▼
                  ┌──────────────────────┐
                  │  Global strategic    │
                  │       thrust         │
                  └──────────────────────┘
                     │               │
                     ▼               ▼
        ┌──────────────────┐  ┌──────────────────┐
        │   Competitive    │◄─►│   Segmentation   │
        │    strategy      │  │    strategy      │
        └──────────────────┘  └──────────────────┘
                     │               │
                     ▼               ▼
                  ┌──────────────────────┐
                  │   Configuring the    │
                  │   global portfolio   │
                  └──────────────────────┘
```

Figure 1 Developing global marketing strategy

the terrain on which to compete has to be made. This defines not only the geographic scope of activities but also with whom the firm competes. Next is the choice of an underlying strategy (i.e. either cost leadership or differentiation or a hybrid of the two appropriate to the firm and industry).

Once the strategy has been established, the next step is to devise a marketing mix that effectively implements the strategy (see THE MARKETING MIX). One of the most basic considerations is whether the firm should standardize all or part of the marketing mix. This entails weighing the barriers to standardization along with the benefits of adapting elements of the mix to local conditions. Finally, as global markets evolve and become more complex and interlinked, and competition becomes more intense, the firm needs to determine how to allocate resources across geographic markets and product businesses so as to establish direction for future growth (see DEVELOPING AND IMPLEMENTING A MARKETING PLAN).

2 Global strategy parameters

The starting point for the development of global marketing strategy is the definition of the business or, in other words, the market arena in which the company will compete. For a domestic market, it is sufficient to define a business in terms of the specific product market or services in which the company is involved; in international markets it is important also to determine the geographic scope of the business. (See Figure 1 for an overview of this process.)

Defining the business

Defining the product market or service
The first step is to define the specific product market or markets in which the company is competing so as to determine the focus and scope of the company's activities. Often this consists of multiple markets and product businesses. General Electric (GE) for example, is strongly committed to global expansion in a number of businesses ranging from aircraft engines, power generators and medical systems to capital services.

Four basic dimensions in defining the business can be identified: customer functions, technologies, customer segments and stages in the value added system. The customer functions indicate the benefits which are provided, as, for example, a fast food outlet provides not only food, but speed of delivery and reliable quality standards. Technology used determines the way in which a function is provided. Thus, for example, automobiles may be powered by internal combustion engines, electric motors or a combination of both. The segment dimension determines the specific customers to be targeted. Ryobi and Makita, for example, target small hand-powered tools to the 'do-it--yourself' amateur segment and professionals such as repair businesses, plumbers and carpenters. The stages in the value added system indicate the degree of vertical integration within the business. Braun, for example, markets high-priced stylish household appliances, but production is farmed out to other companies under highly detailed design specifications.

In applying these dimensions to international markets it is important to note that these may differ from one country to another. In the first place a product or service may not necessarily be used for the same purpose in different countries or geographic regions. For example, while bicycles are predominantly used for recreation in the USA, in China and the Netherlands they are a basic mode of transportation. This implies that the relevant product benefits vary from one country to another. While in the USA factors such as style and design may be crucial, in China and the Netherlands benefits such as economy and durability may be more significant.

The range and availability of different product variants may also differ considerably from country to country. In the USA a wide variety of household detergents are available, including high sudsing and low sudsing detergents, fabric softeners with or without blue, basic bleach or colourfast bleach. In other countries, detergents may be simpler consisting of soap shavings or alternatively bars of soap where clothes are washed on a ridged wooden scrub board or on rocks by the river. Consequently, the specific product benefits vary from an emphasis on high sudsing versus low sudsing detergents or softness to getting the dirt out of clothes.

Differences in relative costs of labour, energy capital or other resources imply that technology varies from one country to another, again affecting the definition of the business. For example, in the rural areas of developing countries where there is no electricity, hand cranked or battery operated equipment and appliances may be required.

Such differences imply that it may be desirable to define the product business by geographic area first. Similarities between product businesses across countries can then be identified. This may in turn lead to a redefinition of the product business depending on the company's desire to target a uniform segment across countries, as opposed to responding to national differences.

Defining geographic market scope
In addition to defining the specific product business, the firm has also to define the geographic scope of the business. This defines the arena in which it will compete as well as establishing basic geographic parameters for allocating resources and developing strategy. Here four major categories of businesses may be identified based on the degree of integration of markets across countries: domestic businesses, interdomestic businesses, regional businesses, and global businesses.

1 *Domestic* businesses are those which are national in scope. Demand within a country is homogeneous and there are substantial barriers between countries. Food items are often domestic businesses, though there is an increasing tendency for various segments, e.g. fast food, soft drinks to become international. Culinary preferences with some notable exceptions tend to be localized.

2 *Interdomestic* businesses are those where products can be sold in other countries with marginal modifications. Many household appliances such as toasters, irons and food mixers are interdomestic as they require only minor modifications in terms of voltage and the configuration of the plugs.

3 *Regional* businesses span a geographic region such as Europe, Latin America and North America. The automobile market is typically regional in scope as models are developed primarily for regional markets. In the past, Ford, for example, has developed models such as the Fiesta, Granada and Sierra specifically for the European market. More recently as markets have become more integrated, economic pressures are resulting in a shift to a more global orientation. With

the 2000 initiative, Ford, like Honda, is moving towards developing a world car.
4. *Global* businesses are those in which the market is the same worldwide, for example, tyres, telecommunications, computers, pharmaceuticals. Such markets are highly integrated worldwide, and hence businesses operate on a global scale. Biro pens provide an example of a global consumer market.

Identifying the company's driving force

The next step is to identify the driving force of the company. This is a key determinant in strategy development, both in providing guidelines for the allocation of resources to different functional areas, and in defining its differential competitive advantage. Six different categories or areas where this may lie have been identified (Day 1984): in products offered, marketing skills, technology, production capability, method of distribution, and control of raw materials.

1. *Products offered*: if a company has certain unique or superior products or product-related advantages, it can seek to exploit these on a global scale and expand into new markets in other countries. Anita Roddick of Body Shop developed a line of environmentally friendly cosmetics, not tested on animals. Following their success in the UK, franchised stores selling the product line were established in other countries with high environmental consciousness.
2. *Marketing skills*: in this case, a company's driving force is its marketing expertise and know-how. Procter and Gamble's success in international markets stems largely from the company's mastery of mass-merchandising techniques, combining heavy media advertising with intensive distribution.
3. *Technology*: here superior technology provides the rationale for product development and identification of target markets. Lucent and Siemens, for example, are at the forefront of new technological development in telecommunications and digital switching.
4. *Production capability*: production-driven businesses focus on efficiency in production and the production process. Japanese competition in the car market is, for example, largely founded on superior production efficiency.
5. *Method of distribution and sale*: here, the unique characteristic of a company is its method of distribution and sales. Avon cosmetics has, for example, successfully utilized its system of employing housewives as sales ladies in many different countries throughout the world.
6. *Control of raw materials*: a final category consists of companies focusing on control of raw materials. This is typically the driving force of petroleum companies such as BP, Exxon and Shell, as well as diamond-mining companies such as DeBeers. Operations in international markets are often dominated by concern with retaining control over key resources and management of conflict with host governments.

In essence, therefore, the identification of a company's driving force determines the specific aspects of strategy on which attention is focused. This does not, however, necessarily imply neglect of other areas. Focus on technology or products offered does not, for example, imply that ability to satisfy market needs and identify key target segments can be ignored. Rather it suggests priorities for allocation of management effort and resources and for the evaluation of new projects.

3 Defining the global strategic thrust

Once the firm has defined the business and its driving force, the next step is to define its strategic thrust and formulate strategy relative to global markets. This should specify first the firm's competitive strategy, thus establishing the basis of a company differential advantage relative to competition; and secondly, the market scope and configuration or target segments.

Competitive strategy

In international markets establishing competitive strategy requires determining, first, the terrain or geographic area in which a company is to compete; and, second, the strategy or tactics to be used in competing on this terrain. These decisions establish the boundaries or limits within which the company's efforts are focused, and provides guidelines for the allocation of those efforts.

Global marketing

Choice of terrain

In entering international markets, an important consideration is the choice of geographic terrain on which a company plans to compete. This requires determining the number and type of countries in which to compete, as well as the geographic scope of operations. An important element affecting this latter decision is whether competition takes place predominantly on a global, regional, interdomestic or domestic scale. However, it is important to note that even though major competitors are global or regional, a company may not necessarily choose to compete at that level. For example, Henkel and Kao compete in the detergent market on a regional scale in Germany and Japan respectively, against global giants such as P&G, Colgate and Unilever.

In determining which countries and on what scale to compete, a key factor is the company's resources and skills relative to those of its competitors. Competing in a global market with a broad product line is likely to require extensive resources and the capacity to operate on a worldwide scale. A small company entering international markets may therefore prefer to concentrate its resources and operate on a more limited scale, focusing on a limited number of countries or regional markets. Increasingly, however, with advances in communications technology shrinking distances worldwide, small and medium-sized firms are able to target niche segments worldwide, as for example, in medical equipment or computer peripherals. Hence the geographic scope of operations is wide, although the range of products or product lines is restricted and focused.

Other aspects to consider in choosing the terrain on which to compete are whether to target a competitor's home market or neutral territory, and the degree of concentration or diversification in the choice of markets. In its home market, a competitor may benefit from a strongly entrenched position due to customer franchise and loyalty, a well-established distribution network, or protection from the home government. However, it may also be more vulnerable in its home market as this may account for a substantial proportion of profits. In the USA, for example, Kodak benefits from a substantial customer franchise, and constitutes a major obstacle to Fuji's expansion in the market. In neutral territory, where there is no major domestic competitor, competition may take place on more equal terms.

Another factor where a firm is entering international markets with a highly innovative product or product line is the threat of competitive entry. If this is high, it may be desirable to enter as many markets as rapidly as possible in order to pre-empt competition.

Choice of competitive tactics

The choice of terrain determines the geographic area in which a company chooses to operate. Next, the firm has to select the strategy with which it will compete on that terrain. Here, three strategic options are typically identified: cost leadership, product differentiation, and a hybrid strategy which is a combination of the first two.

1 *Cost leadership* is often grounded in operating efficiencies which enable a company to offer equivalent product quality at a lower price than competitors. This strategy is frequently followed by Japanese companies such as Casio in calculators, Seiko in watches, and more recently by Korean companies in colour TVs, video cassette recorders, etc. In pursuing such a strategy in international markets it is important to ensure that cost leadership can be sustained in the long run in the face of competition from firms from low cost countries, and is founded in real operating efficiencies. Otherwise, it may stimulate price wars which can erode profit margins dramatically.

2 *Differentiation* focuses on the product and on creating a perception that it is unique, offering certain advantages which are not provided by competitors. A company may, for example, offer a product which is perceived to be of superior quality, as, for example, such as Bang and Olufsen audio equipment and Leica optical products. Alternatively, a company may be perceived as superior in terms of product reliability, service or delivery. IBM, for example, has traditionally held a worldwide reputation for product reliability and service.

Introduction of innovative features provides another means for differentiating products. A company may also be able to develop a strong or unique brand image for its product. Nike has, for example, a certain

Marketing in practice

mystique which to a large extent accounts for its success worldwide. Similarly, Philippe Patek watches and Rolls Royce cars both convey a prestige luxury image, but each is of a somewhat different character.

3 *Hybrid* strategies can be pursued which combine both cost leadership and differentiation strategies. Effectively executed, this will enable the firm to establish a strong position in global markets. Heinz, for example, has spent heavily on advertising to develop strong brand names in many country markets while at the same time managing costs by adapting purchasing and technology to local market conditions.

In essence, therefore, competitive strategy should define the firm's strategic thrust in global markets, based on its core advantage relative to its competitors. At the same time, it provides the basic parameters for developing strategy in international markets, its investment strategy, relative to different business functions and geographic locations.

Market scope and segmentation

The second component of the firm's global strategic thrust concerns the geographic market scope and configuration of target segments. Here, two issues need to be considered: the degree of integration across geographic markets; and the breadth of the target market (see Figure 2). Both issues are closely intertwined with choice of terrain and competitive tactics.

Degree of integration

In considering whether to target the same customer segments worldwide, or to segment on a country by country basis, management needs to examine the similarity of customer behaviour and response patterns across geographic markets, as well as the importance of linkages between markets. Some customers such as business executives, young adults and children have highly similar interests and behaviour patterns irrespective of nationality. Consequently, some products and marketing strategies are effective in targeting such customers worldwide. Similarly, in some business to business markets such as polymers, mainframe computers and medical equipment, customer requirements are essentially the same worldwide. In some cases, separate product lines are developed for specific market segments worldwide. For example, skin care manufacturers market acne products for teenagers, anti-wrinkle collagen products for the middle aged, and environmentally friendly lines for the environmentally conscious. The underlying assumption is that similarity of the skin care needs of these

Figure 2 Global segmentation

segments in different countries outweighs between country differences.

On the other hand, if desired customer benefits or the nature of product market vary substantially from one country to another, product lines and marketing strategy will need to be tailored to specific geographic areas or markets. Differences between countries are thus perceived as greater than those within countries. This may be an appropriate strategy for a food processing company. Findus, Nestlé's frozen food division, has separate product lines in different countries which are adapted to local food tastes. Products such as fish fingers and fishcakes are marketed in the UK, *coq au vin* and *boeuf bourguinon* in France, and dim sum in Singapore.

Increasingly, companies pursue hybrid strategies, marketing some products and brands globally, as well as some tailored to specific regions or local markets. For example, Coca-Cola markets Classic Coke worldwide and a version of diet Coke, often Coke Light in many markets worldwide. It also markets regional brands of soft drinks such as Cappy, a juice drink sold in Turkey, Germany, Hungary, Poland and Romania or Tab Xtra, a sugar free cola sold in the Scandinavian countries. In addition, it markets soft drinks targeted to specific local market tastes, such as Lilt, a soda in pineapple-grapefruit and mango-passion fruit flavours in the UK and Georgia, and a line of canned coffee drinks which is highly successful in Japan.

Breadth of target market
The breadth or scope of the target market has also to be determined. Management may, for example, decide to adopt a broad-line strategy, targeting all segments or potential customers in a given market, or alternatively focus on targeting a specific segment.

In the automobile industry, companies such as GM, Ford and Toyota market a broad-based product line worldwide, while others such as Ferrari and Lamborghini target the luxury sports car segment. A broad-based strategy implies that efforts are targeted towards the entire market. In some cases, this may entail a mass-market approach, with little product differentiation or tailoring of products to individual market segments. In other cases, the firm may have a broad product line, catering to specific individual needs while taking advantage of economies of scope and distribution efficiencies. A focused strategy, on the other hand, targets a specific market segment and is likely to be most appropriate for a company with relatively limited resources, or where distinctive competencies are required to satisfy a specific market segment as, for example, in designer fashion and computer software. Except in the case of globally integrated industries such as aerospace or chemicals, broad-line strategies typically require some adaptation to specific geographic markets or regions of the world, while focused strategies are more readily leveraged worldwide.

Thus, competitive strategy determines the parameters of the company's operations and its driving thrust in global markets, while segmentation defines the spatial configuration of activities. This in turn provides guidelines for the development of the tactics to be used in international markets in relation to each of the elements of the marketing mix. These aspects are next examined in more detail.

4 Establishing the marketing mix

A central issue in determining marketing mix tactics in international markets is the extent to which these are standardized across countries. This depends on the scope of the market, global, regional or domestic; the basis on which the firm competes, cost leadership or differentiation; and the segmentation strategy pursued by a company. Even where the product market is global in character there may be barriers to implementation of a totally standardized strategy such as the nature of the marketing infrastructure or government regulation (see Buzzell 1968). Often this affects the choice of terrain. These relationships are shown in Figure 3.

Although the overall positioning of the product or brand is global or regional, specific elements of the mix or the way in which they are implemented and executed may need to be adapted. For example, the product or service may be the same, but its positioning may differ somewhat from country to country, or alternatively the specific promotional theme or distribution strategy may be different. Similarly, even though the basic promotional theme is the same, the copy execution may need to be adapted to specific national or cultural contexts. Thus, the degree of uniformity versus

Marketing in practice

Figure 3 Global competitive strategy

adaptation may vary all the way from a uniform strategy for all elements of the mix to uniformity with regard to some, but not others, or some degree of adaptation of some or all elements of the mix. This is next considered in relation to the major components of the mix: product, promotion, distribution and pricing.

Product positioning

Product positioning is the cornerstone of the marketing mix. Positioning defines product market boundaries and the relevant competing product set, the specific benefits or attributes to be emphasized, and the segment whose needs and interests the company aims to satisfy. As a result, positioning provides the mechanism to operationalize the firm's competitive strategy.

In establishing positioning strategy, a key issue is whether or not to adopt the same positioning worldwide. A global positioning strategy offers a number of advantages. In the first place, it portrays a uniform image worldwide. Second, cost savings may be achieved since products do not have to be adapted nor separate advertising copy developed for specific markets. Benetton, for example, utilizes the same commercials worldwide, not only saving on production costs, but also reinforcing its global image. Good ideas and know-how, whether for products, advertising or distribution, can be transferred from one country to another, and exploited on a worldwide basis.

On the other hand, even where customer needs and interests are uniform worldwide, there are often a number of barriers to the adoption of global positioning. In the first place, government regulation may impose certain product standards e.g. in safety or environmental pollution, or restrict use of comparative advertising. Second, differences in the marketing infrastructure such as, for example, limited reach of TV advertising or print media, absence of supermarkets or discount outlets may limit the ability to use the same positioning strategy or to execute it in an equivalent manner. Finally, differences in local competition from one market to another may limit the effectiveness of a specific positioning strategy. For example, Perrier's use of a 'health' positioning in international markets prevented Evian from using this, its domestic positioning, internationally.

Such factors may necessitate modification or adaptation of the positioning strategy, whether in relation to most or only certain countries or markets in the world. For example, the positioning strategy of the Renault 5 car was modified in the German market to emphasize engine and safety features to meet competition from Volkswagen, and in Italy to emphasize superior road handling in order to meet competition from Fiat. In some cases, even though the basic product remains the same, positioning strategies may be dramatically changed to emphasize different benefits, and target different segments.

Promotional policy

In the case of promotional policy, substantial benefits can be reaped from standardization in the form of cost savings, uniform image and exploitation of good ideas, etc. However, regulation of promotional copy, budgets, in-store promotions, availability and reach of media, difficulties in interpreting and translating messages all constitute barriers to standardization. For example, in Germany all forms of comparative advertising and mention of competitive brands are banned.

As a result of these obstacles, an intermediate solution is sometimes adopted. A prototype campaign is developed, indicating the key themes and message. This is then executed and adapted to the specific cultural context and infrastructure in each country. Unilever's ice-cream division, for example, adopts a similar positioning for its products worldwide, emphasizing friendliness. Advertising for its house brands shows a salesman selling ice-cream to children clustered around a cart in the street. However, the execution is adapted to the local environment. In the USA, the commercial shows the Good Humour salesman with an ice-cream van and a fast paced jingle. In the Czech republic a Wall's salesman is selling from a pushcart in the streets of Prague, while in China the scenario is similar but features an Asian salesman and children.

Distribution strategy

In the case of distribution strategy, the benefits of a standardized strategy are perhaps least evident. Here, there are substantial differences in the nature of distribution channels, and in the availability of certain types of distribution outlets. This frequently impedes the development of a standardized strategy. A key factor in this context is the relative importance of small independents and other forms of retailing such as kiosks, open markets, itinerants, as opposed to large-scale organized distribution. In many emerging nations, the former account for a significant proportion of distribution.

Fragmentation of retailing typically implies that wholesalers play a key role in the distribution system. In Japan, for example, wholesalers frequently perform not only delivery and warehousing functions, but also finance retailers offering credit terms or selling goods on a consignment basis.

Such differences in the structure of distribution imply that distribution strategies often need to be tailored to the specific characteristics of the distribution system in order to provide the desired level of coverage and control, as well as customer service.

Pricing

The final component of the marketing mix is that of pricing. Again, especially in consumer markets, many factors impede the establishment of a uniform pricing strategy. These include, for example, differences in cost structures from one country to another, in demand response functions, in competitive prices, and in government or trade regulation of prices.

In the case of costs, differences in labour, raw materials management or other operating costs from one country to another, as well as transportation, tariffs, customs and other charges, may result in differences in delivered market costs. Price escalation is often acute when exporting, due to transportation costs, customs and handling dues and agent margins. Retail, wholesale and dealer margins also vary, as well as local taxes, thus resulting in substantial price differences in terms of costs. Differences in demand response functions and competitor prices from one country to another also suggest that it may be preferable to price differentially to be more competitive. In the automobile market, for example, prices frequently differ from country to country due not only to taxes and margins, but also to differences in positioning.

Government or trade regulation of prices, wholesale margins, sales taxes and VAT constitute a final factor hindering uniform pricing. These provide basic parameters for pricing policy. While management has control over other factors such as costs, these essentially constitute 'givens' within which a company has to operate.

The advantages of standardization or uniformity versus adaptation need to be weighed for each of the elements of the marketing mix. Even where the overall positioning is global, this does not necessarily imply that each mix element will or can be uniform, or executed identically in each case. It is, however, important that tactics in each area should be consistent with the overall positioning strategy. For example, a positioning strategy based on product reliability and service should be backed by reliable service, whether provided by the distributor, manufacturer or other intermediary. Similarly, a positioning based on product quality should be accompanied by premium pricing to ensure a coherent image.

5 Configuring the global portfolio

Putting a global strategy in place is an important and critical first step. However, the defining characteristic of global marketing strategy is that it is played out over multiple country markets and product businesses. It is not a single strategy, but a collection of strategies that have to be given coherence and focus. The firm must develop a global portfolio that takes into consideration the degree to which markets and businesses across the globe are interconnected. Further, the composition of the firm's portfolio must be constantly realigned to provide optimal growth and maximum profitability.

The firm needs to consider how to configure its portfolio of countries, product businesses and market capabilities in the light of current trends and changing opportunities. This should provide a guide for establishing investment priorities, determining which businesses and areas of the world to develop, and which to divest. At the same time, management can assess whether its current portfolio is likely to provide the desired direction or rate of future growth, and whether risks are adequately balanced across markets. Once the portfolio is reconfigured to provide the desired direction for growth, management can then consider whether and how to consolidate or integrate operations across geographic areas or product businesses so as to eliminate duplication of effort and streamline operations.

Developing the portfolio structure

As in domestic markets, portfolios can be examined at different levels in the organization, i.e. corporate, product business or product line, and for different units, i.e. products, market segments or business functions. The relevant levels included typically depend on the diversity of the firm's product businesses, product lines and target markets as well as its involvement in different levels of the value chain.

The global corporate portfolio is the most aggregate level of analysis. For example, a diversified company with three product businesses, and operations throughout the world, could examine its position worldwide, by region or by key countries. The next level is the product business or group. Here a company can examine the position of a given product division or group in more detail. This is the level most commonly used.

Construction of the global portfolio must begin at a level meaningful for the planning and execution of marketing strategy. For example, the components of the strategic portfolio unit (SPU) can be defined as product businesses within a specific geographic area. While, in some cases, this corresponds to a country market for a product business, geographic units can be larger or smaller. Certain countries are large enough and diverse enough to be divided into several SPUs. For example, in China, Beijing, Shanghai, and Guangzhou could be separate SPUs.

Once the components have been identified, the next step is to assess interconnectedness of a given product business across geographic units. Next, the interconnectedness across product businesses should be examined.

Geographic market and product business interconnectedness

Given the growth of communication and linkages among countries, assessing interconnectedness across geographic markets is particularly important. It is critical in assessing market expansion and retraction options, as well as whether or not to consolidate operations worldwide or in certain regions.

In assessing geographic market interconnectedness, two different aspects need to be considered (i) the extent to which markets are linked, and (ii) the degree to which they are similar. Markets are *linked* when they share common customers or competitors, have a high volume of trade with each other, can be reached through common distributors or media networks, or when actions in one market affect operations in another. Markets are *similar* where customers have the same tastes, interests, or purchase behaviour, and where market environments are similar regarding, for example, product or advertising regulation or media and distribution infrastructure.

Where markets are closely linked, they should typically be treated as one unit for planning purposes. Even where management cannot achieve cost efficiencies or synergies by integrating operations or pursuing a common strategy, actions by the firm itself, or by competitors, may impact operations in another market. For example, an attack on a competitor in one market may provoke response in another. Where markets are similar, actions in one market will not necessarily affect results in another, but management may achieve efficiencies by applying a common strategy or coordinating operations.

Geographic market interconnectedness
Geographic markets can be linked in a number of ways. Often markets in close proximity are linked. Firms, including customers, suppliers, distributors, and service organizations may expand into neighbouring markets, thereby linking them. Neighbouring markets may also share common media, or have media spill-over. Trade flows and other movements of people, or communication, are often high among neighbouring countries, and are accentuated by trends toward regional market integration. In some cases, though this does not always occur, customers in proximate countries may exhibit similar behaviour patterns.

Geographic market similarity
In addition to considering the interconnectedness of geographic markets, management should also examine market similarity. Similarity of markets suggests opportunities for consolidating operations, particularly in terms of marketing strategy. For example, management may be able to harmonize the product line or brands across similar markets, and adopt a common positioning strategy, thus facilitating use of a similar promotional strategy, advertising copy, and so on. At the same time, such an approach may unleash opportunities for consolidation of production and logistics.

Product business interconnectedness
In addition to assessing geographic market interconnectedness, management should also assess interconnectedness *across* product business. Product businesses may be interconnected in a number of ways – for example, through serving a common target market, sharing common production or distribution facilities, or benefiting from the same R&D information technology or marketing knowledge and experience. Product businesses or lines may benefit from a strong corporate image, utilize a family branding strategy, or share a common sales force or other marketing expenditures. Product businesses may thus be interconnected at different levels of the value chain, both within and across geographic markets. Product businesses with strong and extensive linkages at different stages in the value chain should be treated as one SPU, rather than as distinct SPUs, for planning purposes.

Reconfiguring the portfolio

Once the firm's various portfolios have been assessed based on their interconnectedness, management can then proceed to reconfigure the portfolio. First, management has to decide whether the firm's current portfolio of countries, product businesses, market segments and functions is likely to realize corporate objectives. In particular, it is important to determine whether the portfolio charts the desired direction for future expansion and, at the same time, provides the desired balance between growth and mature markets, as well as the desired level of risk diversification. In addition, management should assess whether or not the strategic portfolio units (SPUs) should be restructured, and operations consolidated or integrated to improve global efficiency and learning.

Expanding the portfolio
In charting direction for future growth, management should determine whether to expand the firm's geographic scope by entering new countries and regions or to enter new product businesses or market segments within the

existing geographic scope of operations. Management can, for example, enter new geographic areas with existing or modified product lines, or extend operations to tap the same or similar target segments in other countries. Alternatively, management can decide to target new market segments, extend the product line, move into new product businesses or add operations at different stages of the value chain *within* existing geographic areas.

Expansion into new geographic markets is a critical issue confronting firms worldwide. As more markets, such as those in Eastern Europe, China or India, open up in different parts of the world, and communication linkages between markets develop, geographic market expansion affords increasingly attractive growth opportunities. Management should, therefore, examine its portfolio to see how it is positioned relative to such markets. If this examination reveals concentration in countries or regions of the world with few or no high-growth markets, management should consider shifting investment to the new rapidly growing markets in order to ensure continued growth in the future.

Geographic expansion options need to be weighed against adding or acquiring new fast growing product businesses in existing markets. As noted earlier, a venture that is related to the firm's core business and is based on the same technology, or can be targeted through the same distribution channels, offers an attractive expansion option. This expansion enables the firm to achieve economies of scope. At the same time, if the business's geographic boundaries coincide with the current boundaries of other businesses, its addition does not increase the level of macroeconomic risk nor the firm's geographic diversification.

Portfolio retraction
Examination of portfolio units may lead management to decide to drop a specific product line, divest a product business, or discontinue selected business operations in a country, region or worldwide. Portfolio units with poor competitive positions in less attractive markets are prime candidates for divestment, freeing up resources for expansion plans. In some cases, divestment may be prompted by adverse conditions, such as increased political or financial risk or foreign government regulation. In other cases, divestment is prompted by low profitability due to aggressive competition, price controls, or simply a decline in demand.

In making retraction decisions, it is important to consider the interconnectedness of different SPUs and, hence, the impact of withdrawing from one SPU on other SPUs in the same geographic area and in other parts of the world. Divestment of a product business in a given country may impact profitability in other product businesses due to shared marketing expenditures or shared production or distribution facilities. Alternatively, withdrawal from one country or region may result in loss of economies of scale, or be detrimental to brand or product image of the business in other countries.

Consolidation
In addition to expanding its international presence aggressively, the firm should examine opportunities for consolidating its global operations. These opportunities can be identified by examining the degree of geographic market or product business interconnectedness and may reveal opportunities for standardizing products or product lines across countries or consolidating R&D or production operations within a region or worldwide. For example, country units for a given product business within a region or worldwide might be grouped into a single SPU. Alternatively, product lines or businesses within the same geographic units might be consolidated into the same SPU.

Synergies can arise not only from scale economies and improved coordination and integration of operations, but also from the transfer or ideas, know-how, and experience from one product business to another, and across country or regional markets. Examination of interconnectedness suggests opportunities for the transfer of R&D experience or ideas for new products, advertising, or other marketing tactics developed in response to conditions in one country or region to another. Similarly, production, management, and marketing skills acquired in a given business or under specific environmental conditions can be transferred to other product businesses or similar operating conditions.

Assessing the global portfolio

The final step is to evaluate the reconfigured portfolio as a vehicle for achieving sustained growth. Two aspects need to be considered – the balance between growth and mature markets, and the degree of interconnectedness between markets. As with a domestic portfolio, achieving a balance between growth and mature markets is important to ensure that the firm is well placed for the future. At the same time, the interconnectedness of these markets has to be considered, as this affects the firm's ability to diversify risk by being in independent markets, as opposed to achieving economies in building a strong competitive position in highly interconnected markets.

Balancing growth and mature markets

As in analysing domestic market portfolios, it is important to consider the balance between presence in high growth and mature markets. In international markets the issue is even more complex, since management has to consider balance in relation to both geographic areas and product businesses. Not only does involvement in mature product businesses have to be balanced with new, rapidly growing product businesses, but also involvement in mature countries and regions of the world such as the USA and Western Europe has to be balanced with that in rapidly growing areas such as China and South East Asia.

While growth opportunities are often more attractive in emerging country markets, such markets are often characterized by a high degree of economic and financial instability. The risks of operating in such markets are typically considerably higher than in mature, well-developed markets. In addition, the costs of entering and operating in these markets are often higher, due to the lack of an efficient distribution structure, and the need for promotional expenditure to generate corporate or brand awareness. Consequently, an appropriate balance between growth and maturity, and the various types of environmental and operating risks, needs to be established.

Concentration and market interconnectedness

In addition to considering the balance between growth and mature markets, management must consider the degree of market interconnectedness. As in the case of market growth, this has to be considered both in terms of geographic units and product businesses. Focus on markets with a high degree of interconnectedness – for example, within a single geographic region – where such markets are characterized by similar demand patterns and market infrastructures, enables the firm to realize substantial economies. Companies with limited resources relative to competition may also prefer such a strategy in order to focus their efforts. It is, however, important to recognize that this strategy is vulnerable to economic trends and market downturns, as well as a concentrated attack by competitors.

Involvement in a number of markets with low interconnectedness, on the other hand, enables management to spread exposure to macroeconomic and competitive risks across a wider range of markets and economic conditions. Companies can counterbalance economic or market fluctuations or foreign exchange risks as well as competitive risks across different markets. Diversification of operations across independent markets or regions also limits vulnerability to competitive threats. An attack in one market or region can be countered by channelling resources from another market to defend its position. At the same time, management must be careful not to spread resources too thinly, as this is likely to result in a weak competitive position.

Analysing the global portfolio thus provides an important tool for managers to chart direction in global markets. It can be used to pinpoint markets to target for future expansion and growth; to determine where resources should be channelled, where operations should be divested, and where opportunities exist for improving efficiency through improved coordination and integration of operations across national boundaries.

6 Summary

As markets worldwide become more competitive and more interlinked, firms hoping to compete successfully must adopt a global perspective and plan their marketing strategy on global basis. This involves a range of issues that go beyond development of strategy on a purely domestic basis. This chapter has attempted to highlight some of the key components of global marketing strategy. Because of space constraints, these issues were not covered in great depth or detail. The reader who is faced with the challenge of developing a strategy in the global arena is encouraged to consult Douglas and Craig (1995), Bradley (1997) and Yip (1995) for more comprehensive treatment of the topics.

SUSAN P DOUGLAS
NEW YORK UNIVERSITY
C. SAMUEL CRAIG
STERN SCHOOL OF BUSINESS
NEW YORK UNIVERSITY

Further reading

(References cited in the text marked *)

* Bradley, Frank (1997) *International Marketing Strategy*, London: Prentice-Hall International.
* Buzzell, Robert D. (1968) 'Can you standardize multinational marketing?', *Harvard Business Review* November–December: 102–13.
* Day, George S. (1984) *Strategic Market Planning: The Pursuit of Competitive Advantage*, St. Paul, MN: West Publishing Co.
* Douglas, Susan P. and Craig, C. Samuel (1995) *Global Marketing Strategy*, New York: McGraw-Hill.
* Yip, George S. (1995) *Total Global Strategy*, Englewood Cliffs, NJ: Prentice-Hall.

See also: DEVELOPING AND IMPLEMENTING A MARKETING PLAN; LOGISTICS AND VALUE CREATION; MARKETING COMMUNICATIONS; MARKET SEGMENTATION; POSITIONING; PRICING; PRODUCT–COUNTRY IMAGES; STRATEGIC ALLIANCES AND SUPPLIER PARTNERSHIPS; THE MARKETING MIX

Marketing ethics

1 Ethics and marketing
2 Ethical issues in marketing
3 Descriptive marketing ethics
4 Normative marketing ethics
5 Potential future developments

Overview

Marketing ethics refers to morally right and wrong action in marketing. It can be defined in two ways. First, it is a discipline that involves the systematic study of the moral evaluation of marketing decisions, practices and institutions. Second, marketing ethics are the standards or 'norms' applied in the judgement of marketing activities as morally right and wrong. More simply, marketing ethics is about the moral problems of marketing managers. It includes, for example, the ethical considerations associated with product safety, truth in advertising, and fairness in pricing. It is an integral part of marketing decision making.

Much of the discussion of marketing ethics, by academics and practitioners, is centered on ethical dilemmas: issues that arise when there is an obligation to one group of people in conflict with an obligation to another, suggesting a difficult choice between alternative courses of action. For instance, a cosmetics company may face demands from animal rights groups that its products not be tested on animals, while consumer interest groups are demanding that the company take every possible step to ensure product safety. Fundamentally, these ethical issues are about the incorporation of values, such as honesty, trust, respect and fairness, into marketing decision making. The end result should be more consistently good, marketing decisions; decisions that promote the welfare of and have respect for those they affect.

Although it is a subset of business ethics, marketing ethics is a subject area in its own right, with frameworks specific to the evaluation of marketing practices and empirical research of ethical decision making in marketing. Building off this literature, this article traces the origins of marketing ethics and its fit within marketing knowledge, identifies some of the major ethical issues in marketing, and provides some approaches for answering the question asked increasingly by marketing managers: What constitutes ethical marketing practice?

1 Ethics and marketing

The development and scope of the field

Ethics is the branch of philosophy concerned with the study of the evaluation of human conduct, particularly the criteria that may be used in judgements of what is good and right for human beings. It is also called moral philosophy. Often the terms 'ethics' and 'morality' are used interchangeably. Ethics is used here to refer to a discipline of study and to moral standards. There are three categories of approaches within ethics:

1 The descriptive approach, a morally neutral attempt to describe the ethics dominant in a society.
2 Meta-ethics, the analysis of the meaning and nature of moral concepts and judgements.
3 Normative ethics, a prescriptive approach identifying moral principles and methods of moral reasoning that justify rules and judgements of what is right and wrong.

Ethics may be applied to the moral problems of specific human activities, such as a profession. Accordingly, in medical ethics, general ethical principles are applied to the practice of medicine. Business ethics is also an example of applied ethics. It involves the systematic study of the moral evaluation of business decisions, practices and institutions. Business ethics was primarily normative (most academics in the field were formally trained moral philosophers). During the mid-late 1990s, however, there has been an increase in descriptive ethics research, with a growing number of empirical researchers attracted to the intriguing and often important questions of business ethics, especially the topic of how managers make business decisions that have ethical content.

Although most business schools now offer courses in business ethics, the discipline is relatively new. The first business ethics texts appeared in the late 1970s. However, concern about the moral problems of business is as old as business itself: Adam Smith's *The Wealth of Nations* is a moral, as well as economic, treatise; Roman philosopher Cicero's *De Officiis* discusses the moral duties of merchants. Prior to business ethics courses, most discussion in business schools of the moral problems of business was in business and society courses. In vogue between the late 1960s and early 1980s, in both these courses and in business itself, was the concept of corporate social responsibility (CSR). Buchholz has summarized the central ideas of the CSR concept:

> While various definitions of social responsibility have been advocated, there seem to be five key elements in most, if not all, of these definitions: 1) corporations have responsibilities that go beyond the production of goods and services at a profit; 2) these responsibilities involve helping to solve important social problems, especially those they have helped create; 3) corporations have a broader constituency than stockholders alone; 4) corporations have impacts that go beyond simple marketplace transactions; and 5) corporations serve a wider range of human values than can be captured by a sole focus on economic values.
> (Buchholz 1991: 19)

Hence, analysis of social responsibility in business was largely concerned with identifying the obligations of business to society. Enlightened self-interest was the rationale to which its proponents appealed, including business leaders. Firms were encouraged to practice corporate social responsibility, even where it could not be clearly justified on the basis of cost and revenue projections, because it was believed to be in their best long-term interest. Many issues of corporate social responsibility have become subsumed within the broader topic of business ethics, though CSR and the related concepts of corporate social responsiveness and corporate social performance remain central considerations within the business and society field. Moreover, in the late 1990s, many businesses have exhibited a renewed interest in CSR under the rubric of 'corporate citizenship', with a focus on giving back to the societies of which they are part through efforts to help solve pressing social problems, such as unemployment and inner-city decay.

A comprehensive review of marketing ethics by Murphy and Laczniak (1981) identified the earliest marketing writings on the topic emerging in the 1960s. They note that in the 1970s, there was a shift from broad observations on marketing ethics to a focus on specific issues. This continued in the 1980s with an increasingly more rigorous treatment of the topic (Laczniak 1993). A major impetus for the development of the entire business ethics field was an overwhelming concern in society about business practices, particularly during the so-called 'greed decade' of the 1980s. This concern focused on misconduct in financial institutions, such as insider trading, and unethical marketing practices, such as bribery and deceptive advertising and sales practices. Interest in marketing ethics grew concurrently with business ethics.

Spurred by developments in business ethics, from the mid-1980s onwards marketing writers began to make substantial use of moral philosophy to develop descriptive and normative theories of marketing ethics, while interest in researching specific issues continued (this literature informs the following section on ethical issues in marketing). While some researchers have continued to address specific issues in marketing ethics (e.g. research on targeting vulnerable consumers with harmful products, by Brenkert 1998 and Smith and Cooper-Martin 1997), others have attempted to develop normative frameworks that might guide marketing decision making, as later discussed. Meanwhile, models that were developed to describe *how* managers make decisions with ethical content are increasingly subject to empirical scrutiny (also discussed below). Many of these empirical studies in marketing of ethical decision making by practitioners are making substantial contributions to the field of business ethics (e.g. research on ethical sensitivity by Sparks and Hunt 1998).

Is marketing unethical?

Recent criticism of the ethics of marketing reflects the increased societal concern about business practices and has focused on specific issues, industries and companies. However, there has been a long-standing suspicion of marketing. Many people associate marketing activities, especially selling and advertising, with hucksterism (a term that dates back to the sixteenth century).

Farmer (1967) asked, 'Would you want your daughter to marry a marketing man?' Proclaiming marketing as unethical, he suggested, 'Too many of us have been "taken" by the tout or "con-man" or "prodded" into buying all sorts of "things" we really did not need, and which we found later on we did not even want.' Ten years later he asked 'Would you want your son to marry a marketing lady?' He remained sceptical of marketing ethics, noting that marketing essentially deals with greed, selfishness and base human desires. This position was largely unchanged in his third and posthumous 1987 critique, though he did identify the beneficial consequences of marketing activities in developed countries that brought peace and prosperity to developing economies through international trade. Farmer and other critics of marketing suggest it employs dubious means to sell products that people do not need. While this criticism is not entirely unwarranted, it should not amount to the view that marketing ethics is an oxymoron.

A basic response offered by many practitioners to criticisms of marketing ethics is *caveat emptor* (let the buyer beware), which implies that consumers can (and should) decide what is in their individual best interests, as well as a need for consumer caution in the marketplace. Where this is insufficient there are often legal safeguards to protect the vulnerable, such as laws prohibiting the sale of tobacco and alcohol to minors. *Caveat emptor* becomes a more adequate response to critics of marketing when the firm's need for repeat purchases and positive word-of-mouth recommendations are also recognized. Firms must provide products of quality at fair prices, with their benefits honestly (albeit persuasively) communicated, or be at a competitive disadvantage. Should a firm resort to deception or manipulation and the consumer not obtain good value, competitive pressures and the imperative of customer satisfaction lower the likelihood of success in the marketplace (aside from any increased exposure of the firm to legal or regulatory actions).

Commentators who suggest that marketing heightens materialism, wastes scarce resources and makes consumption an end in itself, often ignore the role of the consumer in this process and that marketing is a response to consumer preferences. Also frequently overlooked—particularly by critics of marketing's wastefulness—are the intangible benefits that products may provide, including the psychological and social benefits that often accompany marketing activities such as advertising and branding. Hence, an alternative view, often proclaimed by marketing practitioners, is that marketing serves society.

These arguments may be sufficient to counter the charge that marketing in general is unethical. However, they require assumptions that do not always hold. First, not all markets are competitive and not all consumers are well informed. Second, the law has limits and shortcomings. Third, marketing practices (such as advertising) reflect society, yet they also contribute to socialization with possible adverse consequences; for example, the marketing of cosmetics may create an undue concern with appearance, leading to unhappiness or even anorexia. Finally, competitive pressures notwithstanding, marketing managers exercise discretion that by mistake or otherwise may cause harm; for example, an individual marketing manager may decide to adopt a sexist advertising campaign, even though it is rejected by consumers. Accordingly, while marketing in general may not be unethical, the ethics of specific marketing practices may well be questioned.

For these reasons (and others), there are many instances of widely acknowledged unethical conduct in marketing. Indeed, marketing is viewed by many as the worst offender of the business functions. Hence, marketers need to be aware of the ethical issues that often arise in marketing, many of which are identified below. They also need to evaluate their decisions carefully, to prevent instances of bad practice, to make amends when they do occur, and to recognize a responsibility for the sort of society they are contributing towards. Frameworks that may be helpful in the task of determining 'the right thing to do' when faced with such issues are discussed later in this entry, under normative ethics.

Marketing ethics, the law and other related topics

Many instances of alleged unethical conduct in marketing are illegal; many countries have laws prohibiting deceptive advertising, price fixing or bribery, for example. Generally, what is illegal is also unethical. Breaking the law may be regarded as unethical; more importantly, the law acts to proscribe unethical conduct. So deceptive advertising may be unethical as well as illegal because it conflicts with the principles or code of morals of the marketing profession; it is known to be 'wrong' and, for instance, contradicts the American Marketing Association (AMA) code of ethics. More basically, advertising that is untruthful is likely to conflict with the value of honesty.

However, not all widely acknowledged unethical conduct in marketing is illegal. Marketing managers are frequently in a position to make legal decisions which may be unethical. There are issues not yet covered by the law or, because of their complexity or uncertainty about correct conduct, the law cannot or will not prescribe. So, for example, price gouging is usually not illegal, but is often viewed as unethical; television advertising to young children is legal in many countries, yet it, too, is often criticized as unethical. The 'grey areas', where conduct may be legal but unethical or where legality and ethics are uncertain, are often the more challenging, for practitioners and academics.

As well as legal restrictions on marketing, there are other topics closely related to marketing ethics. Social responsibility in marketing may be treated as part of marketing ethics. Marketing ethics includes consideration of the responsibilities of marketing decision makers to various stakeholders affected by marketing practices. Sometimes, social responsibility in marketing is confused with social marketing. Both are concerned with a relationship between society and marketing. However, social responsibility in marketing is concerned with the effects of marketing activities on society, whereas social marketing uses marketing to change behaviours for society and (usually) the target individuals' benefit. For example, advertising offensive to a group in society, such as the elderly, is an issue of social responsibility in marketing. Examples of social marketing include programmes to promote smoking cessation or to discourage drinking-and-driving. As in all other areas of marketing activity, ethical issues arise in social marketing too. Particularly important is the extent to which social marketing programmes involve the informed consent of participants and avoid coercion. Also closely related to marketing ethics are the topics of green marketing and quality-of-life and marketing.

2 Ethical issues in marketing

Many marketing decisions involve ethical considerations. While it is not possible to specify all the various ethical issues that marketers might face, it is possible to identify some of the more frequently occurring questions or criticisms of marketing ethics. One source of information on the ethical issues in marketing is survey research of businesspeople. A classic study by Baumhart (1961) reports the findings of a survey of 1500 US executives. More than half responded to a question asking them to identify the one practice they would most like to see eliminated in their industry. Most of the practices identified involve marketing. Ranked by frequency of citation, they were:

- gifts, gratuities, bribes, and 'call girls' (23%);
- price discrimination, unfair pricing (18%);
- dishonest advertising (14%);
- miscellaneous unfair competitive practices (10%);
- cheating customers, unfair credit practices, overselling (9%);
- price collusion by competitors (8%);
- dishonesty in making or keeping a contract (7%);
- unfairness to employees, prejudice in hiring (6%).

A follow-up study, 15 years later, identified largely similar concerns.

Chonko and Hunt (1985) surveyed marketing practitioners, asking them to describe the job situation that poses the most difficult ethical problem. The issues identified are shown in Table 1. Some issues are not unique to the marketing function, applying to all managers. They fall more appropriately within the broader domain of business ethics; marketing ethics is concerned primarily with the ethical problems of marketing managers in their *marketing* decision making. The most frequently reported ethical conflict in the Chonko and Hunt survey involved attempting to balance the corporate

Table 1 Ethical issues in marketing management: survey findings of Chonko and Hunt (*n* = 281)

Rank	Issue (with illustrations)	Frequency (%)
1	*Bribery* (gifts from outside vendors, 'money under the table,' payment of questionable commissions)	(15%)
2	*Fairness* (manipulation of others, unfairly placing corporate interests over family obligations, inducing customers to use, services not needed, taking credit for work of others)	(14%)
3	*Honesty* (misrepresenting services and capabilities, lying to customers to obtain orders)	(12%)
3	*Price* (differential pricing, meeting competitive prices, charging higher prices than firms with similar products while claiming superiority)	(12%)
5	*Product* (products that do not benefit consumers, product and brand infringements, product safety, exaggerated performance claims)	(11%)
6	*Personnel* (hiring, firing, employee evaluation)	(10%)
7	*Confidentiality* (temptation to use or obtain classified, secret or competitive information)	(5%)
8	*Advertising* (misleading customers, crossing the line between puffery and misleading)	(4%)
8	*Manipulation of Data* (distortion; falsifying figures or misusing statistics or information, internally and externally)	(4%)
10	*Purchasing* (reciprocity in the selection of suppliers)	(3%)

Source: Chonko and Hunt, (1985: 339–59)

interest against the interests of customers (28 percent of cases). This is in keeping with marketing's responsibility for the firm's relationships with its customers. These issues of concern may be organized by the major marketing decision areas (marketing research, market selection, the marketing mix) as discussed below and shown in Table 2, together with other practices that have prompted questions of marketing ethics.

It should be noted that here, as elsewhere in this entry, the ethics of certain marketing practices are treated in a somewhat simplistic fashion, appropriate to the purposes of this introduction to marketing ethics. References to practices as being 'criticized as unethical' or 'generally unethical' often do not refer to considered moral judgements informed by moral philosophy so much as expressions of public or professional opinion and common sense morality. There are good reasons for assuming that there might be a close correlation between the two and definitive ethical evaluations are hard to come by. None the less, there is an important distinction between what a group of people might say is unethical and a judgement based on moral philosophy.

In marketing research and market selection

Various professional bodies, including the UK Market Research Society, the Council of American Survey Research Organizations, and the Professional Marketing Research Society of Canada have developed comprehensive codes of conduct governing marketing research. Generally, these codes are structured according to the rights and obligations of the different stakeholders of marketing research. The primary stakeholders (and participants) in marketing research are the research subjects (typically consumer respondents), research users (clients sponsors) and the researcher, as shown in Table 2. Issues involving consumer respondents are largely violations of generally accepted consumer rights to choice, to be informed, to safety, to respect, and to privacy. Another important topic of concern in marketing research is competitive intelligence gathering.

Marketing in practice

Table 2 Ethical issues in marketing

Marketing research

Issues affecting consumer respondents:
1 Deception (e.g. non-disclosure of study procedures, purpose or sponsor)
2 Respondent anonymity and confidentiality
3 Privacy (e.g. use of covert observation, data-merging)
4 Lack of consideration or concern for the respondent, causing inconvenience, embarrassment or offence (e.g. calls at inconvenient times, lengthy interviews, personal questions)
5 Mental stress/physical harm (e.g. asking difficult questions; food allergies)
6 Sugging/frugging (sales or fundraising under the guise of research)

Issues affecting client sponsors:
1 Research integrity (study reliability and validity)
2 Confidentiality of study and client
3 Researcher conflicts of interest (e.g. with competing clients)
4 Overbilling by researchers

Issues affecting researchers:
1 Client pressure to conduct research to support *a priori* conclusions
2 Illegitimate requests for research proposals (e.g. when client has no intention of using research agency)
3 Disclosure of researcher's specialized techniques
4 Distorted portrayal of research findings

Market selection

Inclusion issues:
1 Harmful products targeted at vulnerable segments (e.g. children, the elderly)
2 Stereotyping the target market (e.g. sex/race/age stereotypes in ads)
3 Privacy concerns (e.g. telemarketing intrusions, database marketing)

Exclusion issues:
1 Consumers denied products (e.g. redlining of financial services, restricted distribution whereby poor pay more for groceries)
2 Advertising spillover effects that frustrate/offend consumers outside the target market (e.g. ads for expensive toys, sexist advertising)

Product policy

1 Product safety
- requires design, manufacture and distribution to minimize harm
- enhanced by careful positioning, safety information on packaging/labels, and product recall planning
2 Adequacy of product benefits
3 Socially controversial or 'unwholesome' products
- that cause harm via misuse/abuse (e.g. alcohol) or used as intended (e.g. cigarettes)
- of doubtful social benefit/taste (e.g. violent toys)
4 'Me-too' products
- that waste resources (e.g. me-too drugs)
- unfair on competitor copied or may infringe copyrights (product counterfeiting in extreme form)
5 Environmental impacts (e.g. pollution)

6 Deceptive packaging/quality specifications
- slack packaging to reduce quantity and avoid price increase; i.e. 'downsizing'
- quality reduction to avoid price increase
7 Planned obsolescence (e.g. through design/style)
8 Arbitrary product elimination
- premature/unannounced product elimination
- failure to ensure replacement parts for eliminated products
- failure to discontinue less safe products when superior products are introduced (e.g. drugs)
9 Respect for persons in service product delivery
- employee respect for customers as persons
- customer respect for employees as persons

Pricing policy

Illegal/unethical practices:
1 Horizontal/vertical price-fixing
2 Price discrimination
3 Predatory pricing
4 Deceptive pricing

Fairness issues:
1 Price may be too low, when there is:
- 'dumping' by competitors (at cost or below)
- failure to include social costs (environmental harm)
2 Price may be too high, when it/there is:
- unwarranted (relative to competitive products)
- used as unjustified signal of quality
- differential pricing
- non-price competition

- price gouging
- limited consumer ability to pay (e.g. life-saving drugs)
- less value than legitimately expected (e.g. Downsizing)

Misleading practices:
1 Non-unit pricing
2 Absence of item marking in retail stores
3 Price advertising that fails to disclose full price (e.g. through disclaimers)
4 Retailer 'high-low' pricing (i.e. use of fictitiously high reference prices for a limited introductory period to establish a subsequent 'discount' or 'saving')

Table 2 Ethical issues in marketing *continued*

Channels of distribution

Issues affecting channel intermediaries:
1 Abuses of power imbalance in channel relationships (e.g. slotting allowances, franchisee–franchisor conflicts)
2 Grey markets
• 'diverting', within markets
• 'parallel imports', across international markets

Issues affecting consumers:
1 Discrimination (e.g. redlining, selective direct marketing)
2 Privacy concerns about direct marketing
3 Lower standards in export markets, esp. LDCs (e.g. infant formula)
4 Restricted availability (e.g. supply shortages, trade sanctions compliance)

Personal selling and salesforce management

Salesperson–customer:
1 Use of gifts/entertainment; commercial bribery
2 Misrepresentation
• beyond permissible puffery
• by omission
3 Questionable/psychological sales techniques (e.g. high pressure selling)
4 Overselling
• overstocking
• overestimating customer's problem or overspecifying product requirement
• overpromising product performance
5 Account discrimination or favoritism, due to
• reciprocity
• personalities
6 Conflicts of interest
• incentives to push products not best suited to customer

Salesperson–company:
1 Equity in evaluation and compensation (e.g. sales territory allocation, sales quotas)
2 Use of company assets (e.g. personal mileage in company car)
3 Padding or falsifying expense accounts and sales reports
4 Compliance with company policy

Salesperson–competitor:
1 Competitive disparagement
2 Tampering with competitor's product
3 Spying
4 Exclusionary behaviour
5 Discussing prices

Advertising and sales promotion

Misleading/deceptive practices:
1 Deceptive advertising (a representation, omission or practice likely to mislead consumers, acting reasonably under the circumstances, in a material way)
2 Misleading advertising (advertising that is unintentionally deceptive)

Social harm of advertising–criticisms:
1 Manipulates behaviour: creates false needs leading to unnecessary/harmful demand; it is a 'hidden persuader'
2 A contributor to socialization, promoting unwholesome values or behaviours; increases materialism
3 Sex/race/age stereotypes
4 Offensive: appeals to base motives; use of vulgarity; 'pollution'; irritating

Social harm of advertising—industry replies:
1 Advertising is misunderstood
2 Advertising creates freedom of choice

Other issues for advertisers:
1 Fairness in agency–client selection/relations
2 Independence of the media (e.g. 'advertorials','infomercials')
3 Bait-and-switch advertising

In sales promotion:
1 Deceptive/misleading practices
2 Fraudulent practices (e.g. coupon fraud by retailers)

In direct marketing:
1 Misrepresentation of products, misleading advertising
2 Unauthorized use of lists
3 Consumer privacy concerns

While research on competitors is generally considered necessary and appropriate, instances of espionage (e.g. electronic surveillance) by some companies have been widely condemned as unethical (see MARKETING RESEARCH; QUALITATIVE RESEARCH IN MARKETING).

Market selection decisions inevitably involve including some consumers and excluding others. Target marketing may thus raise a variety of ethical concerns. 'Inclusion issues' may result when targeted groups are offended or victimized (e.g. Smith and Cooper-Martin 1997); 'exclusion issues' may result when groups of consumers are not targeted and denied access to a product or frustrated or offended by spillover from advertising intended for the target (see ADVERTISING).

In the marketing programme

Ethical issues may arise in product policy throughout the product life-cycle, from development to elimination. Product safety is often a significant ethical issue in product policy (see NEW PRODUCT DEVELOPMENT). There is a legal requirement in most countries to provide products of 'merchantable' quality; that is, worthy of sale and fit for their intended purpose. This requirement encompasses product safety. As well as this 'implied warranty', an absence of 'ordinary care' on the part of sellers (manufacturers, wholesalers and retailers) can give rise to charges of negligence under tort law, with the seller made liable for products proven defective that have caused injury. In addition, sellers must comply with safety regulations established by government agencies. Yet there remain ethical considerations in product safety beyond those established by the law. Marketers have to ask: How safe should a product be? It is not possible to create a risk-free environment, with products incapable of causing harm, largely because product safety is a function of the consumer as well as the product's design and manufacture.

Pricing is the most regulated area of marketing. There are legal prohibitions governing price-fixing, price discrimination, predatory pricing, and deceptive pricing. In some cases, unethical practices may be possible without being illegal. For example, competitors may find ways to signal prices that are legal, yet result in informal price-fixing. Issues of fairness in pricing may occur when prices are perceived to be too low as well as too high. For instance, from a societal perspective, prices may be considered too low and ethically suspect when they fail to incorporate social costs. Pricing decisions may involve misleading practices that are also ethically questionable (see PRICING).

Ethical issues in distribution largely involve conflicts between channel intermediaries, typically reflecting a power imbalance in channel relationships. The size and market power of large retailers, wholesalers or manufacturers, often may be open to abuse. The increasing power of the retailer has resulted in demands of suppliers that not all can meet; for instance, 'slotting allowances' (fees required by retailers for listing a manufacturer's product) have escalated in the grocery trade, with some smaller suppliers crying foul when unable to match fees paid by larger suppliers. Other channel management issues include grey marketing, where some channel intermediaries have been criticized for free-riding on legitimate channel intermediaries who often face higher costs (e.g. because they have to provide higher levels of customer service), and issues affecting consumers, perhaps as a result of restricted product availability (see CHANNELS OF DISTRIBUTION; RETAILING).

The persuasive purpose of the sales task often creates conflicts for the salesperson. In addition to challenges created by the salesperson's advocacy role, the 'boundary-spanning' position and autonomous operation of the salesperson and organizational pressures to 'make the numbers' also increase the likelihood of ethical conflicts involving the salesforce. These conflicts arise largely within three interfaces: the salesperson–customer, the salesperson–company, and the salesperson–competitor interface, as shown in Table 2. The major ethical issues listed under the salesperson–competitor interface are largely illegal under laws prohibiting misrepresentation and unfair competition and antitrust legislation (see PERSONAL SELLING AND SALES MANAGEMENT; SALES PROMOTION).

Commercial bribery is ordinarily illegal, but the potential gains from this generally unethical practice are often so great that it can be found in many markets and in all countries. While there is widespread agreement that a cash payment made to a buyer to influence a purchase decision constitutes a bribe, there is less certainty about gift-giving and entertainment. Standards vary across industries and from country to country; accordingly, industry norms are a key consideration. Recognition of the harmful effects of bribery, particularly the bribery of public officials, has led to increased pressure for international action by bodies such as the OECD (Nichols 1997) (see CULTURAL ASPECTS OF MARKETING; GLOBAL MARKETING).

The visibility of advertising, coupled with its role as persuasive communication, result in it being one of the most frequently criticized areas of marketing. Truth in advertising has been an ethical issue since the earliest use of advertising (see ADVERTISING). In most countries, advertisers are subject to stringent self-regulation by industry bodies and government regulation. Advertisers must be able to substantiate claims about product performance, for example. In the USA, the FTC (Federal Trade Commission) can determine that advertising is deceptive, intentionally or otherwise without requiring evidence that consumers have been deceived (for one definition of deception, see Table 2). It can issue consent or cease-and-desist orders or require advertising substantiation, affirmative disclosure or corrective advertising. Identifying deception in advertising is difficult. An important distinction is between permissible puffery and deceptive advertising. As well as the ethical and legal concerns about deceptive and misleading advertising, there have been many criticisms of the social harm of advertising (see, for example, Pollay 1986, Preston 1994). There are also other issues involving advertisers, such as the use of 'infomercials', and related concerns including deceptive or misleading practices in sales promotion and in direct marketing (see DIRECT MARKETING; SALES PROMOTION).

3 Descriptive marketing ethics

Ethical issues potentially may arise at all stages of the marketing decision-making process, from strategy formulation to implementation, and as part of any marketing practice or institution. Marketing practices that have been frequently criticized or widely acknowledged as morally problematic are identified above. However, the more fundamental problem, of

Figure 1 Corey's force field model of pressures on the marketing manager
Source: Corey (1993: 43)

which the above issues are symptomatic, is the incorporation of values into marketing decision making. If managers were to better reconcile the ethical considerations of marketing decisions, ethical issues would be far less likely to arise. This section is about how managers are believed to make decisions with ethical content. In the following section on normative marketing ethics, approaches to evaluating the ethics of marketing decision making are discussed, including frameworks that managers might find useful.

Conflicting pressures for marketing managers

Changes in society's expectations of business have increased the pressure on marketing managers for ethical conduct. Consumers, the media, interest groups, regulators, and lawyers are all increasingly less accepting of unethical marketing practices. These pressures, coupled with the increased competitiveness of markets have prompted a shift from *caveat emptor* toward *caveat venditor* (seller beware). If ignored, firms risk adverse publicity and consumer boycotts that can damage hard-won reputations and hurt sales, as well as litigation and government regulation (see Smith 1995).

This is not to suggest that, if these pressures did not exist, marketing managers would necessarily behave less ethically. A study by Hunt and Chonko (1984) found that marketing has its share of Machiavellians, but no more than other functions. Most marketing managers attempt to follow their conscience and do the right thing. However, given marketing's boundary-spanning function, agency role and capacity for exercising economic power, this can be difficult. It is possible that the potential and motivation for behaving unethically may 'go with the territory' (Corey 1993). The tension between the external pressures on marketing managers' behaviour and the inner forces affecting their choices is illustrated in Figure 1. The challenge of resolving the conflicting pressures of the marketing function makes ethical reasoning of particular relevance to marketing decision making.

Ethical reasoning

For thousands of years, philosophers have reflected on how to determine the ethics of human conduct. Business academics have developed synopses of important theories in moral philosophy; a useful contribution being to make a distinction between deontology and teleology. Deontological theories employ duty-based analysis: actions are inherently right or wrong, independent of their consequences, because of the kinds of actions they are or because they conform to a formal principle. Judeo-Christian morality, for example, provides a body of moral duties in the Ten Commandments. Teleological theories, in contrast, hold that an action is right because of the goodness of its consequences; hence this approach is often described as consequentialist. Under utilitarianism, for example, an action is judged as right if it produces the greatest good for the greatest number of people. Theories of justice and virtue ethics have also been applied to problems of marketing ethics (see Chonko 1995 and Laczniak and Murphy 1993 for summaries of these and other applicable moral theories).

Hunt and Vitell (1993) have proposed a 'general theory of marketing ethics' that attempts to explain the decision-making process for problem situations having ethical content. The model, shown in Figure 2, describes how an individual might arrive at deontological and teleological evaluations, that would in turn lead to ethical judgements, intentions and behaviour. There is no attempt here to prescribe how deontological and teleological approaches should influence marketing decision making; rather, the purpose is simply to provide a positive theory that shows how these two approaches might be used. A growing body of empirical research has been conducted to validate this model (e.g. Sparks and Hunt 1998). This model is in the realm of descriptive ethics. Other models that describe how managers might make ethical marketing decisions include theories of individual and organizational moral development, reasoned action and contingency-based decision making.

4 Normative marketing ethics

Normative marketing ethics includes guidelines and frameworks that managers can use in making marketing decisions. It addresses the prescriptive concern: 'What constitutes ethical marketing practice?' It has been suggested that

Figure 2 The Hunt and Vitell general theory of marketing ethics
Source: Hunt and Vitell (1993: 776)

Marketing in practice

Figure 3 Fritzsche's ethical decision model
Source: Fritzsche (1991: 349)

one or more of the following maxims often guide managers in their decision making (Laczniak and Murphy 1993):

- The Golden Rule: do unto others as you would have them do unto you.
- The TV Test: would I be embarrassed in front of colleagues/family/friends, if my decision was publicized in the media?
- The Professional Ethic: would the action be viewed as proper by an objective panel of professional colleagues?
- When in Doubt, Don't.

Some business writers have provided decision rules that incorporate major theories of moral philosophy. For example, Fritzsche (1985) has offered a model of ethical decision making that incorporates theories of moral philosophy within a decision-tree approach, as shown in Figure 3. Decisions are subject first to utilitarian analysis, assessing benefits to society. If that screen is passed, the effect on individuals is assessed, requiring an examination of the deontological concerns of rights and justice.

Laczniak and Murphy (1993) incorporate a broader range of ethical theory by applying the following questions in evaluating the ethics of marketing practices:

- Does the contemplated action violate the law? (legal test).
- Is this action contrary to widely accepted moral obligations? (duties test).
- Does the proposed action violate any other special obligations that stem from the type of marketing organization at focus? (special obligations test).
- Is the intent of the contemplated action harmful? (motives test).
- Is it likely that any major damages to people or organizations will result from the contemplated action? (consequences test).
- Is there a satisfactory alternative action that produces equal or greater benefits to the parties affected than the proposed action? (utilitarian test).
- Does the contemplated action infringe upon property rights, privacy rights or the inalienable rights of the consumer? (rights test).
- Does the proposed action leave another person or group less well off? Is this person or group already a member of a relatively underprivileged class? (justice test).

Answering any of the questions affirmatively may suggest that the marketer's decision is unethical and should be revised. However, as Laczniak and Murphy (1993) acknowledge, for

Marketing ethics

- Producer interests favoured
- Consumer interests less favoured

- Producer interests less favoured
- Consumer interests favoured

Caveat emptor school	Industry practice	Ethics codes	Consumer sovereignty school	Caveat venditor school
– profit maximization – subject to legal constraints	– in general – the best companies	– of individual firms – of industries – of professional bodies (e.g. AMA)	– capability – information – choice	– consumer satisfaction

Figure 4 Marketing ethics framework: consumer sovereignty test
Source: Smith (1995: 92)

many marketing practices there may well be conflicting responses to their questions; for instance, perceived good consequences often conflict with widely accepted moral duties. In many respects, this difficulty in applying multiple theories of moral philosophy is not surprising. Indeed, Robin and Reidenbach (1993) have suggested that the 'grand narratives' of moral philosophy are unsuitable for adaptation to marketing and that the field needs to develop its own workable ethical philosophy.

One response to this problem is the contextualist perspective advanced by Thompson (1995) and the normative implication that managers need to foster a caring orientation in marketing relationships (in keeping with the 'ethics of care' approach to moral reasoning established by the psychologist Carol Gilligan). Another response has been to identify heuristics or 'rules of thumb' that might guide decision makers (at least for a given class of ethical issues) and yet can be grounded in theories of moral philosophy. In this vein, Smith (1995) has proposed the consumer sovereignty test (CST) as part of a marketing-specific framework that managers can use to evaluate marketing decisions. Its domain is limited to corporate impacts on customers, therefore, the framework does not directly address marketing impacts on other stakeholders. The CST identifies an obligation to ensure consumer capability, information and choice, even where there is an absence of market pressure to do so. The manager would establish, for example, whether a target market was fully capable of understanding the risks associated with a product, going beyond legal requirements and perhaps to the firm's economic disadvantage by excluding some potential consumers. Figure 4 summarizes the test, including criteria for determining the adequacy of performance along each dimension. In making these assessments, the manager must still exercise judgement, based on his or her values and interpretation of the facts. However, when conscience signals something is not right about a marketing decision, the manager has this and other models with which to explore its ethical dimensions and some indication of the right decision and alternative actions that might be more appropriate.

Ethics in the organization

An individual's good intent may be influenced or frustrated by the organization. Ferrell *et al.* (1989), in keeping with research that predicts unethical behaviour, suggest that decisions about what type of behaviour is appropriate in any given situation are influenced by the opportunity for the individual to engage in ethical/unethical behaviour. Opportunity is a function of organizational culture, professional codes, corporate policy and rewards and punishments.

Laczniak and Murphy (1993) suggest implementing marketing ethics entails policies that promote ethical decisions and a corporate culture conducive to ethical behaviour. This requires the identification of stakeholders, top management leadership, codes of ethics, ethics seminars and other programmes, and ethics audits. Because research on codes of conduct suggests limited effectiveness, Laczniak and Murphy (1993) recommend that codes be regularly communicated, specific, pertinent to the industry, enforced and periodically revised. Research does confirm the importance of top management leadership. Accordingly, Corey (1993) suggests that to create an environment conducive to ethical behaviour, managers at all levels must send signals that clearly underscore the importance of moral conduct. In keeping with his force field model, he recommends that performance measures which take account of ethical conduct and job security be clearly established.

5 Potential future developments

The pressure on marketing managers for ethical conduct continues to grow. With globalization, this pressure seems likely to become ever more widespread, as firms increasingly attempt to manage differences in values across different country markets (Schlegelmilch 1998). The problems of Russia and other former Eastern bloc countries as they attempt the transition to market economies has added to the recognition of the importance of business ethics, with bribery and other forms of corruption identified as a significant stumbling block.

New issues are likely to emerge. More extensive use of relationship marketing and the burgeoning of network organizations are likely to heighten attention to issues of trust in exchange relationships (Gundlach and Murphy 1993). Technological advances have given rise to the development of new marketing techniques, such as interactive marketing, database marketing and marketing via the Internet. These new technologies often raise ethical issues, such as how to realize the potential for more focused marketing efforts while addressing concerns about data privacy.

Public concern about marketing ethics is likely to sustain the growth in research and teaching of the topic. Researchers are likely continue to refine descriptive and normative models of marketing ethics, often with an increasingly empirical component. One promising avenue of research is social contract theory, where a framework known as Integrative Social Contracts Theory (Donaldson and Dunfee 1999) provides opportunities to combine both the normative and empirical streams of marketing ethics research (Dunfee *et al.* 1998). As the teaching of marketing ethics continues to develop, students should be better equipped to deal with the ethical dilemmas that undoubtedly they will face in their marketing careers.

N. CRAIG SMITH
THE MCDONOUGH SCHOOL OF BUSINESS,
WASHINGTON, DC

Further reading

(References cited in the text marked *)

* Baumhart, Raymond C. (1961) 'How ethical are businessmen?', *Harvard Business Review* July/August: 6–19, 156–76.
  Bol, Jan W., Crespy, Charles T., Stearns, James M. and Walton, John R. (eds) (1991) *Readings in Marketing Ethics*, Needham Heights, MA: Ginn Press.
* Brenkert, George G. (1998) 'Marketing to inner-city blacks: powermaster and moral responsibility,' *Business Ethics Quarterly* 8: 1–18.
* Buchholz, Rogene A. (1991) 'Corporate responsibility and the good society: from economics to ecology; factors which influence corporate policy decisions,' *Business Horizons* 34: 19–31.
* Chonko, Lawrence B. (1995) *Ethical Decision Making in Marketing*, Thousand Oaks: Sage.
* Chonko, Lawrence B. and Hunt, Shelby D. (1985) 'Ethics and marketing management: an empirical investigation,' *Journal of Business Research* 13: 339–59.
* Corey, E. Raymond (1993) 'Marketing managers: caught in the middle,' in Smith, N. Craig and Quelch, John A. *Ethics in Marketing*, Homewood, IL: Richard D. Irwin, p. 43.
* Donaldson, Thomas and Dunfee, Thomas W. (1999) *Ties That Bind: A Social Contracts Approach to Business Ethics*, Cambridge, MA: Harvard Business School Press.
* Dunfee, Thomas W., Smith, N. Craig and Ross, William T., Jr. (1998) 'Social contracts and marketing ethics', working paper: The Carol and Lawrence Zicklin Center for Business Ethics Re-

search, The Wharton School, University of Pennsylvania, Philadelphia.
* Farmer, Richard N. (1967) 'Would you want your daughter to marry a marketing man?', *Journal of Marketing* 31: 1–3.
* Ferrell, O. C., Gresham, Larry G. and Fraedrich, John (1989) 'A synthesis of ethical decision models for marketing,' *Journal of Macromarketing* 9: 55–64.
* Fritzsche, David J. (1985) 'Ethical issues in marketing management,' in Laczniak, Gene R. and Murphy, Patrick E. (eds) .*Marketing Ethics: Guidelines for Managers*, Lexington, MA: Lexington Books.
* Gundlach, Gregory T. and Murphy, Patrick E. (1993) 'Ethical and legal foundations of relational marketing exchanges,' *Journal of Marketing* 57: 35–46.
  Holbrook, Morris B. (1987) 'Mirror, mirror on the wall what's unfair in the reflections on advertising?', *Journal of Marketing* 50: 18–36.
* Hunt, Shelby D. and Chonko, Lawrence B. (1984) 'Marketing and Machiavellianism', *Journal of Marketing* 48: 30–42.
* Hunt, Shelby D. and Vitell, Scott J. (1993) 'The general theory of marketing ethics: a retrospective and revision,' in Smith, N. Craig and Quelch, John A. *Ethics in Marketing*, Homewood, IL: Richard D. Irwin, p. 776.
  Hunt, Shelby D., Chonko, Lawrence B. and Wilcox, James B. (1984) 'Ethical problems of marketing researchers,' *Journal of Marketing Research* 21: 309–24.
* Laczniak, Gene R. (1993) 'Marketing ethics: onward toward greater expectations,' *Journal of Public Policy and Marketing* 12; 91–6.
* Laczniak, Gene R. and Murphy, Patrick E. (1993) *Ethical Marketing Decisions: The Higher Road*, Needham Heights, MA: Allyn and Bacon.
* Murphy, Patrick and Laczniak, Gene R. (1981) 'Marketing ethics: a review with implications for managers, educators and researchers,' in Enis, Ben M. and Roering, Kenneth J. (ed.) *Review of Marketing*, Chicago: American Marketing Association, 1981, pp. 251–66.
* Nichols, Philip M. (1997) 'Outlawing transnational bribery through the World Trade Organization,' *Law and Policy in International Business* 28: 305–81.
* Pollay, Richard W. (1986) 'The distorted mirror: reflections on the unintended consequences of advertising,' *Journal of Marketing* 50: 18–36.
* Preston, Ivan L. (1994) *The Tangled Web They Weave: Truth, Falsity, and Advertisers*, Madison, WI: University of Wisconsin Press)
* Robin, Donald P. and Reidenbach, R. Eric (1993) 'Searching for a place to stand: toward a workable ethical philosophy for marketing,' *Journal of Public Policy and Marketing* 12: 97–105.
* Schlegemilch, Bodo (1998) *Marketing Ethics*, London: International Thomson Business Press.
* Smith, N. Craig (1995) 'Marketing strategies for the ethics era,' *Sloan Management Review* 36: 92.
* Smith, N. Craig and Cooper-Martin, Elizabeth (1997) 'Ethics and target marketing: the role of product harm and consumer vulnerability,' *Journal of Marketing* 61: 1–20.
  Smith, N. Craig and Quelch, John A. (1993) *Ethics in Marketing*, Homewood, IL: Richard D. Irwin.
* Sparks, John R. and Hunt, Shelby D. (1998) 'Marketing researcher ethical sensitivity: conceptualization, measurement, and exploratory investigation,' *Journal of Marketing* 62: 92–109.
* Thompson, Craig J. (1995) 'A contextualist proposal for the conceptualization and study of marketing ethics,' *Journal of Public Policy and Marketing* 14: 177–91.
  Tsalikis, John and Fritzsche, David J. (1989) 'Business ethics: a literature review with a focus on marketing ethics,' *Journal of Business Ethics* 8: 695–743.

See also: ADVERTISING; CHANNELS OF DISTRIBUTION; CULTURAL ASPECTS OF MARKETING; DIRECT MARKETING; GLOBAL MARKETING; GREEN MARKETING; MARKETING RESEARCH; QUALITATIVE RESEARCH IN MARKETING; NEW PRODUCT DEVELOPMENT; PERSONAL SELLING AND SALES MANAGEMENT; PRICING; RELATIONSHIPS AND NETWORKS; RETAILING; SALES PROMOTION; STRATEGIC ALLIANCES AND SUPPLIER PARTNERSHIPS; THE MARKETING MIX

Strategic marketing for non-profit organizations

1 Developing a customer orientation
2 Strategic planning and organization
3 Developing and organizing resources
4 Designing the marketing mix
5 Controlling marketing strategies
6 Summary

Overview

The form and layout of this article is determined by the necessary sequence of activities involved in the marketing planning process, combined with the specific strategic requirements of the non-profit sector. Thus, the article is divided into five principal sections:

1 developing a customer orientation;
2 strategic planning and organization;
3 developing and organizing resources;
4 designing the marketing mix;
5 controlling marketing strategies.

The discussion commences with the issue of the cultivation of a corporate customer orientation as this is the essential starting-point and necessary mind-set for the development of an effective marketing strategy.

The principal need of the non-profit sector in the 1990s is not so much for techniques to implement marketing, but for assistance in strategic planning. Many non-profit organizations face significant declines in their traditional sources of revenue, dramatic changes in their customer mix, and bold new competition. Therefore, they need help in rethinking where they are going and what broad strategies they should be using to get there. Consequently, strategic marketing planning occupies a prominent and very important position in the overall marketing process.

If an organization's marketing programme is to make an impact both internally and externally, it must have sufficient financial and personnel resources to do so. Thus, the acquisition, development, and organization of such resources are essential forerunners to the marketing planning process.

All marketing activities must be realistically costed and form part of a planned and timed programme of events. Each individual element of the marketing mix must form part of a coordinated and complementary programme.

Finally, evaluation and control is an essential part of a marketing programme as it provides ongoing feedback on the reactions of the targeted audience and responses to the marketing efforts of one's organization.

1 Developing a customer orientation

Growth and development of the non-profit sector

Marketing is no longer considered a radical approach to solving the problems of public and non-profit organizations. It is well into its maturity as an effective management tool. Economic and social changes and a proven rate of success have led to rapidly broadened and deepened applications. In the 1990s increased privatization of public programmes, renewed interest in voluntarism, growing appreciation of the potential role of marketing in international social programmes, and decreased support from traditional sources have converged to expand dramatically the importance of non-profit marketing.

Although there is now growing interest in voluntarism, non-profits are faced with two realities. First, they cannot rely on traditional sources of support. Second, as they turn increasingly to the marketplace for this support, they find other non-profits there scratching for the same subsistence. The consequence is that in the 1990s the greatest challenges facing non-profit marketers are competitive. Non-profit marketers must therefore learn not only to find and attract new markets, they must also learn how to accommodate their efforts to a flood of competitors. This means that marketing strategy must be the dominant concern of marketing managers in the 1990s.

Thus, our focus, is on approaches and techniques that can improve significantly the practice of marketing management in the non-profit sector on the part of existing and future managers. The emphasis is on the development of:

1 a proper philosophy of marketing;
2 a systematic approach to solving marketing problems;
3 an awareness of and ability to use the very latest concepts and techniques from the private sector.

The starting point for a consideration of strategic marketing in non-profit organizations is a clear perception and understanding of the unique environment in which they operate. Non-profit organizations can be defined legally, but it is more crucial to understand the organization's environment and the specific marketing activities which constitute its mission. The major factors affecting the organization's environment are whether:

1 it is donative or commercial;
2 its performance is subject to public scrutiny;
3 marketing is perceived to be desirable;
4 the organization is largely volunteer;
5 marketing is judged by non-marketing standards.

The missions of non-profit organizations differ depending on the type of demand they seek to influence and the type of activity they are engaged in. The organization's type of activity can be defined in terms of the key concept of exchange. Target customers are asked to 'pay' economic costs; sacrifice old ideas, values, and views of the world; sacrifice old patterns of behaviour; or sacrifice time and energy. In return, they can expect products, services, social or psychological benefits, or some combination of these. Although non-profits seek to influence exchanges of money for goods and services in the same way as for-profit organizations, what makes them unique is their concentration on exchanges involving non-monetary costs on the one hand and social and psychological benefits on the other. Influencing such exchanges requires different perspectives and modified techniques.

Developing a marketing mind-set

The starting point for an effective marketing strategy is the proper marketing mind-set. Historically, marketing has passed through four stages:

1 product orientation;
2 production orientation;
3 selling orientation;
4 customer orientation.

The first three stages are characterized by management putting the organization's own needs and desires at the centre of the strategic process. It is only when management realizes that it is the customer who truly determines the long-run success of any strategy that the non-profit firm can join the ranks of the sophisticated customer-centred marketing strategists typically found in the private sector.

Several clues can be used to identify a non-profit which is still mired in an organization-centred perspective: they see their offering as inherently desirable; they see the ignorance or lack of motivation of their customers as the major barrier to the organization's success; research plays a minor role in strategy formulation; marketing tends to be defined as synonymous with promotion; marketing specialists tend to be chosen for their product knowledge or for their familiarity with communications techniques; a 'one best' strategy is typically used in approaching the market; generic competition is typically ignored in the process.

Indoctrinating a non-profit organization from top to bottom with the proper marketing philosophy is not an easy task. The experience of those who have successfully achieved this objective suggest such strategies as: recognizing the limited understanding of others about what marketing really is; allowing for other pressures on the organization that may temporarily mandate non-customer-oriented approaches; picking visible, short-term projects for the first marketing applications; and recognizing that the introduction of a new philosophy is as much a political exercise as a matter of logic and persuasion. Allies must be sought and enemies deflected. Above all, it is essential to secure top management's commitment to the new way of thinking. Without it a true marketing orientation will not be achieved and customer-centred thrusts in one area will

Marketing in practice

inevitably run foul of organization-mindedness elsewhere.

2 Strategic planning and organization

The strategic marketing planning process

Once management has developed the appropriate marketing mind-set, it must determine the basic direction which the organization will take over the strategic planning horizon. The means by which this is carried out is called the strategic marketing planning process and involves four steps. These are:

1. Identification of the organization's overall mission, objectives and specific goals and an understanding of its basic culture.
2. Analysis of strengths and weaknesses.
3. Analysis of the organization's external environment and identification and understanding of: its key publics; its competitors; the macro-environment.
4. Development of a specific mission, goals and objectives for the marketing department based on the information provided in the earlier steps.

Decisions about the basic mission then lead naturally to the formulation of objectives for the planning period. These can include maximizing surpluses, revenues, usage or budgets. Alternatively, the organization can set objectives in terms of usage targeting, full or partial cost recovery, or satisfaction of its own staff. These objectives must be turned into detailed goals. These goals should give direction to the organization's staff and describe pathways to its future. They should offer benchmarks for measuring progress and provide triggers for contingency plans. Goals should be motivating for staff and should provide a basis for assessing future performance. Finally, goals should communicate the organization's direction to the outside world and indicate needs for developing marketing tracking information systems.

Understanding consumer behaviour

The ultimate objective of all marketing strategy and tactics is to influence target audience behaviour. Sometimes this necessitates changing ideas and thoughts by communicating facts or changing attitudes. However, since the ultimate goal is behaviour change and the proper philosophy is customer-centred, it is essential that all strategic planning starts with customer behaviour (see CONSUMER BEHAVIOUR).

The targets of the influence strategies of non-profit marketers can be extremely diverse. However, in all cases, the marketer's objective is to bring about exchanges wherein target audience members give up some costs in return for some expected positive consequences. Exchanges may involve two or multiple parties and be of fixed or continuing duration. The starting-point for understanding customer behaviour must be an understanding of the exchange relationship to be effected. Most importantly, that exchange must be seen from the target audience's perspective.

Exchanges in the non-profit sector are usually high involvement and often concern target audience behaviours where audience members have little or no experience. In such highly complex decision situations, customers begin by gathering information to form a choice set of alternative behaviours and to determine the criteria which will eventually be used to choose among them. The criteria, in turn, will be affected by the customer's own needs and wants and by the influences of significant others.

The next step in a typical process is for the customer to evaluate the chosen alternatives on the relevant criteria and to form attitudes and behavioural intentions towards each. These behavioural intentions will again be influenced by others. In a similar way, the eventual course of behaviour will be modified by situational factors such as the availability of funds or time. Finally, behaviour will result in experience and subsequent evaluations which will influence both attitudes and behavioural intentions in the future.

Marketers have several options in seeking to influence complex exchanges that are not turning out as a marketer wishes. The marketer can attempt to change the target customers' perceptions of the probable outcomes of choosing the marketer's alternative and/or the alternatives of competitors. Weightings on the criteria can be changed, although this is more difficult, or the customer can be pointed towards new or neglected favourable consequences.

With experience, customers proceed to simplify and then routinize behavioural patterns. In such cases, criteria are relatively fixed and alternatives are considerably narrowed. At the routine stage, behaviour may appear to occur with little conscious thought or even appear probabilistic. In cases of low-involvement decisions, relatively little cognition may be the norm, even when the customer has little experience.

Not all decisions of interest to non-profit marketers are individual. Where one is dealing with households or organizations, it is first necessary to understand the possible roles various members of the group can play. These roles include initiator, influencer, decider, transactor and exchanger. But even for such groups, a given decision may be much like that which occurs for individuals in that it may be complex, simplified or relatively routine.

Developing a core marketing strategy: segmenting the market

Once an organization has analysed its marketing environment and its internal strengths and weaknesses, it needs to develop a core marketing strategy. The core marketing strategy is the single most important element of the organization's strategic marketing planning process. It involves selecting key target segments, carefully positioning the organization, and then coordinating a set of marketing mix elements to implement the positioning to the target segments. The core marketing strategy must be customer-centred, visionary, differentiating, sustainable, easily communicated, motivating and flexible.

Four approaches to market segmentation are mass marketing, differentiated marketing, target marketing and niche marketing. Segmenting the market requires partitioning the market into subgroups which are mutually exclusive, exhaustive, measurable, accessible, substantial, and possessing differential responsiveness. Bases for segmentation are general or specific, objective or inferred. Many marketers think first of simple objective general measures such as age, income, geographic location and marital status. Over the years more complex general objective measures such as social class and family life-cycle and inferred general measures such as values and lifestyles have become more popular.

Specific bases for the segmentation apply to the specific product or service. They include objective measures such as user status, usage rate and loyalty. Inferred specific measures include beliefs, benefits and perceived sacrifices. Organization markets can be segmented by organization size, interest profile, buying process and degree of local autonomy.

Organizations can target their markets by undifferentiated, differentiated and concentrated marketing. Choices among these options depend on an organization's resources, its strengths and weaknesses, the relative homogeneity of the segments and competitive activity. The organization should focus on market segments that have intrinsic attractiveness and which it has a differential advantage in serving.

Developing a marketing strategy: positioning the organization

Organization positioning involves setting the organization apart from competitors to secure a lasting, defensible position in the marketplace. Positioning involves both establishing a unique set of products and services and making sure the target market perceives them (and the organization) as such. This calls for image measurement, two of the most common approaches to which are the semantic differential and direct attitude measurement.

Positioning has been said to be a largely creative exercise and might be achieved by a number of alternative strategies: building on present strengths; creating a niche; repositioning competitors. The positioning strategy chosen sets the parameters for the marketing mix and makes clear that it needs careful coordination (see POSTIONING).

In mature industries the organization must decide whether to pursue a market leader, market challenger, market follower or market nicher strategy. Market leaders have to decide further whether they will emphasize expanding the total market, protecting market share or expanding market share. Challengers must decide whom to challenge: the market leaders, other firms their own size, or firms smaller than themselves. Market followers must decide whether to follow closely, at a distance or selectively. The market nicher must decide on the basis of its niching strategy. The key idea in niching is specialization. The organization must have the required skills and resources to satisfy successfully the specialized requirements of the niche and must be able to defend its position from major competitors. In addition, the niche must be of sufficient size, offer growth potential and be of negligible interest to major competitors. For many multiple-niching is the most effective and safest strategy (see MARKETING STRATEGY; STRATEGIC MARKETING PLANNING).

The positioning strategy makes clear what the principal elements of the organization's marketing mix must be to round out the core marketing strategy. Once the core marketing strategy is set, the strategic marketing planning process is completed by developing an organization structure and management systems to carry out the marketing strategy. Next, specific tactics are established for each element of the marketing mix, and benchmarks set by which progress towards marketing goals is assessed. The final steps then involve implementation of the plan and careful assessment of its overall effects in preparation for the next round of strategic marketing planning.

Acquiring and using marketing information

Most non-profit organizations carry out much less marketing research than they should. This is a consequence of their limited budgets, relative newness in the marketing field and limited expertise. Increasing the amount of marketing research, therefore, calls for both education and motivation, showing non-profit executives what market research can do and how to do it properly as well as encouraging them to do it more often. Non-profits have accepted certain myths: they assume that marketing research should only be used for major decisions; that it involves big surveys and takes a long time; that it is always expensive; that it requires sophisticated researchers; and, when it is finished, that it is usually not read or used. But research using a diversity of techniques, many at low cost, can be extremely valuable to a wide range of decisions. Effective research requires that the non-profit organization have:

1 a marketing research mission;
2 a long-range strategy;
3 a budget;
4 an approach to carrying out individual projects;
5 an organization;
6 a system of evaluation and control.

Eventually, the sophisticated non-profit manager should plan to invest in a marketing information system. A marketing information system has four major sub-systems: an internal records system; a market intelligence system; a marketing research system; and an analytical marketing system (see INFORMATION TECHNOLOGY AND MARKETING; MARKETING RESEARCH).

Research can help managers by describing, explaining or predicting market characteristics. Most non-profit research is applied, and we would argue forcefully that no market research should be undertaken by a non-profit with a limited budget unless it leads directly into a decision. However, where one has a more generous budget, basic or methodological research might be undertaken. The applied nature of the research provides a good framework for decisions about budgets and for designing specific research projects.

The kinds of studies that should be used most heavily by mature non-profits include: determination of market characteristics; short- and long-range forecasting; trend studies; competitive offerings studies; measurements of market potentials; market share analyses; sales analyses.

There are several approaches to budgeting research, including historical increment, percentage of revenues, competitive matching, and affordable budgeting. A cost–benefit approach is preferable, however, because it explicitly takes account of the uses to which the study's results are to be put. The actual amount to be spent would then depend on the likely quality that the expenditure could achieve.

An applied orientation also recommends a 'backward' research design process. Here the research manager first looks to the decisions to be made using the research results and then works backward to design a study that would best inform such decisions. An important step would be deciding what report format would provide the most managerially useful information. The report form would then suggest the type of analysis needed which, in turn, would specify how the data are to be collected and processed.

Research can be quantitative or non-quantitative, high cost or low cost. Qualitative research, such as in-depth interviewing or focus groups, can be useful in identifying a problem, gathering background for later quantitative studies, interpreting past studies, pre-testing advertisements, product concepts, packaging and brochures, and generating ideas for new products, services and advertisements. Other techniques for keeping research costs low are experimentation, low-cost sampling designs, and use of secondary data and volunteer assistance (see QUALITATIVE RESEARCH IN MARKETING; QUANTITATIVE METHODS IN MARKETING).

Non-profit management of individual projects must involve careful attention in advance to potential biases, followed by careful evaluation of accomplishments or failures after the project has been completed. Such evaluation and control is especially essential as the organization develops a continuous programme of strategic research over several years.

Estimating and forecasting markets

Whether a non-profit should venture into a new market or whether it is getting a reasonable share of the existing market are questions that can be answered only after present and future market potential have been carefully determined. Therefore, in order to carry out their responsibilities for marketing planning, execution and control, non-profit marketing managers need measures of current and future market size. We define a market as the set of actual and potential consumers of a market offer. The marketer's task is to distinguish various levels of the market that is being investigated, such as the potential market, available market, qualified available market, target market and penetrated market.

The next step is to estimate the size of current demand. Total current demand can be estimated through the chain ratio method, which involves multiplying a base number by a succession of appropriate percentages to arrive at the defined market. Estimating actual industry sales requires identifying the relevant competitors and using some method of estimating the sales of each. Finally, the organization should compare its sales to industry sales to find whether its market share is improving or declining.

In the vast majority of markets, total market demand and specific organization demand are not stable from year to year, and good forecasting becomes a key factor in effective performance. This is particularly true for non-profits in which these problems are compounded by a lack of good historical data. In such cases, poor forecasting can lead to excess or insufficient personnel and supplies.

For estimating future demand, the organization can use one or any combination of six forecasting methods: buyer intentions surveys; intermediary estimates; expert estimates; market tests; time-series analysis; or statistical demand analysis. These methods vary in their appropriateness with the purpose of the forecast, the type of product, and the availability and reliability of data.

3 Developing and organizing resources

Fundraising

Fundraising is one of the major problems of non-profit organizations and as such is an essential component of all non-profit strategies. Organizations that raise money typically pass through three stages of marketing orientation in their thinking about how to carry out effective fundraising. Non-profit organizations have gradually been moving away from a product orientation to a sales orientation and then to a marketing orientation. A marketing orientation calls for carefully segmenting donor markets, measuring their giving potential, and assigning executive responsibility and resources to cultivate each market. Marketers assume that the act of giving is really an exchange process in which the giver also gets something that the organization can offer.

The first step in the fundraising process is to study the characteristics of each of the four major donor markets: individuals, foundations, corporations and government. Each donor market has its own giving motives and giving criteria, in addition to institutional and behavioural characteristics.

The second step is to organize the fundraising operation in such a way as to cover the different donor markets, organization services, marketing tools and geographical areas.

The third step is to develop sound goals and strategies to guide the fundraising effort. Goals are set on either an incremental basis, need basis or opportunity basis. Strategies require selection of target markets, positioning and coordination of a full marketing mix.

The fourth step is to develop a mix of fundraising tactics for the various donor groups. Fundraising strategy sets the overall parameters for the fundraising effort, which the development officer must fill with specific actions. Different tactics are effective in the four main segments considered by most fundraising organizations: the mass anonymous small-gift market, the members-and-their-friends market, the affluent citizens market and the wealthy donors market.

The fifth step is to conduct regular evaluations of fundraising results in order to improve the effectiveness of strategies. A macro-evaluation consists of analysing the percentage of the goal reached, the composition of the gifts, comparison with competitors and the expense/contributions ratio. Micro-evaluation consists of evaluating the performance of each individual fundraiser.

Acquiring volunteer and corporate support

Non-profits have limited resources – they lack adequate time, workforce, skills and finance to achieve the mission they or society have established for them. As a consequence, they must become experts at securing these additional staffing, skills and financial resources. This, too, is a marketing task. Others must be convinced that the benefits of helping exceed the costs.

Non-profits are unique in needing volunteers to help them accomplish their basic goals. Strategies for recruiting and managing volunteers must take into account changes in the environment. Today's volunteers cover a wider spectrum of people. They are more demanding and have different motivations than they had in the past. More importantly, some groups are challenging the basic value of volunteer service. These trends are putting pressure on non-profit organizations to improve their abilities to recruit volunteers and to manage them more effectively once they are recruited.

Recruiting volunteers is simply another marketing task and should proceed in a planned strategic way. The most important element of this is undoubtedly understanding the target audience. Thus, recruiting volunteers requires getting to know the target audiences through segmentation, prospect, motivational or image studies. The non-profit should also know how to retain volunteers. Studies of former volunteers and the satisfaction and dissatisfaction of present volunteers can be helpful in this regard. Problems that may emerge involve volunteers' expectations, training, supervision and feedback.

Managing volunteers can also be a problem if the organization is not truly professional in its approach. Many volunteers work hard and effectively with little incentive or guidance. Some hardly work at all under any circumstances. Most, however, respond best to being treated as professionals. This means matching responsibilities to skills, setting clear, achievable goals, and then holding volunteers to achieving them.

Non-profits must also secure important outside help in critical skills areas such as advertising and market research. Commercial agencies might be quite willing to help out for both altruistic and self-interested reasons. The Advertising Council is a prime example of such help. Business firms can also help by loaning space, staff, or equipment and by providing specific advice. Recently, affinity cards and cause-related marketing have been major sources of leverage from private sector firms. Faculty and students from local colleges and universities are another major source of assistance. An effective vehicle for coordinating all of these efforts is through a marketing advisory council.

Organizing for implementation

The role of marketing in a non-profit organization typically evolves through three stages. In the introductory stage there is resistance because organization members are opposed to marketing in principle or because they feel they are already doing it. If the organization wishes to proceed without a formal department, it can make use of outside resources. Should a formal marketing function be contemplated, a marketing committee should carefully consider what form it should take and how it should be introduced.

Marketing will clearly be a separate function during the growth phase. At this point, a major issue is whether marketing should be established as a line or a staff function. There may also be a question of what kind of background is appropriate for marketing positions. While it may be expedient initially to use someone with an advertising or journalism background, most organizations eventually turn to individuals with formal marketing training.

Initial projects for the marketing group should have a high economic impact yet be relatively inexpensive to implement. They should be completed in a short period of time and have high visibility if successful.

Once the mature phase is reached, marketing is well established. The organizational question at this stage is what form is best. The major alternatives are a functional orientation, a product/service orientation, a customer orientation, or some mixture. While the specific form chosen should depend on the experience, market conditions and mission of the organization, the customer-centred form most explicitly incorporates the philosophy emphasized by the authors. Even when the customer-centred form is not chosen, it is essential that the organization adopt such a perspective. This can be accomplished by careful hiring and training, explicit top management support, and a reward structure that reinforces customer-centred behaviour.

4 Designing the marketing mix

Planning and budgeting the marketing mix

There are three tasks involved in developing and choosing cost-effective marketing mixes:

1 Choosing between alternative products or programmes: here cost–benefit analysis is helpful. The programmes with the highest benefit–cost ratio are preferred. To calculate benefits and costs, monetary and quantitative measures are preferred, although ultimately non-quantifiable benefits should be taken into account.

2 Deciding on the marketing expenditure level: organizations decide on their expenditure level using one of five methods – affordable, percentage-of-sales, competitive-based, objective-and-task, response optimization.

3 Developing an optimal marketing mix of product, price, place and promotion: the optimal marketing mix can be set if the response function for each separate marketing mix element is known. The appropriate marketing mix varies with the type of buyer (households or organizations), the communication task, the stage of the offer life-cycle and the economic outlook.

Managing products and services

The mix of offerings in many ways defines an organization and establishes its position against competition. While, traditionally, offerings are categorized as products or services, a broader definition focuses on the fact that, from the customer's standpoint, an offer is simply a set of potential positive and negative consequences (benefits and costs). Consequences can be delivered by products or services or by the customer's own actions (e.g. dieting or exercising). Many non-profit organizations promote all three kinds of offerings. Three levels of the concept of the product offering can be distinguished:

1 The core product defines the needs that the product is really meeting.
2 The tangible product is the form in which the product exists. It is comprised of the product's features, styling, quality, packaging and brand names.
3 The augmented product consists of the tangible product and the additional services and benefits such as installation, after sales service, delivery, credit and warranty.

As competition increases, organizations must carefully manage the length width, and depth of their product offerings to compete.

Most non-profit organizations are primarily in the service business. Services can be delivered by people, places and objects or equipment. Services are especially difficult to manage because they are typically intangible, inseparable from the producer, variable in characteristics, perishable, and involve the customer in their production. Services marketers, therefore, must develop ways of making the intangible tangible, such as by using brand names and atmospherics.

Inseparability means that services are often synonymous with the people who deliver them. Service marketers must vigorously pursue internal marketing to ensure that key front-line people have a customer-first attitude and internal systems to empower front-line people to take the actions necessary to meet customer needs and wants.

Variability in service quality can be managed by good personnel selection and careful training along with as much routinization of the service itself as is possible without diminishing it. Perishability requires attention to service demand and supply which can be altered to some extent through creative pricing, marketing campaigns, adjustments of personnel and facilities, and sharing services with other organizations during peak periods. Finally, customer involvement in service delivery can enhance demand and satisfaction if marketers design services so that they are as easy as possible to use and 'train' customers themselves to be effective and appreciative co-producers.

Social marketing

Social marketing is one of the fastest growing sectors of non-profit marketing. Social marketing is the application of generic marketing to a specific class of problems where the object of the marketer is to change social behaviour primarily to benefit the target audience and the general society. Social marketing can seek to influence behaviour that is: low or high involvement; individual or group; one time or continuing. Continuing high involvement behaviour of groups or individuals is the most difficult to influence and often requires legal measures to achieve any major, long-term effect.

Good social marketers accord exchange a central role in their planning, are willing to change their offer (or consumer perceptions of it), seek to develop coordinated programmes, make extensive use of marketing research, segment their markets, have a 'bottom-line' orientation, are committed to planning and are willing to take reasoned risks. Social marketing differs from generic marketing in that it is subject to public scrutiny and extravagant expectations and often must seek to influence non-existent or negative demand of non-literate target audiences. It often deals with sensitive, hard-to-reach issues, invisible benefits or benefits to third parties that are difficult to portray and that are supposed to lead to long-term change. Social marketers, however, have less freedom to change their offerings, more limited budgets, and need to work with others who are often suspicious of marketing.

Social marketers make use of other disciplines, particularly social anthropology, education and mass communication and behavioural analysis. Marketing is accorded the coordinating role. While social marketing can now document a significant number of successes, social marketers have recently turned their attention to the problems of sustaining the behaviour they have attempted to influence and of institutionalizing the process of social marketing itself.

Developing and launching new offerings

To be successful in today's non-profit environment, organizations must learn to launch and develop new offerings effectively and efficiently. These may involve new or existing offerings in combination with new or existing markets. Extensions into new offerings or markets may involve undertakings that are similar to or dissimilar to present marketing programmes.

To be successful in developing new offerings, the organization must be both creative and systematic. The first stage of the process is to generate ideas for new offerings. This can involve careful searching of available information or attempts to create new ideas through a variety of artificial idea generation techniques. Once the ideas have been produced, it becomes necessary to screen them to eliminate those that do not meet established organization goals.

The next stage involves elaborating the idea into a concrete concept that can be subjected to formal testing. The concept, if successful, must then generate a specific marketing strategy which, in turn, must survive a rigorous business analysis. The final stages of the development process then involve specific offer development and market testing, followed by a carefully orchestrated and timed commercialization process. Critical path techniques may be used to

Strategic marketing for non-profit organizations

ensure that the project meets any crucial timing and cost objectives.

New offerings follow an S-shaped pattern over their life-cycle. They move through introductory, growth, maturity and decline stages. In the introductory and growth stages, the manager must first be concerned with securing trials of the new offering. Five customer groups may be identified on the basis of when they are likely to try the new innovation.

1. The *innovators* – this group will try almost anything that is new and are often considered odd by the rest of the population. They can usually be ignored by the new offer manager.
2. The *early adopters* – they cannot be ignored because they are the opinion leaders who influence the next large group.
3. The *early majority* – they follow the opinion leaders and establish the offer's success.
4. The *late majority* – this group pays less attention to others in making their decisions to adopt and must be convinced that the new offering is not a fad.
5. The *laggards* – this last group, can typically also be ignored because they are very tradition-oriented and very slow to try anything new.

There is a clear set of stages through which individuals typically go in adopting some new pattern of behaviour.

| Knowledge | Persuasion |
| Decision | Confirmation |

Innovations that have significant relative advantages over old approaches, which are compatible with the culture, are not complex, which can be communicated easily, and tried out before full adoption will diffuse faster than other innovations.

Managing perceived costs

Non-profit marketers seek to influence exchanges. Costs are the prices that customers perceive they must pay in order to participate. In a great many of the exchanges sought by a non-profit marketer, managing the perceived costs is often much more important than managing the benefits. Furthermore, the nominal money price tag on the exchange may be the least important of the perceived costs about which the consumer is concerned; in social behaviour exchanges there usually is no price tag at all. Thus, costs can be monetary, non-monetary or mixed. Non-monetary costs include psychic pain, the need to change old habits or ideas, expenditures of time and energy and dislocations of social arrangements.

The non-profit manager has a dual task in managing these costs. Some costs must be kept reasonably high to assure continuing revenues to the organization. Other costs must be reduced as much as possible to lower barriers to customer action. The problem in managing costs rather than a cost (singular) is to figure out which of many costs to reduce and how much to reduce them. To make these decisions the marketing manager needs to know relative responses. That is, for a given amount of the marketer's expenditure, which cost or costs should be impacted to yield the largest net gain in the number of exchanges.

In developing a strategy for monetary prices, the organization must first establish objectives. It could seek:

- surplus maximization;
- cost recovery;
- market size maximization;
- social equity;
- market disincentivization.

Its specific strategy to meet these objectives may be primarily cost-oriented, demand-oriented, or competition-oriented. Organizations that are planning to change an existing price should take into account the price elasticity of demand and perceptual factors in the target audience's response.

Managing the marketing channel

Exchanges require that offers be made at a particular time and in a particular place. Thus, the marketer's task is to create time and place utility for the customer. Often, this requires the services of other agencies, who can provide warehouse and transportation facilities and careful coordination of complex interacting systems. While channels may simply be means to facilitate consumers' time and place utilities, they have potential either significantly to augment or effectively to sabotage carefully designed marketing programmes.

To achieve an effective and efficient channel strategy, the non-profit marketer must

Marketing in practice

decide what quality of service to offer and whether marketing will be direct or indirect. Then the marketer must determine the length and breadth of the channel, recruit channel members and assign functions. Finally, the marketer should put in place systems for effective coordination and control among the channel members.

Coordination and control are best achieved by judicious use of the power potentially available to the non-profit marketer. This power can be based on:

1. rewards;
2. coercion;
3. law;
4. social norms;
5. expertise;
6. prestige;
7. control of critical information.

In general, power strategies that rely on simple compliance on the part of intermediaries (for example, those based on coercion or the law), are less effective in the long run than strategies that encourage intermediaries to identify with and internalize the non-profit organization's goals.

Formulating communications strategies

Every contact a non-profit has with its various publics, whether directly or indirectly, is an occasion for influence. Influencing behaviour is largely a matter of communication. It is a matter of informing target audiences about the alternatives for action, the positive consequences of choosing a particular one, and the motivations for acting (and continuing to act) in a particular way. These contacts may be carried out by many different departments or people using diverse vehicles ranging all the way from standard paid and unpaid media to package designs, corporate publicity releases, personal sales presentations and even promotional 'gimmicks' like shopping bags and T-shirts. For programmes to be effective they must be grounded in a clear understanding of influence processes.

Influence typically involves persuasion. This requires the preparation and transmittal of specific messages. Messages must be encoded by the marketer (the sender), communicated through media, and then decoded by the receiver. At each of these stages, considerable noise can be introduced into the communications process such that the accumulated effect of the received message is very different from what was intended. In general, the more parties involved in the communications system and the less control the marketer has over them, the greater the chance for distortion. Marketers use formal and informal feedback to track these effects. Where communication is face to face, feedback can be easily obtained. Where it is not, as in media campaigns, pre- and post-tests of message strategies must always be carried out. Six steps are involved in developing effective messages:

1. Communications objectives must be determined.
2. Messages must be generated. These can be rational, emotional, moral, or they can be generated from a rewards/situations framework.
3. Thought must be given to how these communications can overcome consumers' tendencies selectively to expose themselves or attend to messages in which they are interested. The style, tone, wording, order and format of the messages are critical to getting a message noticed.
4. Thought must be given to constructing the communications to overcome perceptual distortion, the tendency to add and reinterpret what is actually in the message based on the audience member's own experience, motives and biases.
5. A medium must be chosen to convey the message to achieve maximum impact. Often, in the non-profit sector, this means choosing a spokesperson. If a spokesperson is used, the marketer must assure that he/she is trustworthy and that the message is so clear that it cannot be distorted by a target audience.
6. The marketer must evaluate all the possible messages and select the ones that are most desirable, exclusive and believable.

The marketer must recognize that strategies to influence behaviour need not rely on persuasion – that is, in first changing cognitions in order to change behaviour. Other strategies, such as behaviour modification, can simply manipulate rewards. These strategies (such as shaping, the foot-in-the-door and door-in-the-face techniques) rely on a different model, in which it is assumed that changing behaviour without changing cognitions is an adequate goal in itself and that, once behaviour is changed, attitudes and other cognitions may also change.

Managing advertising and sales promotion

Advertising, non-personal communication conducted through paid media under clear sponsorship, must be planned strategically like any other element of the marketing mix. Objectives must be set, budgets determined, messages defined, media selected and a system of evaluation established (see ADVERTISING).

Advertising objectives must fit with prior decisions about the target market, offer positioning, and the nature of the remainder of the marketing mix. It must be clear what response is sought from the target audience. The ultimate response, of course, is behaviour. But in highly involving and infrequent decisions, behaviour is the end result of a consumer decision-making process. Typically, the response is movement forward through six stages:

1. awareness;
2. knowledge;
3. liking;
4. preference;
5. conviction;
6. action.

Budgets can be set by affordable, percent-of-sales or competitive methods, but the objective-and-task method is best. Budgets must be both set in total and allocated among different market segments, geographical areas, and time periods. Budgets must also be allocated across media categories and to specific media vehicles. Choices here depend on the marketer's objectives, the intended target audience, the planned message and media costs.

Managers must also decide on media timing. Advertisements should be scheduled seasonally or cyclically to parallel changes in audience interest. Within seasons, decisions must be made on short-run timing. The major options are to advertise continuously, intermittently or in preplanned bursts. These choices should be based on audience turnover, the frequency of the behaviour to be influenced and forgetting rates.

Evaluation schemes involve pre-testing and post-testing advertising. Pretesting can incorporate comprehension studies, mailed questionnaires, portfolio recall tests, physiological tests, focus group interviews or self-administered questionnaires. Post-tests are usually based on recall, recognition or some direct behavioural response such as enquiries or sales.

Sales promotion involves a wide range of incentives designed to have short-term effects on specific behaviours of consumers, intermediaries or the salesforce. Sales promotion incentives can impel immediate action but there must be careful planning of objectives, recipient, inclusiveness, form and amount and time of payment (see SALES PROMOTION).

Managing public relations

Public relations is a well-established function in profit and non-profit organizations. However, the more recent introduction of marketing into non-profit organizations has raised the question of marketing's relationship to public relations. The authors assume that public relations is a tool used to advance the marketing purposes of the organization. As such, careful long-range and annual planning of the public relations function cannot be emphasized strongly enough.

The task of public relations is to form, maintain, or change public attitudes towards the organization or its products and services. This process consists of seven steps:

1. identification of the organization's relevant publics;
2. measurement of the images and attitudes held by these publics;
3. establishment of image and attitude goals for the key publics;
4. development of cost-effective public relations strategies;
5. preparation for public relations crises;
6. careful choice of specific public relations tools, such as written material, audiovisual material, organization identity media, news, events, speeches and telephone information services;
7. implementation of actions and evaluation of results.

Just as elsewhere in the organization, a customer orientation is the best philosophy to apply to both long-term and short-term public relations strategies.

Managing personal selling

Many organizations utilize sales representatives and assign to them a pivotal role in the creation of sales. The high cost of the sales resource calls for effective sales management, consisting of six steps:

1. establishment of salesforce objectives;
2. design of salesforce strategy, structure, size and compensation;
3. recruitment and selection;
4. training;
5. supervision;
6. evaluation.

As an element of the marketing mix, the salesforce is capable of effectively achieving certain marketing objectives. The organization has to decide on the proper mix of the following sales activities: prospecting, communicating, selling and servicing, information gathering and allocating.

Given the salesforce objectives, the salesforce is then designed to answer the question of what strategy would be most effective (individual selling, team selling), what type of structure would work best (territorial-, product-, customer-structured), how large a salesforce is needed and how it should be compensated.

Sales representatives must be recruited and selected carefully to avoid the high costs of hiring the wrong persons. Their training should familiarize them with the organization's history, products and policies, customer and competitor characteristics and the art of selling. The art of selling itself calls for training in a seven-step sales process:

1. prospecting and qualifying;
2. preapproach;
3. approach;
4. presentation and demonstration;
5. handling objections;
6. closing;
7. follow-up.

The salesperson needs supervision and continuous encouragement. Periodically, the person's performance must be evaluated formally to help him/her do a better job.

5 Controlling marketing strategies

Marketing evaluation and control

The purpose of marketing control is to maximize the probability that the organization will achieve its short-run and long-run objectives in the marketplace. Non-profit managers must therefore have carefully designed measurement systems in place in order to track organizational performance and make appropriate adjustments. Marketing control systems are an intrinsic part of the marketing planning process since they permit such crucial and timely adjustments. There are two broad categories of control systems:

1. Strategic control systems monitor the organization's environment, competitors, publics, strengths and weaknesses and long-run performance.
2. Tactical control systems monitor day-to-day performance for the purposes of fine-tuning current marketing efforts.

Two types of tactical control systems are those that measure organization revenues and those that measure customer satisfaction. In non-profit organizations that have some sort of revenue objective, the three main control tools are: revenue analysis, market share analysis and marketing expenses-to-sales analysis. The first two measures assess effectiveness, the latter efficiency. For non-profits without sales or revenue outcomes, other measures are necessary.

Customer satisfaction should be a major objective of all non-profit organizations. Complaint tracking systems provide one way of assessing this satisfaction over time. However, complaint measures are typically biased both as to types of complaints and persons affected. Periodic direct surveys of customers do not suffer from these biases. They can measure satisfaction directly as problems, indirectly as derived dissatisfaction, or as a combined measure of performance and importance. Studies of problems can be particularly helpful if they also track performance of the organization's complaint-handling activities.

Equally important as a measurement of the effectiveness of the programme is that of efficiency. An effective control system therefore also ought to track costs and relate them to the returns from the programme elements on which they are spent. Where the returns are dollar revenues, this evaluation is usually referred to as profitability analysis. Where the returns involve other measures of satisfaction or attitude change, the evaluation is usually referred to by the more general term of cost–benefit analysis.

6 Summary

Many of the techniques and practices discussed in this article constitute the basic elements of the marketing planning process and are considered, in this instance, in relation to their application in the non-profit sector in order that they may be thoroughly explained and their application demonstrated. However, they are equally applicable to a wide variety of other marketing sectors, and as such, all of these topics are discussed in their own right in greater detail at other points in the Encyclopedia.

PHILIP KOTLER
KELLOGG GRADUATE SCHOOL OF MANAGEMENT
ALAN R. ANDREASEN
GEORGETOWN UNIVERSITY

Note

This article is a summary of *Strategic Marketing for Non-profit Organizations*, 4th edn, Englewood Cliffs, NJ: Prentice-Hall, and was prepared by Ms Claire Currie of the University of Strathclyde.

See also: ADVERTISING; CONSUMER BEHAVIOUR; INFORMATION TECHNOLOGY AND MARKETING; MARKETING RESEARCH; MARKETING STRATEGY; POSITIONING; QUALITATIVE RESEARCH IN MARKETING; QUANTITATIVE METHODS IN MARKETING; SALES PROMOTION; STRATEGIC MARKETING PLANNING; THE MARKETING MIX

Special topics

Total quality management (TQM)

1 Quality
2 Meeting the requirements – the marketing interface
3 Commitment and policy
4 Effective leadership
5 Quality systems in marketing, sales and customer service
6 Current issues and future developments

Overview

In any article on the management of quality, it is first necessary to define what is meant by quality and its related concepts. Juran, one of the pioneers of quality management, first summarized a basic rule which is applicable here:

> Any widespread discipline must identify and clarify the universal concepts which underlie its very existence as a discipline. In addition it must evolve and standardise the key words and phrases through which practitioners of the discipline can communicate with each other.
>
> (Juran 1988)

Quality is not a property which has an absolute meaning and the word quality is often used for several distinct purposes. For these reasons, the meaning of quality, in terms of its management, will be explored. The remainder of the article will be about how to manage in a total quality way. It is structured around five parts of a model for total quality management, or as it is now often known 'business excellence'.

The core of the model is the customer–supplier interfaces, both externally and internally, and the fact that at each interface there lie a number of processes. This sensitive core must be surrounded by commitment to quality through well supported policy and strategy, communication of the quality message through effective leadership, and recognition of the need to change the culture of most organizations to create total quality. These are the 'soft foundations' of TQM, to which must be added the systems, the tools and the teams – the 'hard management necessities'.

The interfaces between quality and marketing activities and systems are clearly established and the essential steps for the successful implementation of TQM are set out. These include the development of a mission statement, identification of critical success factors (CSFs) and critical processes, all linked through a cycle of continuous improvement.

The article concludes with a discussion of current issues and future developments, including the results of recent research linking TQM/business excellence and bottom-line results.

1 Quality

Quality is often used to signify excellence of a product or service – people talk about 'Rolls--Royce quality' and 'top quality'. In some engineering companies the word may be used to indicate that a piece of metal conforms to certain physical dimension characteristics, often set down in the form of a particularly 'tight' specification. In a hospital it might be used to indicate some sort of professionalism. If we are to define quality in a way that is useful in its management, then we must recognize the need to include in the assessment of quality the true requirements of the customer – the needs and expectations.

Quality, then, is simply meeting the customer requirements. There is another word that we should define properly – reliability. Quality and reliability are often used synonymously, sometimes in a totally confused way. Clearly, part of the acceptability of a product or service will depend on its ability to function satisfactorily over a period of time, and it is this aspect of performance which is given the name reliability. It is the ability of the product or service to continue to meet the customer requirements. Reliability ranks with quality in importance, since it is a key factor in many purchasing decisions where alternatives are being considered. Many of the general management issues related

Special topics

Figure 1 The quality chains

to achieving product or service quality are also applicable to reliability.

It is important to realize that the 'meeting the customer requirements' definition of quality is not restrictive to the functional characteristics of products or services. Anyone with children knows that the quality of some of the products they purchase is more associated with satisfaction in ownership than some functional property. This is also true of many items, from antiques to certain pieces of clothing. The requirements for status symbols account for the sale of some executive cars, certain bank accounts and charge cards, and even hospital beds. The requirements are of paramount importance in the assessment of the quality of any product or service.

By consistently meeting customer requirements we can move to a different plane of satisfaction – delighting the customer. There is no doubt that many organizations have so well addressed their capability to meet their customers' requirements time and time again, that this has created a reputation for excellence. But within the same organization there exists in each department, each office, even each household, a series of suppliers and customers. The typist is a supplier to the boss – are his requirements being met? Does he receive error-free typing set out as he wants it, when he wants it?

If so, then he has a quality typing service. Does the air hostess receive from her supplier in the airline the correct food trays in the right quantity?

Throughout and beyond all organizations, whether they are manufacturing concerns, banks, retail stores, universities, hospitals or hotels, there is a series of quality chains of customers and suppliers (Figure 1) which may be broken at any point by one person or one piece of equipment not meeting the requirements of the customer, internal or external. The interesting point is that this failure usually finds its way to the interface between the organization and its outside customers, and the people who operate at that interface – like the air hostess or a sales representative – usually experience the ramifications. The concept of internal and external customers/suppliers forms the core of total quality.

Quality has to be managed – it will not just happen. Clearly it must involve everyone in the process and be applied throughout the organization. Many people in the support functions of organizations never see, experience, or touch the products or services that their organizations purchase or provide, but they do handle or produce things like purchase orders or invoices. If every fourth invoice carries at least one error, what image of quality is transmitted?

Failure to meet the requirements in any part of a quality chain has a way of multiplying. Failure in one part of the system creates problems elsewhere, leading to yet more failure, more problems and so on. The price of quality is the continual examination of the requirements and ability to meet them. This alone will lead to a 'continuing improvement' philosophy. The benefits of making sure that the requirements are met at every stage, every time, are truly enormous in terms of increased competitiveness and market share, reduced costs, improved productivity and delivery performance, and the elimination of waste.

2 Meeting the requirements – the marketing interface

If quality is meeting the customer requirements then this has wide implications. The requirements may include availability, delivery, reliability, maintainability and cost effectiveness, among many other features. The first item on the list of things to do is to find out what the requirements are. If we are dealing with a customer–supplier relationship crossing two organizations, then the supplier must establish a 'marketing' activity charged with this task.

The marketers must, of course, understand not only the needs of the customer, but also the ability of their own organization to meet the demands. If my customer places a requirement on me to run 1500 metres in 4 minutes, then I know I am unable to meet this demand, unless something is done to improve my running performance. Of course, I may never be able to achieve this requirement.

Within organizations, between internal customers and suppliers, the transfer of information regarding requirements is frequently poor to totally absent. How many executives really bother to find out what are the requirements of their customers – their secretaries? Can their handwriting be read, do they leave clear instructions, do the secretaries always know where the boss is? Equally, do the secretaries establish what their bosses need – error-free typing, clear messages, a tidy office? These internal supplier–customer relationships are often the most difficult to manage in terms of establishing the requirements. To achieve quality throughout an organization, each person in the quality chain must interrogate every interface as follows:

Customers

- Who are my immediate customers?
- What are their true requirements?
- How do or can I find out what the requirements are?
- How can I measure my ability to meet the requirements?
- Do I have the necessary capability to meet the requirements? If not then what must change to improve the capability?
- Do I continually meet the requirements? If not then what prevents this from happening, when the capability exists?
- How do I monitor changes in the requirements?

Suppliers

- Who are my immediate suppliers?
- What are my true requirements?
- How do I communicate my requirements?
- Do my suppliers have the capability to measure and meet the requirements? How do I inform them of changes in the requirements?

The measurement of capability is extremely important if the quality chains are to be formed within and without an organization. Each person in the organization must also realize that the supplier's needs and expectations must be respected if the requirements are to be fully satisfied.

Managing process

As we have seen, quality chains can be traced right through the business or service processes used by any organization. A process is the transformation of a set of inputs, which can include actions, methods and operations, into desired outputs which satisfy the customer needs and expectations, in the form of products, information, services or – generally – results. Everything we do is a process, so in each area or function of an organization there will be many processes taking place. For example, a marketing group may be involved in market research processes, segmentation processes, advertising and promotion processes, pricing processes. Each process in each department or functional area can be analysed by an examination of the

Special topics

Figure 2 The systematic approach to process management

inputs and outputs. This will determine some of the actions necessary to improve quality.

The output from a process is that which is transferred to somewhere or to someone – the customer. Clearly to produce an output which meets the requirements of the customer, it is necessary to define, monitor and control the inputs to the process, which in turn may be supplied as output from an earlier process. At every supplier–customer interface then there resides a transformation process (Figure 2), and every single task throughout an organization must be viewed as a process in this way.

Improving the management of processes in many organizations involves replacing a strategy of detection of problems with one of prevention. This concentrates the attention on the front end of any process – the inputs – and changes the emphasis to making sure the inputs are capable of meeting the requirements of the process. This is a managerial responsibility.

These ideas apply to every transformation process, including those in marketing, which must be subject to the same scrutiny of the methods, people, skills, equipment and so on to make sure they are correct for the job. A person giving a sales presentation, whose overhead projector equipment will not focus correctly, or whose materials are not appropriate, will soon discover how difficult it is to provide a presentation which meets the requirements of the recipients.

In every organization there are some very large processes called key or critical or business processes. These are groups of smaller processes or activities which the organization must carry out especially well if its mission and objectives are to be achieved. Understanding these is crucial if the management of quality is to be integrated into the strategy for the organization.

Quality starts with marketing

The author has been asked on more than one occasion if TQM applies to marketing. The answer to the question is not remarkable – it starts there. The marketing function of an organization must take the lead in establishing the true requirements for the product or service. Having determined the need, marketing should define the market sector and demand. This will determine product or service features such as grade, price, quality, timing. Clearly a major hotel chain, before opening a new hotel or refurbishing an old one, will need to consider its location and accessibility, before deciding whether it will be predominantly a budget, first-class, business or family hotel.

Marketing will also need to establish customer requirements by reviewing the market needs, particularly in terms of unclear or unstated expectations or preconceived ideas held by customers. Marketing is responsible for identifying the key characteristics that determine the suitability of the product or service in the eyes of the customer. This may, of course, involve the use of market research techniques, data gathering, and analysis of customer complaints. If possible, quasi-quantitative methods should be employed giving proxy variables that can be used to grade the characteristics in importance, and to decide in which areas superiority over competitors exists. It is often useful to compare these findings with internal perceptions of quality.

Excellent communication between customers and suppliers is the key to total quality. This will eradicate the 'demanding nuisance/idiot' view of customers which pervades some organizations. Poor communications often occur in the supply chain between organizations, when neither party realizes how poor they are. Feedback from both customers and suppliers needs to be improved where dissatisfied customers and suppliers do not communicate their problems. In such cases, non-conformance of purchased products or services is often due to the customers' inability to communicate their requirements clearly. If these ideas are also used within an organization, then the internal supplier/customer interfaces or internal marketing will operate much more smoothly.

All efforts devoted to finding the nature and timing of the demand will be pointless if marketing fails to communicate the requirements promptly, clearly and accurately to the remainder of the organization. The marketing function should be capable of supplying the company with a formal statement or outline of the requirements for each product or service. This constitutes a preliminary set of specifications which can be used as the basis for service or product design. The information requirements include:

1. Characteristics of performance and reliability – these must make reference to the conditions of use and any environmental factors which will be important.
2. Aesthetic characteristics such as style, colour, smell, taste, feel.
3. Any obligatory regulations or standards that govern the nature of the product or service.

Marketing must also establish systems for feedback of customer information and reaction, which should be designed on a continuous monitoring basis. Any information pertinent to the product or service should be collected and collated, interpreted, analysed, and communicated to improve the response to customer experience and expectations. These same principles must also be applied inside the organization for continuous improvement at every transformation process interface to be achieved. If for example the marketing group in a company has problems recruiting the correct sort of staff, and the personnel department have not established mechanisms for gathering, analysing and responding to information on new employees, then frustration and conflict will replace communication and cooperation.

One aspect of the analysis of market demand that extends back into the organization is the review of market readiness of a new product or service. Items that clearly require some attention include assessment of:

- the suitability of the distribution and customer service systems;
- training of personnel in the field;
- availability of spare parts or support staff;
- evidence that the organization is capable of meeting customer requirements.

All organizations receive a wide range of information from customers through invoices, payments, requests for information, letters of complaints, responses to advertisements and promotion. An essential component of any system for the analysis of market demand is that these data are channelled quickly into the appropriate areas for action and, if necessary, response.

There are various techniques of market research that will not be described in detail here for they are well documented elsewhere in this encyclopedia. The number of methods and techniques for researching market demand is limited only by imagination and funds. The important point to stress is that the supplier, whether the internal individual or the external organization, keeps very close to the customer. Market research, coupled with analysis of complaints data, is an essential part of finding out what the requirements are and breaking out from the obsession with inward scrutiny which bedevils quality.

Quality in all functions

For an organization to be truly effective, each part of it must work properly together. Each part, each activity, each person in the organization affects and is in turn affected by others. Errors have a way of multiplying and failure to meet the requirements in one part or area creates problems elsewhere, leading to yet more errors, yet more problems and so on. The benefits of getting it right first time everywhere are enormous.

Everyone experiences – almost accepts – problems in working life. This causes people to spend a large part of their time on useless activities, correcting errors, looking for things, finding out why things are late, checking suspect information, rectifying and reworking, apologizing to customers for mistakes, poor quality and lateness. The list is endless and it is estimated that about one-third of our efforts are wasted in this way. In the service sector it can be much higher.

Quality, the way we have defined it as meeting the customer requirements, gives people in different functions of an organization a common language for improvement. It enables all the people, with different abilities and priorities, to communicate readily with one another, in pursuit of a common goal. When business and industry were local, the craftsman could manage more or less on his own. Business is now so complex and employs so many different specialist skills that everyone has to rely on the activities of others in doing their jobs.

Some of the most exciting applications of TQM have materialized from departments which could see little relevance when first introduced to the concepts. Following training, many examples from different departments of organizations show the use of the techniques. Sales staff can monitor and increase successful sales calls, office staff have used TQM methods to prevent errors in word-processing and improve inputting to computers, customer service people have monitored and reduced complaints, distribution have controlled lateness and disruption in deliveries.

It is worthy of mention that the first point of contact for some outside customers is the telephone operator, the security people at the gate, or the person in reception. Equally the paperwork and support services associated with the product, such as invoices and sales literature, must match the needs of the customer. Clearly TQM cannot be restricted to the production or operational areas without losing great opportunities to gain maximum benefit.

Managements that rely heavily on exhortation of the staff to 'do the right job right the first time', or 'accept that quality is your responsibility', will not only fail to achieve quality but will also create division and conflict. These calls for improvement infer that faults are caused only by the staff and that problems are departmental when, in fact, the opposite is true – most problems are interdepartmental. The involvement of all members of an organization is a requirement of company-wide quality improvement. It must involve everyone working together at every interface to achieve perfection. This can only happen if the top management is really committed to quality improvement.

The total quality management approach

What is total quality management? The answer to this question is often that it is something best left to the experts. But this response is avoiding the issue because it allows executives and managers to opt out, to avoid getting involved. Quality is too important to leave to the so-called quality professionals; it cannot be achieved on a company-wide basis if it is left to the experts. Equally dangerous, however, are the uninformed who try to follow their natural instincts because they 'know what quality is when they see it', or 'it's just basic common sense really'. This type of intuitive approach will lead to serious attitude problems which do no more than reflect the understanding and knowledge of quality that is present in an organization.

The organization that believes that the traditional quality-control techniques, and the way they have always been used, will resolve their quality problems is wrong. Employing more inspectors, tightening up standards, developing correction, repair and rework teams does not promote quality. Traditionally, quality has been regarded as the responsibility of the quality control (QC) department, and it has still not been recognized in some organizations that many quality problems originate in the marketing, sales, service and administration areas.

Total quality management is far more than shifting the responsibility of detection of problems from the customer to the producer. It requires a comprehensive approach which must first be recognized and then implemented if the rewards are to be realized. Today's business environment is such that managers must plan strategically to maintain a hold on market share, let alone increase it. We have known for years that consumers place a higher value on quality than on loyalty to home-based producers and that price is no longer the major determining factor in consumer choice. Price has been replaced by quality and this is true in industrial, service, hospitality, and many other markets.

If definitions are needed, TQM is an approach to improving the competitiveness, effectiveness and flexibility of a whole organization. Essentially it is a way of planning, organizing and understanding each activity, and involving each individual at each level. For an organization to be truly effective, each part of it must work properly together towards the same goals, recognizing that each person and each activity affects and in turn is affected by others. TQM is also a way of ridding people's lives of wasted effort by involving everyone in the processes of improvement, increasing the effectiveness of work so that results are achieved in less time.

The methods and techniques used in TQM can be applied throughout any organization. They are equally useful in marketing, manufacturing, public service, health care, education and the hospitality industries. TQM needs to gain ground rapidly and become a way of life in many organizations.

The impact of TQM on an organization is first to ensure that the management adopt a strategic overview of quality. The approach must focus on developing a problem prevention mentality, but it is easy to underestimate the effort that is required to change attitudes and approaches. Many people will need to undergo a complete change of mind-set to unscramble their intuition which rushes into the detection/inspection mode to solve quality problems – 'we have a quality problem, we had better check every letter – take two samples out of each sack – check every widget twice'.

The correct mind-set may be achieved by looking at the sorts of barriers that exist in key areas. Staff will need to be trained and shown how to reallocate their time and energy to studying their processes in teams, searching for causes of problems, and correcting the causes, not the symptoms, hopefully once and for all. This will require of management a positive, thrusting initiative to promote the right-first-time approach to work situations. Through process improvement teams, which will need to be set up, these actions will reduce naturally the inspection–rejection syndrome. If things are done correctly first time round, the usual problems that create the need for inspection for failure will disappear.

3 Commitment and policy

To be successful in promoting business efficiency and effectiveness, TQM must be truly organization-wide and it must start at the top with the chief executive, or equivalent. The most senior directors and management must all demonstrate that they are serious about quality. The middle management have a particularly important role to play. They must not only grasp the principles of TQM, but go on to explain them to the people for whom they are responsible, and ensure that their own commitment is communicated. Only then will TQM spread effectively throughout the organization. This level of management must also ensure that the efforts and achievements of their subordinates obtain the recognition, attention and reward that they deserve.

The chief executive of an organization must accept the responsibility for and commitment to a quality policy in which he/she must really believe. This commitment is part of a broad approach extending well beyond the accepted formalities of the quality assurance function. It creates responsibilities for a chain of quality interactions between the marketing, design, production/operations, purchasing, distribution and service functions. Within each and every department of the organization at all levels, starting at the top, basic changes of attitude will be required to operate TQM. If the owners or directors of the organization do not recognize and accept their responsibilities for the initiation and operation of TQM, then these changes will not happen. Controls, systems and techniques are very important in TQM, but they are not the primary requirement. It is more an attitude of mind, based on pride in the job and teamwork, and it requires total commitment from the management, which must then be extended to all employees at all levels and in all departments.

Senior management commitment must be obsessional, not lip service. It is possible to detect real commitment: it shows in the salesforce, on the shop floor, in the offices, in the hospital wards – at the point of operation. Going into organizations sporting poster campaigning for quality instead of belief, one is quickly able to detect the falseness. The people are told not to worry if quality problems arise, 'just do the best you can', 'the customer will never notice'. The contrast of an organization where total quality means something can be seen, heard, felt. Things happen at this operating interface as a result of real commitment. Material problems are corrected with suppliers, sales campaigns are properly organized, equipment difficulties are put right by improved maintenance programmes or replacement, people are trained, change takes place, partnerships are built, continuous improvement is achieved.

The quality policy
A sound quality policy, together with the organization and facilities to put it into effect, is a fundamental requirement if an organization is to begin to implement TQM. Every organization should develop and state its policy on quality, together with arrangements for its implementation. The contents of the policy should be made known to all employees. The preparation and implementation of a properly thought-out quality policy, together with continuous monitoring, makes for smoother production or service operation, minimizes errors and reduces waste.

Management must be dedicated to the ongoing improvement of quality, not simply a one-step improvement to an acceptable plateau. These ideas must be set out in a quality policy which requires top management to:

- establish an organization for quality;
- identify the customers' needs and perception of needs;
- assess the ability of the organization to meet these needs economically;
- ensure that bought-out materials and services reliably meet the required standards of performance and efficiency;
- concentrate on the prevention rather than detection philosophy;
- educate and train for quality improvement;
- review the quality management systems to maintain progress.

The quality policy must be publicized and understood at all levels of the organization.

4 Effective leadership

Some management teams have broken away from the traditional style of management, they have made a 'managerial breakthrough'. Their approach puts these organizations ahead of their competitors in the fight for sales, profits, resources, funding and jobs. Many service organizations are beginning to move in the same direction and the successful quality-market based strategy they are adopting depends very much on effective leadership.

Effective leadership starts with the chief executive's vision, capitalizing on market or service opportunities, continues through a strategy which will give the organization competitive advantage, and leads to business or service success. It goes on to embrace all of the beliefs and values held, the decisions taken and the plans made by anyone anywhere in the organization and the focusing of them into effective, value adding action.

Together effective leadership and total quality management result in the company or organization doing the right things, right first time. There are five main things which top management must do to be effective leaders.

Five key leadership points

The mission statement
Clear documented corporate beliefs must be developed and published – a mission statement. Executives must express values and beliefs through a clear vision of what they want their company or organization to be and its

objectives – what they specifically want to achieve in line with the basic beliefs. Together, they define what the company or organization is all about. The senior management team will need to spend some time away from the coalface to do this and develop their programme for implementation.

Clearly defined and properly communicated beliefs and objectives, which can be summarized in the form of a mission statement, are essential if the directors, managers and other employees are to work together as a winning team. The beliefs and objectives should address:

- The definition of the business – for example, the needs that are satisfied or the benefits provided.
- A commitment to effective leadership and quality.
- Target sectors and relationships with customers, and market or service position.
- The role or contribution of the company, organization or unit – for example, profit generator, service department, opportunity seeker.
- The distinctive competence – a brief statement which applies only to that organization, company or unit.
- Indications for future direction – a brief statement of the principal plans which would be considered.
- Commitment to monitoring performance against customers needs and expectations, and continuous improvement.

The mission statement and the broader beliefs and objectives may then be used to communicate an inspiring vision for the organization of where it is going. The top management must then show total commitment to it.

Develop clear and effective strategies and supporting plans for achieving the mission and objectives

The achievement of the company or service objectives requires the development of business or service strategies, including the strategic positioning in the marketplace. Plans can then be made for implementing the strategies. Such strategies and plans can be developed by senior managers alone, but there is likely to be more commitment to them if employee participation in their development and implementation is encouraged.

Identify the critical success factors and critical processes

The next step is the identification of the critical success factors (CSFs), a term used to mean the most important subgoals of a business or organization. CSFs are what must be accomplished for the mission to be achieved. The CSFs are followed by the key or critical or business processes for the organization – the activities which must be done particularly well for the CSFs to be achieved. (This process is described in some detail in Oakland 1998.)

Review the management structure

Defining the corporate objectives and strategies, CSFs and critical processes might make it necessary to review the organizational structure. Directors, managers and other employees can be fully functional only if an effective structure based on process management exists. This includes both the definition of responsibilities for the organization's management and the operational procedures they will use. These must be the agreed best ways of carrying out the critical process.

The review of the management structure should also include the establishment of process improvement teams throughout the organization.

Empowerment – encourage effective employee participation

For effective leadership, it is necessary for management to get very close to the employees. They must develop effective communications – up, down and across the organization, and take action on what is communicated. Good communications should be encouraged between all suppliers and customers.

The foundations of the TQM model

The vehicle for achieving effective leadership is total quality management. We have seen that it involves the entire organization, all the people and all the functions, including external organizations and suppliers. Several facets of TQM have been reviewed, including:

- Recognizing customers and discovering their needs.

Special topics

Figure 3 Deming's Continuous Improvement cycle
Source: Deming (1982)

- Setting standards that are consistent with customer requirements.
- Controlling processes, including systems, and improving their capability.
- Management's responsibility for setting the guiding philosophy and quality policy, providing motivation through leadership and equipping people to achieve quality.
- Empowerment of people at all levels in the organization to act for quality improvement.

The task of implementing TQM can be daunting and the chief executive and directors faced with it may become confused and irritated by the proliferation of theories and packages. A simplification is required. The *core* of TQM must be the customer–supplier interfaces, both internally and externally, and the fact that, at each interface, there are processes which convert inputs to outputs. Clearly, there must be commitment to building-in quality through management of the inputs and processes.

How can senior managers and directors be helped in their understanding of what needs to be done to become committed to quality and implement the vision? Some American and Japanese quality gurus have each set down a number of points or absolutes – words of wisdom in management and leadership – and many organizations are using these to establish a policy based on quality. These have been distilled down and modified here to ten points for senior management to adopt.

Ten points for senior management

1 The organization needs long-term commitment to constant improvement.

There must be a constancy of purpose, and commitment to it must start from the top. The quality improvement process must be planned on a truly organization-wide basis (i.e. it must embrace all locations and departments and must include customers, suppliers, and subcontractors). It cannot start in one department in the hope that the programme will spread from there.

The place to start the quality process is in the boardroom – leadership must be by example. Then progressively expand it to embrace all parts of the organization. It is wise to avoid the 'blitz' approach to TQM implementation, which can lead to a lot of hype but no real changes in behaviour.

2 Adopt the philosophy of zero errors/defects to change the culture to right-first-time.

This must be based on a thorough understanding of the customers' needs and expectations and teamwork, developed through employee participation and rigorous application of Deming's Plan-Do-Act cycle (Figure 3).

3. Train the people to understand the customer–supplier relationships.

   Again the commitment to customer needs must start from the top, with the chairman or chief executive. Without that, time and effort will be wasted. Customer orientation must then be achieved for each and every employee, directors and managers. The concept of internal customers and suppliers must be thoroughly understood and used.

4. Do not buy products or services on price alone – look at the total cost.

   Demand continuous improvement in everything, including suppliers. This will bring about improvements in product, service and failure rates.

   Continuously improve the product or the service provided externally, so that the total costs of doing business are reduced.

5. Recognize that the improvement of the systems needs to be managed.

   Defining the performance standards expected and the systems to achieve them is a managerial responsibility. The rule has to be that the systems will be in line with the shared needs and expectations and will be part of the continuous improvement process.

6. Adopt modern methods of supervision and training – eliminate fear.

   It is all too easy to criticize mistakes, but it often seems difficult to praise efforts and achievements. Recognize and publicize efforts and achievements and provide the right sort of facilitation and supervision.

7. Eliminate barriers between departments by managing the process – improve communications and teamwork.

   Barriers are often created by 'silo management', in which departments are treated like containers which are separate from one another. The customers are not interested in departments – they stand on the outside of the organization and see slices through it – they see the processes. It is necessary to build teams and improve communications around the processes.

8. Eliminate:
   - arbitrary goals without methods;
   - all standards based only on numbers;
   - barriers to pride of workmanship;
   - fiction, get facts by using the correct tools.

   At all times it is essential to know how well you are doing in terms of satisfying the customers' needs and expectations. Help every single employee to know how they will achieve the goals and how well they are doing.

9. Constantly educate and retrain – develop the experts in the business.

   The experts in any business are the people who do the job every day of their lives. The energy that lies within them can be released into the organization through education, training, encouragement and involvement.

10. Develop a systematic approach to manage the implementation of TQM.

    TQM should not be regarded as a woolly-minded approach to running an organization. It requires a carefully planned and fully integrated strategy, derived from the mission. By these means it will help any organization to realize its vision.

Summary of ten points for senior management

- Identify *Customer/Supplier* relationships
- Manage *Processes*
- Change the *Culture*
- Improve *Communication*
- Show *Commitment*

These form the basis of the first part of a model for TQM – the 'soft' outcomes of TQM (see Figure 4). The process core must be surrounded, however, by some 'hard' management necessities:

- *Systems* (based on a good international standard).
- *Tools* (for analysis, correlations, and predictions for action for continuous improvement to be taken).
- *Teams* (councils, quality improvement teams, quality circles, corrective action teams).

The model now provides a multi-dimensional TQM 'vision' against which a particular company's status can be examined, or against which a particular approach to TQM implementation may be compared and weaknesses highlighted.

Figure 4 Total quality management model

It is difficult to draw in only two dimensions, but Figure 4 is an attempt to represent the major features of the model.

5 Quality systems in marketing, sales and customer service

Historically, formal quality systems and procedures were confined to the manufacturing aspects of industry, but in recent years they have extended rapidly into the services sector and functions as organizations seek to enhance their reputations for supplying quality products and services. Against a background of escalating international competition and customer expectations, more and more customers are demanding objective evidence of quality and consistency from their suppliers. This is increasingly taking the form of independent, third party confirmation and certification to recognized standards, in all areas of the business.

The International Standard ISO9000 series on Quality Systems (BSEN ISO in the UK), clearly has its origins in manufacturing industry, yet the principles it embodies are common to services and to the marketing function. Having said that, however, it must be recognized that the interpretation of the standard for these areas is not so simple. It is for this reason that various Guidance Notes have been generated for various sectors, and a separate standard for Marketing Quality Assurance has been written.

Marketing Quality Assurance (MQA)

MQA is a third party certification organization which specializes in providing assessment services to organizations wishing to develop quality systems for their marketing, sales, and customer service activities; in assessing companies in the services sector to the ISO9000 series of Quality System Standards; and in developing third party certification guidelines for specific service areas, such as public relations.

MQA has produced a Quality Assurance Specification for marketing, sales and customer assurance. This is an associated document to the ISO9000 series, and MQA offers registration to ISO9001, BSEN ISO9001 for an organization's marketing, sales and customer service activities. MQA awards a certificate of excellence and the right to use the MQA mark if companies achieve the required standard. The aim is to signal to customers, competitors and employees that the certified organization is one that has achieved independent recognition that it has marketing excellences.

The MQA Specification deals with systems that apply specifically to marketing, sales and customer assurance. It defines a marketing audit, marketing strategy, customer assurance, code of conduct, and a marketing and sales quality system. The requirements of the specification are categorized under 15 areas, which clearly relate to the ISO9000 series:

- quality policy;
- business plans;
- organization;
- management representatives;
- management review;
- quality system;
- marketing and sales plans;
- code of conduct;
- marketing and sales operations;
- customer assurance;
- purchasing;
- resources, personnel, training, organization structure;
- controls and procedures;
- records;
- quality audits;

Briefly, the specification states that business plans must exist and marketing inputs should have contributed to their development. There should be clearly defined processes for the review of market needs which should identify and reassess customer needs and preference. The marketing and sales plans must relate to the business plans, and be understood and agreed by the contributing departments. The requirements under marketing and sales operations call for best practice in all the operational areas, including product or service development, promotion, pricing, selling and distribution. All aspects of customer assurance should be covered to inspire confidence that the stated or implied needs are being satisfied. The specification sets down requirements, under resources, personnel, training and organization structure, for well-trained experienced staff who are responsive to the needs of the marketplace. All this and the more traditional areas are to be in a documented quality system which demonstrates the organization's capabilities in meeting customer requirements.

Figure 5 The Business Excellence Model

Special topics

The business excellence model and self-assessment

Organizations everywhere are under constant pressure to improve their business performance, measure themselves against world class standards and focus their efforts on the customer. To help in this process, many are turning to quality models such as the European Foundation for Quality Management's Business Excellence Model – promoted in the UK by the British Quality Foundation.

As Figure 5 illustrates, the Business Excellence Model includes nine main categories which address areas such as customer satisfaction, people satisfaction and a favourable impact on society achieved through leadership driving policy and strategy, people management, resources and processes, leading ultimately to excellence in business results – both financial and non-financial. Financial measures may include profit, cashflow, sales, value added, working capital, liquidity; non-financial targets may include market share, reduction of non-quality costs, service-level achievements, time to breakeven on new product development, product delivery time, batch processing time and inventory turnover time.

'Self-assessment' to the Business Excellence Model involves an organization in the regular and systematic review of its enablers and results, allowing the identification of strengths and areas for improvement.

Various quality awards have been set up to encourage quality management adoption and provide a platform for measurement against world-class standards. The Malcolm Baldrige National Quality Award was launched in 1987 to encourage United States companies to use total quality management to gain competitive advantage. The award criteria are used to formally examine, through an assessment procedure, companies that apply for the award. The European Quality Award (EQA), which was first awarded in 1992, has many similarities to the Baldrige framework and has stimulated a similar interest in self-assessment. Since 1992, tens of thousands of copies of the guide to self-assessment based on the Business Excellence Model, published by the EFQM, have been distributed in Europe. (See 'EFQM Self-Assessment, Guidelines for Companies, for the latest version). Similarly, the UK Quality Award, now for 'Business Excellence', through the efforts of the British Quality Foundation (BQF), has led to a surge of interest in sound business planning and self-assessment with over 10,000 guides to self-assessment sold in the UK in recent years.

Design, quality and the business excellence model

Design, like quality, permeates many areas of an organization at both the operational and strategic level. While functions like graphics or styling may be largely the preserve of design professionals, design decisions about new products are likely to involve just as many non-designers – from R&D to finance to marketing. The Business Excellence Model provides a framework for just such cross-functional integration. In line with this, it has been widely recognized for many years that success in an organization is more likely to occur when the design, marketing and production functions are well interfaced and coordinated. It is widely recognized that an organization's design capability and quality of product and/or service are inextricably linked. Quality must be 'designed in' to the new product and success and competitive advantage can be sustained only when the design activity is well understood and integrated across the organization's different functions.

6 Current issues and future developments

We often hear expressions such as 'TQM is a journey without a destination', which highlight that the business quest for progress and advancement is never-ending. This sometimes creates, however, a dichotomous situation insofar as managing business organizations is concerned. Many managers, while not denying the need for constant improvements, are presented with a very difficult situation – they are also expected to show consistent results in the marketplace in the short term. Many managers find it difficult to reconcile the short-term benefits with the long-term opportunities for improvement.

Every book, chapter and article on TQM talks about the need for management commitment. Management commitment is, of course, essential for the introduction of TQM, but it may not be enough to generate success in the marketplace. Many failures in TQM implementation have been attributed to factors such as: the executive promotional ladder; executive bonuses and the interest in short-term results; shareholder pressures.

Senior management commitment to TQM is certainly required to overcome the first two factors, but commitment of all employees and their willingness to combat waste, reduce costs and carry out consistent improvement is essential. Commitment of shareholders and financial institutions to taking an interest in longer-term business performance and sustainability, and commitment of governments to preparing the right climate for business, the right incentives and adequate protections, are also crucial for results to be consistently achieved.

The question in relation to TQM and business performance is, therefore, twofold:

1 What are the short-term benefits in enhancing profit levels and initiating growth?
2 What are the long-term benefits through ensuring sustainability and achieving repeated superior performance standards?

In order that TQM can deliver the right answers to these questions, its implementation has to be carried out in a very systematic way, without any wavering in commitment, and without hesitation and deferral in the decision-making process. The following questions must be continually addressed if TQM or business excellence is to lead to pay-offs:

- Does the organization really understand its purpose?
- Is there a clear vision/mission and clear goals?
- Have the vision and TQM plan been communicated effectively?
- Have the goals been deployed effectively?
- Have the people been trained, educated, motivated and really empowered to carry out the improvement efforts?
- Is the organization really customer focused and does it truly understand its customer requirements?
- Does it understand and appreciate what takes place in the marketplace?
- Are systems, tools and teams in place and used in 'anger'?
- Do improvement efforts get measured?

We hear comments such as: 'TQM has failed to help businesses perform in the marketplace'. But what about the question: 'Did businesses fail to introduce TQM effectively, and as such fail to perform in the market?'

Many poor business performances can be traced back to poor implementation of TQM. In many instances, TQM implementation has lacked strategic focus and was introduced as a bolt-on to unchanged business culture. The link between TQM and business performance can only be established if the above questions have been answered in the affirmative.

How does TQM drive business performance?

TQM is a business tool. As such it is about achievements and results. Results are the yardsticks of achievement and progress and, if they are not captured on a regular basis, it becomes very difficult to maintain momentum, commitment and, more importantly, the motivation and desire to achieve higher standards.

Several studies have been carried out, by the author and his colleagues, on companies known to be practising TQM and business excellence. The research has focused on externally reported information which is readily available and recorded continuously which enabled the examination of patterns of behaviour and performance. One of the questions concerning the design of the research was when is it reasonable to expect TQM to start to deliver benefits? From experience and the multitude of case studies of companies that have implemented TQM, it was decided that if TQM is introduced with a sound plan, a clear mission and tangible goals and if the whole process has been deployed in the right way, then it is reasonable to expect benefits to be derived over a period of five years. The sample of companies was chosen carefully, based on good knowledge and understanding of the specific TQM approaches adopted by each individual company and their performance in various award applications.

Seven performance indicators were used for the analysis. The mean for each company was calculated over five years' results for each performance indicator. To establish the extent of enhancements or otherwise, performance under each indicator for each company was compared to the industry median. The results indicate that most of the companies tended to exhibit positive trends in performance, in comparison with their industry average:

- *Profit margin* – the companies studied show healthier profit margins than their industry median.
- *Return on total assets* – the companies show better returns on investment than their industry median.
- *Turnover per employee* – the companies show sales (per employee) higher than their industry median.
- *Profit per employee* – the companies show positive quantums in comparison with their industry median.
- *Total assets per employee* – the companies have at their disposal greater asset value per employee than their industry median.
- *Fixed asset trend* – the companies show a positive pattern of long-term investment in comparison to their respective industry median.
- *Average remuneration* – in the companies studied is higher than their industry median.

The seven indicators chosen for carrying out the various comparisons reflect business performance, both in short-term and long-term perspectives. They also contain 'softer' measures that are people related, such as employee remuneration. In combination, the indicators show a consistent pattern of positiveness in performance between the chosen companies and their industry median.

These patterns of positive business performance suggest that there is a positive association between TQM introduction and bottom-line results. Although the study does not conclude by suggesting direct causation, it is in line with what studies in the USA and Japan have highlighted. Clearly TQM can have a direct impact on bottom-line results, provided its implementation is properly managed and provided that there is strong commitment to sustaining the continuous effort of quality improvement that benefits the end customer.

Developing TQM and business excellence

The above studies do not suggest that TQM leads directly to improvements in bottom-line results. TQM offers companies the opportunity to carry out improvements and presents an opportunity to get closer to customers. It is only a licence to practice. Companies must, of course, have the right strategies in place, the right products and services, the right commitment, and the right investment plans. Senior managers in many organizations recognize the need for change to deal with increasing competitiveness, but lack an understanding of how to implement the changes. Successful organizations in the future will see that change is effected, not by focusing on formal structures and systems, but by aligning process management teams. This starts with writing the mission statement, analysis of the CSFs and understanding the critical or key processes.

Some of the obstacles to TQM implementation and resistance to change still need to be overcome through education, communication, participation, facilitation, and support. The 'blitz' or rapid change approach will be rejected in favour of a slow, planned purposeful one, engaging the top management and using bottom-up involvement.

Successful management teams will achieve process alignment through a self-reinforcing cycle of commitment, communication and culture change. The main steps in this process will always be: gain commitment to change, develop a shared mission or vision of the business or desired change, and define the measurable objectives. The remaining steps will involve developing the mission, really understanding the key or critical processes, gaining ownership, breaking down the critical processes into subprocesses, activities and tasks, and monitoring and adjusting process alignment in response to difficulties in the change process.

Making quality happen requires not only commitment but a competence in the mechanics of TQM/business excellence. Crucial next steps will involve development of the appropriate organization structures, collecting information including costs for prioritizing teamwork, quality systems, training and self-assessment.

Managers must really understand and pursue never-ending improvement. This will involve planning and operating processes, providing inputs, evaluating outputs, examining performance, and modifying processes and their inputs. The three basic principles of continuous improvement – focus on the customer, understand the process, involve the people – will form the core of TQM in the future.

JOHN S. OAKLAND
OAKLAND CONSULTING PLC

Further reading

(References cited in the text marked *)

Caulcutt, Roland (1995) *Achieving Quality Improvement – A Practical Guide*, Chapman & Hall.
* Deming, W. Edwards (1982) *Out of the Crisis*, Cambridge, MA: MIT.
  Deming, W. Edwards (1993) *The New Economics – for Industry, Government, Education*, Massachusetts Institute of Technology.
* European Foundation for Quality Management (1998) *Self-Assessment – based on the European Model for Business Excellence*, EFQM.
  Hammer, Michael and Champy, James (1993) *Re-engineering the Corporation – A Manifesto for Business Revolution*, Nicholas Brearley Publishing.
  Joiner, Brian L. (1994) *Fourth Generation Management – the New Business Consciousness*, McGraw-Hill.
* Juran, J.M. (ed.) (1988) *Quality Control Handbook*, New York: McGraw-Hill.
  Oakland, John S. (1995) *Total Quality Management – Text with Cases* (Guest case study author, Les Porter) Butterworth-Heinemann.
* Oakland, John S. (1996) *Statistical Process Control – A Practical Guide*, 3rd edn, Butterworth-Heinemann.
  Porter, Les J. and Tanner, Steve J. (1996) *Assessing Business Excellence*, Butterworth-Heinemann.
  Senge, Peter M. (1990) *The Fifth Discipline – The Art and Practice of the Learning Organisation*, Century Business.
  Senge, Peter M. et al. (1994/5) *The Fifth Discipline Fieldbook – Strategies and Tools for Building a Learning Organisation*, Nicholas Brearley Publishing.
  Zairi, Mohamed (1996) *Benchmarking – for Best Practice*, Butterworth-Heinemann.
  Zairi, Mohamed (1994) *Measuring Performance for Business Results*, Chapman and Hall.

See also: ADVERTISING; MARKETING RESEARCH; QUALITATIVE RESEARCH IN MARKETING; QUANTITATIVE METHODS IN MARKETING; SALES PROMOTION

Green marketing

1. Environmental protection as a challenge to market-oriented management
2. Approaches to green marketing and prerequisites for its success
3. Situation analysis as a starting point
4. Strategic planning in green marketing
5. Designing an ecologically oriented marketing mix
6. The implementation of green marketing

Overview

During the 1980s there was a growing realization that management was going to have organize to take into account the need for environmental protection. In some cases there would be a legal requirement, but it also became clear that an eco-sensitive approach might be consumer driven.

This article considers how environmental protection challenges the market-oriented approach. It then goes on to discuss how green marketing in itself can be successful and how it can be built into the marketing mix.

1 Environmental protection as a challenge to market-oriented management

Especially during the 1980s people recognized the need to adapt management in such a way as to take account of the problems posed by environmental protection. This marked the beginning of a far-reaching process of evolution in theory and practice. Environmental issues get into the headlines and on to the political agendas of many nations of the world. As Figure 1 shows, a poll of 16 countries (4600 interviews) found that more than four-fifths of respondents identified with the statement: 'I am very worried about the state of the environment'. More than half concurred that 'pollution must be reduced even if it means slower growth'. So environmental issues extend more and more into the mainstream in the consumer's mind.

There is now a growing tendency to stress the need to anchor pollution control as a guiding principle in enterprises (Post and Altman 1992; Schmidheiny 1992; Fischer and Schot 1993; Meffert and Kirchgeorg 1998; Steger 1993; Welford and Gouldson 1993; Winter 1998); and to view it as a task that must be adjusted to every level of functional responsibility.

In this context, attention is focused on two aspects of market-oriented environmental management. On the one hand, commercially oriented marketing often receives a great deal of criticism because it paved the way for our throwaway consumer society. A reorientation in marketing is regarded as an essential prerequisite for transforming the consumer society into a 'sustainable society'. On the other hand, the approaches developed by marketing are considered to be valuable instruments that might be used to accelerate the necessary environmentally oriented change in society. Green marketing or environmental marketing is expected to change the customers' outlook, provide a new direction for competition, and gain market acceptance for innovative environmental solutions.

Within the framework of environment-conscious management, green or environmental marketing has a duty to ensure that environmental pollution is avoided or reduced at every stage of market-oriented activity (planning, coordination, implementation and inspection). The aim is to achieve corporate objectives by permanently satisfying the needs of present or potential clients while exploiting competitive advantages and safeguarding social legitimacy (Meffert and Kirchgeorg 1998).

In the long run ecologically and economically ineffective partial solutions could jeopardize the credibility and legitimacy of the enterprise in the market as well as in the community at large. To avoid this, it is essential that marketing management should develop a specific conception of green marketing. The planning procedure involves the following five steps:

I am very worried about the state of the environment.

[Bar chart showing percentages by country — Strongly agree (upper) / Moderately agree (lower):
- United States: 51 / 37
- Canada: 57 / 30
- Mexico: 66 / 19
- France: 34 / 46
- Britain: 60 / 26
- Germany: 73 / 18
- Spain: 83 / 14
- Italy: 71 / 21
- Russia: 76 / 23
- India: 66 / 23
- Australia: 54 / 28
- Hong Kong: 23 / 62
- South Korea: 45 / 47
- Singapore: 17 / 29
- Taiwan: 35 / 48
- Japan: 53 / 37]

Total average country basis
54% Strongly agree
32% Moderately agree
10% Moderately disagree
3% Strongly disagree

■ Moderately agree
□ Strongly agree

Angus Reid World Poll of 16 countries, 4,600 interviews, in 1992.
Sample sizes differed; 8% margin of error for each country.

Figure 1 Worldwide environmental concern
Source: CNN/Angus Reid World Gorup Poll (1992) cited in Ottmann (1992)

1. Analysing relevant environmental problems that affect the enterprise at present or are likely to affect it at some point in the future. This analysis entails an assessment of opportunities and risks as well as advantages and disadvantages for marketing (informational aspect).
2. Broadening the enterprise's philosophy and objectives. This entails the formulation of environmental principles and goals (philosophical and teleological aspect).
3. Generating and evaluating options. This is to identify target groups and to find the right positioning and competitive strategy for green marketing concepts.
4. Modifying and integrating the utilization of marketing instruments in order to put green marketing principles into practice in horizontal and vertical competition (action and coordination aspect).
5. Supervising and regulating environment-oriented marketing activities as part of an ecological supervision scheme (control aspect).

Product-related environmental benefits as... / Costs	Individual benefits	Social benefits
Price and/or opportunity costs lower than or on a par with those of substitutes	Classical starting points of environmental marketing (I) Securing competitive advantages	Socially oriented image (II) Competitive and environmental advantages
Price and/or opportunity costs higher than those of substitutes	+ Rationalization (III) + Differentiation Eliminating competitive disadvantages	• Marketing for ecology • Instrument of environmental policy (e.g. taxes and fiscal charges) (IV)

Figure 2 Starting points for environmental marketing and prerequisites for its success

2 Approaches to green marketing and prerequisites for its success

Let us begin by considering to what extent green marketing can be implemented by a firm with some chances of success. The feasibility of such an undertaking will depend on the prevailing circumstances under which the firm must manage. As shown in Figure 2, we can distinguish four typical situations in which decisions are taken, and in which green marketing has to prove its worth (Kaas 1992; Meffert 1993).

To begin with we draw a distinction on the basis of whether an environmental benefit provides a surplus for the customer or whether the decision to buy an environment friendly product benefits the community as a whole (social benefit) (Porter and van der Linde 1995). Furthermore, we may make finer distinctions by considering whether environmental advantages are to be gained at a lower, identical or higher price; or at higher costs than traditional products. In addition to the price that must be paid one also has to take account of opportunity costs related to the purchase of environment oriented products (e.g. more time spent and more work involved in collecting information).

Provided that the consumer as an individual derives a benefit from the offer of environment friendly products, and that these goods provide better value than the traditional alternatives (field I, environmental advantages automatically result in competitive advantages, as when energy-saving electrical appliances are offered for sale at very reasonable prices. In addition to finding such solutions, the main task of green marketing must be to guarantee competitive advantage. If what benefits the environment provides a social benefit and not a surplus for the individual consumer but environment friendly products are cheaper than their substitutes, an entrepreneur who applies the principles of green marketing (field II) should have no difficulty in inducing the consumer to buy ecologically oriented products. All the entrepreneur has to do is to highlight the economic advantages of these goods or exploit their prestige value. Good examples of this are provided by the case of CFC-free aerosol cans or products made from reasonably priced recycled materials which are just as good as their traditional alternatives.

```
                    Ecological  ←→  Ecological
                   catastrophes       problems
                              ↘    ↙
                            Ecological
                            awareness
```

```
Ecology │ Government regulations                                                           Market │ Ecology
 Push   │        ←———————— Risks – Opportunities ————————→                                         │  Pull
        │ Criminal │ Liberty   │ Higher    │ Cost-effective │ New        │ Competitive │ New       │
        │ law      │ for the   │ technical │ regulatory     │ social     │ advantages  │ markets   │
        │          │ environment│ standards │ requirements   │ legitimacy │             │           │
```

affect the enterprise's room for manoevre

| Close-down/ interruption of production process | Decline in demand | Threat of substitution by eco-products | Pressure towards product innovation | Pressure towards technological innovation |

Figure 3 Environmental marketing in the tension between 'ecology push' and 'ecology pull'

In reality environment friendly products are often more expensive, and their acquisition entails additional opportunity costs for the consumer (field III). More expensive recycled paper and organic food are familiar examples. If consumers associate individual benefits with environment friendly products, price-linked competitive disadvantages – provided they cannot be reduced by means of rationalization – may be offset with the aid of other green marketing instruments. Green marketing can provide a basis for successful market penetration by highlighting the notion of environmental benefit in advertising campaigns and targeting publicity on various groups of consumers according to their willingness or ability to pay.

The limits of green marketing are shown in field IV. If environment friendly products offer neither extra individual benefits nor economic incentives, we are confronted with a classical phenomenon of market failure. Traditional products are preferred to more environment friendly alternatives. In such a situation environmentally oriented behaviour may be dictated by state intervention and environmental protection acts or encouraged by tax incentives, as in the case of catalytic converters. Another solution is to exploit marketing-for-ecology concepts with a view to changing consumers' attitudes, thereby encouraging environmentally oriented behaviour through knowledge and understanding. In many cases, however, this objective cannot be achieved by the green marketing of a single enterprise. This is particularly true of waste disposal, a typical example being the purchase or use of products with expensive and bulky multi-way packing.

3 Situation analysis as a starting point

An ecologically oriented conception of marketing must be based on external and internal situation analysis. Green marketing lies in an area of tension between 'ecology push' (e.g. EC Directives (Bennett 1992), national environmental legislation, demands made by various social groups (Blumenfeld *et al.* 1992)) and 'ecology pull' (e.g. an increase in the demand for environment friendly products, pollution control as a factor of competition). We must study this area systematically, paying close attention to the determinants underlying the market forces as well as the interconnections that exist between these determinants (Figure 3).

Special topics

Mounting pressures from four directions

Governments: Government regulation supporting a 50% reduction target is likely by the year 2000 — 49% agree

Customers: Consumers will increasingly ask 'How green is your company'? before buying a product — 56% agree

Competitors: Environmental legislation has become a decisive factor in plant location — 72% agree

Employees: Organizations with a poor environmental record will find it increasingly difficult to recruit and retain high-calibre staff — 68% agree

→ Company and/or industry

Figure 4 Empirical results about 'ecology push' and 'ecology pull' factors in worldwide industry
Source: Winsemius and Guntram (1992: 38)

Figure 4 shows that worldwide business leaders recognize that increased societal awareness of environmental problems is exerting ecology push and ecology pull on all sectors of industry from four directions: government regulations, customers, competitors and employees. The observation and analysis of developments in environmental legislation are an essential prerequisite of proactive and holistic green marketing. Abidance by legal requirements is held to be vital to legal legitimacy and cannot be exploited as a means of improving a company's public image. It is incumbent upon the environmental marketer to take the initiative in working out solutions before environmental claims are put forward by the legislator or by various sections of the community.

Green marketing and the situation analysis is centred on the consumer. Table 1 shows the results of a multi-country study conducted in 1992 in 22 countries of the world; 81 per cent of Germans, 57 per cent of Americans and 40 per cent of Japanese have so far actively avoided products perceived as harmful. Other studies from Germany and the USA show results at lower levels. Extensive panel research as well as many opinion poll ratings reveal a well-

Table 1 Personal environmental commitment in different countries of the world

Countries	Avoided environmentally harmful products %	Active in environment group %	Voted/worked for pro-environment candidate %
USA	57	11	19
Canada	77	12	15
Japan	40	4	14
Germany (West)	81	10	18
United Kingdom	75	10	10
Netherlands	68	7	21
Denmark	65	10	18

Source: Gallup, Health of the Planet Survey 1992, cited in Simon (1992)

marked north–south divide in the ecological awareness of European consumers. In the countries bordering on the Mediterranean the ecological awareness of the average household is much less strongly developed than in countries such as Germany, Holland or Norway. Owing to such culture-specific differences in attitude, it may therefore prove quite difficult to work out a standardized strategy for green marketing which will gain acceptance throughout the countries (Simon 1992; Meffert and Kirchgeorg 1998; Brodel 1996). Research has also shown that consumers in every part of Europe are more environment conscious than their actual behaviour would lead one to believe. In Germany, for instance, the percentage of environment-conscious households in 1993 was 60 per cent. Yet only 50 per cent of these households displayed consistently environment-oriented behaviour. Another consumer typology from the USA was published in 1992 by the Roper Organization. They identified five segments within the US population, each with a different level of environmental commitment: active environmentalists 25 per cent (True-Blue Greens 20 per cent and Greenback Greens 5 per cent); the swing group 31 per cent (Sprouts); not active environmentalists 44 per cent (Grousers 9 per cent; Basic Browns 35 per cent). In other words, there is a significant discrepancy between the consumers' intentions and their actual behaviour. Therefore green marketing concepts should be based on a segmentation of the target groups by ecological awareness or environmental commitment and environmentally oriented buying behaviour (McIntyre *et al.* 1993).

There are a great many different obstacles that prevent people from changing their behaviour. Empirical studies show that a reluctance to pay a higher price for pollution control is indeed a serious hindrance, but that there are many other impediments that have mainly to do with knowledge, quality, habits and motivation as well as specific situations (e.g. the availability of ecologically oriented products on the market). All these obstacles have been identified and even explained in terms of behaviour theory (see Monhemius 1992). Hence a great many decision-making situations in green marketing must be assigned to field II or field III in Figure 2.

Particular importance must be attributed to the analysis of the competitive position of the enterprise so that the risks and opportunities of competitive image building as an element of green marketing can be properly assessed. The focus of attention is on the analysis of driving forces that determine the degree of competitive intensity. These forces depend on the following factors (see Meffert and Kirchgeorg 1998; Porter 1984):

- the risk that new competitors will enter the market;
- the threat posed by substitutes;
- suppliers' bargaining power;
- rivalry between enterprises within an industrial sector;
- buyer's bargaining power.

Distributors have assumed an increasingly active role as ecological gatekeepers (Hansen 1992). Since they have been directly affected by environmental problems as a result of their legal liability to take back bottles, packaging and the like, they have distinguished themselves as guardians of the environment in their role as intermediaries between the manufacturer and the consumer (see CHANNELS OF DISTRIBUTION; LOGISTICS AND VALUE CREATION).

As a link between the manufacturer and the consumer, the distributor plays a key role within the context of the situational analysis. For the purposes of green marketing it is therefore necessary to gather information via trade-related data concerning the following elements: the ecological awareness of distributors; their environmental problems; or the extent to which distributors are prepared to cooperate in solving ecological problems.

With the aid of these criteria, a segmentation of impacted present and potential distributors may be helpful in working out appropriate vertical marketing options on the basis of channel-type-specific information.

The strategic market positions of enterprises are now also increasingly influenced by the behaviour of non-market groups like environmental stakeholders (e.g. media reporting, civic action groups and ecological campaigns) (Miles 1987; Dyllick 1989; Ottman 1992), so that classical forms of market research have to be expanded.

Opportunities and risks for the market and the environment must be balanced against corporate strengths and weaknesses. Depending on the particular situation in which an enterprise finds itself, the most relevant internal key factors will be as follows:

- the open-mindedness and flexibility of management with regard to ecological problems;
- damage to the environmental media (i.e. soil, water and air pollution) and consumption of resources associated with the procurement, production sales use and disposal of products;
- the proximity of the firm's range of services to environmental protection markets;
- the firm's public profile or 'visibility';
- the amount of funds available;
- the basic orientation of the marketing and corporate strategy.

Within the context of the internal situational analysis, environmental problems must be considered throughout the products' value chain and at every stage in the life-cycle of the products and services offered by the enterprise (see PRODUCT LIFE-CYCLE MANAGEMENT). In order to develop an integrated pollution control concept we therefore need a green marketing situation analysis which cuts across functional and corporate divisions (e.g. suppliers, distributors and consumers). This makes it possible to identify potential opportunities for differentiation and competitive advantage at every stage in the value chain. Appropriate methodical instruments that might be used here include value chain analyses, product life-cycle analysis or so-called eco-portfolios (see Meffert and Kirchgeorg 1998: 104 ff.; Schaltegger and Sturm 1992; Winsemius and Hahn 1992; Linnanen et al. 1994).

4 Strategic planning in green marketing

On the basis of the situation analysis it is necessary to reconsider and modify corporate objectives and strategic corporate positions.

The 'sustainable development' model is often invoked in this context (Dietz et al. 1992; International Institute for Sustainable Development 1992; Schmidheiny 1992; Enquete-Kommission 1993; Meffert and Kirchgeorg 1998; Gladwin et al. 1995; Hart 1997). In accordance with this model the environmental orientation of an enterprise is to be determined by the principles of a circular flow economy; an approach involving the replacement of non-renewable by renewable resources, various forms of ecologically oriented technical progress, as well as worldwide cooperative action (Pearce and Turner 1990; Kuik and Verbruggen 1991). From these principles we must derive a number of operational environmental objectives for green marketing, objectives which can and must be achieved by a series of small but bold steps. Here are some typical examples of such objective contents:

- cutting down on the use of resources;
- reducing the energy consumption of certain products;
- giving wider publicity to innovations designed to protect the environment;
- investing more time in environmental counselling as after sales service;
- attaining certain return rates by means of retrodistribution;
- increasing the consumer's willingness to purchase more environment friendly products.

When defining the strategic orientation of green marketing, we can draw a distinction between reactive and proactive base strategies. We speak of reactive behaviour when it is only legal requirements that induce a firm to take account of ecological demands made by limited sections of the community. In such a case the company meets minimal ecological demands, but in the long term it forfeits its chance of giving itself a clear image as an ecologically oriented enterprise. Empirical studies confirm that in the long run offensive and innovative environmental strategies offer better chances of market success than passive or selectively oriented strategies. This is particularly true of psychographic success parameters such as competence and image. However, the other side of the coin is that the application of offensive and innovative strategies entails higher risks when a firm is attempting to tap a new market (Kirchgeorg 1990; Arnfalk and Thidell 1992; Meffert and Kirchgeorg 1993c).

When offensive environmental strategies are pursued, special attention must be given to the requirements of the customer and the competitive position of the enterprise in order that actions in favour of the environment can be exploited to gain customer and competitive advantage. Competitive strategies can take several generic forms: quality leadership or differentiation, cost leadership and focusing on a particular niche or submarket. The decision in favour of one of these strategies will inevitably depend on the likelihood of gaining at least an important, obvious and defendable competitive advantage.

Ecologically oriented differentiation strategies aim to outdo competitors in satisfying the customers' demands with regard to the environmental compatibility of products and manufacturing processes. A distinction may be drawn between cases in which a firm merely meets this demand within certain niches and cases where it succeeds in attaining this objective in all of the existing market segments it caters to.

Regardless of whether competitive strategies are oriented towards a global market or a submarket, it is always essential that advantages gained by differentiation should be durable and defendable (Brodel 1996). The success of ecologically oriented competitive strategies depends on the extent to which the ecological advantages of products are anchored at every stage of the corporate value chain.

Holistic eco-strategies that ensure sustainable differentiation advantages must overcome barriers between corporate functions and entities and embrace the entire cycle of production, utilization and disposal ('cradle-to-grave' approach). Differentiation strategies are particularly relevant in the cases indicated in field III of Figure 2 (i.e. in cases where the producers of environment friendly products expect consumers to pay a higher price).

If a firm pursues a cost leadership strategy, what distinguishes it from its competitors is the fact that it can whittle down its unit costs by means of consistent product and process optimization and pass this cost benefit on to the market in the form of lower prices. With regard to the prevailing conditions in green marketing the aim is to exploit cost leadership with a view to gaining a position in field I or field II (see Figure 2). The success of cost leadership strategies depends on whether the enterprise succeeds in wresting sizeable market share from its rivals, thus enabling it to exploit depression and experience curve effects. This strategy, therefore, will only be successful if customers are more responsive to price arguments than to particular utility expectations as purchasing criteria.

Ecologically oriented competitive image-building can be legitimately based on a cost and price leadership strategy if the unit costs of new environment friendly products are lower than those of comparable traditional goods. Such a situation is conceivable if ecologically harmful and expensive raw materials can be replaced by cheaper and more environment friendly raw materials or the amount of expensive raw materials used in the production process can be reduced by employing recycled material.

Most people agree that there is little chance that environment friendly product innovation will result in substantial cost benefits. As a rule, ecologically oriented innovations are accompanied by cost increases which are incompatible with the requirements of successful cost leadership strategies.

When competitive strategies are worked out, the timing of activities with respect to competitors assumes paramount importance. The main question is whether a firm which has devised solutions to environmental problems should enter the market as a pioneer or a market follower. A number of empirical studies have shown that timing, unlike other problems associated with environmental innovation, has been submitted to exceptionally precise and subtle analysis (see Steger 1993). On the one hand, attention is drawn to the fact that eco-friendly products have to contend with considerable market resistance. This is particularly so whenever they have to be offered for sale at prices above those of traditional products. In such a case a firm's rash attempt to distinguish itself in the market may prove counterproductive if it is foiled by competitors and critical consumer groups. On the other hand, pioneers in pollution control have every prospect of creating a durable acceptable image for their products, thereby achieving a kind of success which can only be attained with the aid of a first-to-market strategy.

In green marketing the manufacturer also has to decide whether the application of an environmental strategy necessitates vertical integration in concert with distributors (Meffert and Kirchgeorg 1998). In order to size up the

Special topics

	Manufacturers		
Traders	defensive/reactive	selective	offensive/proactive
defensive	Ignorance		Complete evasion
Selective		Cooperation	Selective evasion
offensive	Complete substitution	Selective substitution	Innovative cooperation

Figure 5 Basic eco-strategies in vertical marketing

situation the producer has to be informed about distributors' basic ecological options. If traders decide in favour of one particular basic eco-strategy this will largely determine the extent to which the manufacturer will be able to gain acceptance for his green marketing concepts. Figure 5 shows basic strategic attitudes which may be adopted by manufacturers and traders. If both manufacturers and traders pursue an offensive pollution control strategy, cooperation may provide further scope for innovation. It often affords opportunities for exploiting ecological know-how at every stage in the distribution process, thereby greatly facilitating the application of integrated solutions to environmental problems. However, manufacturers and distributors may come into conflict with each other in those cases where their environmental strategies diverge.

If the manufacturer pursues an offensive eco-strategy and traders apply a defensive one, pollution control will be a bone of contention between them. In this kind of situation the producer may attempt to circumvent ecologically defensive marketing intermediaries. To this end he may set up his own field organization or look for new marketing intermediaries. If, on the other hand, it is the traders who pursue an offensive eco-strategy, their task will be greatly facilitated by the increase in the number of eco-friendly products now offered in many lines of merchandise. They will find it relatively easy to exclude certain suppliers and replace them by producers pursuing more offensive eco-strategies. This substitution process enables traders to avoid practically all kinds of marketing conflicts by selecting suppliers who share their own ecologically oriented marketing conception.

5 Designing an ecologically oriented marketing mix

Once due consideration has been given to customers, competitors and distributors, an ecologically oriented marketing mix has to be devised as part of a global environmental strategy (Henion and Kinnear 1976; Charter 1992; Ottman 1992; Peattie 1992; Hopfenbeck 1993; Meffert and Kirchgeorg 1998) (see THE MARKETING MIX).

Product policy

A product life-cycle analysis (LCA) (Petersen 1992) can provide a sound basis for more eco-friendly solutions to the problems associated with product and packaging policies. In order to resolve product-related environmental problems, it is necessary to analyse the various spheres of responsibility of the supplier, manufacturer, distributor and consumer. From now on marketing specialists will have to analyse the organization of closed loop value chains with all of its consequences for product design (long-life products, the growing importance of after sales service, the sale of utility instead of products) (see Figure 6). Instruments of product policy include product innovation, product variation, and product elimination designed to bring programmes into line with ecological requirements (see Ostmeier 1990; Türck 1990). While product variations involve modifying existing products in accordance with ecologically oriented demands, ecologically oriented product innovations entail launching entirely new product concepts on the market.

Intelligent product development and closed loop value chain engineering create the necessary conditions for replacing non-renewable resources with renewable resources and increasing ecological effectiveness (Noth 1992: S.49). Possible starting points are (Türck 1990; Oliff 1991; Stahel 1991; Baram and Dillon 1993; Bhat 1993; Rushton 1993):

1. The development of long-life products.
2. Customer service designed to ensure that products can be used for a long time without damage to the environment.
3. Multiple use and utilization strategies ('product stewardship').

If it proves impossible to adapt existing product concepts to ecologically oriented requirements by means of an innovation or variation policy, a product elimination process ought to be initiated as part of a credible green marketing programme. Should any problems arise, particularly at the utilization and disposal stages, recall actions or special disposal services may be necessary.

The introduction of takeback regulation in most European countries obliges both producers and retailers to develop eco-friendly products, packaging and logistic alternatives as part of their product policy. The German Circular Economy and Waste Disposal Law, for example which took effect in October 1996, assigns extended product responsibility to all companies that develop, manufacture, process, or market products. The law, which is based on the principle of sustainable development, aims to ensure that producers will be forced to play an active part in implementing a circular economy. This new definition of product responsibility can be regarded as a further step in the implementation of the prevention and polluter pays principle which have guided environmental policy in Germany and other European countires. The extension of product responsibility is intended to internalize the costs of waste disposal, which have hitherto been

Figure 6 Starting points for product policy in a closed loop value chain carried externally in most cases. Under the Circular Economy Law, enterprises which market products in Germany are required to organize systems for taking back and recycling old and worn products. The end producers are particularly important in respect of product responsibility as this group possesses a high degree of influence on the design and manufacture of products. The design of recycling systems should be undertaken on an interdepartmental basis, and so should the integration of all commercial activities in accordance with recyclable product blue prints. On the way to implement a circular economy it is necessary to rethink the traditional marketing tools.

In order to obtain detailed information about the goals, strategies and schedules for setting up product-related return and recycling systems, the Marketing Institute of the University of Münster, with the backing of the Federal Environment Trust, has conducted personal interviews with 100 German manufacturers as part of an ongoing research project (Kirchgeorg 1998). The following conclusions emerge from this German survey:

Up to now, the organization of product-related substance cycles has been envisaged primarily in terms of cost effectiveness, though considerable importance is also attached to image goals (public image and competitive advantage).

The attainment of the highest possible return rates is one of the main targets aimed at by manufacturers who organize product-related substance cycles.

So far, manufacturers of consumer durables have shown little interest in widely propagated recycling schemes.

Few manufacturers consider the organization of return and recycling systems as a core competence. So they build closed loop value chains as networks. Most of the manufacturers in the survey have teamed up with other businesses, especially recycling firms, to which they have delegated tasks such as the return of used products.

In this context eco-friendly solutions often require a modification of the logistics and goods representation at the point of sale. The preparation of an ecological balance sheet for packaging materials and packaging systems (e.g. non-returnable and multi-way packaging) will ultimately be the only means of finding out which form of packaging can be considered the most environment friendly. Since in some cases packaging cannot be entirely eliminated, recycling and reuse must be envisaged from the outset when packaging is conceived and designed. It is particularly important to create new applications and markets for recycled products in order to ensure that packaging materials returned via retrodistribution channels are reused.

When shaping a brand policy one should consider to what extent a firm's positioning objectives may be attained by means of a different brand image (see BRANDING AND BRAND MANAGEMENT; POSITIONING) or additional markings such as the German 'Blue Angel' eco-label used as a symbol of environmental friendliness in Germany. The Blue Angel eco-labelling scheme was introduced in 1978. In 1995 over 5000 products carried the label; 80 per cent of German households are aware of the eco-label, and it receives widespread support from manufacturers. Since 1991 there exists a new EC eco-labelling regulation. The objectives of this EC regulation are to promote products with a reduced environmental impact throughout their entire life-cycle and to provide better information to consumers on the environmental impacts of products. The EC eco-labelling scheme, issued as a regulation, applies directly to all member states and is EC-wide. It is a voluntary scheme and should be self-financing (Welford 1992).

In order to anchor the environmental utility of products as a confidence characteristic in the consumer's mind, a company may envisage the creation of its own eco-friendly brands or the exploitation of environmental seals or certificates awarded by neutral institutions such as the Federal Environment Office, technical control boards or one of the various environmental associations. An example for helpful consumer environmental information is the consumer guidebook *Shopping for a Better World* in the USA. The guide shows consumers how they can help the environment and contribute to solving various social problems by skewing purchase towards companies with outstanding rewards for green achievement (Tasaday 1991). The shopping guide lists over 2400 brands of consumer products according to their manufacturers' records on eleven social criteria. According to research results 78 per cent of

Environmental Report Card
Burdens from production, distribution, use and disposal.

PRODUCT & PACKAGING:

TYPE OF BURDEN	AMT*
RESOURCE DEPLETION	
WATER	4.8 kg
WOOD	2,800 g
OIL, GAS (non-fuel)	25 g
MINERALS	350 g
ENERGY USE	
TOTAL ENERGY USED	45 MJ
AIR POLLUTION	
CARBON DIOXIDE	3 kg
CARBON MONOXIDE	2 kg
SULFUR OXIDES	20 g
NITROGEN OXIDES	18 g
HYDROCARBONS	15 g
PARTICULATES	6 g
UNCLASSIFIED	0.04 g
HAZARDOUS	5,000 mg
WATER POLLUTION	
TOTAL SOLIDS	8 g
OXYGEN DEPLETERS	7 g
TOXIC	830 mg
SOLID WASTE	
UNCLASSIFIED	500 g
HAZARDOUS	0.3 g

FOR INFORMATION CALL 1-800-ECO-FACTS
SCIENTIFIC CERTIFICATION SYSTEM
* PER 1,120 SHEETS

2 PLY BATH TISSUE FROM NON-INTEGRATED VIRGIN MILL (SYSTEM BOUNDARY EXCLUDES ECOSYSTEM)

Environmental Report Card
Burdens from production, distribution, use and disposal.

PRODUCT & PACKAGING:

TYPE OF BURDEN	AMT*
RESOURCE DEPLETION	
WATER	8 kg
WOOD	0.2 g
OIL, GAS (non-fuel)	18 g
MINERALS	67 g
ENERGY USE	
TOTAL ENERGY USED	21 MJ
AIR POLLUTION	
CARBON DIOXIDE	1.4 kg
CARBON MONOXIDE	1 kg
SULFUR OXIDES	18 g
NITROGEN OXIDES	8 g
HYDROCARBONS	4 g
PARTICULATES	2 g
UNCLASSIFIED	<0.001 g
HAZARDOUS	100 mg
WATER POLLUTION	
TOTAL SOLIDS	3 g
OXYGEN DEPLETERS	4 g
TOXIC	10 mg
SOLID WASTE	
UNCLASSIFIED	75 g
HAZARDOUS	0.3 g

FOR INFORMATION CALL 1-800-ECO-FACTS
SCIENTIFIC CERTIFICATION SYSTEM
* PER 1,120 SHEETS

TREE-FREE 2-PLY 100% RECYCLED BATH TISSUE

Figure 7 Environmental Report Card in the USA
Source: Scientific Certification Systems

readers have changed brands after reading the guide (Ottman 1992).

In the USA there exists also a Green Report Card (Figure 7). This card measures products on life-cycle analysis. The Scientific Certifications Systems Corp. includes subsets under five basic categories: resource, depletion, energy use, air pollution and solid waste. How a product scores in all five areas is clearly displayed on the Green Report Card. So the consumer can get detailed information about products and the burdens from production, distribution, use and disposal (Schlossberg 1993).

In many cases a company's after sales service offers the only chance of exerting direct or indirect influence on the way in which products are used, consumed or disposed of. Preventive customer service may provide some scope for competitive image-building, and it can help to reduce environmental pollution caused at the utilization stage by heating systems, motor vehicles and the like.

Communications policy

Activities associated with product policy should be backed up by an environmentally oriented communications policy. The integration of environmental arguments into product and corporate advertising could improve the corporate image by highlighting the firm's competence in matters relating to the environment. One of the major challenges that must be met by corporate communications experts in this domain is that information about corporate behaviour with respect to the environment is brought to public notice not only via controlled communication channels, but also to an increasing extent through reports presented by the media, environmental organizations and administrative agencies. This being so, the specialists who shape corporate communications policy must take account of such institutions and opinion leaders.

Firms ought to work out holistic, environment friendly solutions to their problems before offering information to the public. Yet even when this necessary condition is fulfilled, problems often arise when companies attempt to apply classical advertising techniques (e.g. emotional and empirically oriented sales messages) to the organization of credible, environmentally oriented communications campaigns. Taking account of a company's initial situation and environmental vulnerability, communications experts must identify the target groups to whom environmentally oriented marketing messages can, must or ought to be transmitted. They must also determine to what extent communication in the relevant sector is dominated by environmental arguments (Peattie 1992).

Content analyses of ecologically oriented advertising in German print media have been made at the Marketing Institute, and the research findings show that since the middle of 1980 there has been an increase in the emotional content of advertising messages. We may therefore conclude that environmentally oriented advertising has recourse to classical activation patterns in order to attract consumers' attention to advertisements amidst the welter of information to which they are exposed on a daily basis. Traditional methods of communication may be complemented by various types of environmental sponsorship (e.g. cooperation with environmental associations demonstrating deep commitment to pollution control; Bruhn 1990) (see ADVERTISING; MARKETING COMMUNICATIONS).

Communications policy must also take account of statutory requirements to furnish information. In this context mention must be made of a Directive issued by the EC Council of Ministers in 1990. This Directive, which relates to free access to corporate information about the environment, is to be incorporated into the law of each European country. Third parties are to be allowed access to corporate environmental information made available to administrative bodies. This means that firms will have to check through their files to find out exactly what corporate data have been transmitted to administrative bodies. Such data may cause considerable embarrassment to the company if they are brought to public notice and it turns out that they are not concordant with the information hitherto provided by the firm as part of its communications policy. In order to avoid such embarrassing situations, companies will have to be less secretive about malfunctions, accidents and other environmental hazards associated with industrial activities. They will have to provide relevant information to all of the social groups concerned (i.e. local residents, environmental associations and the media). Empirical studies relating to the chemical industry demonstrate that confidence in a firm may even be boosted by the proactive publication of information about environmental hazards. However, this is only possible in cases where a company has already acquired a certain reputation and a certain measure of credibility in the eyes of the public. In order to reach a consensus on the acceptance of environmental hazards, industrialists ought to seek a dialogue with all of the social groups concerned, making use of concepts related to citizen participation, citizens' advisory councils, panel discussions and the like (Miles 1987; Jungermann *et al.* 1990).

Distribution policy

The implementation of the closed loop value chain in green marketing forces us to rethink the distribution mix. The packaging regulation, and the amendments to the Waste Disposal Law in particular, have created new conditions for the design of the distribution strategy. In many cases producers have a legal obligation to take back used packaging and products. Just as producers have traditionally had to choose between various kinds of distribution channels, so they now have to concern themselves increasingly with the task of choosing an appropriate retrodistribution channel.

In many cases solutions worked out on a sectoral basis seem to be proving quite efficient, but producers ought to consider setting up their own retrodistribution systems as a competitive strategy, and possibly also for other purposes. By integrating external organizations into retrodistributional logistics and recycling processes one may create hybrid organizations which make coordination quite difficult.

Beyond that, the logistic system ought to be expanded to take account of resource- and environment-related factors (energy and industrial pollution) in addition to cost factors, which have hitherto been the sole preoccupation of the business community. Special attention should also be given to the consequences that the overburdening of the transport systems can have for the logistics of vertical marketing. Logistic operating rates can be lowered by standardizing freight containers, changing the composition of orders (delivery of minimum quantities) or by grouping orders from firms that supply goods to the same customer (see CHANNELS OF DISTRIBUTION; LOGISTICS AND VALUE CREATION; RELATIONSHIPS AND NETWORKS).

Pricing

Decisions relating to pricing are mainly determined by the consumer's sensitivity to price, but the need to integrate the cost of legally stimulated pollution control now plays an increasingly important role in this domain. Thus, for instance, firms mapping out their pricing strategies now have to take account of the packaging regulation and the amendments to the Waste Disposal Law, which necessitate more serious consideration of the costs of recycling and environment friendly waste disposal.

Cost increases due to pollution control can often only be justified by asking environment-conscious buyers to pay a higher price. It has already been emphasized that consumers are still very reluctant to pay a higher price for pollution control. This is especially true in cases where traditional alternatives are available in the market.

Pricing is therefore a matter of paramount importance in green marketing. Pricing strategies should be based on a segmentation of actual and potential target groups classified with the aid of three criteria:

1 ecological awareness;
2 personal affectedness;
3 willingness to pay a price for pollution control.

Segments displaying varying degrees of price sensitivity constitute the basis for price differentiation strategies.

As a matter of principle, lower introductory prices for eco-friendly products help customers to reorient their buyer behaviour, thereby facilitating a more rapid diffusion of eco-friendly products. Combined costing at the expense of non eco-friendly products can ensure a necessary balance here. The return of used packaging and products raises the question of pricing incentives for retrodistribution. For example, retrodistribution rates can be increased by charging deposits, but deposits may also have an inhibiting effect on buyers, thereby limiting total sales. Further points of departure should be examined within the context of terms policy (e.g. special annual quantity discounts or methods of financing eco-friendly product variants). Especially where consumer durables are concerned, green marketing specialists ought to draw the consumer's attention to ways of obtaining compensation through government subsidies for higher expenditure on pollution control (e.g. tax benefits, grants for regenerative power plants).

The examples illustrating various aspects of the marketing mix problem show that better environmental quality only goes hand in hand

Table 2 Environmental best implementation practices

Component	Characteristics of management systems
Senior-level support and commitment	• Top-level commitment, direction and leadership • Senior executive to champion programmes • Adequate environmental funding and commitment
Informational management and communication	• Corporate enviornmental policy statement • Policy goals translated into active procedures • Communication and reinforcement of environmental commitment • Management information system • Systematic feedback/learning
Regulatory knowledge and tracking	• Awareness of the full range of regulatory requirements • Systematic approach to tracking regulatory changes • Regulatory influence on upcoming requirements
Integration of environmental management into business operations	• Consideration of enviornmental issues in key business strategies and major investments • Consideration of environment in market-end pricing analyses • Competitive analysis on environmentally driven costs
Organizational interfaces that promote environmental effectiveness	• Organizational structure that supports effective communication and matches needs and culture of company • Clearly defined environmental roles and responsibilities • Strong horizontal and vertical reporting relationships with complete system of environmental authorities
Employee awareness and training	• Establish ownership for environmental programmes by linking efforts to performance appraisals • Training to convey environmental ethics to workforce • Focus on accident prevention training as well as worker right-to-know programmes
Risk assessment and management	• Environmental compliance audits of facilities • Assessment of raw materials/product/operations health, safety, and environmental risks • Environmental due diligence assessments for property transfers.

with better sales development where environmental requirements are fulfilled within the context of an integrated green marketing programme.

6 The implementation of green marketing

Green marketing must be implemented within the context of an overall concept of ecologically oriented management. In many cases implementation inevitably entails a change in values and cultural conceptions (Hoffman 1993), which affects every corporate function and necessitates a high degree of adaptability in the world of day-to-day realities. Table 2 shows practices for the implementation process.

The successful implementation of environmental concepts will depend to a large extent on a combination of the top-down and bottom-up approaches designed to gain general acceptance for new ideas and make a strong impact on all sections of the community.

Owing to the complexity and the interdisciplinary nature of environmental problems it is particularly important that the function-oriented way of thinking that predominates in many firms should be complemented by a more holistic or integrated point of view. This is closely related to the question of whether pollution control ought to be integrated as an independent organizational form into existing corporate structures. Owing to the numerous tasks and special problems that have to be coped with, it will often be necessary to set up an environmental protection organization in order not to put too great a strain on existing departments. This does not mean that the individual employee no longer shares responsibility for pollution control. He can apply to a staff unit for pollution control if he requires competent advice or information relating collectively to several functions.

In order to coordinate and supervise the implementation of environmental measures we shall have to complement classical controlling with a type of ecologically oriented controlling which will provide decision makers with planning, regulatory and supervisory instruments for working out and applying an environmental strategy. The scope of traditional controlling will have to be widened by attributing particular importance to the recording of information on the quantity structure of corporate activities. At the implementation stage ecological controlling has to fulfil a double function: to show where information and coordination are required, and to ensure close coordination among all those concerned by means of interface management.

HERIBERT MEFFERT AND MANFRED KIRCHGEORG
WESTFALISCHE WILHELMS-UNIVERSITÄT

Further reading

(References cited in the text marked *)

* Arnfalk, P. and Thidell, A. (1992) *Environmental Management in the Swedish Manufacturing Industry*, Lund: Lund University, Dept of Industrial Environmental Economics.

  Ayres, R., Ferrer, T., van Leynseele, T. (1997): 'Eco--efficiency, asset recovery and remanufacturing', *European Management Journal* 15: 557–74.

* Baram, M.S. and Dillon, P.S. (1993) 'Forces shaping the development and use of product stewardship in the private sector', in Fischer, K. and Schot, J. (eds), *Environmental Strategies for Industries*, Washington: Island Press.

* Bennett, E. (1992) 'European industry and the environment: the developing role of the EC and a strategy for industry', *European Environment* 2: 2–4.

* Bhat, V.N. (1993) 'A blueprint for green product development', *Industrial Management* 35: 4–7.

* Blumenfeld, K., Earle, R. III and Annighofer, F. (1992) 'Environmental performance and business strategy', *PRISM* 4th Quarter: 65–85.

* Brodel, E. (1996): *Internationales Umweltmanagement*, Wiesbaden: Gabler-Verlag.

* Bruhn, M. (1990) *Sozio- und Umweltsponsoring*, München: Gabler-Verlag.

* Charter, H. (ed.) (1992) *Greener Marketing*, Sheffield: Greenleaf Publishing.

* Dietz, F.J., Simonis, U.E. and Straaten, J. van der (eds) (1992) *Sustainahility and Environmental Policy*, Berlin: Edition Sigma Bohn Verlag.

* Dyllick, Th. (1989) *Management der Umweltbeziehungen*, Wiesbaden: Gabler-Verlag.

* Enquete-Kommission 'Schutz des Menschen und der Umwelt' des Deutschen Bundestages (ed.) (1993) *Verantwortung für die Zubunft – Wege zum nachhaltigen Umgang mit Stoff – und Materialströmen*, Bonn: Enquete-Kommission.

* Fischer, K. and Schot, J. (eds) (1993) *Environmental Strategies for Industries*, Washington: Island Press.

* Gladwin, T.N., Kennelly, J.J. Krause, T.S. (1995) 'Shifting paradigms for sustainable development: implications for management theory and research', *American Management Review* 20: 72–81.

* Hansen, U. (1992) 'Umweltmanagement im Handel', in Steger, U. (ed.) *Handbuch des Umweltschutzes*, München: Beck Verlag.

* Hart, S.L. (1997): 'Strategies for a sustainable world', *Harvard Business Review* January–February: 67–76.

* Henion, K.E. and Kinnear, T.C. (eds) (1976) 'Ecological marketing', *Educational Workshop Series* 1, Austin: American Marketing Association.

* Hoffman, A.J. (1993) 'The importance of fit between individual values and organisational culture in the greening of industry', *Business Strategy and the Environment* Winter: 10–19.

* Hopfenbeck, W. (1993) *The Green Management Revolution*, Hemel Hempstead: Verlag Moderne Industrie.

* International Institute for Sustainable Development (1992) *Business Strategy for Sustainable Development*, Winnipeg, Manitoba: International Institute for Sustainable Development.

* Jungermann, H., Rohrmann, B. and Wiedemann, P.M. (eds) (1990) *Risiko-Konzepte Risiko-Konflikt, Risiko-Kommunikation, Monographien des Forschungszentrums Jülich 3*, Jülich: Forschungszentrum.

* Kaas, K.P. (1992) *Marketing und Neue Institutionenlehre*, Arbeitspapier Nr. 1 aus dem Forschungsproj ekt Marketing and ökonomische Theorie, Frankfurt a. M.
* Kirchgeorg, M. (1990) *Ökologieorientiertes Unternehmensverhalten*, Wiesbaden: Gabler-Verlag.
* Kirchgeorg, M. (1998): *Marktstrategisches Kreislaufmanagement*, Wiesbaden, Gabler Verlag.
* Kuik, O. and Verbruggen, H. (eds) (1991) *In Search of Indicators of Sustainable Development*, Dordrecht, Boston, London: Kluwer Academic Publ.
* Linnanen, L., Bostrom, T. and Miettinen, P. (1994) *Life Cycle Management*, Espoo: Weilin and Goos.
* McIntyre, R.P., Meloche, M.S. and Lewis, S.L. (1993) 'National culture as a macro tool for environmental sensitivity segmentation', in Cravens, D.W. and Dickson, P.R. (eds), *Enhancing Knowledge Development in Marketing, 1993 AMA Educator's Proceedings*, Chicago: American Marketing Association.
* Meffert, H. (1993) 'Umweltbewulltes Konsumentenverhalten. Ökologieorientiertes Marketing im Spannungsfeld zwischen Individual – und Sozialnutzen', *Marketing ZfP* 1: 51–4.
* Meffert, H. and Kirchgeorg, M. (1993a) 'Das neue Leitbild Sustainable Development – der Weg ist das Ziel', *Harvard Business Manager* 15: 34–45.
* Meffert, H. and Kirchgeorg, M. (1993b) 'Environmental protection and corporate strategy of German companies', in Cravens, D.W. and Dickson, P.R. (eds), *Enhancing Knowledge Development in Marketing, 1993 AMA Educator's Proceedings*, Chicago: American Marketing Association.
* Meffert, H. and Kirchgeorg, M. (1998) *Marktorientiertes Ummeltmanagement*, 3rd edn, Stuttgart: Poeschel-Verlag.
* Miles, R. (1987) *Managing the Corporate Social Environment*, Englewood Cliffs, NJ: Prentice Hall.
* Monhemius, K.Ch. (1992) *Umwelthewußtes Kaufverhalten von Konsumenten*, Frankfurt: Lang-Verlag.
* Noth, K. (1992) 'Environmental business management', *Management Development Series* 30, Geneva.
* Oliff, M. D. (1991) 'Corporate challenges for an age of reconsumption', *The Columbia Journal of World Business* Fall: 7–21.
* Ostmeier, H. (1990) *Ökologieorientierte Produktinnovationen*, Frankfurt a.M.: Lang-Verlag.
* Ottman, J. A. (1992) *Green Marketing*, Lincolnwood IL: NTL Publishing Group.
* Pearce, D. and Turner, R.K. (1990) *Economics of Natural Resources and Environment*, New York: Harvester Wheatsheaf.
* Peattie, K. (1992) *Green Marketing*, London: Pitman.
* Petersen, B. (1992) *Environmental Assessment of Products*, Helsinki: UETP-EEE, The Finnish Association of Graduate Engineers.
* Porer, M. and van der Linde, C. (1995): 'Green and competitive', *Harvard Business Review* September–October: 120–34.
* Porter, M. (1984) *Wettbewerbsstrategie*, Frankfurt: The Free Press.
* Post, J.E. and Altman, B.W. (1992) 'Models of corporate greening', *Markets, Politics, and Social Performance* 13: 3–29.
* Rushton, B.M. (1993) 'How protecting the environment impacts R&D in the United States', *Research Technology Management* 36: 13–21.
* Schaltegger, S.C. and Sturm, A.J. (1992) *Ökologieorientierte Entscheidungen im Unternehmen*, Bern: Haupt-Verlag.
* Schlossberg, H. (1993) 'Hardware industry understands importance of going green', *Marketing News* 27: 10.
* Schmidheiny, S. and the Business Council for Sustainable Development (1992) *Changing Course – A Global Business Perspective on Development and the Environment*, Cambridge: Massachusetts Institute of Technology.
* Simon, F.L. (1992) 'Marketing green products in the triad', *Columbia Journal of World Business* Fall–Winter: 269–85.
* Stahel, (1991) *Langlebigkeit und Materialrecycling*, Essen: Vulkan Verlag.
* Steger, U. (1993) *Umweltmanagement*, 2nd edn, Frankfurt: Gabler-Verlag.
* Tasaday, L. (1991) *Shopping for a Better Environment*, New York: Meadowbrook Press.
* Türck, R. (1990) *Das ökologische Produkt*, Dissertation, Frankfurt a.M.: Campus-Verlag.
* Welford, R. (1992) 'A guide to eco-labelling and the EC eco-labelling scheme', *European Environment* 2: 13–15.
* Welford, R. and Gouldson, A. (1993) *Environmental Management & Business Strategy*, London: Pitman.
* Winsemius, P. and Guntram, U. (1992) 'Responding to the environmental challenge', *Business Horizons* March–April: 37–45.
* Winsemius, P. and Hahn, W. (1992) 'Environmental option assessment', *The Columbia Journal of World Business* Fall–Winter: 249–66.
* Winter, G. (1998) *Business and the Environment*, München: Beck-Verlag.

See also: ADVERTISING; BRANDING AND BRAND MANAGEMENT; CHANNELS OF DISTRIBUTION; LOGISTICS AND VALUE CREATION; MARKET SEGMENTATION; MARKETING COMMUNICATIONS; POSITIONING; PRODUCT LIFE-CYCLE MANAGEMENT; RELATIONSHIPS AND NETWORKS; THE MARKETING MIX

Product–country images

1. Importance and scope of origin images
2. An overview of research
3. Strategic implications of PCI
4. Summary and conclusion

Overview

Products usually carry a 'Made in ...' notation on their label, which for most products is a legal requirement. Rules of origin legislation determines the duty rates assessed on imported products, which can have an important effect on their prices. Therefore, the specification of a product's origin is an important matter to marketers especially in the current, globally competitive environment.

More to the point, however, the 'made-in' specification may also act as an information cue for buyers when they assess a product's overall value, since it is tied to the image of its country of origin as a producer. Many marketers recognize this and feel that, rather than limiting themselves to the legally-mandated notation on obscure made-in labels, actually *stressing* their brands' origins in various parts of the marketing mix can have important strategic benefits. These are often thought to be similar to or greater than other product characteristics that reflect a brand's strengths and can serve as its USP (Unique Selling Proposition). Since the growth of foreign competition also means a potential threat to the importing countries' economies, domestic producers routinely use made-at-home appeals to enhance their products' position among local consumers.

Not surprisingly, given the potential benefits and broad implications from such product–country image (PCI) associations, made-in issues have attracted a lot of attention and Baker and Currie (1993) have even wondered whether they may be 'the 5th element of the marketing mix'. If it is true, as it is often said, that brand names like McDonald's are worth 'millions', then how many *billions* is Germany's image in engineering worth to 'Made in Germany' products? A writer in a popular magazine had this to say about the value of origins in contemporary marketing strategy:

> We need not ask anymore who or what it is that has inherited the earth: we know. It is the walking wallet ... in search of underwear handwoven by Tibetan virgins ... coffee beans certified to have ripened in the very first shaft of morning light at the tippy top of a sacred mountain in Kenya ... bedframes laminated of twigs gathered atop Mount Sinai ... tomatoes from Provence. ... We see [here] the BMW Effect. In the hopes of making whatever they produce as much the wanted thing as the BMW is among cars, manufacturers have streamlined and attempted to imbue with engineering mystique every article ... they turn out.
> (P. Freundlich, *Harper's*, December 1987)

This entry is about the images of product origins and how these may affect the behaviour of buyers. It has three main sections whose objectives are to review the importance and multifaceted dimensions of origin images in marketing, place them in the broader context of buyer behaviour and review relevant research findings, and outline their strategic implications for marketers. Some of the questions that will be addressed are, how do marketers use PCI cues and what is their role in the current globally competitive environment? What factors shape consumer views about foreign versus domestic products? Is the origin effect similarly useful to all brands, in all consumer segments, in, or for, all countries?

Such issues are of vital importance and should be of interest to (i) marketing decision and policy makers in business, government and trade associations who work to enhance the global competitiveness of their organizations or constituents by expanding to foreign markets and/or protecting their domestic consumer franchise; and (ii) students and researchers interested either specifically in this area or in such related disciplines as consumer behaviour, international strategy and international relations.

1 Importance and scope of origin images

Some observers have argued that, since made-in product labels often go unnoticed by consumers, they are not important except in the context of a producer's need to comply with rules-of-origin legislation. These rules are indeed becoming increasingly important, particularly because they can have a significant effect on the prices of 'hybrid' products (those manufactured, assembled or with components made in various different countries). However, such arguments miss the point.

Growing importance of origin images in marketing

The issue is not so much one of little cloth tags on garments or small print on a coffee machine label, but whether buyers are influenced by a product's origin when they can deduce it from their overall knowledge (e.g. Ferrari is Italian), when it is a visible part of the marketing mix, such as in advertising or in a brand's name, or when it permeates all facets of corporate strategy, as in the case of Kentucky Fried Chicken in Japan, whose president, Shin Ohkawara, said that 'We sell the idea of good old America. Green pastures, fresh air, clean water' (Naisbitt and Aburdene 1990: 124) (see CORPORATE IDENTITY; PRODUCT POLICY; THE MARKETING MIX).

The evidence is that origin images are being used more than ever before by sellers and buyers alike (Tse and Gorn 1993, Johansson 1993). There are five key explanations for this:

1 To simplify information processing in complex markets that present them with a growing plethora of goods, consumers increasingly use 'chunking' – that is, they use individual cues, such as a product's origin, as surrogate indicators of product quality and social acceptability (e.g. 'this camera is made in Japan, so it must be reasonably priced, of good quality, technologically advanced, and an overall good buy').

2 Increased exposure to media and other stimuli heightens buyers' awareness of foreign countries, their products, and differences among them (see GLOBAL MARKETING).

3 With modern technology, most products can be made virtually anywhere by many different competitors, and managers are faced with a growing standardization in intrinsic product features. To meet the challenge of differentiating their brands in the eyes of their customers, they increasingly rely on extrinsic identifiers such as product origin or brand name as a means of developing USPs and market positioning strategies (see BRANDING AND BRAND MANAGEMENT; CORPORATE IDENTITY; GLOBAL MARKETING).

4 Governments and industry associations often undertake 'Buy Domestic' campaigns to help protect local producers from foreign competitors. Whether or not they achieve their goal of encouraging a preference for domestic goods, from the buyer's perspective such campaigns accentuate the importance of distinguishing among products based on their origins (see EXPORTING).

5 Marketers and consumers no longer view 'origin' in the strict sense of a product's place of manufacture, and so the globalization of production is not an especially relevant issue in this connection. Origin associations may refer to where the product was assembled, designed, or invented, to the producer's home nation, to the provenance of a key component or ingredient (e.g. 100% Colombian Coffee), and so on. In fact, it may be that the growth of hybrid products actually *broadened* the marketer's range of opportunities for being selective in origin designations in elective parts of the marketing mix (e.g. branding and promotion) as opposed to legally-mandated labelling. Volkswagen, for instance, uses the term German-*engineered*, rather than 'produced', to describe its cars in advertising (see BRANDING AND BRAND MANAGEMENT).

A telling example of the combined effect of factors such as those above comes from a study of Hong Kong tour operators, who were found to be favourably disposed to buying tour buses 'Made in Brazil' partly because of feelings that a country that produced Pelé in soccer and Senna in Formula 1 car racing must be doing something right (Stewart and Chan 1993). And a prime example of how aggressive origin-based marketing strategy can become is a TV commercial by Cadillac dealers in the USA, which begins with 'vintage Second World War footage', shows a Cadillac 'firing bullets from its grille and gunning down Japanese Zero fighter planes', and concludes by stating that 'compared to Cadillac, our competition are real Zeros' (see ADVERTISING).

Marketers' appreciation of the power of origin images can also be seen in the growing incidence of 'borrowed' origin identifiers, or associations of brand images with countries which are thought to be viewed positively by consumers but have little or no actual connection with the product. Examples include the British flag on American Reebok athletic shoes, the US-made Australian Hair Recipe shampoo (complete with a visual of a kangaroo on the package), and the Italian-sounding Cadillac Catera or Nissan Infiniti car models. In these and numerous similar cases, marketers enhance or distinguish their brands by relating them to origin images that carry design strengths, a cosmopolitan appeal or other desireable characteristics.

The growth of this practice represents a challenge to the owners of strong and widely recognized symbols, and governments often take action to protect them. The Reebok case, for example, was taken to court by Britain, on similar grounds to earlier French cases involving Champagne and Cognac. The European Union is also taking several steps in a variety of cases, such as defining the meaning of 'feta' or 'gouda' cheeses to protect Greek and Dutch producers against imitators from other countries.

Development and scope of PCI applications

In earlier times, countries exported and became known mostly for goods reflecting their resource-based comparative advantages (e.g. silk from China, furs from Canada, copper from Chile). As branding evolved, managers often stumbled upon the use of origin symbols as a matter of habitual practice or inertia, frequently resulting in simple descriptive names such as Pan-American Airlines or Norway Sardines. In some instances, it was consumers themselves who made origin notations popular. Hiram Walker's now-famous Canadian Club whisky was called just 'Club' until the 1890s, at which time the company was forced by American distillers to add the origin designator in a move that was aimed to protect their domestic market but in fact led to increased brand sales. Similarly, consumers used the 'Made in Germany' notation to actually identify and buy what they knew to be well-engineered products, although it was imposed on Germany by the victor nations in the aftermath of the First World War to encourage avoidance of German goods.

Today, origin images are used more deliberately and are present in society and marketing in a far broader set of circumstances than most people realize. To fully understand the scope and depth of origin references that are of relevance to marketing, therefore, it is useful to categorize them. This can be done based on the following four dimensions.

Origin cue expressions

Origin cues can take the form of various visual and/or aural stimuli and symbols, including: a nation's name or flag (e.g. the American flag colours in Tommy Hilfiger advertising); representative animals (Australian koala); landmarks (Eiffel Tower, Big Ben); stereotyped ordinary people (e.g. British-accent models promoting tea); personalities strongly associated with a country (e.g. Paul Hogan promoted Australia's Foster beer following the success of his film *Crocodile Dundee*); distinctive national music (Italian arias); or geographic characteristics (landmarks or beaches in tourism promotions).

Origin 'carriers' in the marketing mix

Origin images can be expressed through the marketing mix in a number of ways. A typical case is when they are either directly embedded in the *brand name* (London Fog outerwear, Clearly Canadian bottled water, Yugo cars) or indirectly suggested by it (Italy's Gucci leather goods). The *company name* may serve the same function even when the brand itself does not allude to its home country, as in the cases of cellular phones 'by Ericsson' or steel beams 'by Nippon Steel'. Origin cues are commonly found in *advertising*, where they are used as a USP, most often directly (So French, So Rare by Eugène de Paris cosmetics), sometimes by alluding to a country strength that is not related to the product (Lowenbräu beer advertised in North America as 'Tastefully Engineered in Germany'), and even by playing on negative stereotypes (in Britain, Lowenbräu portrayed a

German in lederhosen with the slogan 'Thankfully they sent us their lager, not their shorts'). Similarly, country images are very often included in *packaging* or on the product itself, through more prominent symbols or words than just on the made-in label (e.g. the Italian flag on some wine brands). Lastly, inventive marketers have used country images in various other parts of the *promotion mix*; for example, Dominos' Pizza delivery personnel in Japan wear American flag-coloured uniforms, to build on the favourable image of the USA there.

Who markets origins, and for what products?
Country images are not, of course, used only by *consumer* goods marketers. They can be found with similar frequency in marketing addressed to *business or industrial* customers (a *Fortune* magazine ad by Credit Suisse was headlined 'Incredibly Swiss. Incredibly American.' and featured a Saint Bernard dog and an American eagle as symbols of the two countries); *services* marketing (e.g. 'Argentine' steakhouses in Holland); *country* marketing (e.g. Spain promoting itself as a tourism destination or Canada as a location for investment); and so on. In fact, governments and trade associations have recently become much more proactive and systematic marketers as they try to protect their domestic markets and/or promote their image abroad (Seringhaus and Rosson 1991). Examples of campaigns of this type include Scotland: The Brand, Support British Industry, Czech Made, Think Canadian, Crafted With Pride in the USA, Buy Greek—You Win, and Swiss Timing. At the same time, there is renewed emphasis on country images in traditional government-supported trade promotion vehicles, such as trade fairs and exhibitions through major retailers ('Italian Week at Harrod's').

What origins are being marketed?
While countries were and continue to be the mainstay of origin-based marketing, it may surprise some to recall how often sub-national regional images are also used. Scotch whisky, Bohemian crystal, Brussels lace, Florida oranges, Bordeaux wines, Silicon Valley technology, and even New Orleans jazz, Liverpool's 'Mersey Beat', and the famous 'I Love New York' slogan, are just a small sample of regions with which marketers commonly associate their brands, in order to draw upon the strong reputation they have built over time. Recently, with the decline in importance of the nation-state and the growth of trade blocs, marketers also commonly use supra-national symbols, such as the 'Euro'-based brand names and advertising that are currently flooding the member countries of the European Union. In the same vein, products that are explicitly promoted as global brands (e.g. United Colors of Benetton) in effect attempt to establish 'world origin' images, as distinct from national ones.

The above dimensions are limited to stimuli provided by marketers. In addition, of course, consumers are exposed to vast amounts of information about countries, and often about their products, through education (e.g. geo-economic maps teaching pupils the 'main products' of each country), the mass media, portrayals of national stereotypes in films and books, etc.

In summary, then, PCI information is provided to buyers in literally millions of ways, directly or through symbolism, by marketers and others, making the images of countries and other kinds of 'places', and their relationship with products, an integral part of daily life.

2 An overview of research

The importance and influence of origin images underscore our need to better understand their nature and role in buyer behaviour. Not surprisingly, therefore, this is one of the most extensively researched fields, with over 500 articles and other publications reporting on hundreds of studies over the past three decades.

This research can be traced in terms of its evolution, and studied in more detail, by reference to several milestone publications. During the first years of research, Schooler (1965) and Reierson (1966) carried out the first systematic PCI studies and showed that origin images affect buyer behaviour; Nagashima (1970) developed a semantic differential scale for PCI surveys which, with various improvements, has been used extensively since; and Bilkey and Nes (1982) critically reviewed the first 25 or so PCI studies in a seminal article that served to awaken broad interest in the field. A number of more elaborate studies that followed helped to address questions raised by Bilkey and Nes or to otherwise advance our understanding of origin images and their effects, including Johansson *et al.* (1985), Chasin and Jaffe (1987), Han

(1989), Hong and Wyer (1989), Papadopoulos *et al.* (1991), Wall *et al.* (1991), Ettenson and Gaeth (1991), Ahmed and d'Astous (1993), and Klein *et al.* (1998). Recently, a significant amount of integrative work has been published, including the first book in this area (Papadopoulos and Heslop 1993), a meta-analysis of PCI findings focusing on experiment-based research (Liefeld 1993) and one focusing on survey-based studies (Peterson and Jolibert 1995) and a taxonomy and paradigm of PCI effects (Nebenzahl *et al.* 1997).

The findings of this research help us to place the origin phenomenon in the context of buyer behaviour and then consider its various facets in more detail. The next paragraphs draw mostly from the principal studies, both by this author and his colleagues and by other contributors to PCI research. A wealth of additional studies that may be of interest to individual readers may be identified through the citations lists of the studies referenced here.

PCI in context

The notion that 'the image is the object' is behind much of the diversity and richness of the human experience, and its importance is well recognized in marketing. Images result from people's perceptions of objects. Since perception can be defined as 'the meaning we attribute to things', and given that it occurs at the individual level, each object has a different image for each individual observer. And, since people act on what they *believe* is true, perception has a major impact on behaviour.

Images and perception are, inevitably, intertwined with stereotyping, the process of generalizing to an entire class of objects a characteristic(s) derived from a limited number of observations. Notwithstanding their occasionally ugly consequences, stereotypes are inherent to the thought processes we use to cope with the world around us, and develop over time as we classify repeated observations into schemata which we then correlate to form our view of the world. Thus images are stereotyped schemata that help us to interpret, understand, categorize, correlate or assess various objects and phenomena. They are part of strong chains of beliefs which, taken together, form personal 'theories' that are the backbone of our actions.

Product images or stereotypes represent bundles of both *intrinsic* and *extrinsic* attributes. Viewing 'products' broadly to include physical goods, services, ideas, people or other entities, intrinsic characteristics can range from technical features, components, performance characteristics, or delivery times, to the architectural design of a company's headquarters building or the physical appearance of a person. Extrinsic characteristics include a product's brand name or price, its warranty or the reputation of its producer and distributors.

The image of places, in their role as origins of products, is one of the extrinsic cues that may become part of a product's total image. Since place images are multi-faceted (more so like brand names than prices, for example), they may carry significant amounts of both 'factual' as well as 'emotional' information. This may range from the producing country's level of industrial development and known areas of manufacturing expertise, to the aura, mystique or overall likeability of a country or people perceived to be 'exotic', 'powerful', 'hardworking' or 'lazy', and 'imperialists' or 'peace loving'.

Key research findings

Origin image research has used a large variety of methodological approaches and taken many forms. Three main distinctions that will be mentioned below, in summarizing various types of findings, are study designs based on (i) *surveys* versus *experiments*, (ii) *single-* versus *multiple-*cue methods (respondents asked to evaluate origins alone or in conjunction with other cues such as brand and price), and (iii) *global* versus *product-specific* assessments (obtaining buyers' views of a country's products in general or in terms of specific product categories).

Use and relative importance of PCI in buyer decisions
Numerous studies have confirmed that people hold stereotyped images of both foreign countries and their own, and of the countries' products, which result in strong beliefs about the countries' strengths and weaknesses as producers and are used as important information and influence buyer behaviour.

Multiple-cue studies, the most appropriate in this instance, show that the relative importance of origin versus other cues varies depending on the particular strengths of the other cues with which it is compared in given settings, such as price, dealer reputation or brand name (Ahmed and d'Astous 1993, Liefeld 1993). That is, origin is sometimes more and sometimes less important in consumer decision making, depending on the situation. Furthermore, the extent to which consumers in different countries seem to care for where a product comes from varies; for example, in one study Canadians were found to be less sensitive to the made-in cue than French consumers (Papadopoulos et al. 1987).

Several studies have shown that national stereotypes influence all types of decision makers, that is, not only end-consumers but also professionals in various settings where country image is an issue. This includes industrial buyers (Ahmed and d'Astous 1995), retail buyers (Sternquist and Tolbert 1986), and business executives selecting country targets for exports (Johansson and Moinpour 1977, Papadopoulos and Denis 1988) or direct investment (Papadopoulos et al. 1997b).

PCI correlates
The findings on demographic and other similar factors that might help to explain why different people hold different country images have been mixed. Some studies have documented perceptual and attitudinal differences in terms of gender (Heslop and Wall 1986), and several researchers have noted a connection between higher education levels and more positive foreign product evaluations. However, the findings on other hypothesized relationships with income, age or household size have been inconsistent and point to the need for more research.

Variations in origin images
The product-specific and global images of a country are congruent. In other words, although, naturally, the images of specific product categories from the same country vary depending on its perceived competence in various areas, the evidence is that each category is evaluated higher or lower in line with the country's global image (e.g. Reierson 1966; Papadopoulos et al. 1997a). This does not mean, for example, that wines from Japan might be judged to be better than those from France, but that the stronger Japan's image is overall, the higher the evaluations of its wines will be.

Various studies have shown that origin images tend to be consistent among consumers worldwide, although, naturally again, some variations have been observed. Products from highly developed major exporters, like the USA, Germany and Japan, are usually evaluated highly in most countries, niche exporters of recognizable brands like Sweden follow, and other countries are less well known and/or receive less positive assessments of their products.

While most studies have looked at country images internationally, a few have focused on, and have found, intra-national differences. Consumers in various parts of a country may hold different views of a given foreign origin, and they also hold distinctly different views for products from various regions within their own country (McDougall and Rawlings 1979, Heslop et al. 1998).

Several researchers have reported that made-in images do change over time, suggesting that producers who are presently successful in international markets cannot afford to rest on their laurels. Favourable product–country stereotypes may deteriorate if buyers perceive a given origin to be 'slipping'. Of course, unfavourable images may also change for the better and begin threatening well-heeled producers who presently dominate a given foreign market. Japan's successful drive to change its image from the low-cost, low-quality stigma of the 1950s is a prime example of this, and South Korea is a more recent case in point. At the same time, entrenched opinions are hard to change, as shown by consumers' continuing reluctance to buy goods made in East European countries several years after the fall of communism (Papadopoulos et al. 1997a).

Origin images affect consumers' price expectations. Seaton and Vogel (1981) found that, other things being equal, a US-produced Volkswagen has a lower preference utility than when it is made in Germany. Nebenzahl and Jaffe (1993) confirmed this finding and were able to estimate the price effect of various origin locations. In essence, the lower the image of an origin is, the greater is the price discount that consumers expect to receive if they are to consider buying its products versus identical ones from countries with a stronger image.

How PCI works

The country–product image interface works either as a *halo* construct, when little is known about a country's products and consumers use its image to assess them, or as a *summary* construct, when more is known about the products than the country, and its image is formed from the former (Han 1989). For example, respondents in several studies have rated Canadian products quite highly although they state that they know little about them, by transposing onto these products their positive views of Canada and its people. Conversely, today's positive image of Japan emerged slowly from its products and improved as they did over time.

Research has confirmed that each of the cognitive (beliefs), affective (emotions) and conative (predispositions to act) components of attitude plays a distinct role in origin evaluations as in other parts of marketing, thus making consumer behaviour less predictable than marketers might like. Inconsistency among these components helps to explain why imports in industrialized countries continue to rise in spite of 'Buy Domestic' campaigns; consumers may like and want to support their home country (affect) but, in many cases, simply believe that foreign products are better (cognitive component).

In choosing between domestic and foreign products, buyers attempt to balance several competing influences. In countries that are highly developed, where national pride is reported to be stronger, and/or where foreign competitors are not perceived as a serious threat to domestic employment or the economy in general, consumers may be more likely to opt for domestic goods, other things being equal – and vice versa. Overall, however, while an attitudinal bias in favour of domestic goods is often found, the evidence is that a preference for them is far from universal and that consumers may well choose foreign products if they judge them to be superior.

The images that buyers hold have been found to consist of groups of distinct underlying constructs. For products, these include 'product integrity' (workmanship, quality, after-sales service, and other technical characteristics); their 'price-value' relationship; their 'presence', or degree of visibility and availability in the consumer's home market; and the consumer's 'responses' to them, including one's pride in owning them, satisfaction from their performance, and continuing willingness to buy them (Papadopoulos et al. 1991). For the origin countries themselves, three constructs have been identified: (i) beliefs about a country's degree of industrial development and ability to produce advanced goods; (ii) affective feelings toward the country and its people; and (iii) consumer views about whether or not they would like to have closer ties with the country being evaluated (Heslop and Papadopoulos 1993).

Several studies have tried to integrate various research findings into a comprehensive model of PCI effects. Although there are significant variations among individual studies, the hierarchy of effects model in Figure 1 is fairly representative of the basic thrust of most such efforts. The model draws on structural analysis of the views of buyers from various countries. It suggests that consumer beliefs about a country's products are influenced by the characteristics and perceived competence of the country and its people and by their degree of familiarity with them. Product beliefs in turn influence product evaluations and, ultimately, behaviour. The bi-directional arrows between country and product beliefs and evaluation suggest the potential halo versus summary hypotheses that were discussed above. In organizational buying situations involving industrial buyers or intermediaries buying for resale, product beliefs and evaluation would be influenced by an additional construct that might be entitled 'Business Evaluation' and refer to such elements as profit margins, supplier service, and so on.

These key research findings have several strategic implications for marketers.

3 Strategic implications of PCI

The preceding discussion outlined what the PCI phenomenon is all about: a pervasive influence, of more interest to some than to others, based on long-ingrained and deeply-held beliefs about the images of places, and playing an increasingly important role in buyer decision making in today's complex markets. The findings suggest the need to take into account and learn more about origin images and to incorporate

Special topics

```
┌─────────────────────┐      ┌─────────┐      ┌──────────┐      ┌──────────┐
│  Characteristics and│      │ Product │      │ Product  │      │ Purchase │
│ perceived competence│◄────►│ Beliefs │◄────►│Evaluation│─────►│Behaviour │
│of a country and its │      │         │      │          │      │          │
│       people        │      └─────────┘      └──────────┘      └──────────┘
└─────────────────────┘           ▲
                                  │
                             ┌─────────┐
                             │ Product │
                             │Familiarity│
                             └─────────┘
```

Figure 1 A basic model of country image effects

this knowledge in the development of international marketing strategies, whether the 'product' is a physical good, a service, an industry association or a country. This section highlights the main implications of the PCI phenomenon along four main dimensions.

Origins in marketing strategy

The frequent use of origin images as key elements in marketing strategy suggests that many producers believe that their target consumers recognize the origin being promoted, have a positive image of it, and consider it a distinct, meaningful, and useful product attribute in making brand choices – in short, that they share the manufacturer's enthusiasm about its reputation. Ascertaining whether or not such beliefs are actually shared by consumers is a key challenge facing marketers. The research tells us that some consumers are indifferent to where a product comes from, and that those who do care may in fact harbour negative stereotypes about some origins, or have generally positive feelings about others but are not willing to translate these feelings into action, or think that the product is too highly priced given its place of manufacture.

In other words, consumers' beliefs about countries mean that origin should not be considered as 'just another product characteristic' which may be used as a USP. Incorporating origin notations in a brand's name is a particularly risky strategy since it is not easy to change (Yugo cars might have had a somewhat better chance of success in foreign markets if they were not so strongly identified with a country not known as a major car manufacturer). Drawing from case-specific research and depending on the situation, various producers may decide to aggressively promote, strengthen, simply present, or even make every effort to conceal, their product's origin.

This matter may be of particular relevance to manufacturers considering a shift in the location of production. Such shifts often occur from high- to low-cost labour countries that typically have a lower caché, and many producers may be unable to use Volkswagen's 'German--engineered' approach to retain the allure of the original home country. In such cases, the cost savings may be outweighed by losses in profit margin. The reverse scenario may have the opposite implications. For example, a production or assembly move by Hyundai from South Korea to Britain may enable the brand not only to cash-in on a more prestigious image but also to lay claim to 'home-made' status that may appeal to British consumers, thereby more than countering the associated extra cost.

Coupled with the growth of hybrid products, the practice of borrowed origin identifiers presents marketers with a broad range of potential opportunities. The exciting possibilities that are available are exemplified by the enormous success in Canada of a series of 'foreign recipe' packaged dinners by Loblaw, a major supermarket chain. Although mostly made in Canada with local ingredients, these products carry a strong identification with the often-exotic countries of origin where the recipes were invented (e.g. from 'Swedish meatballs' to 'Shanghai Stir Fry' and 'Memories of Kobe burgers'). Such approaches, which can be operationalized in branding, advertising and packaging, are available to virtually all the products that use ingredients or components from, are partly made in, or were otherwise inspired by the practices and the reputation of various different countries. The other side of this coin represents a threat to the domestic producers and governments in the originating countries, who may need to take steps at home and/or abroad to safeguard the equity represented by their image.

Past research also points to the fact that origin identifiers need not be restricted to country images. There is a broad range of opportunities for using the images of cities, regions, areas, states, provinces, continents, trade blocs and so on. Such associations may be particularly useful as competition intensifies and companies look for new ways to position their products internationally.

In using PCIs, marketers must be very careful to establish a meaningful connection between origin image components and product attributes. As shown in the model in Figure 1, country images do not impact behaviour directly but through product beliefs. Consumers will not buy a country's products just because they 'like it' or appreciate its industrial competence, and therefore image claims must be linked to product attributes. For example, if research finds that consumers consider a country's people 'highly trustworthy' or 'future-oriented', this can be translated into advertising claims of, respectively, product reliability and innovativeness.

The relative importance of origin cues varies across different types of buyers, and research tells us that there are also variations in the images of various origins. This calls for careful market segmentation as an input to origin-related strategic decisions. Consumers in the north of France may hold different views of British products than those in the south, and in one study male buyers were found to be more reluctant than women to purchase goods from a communist country (Heslop and Wall 1986). Thus 'Made in Britain' or 'Made in China' products may be evaluated differently by different market segments within the same target country (see MARKET SEGMENTATION).

Lastly, the strength and universality of country images varies and may affect the extent to which marketers may be able to standardize their strategies across different country targets. While Japan has been found to have a universally positive image, views of such countries as Sweden and Canada vary by target country depending, at least in part, on the degree of interaction between seller and buyer countries and therefore the consumers' familiarity with the exporters' products. Therefore, a 'Made in Sweden' or 'Made in Canada' USP may work better in Finland and the USA, respectively, than elsewhere.

PCI use by various types of firms

The importance of origin images has different implications for different kinds of firms. PCIs are of the most immediate interest for products intended for export. Exporters face established images of their home country in the minds of target customers, regardless of whether or not they have taken an active part in creating them. These images can act as significant barriers to or facilitators of foreign market entry. In deciding what market penetration strategies to use, exporters need to know what images consumers hold about the origin country, what the components of these images are, and how they compare to the images of both competing exporters and domestic producers. For example, retailers in a highly developed market may think twice before committing to buy from a country that has a reputation of shoddy workmanship or poor supplier service.

Importers, who may include agents, retailers and wholesalers, industrial distributors, and other firms who import goods for resale or their own use, face similar challenges to exporters, but in many cases they have a greater amount of latitude since they can be selective about where they buy from. Where variants of the same product can be procured from different countries, assessing the images of these countries can serve as a significant input to sourcing decisions and determining appropriate trade-offs among intrinsic features, price, brand name, origin and so on.

Although trade is not a zero-sum game, exporters' and importers' gains represent, essentially, domestic producers' losses. Foreign producers enjoying a favourable country image may have an advantage over domestic manufacturers, especially in comparatively less advanced markets. Conversely, if all of the factors mentioned earlier are present (high home-country industrial and market development, perceived economic vulnerability, high degree of nationalism, and favourable alignment of all three attitude components), then domestic producers promoting a home-made appeal have an advantage. However, both research and import statistics show that such factors rarely converge and that there is no *de facto* preference for domestic goods. No matter how many 'Buy Domestic' campaigns are launched in consuming countries, challenging, for example, Japan's dominance in consumer electronics will remain a tall order unless domestic producers somehow succeed in offering similarly-valued products.

PCI use by type of country

Producers from different types of nations face different strategic problems. Developed nations presently hold enviable positions, but their manufacturers face ever-growing challenges to their dominance in markets and customers' minds. There is no reason to believe that the example of Japan, already followed by the original four 'Asian Tigers' (Taiwan, South Korea, Singapore, Hong Kong), will not be duplicated soon by additional ones, such as Malaysia and Thailand, as they develop their ability to compete globally. The main issue facing developed nation producers is how to build on their competitive advantages to protect and enhance their existing strong image franchises.

'Developing' and 'Emerging' nations are the current challengers to the world's major exporters. The collapse of communist regimes is changing the way Eastern and Central European countries are viewed, and these countries, along with the Asian Tigers and other major nations such as China, India and Brazil, are fairly advanced and are already making significant inroads into many markets. However, as noted above, existing perceptual barriers are hard to overcome. To develop a preference for products from these countries, consumers expect both quality and a value component in the form of lower prices. Strategies focusing on a limited range of goods that offer high value may, in line with the 'summary construct', help to spearhead image improvements and establish these countries as competitors on an equal footing with the major exporters.

Less-developed nations face the biggest challenge as consumers hold negative stereotypes about them. Their products are often seen as poorly made, low in technology, of a low price but also lower value, and unreliably serviced. Consumers, however, generally have less difficulty buying low-risk products (e.g. T-shirts) than high-risk ones (e.g. electronics, pharmaceuticals) from such countries. Therefore, an initial focus on penetration-priced, medium-quality, low value added products, moving gradually towards higher quality and greater technological sophistication, may offer the best chance of successful exports for nations in this stage of their economic development.

More generally, niche marketing is the indicated strategy for producers from any but the largest and most advanced exporting nations. To illustrate the potential positive effects of this strategy on consumers, in a study asking respondents to name typical products from various countries the number of mentions accounting for the greatest proportion was four for Japan versus about 15 for each of the USA and UK (Heslop and Papadopoulos 1993). Identifying weak points that may be used by niche marketers to challenge major competitors requires case-specific research (existing research shows, for example, that high prices and a lack of innovativeness are perceived as weak points of, respectively, Germany and Japan).

The government–public policy perspective

As was seen above, governments and trade associations are also heavy users of origin appeals when promoting domestic goods among foreign or, more commonly, local consumers. In the current environment of ever-lower import tariffs and freer trade, developed nations are in fact taking the lead in arguing for their products on their merits rather than through protectionist legislation. The research, however, shows that 'Buy Domestic' campaigns, or those aimed at attracting tourism and investment, have yielded mixed results at best. Public policy makers, therefore, need to consider PCIs more carefully by:

1 Recognizing that their country's or region's image may have far-reaching implications going well beyond the traditional PCI domain. In addition to tourism and investment, the origin image issue can be viewed even from the perspective of groups of employers (the 'product') trying to attract qualified employees (the 'buyers'). For example, the strong technology images of southern France and Silicon Valley in the USA act like magnets for computer personnel and

help companies meet their staffing needs. By contrast, companies in other technology regions with weaker images are not readily a part of the buyers' set of options, and have a chronic staffing problem in spite of their governments' efforts to attract software and other engineers from other regions or countries.

2. Developing better and more co-ordinated strategies that may be undertaken in conjunction with major firms and/or industry associations. *Ad hoc* efforts undertaken only when the domestic economy is threatened, or disparate campaigns by various agencies, will be less effective than comprehensive strategies that begin from a view of the country as a corporate entity whose individual industries are akin to a firm's product lines. Graby (1993) has discussed this concept in detail, and the multifaceted, well coordinated I Love New York campaign by various New York City groups is a good example.

3. Considering the implications of research more carefully. Many governments are indifferent to whether or how their firms use country identifiers. This stance, however, is based on the 'halo' hypothesis, considering national image as a given which is transposed to products. This does not account for the 'summary' construct view, which may be more relevant in some situations. In such cases, where target consumers know little about the country, there may be a greater need to encourage a nation's firms to identify themselves with their origin, through incentive-based and other programmes, when marketing abroad.

4. Protecting their national image against 'borrowers', at least to the furthest extent possible. While government interference with free market forces is generally unwelcome, unwitting 'lenders' may end up losing control over their national image if they do not pro-actively support it. This may in some instances involve court action, as in France's Champagne case, but in most instances it is a matter of marketing strategy. There is little reason to believe that places cannot see their images in the same way that companies view their brands, and take similar steps to distinguish 'the real thing' from imitators.

5. Perhaps most importantly, there is a need to align image claims with a place's actual capabilities, and to appreciate that foreign (and even domestic) consumers may not share a nation's view of its products. As business marketers know well, attempting to build a brand image that exceeds its performance has more chances of backfiring than succeeding (e.g. the Czech Made designation may in fact act more as a deterrent than as a reason to buy for some consumers in major developed markets). As in business marketing, national image building will be more effective if it focuses on what a country can do best, rather than if it claims to be best in everything (tourism and investment promotion often suffers from 'all-round best' claims, which disappoint buyers, reduce repeat purchase rates and lead to negative word-of-mouth effects).

4 Summary and conclusion

This entry has attempted to portray the importance and complexity of the PCI phenomenon, and to outline some of the significant implications that arise from it. Both business and other managers need to consider PCIs carefully in marketing decisions, especially since the use and impact of origin images is likely to grow in the future. The significance of origin claims should neither be exaggerated nor ignored. As with other extrinsic cues that affect purchase decisions, PCI will be less important in some situations than in others. What makes PCI a strong candidate for careful consideration, however, is that, unlike some other cues like warranty, price, or even brand name, people carry place images in their minds even if the marketer chooses not to use them as a central strategic element.

Before concluding it should be noted that, notwithstanding the large number of PCI studies to date, research has yet to address several specific issues in depth. A major limiting factor has been the narrow focus of some researchers and managers on 'made-in labels' as the main carrier of origin information. This has meant that detailed knowledge on the role of origin cues provided through other means is missing. An additional area of interest in domestic rather than international marketing is differences in intra-regional images. For geographically dispersed countries like the USA, Brazil or Russia, or those with several distinct regional and/or cultural identities, like the UK, Belgium, or Indonesia, such differences can be an important factor in marketing strategy. Lastly, there clearly is tremendous scope for looking more carefully at the knowledge base that has been developed in several related disciplines and can help to develop an even better undestanding of how place images work: these include, as a small sample, nationalism and ethnocentrism, cross-cultural psychology, international relations, tourism and, within marketing itself, brand image and brand equity.

NICOLAS PAPADOPOULOS
CARLETON UNIVERSITY

Note

I am indebted to my colleague and co-investigator, Professor Louise A. Heslop, with whom some 60 field studies in about 20 countries have been carried out in the past 15 years, involving approximately 16,000 respondents. This work is co-ordinated through our IKON Research Group at Carleton University and has also involved our co-researchers in various countries and our students, whose contributions are also gratefully acknowledged.

Further reading

(References cited in the text marked *)

* Ahmed, Sadrudin A. and d'Astous, Alain (1993) 'Cross-national evaluation of made-in concept using multiple cues', *European Journal of Marketing*, 27: 39–52.
* Ahmed, Sadrudin A. and d'Astous, Alain (1995) 'Comparison of country-of-origin effects on household and organizational buyers' product perceptions', *European Journal of Marketing*, 29: 35–51.
* Baker, Michael J. and Currie, C. (1993) 'Country of origin — the 5th element of the marketing mix?', Marketing Education Group Conference, Loughborough, July.
* Bilkey, Warren J. and Nes, Erik (1982) 'Country-of--origin effects on product evaluations', *Journal of International Business Studies*, 8: 89–99.
* Chasin, J.B. and Jaffe, Eugene D. (1987) 'Industrial buyer attitudes towards goods made in Eastern Europe: an update', *European Management Journal*, 5: 180–9.
* Ettenson, Richard and Gaeth, Gary (1991) 'Consumer perceptions of hybrid (bi-national) products', *Journal of Consumer Marketing*, 8: 13–18

Gold, John R., and Ward, Stephen V. (1994) *Place Promotion: The Use of Publicity and Marketing to Sell Towns and Regions*, New York: John Wiley & Sons. (Discusses place-driven promotion strategies and tactics.)
* Graby, Françoise (1993) 'Countries as corporate entities in international markets', in Papadopoulos, N. and Heslop, L.A. (eds), *Product–country Images: Impact and Role in International Marketing*, Binghamton, NY: The Haworth Press, 257–84.
* Han, Min C. (1989) 'Country image: halo or summary construct?' *Journal of Marketing Research*, XXVI: 222–9.
Head, David (1992) *Made in Germany': The Corporate Identity of a Nation*, London: Hodder & Stoughton. (Chronicles the evolution of Germany's image and identity).
* Heslop, Louise A. and Papadopoulos, Nicolas (1993) '"But who knows where or when": reflections on the images of countries and their products', in Papadopoulos, N. and Heslop, L.A. (eds), *Product–Country Images: Impact and Role in International Marketing*, Binghamton, NY: The Haworth Press, 39–77.
* Heslop Louise A. and Wall, Marjorie (1986) 'Two views of the world: differences between men and women on perceptions of countries as producers of consumer goods', in Muller,T.E. (ed.) *Marketing*, Whistler, BC: Administrative Sciences Association of Canada Proceedings, Marketing Division, 123–132.
* Heslop, Louise A., Papadopoulos, Nicolas and Bourk, Margie (1998) 'An inter-regional and inter-cultural perspective on subcultural differences in product evaluations', *Canadian Journal of Administrative Sciences*, 15.
* Hong, Sung-Tai and Wyer, Robert S. Jr. (1989) 'Effects of country-of-origin and product-attribute information on product evaluation: an information processing perspective', *Journal of Consumer Research*, 16: 175–87.
* Johansson, Johnny K. (1993) 'Missing a strategic opportunity: managers' denial of country-of-origin effects', in Papadopoulos, N. and Heslop, L.A. (eds), *Product–Country Images: Impact and Role in International Marketing*, Binghamton, NY: The Haworth Press, 77–86.
* Johansson, Johny K. and Moinpour, R. (1977) 'Objective and perceived similarity of Pacific rim countries', *Columbia Journal of World Business*, Winter, 65–76.
* Johansson, Johnny K., Douglas, Susan P. and Nonaka, I. (1985) 'Assessing the impact of country of origin on product evaluations: a new methodological perspective', *Journal of Marketing Research*, 22; 388–96.
* Klein, Jill G., Ettenson, Richard and Morris, Marlene D. (1998) 'The animosity model of foreign prod-

uct purchase: an empirical test in the People's Republic of China', *Journal of Marketing*, 62: 89–100.

Kotler, Philip, Haider, Donald H. and Rein, Irving (1993) *Marketing Places: Attracting Investment, Industry, and Tourism to Cities,* States, and Nations, New York, NY: The Free Press. *(Discusses broader place-driven marketing strategies for the purposes* identified in the title.)

* Liefeld, John P. (1993) 'Consumer use of country-of-origin information in product evaluations: evidence from experiments', in Papadopoulos, N. and Heslop, L. (eds), *Product–Country Images: Impact and Role in International Marketing*, Binghamton, NY: The Haworth Press, 117–56.
* McDougall, Gordon H.G. and Rawlings, B.J. (1979) 'Canadian advertising appeals: or will 'Oh Canada' sell beer?', *Business Quarterly* Autumn, 39–45.
* Nagashima, Akira (1970) 'A comparison of Japanese and U.S. attitudes toward foreign products', *Journal of Marketing* January, 260–6.
* Naisbitt, John and Aburdene, Patricia (1990) *Megatrends 2000*, New York, NY: Avon.
* Nebenzahl, Israel D. and Jaffe, Eugene D. (1993) 'Estimating demand functions from the country-of-origin effect', in Papadopoulos, N. and Heslop, L. (eds), *Product–Country Images: Impact and Role in International Marketing*, Binghamton, NY: The Haworth Press, 159–78.
* Nebenzahl, Israel D., Jaffe, Eugene D. and Lampert, Shlomo I. (1997) 'Towards a theory of country image effect on product evaluation', *Management International Review*, 37: 27–49.
* Papadopoulos, Nicolas and Denis, Jean-Emile (1988) 'Inventory, taxonomy and assessment of methods for international market selection', *International Marketing Review*, 5: 38–51.
* Papadopoulos, Nicolas, and Heslop, Louise A. (eds), (1993) *Product–Country Images: Role and Implications for International Marketing*, New York, NY: The Haworth Press.
* Papadopoulos, Nicolas, Heslop, Louise A., Graby, Françoise and Avlonitis, George (1987) 'Does country-of-origin matter? some findings from a cross-cultural study of consumer views about foreign products', Working Paper no. 87-104, Cambridge, MA: Marketing Science Institute, Cambridge.
* Papadopoulos, Nicolas, Heslop, Louise A. and Bamossy, Gary J. (1991) 'A comparative analysis of domestic versus imported products', *International Journal of Research in Marketing* 7: 283–94.
* Papadopoulos, Nicolas, Heslop, Louise A., Szamosi, Leslie, Ettenson, Richard and Sullivan-Mort, Gillian (1997a) '"Czech Made" or check mate?

an assessment of the competitiveness of East European products', in Wong, V. and Shaw,V. (eds), *Marketing: Progress, Prospects, Perspectives*, Warwick, UK: European Marketing Academy Proceedings, May, 993–1012.

* Papadopoulos, Nicolas, Jog, Vijay M., Heslop, Louise A. and D'Souza, Ritoo (1997b) 'The investment climate in Canada: foreign investor experiences and perceptions', in Preece, S. and Woodcock, P. (eds), *International Business*, Vol. 18, St. John's, Newfoundland: Administrative Sciences Association of Canada Proceedings, International Business Division; June, 37–47.
* Peterson, Robert A. and Jolibert, Alain J.P. (1995) 'A meta-analysis of country-of-origin effects', *Journal of International Business Studies*, 26: 883–900.
* Reierson, Curtis C. (1966) 'Are foreign products seen as national stereotypes', *Journal of Retailing*, 42; 33–40.
* Schooler, Robert D. (1965) 'Product bias in the Central American Common Market', *Journal of Marketing Research*, II: 394–7.
* Seaton B. and Vogel, R.H. (1981) 'International dimensions and price as factors in consumer perceptions of autos', presented to the Academy of International Business Conference, Montreal, October.
* Seringhaus, F.H. Rolf and Rosson, Philip J. (1991) *Export Development and Promotion: The Role of Public Organizations*, Boston, MA: Kluwer Academic Publishers.
* Sternquist B. and Tolbert, S. (1986) 'Survey: retailers shun apparel industry's Buy American program', *Marketing News*, 23 May: 8.
* Stewart, Sally and Chan, Edmen (1993) 'Influence of place-of-production on industrial buyers' perceptions', in Papadopoulos, N. and Heslop, L. (eds), *Product–Country Images: Impact and Role in International Marketing*, Binghamton, NY: The Haworth Press, 223–44.
* Tse, David K., and Gorn, Gerald J. (1993) 'An experiment on the salience of country-of-origin in the era of global brands', *Journal of International Marketing* 1: 57–76.
* Wall, Marjorie, Liefeld, John P. and Heslop, Louise A. (1991) 'Impact of country-of-origin cues on consumer judgement in multi-cue situations: a covariance analysis', *Journal of the Academy of Marketing Science* 19: 105–13.

See also: ADVERTISING; BRANDING AND BRAND MANAGEMENT; CORPORATE IDENTITY; EXPORTING; GLOBAL MARKETING; MARKET SEGMENTATION; PRODUCT POLICY; THE MARKETING MIX

Corporate identity

1 Introduction
2 What is corporate identity?
3 Historical perspective
4 Corporate identity management
5 Towards a theory of corporate marketing

Overview

Corporate identity is a topic which has received increasing attention in the last ten years, evidenced by a wide range of published material on the subject. This aspect of management is developing quickly at the present time and the entry seeks to discuss the implications of corporate identity for marketing in particular. First, a working definintion of corporate identity must be established. The definition that is currently most frequently used by practitioners and managers is that corporate identity describes the distinct attributes of an organization, that is to say it is concerned with what an organization 'is'. However, a concept as broad as corporate identity must draw on a number of disciplines; in this case, for example, psychology, strategy, philosophy and history. It must also take into account the scope of the business and the range and type of products and services it offers, not forgetting the values held by staff within the organization and all the things which the organization says or does.

The development of corporate identity since the 1950s is considered, from the idea of identity as image to the more cross-disciplinary approach of the present day. Four main schools of thought have evolved over the issue of corporate identity: the strategic school, the behavioural school, the total communications school and the visual school. The position of each is discussed in turn and models derived to illustrate those elements which each school believes require attention in corporate identity management.

What, then, is the role of corporate identity in the marketing mix? A final model is offered – that of the ten Ps of corporate marketing: philosophy; personality; people; products; price; place; promotion; performance; perception; and positioning.

Introduction

The last decade has witnessed increased international academic interest in corporate identity from scholars from a variety of disciplines including marketing (Baker and Balmer 1997; Dowling 1994), organizational behaviour (Albert and Whetten 1985; Hatch and Schultz 1997), strategy (Morison 1997; Gray and Balmer 1998) and from corporate communications (Van Riel 1995).

All the above scholars attach a good deal of importance to the identity concept and some, such as Van Riel (1995: 26) have argued that corporate identity is 'central' to an understanding of their discipline. This heightened interest in the area is also reflected in special editions of academic journals being devoted to the area: *European Journal of Marketing* (1997), *International Journal of Bank Marketing* (1997), *International Studies of Management and Organization* (1998), and *Academy of Management Review* (1999) and in recent tomes dealing with business and management (Tyrrell 1995). An international group of academics, managers and consultants having an interest in furthering their understanding of corporate identity (the International Corporate Identity Group) was formed in 1997. Furthermore, the Department of Marketing at the University of Strathclyde has recognized the importance of the area by establishing a research centre focusing on corporate identity. A number of Business Schools worldwide also include corporate identity as a subject on their degree programmes including Harvard (USA), Erasmus (Netherlands), Queensland University of Science and Technology (Australia), Strathclyde (UK), and Waikato Business School (New Zealand). Questions of corporate identity are frequently covered in the quality broadsheets and business press, a case in point being British Airways new global positioning strategy which has resulted in a variety of visual identities.

This entry on corporate identity aims to provide the reader with a broad introduction to this rapidly evolving area of management. The entry is broken down into four distinct sections. The next section, 'What is corporate identity?', outlines the underlying tenets, disciplines and objectives of corporate identity management and reproduces the ICIG's (International Corporate Identity Group's) influential 'Strathclyde Statement' on corporate identity. The following section, 'Historical perspectives', articulates the four evolutionary stages which have characterized our current understanding of the area. The subsequent section, entitled 'Corporate identity management', describes the various disciplinary approaches which have resulted and lead to a broader and wider appreciation of the elements requiring senior management attention. Finally, the last section 'Towards a theory of corporate marketing', the author anticipates future developments and postulates that we are, at present, witnessing the emergence of a new, cognate area of management, which derives much from marketing management. As such the author argues that the basic marketing mix needs to be re-appraised and extended in order to embrace the many elements which fuse to form what he calls the 'corporate marketing mix'.

2 What is corporate identity?

Corporate identity is a subject which is widely talked about, but is so little understood. As with marketing, there are a plethora of definitions. The definition of corporate identity favoured by the writer, and one that is increasingly used by a number of practitioners and managers working in the area, is that it refers to the distinct attributes of an organization, or, explained very simply, is concerned with what an organization 'is' (Balmer 1995). This view of corporate identity may be contrasted with other, influential, definitions of corporate identity which refer to the systems of visual identification. As this entry will reveal, both approaches may be seen to be complementary, since the modern understanding of corporate identity does, in part, grow out of graphic design.

The distinguishing features of corporate identity may be outlined as follows. First, corporate identity is eclectic in nature and draws on several management and non-management disciplines, such as psychology, and encompasses corporate strategy, corporate philosophy, corporate history, business scope, the range and type of products and services offered, (Balmer 1995; Moingeon and Ramanantsoa 1997; Schmidt and Ludlow 1995; Van Riel and Balmer 1997). Second, the 'soul' of a corporate identity is to be found in the mix of values held by staff within the organization (Balmer 1995; Balmer and Wilson 1998; Hatch and Schultz 1997). In the author's view this refers to 'The corporate personality'. Third, an organization's identity is revealed through everything the organization says, makes or does – this gives rise to the concept of total corporate communications (Balmer 1995).

In answering the question, What is the purpose of corporate identity management? Balmer and Stotvig provided the following definition:

> The main objective of corporate identity management is to ensure that an organisation's key stakeholders and stakeholder groups are favourably disposed towards the organisation. As such, it is presumed that such groups are predisposed towards the organisation's products or services (retail customers), to trade with the organisation (industrial customers), to purchase stock in the company (stockholders), to work for the company (employees), to provide a sympathetic legal framework (government), and to speak well of the organisation (the media and local communities).
> (Balmer and Stotvig 1997: 170)

The task of managing an organization's identity is complicated. It involves:

- understanding the company's philosophy, personality, (sub-cultures), identity, image and reputation;
- examining the above with internal–external environmental interfaces for signs of inconsistency and incompatibility;
- managing the organization's identity on an ongoing basis by senior management, with the Chief Executive taking an important role.

Corporate identity management can, quite often, result in major organizational change, including:

Figure 1 The basic tenets, disciplines and objectives involved in corporate identity management

- the repositioning of the organization;
- the nurturing of a new corporate personality (mix of internal value systems within the organization);
- altering the organization's corporate architecture, i.e. relationship between subsidiaries and business units and the organization's parent;
- improving the organization's corporate communications and visual identity;
- beginning the task of changing the image (and over time reputation) held of an organization by stakeholder groups both within and outwith the organization.

Figure 1 outlines the basic tenets, disciplines and objectives involved in corporate identity management.

Also of interest is a statement on corporate identity penned by a group of consultants and academics under the auspices of the International Corporate Identity Group (ICIG): an organization which aims to promote the strategic nature of corporate identity. This is known as the 'Strathclyde Statement':

> Every organisation has an identity. It articulates the corporate ethos, aims and values, and presents a sense of individuality that can help to differentiate the organisation within its competitive environment.
> When well managed, corporate identity can be a powerful means of integrating the many disciplines and activities essential to an organisation's success. It can also provide the visual cohesion necessary to ensure that all corporate communications are coherent with each other and result in an image consistent with the organisation's defining ethos and character.
> By effectively managing its corporate identity, an organisation can build understanding and commitment amongst its diverse stakeholders. This can be manifested in an ability to attract and retain customers and employees, achieve strategic alliances, gain the support of financial markets and generate a sense of direction and purpose. Corporate identity is a strategic issue.
> Corporate identity differs from traditional brand marketing since it is concerned with all of an organisation's stakeholders and the multifaceted way in which an organisation communicates.

3 Historical perspective

In this section the evolution of the theory relating to corporate identity since the 1950s will be briefly outlined. What becomes apparent is that different disciplines and national groups have made distinct contributions to this evolving area of management. Figure 2 outlines the main developments in the theory of corporate identity management.

Stage one – 1950s–1970s

For the main part, the focus was on the concept of the corporate image during this period, with North American writers undertaking a good deal of the seminal work in the area. They have remained influential ever since. Of particular influence were Boulding (1956) and Martineau (1958). The former, an eminent philosopher, noted in his text, *The Image*, that humans have to rely on images and concluded that there was an *a priori* link between an individual's image of an organization and that person's behaviour towards the organization. For his part, Martineau pointed out that if image was of such importance it deserved the attention of senior managers. His paper triggered a great deal of interest in the concept of corporate image by academics in the 1960s. See Bolger (1959), Bristol (1960), Budd (1969), Crespi (1961), Swanson (1957) and Tyler (1957).

In retrospect, a review of the literature reveals that there are three distinct disciplinary approaches to corporate image; the psychological paradigm, the graphic design paradigm, and the marketing and public relations paradigm. They are articulated below:

- *Psychology paradigm* – seen as a mental image or idea that is a visual, sensory or spatial analogy of reality (Grunig 1993).
- *Graphic design paradigm* – focuses on how an organization communicates an image through a name and/or icon (Baker and Balmer 1997).
- *Marketing and public relations paradigm* – views the concept from customers and other stakeholder groups and deals with image formation which is based on, 'the experiences, impressions, beliefs, feelings and

STAGE 1 - 1950s to 1970s

Concern with Corporate Image (perception of External Stakeholders) and with graphic design. Hegemony of the USA. Writings of Boulding (1956), Martineau (1958), and graphic design consultancies are influential.

1964

The concept of Corporate Identity coined by the graphic design consultants Lippincott and Margulies.

STAGE 2 - 1970s and early 1980s

Growing importance of graphic design consultancies in USA. British design, image research, and marketing communications consultants show interest in the area (Bernstein, 1986; Olins, 1978; Worcester, 1986). Increasing concern with the internal environment, with corporate communication and with the concepts of corporate personality and in particular corporate identity. Academic research reveals importance of personnel in image formation (Kennedy, 1977).

STAGE 3 - Late 1980s to present

Growing academic interest from marketers (Abratt, 1989; Dowling, 1986; Balmer, 1995; Van Riel, 1995), strategists (gray and Smeltzer, 1986), organizational behaviourists (Albert and Whetten, 1985; Fombrun and Shanley, 1990; Mael and Ashforth, 1991; Hatch and Schultz, 1997), psychologists (Bromley, 1993), public relations (Grunig, 1993). Greater emphasis given to the behavioral aspects of identity and, in particular, to organizational identity in N. America and Europe.

STAGE 4 - The present

Increasing international and interdisciplinary contact between academics: multidisciplinary nature of areas being recognised. Area frequently referred to as Corporate Brand Management (Balmer, 1995; Ind, 1997). Academic literature from mainland Europe becomes more widely known in Anglophone nations. Underlying rationale of corporate identity management starts to be formulated. Launch of the International Corporate Identity Group at the House of Lords (1996), with aims to provide a bridge between academic, managers and consultants is indicative of the fact that the area has "come of age".

STAGE 5 - 2000?

Establishment of Corporate Identity as a cognate area of management which may in time be known as 'Corporate Marketing'?

Hegemony returns to the USA?

Major general management consultancies fill void left by design consultancies?

Degree courses in Corporate Identity/Corporate Marketing offered by leading business schools?.

Figure 2 The main developments in the evolution of corporate identity management knowledge that people have about a company' (Bevis in Bernstein 1984: 125).

Whilst interest in the concept of corporate image has remained a dominant feature of the literature, there are a number of problems associated with the concept. Five will be articulated here.

1. There are a multiplicity of interpretations assigned to the concept. For instance, Kennedy (1977) identified 21 definitions of corporate image.
2. It has negative associations. Bernstein (1984) stated that image, in common parlance, means falsehood, whilst Olins (1979) remarked that it implies the use of sophisticated techniques of manipulation.
3. 'Corporate Image Management' is open to question. Kennedy's 1977 research repudiated the notion of 'Corporate Image Management.'
4. Different individuals and/or stakeholder groups may have different perceptions of the organization.
5. Not all stakeholder groups are of equal importance. The stakeholders for a holding company, conglomerate or subsidiary not only vary, but vary in importance.

The above explains why the concept of corporate image is so problematic. Indeed, Grunnig refuses to refer to the concept in his lectures to students.

In recent years, the concept of corporate image has partly been eclipsed by the distinct but related concept of corporate reputation. The distinguishing features of corporate reputation are that it is built up over a period of time (Gray and Balmer 1998) and focuses on the more tangible aspects of an organization, (what it does and how it behaves). Images can change quickly – reputations are more enduring. However, image and reputation can be damaged in a short space of time.

The following definitions of corporate reputation illustrate the fundamental differences between corporate image and reputation. It refers to the attributes or distinctivenesses which are found over a period of time:

> a corporate reputation is a set of attributes ascribed to a firm from a firm's past actions.
> (Weigelt and Camerer 1988: 1)

> corporate reputation is formed by the aggregate of messages and experiences received about an organisation's products and services by an individual, group or groups over a period of time.
> (Balmer 1997)

The concept of the corporate reputation is a useful development of the image concept. It has been argued that a positive reputation can act as a standard by which decisions, actions, communications and behaviour are evaluated. It is suggested by the author that managers should ask the question, 'Would this decision/action undermine our reputation?'

The basic building blocks of reputation as a control mechanism are illustrated in the 'DEAR' principle (Balmer 1998):

D = DECISIONS
E = EVALUATED
A = AGAINST
R = REPUTATION

Stage two – 1970s–1980s

The second stage which covers the period from the early 1970s to the 1980s witnesses the ascendancy of the concepts of the corporate identity and corporate personality and sees a growth of interest in the United Kingdom. British graphic design, image research and corporate communications consultants play an important role in disseminating knowledge about corporate identity, corporate image, and corporate visual identification through their consultancy work and publications.

This period saw a gradual change of emphasis away from questions of perception from the perspective of customers, to internal concerns and the role of personnel. Kennedy's (1977) research may be seen to provide an important bridge between Stages one and two. The findings of her research revealed that personnel were of pivotal importance in corporate image formation. At about the same time, the leading British identity consultant Wally Olins articulated a hypothesis of corporate identity management in his book, *The Corporate Personality: An Inquiry into the Nature of Corporate Identity* (1979). Olins' hypothesis was that organizations in their formative years develop a personality which mirrors that of the founder. Recent examples of this include

Richard Branson (Virgin Group), Anita Roddick (Body Shop), Bill Gates (Microsoft). Olins calls this stage of development the 'heroic' identity. He postulates that when such leaders depart it is left to his or her successor to place particular importance on the organization's personality and resulting identity since there is no longer a natural focus for the organization's identity. He calls this stage the 'technocratic' identity.

Recent research undertaken by Balmer (1998) concludes that the kernel of an organization's identity rests in the organization's personality which (after the founder has left) consists of the mix of sub-cultures. These include both corporate cultures, as well as other types of cultures such as professional and national/regional cultures.

The marketing concept of the corporate personality has a strong relationship with the concept of organizational identity, which is favoured by organizational behaviourists. Hatch and Schultz (1997) state that organizations' identities refer to what employees feel and think about their organization. It relates to the collective, commonly shared understanding of the organization's distinctive values and characteristics.

Stage three – 1980–present

The third stage, from the late 1980s to the present sees heightened interest in the concept of corporate identity in Europe. In Germany, according to Van Riel (1995), the writings of the consultant Birkigt and Stadler (1986) were influential. In addition, academics began to pay more attention to the topic throughout the UK, the British Commonwealth and in mainland Europe. Academic writers of note are the South African Russell Abratt (1989) who provides a comparative literatures review of corporate identity and provided a conceptual model which, for the first time, integrated the concept of corporate personality, corporate identity and corporate image. Other academics took a different stance. Cees van Reil (1995) integrated the concept of corporate identity, image and reputation within a broad framework of corporate communications management. Organizational behaviour theorists were also influential (Albert and Whetten 1985; Dutton and Dukerich 1991; Hatch and Schultz 1997).

One characteristic of the third stage was the emphasis given to the corporate identity/corporate image interface by a number of writers such as Abratt (1989), Stuart (1994) and Balmer (1997) and which built on the work of Kennedy (1977). The importance of the interface was noted by Stuart (1994) who stated that it represents a 'moment of truth' for an organization, in that it reveals discrepancies between what the organization is (identity), and how it is perceived. Balmer (1997) is of the view that the interface concept has great potential in focusing the minds of consultants and managers on three areas which can undermine the organization's attempts to secure a distinct position and strategic advantage in the marketplace. Balmer expanded the image–identity interface to cover other areas. Figure 3 replicates these interfaces. Figure 3 also includes a number of environmental interfaces since demographic, economic, natural, technological, political and cultural forces impinge upon the various facets of corporate identity management.

Stage four – The present

Stage four, covering the present period, is notable for the cross-disciplinary emphasis of the area, and a breaking down of barriers caused by national and linguistic factors. This has lead to an increased consensus on the fundamental tenets of corporate identity formation and management and greater clarity between the concepts of corporate personality, identity, image and communication.

In the marketing literature there has been an increased reference to the concept of 'The corporate brand' (Balmer 1995; King 1991; Olins 1995; and Ind 1997). The concept of the corporate brand has the distinct advantage that it is not confused with visual identification. King (1991), in discussing the differences between traditional product brands and company brands, observed that with the company brand there are more stakeholders, there are more points of contact, staff are important, and that the personnel directors have a role in its management. However, whilst there is an inextricable link between corporate identity and corporate branding they should be treated as distinct concepts. As with so many aspects of this evolving discipline, there is scope for a

Figure 3 Key interfaces in corporate identity management

clearer articulation of the differences between the concepts.

The work of Van Riel (1995) has highlighted another difference between traditional product brands and corporate brands with regard to communication. Van Riel breaks corporate communications into three categories:

1. marketing communications;
2. management communications (management actions and communication);
3. corporate communications (controlled communications).

There is, however, a broader interpretation of what is meant by corporate communication, in that organizations need to consider not only the multifaceted channels through which they communicate (staff, products, buildings), but to take into account that there are groups other than customers which are important to them. This has led to a new umbrella term which covers the complement of corporate communications which led to the author coining the phrase, 'total corporate communications' (Balmer 1995). Bernstein appears to have anticipated this view in the following quotation:

Special topics

A company needs to take a holistic view of communications because it communicates all the time (even if it doesn't want to or doesn't realize it) to all of its publics. The communication which is taking place even if unplanned or unconscious, is creating impressions, and images are being formed.

(Bernstein 1994: 118)

Figure 4 shows what the author calls 'The triple diamond of total corporate communications'. This model attempts to show:

- The complexity of corporate communications.
- The importance of vertical as well as horizontal communication channels, in that stakeholders communicate to each other about the organization, and that product/service experience (communication) may be at variance with formal communication messages.
- The importance of appreciating the above in relation to determining the anticipated feedback from targeted and non-targeted stakeholder groups.
- The need to understand and bridge the communications gap/target-response gap by senior management.

4 Corporate identity management

Schools of thought

In 1995 the present author identified seven schools of thought with regard to corporate identity management (Balmer 1995). There is still a view that each school of thought is mutually exclusive, but the author is of the view that the schools of thought reveal something of the totality of corporate identity management. The aim of this section is to explain the elements requiring attention in corporate identity management, drawing on the four main schools of thought.

The strategic school

Corporate identity can be regarded as strategic because:

- It is concerned with the positioning of an organization in its market or markets.
- It is concerned with questions of organizational design, that is the type of structural and management relationship between the parent organization and its business units and/or subsidiaries (see Kammerer 1989).
- It is concerned with responding to changes in the environment in order to maximize the market opportunities with the capabilities of

Figure 4 The triple diamond of total corporate communications the organization, with the needs of its stakeholders, and taking account of the characteristics of the organization's corporate brand or brands as evinced in its image and reputation.

The author concludes that this school of thought has gone through three phases, as evinced by three questions posited by authors in the 1950s, 1980s and, more recently, in the 1990s. Drucker's (1955) question, 'What is our business?'; Gray and Smeltzer's (1985) question, 'What is our image?'; and Balmer and Stotvig's (1997) question, 'What is our identity?'. In this article the author suggests another part to the triumvirate, namely, 'What is happening in the environment?'. Figure 5 shows what may be seen to be the foundations of corporate identity management. However, the model is incomplete since it fails to deal with: (i) questions of culture, (ii) questions of communication, and (iii) questions relating to branding and graphic design.

The behavioural school
This may be seen to encapsulate the work of organizational behaviourists such as Hatch and Schultz (1997), as well as the work of marketers such as Balmer and Wilson (1998). The behavioural school emphasizes the cultural aspects of corporate identity. In addressing this issue, Balmer (1997) states that managers might usefully address five issues:

1 Define the organization's mission and philosophy established by the founder or board of management.
2 Show sensitivity to the multiple sub-cultures present in the organization.
3 Evaluate dominant sub-cultures *vis-à-vis* the corporate mission and philosophy.
4 Nurture those sub-cultures which underpin the corporate mission and philosophy, or alter the mission in the light of the sub-cultures (and other considerations such as organizational competencies and environmental conditions).
5 Who is responsible for managing the above?

Figure 6 adds the behavioural element to strategic issues to be considered in corporate identity management. This still leaves us with questions relating to communications, branding and graphic design.

The total communications school
The third school is concerned with the multifaceted ways in which organizations communicate by controlled and uncontrolled means, and how such messages are interpreted by an organization's stakeholders. A useful introduction to the complexity of communications is described by Bernstein (1984) by making reference to his communications wheel. However, the following questions provide a start to addressing this difficult and complex area:

Figure 5 Foundations of corporate identity management: the strategic school
Source: Balmer (year?)

Special topics

Figure 6 Corporate identity management adding the behavioural dimension
Source: Balmer (year?)

1 Who are the organization's most important internal and external stakeholders?
2 Why are they important?
3 What are the most effective means of communicating with each stakeholder group?
4 How does the organization communicate with such groups at present?
5 What is the communication impact of managerial actions, staff behaviour, product and service quality, industry image and country of origin?
6 What is the communications impact of controlled communications such as advertising, public relations, sales promotions, annual reports and other publications?
7 Who is responsible for the above?

Figure 7 adds total communications to the list of issues involved in corporate identity

Figure 7 Corporate identity management: adding total corporate communications
Source: Balmer (year?)

management. The final areas which now need to be considered are questions relating to branding and to graphic design.

The visual school(s)
The fourth school of thought encompasses branding and graphic design issues. The author is of the view that the role of graphic design has been overplayed, but what is certain is that a visual audit can be a most effective means of highlighting problems with an organization's strategy, culture, communications and branding policies. A new visual identity can also communicate a change of direction. The following questions provide a basic checklist of the issues to be addressed in relation to graphic design and to branding:

1. Does the visual identity system reflect the organization's espoused mission and philosophy?
2. Does the visual identity system reflect the cultural focus in the organization?
3. Does the visual identity system reflect the organization's corporate communications strategy?
4. What is the organization's branding system? (monolithic, endorsed, branded – see Van Riel 1995).
5. Which system should the organization use?
6. Who is responsible for the above?

Figure 8 shows the issues to be addressed in corporate identity management. As such, corporate identity management requires managers to address seven issues or the 'seven deadly sins of corporate identity management'.

1. Strategy (what is our business?)
2. Reality (what is our identity?)
3. Stakeholder perception (what is our image?)
4. Employee behaviour (what is our culture?)
5. Expression (what are our communications?)
6. Branding architecture (what is our visual identity?)
7. Political, economic, ethical, social and technological issues (what is going on in the environment?)

5 Towards a theory of corporate marketing

The relationship between corporate identity and marketing is one that is unresolved. Certainly there are problems, for corporate identity – as its title suggests – is a corporate and strategic concern aimed at the positioning of organizations rather than of products or services.

Professor Baker, in the opening article, 'Marketing – philosophy or function?' states that the true essence of marketing is based on mutually satisfying exchange relationships and its evolution over time is in parallel with stages of economic growth and development. The

Figure 8 The seven elements of corporate identity management

Special topics

same may be said about corporate identity, in that corporate identity is concerned with mutually satisfying exchange relationships with the important difference that it is concerned with all, and at a minimum with the, key stakeholder groups of an organization. The evolution of corporate identity, as with marketing, appears to have reflected changes in economic growth. The emphasis placed on graphic design and image by graphic design consultancies in the 1950s appears to be mirrored by companies in emerging countries at present.

The current understanding of corporate identity also appears to reflect the Alpine and German models of marketing which emphasize the importance of long-term relationship marketing. Here, there is an obvious link with the related concept of corporate reputation, which is based on the notion of long-term relationships.

There have been attempts in the literature to treat corporate identity as a management function by providing, as with marketing, a distinct corporate identity mix. The most famous of these is Birkigt and Stadler (1986), whose corporate identity mix encompasses personality, communication, behaviour and symbolism. This entry has built on this work. Recently Balmer (1997) has extended the marketing mix to encompass the marketing of organizations. This not only requires an extension of the mix as applied to organizations in their totality, but also a rethinking of the elements of a mix. The so-called corporate marketing mix (see Figure 9), encompasses the following:

1. *Philosophy and ethos* – what the organization does, stands for, and the way it undertakes its work.
2. *Personality* – the mix of sub-cultures present within the organization and which are necessary to underpin the corporate philosophy and ethos.
3. *People* – a recognition of the importance of personnel in contributing to the identity, and their role in communicating the identity.
4. *Products* – what an organization makes or does.
5. *Price* – what an organization charges for its products and services, including the 'added value' and the 'goodwill' element in the valuation of its corporate brands, what it pays its personnel, its share price.
6. *Place* – distribution channels, a company's relationship with distributors, franchising arrangements, etc.

Figure 9 The ten Ps of the corporate marketing mix

7 *Promotion* – branding policy, visual identity and organizational symbolism. A concern with total corporate communications.
8 *Performance* – how the organization's performance is rated by its key stakeholders *vis-à-vis* the organization's espoused philosophy and ethos as well as that of competitors.
9 *Perception* – questions relating to the corporate image (the mental picture of an organization) and corporate reputation (a value judgement of the organization's attributes by stakeholders and stakeholder groups). Also takes into account the perception of country of origin (national identity), industry sector (generic identity), and main activity(ies) of employees (professional identity).
10 *Positioning* – (i) in the minds of important stakeholders, (ii) in relation to competition in the market, and (iii) in relation to the external environment.

Should the area of corporate marketing be accepted as a distinct marketing school in a way that services marketing, internal marketing and industrial marketing have, there will still be a need to re-appraise how the area is managed. This is because the area is too wide for a director of marketing, and is more appropriately a senior board position such as deputy chief executive. What is clear is that corporate marketing, if it does secure a place as a distinct branch of marketing, will draw heavily on corporate identity theory and will place the marketing concept firmly at the heart of corporate strategy formulation.

JOHN BALMER
UNIVERSITY OF STRATHCLYDE BUSINESS SCHOOL

Further reading

(References cited in the text marked *)

* Abratt, R. (1989), 'A new approach to the corporate image management process', *Journal of Marketing Management* 5: 63–76.
* Albert, S. and Whetten, D. (1985), 'Organisational identity', in Cummings, L.C. and Staw, B.M. (eds), *Research in Organisational Behaviour*, 7: 263–95, JAI Press, Greenwich, CT.
* Baker, M.J. and Balmer, J.M.T. (1997), 'Visual identity: trappings or substance?' *European Journal of Marketing* (special edition on corporate identity) 31: 366–82.
* Balmer, J.M.T. (1995) 'Corporate branding and connoisseurship', *Journal of General Management* 21: 22–46.
  Balmer, J. M. T. (1998) 'Corporate identity and the advent of corporate marketing', *Journal of Marketing Management* Autumn, forthcoming.
* Balmer, J.M.T. and Wilson, A. (1998), 'Corporate identity: it is more than meets the eye', *International Studies of Management and Organisation*, forthcoming.
* Bernstein, D. (1984) *Company Image and Reality*, Eastbourne: Reinhart and Winston.
* Birkigt, K. and Stadler, M. (1986) *Corporate Identity, Grundagen, Funktionen Fallbeispiele, Verlag, Moderne Industrie*, Landsberg an Lech, 19–63.
* Bolger, J.F. (1959) 'How to evaluate your company image', *Journal of Marketing* 24: 7–10.
* Boulding, K. (1956) *The Image*, Ann Arbor: University of Michigan Press.
* Bristol, L.H. (1960) *Developing The Corporate Image, a Management Guide to Public Relations*, Scribner: New York.
  Bromley, D.D. (1993) *Reputation, Image and Impression Management*, Chichester: John Wiley & Sons.
  Brown, T.J. (1998) 'Corporate associations in marketing: antecedents and consequences', *Corporate Reputation Review* 1: 215–33.
* Budd, J. (1969) 'A mirror on the corporate image', *SAM Advanced Management Journal* 34: 45–50.
* Crespi, L.P. (1961) 'Some observations on the concept of image', *Public Relations Quarterly* 25: 115–19.
* Dowling, G. (1994) *Corporate Reputations, Strategies for Developing the Corporate Brand*, London: Kogan Page.
* Drucker, P.F. (1955) *The Practice of Management*, Oxford: Butterworth-Heinemann.
* Dutton, J.E. and Dukerich, J.M. (1991) 'Keeping an eye on the mirror: image and identity in organizational adaption', *Academy of Management Journal* 34: 517–24.
* *European Journal of Marketing* (1997) Special edition on corporate identity, 31.
  Fombrun, C. and Van Riel, C. (1997) 'The reputational landscape', *Corporate Reputation Review* 1 & 2: 6–13.
* Gray, E.R. and Balmer, J.M.T. (1998) 'Managing image and corporate reputation', *Long Range Planning* 31: 685–92.
* Gray, E.R. and Smeltzer, L.R. (1985) 'Corporate image – an integral part of strategy', *Sloan Management Review* Summer: 73–7.
  Greyser, S. A. (1998) 'Advancing and enhancing corporate reputation', The First Lord Goold Me-

morial Lecture, 4th International Corporate Identity Conference, London, 18 June.
* Grunig, J.E. (1993) 'Image and substance: from symbolic to behavioural relationships', *Public Relations Review* 19: 121–39.
Hall, R. (1993) 'A framework linking intangible resources and capabilities to sustainable competitive advantage', *Strategic Management Journal* 14: 607–18.
* Hatch, M.J. and Schultz, M. (1997) 'Relations between organisational culture, identity and image', *European Journal of Marketing* Special edition on corporate identity, 31: 356–65.
International Centre for Corporate Identity Studies, Department of Marketing, University of Strathclyde. Working Papers (1997–).
* Ind, N. (1997) *The Corporate Brand*, Oxford: Macmillan.
* *International Journal of Bank Marketing* (1997) Special edition on corporate identity in financial services, 15(5).
* Kammerer, J. (1989) *Bietrag der Produkpoltik Zur Corporate Identity*, München: GBI-Verlag.
Kay, J. (1995) *The Foundations of Corporate Success*, Oxford: Oxford University Press.
* Kennedy, S.H. (1977) 'Nurturing corporate images: total communication or ego trip', *European Journal of Marketing* 11: 120–64.
* King, S. (1991) 'Brand building in the 1990's', *Journal of Marketing Management* 7: 13.
* Martineau, P. (1958) 'The personality of the retail store', *Harvard Business School Press* January–February: 47–55.
* Morison, I. (19997) 'Breaking the monolithic mould', *International Journal of Bank Marketing* Special edition on corporate identity, 15: 153–62.
* Olins, W. (1978) *The Corporate Personality: An Inquiry into the Nature of Corporate Identity*, London: Design Council.
* Olins, W. (1995) *The New Guide to Corporate Identity*, Aldershot: Gower.
Ries, A. and Trout, S. (1986) *Positioning: The Battle For Your Mind*, New York: McGraw-Hill.
Saatchi, Lord (1998) 'Perception is reality' *The Times* lecture given at Worcester College, Oxford, *The Times*, 1 May; 23.
Schmidt, C. and Ludlow, C. (1995) *The Quest for Identity*, London: Cassell.
* Stuart, H. (1994) 'Exploring the corporate identity/corporate image interface', Paper presented at The Department of Marketing's First Symposium on Corporate Identity Management, University of Strathclyde, Scotland.
* Swanson, C.E. (1957) 'Branded and company images changed by advertising', *ADMAP* 302–18.
* Tyler, W.P. (1957) 'The image, the brand and the consumer', *Journal of Marketing*, 22: 162–5.
* Tyrrell, T. (1995) 'Managing corporate identity', in *The Financial Times Handbook of Management*, London: Pitman.
* Van Riel, C.B.M. (1995) *Corporate Communications*, London: Prentice Hall.
* Van Riel, C.B.M. and Balmer, J.M.T. (1997) 'Corporate identity: the concept, its management and measurement', *European Journal of Marketing* Special edition on corporate identity, 31: 340–55.
* Weigelt, K. and Camerer, C. (1988) 'Reputation and corporate strategy: a review of recent theory and applications', *Strategic Management Journal* 9: 433–55.

See also: BRANDING AND BRAND MANAGEMENT; CULTURAL ASPECTS OF MARKETING; ENVIRONMENTAL ANALYSIS; POSITIONING; THE MARKETING MIX

Internal marketing – a relationship perspective

1 What is internal marketing?
2 The development of internal marketing
3 A relationship-based view
4 Internal customization
5 Internal customers and suppliers
6 Strategic and operational visions

Overview

Internal marketing as a concept emerged as part of the research into service marketing. Internal marketing is perceived differently by different scholars, but may be regarded as an umbrella concept for a variety of internal activities. In this entry a relationship-oriented perspective of internal marketing is presented. When organizations change and transform towards more virtual and imaginary organizations, internal marketing should also develop to meet the demands of the organizations of the twenty-first century.

1 What is internal marketing?

Ever since the early 1970s, when Rathmell (1974) wrote the first book that discussed service marketing, the subject has fascinated researchers. During the past 20 years, service marketing has developed quickly and substantial progress has been made in research. One of the subcategories that grew out of this research is the concept of internal marketing. Internal marketing first emerged in the service marketing literature and later in the service management, industrial marketing and relationship marketing literature (see, for example, Grönroos 1978; 1981; Grönroos and Gummesson 1985; Gummesson 1995; Berry 1981; George 1984).

An examination of the literature reveals that internal marketing as a concept engaged researchers mostly in the 1980s, even though the term *internal marketing* was introduced as early as the late 1970s. Without using the concept itself, Eiglier and Langeard had already discussed the need for marketing services internally in organizations as long ago as 1976. A central element in internal marketing has been the concept of the internal customer, a concept which originally emerged in the service sector where it was manifested in the idea of selling jobs so that they would appear attractive to the employees (Sasser and Arbeit 1976). This idea has been developed further by several scholars (e.g. Berry 1981; Gummesson 1990). For example, Grönroos (1990: 230) has called this phenomena the internal marketing product.

> The internal product consists of a job and a work environment which motivates the employees to respond favourably to management's demands for customer orientation and good interactive marketing performance as 'part-time marketers' and which, moreover, attracts and retains good employees.

Internal marketing has been considered a management strategy, where the focus is on how to develop customer-conscious employees. According to Grönroos (1990: 222) 'goods and services as well as specific external marketing campaigns have to be marketed to employees before they are marketed externally'. Other scholars (Piercy and Morgan 1991; Carlzon and Hubendick 1983) also stress the use of a marketing-like internal approach which is done by using marketing-like activities internally.

2 The development of internal marketing

When trying to understand how internal marketing has developed since the late 1970s, it is essential to acknowledge that the development has been very context based. When internal marketing as a concept emerged in the late 1970s and early 1980s, the research context was completely different from the relationship emphasis in research today. External marketing was more or less totally based on the marketing mix and its model of the 4 Ps (product, price, place and promotion), which also had its effect on the development of internal marketing. The origins of internal marketing can therefore be found in a transaction-based approach to marketing, which can also be seen in the development of the theoretical framework of internal marketing.

3 A relationship-based view

It is difficult to analyse the development of internal marketing because the concept has so many dimensions. When the internal marketing concept first emerged many scholars (Grönroos 1983; Carlzon and Hubendick 1983; Stubert 1983) saw internal marketing as a means of motivating employees to become service-oriented and customer conscious. However, later on, other views of internal marketing emerged that had evolved from the idea of employees being the first, internal market. Instead of emphasizing the importance of motivating employees to become more service-oriented, the focus has been transferred to perceiving organizations as internal markets with internal customers and suppliers (see Albrecht 1988; Reynoso and Moores 1995; Christopher *et al.* 1991; Pfau *et al.* 1991).

If these two views of internal marketing are analysed in more detail it can be seen that the focus and interest has increasingly been put on the internal market approach with internal customers and suppliers. This view has probably also emanated from the traditional internal marketing concept and a debate continues as to whether it can be perceived as internal marketing or not. Gummesson (1995) argues that there are several phenomena that could be called internal marketing, although internal marketing has traditionally been perceived as marketing to the employees. He presents in his book, *From 4P to 30R*, seven so-called 'nano--relationships', which could all be perceived in some way as part of or aspects of internal marketing.

Although internal marketing originated from a more transaction emphasizing surrounding, the concept has, over the years, developed towards a more relational approach. Whether internal marketing is perceived as motivating employees to become more service-oriented, or as managing an internal market with internal customers and suppliers, more and more relational approaches have been presented. Gummesson (1995) has called the traditional internal marketing concept 'a relationship to the employees'. He also stresses the importance of relationships in internal marketing, but he does not suggest that the means used by management to succeed in their task of motivating employees and marketing to the employees should be changed to being more relationship enhancing.

When internal marketing is perceived in terms of relationships, it could be argued that it may be perceived as an umbrella concept for a variety of internal activities, on many different levels. When this view is taken the relational definition of internal marketing could state that:

> Internal marketing from a relational perspective can be defined as the process of identifying and establishing, maintaining, and enhancing, and when necessary terminating relationships with employees and all other internal customers, on all company levels, so that the objectives of all parties involved are met, where this is done by a mutual giving and fulfilment of promises.

This definition is a modification of the definition of marketing from a relationship perspective presented by Grönroos (1995). The definition of internal marketing highlights two important aspects. Not only should internal marketing from a relational perspective be perceived as a relationship between the management and the employees but internal marketing should also be perceived as management of all the relationships that exist in the internal market, on all company levels.

4 Internal customization

Management should focus on recruiting the best employees and use different bonds in order to bind these good employees to the company. The bonds used can be of different kinds, for example legal bonds, financial bonds, social bonds, etc. The bonds used in a relationship should not be perceived by the employees as suffocating, but instead they should be customized to reflect what the specific employee values are. If the employee has bought a new house and is in desperate need of a higher salary, the financial aspect may be used to bind the employee to the company. If, on the other hand, the employee has no family, that employee may perceive a good social atmosphere to be the most important aspect, and this may be used to bind the employee to the company.

When internal marketing is perceived in terms of relationships, it becomes important to understand the different aspects present in a relationship. The relationship between management and employees should be customized so that the employees feel their needs and expectations are taken into consideration. In the same way as the needs and expectations of external customers are perceived to be important and the organization seeks to fulfil them, so the needs and expectations of employees should be perceived as important too. It is obvious that it is impossible to fulfil all the demands of the employees but the company and its management should try to nurture the relationship with employees so that both parties find the relationship rewarding. However, it is important to recognize that no relationships with employees are isolated, because all relationships affect each other. So if a rise in salary is given to one employee, it is possible that – although this employee is satisfied – other employees may feel dissatisfied because they believe they also deserved a rise.

5 Internal customers and suppliers

When internal marketing is perceived from a relational perspective the concept of the internal customer and supplier becomes important. An organization can be perceived as an internal market which consists of several relationships that are interconnected and affect one another. In contrast to relationships in consumer markets, the relationships within the internal market cannot be perceived in isolation. Relationships can be identified on several different company levels, dependent on the size of the company. All actors in the internal market, independent of the company level at which they are identified, are often both internal customers and suppliers.

The relationships in the internal market should be managed so that they support the external relationships and their profitability. Christopher et al. (1991) argue that if the links between internal customers and suppliers are traced from their starting point with the external customer, real opportunities for quality improvement can be achieved. They also state that 'by carefully defining the way customers use the firm's offering, large or small modifications can be made within the firm in terms of job designs, work environments, work processes, and training, to mention some key areas.'

The importance of satisfying the needs and expectations of both external and internal customers is becoming more and more important. Internal customers and suppliers can be perceived as a long chain of actors performing different activities, or as a process, where the quality of the outcome of the process is dependent on the quality of the different activities in the process. If one internal supplier cannot deliver, for example, important information on time, that internal customer cannot satisfy the needs of the next internal customer in the chain of actors. Pfau et al. (1991) point out that companies can begin to adopt an internal service focus by helping their employees in internal-supplier functions identify just who their customers are. It is very difficult for internal suppliers to satisfy the need of internal customers if they do not know who those customers are or what their needs and demands are.

Therefore it becomes important to identify who the internal customers are in order to make it possible to understand the internal customers' needs and expectations. In this way it becomes possible to identify the extent to which the needs and expectations of internal customers are being met.

6 Strategic and operational visions

The new relational approach to internal marketing suggests that the ultimate strategic goal for internal marketing is profitable external relationships. Profitable external relationships are the strategic foundation on which the whole internal market should be built. Even though attitude management and communications management (see Grönroos 1990) can be seen as two important aspects in internal marketing, it is argued that actors on the internal market possess two different types of visions. The most important vision is the strategic vision, which stresses that the goal of the organization is profitable external relationships. This vision permeates throughout the whole organization starting at the top management level. All actors in the internal market should be aware of this strategic vision in order to be able to do their best to accomplish it.

After this strategic vision is shared with all actors in the internal market, the operational visions come into play. These are the visions that different actors in the internal market have, of how the strategic vision might be achieved. What this means is that in order for top management to succeed in implementing the strategic vision of profitable external relationships, it is necessary for the management to be given the tools to bring this about. The operational visions are these tools. Different actors in the internal market have different operational visions; operational visions can exist at different company levels. A visual illustration of the visions on the individual level is presented in Figure 1.

Figure 1 illustrates that employees who are close to the customer and are aware of what the customer wants can communicate this operational vision to middle management (MM), which sees the operational vision of that employee in a broader context. Middle management then communicates another operational vision to the next level in the company, and in this way the operational visions, one step at a time, become strategically more important. The gradual transformation process of operational visions to strategically more important visions that support the implementation of the strategic vision can be seen in the way the arrows are shaded in Figure 1. Strategic visions and operational visions support each other, and it is through the operational visions that the implementation of the strategic vision becomes possible.

All operational visions are important, but the strategic importance of these visions can be seen only when viewing them in a broader context. The broader the scope of perception that an actor in the organization has, the more capable he or she will be of judging the importance of an operational vision. Top management should have the broadest scope of perception, and should also be responsible for using the strategically important operational visions so that they support the goal of profitable external relationships. The focus and starting-point are, at all times, the profitable external relationships, and the operational visions are the means of achieving the goal of profitable external relationships.

After all actors in the organization have adopted the strategic vision of profitable external relationships, the focus should be placed on managing internal relationships profitably so that the strategic vision is achieved. However, because it is impossible for management to manage all internal relationships in a large company, the strategic vision should include the vision of responsibility. The vision of responsibility states that all actors have the responsibility for managing their own set of relationships so that the internal relationships support the profitable external relationships.

This suggests that managing internal relationships profitably is no longer an issue for top management alone. Instead, all actors in the

Figure 1 Strategic and operational visions on the individual level internal market should take responsibility for managing internal relationships. It should, however, be taken into consideration that the *main* responsibility for managing internal relationships lies with top management, because they have the broadest scope of perception and therefore the ability to see which relationships within the internal market are the most important from a holistic point of view.

If an internal customer, for example a department, feels that the service they get from another department is of low quality, that original department should take responsibility for trying to manage the relationship so that the quality of the service improves. However, it is possible that management is aware of the situation but through the broader scope of perception knows that the quality of the service is poor because another internal relationship is seen as more important from the point of view of the external customer, and therefore the resources are concentrated on this relationship.

PÄIVI VOIMA AND
CHRISTIAN GRÖNROOS
CERS CENTRE FOR RELATIONSHIP MARKETING
AND SERVICE MANAGEMENT
HANKEN SWEDISH SCHOOL OF ECONOMICS
FINLAND

Further reading

(References cited in the text marked *)

* Albrecht, K. (1988) *At America's service*, Homewood: Dow-Jones-Irwin.
* Berry, L.L. (1981) 'The employee as customer', *Journal of Retail Banking* 3: 33–40.
* Carlzon, J. and Hubendick, U. (1983) 'Intern marknadsföring som ledningsinstrument vid stora förändringar', in I: Arndt, J. and Friman, A. (eds) *Intern marknadsföring*, Malmö: Liber, 96–110.
* Christopher, M., Payne, A and Ballantyne. (1991) *Relationship Marketing – Bringing quality, customer service, and marketing together*, Oxford: Butterworth-Heinemann Ltd.
* George, W.R. (1984) 'Internal marketing for retailers. The junior executive employee', in Venkatesan, M. *et al.*, (eds), *Creativity in Services Marketing*, Chicago: American Marketing Association.
* Grönroos, C. (1978) 'A service-oriented approach to marketing of services', *European Journal of Marketing* 12: 588–601.
* Grönroos, C. (1981) 'Internal marketing – an integral part of marketing theory', in Donnelly, J.H. and George, W.E. (eds), *Marketing of Services*, Chicago: American Marketing Association, 236–38.
* Grönroos, C. (1983) 'Intern marknadsföring – teori och praktik', in Arndt, J. and Friman, A. (eds*), Intern marknadsföring*, Malmö: Liber, 8–30.
* Grönroos, C. (1990*) Service Management and Marketing: managing the moment of truth in service competition*, Lexington, MA: Lexington Books.
* Grönroos, C. (1995) 'The Rebirth of Modern Marketing – Six Proposals About Relationship Marketing', Working paper, Helsingfors: Swedish School of Economics and Business Administration.
* Grönroos, C. and Gummesson, E. (1985) 'Service Marketing – Nordic School Perspective.', Reserch report, Stockholm University.
* Gummesson, E. (1991) 'Marketing-orientation revisited: the crucial role of the part-time marketer', *European Journal of Marketing* 25: 60–75.
* Gummesson, E. (1995) *Relationsmarknadsföring: Från 4 P till 30 R.*, Malmö: Liber-Hermods.
* Pfau, B., Detzel, D. and Geller, A. (1991) 'Satisfy your internal customers', *Journal of Business Strategy* November/December: 9–13.
* Piercy, N. and Morgan, N. (1991) 'Internal marketing the missing half of the marketing programme', *Long Range Planning* 24: 82–93.
* Rathmell, J.R. (1974) *Marketing in the Service Sector*, Cambridge, MA: Winthrop.
* Reynoso, J. and Moores, B. (1995) 'Towards the measurement of internal service quality', *International Journal of Service Industry Management* 6: 64–83.
* Sasser, W.E. and Arbeit, S.F. (1976) 'Selling jobs in the service sector', *Business Horizons* June: 61.
* Stubert, H. (1983) 'Att marknadsorientera i praktiken', in Arndt, J. and Friman, A. (eds), *Intern marknadsföring*, Malmö: Liber, 111–22.

The assessment of marketing performance

1. Introduction
2. What do we mean by 'effective marketing'?
3. Brand equity
4. Some approaches to measurement
5. Managerial implications
6. Conclusions

Overview

It is relatively rare for organizations to assess the performance of their marketing efforts, either in terms of financial effectiveness or profit contribution. In some cases, marketing performance is seen to be synonymous with the organization's performance – if the firm is doing well then the marketing must be successful – but this approach will not define the net profit contribution of marketing nor the return on investment. So how can marketers justify the marketing budget? This entry considers marketing performance assessment, starting with what constitutes effective marketing. It then goes on to discuss the concept of brand equity from both financial and customer-based perspectives. A number of key approaches to performance measurement are reviewed, and their implications for management considered. The entry concludes by suggesting that trying to justify marketing expenditure in terms of return on investment may not be the right approach, the results of performance measurement may not, in fact, be as important as the process of the assessment itself.

1 Introduction

Marketing is such a numerate discipline that it is perhaps surprising how little quantification there is of overall marketing performance. Firms rarely if ever assess the profit contribution of Finance or Human Resources either. Functions only come under the spotlight when their contribution is in doubt. One response is that marketing is not a separate function or activity; it is the whole company effort to win and retain customer preference and thereby achieve its own ends. Marketing performance is therefore the same as the company's. We call this perception 'pan-company marketing'.

This perception is not what people mean when they question the value, i.e. net profit contribution, of marketing. Questioning concerns the return on investment of the marketing budget as a whole, including the marketing department, or part by part, i.e. the elements of the marketing mix (see THE MARKETING MIX). To a greater extent than other costs the marketing budget is seen as discretionary, and it has fewer board level champions to defend it (IPA KPMG 1996). Marketers are seen as poor internal communicators and even somewhat externalized; their existence is seen to be justifying, and then spending, extravagant sums on intangible, ephemeral activities. Marketing, in short, is seen as added overhead, something to do when it can be afforded (see THE ECONOMICS BASIS OF MARKETING).

These charges, rarely so baldly expressed, condition the culture in which many marketers have to operate. Winning marketing resources may need simple answers but the reality is more complex. We unravel marketing performance assessment as follows:

- How performance is defined and what 'effective marketing' is.
- Whom a company should seek to satisfy.
- Performance benchmarks.
- The relations between different performance measures.
- Brand equity. Expenditure today may produce sales in the next accounting period, or several thereafter. Marketing inputs can be matched with results if and only if brand equity is brought into the equation.
- Brand equity measurement.
- Financial approaches to brand equity.
- Customer based brand equity.
- Insufficiency of financial measures. Marketers and accountants would be equally delighted if marketing assessment could all be expressed in financial terms. In particular, if marketing assets (brand equities) could be

valued in money terms, then the surplus of income over marketing expenditure for any period could be identified, allowing for the gain or reduction in the net assets. If the company's ends can be identified solely in financial terms, and that is a big 'if', that part of the puzzle may be met by the company's accounting systems. Unfortunately, the customers' preferences are not expressed in financial language, and still less in internal accounting systems. *Marketplace* measures are essential to performance assessment but cannot be expressed in financial terms.

- Some approaches to measurement. There are several approaches to marketing performance assessment and several measures of marketing performance. We do not attempt a comprehensive review here but assemble some key metrics and measurement frameworks.
- Managerial implications. Practitioners may find it hard to identify with the more esoteric academic approaches noted thus far. The evidence that marketing performance assessment necessarily leads to success is not compelling. On the other hand, the evidence that market orientation is associated with performance is there and it seems reasonable that market orientated executives will want the state of the art system for performance assessment. We do not believe that one size fits all, but some inferences for practitioners can be deduced.
- Finally, we draw conclusions. Those demanding justification for marketing expenditure or questioning pan-company marketing, may be asking the wrong question. We know that market orientation is associated with improved profit performance and orientation, and, in turn, predisposes what measures are tracked. Therefore, the tracking of marketing performance itself is associated with better performance. In other words, the information provided by the measures may be less important than the fact that the firm is measuring the market at all.

2 What do we mean by 'effective marketing'?

Recent years have witnessed a renewed emphasis on delivering superior quality products and services to customers. As cost cutting and downsizing produce diminishing returns, the corporate spotlight has returned to marketing. Product, packaging and distribution innovation, increasing markets, increasing share of market and customer value so that higher prices can be justified, are all the province of marketing. Effective marketing can be defined as success in winning and retaining customer preference, and thereby achieving the firm's long-term goals. Putting the customer first in every business activity is claimed to be the key to sustained competitiveness (Kotler 1997).

Market orientation, i.e. the organization-wide generation of market intelligence, dissemination of the intelligence across departments and organization-wide responsiveness to it (Kohli and Jarowski 1990), leads to greater customer satisfaction and thus provides competitive advantage and enhances business performance (Narver and Slater 1990). Thus effective marketing does not imply a trade-off for suppliers against customers; *both* should achieve their objectives from the relationship.

Neo-classical marketing, based on microeconomics, tended to examine the individual exchange transaction but we now recognize that most marketing transactions form a dynamic continuum over considerable periods of time. The relationship between a consumer of Nescafé and the brand may have built up over 30 years. We deal with the problems of accounting for marketing performance over long-term time periods in the brand equity section but first we need to develop the question of stakeholders, i.e. who is the company for, a little further. This section then addresses the benchmarks of performance and the relations between performance measures.

Stakeholders

The shareholder versus stakeholder debate has been running for over 30 years (Ambler and Wilson 1995). One extreme is that companies should single-mindedly seek to benefit their shareholders (Friedman 1962) and the other is that, like it or not, companies have to meet the diverse interests of their stakeholder groups: consumers, consumer advocate groups, competitors, employees, unions, government, political groups, activist groups, financial community, trade associations, suppliers *and* shareholders (Freeman 1983). Both may amount to the same thing: stakeholders have to be satisfied in order that shareholders can profit over the longer term. Conversely, failing to satisfy shareholders may not keep the company in business, thereby disappointing the other stakeholders.

Two theories address the way companies deal with diversity of stakeholder interests. The value exchange model proposes that the company is faced with planning a balance between its own set of values and needs, and the set of values and needs of each stakeholder group (Miller and Lewis 1991). In this conceptualization, a balance should be pursued by developing exchange relationships with each stakeholder group. The second approach proposes a balance between internal and external stakeholder groups resulting from the difference of power that different sources exert over the company (Mintzberg 1983). Companies will not seek to optimize the satisfaction of each stakeholder group, but will react to those groups that wield the most power. Freeman and Liedtka (1992) conclude in seeing 'the corporation as a network of relationships' which make possible 'a social world in which "caring" has primary significance'. This extends the Coase (1937) view of the corporation as a 'nexus of contracts', both real and implicit, between the equivalent of stakeholder groups.

To the extent that stakeholder and shareholder interests are ultimately identical, 'success' can be based on meeting either set. Ultimately this may be a long way off: clearly there are short-term gains for shareholders in pricing experience goods high and reducing product costs. Conversely, customers may be delighted by price reductions which hurt the shareholders.

For the purpose of this entry, we define the stakeholder set for which performance should be assessed as being first the customers, both immediate trade customers, where applicable, and end users, and secondly the shareholders.

Benchmarks

Most firms now operate in a rapidly changing environment in which uncertainty, complexity and risk are fundamental issues. In performance evaluation, benchmarking constitutes a primary activity, involving both business results (e.g. profitability, quality) and processes (e.g. internal communications).

There are four types of benchmarking activity: internal, functional, competitive and generic (Dence 1995). Benchmarking therefore involves multiple comparisons against past performance, business plan and goals set, performance and procedures of other units in the company, performance of similar units in other organizations, against specific competitors and other industries. Although plans are the most popular managerial benchmark, they are rarely used in academic research and performance tends to be evaluated against subjective criteria (Ambler and Kokkinaki 1997).

One issue is whether internal benchmarking suffices or whether external benchmarking is also required. Internal benchmarks may be more or less demanding than external comparisons. Both are needed. In practical terms, performance needs to be at least compared (internally) with plan and/or prior year and externally against the market as a whole (e.g. market share or relative price) and/or the leading competitor.

The relations between performance measures

Strategy research has becoming increasingly a matter of belief rather than science according to Venkatraman and Grant (1986) who emphasize the need to include and improve validity checks of measurement instruments. More rigour is needed to define the measures of success and then ensure their validity and consistency. In proposing a definition for 'metrics' below as the key strategic measures, we are mindful of the need to align company strategy, marketing and measurement.

Murphy *et al.* (1996) in a review of performance measurement in entrepreneurship research found the majority of performance measures to be related to one of eight dimensions: efficiency, growth, profit, size, liquidity, success/failure, market share and leverage.

Other researchers have examined the relations between performance measures, e.g. between market share and profitability. Building market share has long been seen as leading to superior financial performance (e.g. Buzzell and Gale 1987). Practitioner scepticism has since been justified by Gale (1994) who, in a remarkable recantation, found the correlation was attributable to them both being driven by perceived quality. Thus gaining market share by discounts or promotions, as any practitioner knows, is indeed likely to damage profitability both long and short term (Jacobson 1988). Anderson *et al.* (1994) found a positive impact of quality on customer satisfaction, and in turn, profitability. However, customer satisfaction was inversely related to market share.

Aaker and Jacobson (1994) found the firm's stock price to be associated with information contained in perceived quality measures. The explanatory power of product quality compared favourably to that of return on investment (ROI), but had the advantage of reflecting the long-term effects of marketing rather than current-term financial performance. They suggest that managers should convey information to the stock market, such as the brand's quality image, useful in depicting the long-term prospects of the business. By so doing they would be freer to undertake strategies necessary for ensuring the long-term viability of their firms.

So far we have not specifically considered innovation which some consider the defining characteristic of marketing (e.g. Simmonds 1986). Continuous innovation, in this perception, is what holds commoditization at bay. By providing ever fresh differentiation, competitors are sustainably disadvantaged. Clearly innovation aimed at improving customer value falls within 'pan-company marketing' but not all companies see product, service and distribution innovation as falling within the narrower (budget) view of marketing since the costs may be charged elsewhere in the organization. Nevertheless, innovation is an important dimension of marketing performance. It may be measured indirectly by enhanced perceptions by customers but we believe it should be treated as a separate dimension of marketing assessment. Some companies, for example, measure the proportion of turnover due to products introduced in the previous three or five years.

Our conclusions thus far are:

- Performance assessment should be from both customers' and the firm's own points of view.
- Benchmarks should be both internal (plan/prior year) and external (market/competitor).
- Measures should include innovation and the extent to which the objectives of stakeholders, i.e. end user, immediate trade customer/retailer (where applicable) and the firm itself, have been achieved within the context of the environment, i.e. relative to competition.
- The relation between performance indicators is complex and not fully explored. Until convergence can be established, multiple, diverse measures will be needed to assess marketing performance.

3 Brand equity

Our awareness and memory associations of, and attitudes towards, the brands we use, or might use, extend back over many years. Measuring long-term effects of marketing has long been seen as a problem. Dekimpe and Hanssens (1995) introduced 'persistence modelling', in which a 'persistent effect' sets a new trend in performance. On the other hand, marketing has only a temporary effect, if after a number of periods, the brand returns to its pre-expenditure performance level. To establish persistence, one must determine if sales are stable or evolving. Stable sales fluctuate temporarily around a fixed mean, while evolving sales have no fixed mean and can deviate permanently from previous levels, in which case, were they caused by marketing efforts? Persistence modelling quantifies the long-run impact of specific marketing actions, distinguishes long-run effectiveness in stable versus evolving environments and provides a formal link between marketing's short- and long-run effects.

The performance in any one period results partly from marketing in prior periods, and partly from efforts in prior periods. An 'asset', called 'brand equity', was brought forward at the beginning of the period, say a year. Aaker (1991) defines brand equity as 'a set of assets and liabilities linked to a brand, its name and symbol, that add to, or subtract from, the value provided by a product or service to a firm and/or that firm's customers'. To establish whether performance is due to current marketing one also has to look at the state of brand equity carried forward. Thus brand equity is used to compartmentalize time into:

755

- the past (represented by brand equity brought forward);
- current year's financial and other investments (energy, managerial time, enthusiasm, teamwork); and
- the future (represented by brand equity carried forward).

A single period's performance, from the firm's point of view, can be assessed from the progress towards its objectives, less the financial and other resource costs and adjusted by the change in brand equity, i.e. the measures carried forward less those brought forward.

Brand equity is thus a key concept in business practice because it represents the accumulated competitive advantage for the brand. The competitive advantage of firms that have brands with high equity includes the opportunity for successful extensions, resilience against competitors' promotional pressures, and creation of barriers to competitive entry.

The actual term 'brand equity' began to be used widely by US advertising practitioners in the early 1980s and led to academic interest. Irmscher (1993) contrasts financial, primarily seen as the DCF model, and marketing perspectives of brand equity. The marketing perspective is 'equivalent to the multi-dimensional construct of brand knowledge' and this is seen as the source of brand equity in the financial sense. Brand equity is presented normatively as a 'corporate controlling instrument'. Brand equity has mostly been examined from these two different perspectives – financial value and customer value.

Financial approaches to brand equity

Simon and Sullivan (1993) define brand equity as the incremental cash flows which accrue to branded products over and above the cash flows which would result from the sale of unbranded products and follow a financial approach in measuring brand equity. In implementing their definition, they extract the value of a firm's brand equity from the value of the firm's other assets. The result is an estimate of brand equity based on the firm's future cash flows. This methodology has three important implications:

1. Brand equity is treated as an asset of the firm and the methodology objectively separates brand equity from other assets of the firm.
2. Brand equity is measured in a forward-looking perspective, since market value of the firm's traded securities reflect an unbiased estimate of future cash flows.
3. The value of a firm's brands changes as new information becomes available in the market.

Ambler and Barwise (1998) support these three implications but have two important differences: the valuation of the brand (money) should not be confused with brand equity (the intangible asset) and the brand concept includes the product(s), be they goods and/or services, on which it is based. They show little consistency in the usage of the term brand including or excluding products though there is a tendency for the former in Europe and the latter in the USA. Whether brand does, or does not, include the product, brand equity is an *asset,* not the financial value of that asset.

We noted earlier that, from the firm's point of view, the costs of, and returns from, marketing can be expressed financially. If the marketing asset, brand equity, could also be valued at the beginning and end of each year, then the brand stewardship could more easily appear in the notes, if not the accounts, within annual reports. However, the purposes of valuation make a difference to the result.

Different asset valuation methodologies for different purposes (sale, insurance, probate, amortization) have been commonly used. Using brand valuation to justify existing balance sheet figures is wise. Similarly, most firms will review alternative investments, such as advertising, against likely future cash flows. The expected, risk adjusted, paybacks form sensible comparisons. The issue here however is whether brand valuation provides a single number measure of brand equity brought or carried forward.

We would not accept a single indicator – pulse or temperature say – of our own health. The relationships of brands with consumers is even more complex and a single number is unlikely to provide the richness we need. The last section noted the need for multiple measures. The International Accounting Standards Committee has been seeking to harmonize intangible asset accounting standards. Its Secretary-General, Sir Bryan Carsberg (1998) wrote 'we do not account for intangibles very well and perhaps cannot do so under traditional accounting'. The UK Accounting Standards Board (1997) has some tough comments on brand valuation, e.g. 'It is not possible to determine a market value for unique intangible assets such as brands and publishing titles' (Para.12).

Customer-based brand equity

Brand equity, the company asset, exists in the minds of various stakeholders, shareholders, employees, end users and distribution channel members in particular. The customer (meaning end user) part of that dominates most analysis and has been defined as the differential effect of brand knowledge on consumer response to the marketing of the brand (Kakamura and Russell 1993). Table 1 summarizes the components of customer-based brand equity from the academic literature. Aaker (1991) describes five components of the brand equity: brand loyalty; name awareness; perceived quality; brand associations in addition to perceived quality; and a bundle of intellectual properties such as patents, trademarks, and channel relationships. This conceptualization prompts repurchase rates, switching costs, level of satisfaction, preference for the brand and perceived quality on various product and service dimensions as potential measures, among others.

In their customer-based brand equity measurement scale, Lassar et al. (1995) replace perceived quality with perceived performance, limit the image concept to social image and distinguish between commitment as a feeling versus commitment as action. They also define value as 'the perceived brand utility relative to

Table 1 Components of customer-based brand equity

Memory association characteristics (e.g. size, valence, uniqueness)	Krishnan 1996
Brand images and association	Dyson et al. 1996
Awareness, perceptions and attitudes, preferences, choice intentions, actual choice	Agarwal and Rao 1996
Loyalty, perceived quality/leadership, associations/differentiation, awareness, market behaviour	Aaker 1996
Perceived performance, value, social image, trustworthiness and commitment (feeling and action)	Lassar et al. 1995
Attribute-based (differences between subjectively perceived attribute levels and objectively measured attribute levels) and non-attribute based (a brand's overall preference unrelated to product attributes)	Park and Srinivasan 1994
Brand awareness and brand image	Keller 1993
Tangible equity, relating to the physical attributes of the product, and intangible equity, relating to that component of brand value that cannot be attributed to the products' physical attributes.	Kamakura and Russell 1993
'Equalization Price' derived from a combination of measures of brand preference with responses to a series of experiments where respondents choose between existing brands and/or brand extensions at different (actual market) prices	Swait et al. 1993
The incremental cash flows which accrue to branded products over and above the cash flows which would result from the sale of unbranded products	Simon and Sullivan 1993
Brand strength (brand associations) and brand value	Srivastava and Shocker 1991
Brand loyalty, name awareness, perceived quality and other brand associations	Aaker 1991

Table 2 Marketing service companies' measures of brand equity

Measure	Components	
Brand dynamics (Millward Brown)	Presence (familiarity), relevance to consumer needs, product performance, competitive advantage, bonding (endorsement on key attributes)	Cooper 1998
Equitrend (total research)	Salience, perceived quality, user satisfaction	Cooper 1998
Brand Asset$_{TM}$ Valuator	Differentiation, relevance, esteem, familiarity (since revised to knowledge)	Young and Rubicam 1994
Consumer Brand Equity (Leo Burnett Brand Consultancy)	Sales, price paid, distribution	Broadbent 1992
Equity Monitor (Yankelovich, Clancy, Shulman)	Factors that create equity; attitudinal equity; behavioural equity; economic equity	Winters 1991; Yankelovich and Partners 1994
Brand Equity Index (Longman-Moran Analytics Inc.)	Market share × relative price × durability index (consumers future expectations of the brand)	Moran 1994
Image Power (Landor Associates)	Familiarity; esteem	Winters 1991
The Conversion Model (Market Facts Inc.)	Willingness to continue purchasing a brand	Winters 1991
DDB Needham Worldwide	Brand awareness × liking (10-point scale) × perceived quality (10-point scale)	Winters 1991

its costs, assessed by the consumer and based on simultaneous considerations of what is received and what is given up to receive it' and trustworthiness as 'the confidence a consumer places in the firm and the firm's communications, and as to whether the firm's actions would be in the consumer's interest' (Lassar *et al.* 1995: 13).

Agarwal and Rao (1996) reviewed eleven consumer-based measures of brand equity falling in one of the following dimensions: awareness (unaided recall and familiarity), perceptions and attitudes, preferences, choice intentions, actual choice. At the aggregate level, brands differed in their strength on any given measure and there was no unanimity across the measures as to which brands were the strongest. Two factors explained 91 per cent of the variance, unaided recall being one and the second was a composite of all other measures. Thus, apart from unaided recall, there appears to be high convergent validity among the remaining measures.

Some marketing measures of brand equity have their origin in decision making and loyalty research (e.g. Rangaswamy *et al.* 1993). These and others have also been developed, or branded, by advertising agencies and consultancies. Winters (1991) provided a valuable overview which is summarized, with later additions, as Table 2.

4 Some approaches to measurement

Financial approaches to measurement: the insufficiency of financial measures

A number of writers have taken the financial approach to marketing performance. Such approaches include:

- marketing profitability analysis (Sevin 1965) and Goodman's (1972) marketing accounting scheme;
- marginal revenues/marginal costs approach (Feder 1965);
- Anderson and Weitz's (1986) vertical integration measures {net effectiveness = revenue − direct cost; efficiency = net effectiveness / administrative overhead};
- sales analysis (e.g. McNiven 1980);
- marketing budgeted variances (Hulbert and Toy 1977); particular focus on market share, market size and market growth;
- cash flow potentials relative to those outside the organization (Buzzel and Chussil 1985). The final performance measure expresses performance as a percentage of potential: (Actual cash flows + actual market value)/(potential cash flows + potential market value). Comparison of strategic 'look-alikes' from the PIMS database.

Accounting measures are in the main short-term and take little account of the value to the firm of long-term customer preference, or the marketing investment which created it. Most companies recognize that financial numbers do not tell the whole story. Annual reports now discuss their intangible assets are instrumental in achieving success. For many corporations, intangible have become more significant than tangible assets. More than 90 per cent of the stockmarket value of Coca Cola lies in its brands. Shareholders will increasingly demand better accounting for the stewardship of these assets in firms' annual reports. Although the CEO/president's letter to shareholders and the review of operations make reference to intangible assets, such as brand equity and brand leverage, the financial statements and notes rarely include such assets (Herremans and Ryans 1995).

Financial performance measures are necessary but not sufficient to define overall business performance (Ambler and Barwise 1998). Beyond valuation lie non-financial performance indicators, such as product quality and customer satisfaction, that define a broader conceptualization that leads to financial performance in the long-term but is measurable now. Other writers have therefore taken a broader perspective in performance measurement.

Non-financial approaches to measurement

Non-financial approaches to measurement include Mehrotra's (1984) 'brand franchise' which was a pre-cursor of brand equity. Brand franchise consists of the number of consistent high-probability buyers. Then, sales = [P (buy if committed) number of committed buyers] + [P (buy if uncommitted) number of uncommitted buyers]. This approach allows one to see whether consumers buy a product because they are committed to it or because they are committed to get a low price.

A number of writers have sought to use ratios to quantify marketing effectiveness and efficiency. Gross (1981) defined functional productivity as functional efficiency × functional effectiveness. Then (marketing activity/marketing resources) (functional results/marketing activity) = (functional results/marketing resources) and market effectiveness × functional effectiveness × functional efficiency = marketing productivity.

Bonoma and Clark (1988) proposed a model based on psychological variables. Marketing performance was expressed as a function of the ratio of management's satisfaction with the results of marketing efforts to the efforts expended to attain these results and the impact of actions external to the organization. The basic model is represented in the following equation:

$$MP = \frac{SAT}{EFF} \times EXT$$

where MP = marketing performance
SAT = management's satisfaction from the results of marketing programme efforts
EFF = the effort expended to attain these results
EXT = the impact of actions external to the organization on marketing efforts.

Kaplan and Norton's (1992) 'Balanced Scorecard' integrates traditional financial indicators, customer-based performance measures, measures for internal processes and innovation and improvement activities. This updates Drucker's (1974) multiple-criterion measure based on market share, innovative performance, productivity performance (the real value added of a company's output divided by the amount of capital, materials and labour the company uses), cash flow and profitability (36-month moving average of operating profit).

Finally, a number of writers (Kotler *et al.* 1977, 1989; Parkinson 1995) have proposed checklists for marketing audit purposes. This typically covers: customer orientation, organization, information used (measures), strategic orientation, and operational efficiency.

We define a 'metric' as a measure of sufficient importance for performance assessment that it should be reviewed by the top management committee of the firm. The set of appropriate metrics will be of two types: short term costs and performance and brand equity. The word 'metric' is from music and verse and means the underlying rhythm, or measure which consistently repeats. In marketing, a metric is a measure which is used on a regular basis and which is both precise and consistent:

- between marketers;
- from accounting period to period;
- with finance and accounting measures;
- with other marketing metrics, e.g. the same 'market' is used in measuring market share and relative price;
- understood across functions, especially finance and accounting.

Examples of metrics include market share, relative price, share of voice, brand loyalty, and penetration. Such metrics can be classified into the following categories:

- consumer or end user;
- immediate trade customer or retailer, perhaps the manager of a branded chain store;
- competition;
- innovations;
- shareholder or financial.

Metrics indicate progress towards objectives. As these differ from firm to firm, so will the selected metrics. As such they always concern effectiveness, not necessarily efficiency. Ideally, a firm's set of marketing metrics are:

- sufficient, i.e. they are comprehensive;
- synchronized with the firm's objectives;
- necessary, i.e. there is minimal internal redundancy of measurement. Metrics which co-vary can be reduced to whichever representative measure is sufficiently, but not excessively, sensitive.

We have set out some metrics in common use as an Appendix. In order to keep the list reasonably short we have *not* included:

- Year-to-year and plan comparisons. Metrics will naturally be tracked to show growth, etc.
- Varying periods. Year-to-date, moving annual totals, quarterly and monthly metrics are usual cycles as well as specific pre- and post-campaigns.
- Ratios. Where two metrics are included, we exclude the third, even though it may be widely used, so that a ratio standard can be calculated (e.g. we have turnover and market share (value) but not total market value).
- Diagnostics. Whereas metrics should be considered by top management, analyses by region, by channel, by segment, etc., i.e. diagnostics, will be used by middle management to explain variances in metrics.

5 Managerial implications

To assess marketing performance, management should begin at the beginning with some basic questions:

- What does 'marketing' include? Pan-company or departmental expenditure or both?
- What is the orientation of this firm? Which groups of stakeholders are we most keen to satisfy? Customers first? If so, which group of customers in particular? If no stakeholders matter save shareholders, then the company is not 'marketing' at all. In these circumstances, marketing performance cannot be assessed if customer benefits are not considered. Advertising and promotions may be expended but performance measurement would be akin to judging a 1500 metre runner on her performance over the first 100.
- What internal and external benchmarks are key? Is plan more important than prior year? Should performance be measured against the market as a whole? If so, which product category, customer segments, geographic territory? History is littered with examples of companies where performance was flattered by the wrong market benchmark. Or should the external benchmark be a specific competitor?

The quality of strategic thinking at this level sets the context for all that follows. Several approaches to the assessment of marketing and business performance have been put forward. Earlier approaches were mainly focused on financial measures. However, in recent years more complex frameworks, which integrate other indicators of success, have been developed. Eccles and Pyburn (1992), for example, provided a performance model with increased customer satisfaction from improved product quality, leading in turn to enhanced profitability. Traditional financial measures are too limited to direct decision making and assist with effective performance measurement. Non-financial data, on the other hand, are isolated and enter manager's choices in a piecemeal fashion. Without a comprehensive measurement framework, these disaggregated indicators may distort decision making and lead to unanticipated consequences.

Thus the next stage is to define the metrics, the top level marketing indicators, that are appropriate for that firm, given its sector, environment, competition, etc. Essentially performance indicators are of two types: short-term which deliver within this accounting period, say one year, and brand equity, stored for future periods. Most firms express their orientation in long standing measurement preferences, but this is the time to review a long list of options, such as the Appendix, which is itself not comprehensive. The choice will be rightly influenced by the key stakeholder relationships. For example, if 20–30 year-old female consumers are the primary market, then data from other groups may be cheaper and more accessible but less relevant. Syndicated market research is cheaper than bespoke, but has to conform to the supplier's assessment of the joint requirement.

A long list of potential metrics is relatively easy to derive, though third party facilitation may be needed. More difficult is to reduce that to a short, say 10–20, list which truly conforms to the definition of 'metric' given above. Ideally, they should be sensitive and predictive. Though the literature is not short of the measures that matter (see Tables 1 and 2 above) company circumstances vary too widely to generalize. The metrics for any company are best derived empirically. Not all companies have the past data to test sensitivity and predictivity and may have to use new research, or deduce likelihoods from other data or wait for new information to arise in trade. The principle remains the same: use theory to build the long list of metrics for consideration and then use actual results, incrementally if not immediately available, to reduce the long list to a manageable set.

Leading firms, such as Diageo, have a battery of indicators used collectively to monitor brand equity. They are selected to be objective with as little room as possible for brand managers to arrange them to give a partial view. Year-to-year consistency, both in which indicators are used and how they are measured, is important since it is the change, not the snapshot, that is important. For the same reason, the indicators should not just reflect current strategy. Strategy changes but metrics should be stable.

Forget the idea of using just one number for brand equity, be it a financial valuation or an index number. Brand equity is essentially multidimensional, e.g. what immediate trade customers think of the brand is different to end-user brand memories. Brand valuation, or a number of valuations using improving methodologies, should be part of the total set of measures. Ambler and Barwise (1998) suggested that, for the purpose of marketing performance assessment, current valuation methodologies are flawed, not that they are wrong. This is an imperfect world and most firms should be satisfied by metrics each of which may be flawed in itself but, taken together, provide a reliable picture.

6 Conclusions

Research (Swartz et al. 1996) confirms that firms tend to perform better on those measures which are most visibly tracked. For whatever reasons, companies get what they measure. Market share, for example, tends to increase where that is the dominant focus and customer satisfaction where that is the most actively tracked measure. This indicates that formalization of the measurement of marketing performance pays off.

The relationships between a firm's objectives, how they measure progress towards those objectives, how budgets are set, the impact of measurement on performance, the significance of the frequency of reporting (what), the ability of indicators to predict performance outcomes and relating specific expenditures with results are issues substantive to business success. The changes in the world economy increase the complexity of markets and marketing and hence the complexity of performance tracking. New technologies are opening up new forms of consumer behaviour, marketing tools and measurement techniques.

TIM AMBLER AND FLORA KOKKINAKI
LONDON BUSINESS SCHOOL

Further reading

(References cited in the text marked *)

* Aaker, D.A. (1991) *Managing Brand Equity*, New York: Free Press, p.15.
* Aaker, D.A. (1996) *Building Strong Brands*, New York: Free Press. (A prescriptive book on brand management illustrating successful brand building cases.)
* Aaker, D. and Jacobson, R. (1994) 'The financial information content of perceived quality', *Journal of Marketing Research* 31: 191–201.
* Accounting Standards Board (1997) *Goodwill and Intangible Assets*, Financing Reporting Standard 10, December, London.
* Agarwal, M. K. and Rao, V. R. (1996) 'An empirical comparison of consumer-based measures of brand equity', *Marketing Letters* 7: 237–47.
* Ambler, T. and Barwise, P. (1998), 'The trouble with brand valuation', *Journal of Brand Management* in press.
* Ambler, T. and Kokkinaki, F. (1997), 'Measures of marketing success,' *Journal of Marketing Management* 13: 665–78.
* Ambler, T. and Wilson, A. (1995) 'The problems of stakeholder theory', *Business Ethics* 4: 30–5.
* Anderson, E. and Weitz, B.A. (1986) 'Make-or-buy decisions', *Sloan Management Review* 27: 3–19.
* Anderson, E.W., Fornell, C. and Lehmann, D.R. (1994) 'Customer satisfaction, market share, and profitability: Findings from Sweden', *Journal of Marketing* 58: 53–66.
* Bonoma, T.V. and Clark, B. (1988) *Marketing Performance Assessment*, Cambridge, MA:Harvard Business School.
* Broadbent, S. (1992) 'Using data better' *Admap* (January): 48–54.
* Buzzell, R.D. and Chussil, M.J. (1985) 'Managing for tomorrow', *Sloan Management Review* 26: 3–14.
* Buzzell, R.D. and Gale, B.T. (1987) *The PIMS Principles*, New York: Free Press.
* Carsberg, B. (1998) 'Future directions of financial reporting', *Performance Measurement in the Digital Age*, London: Institute of Chartered Accountants in England and Wales.
* Coase, R.H. (1937) 'The nature of the firm', *Economica* 386–405.
* Cooper, A. (1998) 'Brand equity – a lifestage model', *Admap* (January): 32–5.
* Dekimpe, M.G. and Hanssens, D.M. (1995) 'The persistence of marketing effects on sales', *Marketing Science* 14: 1–21.
* Dence, R. (1995) 'Best practices benchmarking', in Holloway, J., Lewis, J. and Mallory, G. (eds), *Performance Measurement and Evaluation*, London: Sage.
* Drucker, P. (1974) *Management: Tasks, Responsibilities, Practices*, New York: Harper and Row.
* Dyson, P., Farr, A. and Hollis, N.S. (1996) 'Understanding, measuring and using brand equity', *Journal of Advertising Research* 36: 9–21.
* Eccles, R.G. and Pyburn, P.J. (1992) 'Creating a comprehensive system to measure performance', *Management Accounting* 74: 41–4.
* Feder, R.A. (1965) 'How to measure marketing performance', *Harvard Business Review* 43: 132–42.
  Freeman, R.E. (1984) *Strategic Management: A Stakeholder Approach,* Boston, MA: Pitman.
  Freeman, R.E. and Liedtka, J. (1991) 'Corporate social responsibility: A critical approach', *Business Horizons* 34: 92–8.
* Friedman, M. (1962) *Capitalism and Freedom*, Chicago: The University of Chicago Press.
* Gale, B.T. (1994) *Managing Customer Value,* New York: Free Press.
  Goodman, S.R. (1967) 'Improved marketing analysis of profitability, relevant costs, and life cycles', *Financial Executive* 35: 28–34.
* Gross, I. (1981) 'Advertising productivity', *Advertising Age* 52: S1–S12.
* Herremans, I.M. and Ryans, J.K. Jr. (1995) 'The case for better measurement and reporting of marketing performance,' *Business Horizons* (September–October): 51–60.
  Holloway, J., Lewis, J. and Mallory, G. (eds) (1995) *Performance Measurement and Evaluation*, London: Sage. (A wide variety of articles on academic frameworks and management applications on performance measurement.)
* Hulbert, J.M. and Toy, N.E. (1977) 'A strategic framework for marketing control', *Journal of Marketing* 41: 12–20.
* IPA KPMG (1996) *Marketing Effectiveness: A survey of finance directors*, London: Institute of Practitioners in Advertising.
* Irmscher, M. (1993) 'Modelling the brand equity concept', *Marketing and Research Today* 21: 102–10.
* Jacobson, R. (1988) 'Distinguishing among competing theories of the market share effect', *Journal of Marketing* 52: 68–80.

The assessment of marketing performance

* Kamakura, W.A. and Russell, G.J. (1993) 'Measuring brand value with scanner data', *International Journal of Research in Marketing* 10: 9–22.
* Kaplan, R.S. and Norton, D.P. (1992) 'The balanced scorecard: Measures that drive performance', *Harvard Business Review* 70: 71–9.
* Keller, K.L. (1993) 'Conceptualising, measuring and managing customer-based band equity', *Journal of Marketing* 57: 1–22.
* Kohli, A.K. and Jaworski, B.J. (1990) 'Market orientation: the construct, research propositions, and managerial implications', *Journal of Marketing* 54: 1–18.
* Kotler, P. (1997) *Marketing Management: Analysis, Planning Implementation and Control*, 9th edn, Englewood Cliffs, NJ: Prentice-Hall. (Top graduate-level marketing textbook..)
* Kotler, P., Gregor, W. and Rodgers, W. (1977) 'The marketing audit comes of age', *Sloan Management Review* 18: 25–43. (Rigorous presentation of the marketing audit. Updated in 1989, in *Sloan Management Review* 30: 49–62).
* Krishnan, H.S. (1996) 'Characteristics of memory associations: A consumer-based brand equity perspective', *International Journal of Research in Marketing* 13: 389–405.
* Lassar, W., Mittal, B. and Sharma, A. (1995) 'Measuring customer-based brand equity', *Journal of Consumer Marketing* 12: 11–19.
* McNiven, M. (1980) 'Plan for more productive advertising', *Harvard Business Review* 58: 130–6.
* Mehrotra, S. (1984) 'How to measure marketing productivity', *Journal of Advertising Research* 24: 9–15.
* Miller, R.L. and Lewis, W.F. (1991) 'A stakeholder approach to marketing management using the value exchange models', *European Journal of Marketing* 25: 55–68.
* Mintzberg, H. (1983) *Structure in Fives: Designing Effective Organisations*, Englewood Cliffs, NJ: Prentice-Hall.
* Moran, W.T. (1994) 'Marketplace measurement of brand equity', *Journal of Brand Management* 1: 272–82.
* Murphy, G.B., Trailer, J.W. and Hill, R.C. (1996) 'Measuring performance in entrepreneurship research,' *Journal of Business Research* 36: 15–23.
* Narver J.C. and Slater S.F. (1990) 'The effect of a market orientation on business profitability', *Journal of Marketing* 54: 20–35.
* Park, C.S. and Srinivasan, V. (1994) 'A survey-based method for measuring and understanding brand equity and its extendibility', *Journal of Marketing Research* 31: 271–88.
* Parkinson, S. (1995) *Manufacturing the Marketing Solution*, Maidenhead: The Chartered Institute of Marketing.
* Rangaswamy, A., Burke, R. and Oliva, T.A. (1993) 'Brand equity and the extendibility of brand names', *International Journal of Research in Marketing* 10: 61–75.
* Sevin, C.H. (1965) *Marketing Productivity Analysis*, New York: McGraw-Hill.
* Simmonds, K. (1986), 'Marketing as innovation. the eighth paradigm', *Journal of Management Studies* 23: 479–500.
* Simon, C. J. and Sullivan, M. W. (1993) 'The measurement and determinants of brand equity: a financial approach', *Marketing Science* 12: 28–52.
* Srivastava, R.K. and Shocker, A.D. (1991) 'Brand Equity: A Perspective on its Meaning and Measurement', Working Paper No. 91–124, Cambridge, MA: Marketing Science Institute
* Swait, J., Erdem, T., Louviere, J. and Dubelaar, C. (1993) 'The equalization price: A measure of consumer-perceived brand equity', *International Journal of Research in Marketing* 10: 23–45.
* Swartz, G., Hardie, B., Grayson, K. and Ambler, T. (1996) *Value for Money? The Relationships Between Marketing Expenditure and Business Performance in the UK Financial Services Industry*, Maidenhead: The Chartered Institute of Marketing.
* Venkatraman, N. and Grant, J.H. (1986) 'Construct measurement in organizational strategy research: a critique and proposal', *Academy of Management Review* 11: 71–87.
* Winters, L.C. (1991) 'Brand equity measures: some recent advances', *Marketing Research* 3: 70–3.
* Yankelovich Partners (1994) *Brand Equity: Its Meaning, Measurement and Management*, New York: Yankelovich Partners.
* Young and Rubicam (1994) *Brands Need Not Die*, Press presentation, London ,14 June.

See also: THE ECONOMICS BASIS OF MARKETING; THE MARKETING MIX

Appendix: Marketing metrics

Consumer/end user intermediate

Satisfaction
Perceived quality/service
Reputation
Awareness
Salience
Perceived differentiation
Purchase intent
Overall image
Attitude/liking
Attributes
Ad awareness
Ad comprehension

Special topics

Consumer/end user behaviour

Total number of consumers/customers
Loyalty/retention
Loss/switching
Repurchase rates
Penetration/new consumer/customer acquisition
Number/range of products per consumer/customer
Number of new customers
Number of leads generated/direct marketing response
Conversions (leads to sales)
Media reach (percentage target market reached)
Media frequency/opportunities to see
Demographics/psychographics of users
Usage patterns
Purchase patterns
Expressed complaints/dissatisfaction
Warranty expenses

Relative to competitor

Market share volume (SOM Vol)
Relative price (SOM Val/SOM Vol)
Response time to price changes of competitors
Relative perceived quality
Share of voice

Innovation

Number of new products
Satisfaction from new products
Perceived quality of new products
Revenue of new products
Margin of new products
Diffusion parameter (indicator of speed of market take-up)
Delivery rates/percentage on-time delivery
Quality/performance/superiority
Range of products/product mix
Revenue/development cost (per product)
Order fulfilment

Financial

Revenue/income/turnover (value of sales)
Average percentage discount
Sales volume
Gross margins
Gross margins of new customers
Cost/cost structure
Cost of new customer acquisition
Cost of retention
Quality of lending book
Marketing spend
Profit/Profitability (specify level: contribution, trading, NPBT, NPAT....)
ROI
EPS/EVA
Stock cover
Value of the rental base
Number of units on rent

Qualitative research in marketing

1 Definitions of qualitative research
2 The scope of qualitative research in marketing
3 Different philosophical orientations used by different researchers in qualitative research
4 The principal methods of inquiry used in qualitative research
5 The use of computers in qualitative research
6 Future trends in qualitative research

Overview

One of the main motivations for writing this entry has been the attempt to document and explain some of the subtle and implicit aspects of research craftsmanship to be found amongst competent qualitative researchers. These important research skills have frequently been omitted or undervalued in standard text books on marketing research for two main reasons. First, this is to do with lineage of the dominant research methodologies which academic marketing has developed rather than the utility of qualitative research methods *per se*. The academic discipline of marketing has its origins in economics and psychology. Both of these disciplines are based on deductive research philosophies. These traditions have been perpetuated by the majority of academics working in the area of marketing research. In contrast, qualitative research is predominantly concerned with inductive rather than deductive research philosophies. Secondly, qualitative research is a highly creative process and requires the researcher to use both intuition as well as intellect. Detailed insight showing exactly how this process works is very difficult to express with clarity within the text book format, and has therefore been overlooked by most of the standard texts on marketing research.

The entry is organized into five main sections; definitions of qualitative research, the scope of qualitative research in marketing research, discussion of the key concepts used in qualitative research, the principal methods used, and use of computers in the analysis of qualitative research.

1 Definitions of qualitative research

Qualitative research has been defined from the academic perspective by Van Maanen (1983) as 'an array of interpretative techniques which seek to describe, decode, translate and otherwise come to terms with the meaning not the frequency, of certain more or less naturally occurring phenomena in the social world.'

Qualitative research is explained from the commercial practitioner perspective by Gordon and Langmaid (1988) as being 'best used for problems where the results will increase understanding, expand knowledge, clarify the real issues, generate hypotheses, identify distinct behavioural groups, provide input to a future stage of research or development.'

Both of these slightly different perspectives have at least one major theme in common. Qualitative research offers the possibility to clients of market research to open the agendas of their customers to different perspectives which other research methodologies are not able to do. This is especially important when dealing with new product development, diagnostic studies, creative development and tactical research projects. This is in sharp contrast to the minimal coverage which qualitative research receives in several of the main textbooks on market research such as McDaniel and Gates (1995), Kinnear and Taylor (1996), Chisnall (1996), Holbert and Spence (1993), Tull and Hawkins (1994) and Parasuraman (1991). Not one of these textbooks devotes more than 5 per cent of its content to the explanation of qualitative research. The textbooks in marketing research refer to qualitative research as 'exploratory', 'descriptive' or 'unstructured'. The authors of these books are rather patronizing in their approach to qualitative research. This is because they take the view that qualitative research is something which precedes the main scientific market research which must involve deterministic deductivism. They make erroneous comparisons between qualitative and quantitative research by adopting the same criteria for both methodological approaches. Inductive research should never be evaluated by criteria that relate to deductive research. In this entry the author will demonstrate that qualitative research can be more than just exploratory in nature and has the potential to generate robust scientific theories in its own right.

2 The scope of qualitative research in marketing

Qualitative research is now big business. Three decades ago in the 1970s there was an explosion in the commercial qualitative research business culminating in the establishment of the Association of Qualitative Research Practitioners in the UK in the 1980s (AQRP). The AQRP now has around 1000 members. This would not have happened without the client-driven demand for such services. The wider business community realizes the importance of discovering the agendas of their different constituencies of customers by commissioning qualitative market research.

Commercial market research has employed qualitative methods to help develop new insights into the following range of marketing problems; fundamental exploratory studies, new product development, diagnostic studies, creative development and tactical research projects.

Exploratory studies

With each generation comes new lifestyle preferences. One such emerging preference is called 'cocooning'. This concept explains the phenomena where occupants of urban households increasingly prefer to barricade themselves inside their homes and have as many of their service requirements fulfilled by external delivery services. This goes far beyond dial-a-pizza! The Internet now makes it possible for people to do much of their work and leisure activities 'cocooned' at home. Now that the concept of 'cocooning' is widely understood the intelligent thing for companies to do is establish in which manifestations of 'cocooning' are latent needs of urban householders being mostly unsatisfied. Exploratory qualitative research can trigger indicators of fundamental unsatisfied needs which can be commercialized.

New product development

The possibilities for introducing new products and services is happening at an ever increasing rate. In order to attempt to establish which product or service offerings are likely to deliver commercially acceptable results, different types of qualitative research are very frequently employed. A typical market research problem for all new products and services is where should the new entrant be positioned in relation to the existing competition? The UK-based First Direct retail bank company carried out a series of focus group interviews prior to its UK launch in 1989. The exploratory qualitative research was able to indicate that retail banking customers were equally underwhelmed by all current retail banking service providers. In addition to this, customers of existing banks disliked queuing and the opening hours associated with the traditional bank branch networks. Armed with this information it was decided to deliberately launch this retail bank as a bank without branches. First Direct was the first genuine 24-hour retail telephone bank in the UK. Although it was owned by an existing major bank, First Direct was originally marketed with its enigmatic name. It became the first retail bank in the UK to declare itself a rather special new form of financial service provider rather than be considered as a retail bank. The strategy worked, and First Direct was in a fully profitable situation within four years of the launch. In 1990 First Direct had 50,000 customers and by May 1997 it had in excess of 700,000 customers.

Diagnostic studies

Existing brands which have been very successful for many years sometimes appear to flounder for no apparent reason. In such situations qualitative research can be helpful in explaining the unexplainable. This aspect of brand fatigue can be addressed by using a wide range of qualitative research methods to discover the fundamental basic social processes which have caused such unpredictable changes in customer behaviour.

Creative development

The dilemma facing any company wishing to communicate with its customers through advertising and other promotional media is: What should the overall message convey? Which vocabulary would be most appropriate both for the product or service as well as the customer? The answers to these types of questions can frequently be derived from the lips of customer members in focus group interviews.

Tactical research projects

Having understood what the positioning strategy of a particular brand should be, companies are then faced with several other problems such as; pack design alternatives, promotional mix, and the celebrity endorsement preference. Qualitative research approaches are able to resolve all such issues.

An interesting contrast has developed between the relative importance ascribed by commercial clients of marketing research to qualitative research as compared to that published in academic journals and academic text books on marketing research. The Market Research Society acknowledges that the client spend in marketing research is greater on qualitative research than quantitative research. This author contends that the main reason for this is that the academic discipline of marketing has been developed by economists and psychologists, both of whom come from deductive rather than inductive research traditions. Academics have tended to perpetuate their professional research agendas rather than being driven by the real marketing problems which are confronting the commercial world.

Before discussing qualitative research methods in more detail it is vital to understand why it is that there appears to be a range of different approaches used in this research tradition.

3 Different philosophical orientations used by different researchers in qualitative research

Research which is labelled qualitative can vary quite considerably. In one extreme it is highly deductive and treats words as data to be measured for the frequency of their occurrence. Techniques such as content analysis are typical of this approach. They are principally influenced by deduction and therefore seek to collect data which is used in an evidentiary manner. This is the line argument adopted by McDaniel and Gates (1993), Kinnear and Taylor (1996), Chisnall (1996) Holbert and Spence (1993), Tull and Hawkins (1994) and Parasuraman (1991). The author of this entry is of the opinion that they miss more than they reveal by adopting this approach. There are market research books which do take a more comprehensive view of qualitative research, they include Crimp (1995) and Gordon and Langmaid (1988). It is interesting to note that both these authors come from commercial marketing research rather than academic marketing research backgrounds.

The two approaches to qualitative research in marketing can be summarized at one extreme as saying that it can only be descriptive, and at the other extreme as saying that qualitative research is a powerful device for facilitating the emergence of patterns of complex human behaviour. The problem is that both extremes have assumed that both deductive and inductive research approaches are mutually exclusive; they are not.

To be successful qualitative research demands that the researcher is able to tolerate extended periods of psychological regression as a necessary prerequisite to fully understanding the nature of the data being analysed. It is a delayed action phenomenon; difficult to document but instantly recognizable once understood.

Discussion of the key concepts and ideas associated with qualitative research

A particular characteristic of being successful as a qualitative researcher which is rather different from other kinds of research approaches is the requirement to engage more than just one's intellect in the research process. An awareness of one's own morality and intuition is essential. and has been referred to as intellectual craftsmanship. These special qualities of intellectual craftsmanship, required by the qualitative researcher, are brilliantly captured by C.W. Mills (1970). He refers to eight main precepts which are the hallmark of intellectual craftsmanship:

Special topics

1. Develop and use one's own sociological imagination.
2. Avoid the Byzantine oddity of associated and disassociated concepts, the mannerisms of verbiage.
3. Take as your task the defining of this reality; formulate your problems in its terms; on its level try to solve these problems and thus resolve the issues and the troubles they incorporate.
4. Do not study merely one small milieu after another: study the social structures in which the milieu are organized.
5. Realize that your aim is a fully comparative understanding of the social structures which have appeared.
6. Always keep your eyes open to the image of man – the generic notion of his human nature – which by your work you are assuming and implying.
7. Know that you inherit and are carrying on the tradition of classic social analysis; so try to understand man not as an isolated fragment, not as an intelligible field or system in awe of itself.
8. Do not allow public issues as they are officially formulated, or troubles as they are privately felt, to determine the problems that you take up for study.

There is no more to research than the systematic application of appropriate methodology to a problem. The more systematic one is in executing the chosen methodology in one's research project, the more likely it is that one's work will be of relevance to those whom the research addresses. All systematic research methods have the potential to yield useful results. It does not really matter which research method is being used. Providing it does not violate the tenets of orthodoxy and is appropriate to the problem central to the research, interesting interpretations will be forthcoming. The real challenge is to understand which type of research method is best suited to which type of problem. It is assumed by many that qualitative research stems from the inductive research tradition. An argument in support of this notion is given in Easterby-Smith *et al.* (1991).

Is qualitative research always inductive?

The answer to this question is not a simple one. Qualitative research is heavily influenced by inductive thinking but is also reliant on deductive thinking. It is equally misleading to assume that quantitative research is purely based on deduction. Quantitative research has elements of induction and qualitative research relies on the logic of deduction. In quantitative research the researcher's own agenda is adopted as the legitimate point of departure and seeks to prove or disprove a hypothesis. Quantitative research appears to be quite difficult to some because it often involves learning more about statistical analysis. However, in a way this kind of research is relatively straightforward because it involves remembering a series of well documented procedures. Whereas qualitative research appears to be easy because most of the research methods used by this approach are simply listening and watching other people's behaviour. Those with experience of qualitative research will appreciate that it is often much more difficult to do than quantitative research because the researcher must act as arbiter and interpreter in creating interpretative frameworks. This is a highly creative process to which not everyone is emotionally and intellectually suited. This type of research seeks to generate a hypothesis by discovering the agenda of those being researched.

There is no such thing as pure deduction or pure induction. Deductivists choose their own research hypotheses. They claim this is done after having completed a rigorous review of the literature. Since the researcher is free to read whatever he or she may wish the choice in reading will largely be based on the researcher's own influences and preferences. This is an intuitive and inductive process. Once the primary data have been collected, analysed and synthesized they have to be interpreted. Interpretation is an inductive process. In inductive research, once data have been generated they have to be analysed and synthesized, these are deductive processes. It is therefore very misleading to believe that either pure deduction or pure induction actually exist. All that one can say is that the main research emphasis is either deductive or inductive.

Data collection or generation?

This type of research is based on the assumption that theoretical explanations of the world we live in can best be achieved by explaining social phenomena which already exist in abundance around us. Unlike deductive research, this approach uses subjectivity as an important resource to be mobilized in the pursuit of understanding. The inductive researcher should go directly to the real world and generate data so that the implicit patterns of the human world can be understood and then explained. This means that the inductive researcher has to be able to translate, decode, interpret and explain rather than measure the frequency of instances occurring. The inductive researcher does not collect data, he or she generates them. In generating the data the researcher decides on his or her own intuition and subjectivity what to focus on and what to leave alone. One of the leading philosophers who promulgates this perspective is Popper (1959). He demonstrated that it was logically inconsistent for deductivists to claim to have exclusive access to fundamental scientific laws. The basis of his argument is that deductive research relies on verification as the final proof of a scientific theory. Instead, Popper (1959) demonstrates that real scientific advances are made when researchers use falsification in preference to verification. Inductive research is also known as qualitative research and phenomenological research.

One of the most powerful forms of inductive research is the 'grounded theory' research method. This approach was invented in 1967 by Glaser and Strauss. In common with all inductive methods, grounded theory begins with the agenda of those being studied. It seeks to discover and explain the main issues of concern in the context of the research rather than to impose and force the researcher's own agenda on those being studied. This can be a little unnerving to the novice researcher because the inductive researcher does not have the safety net of the preliminary literature review from which to extract ideas and general themes. Instead the researcher goes directly into the context of the research in order to discover the main issue of concern to those being studied. After following the orthodox tenets of the research method being used the inductive researcher generates his or her own theory from the data generated. One of the main implicit assumptions of all inductive research is that the world is socially integrated. Patterns of behaviour exist whether they are researched or not. It is the inductive researcher's task to discover these patterns by emergence rather than forcing a preconceived agenda onto the data. In order that patterns might emerge and be revealed to others, data must be categorized by analysis and then sorted by synthesis before they can be explained.

There is an implicit paradox of categorization which has been explained by Seyle in the following terms:

> The human brain is so constructed that it refuses to handle thoughts unless they can be wrapped into more or less neatly individual IDEA PACKAGES. It is astonishing how much confusion has been caused by the failure to understand the following three simple concepts – thoughts, like fluids, can be adequately handled only when put in individual containers – the thought packages contain previous experiences: only the selection within the wrappings can be new. We have no new thoughts of things whose likeness we have never perceived before – the idea packages are loosely bound together and their contents are not homogeneous.
>
> (Seyle 1964)

When the qualitative researcher acknowledges this paradox there is the possibility that through humility the researcher can develop a new form of openness through which previously hidden patterns of behaviour might be revealed. One of the most useful research methodologies to emerge which has direct relevance to qualitative market research is the grounded theory method. A key element of this research method is the use of a device called the theoretical memo. This is a useful device which encourages the researcher to have a reflective conversation with the data. These theoretical memos are the conceptual building blocks through which new ideas can emerge. A comprehensive explanation of this technique is given in Glaser (1978). The grounded theory method has been highlighted in this entry because there are several general methodological issues raised by its explanation which are relevant across the range of qualitative approaches. In particular, grounded theory highlights the importance of following:

1 The necessary requirement for the researcher to deal effectively with psychological regression.
2 The importance of not preconceiving the problem prior to the commencement of the research project.

Special topics

3. The need to understand the importance of revealing the issues of main concern to those in the substantive area of the study rather than merely pursuing the professional research agenda of the researcher.
4. The importance of high ethical and moral standards when investigating issues which will impact on people's lives.
5. The requirement to focus on process analysis rather than unit analysis.
6. The simultaneous collection, analysis and synthesis of data.
7. The need to follow an orthodox method of scientific inquiry in qualitative research.
8. The necessity to ensure that appropriate criteria are used to evaluate the research.

A more comprehensive discussion of these issues appears later in the entry.

4 The principal methods of inquiry used in qualitative research

Although there are five main methods of inquiry which are employed in qualitative research they all can be used quite differently according to the deductive or inductive emphasis used by the researcher. The five main methods are:

1. in-depth interviews;
2. focus group interviews;
3. participant observation;
4. case studies;
5. projective techniques.

One of the key issues involved in all the methods of inquiry used in qualitative research is how to gain and sustain access within the context being researched. This issue has been comprehensively dealt with by a number of different authors (Bogdan and Taylor 1975; Cassell *et al.* 1994; Coffey and Atikinson 1996; Denzin *et al.* 1994; Easterby-Smith *et al.* 1991; Guthrie and Lowe 1998). Very useful information has been collated by the European Society for Opinion Research and Marketing Research (ESOMAR) (1997) giving ethical guidance to practitioners, clients and participants in qualitative research projects.

In-depth interviews

The rationale for in-depth interviews has been explained by Burgess (1982) in the following terms: 'It is the opportunity for the researcher to probe deeply, to uncover new clues, to open up new dimensions of a problem and secure vivid, accurate, inclusive accounts that are based on personal experience.' An often neglected but important issue concerning in-depth interviews relates to the philosophical perspective being adopted by the researcher. If a deductive and evidentiary approach is being used, as advocated by Miles and Huberman (1984), then as many in-depth interviews as the budget will allow are recommended. The belief here is that data should first be collected en masse, then they can subsequently be analysed, synthesized and interpreted. If a more inductive approach is being used, as advocated by Van Maanen (1983), then the researcher should generate data slowly and incrementally. There must be a time gap between each interview to permit the researcher to carefully analyse, synthesize and interpret each individual interview prior to carrying out more. The detailed skills which need to be mastered in the in-depth interview are concisely and authoritatively articulated by Burgess (1982).

Focus group interviews

The focus group interview is the most widely used method of inquiry in commercial qualitative research and is gaining increased favour amongst the academic research communities. This method of inquiry should be regarded as a loosely structured steered conversation conducted by a trained moderator among a small group of people. The main reason for its popularity amongst the constituencies of corporate clients of research is that it directly engages a real time dialogue with real customers which can be covertly and vicariously observed by video links. Gordon and Langmaid (1988) provide a useful and wide ranging explanation of the use of the focus group interview within the setting of marketing research. These authors wisely advise those planning focus group interviews not to underestimate the importance of the use of fully trained moderators. Further explanation of the use of this method is skilfully documented by Walker (1985).

Participant observation

When participant observation is being carried out the researcher participates, overtly or covertly, in people's daily lives for an extended period of time, watching what happens, listening to what is said, asking questions: in fact generating whatever data are available to illuminate issues with which the research is concerned. Although participant observation has its roots in ethnographic studies from the discipline of anthropology it has great relevance in marketing research. Commercial qualitative market researchers describe participant observation as 'mystery shoppers'. They do this because with this method researchers often covertly pretend to be customers and experience the authentic service level or product quality without the company employees being aware. In this way it is argued that the actual performance of the company's product and service range can be more effectively evaluated. In academic terms Junkers (1960) has developed a detailed typology of participant observation which takes account of the degree of covertness and involvement of the researcher. Probably more than any other qualitative method of inquiry, a series of ethical dilemmas are raised by this useful but invasive approach to generating qualitative data. The ESOMAR (1997) guidelines are very useful in explaining how the researcher can achieve the data required without compromising his or her standing with those being researched.

Case studies

Of all the qualitative research methods of inquiry used in academic marketing, case study research is perhaps the most poorly executed. Partly this is because those doing the case study research have adopted a rather schizophrenic approach to their methodological orientation. This perspective is expertly articulated by Bonoma (1985). Writing in the *Journal of Marketing* he explains an interesting dichotomy. Why is it, he asks, that although the case study approach is so universally adopted by marketing academics as a research approach they have failed to get beyond a descriptive scenario when explaining their findings. He cites the examples of the case study research method as used by clinicians and demonstrates that academics in marketing have much to learn about how to operationalize such data. Other authors who give useful contributions to the clarification of case study research include the following: Gummesson (1988), Yin (1984), Patton (1980) and Schwartz and Jacobs (1979).

Projective techniques

Although this is a deductive approach to research it is considered by many to be properly labelled qualitative. It is deductive in nature because its origin is derived from clinical and experimental psychology. Much of the literature surrounding its justification and use is rather impenetrable, but its use by both focus group members and moderators is usually enjoyable and sometimes very useful. Typically, members of focus group interviews might be asked to react to a physical object or drawing. They are invited to project their emotions, thoughts and desires onto the objects before them. The skilled researcher then documents the manner in which the respondent reacts at face value to the situation that confronts them. Often non-verbal communication can be more revealing than spoken words. Projective techniques are most frequently used in five main ways: association, completion, construction, expression and choice-ordering. For comprehensive discussions of projective techniques both Gordon and Langmaid (1988) and Worcester and Downham (1986) provide intelligent and accessible insights.

Before any form of data collection takes place in a qualitative research design, fundamental decisions have to be made as to the particular research tradition to be used. Since very little has been previously written in an accessible format about the detailed processes involved in inductively based qualitative research methods, this author has chosen to give some further insights into the Grounded Theory Method. Any kind of data can be used in grounded theory research which might have been generated by in-depth interview, focus group interview, participant observation or case study.

An explanation of grounded theory

The purpose of grounded theory is to explain the prime movers which continually resolve the issues of concern to those in the substantive area of a research project. The methodology was formulated by Glaser and Strauss (1967) and was further elaborated in Glaser (1993, 1994). This research method is ideal for explaining issues where the consequences of error can result in very high human and economic costs. Grounded theory is very effective in dealing with contexts with high consequence impact. Within the field of management and marketing research its use is growing in importance (Gummesson, 1988; Haslam, 1997; Lowe and Glaser, 1995).

Philosophical assumptions of grounded theory
The basic philosophical approach underpinning the theory is that the social organization of the world is integrated. The grounded theorist's job is twofold. First, to discover which patterns of behaviour exist, and secondly how these processes of socialization are sustained. To be able to discover patterns of behaviour requires a combination of creativity and theoretical sensitivity. To understand the processes of socialization the researcher must go beyond unit analysis and move towards process analysis. The grounded theory analyst transcends both the research agendas of the professional research community and the contextual data. This is done by revealing and communicating the conceptual issues which are of importance to the substantive area of study but which lie buried in the mass of data. In order to do this the researcher has to be able to recognize a number of different indicators which, when synthesized, can explain most of the variation in the data. Most people already have the talent to enable them to make leaps between their intellect and intuition. This talent is called creativity. The problem is that people are afraid to use it because of their combined fear of uncertainty and regression. Glaser (1978) suggests ways in which our latent creativity can be activated and then enhanced. Since everything is considered data in grounded theory it is inappropriate for it to be used as a kind of proof of a theory, rather it is used as an occasional illustration of the emerged theory as necessary.

There is no need for preconceived theorizing because all the theoretical explanations are already present. There are two hidden subtleties which need to be explained before beginning to explain how grounded theory is actually carried out; mobilizing one's creativity and dealing with regression.

Mobilizing creativity
Everyone has the potential to utilize their creativity much more than they often realize, but for this to happen there are two main requirements; a tolerance for chaos and an ability to deal with regression. Not everyone can become grounded theory analysts. It demands that our normal aversion to chaos be held in suspension. People like to be in control. When doing grounded theory this is the first thing which must be surrendered. The data have to be in control, not the researcher. The researcher's task is to be able to follow where the data lead. At the outset and for a considerable time afterwards the precise destination remains unknown. Many people will have great difficulty in remaining in a state of uncertainty for extended periods of time. This is one of the challenges of mobilizing one's own creativity.

Dealing with regression
The next big issue in being able to sustain one's creativity is being able to deal with one's own regression. This is the tendency to feel stupid and almost childlike when surrounded by one's confusion in the early stages of mobilizing creativity. It is better to remain in a temporary state of confusion rather than to produce a controlled and forced interpretation which remains permanently false. A regression coping strategy which works for many people is to prepare oneself in advance so that when regression symptoms occur they are recognized. When they manifest, they can simply be treated as regression symptoms and noted for what they are without emotional involvement.

The evaluation of inductive qualitative research which goes beyond descriptive exploration

There are four main criteria for evaluating qualitative research which generates robust conceptual processes; fit, workability, relevance and modifiability

Fit is another word for validity. Does the concept adequately explain the data that the theory purports to express? As the researcher constantly codes, analyses and collects the data he or she is constantly testing the concepts to see it they fit the data as they reoccur before they saturate. This is automatic if grounded theory is done correctly. A concept which fits has to earn a place in the theory by pulling its weight. Workability answers the following question. Do the concepts begin to account for how the main concern is being continually resolved? For example, in Lowe (1998) are all the variables in default remodelling necessary for the process to be completed? It was found that merging organizations redesign their business relationships by reverting to the values that they know best and then implementing a systematic process of socialization to ensure compliance. Relevance is very important because so much of which is studied means very little to those whence the data originated. It should be very relevant for the people involved. For example, in Lowe (1998), the organization had been studied in great detail prior to the merger as to how it might be accomplished, but they did not understand the consequences of their actions on their business relationships with many of their clients. That is, until they read the study. Then they realized the relevance instantly. Modifiability deals with the question of: How capable is the theory of incorporating new concepts from data which is generated after the completion of the study? The data might be generated by the same researcher or others working in quite different fields. It does not matter – the principles remain the same. When someone comes along with new data about an existing grounded theory the researcher should just treat it as one more incident, and compare and then modify the theory to include these new variables. When new challenges to existing grounded theories happen it is not the theory that is wrong, it is not the data which are wrong. All that is needed is a new analysis of new data. So the theory grows to include another variable.

5 The use of computers in qualitative research

The use of computers in qualitative research has become much more popular amongst academics in marketing than amongst researchers working with commercial research organizations. This reflects the previously mentioned preference in academia for the use of deductive methodologies interpreting qualitative research in academic marketing research. Clearly, computers are extremely useful in handling large quantities of data systematically. Any research approach which is consistently systematic and which undergoes a known series of iterations will yield results which are useful. The reader should also understand that the type of interpretation that will result from the computerized analysis of qualitative data will be evidentiary in nature and will not necessarily reflect the nature of the data themselves. Providing the researcher understands this then there is much to commend the use of computers.

The most useful publication, which provides both intellectual and practical insights into a wide range of computerized software tools is outlined in Tesch (1990). An interesting compilation of specific examples of qualitative data which has been analysed by a series of different computer packages can be found in Fielding and Lee (1991).

6 Future trends in qualitative research

All major customer-oriented organizations are already heavily engaged in interacting with key groups of their customers on a regular basis. This happens in major global airline companies with their club class customers, as it does with the main banking service providers who are busily wooing and retaining their high net worth individuals. The device used is the focus group interview. It is probably the most ubiquitous research technique favoured by clients of commercially focused market research organizations.

In the future this reality will be mirrored by the academic community's increased involvement in qualitative marketing research. The change will be very gradual and will not happen until the gatekeepers of refereed academic journals widen their vision and become more tolerant of research methodologies which emanate from different traditions than those to which they themselves have been exposed.

Literature sources

Readers who wish to keep abreast of interesting developments in the use and evolution of qualitative research should go to the following web site – http//www.sociologypress.com. The site is maintained by Dr Glaser, the originator of grounded theory and the founder of the *International Grounded Theory Review*. It contains a rich source of information about qualitative research techniques in addition to a range of relevant publications.

Earlier in this paper references were made to the book written by Gordon and Langmaid (1988). This publication, although written in the 1980s, is still an excellent source book for those wishing to understand the practical issues involved in carrying out qualitative research.

For those who prefer a more academic perspective on issues in qualitative research, the book by Van Maanen (1983) remains a very useful source book. Denzin *et al.* (1994) has produced an encyclopaedic publication which examines the range and variety of qualitative research approaches which some readers will find useful. For practical advice for both practitioners and academics alike, the highly relevant ESOMAR (1997) international code of marketing and social research practice should not be overlooked.

ANDY LOWE
UNIVERSITY OF STRATHCLYDE, GLASGOW

Further reading

(References cited in the text marked *)

* Bogdan, R. and Taylor, S.J. (1975) *Introduction to Qualitative Research Methods*, New York: Wiley.
* Bonoma, T.V. (1985) 'Case research in marketing; opportunities, problems, and a process', *Journal of Marketing Research* 22: 199–208.
* Burgess, R. (1982) *Field Research: A Source Book and Field Manual*, London: Allen and Unwin.
* Cassell, C. and Symon, G. (1994) *Qualitative Methods in Organisational Research*, London: Sage.
* Chisnall, P.M. (1996) *Marketing Research*, London: McGraw-Hill.
* Coffey, A. and Atikinson, P. (1996) *Making Sense of Qualitative Data*, London: Sage.
* Crimp, M. (1995) *The Marketing Research Process*, London: Macmillan.
* Denzin, N.K. (eds) (1994) *The Handbook of Qualitative Research*, Thousand Oaks: Sage.
* Easterby-Smith, M., Thorpe, R. and Lowe ,A. (1991) *Management Research: An Introduction*, London: Sage.
* ESOMAR (1997) International Code of Marketing and Social Research Practice; Tape and Video Recording and Client Observation of Interviews and Group Discussions; Guidelines on Mystery Shopping, London: ESOMAR.
* Fielding, N.G. and Lee, R.M. (1991) *Using Computers in Qualitative Research*, London: Sage.

* Glaser, B.G. and Strauss, A.L. (1967) *The Discovery Of Grounded Theory*, Chicago: Aldine.
* Glaser, B.G. (1978) *Theoretical Sensitivity*, Mill Valley, CA: Sociology Press.
* Glaser, B G. (1993) *Examples Of Grounded Theory: A Reader*, Mill Valley, CA: Sociology Press.
* Glaser, B G. (1994) *More Grounded Theory Methodology: A Reader*, Mill Valley, CA: Sociology Press.
* Gordon, R. and Langmaid, R. (1988) *Qualitative Market Research*, Aldershot: Gower.
* Gummesson, E. (1988) *Qualitative Methods in Management Research*, London: Sage.
* Guthrie, W. and Lowe, A. (1998) 'The basic social process of infiltration', *The Grounded Theory Review* forthcoming.
* Haslam, S. (1997) 'Personal legitimising: a perspective of marketing management', *Journal of Marketing Management* 13.
* Holbert, N.B. and Spence , M.W. (1993) *Practical Marketing Research; An Integrated Global Perspective*, New York: Prentice-Hall.
* Junkers, B.H. (1960) *Fieldwork: An Introduction to the Social Sciences*, Cambridge: Cambridge University Press.
* Kinnear, T.C. and Taylor, J.R. (1996) *Marketing Research an Applied Approach*, New York: McGraw-Hill.
* Lowe, A. and Glaser, B.G. (eds) (1995) *The Potential of Grounded Theory for the Development of Relationship Marketing Theory in Grounded Theory 1984–1994*, Mill Valley, CA: Sociology Press.
* Lowe, A. (1998) 'Default remodelling – managing the post merger aftermath', *Management Decision* 36: 102–10).
* McDaniel, C. and Gates, R. (1995) *Contemporary Marketing Research*, New York: West Publishing.
* Mills, W.C. (1970) *The Sociological Imagination*, Oxford: Oxford University Press.
* Miles, N.B. and Huberman, A.M. (1984) *Qualitative Data Analysis: A Source Book of New Methods*, London: Sage.
* Patton, M.Q. (1980) *Qualitative Evaluation Methods*, Beverly Hills, CA: Sage.
* Parasuraman, A. (1991) *Marketing Research*, Reading, MA: Addison-Wesley.
* Popper, K. (1959) *The Logic of Scientific Discovery*, London: Hutchinson.
* Seyle, H. (1964) *From Dream to Discovery; On Being a Scientist*, New York: McGraw-Hill.
* Schwartz, H. and Jacobs, J. (1979) *Qualitative Sociology – A Method to the Madness*, New York: The Free Press.
* Tesch, R. (1990) *Qualitative Research; Analysis Types and Software Tools*, New York: The Farmer Press.

* Tull, D.S. and Hawkins, D.I. (1994) *Essentials of Marketing Research*, New York: Macmillan.
* Van Maanen, J. (1983) *Qualitative Methodology*, London: Sage.
* Walker, R. (1985) *Applied Qualitative Research*, Basingstoke: Gowe.r
* Worcester, R. and Downham, J. (1986) *Consumer Market Research Handbook*, London: ESOMAR.
* Yin, R. K. (1984) *Case Study Research*, Beverly Hills, CA: Sage.

See also: INFORMATION TECHNOLOGY AND MARKETING; MARKETING THEORY; NEW PRODUCT DEVELOPMENT; QUANTITATIVE METHODS IN MARKETING; THE PSYCHOLOGICAL BASIS OF MARKETING

Strategic alliances and supplier partnerships

1 Introduction
2 Alliances: causes, motives and benefits
3 Approaches to successful alliances and partnerships
4 An alliance model: the virtuous circle
5 Conclusions

Overview

The phenomenon of strategic alliances and partnerships is one that has attracted considerable interest during recent times. To be sure, the usage of cooperative strategies is not a new development. Early oil exploration firms used joint ventures as a means of spreading risks, and so have many trading and merchant firms. However, the increased usage and reliance is unprecedented in both scale and intensity. For the past two decades or so, marketing academics and experts who recognized the need to study the phenomenon in more detail urged others to consider undertaking in-depth research on alliances (Arndt 1979; Baker 1995; Sharma and Sheth 1997; Sheth and Sharma 1997; Webster 1992). Business literature has so far largely focused on the concept of competition (Porter 1980; 1985) and its effects (Culpan 1993) and it is only recently that the focus is shifting to collaboration and its benefits.

Now, more than any other time, there is a need for an in-depth understanding of the field of cooperation. In a business world that is characterized by change rather than stability, and novelty in place of tradition, pressures and pace of activity increasingly mandate that firms should operate within the boundaries of core competence (Prahalad and Hamel 1990), and at the same time build cooperative relationships with other firms. While competition will continue to play its part in the future, it is expected that it is the resurgence of interest in cooperative strategies and their impact on business that will capture the interest of practitioners and academics. Companies that know why to partner, with whom and how, might well be the ones that will reign supreme in the future business contests that are already starting to unravel as we move into the new millennium.

1 Introduction

This entry aims to outline some of the strategic issues involved in building competitive advantages through the route of cooperative relationships in a business-to-business context between customers and suppliers. This is carried out with a view to furnishing the reader with an overall picture concerning the field of strategic alliances and supplier partnerships. While the focus here is very much on the alliances between suppliers and customers, the processes of building relations and implications thereof have broader applicability to other links that corporations need to have, for example, with their intermediaries, end-users and not uncommonly even with firms with whom they compete.

The concept of customer–supplier alliances is used here as a generic model for relations between companies. For example, the manufacturer–supplier and the manufacturer–distributor relations may both be classified as dealings between customers and suppliers. For that matter, a simple licensing agreement involving technology transfer could also be classified using such a generic framework. Admittedly, more complex arrangements, such as a joint venture or a loose arrangement between firms in the same or related industries, such as the ones between General Motors and Toyota, and Ford and Mazda are difficult to box into one group or another. None the less, the various strands that constitute the 'link' represent identifiable and discrete units of interactions that could readily be analysed using the customer–supplier alliance framework. In our view, this allows us to readily apply some of the concepts that exist in the marketing and strategy literature, and facilitates understanding and implementation of the strategic concepts and processes associated with collaborative relationships.

Business success and competitive advantage are products of organizing, managing and integrating different businesses meaningfully. Closer relations, when pursued and invested in, lead to the building of alliances and partnerships. Our main argument here is that the highway of alliances and partnerships leads to the generation of lasting strategic gains thereby creating a virtuous network of linked corporations (see RELATIONSHIPS AND NETWORKS).

This entry will detail the reasons as to why firms are seeking alliances and also the processes that allow partners to achieve advantages that can accrue from alliance activities. The next section highlights the changes in the competitive environment that are inducing firms to seek avenues for collaboration and the various associated benefits and disadvantages. The following section outlines the approaches for building successful alliances and partnerships. This section emphasizes the need to be selective when forging cooperative relationships with other firms. The penultimate section builds on the wide-ranging review of literature presented in the previous two sections. A 'Strategic Alliance' model is offered that may help explain details of the alliance phenomenon and guidelines in a parsimonious way. Finally, a few conclusions as well as some positive speculations about the progress of research on alliances are offered.

2 Alliances: causes, motives, and benefits

Drivers of alliance formation

Rapid changes in technology, shortened product life cycles, and increased competition owing to reduced barriers to international trade (Ohmae 1985) have all contributed to the need to have distinctive capabilities. A firm may be considered to have a competitive advantage when its products and services deliver superior value to customers compared to the offerings of competing firms. Distinctive capabilities or core competencies when successfully applied to a firm's markets become competitive advantages (Kay 1993). If the generation of competitive advantage is in itself a formidable task, sustaining it is a tougher proposition by any standards. It is reported that most product and even process innovations are replicated by the competition in about one year's time from the date of introduction (Slater 1996). Competitive advantages vary in terms of their degree and ease of replication. The list of competitive advantages ranges from being ones that are easily reproduced to those that are difficult to replicate. *The more embedded an ability is, the harder it is for other firms to imitate.* The array of dimensions on which firms compete today is quite large and varied. The original Porter framework lists three broad advantages: cost, differentiation and focus (Porter 1980). In recent years, the qualitative as well as quantitative increases in the number and type of firms competing have rendered some of the traditional advantages such as cost, quality, speed of delivery and service as what could be termed entry fees or *sine qua non* for competition.

While it is necessary for firms to possess these traditional strengths to compete in the marketplace, and most firms do have them, successful outcomes depend on whether firms have other competitive advantages that are unique and exclusive. Customers have come to treat the traditional attributes as given and hence firms find it hard to differentiate themselves on those parameters and strive continually to upgrade and leapfrog ahead of competitors. *Higher order abilities such as partnering, learning and innovation abilities are more difficult to imitate.* The uniqueness and exclusivity of competence lies in its being harder to replicate, allowing time for firms to utilize it in their chosen markets, and build on them as a foundation for the next stage of development of competitive advantage. The process of developing and sustaining competitive advantages is best viewed as dynamic and amenable to continuous up-grading and renewal. Indeed, in future, the growth and prosperity of firms is likely to be a function of their ability to build new businesses rather than to sustain old businesses (Hamel and Prahalad 1994).

Technological developments in the communication and transport fields have significantly eroded the way we perceive distances and time (McKenna 1997) and have steadily been chipping away at the forces that bind us to remain local. The integration of economies, regional agreements, monetary unions and converging consumer tastes and living standards makes firms that are merely reliant on geographically bound ideas, markets, products and facilities redundant. The Asian monetary crisis in 1997 has sent shock waves all across the world,

Special topics

highlighting the interwoven nature of business. The introduction of the euro, a single currency for a number of European countries in 1999 is another significant development. This is a step that takes the common market forward from the establishment of European Union. Firms that collaborate with suppliers, customers and even competitors across and within regions will have established a competitive position that will be hard to rival.

Generating and successfully sustaining competitive advantages all by oneself may not be viable in many instances, if not entirely infeasible. Products and innovations that reach the market later than scheduled may fail to deliver profits and might even result in the incurring of losses if competing products are launched and marketed aggressively. Some high technology industries are known to be prone to excessive rates of obsolescence and volatility, and efforts designed simply to keep in step with the competition require large resources. Research and development costs have risen sky high, and the time to recoup investments is considerably shorter than ever before. Figure 1 depicts the options that a firm has available to respond to the increasingly complicated and competitive business situations that prevail in most industries. As may be evidenced, firms have a wide range of options to choose from, and opting for the appropriate alternative course of action is a highly strategic decision.

Collaboration is 'the' solution

Although the range and forms that inter-firm cooperation can take are numerous and deliver tangible benefits and advantages, managers and practitioners alike appear to have a tendency to resort to mergers and acquisitions as a means for growth and profitability. This is evidenced in the number of mergers and acquisitions that are announced in financial daily newspapers. This happens despite the fact that all available evidence suggests that mergers rarely if ever result in profitable long-term returns. Neither do acquisitions end in complete successes owing to a number of difficulties in finding the appropriate partners at the right prices. Indeed, it has been argued that 'managers often over-integrate because they fail to consider the rich array of quasi-integration strategies such as long-term contracts, joint ventures, strategic alliances, preferred-supplier partnerships, technology licenses, asset ownership and franchising which tend to involve lower capital costs and greater flexibility than vertical integration' (Stuckey and White 1993).

The risks of total and complete reliance on internal growth and development may be so high as to outweigh any possibility of gaining reasonable returns (Buzzell 1983). If they fail to bear fruit, some investment-intensive ventures may pose a disproportionate and inordinate threat to the very survival of sponsoring firms. In which case, it is not surprising that

Figure 1 Drivers of alliance formation

'collaboration' is being suggested by academics, consultants and practitioners as the solution for success in the increasingly complex business context. Several authors mention that the ability to form and successfully manage alliances for creating scale, scope and sequence advantages is important in an era marked by globalization, increased competition and a rapidly changing technological environment (Ohmae 1985) The ability to form and manage alliances is emerging as an important capability, and one that all firms need to develop and few can afford to ignore. The art of alliance management is a distinctive capability that firms need to develop in order to stay ahead of their rivals in the increasingly competitive environment that prevails in most industries.

Alliance objectives are strategic

The proliferation of alliances and partnerships is now a widespread phenomenon, but one that is little understood. Our knowledge of alliance activity is still in a nascent stage and clear normative guidelines are only now beginning to emerge, and the process of research is far from over. Companies cooperate in two broad ways (Kay 1993; Stafford 1994). They may either (i) pool resources with a view to attaining mutually agreed objectives; or (ii) exchange resources in order to acquire complementary strengths. The objectives and goals, among others, include access to hitherto unexplored markets and customers, introduction of new or better products, access to technology and know-how, reduction of costs and attendant risks, and productivity or efficiency gains.

Efficiency gains and process improvements, although of great importance by themselves, are at the operational level only, while others, such as market development and acquisition of new skills, are of strategic importance to corporations (Porter 1996). The real test of an alliance is whether it is of sufficiently strategic importance for all the partners involved. The acid test is the marketplace and the judge and the jury are the consumer or end-user. Accordingly, strategic alliances and partnerships should favourably affect the partners involved and lead to the generation and sustenance of competitive advantages for all of them.

The continuum of inter-firm relations ranges from arm's-length dealings, as in market transactions, to total integration as in a merger. Figure 2 depicts the range of all possible inter-firm relationships as a stepwise progression. As objectives of collaboration become more strategic from being merely operational, so do the needs for investment, attendant risks, and more importantly the time lag for reaping the rewards of association. Strategic alliances are not a quick and easy fix for inherent weaknesses in firms entering into collaborative efforts.

Figure 2 The ladder of inter-firm relations
Source: Adapted from Lorange and Roos (1992) and Webster (1992)

Unlike some of the forms of cooperation shown in Figure 2 at the bottom of the ladder, 'strategic alliances lay more emphasis on the future aspects of the association and the results of collaboration have a comparatively longer developmental period. As a result, the risks of association and the exit costs are much higher' (Baker and Srivastav 1997). For the sake of being complete, Figure 2 also illustrates higher forms of collaboration – networks, clusters, and mergers – that lead to total integration. Clearly, not all forms of cooperation could be classified as strategic alliances and there exist significant differences between various forms of cooperation which entail entirely different implications for partnering firms. However, writings in the field of management literature, although replete with various classifications of interfirm cooperation, show a remarkable lack of agreement and uniformity.

The treatments of classification normally employed in the strategic alliance literature tend to be based on the presence or absence of equity investments, and variations in structural forms, say a joint venture or a licensing agreement (Borys and Jemison 1989; Contractor and Lorange 1988; Culpan 1993; Frear and Metcalf 1995; Gerlach 1987; Harrigan 1988; Houston *et al.* 1992; KPMG Report 1996; Lewis 1990; Rangan and Yoshino 1996; Varadarajan and Cunningham 1998). Although a large body of literature on strategic alliances exists, as indicated by the aforementioned citations, we feel that there is still a need to develop rigorous taxonomic models that delineate various forms of collaboration and highlight differences between them.

Indeed, Baker and Srivastav note

Much of the literature relating to relationships and alliances conceives of these as 'either/or' alternatives. For our part, we conceive of collaboration between partners existing along a continuum with associations at one end and strategic alliances the other end of the continuum. It is argued that the relationship between two partners is clearly a matter of degree and moves from 'association' into more strategic perspectives depending on the success of the intervening operational dimensions. To this extent we think that successful alliances must evolve, and an association between partners should be a necessary precursor to a strategic alliance. This is necessary because strategic alliances involve commitments of a much higher order such as sharing technology, joint product development, substantial resource obligations etc. In our view, it could well be that the reason for the high failure rate of strategic alliances reported in the management literature may well be a consequence of the partners failing to get to know each other through a series of increasingly closer relationships.

(Baker and Srivastav 1997)

Customer–supplier partnerships are those cooperative efforts that lead to operational gains whereas alliances aim at achieving strategic objectives. At a detailed level, an inter-firm partnership may be defined as an agreement between a buyer and a supplier that involves a commitment on a long-term contractual basis, and includes the sharing of information, risks and rewards of the relationship. Relations marked by partnership offer significant benefits and synergies for the parties involved. As indicated earlier, partnerships could over time evolve to become true alliances or even a merger of cooperating firms. However, both alliances and partnerships require a great deal of investment and hence a firm will have to exercise the tools of collaboration judiciously.

Transaction orientation is giving way to partnership-orientation

The proliferation of alliances and partnerships is now an accepted fact of business, and current trends indicate further growth in the number as well as the scope of alliances. Alliances involving vertical relationships in the value chain, such as those between manufacturers and suppliers or distributors, are being accorded greater attention as their significance is being more widely recognized. The concept of a boundary-less organization with a network of connections is becoming increasingly visible in practice, contributing to a growth in alliances and a reliance on partner networks. Customer–supplier relations through alliances and partnerships are seen as an important source of various advantages that lead to competitive advantage.

The traditional supplier–buyer links were largely non-equity ties and these relations were often characterized by arm's-length transactional orientations, and even an adversarial spirit. Buyer–supplier transactions, involving outside specialist suppliers compete with the closeness, reliability, continuity and other advantages entailed by in-house production. Although many Japanese firms have been deriving the benefits of closer cooperation with suppliers, it is only recently that companies in North America and Europe have begun to actively seek to develop close cooperation with suppliers and to build partnership association or networks. It is evident that the trend for the future is clearly more outsourcing and less integration within an organization, and that the erstwhile discrete and bipolar choices of build or buy are giving way to the formation of alliances involving close relations, and in some cases even equity investments. In recent years, close inter-firm relationships at various stages of the value chain have become popular and a number of studies have been published highlighting the beneficial aspects of forging and maintaining close relationships (Anderson and Narus 1990; Morgan and Hunt 1994). These writings and many other similar works highlight the fact that customer–supplier alliances and partnerships are now increasingly seen as an important route for deriving a range of advantages.

Motives of alliances

Organizations can create the highest value for customers and other stakeholders by selectively sharing and trading control, costs, capital, access to markets, information and technology with competitors, customers and suppliers alike (Bleeke and Ernst 1991). The keys to success in alliances are complementary activities, well-matched functional strengths, and a solid business rationale rather than the self-improvement of partners. Several authors have written that 'managers prefer to manage what they own' (e.g. Spekman *et al.* 1996). Cooperation increases interdependence and the need to share control, which may not be to the liking of all firms. Alliances require that one firm takes into consideration the needs and requirements of another firm in plotting its own future. 'As the ways to combine resources increase, the ability to command decreases' (Kanter 1989) It may be important to recognize that alliances are a tradeoff between a need for resources and the control associated with ownership.

Firms may decide to cooperate to exchange or pool resources for either higher or quicker value creation through joint innovation; to increase the organizational knowledge pool through learning; acquire new competencies or skills; access markets and customers; internationalize operations (Bleeke and Ernst 1991; Ohmae 1985); diffuse technologies (Lorange and Roos 1992); block or preempt competition (Porter 1986; Stafford 1994); derive cost advantages or gain productivity enhancements; share risks and costs (Ohmae 1985, 1989), increase the flexibility of operations; destabilize and create new market values (Newman and Chaharbaghi 1996); improve products and services; offer complementary products or services of partners such as system deals (Bronder and Pritzl 1992); shape industries (Porter 1986); influence policy making bodies; or even as a prelude to full cooperation, usually a merger, sale or acquisition (Bleeke and Ernst 1991; Bronder and Pritzl 1992; Kanter 1994).

Bronder and Pritzl (1992) offer one of the most comprehensive classifications of the benefits of collaboration:

- Time advantages can arise from faster responses to changes in the environment. Implementing cooperative R&D programmes can substantially reduce development times.
- Know-how advantages: the complexity of product technology increases dramatically while product and other life-cycles become shorter. Mutual learning within a strategic alliance can help to overcome knowledge deficits due to these technological changes.
- Access to markets as an objective is getting more and more important due to increased global protectionism.
- Cost advantages from external synergy can arise through combining value chain activities.
- System competence: through strategic alliances, companies can achieve system competence in certain markets even though their own core competencies are focused on specialized areas.

Collaborations involving many companies in the same industry or similar industries collectively endeavouring to shape industry competition are not uncommon. Indeed, many authors suggest that firms in the same industry are ideal for forging collaborative partnerships owing to their similarities (Hamel et al. 1989). Collaborating with competitors helps companies to counter bigger competitors, define industry standards, share development and marketing costs, expand their product range, and influence governments in their favour.

As indicated earlier, firms need to collaborate for a variety of reasons such as needs for resource exchange, sharing investment, reducing risks, gaining market access, pre-empting competitors, and shaping industry competition. Lewis (1995) asserts that relations with other firms extend scale and scope, virtually doubling an organization's resources. The extended organization is increasingly seen as a path to future prosperity and a significant means for achieving the same is customer–supplier alliances. The reasons, motives and benefits cited support the need for alliances and partnerships. An important and growing area of significance – customer–supplier alliances – is discussed in detail next.

Customer–supplier alliances

Customer–supplier alliances offer and hold great potential for companies. A typical firm – and this is especially the case when large organizations are considered – derives about one-half or more of its turnover from supplies sourced externally (Baker and Srivastav 1997; Lewis 1995). Baker and Srivastav put forward the view that the cost reductions and other improvements that may be gained from customer–supplier alliances are more likely to contribute to a firm's profits than the uncertainty that is associated with affecting sales growth. These views further buttress our view of the need for a closer and more integrated approach towards collaborators, including suppliers.

Traditional customer–supplier alliances involved the exchange of goods or services for a price. The focus was mostly on the price of the items bought. Arm's-length transactions might work best in perfect market conditions. Perfect market conditions are created by the existence of a large number of companies signifying low barriers to entry and exit, the absence of differentiated products, an inability on the part of any of the firms to influence prices of goods, and the non-existence of economies of scale. Imperfect market conditions coupled with occasional misrepresentation and deception interfere with the efficient working of markets (Rugman 1981; Williamson 1975, 1985). The implication is that it may not be entirely prudent to rely solely on either market mechanisms or internalization strategies to aid the working of an organization. Gaining economies of scale and scope, and other important competitive advantages all by oneself is a difficult task. Excessive vertical integration may leave a firm in no position to be flexible in its responses to the innovations of competitive firms. Forging alliances with partners could help an organization – in terms of capital and human resources – to focus on core areas of operation.

The adversarial relations that once characterized customer–supplier dealings are gradually giving way to partnership and trust. Lewis (1995) suggests that companies have paid attention to customers all along, whereas the other half of the competitive-resource equation, the supplier, has not received the focus that it so richly deserves. Integrating suppliers and leveraging their strengths for mutual benefit are areas that no company can easily ignore.

Customer–supplier alliances aim to achieve more than that expected from a transactional orientation. While market based dealings with suppliers may work well under perfect market conditions; such dealings may not work as well in real conditions. Alliances should aim to maximize benefits through close coordination and a sharing of resources, including technology. Though market based dealings aim to maximize efficiencies in most cases, an absence of shared information and close links between customer and supplier is likely to lead to under-performance relative to market players who have forged strategic alliances and partnerships. The sharing of information and other forms of cooperation are the underlying pillars that support the strength and higher value creation potential of alliances. True buyer-supplier relations are governed by mutual dependence, expectation of continued relations and trust. Collaboration and cooperation with other firms to maximize customer benefits is an appropriate route to corporate success when a continued relationship is likely to lead to higher value creation as opposed to market based or internalization strategies.

Companies that were earlier known for fiercely defending total reliance on internal development are now turning to various forms of collaboration. IBM has successfully made the transition from being a totally integrated firm to a firm that now relies on a number of suppliers and partners. Ford is in the process of rationalizing its worldwide operations and its number of suppliers with a view to forging solid links with a smaller number of firms. It is reported that Ford is reducing the number of suppliers it has by one-half by the turn of the century. Lewis (1990; 1995) provides a host of examples of companies that are turning to customer–supplier alliances. Some of the most successful Japanese style partnerships are characterized by fewer direct suppliers, customized investments by suppliers and forced competition (Dyer and Ouchi 1993). Fewer direct suppliers allow the focus to be put on procurement of systems and not on individual components, thereby leading to cost reductions and quality improvements. Suppliers, when given the opportunity and assurance of a stable, and long-term relationship, are likely to invest more in site-specific (closer to the location of customer), customer-specific equipment and in learning more about the operations and needs of customer. This is a growing phenomenon that needs to be taken note of by all companies. Increasingly firms are moving toward establishing more solid relations but with a shrinking number of companies. A firm that does not substantially add value faces the danger of being left out in the cold.

Focusing on core competence

Sourcing supplies from other firms could benefit a company in many ways. Considering that resources for any firm are limited, it is necessary to collaborate with other firms. Modern business calls for a focus on core areas wherein competitive advantages could be developed (Prahalad and Hamel 1990). A firm needs to invest its resources in its area of core operations. Non-core areas could easily be outsourced or alliances with other firms could produce the desired results. Even within core areas of operation, there could exist avenues for cooperation when going alone may either take too long, or when internal resources are simply inadequate. To be the first in the marketplace with new or improved products and services is an important advantage that firms cannot easily ignore. Focusing on core areas and collaborating with others who specialize in complementary fields allow a firm to simultaneously reap the benefits of economies of scale, and a differentiated or extended product range. Alliances and partnerships could free scarce resources for core functions to be performed within the organization rendering a better focus on core areas. It is important to realize that others who have already built up expertise in that area could perform some functions better. Duplication of others' areas of expertise and reinventing the wheel are not likely to significantly contribute to a firm's growth and profitability. Although it is a paradoxical outcome in most situations, interdependence could well contribute to independence (Lewis 1995). Going alone or relying on internal or organic growth is just one of the options. The range of options on the continuum, formed by total self-reliance at one end and reliance on external sources at the other end, is quite varied. A firm needs to consider all options and select the best option that could help it to develop and sustain long-term competencies in its core areas of operations.

Alliances and partnerships yield efficiencies and cost reductions

Strategic sourcing through alliances and partnerships is the process of creating value adding supply relationships to provide a competitive advantage (Spekman et al. 1994). Apart from contributing to cost control, sourcing also improves overall performance in quality, dependability, flexibility and innovation. Strategic outsourcing provides four main benefits. According to Quinn and Hilmer (1994), these benefits are:

First, firms maximise returns on internal resources by concentrating investments and energies on what the enterprise does best. Second, well developed core competencies provide formidable barriers against present and future competitors that seek to expand into the company's areas of interest, thus facilitating and protecting the strategic advantages of market share. Third, perhaps the greatest leverage of all is the full utilisation of external suppliers' investments, innovations, and specialised professional capabilities that would be prohibitively expensive or even impossible to duplicate internally. Fourth, in rapidly changing marketplaces and technological situations, joint strategies decrease risks, shorten cycle times, lower investments, and create better responsiveness to customer needs.

Organizations outsourcing activities in which they cannot develop strategic advantages can:

- achieve an improvement in the performance of those service areas;
- reduce overheads;
- improve their focus on the development of core abilities;
- lever those competencies; and
- achieve a more compact, less hierarchical organization (Quinn and Hilmer 1994).

Narus and Anderson (1996) argue that cooperative arrangements, strategic alliances and partnerships leverage resources and share capabilities to improve the quality of service throughout their supply chains. As the focus shifts from products to services, suppliers need to strengthen and increase their service levels substantially, or face the prospect of being left out due to the shrinking number of suppliers on the lists of manufacturers. Anderson *et al.* (1994) suggest that firms that see themselves as 'embedded in webs of capabilities can augment their own capabilities with those of other members and broaden their offerings'. A comprehensive list of benefits offered by Frankel *et al.* (1996) suggests that the following benefits accrue to alliances in general:

- reduced cost through specialization;
- improved synergistic performance;
- increased information to support joint planning;
- enhanced customer service;
- reduced risk and uncertainty;
- shared creativity; and
- competitive advantage.

Williamson (1985) contends that transaction costs are inefficiencies directly attributable to commerce between firms, and costs of creating contracts and monitoring trading partners activities. Williamson maintains that minimization or the lowering of transaction costs is very important in the formation stages of a relationship. Alliances should focus not just on cost reductions but on developing true competitive advantages in terms of innovation leading to new products or higher value creation, customer satisfaction and in developing competitive advantages in the marketplace (Porter 1996). However, it is likely that operational gains such as cost reductions, improvements in quality and the like may help a partnership grow to include a focus on other more strategic parameters (Baker and Srivastav 1997).

Customers' costs consist of four main elements: invoice costs, acquisition costs, possession costs and usage costs. Alliances and partnerships due to the nature of long-term arrangements optimize the total cost of doing business. One major friction point is inventory costs. While it is suggested that suppliers are being forced to carry the burden of inventory costs, the same may be due to the genuine pressures that customers face or because they are simply not able to forecast proper or varying quantities (Bowersox 1991). Fisher *et al.* (1994) suggest that customers and suppliers gain by filling non-reactive capacity as much as possible in advance, and use the reactive capacity to incorporate the most recent information, such as market trends etc. This method may help in controlling and eliminating the costs of carrying inventories, stock-out costs and mark-downs or damaged goods.

The above technique of sharing of information is consistent with Gentry's (1996) suggestion that increased information sharing may substitute for inventories leading to a reduction in possession costs. This finding is in contrast to the finding of Noordewier *et al.* (1990) that only acquisition costs not possession costs could be lowered through long-term relations.

Kalwani and Narayandas (1995) found that suppliers benefit through establishing long-term relationships with customers. They suggest that suppliers in partnerships face price pressures and hence decreased gross margin levels. Customers who engage in partnerships are generally very demanding in expecting short-term price concessions and long-term orientation simultaneously. The study, however, suggests that partnerships and long-term alliances help suppliers to considerably reduce their selling and other administrative expenses resulting in increased profits and return on investments (ROI). Customer loyalty and continuity of relationship could benefit supplier firms through increased long-term profits, and improved efficiencies due to developing a better understanding of customer needs. Overall, the view that partnerships result in reduced inventories does find some support in the literature. This is especially so when information exchange is regular. Apart from the inventory reduction, improvements actually gained by firms involved in partnership sourcing have been examined in a number of studies (Baker and Srivastav 1997; Kalwani and Narayandas 1995).

Potential drawbacks of alliances

Some potential drawbacks are the difficulties and risks involved in coordinating different firms, unequal gains, culture clashes, role ambiguities, the possibilities of a partner allying with competitors, and the chances of facing anti-trust charges (Culpan 1993: 27–8). Porter (1986) identifies three broad categories of costs associated with coalitions: coordination, erosion of competitive position and creation of an adverse bargaining position. Jain (1987) mentions a potential imbalance in benefits, an imbalance in commitment and motivation, difficulties in arriving at agreement, communication problems, possible conflict between partners, and retaliation from government and competition as significant likely drawbacks. Undue reliance or dependence on others is also a drawback.

It is important to note these drawbacks and disadvantages. Firms that enter into alliances should take into account these issues and ensure that safeguards are available. The importance of adopting a selective approach to relations cannot be exaggerated. Only when the benefits outweigh the risks should alliances be entered into. The next section details processes that are likely to ensure the success of alliances. This is done with a view to deriving guidelines which when implemented could enhance the chances of success.

3 Approaches to successful alliances and partnerships

Relational orientation is not a panacea

The field of marketing is witnessing a paradigm shift through an embracing of the concept of inter-organizational cooperation and relationships (Morgan and Hunt 1994; Webster 1992). The role of marketing in the corporation is evolving from the traditional focus of selecting target markets and developing a marketing mix (Osland and Yaprak 1995). According to Osland and Yaprak, some of the new roles include deciding when and how to partner with other firms to enhance distinctive competencies, and to achieve higher market share, long-term profitability and a better defined set of core competencies.

The concept of relational orientation as put forward by various writers is essential for the success of alliances. However, adoption of such an orientation may not be appropriate to all customer–supplier relations. Wray *et al.* (1994) assert that increasing of relational orientation may only be appropriate when purchases involve a high level of risk and relationship acts as a manager of risk exposure. They further suggest that relationship building may also be necessary 'where a stream of benefits is produced and consumed over a period of time or where they can reduce transaction costs associated with repeated purchase routines'.

Noordewier *et al.* (1990) found empirical support for their premise that the purchasing performance of firms could be enhanced by increasing the relational content of the exchange structure when uncertainty is high. The study suggests that not all transactions and sourcing need to have relational elements. They conclude that increasing relational content when uncertainty is low has no effect on performance. Kumar (1996) conducted an empirical survey to measure the impact of trust and found that customer–supplier relations characterized by trust are mutually beneficial in terms of sales, profits, higher dedicated investments and adaptability to changing market conditions. The author, however, suggests that there are limits to the application of trust strategy, and that employing trust based relationships works best with those partners who are willing to play the trust game. It is likely that indiscriminate use of alliances may expose firms to exploitation by opportunistic partners.

Krapfel *et al.* (1991) put forward the view that not all transactions require approaches characterized by high relationalism. They suggest that relations could be classified into four categories according to the levels of two parameters: relationship value and interest commonality. This classification treats partners and rivals as high value relationships but with different levels of commonalties between partners having high commonality and rivals having low interest commonalties. Similarly, friends and acquaintances are low value relationships but with different levels of commonalties with friends having high commonality and acquaintances having low interest commonalties. The authors contend that different classes of relationships require different levels of resources, stability and governance structure, and consequently hold varying profit potential. Further, the authors suggest that each relation may potentially evolve into one of the other three forms over time due either to changes in environment or by design of partners. However, firms intending to maximize profits may also influence the process of evolution of other firms to some extent. In some situations acquaintances or rivals may hold more profit potential and need to be treated accordingly. Firms have to balance their resources with the commonalties of interest and values they derive from a relationship in order to maximize profits by having a portfolio of relationships rather than a single approach such as either all market orientation (transactional orientation) or relational orientation.

Information exchange

The driving forces behind an alliance should be the top management of partners. The top executives should not only be convinced of the business rationale and commercial logic of an alliance, but they should also establish good personal relations to ensure that the alliance succeeds and overcomes any teething problems, conflicts and disagreements between operating managers and employees from different firms. While an alliance manager normally oversees day-to-day functioning of the alliances and is responsible for resolving issues and problems, the importance of top management's role should not be underestimated. The role of political blessing and stakeholder involvement is crucial to the success of an alliance (Lorange and Roos 1992). In fact, many authors have attributed the success of alliances to the chemistry or good interpersonal relations and regular exchange of information between partnering firms' top executives (Kanter 1994; Ohmae 1985; 1989).

There are various accounts of failed alliances that focus excessively on commercial issues at the expense of interpersonal issues. There appears to be a strong consensus in the literature that absence of interpersonal relations may have a negative effect on even those alliances that have strong commercial logic (Spekman *et al.* 1996). It is also essential that alliance vision be understood throughout cooperating organizations so they participate and contribute to the success. This could be achieved through establishing contacts at multiple levels. Good interpersonal relations and information exchange not only at top levels but also at multiple levels are key to the success of an alliance.

Dyer (1996) notes that Chrysler had managed to increase its market share and profits dramatically through its partnerships with suppliers. The reduced number of suppliers get more work from the company than before and participate in the design stages of a vehicle right up to delivery of parts. Chrysler managed to cut costs, increase quality, reduce defect rates, develop innovative products, reduce development times, and increase efficiency of its production lines. Most suppliers have made dedicated investments and report increased satisfaction and make suggestions for saving costs or for improving products. Chrysler has adopted more oral agreements than ever before. Interpersonal relationships between executives of Chrysler and supplier personnel have substantially contributed to the process of building partnerships.

Trust is considered an essential ingredient for success (Ford 1980). Trust develops with more communication and cooperation (Anderson and Narus 1990; Ohmae 1985). Elaborate contracts and the associated effort in drawing them up, plus the costs of enforcing them are part of the transaction costs related to an exchange of goods (Williamson 1975, 1985). Trust could obviate or reduce the need for contracts and considerable related expenses. Further, trusting and cooperative behaviour leads to satisfaction in organizational relationships

(Osland and Yaprak 1993). Marketing theories suggest that satisfaction leads to loyalty, and commitment to alliance and its purpose. Trust is more likely to develop when one partner takes the initiative and exercises trusting behaviour (Gulati et al. 1994; Osland and Yaprak 1993). Gulati et al. (1994) argue that unilateral commitment by one partner may act as a catalyst and enhance the possibility that other partners cooperate in making a venture successful. They argue that if companies form an alliance but do not cooperate with each other, then the result could be loss for all parties. This argument is in line with Bleeke and Ernst's (1991) findings that unsuccessful alliances result in failure for all partners. It is important for partners of an alliance to take effective, sometimes unilateral actions to ensure that an alliance stays on course, and also to signal their commitment to other partners. According to Morgan and Hunt (1994) relationship commitment and trust develop when firms attend to relationships by:

- providing resources, opportunities, and benefits that are superior to the offerings of alternative partners;
- maintaining high standards of corporate values and allying oneself with exchange partners having similar values;
- communicating valuable information, including expectations, market intelligence, and evaluations of the partner's performance; and
- avoiding malevolently taking advantage of their exchange partners.

Information exchange is considered an important determinant of customer–supplier partnerships (Gadde and Hakansson 1994; Hakansson 1982; Metcalf et al. (1992) found that exchange of information and interpersonal contacts produce a cooperative atmosphere between partners, which in turn influences adaptation. Interpersonal exchange generates attitudes of mutual trust and produces an atmosphere of cooperation which influences investments that generate higher sales, cost reductions or new innovations. Their findings reinforce the need for a coordinated set of communications at multiple levels, and formalized systems such as committees for regular meetings to exchange information, and frequency of contact. It is clear that this important attribute of information exchange contributes to the development of strong relationships and accordingly firms need to build channels for communication with partners.

Strength of relationship

Webster and Wind (1972) suggests that source loyalty may reduce the costs associated with frequently changing suppliers. The authors recognize that buying decisions might result in organizational satisfaction and possible source loyalty to vendors. Barclay (1992) posits that this could make acceptance of new vendors more difficult. Vendors once selected may expect to continue for a reasonable length of time and generally enjoy benefits of continuity. Expectations of long-term cooperation and mutual trust enhance the possibilities of a favourable decision in industrial purchasing (Laios and Xideas 1994). Possible disadvantages might be higher expectations and dependence.

Heide and John (1988) found that firms which were dependent on other companies due to their dedicated assets could reduce an imbalance in dependence by establishing closer bonds with end-users, thereby locking in other companies such as suppliers and manufacturers. Heide and John also suggest that partner opportunism is reduced when organizational boundaries are interpenetrated. On the other hand, a firm's relation-specific investments signal dependence and a tendency to maintain a relationship (Anderson and Narus 1990). Ganesan (1994) suggests that long-term orientation of a relationship is a function of mutual dependence and trust. In turn, relation-specific investments, uncertainty, reputation of partners, and satisfaction with outcomes influence mutual dependence and trust. Long-term orientation requires building of technological capabilities through sharing and investments in developing strengths. Monczka et al. (1995) found empirical support for their premise that 'overall satisfaction with a relationship and exchange of information were affected by cooperative behaviours, lower transaction costs, greater dependence, better quality, greater economic satisfaction, longer business relationship, more specific investments and joint programs'. Relative dependence could be used to influence partners to act in a mutually beneficial fashion.

787

Relation-specific investments help bond a relation but may be construed as a cause of overdependence. Reciprocation of specific investments by partners to an alliance redresses potential situations of imbalance in contributions and mutual interest. In any case, partnerships entail interdependence and need trust for successful functioning.

Satisfaction with a partnership is treated as a focal construct in various studies. Anderson and Narus (1990) contend that satisfaction is 'not only a close proxy for perceived effectiveness, but also may be more predictive of future actions by partner firm managers'. This view is consistent with the views expressed elsewhere in marketing theory that satisfaction leads to repeat transactions and long-term relationship. Wray et al. (1994) view relationship quality as a two-dimensional construct: consisting of satisfaction and trust. Their research found that the expertise of the seller contributes to the satisfaction of the customer and the duration of a relation leads to the generation of trust. Shamdasani and Sheth (1995) contend that examining member satisfaction and continuity decisions should receive focal attention, as dissatisfaction with an alliance relationship is cited in the literature as one of the major reasons for the failure of alliances. The authors suggest that dissatisfaction is a product of both financial outcomes and relational outcomes. 'While satisfaction reflects existing feelings about alliances based on evaluation of outcomes and experiences received in the past, continuity decisions reflect expectations of future cooperation' (Shamdasani and Sheth 1995). Gentry (1996) identified that successful buyer–supplier relationships have four partnership dimensions: (i) long-term commitments, (ii) open communications and information sharing, (iii) joint problem solving and continuous improvements and (iv) shared risks and rewards. Constructs such as economies of scale, cost reduction potential and innovation ability indicate the need for continuity in a partnership arrangement. Satisfaction with relation and continuity decisions are strongly related to the quality improvements and cost reductions that may be gained through alliances and partnerships.

Alliance guidelines

Partnerships entail 'mutual recognition and understanding that the success of one firm depends in part on the other firm, with each firm consequently taking actions so as to provide a coordinated effort focused on jointly satisfying the requirements of the customer market place' (Anderson and Narus 1990). The main rationale of an alliance should be the market impact through the competitive advantage that it generates. Short-term cost reductions may lead to the generation of long-term competencies, but it is not always necessarily so. Hence, it is important to keep in mind that alliances and partnerships generally yield their benefits after a long duration, and need to be nurtured through careful investments in the forms of both physical and social capital, particularly in the initial years. Indeed, we feel that it may well be totally inappropriate to use generally used accounting and other financial measures to evaluate the performance of alliances. More strategic and often intangible measures could often prove to be suitable indicators. Bowersox (1991) suggests the following five guidelines that help to make alliances and partnerships work.

1 View the arrangements as the implementation of a strategic plan. Encourage the participants involved to consider their roles in terms of a value-added process.
2 Seek an arrangement that achieves scale-economy benefits while spreading risks.
3 Recognize that the benefits can be gained only through a long-term relationship in which the parties are interdependent; make sure that the information necessary to function well is shared between them.
4 Build trust between the organizations by setting unambiguous goals, establishing clear roles, laying down firm rules and measuring performance rigorously.
5 Start the venture on a realistic course by acknowledging that eventually the alliance may have to be terminated.

A study by Bleeke and Ernst (1991) revealed the following in relation to alliances.

1 Alliances are effective for related businesses or expanding into new geographic markets.
2 Alliances between strong and weak companies rarely work.

3 The hallmark of successful alliances is their ability to evolve beyond initial expectations and objectives.
4 Alliances with an even split of financial ownership are more likely to succeed than other dominant ventures.
5 Three-fourths of the alliances that terminated ended with an acquisition by one of the parents.

4 An alliance model: the virtuous circle

The three 'I's of strategic alliances and partnerships

True alliances go beyond achieving the benefits of efficiencies and cost reductions possible in dealings through arm's-length relations with multiple suppliers. Traditional relations characterized by price and reliability do not maximize opportunities to innovate and thereby create higher value through collaboration. The historical relations were largely adversarial and involved an exchange of goods for money and as little interaction as necessary. As opposed to the arm's-length transactional orientation, alliances are built on relational orientation with a view to maximizing mutual benefits.

We propose a model that takes into account all the information presented earlier in this entry and offer a parsimonious model of three 'I's. To be successful an alliance needs three main elements to be present. The maximization of mutual benefits can be achieved through *interaction* between alliance entities, *investments* both physical ones in capital equipment and in developing mutual understanding, and by creating an atmosphere that encourages and fosters *innovation*. The three 'I's of strategic alliances are inter-related and mutually reinforce each other in a virtuous cycle.

The 'Strategic Alliance' model derived from the literature review that was detailed earlier is depicted in Figure 3.

The level of *interaction* between firms in a customer–supplier alliance at all relevant key managerial levels is vital to forging successful partnerships. The essential first step has to be taken by top management itself in nominating a lead executive to nurture the relationship in order to reap the full benefits of the alliance and also to build communication channels with partners.

Customer–supplier alliances in their true sense are not an easy and quick way either to sell products or to reduce costs. To forge a powerful partnership, firms need to invest in each other. Most important is the need to invest in building solid relationships in which both parties respect and trust each other's needs. Margins, confidential technologies, cost data and the need for independence are all ingredients that help in generating competitive advantage

Figure 3 The three 'I's of strategic alliances

in the marketplace. Sometimes customer and supplier may be required to make company-specific investments. The amortization and sharing of costs have to be done in an equal and just fashion to build a win–win situation. Opportunistic behaviour by one or all partners involved, such as using knowledge of supplier's cost data to manipulate or to knock down prices to gain unilateral gains, are not likely to lead to the commitment of partners that is essential for the success of alliance. The sources of cost reductions are numerous and joint cost reduction exercises and strengthening interfaces are some of them. Having said that, it has to be emphasized that too much focus on cost reduction alone can harm relationships. The aims of alliances should include higher value creation, end-consumer satisfaction and creation of competitive advantage.

A direct consequence of looking ahead of cost reduction leads to the area of *innovation*. Parties to an alliance need to focus on maximizing their innovation abilities and leveraging them to increase customer satisfaction. Innovation comes not only from within but also from interaction with other firms. To this extent, focused competition and multiple sourcing alternatives help firms to move ahead rather than to continue to depend on existing products, and inevitably stagnate in the end. Dealings with various customers and suppliers help advance the process of learning from important external sources that may facilitate knowledge accumulation.

5 Conclusions

Alliances and partnerships have existed for a long time but our understanding of them is still in its infancy. A detailed understanding is necessary to ensure that a firm gets what it hopes to achieve from a collaborative effort. It is estimated that over one-half of all alliances are unsuccessful. Non-materialization of desired objectives could mean squandered resources for companies. For certain firms, a loss of significant magnitude could have devastating consequences, even threatening its existence. An all or nothing attitude when investing in collaborations may prove dangerous. The high rate of failure emphasizes the need for developing a thorough understanding of the mechanisms for structuring, implementing and managing alliances.

Alliances allow a company to focus on its core activities where it can develop and sustain competitive advantages or core competencies. Scarce resources could be deployed for focused attention on priority areas. Focused collaborations hold a great potential to deliver sustainable competitive advantages to firms (Anderson and Narus 1991; Baker and Faulkner 1991; Dyer *et al.* 1998; Kapoor and Gupta 1997). Diffused and diverse efforts are a sure recipe for failure given the present competitive business environment. Collaboration and interdependence could contribute to the independence of a firm by allowing it to leverage others' areas of expertise for its own benefit. Customer–supplier alliances need to be built with a long-term outlook, and with a view to building solid relations based on trust and team spirit. Building networks and creating an extended organization that adds value internally and externally are essential prerequisites for future success in business (Hakansson and Sharma 1996).

Marketing academics and experts are starting to contribute to the field in general and in particular through contributions to theoretical guidelines, which yield normative prescriptions. The model building approaches in marketing (Lilien *et al.* 1992) are proving to be of aid in understanding business relationships (Wilson 1995) and hold great potential for the study of alliances in the future.

The concepts and ideas discussed so far could lead to the success of an alliance when thoughtfully executed and customized to specific needs. In particular, our aim was to offer some balanced views as to the benefits and drawbacks of alliances, and managers need to take these factors into account when forging alliances. A selective orientation is necessary, as a relational orientation is not a panacea for all problems. Every alliance is unique in its own right. There are no formulae for success, but the guidelines and the approaches offered in this entry can, when tailored to the needs of an alliance, significantly enhance chances of success.

PRATHAP OBURAI AND MICHAEL J. BAKER
UNIVERSITY OF STRATHCLYDE

Further reading

(References cited in the text marked *)

* Anderson, J.C. and Narus, J.A. (1990) 'A model of distributor firms and manufacturing firm working partnerships', *Journal of Marketing* 54: 42–58.
* Anderson, J.C. and Narus, J.A. (1991) 'Partnering as a focused market strategy', *California Management Review* 33: 95–113.
* Anderson, J.C., Hakansson, H. and Johansson, J. (1994) 'Dyadic business relationships within a business network context', *Journal of Marketing* 58: 1–15.
* Arndt, J. (1979) 'Toward a concept of domesticated markets', *Journal of Marketing* 43: 69–75.
* Baker, M.J. (1995) 'The future of marketing', in Baker, M.J., (ed.) *Companion Encyclopedia of Marketing*, 1st edn, London; New York: Routledge, pp. 1003–18.
* Baker, M.J. and Srivastav, A. (1997) 'Supplier partnering', A Working Paper, Department of Marketing, University of Strathclyde, Glasgow, UK.
* Baker, W.E. and Faulkner, R.R. (1991) 'Strategies for managing suppliers of professional services', *California Management Review* 33: 33–45.
* Barclay, D.W. (1992) 'Organisational buying outcomes and their effects on subsequent decisions', *European Journal of Marketing* 26: 48–64.
* Bleeke, J. and Ernst, D. (1991) 'The way to win in cross–border alliances', *Harvard Business Review* November–December, 127–35.
* Bleeke, J. and Ernst, D. (eds) (1993) *Collaborating to Compete : Using Strategic Alliances in the Global Marketplace*, New York: John Wiley & Sons. (A book by a group of McKinsey consultants that explores the range of options that firms employ for growth and expansion.)
* Borys, B. and Jemison, D.D. (1989) 'Hybrid arrangements as strategic alliances: Theoretical issues in organisational combinations', *Academy of Management Review* 14: 234–49.
* Bowersox, D.J. (1991) 'The strategic benefits of logistics alliances', *Harvard Business Review* July–August: 36–45.
* Bronder, C. and Pritzl, R. (1992) 'Developing strategic alliances: A conceptual framework for successful cooperation', *European Management Journal* 10: 412–21.
* Buzzell, R.D. (1983) 'Is vertical integration profitable?', *Harvard Business Review* 92–102.
* Contractor, F. and Lorange, P. (eds) (1988) *Cooperative Strategies in International Business*, Lexington: Lexington Books.
* Culpan, R. (ed.) (1993) *Multinational Strategic Alliances*, Binghamton, New York: International Business Press.
* Dyer, J.H. (1996) 'How Chrysler created an American Keiretsu', *Harvard Business Review* July–August: 42–56.
* Dyer, J.H. and Ouchi, W.G. (1993) 'Japanese-style partnerships: Giving companies a competitive edge', *Sloan Management Review* 35: 51–64.
* Dyer, J.H., Cho, D.S. and Chu, W. (1998) 'Strategic supplier segmentation: the next 'best practice' in supply chain management', *California Management Review* 40: 57–77.
* Fisher, M.L., Hammond, J.H., Obermeyer, W.R. and Raman, A. (1994) 'Making supply meet demand in an uncertain world', *Harvard Business Review* May–June: 83–93.
* Ford, D. (1980) 'The development of buyer–seller relationships in industrial markets', *European Journal of Marketing* 14: 339–53.
* Frankel, R., Whipple, J.S. and Frayer, D.J. (1996) 'Formal versus informal contracts : Achieving alliance success', *International Journal of Physical Distribution & Logistics Management* 26: 47–63.
* Frear, C.R. and Metcalf, L.E. (1995) 'Strategic alliances and technology networks', *Industrial Marketing Management* 25: 379–90.
* Gadde, L.–E. and Hakansson, H. (1994) 'The changing role of purchasing: reconsidering three strategic issues', *European Journal of Purchasing and Supply Management* 1: 27–35.
* Ganesan, S. (1994) 'Determinants of long-term orientation in buyer–seller relationships', *Journal of Marketing* 58: 1–19.
* Gentry, J.J. (1996) 'Carrier involvement in buyer–supplier strategic partnerships', *International Journal of Physical Distribution & Logistics Management* 26: 14–25.
* Gerlach, M. (1987) 'Business alliances and the strategy of the Japanese firm', *California Management Review* 30: 126–42.
* Gulati, R., Khanna, T. and Nohria, N. (1994) 'Unilateral commitments and the importance of process in alliances', *Sloan Management Review* 35: 61–70.
* Håkansson, H. (ed.) (1982) *International Marketing and Purchasing of Industrial Goods: An Interaction Approach*, New York: John Wiley & Sons.
* Håkansson, H. and Sharma, D.D. (1996) 'Strategic alliances in a network perspective', in Iacobucci, D. (ed.) *Networks in Marketing*, London: Sage Publications, pp. 108–124. (An excellent work that examines alliances from a Network perspective.)
  Hamel, G. and Prahalad, C.K. (1994) 'Competing for the future, 1994', *Harvard Business Review* July–August: 122–8.
* Hamel, G., Doz, Y.L. and Prahalad, C.K. (1989) 'Collaborate with your competitors – and win', *Harvard Business Review* January–February, 133–9.

Special topics

* Harrigan, K.R. (1988) 'Joint ventures and competitive strategy', *Strategic Management Journal* 9, 141–158.
* Heide, J.B. and John, G. (1988) 'The role of dependence balancing in safeguarding transaction specific assets in conventional channels', *Journal of Marketing* 52: 320–58.
* Houston, F.S., Gassenheimer, J.B. and Maskulka, J.M. (1992) *Marketing Exchange Transactions and Relationships*, Westport, Connecticut: Quorum Books.
* Jain S.C (1987) 'Perspectives on international strategic alliances', in Jain S.C. (ed.) *Advances in International Marketing*, New York: JAI Press
* Kalwani, M.U. and Narayandas, N. (1995) 'Long term manufacturer–supplier relationships: Do they pay off for supplier firms', *Journal of Marketing* 59: 1–16.
* Kanter, R.M. (1989) 'The new managerial work', *Harvard Business Review* November–December, 85–92.
* Kanter, R.M. (1994) 'Collaborative advantage', *Harvard Business Review* July–August: 96–108.
* Kapoor, V. and Gupta, A. (1997) 'Aggressive sourcing: a free–market approach', *Sloan Management Review* **39**, 2, 21–31.
* Kay, J.A. (1993) *Foundations of Corporate Success: How Business Strategies Add Value*, Oxford: Oxford University Press.
* KPMG Report (1996) *Alliances and Networks: the Next Generation*, Amsterdam: KPMG.
* Krapfel, R.J.E., Salmond, D.J. and Spekman, R. (1991) 'A strategic approach to managing buyer–seller relationships', *European Journal of Marketing* 25: 22–37.
* Kumar, N. (1996) 'The power of trust in manufacturer–retailer relationships', *Harvard Business Review* November–December: 92–106.
* Laios, L. and Xideas, E. (1994) 'An empirical investigation of institutional and industrial purchasing structure', *European Journal of Marketing* 28: 20–38.
* Lewis, J.D. (1990) *Partnerships for Profit*, New York: Free Press.
* Lewis, J.D. (1995) *The Connected Corporation: How Leading Companies Win through Customer–Supplier Alliances*, New York: Free Press. (A highly readable and interesting account of alliances that provides valuable insights.)
* Lilien, G.L., Kotler, P. and Moorthy, S.K. (1992) *Marketing Models*, New Jersey: Prentice-Hall.
* Lorange, P. and Roos, J. (1992) *Strategic Alliances: Formation, Evolution and Implementation*, Cambridge, MA: Blackwell. (A sound basic introduction to the topic and has a number of case studies. A nice text book for both undergraduate and graduate students.)
* Macbeth, D.K. and Ferguson, N. (1994) *Partnership Sourcing: An Integrated Supply Chain Management Approach*, London: Pitman Publishing. (A very useful practical guide on Partnership Sourcing that explores best practices in a number of UK firms.)
* McKenna, R. (1997) *Real time: Preparing for the Age of the Never Satisfied Customer*, Boston, MA: Harvard Business School Press.
* Metcalf, L.E., Frear, C.R. and Krishnan, R. (1992) 'Buyer–seller relationships: An application of the IMP interaction model', *European Journal of Marketing* 26: 27–46.
* Monczka, R.M., Callahan, T.J. and Nichols, E.L.J. (1995) 'Predictors of relationships among buying and supplying firms', *International Journal of Physical Distribution & Logistics Management* 25: 45–59.
* Morgan, R.M. and Hunt, S.D. (1994) 'The commitment – trust theory of relationship marketing', *Journal of Marketing* 58: 20–38.
* Narus, J.A. and Anderson, J.C. (1996) 'Rethinking distribution', *Harvard Business Review* July–August: 112–20.
* Newman, V. and Chaharbaghi, K. (1996) 'Strategic alliances in fast-moving markets', *Long Range Planning* 29: 850–856.
* Noordewier, T.G., John, G. and John, N.R. (1990) 'Performance outcomes of purchasing arrangements in industrial buyer–vendor relationships', *Journal of Marketing* 54: 80–93.
* Ohmae, K. (1985) *The Triad Power: The Coming Shape of Competition*, New York: Free Press.
* Ohmae, K. (1989) 'The global logic of strategic alliances', *Harvard Business Review* March–April: 143–54.
* Osland, G.E. and Yaprak, A. (1993) 'A process model on the formation of multinational strategic alliances', in: Culpan, R. (ed.) *Multinational Strategic Alliances*, New York: International Business Press.
* Osland, G.E. and Yaprak, A. (1995) 'Learning through strategic alliances: Processes and factors that enhance marketing effectiveness', *European Journal of Marketing* 29: 52–66.
* Porter, M.E. (1980) *Competitive Strategy*, New York: Free Press.
* Porter, M.E. (1985) *Competitive Advantage*, New York: Free Press.
* Porter, M.E. (1986) *Competition in Global Industries*, Boston: Harvard Business Schools Press.
* Porter, M.E. (1996) 'What is strategy?', *Harvard Business Review* November–December: 61–78.
* Prahalad, C.K. and Hamel, G. (1990) 'The core competence of the organisation', *Harvard Business Review* May–June.
* Quinn, J.B. and Hilmer, F.G. (1994) 'Strategic outsourcing', *Sloan Management Review* 35: 43–55.
* Rangan, S.U. and Yoshino, M.Y. (1996) 'Forging alliances: a guide to top management', *Columbia Journal of World Business* XXXI.

* Rugman, A. (1981) *Inside Multinationals*, London: Croon Helm.
* Shamdasani, P.N. and Sheth, J.N. (1995) 'An experimental approach to investigating satisfaction and continuity in marketing alliances', *European Journal of Marketing* 29: 6–23.
* Sharma, A. and Sheth, J.N. (1997) 'Relationship marketing: an agenda for enquiry', *Industrial Marketing Management* 26: 87–9.
* Sheth, J.N. and Sharma, A. (1997) 'Supplier relationships: emerging issues and challenges', *Industrial Marketing Management* **26**, 91–100.
* Slater, S.F. (1996) 'The challenge of sustaining competitive advantage', *Industrial Marketing Management* 25, 79–86.
  Spekman, R., Kamauff, J.W. and Salmond, D.J. (1994) 'At last purchasing is becoming strategic', *Long Range Planning* 27: 76–84.
* Spekman, R., Isabella, L.A., MacAvoy Tomas C. and Forbes, T.I. (1996) 'Creating alliances which endure', *Long Range Planning* 29: 346–57.
* Stafford, E.R. (1994) 'Using cooperative strategies to make alliances work', *Long Range Planning* 27: 64–74.
  Stuckey, J.A. (1983) *Vertical Integration and Joint Ventures in the Aluminium Industry,* Cambridge, MA: Harvard University Press. (A good book for those interested in understanding alliances in continuous process and mineral/metal based industries.)
* Stuckey, J.A. and White, D. (1993) 'When and when not to vertically integrate', *Sloan Management Review* 34: 71–83.
* Varadarajan, R.P. and Cunningham, M.H. (1998) 'Strategic alliances: a synthesis of conceptual foundation', *Journal of the Academy of Marketing Science* 23: 282–96. (An article that looks into the theoretical aspects and explains the role of marketing in strategic alliances.)
* Webster, F.E. (1992) 'The changing role of marketing in the corporation', *Journal of Marketing* 56: 1–17.
* Webster, F.E. and Wind, Y. (1972) 'A general model for understanding organisational buying behaviour', *Journal of Marketing* 36, April, 12–19.
* Williamson, O.E. (1975) Markets *and Hierarchies: Analysis and Antitrust Implications*, New York: Free Press.
* Williamson, O.E. (1985) *The Economic Institutions of Capitalism: Firms, Markets, Relational Contracting*, New York: Free Press.
  Williamson, O.E. (1996) *The Mechanisms of Governance*, New York: The Free Press. (A theoretical book that investigates alternative forms of organisation of work. This book brings together in one place the work of transaction cost economics.)
* Wilson, D.T. (1995) 'An integrated model of buyer–seller relationships', *Journal of the Academy of Marketing Science* 23: 335–45. (Good source for a synthesis of literature and for references to empirical works in the marketing field.)
* Wray, B., Palmer, A. and Bejou, D. (1994) 'Using neural network analysis to evaluate buyer–seller relationships', *European Journal of Marketing* 28, 10, 32–48.
  Yoshino, M.Y. and Rangan, S.U. (1995) *Strategic Alliances: An Entrepreneurial Approach to Globalization*, Boston, MA: Harvard Business School Press. (Although conceptual in content, this book is also managerial in nature. A must read for those who wish to explore the field in some detail.)

See also: RELATIONSHIPS AND NETWORKS

Marketing theory

1 Why we need theory in marketing
2 Is it a wild goose chase? Can we have scientific theory in marketing?
3 What's gone wrong?
4 Where to now?

Overview

1 Why we need theory in marketing

The roots of the argument for the need for a theoretical development of the discipline can be traced back to the 1940s in articles by Lyndon Brown (1948) and Wroe Alderson and Reavis Cox (1948). The reasons for the emergence of this interest in theory at that time were explained by Alderson and Cox as partly intellectual curiosity and partly 'follow-the-leader': 'When some people become avidly and outspokenly interested in anything, others will take a look and see what is going on' (Alderson and Cox 1948: 138) More fundamentally, they argue that underlying foundations of this interest in theory consisted of two core elements: (i) students of marketing, for all their efforts, have produced very few accurate, comprehensive and significant generalizations, principles or theories; (ii) the belief that they have achieved little even in setting themselves fundamental problems and less still in developing procedures for solving such problems. They complain that 'the multitude of facts thus far assembled seems to add up to very little' (1948: 138). A sound theory is needed, not simply to produce immediate generalizations, but because it helps marketers to better initiate and direct their inquiries.

Alderson and Cox's fundamental rationale for their call in 1948 for better theory was that it would help identify salient problems to be solved and thus direct the researcher towards an understanding of which facts to assemble and how to analyse them. 'Only a sound theory of marketing can raise the analysis of such problems above the level of an empirical art and establish truly scientific criteria for setting up hypotheses and selecting the facts by means of which to test them' (1948: 139). This reasoning was subsequently endorsed by William Baumol (in Halbert 1965), *inter alia*, who stated succinctly that 'facts are silent' and therefore theory is needed to describe and explain the workings of facts.

The Marketing Science Institute was established in 1961 to 'create knowledge that will improve business performance' (Lehman and Jocz 1997: 141). They established four 'position studies', which went some way to setting out the 'fundamental problems' that Alderson and Cox cited and one of these was to conduct long-term research on marketing theory and its application in order to provide the 'concepts, methods and opportunities for more creative and imaginative solutions for more difficult and important problems' (Lehman and Jocz 1997: xiv). Several reasons for the importance of this effort to improve the theory were presented in their report by Michael Halbert (1965):

1 Theoretical rules are a prerequisite for learning. 'It is said that we learn by experience, but we really learn only by the analysis of experience...But without a theoretical base, we cannot analyse, for the rules of proper analysis are theoretical rules; we cannot be selective about which experiences are relevant, for the criteria of relevance are theoretical criteria' (Lehman and Jocz 1997: xiv). There is a great deal of data and knowledge available about the operation of the marketing system but theory is needed to provide a formal structure for organizing, analysing and evaluating this knowledge. Adequate theories would also help present a much more 'coherent, understandable and useful picture' of the entire marketing process.

2 Practitioners need theory in order to make better decisions. As well as facts, the executive's informational needs also include marketing theory 'because it can reduce the cost and uncertainty of decision making while increasing the productivity and assurance of decision makers'. Examples given here are theory concerning how pricing affects distribution and what

happens if advertising spend doubles (Lehman and Jocz 1997: xxii).

3 Marketing cannot rely on borrowing from other disciplines. Not all borrowing is bad, but one must distinguish between three classes of borrowing: (i) of content, which presents few problems, (ii) the adaptation of techniques and methods from other subjects, which is acceptable if properly applied, and (iii) the borrowing of theories and concepts from other disciplines, which is 'dangerous at best and larceny at worst ... often semantic similarity is mistaken for formal appropriateness' (Lehman and Jocz 1997: xxvi). It is seldom that a theoretical structure from one area is directly applicable to another and the many problems associated with marketing's reliance at that time on borrowing particularly from economics, behavioural sciences, and law are examined in the report.

In his influential text *Marketing: Theory and Practice* (1975, 1983, 1995) Michael Baker devotes a whole chapter to 'The need for theory in marketing'. Taking a marketing-as-exchange position along with Bagozzi (1978), Baker presents the core reason as 'the recognition and acceptance of the need to improve our understanding of the manner in which the [marketing] system works which underlies the need to develop a workable theory of exchange' (Baker 1983: 19). The benefits resulting from this he agrees with Halbert (1965) will be (i) the satisfaction of intellectual curiosity and (ii) improved operational performance. By solving immediate operating problems, the latter would permit marketing academics to concentrate on the more fundamental problems underlying them. This would also liberate marketing practitioners from 'fire-fighting' activities in order to concentrate on anticipating and avoiding marketing problems in an increasingly complex business world.

The need for marketing theory is now largely accepted (Kerin, 1996). In order to summarize all the arguments put forward above, they can be grouped into four main categories – practical, knowledge, academic and intellectual needs.

1 *Practical value*: Better theories will improve managerial decision making and problem solving.

2 *Knowledge creation*: Theory provides direction and structure to academic inquiry and helps 'make sense of facts'.

3 *Academic status*: Marketing as an academic discipline requires its own theory. It cannot rely on borrowing from other disciplines.

4 *Intellectual curiosity*: Only theory can provide the basis for understanding how the marketing system works and explaining the underlying foundations and forces.

In true demand-pull fashion, the early identification of a need for theory stimulated the start of its production by academics such as Alderson himself in 1957, McGary (1953 – both functionalist), Bartels (1968 – general theory), and McInnes (1964 – SYSTEMS model), which, as we shall see in the next sections, spawned over 40 years of debate as to what marketing theory should be like and, indeed, whether it is possible at all.

2 Is it a wild goose chase? Can we have scientific theory in marketing?

Marketing would appear to be primarily an area for application of findings from the sciences (primarily the behavioural sciences) and not a science in itself. Should then the attempt to make it a science be abandoned as a wild-goose chase?

(Buzzell 1963: 34)

So Robert Buzzell in his *Harvard Business Review* article 'Is Marketing a Science?' expressed the question, over which marketing theorists have locked in debate (in one form or another), ever since Alderson and Cox made their 'call to arms' 50 years ago. Indeed only six months after their article appeared Roland Vaile (1949) published a direct commentary on it in the *Journal of Marketing*, in which he took the contrary view that 'marketing will remain an art' (Vaile 1949: 522). Thus began the 'marketing as science versus art' controversy which filled the journals up until the mid 1960s and still echoes on today. Those who began the need for theory tended to recommend a scientific approach to its development and evaluation, at least along the positive lines of the social sciences, if not akin to the physical sciences (Bartels 1951; Alderson and Cox 1948). Those who responded from the managerial, normative perspective regarded marketing as a vocation, an application of scientific principles, like engineering or medicine (Vaile 1949). Managers certainly do not regard marketing as scientific 'The businessman's practical wisdom is of a completely different character than scientific knowledge. While it does not ignore generalities, it recognizes the low probability that given combinations of phenomena can or will be repeated. ... In place of scientific knowledge, then, the businessman collects lore' (Ramond 1962).

Few would disagree with this today, especially given the recent anthropological attention to management behaviour, but adducing the paucity of managers' use of marketing models and theories is not sufficient to refute the possibility of the development of scientific theories in marketing. To do so requires detailed attention as to exactly what constitutes a theory. Vaile (1949) raised this issue initially in his critique of Alderson and Cox (1948) who had proposed that a systematic theory of marketing can and should be developed and that it may become scientific. He pointed out that this requires a definition of the term 'theory' which they do not provide. Vaile suggests a dictionary definition of theory as 'a coherent group of general propositions used as principles of explanation for a class of phenomena'. Marketing theory cannot exist he argues because (i) marketing has many, not one, coherent groups of propositions, and (ii) marketing must do more than explain, it also must make judgements about marketing policies.

Buzzell (1963) also argued that marketing is not a science because it does not meet his definition. In order to qualify as a distinct science in its own right, marketing would have to meet some rather stringent requirements. It is generally agreed that a science is 'a classified and systematized body of knowledge, organized around one or more central theories and a number of general principles, usually expressed in quantitative terms, knowledge which permits the prediction and, under some circumstances, the control of future events. Few believe that marketing now meets these criteria' (Buzzell 1963: 33).

Shelby Hunt (1971), the leading proponent of the 'marketing-is-science' school, argued that these definitions are over-restrictive and, following Rudner (1966), proposed that:

'Theories are systematically related sets of statements, including some law-like generalizations, that are empirically testable. The purpose of theory is to increase scientific understanding through a systematized structure capable of both explaining and predicting phenomena' (Hunt 1971: 65). This avoids the central theory requirement, which, even today, for marketing is clearly untenable and by 1983 Hunt was able to assert that 'both philosophers of science and marketing theorists agree on the nature of theory' (Hunt 1983). He cited the definitions adopted by many of the marketing-is/not-science writers such as Alderson (1957), Zaltman et al. (1973), Bagozzi (1980), Ryan and O'Shaunessy (1980) and even Keat and Urry (1975) to demonstrate that both advocates and critics 'basically concur as to the general characteristics of theory' (Hunt 1983: 10).

In reviewing the *Journal of Marketing*'s 60 year pursuit of the 'ideal' of advancement of science and practice in marketing Roger Kerin argues that by 1965 marketing literature had become more scientific, particularly in terms of quantitative analysis as an integral element. 'Marketing phenomena, originally addressed by intuition and judgement, were increasingly studied with fundamental tenets of the scientific method' (Kerin 1996: 5).

The debate about whether it is possible to have scientific theories in marketing has now moved on from the 'definition' issue to the question of what marketing theory should be like.

What form should marketing theory take?

The Fall 1983 edition of the *Journal of Marketing* began the next 'round' in the contest about the nature of marketing theory (Kavanagh (1994) likens the debate to a boxing match). In this edition Paul Anderson questions particularly Hunt's positivistic concept of the scientific method. 'Despite its prevalence in marketing, positivism has been abandoned by these disciplines [philosophy and sociology of science] over the last two decades in the face of overwhelming historical and logical arguments that have been raised against it' (Anderson 1983: 25). Thus, the debate moved from whether marketing can have scientific theory to what form of scientific theory is appropriate. It is argued that there is no longer one 'correct' method for evaluating theory and different research disciplines will adopt different methodologies, ontologies and epistemologies. These marketing theorists draw on Kuhn's (1962) revolutionary view of scientific progress in terms of competing paradigms (see Dholakia and Arndt 1985), which within any discipline are 'incommensurable' – i.e. scientists of each persuasion have different 'world--views' and are unable to agree on salient problems, theories or terminologies to be employed and thus could never agree on any 'experiments' or data that would resolve their differences. In marketing Anderson (1983) cites the theory of consumer behaviour and the theory of the firm as incommensurable. With no agreed or agreeable 'demarcation criterion' between theory and non-theory or even science and non-science in marketing, Anderson concludes that a relativistic approach is the only viable one.

Hunt (1984) was quick to counter-attack Anderson's naive relativist advocacy, which can easily be forced to its (il)logical conclusion of nihilism, ontological solipsism (death of the *object*) and epistemological anarchy (can't know anything or can know everything). Interestingly, both Hunt and Anderson moved their positions somewhat after each other's attack in this 'round' in order to defend their 'weak flanks'. Hunt moved from logical empiricism to scientific realism, in which he accepts a critical realist position that some of our perceptions may be illusions and certainly some are more accurate than others (thus moderating pure empiricism). Therefore the job of science is to develop theories that have 'long-run predictive success' (Hunt 1990) in explaining behaviour, 'even if we cannot finally 'know' whether the entities and structure postulated by the theory actually exists' (McMullin, 1984: 26). Anderson (1986) meanwhile was adopting critical relativism, which accepts the possibility of a single pre-existing 'reality', but rejects the notion that it can be discovered via a particular scientific method. So, it seemed for a while that boxing had brought them closer together!

This debate between realism and relativism in marketing theory mirrors debate which had been going on in the social sciences (see Burrell and Morgan 1979) about how we can *know* the world; is reality out there or a product of one's mind? As Kavanagh (1994) rightly observes epistemology and ontology tend to be conflated in all these debates – i.e. 'being is reduced to knowledge and knowledge is reduced to being'. Although this certainly all follows from the Cartesian dictum *cognito ergo sum*, the question for marketing theory is that we need to be able to know more about reality beyond one's own existence.

In one of his rigorously produced refutations of all forms of relativism, Hunt (1976) argues that the knowledge claims of any theory must be *objective* in the sense that 'its truth content must be intersubjectively certifiable' and that 'requiring that theories, laws and explanations be empirically testable ensures that they will be intersubjectively certifiable since different (but reasonably competent) investigators with differing attitudes, opinions and beliefs will be able to make observations and conduct experiments to ascertain their truth content.'(Hunt 1976: 27). He challenges all those academics in what he calls marketing's 'crisis literature' who have questioned the very possibility of objective marketing research e.g. 'Objectivity is an illusion' (Peter and Olson 1983: 385); 'objectivity is impossible' (Mick 1986: 207); 'Researcher objectivity and intersubjective certifiability are chimeras – they cannot be achieved' (Fullerton 1986: 433). Hunt categorizes and articulates the five 'primary arguments' which marketing writers have employed 'ostensibly implying the impossibility of objective marketing research' (Hunt 1993: 80). He summarizes these along with their original philosophical sources (see Table 1) and then refutes each argument from a scientific realist perspective, often asserting that the marketing authors have misconstrued, misunderstood or misapplied the ideas from the philosophy of science literature.

Following the discussion above of the influence on marketing theory of Kuhnian ideas about the progress of science (see also Dholakia and Arndt 1985), take for example Hunt's refutation of argument 2 in Table 1. This had been used by Anderson *inter alia*, to show that objectivity is impossible because the paradigms that researchers hold are incommensurable. Countering it, Hunt (1993) makes two points; first that it is 'simply incoherent 'to compare and contrast different paradigms in marketing and then to claim that they are incommensurable

Table 1 Objectivity and marketing research

Arguments against objectivity	Philosophy and history of science sources
1 Objectivity is impossible because the language of a culture determines the reality that members of that culture see	Sapir (1949), Whorf (1956)
2 Objectivity is impossible because the paradigms that researchers hold are incommensurable	Kuhn (1962), Feyerabend (1975)
3 Objectivity is impossible because theories are undermined by facts	Kuhn (1962), Feyerabend (1975), Goodman (1973)
4 Objectivity is impossible because the psychology of perception informs us that a theory-free observation language is impossible	Hanson (1958), Kuhn (1962), Feyerabend (1975), Goodman (1978), Churchland (1988)
5 Objectivity is impossible because all epistemically significant observations are theory-laden	Kuhn (1962), Feyerabend (1975), Brown (1977)

Source: Adapted from Hunt 1993.

because they are 'non-comparable' and secondly, that for incommensurability to bar objective choice between two paradigms implies that they are *rival,* but most of the so-called paradigms identified by marketers are simply *different*, not necessarily putting forward conflicting knowledge claims. Going on to counter all five arguments, Hunt concludes that 'there is nothing, absolutely nothing, in modern philosophy of science or psychology that makes objectivity either impossible or undesirable' (Hunt 1993: 87).

Whether Hunt is correct or not about 'rival' or 'different' paradigms in marketing there certainly are a lot of them. Carmen (1980) identifies six (microeconomic, persuasion/attitude change, conflict resolution, generalist system, functionalist and social exchange paradigms). Fisk and Meyers (1982) classify another six (network flow, market scarcity, competitive marketing management, evolutionary systems change, general systems and dissapative structures paradigms). Sheth and Gardener (1988) list twelve 'schools of thought' in marketing (commodity, functional, functionalist, regional, institutional, managerial, buyer behaviour, activist, macromarketing, organizational dynamics and social exchange schools). Kerin (1996) chooses six 'metaphors' that characterize marketing science and practice in each of the six decades since the launch of the *Journal of Marketing* in 1936. These are marketing as: applied economics, a managerial activity, a quantitative science, a behavioural science, a decision science and an integrative science.

Of course, taking Hunt's point about interpreting Kuhn's ideas correctly, many of the above are not strictly 'paradigms' and it can be seen that they are by no means all posited as such. Indeed, as so often happens with even the supposedly technical language of science (cf. argument 1 in Table 1), a term loses its 'original' meaning in the noise of academic discourse. The word ' paradigm' is (adopting the vernacular) an excellent paradigm of this phenomenon. Even those who take an 'alternative paradigm' approach to marketing theory recognize this. 'It is commonly agreed that the paradigm concept itself remains somewhat vague and unclear. This is partly because [it] has taken on different meanings over time' (Arndt 1985). Even in its original formulation the notion was ambiguous and Kuhn has been accused of using the paradigm notion in many different ways (Morgan 1980).

Arndt (1985) attempted to make sense of the concept for use in marketing theory by adapting Morgan's (1980) hierarchy, which distinguishes paradigms (alternative realities or world-views) at the second level from *orientations* (perspective of the researcher relating to the role of data, theory and values) above it at level 1 with *metaphors* (basis for schools of thought) at level 3 and *puzzle-solving* (based on specific tools or procedures) at level 4. Using Morgan's framework, Arndt analyses and categorizes the different paradigms and metaphors in marketing theory, identifying four main paradigms based on different (and indeed one would have to say *conflicting*) world-views.

Marketing theory

Figure 1 Paradigms and metaphors in marketing
Source: Arndt 1985.

Diagram description (quadrants formed by Objective–Subjective axis and Harmony–Conflict axis):

- **Logical empiricist paradigm** (Objective/Harmony): Microeconomic theory; Marketing management; Broadening marketing; Consumer behaviour. Metaphors: Instrumental man, Organism, Marketing warfare, Brand loyal consumer.
- **Subjective world paradigm** (Subjective/Harmony): Motivation research; Interpretive studies; Symbolic interactionism. Metaphors: Language and text, Experiencing man, Irrational man.
- **Sociopolitical paradigm** (Objective/Conflict): Conflict theory; Environmentalism. Metaphors: Spaceship Earth, Political economy, Political marketplace.
- **Liberating paradigm** (Subjective/Conflict): Action research; Critical research. Metaphors: Victimized consumers, Alienated man.

These contain 'different metatheoretical assumptions about the nature of science, the subjective–objective dimension and the explicitness of long-term conflicts in society. There are also assumptions about the nature of the marketing discipline and the study of marketing phenomena.' (Arndt 1985: 15). These are shown in Figure 1, classified on two dimensions – objective/subjective and harmony/conflict. Arndt thus classifies four paradigms in marketing along these dimensions: (i) logical empiricist; (ii) sociopolitical; (iii) subjective world; and (iv) liberating paradigms.

The *logical empiricist paradigm* emphasizes measurability and intersubjective certification. It takes a mechanistic approach, assuming that marketing relations have a real existence independent of the observer and a systematic character resulting in regularities in marketing behaviour and equilibrium-seeking marketing systems. Neoclassical economics provides the basis for many of its typical metaphors such as *instrumental man* with rational decision making and the *organism metaphor* for the organized behaviour and environmental learning of the marketing system.

The *sociopolitical paradigm* is similarly based on the assumption of a real and measurable world of marketing phenomena and predictable uniformities in marketing behaviour. Unlike the value-free and equilibria assumptions of logical empirical theories, however, this paradigm explicitly recognizes conflicts of interests, resources and relations in marketing exchanges and systems. The metaphors of this paradigm constitute the *political markets and*

799

economies and even spaceship *earth*, the global, ecological approach of much of what would nowadays be called green marketing.

The *subjective world paradigm* rejects the existence of social reality in any concrete, verifiable or concrete sense. It is the product of the subjective experiences and inter-experiences of individuals and therefore marketing phenomena cannot be understood from the perspective of an external observer, but must be studied from the viewpoint of the participant. It thus incorporates the interpretivist and social constructionist approaches and adopts the motivational and psychology-based metaphor of *irrational man*, the phenomenological metaphor of *experiencing man* with an existential and semiological basis and the *language and text* metaphor for understanding the behaviour of marketing actors from stories, myths, rhetoric and discourse.

The *liberating paradigm* also takes a social constructionist perspective regarding the ontological status of reality but focuses on the social, economic and technological processes that constrain and control human beings in the marketing system. The role of theoretical inquiry is to identify and analyse the conflicts and contradictions in the system and point the way to emancipation. Critical theory adherents within this paradigm often take *alienation* and *victimization* as metaphors for the oppressed groups in modern mass consumer society.

A strong case is made by Arndt (1985) that marketing has been dominated by one paradigm – i.e. logical empiricism:

> Even a cursory perusal of scholarly articles in marketing journals is bound to confirm the dominant status of logical empiricism. The principles of empiricism appear to be treated synonymously with the scientific method as such. ... The control technology and instrumentalist of the logical empiricist paradigm may well be compatible with the problem solving needs and pragmatism of marketing practitioners.
>
> (Arndt 1985: 19)

This is directly opposed by Hunt's (1991) contention that to even ask the question 'what philosophy dominates marketing?' *presumes* that marketing is *dominated* (which carries pejorative overtones) by one view and that, on the contrary, the marketing discipline has been amazingly eclectic. The most accurate answer is: 'No single philosophy dominates marketing'(Hunt 1991: 398).

Arntd makes a strong case for pluralism in orientations and paradigms for the development of marketing theory. 'by limiting itself to the empiricist orientation and logical empiricist paradigms such as instrumental man, marketing has remained essentially a one-dimensional science concerned with technology and problem solving.' Adopting other paradigms and metaphors will result in the asking of quite different research questions 'The *notion* of paradigms should be viewed as an argument for paradigmatic tolerance and pluralism' (Arndt 1985: 21). Perhaps this explains one reason why Hunt goes to such great efforts to reject the notion itself for marketing theory?

Despite the length and intensity of the debate regarding the appropriate characteristics and scientific underpinning for the development of marketing theories and despite the coalescence of key positions around the two poles of relativism and realism, there is no consensus as to what marketing theory should be like. We do have several competing schools of thought, if not exactly 'paradigms'. Attempts at constructing 'general/generic' theories of marketing (Kotler 1972, Bartels 1968, Alderson 1957) have not led to any shared, let alone agreed theoretical basis for the discipline. Worse still, whether it is because of over-emphasis on empirical research at the expense of theory generation by positivists (Peter 1992; Deshpande 1983) or because of the advocacy of loosely thought-out epistemological 'anarchy' by relativists (Hunt 1994), the one thing that most authors on both sides agree about is that, since Alderson and Cox's call 50 years ago, marketing theory has not advanced as well as it should have done – or even satisfactorily. The next question then is: 'What's gone wrong?

3 What's gone wrong?

The American Marketing Association (AMA) set up a task force in 1984 to investigate the development of marketing thought. Its report (*Journal of Marketing* 1988) recognized that 'the marketing discipline has come a long way since 1959. Nevertheless the task force believes that our self-evaluation of how marketing develops, disseminates and utilizes marketing knowledge indicates that, as a discipline, we still have a long way to go' (*Journal of Marketing* 1988: 24). An earlier commission set up under the auspices of the AMA to assess the effectiveness of research and development for marketing management had concluded that marketing research 'has had relatively little impact on improving marketing management practice' (Myers *et al.* 1980: 280). The AMA task force identified six principle barriers:

1 insufficient resources devoted to marketing knowledge and development;
2 too few people generating and disseminating knowledge;
3 the premature end to too many research careers at pre-tenure and post-tenure stages;
4 senior faculty do not devote sufficient time to knowledge generation;
5 restrictions against practical, innovative and long-term projects and reports by journals and doctoral programmes;
6 extremely limited dissemination of knowledge.

They made recommendations for overcoming these barriers involving more effort, more resources and more encouragement for researchers in marketing to develop and communicate knowledge.

Other causes have been identified and discussed in the literature, which point to failings in the research approach of the discipline.

Lack of attention to history

In a recent book reflecting on the future of marketing, Stephen Greyser (1997) – one of the original AMA Commission authors – endorses Michael Baker's observation that what is regarded as history by a new generation was an important element in the education and experience of the old. This carries with it, Baker (1995) cautions, a grave danger for the new generation of marketing scholars in their rush to make their own impact that they may overlook or, even worse, ignore the lessons of the past. 'Will our concern for recency blur our vision of what is relevant? In ignoring the past will we reinvent what is already known...?' (Baker, 1995: 1004).

This may be one reason for the subject's lack of progress in developing marketing theory according to Savitt (1980). He argues for more attention to and awareness of marketing's history

and theoretical foundations in order for marketing scholars to gain a better understanding of the discipline's origins and patterns of change. Cunningham and Sheth (1982) similarly argue that; 'An effective theory paper begins with an exhaustive and critical historical review of past work. Marketing theory is made up of a set of building blocks. Readers of a theoretical paper should be able to see how the new theory builds on past theoretical work' (Cunningham and Sheth 1982: 11)

There has recently been much more attention to historical research in marketing which is reviewed elsewhere in this volume. The application of the historical approach has resulted in some significant shifts in academic thinking about the framework of evolution marketing (notably Fullerton's (1988) reassessment of the 'marketing era'). It has also provided an alternative technique for the analysis of practice and, potentially, for the development of theory. Nevett (1991) emphasizes the advantages of an historical approach to establishing facts, relevance and causality, which is more impressionistic and intuitive than positivist 'scientific' analysis.

Too much attention to quantitative methods

Venkatesh (1985) presents one reason for the lack of successful development of marketing theory because of a lack of skills or training in marketing researchers, which was also highlighted by the AMA task force (*Journal of Marketing* 1988). Training in theory development is not available to most academic marketers who come out of traditional marketing departments 'where the emphasis is on empirical research, data analysis, and quantitative modeling. These areas offer little potential for theory generation' (Venkatesh 1985: 62). Deshpande (1983) makes the same point that quantitative methods are more suitable for theory testing than theory generation. He recommends the use of qualitative methods to generate new theory and furthermore to use them for triangulation in theory testing as well as quantitative methods. In consumer behaviour, Belk (1986) shows how art can be used to suggest and inspire hypotheses and theories. Anderson (1994) considers that progress has been impeded by the disciplines' quantitative bias. The analytical and empirical 'toolkit' has become ever more sophisticated with far less attention to techniques of theory development.

Following an analysis of criteria for getting work published in marketing journals, Armstrong (1982) proposes an 'author's formula' for a successful publication strategy as:

1 Do *not* pick an important problem.
2 Do *not* challenge existing beliefs.
3 Do *not* obtain surprising results.
4 Do *not* use simple methods.
5 Do *not* provide full disclosure.
6 Do *not* write clearly.

Even Shelby Hunt laments the paucity of qualitative research publications:

> Numerous marketers have pointed out over the last decade that research using qualitative methods could usefully complement our quantitative analyses. I have never heard anyone dispute the potential value of qualitative research – but qualitative works in marketing are few. Why are our major journals almost exclusively devoted to studies using quantitative methods?
> (Hunt 1994: 13)

Following his familiar *modus operandi*, Hunt proceeds to answer his own question by constructing a step-by-step refutation of the arguments of relativists, constructionists and subjectivists who according to him, proffer their standard (and to Hunt totally false) reasoning as a basis for advocating the use of qualitative methods. 'Is it any wonder then', he concludes, 'that mainstream marketers have been reluctant to accept qualitative methods when their advocates have explicitly grounded them in relativism, constructionism and subjectivism? How could marketers trust the output of such research methods?'(Hunt 1994: 21).

There is, then, little disagreement about the *need* for increased and appropriate application of qualitative, as opposed to quantitative, techniques for research leading to theory generation in marketing.

Lack of impact on practice

In advocating a theory-in-use approach, Heffring (1985) asks what accounts for 'this seemingly dismal performance of marketing theory?'(Heffring 1985: 106). The dismal performance to which he is referring is the conclusion of Myers *et al.* (1979) that marketing knowledge development, model building and theorizing has had little impact on the practice of marketing. 'There isn't a single problem area with regard to the practice of marketing and management that marketing research or the world of technology and concepts has mastered.' (Myers *et al.* 1979: 280).

Heffring (1985) gives three broad explanations.

1 Marketing theories reflect the realities of the builder, not the user. Managers *do* have principles and theories that they have acquired over time and use when approaching marketing decisions They are guided by their *own* theories – in- use. The trouble is that many of the academic theories do not reflect managers' language nor their business realities.
2 Marketing theory provides complex answers to marketing problems. On the contrary, managers want complex problems to be solved as simplified representations and with clarity. Concepts like the product lifecycle and the product portfolio matrix have been adopted so quickly primarily because they are simple representations of marketing phenomena that can help managers' with their decisions.
3 Marketing theories may be logically correct but practically incorrect. Managers have several problems with this: (i) many theories focus on strategy not tactics and do not give guidance for their implementation; (ii) theory is judged by academics by process not the relevance of the content; (iii) theory focuses on problem formulation whereas mangers are concerned with problem solving; (iv) pro-theory bias. It is assumed that theory is good, that it improves manager's decision making and that to have any theory is better than to have none. Managers in fact are often confused by theories that they find difficult to interpret.

Other authors have blamed the academic system for this state of affairs with its emphasis on research and publication regardless of their significance for managers (Anderson 1992; Mason 1990). Venkatesh describes this as the 'Crisis of Relevance' (Venkatesh 1985: 63) and considers that theories of researchers are not perceived as useful because practitioners want their everyday problems solved and marketing academics *cannot* perform this function.

Indeed, some would argue that they *should* not – including a member of the AMA Task Force, Morris Holbrook (1989) in an article entitled 'Aftermath of the Task Force: Dogmatism and Catastrophe in Marketing Thought'. Holbrook employs 'cat' and 'dog' metaphors to argue that the pur(r)suit of managerially relevant applied research tends towards the dogmatic, whereas basic or pure research is best carried out by the curiosity-driven and self-directed academic, free from the constraints of relevance. The development of theory is clearly basic and creative in nature, rather than applied research, and therefore the conditions best suited to theory development are those of 'pure' academic freedom.

The concern throughout the business academy about the paucity of the impact of theory on practice does suggest however that this issue is a problem – and a wider problem than just for marketing theory. 'What is the impact of business school research on the practice of business and management? The apparent answer is not much... If impact is measured in terms of whether managers are directly influenced in their day-to-day actions by the latest research articles and scholarly books, then one would have to conclude that such effects are virtually nil'(Porter and McKibben 1988: 180).

Of course, academic theory does not normally produce immediate impact and relevance is itself a problematic construct (try defining it). There is, nevertheless, a serious issue for marketing theory in this regard and indeed for the academy's understanding of its role. In the recent debate about the 'gap' between the approach and concerns of marketing practitioners and academics, between theory and practice, it is perhaps not surprising that the two 'worlds' are regarded as 'separate'. But the paradox is, as Halbert (1965) put the argument, that 'the criteria for relevance are theoretical criteria'. If we all, academics and managers, need theory (or at least if it is *implicit*, if not explicit) in order to distinguish salient facts and to learn from experience, then what exactly are the reasons for the long-term continuance of this vast gap between the two 'world-views'? The answer may be that it has been constructed and maintained by the marketing academy itself (Brownlie and Saren 1996).

4 Where to now?

It was concluded in the first section here that despite earlier debates the need for marketing theory is now well accepted (Kerin 1996). As we have seen, however, it has largely failed to live up to its potential to the satisfaction of either academics or practitioners. The need for theory may be even more important today than it was at the time of Alderson and Cox (1948) for two principal reasons.

First, there has been more emphasis and awareness of 'the power effects of knowledge' (Morgan 1992: 151) – i.e. what knowledge *does*. The Foulcauldian synonymity of knowledge and power (Foucault 1980) implies that 'doing-in-the-world' (after Heideggar 1962) is inexorably intertwined and embedded in 'knowing-the-world' in a particular way. If theory helps create knowledge, as most marketing academics accept, then theory also helps create power. This underlies and reinforces both mangers' and academics' need for marketing theory in order to increase their relative *professional power* over competitors (and colleagues!).

Secondly, in an increasingly information-saturated world, knowledge needs to be firmly rooted in order to be distinctive and meaningful. It has been argued that information is now packaged, mediated and re-presented in various forms and that *marketing* knowledge has become a 'commodity' to be shaped, packaged, distributed and marketed like any other (Brownlie and Saren 1995). Academics are now not only producers of marketing knowledge, but also merchandisers, retailers and consumers of it as authors, researchers, teachers and consultants. One effect of this process is that the product life-cycle of marketing knowledge is shortening, and its velocity of circulation is accelerating. The capital value of marketing knowledge has a shorter shelf life. Under these conditions the need for theory is now even greater in order to provide an anchor and a referent for marketing information and knowledge and to differentiate it and set it in context.

But where are the advances in the theory of marketing going to come from in the future? There are a number of possibilities.

New regions, new theories

Marketing theory as it has developed (or not) over the past 50 years has had a clear North American flavour. The overwhelming majority of the authors are US based, the leading journals are all American. and all the main theories were developed there. One solution may be the generation of new ideas and new theories from marketing academics in other parts of the world. Grönroos (1989) points out that the north American marketing environment is quite specific in many respects with a huge domestic market, a unique media structure and a non-oligopolistic, highly competitive distribution system. 'This marketing model may cover many marketing situations in North America, but its general validity has more been taken for granted than formally proved. In spite of this we have, for instance, no European marketing theory or model geared to European conditions' (Grönroos 1989: 53).

Grönroos envisages the development of a distinct Nordic or Northern European approach to marketing theory as a whole emerging from their unique research approach in the areas of industrial and services marketing. The research tradition in the Nordic school relies on a close contact between researchers and actors in the marketplace and on case study methodology. The basic view of the marketing function also differs from that of the North American theories. In services marketing the term *Nordic School* has been used widely to distinguish the conceptualization and methods of scholars such as Grönroos and Gummesson (1985). Some of the new ideas and approaches to marketing which have emanated from the Nordic approach since Grönroos (1989) posited this distinct tradition will be discussed later and can be seen in their impact on the development of relationship marketing.

North American and North European approaches to marketing theory are only two perspectives. And they may have more in common than differences according to Bernard Cova (1997) who distinguishes between both of them and what he terms the 'Latin approach' of some southern European researchers in France, Italy and Spain. Their common thinking about marketing derives from their conception of 'Societing', as distinct from Anglo-Saxon theorists. The Southern European view of Societing holds that people like to gather together in tribes and such social, proximate communities are more affective and influential on people's behaviour than either marketing institutions or other 'formal' cultural authorities. There is also an element of resistance and reappropriation to the acts of being, gathering and experiencing *together*. This Latin view of the shared experience of 'tribes' sets it apart from both 'Anglo-Saxon' notions of one-to-one relationships and atomistic markets.

Taking Grönroos's point about the limited contextual, environmental and institutional base from which North American marketing theories developed, one could further envisage the development of other contingent area-based theories emerging from other regions of the world where different conditions hold. Japanese business methods and ideas of collaboration, quality control, employee relations and procurement practices have all had an enormous impact on business methods and thinking in the West. So, what about Asian-based marketing theory in future for example? Or, African or Latin American approaches?

Sub-disciplinary fields

Several specialist areas within the discipline have developed theories and theoretical approaches that may have potential for development as general theories of marketing. Although there may be many such fields with potential (e.g. communications, retailing, entrepreneurship) the contributions of three particular areas are considered here: strategic marketing, consumer behaviour and relationship marketing.

Day and Wensley (1983) argued that a paradigm shift had occurred in the 1980s which placed the *strategic* role of marketing as central with a long-run competitive, rather than a short-term customer, orientation, a constituency-based theory of the firm and marketing's role in organizational innovation and adaptation. The development of marketing theory with a strategic orientation will provide better explanations and understanding than previous approaches. Barely 10 years later, however, Day (1992) concludes that the contribution of marketing academics 'to the development, testing and dissemination of strategy theories has been marginalized during the past decade' (Day 1992: 328). Looking ahead, the prognosis for marketing, he forecasts, 'is not encouraging'. If strategic marketing theories cannot even contribute effectively to strategic thinking there would appear to be little prospect of them providing a theoretical base for the entire marketing discipline.

Consumer behaviour research is in a unique position in marketing theory development according to Zaltman *et al.* (1973). They argue that as opposed to the conflicting and partial explanations of theories in marketing as a whole, the field of consumer behaviour alone contains several grand theories claiming to hold the key to explaining consumer behaviour. Twenty-five years later however there is still little agreement amongst consumer researchers who, if anything have now diverged their methodologies and research orientations *further*, making agreement about theories or even core problems less likely. Moreover, Anderson (1994) contends that indeed there are implications for marketing theory from consumer research but he is far less sanguine as to their interpretation. 'Consumer behavior research provides compelling evidence that marketing's lack of progress in theory development is largely caused by the nature of phenomena endemic to the discipline '(Anderson 1994: 10). Although it is unlikely that consumer research can provide the basis for a theory of marketing, the area has undoubtedly provided an extremely fruitful ground for the application and refinement of methods and research techniques, particularly from anthropology, semiotics and sociology (see Hirshman, Holbrook, Mick, Belk, Firat, Venkatesh) which can also make an enormous contribution to research in other marketing fields.

It is far from clear whether relationship marketing is even a unified paradigm (Mattson 1997). One review identified at least 36 separate definitions of the field (Harker 1998). Nevertheless, some of the leading US marketing theorists (Sheth, Hunt, Webster) have enthusiastically embraced the 'new paradigm' with its roots in the Nordic School of industrial and services marketing. Perhaps they hope that it might provide potential for the development of a unified general theory of marketing beyond the marketing-as-exchange view. In contrast to traditional marketing's microeconomic base, the relational approach emphasizes long-term collaboration as opposed to competition between market and social actors.

Conceivably, all marketing activities, problems, systems and behaviour can be conceptualized and researched taking the unit of analysis as the relationships in which they occur. Even the product concept can be redefined in this way (Saren and Tzokas 1998). At the micro-level dyadic relational theory is being developed from social psychology and human relations literature. There is a strong philosophical underpinning in the 'I–Thou' ontology originated by Feuerbach (1904) and Buber (1937) which defines human existence in terms of relations with others. At the macro-relational level social network theory has been well applied and refined towards a theory of industrial marketing by the north European IMP group (Mattsson 1985; Ford 1990). This enables the behaviour of marketing systems to be explained analysed in terms of networks of relationships using sophisticated sociometric methods, agency theory, exchange theory and even chaos theory, which has enormous potential for marketing theory generally beyond the confines of industrial networks. Relationship marketing may not yet be a new marketing paradigm in the Kuhnian sense, but of all the expanding areas of knowledge within the discipline it has by far the best prospect for providing the basis for a new theory of marketing.

Radical approaches

There are two prominent approaches to marketing that can be regarded as 'radical' – postmodernism and critical theory. Those marketing academics who have introduced the former into marketing make a strong case that marketing is *the* epitome of the postmodern condition (e.g. Venkatesh 1989; Sherry 1990; Firat 1990, 1991; Hirchman and Holbrook 1992; Brown 1995; Cova and Badot 1995). 'Marketing has always been a postmodern institution in its fundamental tendencies ... it can be expected that marketing, the ultimate postmodern practice, will be the first institution to adapt to postmodernism' (Firat and Venkatesh1993: 246). There is no doubt that some of the concepts and ideas of writers who are labelled as postmodern are enormously powerful and directly applicable to marketing. Jean Baudrillard's (1981) notion of consumption as 'the mirror of production' in which the *system* of objects and exchanged items as 'signs' has made an enormous contribution. Although it may ignore important material and experiential aspects of consumption (Fitchett and Saren 1998)}, one could nevertheless envisage *all* marketing behaviour and systems being conceptualized in terms of semiotic exchanges. Even if it were possible to construct a new marketing theory on this basis, however, Baudrillard's 'critique of the political economy of the sign' is essentially *structuralist* (Marxist even), unlike his later ideas (such as hyperreality, fragmentation, simulation and free-floating signifiers), which can more easily be labelled *postmodernist*. And overall, as Hetrick and Lozada (1998) point out, postmodernism is essentially 'anti-theory' with its denial of the grand narrative. A postmodern marketing *theory* would appear to be an oxymoron (although I suppose its advocates would say that is precisely the point – and I've missed it!) and therefore postmodernism is unlikely to be capable of providing a general theory of marketing.

Critical theory attempts to look beneath the explanations and arguments of traditional marketing theories in order to unveil a 'deeper' reality and structures. Based on the Frankfurt school, particularly the ideas of Jurgan Habermas and Herbert Marcuse, this approach has had some impact on theory in marketing communications, consumer behaviour, marketing ethics and green marketing in particular. Following Habermas (1971), critical theory distinguishes between: (i) empirical–analytical knowledge, concerned with prediction and control; (ii) historical–hermeneutic knowledge, concerned with communicative interpretation in culture and discourse; and (iii) critical–emancipatory knowledge, concerned with self-reflection, power relations and liberation. There are many areas of marketing where the critical theory approach can help researchers go beyond the 'one-dimensional' (Marcuse 1964) perspective of existing theories and methods and ask deeper questions, but, like postmodernism, it is unlikely to provide the basis for a complete marketing theory.

With so many different approaches, methods and theories in the discipline and yet with so little agreement about marketing research in the academy, it may be that 'better theory' in the subject will inevitably be partial. Alternatively, it may be that the seeds of an agreed general theory are emerging with the adoption of the relationship marketing approach. In either case, several European academics (Brownlie *et al.* 1998) have concluded that with so many new ideas being applied in so many different fields from consumer behaviour to marketing ethics there is now a strong case for 'rethinking marketing' as a first step to realigning the development of theory in the future.

MICHAEL SAREN
UNIVERSITY OF STRATHCLYDE

Further reading

(References cited in the text marked *)

* Alderson, W. (1957) *Marketing Behaviour and Executive Action*, Homewood, IL: Richard D Irwin.
* Alderson, W. and Cox, R. (1948) 'Towards a theory of marketing', *Journal of Marketing* 13: 137–52.
* American Marketing Association (AMA) (1988) 'Task force on the development of marketing thought. "Developing, disseminating and utilizing marketing knowledge"', *Journal of Marketing* 52l: 1–25.
* Anderson, P.F. (1983) 'Marketing, scientific progress and scientific method', *Journal of Marketing* 47: 18–31.
* Anderson, P.F. (1986) 'On method in consumer research: a critical relativist perspective', *Journal of Consumer Research* 13: 155–73.
* Anderson, M. (1992) 'What! Me Teach? I am a Professor' *Wall Street Journal* 8 September: 16.
* Anderson, J.M. (1994) 'Marketing science: where's the beef?', *Business Horizons* January/February: 8–16.
* Armstrong, J.S. (1982) 'Barriers to scientific contribution- the author's formula', *Behavioural and Brain Sciences* 5: 197–9.
* Arndt, J. (1985) 'On making marketing science more scientific: role of orientations, paradigms, metaphors, and puzzle solving', *Journal of Marketing* 49: 18–23.
* Bagozzi, R.P. (1978) 'Marketing as exchange: a theory of transactions in the marketplace', *American Behavioural Scientist* 21: 535–56.
* Bagozzi, R.P. (1980) *Causal Models in Marketing*, New York: Wiley.
* Baker, M. (1975, 1983, 1995) *Marketing: Theory and Practice,* London: Macmillan Press.
* Bartels, R. (1951) 'Can marketing be a science?' *Journal of Marketing* January: 319–28.
* Bartels, R. (1968) 'The general theory of marketing', *Journal of Marketing* 32: 29–33.

Baumol, W. (1957) 'On the role of marketing theory, *Journal of Marketing* April: 413–18.

* Baudrillard, J. (1981) *For a Critique of the Political Economy of the Sign*, (translated by Levin, C.), USA: Telos Press.
* Brown, L.Q. (1948) 'Toward a profession of marketing', *Journal of Marketing* 13: 27–31.
* Brown, S. (1995) *Postmodern Marketing*, London: Routledge.
* Brownlie, D. and Saren, M. (1995) 'On the commodification of marketing knowledge', *Journal of Marketing Management* 11: 619–28.
* Brownlie, D. and Saren, M. (1996) 'Beyond the one-dimensional marketing manager: the discourse of theory, practice and relevance', *International Journal of Research in Marketing* 14: 147–61.
* Brownlie, D., Saren, M., Wensley, R. and Whittington, R. (eds) (1998) *Rethinking Marketing: Towards Critical Marketing Accountings*, London: Sage Publications.
* Buber, M. (1937) *I and Thou*, Edinburgh: T & T Clark.
* Burrell, G. and Morgan, G. (1979) *Sociological Paradigms and Organisational Analysis*, London: Heinemann.
* Buzzell, R. (1963) 'Is marketing a science?' *Harvard Business Review* January–February: 32–48.
* Carmen, J.M. (1980) 'Paradigms for marketing theory', in Sheth, J.N. (ed.) *Research in Marketing* Vol. 3, Greenwich, CT: JAI Press.
* Cova, B. and Aubert-Gamet, V. (1997) 'Exit, voice, loyalty and twist! consumer behaviour in search of the subject', presented at EIASM Workshop on Interpretive Consumer Research, April, Oxford, England.
* Cova, B. and Badot, O. (1995) 'Marketing theory and practice in a postmodern era', in Baker, M.J. *Marketing: Theory and Practice* 3rd edn, London: Macmillan Press.
* Cunningham, W. and Sheth, J.N. (1982) 'From the Editor' *Journal of Marketing*, Spring: 11–12.
* Day, G.S. (1992) 'Marketing's contribution to the strategy dialogue', *Journal of the Academy of Marketing Science* 20: 323–30.
* Day, G.S. and Wensley, R. (1983) 'Marketing theory with a strategic orientation', *Journal of Marketing* 47: 79–89.
* Deshpande, R. (1983) 'Paradigms Lost: on theory and method in research in marketing', *Journal of Marketing* 47: 101–10.
* Dholakia, N. and Arndt, J. (eds) (1985) *Changing the Course of Marketing: Alternative Paradigms for Widening Marketing Theory (*Research In Marketing Supplement 2) Greenwich, CT: JAI Press.
* Feuerbach, L. (1904) *Selected Correspondence* (ed. Schuffenhauer, W.) Berlin: Wilhelm Bolin.
* Firat, A.F. (1990) 'The consumer in postmodernity', in Holman, R.H. and Solomon. M.R. (eds), *Advances in Consumer Research*, Provo, UT: Association for Consumer Research.

* Firat, A.F. (1991) 'Postmodern culture, marketing and the consumer', in Childers, T.L. *et al.* (eds), *Marketing Theory and Application*, Chicago, IL: AMA.
* Firat, A.F. and Venkatesh, A. (1993) 'Postmodernity: the age of marketing', *International Journal of Research in Marketing* 10: 227–49.
* Fisk, G. and Meyers, P. (1982) 'Macromarketers' guide to paradigm' in Bush, R. and Hunt, S.D. (eds), *Marketing Theory: Philosophy of Science Perspectives*, Chicago: AMA.
* Fitchett, J. and Saren, M. (1998) 'Baudrillard in the museum: the value of dasein', *Consumption, Culture and Markets* 2, part 3.
* Ford, I.D. (ed.) (1990) *Understanding Business Markets: Interaction, Relationships and Networks*, New York: Academic Press.
* Foucault, M. (1980) *Power/Knowledge: Selected Interviews and Other Writings*, (ed. Gordon, C.) New York: Pantheon Books.
* Fullerton, R. (1986) 'Historicism: what it is and what it means for consumer research', in Wallendorf, M. and Anderson, P. (eds.) *Advances in Consumer Research* 14, Association for Consumer Research: 431–4.
* Fullerton, R. (1988) 'How modern is modern marketing? marketing's evolution and the myth of the production era', *Journal of Marketing* 52: 108–25.
* Greyser, S. (1997) 'Janus and marketing : the past, present and prospective future of marketing', in Lehman, D.R. and Jocz, K.E. *Reflections on the Futures of Marketing: Practice and Education*, Cambridge, MA: Marketing Science Institute.
* Grönroos, C. (1989) 'Defining marketing: a market-oriented approach', *European Journal of Marketing* 23: 52–60.
* Grönroos, C. and Gummesson, E. (1985) *Service Marketing: Nordic School Perspectives*, Stockholm: Stockholm University.
* Habermas, J. (1971) *Towards a Rational Society*,Oxford: Heinemann.
* Halbert, M. (1965) *The Meaning and Sources of Marketing Theory*, New York: McGraw-Hill.
* Harker, M. (1998) 'Relationship marketing defined', presented at UK Academy of Marketing Doctoral Colloquium, July, Sheffield Metropolitan University, England.
* Heideggar, M. (1962) *Being and Time* (Trans. McQuarrie, J. and Robison, E.) New York: Harper Row.
* Heffring, M. (1985) 'A theory-use approach to developing marketing theories', in Dholakia, N. and Arndt, J. (eds), *Changing the Course of Marketing: Alternative Paradigms for Widening Marketing Theory*, (Research in marketing Supplement 2) Greenwich, CT: JAI Press.
* Hetrick, W. and Lozada, H. (1998) 'From marketing theory to marketing anti-theory: implications of

ethical critique within the (post) modern experience', in Brownlie, D., Saren, M., Wensley, R. and Whittington, R (eds), *Rethinking Marketing: Towards Critical Marketing Accountings*, London: Sage Publications.
* Hirschman, E. and Holbrook, M. (1992) *Postmodern Consumer Research: The Study of Consumption as Text*, London: Sage Publications.
* Holbrook, M (1989) 'Aftermath of the task force: dogmatism and catastrophe in marketing thought'.
* Hunt, S.D. (1971) 'The morphology of theory and the general theory of marketing', *Journal of Marketing* 35: 65–8.
* Hunt, S.D. (1976) 'The nature and scope of marketing', *Journal of Marketing* 40: 17–28.
* Hunt, S.D. (1983) 'General theories and the fundamental explananda of marketing', *Journal of Marketing* 47: 9–17.
* Hunt, S.D. (1984) 'Should marketers adopt relativism?' in Anderson, P.F. and Ryan, M.J. (eds), *Scientific Method in Marketing: AMA Winter Educators Conference Proceedings*, Chicago: American Marketing Association, 30–4.
* Hunt, S.D. (1990) 'Truth in marketing theory and research', *Journal of Marketing* 54: 1–15.
* Hunt, S.D. (1991) *Marketing Theory: Conceptual Foundations of Research in Marketing*, Homewood, IL: Irwin.
* Hunt, S.D. (1993) 'Objectivity in marketing theory and research', *Journal of Marketing* 57: 76–91.
  Hunt, S. (1994) 'On rethinking marketing: our discipline, our practice, our methods', *European Journal of Marketing* (special edition on the New Marketing Myopia: Critical Perspectives on Theory and Research in Marketing) 28: 13–25.
* Kavanagh, D. (1994) 'Hunt versus Anderson: Round 16', *European Journal of Marketing* 28: 26–41.
* Keat, R. and Urry, J. (1975) *Social Theory as Science*, London: Routledge and Kegan Paul.
* Kerin, R. (1996) 'In pursuit of an ideal: the editorial and literary history of the *Journal of Marketing*', *Journal of Marketing* 601: 1–13.
* Kotler, P. (1972) 'A generic concept of marketing' *Journal of Marketing* 36: 46–54.
* Kuhn, T. (1962) *The Structure of Scientific Revolutions*, Chicago, IL: University of Chicago Press.
* Lehman, D.R. and Jocz, K.E. *Reflections on the Futures of Marketing: Practice and Education*, Cambridge, MA: Marketing Science Institute.
* Marcuse, H. (1964) *One-Dimensional Man: Studies in the Ideology of Advanced Industrial Society*, London: Routledge and Keagan Paul.
* Mason, J.B. (1990) 'Improving marketing education in the 1990s: A Dean's perspective', *Marketing Education Review* November: 10–21.
  Matheson, L.G. (1997) 'Relationship marketing and markets–as–networks approach: a comparative analysis of two evolving streams of research' (Guest Lecture, 20 February, University of Auckland, New Zealand.
* Mattsson, L.G. (1985) 'An application of the network approach to marketing', in Dholakia, N. and Arndt, J. (eds), *Changing the Course of Marketing: Alternative Paradigms for Widening Marketing Theory*, Greenwich, CT: JAI Press.
* McGary, E.D. (1953) 'Some new viewpoints in marketing', *Journal of Marketing* XVIII: 33–40.
* McInnes, W.C. (1964) 'A conceptual approach to marketing', in Cox, R., Alderson, W. and Shapiro, S. (eds), *Theory in Marketing* 2nd Series, Homewood, IL: Richard D Irwin Inc.
* McMullin, E. (1984) 'A case for scientific realism', in Leplin, J. (ed.), *Scientific Realism*, Berkeley: University of California Press.
* Mick, D.G. (1986) 'Consumer research and semiotics: exploring the morphology of signs, symbols and significance', *Journal of Consumer Research* September: 196–213.
* Morgan.G. (1980) 'Paradigms, metaphors and puzzle-solving in organisation theory', *Administrative Science Quarterly* 25: 605–22.
* Morgan, G. (1992) 'Marketing discourse and practice', in Alvesson, M. and Wilmott, H. (eds), *Critical Management Studies,* London: Sage Publications.
* Myers, J.G., Greyser, S. and Massey, W. (1979) 'The effectiveness of marketing's R&D for marketing management: an assessment', *Journal of Marketing* January: 17–29.
* Myers, J.G., Massey, W. and Greyser, S. (1980) *Marketing Research and Knowledge Development: An Assessment for Marketing Management*, Englewood Cliffs, NJ: Prentice-Hall.
* Nevett, T. (1991) 'Historical investigation and the practice of marketing', *Journal of Marketing* 55: 13–23.
* Peter, P.J.and Olson, J.C. (1983) 'Is Science marketing?', *Journal of Marketing* 47: 111–25.
  Peter, P.J. (1992) 'Realism or relativism for marketing theory research: a comment on Hunt's "Scientific realism"', *Journal of Marketing* 56: 72–9.
* Porter, L. and McKibben, L. (1988) *Management Education and Development: Drift or Thrust into the 21st Century?*, New York: McGraw-Hill.
* Ramond, C. (1962) Speech to the American Psychological Association – 5th September , quoted in Buzzell, R. (1963) 'Is marketing a science?' *Harvard Business Review* January–February: 32.
* Rudner, R. (1966) *Philosophy of Social Science*, Englewood Cliffs, NJ: Prentice-Hall.
* Ryan, M. and O'Shaunessy, J. (1980) 'Theory development, the need to distinguish the levels of abstraction', in Lamb, C. and Dunne, P. (eds), *Theoretical Developments in Marketing*, Chicago, IL: AMA.
* Saren, M. and Tzokas, N. (1998) 'The nature of the product in market relationships: a pluri-signified

product concept', *Journal of Marketing Management* 14: 445–64.
* Savitt, R. (1980) 'Historical research in marketing', *Journal of Marketing* 44: 52–8.
* Sherry, J.F. Jr. (1990) 'Postmodern alternatives: the interpretive turn in consumer research', in Kassarjian, H. and Robertson, T. (eds), *Handbook of Research*, Englewood Cliffs, NJ: Prentice-Hall.
* Sheth, J.N. and Gardener, D.M. (1988) 'History of marketing thought: an update', in Bush, R. and Hunt, S.D. (eds), *Marketing Theory: Philosophy of Science Perspectives*, Chicago: AMA.
* Vaile, R. (1949) 'Towards a theory of marketing – a comment', *Journal of Marketing* 14: 520–2.
* Venkatesh, A. (1985) 'Is marketing ready for Kuhn?', in Dholakia, N. and Arndt, J. (eds), *Changing the Course of Marketing: Alternative Paradigms for Widening Marketing Theory* (Research in marketing Supplement 2) Greenwich, CT: JAI Press.
* Venkatesh, A. (1989) 'Modernity and post modernity: a synthesis or antithesis', in Childers, T.L. *et al.* (eds), *Marketing Theory and Application*, Chicago, IL: AMA.
* Zaltman, G., Pinson, C. and Angelmar, R. (1973) *Metatheory and Consumer Research*, New York: Holt Rinehart and Winston Inc.

See also: CONSUMER BEHAVIOUR; GREEN MARKETING; HISTORICAL RESEARCH IN MARKETING; MARKETING – PHILOSOPHY OR FUNCTION?; POSTMODERN MARKETING; QUALITATIVE RESEARCH IN MARKETING; QUANTITATIVE METHODS IN MARKETING; THE SOCIOLOGICAL BASIS OF MARKETING

Postmodern marketing

1 **Abrandon hope all ye who enter here**
2 **Post no bills**
3 **Not to be taken internally**
4 **This is not an exit**
5 **The biter bit**

Overview

Is there such a thing as postmodern marketing? If it were to exist, could it be defined? Is postmodern marketing simply a paradox? Does it provide a new method, or seek only to attack established methods? Is there such a thing as a postmodern consumer? Does postmodern marketing seek to supply what the consumer does want, or identify what he or she does not want? If postmodernism questions conventional marketing research, how are these questions to be answered?

1 Abrandon hope all ye who enter here

For some people, postmodern marketing is just one among many conceptual brands on the well-stocked shelves of the scholarly supermarket, to be considered, chosen or discarded as the purchaser sees fit. For others, it is a prestigious intellectual label – the Versace, the Valentino, the Louis Vuitton of the academy – direct from the cerebral catwalks of Paris, Milan and New York. For yet others, postmodernism is the 'category killer' of the ivory tower, an aggressive interloper that has cut a swathe through adjacent academic disciplines like anthropology, sociology, history, geography, politics, cultural studies ... and is heading our way.

Postmodern marketing is none and all of these things. Or is it? Is it even an 'it'? Indeed, is it 'is' or 'was'? The anthologization process, after all, implies that the postmodern moment has been and gone. By their very nature encyclopaedias are records of past achievement not current endeavour. Like 'readers', 'companions', 'guides', 'compendia', 'collections' and 'treasuries', encyclopaedias are the fast food franchises of academe. They purvey bland, bite-sized, ready-salted, extra-mayonnaise, hold-the-pickle nuggets of McMarketing scholarship, suitable only for filling the bellies of lazy students and even lazier lecturers. At least, that's what my encyclopaedia says about encyclopaedias ...

It follows, then, that the very act of writing this pen-portrait of postmodern marketing is an act of betrayal. It intimates that postmodernism *can* be defined, pigeon-holed and allocated a slot in the great marketing scheme of things (adjacent, naturally, to Green marketing, Telemarketing and other slightly suspicious, somewhat illegitimate and decidedly 'iffy' perspectives). The unstable is thereby stabilized, the threat nullified, the neutron bomb defused. Mainstream marketers can sleep easy in their beds, confident that the postmodern barbarians at the gates of Castle Kotler have been repulsed, or, rather, that they are being permitted to enter the Kotlerite citadel, one at a time, in an orderly line, check your weapons at the wicket. As any conspiracy theorist worth their salt will testify, the sad fact is that no matter how carefully worded the contribution, or qualified the 'definition', or even how exemplary the 'entry' turns out to be, the primary outcome of the anthologization process is a disciplined discipline.

Set against this, however, the alternative option of resisting recuperation, of eschewing encyclopaediation, of refusing to succumb to soundbite scholarship, is equally unsatisfactory. The anthologization process is not just about definition, delineation and control, it is about legitimization. Inclusion serves as a sort of seal of disciplinary 'approval', an official acknowledgement that something called postmodern marketing actually 'exists', that it is a topographical feature of the academic landscape, albeit of the 'there be dragons' variety. In this regard, it is no accident that the spatial structure of companions, collections, readers and the like unfailingly reflects the scholarly standing of its constituent parts. The contributions furthest from the front are the least well established disciplinary subfields and as their

Postmodern marketing

acceptability increases (by dint of downright durability, as much as anything else), so too they break out of the 'miscellaneous' section at the back of the book and advance slowly but inexorably through the text. A kind of *cordon sanitaire* of cerebration thus exists; a period of intellectual quarantine clearly obtains; only 49 steps to go before postmodern marketing is sufficiently sanitized to circulate unchaperoned in polite scholarly society.

It essence, then, the choice facing any would-be encyclopaedist of postmodern marketing is between prostitution and illegitimacy, between bastard and whore, between the Dell and the Big Blue Sea, as it were. So, am I going to betray my calling? To renege on my fellow postmodern marketers? To reveal that I have no moral or intellectual fibre, that I have no scruples? Of course I am! I'm a postmodernist, after all! What do you want from me – integrity?, honesty?, the truth? Get real! I put the dupe into duplicitous, the art into artifice, the post into impostor. If you believe a single word of this 'entry', you have no one to blame but yourself. And if you don't believe me when I say don't believe me, then you really are in trouble. Believe me.

2 Post no bills

This ostentatious agonizing over participation or abstention may strike many readers as a tad excessive, not to say histrionic, but it is directly relevant to the inessential essence, the nubless nub, the core-free core of the postmodern condition. Postmodernism, as many commentators have observed, comprises a 'crisis of representation', a deep sense of disillusion with the way things are, whether these 'things' be theories, methods or modes of discourse (e.g. Denzin 1997; Dickens and Fontana 1992). Yet as this purported crisis of representation is itself a representation of crisis, it is impossible to avoid being implicated in the very thing that is being contested, to prevent being hoist by one's own petard, to get out of the glasshouse so that one can safely throw stones (Brown 1995a). Linguistic meaning may well be indeterminate, as post-structuralist philosophers suggest, but determining its indeterminacy presupposes linguistic meaning of some sort. You work it out ...

It is paradoxes like this that give postmodern marketing its dilettantish air. The horny-handed pragmatists of mainstream marketing research – the brutes who put the brute into brute empiricism – are understandably infuriated by such flagrant acts of textual exhibitionism. In the recent words of one broad-minded member of marketing's community of scholars, 'conventions of decency in language and the laws of libel preclude me from making any comment whatsoever about the practical implications of postmodernism to marketing' (Piercy 1997: 11). Certainly, it is a world away from the good old days of the marketing management paradigm, when there were 4Ps, three generic strategies, two by two matrices and one size fits all (beware of imitations, accept no substitutes) marketing philosophy. Let's not forget, however, that it was also the not-so-good days of rationing, rickets, radiograms, slide rules, Reliant Robins, Red Barrel and entirely unwarranted respect for our academic elders and betters.

Yet, despite their penchant for textual extravagances, embellishments, exaggerations and pretentious words like 'penchant', the postmodern marketers do have a point. Their disillusionment is not an illusion. As the journals clearly demonstrate, many of marketing's most illustrious intellectual luminaries – Kotler, Webster, Sheth, Baker, McDonald, etc. – readily accept that the traditional concepts no longer appear to 'work', no longer reflect the marketing world as it really is, no longer help managers cope with decentred, delayered, downsized, reengineered, ever accelerating, global–local marketing milieux (see Brown 1997). Existing frameworks and models seem simplistic, reductive and static, Ps are passé, generic strategies are geriatric, matrices cease to mesmerize and the marketing philosophy has gone the way of phologiston.

The real 'problem' with postmodern marketing escapades is not that they are incomprehensible or pretentious, though they can of course be that. Nor are they simply a side-effect of late-twentieth century apocalypticism, *fin de siècle* fever or pre-millennial marketing madness, as some eccentrics have suggested (Brown *et al*, 1996). Nor, for that matter, is the postmodern marketing imbroglio an artefact of the changing of the academic guard, a sort of smart weapon or scholarly Exocet that

811

'encourages' the older generation of researchers to release the reigns of disciplinary power.[1] The real difficulty with postmodernism is that it is, in Rorty's (1980) words, an edifying rather than a systematic philosophy. It is an attack not an alternative, it dissembles instead of assembles, it offers deconstruction not reconstruction. It clears a space, no more no less. It is the wrecking ball of the marketing academy. It is a trendy, touched-up, nip and tucked, lightly airbrushed, shamelessly spin-doctored, once more with feeling, 1990s version of nihilism. Neo-nihilism, in short.

3 Not to be taken internally

So what exactly is postmodern marketing? According to the foremost academic commentators on postmodern (consumer) society, it is characterized by five key features: hyperreality; fragmentation; reversed production and consumption; decentred subjects; and the juxtaposition of opposites (Firat and Venkatesh 1995).

Hyperreality

Exemplified by the virtual worlds of cyberspace and the pseudo worlds of theme parks, hotels and heritage centres, hyperreality involves the creation of consumption sites and marketing phenomena that are 'more real than real'. The distinction between reality and fantasy is momentarily blurred, as in the back lot tour of 'working' movie studios in Universal City, Los Angeles. In certain respects, indeed, hyperreality is superior to everyday mundane reality, since the aversive side of authentic marketplace experiences – anti-tourist terrorism in Egypt, muggings in New York, dysentery in Delhi – magically disappears when such destinations are recreated in Las Vegas, Busch Gardens, Walt Disney World or the manifold variations on the theme park theme. Ironically, however, the perceived superiority of the fake is predicated upon an (often) unwarranted stereotype of reality, and the reality of the fake – e.g. the queues in Disneyland – may be much worse than anything the average visitor would actually experience in Egypt, New York, Delhi or wherever. Doubtless some enterprising theme park developer is currently working on a theme park of a theme park only without the queues, screaming kids and general unpleasantness (or, alternatively, with pseudo queues, unspeakable animatronic children, overpriced holographic hamburgers and general ersatz unpleasantness – just to ensure visitors get a genuine sense of the 'real' theme park experience).[2]

Fragmentation

Marketing in postmodernity is unfailingly fast, furious, frenetic, frenzied, fleeting, hyperactive. It is akin to zapping from channel to channel, or flicking through the pages of the glossies, in search of something worth watching, reading or buying. Shopping on Speed. This disjointedness is partly attributable to the activities of practitioners with their ceaseless proliferation of brands, ever-burgeoning channels of distribution, increasingly condensed commercial breaks and apparent preparedness to accept almost any form of payment from cowrie shells to plastic (plastic cowrie shells, perhaps?). It is also due to the disconnected postmodern lifestyles, behaviours, moods, whims and vagaries of contemporary consumers. A product of profusion with a profusion of products, the postmodern consumer performs a host of roles – 'wife and mother', 'career woman', 'sports fanatic', 'fashion victim', 'DIY enthusiast', 'culture vulture', 'earnest academic', 'windswept and interesting postmodern marketer', etc. each with its appropriate brand name array (Gergen 1991). These identities or selves, furthermore, are neither sequential nor stable, but fluid, mutable and, not least, negotiable. A cascade of complementary, occasionally incommensurable, lifestyle options typically obtains. The possibilities, if not exactly endless, are certainly plentiful, verging on abundant.

Reversed production and consumption

The postmodern consumer, it must also be stressed, is not the unwitting dupe of legend, who responds rat-like to environmental stimuli of Skinnerian caprice. Nor is the postmodern consumer transfixed, rabbit-like, in the headlights of multinational capital. Nor, for that matter, is he or she likely to be seduced by the sexual textual embeds of subliminal advertisers, though (s)he might pretend to be. On the contrary, the very idea that consumers have something 'done' to them by marketers and advertisers no longer passes muster. Postmodern consumers, in fact, do things with advertising; they are active in the production of meaning, of marketing, of consumption. As Firat and Venkatesh rightly observe:

> It is not to brands that consumers will be loyal, but to images and symbols, especially to images and symbols that *they* produce while they consume. Because symbols keep shifting, consumer loyalties cannot be fixed. In such a case a modernist might argue that the consumers are fickle – which perhaps says more about the modernist intolerance of uncertainty – while the postmodernist interpretation would be that consumers respond strategically by making themselves unpredictable. The consumer finds his/her liberatory potential in subverting the market rather than being seduced by it.
> (Firat and Venkatesh 1995: 251)

Decentred subjects

This idea of a multiphrenic, fragmented, knowing consumer is further developed in Firat and Venkatesh's notion of decentred subjectivity. The centredness that is characteristic of modernity, where individuals are unambiguously defined by their occupation, social class, demographics, postcode, personalities and so on, has been ripped asunder in postmodernity (Bocock 1993). Traditional segmentation criteria *may* be applied to such people, and marketing strategies formulated, but it is increasingly accepted that these fleetingly capture, or freeze frame at most, a constantly moving target market. Even the much-vaunted 'markets of one', in which marketing technologies are supposedly adapted to the specific needs of individual consumers, is doomed to fail in postmodernity, since each consumer comprises a multiplicity of shopping homunculi, so to speak. The harder marketers try to pin down the decentred consuming subject, the less successful they'll be. Today's consumers are always just beyond the reach of marketing strategists, marketing tacticians, marketing technologists, marketing notaries, votaries, proselytes and zealots. In the immortal words of Douglas Coupland (1991), whose writings defined the disaffected, decentred, slacking, rebellious, couldn't-care-less, anti-authoritarian attitudes of postmodern Generation X, 'I am not a target market'.

Juxtaposition of opposites

Although it is well-nigh impossible to 'target' or 'capture' the inscrutable, amorphous entity that is the postmodern consumer, it is still possible to engage with, appeal to, or attract them. The key to this quasi-conversation is not ever more precise segmentation and positioning, but the exact opposite. An open, untargeted, ill-defined, imprecise approach, which leaves scope for imaginative consumer participation (e.g. ironic advertising treatments where the purpose, pitch or indeed 'product' is unclear), is typical of postmodern marketing. This sense of fluidity and porosity is achieved by pastiche, by bricolage, by radical juxtaposition, by the mixing and matching of opposites, by combinations of contradictory styles, motifs and allusions, whether it be in the shimmering surfaces of pseudo-rococo shopping centres or the ceaseless cavalcade of contrasting images that are regularly encountered in commercial breaks, shop windows or roadside billboards (Brown 1995b). Occasionally, these succeed in exceeding the sum of their parts and combine to produce a sublime whole, an ephemeral spectacular, a fleeting moment of postmodern transcendence, as in *Riverdance the Show*. This staggeringly successful example of services marketing, at its very best, comprises a *siècle*-surfing stew of contrapuntal terpsichorean traditions – Irish, Scottish, Spanish, Russian, American tap, square dance, break dance, Hollywood musical, etc. – which, despite its ostensible ethnocentrism, has proved to be an unalloyed international triumph (Brown 1997).

4 This is not an exit

Irrespective of the accuracy or comprehensiveness of Firat and Venkatesh's (1995) summary of consumption in postmodernity, it has major implications for the practice of marketing in this the twilight of the twentieth century. As with the 'crisis of representation' paradox, it is important to appreciate that marketing is a part of, not apart from, the contemporary sociocultural matrix. It affects society, it reflects society, it affects its reflected effects, effects its affected reflections and on and on and on in a marketing maelstrom of infinite regress. It is caught up in what it conveys. The old idea of finding out what customers want and delivering it to them in an efficient, timely and, above all, profitable manner, no longer seems to connect. Truth to tell, people often don't know what they want – though they know it when they see it – or, to be more precise, they know what they don't want, as in 'I wouldn't be seen dead in that' (Douglas 1997). Perhaps marketing in a postmodern age should be devoted, not to fulfilling consumers' unexpressed and inexpressible needs, but to finding out what they don't want and giving them less unacceptable alternatives.

Postmodern marketing, to be sure, is not just about finding out what customers don't want and not giving it to them (marketing sadomasochism?). It also has major methodological implications. The essence of the issue is simplicity itself: how is it possible to understand, represent or describe postmodern marketing and consumption phenomena, when postmodernism challenges the very premises of conventional marketing research? The logic, order, rationality and model building modalities of the modernist research tradition seem totally inappropriate when addressing postmodern concerns. Now, this is not to suggest that established tools and techniques *cannot* be applied to postmodern artefacts and occurrences. There are any number of essentially modernist portrayals of the postmodern marketing condition – what is it?, what are its principal characteristics?, what can we 'do' with it? (e.g. Cova 1996; Elliott 1993; Firat and Venkatesh 1993; van Raaij 1993). Yet the relevance of such approaches remains moot. Is it *really* possible to capture the exuberance, the flamboyance, the incongruity, the energy, the playfulness of postmodern marketing in a standard, all-too-standard research paper?

On the surface, this may seem like a comparatively trivial matter – if we jazz up our manuscripts and use expressive language, everything will be okay – but it goes to the very heart of why we do what we do, how we do it and who we do it for. The decision facing marketing and consumer research, as it has faced other academic disciplines grappling with postmodern incursions, is whether we should strive to be postmodern marketing researchers or researchers of postmodern marketing. The former implies that the traits, features and peculiarities of postmodernism should be imported into marketing research, that we should endeavour to 'walk the talk', to *be* postmodern. The latter intimates that researchers should confine themselves to applying proven tools and techniques to this (not so) brave (not so) new world of postmodern consumption. Just because marketing conditions have changed, or are supposed to have changed, it does not necessarily follow that tried and trusted methods of marketing research must change as well.

Although this choice is nothing if not clear cut, a moment's reflection reveals it to be deeply divisive at best and potentially ruinous at worst. After all, if one group of marketing academics works in a postmodern mode, a mode that is unlike anything that has gone before, it is fated to 'fail' when conventional standards of assessment are applied. Postmodern marketing scholarship *cannot* meet the criteria – rigor, reliability, trustworthiness and so on – that are accepted, indeed *expected*, by champions of established methods and used to judge the worth, the contribution, the success or otherwise of a particular piece of work. For many commentators, then, postmodern marketing research does not constitute 'research' as such. It is regarded rather as 'journalism', 'light reading', 'unscientific', 'comical', or something equally derogatory, albeit postmodernists do not consider such terms pejorative. On the contrary, they contend that journalists, comedians, columnists and so on, can offer insights into marketplace phenomena that are infinitely superior to those emanating from heavy-weight marketing scientists and analogous self-appointed defenders of the marketing faith (insights, incidentally, which no manager finds of use and, abstract excepted, almost no one bothers to read).

5 The biter bit

Tolerated by some, ridiculed by many and distrusted by all and sundry, postmodern marketing researchers refuse to bend the knee to conventional forms of academic discourse. Although there are many distinguishing features of the postmodern condition, perhaps the clearest indicator of 'postmodernists at work' is the convoluted, hyperbolic, well-nigh incomprehensible language in which their arguments are couched. And, of course, it is the outrageousness of postmodern modes of textual expression – four letter words, first person narratives, self-conscious running commentary and the like are very much to the fore – that drives more sober-sided scholarly citizens into paroxysms of refutational rage. Postmodernists, however, maintain that such acts of textual promiscuity are more than mere affectation or ostentation, because their very 'inappropriateness' in intellectual discourse serves to throw the 'conventionality' of textual norms into sharp relief. Why, they ask, do we write about marketing the way we do? Where does it say that there is a 'right' way of writing about marketing artefacts? Who is the arbiter of these things – academics?, practitioners?, students?, publishers? What criteria should we use to evaluate postmodern marketing texts? Reliability? Validity? Truth? Please! When and how is he going to work 'when' and 'how' into this concluding list of rhetorical questions?

Postmodernism, in sum, not only bites the hand that feeds it, it also bites the biter.

Notes

1 Inter-generational power struggles in intellectual life rarely involve head-to-head conflict – unlike intra-generational manoeuvring – since the older generation's decision to step down, as it were, is often precipitated by their own, internalized sense of being 'out of touch' with the (theoretical, mathematical, methodological or whatever) argot of the young turks of the field. In effect, they no longer speak the language.
2 You know, I reckon the most horrendous hyperreal happening that could befall anyone is to be mugged in the New York-New York theme hotel in Las Vegas by an Elvis impersonator brandishing a fake weapon. Do you think he'd accept an IOU?

STEPHEN BROWN
UNIVERSITY OF ULSTER AT COLERAINE

Further reading

(References cited in the text marked *)

* Bocock, R. (1993) *Consumption*, London: Routledge.
* Brown, S. (1995a) 'Life begins at 40: further thoughts on marketing's mid-life crisis', *Marketing Intelligence and Planning* 13: 4–17.
* Brown, S. (1995b) *Postmodern Marketing*, London: Routledge.
  Brown, S. (1996) *Marketing Apocalypse*, London: Routledge.
* Brown, S. (1997) *Postmodern Marketing Two: Telling Tales*, London: ITBP.
  Brown, S. (1998) *Romancing the Market*, London: Routledge.
* Brown, S., J. Bell and D. Carson (1996) 'Apocaholics anonymous: looking back on the end of marketing', in Brown, S. *et al.* (eds), *Marketing Apocalypse: Eschatology, Escapology and the Illusion of the End*, London: Routledge, 1–20.
* Coupland, D. (1991) *Generation X: Tales for an Accelerated Culture*, London: Abacus.
* Cova, B. (1996) 'What postmodernism means to marketing managers', *European Management Journal* 14: 494–9.
* Denzin, N.K. (1997) *Interpretive Ethnography: Ethnographic Practices for the 21st Century*, Thousand Oaks: Sage.
* Dickens, D.R. and Fontana, A. (1994) 'Postmodernism in the social sciences', in Dickens, D.R. and Fontana, A. (eds), *Postmodernism and Social Inquiry*, London: UCL Press, 1–22.
* Douglas, M. (1997) *Thought Styles: Critical Essays on Good Taste*, London: Sage.
* Elliott, R. (1993) 'Marketing and the meaning of postmodern consumer culture', in Brownlie, D. *et al.* (eds), *Rethinking Marketing*, Coventry: Warwick Business School Research Bureau, 134–42.
* Firat, A.F. and Venkatesh, A. (1993) 'Postmodernity: the age of marketing', *International Journal of Research in Marketing* 10: 227–49.
* Firat, A.F. and Venkatesh, A. (1995) 'Liberatory postmodernism and the reenchantment of consumption', *Journal of Consumer Research* 22: 239–67.
* Gergen, K.J. (1991) *The Saturated Self: Dilemmas of Identity in Contemporary Life*, New York: Basic Books.
* Piercy, N.F. (1997) *Market-Led Strategic Change*, Oxford: Butterworth-Heinemann.
* Rorty, R. (1980) *Philosophy and the Mirror of Nature*, Oxford: Blackwell.
* Van Raaij, W.F. (1993) 'Postmodern consumption: architecture, art and consumer behaviour', in van Raaij, W.F. and Bamossy, G.J. (eds), *European Advances in Consumer Research, Vol. I*, Provo: Association for Consumer Research, 550–8.

See also: ADVERTISING; BRANDING AND BRAND MANAGEMENT; CHANNELS OF DISTRIBUTION; THE SOCIOLOGICAL BASIS OF MARKETING

The future of marketing

1 Where are we now?
2 Alternative perspectives
3 Evolution not revolution
4 The futures of marketing

Overview

In the call for papers for the AMA's 1994 Winter Educators' Conference the organizers set the theme as 'Renaissance in Marketing Thought and Practice' and observed:

> The ongoing interplay of marketing theory and practice has led to several new research areas. As a field, our agenda now features topics such as Relationship Marketing, Strategic Alliances, Managing Brand Equity, Total Quality Management and Market-oriented Management, among others.
>
> The emergence of such topics raises at least two provocative issues for marketing scholars. First, are we reinventing the wheel? Even though the general topic headings may be new, how new are the specific research questions related to each area? ... Second, interest in many of these emerging topics extends beyond the traditional domain of marketing. Unfortunately, interdisciplinary collaboration in the conduct of research in marketing is rare.

A very similar view was expressed in the *Journal of Marketing Management* (9.2, 1993) in which the Editor wrote:

> As a confirmed supporter of the concept of the product life cycle (PLC) it is interesting to speculate on its application to the study of marketing as a business discipline. While the establishment of the first chair in the subject can be dated to the 1880s most would agree that marketing only really took off in the mid 1950s to early 1960s with a number of seminal contributions by authors such as Peter Drucker, Joel Dean, Ted Levitt and Eugene McCarthy. Since that time the number of students opting to study the subject at the undergraduate and postgraduate levels has accelerated rapidly and resulted in a significant expansion in the number of academics researching and teaching the subject. The question is, however, at what stage will growth begin to slow and the 'market' approach saturation and maturity? The question is prompted not by a concern with the quality of contributions to *JMM* but a more broadly based awareness that research and publication in marketing might be approaching a plateau. Two factors prompt this observation. The first is the decline in the incremental value added by current research/publication. The second is the trend towards increasing marketing's domain to the point when it will subsume other fields whose practitioners might legitimately consider to be quite distinct from marketing.
>
> The decline in incremental value added is noticeable everywhere To a marked degree it is fuelled by the feeling that one should only cite the latest work relating to one's topic. As a result earlier path breaking and insightful contributions tend to be overlooked or ignored and much of what passes for original work is a weak replication of seminal contributions published 30 or 40 years ago. The extension of marketing's domain is apparent in the flurry of publication about internal marketing and relationship marketing. To an old-fashioned marketer like myself much of this writing gives a distinct impression that the authors have just discovered the subject of human resource management, and concepts such as motivation and leadership. While I am all for this, I am not sure we are not doing marketing a disservice if we seek to take over rather than integrate these concepts. Either way both phenomena are symptomatic of the 'hunting' behaviour observed in biological life cycles when an organism perceives a limit to growth and searches frantically for a means to get round it.

Perhaps it is a symptom of advancing years that what is regarded as history by a new generation was an important element in the education and experience of the old. For the older generation nostalgia and resistance to change may cause them to cling to the old-fashioned and outmoded ways of yesteryear. For the new generation a desire to think for themselves and make their own impact on the affairs of the world may lead them to overlook, or, worse still, ignore, hard-won lessons of the past.

Such oversight or ignorance may well lead to a condition first diagnosed almost 40 years ago by one of marketing's most influential scholars and authors, Ted Levitt, in his seminar 'Marketing myopia' (1960). Levitt along with Keith (1960) is widely regarded as one of the founding fathers of the 'marketing management' model which has dominated much of marketing education and practice for the past 30 years or so. While this model has been subject to much criticism in recent years (Webster 1992; Marion 1993; Gummesson 1993; Grönroos 1993 – with its emphasis on the Four Ps of Product, Price, Place and Promotion – McCarthy 1960; Kotler 1967), one feels bound to question whether or not it is myopic to discard it in favour of a new-found enthusiasm for relationship marketing, etc.? Will our concern for recency (no citation more than ten years old is worth citing – possibly true for much of the physical sciences) blur our vision of what is relevant? In ignoring the past will we reinvent what is already known or, by taking cognisance of the past, will we see a renaissance in marketing theory and practice which properly reflects our rich inheritance?

In other words, what is the future of marketing? To answer this question it will be helpful to take stock of where we are currently.

1 Where are we now?

In the opening paragraph I cited the AMA Conference Chairman's question concerning the possible reinvention of currently fashionable topics. To address this issue Park and Smith asserted that: 'Answers to these questions call for the benchmarks provided by state-of-the-art reviews in traditional areas of inquiry. However, there is a noticeable shortage of such progress updates'.

In and of itself this shortage is indicative of a lack of interest in the past. In building our new temple of knowledge we bury the foundations of the old with scarcely a thought as to their ability to support the new edifice. If we are wrong then, surely, the whole structure is liable to topple about our ears. Given the scope and complexity of modern marketing no single article could define fully the foundations of modern marketing thought. None the less, it will be useful to sketch some of the outlines of our subject to establish the present *status quo* before attempting to address the more challenging question *Quo vadis*?

As a basis for answering our first question – where are we now – as good a place to begin as any is the plenary session of the 1993 AMA Winter Educators' Conference. At that meeting a distinguished panel consisting of Hal Kassarjian, Sidney Levy and Stephen Greyser under the chairmanship of Jagdish Sheth offered their 'Reflections on the Evolution of the Field of Marketing'.

Hal Kassarjian opened the session by giving a broad perspective of the evolution of marketing during this century. In his view, prior to the Second World War, most professors of marketing were trained as economists and research on the subject was largely of a narrative nature with some underpinning of economic theorizing. Interestingly, in his view, it was the migration of Europeans to the USA that introduced behavioural concepts into the marketing repertoire. Thus it was George Katona whose psychological analysis of economic behaviour broke the mould and paved the way for the development of media studies and motivation research associated with the names of Gallup, Nielsen, Kantril, Lazerfeld, Dichter, Hertzog, and many others.

The 1960s saw the growth of cognitive research and the migration of scientific ideas from other disciplines. Again, many of the scholars such as Bass, Levy and Silk, who were prominent in this field, were strongly linked to the positivist influence of Europeans.

During the 1970s marketing came to be seen as the handmaiden of the industrial/militaristic complex. This association prompted many marketing scholars to seek methods for broadening the base of their subject into other areas and saw the introduction of social marketing and marketing for non-profit organizations. Consumerism re-emerged as a potent force. However, the emphasis upon the consumer in the 1970s saw something of a counter revolution in the 1980s with many challenging the concept of the learning consumer and the emergence of ideas of low involvement and muddling through.

As for the 1990s, in Kassarjian's view it is clear that we are headed for information processing models and he speculated that Clinton's administration would lead to the return of Kennedy's 'Camelot', with a strong emphasis on consumerism.

Sid Levy echoed many of Kassarjian's themes in a presentation which strongly emphasized the need for present-day scholars to be aware of the contributions of those who had preceded them. As he observed, 'Companies tend to lack memory'. Parenthetically, he clearly believes that many marketing researchers suffer from the same problem. He certainly struck a receptive chord with the author when he observed that 'when you get this old you suffer from the disease of reminiscence'. That said, it is clear that while fashions and theory ebb and flow there is a strong central current so that most arguments are very similar but appear in different guises, reflecting the original distinctions introduced by Aristotle and Plato.

Levy, too, was of the opinion that Europeans have always been more willing to pursue a greater in-depth approach to research than their American colleagues. Finally, he identified the current hot topics as:

- consumer satisfaction (it always was);
- internationalism – with everything;
- environmentalism;
- ethics.

Steve Greyser took as his theme 'Marketing and Public Policy'. Tracing developments over the course of the century Greyser summed up by seeing the 1970s as a period of hyperactivity, the 1980s as a period of remission, and he anticipated that the 1990s would offer tremendous potential for a revival of interest in marketing and public policy as the pendulum swings yet again.

Finally, Jagdish Sheth spoke on the theme of 'Marketing Theory: A Metatheory Assessment'. In classifying marketing schools of thought Sheth argued that evolution has gone back and forth between non-interactive and interactive perspectives. Starting with an economic and non-interactive perspective in the 1950s, interest in the 1960s shifted to an interactive perspective but still underpinned by economic considerations. In turn this led, in the 1970s, to an emphasis upon non-economic factors but in a non-interactive perspective which, in the 1980s, moved into an interactive and non-economic perspective. Based on his analysis Sheth argued that today's marketing theory depends largely on borrowed constructs and depends heavily on context. In future he sees it moving towards a discipline based upon its own indigenous constructs which, in turn, represents a move from the existence of an invisible hand to the visible hand of managed competition.

Sheth concluded that marketing will not be a discipline so long as it is treated as context and relies on borrowed constructs and theories. Clearly, he sees 'relationship marketing' as providing the opportunity to develop this distinctive set of constructs which will enable marketing to emerge as a discipline.

From these presentations by distinguished marketing scholars the author drew three broad conclusions. First, marketing thought and research is largely distinguished by its micro perspective with an emphasis upon the individual and the firm. Second, from decade to decade the emphasis on firm and individual swings from one to the other with the common thread being the interaction between these parties to exchange. Third, there are some significant differences in the approach taken by North American and European researchers, a need to improve communication between these schools and considerable potential for integrating them into a single holistic approach to the subject.

It must be emphasized that the above represents the author's interpretation of what the distinguished panel said and, in the absence of a written transcript, one is conscious of the ever-present dangers of selective perception and hearing what one wants to hear. However, for an authoritative and widely accepted written statement on the current status of marketing we do not have to look far. In 'The Changing Role of Marketing in the Corporation', Fred Webster Jr. set out 'to outline both the intellectual and pragmatic roots of changes that are occurring in marketing, especially marketing *management*, as a body of knowledge, theory, and practice and to suggest the need for a new paradigm of the marketing function within the firm' (1992: 1).

Webster dates the early roots of the development of marketing as an area of academic study to around 1910 with a growing interest in the marketing of agricultural products in the midwestern land grant universities. Three separate schools may be identified:

1 focusing on the commodities themselves;
2 focusing on the institutions involved;
3 focusing on the functions performed by these institutions.

All three schools tended to be descriptive rather than normative with the functional being the most analytical and providing the basis for conceptual development. Relatively little attention was given to managerial factors or orientation and 'marketing was seen as a set of social and economic processes rather than as a set of managerial activities and responsibilities' (Webster 1992: 2). This perspective began to emerge in the late 1940s and early 1950s and, in Webster's view, 'the managerial approach brought relevance and realism to the study of marketing, with an emphasis on problem solving, planning, implementation, and control in a competitive marketplace' (Webster 1992: 2).

The new managerial school, represented by scholars such as Howard (1957), McCarthy (1960) and Kotler (1967), looked upon marketing as a problem-solving and decision-making process and drew heavily on analytical frameworks from economics, psychology, sociology and statistics. It was during the 1950s that the marketing concept was articulated, by writers such as Drucker (1954), McKitterick (1957) and Levitt (1960), emphasizing customer satisfaction as the primary objective of the organization with profit being seen as the reward.

Unsurprisingly, proponents of the institutional/functionalist view were not ready to discard lightly the accumulation of 50 years of writing and research and the managerial approach was not received with universal enthusiasm. However, as calls for greater rigour in approaches to management education gathered momentum in the late 1950s and early 1960s so the managerial school became dominant and was to remain so for nearly three decades.

The foundation of the managerial school was the basic micro-economic paradigm emphasizing profit maximization and the nature of transactions between buyer and seller. 'Behavioural science models were used primarily to structure problem definition, helping the market researcher to define the questions that are worth asking and to identify important variables and the relationships between them' (Webster 1992: 3). To measure and analyse these relationships sophisticated statistical analysis was called for and the marketing function grew within major organizations as groupings or departments containing individuals with the requisite expertise and professionalism – a development well suited to the culture of large, divisionalized, bureaucratic and hierarchical organizations. Such organizations were the 'engines of economic activity' (Miles and Snow 1978) for more than a century and were the dominant organizations as the managerial approach to marketing developed in the 1950s and 1960s. Often marketing departments evolved from sales departments as these large organizations moved slowly to adopt the greater rigour and discipline offered by the new managerial orientation.

In the large, divisionalized corporations where size and economies of scale and experience were seen as leading to competitive success, 'the task of the marketing function was first to develop a thorough understanding of the marketplace to ensure that the firm was producing goods and services required and desired by

1. Transactions →→→→→
2. Repeated transactions →→→→→→
3. Long-term relationships →→→→
4. Buyer-seller partnerships (mutual, total dependence) →
5. strategic alliances (incl. joint ventures) →→→→→→
6. Network organizations →→→
7. Vertical integration

Figure 1 The range of marketing relationships

the consumer' (Webster 1992: 4). Having done so, marketing was responsible for creating and sustaining consumer preference through manipulation of the mix variables – product, price, promotion and distribution. Centralized, corporate marketing departments were the order of the day.

During the late 1970s and early 1980s the move towards decentralization began to gather momentum as the concept of the strategic business unit (SBU) with profit and loss responsibility found favour with corporate management. Inevitably, decentralization led to duplication and excessive numbers and layers of middle management. Faced with increased competition both domestically and internationally cost containment became an imperative and 'down-sizing' the consequence. However, down-sizing was only a partial solution and more radical restructuring was clearly required.

> The new organizations emphasised partnerships between firms; multiple types of ownership and partnering within the organisation (divisions, wholly owned subsidiaries, licensees, franchises, joint ventures, etc.); teamwork among members of the organisation, often with team members from two or more co-operating firms; sharing of responsibility for developing converging and overlapping technologies; and often less emphasis on formal contracting and managerial reporting, evaluation and control systems.
> (Webster 1992: 4)

Various names have been coined for these more flexible and adaptable organizational forms ('networks', Miles and Snow 1978; 'value adding partnerships', Johnston and Lawrence 1988; 'alliances', Ohmae 1989; and 'shamrocks', Handy 1990).

> All are characterised by flexibility, specialisation, and an emphasis on relationship management instead of market transactions. They depend on administrative processes but they are not hierarchies (Thorelli 1986); they engage in transactions within ongoing relationships and they depend on negotiation, rather than market-based processes, as a principal basis for conducting business and determining prices, though market forces almost always influence and shape negotiation. The purpose of these new organisation forms is to respond quickly and flexibly to accelerating change in technology, competition, and customer preferences.
> (Webster 1992: 4–5)

Although Webster perceives no strong consensus in the terminology and typology for describing the new organization forms he proposes-a continuum from pure transactions to fully integrated organizations, as depicted in Figure 1.

As one moves along this continuum the role of the marketing function will change and Webster describes each of these phases in some detail. Based on his analysis of the evolution of exchange relationships he states (1992: 10): 'The intellectual core of marketing management needs to be expanded beyond the conceptual framework of micro economics in order to address more fully the set of organizational and strategic issues inherent in relationships and alliances'.

To do so will require closer consideration of phenomena which, traditionally, have been 'the subject of study of psychologists, organizational behaviourists, political economists and sociologists. The focus shifts from products and firms as units of analysis to people, organizations, and the social processes that bind actors together in ongoing relationships' (Webster 1992: 10).

In order to consider the role of marketing in the evolving organization Webster argues that it is essential to recognize that marketing really operates at three strategic levels – corporate, business or SBU, and the functional or operational level. He further states that it is a failure to distinguish clearly these three levels which underlies much of the misdefinition and misunderstanding of the marketing concept over the years: 'In addition to the three levels of strategy we can identify three distinct dimensions of marketing – marketing as *culture*, marketing as *strategy*, and marketing as *tactics*' (original emphasis, Webster 1992: 10). Marketing as culture is the responsibility of corporate and SBU levels, marketing as strategy is the emphasis of the SBU level, and marketing as tactics is the focus at the operating level responsible for managing the marketing mix. Webster elaborates on each of these propositions and reiterates his view that 'the political economy and organizational behaviour models seem to be more appropriate for a *strategic* view of the marketing function as distinct from the *sales* or demand stimulation function, for which the micro-economics paradigm is still more fitting'(Webster 1992: 13).

In conclusion, Webster offers us a definition and an opinion. Marketing 'is the management function responsible for making sure that every aspect of the business is focused on delivering superior value to customers in the competitive marketplace' (Webster 1992: 14). 'Marketing can no longer be the sole responsibility of a few specialists. Rather, everyone in the firm must be charged with responsibility for understanding customers and contributing to developing and delivering value for them' (Webster 1992: 14).

Clearly, there is considerable correspondence between Webster's views and those cited earlier. If nothing else it seems reasonable to accept them as the dominant and prevailing school of thought in the USA. That said it must be recognized that there are dissident voices or at least alternative perspectives within the USA while in Europe, Japan and many other countries there is a sense of some surprise that it has taken the Americans so long to reach a conclusion they had arrived at some time ago. (Perhaps it is not so surprising when one appreciates how limited is the American scholars' awareness of non-American sources. For example. Webster's 1992 article contains over 70 references. Only six of these are non-American and five of these six are by American authors. A clear case of acute research myopia.)

2 Alternative perspectives

One of the key tenets of the marketing management faith is that the articulation of the marketing concept and its implementation through the development of marketing management occurred with the transition from a production and sales orientation/era which had preceded the marketing era. This belief, enshrined in the traditional three eras conceptualization of marketing, was challenged seriously by Ronald A. Fullerton in his article 'How Modern is Modern Marketing?' (1988).

Fullerton attributes the source of the three eras approach to a seminal article by Keith (1960) in which he described the evolution of marketing in the Pillsbury Company as having followed a production, sales and marketing stage. While this conceptualization has pedagogical advantages in summarizing the changes in the dominant orientation of business management it is singularly deficient in analysing the much more complex processes which underlay and resulted in these changes. Such an analysis is properly the domain of the business historian following the requirements of rigorous historical research. It is this which Fullerton sets out to achieve and we summarized the key arguments in the opening article.

Fullerton's thesis about the evolutionary nature of marketing receives considerable support from the work of another American historian – Richard S. Tedlow (1990; Tedlow *et al.*1993). He identifies three phases in the history of consumer product marketing in the USA: fragmentation (lasting until the 1880s); unification (1880s–early 1950s); and segmentation (1950s–late 1980s/early l990s). He speculates that we are now entering a fourth phase of micromarketing or hyper-segmentation based upon developments in information technology. Inevitably this implies the establishment of closer relationships between producers and consumers and lends support to Webster and Sheth, *inter alia*, that we are on the threshold of a new era in marketing.

It is here, however, that American scholars and researchers are seen as latecomers to a perspective of marketing which has enjoyed considerable support for decades amongst other international researchers. In the opinion of one leading French researcher, Giles Marion, (see MARKETING – PHILOSOPHY OR FUNCTION?) although the normative theory of marketing management may well have had a useful impact on managerial thinking and practice, 'there has been nothing new since the 1960s or even well before' (Marion 1993: 166).

Since the 1960s generations of managers have been educated in the 'marketing management' school popularized by McCarthy (1960) and Kotler (1967) and their numerous disciples. This positivist approach – analysis, planning and control – has been the dominant paradigm for over 30 years. But, because many managers have experienced difficulty in implementing the 'marketing orientation' its nature and validity have come into question (see Swartz 1990).

In Marion's view the marketing management school is founded largely on myth and rhetoric. Three essential ideas are cited as central to the contributions of Drucker, McKitterick, Keith and Levitt:

> which appear as the basis of all textbooks on marketing management:
> 1 That it is the customer who ultimately determines the purpose of companies and even of organizations, in other words, the marketing concept;
> 2 That all companies, and even all organizations will eventually adopt this concept;
> 3 That the 'opponents' of this concept cannot and must not succeed because the company would not survive.
> (Marion 1993: 157)

Marion points out that the first proposition is simply a definition of a market economy and is an idea which is axiomatic in economics and one which was articulated as long ago as 1933 by Tosdal when specifically discussing marketing management:

> The first, and one of the most significant and striking changes of the last dozen years, stressed particularly since 1929, is the increased emphasis placed upon consumer wants and needs as a guide to good marketing management. While serious students of marketing have continuously recognised this viewpoint, here is good reason to agree ... that manufacturers as a whole have been giving only lip service to the consideration of consumer wants and needs.

and:

> The idea that consumer needs and wants should be the starting pomt for business thinking is certainly not revolutionary. For a century or more, economists have made assertions that the aim of our economic and business structure and its functioning was the satisfaction of consumer needs.
> (Tosdal 1933: 157)

Perhaps Tosdal had in mind the oft-quoted observation in Adam Smith's Wealth of Nations (1776) that 'consumption is the sole end and purpose of production'.

While few would challenge the central role of economic thinking in the development of marketing theory, proponents of the marketing management school are seen as promoting the satisfaction of consumer needs as the very *raison d'être* of the organization. But Marion, *inter alia*, rightly points out that other motivations underlie organizational and managerial behaviour which is why single factor explanations have been singularly unsuccessful in explaining competitive performance (Baker and Hart 1989).

To overcome the failings of the normative theory of marketing management with its assumptions that needs are given so that consumer sovereignty and managerial rationality are the foundation of exchange behaviour, Marion argues that one must consider simultaneously both parties to the relationship. Doing so enables one to reconcile the views of those like Galbraith, who used the same assumption of exogenous preferences, to argue for producer sovereignty. Thus Marion (1993) is proposing a model based on interactive rationality according to which 'the origin of preferences is endogenous, they are built by the actors' interaction before becoming exogenous and growing into a set of constraints'.

Such a model is in keeping with the Scandinavian School dealing with interorganizational exchanges in an industrial environment (the 'interaction' approach), with channel theory, and more broadly based theories of organizational behaviour such as those proposed by March and Simon (1958), Cyert and March (1963), and others.

Marion argues that 'marketing as a discipline, should show greater humility by presenting its prescriptions in a more prudent manner, and by describing more systematically the interaction between supply and demand and the organizational consequences that follow' (1993: 166). In conclusion Marion expresses the view that, while the normative theory of marketing management may well have had a useful impact on managerial thinking and practice, there has been nothing new for some decades.

While Marion's critique strikes at the very heart of the marketing management school promoted by Americans (see MARKETING – PHILOSOPHY OR FUNCTION?), it is comparatively mild compared with the trenchant criticisms expressed by Evert Gummesson and Christian Grönroos, leading members of the Scandinavian School.

3 Evolution not revolution

At this juncture it will be helpful to summarize the arguments presented in the preceding sections, suggest some conclusions and propose at least a partial answer to the questions implicit in the title of this article.

Whatever their perspective, all the authorities cited appear to agree that between 1960 and 1990 the dominant paradigm in marketing theory and practice can be identified as the 'marketing management model' of which Philip Kotler has been the most influential exponent.

However, there is considerable diversity of views about the emergence of this model as the natural consequence of a shift in business orientation from a production or sales orientation to a marketing orientation. While the distinguishing of these three stages or eras is a useful pedagogical device to highlight differences in emphasis in management thinking and practice, the chronology proposed in most marketing management textbooks is severely flawed as evidenced by the work of business historians.

Further, in promoting the marketing management model as a 'new approach' its proponents have been guilty of ignoring or overlooking the roots or foundations of marketing which are to be found originally in the writings of the political economists of the nineteenth century. (This view is inferred by the author and is not made specifically by the sources quoted. In my opinion political economy was/is a behavioural theory of production, consumption and exchange and it is only the more recent preoccupation with quantification – presumably in pursuit of an unattainable 'scientific' rigour – which has disguised and distorted this fact. *Caveat* marketer!) Certainly, there is little 'new' in the marketing management model as articulated from the 1960s onwards.

The marketing management model is production orientated due to its preoccupation with what marketers 'do' to consumers. Its emphasis is essentially short-term and transactional. Furthermore it is concerned primarily with the production and sale of fast-moving consumer goods which represent only a fraction of all commercial exchanges.

With its emphasis on the manipulation of the marketing mix of product, price, place and promotion (the Four Ps) the marketing management model ignores the influence and impact of numerous other factors which are involved in exchange relationships. Attempts to explain competitive performance solely in terms of marketing factors are doomed to failure.

While the marketing management model has been the dominant model, alternative explanations of marketing are to be found in the interaction, services and now relationship approaches developed in Europe from the 1960s onwards, particularly by the so-called Scandinavian School. The relationship marketing approach has been recognized and

Anglo Saxon		**Germanic-Alpine**
	Basic principle	
Free competition		Controlled competition
	Power centres	
The stock exchange		The Bank
Customer (as consumer)		Company over customer
		Management over shareholder
	Time perspective	
Short term		Long term
The tyranny of the quarterly report		Development as opposed to profit
	Types of business relationship	
Ad hoc transaction		Long-term relationship
	Social involvement	
Weak		Strong

Figure 2 Major differences between the two models
Source: Dussart (1994)

enthusiastically promoted in the USA since the early 1990s (particularly by Sheth and Webster). It is now widely seen as both an alternative to and replacement for the marketing management model.

The relationship marketing model can trace its lineage directly to the work of European economists from the 1930s onwards (the Copenhagen School's parameter theory). It is also implicit in the Germanic/Alpine model of capitalism that contrasts strongly with the Anglo-Saxon model of capitalism which dominates thinking in the free market economies of the USA and UK. The essence of these two models of capitalism is summarized in Figure 2.

From the evidence presented there can be little doubt that most marketing scholars are guilty of research myopia in that they fail to consider earlier research within their own discipline, parallel research activity by scholars in other geographical areas, and complementary research by scholars in other disciplines. In large measure the failure to consider earlier research is attributable to a preoccupation with recency (you will note there are very few 'dated' references in this article!). It seems inevitable, therefore, that we will frequently be guilty of reinvention. For example, a major preoccupation of marketers in recent years has been 'time to market'. Robert Weigand addressed this very topic in the *Journal of Marketing* in 1962, but is seldom if ever cited. The importance of parallel processing, concurrent engineering and simultaneity are seen as vital but few researchers appear to be aware of the PERT and CPA techniques first articulated in the late 1950s. Competitiveness is of central concern to us all but how many readers are aware of, let alone have consulted the analysis by Carter and Williams (1959) of the characteristics of technically progressive firms. And so I could go on.

If these indictments are correct then the relevance of much of what we do must also be called into question. If productivity, on which academic recognition and preferment are judged, is to be measured in terms of frequency and recency rather than quality and importance then the proliferation of trivia can only gather momentum to the neglect of true knowledge.

What is called for is a renaissance in marketing thinking and research. The time may now be right for this to occur. Given that renaissance was the theme of the 1994 AMA Educators' Winter Conference, and given the widespread enthusiasm for relationship marketing in place of the marketing management model which has dominated our thinking for the past 30 years or more, the opportunity for a fundamental reappraisal of marketing thinking could not be better. Now is the time for all of us to revisit the marketing classics of the 1950s and early 1960s for it was these that influenced and challenged the senior scholars at the top of our profession today. Now is also the time to reaffirm that marketing like architecture, engineering and medicine is a synthetic discipline which draws upon contributions from many other disciplines and integrates these into a body of knowledge which is relevant to a craft or professional practice. Unlike many of the core disciplines, such as economics, psychology and sociology, on which it draws, marketing cannot afford to become enmeshed in a scientific rigour that requires one to control or assume away the complexity which is the real world of practice. As with architecture, engineering and medicine the acid test should be 'does it work?' What we need are more basic principles and rules of thumb – what at Harvard Business School in my day were called 'currently useful generalizations' (CUGs) – and fewer esoteric irrelevancies which are fit only to grace the pages of the *Journal of Obscurity*.

Further, in creating our vision of the future perhaps what we need most of all is a greater awareness of our past. Business history and the works of the political economists of the eighteenth and nineteenth centuries should be required reading for us all. That said, help is nearer to hand. As noted in the Preface to this Encyclopedia, this work represents the distilled wisdom of many of the world's leading authorities, each of whom is recognized internationally as an expert in their field. While the contributing authors have concentrated on specific topics, many of the themes addressed here are to be found in their individual articles and it is to these that the reader should turn first for enlightenment.

At the time of preparing the first edition in 1995 this article concluded by citing the Editorial for volume 10.8 of the *Journal of Marketing Management* by David Carson and Stephen Brown of the University of Ulster. David and Stephen and their colleagues were responsible for organizing the annual conference of the UK Marketing Education Group and it fell to them to select a cross-section from over 200 papers presented to provide a flavour of the Conference and its theme 'Unity in Diversity'. In their editorial Carson and Brown echo many of the issues and themes touched on in this article which speculated on the current state and future development of marketing thought and practice:

> Although the marketing function has been performed since the dawn of civilization, the modern marketing concept, or philosophy, dates from the early 1950s and Peter Drucker's (1954: 36) famous contention that, 'Marketing ... is the whole business seen from the point of view of its final result, that is, from the customer's point of view'. Forty years on from Drucker's seminal insight – and the dangers of disciplinary anthropomorphism notwithstanding – it is perhaps only to be expected that marketing is in the throes of its 'mid-life crisis'. As a glance at the journals amply testifies, doubts are increasingly being cast on the veracity of the marketing concept; marketing principles no longer seem relevant to the real world of practitioners; leading figures in the field are marketing's most outspoken critics, and the sense of academic cohesion, solidarity and commitment to the marketing cause has been torn asunder by a series of bitter philosophical disputes and declarations of epistemological independence (Brady and Davis 1993; Freeling 1994; Wilson and McDonald 1994).
>
> Rather than dwell on marketing's current crisis of relevance and representation, it may be more appropriate to remind ourselves of several salient facts. First, 'crises' in marketing are not exactly new. More than 30 years ago, for example, Bartels (1962) was discussing the then crisis in marketing. Twenty years or so ago, Bell and Emory (1971) were saying something similar. And, it is more than 10 years now since Bennett and Cooper (1981) were also crying crisis. Second, crises in marketing are not necessarily unhealthy. As the 'broadening' convulsions of the early 1970s and the philosophical 'crisis' literature of a decade ago clearly demonstrate, periods of instability impel everyone, not just the protagonists, to reflect on their own position, consider alternative approaches or embrace novel perspectives, the ultimate consequence of which is an all-round improvement in academic standards. Third, and most importantly, marketing's current bout of self-abasement should not tempt us to forget the enormous strides that it has made in the post-war era. As Baker and Hart (1989) have shown, there is considerable evidence that a marketing orientation is the key to long-term business success. The marketing concept has been enthusiastically embraced in fields as diverse as health care, public administration and the not-for-profit sector. It is rapidly colonising the erstwhile command economies of eastern Europe, where the market is supplanting Marxism as the societal touchstone, albeit not without privation. And, the proliferation of publications, professorships, degree programmes, university departments and professional societies testifies to the fact that marketing is in the ascendant as an academic discipline.
>
> It is important, therefore, in these uncertain times and in this the 40th anniversary of Drucker's acclaimed contribution, to remember that we have indeed come a long way baby! In today's fragmented marketing world of realism and relativism, positivism and post-positivism, micro-marketing and macro-marketing, scientists and semiologists, transactions and relationships, myths and metaphors, modernists and post-modernists, where all manner of shortcomings are being identified, putative solutions to our ills proposed and the possibility of disciplinary disintegration looms large, it is equally important to remember that marketing is a very broad church. Marketing is and always has been a remarkably diverse discipline, drawing from and, increasingly, contributing to cognate academic specialisms. Indeed, it is arguable that now, more than ever, is the time to abandon our long-standing lack of scholarly selfesteem, the utterly erroneous but depressingly widespread view that marketers cannot make an original contribution to knowledge, that we are forever condemned to live off the scraps from the tables of our academic elders and betters (Brown 1994).

Despite its rich, welcome and ever-increasing diversity, marketing still possesses an underlying unity. This unity, however, does not derive from the phenomena we study, the subject matter of our investigations. Marketing does not 'own' new product development; it does not possess a monopoly on distribution channels or pricing strategies; and, only the most reactionary or recidivist scholar would consider advertising and promotion to be marketing's disciplinary preserve. Nor, for that matter, is marketing unified by a distinctive methodology, a particular scale of analysis, or, arguably, a core concept such as 'exchange'. Marketing, rather, seems to be held together by the, sometimes divergent, often overlapping, belief systems of those that consider themselves marketers. *Marketing*, to modify the venerable neologism, *is not what marketers do; marketing is what marketers perceive it to be* [my emphasis].

(Carson and Brown, 1994)

Given this 'unity in diversity' perhaps it would be more appropriate to consider the future*s* of marketing?

4 The futures of marketing

In 1997 the Marketing Science Institute of Cambridge, Massachusetts published a book entitled *Reflections on the Futures of Marketing* edited by Donald R. Lehmann and Katherine E. Jocz. In the opening article of the book by Stephen A. Greyser, specific reference is made to the content of this article in the first edition of the Encyclopedia. Like myself, Professor Greyser shares the view that if we are to understand the present and prospective future of marketing then it is important to begin with reflections on its past. That we should share the same views is probably unsurprising as Ray Bauer and Steve Greyser were responsible for the Research Methodology course when I was a doctoral candidate at the Harvard Business School in the late 1960s.

While *Reflections on the Futures of Marketing* is concerned with a number of issues and dimensions of the subject, two articles in particular resonated strongly with what I attempted in the first edition of this book. These are chapter 3 'The future role of marketing in the organisation' by Frederick E. Webster Jnr. and chapter 6 'Some thoughts on the futures of marketing' by one of the editors, Donald R. Lehmann, which draws on the contributions of his other distinguished colleagues.

In common with his other seminal contributions to the literature of marketing Webster's article is a model of content and clarity. In many ways, Webster's article may be seen as a response to the frequently posed and not always rhetorical question 'Has marketing a future?' For the past decade or so many informed commentators (and even more uninformed ones) have raised this question explicitly or implicitly. Two major international consultancies have provided at least a partial answer to the question. First, in 1993, McKinsey & Co. published a report on 'Marketing's mid-life crisis which argued that marketing departments are 'Often a millstone around an organization's neck' while, in 1997, KPMG Management Consulting produced a research report entitled 'The future of marketing is on the line'. (Further reference to these reports will be made later).

In his incisive response to the unstated question Webster, like Greyser in an earlier article, feels it important to trace the evolution of marketing in the organization as background to speculating on its future. The opening sentence of his essay sets the scene. 'Among the several management functions, marketing has the most difficulty defining its position in the organization because it is simultaneously culture, strategy, and tactics.'

This threefold distinction is useful because it extends the more unusual discussion of the marketing concept (culture) as a philosophy of business which should pervade the whole organization and the marketing function (strategy and tactics) which are concerned with the conversion of the philosophy into practice. As will be seen, one of the reasons for the role of marketing becoming blurred is that as the philosophy of serving customers' needs has become the dominant culture in successful organizations, so it has come to be seen as 'everybody's business'. The result is that this common ownership dilutes the claim of marketing to be its sponsor and custodian. Similiarly, as the philosophy has become widely accepted so, too, has the need to convert this into a strategy which manages the interface between the organization and its various constituencies. The result is that strategy, too, becomes a shared activity.

As a result of these changes, the third element of marketing becomes dominant in people's perceptions and confirms their suspicions that marketing really is just a superior form of selling supported by advertising and promotion.

As organizations have mutated in order to adapt themselves to a rapidly changing environment so has the role of marketing in the organization become blurred. In Webster's opinion 'If marketing is to survive into the 21st Century as an identifiable (although not necessarily *distinct*) management function, it must address some shortcomings in its ability to contribute to the strategy and business design dialogue within the firm by integrating its culture, strategic and tactical dimensions.' The challenge implicit in this statement is that integration of the three dimensions of marketing may result in its ultimate objective – the customer orientated firm – it may also result in the disappearance of marketing as a distinguishable discipline. Our own view is that this is unlikely to happen. While all may share the vision and espouse the culture, the management of the interface and the creation and delivery of customer value will still remain the responsibility of what we currently recognize as marketing.

Webster traces the evolution of marketing's organizational positioning since it first emerged as a separate business function in the 1920s. Initially, marketing evolved out of, and in support of, the sales function. In increasingly competitive markets a more sophisticated understanding of consumer behaviour was called for, supported by enhanced performance in the management of the marketing mix. While no single form of marketing organization emerged to take responsibility for these roles, Webster distinguishes five assumptions on which the design of traditional marketing organizations was based. Included within these were the assumptions that:

- both strategy and structure should have some long-term permanence;
- there is a definable set of business functions that are the legitimate domain of professional marketing managers;
- the fundamental purpose of the marketing department is to generate and stimulate demand for the firm's production.

As the history of competition in the second half of this century clearly demonstrates there is an intrinsic conflict between the first of these assumptions and the other two. Long-term strategy suggests the establishment of relationships with both suppliers and customers to create and deliver value. By contrast, the need to generate and stimulate demand for the firm's production may well require the marketing function to bend demand to the will of supply. Such an approach inevitably leads to a short-term and transactional approach to customer relations. In turn, the 'tyranny of the quarterly report' inevitably leads to an emphasis on short-termism and an emphasis upon the shareholder to the disadvantage of the customer.

The articulation of the marketing concept in the 1950s was a clear recognition of this tendency to stray from the philosophy of marketing but, the dominance of the marketing management school from the 1950s to the mid-late 1980s shows that, at best, only lip service was paid to these exhortations.

In Webster's view this resulted in marketing failing to perform its basic strategic management functions in at least three areas:

1. Market segmentation and targeting – analysing markets to define differences in customer needs, preferences, and priorities and selecting those segments where the firm is best able to achieve unique competitive advantage.
2. Developing the value proposition – matching the firm's resources, capabilities and 'distinctive competence' with a carefully defined set of customer needs; positioning the firm in the value chain.
3. Supply chain design and management – developing and managing relationships with various resource providers, including resellers and product/service vendors, in order to provide a total product/service offering that is consistent with the firm's value proposition.

In part, due to this neglect, many firms lost their competitive edge during the 1980s in the face of increased global competition. Diagnosis of the possible causes pointed clearly to short-termism and the lack of customer orientation as causal factors. This diagnosis was lent considerable additional weight with the collapse of Communism and the command-controlled economies of the Soviet Bloc in the late 1980s.

Traditionally, thinking about alternative forms of political and economic organization had been polarized between capitalism and communism. However, as Michel Albert pointed out, as a result of the dominance of the United States and Russia as great powers, it was their interpretation of capitalism and communism which dominated the debate. With the removal of communism as a serious contender as an alternative form of economic organization more attention was focused on different interpretations of capitalism. It was this that led Albert, Dussart and others to point out that capitalism, as practised in the USA, was a somewhat extreme form at variance with the approach followed in many other market-based economies. In short, the 'Anglo-Saxon' variant of capitalism as practised in the United States and, to a lesser extent, the United Kingdom emphasized the interplay of free market forces as the sole determinant of economic efficiency. It is this interpretation of capitalism which is mirrored in the marketing management concept.

Closer inspection revealed that while the United States and the United Kingdom, which practised Anglo-Saxon capitalism, had experienced declining competitiveness in the period following the Second World War, other market-driven economies had demonstrated superior growth and performance. Japan and West Germany fall into this category and evaluation of their underlying economic/political philosophy indicates a significant difference between what has been termed the Germanic-Alpine model of capitalism and the Anglo-Saxon version. These essential differences are summarized in Figure 2. In turn, these differences may be summarized as those that distinguish between an emphasis on the marketing management approach with its focus on the short-term transactional approach and the longer-term customer orientated philosophy which has been designated as relationship marketing.

During the 1990s the relationship marketing model has been seen increasingly as reflecting the essence of the marketing concept and the integration of culture, strategy and tactics. It is in this context that Webster sees the concept of customer value providing a mechanism for the integration of the three dimensions of marketing.

Webster claims that 'Marketing can be thought of as the design and management of all of the business processes necessary to define, develop, and deliver value to customers.' He then goes on to list those marketing processes in three major categories – value defining, value developing, and value delivering. Figure 3 summarizes the processes which Webster perceives as falling within these three categories.

In order to develop and manage these processes effectively calls for a highly flexible and dynamic organizational structure. It seems likely that traditional structures built around functions, products or markets are unlikely to meet these criteria particularly, as in the New

Value Defining Processes	Value Developing Processes	Value Delivering Processes
Market research – studies of customer needs, preferences, buying behaviour, product use, etc. Analysis of core competencies Strategic positioning of the firm in the value chain Economic analysis of customer use systems	New product development Design of distribution channels Development of procurement strategy Vendor selection Strategic partnering with service providers (e.g. Credit, database management, product service and disposal) Developing pricing strategy Developing the value proposition	Managing distribution in logistics Deployment of the field sales source Order entry, credit and post sales service Advertising and sales promotion Applications engineering Product upgrades and recalls Customer training

Figure 3 The three major categories of marketing processes
Source: Webster (1992)

Age, it is highly unlikely that any single organization will possess all the skills and resources necessary to maintain a sustainable competitive advantage. This being the case then organizations need to develop relationships not only with their customers but also with their suppliers and other interested constituencies.

While Webster does not explicitly say so his recommendations for future marketing organizations appear to be for a project-based structure. Under this concept teams would coalesce and form to address particular marketing challenges and opportunities and be responsible for the management of a product/market as it progresses through its life-cycle. Under such an organizational structure the skills and competencies of the project leader will be paramount. If, by education, training and experience, marketers are best suited to lead and manage interdisciplinary teams of other specialists, then in future perhaps the leaders of such teams will consider themselves to be 'marketers'. Ultimately, however, on the same basis that 'a rose by any other name would smell as sweet' perhaps those who believe in a customer orientation and the practice of marketing would feel more comfortable if they knew a less narrowly perceived label was attached to the project leader.

Even if the marketer or marketing specialist does not emerge as the project leader they will still have an important contribution to make in promoting a consumer orientation and implementing value delivery. Webster cites the work of management consultants, A.T. Kearney, who identified four key marketing processes based on their research at 26 major US companies. These processes are:

1. establishing a competitive position;
2. defining target markets and designing products/services to serve these markets;
3. delivering products/services to target markets;
4. creating and managing demand.

Webster also cites contributions by Thomas M. Beddow of the 3M Company at an MSI Seminar convened to discuss the futures of marketing. In the view of Beddow marketing 'competencies' encompass both process and capability and may be listed as follows:

Core marketing competencies

- *Planning* – defining the business and its customers.
- *Product development* – strategy for business unit growth.
- *Value pricing* – understanding the utility the customer places on the company's products and services.
- *Channel management* – developing and managing the institution through which the company goes to market.
- *Customer analysis* – analysing individuals, organizations, and institutions in terms of needs, desires and ability to buy.
- *Research* – gathering and interpreting market information for marketing decision making.
- *Brand management* – developing and managing strong global brands and corporate assets.

Advanced marketing competencies

- *International* – marketing products and services across national borders.
- *Financial analysis* – identifying profitable strategies that increase the lifetime value of the customer.
- *Strategic planning* – developing strategic fit between organizational goals and capabilities and changing market opportunities..
- *Quality function deployment* – translating customer inputs into design requirements.
- *Process management* – interrelating critical organizational functions in products development, manufacturing, selling and distribution.
- *Value added* – continually improving customer value.
- *Customer focused selling* – demonstrating a consistent ability to meet and exceed customer expectations.

Complementary marketing competencies

- *Team work* – ability to function as a member of a cross-functional team.
- *Interpersonal skills* – ability to listen and understand the needs of others, to manage conflict, and to convey information.

- *Marketing communications* – exchange of product information between buyers and sellers.
- *Computer literacy* – ability to use data retrieval systems, develop databases, apply computer-based models, etc.

Beddow's trilogy of competencies summarizes well current thinking on the future of marketing as we approach the millennium and reinforces Carson and Brown's neologism that 'marketing is what marketers perceive it to be'. Few, if any, would argue that the Core Marketing Competencies define the essence of the marketing function and the management of the marketing mix. However, the Advanced Marketing Competencies overlap the domain of other business disciplines and reflect a philosophy of business which is market oriented and customer driven. Acceptance and pursuit of these goals cannot be restricted solely to those who profess to be marketers. Similarly, the Complementary Marketing Competencies are fundamental to effective managerial practice irrespective of functional affiliation.

Given the scope and content of this Encyclopedia it is clear that managing the marketing function is more than enough to ensure marketing and marketers have a challenging future ahead of them. As to whether 'marketing' will be seen as the primary source of strategic thinking and business leadership that must surely depend both on what marketers perceive it to be *and* on what they do.

MICHAEL J. BAKER
UNIVERSITY OF STRATHCLYDE

Further reading

(References cited in the text marked *)

* Baker, Michael J. (ed.) (1993) *Perspectives on Marketing Management*, Vol. 3, Chichester: John Wiley & Sons.
* Baker, Michael J. and Hart, Susan J. (1989) *Marketing and Competitive Success*, London: Philip Allen.
* Bartels, R. (1962) *The Development of Marketing Thought*, Homewood: Richard D. Irwin.
* Bell, M.L. and Emory, C.W. (1971) 'The faltering marketing concept', *Journal of Marketing* 35: 37–42.
* Bennett, R.C. and Cooper, R.G. (1981) 'The misuse of marketing: an American tragedy', *Business Horizons* 24: 51–61.
* Brady, J. and Davis, l. (1993) 'Marketing's mid-life crisis', *McKinsey Quarterly* 2: 17–28.
* Brown, S. (1994) 'Sources and status of marketing theory', in Baker, M.J. (ed.), *Marketing: Theory and Practice*, 3rd edn, London: Macmillan.
* Carson, D. and Brown, S. (1994) 'Editorial', *Journal of Marketing Management* 10.8.
* Carter, C.F. and Williams, B.R. (1959) 'The characteristics of technically progressive firms', *Journal of Industrial Economics* March.
* Cyert, R.M. and March, J.G. (1963) *A Behavioural Theory of the Firm*, Englewood Cliffs, NJ: Prentice-Hall.
* Drucker, Peter (1954) *The Practice of Management*, New York: Harper & Row.
* Dussart, Christian (1994) 'Capitalism versus capitalism', in Baker, Michael J. (ed.), *Perspectives on Marketing Management*, Vol. 4, Chichester: John Wiley & Sons.
* Freeling, A. (1994) 'Marketing is in crisis – can market research help?', *Journal of the Market Research Society* 36: 97–104.
* Fullerton, Ronald A. (1988) 'How modern is modern marketing?', *Journal of Marketing*.
* Grönroos, Christian (1993) 'Quo vadis, marketing', invited paper, European Marketing Academy, Annual Conference, Barcelona, May.
* Gummesson, E. (1993) 'Broadening and specifying relationship marketing', invited paper, Monash Colloquium on Relationship Marketing, Monash University, Melbourne, Australia, 1–4 August.
* Handy, Charles (1990) *The Age of Unreason*, Boston: Harvard Business School Press.
* Howard, J.A. (1957) *Marketing Managemement: Analysis and Planning*, Homewood, IL: Richard D. Irwin, Inc.
* Johnston, Russell and Lawrence, Paul R. (1988) 'Beyond vertical integration – the rise of the value-adding partnership', *Harvard Business Review* 66: 94–101.
* Keith, R.J. (1960) 'The marketing revolution', *Journal of Marketing* 24: 35–8.
* Kotler, Philip (1967) *Marketing Management: Analysis, Planning and Control*, Englewood Cliffs, NJ: Prentice-Hall.
* Lehmann, Donald R. and Jocz, Katherine E. (eds) (1997) *Reflections on the Futures of Marketing*, Cambridge, MA: Marketing Science Institute.
* Levitt, T. (1960) 'Marketing myopia', *Harvard Business Review* July–August.
* McCarthy, E. Jerome (1960) *Basic Marketing: A Managerial Approach*, Homewood, IL: Richard D. Irwin, Inc.
* McKitterick, J.B. (1957) 'What is the marketing management concept?', in Bass, F.M. (ed.), *The Frontiers of Marketing Thought and Science*, Chicago: American Marketing Association: 71–82.

* March, J.G. and Simon, H.A. (1958) *Organization*, New York, NY: John Wiley.
* Marion, G. (1993) 'The marketing management discourse: what's new since the 1960s?', in Baker, Michael J. (ed.), *Perspectives on Marketing Management*, Vol. 3, Chichester: John Wiley & Sons.
* Miles, R.E. and Snow, C.C. (1978) *Organizational Strategy, Structure and Process*, New York, NY: McGraw-Hill.
* Ohmae, Kenichi (1989) 'The global logic of strategic alliances', *Harvard Business Review* 67: 143–54.
* Swartz, G.S. (1990) 'Organising to become market-driven', Conference Summary, Marketing Science Institute, Cambridge, MA., 13–14 September.
* Tedlow, Richard S. (1990) *New and Improved: The Story of Mass Marketing in America*, Oxford: Heinemann.
* Tedlow, Richard S. and Jones, Geoffrey (eds) (1993) *The Rise and Fall of Mass Marketing*, London: Routledge.
* Thorelli, Hans R. (1986) 'Networks: between markets and hierarchies', *Strategic Management Journal* 7: 37–51.
* Tosdal, H.R. (1933) 'Some recent changes in the marketing of consumer goods', *Harvard Business Review* 2, January.
* Webster, F.E. Jr. (1992) 'The changing role of marketing in the corporation', *Journal of Marketing* October: 1–17.
* Weigand, Robert (1962) 'How extensive is the planning and development program?', *Journal of Marketing* 3: 55–7.
* Wilson, M. and McDonald, M. (1994) 'Marketing at the crossroads – a comment', *Marketing Intelligence and Planning* 12: 41–5.

Index

Aaker, D.A. 757
academic status 795
Academy of Marketing Science (AMS) 26
Academy of Marketing, UK 558
accomplishment 62
accumulation behaviour 61–2
Achrol, Ravi S. 199, 201, 202
acquisition
    government 423
    manufacturing 423
    retail 458
ACR *see* Association of Consumer Research
added value
    advertising 498, 501
    Internet 480
    packaging/design 368
administration, organizational services 605
advanced marketing 829
advantage, sustainable 162, 463
advertising 39, 41, 319, 475–8, 486, 488, **494–504**, 496, 539–40
    banner 482
    buying 494
    controls 503–4
    direct marketing 466, 469
    economy 503
    effects 87
    ethical issues 659, 661
    false 251
    generic 587
    history 21, 23–4
    image 475, 478
    influence of 45–6
    management 679
    micromarketing 229–31
    PCI 721
    people involved 495
        advertiser 495
        advertising agency 496
        media 496
        research 496
    planning 494
    pricing 401
    process 498
        budget setting 499–500
        campaign evaluation 502–3
        creativity/creative brief 500
        developing/pre-testing 500–1
        media brief/planning/buying 502
        production 501–2
        strategy 498–9
    profitability 467
    promotions 510
    public opinion 503
    retail 456
    statistics 494–5
        international comparisons 496
advertising agencies 495–6, 497
advertising associations 504
Advertising Council 674
Advertising Standards authority 503–4
affiliation group retailers 448–9
affordability 507
after sales service, green marketing 714
Agarwal, M.K. 758
agencies, advertising 495–6, 497
agricultural commodities 582
AID *see* automatic interaction detection
AIDA *see* Attention Interest Desire Action
Alderson, Wroe 65
alienation 800
Alldays 447
alliances 820
    collaboration 778–9
    customer-supplier 782–3
    drawbacks 785
    efficiencies/cost reductions 783–5
    formation drivers 777–8
    motives 781–2
    objectives 779–80
    strategic 776–90
Alpine model, marketing 744
Alpine/Germanic capitalism model 13
AMA *see* American Marketing Association
AMA Winter Educators' Conference 816, 817
Amazon.com 478, 480, 481
American Marketing Association (AMA) 20, 26, 332, 558, 800–1, 816
AMS *see* Academy of Marketing Science
analogue methods, retail location 454
analysis
    competitor 257–8
    conjoint 96, 399
    correspondence 14

Index

cost reduction 418
cost-benefit 672
customer 829
green marketing 703
new products 345–6
regression 90–1, 94, 772
situational 176–8, 705–8
statistical 819
transaction cost 39
vulnerability 179
Anderson, Erin 196
Anderson, J.C. 784
Anglo-Saxon capitalism model 13, 828
Ansoff, H.I. 245, 247, 340
anti-theory 806
Apple Computer example 380
AQRP *see* Associationn of Qualitative Research Practitioners
Aquillar, F.S. 243–5
archetypal organizational forms 196
arm's length relationships 144
Arndt, J. 798–800
Arndt, Johan 66, 122
assets
   goodwill 537–8
   intangible 759
   specificity 44
   TQM 700
   transaction specific 105–6
Association of Consumer Research (ACR) 26
Associationn of Qualitative Research Practitioners (AQRP) 766
assortment convenience, wholesalers 438
Attention Interest Desire Action (AIDA) model 488, 510–11
attitudes, public relations 533–4, 535
audits
   market 268
   marketing 268–77, 571–2, 574
Austin, Nancy 463
automated information capture 227
automatic interaction detection (AID) 94–5
Avis 538

backward research 672
Bagozzi, Richard P. 36
bahavioural school, corporate identity 741
Baker, Michael J. 4, 7, 10, 13, 743, 780, 795
Balanced Scorecard 759–60
Baldridge National Quality Award, USA 609–10, 698
Balmer, J.M.T. 737, 738
banking, franchising 608

Banks, Seymour 469–70
barriers, TQM 695
Bartels, Robert 35
Baudrillard, Jean 805–6
Beare, S. 587
Beddow, Thomas M. 829
behaviour
   channel management 418
   company 535–6
   consumer 670–1
   customer 257
   elementary 52–3
   opportunistic 105
   patterns 769
Behavioural Perspective Model 57–8
   application of 60–3
   hierarchy of consumer lifestyles 58–60
benchmarks 754
benefits, environmental 704–5
Benetton 458
Berry, L.L. 557
BFA *see* British Franchise Association
Birkigt, K. 744
black economy 73
Blackwell, R.D. 115, 116–18
Bleeke, J. 788
BMW 378, 384
boardrooms
   reputation appraisal 536–7
   TQM 694–5
Borden, Neil 10–11, 319
Boston Consulting Group (BCG) 180, 193, 356, 377
boundaries, environmental 246
boundary-less organization 780
bounded rationality 41–2
Box-Jenkins procedure, sales forecasting 280
Boyatzis, R.E. 558
BQF *see* British Quality Foundation
brand equity 41, 761
   customer-based 757–8
   financial approach 756–7
   performance 755–8
brand franchise 759
brand loyalty
   consumer 505–6
   declining 507
brand management 496, 829
brand mix
   coherent 380
   information hierarchy 381–2
   service industries 386
brand names 41, 719

Index

PCI 721
brand value 537–8
branding **376–88**
   commodities 590
   corporate 385
   service industries 386
brands 376
   added value 368–9
   advertising 498
   concept management 40
   consumer problem solving 119
   corporate 738
   cross-country harmonization 374
   differentiation 165
   features
      coherent mix 380
      distinctive added value 379–80
      highest common factors 378–9
      spiritual reward 379
      summary 381
      value performance 377–8
   future 388
   hierarchy of information 381–2
   history review 500
   loyalty 121
   management 386–8
   packaging/design equities 371–2
   positioning 370–1
   price promotion 402
   product life-cycle 359
   qualitative research 766
   range extension 382–4, 385–6
   retail 455
   stretch 383–4
   structures 384–6
   value
      companies 377
      consumers 376–7
break-even analysis, pricing 392
briefs, advertising 500, 502
British Airways 534
British Franchise Association (BFA) 608
British Quality Foundation (BQF) 698
Bronder, C. 781
Brown, S. 453, 825–6
Bucklin, L.P. 332–3
budget management 679
budget setting
   advertising 499
      broad history review 500
      ratio to sales 500
      reviews 499–500
budgeting
   approaches 672
   baseline establishment 213–15
   behavioural issues 218–19
   dangers 219–20
   flexible 217–18
   locating 210–13
   master budget development 215–16
   planning 675
   scope/nature of 208–10
budgets marketing communications 490
bulk-breaking, wholesalers 438
Bulkeley, William M. 471
bundling, commodities 589
bureaucratic structures 196
business analysis, new products 345–6
Business Excellence Model
   design/quality 698
   self-assessment 698
business format franchising 616–17
business market
   characteristics 592–5
   defined 592–4
business marketing **592–602**
   relationships 594–5
business planning 573–5
business portfolio 337–9
   cash cow 338
   dogs 338
business processes, marketing strategy 172–3
businesses
   definition 640–1
   domestic 641
   global 642
   interdomestic 641
   regional 641–2
   success 776
   wholesaler relationships 437–9
buyer behaviour, pricing 392–5
buyer-seller relationship 594–5, 596
buyer-supplier link 780–1
buyers 13
   PCI 723–4
buygrid 131
buying
   advertising 494, 502
   influences 133
      environmental 133–4
      individual 136
      interpersonal 135–6
      organizational 134–5
   modified rebuy 131–3
   newbuy 131–3
   organizational behaviour **128–36**

835

Index

retail 454–5
straight rebuy 130–3
TQM 695
buying centre 139
Buzzell, Robert D. 336, 795

c-stores *see* convenience stores
CAD *see* computer-assisted design
Cadbury, Sir Adrian 535
CAM systems 13
campaigns
    delegation 492–3
    evaluation 502–3
    marketing communications 488–90
CAP *see* Common Agricultural Policy
CAPI *see* computer aided personal interviewing
capital projects, exports 632–3
capitalism, Anglo-Saxon 828
Caples, John 469
capture the client strategy 304
Carson, D. 826
case studies 771
cash cows
    business portfolio 338
    product life-cycle 360
CASI *see* computer aided self completion interviewing
catalogues
    home shopping 459
    printing 481
    showroom 459–60
Cateora, Philip R. 47
Caterpillar Tractor Corporation 410
CATI *see* computer aided telephone interviewing
causal relationships, budget planning 220
cause-and-effect relationships, true experiments 468–70
cellular organizations 202
central route to persuasion 475–8
centralization, purchasing 141–2
change, social 72–3
channel design 411
    alternative structures 412
    optimal structure 412–13
    setting objectives 411
    specifying functions 411–12
channel functions *see* distribution functions
channel management **407–18**, 829
    basic areas 408–9
        coordination with marketing mix 415–16

    design structure 411–13
    evaluation of member performance 417
    member motivation 414–15
    member selection 413–14
    strategy formulation 409–10
    nature of 407
    perspectives 408
    trends 417
        behavioural perspective 418
        cost reduction analysis 418
        partnerships/alliances 418
        strategy 417–18
        technology 418
channel members
    leadership 415
    motivation 414
    needs/problems 414–15
    performance evaluation 417
    selection criteria 105, 413–14
    support for 415
channel partnerships 234
channel strategy 409
    competitive parity 410
    distribution neglect 410
    synergy 410
    target market 409–10
channels of distribution 43, **100–12**
    defined 100–1
    determinants 103–6
    electronic 109–10
        advantages/disadvantages 110
    ethical issues 659
    flows 107–8
    information technology 231
    management 407–18, 677–8
    relationships 151–2
    as social systems 108–9
    structure 101–2
        intensity 103, 412
        length 102–3
        types of intermediaries 103
    trends 110–11
        partnerships/strategic alliances 111
        retailers 111
        role of technology 111–12
        strategic emphasis 111
        vertical marketing systems 111
    wholesalers 432–42
Chartered Institute of Marketing 532, 558
check-out scanning, retail 457
checklists
    marketing audit 270–1
    retail location 454

chief executives, TQM 691–2
chief marketing executive (CME) 192–3
China 82
choice 4, 41–2
  consumers 37
Christiansen, Clayton M. 166
Chrysler 786
Churchill, G.A. 529
Citibank 303–4
Claritas Prizm lifestyle segmentation 304
Clarke, Darral G. 474
classification, strategic alliances 780
classified advertising 495
client-server systems/groupware 226–7
closure, consumer behaviour setting 60–1
clubs 509
cluster analysis 96
CME *see* chief marketing executive
Coca-Cola example 376
cocooning 766
Code of Ethics, BFA 619
cognitive psychology 42, 52, 52–3
collaborations 778–9, 781
Collins, Tom 466
comfort level, franchisees 620
commercial bribery 660–1
commercial success, corporate reputation 533
commercialization, new products 347
commitment, TQM 691–2
commodities **579–90**, 803
  agricultural 582
  defined 579–80
  development 581–2, 588–90
  futures 584–5
  marketing 583–4
  promotion 586–8
  trading 582–3
Common Agricultural Policy (CAP) 582
communication 777, 830
  advertising 498
  campaign 488–90
  direct marketing 462–3
  exhibitions 543
  green marketing 714–15
  integrity in 534
  Internet 483
  marketing 486–93
  marketing channels 107–8
  non-profit organizations 678–9
  positive 527–8
  product/corporate brand distinction 739
  promotion instruments 323, 326
  promotions 510, 512

TQM 689, 695
companies
  behaviour 535–6
  driving force, identification of 642
  export decisions 626–9
  internationalization process 626–7
  PCI 727–8
  strategic marketing planning 178–9
  support 535
company name, PCI 721
competencies
  advanced marketing 829
  complementary marketing 829–30
  core 148, 172, 203, 777, 783, 829
  marketing 558–9
  world class logistics 428–9
competition 166–7, 827
  channel strategy 410
  differentiation 166
  global 639
  green marketing 707, 709
  monopolistic 38
  new products 343
  non-profit organizations 668
  pricing 166, 395–6
  product life-cycle 361
  public relations 536
  spatial 42
  strategic marketing planning 178
competitions 508
competitive advantage 776, 777–8
  achieving 163–4
  building 162–3
  green marketing 708
  logistics 431
  positioning 313
  pricing 395–6
  sustainable 38, 162
competitive strategies
  direct marketing 464–5
  international markets 642–4
competitors
  analysis 257–8
  depositioning 314–15
  metrics 764
  sales forecasting 283
  strategic triangle 165–7
complementary marketing 829–30
complementary pricing 398
complements, product 40
complex approach, environment 196
complex flux model 9–10

837

Index

computer aided personal interviewing (CAPI) 261
computer aided self completion interviewing (CASI) 261
computer aided telephone interviewing (CATI) 261
computer intensive quantitative methods 97–8
computer literacy 830
computer-assisted design (CAD) 13, 228
computers, qualitative research 773
concentration, global markets 651
concentric networks 202–3
concepts 64
concessions, retail 458
conflict
   distribution channels 109
   ethical 660, 662, 665
   franchisor/franchisee relationship 618–19
   personal selling 518
   social 72
conjoint analysis 96
   price setting 399
consolidation, global marketing 650
consortia 631–2
consumer behaviour **114–25**
   costs, rewards, exchange 53–7
   decision making 116–18
      levels of complexity 118–22
      purchasing 122–3
   elementary 52–3
   environmental concern 124–5
   future developments 123–5
   macro-level 114
   management of 60–1
   micro-level 114
   purchasing 122–3
   research 114–16
consumer goods, wholesalers' approach 439–41
consumer public relations 538
consumer sovereignty test (CST) 665
consumers 37–8, 41, 822
   behaviour 670–1
   brand loyalty 377, 378
   choice 37
   green marketing 707, 712–13
   heterogeneity 394–5
   hierarchy of lifestyles 58–60
   Internet relationships 479–80
   metrics 763–4
   price perceptions 390, 392–3, 393–5
   sales promotions 505–6
   targeting 515

   wholesalers 432
consumption 43
   psychology of 54–7
   reversed 812–13
   theory 805–6
contact efficiency 105
content analysis 767
context, marketing communications 490
contingency models 196
contingency planning 184–5
Continuous Improvement cycle 694
contracts
   commodities 589
   franchisor/franchisee relationship 618–19
control 668
   advertising 491
   green marketing 717
   marketing channel 678
   marketing strategies 680–1
   strategic marketing 673
convenience stores 447–8
conversion studies, tracking systems 466–8
Cook, Victor 336
cooperation 776
   motives 781–2
cooperative societies 449
coordinating flows, distribution channels 108
coordination
   advertising/public relations 539–40
   direct marketing 473–4
   green marketing 717
   logistics 424
   marketing channel 678
   markets 151
   networks 154
Copeland, Melvin T. 332
Copenhagen School 12
core competencies 148, 203, 777
   marketing strategy 172
   strategic alliances 783
core marketing 829
core strategy, development 671–2
Corey, Edward R. 189
corporate brand 385, 738
corporate identity **732–45**
   behavioural school 741
   defined 733
   development 737–8
   European 738
   historical perspective 735–40
   management 733–5, 740–3
   purpose 733
   strategic school 740–1

Index

theory 743–5
total communications schol 741–3
visual school 743
corporate image 732, 735, 737
corporate personality, projection 532
corporate planning 573–5
corporate projection 538
corporate reputation 737
   commercial success 533
corporate support, non-profit organizations 674
corporate/industry marketing, history 24
corporations
   new product prosperity 342–3
   reputations 536–7
   strategic triangle 167–8
correspondence analysis 14
cost leadership
   international markets 643
   product policy 333
   success 709
cost reductions 790
   partnerships/alliances 783–5
cost-benefit analysis 672
cost-effectiveness
   advertising 507
   marketing communication 491
costs
   channel management 418
   customers 784
   fixed/variable 167–8
   perceived 677
   pricing 391–2, 395
   psychology of 53–7
Council of American Survey Research Organizations 657
Council of Logistics Management 420
countertrade 632
countries, PCI 728
coupons
   gift 508
   money-off 507
CP *see* customer portfolio
craft industry 6
creative brief, advertising 500
creativity
   advertising 500
   grounded theory 772
credit, wholesalers 438
crisis of representation paradox 813
critical processes
   identification 693
   TQM 688

critical success factors (CSFs) 179, 685
critical theory 806
cross-border alliances, retail 458
cross-functional teams, new products 351
CST *see* consumer sovereignty test
culture **76–84**, 820
   corporate 203
   defined 76
   dynamic 82–3
   and globalization of markets 81–2
   overcoming problems of 77–9
   problems of 76–7
   respect for 79–80
   utilization of 80–1
customer analysis 829
customer care/satisfaction **550–60**, 680
   balanced 555
   core/peripheral product 556
   dimensions 553–4
   expectations 553
   future 558–60
   implementation 557–8
   integrated 559–60
   internal customers 557
   key components 556
   measurement 554–5
   origins 550–1
   peripheral aspects 556
   relationship marketing 557
   scope 551–5
   service 608
   TQM/total systems 557
   variables 556
customer focused selling 829
customer needs, new products 343
customer orientation
   exhibitions 542
   strategic marketing 668–9
customer portfolio (CP), management 597–602
customer relations 538
customer response model 472
customer satisfaction *see* customer care/satisfaction
customer service
   logistics 427
   TQM 696
   wholesalers 438
customer-marketer IMC relationship 474–5
   central route to persuasion 475–8
   exposure to advertising 475
customer-supplier alliances 776, 780, 782–3
   three 'I's 789–90

Index

customer-supplier relationship 598, 685
customers
    attitutes towards 534
    best 464
    brand equity 757–8
    costs 784
    interaction 607
    internal 749
    Internet 482
    long-term relationships 463–4
    new offerings 677
    new products 351
    PCI 722
    personal selling 520
    product life-cycle 360–1
    requirement logistics 420–1, 430
    requirements, quality 685–6, 687, 690
    research 256–7
    response to inquiries 477–8
    sales forecasting 283
    service delivery involvement 676
    strategic marketing planning 177
    strategic triangle 164–5
    wholesalers' support 437

DAGMAR 488
data collection
    cross-sectional data 90
    interpretation 179–80
    primary research 260
        diaries 261
        electronic 261–2
        group discussions 261
        Hall tests 262
        Internet 262–3
        interview 260–1
        mail questionnaire 261
        observation techniques 262
    qualitative research 768–70
    secondary research 259–60
    time-series models 90
data evaluation, performance monitoring 467–8
data mining 304
database marketing 229–30
Davidson, W.R. 447
Day, George 186, 194
Dean, Joel 10
Debenhams 451
decentralization 820
decentred subjects 813
decision making
    attitudes 533–4
    complex approach 116–18

    levels 118–22
computer assisted 232–3
consumer behaviour 116–18
ethical 663
non-profit organization 671
PCI 723–4
positioning 312–13
segment identification 294–6
deductive research 767, 768
DeFillippi, R.J. 169
delegation, campaign management 492–3
delivery quality 609
delivery services 607–8
Dell Corporation 410, 478, 479–80, 601
Delphi method, sales forecasting 279–80
demand 9
    commodities 581–2
    non-profit organizations 673
    product life-cycle 359
    and supply 40–1, 43, 44
demarketing 320
Deming, W. Edwards 694
deontological theories 662
department stores 451
dependent variables 220–2
deregulation, public services 605, 612
design **368–74**
    added value 368
    agencies 373–4
    category rules 369
    equities protection 371–2
    experts 373–4
    quality 609
    services 608
    TQM 698
development
    new products 346
    sales promotion 506–7
Dewbre, J. 587
Dhalla, G.S. 337
diagnostic studies 766
differentiation
    brand 165
    commodities 579–80, 589–90
    competitive 166
    green marketing 708, 709
    international markets 643–4
    new product failure 350
    new product success 350
    product policy 333
diffusion of innovations 72–3, 115
direct marketing 231–2, **462–84**, 486
    benefits/opportunities 463–73

840

Index

defined 462
design/implementation 478–84
problems 473–5
strategies 462
Direct Marketing Association 462
direct price discrimination 397
direct response
   advertising 476–7
   mechanisms 462–3
direct salespeople 520–1
discount pricing/sales 507
discounters 452–3
Disneyland, Paris 611
display advertising 495
distribution 9, 12
   chains 442
   channel strategy 410
   channels *see* channels of distribution
   ethical concerns 660
   green marketing 715
   industrial 441–2
   intensive/selective/exclusive 412
   international marketing 647
   logistics 427–8
distribution functions 103–4
   assortment 104
   discrepancies, quantity 104
   economics 105
      specialization/division of labour 105
      transaction efficiency 105
   management control of 105–6
   space 104–5
   time 104
distributors, green marketing 707
diversification 181
divestment strategy 182
   decline phase 366
division of labour 44, 105
documents, franchising 617
dogs
   branding 377
   business portfolio 338
domestic business 641
down-sizing 820
Doyle, Peter 188
Drucker, Peter 10, 13, 39, 338, 407
Dulux example 381–2
Dunhill example 380, 383
dynamic psychology 52
dynamics, pricing models 400–1

early adopters group 677
early majority group 677

ecological model 563
ecological psychologists 60
ecology, green marketing 705, 708, 709–10, 712
economic growth, Rostow's stages 4–5
economics 35, **35–47**, 822
   as foundation of marketing 35–6
   go/kill decision models 347–9
   history of development 24
   of information 41–2
   laws of 5
   primary commodities policy 582
economies of scale, commodities 580
economies of scope 105
ECR *see* efficient consumer response
EDI *see* electronic data interchange
education, TQM 695
effective marketing, definitions 753–5
effectiveness
   leadership 692–6
   marketing communication 257
   measurement 680–1
   of networks 203
   packaging 373
   sales promotions 516
efficiencies 44
   partnerships/alliances 783–5
efficiency gains, alliances 779
efficient consumer response (ECR) 112
El Corte Inglés 451
elasticities
   customer 165
   price 43
electronic commerce 601–2
electronic data collection 261–2
electronic data interchange (EDI) 227
   distribution channels 109–10, 112
electronic point-of-sale (EPOS) 262
electronic shopping 460
   future possibilities 461
   interactive cable television systems 460
   Internet sites 460
   shopping channels 460
   Videotex Services 460
elementary marketing behaviour 52–3
employees
   empowerment 693
   internal relationships 748–9
   vision 749–51
empowerment
   effective 693
   employees 610
end users, metrics 763–4

Index

enduring involvement, consumers 120
Engel, J.F. 115, 116–18
enhanced purchase consumption experience 477
entry model 86
entry strategies
   retail internationalization
      acquisition 458
      concessions 458
      franchising 458
      joint venture 458
      self-start 458
environment
   analysis **238–50**
   green marketing 712–16, 717
   influence on buying process 133–4
   information needs 241–3
   marketing organization 186, 196
   non-profit organizations 669
   pricing 390–1
   product policy 334
   sales forecasting 283
   selling 456
   services marketing 607
   volatile 200–1
environmental benefit 704–5
environmental concern, consumer behaviour 124–5
environmental contingencies 196
environmental factors, franchising 615
environmental packaging 372, 373
environmental protection 702–3
environmental scanning 238
   contribution 239
   development 243–5
   models
      continuous 245
      irregular 245
      periodic 245
   paradox 245
   procedures/pitfalls 245–6
      appropriate time horizon 246–7
      defining boundaries 246
      degree of formality 248–9
      responsibility 247–8
      strategy making 249–50
   scope of 239–41
EPOS *see* electronic point-of-sale
EPS *see* extended problem solving
EQA *see* European Quality Award
equities, packaging/design protection 371–2
Ernst, D. 788
estimation
   model 90–1
   strategic marketing 673
ethical reasoning 662
ethics
   conflicts 660, 662, 665
   marketing 653–66
   organizational 665–6
ethos factor 744
EU *see* European Union
European Foundation for Quality Management 698
European Quality Award (EQA) 698
European School 11
European Union (EU)
   commodities 582
   franchising 608
   service infrastructure 611
evaluation 668, 679, 680–1
   advertising campaigns 502–3
   channel members 417
   exhibitions 546–7
   media 475
   sales promotions 516
   salesforce performance 528–9
   strategic marketing 673
evaluation of strategies 183
   commercial viability 184
   desirability 183–4
   practical feasibility 184
evolution
   future prospects 823–6
   markets 360–2
      decline 364–6
      emerging 363
      high growth 363–4
      mature 364
exchange 5, 7
   marketing as 36–7
   non-profit organizations 670
   psychology of 53–7
   relationship approach 150, 151, 156
   social 65–6
exhibitions **541–8**
   communication tool 543
   evaluation difficulties 547
   export tool 544
   globalization 547–8
   importance 543
   information 548
   role 542
      market research 543
      relationship building 542–3
      selling 542

strategy 544
   evaluation 546–7
   post-show activity 546
   pre-exhibition activity 545
   selecting 544–5
   setting objectives 544
   special in-booth promotions 545–6
   staffing 545
technological change 547
types 541
   customer orientation 542
   geographical reach 541–2
   market coverage 542
experience curve
   costs dynamics 166
   pricing 397
experiencing man 800
experimentation, causal relationships 220–2
experiments, PCI 723
expert systems 233
experts
   design/packaging 373–4
   sales forecasting 279–80, 285–6
exploratory studies 766
exporters 626
exporting **624–35**
   capital projects 632–3
   company decisions 626–9
   consortia 631–2
   defined 624–5
   documentation 624
   exhibitions 544
   franchising 633–4
   government support 629–31
   growth 624
   involvement 625–6
   market choice 627
   market entry method 627–9
   over time 629
   research 625
   success 634
exports
   barriers/motivators 626
   franchising 633–4
extended problem solving (EPS) 119
external environment 177
external influences, franchising 621–2
external marketing 747

facilitating factors, internationalization 458
factor analysis 96
Factory Outlet Centres 451
facts, budgets 218

failures
   alliances 786
   new products 343, 349–50
false advertising 251
family, decision-making unit 115–16
fast moving consumer goods (FCMG) 506
FCMG *see* fast moving consumer goods
Federal Trade Commission (FTC) 251–2, 661
film production commercials 502
finance, wholesalers 438
finance flows, distribution channels 107
financial analysis 167–8, 829
financial approach, brand equity 756–7
financial approaches, marketing performance 758–9
financial flows, logistics value chains 424–5
financial metrics 764
financial options 169
financial performance, measurement 754–5
financial summary 566
Firat, A. Fuat 22, 813
First Direct 539
fit 772–3
flexibility, new product development 353
flexible manufacturing 13
flexible organization 201, 820
flowcharts
   new product development 353
   service 608
flows 107
   coordinating 108
   finance 107
   information 107–8
   inventory 422, 423–4
   material 139
   negotiation 107
   product 107
   promotion 108
   retail 457
   title 107
   wholesalers' participation 432, 435
FOB strategy 397
focus, involvement 120
focus group interviews 770
focus strategies, new products 350, 353
Ford 377, 384
Ford, Henry 7
forecasting
   estimation prediction intervals 287
   evaluating/selecting methods 286–7
   implementation 287
      acceptance 287–8
   methods 278

Index

bootstrapping 280
Delphi procedure 279–80
econometric 281
expert systems 280, 281
extrapolation 280
intentions studies 278–9, 280
multivariate time-series 281
role-playing 279
rule-based 280–1
non-profit organizations 673
sales 278–88
foreign markets
entry methods 627–9
franchising 621–2
Four Ps 11–12, 12, 13, 486, 491, 606
basic typology 322–3
explications/extensions 326–7, 606
Foxall, G.R. 63, 116
fragmentation 812
franchisees
associations/councils 620–1
comfort level 620
multi-unit 620
perspective 615, 616
selection 617
franchises 449
franchising **613–22**
components 617
documents 617
ongoing support 617–18
'pilot' 617
selection 617
defined 613
downside 616
exports 633–4
external influences 621–2
future 621–2
history/development 613–15
internal influences 622
retail 458
services 611
socioeconomic influences/third parties 615–16
trends 620–1
franchisor/franchisee relationship 618
conflict/contract 618–19
protection 619–20
franchisors
perspective 615, 616
recruitment/funding criteria 621
Frankel, R. 784
frequency marketing 464
Fritzsche, David J. 663

front-line, service 607
FTC *see* Fderal Trade Commission; Federal Trade Commission
Fullerton, Ronald A. 8–10, 22, 821
functional productivity 759
functional quality 608
funding, franchisors 621
fundraising, non-profit organizations 673–4

Galbraith, John Kenneth 7, 44, 45–6
game theory 39
Ganesan, S. 787
gaps model 609
Gatignon, Hubert 40
GATT *see* General Agreement on Tariffs and Trade
General Agreement on Tariffs and Trade (GATT) 630
General Electric (GE) 180, 247
generic marketing
commodities 587
competition strategies 182
customer-supplier alliances 776
mix functions 320–1
services 606, 610
geographic information, retail location 454
geographic market
interconnectedness 648–9
scope 641–2
similarity 649
geographic pricing 397
geographical reach, exhibitions 541–2
geographical salesforce specialization 521
geography, promotion 515
German Circular Economy and Waste Disposal Law 711
German Historical School of Economics 35
German model, marketing 744
Ghemawat, P. 169
Gibson, Helen *et al* 14–15
gift coupons 508
Glaser, B.G. 769
global business 642
global marketing **639–52**
consolidation 650
developments 639–40
strategy 640–2
global portfolio, configuration 648–51
global sourcing 639
global strategic thrust
competitive strategy 642–4
defined 642–5
market scope/segmentation 644–5

global strategies, evolutionary 46
globalization 46–7
    culture 81–2
    design/packaging 374
    exhibitions 547
    segmentation 303–5
glocalization 374
go/kill decision points 347–9
goals *see* objectives
Goldberg, R.A. 589
goods, services distinction 605
goodwill, public relations 537
Gordon, R. 765
governments
    exporting role 629–31
    PCI 728–9
Grabowski, Henry G. 45
graphic design, corporate image 735
green marketing 124–5, **702–17**
    approaches 704–5
    implementation 716–17
    strategic planning 708–10
Green, P.E. 123–4
Green Report Card, USA 712
Greyser, Stephen 193, 818
Grönroos, Christian 11, 12, 13, 609, 804
grounded theory 769, 771–2
    mobilizing creativity 772
    philosophical assumptions 772
    regression 772
growth
    global markets 651
    retail cycles 445–7
    strategy 181
growth vector matrix, product policy 339–41
guarantees 509
Gummesson, Evert 11, 609

Hair, J.H. 231
Hakansson, H. 171
halo constructs, PCI 725
Hamel, G. 172
Hannaford, W.J. 439
Hanson, Lord 534
Harley-Davidson 80–1
harvesting strategy 182
    decline phase 365
Haynes 410
Hayward, Roger 534
Heeler, Roger M. 41
Heide, J.B. 787
Heilbronner, Robert L. 43
Henderson, Sir Denys 534

heterogeneity
    markets 151
    networks 153–4
    services 605
hierarchies
    brand information 381–2
    breaking 198
Hierarchy of Effects 488
Hilmer, F.G. 783–4
historical research 18, **18–26**
    early period 20
    as emerging discipline 21–2
    foundations 20
    future of 26
    marketing history 23–4
    marketing thought 19–20
    methodology 19, 22
    omissions 18–19
historical review
    brands 500
    strategic planning 176–9
history 801
HJ Heinz 377, 384
hollow corporation 199, 201
home shopping 459–60
Honda motors 409–10
Hong Kong 82–3
horizontal shows, exhibitions 542
Howard, J.A. 119
Hudson, M.A. 588–9
human resources, retail 456
Hunt, S.D. 787, 797–8
Hunt, Shelby D. 662
hybrid strategies, international markets 644
hypermarkets 451–2
hyperreality 812

IBM 179–80, 193, 535
idea generation, new product process 345
identity, corporate **732–45**
image, corporate 732, 735, 737
image advertising 475, 478
image pricing 397
image-building, green marketing 709
image/identity interface 738
images, product origins 719–30
IMC *see* integrated marketing
    communications
IMP *see* Industrial Marketing and Purchasing
implementation, strategic marketing 674–5
improved payment terms 508
impulse purchasing 507
in-depth interviews 770

Index

inbound logistics 423–4
independent
  agents 520–1
  retailers 447
  variables 220–2
indifference curve 37
inductive research 768, 769, 772–3
industrial goods, wholesalers' approach 441–2
Industrial Marketing and Purchasing (IMP) 12
industrial markets 593
  analysis 263–5
industrial organization (IO) 38–9
Industrial Revolution 6–7, 10
infant formula selling 79–80, 84
influence
  franchising 621–2
  promotion of 45–6
information
  asymmetrical 41
  commodities 585–6
  creation/scheduling 62
  customer processing 477–8
  economics of 41–2
  environmental 241–3
  exhibitions 548
  geographic 454
  green marketing 712
  Internet 482–3
  marketing audit 271–4
  for marketing planning 256–8
  new economics of 198
  promotion of 45
  promotional 508–9
  retail 456–7
  segmentation strategies 304
  sharing 784, 786–7
  strategic marketing 672–3
  TQM 689
  wholesalers 437
information flows
  distribution channels 107–8
  logistics value chains 424
information processing, and marketing organization 189
Information Resources Incorporated 232
information technology (IT) 13, 195, **225–35**
  automated information capture 227
  client-server systems/groupware 226–7
  consumer behaviour 124
  distribution channels 231
  electronic data interchange (EDI) 227
  future of marketing 234–5
  growth in direct marketing 231–2
  Internet 227–8
  key developments 225
    data storage 226
    display 226
    networks 226
    processing 226
    software 226
    wireless systems 226
  marketing decision support systems 232–3
  marketing programmes 228
    advertising/promotion 229–31
    pricing 228–9
    product design/development 228
    salesforce 'automation' 229
  purchasing management 148
  redesigning processes 233
    channel partnerships 234
    new product development 233–4
  salesforce operations 523
infrastructure, service 611
innovation 677, 790
  diffusion of 72–3, 115
  measurement 755
  metrics 764
  new product 352
  new products 352–3
  packaging 369–70
innovativeness 151
  heterogenous networks 154
innovators, non-profit organizations 677
input-output relationships, budgets 212
inseparability, services 605
insourcing 148, 154
instrumental man 799
intangibility, services 605
intangible assets 759
integrated approach, Internet 481–2
integrated logistics 424, 429
integrated marketing communications (IMC) 462, 463, 469
  agencies 492
  benefits/opportunities 463–73
  design/implementation 478–84
  problems 473–5
integrating multiple media 462–3
integration 644–5
  customer care 559–6
  customer relations/consumer public relations 538
  economies 777
  marketing responsibilities 192
  mergers 779

Index

vertical 143, 181, 709
Integrative Social Contracts Theory 666
intellectual curiosity 795
intentions surveys 278–9, 285
inter-firm partnerships 780
inter-organizational relationships 198–9
interaction, services 607
interaction/network approach 12–13
interactive cable television systems 460
interconnectedness
    geographic market 648–9
    market 651
    product business 648–9
interdomestic business 641
intermarket networks 202–3
intermediaries
    channel design 412, 413
    channel structure 103, 104
    enhanced strategic triangle 170–1
    sales forecasting 283
    sales prediction models 283–4
    sales promotions 506
    title transfer 100
    wholesaling 432–43
internal customers 557
internal customization 748–9
internal influences, franchising 622
internal market, networks 202
internal marketing 557, 610–12, **747–51**
    definitions 747, 748
    development 747–8
    relationship-based view 748
    strategic/operational vision 749–51
internal organization 195–7
    environmental/strategic change 197, 198
International Association of Department Stores 451
International Coffee Agreement 587
international comparisons
    advertising 496
    advertising statistics 496
international marketing 46
    macro issues 46
    micro issues 46–7
international markets
    competitive strategy 642–4
    competitive tactics 643–4
    geographic terrain 643
international research 265
International Standard on quality *see* ISO9000
International Trade Centre (ITC) 630
International Wool Secretariat 587
internationalization, retailing 457–9

internationalization process 626–7
Internet 162, 227–8, 478–9, 487, 766
    challenges 482
        communication 483
        privacy/control 482–3
    home shopping 460
    integrated approach 481–2
    marketing research data collection 262–3
    opportunities 479
        consumer relationships 479–80
        convenience 480–1
        cost savings 481
        global audience 479
    potential 484
interpersonal skills 829
interpretative model 562–3
interviews
    focus group 770
    in-depth 770
inventory flows, reverse logistics 422
inventory management
    logistic activities 427
    minimum inventory 425
inventory-holding, wholesalers 437
investment
    analysis 169
    objectives 181
    sales promotion 512
involvement
    consumer decision making 119–22
    consumers 119–22
    direction/focus 120
    intensity 120
    persistence 120
IO *see* industrial organization
irrational man 800
ISO9000 696–1
    service quality 610
IT *see* information technology
ITC *see* International Trade Centre
iterative process 92

Jack Daniels 465–6
Japan 77–9
Jaworski, Bernard J. 188
JIT *see* just-in-time
John, G. 787
John Lewis 451
Johnson & Johnson 377
joint venture, retail 458
just-in-time (JIT) 138, 145, 594
    wholesalers 438
juxtaposition of opposites 813

847

Index

kaizen 608
Kalwani, M.U. 784
Kamakura, W. 165
Kaplan, R.S. 759–60
Kassarjian, Hal 817–18
Keep, W.W. 231
Keith, Robert 8
Kellogg 377, 384
Kennedy, S.H. 737
Kent, R.A. 12
key account selling 522
key processeses, TQM 688
knowledge
    creation 795
    direct marketing 474–5
    dissemination 737
    theory 803
Kodak 385
Kohli, Ajay K. 188
Kohls, R.L. 585
Kollat, D.T. 115
Kotler, Philip 10, 11, 43, 606
Krapfel, R.J.E. 786
Kuhn, Thomas 797, 798
Kumar, N. 785

Laczniak, Gene R. 663–4
laggards group 677
Lancaster, Kelvin 39–40
Langmaid, R. 765
Lasser, W. 757–8
late majority group 677
Latin approach 804
law
    advertising controls 503–4
    ethics 655–6
    franchisor/franchisee relationship 619–20
    green marketing 706, 711–12
    pricing 396
    relationship to marketing 251
    retail 454–5
Lawless, M.W. 589
LDCs *see* less developed countries
leadership
    channel members 415
    decline phase 365
    effective 692–6
    key points 692–3
    TQM 693–6
    visionary 563
learning, socialization 72
learning organizations 198
Leeflang, P.S.H. 165

less developed countries (LDCs), primary commodities 582, 583
Levitt, Theodore 7–8, 10, 46–7, 81–2, 84, 463
Levy, Sid 818
Lewis, J.D. 782, 783
liberating paradigm 800
life-cycle
    classification, customer relationships 598
    retail 445–7
life-cycle support, logistics 426–7
limited problem solving (LPS) 120
Little, J.D.C. 85–6, 232
local area marketing 230
location, retail stores 453–4
logical empiricist paradigm 799
logical incremental model 563
logistics **420–31**
    activities 427
        customer service 427
        distribution operations 427–8
        inventory management 427
        transportation 427
    competency model 428–9, 430
    definition 420–1
    production 639
    retail 456–7
    role 420
    value chain
        capabilities 423–5
        creation 421–3
        objectives 425–7
logit analysis 94
long-term relationships 594–5
LPS *see* limited problem solving
Lucozade 383

McCarthy, E. Jerome 10, 11, 12, 40, 322–3
McDonald, M.H.B. 564
McDonald's examples 386
McGoldrick, P.J. 453
McKinsey portfolio 356
made-in images, PCI 724
maintenance selling 519–20
make-or-buy decision 143–4
management
    agenda for marketing organization 203–4
    alliances 786
    competence 537
    competencies 558–9
    control of distribution functions 105–6
    ethical conflict 662
    global segmentation decisions 303–4
    market performance implications 760–1

marketing organization **186–204**
mind-set 691
network approach implications 203
services marketing 607–11
structure 693
TQM 690–1, 698–9, 700
management information systems (MIS) 471
managerial approach 819
managing, sales promotions 513–15
manufacturers
   green marketing 707
   logistics 423
manufacturing, logistics support 423
marginal utility, diminishing 5, 37
Marion, G. 822
Marion, Giles 11
market
   coverage, wholesalers 437
   evolution
      competition 361
      customers 360–1
      new entrants 361–2
      substitute product/technologies 362
      supply relationships 362
   interconnectedness 651
   measurement 256
   offerings, competitive target marketing 595–7
   orientation 188–9
   position 309–15
      strategic historical analysis 168
   scope 644–5
   selection, ethical issues 657–9
   strategic marketing planning 177
   structure 189
market analysis 85, 94–7
   criterion/predictor variables 94–5
   non-partitioned approaches 96–7
   summary 97
market attractiveness, new products 351
market audit 268
market construct 43
market modelling
   data collection 90
   entry 86
   estimation 90–1
   objective specification 88–90
   objectives 86–7
   optimization 92
   subjective specification 87–8
   summary 92–3
   tracking 92
   validation 91–2

market orientation 38, 753
market overview 566–7
market research 85
   ethical issues 657–9
   exhibitions 543
   TQM 689–90
   validation in 93
Market Research Society 657
Market Science Institute 794
market scope, geographic 641–2
market segmentation 38, 116
   customers 164–5
market share
   measurement 754–5
   sales forecasting 283
market specialization, salesforce structuring 522
marketing
   alternative perspectives 821–2
   as business function 13
   change, marketing organization 195–7
   corporate image 735, 737
   current state 817–21
   defined 532, 669
   definitions 3, 5, 14–15
   departmentation of 190
   development 818–19
   era 8–9, 10
   essence 743–4
   ethical issues 656–7
   evolution 20, 821
   evolution/revolution 822–6
   external 747
   failure 827
   functions, wholesaling 437
   future 826–30
   history of 21, 23–4
   instruments 319
   interface, TQM 688–90
   internal 747–51
   as management orientation 66–8
   mid-life crisis 826
   mind-set, development 668, 669–70
   myopia 7, 8
   neo-classical 753
   overview 816–17
   performance assessment 752–62
   philosophy 669, 826
   as philosophy of business 13
   rediscovery of 7–10
   relationship/network relationships 154–5
   segmentation 292–3
   services 604–12

Index

theory 794–806
marketing audit **268–77**, 571–2, 574
  checklist approach 270
    supplementary questions 270–1
  definitions 268
  identifying respondents 270
  mechanics 274
  obtaining information 271
    mail interrogation 273
    method choice 274
    self-analysis 272–3
    visits/interviews 273
  personnel choice 274–5
  process 276–7
  report 275
  technique 268–9
marketing boards, commodities 586
marketing campaigns, and culture 80–1
marketing channels
  design 43–4
  management 43
marketing coalition company 199
marketing communications **486–93**
  activities 486
    advertising 486
    direct marketing 486
    packaging 486
    personal selling 486
    publicity 486
    sales promotion 487
    sponsorship 486–7
  campaign planning 488–9
    budget 490
    context 490
    objectives 490
    strategy 490
  defined 486–7
  delegation of campaign management 492–3
  deployment of mix 490–1
  in practice 487–8
marketing concept 76
  history 25
marketing ethics **653–66**
  descriptive 661–2
  future developments 666
  general theory 662–3
  normative 662, 664–6
marketing exchange company 199
marketing focus 66–8
marketing functions *see* distribution functions
Marketing History Conferences 18, 21–2, 26

marketing management 8, 10–11, 60, **161–315**
  consumer behaviour setting 60–1
  European perspective 11–13
  rewards 61–2
marketing management model 822, 823–4
marketing mix 10–11, 12, 41, 150–1, **319–575**
  channel strategy 415–17
  classification 324–5
  concept 329
  criticisms 327–9
  design 675–80
  ecological 710–16
  expanded 606
  explications/extensions 326–7
  extensions 744–5
  four P classification 322–3, 326, 329
  generic functions 320–1
  global 645–8
  instruments 321–2, 323, 326
  international markets 645–8
  logistics 421
  nature/scope 319–20
  origin carriers 721–2
  packaging 368–9
  pricing 390
  promotions 509–10, 511
marketing modelling 85
marketing performance assessment
  approaches 758–60
  benchmarks 754
  brand equity 755–8
  managerial implications 760–1
  relations between measures 754–5
  stakeholders 753–4
marketing planning 155, **562–75**
  defined 564–9
  importance 563–4
  information for 256–8
  new products 351
marketing productivity, history 25
marketing programme, ethical issues 660–1
marketing public relations 533
marketing quality assurance (MQA) 696–8
marketing research 40, **255–67**
  competitor analysis 257–8
  customer research 256–7
  data collection methods 259
    analysis 264
    geodemographic/lifestyle 264
    primary research 260–3
    questionnaires 263

sampling 263–4
secondary research 259–60
forms
ad hoc surveys 259
continuous consumer panels 258
omnibus surveys 259
retail audits 258–9
syndicated surveys 259
industrial markets 264–5
international 265
knowledge-base 255
market measurement 256
objectivity 798
research companies 265–6
users 255–6
Marketing Science Institute (MSI) 336
marketing strategy **161–73**
analysis of history 168–70
basic principles 162–4
as determinant of organization 187
economics 38–9
implementation 187
meaning of 161–2
as part of organization 187–8
product policy 366
recent issues 170–3
strategic triangle 164
marketing systems, history 24
marketing thought
classification/evalutiona 25
historical research 19–20
history 24–5
history of 21
markets
creation of 6
dynamic 82–3
PCI 722
Marks & Spencer 382, 386, 451
Marlboro 380
Mars example 376, 382
Maslow, Abraham 4, 7
mass
assembly 7
consumption 7
markets 12, 67
media 12
material flows, purchasing management 139
Mattsson, L.-G. 171–2
mature markets 651
maximization 4, 36–7, 39
MDS *see* multidimensional scaling
measurable response, direct marketing 466
media 497

brief 502
evaluation 475
integrating multiple 462–3
planning 502
research 257
mental screening strategy 181
Mercedes example 378, 384
metrics 760, 761, 763–4
microeconomics 37, 38, 39, 42
micromarketing 229
database 229–30
local area 230
occasion-based 230
outside North America 231
privacy issues 230–1
sales promotions 507
Mighty Dog strategy 464–5
migrated marketing 193
military strategies 366, 669
mind-set
development 668, 669–70
TQM 691
Miniard, P.W. 116–18
minimum inventory, value chains 425–6
minimum variance, value chains 425
MIS *see* management information systems
mission statement 535, 536, 566, 692–3
mix instruments 320
multiple functions 321–2
Mobil 535
modelling, customer/marketer IMC
relationships 474–8
models
alliance 789–90
Alpine 744
Anglo-Saxon capitalism 828
customer response 472
ecological 563
entry 86
generic 776
German 744
interpretative 562–3
logical incremental 563
marketing management 822, 823–4
PCI 725
planning 562
political 563
visionary leadership 563
modularity 198
Moët & Chandon example 382
Monczka, R.M. 787
money-off coupons 507
monitoring 470–3

sales promotions 516
monopolistic competition 38
Morgan, R.M. 787
motivation, salespeople 526–8
MQA *see* marketing quality assurance
multi-firm network 202–3
multi-functional team, new product development 353
multidimensional scaling (MDS) 96–7
multipacks/multibuys 508
multiple retailers 447
multiple-cue studies, PCI 723, 724
Murphy, G.B. 754
Murphy, Patrick E. 663–4

NAFTA *see* North American Free Trade Agreement
Nagle, Thomas 41
Narayandas, N. 784
Narus, J.A. 784
Narver, John C. 188
needs 4, 7
negotiation flows, distribution channels 107
neo-classical marketing 753
Nestlé 79–80, 84
network
    effectiveness 203
    implications of 203
    intermarket/concentric 202–3
    internal market 202
    multi-firm/multiple industry 202–3
    opportunity 203
    social 72
    value-added 202
    vertical market 202
    virtual 202
network approach *see* interaction/network approach
networking, customer care 559
networks **150–6**
    boundaries 153
    central concepts 200
    classification 200–1
    customer/supplier 598
    formation process 200
    heterogeneity in 153–4
    hollow 201
    marketing coalition company 199
    marketing exchange company 199
    marketing management implications 154–6
    marketing strategy 171–2
    markets-as-networks 152–3, 156
    value creating 600–1

Nevett, Terence 22, 23
New Age 828–9
new business selling 519–20
new entrants, market dynamics 361–2
new offerings, non-profit organizations 676–7
new products
    adoption rate 134
    cycle time 352–3
    definition 343–4
    development 233–4, **342–53**
        qualitative research 766
    drivers 342–3
    failure factors 343
        lack of differentiation 350
        lack of market orientation 349
        lack of resources 350
        moving too quickly/slowly 349
        no focus 350
        not enough homework 349–50
        poor quality of execution 349
        technical problems 350
        too many projects 350
    go/kill decision points 347–9
    impact 342
    introduction 40
    launch 351–2
    process 344–5
        business analysis 345–6
        commercialization 347
        development 346
        idea generation/exploration/screening 345
        testing/validation 346–7
    sales forecasting 284–6
    success factors 350–2
niche marketing 80
niche position, decline phase 365
niche strategies, core 671–2
Nike 146–7
non-exporters 626
non-financial approaches, marketing performance 759–60
non-partitioned approaches 96
    cluster analysis 96
    conjoint analysis 96
    factor analysis 96
    multi-dimensional scaling 96–7
non-profit organizations
    development 668–9
    environment 669
    mission 669
    strategic marketing **668–81**
non-store retailing 459

Index

electronic shopping 460–1
home shopping 459–60
Noordewier, T.G. 785
normative marketing ethics 662–6
normative theory 822
North American Free Trade Agreement (NAFTA) 611
Norton, D.P. 759–60

objective specification 88–90
objectives 761
   alliance 779–80
   budget management 218, 219
   channel distribution 411
   effective 693
   exhibition 544
   green marketing 712
   marketing 569–70, 574
   marketing communications 490
   model 86–7
   organization 670
   pricing 391–2, 396–7
   TQM 695
occasion-based marketing 230
Ogilvy, David 469
oligopoly 39
Olins, Wally 737–8
OPEC *see* Organization of Petroleum Exporting Countries
operating budget 209–10
operational fulfillment systems, logistics 424
operational marketing plan 564–5
operational vision 750–1
opinion leaders 73
opportunity costs 37, 214
opportunity networks 203
opportunity-based value adding promotions 508–9
opposites, juxtaposition 813
optical scanners 232
optimization methods, pricing 398–9
optimization model 92
order processing, wholesalers 437
organization
   assumptions 827
   boundary-less 780
   cellular 202
   characteristics of success 193–5
   commodities 586
   ethics 665–6
   evolution 186–7
   flexible 201
   functional issues 190, 191

   future of 193–5
   identity *see* corporate identity
   key processes 198
   learning 198
   management agenda 203–4
   market-based 190, 191
   matrix structures 190, 191
   product-based 190, 191
   public relations 532–5
   services 610–11
   status quo of 192–3
   strategic marketing 668, 670–2
   TQM 690
   transactional 198
Organization of Petroleum Exporting Countries (OPEC) 582
organizational
   culture, budget management 218–19
   dimensions 187–90
   forms 190–5, 197–203
organizational buying behaviour **128–36**
   decision making 128
   process 130–3
      influences 133–6
   purchasing
      behaviour 130
      function 129–30
orientation, market 753
origin carriers 721–2
origin cues 721
origin images 719
   carriers in marketing mix 721–2
   cue expressions 721
   importance 720–1
   marketing 722
   marketing strategy 726–7
   slipping 724
   usage 720–1, 722
   variations 724–5
out-of-stock conditions, retail 457
out-of-town retail development 450–1
outcome quality 608–9
outsourcing 148, 154
over-demand 60
Oxfam example 376
OXO example 379

packaging **368–74**, 486
   added value 368–9
   agencies 373–4
   category rules 369
   effective 373
   equities protection 371–2

Index

experts 373–4
green marketing 715
innovation 369–70
PCI 722
point-of-sale 372–3
valued 508
pan-company marketing 752, 755
paradigms 799-800, 804–5
parallel processing, new product development 353
parameter theory 12
participation observation 771
partnerships 780
   channel 234
   channel management 417, 418
   distribution channels 106, 111
   efficiencies/cost reductions 783–5
   satisfaction 788
   supplier 776–90
payment, improved terms 508
PCI *see* product-country images
peak-load pricing 397
Peattie, S. & K. 514
penetration pricing 397
people factor 744
perceived value pricing 41, 399–400
perceptions 745
   corporate reputations 536
perfect competition 12, 39
performance 745
   assessment **752–62**
   channel members 417
   customer care 557–8
   export 634
   measurement, relations between 754–5
   salesforce evaluation 528–9
   TQM 695, 699–700
   values 466
performance tracking systems 466–73
perishability, services 605
Persil example 379
personal selling 486, **518–30**
   ethical issues 659
   importance 518–20
   management 680
   types 519–20
personality, corporate 532
personality factor 744
persuasion
   advertising 475–8
   promotions 510, 512
Peters, Tom 463
Philips 539

philosophical orientations, qualitative research 767–70
philosophy 744
   marketing 826
physical distribution
   logistics 423–4
   wholesalers 439–40
physiological psychology 53
Piercy, Nigel 192
Pillsbury Company 8
pilots, franchising 617
place of distribution 744
place of purchase 11, 43–4
   promotions 510
Plan-Do-Act cycle 694
planning 829
   advertising 494, 502
   assumptions 568–9
   direct marketing 473–4
   green marketing 708–10
   logistics 424
   marketing communications campaign 488–90
   new product development 353
   rationality in 175
   sales promotions 513–15
   TQM 697
planning gap
   calculation of 180
   problem diagnosis 180
   strategies 180–2
planning model 562
planning time horizons 507
PLC *see* product life-cycle
pleasure 61–2
point-of-sale (POS) 510
   packaging 372–3
policy
   public relations 534–5
   shaping of behaviour 535–6
   TQM 691–2
political markets 799–800
political model 563
Pollay, Richard 23–4
Polli, Roland 336
pollution, green marketing 707, 711–12, 715, 717
Porter, Michael E. 38, 180, 182, 333, 362, 365
portfolios
   brands 377
   business 337–9
   customer 597–602
   expanding 649–50

global 648–51
　reconfiguring 649–51
　retraction 650
　structure 648
　summary 568
positioning 165, 168, **309–15**, 745
　brand 370–1
　company competitive 309
　decision making 312–13
　effective 310
　future directions 315
　global 645–6
　green marketing 707
　key concepts/ideas 309–10
　organization 671–2
　product 40, 491, 646–7
　product/brand 309, 311–12
　segmentation implementation 303
　strategy 313
　　competitor depositioning 314–15
　　incremental 314
　　radical 314
　　reinforcement 314
post-functional marketing 186
post-industrial society 3, 4
posthoc sales 488
postmodern marketing **810–15**
　acceptance/dismissal 813–14
　characteristics
　　decentred subjects 813
　　fragmentation 812
　　hyperreality 812
　　juxtaposition of opposites 813
　　reversed production/consumption 812–13
　crisis of representation 811
　outrageousness 814–15
　participation/abstention 810–11
　problem 811–12
postmodernists 806
power
　budget management 218
　and culture 79–80
　distribution channels 108–9
　and marketing organization 189
　retailer 444–5
　social 72
PR *see* public relations
practice, impact of theory 802
Prahalad, C.K. 172
pre-testing, advertising 500–1
premium pricing 397
premiums 508

price 11, 40–1, 744
　commodities 581, 584
　competition, adoption 40
　futures market 584–5
　and information 41–2
　quantity discounts 41
　segmented 42–3
　and spatial competition 42
price bundling 397–8
price elasticity 43
price signalling 397
price skimming 397
price-based value increasing promotions 507–8
price-quality effect 41
price-quantity discounts 397
price-volume relationship 392–3
pricing **390–403**
　analysis, company goals/strategies/costs 391–2
　brand mix 380
　buyer behaviour 392–5
　channel management 416
　competition 395–6
　concepts/issues 390–1
　discount 507
　environmental analysis 390–1
　ethical concerns 660
　ethical issues 658
　green marketing 715–16
　implementation 398
　　dynamic models 400–1
　　methods/techniques 398–400
　　structure 398
　IT systems 228–9
　legal constraints 396
　multidimensional character 390
　objectives 396–7
　PCI 724
　perceived value 393–4, 399
　promotions 401–2
　psychological aspects 394
　retail 455–6
　segmented 42–3
　strategies, international marketing 647–8
　strategy 397–8
　strategy vs tactics 401
　value 829
Pritzl, R. 781
privacy
　Internet 482–3
　micromarketing 230–1
probit analysis 94

855

Index

problem solving, consumer decision making 118–19
process improvement, alliances 779
process management 687–8, 829
process quality 608
Procter & Gamble (P&G) 193, 376, 383, 386, 410, 592
　in Japan 77–9
　Vizir launch 76–7
procurement, logistics 423–4
product
　communication medium 462
　innovation 352–3
product business interconnectedness 648–9
product flows, distribution channels 107
product life-cycle analysis (LCA) 710
product life-cycle (PLC) 12, 334–7, **356–67**, 816
　alternative concepts 358
　cycles of confusion 356–9
　ethical concerns 660
　green marketing 708
　implications for marketing 357
　pricing 393
　stage 515
　theory 803
　weaknesses
　　no common shape 359
　　not exogenous 359–60
　　product oriented 360
　　unclear implications 359
　　undefined 359
　　unpredictable turning-points 359
product-based value increasing promotions 508
product-country images (PCI) **719–30**
　buyer decisions 723–4
　context 723
　correlates 724
　development/scope 721–2
　government/public policy 728–9
　practice 725
　research 722–5
　strategic implications 725–9
　usage 727–8
product-specific assessments, PCI 723
production 8–9, 43
　advertising 501–2
　factory 6–7
　logistics 639
　reversed 812–13
　services 607–8
production quality 609

productivity
　functional 759
　services 608–10
products 39–40
　advertising 498
　availability, wholesalers 438
　bundles of attributes 40, 45
　channel management 416
　characteristics 140–1
　commodity 580
　complements 40
　computer design/development 228
　core/peripheral 556
　country images 719–30
　definitions 331–4
　deletion 334
　development 829
　ecological 707, 710–14
　ethical issues 658
　improved quality/features 508
　increased quantity 508
　joint development 145
　management 675
　market readiness 689
　nature of 515
　policy **331–41**
　portofolio 337–9
　positioning 40, 309, 311–12, 491
　pricing 395–6
　purchasing management 140–1
　retail selection 454–5
　salesforce specialization 521–2
　samples 508
　situational involvement 120
　substitutes 40
　TQM 695
Professional Marketing Research Society 657
profit
　five forces 182
　maximization 36–7, 39
　measurement 754
　TQM 700
programming 222–3
projective techniques 771
promotion 11, 44–5, 486, 509–10, 745
　channel management 416
　commodities 586–8, 587
　export 631
　history 21
　as influence 45–6
　as information 45
　instruments 323, 326
　marketing 538

Index

as means of communication 510, 512
PCI 722
price 401–2
selecting 515
tactical/strategic dimensions 512
promotion flows, distribution channels 108
promotional
    discounts 43
    policy, international marketing 647
prospect theory 42
protectionism
    brand equities 371–2
    commodities 582–3
Prudential Securities 480
psychographics
    consumer behaviour theory 115–16
    green marketing 708
    profile 490
psychological variables 759
psychology 52, **52–63**
    Behavioural Perspective Model 57–8
        hierarchy of consumer lifestyles 58–60
    corporate image 735
    and marketing 52
        costs, rewards, exchange 53–7
        elementary behaviour 52–3
    pricing 394
public opinion 503
public policy
    future 252–3
    high-water mark 251–2
    law 251
    marketing **251–4**
    time of remission 252
    world views 253–4
public relations (PR) **531–40**
    attitudes 533–4, 535
    consumer 538
    corporate image 735, 737
    defined 531
    development 538–40
    effective 537–8
    management 679–80
    marketing communications mix 487
    organizational 532–5
    policy 534–5
    reputation 535–7
    sales promotions 510
public services 605–6
publicity 486
    costs 491
purchasing
    consumer behaviour 122–3

historical development 129–30
organization 141–2
organizational
    behaviour 130–1
    function 129–30
psychology of 54–7
purchasing management **138–48**
    conditions 140
        external 140–1
        internal 141–2
    current issues 148
    significance 138–9
    strategic issues 142–3
        configuration of supplier base 146–7
        make-or-buy 143–4
        supplier relationships 144–6
    strategic roles
        development 139
        rationalization 139
        structural 139
push and pull
    ecology 705
    factors 458
    Internet 480
    promotions 416
    sales promotions 505, 506

QC *see* quality control
qualitative research 673, **765–74**
    computer research 773
    computers 773
    definitions 765–6
    future trends 773–4
    literature sources 773–4
    methods 770
        case studies 771
        evaluation 772–3
        focus group interviews 770
        grounded theory 771–2
        in-depth interviews 770
        participant observation 771
        projective techniques 771
    philosophical orientations 767
        data collection/generation 768–70
        inductive 768, 772–3
        key concepts/ideas 767–8
    scope 766
        diagnostic studies 766–7
        exploratory studies 766
        new product development 766
        tactical research projects 767
quality
    brand equity 757

857

Index

customer care 559
defined 685–7
products 508
service 608–10
TQM 685–701
see also total quality management
quality assurance 138
quality chains 686, 687
quality control (QC) techniques 691
quality function deployment 829
quality policy 692
quality systems 696
quantitative methods 85, **85–98**, 801–2
    computer intensive 97–8
    market analysis 94–7
    market modelling 85–93
    validation measures 93–4
quantitative research 673, 768
quantity, increased products 508
quasi-experiments 472
Quinn, J.B. 783–4

rack jobbers 440
radical approaches, theory 805–6
radio commercials 502
railroad industry, US 7–8
random discounting 397
Rao, V.R. 123–4, 758
rapid response, value chains 425
Rapp, Stan 466
ratio to sales, advertising 500
rational quality 608
rationalism 37
re-engineering 198
realism/relativism debate 796–800
recruitment
    franchisors 621
    salesforce 525–6
recycling systems, green marketing 712
Reed, R. 169
refunds 508
regional business 641–2
regression analysis 90–1, 94
    grounded theory 772
regression models, retail location 454
relational forms 196
relational orientation, alliances/partnerships 785–6
relationship approach, internal marketing 748, 749
relationship building
    continual monitoring 470–3
    customer 463–4

exhibitions 542–3
relationship marketing 12, 13, 15, 152, 195, 478
    customer care 557
    direct marketing 463
    expanded 606–7
    management implications 154–6
    salespeople 519
    services 606–7, 611
    theory 805
relationships **150–6**
    business marketing 599–600
    consumer 151–2
    establishing/managing 203
    exchange 151
    inter-organizational 198–9
    Internet 479–80
    marketing strategy 171–2
    purchaser-supplier 144–7
    social 71–2
reliability 685
reputation 535–6
    appraisal 536–7
    building 537
    corporate 737
research 829
    advertising 497
    consumer behaviour 114–16
    deductive 767, 768
    inductive 768
    non-profit organizations 672–3
    product-country images 722–3
        context 723
        key findings 723–5
    qualitative 15, 765–74
    quantitative 15, 768
    segmentation
        classification 299–300
        database management 301
        discrimination 300
        linking findings with management subjective judgements 302
        selection 296–7
        simulation/optimization 301–2
        simultaneous evaluation 300–1
    TQM performance 699–700
research companies
    controlling process 266
    proposal 266
    research brief 266
    working with 265–6
research and development (R&D) 778
    new products 342–3

Index

resources 537
　allocation among segments 299
　marketing strategy 172, 173
　non-profit organizations 673–5
　ownership 143–4
　requirements 570
responsibility
　campaign management 492
　environmental scanning 247–8
responsibility accounting 213
retail
　audits 258–9
　density 447
　formats 449–50
　　department/variety stores 451
　　discounters 452–3
　　shopping centres/parks 450–1
　　superstores/hypermarkets 451–2
　outlets 444
　parks 450–1
　structures 448
　theories of change 445, 447
retail functions 453
　advertising 456
　brands 455
　human resources 456
　information/logistics 456–7
　location 453–4
　pricing 455–6
　product selection/buying 454–5
　selling environment 456
retail life-cycles 445–7
retail organization
　cooperative societies 449
　franchises 449
　independents/multiples 447–8
　voluntary groups 448–9
retailers
　advertising 498
　competitive advantage 395–6
　power 444
　power increase 111
　sales promotions 506
retailing **444–61**
　definition/scope 444
　evolution 444–7
　history 24
　internationalization 457–8
　　entry strategies 458–9
　　motives 458
　non-store 459–61
retraction decisions 650
retraining, TQM 695

return on investment (ROI) 755, 785
return rates, green marketing 712
returns, TQM 700
reversed production/consumption 812–13
rewards
　effectiveness enhancement 61–2
　increasing quality/quantity of 62
　management of 61–2
　monetary 527
　psychology of 53–7
　scheduling 62
　spiritual 379
Robertson, Thomas S. 40
Robinson Patman Act 454
Rogers, E. 115
ROI *see* return on investment
roles
　sales promotion 505–6
　salespeople 518–19
Rolex example 379
Rostow, W.W. 4–5, 7
routine problem solving (RPS) 118–19
RPS *see* routine problem solving
Rubbermaid Inc 189
rules, theoretical 794
rules of thumb, price setting 399
Russell, G.J. 165

S-O-R approach 150–1
sales 8, 9
　advertising effects 503
　discount 507
　posthoc 488
　TQM 696
　wholesalers contact 437
sales forecasting **278–88**
　causal approaches 282–3
　　company 283
　　competitors 284
　　customers 283
　　environment 283
　　intermediaries 283–4
　　market share 284
　direct extrapolation 281–2
　new products 284–6
sales management **518–30**
　role 520
SALES model 470–1, 472
sales promotion 487, **505–17**
　defined 505
　development 506–7
　ethical issues 659
　evaluation of effectiveness 516

859

Index

future of 516–17
management 679
managing/planning 513–15
pitfalls 512–13
role 505–6
selecting 515
trade 515–16
types 507
    opportunity-based value adding 508–9
    price-based value increasing 507–8
    product-based value increasing 508
    tangible value adding 508
salesforce
    'automation' 229
    ethical issues 659
    sales promotions 506
    segmentation 305–6
    size 523–4
    structure 521
        combined methods 522
        geographical specialization 521
        information technology 523
        key account selling 522
        market specialization 522
        product specialization 521–2
        team selling 522–3
        telesales 522
    territory management 524–5
salespeople
    deployment 520–5
    motivation 526–8
    organization 520
        direct vs independent 520–1
    performance evaluation 528–9
    recruitment 525
    training 525–6
Samuelson, Paul A. 42
saturation effects 87
Savitt, R. 22
SBU *see* strategic business unit
Scandinavian School 11, 822
scanning equipment, retail 457
scarcity 4
Scheuing, E.E. 336
Schultz, Don 469
Schwartz, George 21
Scitovsky, T. 41
Sears 386
segment
    allocating resources among 299
    identification decision 294–6
    target selection 297–8
segmentation 182, **291–307**, 644–5

bases 671
best practice/new developments 291–2
branding 377
business markets 597
concept extension 205–6
differentiation 166
global 303
    data mining 304
    globalization 304–5
    information strategies 304
    management decisions 303–4
green marketing 707
implementation decisions 294–9
PCI 727
problems 302
    poor integration with strategy 303
    static/deterministic perspective 302–3
    too narrow a focus 302
research 296–7, 299–302, 306–7
uses 292–3
segmented pricing, economics 42–3
selection criteria
    channel members 413–14
    customer 470–1
    ethical issues 657–9
    exhibitions 544–5
    franchisees 617
self-analysis questionnaires 272
    plus independent evaluation of analysis 272–3
self-assessment, business excellence model 698
self-managing teams 198
self-regulation, franchisor/franchisee relationship 619–20
self-start, retail 458
sellers 13
selling
    customer focused 829
    exhibition 542
    personal 486, 518–30
    promotions 510
    retail environment 456
senior management, TQM 694–5, 699
sensitivity analysis, budgeting 220
service marketing, Four Ps 327
service relationships 152
service selling 520
services **604–12**
    characteristics 605
    development/design 608
    emergence 604
    future 611–12

infrastructure 611
management 675–6
marketing organization 610–11
productivity 608–10
quality 608–10
TQM 695
types/perspective 605–6
settings, consumer behaviour 60–1
Seyle, H. 769
Shapiro, S.J. 40
Sheth, Jagdish 818
Sheth, J.N. 558
shops, shopping centres 444, 450–1
silo management 695
simulation techniques, price setting 399
simultaneity, services 605
situational analysis 176–7
company 178–9
competition 178
customer 177
external environment 177
green marketing 705–8
market 177
situational involvement, consumers 120
Six Ps, brand mix 380–1
skills, direct marketing 474–5
Slater, Stanley F. 188
small numbers market 67
Smith, Adam 6, 38
SmithKline Beecham 377
smoke and mirrors, publice relations 534
SMP *see* strategic market planning
snowball effect 507
social
exchange 65–6
marketing 676
organization 66
phenomena, qualitative research 768–9
social systems
change 72–3
conflict 72
culture 70–1
distribution channels 108–9
family life-cycle 70
family/household 70
groups 69–70
lifestyle 70
network 72
norm 69
power 72
relationships 71–2
role 68
social class 70

socialization 72
status 68
subculture 71
socio-technical systems, marketing strategy 172–3
socioeconomic factors, franchising 615–16
sociology 64, **64–74**, 65–6, 73–4
sociopolitical paradigm 799
sourcing, global 639
spatial competition, economics 42
specialization 44
geographical 521
market 522
product 521–2
specialization economies of scale 105
spider web company 201
split-run tests 469
sponsorship 486–7
Srivastav, A. 780
Stadler, M. 744
staffing
exhibition booths 545
green marketing 717
levels 60
requirements 203
TQM 690, 700
stage-gate systems, new products 352
stakeholders 753–4
segmentation strategy 306
Star, Steven H. 189
stars, branding 377
statistics, advertising 494–6
stochastic models, consumer behaviour 124
strategic alliances **776–90**
channel management 418
classification 780
distribution channels 106, 111
future prospects 780
three 'I's 789–90
strategic business unit (SBU) 820
strategic control systems 680
strategic decision making 562–3
strategic intent, role of 169–70
strategic marketing
non-profit organizations **668–81**
planning process 670
strategic marketing plan 562, 564
contents 565
strategic marketing planning (SMP) **175–85**, 573, 668
checklist 178
current issues 185
data interpretation 179–80

Index

    defined 175–6
    historical review 176–9
    process 670
    setting tentative objectives 176
    strategy evaluation 183–4
strategic planning 829
strategic school, corporate identity 740–1
strategic triangle
    competitors 165–6
        differentiation 166
        price 166
        subgroups 166–7
    corporation 167
        financial analysis 167–8
        SWOT analysis 167
    customers 164
        market segmentation 164–5
    enhanced 170–1
strategic vision 749–50
strategies 39, 820
    advertising 498–9
    channel 409–11
    channel management 106, 417–18
    communication 678–9
    competitive 464–5
    defined 161–2
    distribution 647
    effective 693
    entry 458–9
    environmental scanning 249–50
    exhibition 544–7
    global 639–42
    green marketing 708–10
    growth 181
    identification of 180–2
    marketing 154–5, 161–73, 569–70
    marketing communications 490
    marketing planning 175–85
    mental screening/evaluation 181
    military 366
    PCI 726–7
    pricing 391–2, 397–8
    product policy 333–4, 366
    promotions 512
    public relations 536–7
    purchasing 142–3
    quality 761
    segmentation 292–9
structures
    brand 384–6
    bureacratic 196
    channel 412–13
    organic 196

stubstitutes, product 40
sub-disciplinary fields, theory 804–5
subjective specification 87
    advertising effects 87
    saturation effects 87
subjective world paradigm 800
subjective-objective dimension 799
substitute products, market dynamics 362
success
    alliances 786
    exporting 634
    factors, identification 693
summary constructs, PCI 725
superstores 451–2
supervision, TQM 695
supplier partnerships **776–90**
supplier-buyer link 780–1
suppliers
    base configuration 146–7
    design/packaging 373–4
    environmental influences on buying
        process 133
    high-involvement relationships 144–6, 147
    internal 749
    low-involvement relationships 144, 147
    organizational buying behaviour 130,
        131–3
    purchasing management 139–40
    quality 687
supply
    and demand 40–1, 43, 44
    market dynamics 362
supply chain management 112
    channel strategy 410
support
    franchising 617–18
    non-profit organizations 668, 674
surplus 5
surveys, PCI 723
sustainability, analysis 168–9
sustainable competitive advantage (SCA) 162
sustainable strategic advantage, direct
    marketing 463
SWOT analysis 167, 179, 567
symbol group retailers 448–9
synergy
    channel strategy 410
    global marketing 650
    marketing communication 491
    new product success 351
systems, TQM 695
systems selling, wholesalers 439

Index

tactical control systems 680
tactical marketing 165
    pricing 401–2
tactical marketing plan 564–5
    contents 565–9
tactics 820
    promotions 512
takeback regulation 711
tangible asset value 537–8
tangible value adding promotions 508
target audience 670
    marketing communication 490–1
target market 645
target marketing
    competitive 595–7
    ethical concerns 660
target markets 597
    channel strategy 409–10
    new product success 351
    positioning 313
target segments 297–9
targeting
    consumers 515
    promotions 510
targets, advertising 498–9
task specialization 5, 7
TCA *see* transaction cost approach
team selling 522–3
team work 829
technical problems, new products 350
technical support, wholesalers 438–9
technological capabilities, new products 352
technology 47
    channel management 418
    developments 777
    exhibition presentations 547–8
    market offering 595
    product life-cycle 359
    role 111–12
Tedlow, Richard S. 23
telemarketing 481
teleology 662
telephone shopping 459
telesales 522
television commercials 502
Tennessee Squires example 465–6
territory management, salesforce 524–5
testing, new products 346–7
theory **794–806**
    academic status 795
    attention to history 801
    form 796–800
    future 803

    new regions/theories 804
    radical approaches 805–6
    sub-disciplinary fields 804–5
    impact on practice 802–3
    intellectual curiosity 795
    knowledge creation 795
    normative 822
    practical value 795
    problems 800–1
    quantitative methods 801–2
    realism/relativism debate 796–800
    reasons 794–5
    rules 794
    scientific 795–6
third parties, franchising 615–16
three Is 789–90
through-the-line operators 492
time dimension, budget planning 212
time horizon, environmental scanning 246–7
time stability 168
Timex watches example 410
title flow, distribution channels 100, 107
TOMA *see* top-of-mind-awareness
top-of-mind-awareness (TOMA) 475
Tosdal, H.R. 822
total communications school, corporate
    identity 741–3
total corporate communications 739–40
total quality management (TQM) **685–701**
    customer care 557
    definitions 691
    development 698–701
    foundation 693–4
    impact 691
    implementation 694
    logistics 426
    marketing change 195
    methods/techniques 691
    positioning 315
    see also quality
total systems, customer care 557
TQM *see* Total Quality Management
tracking systems 92
    direct marketing 466–73
Trade Descriptions Act 503
trade promotions 515–16
trade shows 543
trading, commodities 582–3
trading companies 631
trading relationship 100
training
    salesforce 525–6
    TQM 690, 695

863

Index

transaction cost analysis 39
transaction cost approach (TCA) 44, 46, 47
transaction efficiency 105
transaction orientation 780–1
transaction utility 42
transactional, organizations 198
transactional forms 196
transnational retailing 458–9
transportation 777
    logistics 426, 427
Treacy, Michael 182
true experiments 468–70, 472–3
trust 786–7
Tull, Donald S. 192
turnabout/turnaround objective 181–2
Turner, R.E. 43
turnover, TQM 700
Tzokas, 331–2

Uhl, J.N. 585
uncertainty reduction 151, 154
UNCTAD *see* United Nations Committee on Trade and Development
unethical practices 663
    legal aspects 655–6, 657
    marketing 654–5
uniform delivered prices 397
Unilever 193, 376
United Nations Committee on Trade and Development (UNCTAD) 630
Uppsala internationalization theory 627, 629
utilities 47

validation 93–4
    model
        face 91
        hold-out sample 91
        U-method 91–2
    new products 346–7
validation measures 85, 93
    summary 93–4
validity 772
value
    brand image 379–80
    market offering 596
    non-functional 379
value adding 829
    logistics 422
    sales promotions 506
    wholesalers 432
value chains 602
    green marketing 708
    logistics 421–7

value creation **420–31**
value curves
    branding 378
    highest common factors 378–9
value enhanced products, commodities 590
value networks 600–1, 602
value performance, brands 377–8
value pricing 829
value-added networks 202
valued packaging 508
values, performance 466
Van den Bulte, C. 327–9
Van Maanen, J. 765
Van Riel, C.B.M. 739
variables
    budget management 220
    customer care 556
    psychological 759
    qualitative research 772–3
variance, logistics systems 425
variety stores 451
Venkatesh, A. 813
vertical, relationship 780
vertical integration 143, 181
    channel management 106
    green marketing 709–10
vertical market networks 202
vertical marketing systems (VMS), growth in 111
vertical shows, exhibitions 542
victimization 800
Vidal Sassoon 383
Videotex, home shopping 460
virtual information, Internet control 482–3
virtual network 202
virtuous circle 789–90
vision
    operational 750–1
    strategic 749–50
    TQM 695
visionary leadership model 563
visual school, corporate identity 743
Vitasoy 83
Vitell, Scott J. 662
VMS *see* vertical marketing systems
voluntary group retailers 448–9
volunteer support, non-profit organizations 674
vulnerability 165
    analysis 179

warehouse clubs 452–3
waste disposal, green marketing 711–12

Webster, Frederick E. 186–7, 190, 193, 195, 198
Webster, Frederick E. Jr 11, 39, 787, 818–19, 820–1, 827–9
Weitz, Bart 196
Wells, W.D. 122–3
wholesalers
   business user relationship 437–9
   existence rationale 432–3
   marketing functions 439
   participation in marketing flows 432, 435
   retailer relationship 436–7
   selecting/using 434–9
   supplier relationship 434, 436
wholesaling **432–43**
   assessment 439–42
   structure 433–4

Wiersema, Fred 182
Williams, J.R. 168–9
Williamson, Oliver E. 44, 784
Wind, J. 123–4
Wind, Yoram 306, 787
Wittink, D. 165
Woolite example 409
World Trade Organization (WTO) 630
World Wide Web 487, 601, 602
WTO *see* World Trade Organization

Yupseh, S. 337

Zeithaml, Valerie A. 609
Zeneca 534
zero errors/defects 138, 694
zero-sum 144
zone pricing 397